Estate Planning And Taxation

1998 ANNUAL EDITION

Estate Planning And Taxation

1998 ANNUAL EDITION

The **CHRIS J. PRESTOPINO** text

continued by **JOHN C. BOST,** J.D., M.S.(Tax)

Associate Professor of Finance
San Diego State University

KENDALL/HUNT PUBLISHING COMPANY
4050 Westmark Drive   Dubuque, Iowa 52002

DEDICATION

To Chris' students, who were his ongoing inspiration, and to his wife Nancy, and their two children, Matt and Julie, whose patience and understanding were lovingly appreciated by the late Professor Chris J. Prestopino.

To students of estate planning, past, present and future, for whom this text was created and for whom it continues; and to my wife, Jennifer, and our two children, Heather and Laura, my personal reason for learning about estate planning. JCB

Chris J. Prestopino
1943 - 1994

This text is dedicated to Chris J. Prestopino, an outstanding leader in the field of estate planning and estate planning education. He was well loved by his students and colleagues at California State University, Chico, where, in over 20 years of teaching estate planning courses, he won numerous teaching awards.

This textbook, first published in 1987, became the leader in the growing field of estate planning education, as the only book truly aimed at university level academic programs. Its success is a testament to Professor Prestopino's foresight and hard work. He believed in examples, examples, and more examples, a tradition that will be continued in this and future editions of the book.

Professor Prestopino received his A.B. in Economics from Cornell University, an M.B.A. and a Ph.D. in Finance from the University of Pennsylvania's Wharton School of Business; an M.B.A. in taxation from Golden Gate University in San Francisco. He served as an associate editor for tax and estate planning for the Financial Services Review (the journal of the Academy of Financial Services); he served on exam question audit committees for the CFP Board of Standards; and was the Program Director for the CFP education program at Chico State.

Perhaps, those of us who work and study in the area of estate planning think about death and dying more than most people. Nevertheless, when someone as young as Chris dies just as he is reaching the pinnacle of his profession, just as his children are entering young adulthood, we deeply feel the loss. He will be missed. It is to Chris and students everywhere that this promise is made: to continue his tradition of excellence in our teaching, in our learning, and in this textbook.

Contents

Introduction to Charitable Giving. Tax Consequences of Charitable Trusts. Gifts of Split Interests. Appendix 14A: Defective Incomplete Transfers. Overview. Interest-Free Loan. *Gift Tax Consequences. Income Tax Consequences. Estate Tax Consequences.* Short-Term Trust. *Gift Tax Consequences. Income Tax Consequences. Estate Tax Consequences to the Grantor.* Spousal Remainder Trust. Sale of a Remainder Interest and Joint Purchase. The Family Estate Trust: A Trap for the Unwary.

Illustrations

Preface

Professor Prestopino's *Estate Planning and Taxation* really began in 1974, after his first unsuccessful search for a textbook. For the next eight years, each time he taught estate planning in the undergraduate or graduate business curriculum, he had to settle on a book not designed primarily for students. The options were limited to three types of publications: simple primers and paperbacks intended for the lay reader; technical references suited for the informed professional; and treatises written for the third-year law student. In 1987 Professor Prestopino published the first edition of this book.

Estate Planning and Taxation offers an alternative, one having a different format. It is a textbook, designed to be used in an academic program. Its concepts are introduced logically rather than encyclopedically; and as the reader's knowledge grows, more advanced principles are covered.

Estate Planning and Taxation is for the professional or student pursuing a career in financial services, taxation, or law in which estate planning and estate and gift taxation is but one of several principal areas of practice. Applicable careers include law, tax accounting, financial planning, insurance sales, paralegal work, banking, trust management, investment brokerage and management, and real estate. Since much of the subject matter is Internal Revenue Code driven, the textbook draws heavily on primary sources of the law, both Code and cases. The textbook is adaptable to law school courses in estate planning and taxation, giving the law student a strongly quantitative slant that is often overlooked in traditional law books, even those dealing with taxes.

The book is divided into three parts. The first two present the basic language and constraints found in estate planning, including the underlying tax and nontax laws that serve as the basis for planning. The third, and largest, part surveys the major estate planning strategies used currently by practitioners. Tax analysis is emphasized. This sequential approach aids learning because estate planning techniques presuppose a familiarity with many fundamental legal concepts, including tax principles.

The organization of *Estate Planning and Taxation* seeks to present a concise, integrated overview, highlighting the essence of concepts without confusing the reader with every technical qualification and reference, a problem which has impaired the readability of many books in the field. For example, the text expects the student to learn only those case names and Code section numbers that have attained the status of common industry jargon (chapter endnotes cite many others). Nonetheless, the book's content is comprehensive. For example, with its quantitative orientation, it demonstrates numerically, wherever possible, the consequences of planning, and of the failure to plan, on family wealth.

Many pedagogical devices are used to aid comprehension. Numerous examples are included in each chapter to clarify concepts. Each chapter contains end-of-chapter questions and problems, many with solutions. Appendixes include a glossary, sample tax returns, tax and valuation tables, as well as those sections of the Internal Revenue Code most relevant to estate planning. A manual containing a test bank is available to instructors who adopt the book.

Estate Planning and Taxation can be used in a two-hour or three-hour quarter or semester introductory college undergraduate course, or graduate or law school course. It can be read in conjunction with a correspondence, certificate-type course offered to the financial services industry; and it can be read independently by anyone seeking a moderately technical overview, including the practitioner in accounting or financial services, the law student, the attorney in general practice, and the very determined lay reader.

ACKNOWLEDGMENTS

For their suggestions and help with the present edition, I wish to thank the following people: Texas Tech University adjunct faculty and attorney, Robert E. Barnhill for keeping chapter 8 up to date; Academic Assistant at National Endowment for Financial Education (NEFE) and attorney, Gregg A. Parish for continued encouragement and suggestions; and fee-only financial consultant Daniel J. Burnside, Binghamton, New York, for ten pages of thoughtful suggestions.

Individuals previously thanked by Chris J. Prestopino and myself, and whose many contributions continue to be reflected in the text: Michael Ahearn, Martin Anderson, Robert Barnhill, Russell L. Block, Karen Booth, J. Buckhold, Paul M. Cheverton, Neil Cohen, Larry Cox, Mariel Damaskin, Jeffrey Dennis-Strathmeyer, D. J. Devin, Mark Dorfman, W. W. Dotterweich, Jon Gallo, Keith Fevurly, Mark Greene, Benjamin Henszey, Carole Hill, Jerry Kasner, Fred Keydel, Georgina Knowles, James K. Leese, H. Russell May, Shekhar Misra, Karen Molloy, Burton Nissing, Gregg Parish, Mary Reese, Phelder St. Germain, Janice Samuells, John Schooling, Jack Stephens, and Richard Wellman.

Thank you all for your suggestions.   John C. Bost

ETAX Program Information

On disk you will find ETAX96.wb2 for use with QUATTRO PRO and ETAX96.xls for use with EXCEL. ETAX96 is an estate and gift tax spreadsheet program designed for educational use only. It will do basic estate taxes, the state death tax credit, and to a limited degree the cumulative gift tax calculations. It will not add in the gift taxes paid on gifts made within three years of death, nor will it work with pre-1977 estate or gift tax calculations.

Before working with the ETAX program, you should create a backup disk. You can only input data into certain **cells**:

- Estates: the **year of death**, the **gross estate**, and **deductions** (you will have to do your own total for marital, charitable, debts and expenses).
- Gifts: the **year of the current gifts**, the **year of prior gifts**, the **current year's gifts** (you must first subtract the annual exclusions) and **prior year's gifts** (the taxable amount, i.e., after subtracting the annual exclusions)
- After entering the data hit calculate. Your spreadsheet setup should be set for at least five iterations, ten if you want to try to do inter-related calculations such as net gifts. To determine whether you have the iterations set high enough, enter figures high enough to generate a tax at the cells for prior gifts, current gifts, and the gross estate and see whether the resulting tax amounts change after you hit calculate a second time. If they do, notice how many times you must hit calculate before they don't change and set the iterations accordingly.

PART 1

Overview and Conceptual Background

— 1

Introduction to Estate Planning

WHAT ESTATE PLANNING IS ABOUT

Estate planning is the study of the principles of planning for the use, conservation, and efficient transfer of an individual's wealth. Its concepts are based on the premise that people do not live forever; sooner or later, death will bring about a fundamental shift in the possession and ownership of family wealth. Estate planning seeks to arrange future wealth transfers to maximize financial well being, both for the client and the client's survivors. Other definitions of estate planning include the accumulation of wealth as an estate planning activity, however, this definition unrealistically broadens the subject's scope by adding investment management— another specialty of great scope, and one better left for textbooks devoted just to investment analysis. Many estate planning practitioners give little or no investment advice. Therefore, the focus of this text is estate planning as *the study of financial planning in anticipation of death.*

Planning for future wealth transfers usually requires the preparation of contracts, such as life insurance policies, and other documents including wills, trusts, deeds, and powers of attorney. These documents implement the plan by arranging, in writing, the future financial affairs of the individual.

Learning how to use these documents to plan wealth transfers requires an understanding of many law-related subjects, including the law of property, wills, trusts, future interests, estate administration, intestacy, insurance, income taxation, gift taxation, and estate taxation.

How can knowledge of such an extensive subject benefit you, the reader? In your role as a planner, you can help clients avoid the adverse consequences of inadequate planning. Here are some common situations that arise without proper planning.

EXAMPLE 1 - 1. Joanne died last week, survived by her husband and their two young daughters. Because Joanne did not write a will, the intestate laws of her state require that two-thirds of her $300,000 estate *pass to her daughters*, who will each receive the property outright from their guardian-father on their 18th birthdays. The other one-third passes to Joanne's husband, who is shocked that he is not inheriting it all and that as guardian of the daughters estate he must file annual accountings with the court. In addition to the problem of inefficient distribution, both state and federal taxes on the estate may be due—taxes which could have been minimized with advance planning.

EXAMPLE 1 - 2. Marge and Henry, parents of five-year-old twins, had done no estate planning. After they were killed in an auto accident, a court choose Marge's sister Julie as *guardian* for the twins, since the parents left no written evidence of any preference. Marge and Henry had been quite critical of how Julie and her husband were raising their own children, but had not expressed their concerns to anyone.

EXAMPLE 1 - 3. Maggie was 80 when she died leaving an estate with a net value of $300,000. Six weeks prior to her death, she gave ABC common stock worth $90,000 to her son, Charlie. Because Maggie's $14,000 basis in the stock becomes Charlie's basis, he had to pay *income tax* of over $22,000 after selling the stock for $95,000. No one told Maggie that had she kept the stock until her death, giving it to Charlie at that time, he could have sold it at little or no income tax cost because his basis would have become its date of death value.

EXAMPLE 1 - 4. Shortly before Christine died at the age of 75, her family lawyer drafted a *simple will*, leaving her wealth (estimated to be worth a net value of $500,000) to her husband Evan. Since his own estate was worth about the same as Christine's estate, Evan now realizes that as owner of all of the family wealth, his death will incur estate taxes in excess of $150,000 that could have been eliminated had Christine's will incorporated a more sophisticated estate planning device known as a *bypass trust*.

EXAMPLE 1 - 5. Suppose that, instead of receiving the property by will (as in the preceding example), Evan received it as surviving *joint tenant*. Evan's estate would be faced with the same estate tax problem at his death.

EXAMPLE 1- 6. Leslie, the founder of a highly successful real estate sales company, died last year without doing any estate planning. Her children are struggling with several problems, including how to generate sufficient *liquidity* to pay the death taxes and whether or not to sell the business, which they fear will sell for much less than its pre-death value.

EXAMPLE 1 - 7. Elmer, a wealthy man, had a severe stroke three months ago. Unable to communicate, he is hooked up to machines that keep him alive, and the doctors say his prognosis is very poor. His family realizes that they should have encouraged Elmer to consult an estate planner years ago while he was still able to express his desires. Documents could have been drafted that would have nominated a person or persons to manage his wealth in the event of his incapacity, stipulated the degree of life-sustaining medical intervention in a situation such as he is now in, and would have directed the eventual distribution of his wealth after his death. Whether the decision of the doctors and the family concerning his care, and the *laws of intestate succession* which will control distribution of his estate really match what he would have planned may never be known. In addition, if the family cannot reach agreement on treatment, a costly court battle could ensue.

EXAMPLE 1 - 8. Several years before he died, at the advice of a friend, Marty executed a revocable living trust leaving all his property to several close friends rather than to the few relatives that had been rather cool to him for years. The trust was completed by filling in the blanks of a form photocopied from the pages of a popular "how to" book. Thinking that the trust took care of his estate, Marty tore up the old will that had also left everything to the same set of friends. He did not make a new will, although a careful reading of the how-to book would have explained the importance of something called a *pour-over will*. Marty did not realize that the trust was ineffective in avoiding probate, and did not control who would receive his estate because he did not transfer his property to the trustee of the trust. Without a will, Marty's estate will be distributed to his relatives in a manner specified in his state's intestate succession laws.

EXAMPLE 1 - 9. At his death, Coldwell owned real estate in six states, including his state of residence. In addition to the *probate* in his state of domicile, there were five ancillary probates, forcing Coldwell's family to pay court filing fees and to hire probate attorneys in all six states. Had Coldwell's estate plan used a *living trust*, these probates and their associated expenses might have been avoided.

These and other problems occur because most people put off effective estate planning. Lay people have many misconceptions about estate planning because it is a fairly technical and often changing subject. Many people choose to ignore their estate planning needs because estate planning forces them to discuss matters related to their own death. Thus, estate planning requires thoughtful, sensitive encouragement from estate planning professionals.

DEVELOPING AN ESTATE PLAN

Developing an estate plan should result in a set of recommendations and related documents that skillfully allow for the best use, conservation, and transfer of the client's wealth. In 1996 the CFP Board of Standards identified the following steps in the financial planning process: (1) establishing and defining the client-planner relationship; (2) gathering client data, including goals; (3) analyzing and evaluating the client's financial status; (4) developing and presenting financial planning recommendations and/or alternatives; (5) implementing the financial planning recommendations; and (6) monitoring the financial planning recommendations.

Establishing the Client-Planner Relationship

The planner must take the lead in explaining to the client the financial planning process. Some of the issues and concepts will already be familiar to the client such as the purpose of a will, but other matters such as estate taxation or the use of trusts may be quite foreign. The role of the estate planner should be made clear and should be memorialized in an engagement letter that spells out the services to be performed. The cooperation of the client is important to building a successful plan, so the planner must make the client aware of his or her responsibilities including gathering information, working with the planner to implement a plan, and keeping the planner informed as to changes that might require modification of the plan.

Acquiring Client Facts and Goals

To make meaningful recommendations, the planner must acquire sufficient information about the client and the client's family. Essential information includes the client's financial and personal situation, and the client's objectives.
The client's financial situation and objectives. To understand the client's

financial situation, the planner will require several types of statements. First, he or she will need a current *balance sheet*, showing the fair market value of all assets and liabilities. Information on each asset should include the form in which title is held, date of acquisition, and current adjusted tax basis.

> EXAMPLE 1 - 10. Relying on the client's oral comment that she owned a parcel of investment property as an individual, an inexperienced planner didn't *examine the actual deed*. Two years after executing a will that left all property to her husband, the client died, at which time it was discovered that the parcel was held in joint tenancy with the client's niece, who became the sole owner.

For liabilities, the client should list the lender and the loan terms (maturity, payment schedule, interest rate, collateral, etc). In addition to a description of assets and liabilities, the planner will need a *cash flow statement*, describing sources of income and major categories of expenses.

The planner will also need other facts, such as information about the client's expectation of receiving significant gifts or inheritances, and the names of all the client's other advisors including their accountant, lawyer, investment broker, life underwriter, real estate agent, physician, and religious advisor. Further, the planner will need a description of the client's and the spouse's financial objectives, a self-appraisal of their ability to manage their finances, and the location of any estate planning documents such as wills.

The client's personal situation and objectives. The planner must also acquire personal nonfinancial information, including the names of all of the members of the family, their ages, their health, and their station in life (occupations, etc.).

The planner also needs an understanding of the client's personal objectives, especially with regard to dispositive preferences for the spouse and the children before and at the client's death, as well as any interests in charitable donations.

Many planners, often with the help of financial institutions, develop customized questionnaires and checklists to help them acquire this information as efficiently as possible. An example of a questionnaire can be found in Appendix 1A at the end of this chapter.

In addition to using the checklist, the planner should routinely examine existing documents, such as the will and evidence of title to property. Too often, checklist information is inaccurate, as Example 1 - 10 illustrated.

Analyzing and Evaluating the Client's Financial Status

After acquiring the necessary facts, the planner will review the facts and prepare a plan incorporating preliminary recommendations and, where appropriate, alternatives. The most common recommendations fall into two areas: financial planning for property transfers, and personal planning for the client's incapacity and death.

Developing and Presenting Recommendations and/or Alternatives

Financial planning for property transfers. The major purpose of the plan is to efficiently distribute the client's wealth to the proper persons, in the proper amount, and at the proper time. To do this, the planner must keep in mind the following considerations that relate to more specific estate planning goals:

- Deciding whether or not to *avoid probate* as a means of transferring property at the death of the client;
- Examining alternatives to reduce and possibly eliminate *transfer taxes* at the death of the client and the client's spouse;
- Considering *lifetime transfers*, partly to reduce transfer costs and partly to shift taxable income to a lower tax bracket;
- Arranging to provide the *liquidity* needed at the client's disability or death;
- Devising a strategy to unwind the client's *business affairs* in a manner which can maintain the greatest income and value for the survivors.

Personal planning for incapacity and death. The major areas in personal planning for client incapacity and death include arranging for someone to care for the client and the client's property at the onset of incompetence, and arranging for someone to care for the client's children if both parents die or become incapacitated before the children reach adulthood.

Because this text is primarily devoted to these and other objectives and techniques, further explanation will be covered in subsequent chapters.

Implementing the Plan

After the specifics of a plan are agreed upon, the planner and client should move to implement it. Transfer documents are drafted by the attorney and executed by the client. An insurance agent may be needed to secure the appropriate insurance contracts. If a trust is included in the plan and the client wants a bank trust-department named either as initial trustee or as a successor trustee, one of the bank trust officers should be contacted for authorization and advice before the trust document is completed. The client should feel comfortable with the bank's trust-department's management style, including how it interacts with trust beneficiaries and its investment philosophy.

Clients "execute" a document by completing it; that is, doing what is necessary to render it valid. For example, execution of a will normally requires, among other things, that the client sign the will in the presence of witnesses, (who also sign), attesting to the authenticity of the client's signature.

Monitoring the Financial Planning Recommendations

An indispensable part of the estate planning process is following up. Since laws change, the client's personal situation and objectives may change. By keeping up-to-date, the planner can periodically suggest appropriate revisions to the plan. Events which are likely to require plan revision include marriage, divorce, birth of a child, new legislation, and new court decisions.

For example, in 1981, Congress made many significant changes in federal transfer taxation law. One major change involved the taxation of property passing at death to a surviving spouse. Prior to the change, wills and trusts of wealthy individuals were likely to contain a provision that had the effect of passing to the surviving spouse only half of the decedent's estate, because that was the maximum amount that qualified for the marital deduction. However, under the new law, the maximum amount was increased to allow the client's *entire* estate to qualify for the marital deduction. Concerned that many clients whose estate plans incorporated such a provision might not want to leave their entire estate to their spouse, Congress included a transition rule that had the effect of limiting, for most estates, the transfer to the surviving spouse of half of the decedent's estate if the plan used words like "I leave to my spouse the maximum amount that qualifies for the marital deduction." The 100% marital deduction became available to those who revised their plans after the law changed, and those people living (dying) in states that passed legislation that said "maximum marital deduction" clauses in estate plans should be interpreted to mean the maximum under the new federal law. Thus, most transfer documents had to be revised to take advantage of the new, more beneficial tax provisions; most planners contacted all of their affected clients to make the necessary changes.

For a discussion of the use of disclaimers and post-mortem tax planning techniques to remedy this problem for clients who died without revising their pre-ERTA estate plans, see Chapter 18.

THE ESTATE PLANNING TEAM

Generally, estate planning is not conducted by just one professional; the job requires the diverse knowledge and skills of a number of practitioners including attorneys, accountants, life underwriters, trust officers, and financial planners. These professionals are referred to as the *estate planning team*. Next, we describe the unique contribution each team member makes to the overall planning process.

Attorney

In most states the only professional who may legally accept payment for drafting estate planning documents and rendering legal advice is an attorney. This makes the attorney an indispensable team member in the estate planning process. Document preparation requires the ability to make precise legal distinctions. Many years may pass before these documents become the final authority—and will generally be taken as the literal expression of the clients estate planning objectives. Thus, by putting an estate plan in print, the attorney places his or her professional reputation on the line for all to see, criticize, and even second guess.

Most attorneys accept the responsibility of coordinating the actions of the other members of the estate planning team. This is especially common among lawyers specializing in estate planning and taxation.

The attorney's role might not end at the client's death. He or she may be hired to advise the executor of the deceased client's estate or the trustee; that is, to complete the process involving the legal transfer of the client's assets to surviving beneficiaries. In addition, the attorney may engage in postmortem tax planning, a job which, as we shall see in Chapter 18, entails choosing certain tax options available after the client's death and, if necessary, preparation of estate tax returns.

Accountant

By preparing the client's financial statements and tax returns, the accountant is often the professional having the earliest and most frequent contact with the client. Typically, these forms are so financially revealing to accountants that financial planners have described them as the client's "personal annual business report."

The accountant is often able to spot specific financial problems requiring attention, especially with regard to the client's business interests. Perhaps the accountants most important service to the client, insofar as estate planning is concerned, is in encouraging the client to enter into the estate planning process. Once the process begins it is generally the duty of the accountant to prepare the client's financial balance sheet and cash flow statement. After the client's death, the accountant may be called on to complete any necessary income tax and death tax returns.

Life Underwriter

The life underwriter's crucial role is to provide insurance contracts to meet liquidity requirements expected to arise at the client's disability or death. The efficient use of life insurance requires an understanding of estate planning because proper planning will minimize transfer costs and provide an appropriate level of financial support for the client's surviving beneficiaries.

As an active solicitor, the life underwriter is often the first professional to recommend estate planning to the client, and may therefore be in a position to select the other members of the client's estate planning team.

Trust Officer

A skilled professional executor and trustee, the trust officer performs fiduciary services for clients and estates. A *fiduciary* is a person having a legal duty to act for the benefit of another. (See Chapter 2 for a further discussion.)

If selected to serve as the *executor* of the client's estate, the trust officer manages assets that are transferred through the probate process. Similarly, if selected to serve as *trustee* of a trust created by the client, the trust officer manages those assets placed in the trust. Thus, the trust officer can be particularly helpful in the planning stage by offering advice in the area of planning for long term management of assets, and by advising as to what parameters have been set by the trust department with regards to the trusts or estates it is willing to handle. Some bank trust-departments will not accept a fiduciary position for estates below a certain size, such as those below $300,000, or may be reluctant to serve as trustee if too much supervision of a beneficiary is expected.

> EXAMPLE 1 - 12. Without consulting the trust department, Martha's trust named her local bank to serve as successor trustee of her living trust. After her death, the trust was to provide income for the life of her son, Curtis, and after his death be distributed to his issue (children, grandchildren, etc.) if any, otherwise it would be distributed to Martha's brother William, or William's issue. Because Curtis had a long history of substance abuse, the trust had a clause that required the trustee withhold distribution of income if Curtis failed to stay free of drugs and alcohol. It also allowed the trustee to distribute *trust corpus* (trust principle) if the trustee thought it would contribute to Curtis' well-being. When Martha died, Curtis was 50, unemployed, and childless. The bank refused to serve as trustee because it did not want the responsibility of deciding when and whether to distribute income and corpus to Curtis. *** *Query 1. What risk would the bank take if it accepted the job of trustee?*

Financial Planner

The financial planner is the newest member of the estate planning team. As the professional with the greatest potential of being in the position of recommending an integrated financial plan that includes recommendations concerning insurance, investments, retirement planning, and income tax planning, as well as estate planning, he or she may serve as the team captain, coordinating the work of the others. The financial planner does not, however, draft the legal documents. As stated earlier, in most states only an attorney is legally permitted to accept payment for doing that. As the profession matures, it is expected that the financial planner's role will increase.

THE NEED TO ENCOURAGE PLANNING

Many individuals need estate planning but fail to seek it. Many simply ignore issues involving their own death, refusing to face the fact that they could die soon, and that all of us must die someday. Others are so busy pursuing their careers that they do not make time for planning. Still others lead lives that seem too unsettled to undertake long-range planning. Finally, some fear the family conflicts and expenses that may arise at death as a result of their planning—unaware that good planning is likely to minimize the potential problems.

For these reasons, members of the estate planning team should actively encourage individuals to plan their estates. As mentioned earlier, good planning will help dispose of assets fairly, minimize taxes and expenses at death, provide for the care of disabled family members, generate sufficient liquidity, provide for continued income for dependent survivors, and arrange for efficient business succession.

Next, we turn to the organization of this text.

ORGANIZATION OF THE BOOK

This book is divided into three parts. Part 1 includes this introductory chapter and Chapter 2, which introduces the major concepts that will be used throughout the text. It describes the basic concepts of estate planning and defines many estate planning terms, such as *fee simple, life estate, remainder, probate, trust, irrevocable*, and *insured*.

Part 2 (Chapters 3 to 8) provides a more detailed background knowledge required to understand the techniques of estate planning. It introduces the constraints in planning, and the basic principles of tax and property law on which estate planning rests.

Chapter 3 explores the rudimentary contents of wills and trusts, the two major documents of property transfer. Sample forms illustrating the simple will, living trust, and trust-will are examined to give the reader an early concrete awareness of the focus of planning.

Chapter 4 explains how property is actually transferred and features the probate process. Included are discussions of supervised probate, probate alternatives in states adopting the Uniform Probate Code, and some examples of summary probate.

Chapter 5 introduces federal wealth transfer taxation, describing the computation of both the gift tax and the estate tax. It also discusses death taxes imposed by states, and the computation of the federal state death tax credit. Since basis in property is determined by how the owner acquired the property, the rules for determining basis are discussed.

Continuing the material on wealth transfer taxation, Chapter 6 contains a thorough examination of the federal estate tax, exploring three major areas: components of the gross estate, estate tax deductions, and estate tax credits.

Chapter 7 covers the federal gift tax and the basis rules. It also introduces the special valuation rules under Internal Revenue Code §2701-§2704 and the generation-skipping transfer tax.

Chapter 8 is an introduction to the federal income taxation of estates, trusts, and their beneficiaries.

Part 3 utilizes the material in Parts 1 and 2 to survey the actual techniques used in planning. It begins with Chapter 9's survey of the principal goals of estate planning. Examples include minimizing the costs of the property transfer process, shifting taxable income to lower bracket taxpayers, and reducing and/or freezing the taxable estate.

Chapter 10 examines the decision whether to have one's estate avoid probate, and to consider the probate alternatives, including the revocable living trust which seems to be growing in popularity.

Chapters 11 and 12 focus on planning for those transfers at death that can defer, completely eliminate, or reduce a wealthy client's death taxes. The emphasis here is on estate planning for wealthy married couples. We will see that the major transfer strategies incorporate the estate tax marital deduction and the bypass trust. We will also explore techniques used to avoid or lessen the impact of the generation-skipping transfer tax.

Chapters 13 and 14 explore various aspects of planning lifetime transfers. Chapter 13's discussion of gift planning shows that, although gifts can save both income and transfer taxes, the requirement of relinquishment of control over the assets given causes many clients to choose other forms of property transfers. Chapter 14 describes lifetime transfers where the donor retains some control over the gift property and lifetime transfers where the donor receives some consideration in exchange. The chapter also covers charitable transfers. An Appendix to Chapter 14 summarizes several once popular lifetime transfers, such as the short-term trust, that have lost their appeal due to changes in the tax law.

It also describes some dubious estate planning devices.

Chapter 15 assesses common methods of providing the client's estate with adequate liquidity to fund expenses that are associated with dying, such as death taxes and the cost of transferring property. Topics include sale of assets before death, life insurance, liquidity planning devices unique to business owners, and valuation discounts.

Chapter 16 explores the principles of planning for closely held business interests. Their owners have special estate planning problems, including maintaining sufficient income after withdrawing from the business, and transferring to their chosen beneficiaries the maximum value attributable to that business. In addition to an extended discussion of these problems, the chapter covers several specific techniques, including sale of the business during the owner's lifetime, the business buy-out, family limited partnerships, limited liability companies, and business estate freeze techniques.

Chapter 17 covers miscellaneous techniques that estate planners routinely employ, including providing for minor children, selecting a trustee, planning for nontraditional relationships, and planning for the client's incapacity through the use of durable powers of attorney.

Chapter 18 examines the principles of post-mortem tax planning, showing that income tax and estate tax planning occurs even after the client's death. Major topics include decisions related to expense deduction elections, disclaimers, and marital deduction planning.

Finally, Chapter 19 presents a hypothetical estate planning case study, with questions for review. The case appeared in one of the early certification examinations of the Certified Financial Planner (CFP) Board of Standards. It was then released as an educational aid. The chapter concludes with the estate planning portion of the CFP's Job Knowledge Requirements (often referred to as the topics list) as determined by the Board of Standards 1994 jobs-analysis survey.

QUERIES ANSWERED:

1. The bank's risk is that if it doesn't monitor Curtis properly, and wrongly makes distributions while he is having drug problems, it might be sued by Curtis for allowing his condition to worsen, it might be sued by someone injured by Curtis, or by the remaindermen whose remainder interests are

diminished. Although the likely success of such suits may be low, and the cost of defending the suits will probably be chargeable to the trust, most trust-departments would rather not take on a trust where its terms greatly increase the likelihood of a law suit.

QUESTIONS AND PROBLEMS

1. At a dinner party, one of your clients asks you what estate planning entails. Define estate planning for her, and name the areas of the law embraced by it.

2. A man comes into your office to inquire about your services. You find out that he owns a closely held business and has a wife and two young children. He has not yet done any estate planning. Explain briefly how failure to plan could lead to adverse consequences.

3. Fill in the questionnaire in Appendix 1A with information about yourself. Which items are likely to be the most difficult to complete? Why?

4. Outline the steps required to develop an estate plan.

5. Explain the unique contribution made by each member of the estate planning team.

ANSWERS TO QUESTIONS AND PROBLEMS

1. Estate planning is the study of the principles of planning for the use, conservation, and efficient transfer of an individual's wealth. It embraces the law of property, wills, trusts, future interests, estate administration, intestacy, insurance, income taxation, gift taxation, and death taxation.

2. Examples of how failure to plan could lead to adverse consequences include the following:

   a. Premature death of husband and wife in a common accident resulting in the court appointing an undesirable parental guardian for the children.

   b. Inability to sell the business after the premature death of the owner.

   Please refer to examples 1-1 through 1-8 for common illustrations of the failure to plan.

3. Items in the questionnaire probably most difficult to acquire include how title to property is actually held, correct fair market values, and the composition of employee benefit plans. Individuals with minor children often find it difficult to choose a personal guardian.

4. Steps required in developing an estate plan: The following is taken from the CFP Board of Standards definition of the financial planning process adopted 9/14/96:

   i. Establishing and defining the client-planner relationship;
   ii. Gathering client data including goals;
   iii. Analyzing and evaluating the client's financial status;
   iv. Developing and presenting financial planning recommendations and/or alternatives;
   v. Implementing the financial planning recommendations; and
   vi. Monitoring the financial planning recommendations.

5. Unique contribution made by each member of the estate planning team:

a. Attorney: drafting legal documents.

b. Accountant: preparing the client's financial statements and tax returns often gives her or him the greatest and earliest financial contact with the client.

c. Life Underwriter: providing insurance contracts to meet liquidity needs at the client's death.

d. Trust Officer: as an experienced trustee and executor, capable of providing fiduciary services and advice.

e. Financial Planner: potentially capable of creating a complete financial plan, one including recommendations concerning insurance, investments, retirement planning, income tax planning and estate planning.

Sample Client Fact-Finding Questionnaire

Susan R. Goodall
5556 Long Street, Suite 245
Anytown, ST 54321
888/555-3456

DATE SHEET FOR ESTATE PLAN
Married Persons
(With Minor Children)

Please print or type the following information. If you need more space, use reverse side (include number of question). If you are not certain about an answer, put a question mark. If you have questions, write them down at the end of this data sheet.

1. Husband (H) full name _____
    Name used on real estate documents _____
    Other or former names _____
    Wife (W) full name _____
    Name used on real estate documents _____
    Other or former names _____

2. a. Residents of _____ County.
    b. Address _____
        _____
    c. Home phone # _____   Business # _____

3. Date of Birth: (H) _____ (W) _____
   Place of Birth: (H) _____ (W) _____
   Date of Marriage: _____ Place: _____
   Approximate date moved to California (H) _____ (W) _____
   Social Security #: (H) _____ (W) _____
   Occupation: (H) _____
               (W) _____

4. FAMILY:
   a. Children of this marriage:

Name	Birth date	Residence (If still living with you, put "Home"
_____	_____	_____
_____	_____	_____
_____	_____	_____

   b. Are there children by prior marriage? Yes/no. If yes, please give full information below:

Name	Birth date	Residence (If still living with you, put "Home"
_____	_____	_____
_____	_____	_____
_____	_____	_____

   c. If there are deceased children who left issue, please give information below:

   _____
   _____

   d. Living parents (names/addresses):
   (H) _____
        _____
   (W) _____
        _____

e. Brothers and Sisters (names/addresses):

(H) _____

_____

(W)_____

_____

f. Should you or your children adopt a child (or children)should they inherit on the same basis as natural children and/or grandchildren? _____

5. Friends to whom you intend to leave bequests (names/addresses):

a. _____

b. _____

6. Estate information (to nearest $10,000)

a. The <u>net</u> value of our assets is approximately $ _____.

b. Our three major assets and their approximate <u>net</u> values are:

(1) _____ (value $_____)

(2) _____ (value $_____)

(3) _____ (value $_____)

7. How is title to your property actually held? Bring title documents with you when you come to see me.

8. Give the following information about your life insurance.

Whose Life? H or W	Company/ Policy No.	Owner H/W/Both	Beneficiary & 1st Alternate	Amount
____	____	____	_____	____
____	____	____	_____	____
____	____	____	_____	____
____	____	____	_____	____

9. Have you entered into a community property agreement? Yes/no
Have you entered into a prenuptial or postnuptial agreement? Yes/no

10. Distribution. Put your thoughts in general terms at part (b). We will discuss details at the time of interview.

    a. Specific gifts (show gift, i.e., heirlooms/money, etc. and the beneficiaries name and address).

        1. _____
           _____
        2. _____
           _____
        3. _____
           _____
        4. _____
           _____

        For specific gifts, indicate which alternative:
        1st alternative: Property left free and clear _____
        2 nd alternative: Property left with encumbrances _____

    b. Residue (1st) _____
        _____
        (2 nd) (if people in 1 predecease me) _____
        _____
        (3 rd) (if people in 1 & 2 predecease me) _____
        _____

11. Please circle the answer to the following questions. (If yes, give details and, if appropriate, approximate values on reverse side)

    a. Have you made gifts of more than $3,000 prior to 1982, or $10,000 after 1981, in any one year to anyone? (H)Yes/no (W) Yes/no

    b. Do either of you expect to inherit or receive gifts totaling in excess of $100,000 from your parents and/or from others?
        (H) Yes/no (W) Yes/no   If yes, we should discuss.

    c. Do you have powers of appointment? (H) Yes/no (W) Yes/no

   d. Do you have Wills already drawn? (H) Yes/no (W) Yes/no
      (If yes, attach a copy of it to this Data Sheet).

12. If a Trust is contemplated: Proposed Trustee (give the relationship, name and address if not already listed):
    1st choice: _____
    2 nd choice: _____
    3 rd choice: _____

13. Proposed Guardian (relationship/name/address if not already listed):
    1st choice: _____
    2 nd choice: _____
    3 rd choice: _____

14. Proposed Executor (relationship/name/address if not already listed):
    (H) 1st choice: _____
        2 nd choice: _____
        3 rd choice: _____

    (W)1st choice: _____
        2 nd choice: _____
        3 rd choice: _____

15. Are specific burial instructions available to the executor? If yes, explain:
    (H) _____
    (W) _____

16. Do you have a safe deposit box? Yes/No
    a. Where? _____
    b. Who has access? H ____ W ____ Other _____

17. Where shall the original of the Will be kept? (check one)
    a. Client's (your) safe deposit box _____
    b. Other place _____ Where _____

18. How many photocopies of each Will do you want, i.e., in addition to the original? H _____ W _____ (Giving a copy to your executor is optional)

19. Questions to ask attorney:

    a. _____
       _____
    b. _____
       _____
    c. _____
       _____
    d. _____
       _____

Survey of the Basic Concepts of Estate Planning

OVERVIEW

This chapter introduces many basic concepts regularly employed in estate planning. Because they will be referred to throughout the text, the reader is advised to study them carefully. Some of these concepts are so straightforward that mere use of them in a sentence will make their meaning clear. More involved terms are defined and illustrated. These terms, along with others introduced in later chapters, are included in the Glossary at the end of this book.

The discussion of these terms is tied to the various estate planning areas with which they are most likely to be associated even though there is considerable overlap.

CONCEPTS DEALING WITH ESTATES

An *estate* is a quantity of wealth or property. *Property* represents things or objects over which the owner may lawfully exercise the right to use, control, or dispose. More simply, property is anything that can be owned.

Ordinarily, for a person or for a family, an estate represents the total amount of property owned. However, the word *estate* is often used in several other contexts in estate planning to mean some other amount. First, in certain situations, estate means the *net* value of property owned, calculated by subtracting the amount of the estate owner's liabilities from the value of all property owned. Second, estate can be limited to the *probate estate*, which constitutes all of the property that passes to others by means of the probate process after the death of the owner. Third, estate may mean the *gross estate* or the *taxable estate*, two concepts used only in connection to taxation at death. As we will see later, the probate estate and the tax-related estate may be very different in size and composition. The net estate and the probate estate are generally less than all property owned; the net estate because liabilities are subtracted; and the probate estate because many things owned, such as those held in joint tenancy and life insurance, pass outside the probate process. The gross estate is likely to equal or exceed the value of all property owned because it includes all things owned, but may also include things that are not owned, such as vested interests in trusts. In Chapter 6 we will cover the concept of the gross estate and of the taxable estate in detail.

CONCEPTS DEALING WITH TRANSFERS OF PROPERTY

One of the primary areas of emphasis in estate planning is on how property is transferred. This section will cover the terminology used in this area.

Transfers of Legal, Beneficial, or Legal and Beneficial Interests

A *transfer* or *assignment* of property refers to any type of passing of property in which the *transferor* gives up an *interest* to the *transferee*. The interest transferred can be purely legal, purely beneficial, or both legal and beneficial. *Legal interest* refers to a situation where title passes. For example, the typical trustee of a trust receives title alone, to be able to manage property but not to enjoy it. Another example of someone with a purely legal interest is a stockbroker holding customer shares in street name. The customer, of course, owns the beneficial interest.

On the other hand, a purely *beneficial interest* occurs when the transferee receives something that carries an economic benefit, but not title. Examples of beneficial interest in property include the temporary or permanent right to possess, consume, pledge or otherwise benefit from property. As we shall see, a trust beneficiary's rights are purely beneficial.

Finally, an interest given up by the transferor can be both legal and beneficial, such as where the transferee receives both title and the beneficial interest. An *outright transfer* occurs when one transferee receives both legal and beneficial interests, without restrictions or conditions, as typically happens when one person gives another a birthday present.

Complete Versus Incomplete Transfers; Property in General Versus a Specific Property Interest

Complete versus incomplete transfers: overview. Speaking generally, a transfer of property is said to be *complete* and *irrevocable* when it is no longer rescindable or amendable, (i.e., when the transferor has totally relinquished all dominion and control over that property). For example, after purchasing this book, at the expiration of the returns period, you made a completed transfer of money. On the other hand, a transfer is said to be *incomplete* and *revocable* while it is still rescindable or amendable, (i.e., made without total relinquishment of dominion and control over that property).

Property in general versus an interest in property. To fully distinguish between complete and incomplete transfers, one must grasp the difference between property in general and a specific interest in property. *Property in general*, such as 100 shares of ABC stock, means the entire asset, whether physical or intangible, including all rights and interests that go with ownership. In contrast, an *interest in property* means one or more rights to property, such as the right to the first five years of dividends from the 100 shares of ABC stock.

In estate planning, more than one interest in a given item of property may be transferred in a way that highlights the divisibility of the bundle of interests associated with property ownership.

> EXAMPLE 2 - 1. Tom transfers 100 shares of stock in trust, giving Alan the right to receive all income for five years, followed by Barbara having the right to receive income for ten years, and finally, after 15 years, the trust is to terminate with the trust assets distributed to Carl. Each has received an "interest" in the stock. We'll take a more detailed look at trusts later in the chapter.

Complete, incomplete, and partially complete transfers. A transfer of each specific interest in property is either complete or incomplete, while the transfer of more than one interest can be either *totally complete, partially complete, or totally incomplete.* Continuing with the same facts as above, if Tom retained the right in general to revoke or amend the trust, Tom's transfers of Alan's, Barbara's and Carl's specific interests would each be incomplete, and Tom's transfer of the stock in general would be totally incomplete. On the other hand, if T retained the right to revoke or amend only Alan's interest, the transfer of Alan's interest would be incomplete, the transfer of Barbara's and Carl's interests would be complete, and Tom's overall transfer of the stock would be said to be partially complete. Finally, if Tom retained no rights whatsoever over the stock, the transfers of interest to Alan, Barbara, and Carl would all be complete, as would be the transfer of stock in general. As we shall see when we study gift taxes, this issue is important because gift tax law treats complete transfers of specific interests as gifts subject to gift taxation.

Sale Versus Gift

Most commonly, completed transfers of property interests are undertaken by sale, by gift, or by a combination of both sale and gift. A *sale* is a transfer of property under which each transferor exchanges *consideration* that is regarded as equivalent in value. By contrast, a gift is generally thought to be a transfer of property for which the transferor receives nothing of economic value in exchange. The most common methods of making gift transfers are *outright* and *in trust*.

A Bargain sale is a gift. A bargain sale occurs when a person (the transferor) transfers property in exchange for property with an economic value to the transferor that the transferor knows is less than the worth of the property he or she is giving up. A bargain sale involves a transfer that is part sale and part gift. The notion of the bargain sale requires us to define a gift somewhat more broadly than in the last paragraph. While the above idea of a gift (something given with nothing given in return) is probably the most common type of gift, it must be recognized that a bargain sale is also a gift, even though property is received in exchange. Federal tax law treats the actual amount of the gift as the difference between the respective values of the consideration exchanged. Thus, a transfer during the life of the transferor will be either a gift or a sale, with a gift defined to include a *bargain sale*: (i.e., an exchange of considerations of unequal value, where the parties know and intend it to be unequal).

Inter Vivos Transfer Versus Transfer at Death

A transfer of property can be *inter vivos*, meaning that it is made while the transferor is alive, or it can be made at death. Inter vivos is Latin for "among the living." Transfers at death may be made pursuant to a valid document, also called an *instrument*, prepared by the owner before death (e.g., will, trust, title by joint tenancy, or insurance beneficiary designation), or pursuant to state law (intestate succession) in the event that no such document exists.

Fair Market Value of Transfer

The value of a transfer is measured by its fair market value at the time of the transfer. Determining fair market value is the subject of several sections in the text. A generally accepted definition of *fair market value* is, "the price at which the property would change hands between a willing buyer and a willing seller, neither being under any compulsion to buy or to sell and both having reasonable knowledge of the relevant facts." The IRS uses this definition in the regulations for valuing estates and gifts.[1]

BENEFICIARIES

A *beneficiary* or *donee*, is a person who receives or will receive a gift of a beneficial interest in property from a transferor, who is also known as a *donor*. Although in the most general sense, donee and beneficiary are synonymous, in certain contexts one or the other term is used more commonly. For example, the recipient of an outright *inter vivos* gift from the donor is usually called a donee. On the other hand, the recipient of a bequest by a will or an interest in a trust, whether the trust was created *inter vivos* or funded at death (see following section), is usually called a beneficiary. Occasionally, the term *donee* is used to describe one who has received something without also receiving any beneficial interest, such as where one is given a limited power of appointment, an estate planning tool discussed later.

WILLS, TRUSTS, AND PROBATE

In estate planning, a *decedent* is a person who has died. When a person dies, property owned by the decedent must be transferred. Each state takes special interest in ensuring that all property owned by the decedent is transferred to the proper parties. States accomplish this in two basic ways. First, state law recognizes certain documents prepared by the decedent (wills, trusts, joint tenancy arrangements, life insurance policies, etc.) as valid legally binding guides for the proper disposition of the decedent's property. A *will* is a written document that expresses a person (*the testator*)'s desired distribution of his or her property at death. The will is said to make *testamentary* transfers, however the actual process by which transfer is accomplished is the probate process. The will controls only property for which there is no superior mechanism of transfer. Thus, the will controls property in the decedent's name alone but not property held in trust, nor that held in joint tenancy.

A trust is "a fiduciary relationship in which one person (the trustee) is the holder of the title to property (the trust estate or the trust corpus), subject to an equitable obligation to keep or use the property for the benefit of another (the beneficiary)." The *trust instrument* is the written agreement between the settlor (also called the trustor) and the trustee that sets forth for whose benefit the trust is created, how the trust estate is to be managed, its duration, and to whom the corpus must be given when the trust terminates. Trusts are described in greater detail later in the chapter.

Intestate, testate, and partially intestate. If a valid will is found, the decedent is said to have died *testate*. If the document does not dispose of all of the decedent's property, the decedent is said to have died *partially intestate*. If no will is found, the decedent is said to have died *intestate*. However, if all of the decedent's property is disposed of by alternative means, (e.g., trusts, joint tenancy), a will may not be necessary, and the absence of a will would not cause any problems as there would be no property subject to its control.

In some cases, the moment that death occurs may have some significance because it might determine the rights of beneficiaries and/or the liabilities of the estate. The Uniform Determination of Death Act, adopted in at least 15 states, addresses this issue by defining death as occurring when the person is brain dead, meaning the absence of brain waves, as well as "cessation of circulatory and respiratory functions."

Probate and the personal representative. *Probate* is the legal process of administering the estate of a decedent. The probate estate consists of all property belonging to the decedent for which there is no other mechanism of transfer. Thus, the probate estate is that property whose disposition is guided by either the decedent's will or by the state laws of intestate succession. Typical *probate assets* fall into one of three groups: property owned by the decedent as an individual, interests of the decedent held with others as "tenants-in-common," and, in some community property states, the decedent's one half interest in community property. Some community property states, such as California, no longer require a probate for property going to the surviving spouse whether that property is the decedent's half of the community property or is the decedent's separate property. *Non-probate assets* include property held in trusts and in joint tenancy, most insurance policies on the life of the decedent (unless payable to his or her estate), and most retirement plan assets. Many of these terms will be described later in the chapter.

Essentially, in probate administration, the governmental unit, often the county court, determines the validity of the will, if any, and authorizes distribution of the probate estate to creditors and beneficiaries. The court appoints a *personal representative* to act as fiduciary to represent and manage the probate estate. If the court appoints the person nominated in the will to be personal representative, that person is called the *executor*. In some states, a female personal representative is called an *executrix*, however the trend is to use the term executor to refer to either gender. An *administrator* is a person appointed by the court to represent the estate of a person who died intestate or where the court appoints someone other than the persons nominated in the will. The person nominated may have predeceased the testator or may be incapacitated, or perhaps is unfit, (e.g., is serving time in prison for bank robbery). If the decedent died testate but the court appoints someone other the person nominated in the will, once the will is admitted for probate, the personal representative is called an *administrator with will annexed*.

The word fiduciary is derived from the Latin word for "trust." A *fiduciary* is a person in a position of trust, loyalty, and confidence, who has the legal duty to act for the benefit of another, putting that other person's interests above his or her own. Besides personal representatives, fiduciaries include trustees, guardians, and agents.

Recipients of probate property. Beneficiaries of a decedent's probate property are called heirs, devisees, or legatees. An *heir* is a person who inherits property from a decedent whether by will, intestate succession, or any other mechanism of transfer such as through a trust or by joint tenancy. *Heir at law* refers to the person (or persons) who have a right to an intestate decedent's property. A *devisee* is a beneficiary, under a will, of a gift of real property. A devisee is said to receive a *devise*. A *legatee* is a beneficiary, under a will, of a gift of personal property. A legatee is said to receive a *legacy* or a *bequest*. The trend in modern usage is to use the term bequest for any testamentary gift, whether of real or personal property. The Uniform Probate Code, discussed in the next chapter, uses the term "devise" both as a noun and a verb, to mean a bequest or the act of making a bequest (in the broad sense) in connection with transfers by will.

Issue refers to a person's offspring or progeny, including children, grandchildren, great-grandchildren and the like. A descendant is one who is descended from a specific ancestor (i.e., an offspring). Thus, the terms issue and descendants are used interchangeably. Most state succession statutes treat adopted children as though naturally born to their adoptive parents, this is usually accomplished by defining them as included in the issue of the adoptive parent. Degrees of blood relationship, which are important in determining heirs at law, will be covered in Chapter 4.

Types of bequests. Bequests are categorized as specific, pecuniary, general, residuary and/or class gifts. A *specific bequest* is a gift of a particular item of property which is capable of being identified and distinguished from all other property in the testator's estate (e.g., "I leave all my household furnishings to Sally Ann," and "I leave my high school ring to my brother Bill.") If the property subject to a specific bequest is sold, given away, or lost before the testator's death, under the common law doctrine of *ademption* (from the Latin *ademption* - a taking away) the bequest fails, meaning that the person does not receive anything to replace the missing property. Although most states follow the common law doctrine, some state's statutes have exceptions that do not result in ademption in certain circumstances (e.g., an asset was acquired by the decedent in a manner that made it clear that it was intended to replace property, specifically, devised real or tangible property).[2] A *general bequest* is a gift payable out of the general assets of the estate, but not one that specifies one or more particular items. For example, the bequest "I leave ten percent of my estate to..." is a general bequest because it can be paid from more than one asset.

At common law the term *legacy* meant a testamentary gift of money, however, it has come to mean any bequest. *Pecuniary bequest* is the term used to describe a bequest expressed as a specific dollar amount. It is called a pecuniary bequest even though the executor has the option of satisfying it with cash or with assets worth the specified dollar amount. Since the bequest could be paid from any account, or could come from assets sold by the executor, a pecuniary bequest is a type of general bequest. Pecuniary bequests are commonly found in complex estate plans aimed at minimizing death taxes. The bequest is likely to be expressed in terms of a *formula*, such as "I leave to my spouse the least amount needed to reduce my death taxes to zero." A pecuniary bequest is distinguished from a *fractional share bequest*, which uses fractions (or percentages) in defining the interests of beneficiaries to certain property or to a portion of the estate (e.g., "I leave 65 percent of the residue of my estate to my sister Gladys, and the other 35 percent to my brother Marco.")

What remains after all bequests are taken into account is called the *residue* of the estate. A *residuary bequest* is a gift of that part of the testator's estate not otherwise disposed of by the will (e.g., "I leave the rest of my estate to Robert Moon.") Generally, debts are paid out of the residue and not charged against the specific bequests.

A *class gift* is a gift to a group of individuals that may not be completely defined at the time the gift is made (e.g., "I leave the residue of my estate to my grandchildren living at the time of my death.")

Occasionally, a testator dies leaving insufficient assets to satisfy all bequests and pay all creditors. Under the procedure called *abatement*, bequests are eliminated or reduced so that all debts (and administration expenses) are paid in full, or else the estate is exhausted. In those states that follow the Uniform Probate Code (UPC), shares of the beneficiaries abate in the following order: (1) probate property not disposed of in the will, (2) residuary bequests, (3) general bequests, and (4) specific bequests. Some state statutes abate gifts to a spouse or to issue only after abatement of gifts to persons not related to the decedent.

EXAMPLE 2 - 2. Lawrence died in a UPC state. Lawrence's will leaves his car to his son, Sam, $20,000 cash to his daughter, and the residue of his estate to his wife. Assume that at his death Lawrence owned only the car and $10,000 cash, and he owed $6,000 in debts. In many states abatement would require paying the $6,000 debt in full, with nothing to his wife, $4,000 cash to his daughter, and the car to his son.

Disclaimer

Most people would welcome a large bequest, especially if it came from a distant relative. After all, such gifts should make for financial security. Yet there are times when it makes sense for a beneficiary to refuse a gift or bequest. Disclaiming may be preferable, such as when it avoids, reduces, or delays transfer taxes. Usually, a person will disclaim property only if it will then pass to a person the disclaimant wants to have it.

A *disclaimer* is an unqualified refusal to accept a gift. To be *tax-effective,* it must meet the requirements of both state property law and federal tax law. Under property law, a disclaimant is treated as having *predeceased* the decedent-donor. Consequently, the disclaimed property will pass under one of two possible sets of legal guidelines. Either it will pass to the "alternate taker" in accordance with the terms of the decedent's transfer document (which is usually the will or trust) or, if no such document exists or if the document does not name an alternate taker, the property will pass under laws of intestacy.

EXAMPLE 2 - 3. Barry died recently, and his twenty year old will left Barry's valuable super bowl ring to his football loving father-in-law, Bob, and the residue of his estate to his grandson Mike. Bob, age 87 and in poor health, validly disclaims the ring, which will instead pass under the will to Mike.

EXAMPLE 2 - 4. Changing the facts in the previous example a bit, assume Barry's will did not have a residuary clause, that is, the residue of his property was not disposed of in the will. The ring will pass under the state's laws of intestacy.

A disclaimer is considered to be tax-effective if it avoids being treated as a gift by the disclaimant. It will be considered tax-effective if it complies with requirements set forth at IRC §2518. When we take up estate and gift taxes we will cover in detail the requirements for a tax-effective disclaimer, and in later chapters, we will illustrate ways in which disclaimers can be used to correct some inefficient or obsolete estate plans.

LIFE INSURANCE

A *life insurance* policy is a contract in which the insurance company, in exchange for the payment of premiums, agrees to pay a cash lump-sum amount (called the *face value* or *policy proceeds*) to a person designated in the policy to receive it (the *beneficiary*) upon the death of the subject of the insurance (the *insured*). Usually, the policy names alternate beneficiaries who will receive the proceeds if the named beneficiary dies. One other important party in the life insurance contract is the *owner*, who has title to the policy, and who generally possesses both legal and beneficial interests in the policy. As present beneficial owner, the policy owner has the right to benefit from the policy. Beneficial rights usually include the right to receive policy dividends, the right to designate and to change the beneficiary, and the right to surrender the policy. These rights can have economic value, even before the death of the insured. Whether or not a life insurance policy has economic value prior to the insured's death depends upon the type of policy. If the owner holds title to the policy as the trustee of an irrevocable life insurance trust, then the owner will have legal title but will most likely not have a beneficial interest. Irrevocable life insurance trusts are used to keep life insurance proceeds out of the estate of the insured.

Most *term life insurance* policies have minimal cash value prior to the death of the insured because the premium charged, which increases over time along with increasing risk of death, simply buys pure protection. If the insured dies during the policy term, the company will pay the face value; otherwise, it will pay nothing. Some multi-year term policies (called *level term*) have a constant premium for a stated period (e.g., five or ten years). This requires a cash build-up during the early years of the period that is used to pay the higher mortality risk in the later years.

In contrast to a term policy, a *cash value* policy accumulates economic value because the insurer charges a constant premium that is considerably higher than mortality costs require during the earlier years. Part of this overpayment accumulates as a *cash surrender value*, which, prior to the death of the insured, can be enjoyed by the owner in one of two ways: (1) at any time the owner can surrender the policy and receive this value in cash or, (2) the owner can request a policy loan and borrow up to the amount of this value.

Because life insurance policies can have value prior to the insured's death, and because the insured's death results in the payment of the face amount of the policy in cash to the beneficiaries, life insurance makes a significant contribution to estate planning. It is said to be the only asset that can create an *instant* estate of substantial magnitude for a person of otherwise modest wealth. For a family with dependent children, this may be an important means of assuring the financial well-being of the surviving family members if the primary wage earned dies. For the wealthy family, life insurance may provide needed cash to pay the death taxes. A discussion of the types of life insurance, and more about irrevocable life insurance trusts is found in Chapter 15. To use life insurance properly, the planner must be aware of the impact of taxes, a subject to be introduced briefly next and explained in detail in Chapters 5 through 8.

TAXATION

In estate planning, the two principal types of taxing authority are the individual states and the federal government. The four major types of taxes are gift tax, death tax, generation-skipping transfer tax, and income tax.

A *gift tax* is a tax on a lifetime gift; that is, a lifetime transfer of property for less than full consideration.

A *death tax* is essentially a tax levied on certain property owned or transferred by the decedent at death. Death taxes have two basic forms: estate tax or inheritance tax. An *estate tax* is a tax on the decedent's right to transfer property, while an *inheritance tax* is a tax on the right of a beneficiary to receive property from a decedent. Either way, their net effect is essentially the same: they are both considered death taxes, because the tax is paid by the executor out of the decedent's estate before the property is transferred to the heirs. With an inheritance tax, the amount of death tax paid on any given size inheritance is likely to be greater for remote relatives as compared to close relatives, and greatest for non-relatives. For example, amounts going to a surviving spouse might not be taxed at all, and bequests to a child might have a high exemption amount and/or a lower tax rate than property going to a non-relative. The federal death tax is referred to as the federal estate tax. The characteristic of an estate tax is that for any given size net estate the tax will be the same regardless of who receives it. For example, the federal tax on a $5 million bequest after applying a $391,600 federal state death tax credit would be $1,806,400, whether the estate went to the decedent's children or went entirely to strangers (non-relatives). However, the federal estate tax is not a pure estate tax in that two deductions are based upon the relationship or nature of the beneficiary. A complete marital deduction is allowed for all property going to a surviving spouse (for a non-USA citizen spouse a special trust might be required, but we'll save that until later), and a complete charitable deduction is allowed for property going to qualified charities. Since these are complete (100%) deductions, subtracted from the gross estate before arriving at the taxable estate, and they are the only two deductions that are based upon the character of the beneficiary, little is lost in thinking of the federal death tax as an estate tax. At the state level, some states impose an estate tax and others have an inheritance tax. The trend is to impose an estate tax that results in no additional cost to the estate because, although it is paid to the state, the state death tax statute sets the death taxes as being equal to the state's allowable share of the federal state death tax credit. This so-called *"pick-up tax"* reduces the federal death tax by an equivalent amount, thus there is no increase in the over-all taxes. More than half of the states (including California, Florida and Nevada) use the "pick-up tax." The calculation for the "pick-up tax" is explained in Chapter 5. *** *Query 1. What is the death tax collected by the State of Florida if one of its citizens dies leaving a taxable estate of $5 million (the federal tax after applying a $391,600 federal state death tax credit would be $1,806.400)?*

A *generation-skipping transfer tax* (GSTT) is a tax on certain property transferred to a "skip person," that is, for the benefit of someone who is more than one generation younger than the donor. Thus, the surviving spouse and the children of a decedent are not skip persons, but grandchildren and great-grandchildren are. Without this tax, wealth could skip several generations and escape one level of transfer tax. For example, a gift or estate transfer of a $10 million parcel of land to a grandchild would be subject once to a gift tax or death tax, but it would not be taxed twice, as it would have if the property first passed from the client to the child, and then from the child to the grandchild. Chapters 7 and 12 cover the GSTT in more detail. It is enough to say here that the federal generation-skipping transfer tax has a $1 million exemption per transferor, making careful planning in this area necessary only for clients with fairly substantial estates.

An *income tax* is essentially a tax levied on income earned by a taxpayer during a given year. Income tax laws usually distinguish five different taxpayers or entities that must report income by filing income tax returns: individuals, partnerships, corporations, estates, and trusts. Principles of taxation can differ substantially for each. For instance, partnerships generally do not pay income taxes because the partnership is treated as a *pass-through* entity, meaning that its income and deductions are passed through to be reported by the individual partners. Each taxpayer, including partnerships, must submit an annual income tax return that reports certain items including income, deductions, credits, and the tax due (calculated by using tax tables applicable to that entity.) Married individuals may file a *joint income tax return*, in which they report their combined income, deductions, and other information on one return. This textbook will not try to cover income taxes in detail as it is far beyond the scope of this course. An extensive introduction to the income taxation of trusts and estates will be found in Chapter 8.

PROPERTY INTERESTS

Estate planning seeks to preserve and efficiently transfer an individual's wealth. Wealth is generally thought of as the property a person owns. This section will describe some of the ways in which property can be owned. Essentially, ownership can be classified in the following ways: extent of interests in property (e.g., fee simple); physical characteristic of property (e.g., real versus personal); number of owners and type of co-ownership (e.g., individual versus tenants in common); legal versus beneficial interests (e.g., property held in the name of the trustee versus a trust beneficial interest); present versus future interests (e.g., an income interest in a trust versus a remainder interest); and vested versus contingent interests (e.g.. ownership of land versus a contingent remainder interest, where the remainderman must out live the income beneficiary otherwise the trust property reverts back to the trustor's estate).

Classification of Property by Physical Characteristics

Property is classified as real or personal. *Real* property includes ownership interests in land and any improvements, such as buildings, fences, trees, and the like, that are attached to the land. Curiously, an interest for years (a leasehold) in real estate is considered personal property. Accordingly, a good functional definition of *personal property* is all property except interests in land and its improvements.

Property is further divided into tangible and intangible property. Something is tangible if it can be apprehended by the senses as having a physical existence. *Tangible personal property* is personal property whose utility comes primarily from its physical characteristics rather than the legal rights conferred upon the owner or possessor of the property. Conversely, *intangible personal property* derives its value from the legal rights it represents. Thus, a newspaper is tangible personal property because its value is based on the news printed there. Initially one might pay 35 cents to read it, a few days later the value may drop to almost nothing, being useful to wrap dead fish or as recycled newspaper, yet a very old paper with an article on the front page of historical significance may be worth a lot to collectors of old newspapers. On the other hand, a stock certificate is valuable to the owner of the certificate if the company is a going business, not because of the physical characteristics of the paper its printed on, but because of the rights it represents, such as the right to vote for the board of directors, the right to dividends when they are declared, and certain liquidation rights. If the company has gone out of business then the stock certificate has become tangible personable property, and the certificate may be worth only the value of the paper it is printed on, or, if it is old or unusual for some reason, it may be of some value as a collectors item.

Intangible personal property includes a *chose in action*, which is a claim for money or property that could be recovered from another in a lawsuit, if such is necessary. A chose in action, pronounced "shows," represents right to money or property that is owed to the holder of the chose. That right can be transferred, sold, or assigned to another, who can then act on it in his or her own name. The person holding the chose as a result of a transfer is entitled to keep any recovery.

EXAMPLE 2 - 5. Betty borrowed $9,000 from Lenny, agreeing to pay it back by December 31 of this year. Lenny signs a piece of paper assigning to his daughter, Christine, his right to collect the debt. Since the debt could be collected by a law suit if necessary, it is considered to be a chose in action, and the assignment to Christine gives her the right to collect it.

Basic Interests in Property

The three basic interests in property are fee simple, life estate, and estate for years.

Fee simple. A fee simple interest, often called a *fee* or a *fee simple absolute*, represents the greatest interest that a person can have over *real* property and corresponds to our usual notion of full ownership. Common rights include the right to possess, use, pledge, or transfer the property. If you own a house, even if it is subject to a mortgage, you probably have it in fee.

Life estate. A *life estate* interest in property, like a fee simple, is a powerful form of ownership, but is different in that the interest ceases upon someone's death. Ordinarily, the *measuring life* is that of the owner of the interest. However, it could be any other person.

> EXAMPLE 2 - 6. Doctor Bud assigns his interest in a house to his widowed mother for her to use and enjoy until her death. Mother has received a life estate in the house. Her own life is the measuring life.

A life estate for the life of someone other than the owner of the interest is called an estate *for the life of another*. These are rarely used.

> EXAMPLE 2 - 7. Facts are similar to previous example, except that Mother's interest will cease upon the death of Bud. Mother still has a life estate in the house but now Bud's life, rather than her life, is the measuring life. She has an estate for the life of another.

Ordinarily, the owner of a life estate enjoys, for the length of a measuring life, a complete ownership; one that is nearly equivalent to a fee, except that it will end upon the life tenants death. However, life estates are sometimes created so that the recipient enjoys only a partial present interest in the property.

> EXAMPLE 2 - 8. Aunt Jane, owner of dividend-paying common stock, gives to her niece Barbie the right to receive the dividends for as long as Barbie lives. Barbie has received a life estate in the income of the stock. Under the customary arrangements, Barbie does not have many rights in the stock itself. For example, she does not have the right to possess or sell the stock, or to use it as collateral against a loan. The stock will be held by someone else, either the original owner or, more commonly, a trustee under a trust arrangement.

Trusts are used extensively in estate planning, so they will be discussed in almost every chapter of this textbook. An introduction to trusts follows this discussion of property.

Interest for years. Often, a person transfers possession and/or enjoyment of property to another for a fixed period. This is called an *estate for years*—even if the fixed period is something other than a certain number of years.

> EXAMPLE 2 - 9. Professor Jackson rents his cottage to Dr. Johnson, a visiting professor, for the Spring semester. Dr. Johnson has an estate "for years" even though the semester is only four months long.

> EXAMPLE 2 - 10. Mary is presently enjoying a life estate, for her life, in the income from certain common stock. Today Mary transfers to Mark her interest for the next two years. If Mary does not survive the full two years, Mark's interest will be cut off upon Mary's death. Mary cannot transfer any greater interest than she actually owns, and Mark's interest is limited to that which Mary can legally give; thus, Mark has an income interest in the stock, ending at the earlier of two years or Mary's death.

A common example of an interest for years is a *leasehold*, which entitles the lessee to possess and use the property (e.g., a house or computer) for a specified time, usually in exchange for a fixed series of payments. Leasehold interests can amount to a valuable part of a lessee's wealth if the fixed payments are below current market rates, and if the lessee is permitted to "sublet" the property.

> EXAMPLE 2 - 11. For the past two years, Freda has owned a ten year leasehold interest in a commercial building, and is obligated to pay $15,000 per year for the entire period. If the rent for comparable buildings is expected to be $25,000 per year for the next eight years, and assuming a discount rate of 10 percent, the value of Freda's leasehold is the present value of $10,000 for eight years, discounted at 10 percent, or $53,349. Freda could possibly sell her interest for that amount.

Concurrent Ownership

Property may be owned individually, in which case one person owns and uses it, or it may be owned concurrently, by two or more persons. Where there is *concurrent ownership*, title may be taken as joint tenancy, tenants by the entirety, tenants in common, or as community property.

A common characteristic of all types of concurrent ownership is the *undivided* right to use the entire property, not just a physically identifiable portion. In addition, the co-owners usually each have the right, in the event of a dispute, to have the property physically divided, at which time concurrent ownership ends.

Joint tenancy interests. When two or more persons own an equal undivided interest in and right to possess property that, upon death of one owner, automatically passes to the surviving owner(s), they are said to hold title in *joint tenancy* or that they are *joint tenants*. Note that their interest must be equal, and their share must not be stated as part of the title; thus, "Jim, John, and Jose, as joint tenants," not "Jim, John, and Jose, as joint tenants each owning a one-third share." Because tenants in common can own unequal shares, the share of each is usually expressed in the title; therefore the second statement, with the shares defined as "one-third" might result in a claim by the heirs of a deceased co-owner that tenants in common was actually intended, and that the one-third interest belonged to them not to the surviving co-owners.

> EXAMPLE 2 - 12. John and Mary own a house as joint tenants. At John's death, Mary automatically becomes the sole owner of the house.

Under joint tenancy, ownership passes to the surviving co-tenants automatically at a cotenant's death by what is called *operation of law* and does not legally depend upon physical transfer of title. However, some authorities, such as banks, will require document revision in order to transact further business. A title company will want proof of the death of a joint tenant before it will issue title insurance should the survivors try to transfer title to someone else.

Joint tenancy interests in real estate can only be created by a written document. In most states, one co-tenant can unilaterally "sever" the joint tenancy without the knowledge or consent of the other tenant(s).

> EXAMPLE 2 - 13. Oscar, Ray, Sam, and Clark own Green Acre Ranch as joint tenants. Without telling the other three, Sam deeds his interest to his friend Ed. Sam has broken the joint tenancy insofar as his interest in concerned. Ed owns a one-fourth interest as a tenant in common with the other three holding title to three-fourth as joint tenants. If Ray then dies, Oscar and Clark will own the three-fourths as joint tenants, and Ed will continue to own one-fourth. If Ed dies, his share will go to his heirs, not to the other co-owners.

The automatic right of survivorship inherent in joint tenancy prevails over other means of transfer at death, including the will and the trust instrument.

> EXAMPLE 2 - 14. Continuing Example 2-12, if, prior to his death, John had executed a will that left his one half interest in the house to his son, Mary would still receive it by right of survivorship. The joint tenancy designation supersedes the will.

However, in certain jurisdictions, agreements can be executed between joint owners to nullify a joint tenancy designation.

> EXAMPLE 2 - 15. Continuing Examples 2-12 and 2-14 above, if John and Mary were to execute a written *agreement* stating that it is their intention that the house, presently held in joint tenancy, is in fact to be held by them as community property or as tenants in common (see description below), many jurisdictions will honor the agreement, and the house would not pass to Mary by automatic right of survivorship.

Joint tenancy's are most commonly created among family members, who often wish to transfer property at their death to co-owning relatives.

Interests by the entirety. An *interest by the entirety* is like a joint tenancy in that it carries with it that key characteristic of joint tenancy, the right of survivorship; however, an interest by the entirety can be created only between husband and wife. And unlike joint tenancy, neither spouse may transfer or encumber the property without the consent of the other. Tenants by the entirety is a common law concept, generally not recognized in the community property states. In addition, a few of the common law states no longer recognize this form of ownership, and will treat an attempt to create it as merely joint tenancy. Where it is recognized, since it is available only to married couples, a divorce will cause the title to automatically transmute into tenants in common.

Tenants in common. Like joint tenancy, *tenants in common* are held by two or more persons, each having an equal undivided right to possess property. Unlike joint interests, however, interests in common may be owned in unequal percentages, and when one owner dies the remaining owners do not automatically succeed in ownership. Instead, the decedent's interest passes through his or her estate, by will, by some other document, or by the laws of intestate succession.

> EXAMPLE 2 - 16. Jack owns a 16 percent real estate interest in common with two

other individuals who, combined, own the other 84 percent. Jack's will leaves his entire estate to his wife, Deanna. Upon Jack's death, his will determines who will get his interest, therefore, the 16 percent interest will pass by the probate process to his wife, Deanna, not to the other co-tenants.

In contrast to joint tenancy interests, interests in common are the title of choice for non-related parties, as a means of enjoying common ownership without losing the right of disposition at death.

Community property interests. In the eight states recognizing it, *community property* is that property acquired by the efforts of either spouse during their marriage while living in a community property state, and such other property which by the agreement of the spouses is converted from separate property into community property. *Separate property* is all other property owned by the spouses (e.g., acquired by only one of the spouses by gift, devise, bequest or inheritance, or by a spouse domiciled in a common law state, or acquired by either spouse prior to their marriage). The traditional community property states are Arizona, California, Idaho, Louisiana, Nevada, New Mexico, Texas, and Washington. In addition, Wisconsin recently adopted a form of community property known as "marital property", based on the Uniform Marital Property Act (UMPA). Most of the community property states follow what is sometimes referred to as the California rule, which is that income from community property is community property, as is anything bought with it, and income from separate property is separate property, as is anything bought with it. Three community property states, Texas, Idaho, and Louisiana, treat income earned from separate property during the marriage as community property, however, even these three states treat the gain on separate property that is sold as separate property, and anything bought with the proceeds of the sale will continue to be separate property.

Community property is owned equally by both spouses. Generally, both spouses must consent to a gift of community property. Community property states allow couples to convert community property to separate property, and vice versa, although some states require a written agreement wherein the spouse whose interest is reduced acknowledges the fact that something has been lost. Separate property is considered entirely owned by the acquiring spouse. In states without community-property provisions, of course, all property is separate property. In those states, it would simply be referred to as "the property owned by" Sam, Wanda, or whomever.

EXAMPLE 2 - 17. Pat and Mary live in the community property State of New Mexico. When they married two years ago, Pat owned a sports car, that Mary also uses. Pat works as a shoe salesman and Mary as a bank teller. Last year Mary's father gave her 100 shares of XYZ stock, which pays a quarterly dividend. Mary used the last dividend check to buy a bicycle. Pat bought a rowboat from money saved from his July paycheck. The stock and bicycle are Mary's separate property. The car is Pat's separate property. All of the other assets, including both salaries, are community property. ***Query 2-2. If Louisiana was their home, what difference would it make insofar as property ownership goes?*

Community property laws represent certain state government attempts to impose greater fairness in property ownership between married couples. Under old English common law, the husband owned all property that either husband or wife acquired during their marriage. Even after most states recognized the right of married women to own property, during pre-World War II America, the husband typically earned most of the outside income while the wife performed the non income-producing household chores; therefore, husbands usually acquired all title to the family wealth. At common law, a wife was entitled to own none of this property until her husband's death, at which time she received a life estate in one-third of her husband's real property. Called a "dower" interest, it has been modified by most common law states, however, it seldom gives the non-working spouse the advantages inherent in the law of community property, which automatically gives both spouses an immediate equal share in all of the property acquired by their efforts during the course of their marriage.

Arizona, California, Idaho, Washington, and Wisconsin have a concept called *quasi-community property*, which is defined as property acquired by their residents while domiciled elsewhere in a non-community property state, that would have been community property had they been domicile in a community property state. For example, if a married couple moves to California owning common stock acquired with salary earned during the marriage, while they were residents of New York; the stock is quasi-community property. Essentially, quasi-community property is treated as separate property of the acquiring spouse until divorce or death. If the parties divorce, the property is divided in a manner similar to community property. Treatment at death depends on which spouse dies first. If the acquiring spouse dies first, the surviving spouse is entitled to one half of the property. On the other hand, the non-acquiring spouse's rights to the property cease at his or her earlier death.

As different types of co-ownership of property, joint tenancy (JT) and community property (CP) have several major similarities and differences that are summarized in the outline below.

1. Major Similarities:
   a. Both involve ownership by more than one person.
   b. The owners have equal ownership rights and equal rights to use the entire property. Their interests are undivided.
   c. Any owner may demand a division of the property into separate, equal shares.
2. Major Differences:
   a. CP exists only between spouses. JT can exist between any two or more persons.
   b. CP rights arise automatically, by operation of law under state statute. Hence, they are created immediately upon acquisition of the property. JT rights usually arise at the time of the agreement between the parties and are not governmentally imposed.
   c. JT includes automatic right of succession to ownership (right of survivorship) by surviving joint owners. This right takes priority over any will. In contrast, CP includes no automatic succession to ownership of the decedent's share by the surviving spouse. Therefore, at death, a spouse can transfer his or her share of CP, by will, to someone other than the spouse. However, intestacy will ordinarily result in succession by the surviving spouse under most state laws of intestate succession.
   d. Property held in JT will not be subject to the probate process. In contrast, the decedent's share of CP may be subject to probate. Some CP states no longer require a probate if the property is left to the surviving spouse or if, because of intestacy, the surviving spouse will receive the property by the laws of intestate succession.

It's important to make two observations regarding item 2c: First, some states, such as New York, recognize an agreement between the spouses declaring that specified property is held in joint tenancy "for convenience only;" and second, Arizona, Idaho, Nevada, and Washington have enacted statutes that allow the designation "community property with right of survivorship." This results in the property being treated like joint tenancy in that the decedent spouse's will does not control disposition, and the property transfers to the surviving spouse by operation of law, meaning that there is no need for probate.

Legal Versus Beneficial Interests: Introduction to the Trust

Usually, the owner of property has all the rights to possess and enjoy it; however, these interests can be divided such that one party has just the "bare legal title," responsible solely for preserving and managing property for the benefit of another, who is entitled to enjoy the property in specified ways. The former holds the *legal interest* while the latter holds a *beneficial interest*, also called an *equitable interest*, in the property. Trusts are the most common legal arrangement to employ this division.

There are three major parties to the trust: trustor, trustee and beneficiary. The *trustor*, also called *grantor*, *creator*, or *settlor*, is the person who creates the trust, and whose property is used to *fund* the trust. The property held in a trust is called the *principal* or the *corpus*. The *trustee* is the person, persons, or entity (e.g., bank trust department) who takes legal title to the trust property. Usually the trust instrument names an initial trustee and several alternates. The trust *beneficiary* is the person or persons who are named to enjoy beneficial interest in the trust. Placing property in a trust is called *funding* the trust. Funding is accomplished by transferring title of the property into the name of the trustee. Figure 2-1 illustrates the relationship between the parties to the trust.

A trust can be *living* or *inter vivos*, meaning it is funded during the life of the trustor, or it can be *testamentary*, to take effect at the trustor's death with the funding mechanism being the probate process. A testamentary trust is one created by the trustor's will. An example of the provisions of a testamentary trust can be found in Chapter 3, Exhibit 3-3.

> EXAMPLE 2 - 18. On November 23, 1996, trustor Harold Stuart transfers 1,000 shares of ABC stock in trust to Uncle Jay as trustee, with the income payable to Harold's son, Chet, for 11 years, after which the corpus of the trust reverts to Harold. Jay receives only legal title which would probably read, "Jay Stuart, as trustee of the Chet Stuart Trust, dated 11/23/96." Jay is responsible for managing the property during the term of the trust. He can sell the stock and buy other investments in his name, as trustee, but he may not use trust assets for his own benefit, and he is required to distribute all income to Chet, the income beneficiary. Chet has a beneficial interest, that is, an estate for years in the income of the trust.

FIGURE 2-1 The Parties To a Trust

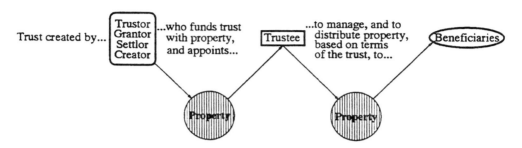

Reasons for creating trusts. Clients may wish to include trusts in their estate plans for five principal reasons: to provide for multiple beneficiaries, to manage their property if they become incapacitated, to protect beneficiaries from themselves and others, to avoid probate, and to avoid or reduce taxes. Since these factors are discussed in detail in numerous sections of the text, the following exposition will be brief.

First, clients may wish to *leave their property to more than one person*, either at the same time or successively, over a period of time, and may need an arrangement that will fairly protect each beneficiaries' individual property rights.

> EXAMPLE 2 - 19. After his death, Constantine wants to let his second wife enjoy the use of his property for the rest of her life. After her death, Constantine wants the income from his property to be payable to the children of his first marriage until they reach age 30, at which time he wants them to receive the principal outright. By executing a trust, Constantine can appoint a responsible trustee to manage the property for what may turn out to be a very long time. The trustee can be charged with preserving a proper balance between the differing interests of the beneficiaries.

A transfer into a trust is sometimes called a *split interest* transfer, because it divides rights to the corpus into two or more interests, usually an income interest for a specified period of years or for the beneficiary's life, and a "remainder" interest in the principal. Remainder interests will be described shortly. Discussions of income versus principal interests will be covered later.

Second, clients may create trusts to *manage their property if they become incapacitated.*

EXAMPLE 2 - 20. Several years ago, Linda Smith created a *revocable living trust*, changing the title of all her property to read "Linda Smith, trustee of the Linda Smith Revocable Living Trust, dated March 19, 1992." The terms of the trust provide that if Linda becomes incapacitated during her lifetime, her brother Tom will become successor trustee. Linda has taken steps to prevent the need for expensive court procedures to determine who should be appointed guardian or conservator of her property if she becomes incapacitated before death.

Third, clients may wish to create trusts to *protect beneficiaries from themselves and others.*[3] As we shall see in the next chapter, trust documents typically contain provisions restricting use of the property by beneficiaries. For example, trust instruments often provide that the trustee's discretion will determine the amount and timing of distributions to beneficiaries. In addition, they often prohibit any beneficiary from pledging his or her interest in the trust property as collateral for a loan. Many other restrictions can be included.

Fourth, a trust that is funded during the trustor's lifetime allows the property that is placed in the trust to *avoid the probate process.* Trusts funded while the trustor is alive are called *living trusts.* Trusts can also be funded through the probate process, either by means of a *pourover will* (a will that has a previously established trust as its primary beneficiary) or by means of a *testamentary trust* (a will that incorporates a trust within the body of the will). The probate process and means of avoiding probate are discussed in much more detail in Chapter 10.

Fifth, clients may wish to use trusts to *avoid or reduce taxes.* This text will have a great deal to say about tax planning with trusts after examining the taxation of gifts, estates, trusts, and beneficiaries in Chapters 5 through 8.

Power of Appointment

In arranging property transfers into trust or otherwise, clients can add considerable flexibility to their estate plans by granting a power of appointment. A *power of appointment* is a power to name someone to receive a beneficial interest in property. The grantor of the power is called the *donor.* The person receiving the power is called the *holder* or *donee.* The parties whom the holder may appoint by *exercising* the power are called the *permissible appointees,* and the parties whom the holder actually appoints are called the *appointees.* In addition, the persons who receive the property if the holder permits the power to *lapse* (i.e., does not exercise the power within the permitted period) are called the *takers in default.* The holder of a power of appointment can *release* the power by formally relinquishing the right to exercise the power.

A power of appointment can be exercisable either during lifetime or at death, or both during lifetime and at death. If exercisable during lifetime, it is exercisable either sometime during the holder's entire lifetime, or only for a stated period. If it is exercisable at this very moment, it is said to be "presently exercisable." A *testamentary* power is only exercisable at death, by a provision in the holder's will. The broadest powers allow the holder to exercise both during lifetime and at death.

> EXAMPLE 2 - 21. Assume that Anna transfers to Burt a power of appointment over her 100 shares of IBM stock, permitting Burt to appoint Carol, Dan, or Edward. If Burt eventually appoints Dan to receive the stock, then Anna is the donor, Burt is the holder (of the power), Carol, Dan, and Edward are the permissible appointees, and Dan is the appointee (of the stock). There are no takers in default because the holder did not permit the power to lapse.

Figure 2-2 illustrates the relationship between the parties involved in the power of appointment.

FIGURE 2-2   The Parties to a Power of Appointment

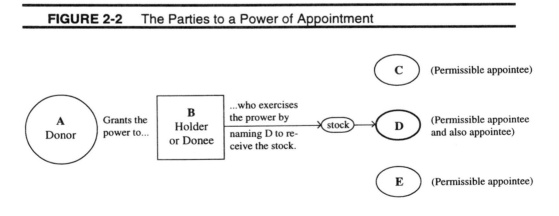

Powers of appointment are most often established within the framework of a trust. Comparing the relationship between the parties to a power of appointment with the parties to a trust, the donor of the power is usually the trustor. The holder is commonly the trustee but may also be one or more beneficiaries or a trusted friend of the trustor. The permissible appointees are usually the trust's beneficiaries. Trustee powers of appointment may be over trust income, principal, or both income and principal. Trustees may also be granted the power to *distribute income* amongst a group of beneficiaries, which is referred to as "sprinkling the income" or the trust. Where the trustee has this discretion, the trust is referred to as a "sprinkling trust." Almost humorously (we estate planners are always looking for a good laugh), the term "spray" is used to describe a trust clause that gives the trustee discretion in the *distribution of principal* in different amounts among permissible beneficiaries. Trust powers of appointment are extremely important estate planning tools, and will be discussed frequently in this book.

In the chapter on estate taxes, we shall see that death taxes play an important role in the use of powers of appointment—so much so that we commonly classify two types of powers using Internal Revenue Code clarifications. Under the Code, a power of appointment is either a *general* power of appointment or a *non-general* power of appointment, also called a *limited* or *special* power of appointment. We'll define these terms in greater detail when we start working on estate taxes, noting how the wording of a power can cause property to be included in the holder's estate. The next example shows a common use of a power of appointment.

> EXAMPLE 2 - 22. Charles, a single parent, died recently, and his will placed some of his property in trust for the benefit of his children. A bank is named trustee and is given a non-general power of appointment over the corpus. The bank has, among other things, discretion to distribute corpus to the children in accordance with their needs "for their proper support, health, and education." This year, the trustee has distributed $6,000 to one son and $4,000 to a daughter to pay their college tuition.

Powers of appointment add great flexibility to a client's estate plan by enabling someone to direct trust dispositions after taking into account changes in circumstances that occur long after the trustor's death. This flexibility is enhanced by a widely accepted rule of local property law, under which the property subject to a power of appointment is not considered legally owned by the holder, rather, the holder is simply treated as an agent for the donor. As Chapter 6 explains, however, federal tax law is not nearly as liberal if the power is a general one.

Present Versus Future Interests and Vested Versus Contingent Interests

A beneficial interest in property may be classified as a present interest or a future interest, depending upon whether or not the owner has the immediate right to possess or enjoy the property. We shall see later that this distinction is of great importance in connection with the $10,000 annual gift tax exclusion.

An owner of a *present interest* has an immediate right to possess or enjoy the property while an owner of a *future interest* does not, because the latter's right to possess or enjoy the property is delayed, either by a specific period of time or until the happening of a future event. The most common types of future interests are reversions and remainders. A *reversion* is a future interest in property that is retained by the transferor after the transferor transfers to another some interest in the property. The reversion will become a present interest of the transferor, or the transferor's estate, at the termination of all interests that were transferred.

> EXAMPLE 2 - 23. Jerry transfers property to Eve for her life. It will become Jerry's (or his estate's) present interest at Eve's death. Jerry has implicitly retained a reversion, also called a reversionary interest.

Technically, in the law of future interests, a *remainder* is the right to use, possess, and enjoy property after a prior owner's interest ends, in a situation where both interests were created at the same time and in the same document. It is a type of future interest held by someone other than the transferor and will become a present interest when all other interests have ended. The preceding definition of remainder is unnecessarily technical for our purposes, because most remainders in estate planning are quite simple. In estate planning, remainders usually arise in the context of trusts, where the remainderman is entitled to the remaining trust assets at the termination of the trust. In many, if not most, trust situations, the remaindermen are the clients' children or grandchildren, who will receive the remainder at the death of both client-spouses, and who are likely to have had joint life estates in a revocable trust. In some of these estate plans, the trust changes at the death of one spouse into several trusts, including one or more irrevocable trusts. Where multiple trusts are formed at the death of one spouse, the survivor probably will be the income beneficiary, and the children wait as remaindermen until the surviving spouse dies.

EXAMPLE 2 - 24. George irrevocably transfers property to Sally for her life, then to John or his estate. John's future interest in the property is a remainder. It is not a reversion because John was not the transferor.

A *vested remainder* is a remainder that is non-forfeitable; it is a remainder whose possession and enjoyment are delayed *only by time*, and are not dependent upon the happening of any future event.

EXAMPLE 2 - 25. With regard to the transfer by George in previous example, John's remainder is vested. Nothing prevents him or his estate from receiving possession, except the passage of time. Morbidly but accurately speaking, eventually Sally will die.

A *contingent remainder* is a remainder that is not vested; that is, it is a remainder whose possession and enjoyment are dependent upon the happening of a future event, not on just the passage of time.

EXAMPLE 2 - 26. Catherine transfers property to Flo for her life, then outright in fee simple to Jason, if alive, otherwise to Chris, if alive. Jason and Chris each have a contingent remainder interest in the property. Both interests are dependent on each of them living long enough. From today's perspective, each may or may not survive the required period; either Jason's or Chris's or both of their interests will be cut off by the happening of an event: (their own death prior to the transfer of interest).

A vested remainder is usually enforceable in court, while a contingent remainder is usually not. Both, however, may be subject to transfer taxation.

A few more examples, presented in the context of common transfer devices, should help to clarify these distinctions.

EXAMPLE 2 - 27. When Gary died, his will created a trust funded with his entire estate. The terms of the trust give income to his wife, Joan, for her life. At Joan's death, the trust will terminate and the property will pass outright in fee to Gary's son Max, if still alive, otherwise to the Salvation Army. At Gary's death, Joan received a present interest called a life estate in the income, and Max and the Salvation Army each received a future interest, called a contingent remainder. Max and the Salvation Army share something in common; only one of the interests can ever become a present interest since an event will occur which will defeat one or the others interest. Max's interest will cease if he predeceases Joan. The Salvation Army's interest will cease if Max survives Joan. Therefore, both have contingent remainder interests because possession is dependent upon the happening of a future event, not on just the mere passage of time.

EXAMPLE 2 - 28. Sam left property in trust, giving his wife, June, income for life with the remainder going to Sam's son, Kurt, or his estate. Kurt has a vested remainder in the property. Although initially a future interest, it is certain that it will become a present interest someday; it cannot be defeated. Only the passage of time keeps Kurt's interest from being a present interest. Of course, Kurt may not be alive to enjoy the property, but the beneficiaries of his estate will.

We have seen that the transfer of property in trust results in a division into two interests, with the trustee receiving the legal interest and the beneficiaries receiving the beneficial interests. In addition, transfers into trust typically result in a second type of division of interests when the beneficial interests are split among two or more beneficiaries. Ordinarily, one group of beneficiaries, called the *income beneficiaries,* receive a life estate or estate for years in the trust income, while the other group, called the *remaindermen*, receive the remainder at the termination of the income interests. The many reasons for splitting beneficial interests into a life estate, or into an estate for years and a remainder, will be explained in later chapters. At present, the reader should simply be aware of the interest-splitting nature of the trust. You should recognize that, at the time of the transfer into the trust, the life estate and estate for years are usually, but not always, present vested interests; the remainder is a future interest, either vested or contingent.

Mathematics of Remainders, Reversions and Income Interests

The previous section described the nature of remainders, reversions, life estates, and interests for years. These concepts are important to understanding later chapters, because many common estate planning techniques require their creation.

Up to now, the description of these interests has been qualitative rather than quantitative. But most of the chapters to come emphasize numerical analysis. Estate planning is inherently "numbers oriented," for two principal reasons. First, estate planning decisions often have a sizable impact on *family wealth*, and clients want to discuss that effect with the planner. Second, property transfer decisions often have *tax consequences* that must be projected and evaluated.

Thus, it is important to understand the quantitative nature of remainders, reversions, life estates, and interests for years. This section demonstrates how they are calculated.

Overview of IRS valuation tables. The calculations can be most easily performed with the help of tables published by the Internal Revenue Service. The Service's complete "Alpha" volume runs 795 pages and costs about $32.[4] It includes six different tables and lists tens of thousands of values, most of which are derived from discount rates ranging from 2.2 percent to 26 percent, at two tenths of one percentage point intervals. This conforms precisely with Internal Revenue Code valuation rules, often requiring the use of a current monthly discount rate that is equal to 120 percent of what is called the "applicable federal mid-term rate" (AFMR), which, in turn, is derived from the average market yield on U.S. Treasury obligations of maturities of three to nine years.[5] The rate, often referred to as the §7520 rate, has been rounded to the nearest two tenths of a percentage. Since these rates are published monthly by the Treasury Department, you do not have to figure out the rate. If a rate is given in an example or in problems at the end of the chapters, use that rate to determine the appropriate table to use.

For obvious practical reasons, this text can not include all pages from the IRS volume but reproduces many of the most useful ones. Appendix A includes part of IRS Tables "S," "B," "K," and "80CNSMT," the four most commonly used tables in estate planning. Appendix Table S and Table B are abridged to just list present values factors for discount rates of 6, 8, 10, and 12%. Table K gives adjustment factors where payments are made other than annually. Tables S and B assume an annual payment, with the first payment at the end of the first year. We will be using the factors for various rates in examples and problems. They offer a clear idea of the magnitude the values can take and can be especially helpful in the *planning* stage, when estimates are useful in calculating the values of life estates, remainders, and the like. Table 80CNSMT is a one page mortality table, useful for valuing interests that are contingent upon survival.

The following series of examples will illustrate the use of these four tables for the valuation of four basic property interests: remainders, reversions, annuities for life and annuities for a *term certain*. The discussion makes it clear that the choice of table for a particular problem depends in part upon whether the interest to be valued is predicated on the fact that someone will be paid either all income or a fixed annuity (1) for a fixed number of years, or (2) for life. All examples will assume, unless otherwise stated, that the appropriate rate is 10%, payments are annual, and that the first payment is at the end of the first year.

Valuations predicated on income for term certain: IRS Table B. Each of the next four examples calculates the value of an interest which is (directly or indirectly) dependent upon the fact that someone will be paid income for a *fixed number of years*, also called a *term certain*. Where a term certain is involved one must use the IRS Table B with the appropriate percentage rate.

Valuation of income for term certain. IRS Table B indicates what percentage of a given quantity of property reflects the value of a beneficiary's income for a term certain.

> EXAMPLE 2 - 29. Today Dana creates an irrevocable trust, transferring $200,000 in property to the trustee. The trustee is required to distribute annually all income earned from the property to Harry (or his heirs) for a period of ten years. Then, the trust terminates, and all trust principal will be distributed to Stephen (or his heirs). The current value of Harry's ten year annuity for a term certain is calculated as follows: Using Table B (10%), the income interest factor for to 10 years is 0.614457. Thus, the current value of Harry's income interest is $122,891 [$200,000 * 0.614457].

Valuation of vested remainder after income for term certain. Similarly, IRS Table B allows us to determine portion of the property's value reflects the value of a beneficiary's vested remainder interest at the termination of income for a term certain.

> EXAMPLE 2 - 30. Continuing as in previous example, the current value of Stephen's vested remainder interest can be calculated starting with the same table. The remainder factor found in Table B (10%) corresponding to 10 years is 0.385543. Thus, the present value of his vested remainder interest is $77,109 [$200,000 * 0.385543].

In the previous two examples, since Harry's and Stephen's interests represent the only two interests in the trust assets, it is logical that the sum of their current values should total $200,000, the current total value of the trust principal. And for the same reason, it's also logical that the sum of the two table values should add up to one. Consequently, each table value can be determined in a slightly different way. If one value is known, the other can be determined by simply subtracting the known value from 1.0. Thus, the table value for Stephen's interest, 0.385543, could have been calculated by subtracting the table value for Harry's interest, 0.614457 from the number 1.0; or, the remainder value could have been determined by subtracting the value of the income interest from the value of the whole trust ($200,000 - $122,891 = $77,109).

Valuation of reversion. Reversions are calculated the same way as remainders.

> EXAMPLE 2 - 31. Revising the terms of the trust in the above ongoing example, assume that at the end of 10 years, the trust will terminate and trust principal will be distributed back to the trustor Dana (or her heirs). The initial value of Dana's *reversion*, $77,109, is exactly equal to the value of Stephen's remainder, calculated using Table B (10%).

Valuation of remainder (after term certain) contingent upon survival. A remainder after a term certain that is contingent on the remainderman's survival of the term is calculated by multiplying the value of the vested remainder by the probability of the remainderman being alive at the end of the trust. IRS mortality Table 80CNSMT, reprinted in Appendix A, shows the number of people expected to be living at each age based upon statistics for the 1980 census. For example, out of 100,000 people born alive (age 0 = birth), only 94,926 of them are expected to be alive at age 40. Calculating the probability of a person age x surviving to age y involves simply dividing the number of people alive at age y by the number alive at age x. Thus, the probability of a newborn reaching age 40 alive is 0.94926 [94,926 ÷ 100,000].

> EXAMPLE 2 - 32. Revising the facts again in this on going example, assume that Stephen is currently age 40, that his remainder is contingent upon his surviving the ten year period, and that if he fails to survive, the trust principal will pass to someone else. The probability of Stephen surviving to age 50 is calculated, using Table 80CNSMT, by dividing 91,526 (the number alive at age 50) by 94,926 (the number alive at age 40). This quotient equals 0.964183. Thus, the value of Stephen's *contingent remainder* is $74,347 [0.964183 x $77,109].

Valuation of annuity for term certain. Now consider a new example in which the annual annuity payment for a term certain is known.

> EXAMPLE 2 - 33. A trust provides for an annual distribution to Brett of $4,000 per year for 15 years, with the first payment to be made exactly one year after the trust is established. The current value of Brett's 15 year annuity interest is calculated in the following manner: Using IRS Table B (10%), the annuity value

corresponding to 15 years is 7.6061. Thus, the current value of Brett's annuity interest is $30,424 [$4,000 x 7.6061]. The values in the annuity column are simply the present value factors for an annuity of $1.

All of the calculations in the above examples in some way involve an income interest or an annuity for a fixed number of years. The next section deals with examples involving a different inherent property interest: an income interest or an annuity for life.

Valuations predicated on income interest for life: IRS Table S. Each of the next three examples calculates the value of an interest which is (directly or indirectly) dependent upon the fact that someone will be paid an income or an annuity for life. In each case, use IRS Table S for the appropriate interest rate, see Appendix A.

Valuation of life estate. IRS Table S indicates what portion of a property's total value is reflected in the value of a beneficiary's income or annuity interest for life. The regulations do not allow the use of Table S where the person with the measuring life (e.g., the person with a life estate) is terminally ill at the time the interest is being valued. The regulations define terminal illness as "an incurable illness or other deteriorating physical condition...if there is at least a 50 percent probability that the individual will die within 1 year." However, if the person actually lives 18 months or longer, there is a presumption that the person was not terminally ill, unless the contrary is established by clear and convincing evidence.[6] In the examples that follow, unless stated to the contrary, we will assume that the person was not terminally ill, and that Tables S could be used to value the interests.

EXAMPLE 2 - 34. A trust containing $100,000 in principal provides for payment of a life estate in the trust income to Charles, age 50, and at Charles' death, distribution of the remainder to Samuel (or his heirs). The current value of Charles' life estate in the income of the trust is calculated in the following manner: Using IRS Table S (10%), the "life estate" value corresponding to age 50 is 0.86818. Thus, the current value of Charles' life estate interest is $86,818 [$100,000 x 0.86818].

Valuation of vested remainder after life estate. Similarly, IRS Table S indicates what portion of a property's total value should be allocated to a beneficiary's vested remainder after the termination of an annuity for life.

EXAMPLE 2 - 35. Continuing the previous example, the current value of Samuel's remainder interest after Charles' life estate can be calculated starting with the same table. For 10%, the "remainder" value corresponding to age 50 is 0.13182. Thus the current value of Samuel's vested remainder interest is $13,182 [$100,000 x 0.13182].

Similar to the earlier discussion, since Charles' and Samuel's interests represent the only two interests in the trust assets, it is logical that the sum of their current values should total $100,000, the current total value of the trust principal. And, again, for the same reason, the sum of the two table values add up to 1.0. Finally, we can determine each of the table values subtracting the known table value from the number 1.0.

Valuation of reversion after life estate. As with reversions after an income interest or an annuity interest for a term certain, reversions after a life estate are calculated in exactly the same manner as remainders.

Valuation of annuity for life. Now consider a different example in which the *actual* annuity payment is known.

EXAMPLE 2 - 36. Muhammad, age 40, is the beneficiary of a testamentary trust which is required to pay him the amount $10,000 per year for life, with the first payment to be made in exactly one year. Again, using IRS Table S (10%), the "annuity" value corresponding to age 40 is 9.2945.[7] Thus, the current value of this life estate is $92,945 [$10,000 x 9.2945].

These IRS tables will be used to value property interests in several sections of the text, covering such estate planning techniques as annual exclusion gifts (Chapter 7), minor's income trusts (Chapter 13), private annuities (Chapter 14), and charitable remainder trusts (Chapter 14).

OVERVIEW OF GOALS OF ESTATE PLANNING

Finally, let's summarize the major goals of estate planning. These goals, outlined below, are described in detail in Chapter 9 as an overview of the specific techniques detailed in Chapters 10 through 18.

A. Nonfinancial Goals
   1. Caring for future dependents.
   2. Accomplishing fair and proper distribution of property.
   3. Attaining privacy in the property transfer process.
   4. Attaining speed in the property transfer process.
   5. Maintaining control over assets.
B. Financial Goals
   1. Non-tax financial goals
      a. Minimizing non-tax estate transfer costs.
      b. Maintaining a satisfactory standard of living.
      c. Ensuring proper disposition by careful drafting.
      d. Preserving business value.
      e. Attaining pre- and postmortem flexibility.
      f. Maximizing benefits for the surviving spouse.
   2. Tax saving goals
      a. Income tax saving goals
         1) Obtaining a stepped-up basis.
         2) Shifting income to a lower bracket taxpayer.
         3) Deferring recognition of income.
      b. Transfer tax saving goals and planning
         1) Reducing the estate tax value.
         2) Freezing the estate tax value.
         3) Leveraging the use of exclusions, exemptions, and the unified credit.
         4) Delaying payment of the transfer tax.
         5) Minimizing the generation-skipping transfer tax.

The next chapter will apply many of the concepts introduced in this chapter to describe the provisions of the major documents utilized in the property transfer process.

IMPORTANT CONCEPTS AND TERMS COVERED IN THIS CHAPTER

Estate	Personal representative	Personal property
Property	Fiduciary	Tangible personal property
Probate estate	Executor	Intangible personal
Gross estate	Administrator	property
Taxable estate	Heir	Chose in action
Transfer	Devisee	Concurrent ownership
Assignment	Legatee	Joint interest
Transferor	Legacy	Joint tenancy
Transferee	Issue	Interest by the entirety
Legal interest	Descendant	Tenants in common
Beneficial interest	Specific bequest	Community property
Transfer	Ademption	Separate property
Outright gift	General bequest	Trust
Complete (transfer)	Pecuniary bequest	Trustor, grantor, creator
Irrevocable (transfer)	Residuary bequest	or settlor
Incomplete (transfer)	Residue	Trust principal or corpus
Revocable (transfer)	Class gift	Trustee
Interest in property	Abatement	Trust beneficiary
Partially complete (transfer)	Disclaimer	Living trust
Sale	Life insurance	Testamentary trust
Consideration	Insured	or trust-will
Gift	Term life insurance	Power of appointment
Bargain sale	Level term life insurance	Donor or creator (of a power)
Inter vivos	Cash surrender value	Holder or donee (of a power)
Instrument	Cash value life insurance	Permissible appointee
Beneficiary	Unified transfer tax	Appointee
Donee	Gift tax	Exercise (a power)
Donor	Death tax	Release (a power)
Decedent	Inheritance tax	Lapse (of a power)
Will	Estate tax	Taker in default
Testamentary	Generation-skipping	Present interest
Executed	transfer tax	Future interest
Testator	Fee simple	Reversion
Trust	Life estate	Remainder
Intestate	Measuring life	Vested remainder
Testate	Interest for years	Contingent remainder
Partially intestate	Leasehold	Income beneficiary
Probate	Real property	Remainderman

QUERIES ANSWERED:

1. Since Florida is a "pick-up tax" state, its death taxes equal the federal state death tax credit of $391,600. Thus, for a $5 million dollar taxable estate, the total taxes in Florida would be $2,198,000 ($391,600 + $1,806,400 = $2,198,000).

2. The bicycle would be community property because, like Texas and Idaho, Louisiana treats income from separate property as community property.

QUESTIONS AND PROBLEMS

1. Describe four different meanings of the concept "estate".

2. (a) Contrast a legal interest from a beneficial interest. (b) Why might a person want to transfer such interests in the same property to different individuals, rather than outright to one person?

3. Kasner "sells" a $10,000 car to his son for $4,000. Technically speaking, is this more of a sale or a gift? Why?

4. One of your clients shows you the following clipping from a trade journal:

"John Smith, the prominent local celebrity, died on Thursday. His generosity was legendary. Last year, he made a large *outright inter vivos gift* to his alma mater, and to another charitable *donee*. In addition, in a lengthy handwritten *will executed* last year, the *decedent* made several large *general bequests* and *specific devises* to the local orphans' fund, including a *transfer* into a *testamentary trust*. Finally, as *holder* of a *power of appointment* over several parcels of land on the outskirts of town, Smith *exercised* the power in favor of several *permissible appointees*, one of whom is a grandson of the *donor*. To the surprise of almost everyone in the family, two *appointees* refused some of the gifts by exercising valid *disclaimers*. And interestingly, no *residuary bequest* was included in the will, which means that the *testator* died *intestate* with regard to a considerable portion of his *estate*. Smith nominated as *executor* of his *probate* estate several of his surviving *issue*..."

Explain to your client the meaning of each highlighted word.

5. (a) What is probate? (b) What types of assets are subject to probate administration? (c) What types of assets are not subject to probate? (d) Does having a will avoid probate?

6. Contrast the insured, the owner, and the beneficiary of a life insurance policy.

7. At the moment of Lou's death, a life insurance policy was in force in the amount of $250,000, which had a cash surrender value of $60,000. Lou had the power under the policy to change the beneficiary. After Lou's death, his wife, Mary, received a check from the insurance company.
   a. Explain who were the likely parties to this policy:
      1. Insured
      2. Beneficiary
      3. Owner
   b. Did Lou's wife receive $60,000, $190,000, $250,000, or $310,000? Why?
   c. Why will this policy likely help in estate planning for Lou's family?

8. (a) Why is a fee simple interest greater than a life estate or an interest for years? (b) Can you think of any sense in which all three interests can be considered nearly equal?

9. Compare and contrast joint tenancy with tenants in common.

10. Beth tells you that she has a property interest having all of the following characteristics: concurrent ownership with two of her friends automatic right of succession to ownership and all three owners are allowed to own unequal percentages. Why must she be mistaken? Explain.

11. Define community property and separate property.

12. Compare community property with joint tenancy.

13. Cindy and Dennis, residents of a community property state, were married in 1980. At that time, they each owned a car and some furnishings. Since then Dennis has been working full-time and Cindy has been working as the mother and homemaker. In 1982, Dennis was given 100 shares of IBM stock. In 1983, Cindy inherited her father's computer. This year, Dennis put one half of a year's salary as down-payment on a house for his family. Making your own assumptions when necessary, identify the community property and the separate property.

14. Continuing the problem immediately above, suppose Dennis paid the down payment on the house with dividend income from the IBM stock, but the house payments were made from Dennis' salary. Is the house community property, separate property, or part community and part separate property?

15. One day your client, Pedro Espinosa, asks you "Why do estate planners recommend trusts?" Briefly answer his question.

16. If you are the holder of a power of appointment, how might you be assisting in the donor's estate plan?

17. Contrast a present interest with a future interest.

18. (a) If Cheryl named Paul today to be the remainder beneficiary of her probate avoiding trust, is Paul's interest most likely a present or future interest? (b) If future, is it most likely to be a vested or contingent one? (c) If contingent, when will it vest, if ever? Explain each answer carefully.

19. Today Edward transfers $300,000 to an irrevocable trust, whose terms provide that all income will be payable annually to son Dale (or his heirs) for a period of twenty years. At the end of that period, the trust will terminate and all corpus will be distributed to grandson Kevin, age 14 (or his estate). (a) At a rate of 8%, calculate the current value of Dale's and Kevin's property interests. (b) Recalculate Kevin's remainder interest if it was contingent upon his surviving the income period.

20. Roberta died recently, leaving $500,000 in trust. Roberta's husband Mo, age 65, will receive a life estate in all of the income, payable annually. At his death, all principal will pass outright to Roberta's daughter Sherrie (or her estate). (a) At a rate of 6%, calculate the current value of Mo's and Sherrie's property interests. (b) Also, calculate the values at 12 %. (c) Comment on the influence of a higher discount rate.

21. Thomas Smith, age 30, is beneficiary of a trust which will pay him $3,500 a year for life. At 12%, calculate the current value of this life estate.

ANSWERS TO QUESTIONS AND PROBLEMS

1. Four different meanings of the concept "estate":

   a. Estate: A quantity of wealth or property.
   b. Net Estate: Property owned reduced by the estate owners liabilities.
   c. Probate Estate: Property passing through the probate process.
   d. Gross Estate and Taxable Estate: Property subject to death taxation.

2. a. Legal Interest: Ownership of bare legal title. Beneficial interest: Ownership of an economic benefit.

   b. A person might want to transfer legal and beneficial interests to different individuals for any of the following reasons:

      1. To provide for multiple beneficiaries.
      2. To have their property managed for them if they become incapacitated.

3. To protect beneficiaries from themselves.
4. To avoid or reduce taxes.

3. Kasner has undertaken a *bargain sale*, which is a hybrid of gift and sale but is commonly classified as a gift. While a sale is a transfer in exchange for full consideration, a gift (and a bargain sale) is a transfer for *less than* full and adequate consideration.

4. Terms from the article:

- "Outright": subject to no restrictions or conditions; the transferee receives both legal interest and all beneficial interests in the property.
- "Inter vivos": during the transferor's lifetime.
- "Gifts": transfers for less than full consideration.
- "Donee": a person who is receiving or will receive a gift of a beneficial interest in property.
- "Will": a written document disposing of a person's probate property at death.
- "Executed": completed, that is, signed in the presence of witnesses. More generally, to execute is to do what is necessary to render the document valid.
- "Decedent": a person who has died.
- "General bequests": gifts payable out of the general assets of the estate, but not ones that specify one or more particular items.
- "Specific devises": gifts of specific real property.
- "Transfer": the passing of property where the transferor gives up some kind of interest to the transferee.
- "Testamentary trust": a trust that takes effect at the death of the trustor.
- "Holder" (of a power of appointment): the person receiving the power.
- "Power of appointment": a power to name someone to receive a beneficial interest in property.
- "Exercised": invoked the power by appointing a permissible appointee.
- "Permissible appointees": the parties whom the holder may appoint by exercising the power.
- "Donor": a person making a gift.
- "Appointees": the parties whom the holder actually appoints.
- "Disclaimer": An unqualified refusal to accept a gift.
- "Residuary bequest": a gift of that part of the testator's estate not otherwise

disposed of by will.

- "Testator": the person who executed a will.
- "Intestate": Having died leaving property not disposed of by a valid will.
- "Estate": the decedent's property owned at death.
- "Executor": a personal representative who was nominated in the will.
- "Probate": the court process of administering the estate of a decedent.
- "Issue": a person's direct descendants.

5. a. Modern usage: the entire court process which oversees the transfer of assets after a person dies. It is intended to protect estate beneficiaries and creditors.

   b. Assets subject to probate administration fall into one of three groups: property owned by the decedent as an individual, interests of the decedent held in common with others, and, in community property states, the decedent's one half interest in community property.

   c. Assets not subject to probate administration are those for which some other mechanism of transfer is legally recognized as controlling. This includes property held in trusts and in joint tenancy, most insurance policies on the life of the decedent (unless payable to his or her estate), and most retirement plan assets.

   d. Having a will does not avoid probate. The will acts as a guide for distribution rather than having intestate succession control.

6. Insured: the subject of the insurance; that is, the one whose death triggers payment of the proceeds.

   Owner: usually the possessor of both legal and beneficial interests in the policy. Commonly held "incidents" of ownership include the right to dividends, to surrender the policy, to pledge the policy, and to change the beneficiary.

   Beneficiary: the person who is named to receive the proceeds.

7. a. 1. Insured: Lou, because his death apparently triggered the payment of the policy proceeds.

      2. Beneficiary: Lou's wife, who received the proceeds.

      3. Owner: Probably Lou-- he had the power to change the beneficiary and, presumably, owned the other rights as well.

b. Lou's wife received $250,000. With most cash value policies, the cash value disappears as an economic benefit at the insured's death.

c. This policy will likely help in estate planning for Lou's family to help pay for death taxes and other cash obligations arising at Lou's death. Death often triggers *obligations*, and, with the ownership of life insurance, it can also trigger the *liquidity* to cover these obligations.

8. a. A fee simple interest is greater than a life estate or an estate for years because a fee simple interest does not cease after the passage of time or the happening of a future event.

b. All three interests can be considered equal in that while the owners enjoy them, they have virtually the same right to use them. Of course, only the fee owner can freely act to destroy or modify the nature of the property.

9. Joint interests (JT) and interests in common (TIC) contrasted:

Differences:
a. JT: equal ownership; TIC: can be unequal.
b. JT: automatic survivorship; TIC: no automatic survivorship.

Similarities:
a. both held by two or more persons.
b. both involve an undivided right to possess the property.

10. No valid type of property ownership includes all three characteristics mentioned by Beth. Joint tenancies and tenancies by the entity both require equal percentage ownership. And tenancy in common does not include automatic right of succession to ownership.

11. *Community property* is any property acquired by the efforts of either spouse during the marriage while domiciled in a community property state. It also includes any property which by agreement of the couple they convert from separate into community. Some states require said conversion to be in writing. Excluded is property acquired by gift, devise, bequest or inheritance, and the income from separate property. Texas, Idaho, and Louisiana treat income from separate property as community property.

Separate property is defined as any property that is not community property, i.e., all property acquired by a person not during marriage, or during marriage in a common law state, and property acquired during a marriage by gift, devise, bequest or inheritance, or often, income earned on property so acquired.

12. Community property vs joint tenancy interests:

    Major similarities:
    a. Ownership by more than one person.
    b. Owners have equal ownership rights which are undivided, i.e., exercisable over the entire property.
    c. Any owner may demand a division of the property into separate, equal shares.

    Major differences:
    a. CP exists only between spouses. JT can exist between any two or more persons.
    b. CP rights arise automatically (i.e., by operation of law).
    c. JT includes automatic right of succession to ownership by surviving joint owners, a right that takes priority over the will. CP does not, which means that CP can be disposed of by will.

13. Community property: house and salary. Acquired during the marriage not by gift, inheritance, or the income there from.

    Separate property: the cars, the furnishings, IBM stock, computer. Either acquired before the marriage, or during the marriage by gift or inheritance.

14. In most community property states, the house would be part community, part separate, because it was acquired partly with community property and partly with separate property. However, in Texas, Idaho and Louisiana, it would be entirely community property.

15. Estate planners recommend trusts for many reasons, which can be reduced to four major ones: to provide for multiple beneficiaries, to manage the client's

property if they become incapacitated, to protect beneficiaries from their imprudence, and to avoid or reduce taxes. This text will have a lot to say about the use of trusts to meet client goals.

16. By acting as the holder of a power of appointment, you might be assisting in the donor's estate plan in several ways, including making gifting decisions on behalf of the donor (of the power) for possibly a period of many years after the donor's death. Later in the text, students will learn that a power of appointment holder is one type of *surrogate decision maker*.

17. The owner of a present interest has an immediate right to possess or enjoy the property, while the owner of a future interest does not, because possession or enjoyment is delayed, solely in time, or until the happening of a future event.

18. a. Paul would have a future interest, because possession or enjoyment is delayed until Walsh's death.
    b. Paul's interest is contingent because possession or enjoyment is dependent upon the happening of a future event, rather than merely the passage of time. The event is Walsh's death occurring without changing the terms of his will and, possibly, Paul surviving Walsh.
    c. Paul's interest will vest at Walsh's death. Note: If the bequest is "to Paul or his estate," then his or his estate's interest would vest at Walsh's death, even if Paul predeceases him.

19. a. Dales interest: Change such that the period is 20 years:

    Using IRS Table B (8%), the appropriate "income interest" corresponding to 20 years is 0.785452. Thus, Dale's interest is currently worth $235,636 [$300,000 x 0.785452]. This assumes that the first income distribution will be made exactly one year from now.

    Kevin's (vested) interest: One method of calculating it: Using the same table, at 8% the appropriate "remainder" corresponding to 20 years is 0.214548. Thus, Kevin's interest is currently worth $64,364 [$300,000 x 0.214548].

Another way: Subtract Dale's table value from 1.0: Thus, 1.0 - 0.785452 = 0.214548. Then perform the same multiplication as in the first method or simply subtract Dale's interest from the value of the trust as a whole: $300,000 - $235,636 = $64,364.

b. Recalculation of Kevin's remainder interest if it were contingent upon his surviving the income period: Kevin's probability of surviving to age 34 is expressed by the fraction 95951/98248, which is the ratio of the number alive at age 34 to the number alive at age 14. Thus, the value of Kevin's contingent remainder interest is $62,860 [$64,364 * (95951/98248)].

20. a. At 6%:

Mo's interest: Using IRS Table S (6%) the appropriate "income interest" corresponding to age 65 is 0.56599. Thus, Mo's interest is currently worth $282,995 [$500,000 x 0.56599]. This assumes that the first income distribution will be made exactly one year from now.

Sherrie's interest: One method of calculating it: Using the same table as above, at 6% the appropriate "remainder" corresponding to age 65 is 0.43401. Thus, Sherrie's interest is currently worth $217,005 [$500,000 x 0.43401].

Another way: Subtract Mo's table value from 1.0: Thus, 1.0 - 0.56599 = 0.43401. Then perform the same multiplication as in the first method. Or stated another way, simply subtract Mo's life estate value from the total value of the trust to arrive at Sherrie's remainder interest: $500,000 - $282,995 = $217,005.

b. At 12%: Mo's interest: $500,000 x 0.75746 = $378,730.   Sherrie's interest:$500,000 x 0.24254 = $121,270.

c. As the discount rate increases, the value of the remainder interest drops and the value of the life estate rises because discounting has an over proportionately depressing effect on the more distant cash flows, due to the exponential nature of the mathematical equation for time value of money discounting. Finance oriented types might grasp the reason from this simplified analogy: $1/(1.06)^{20}$ (which equals 0.3118) is considerably less than one half of $1/(1.06)^{10}$ (which equals 0.8900).

21. Using IRS Table S (12%), the appropriate "annuity" corresponding to age 30 is 8.1208. Thus, Thomas Smith's interest is currently worth $28,443 [$3,500 x 8.1208]. This assumes that the next income distribution will be made exactly one year from now.

ENDNOTES

1. IRS Reg. 20.2031-1(b).

2. For the Uniform Probate Code's six exceptions, see UPC §2-606.

3. Somewhat humorously, Edward Schlesinger has described the trust as capable of protecting assets from "inability, disability, creditors and predators."

4. The Alpha volume, Publication 1457, can be purchased from the U.S. Government Printing Office. These tables are also available in the form of easy-to-use computer software. For example, *Tiger Tables*, available from Lawrence P. Katzenstein at (314) 231-2800, computes all Alpha values plus many other factors, including unitrust remainder factors for from one to ten lives, probabilities of survival, annuity adjustment factors for annuities due, the value of an income beneficiary's interest in a trust with a 5 and 5 power, and commutation tables.

5. See Internal Revenue Code §7520 (see App. A) and §1274(d)(1). Current AFMR rates are released regularly by popular income tax report publishers, such as Prentice Hall and Commerce Clearing House (CCH). CCH reports the monthly changes in the "New Developments" volume of the *Standard Federal Tax Reports*. In that volume, see "New Matters....Cumulative index to 199_ developments," under §7872, under "Applicable Federal Rates Established for (Month), 199_ Rulings" section. CCH also reports these rates in the "Cumulative Index" of its *Federal Estate and Gift Tax Reports*, again under Code §7872. Look for "Applicable Federal Rates..." Monthly news releases are usually issued by the IRS one to two weeks prior to the beginning of the current month, and are

published in the report of the first week of that month. The AFMR rates also appear under the heading "Credit Markets" in Section C of the *Wall Street Journal* between the 17th and the 22nd of each month.

6. §§1.7520-3(b)(3); 20.7520-3(b)(3)(i); 25.7520-3(b)(3)

7. Students of finance may notice that traditional financial mathematics can *not* derive this number. It is based not only on the time value of money, but also on a life expectancy.

PART 2

Constraints in Planning

— 3

Introduction to Property Transfers I: The Documents of Transfer

OVERVIEW

Estate planning seeks to facilitate the transfer of the client's wealth as efficiently as possible. Efficiency in estate transfer usually requires the preparation of one or more formal documents that will be accepted by those authorities that ultimately authorize and make the transfers. For example, the proper preparation and execution of a will is essential to the efficient disposal of any probate property. The will must be drafted correctly to ensure proper disposition, and it must be signed and witnessed according to law so that officials, such as the probate judge, the court clerk, the county recorder, and the bank officer, will accept it as the guide for the title transfer process.

This chapter, the first of two introducing the principles of property transfer, explores the *documents* used in the process of transferring wealth. Specifically, it examines the creation of four common property transfer mechanisms: joint tenancy, property disposition by contract, the will, and the trust instrument. Appendix 3A at the end of the chapter covers in greater detail the *rule against perpetuities*, a legal doctrine that acts to prevent a transferor from controlling the disposition of property for an unreasonably long time after making the transfer. The next chapter examines the actual *process* of transfer of property disposed of by these documents, with emphasis on the probate process. Because probate also administers the decedent's intestate property, this chapter also surveys the law of intestate succession.

Property transfers are regulated by state, not federal, law. State laws in this area vary greatly, making generalization difficult. However, more than half of the states have adopted all or a significant part of the Uniform Probate Code (UPC) and, therefore, have many property distribution laws in common. The UPC was introduced in 1966, partly in answer to the criticism that probate procedures in the United States were too costly, too time-consuming, and too complicated. Idaho was the first state to adopt it in 1972; since then, a total of 28 states have adopted the UPC in whole or in large part.[1] In presenting the material in this and the next chapter, we will often refer to the laws of those states which have adopted the UPC, especially in three major areas: will execution, intestate succession, and probate administration.

JOINT TENANCY ARRANGEMENTS

The acquisition of title in joint tenancy is ordinarily a simple matter, requiring the completion of one or two preprinted forms. Ordinarily, an attorney is not needed. Title to real property is usually completed in the real estate agent's or title company's office. Similarly, written title in joint ownership of personal property, when it can easily be created, is completed in the office of the professional who helps to acquire it. Examples include title to securities by the investment broker, to a car by the motor vehicle bureau, and to a bank account by the bank.

Later in the text the reader will learn several significant disadvantages to taking title in joint tenancy. Deciding whether joint tenancy is appropriate is not always clear, however, our focus here is on how title in joint tenancy is taken, not whether it should be taken.

PROPERTY DISPOSAL BY CONTRACT

There are a number of significant ways in which property can be transferred pursuant to a contract. Life insurance, pension, and profit sharing plans are common examples.

Life Insurance

Wealth derived from life insurance comes in two forms: the policy death proceeds, and the policy itself. Each of these transfers requires different arrangements.

During the policy application process, the applicant designates the beneficiary who will receive the proceeds at the insured's death. Once the policy is issued, up until the death of the insured, the policy owner can easily change the beneficiary designation by giving the company written notice using its beneficiary designation form. Very rarely, policies are issued with the beneficiary irrevocably designated, i.e., the designation cannot be changed without the beneficiary's consent. Such may be the result of a divorce decree or as one condition of a personal loan. Once certain conditions are met the owner-insured is free to change beneficiaries, e.g., the children are grown or the loan is repaid.

Arranging the transfer of title to a life insurance *policy itself* is simple. All that is required is the completion of a short assignment form that can be obtained from the insurance company.

Pension and Profit Sharing Plans

Pension and profit sharing plans are contracts between the employee-client and the employer. Ordinarily, the employer requests that the employee fill out a written form designating the beneficiary, the party who will be entitled to any benefits paid after the employee's death. Thus, the actual process of beneficiary designation for most retirement plans is simple and straightforward.

WILLS AND TRUSTS

In contrast with the above transfer arrangements, the document preparation process for the will and the trust are not simple, for two reasons. First, unlike joint tenancy and written contracts, the will and the trust are capable of disposing of *nearly all* of the client's estate, as well as providing for the care of the client's minor children. Thus, the will and the trust will inevitably be more complicated. Second, unlike insurance and retirement contracts, which are drafted by the insurer or the employer, the *responsibility for drafting* the will and the trust falls on the individual client.

The following material presents an overview of will and trust construction. Major topics include the legal requirements for a valid will, common will provisions, essential characteristics of trusts, and common provisions of the living trust and the testamentary trust.

The Will

Many people die leaving no formal directions as to the disposal of their probate property or who should care for their minor children. In such cases, the state seeks to make these decisions equitably and sensibly, using statutory rules tailored according to the surviving family situation. However, state law may conflict with the wishes of a decedent, whether unstated or even as recollected by the survivors. Compared to a properly planned estate, intestacy can result in unsuitable property disposition and higher taxes. Individuals can avoid an undesirable outcome by expressing their wishes while still alive, in a legally acceptable document that serves as a direction and guide for those who survive. The will is the most common formal document for this purpose.

A will is a legally enforceable document that expresses the testator's directions for disposing of his or her probate property at death. In many states, wills can be *oral*, but laws usually greatly restrict the scope of their ability to dispose of wealth, generally limiting their application to personal property worth no more than some modest amount, such as $2,000. In addition, the testator, on execution, is often required to be a member of the armed forces or in peril of death. Practically speaking, wills prepared in the estate planning process are written.

Who May Execute a Will

In most states, any individual 18 or older who is of sound mind may dispose of his or her property by will. The implications of this are twofold. First, individuals under the age of 18 cannot transfer property by will unless they are emancipated minors. Thus, a deceased minor's probate property will pass according to the laws of intestate succession, which will usually be to the parents. Second, a will can be denied probate if it can be established that the testator, at date of execution of the will, lacked testamentary capacity, was subject to undue influence or to fraud, or acted mistakenly. These four concepts are discussed next.

Testamentary capacity. *Testamentary capacity* concerns the testator's mental ability to validly execute a will. A testator has testamentary capacity if he or she possesses each of the following three attributes:

1. Sufficient mental capacity to understand the *nature of the act* being undertaken (executing a will).
2. Sufficient mental capacity to understand and recollect the general nature of his or her *property*.
3. Sufficient mental capacity to remember and understand his or her relationship to the *persons* who have natural claims on his or her bounty and whose interests are affected by the provisions of the will.

Essentially, in addition to being an adult, testators must know that they are executing a will, they must be aware of what they own, and they must be cognizant of family and friends. On its face, this test seems quite severe; strictly construed, it might prevent many older testators from executing a valid will. However, because the law holds that mere age and physical disability do not negate testamentary capacity, probate courts are not so strict, and have admitted to probate wills executed by individuals who were forgetful, absent-minded, alcoholic, or have behaved peculiarly—even persons declared mentally incompetent, insane, under conservatorship, or who committed suicide shortly after executing a will. Nonetheless, failure to meet one or more of these three requirements will result in a finding of insufficient testamentary capacity. Examples of sufficient evidence of incompetence include senility, ongoing hallucinations and irrational beliefs combined, irrational behavior, and totally groundless beliefs about the testator's spouse, children, or siblings. Generally, the outcome hinges on whether or not, at or about the specific time the will was executed, the three-prong test was met. Appellate courts do not like "setting aside a will" and have reversed many jury set-aside decisions. As a consequence, affirmed findings of testamentary incapacity are very rare.

Anticipating the possibility of a will contest based on lack of testamentary capacity, some attorneys *videotape* the will execution of a testator who may have questionable capacity, believing that the taping will make capacity more credible. Others believe that videotaping can enhance the success of a contest, reasoning that testators may look terrible on the screen (especially if they are shown lying in a hospital bed), and that the taping constitutes evidence that even the will drafting attorney lacked confidence in the testator's capacity.

Undue influence. A will executed by a testator who was subject to undue influence by someone who stands to benefit may also be denied probate. Undue influence is influence by a confidante that has the effect of impeding the testator's free will. Examples include threats, the use of force (duress), and the use of over persuasion and psychological domination, as when "Snake Oil Sam," the smooth-talking newcomer, makes a romantic play for the 92-year-old widow, "encouraging" her to disinherit her children and leave her entire estate to him.

Winning an undue influence case can be difficult. In because these cases typically involve a weak, unsound or impaired mind, or a will procured by one who occupied a fiduciary relationship to the decedent who was not the natural object of the decedent's bounty and who benefited substantially under the will. An element of fraud or deceit is a common thread in these cases. Juries tend to side with family members against meddling non-relatives and "rewrite" a will that reflects what the jurors think is fair to the family. But, unless the evidence of undue influence is clearly in the record, appellate courts will reverse such jury verdicts.

Fraud. Fraud involves deception through false information. For example, fraud exists if a niece tells her great uncle that she is penniless when, in fact, she is wealthy, or a daughter incorrectly tells her mother that only her sister instigated a conservatorship proceeding, when actually they both did.

Mistake. A will can also be contested on the basis of a mistake. Examples include: (*a*) the testator leaves her estate to only one son, mistakenly believing that the other is wealthy; (*b*) the testator mistakenly leaves out an intended clause; or (*c*) the will mistakenly includes an unintended clause.

Ordinarily, a finding of lack of testamentary capacity will invalidate the entire will, while a finding of undue influence, fraud, or mistake might invalidate only those provisions that relate to the specific problem.

Statutory Requirements for Wills

Most states, including those that have adopted the Uniform Probate Code, recognize at least two types of wills, the *witnessed will* and the *holographic will*.

Witnessed will. Although state laws vary, a witnessed or "attested" will must usually meet the following three requirements:

1. It must be *in writing* (handwritten, typed, etc.).
2. The *testator must sign* the will in the presence of *two witnesses* (three in a few states).
3. The *witnesses must sign* their names to the will, understanding that the instrument they sign is the testator's will. The main purpose of requiring witnesses is to prevent forgery and coercion of the testator.

Beneficiaries should not be witnesses to a will because that could imperil their right to receive some or all of their bequest. In most states, a bequest to a witness is void, unless the witness is an heir. And in that case, the witness can take no more than his or her intestate share. In some other states, if challenged, an "interested witness" may take more than the intestate share only if he or she is able to rebut a statutory presumption that the devise was procured by duress, menace, fraud, or undue influence. Although inability to rebut this presumption will not totally invalidate the will, it will invalidate some or all of the bequest to that witness.

Holographic will. If a written will does not meet all of the requirements for a witnessed will, in many states, including those adopting the UPC, it can still be admitted to probate if it meets the requirements for a holographic will. Typical state requirements for a holographic will are:

1. Signature is in the testator's handwriting.
2. All of the "material provisions" of the will are in the testator's handwriting.

Years ago, the courts of most states applied will format and formality requirements more strictly than they do today. Let's consider two examples.

First, courts often refused to admit to probate holographic documents written on printed stationery, such as letterhead. This restriction is less common today. In determining what parts of the will must be in the testator's handwriting, some states currently use the following test: If the non-testator's portion is excluded, will the remaining handwritten portion make sense? Reflecting the position of perhaps a minority of states, an Arizona court recently concluded "no" in a situation where the testator completed a preprinted will purchased at a retail store.[2] However, the modern trend is to admit documents that reflect "substantial compliance." The "material provisions" requirement of some state holographic will requirements described above reflect this trend. UPC §2-503 was recently added to recognize imperfect documents intended by the decedent to be his or her will, implicitly accepting the premise that a "harmless error" will be disregarded.

Second, most states have required the testator's signature to be placed at the end of the will. But one state in a recent case approved a will in which the testator had simply written her name at the beginning.[3]

Holographic wills are recognized in about 40 percent of the states.

Contrasting witnessed and holographic wills. There are two major differences between the two sets of formal requirements: First, the witnessed will requires the performance of certain activities by two witnesses. In contrast, the holographic will may, but need not, be witnessed. Second, the holographic will requires that all material provisions of the will be in the testator's handwriting. In contrast, the witnessed will requires that only the testator's signature be handwritten, and even this may be unnecessary when a proper authorization is arranged.

No Contest Clause

In the last few pages, we have described several technical requirements for a valid will including testamentary capacity, absence of undue influence, fraud, mistake, and certain specific execution requirements such as signatures by witnesses and the testator. Anticipating that dissatisfied persons may claim that one or more violations of these requirements has occurred, as a pretext for obtaining more of the estate, testators may insert in their will a "no contest" clause like the one that follows:

> *I have purposely made no provisions herein for any other person or persons, other than as set forth in this will, and if any person contests this will, I revoke any share or interest given such person, and said share or interest shall be disposed of as though said person predeceased me without leaving issue.*

It usually discourages will contests, but not always, for several reasons. First, it will discourage only beneficiaries named in the will, not disinherited persons who stand to lose nothing by contesting. Second, beneficiaries may still wish to contest if they expect to gain considerably more than they'll lose. Finally, courts in most jurisdictions narrowly construe no contest clauses, and will not enforce them if the contestant acted in good faith or with probable cause. Perhaps most testators would desire this result, anyway.

What situations tend to invite will contests? The most common are where the testator chooses to disinherit family members in favor of a friend, a charity, a spouse married shortly before death, or where a testator treats children unequally. If the testator is very old or is ailing physically or mentally, a contest is even more likely.

Will contests are infrequent, and *successful* contests are very uncommon. Fewer than one percent of wills offered for probate are challenged, and over two-thirds of these challenges are unsuccessful. However, recently will contests have probably become more common for at least three reasons: First, during recessionary periods, more claimants will look to estates as a source of funds. Second, as the general population continues to age, more elderly people of means will acquire 'friends' who offer to assist them in their finances. And third, a higher divorce rate has increased the number of children of former marriages, a group that is less likely to get along with the surviving spouse of a later marriage. When any of these situations or factors apply to a particular client, attorneys should take special precautions in drafting and executing the will.

The Simple Will

Wills can be quite lengthy and complex, but this section focuses on a relatively simple will. A *simple will*, as it is generally called, is a will prepared for a family having a small, or even a modest estate, where death taxes are not a significant concern (generally, these are estates less than $600,000.)

The simple will usually includes all of the following: nominating an executor and, if there are minor children, a guardian, a waiver of the probate bond, and, in most cases, it gives the testator's property to the spouse, if alive, otherwise to the children by right of representation.

Exhibit 3-1 presents a simple will that demonstrates the essential nature of this probate property transfer document. The reader is encouraged to study it carefully, so that the analysis that follows is more readily understood.

EXHIBIT 3-1 Simple Will

WILL
OF
WILLARD THOMAS SMITH

I, Willard Thomas Smith, a resident of Mytown, Anystate, declare this to be my will. I revoke all prior Wills and Codicils.

First: Family and Guardian I am married to, Sue L. Smith, referred to in this will as "my wife." I have three children, all from this marriage, whose names and birthdays are:

Kristi M. Smith   June 27, 1987
Heather L. Smith   April 19, 1989
Todd R. Smith   May 11, 1991

Reference to "my children" or to "my child," shall include children born later and children adopted by me. I have no deceased children.

If my wife does not survive me, and it is necessary to appoint a guardian, I appoint Curtis J. Quint guardian of the person and estate of each such minor child. If for any reason Curtis J. Quint does not act as guardian, I appoint Maria S. Cruise as guardian of the person and estate of each such minor child.

Second: Executor The executor shall serve as follows:

A. *Designation* I appoint my wife as my executor. If for any reason she does not so act, I appoint James A. Reliable to be my executor. If for any reason neither my wife nor James A. Reliable acts as executor, I appoint Third National Bank of Mytown to be my executor.

B. *Bond waiver* No bond, surety, or other security shall be required of my executor.

Third: Disposition of Property I make the following gifts of property:

A. *Tangible personal property* If my wife survives me by 30 days, I give her all of my interest in our tangible personal property. If my wife does not survive me by 30 days, I give my tangible personal property to my issue, by right of representation, provided they survive me for that period. My executor shall consider their personal preferences in making the division. My executor has my permission to sell any of that property and distribute the proceeds to equalize the shares. My executor shall be discharged for all tangible personal property so given to any minor child if the child, or adult having the child's custody, gives a written receipt to my executor.

B. *Residue* If my wife survives me by 120 days, I give her the residue of my estate. If my wife does not survive me by 120 days, I give the residue to my issue, by right of representation, provided they survive me for that period. If neither my wife nor any of

EXHIBIT 3-1 Simple Will *(continued)*

my descendants survives me by 120 days, I give the residue of my estate according to Mystate's laws of descent and distribution, one half as if I had died with no will on the last day of that 120 day period, and one half as if it were my wife's estate and she had died with no will on that last day.

C. *Taxes from residue* All death taxes imposed because of my death and interest and penalties on those taxes, whether on property passing under this will or otherwise, shall be paid by my executor from the residue of my estate.

Fourth: Powers of Executor My executor shall have unrestricted powers, without court order, to settle my estate as this will provides. In addition, my executor shall have the following powers:

1. To make interim distributions of principal and income on an interim basis to those entitled to it.
2. To sell, exchange, mortgage, pledge, lease or assign any property belonging to my estate.
3. To continue operation of any business belonging to my estate.
4. To invest and reinvest any surplus money.

I have signed my name to this instrument on March 19, 1996, at Mytown, Anystate.

_____(Signature)_____

Statement of Witnesses The undersigned witnesses declare under penalty of perjury under Anystate law, on March 19, 1996, that we are over twenty-one, that the testator declared to us that this instrument is his will, that he signed this will, and that he requested us to act as witnesses to it. Whereupon he signed in our presence, and we now, in the presence of each other, subscribe our names as witnesses. In doing so, we attest that we believe that the testator is of sound mind, and did not act under fraud, duress or undue influence.

_____(Signature)_____   _____(Signature)_____

_____(Address)_____   _____(Address)_____

Analysis of the Simple Will. Let's analyze the major provisions of this will, section by section.

Will of Willard Thomas Smith. In this introductory paragraph, the testator "declares" the document to be his will, satisfying the legal requirement that to be a will there must be evidence of testamentary intent.

A *codicil* is a separate written document that amends or revokes a prior will. It is executed if the testator wishes to make one or more brief changes or additions to the will. It must meet all of the legal requirements of a will, including subscription by witnesses, although in states that recognize holographic wills, a holographic codicil even to a witnessed will is acceptable if the codicil meets that state's requirements for a holographic will.

One of the more common methods of *revoking* a prior will is by executing a later will that declares such revocation as is done in the Smith's will. Revocation by "cancellation" with a "subsequent instrument," as it is termed, can also be undertaken in any other signed, witnessed statement. A will can also be revoked by a physical act, such as by burning, tearing, canceling, obliterating or destroying it, when such is done by the testator with an intent to revoke.[4]

Revoking all prior wills and codicils eliminates the danger that provisions in prior wills that are inconsistent with the present will may have to be construed together with the current will. Without a revocation clause, needless litigation might arise over whether or not the provisions in two or more wills are inconsistent. For example, in one state supreme court case, a decedent-testator had written two "last" wills within three weeks. The first simply left "a tract of land" to a friend. The second contained no revocation clause and left "all my effects" to siblings Y and Z. The court permitted a trial to determine whether the first will should be construed along with the second, reasoning that they were not necessarily inconsistent because the testator could have used the word "effects" to mean only personal property.[5] If the testator's intent was to leave everything to Y and Z, inclusion of a revocation clause would have assured this result, and if the intent was to preserve the gift of the land to the friend, then that should have been clearly stated in the second will.

First: Family and Guardian. Naming all members of the immediate family assists the personal representative in finding relatives and locating assets.

Including *after born children* in the will prevents a child born after the execution of the will and, therefore, not provided for in it, from being left to inherit under the laws of intestate succession, a consequence which might conflict with the testator's intent.

A minor child who out-lives both parents is required by law to have a *guardian* of the person and of the estate appointed. A guardian of the person is responsible for the minor child's care, custody, control and education, while a guardian of the child's estate is responsible for managing the minor child's property. A testator's nomination carries great weight and is usually followed, however the probate judge does have the power to appoint someone else. Nominating an alternate guardian increases the likelihood that the testator's preferences will be followed.

Second: Executor. Similar to the nomination of a guardian, the nomination of an executor and an alternate executor is helpful to the probate court in its selection process.

Unless the bond is waived in the will, the executor is required to post a *fiduciary bond*. A bonding company, for a fee, insures the estate assets against loss if such is caused by the executor's breach of fiduciary obligations. The will can waive the bond requirement. The testator may consider a bond unnecessary because it results in additional expense to the estate, and/or because the executor is likely to be not only a highly trusted member of the testator's family, such as the surviving spouse, but is also likely to be one of the major beneficiaries of the estate. Ordinarily, the bond amount will be set by the court to be equal to the total value of the personal probate property, plus one year's estimated income from all of the probate property; the idea being that the personal representative could run off with everything but the real property.

Third: Disposition of property. This simple will essentially leaves all property to the testator's spouse, if surviving, otherwise to the children. The interest of the children is sometimes referred to as a "gift-over" to the children. The will distinguishes the tangible personal property from the residue, which consists of all other probate assets. Thus, the spouse must survive by 30 days to take tangible personal property and 120 days to take the residue. If the spouse does not survive the requisite time period, the property passes to the children who do so survive.

Inclusion of a survival requirement, such as 30 days or 120 days, reduces the likelihood that the death of both spouses in a common accident will result in subjecting some of the family property to two successive probates. This *survival clause*, as it is called, helps in situations not covered by the Uniform Simultaneous Death Act (USDA).

Enacted by *every* state, the USDA provides that when transfer of title to property depends on the order of deaths, and when no sufficient evidence exists that two people died other than simultaneously, the property of each is disposed of as if each had survived the other. Thus, in the case of a married couple, the husband's estate would likely pass to his blood relatives and the wife's estate would likely pass to her blood relatives. This statute is of limited value, however, because it does not avoid double probate when the order of deaths can in fact be established. In some states, if it *can* be established that one spouse survived the other, even only by seconds, then the USDA will not apply and, absent a survival clause, there will be a *double probate* of the property owned by the first spouse to die. Perhaps worse, *all* of the property may ultimately pass to that spouse's in-laws, rather than the surviving relatives. Some states, including California, have legislated safeguards against inheritance by in-laws by requiring that the portion of the decedent's estate attributable to the predeceased spouse pass, in some circumstances, to the predeceased spouse's children, parents, or other kin.[6] The Uniform Probate Code's version of the USDA, in Section 2-104, provides that the property of each is disposed of as if each had survived the other when it cannot be established that the other person survived by *120 hours*.

With regard to *insurance* on the life of a decedent, the USDA states that in the event of an apparent simultaneous death of the insured and the beneficiary, the policy proceeds are to be distributed as if the insured survived the beneficiary. Thus, the proceeds will be paid to the contingent beneficiary, and if none, then to the owner's probate estate.

Section B covering the "residue" is called the *residuary clause*. Failure to include it in a will can result in *partial intestacy*. In a recent case, the attorney who had drafted the decedent's will admitted that he mistakenly omitted the residuary clause, but indicated that the decedent wanted the residue to go to a friend. The court would not allow admission of this evidence, ruling that extrinsic evidence is admissible to explain what is *in* the will, not to *add* to the will.[7]

Disposing of estate property by differentiating the tangible personal property from the residue can speed up probate distribution and can often save income taxes. In the chapter on fiduciary income taxes, the concept of distributable net income, DNI, is discussed. A *specific bequest* of property, such as when the testator specifies the tangible personal property, prevents the distribution from being labeled DNI. This generates less taxable income to the distributee (often the spouse), and correspondingly more taxable income to the estate, which is (hopefully) in a lower rate bracket.

Instead of "tangible personal property," some wills ill-advisedly use the term "personal effects," which really means "tangible personal property, worn or carried about the person or having some intimate relation with the person." Since automobiles and some other property are not considered "personal effects," the broader term *tangible personal property* is preferred.

Distribution by right of representation, or as it is also called *per stirpes*, is a method of allocating a bequest of the decedent's property such that it follows the natural line of descent (e.g., the children of a predeceased child share that child's portion of the estate.)

The laws of intestate succession, also known as "laws of descent and distribution," vary somewhat from state to state. They spell out the priority of succession rights of the decedent's spouse and kin in the event of intestacy. In the event that his wife and all of his descendants fail to survive him by 120 days, the testator has generously chosen to divide his property in halves, with one half going by intestate succession to his relatives and the other half going by intestate succession to his wife's relatives.

Declaring that all *death taxes* be paid from the residue of the estate may be the fairest plan, and one that can minimize administrative delay. It relieves recipients of specifically bequeathed property from having to share in this burden. In addition, it relieves the executor from the responsibility of *seeking reimbursement* from individuals who may have received non-liquid assets, such as a painting or a piano. And reimbursement for death taxes can be difficult to obtain from individuals not at all connected with the probate process, such as those succeeding to ownership as former joint tenants with the decedent, and beneficiaries of a life insurance policy on the life of the decedent. In some circumstances, however, fairness would dictate apportioning the taxes among all beneficiaries in direct proportion to their share of the taxable estate.

Fourth: Powers of Executor. Granting explicit powers to the executor can eliminate the need to secure permission of the probate court to undertake certain administrative actions. Ordinarily, testators would like their executors to act without undue delay.

Signature Clause and the Statement of Witnesses. Every state imposes formal requirements regarding the signing of the will and the role of witnesses. The sentences including the statement of witnesses offer some additional evidence of the testator's capacity to execute a will. It also increases the likelihood of compliance with these formal requirements by explicitly stating them, which the witnesses acknowledge by signing. The Statement of Witnesses is also referred to as the *attestation clause*. When a will is signed and witnessed in the proper manner, such that it is a valid will, it is said to be executed.

Other aspects of the simple will. Simple wills are most commonly drafted by attorneys for clients with smaller estates. If two such clients are married, a simple will is usually prepared for each spouse. In most cases, the dispositive clauses are identical. Thus, the husband's will leaves all to his wife, if she survives, otherwise to their children. And the wife's will leaves all to her husband, if he survives, otherwise to their children. Such simple wills are commonly called *reciprocal wills*, *mirror wills*, or *mutual wills*.

Occasionally clients will want *contractual wills*, ones which cannot be revised once one of the parties (usually spouses) dies. Sometimes, these are done in the form of a single will for two people, called a *joint will*, although a joint will need not be contractual. Contractual wills are rare because most clients want the flexibility of changing their estate plan after one spouse dies. Joint wills should be avoided unless the clients really want a contractual will, because even if the clients did not intend the joint will to be irrevocable once one of the testators dies, a court may rule that this was the intent because there can be little other reason to create one document for two people.

Wills that are more complex are hardly ever found to be reciprocal in content. Typically, they are prepared by attorneys specializing in estate planning to reflect the inherently different preferences and different financial and tax circumstances of the spouses. This text will highlight many of these differences in later chapters.

Where should the original copy of the will be kept? The client's safe deposit box makes good sense only in those states (e.g., California) that do not *seal* boxes at the owner's death. In states where safe deposit boxes are sealed at the owner's death execution of the will is delayed until a state official can join the prospective executor in inventorying the contents, so as to ensure that the estate includes any jewelry, bearer bonds, and the like that might be there, as such may enhance the state's share of death taxes. Some attorneys recommend their own safe, but this might be viewed as self-serving, since the executor will have to come to the attorney's office to take charge of the will, thus giving the attorney a good chance of serving as the probate attorney. However, given the testator picked that attorney to help with his or her estate plan, it would seem reasonable to go back to that attorney for help with the decedent's estate. Some attorneys simply recommend a secure, handy place in the client's home.

Next, we examine the trust, the other major planning document of transfer.

THE TRUST

The principal parties to a trust are the trustor, the trustee, and the beneficiary. As a legal arrangement, a trust is created by the trustor and divides and transfers interests in property between two or more people. Any interests or control over the trust not given to the beneficiaries are either retained by the trustor, granted to the trustee, or exercised by both.

A trust can take effect during the lifetime of the trustor, or it can take effect at the trustor's death. As we have seen, the former is called a *living* (or *inter vivos*) *trust*, while the latter is called a *testamentary trust*, that is, a trust created in a complex will that professionals also call a "trust-will." The testamentary trust document is covered later in the chapter.

At any given moment, a trust is either revocable and amendable, in which case the trustor is capable of voiding or amending it, or it is irrevocable, that is, not voidable or amendable. A living trust usually contains specific language stating whether it is revocable or irrevocable. A revocable living trust usually, but not always, becomes irrevocable at the death of the trustor(s). Like the contents of most wills, the provisions of a testamentary trust can be amended or revoked before the testator's death by codicil, revocation, or destruction of the testamentary trust. At the testator's death, a testamentary trust takes effect and becomes irrevocable, since the only person capable of amending or revoking it, the testator, is, of course, permanently unavailable.

A trust usually contains two different legal types of property, principal and income. The *principal* of a trust is its invested wealth, and its size will fluctuate as additions are made to it and as charges are made against it. Additions to principal accrue from such things as asset appreciation and stock share dividends. Charges against principal include costs of investing the principal (commissions, legal fees, etc.) and transfer taxes.

In contrast with trust principal, the *income* of a trust is the return in money or property derived from use of the trust principal. Examples of income include cash dividends, rent, and interest. Trust income also has charges against it, most of which reflect expenses incurred in managing the trust property (e.g., insurance premiums and some portion of the trustee's fee). Any trust income not distributed to beneficiaries is said to be *accumulated* in the trust and is generally accounted for as retained income, not principal.

The accounting distinction between principal and income is particularly important, because most trusts contain provisions that bestow rights to principal and income to different beneficiaries. In the chapter on fiduciary income taxes, we'll see that the distinction between principal and income will influence trust income taxation.

The beneficiaries of an irrevocable trust are usually either *income beneficiaries* (i.e., those having an interest in the income) or *principal beneficiaries* (for example, a remainderman, one who stands to receive principal outright when the trust terminates). These two types of beneficiaries may have conflicting or "adverse" interests, because the increased distributions to one may decrease the distributions to the other. For example, high yield-low growth stock would tend to benefit the income beneficiaries more than the remaindermen whereas low yield-high growth stock would favor the remaindermen more than the income beneficiaries.

There are other ways of classifying trusts, especially in connection with tax planning. The chapters in Part 3 introduce several tax-saving trusts, including the bypass trust, the Crummey trust, and the QTIP trust. First, however, we will explore the laws of estate, gift, and income taxation to understand how to save taxes. The purpose of focusing on trusts in the present chapter is more basic: to enable the reader to learn the essential structure of the two principal documents creating the trust. The following material describes a living trust and a testamentary trust. Keep in mind these trusts vary greatly, so it is a stretch to call any one trust typical.

Living Trust Instrument

A living trust is created by a document of agreement between the trustor (or settlor) and the trustee. Before we examine the actual instrument, let's compare and contrast the characteristics of that document with the will, which is the document most people think of when considering how transfers at death are guided.

Similarities. The will and the living trust instrument are similar in three important ways. First, both serve as the guide to the disposition of the one's property at his or her death. Second, both have a fiduciary (the executor or the trustee) who is responsible for managing property for a period of time until the transfers can be completed. Third, both instruments are generally amendable and revocable, at least until the person creating the instrument dies. The will can nearly always be amended by a codicil, or revoked by its destruction or by execution of a later will that explicitly revokes it. One exception, of course, is the *contractual will*, which becomes irrevocable after the death of the first co-testator. The living trust is either revocable or irrevocable. In most states, a trust must state that it is revocable, otherwise it becomes irrevocable upon execution. In the other states, the opposite rule is in effect, such that a trust is revocable unless stated to be irrevocable.

Differences. The will and the living trust instrument are different in three important ways. First, they dispose of a totally different set of property. A living trust instrument disposes of property owned by the trustee, while a will disposes of probate property owned by the decedent at death. Thus, with regard to property transfers, the living trust instrument and the will are mutually exclusive; property owned by the trustee is not probate property, while probate property is owned by the decedent, not the trustee. Of course, the decedent's will can transfer property, by way of the probate process, to the trustee of his or her living trust, or even to the trustee of a trust he or she did not create, such as one created by one's spouse. Wills that transfer property to a trustee are called *pour-over wills,* because they "pour" property into the trust.

Second, with regard to choosing a fiduciary, a living trust instrument *appoints* a trustee whereas a will *nominates* an executor. Of course, a testamentary trust must nominate both an executor and a trustee. Since the trustor of a living trust is alive when the trustee is appointed, the trustor has control over the appointment. The trust instrument is a legal *contract* between the trustor and the trustee. On the other hand, the probate judge appoints the executor of a will after the testator's death. The judge may appoint someone else for any number of reasons, including the nominee's inability to serve due to death, disability, or incompetence.

Third, while the formal execution requirements for writing a will are quite strict, the requirements for properly executing a trust instrument are simple to meet. In most cases, the trust document is simply dated and signed by the trustor and the trustee. Witnesses are not required, however some attorneys have the trustor's signature notarized to assure others of its validity, especially those who might have to rely on the document at a time when the trustor is incapacitated or deceased. Although the formalities surrounding the execution of a trust document are simpler than those for a will, the mental capacity necessary is set at a higher standard. The settlor must have contractual capacity. Given the nature of the trust document, this would be, in addition to testamentary capacity, the ability to understand and enter into a bilateral contractual agreement. In most states, one contesting a settlor's (or a testator's) capacity has the burden of proving the lack of capacity by "clear and convincing" evidence. This is a more difficult (i.e., higher) standard than the typical "preponderance" of evidence burden generally placed on the plaintiff in a civil case.

Exhibit 3-2 presents a living trust that is fairly simple since it is not designed to save taxes. Trusts designed to save taxes break into several irrevocable trusts at the trustor's death.

EXHIBIT 3-2 Living Trust Instrument

JOHN C. JONES

Revocable Living Trust

Dated March 19, 1996

TRUST AGREEMENT made March 19, 1996, between John C. Jones, as trustor, resident of Common County, Mystate, and John C. Jones, resident of Common County, Mystate, as trustee.

1. Trust property. The trustor has set aside and holds in trust the property described on Schedule One, attached to this instrument. The trustee agrees to hold such property and any later accepted property, in trust, under the terms and conditions provided herein.

2. Successor trustee. If John C. Jones for any reason ceases to act as trustee, my wife, Sarah E. Jones, shall serve as trustee. If Sarah E. Jones is unable or for any reason ceases to act as trustee, then First National Bank of Anytown shall serve as trustee.

3. Power to amend or revoke. The trustor reserves the right at any time to amend or revoke this trust, in whole or in part, by an instrument in writing signed by him and delivered during his lifetime to the trustee.

4. Operation of trust during trustor's lifetime. During the trustor's lifetime, the trustee shall administer and distribute the trust as follows:

a. Trust income. The trustee shall pay the net income to the trustor at convenient intervals but at least quarter-annually.

b. Trust principal. The trustee shall pay to the trustor from time to time such amounts of the principal of this trust as the trustor shall direct in writing or as the trustee deems advisable for the trustor's support and comfort.

5. Operation of trust after trustor's death. Upon the death of the trustor, the trust estate shall be held, administered, and distributed as follows:

a. Wife survives by four months. If the trustor's wife survives trustor by four months, the trustee shall distribute the entire trust estate to the trustee of her revocable trust, dated the same date as this trust, to be held and administered according to its

EXHIBIT 3-2 Living Trust Instrument *(continued)*

terms. If said trust is no longer in existence, then distribution shall be to trustor's wife, free of trust.

   b.   Wife does not survive by four months. If the trustor's wife does not survive the trustor by four months and if no then-living child of the trustor is under age twenty-one, then the trustee shall divide the trust into as many equal shares as there are children of the trustor's then living and children of the trustor's then deceased with descendants then living. Each share set aside for a child then deceased with descendants then living shall be further divided into shares for such descendants, by right of representation. The trust estate shall be held, administered, and distributed in the manner described in subsections 5(b)(2)(a) and (b), below.

   If neither the trustor's wife nor any of the trustor's descendants survive the trustor by four months, the trustee shall distribute the entire trust estate according to Mystate's laws of descent and distribution, one half as if the trustor had died with no will on the last day of the four-month period and one half as if it were the trustor's wife's estate and she had died with no will on the last day. If the trustor's wife does not survive the trustor by four months and if any then-living child of the trustor is under age twenty-one, then the trust estate shall be held, administered, and distributed as follows:

   (1) *Any child under age* twenty-one. So long as any of the trustor's children are living who are under twenty-one, the trustee shall pay to or apply for the benefit of all of the trustor's children as much of the net income and principal as the trustee in the trustee's discretion deems necessary for their proper support, health, and education, after taking into consideration, to the extent that the trustee considers advisable, the value of the trust assets, the relative needs, both present and future, of each of the beneficiaries, and their other income and resources made known to the trustee and reasonably available to meet beneficiary needs. The trustee may make distributions under this provision that benefit one or more beneficiaries to the exclusion of others. Any net income not distributed shall be accumulated and added to principal.

   (2) *Youngest child reaches age twenty-one.* When the youngest of the trustor's then-living children reaches the age of twenty-one, the trustee shall divide the trust into as many equal shares as there are children of the trustor's then living and deceased children who left issue. Each share set aside the issue of a deceased child shall be further divided into shares, by right of representation, for such descendants. Each such share shall be distributed, or retained in trust, as hereafter provided.

   (a) Each share set aside for a descendant shall be distributed to that descendant free of trust when he or she reaches the age of twenty-one.

   (b) Each share set aside for a descendant who had not then reached age twenty-one shall be retained in trust. The trustee shall pay to or for the benefit of that descendant as much of the income and principal of the trust as the trustee, in the trustee's discretion, considers appropriate for that descendant's support, health, and education. When that descendant reaches age twenty-one, the descendant's share shall be distributed to that descendant, free of trust. If that descendant dies before receiving distribution of that descendant's entire share, the undistributed balance of that descendant's share shall be distributed, free of trust, to that descendant's then-living descendants, by right of representation, or if there are none, to the trustor's then-living

---

EXHIBIT 3-2 Living Trust Instrument *(continued)*

descendants, by right of representation. The share of a descendant for whom there exists a trust created by this instrument, shall augment that descendant's trust.

6. Restriction against assignment, etc. No interest in the principal or income of this trust shall be anticipated, assigned, encumbered, or subject to any creditor's claim or to legal process before its actual receipt by the beneficiary.

7. Perpetuities saving. Any trust created by this will that has not terminated sooner shall terminate twenty-one years after the death of the last survivor of the class composed of my wife and those of my descendants living at my death.

8. Powers of trustee. To carry out the purposes of this trust, the trustee is vested with the following powers with respect to the trust estate and any part of it, in addition to those powers now or hereafter conferred by law:

a. To continue to hold any property, including shares of the trustee's own stock, and to operate at the risk of the trust estate any business that the trustee receives or acquires under the trust as long as the trustee deems advisable.

b. To manage, control, grant options on, sell (for cash or on deferred payments), convey, exchange, partition, divide, improve, and repair trust property.

c. To lease trust property for terms within or beyond the term of the trust and for any purpose, including exploration for and removal of gas, oil, and other minerals and to enter into community oil leases, pooling, and unitization agreements.

d. To borrow money, and to encumber or hypothecate trust property by mortgage, deed of trust, pledge, or otherwise.

e. To invest and reinvest the trust estate in every kind of property, real, personal, or mixed, and every kind of investment, specifically including, but not by way of limitation, corporate obligations of every kind, stocks, preferred or common, shares of investment trusts, investment companies and mutual funds, and mortgage participations, which men of prudence, discretion, and intelligence acquire for their own account, and any common trust fund administered by the trustee.

f. In any case in which the trustee is required, pursuant to the provisions of the trust, to divide any trust property into parts or shares for the purpose of distribution, or otherwise, the trustee is authorized, in the trustee's absolute discretion, to make the division and distribution partly in kind and partly in money, and for this purpose to make such sales of the trust property as the trustee may deem necessary on such terms and conditions as the trustee shall see fit.

IN WITNESS THEREOF this instrument has been executed as of the date set forth on the first page of this instrument.

_____(Signature of Trustor)_____   _____(Signature of Trustee)_____

John C. Jones, Trustor   John C. Jones, Trustee

Analysis of the living trust instrument. Let's examine the major provisions of this living trust instrument, section by section.

Trust Agreement. A trust is, in effect, a contract or agreement between two parties, the trustor and the trustee. Both sides agree to perform certain tasks: among other things, the trustor agrees to deliver property described in Schedule One (not shown) to the trustee, and the trustee agrees to hold, administer, and distribute the trust property in keeping with the terms of the trust.

In this living trust instrument, the trustor names himself to be initial trustee, and names alternate successor trustees to take over when he is incapable of performing, either because of his death, or earlier. He might want to travel without worrying about managing the trust property or he might be come too ill to manage it.

1. Trust property. The instrument specifies that additional assets may be put in trust in the future, even after the trustor's death. For example, a decedent's will can be directed to "pour over" probate property into a trust after the trustor-testator's death.

2. Successor trustee. Since the trust instrument states the trustee's name in the opening paragraph, this section need only name successor trustees. It is not unusual to name one or more of the remaindermen, if they are adults, as a successors, since the person or persons have a vested interest in managing and transferring the property efficiently. Some times, the children are named as successor trustees, with a contingency that they must have reached a certain age, (e.g., twenty-five), in order to serve. Naming a bank, or other corporate entity, as a successor trustee virtually ensures that an experienced trustee will be available to serve for the duration of the trust. Some corporate fiduciaries will not assume the position of trustee unless the corpus is some minimum value. In any case where a corporate trustee is being considered, a meeting with the trust officers should be arranged to decrease the likelihood that trust position will be refused later.

3. Power to amend or revoke. This trust can be amended or revoked by a written document signed by the trustor and delivered to the trustee. An amendment is similar to a codicil to a will, but without the strict formal execution requirements.

4. Operation of trust during trustor's lifetime. During the trustor's lifetime, the trustee is required to pay to the trustor all income at least quarterly, and any principal as requested. The reader will notice that the wording assumes that the trustor and the trustee are *different parties.* However, as mentioned above, many, perhaps most living trust agreements name the trustor to be trustee. Then, as in

Exhibit 3-2, this paragraph would still be used, but would be meaningful only if the client became incompetent, thus requiring the appointment of a different successor trustee.

5. *Operation of trust after trustor's death.* This section is substantially longer than the Disposition of Property section in the simple will. It provides for several alternative outcomes depending upon who survives. First, the trust terminates if the trustor's *spouse survives* the trustor by four months, and all trust property passes to her revocable trust or, if it is no longer in existence, then outright to her.

Second, if the trustor's spouse does not survive by four months and all of the trustor's children are over the age of twenty-one, the trust will terminate and distribute free of trust to the children. However, if one or more of the trustor's living children is *under twenty-one*, the trust continues as one trust. The trustee is instructed to collectively use trust principal and income to provide for all the children's support, education, and other reasonable needs. Thus, the trustee has a limited power of appointment over the entire trust income and principal, with all living descendants named as permissible appointees. Then, when the youngest child reaches twenty-one, the trust is divided into equal shares, one for each child then living, and one for each deceased child for whom there are living descendants. The trust directs distribution to the younger generations by right of representation, also called "traditional *per stirpes*," a concept more fully explained in a later chapter. Each share is then distributed outright to each descendant when he or she reaches age twenty-one. Thus, at the time of the splitting of the corpus, each child and any other descendant beneficiary at least age twenty-one will immediately receive one share.

Third, if the trustor's spouse fails to survive the trustor by four months and if no living child is under age twenty-one, the trust may or may not terminate, depending upon whether there are underage descendants of deceased children. In any event, however, the trust estate is immediately divided into shares, and each child immediately receives one share. The balance of the trust corpus (held for these underage descendants of deceased children) will be administered in a manner (described below) quite similar to the way it is administered for a living child when under twenty-one. As each of these descendants reaches age twenty-one, he or she will receive an outright distribution of his or her share. Accordingly, the trust will terminate when the youngest living descendant of deceased children reaches age twenty-one.

Finally, if the trustor is survived neither by a spouse nor any descendants, the trust terminates and the trust property passes by *intestate succession*, with one half to the trustor's relatives and the other half to the trustor's spouse's relatives. The laws of intestate succession are covered in the next chapter.

The above disposition, via trustee, has much to recommend it over the will's provisions making outright gifts to the minor children, via a property guardian. We'll defer describing these advantages, however, until Part 3.

6. Restriction against assignment. This is an example of a *spendthrift clause*. Without it, the laws of many states would allow trust beneficiaries to transfer and encumber their interests in the trust property, and would enable the beneficiaries' creditors to seize trust assets to satisfy their claims. For example, beneficiaries could mortgage their share of trust property, sell a future interest in it, and devise it. A spendthrift clause restricts such transfers. However, it only protects trust property while held by the trustee, not after it has been transferred outright to the beneficiary.

7. Perpetuities saving. This clause is included to prevent a contingent gift from being ruled invalid because it violates a law found in almost all states that requires interests to vest within some reasonable time after the transfer. This law is called the rule against perpetuities. It is discussed in more detail in the Appendix 3A, which immediately follows this chapter.

8. Powers of trustee. Since a trustee is likely to manage trust property for a considerably longer period than an executor is likely to manage an estate, the powers granted to the trustee are usually stated in more detail than those granted in a will to an executor. In addition to these powers, both the executor and trustee automatically have other implicit powers derived from statutory law and from case law, unless the document specifically prohibits such powers. For example, trustees have the power to defend against claims brought against the trust property, whether or not that power is specifically granted in the document.

This living trust is uncomplicated primarily because it does not attempt to save estate taxes. If the other spouse survives the trustor spouse by four months, all corpus will pass to the surviving spouse's revocable trust or outright to her. Like the simple will, it is created for families with modest estates, for whom death tax planning is not a significant concern. We'll introduce a more complicated tax-saving living trust in the two chapters that deal with estate plans for the wealthy, where estate taxes are a concern.

The third and final document, covered next, combines the disposition characteristics of a will with the many benefits of a delayed trust, one that takes effect after the client's death.

THE TESTAMENTARY TRUST

The testamentary trust, or trust-will, is the third principal document of property disposition commonly prepared by attorneys in the estate planning process. In essence, a testamentary trust is actually one type of *will*; it serves as the guiding document for the distribution of the testator-trustor's probate property at death. In addition, it disposes of some, or all, of the probate property to the trustee of a trust that is newly created according to trust terms that are set forth in the document. This trust takes effect after the testator's death at the end of the probate process. The actual creation of the trust, and the funding mechanism, is the order for distribution. The order names (appoints) the trustee, sets forth all of the terms of the trust (generally quoting verbatim from the testamentary trust document), and orders the executor to distribute the estate to the trustee. The trustee uses the order as the governing document when dealing with third parties, such as banks, brokers, and title companies, rather than the original trust-will. Recording a certified copy of the order in those counties where real property is located, serves to transfer the property from the estate to the trustee.

As a will, the testamentary trust must conform to all of the formal legal requirements for the execution of wills. It, therefore, contains all essential provisions found in any will, such as nomination of a guardian of the person and estate of the testator's minor children, nomination of executors, and a section for the attestation by witnesses. It may also have provisions that make outright gifts of certain property, (e.g., the tangible personal property may be given to the spouse or children free of trust).

In addition to containing all of the provisions customarily found in other wills, the testamentary trust, like the living trust, must include *other unique clauses* that relate to the trust itself. Thus, it will include provisions for distributing probate property into the trust, for naming one or more trustees, for indicating who will be the trust beneficiaries, for specifying how much income and principal they will receive and when they will receive it, and for describing the trustee's duties and powers in connection with managing the trust property. Of course, all but the first clause just mentioned are also included in a living trust.

It should be noted that being a will, the testamentary trust is not an "agreement" between testator and future trustee. In fact, the potential trustee may not even be aware that he or she may be performing this task, and may not even be born at execution date of the testamentary trust. Before the court order of distribution, the nominated trustee will have to file with the court a consent to serve as trustee.

Exhibit 3-3 presents a relatively uncomplicated testamentary trust.

EXHIBIT 3-3 Testamentary trust (Trust-Will)

WILL

OF

WILLARD THOMAS SMITH

I, Willard Thomas Smith, a resident of Mytown, Anystate, declare this to be my will. I revoke all prior Wills and Codicils.

First: Family and Guardian I am married to, Sue L. Smith, referred to in this will as "my wife." I have three children, all from this marriage, whose names and birthdays are:

Kristi M. Smith   June 27, 1987
Heather L. Smith   April 19, 1989
Todd R. Smith May 11, 1991

Reference to "my children" or to "my child," shall include children born later and children adopted by me. I have no deceased children.

If my wife does not survive me, and it is necessary to appoint a guardian, I nominate Curtis J. Quint guardian of the person and estate of each such minor child. If for any reason Curtis J. Quint does not act as guardian, I nominate Maria S. Cruise as guardian of the person and estate.

Second: Selection of Fiduciaries I nominate the following fiduciaries:

A. *Designation of Executor* I nominate my wife as my executor. If for any reason she does not so act, I nominate James A. Reliable to be my executor. If for any reason neither my wife nor James A. Reliable acts as executor, I nominate Third National Bank of Mytown to be my executor.

B. *Designation of trustee* I nominate such of my children as are over the age of twenty- five as co-trustees. If my children are unable to serve as trustee, then I nominate James A. Reliable as the trustee of all trusts provided for under this will. If for any reason neither my children nor James A. Reliable are available to serve as trustee, I nominate Third National Bank of Mytown as trustee.

C. *Bond waiver* No bond, surety, or other security shall be required of my executor or of my trustee.

Third: Disposition of Property I make the following provisions for my probate property:

A. *Tangible personal property* If my wife survives me by 30 days, I give her all

---

EXHIBIT 3-3 Testamentary trust *(continued)*

---

of my interest in any tangible personal property. If my wife does not survive me by 30 days, I give my tangible personal property in equal shares to those of my children who survive me by 30 days. My executor shall consider their personal preferences in making that division. If my children are still minors, my executor has my permission to sell any of that property and distribute the proceeds to equalize the shares. My executor shall be discharged for all tangible personal property so given to any minor child if the child or adult having the child's custody gives a written receipt to my executor.

B. *Residue* If my wife survives me by four months, I give her the residue of my estate. If my wife does not survive me by four months and all of my children are then over the age of twenty-one, I give the residue in equal shares: one to each child who survived me by four months, and one share for each deceased child whose issue is then living.

If my wife does not survive me and if any child of mine is under age twenty-one, then the residue of my estate shall not vest in the children as provided above; rather, such property shall be distributed in trust to the trustee named above, to be held, administered, and distributed as follows:

1. *Any child under age twenty-one* So long as a child is under age twenty-one, the trustee shall pay to or apply for the benefit of all of my children, as much of the net income and principal as the trustee in the trustee's discretion deems appropriate for their proper support, health, and education, after taking into consideration, to the extent that the trustee considers it advisable, the value of the trust assets, the relative needs, both present and future, of each of the beneficiaries, and their other income and resources made known to the trustee and reasonably available to meet beneficiary needs. The trustee may make distributions under this provision that benefit one or more beneficiaries to the exclusion of others. Any net income not distributed shall be accumulated and added to principal.

2. *Youngest child reaches age twenty-one* When the youngest child reaches the age of twenty-one, the trustee shall divide the trust into as many equal shares as there are children of mine then living and children of mine then deceased with descendants then living. Each share set aside for a child of mine then deceased with descendants then living shall be further divided into shares for such descendants, by right of representation. Each such share shall be distributed, or retained in trust, as hereafter provided.

a. Each share set aside for a child, or for the descendant of a deceased child who has reached the age of twenty-one, shall be distributed free of trust.

b. Each share set aside for a descendant who has not reached age twenty-one shall be retained in trust. The trustee shall pay to or for the benefit of that descendant as much of the income and principal of the trust as the trustee, in the trustee's discretion, considers appropriate for that descendant's support, health, and education. When the descendant reaches age twenty-one, that descendant's entire share shall be distributed to that descendant, free of trust. If that descendant dies before receiving distribution of that descendant's entire share, the undistributed balance of that descendant's entire share shall be distributed to that descendant's then-living descendants, by right of representation, or if there are none, to my then-living issue, by

---

EXHIBIT 3-3 Testamentary trust *(continued)*

---

right of representation. In the latter event, the share, of a descendant for whom there exists a trust created by this instrument, shall augment that descendant's trust.

C. *Taxes from residue* All death taxes imposed because of my death and interest and penalties on those taxes, whether on property passing under this will or otherwise, shall be paid by my executor from the residue of my estate.

D. *Restriction against assignment, etc.* No interest in the principal or income of this trust shall be anticipated, assigned, encumbered, or subject to any creditor's claim or to legal process before its actual receipt by the beneficiary.

E. *If all beneficiaries die before full distribution* If neither my wife nor any of my descendants survives me by four months, I give the residue of my estate according to Mystate's laws of descent and distribution, one half as if I had died with no will on the last day of that four-month period, and one half as if it were my wife's estate and she had died with no will on that last day.

F. *Perpetuities saving* Any trust created by this will that has not terminated sooner, shall terminate twenty-one years after the death of the last survivor of the class composed of my wife and those of my issue living at my death.

Fourth: Powers of Executor My executor shall have unrestricted powers, without court order, to settle my estate as this will provides. In addition, my executor shall have all powers my executor thinks necessary or desirable to administer my estate, including the following:

A. To make distributions of principal and income on an interim basis to those entitled to it.

B. To sell, exchange, mortgage, pledge, lease or assign any property belonging to my estate.

C. To continue operation of any business belonging to my estate.

D. To invest and reinvest any surplus money.

Fifth: Powers of Trustee To carry out the purposes of any trust created under this paragraph third, and subject to any limitations stated elsewhere in this will, the trustee is vested with the following powers with respect to the trust estate and any part of it, in addition to those powers now or hereafter conferred by law:

A. To continue to hold any property, including shares of the trustee's own stock, and to operate at the risk of the trust estate any business that the trustee receives or acquires under the trust as long as the trustee deems advisable.

B. To manage, control, grant options on, sell (for cash or on deferred payments), convey, exchange, partition, divide, improve, and repair trust property.

C. To lease trust property for terms within or beyond the term of the trust and for any purpose, including exploration for and removal of gas, oil, and other minerals and to enter into community oil leases, pooling, and unitization agreements.

D. To borrow money, and to encumber or hypothecate trust property by mortgage, deed of trust, pledge, or otherwise.

E. To invest and reinvest the trust estate in every kind of property, real, personal, or mixed, and every kind of investment, specifically including, but not by way of

---

EXHIBIT 3-3 Testamentary trust *(continued)*

limitation, corporate obligations of every kind, stocks, preferred or common, shares of investment trusts, investment companies and mutual funds, and mortgage participations, which men of prudence, discretion, and intelligence acquire for their own account, and any common trust fund administered by the trustee.

F.   In any case in which the trustee is required, pursuant to the provisions of the trust, to divide any trust property into parts or shares for the purpose of distribution, or otherwise, the trustee is authorized, in the trustee's absolute discretion, to make the division and distribution in kind, including undivided interests in any property, or partly in kind and partly in money, and for this purpose to make such sales of the trust property as the trustee may deem necessary on such terms and conditions as the trustee shall see fit.

I have signed my name to this instrument on March 19, 1996, at Mytown, Anystate.

_____
(Signature)

Statement of Witnesses

The undersigned witnesses declare under penalty of perjury under Anystate law, on March 19, 1996, that we are over twenty-one, that the testator declared to us that this instrument is his will, that he signed this will, and that he requested us to act as witnesses to it. We believe that the testator is of sound mind and did not act under fraud, duress or undue influence.

_____   _____
(Signature)   (Signature)

_____   _____
(Address)   (Address)

Notice that, unlike the living trust shown in Exhibit 3-2, this particular testamentary trust provides only a *contingent trust*, (i.e., a trust that comes into effect only if both the testator's wife fails to survive and one or more living children are under age twenty-one). Not all testamentary trusts are contingent. For example, a testamentary trust could provide that a trust be created that gives the surviving spouse a life estate, followed by a life estate for the children, with the remainder going to the grandchildren.

This chapter has introduced the documents used in the transfer of an estate, with particular emphasis on the simple will, the living trust, and the testamentary trust. The next chapter focuses on the actual process of transfer of the property disposed of by these documents, with particular emphasis on the probate process and its handling of intestate succession. Later chapters will again discuss trusts in connection with saving estate taxes, with special emphasis on what are called bypass trusts and marital deduction trusts.

QUESTIONS AND PROBLEMS

1. (*a*) Name the major documents used in the estate planning process to transfer wealth. (*b*) Do they all require the same effort in their preparation? Why or why not?

2. Describe the five major reasons why a will might not be admitted to probate.

3. Name and describe the two different types of wills recognized by many states.

4. Can a valid will meet the typical statutory requirements for both the witnessed will and the holographic will? Why or why not?

5. (*a*) What is a simple will? (*b*) List its major sections.

6. (*a*) What is a codicil? (*b*) Why is it mentioned in the typical will?

7. (*a*) Why does the will nominate two types of guardians? (*b*) Must the probate judge follow the testator's nominations?

8. Why might it be a mistake to waive (as part of one's will) the requirement of an executor's bond? When does waiving one make the most sense?

9. What is the purpose of a clause directing that all death taxes be paid from the residue?

10. Why does the disposition section in a will contain a survival clause?

11. Describe the contents of the "Statement of Witnesses" section of a will.

12. (*a*) Distinguish between a living trust and a testamentary trust. (*b*) Are all testamentary trusts established in wills?

13. (*a*) Of the three documents highlighted in this chapter, how many are wills? (*b*) How many create trusts?

14. Contrast the living trust in Exhibit 3-2 with the testamentary trust in Exhibit 3-3 in terms of:
  a. When the trust takes effect.
  b. Who is the appointed or nominated trustee.
  c. Whether the trust principal is subject to probate administration at the trustor's death.
  d. Who are the income beneficiaries.
  e. Who are the remaindermen.

15. (*a*) Describe, in general, how the living trust included in Exhibit 3-2 disposes of income and principal. (*b*) Which parties stand to receive a contingent future interest? (c) When, if ever, will each future interest become vested?

16. List the sections of a testamentary trust that are common to all witnessed wills and the sections that are found only in testamentary trusts.

17. Finnegan, a widower, died last week. He is survived by the following family members (current ages in parentheses): Two children, Joe (30) and Gary (27). Joe has four children, Jackie (5), John (3), Carol (2), and Bob(1). Finnegan is also survived by three other grandchildren: Floyd (4), Fred (3), the sons of Finnegan's deceased daughter, Kerri, and Kitty (9), the daughter of Finnegan's deceased daughter, Shirley. Kerri's and Shirley's husbands, Kurt (29), and Rolf (31), are still alive. Joe has come to your office requesting some information. Assuming that Finnegan's large estate will be distributed in accordance with the testamentary trust contained in Exhibit 3-3 answer the following: (a) *Who* will receive the property (i.e., principal), and (b) assuming no more family members die at a young age, *when* will they receive it?

The Rule Against Perpetuities

The rule against perpetuities (the Rule) originated in English common law. The statutes of all states except Idaho, Wisconsin, North Dakota, and South Dakota contain some variation of this rule. Charitable trusts are exempt from the Rule, making them potentially infinite in duration.

The Rule acts to prevent a transferor from controlling the disposition of property for an unreasonably long period after making the transfer. The classic, concise statement of the Rule, with this author's emphasis added, is:

No *interest* is good unless it must *vest*, if at all, not later than twenty-one years after some *life in being* at the creation of the interest.

In simpler though a bit less exact language, the Rule has the effect of invalidating a future contingent interest which does not vest within twenty-one years after the death of certain people alive at the time the document creating the interest became irrevocable. This requires some explanation.

In estate planning, an interest in property can take effect during the transferor's lifetime, or it can take effect at the transferor's death. A transfer into an irrevocable living trust is an example of the creation of a property interest that will take effect during the transferor's lifetime, while a transfer into the typical revocable living trust and a transfer by will are examples of transfers creating interests that take effect at the transferor's death.

Thus, to satisfy the requirements of the Rule, the interest must *vest*, if at all, within twenty-one years after the death of someone alive at the moment of transfer into an irrevocable trust, or at the moment of the transferor's death, for interests created by will or by revocable living trust.

Interests that vest immediately when they take effect will automatically meet the requirements of the Rule. Thus, a transfer in a will "to John, for his life, then to Mary or her estate" creates vested interests for both John and Mary at the testator's death. Nothing (except perhaps the passage of time) will prevent them from receiving possession of the property. Therefore, the Rule need only be used to determine the validity of contingent future interests, that is, interests that are *not vested* when created.

The requirement that the interest must vest, "if at all," means that a contingent future interest will not violate the Rule merely because it failed to vest because the happening of the contingency did not work favorably for the named party. Thus, the transfer "to Jane if she survives Margo" gives Jane a contingent future interest that must vest or fail to vest within the permitted time. Failure to vest will not violate the Rule, so long as that failure (along with vesting) must occur within the required period. Thus, Jane will or will not survive Margo. What is required is that the interest must either vest or fail to vest within the required period. If we can't be sure that either of these will happen, then the interest violates the Rule.

To qualify under the Rule, an interest must vest or fail to vest "not later than twenty-one years after some life in being at the creation of the interest". The "life in being" concept is difficult to explain precisely. For our purposes, however, we can say that the persons permitted to be "lives in being" are usually those mentioned or implied in the transfer document itself. Thus, for the transfer "to Carrie for her life, then to Carrie's living children," Carrie would be the sole measuring life. She is alive at the creation of the children's interest, and the length of her life span will determine the devolution of the property. Taking a second example, the provision that a trust will terminate no later than "twenty-one years after the death of the last survivor of the class composed of my wife and those of my issue living at my death" explicitly creates the measuring lives to be used in the test. This "perpetuities saving clause," included in the testamentary trust in Exhibit 3-3, is a clause that can further protect an interest from vesting too remotely. It will be discussed further, shortly.

The requirement of vesting within "twenty-one years" after the death of a life in being, was originally included to enable the transferor to control the disposition of property for his or her life, for the lives of the children, and for the period of the grandchildren's minority, but no longer. For those individuals, all interests created which are contingent solely upon *parent survival* will usually vest within the required period. The children's interest will vest by the time of the death of the transferor, and the grandchildren's interest will vest within twenty-one years of the death of the last surviving child. All of their interests will vest within the required period. On the other hand, a great-grandchild's interest will typically (but not always) vest *after* the twenty-one year period, and thus will usually fail.

A violation of the Rule will cause that particular interest to be void. The interest will then revert to the transferor or the transferor's successors.

Let's consider some examples. In each case, assume that the transferor has died, leaving a will containing the disposition clause shown as the initial quote.

EXAMPLE 3A-1. "To my wife, Mary, for her life, then to Bill or his estate." Both Mary's and Bill's interests vested immediately when the will took effect (at Ted's death) because at that point, nothing except the passage of time could delay their possession or enjoyment. Therefore, neither interest is at any time contingent, that is, dependent upon the happening of a future event, other than the passage of time. Applying the Rule, their interests "must vest...not later than....". Thus, both interests are valid under the Rule.

EXAMPLE 3A-2. "To my husband, Bert, for his life, then to my son James, if still living, otherwise to Ron or his estate." Bert's vested interest is valid under the rule, for the same reason that Mary's was, in the preceding example. Both James and Ron have contingent interests in the property. Thus, we must ask whether they must vest within the specified time. Both James's and Ron's interests will vest, if at all (either one or the other will never vest, depending upon whether or not James survives Bert), within "twenty-one years after some life in being". Bert is "a life in being" at the time of Theresa's death, and both interests will vest or will fail to vest at his death, obviously well within the time limit of the rule. Therefore, both James's and Ron's interests are valid under the Rule.

EXAMPLE 3A-3. "To my wife Sarah, for her life, then to my son Greg, for his life, then equally to Greg's living children when the youngest child reaches age 25." Are Greg's children's interest valid under the Rule? Sarah, Greg and any children alive when the trust became irrevocable at Tom's death are "lives in being" at the creation of the interest. But more children could be born to Greg, and they would not be lives in being at the time the trust became irrevocable, yet they would (by the terms of the trust) each have an interest that could vest, more than twenty-one years after the deaths of Sarah, Greg and any of the children that were born when the trust became irrevocable. Therefore, all of the grandchildren's interests are void, and Tom or his successors would receive a reversionary interest in them, which would probably mean that Greg would have the interests in fee. Note that had the trust called for the interests to vest when Greg's oldest living child reaches age twenty-one, then all the children's interests would vest within a life in being plus twenty-one years, even if none of the children were born when the trust became irrevocable, since all children would be born within Greg's life time. The law tacks on the period of gestation to the twenty-one years.

> EXAMPLE 3A-4. Continuing with Example 3A-1, assume the following is also included in Ted's will: "...then to my great, great, great-grandchildren..." Assuming that Ted is survived only by children and grandchildren, it is possible that the great, great, great-grandchildren's contingent interest will vest after twenty-one years after the death of all children and grandchildren, who are the only apparent lives in being at Ted's death. Thus, their interests are void.

Here are two general *rules of thumb* when applying the Rule to transfers of interests to surviving issue:

1. Transferors usually can create valid contingent interests for their *grandchildren*, as long as the interests must vest by the time their grandchildren reach age twenty-one.
2. Transferors usually can create valid interests for their *great-grand-children,* only if they outlive all of their children.

Today, not all dispositions in violation of the Rule are invalid. Two types of *safeguards* designed to overcome the Rule are available to transferors. First, most states have enacted *statutes* that limit application of the Rule, or even invalidate it entirely. For example, many states have enacted a "wait and see" statute which, in effect, finds an interest void only if the interest turns out *in fact* not to vest within the required period. In addition, some states have a type of wait-and-see statute stating that any interest which actually vests within a certain period of time (e.g., 60 years) after its creation cannot be declared void, even if it violates the Rule. In 1986 the National Conference of Commissioners on Uniform State Laws approved the Uniform Statutory Rule Against Perpetuities, recommending that all states enact it. It includes a wait-and-see period of 90 years after creation.

Another statutory safeguard is the application of the *"cy pres"* rule to enable the courts to correct violations of the rule, if at all possible, so that the transferor's intentions can be respected. *Cy pres*, French for "as near as possible," is a principle used primarily in the context of charitable bequests, to permit the substitution of one beneficiary for another when the original charitable purpose is impossible, illegal, or impractical to carry out. For example, over a century ago, one testator left property in trust to fight for the cause of abolition. After the

13th Amendment freed the slaves, a court applied *cy pres* to permit the trust to continue by assisting freed slaves.

A second type of safeguard against a perpetuities violation involves the lawyer's insertion in the document of the earlier mentioned *perpetuities saving clause*, similar to the one in the *testamentary trust* in Exhibit 3-3. Such a provision, however, may act to prevent the client from making an otherwise valid transfer, perhaps simply because the attorney chose not to test the interest against the Rule. In fact, none of the above safeguards is as effective as the thoughtful analysis and planning of an expert.

Yet, one must have some sympathy for the lawyers who use the clause. The Rule often requires complex analysis to test a given interest, and it can even puzzle experts. One state supreme court called it "a dangerous instrumentality in the hands of most members of the bar." It held that even though an attorney sued by a client for malpractice did in fact violate the Rule, he was innocent because he did not fail to use ordinary skill commonly exercised by lawyers![8]

The purpose of this appendix has been to present an overview of the rule against perpetuities, without exploring the complexities occasionally encountered by attorneys. This author believes that all members of the estate planning team should acquire a general understanding of the Rule, primarily because it constitutes a material constraint on the temporal boundaries of intelligent planning.

QUESTIONS AND PROBLEMS FOR 3A

1. What is the purpose of the Rule Against Perpetuities?

2. Helen's will leaves one half of her wealth outright to Vinnie and the other half in trust for Johnny, with all income payable annually to Johnny and, at the earlier of Johnny's death or his reaching age twenty-one, corpus to Johnny or his estate. Does this will violate the Rule? Why or why not?

3. Holly's will leaves all of her property in trust, with income to her living children for life, then income to her then-living grandchildren for their lives, and then remainder over to her then living great-grandchildren. Who will get Holly's property?

4. Generally, how do drafters of trust documents avoid violation of the Rule today?

ANSWERS TO QUESTIONS AND PROBLEMS (Chapter, then appendix 3A)

1. a. The major documents used in the estate planning process to transfer wealth include the will, the trust, joint tenancies, and contractual arrangements, including life insurance and pension and profit sharing plans.

   b. Not all of them require the same effort in preparation. The will and the trust require more effort in preparation, primarily because they are custom-drafted for each client. The other documents are considerably simpler and do not require an attorney's help. However, as we'll see, clients anticipating a potential death tax will do well to seek competent advice.

2. Five major reasons why a will may not be admitted to probate:

   a. Lack of testamentary capacity: that is, failure to be aware: 1) that they are executing a will; 2) of what they own; 3) of their heirs.
   b. Undue influence, or over persuasion.
   c. Fraud.
   d. Mistake.
   e. Format (formality) problems, e.g., one witness where the state of domicile requires two.

3. Two different wills recognized by many states:

   a. The witnessed will. Typical requirements: 1) must be in writing; 2) testator must sign in the presence of two witnesses.
   b. The holographic will. Typical requirements: 1) signature in testator's handwriting; 2) all or all of the material provision in testator's handwriting.

4. In many states, a valid will can theoretically meet the typical requirements for both the witnessed will and the holographic will because the formal requirements are not usually mutually exclusive. Such a will would usually have to be written, with all material provisions written in the testator's hand, and signed in the presence of two witnesses.

5. a. A simple will is one prepared for a family having a modest estate, one for which death tax planning is not a significant concern, and one in which all property is usually devised to the surviving spouse, and if no surviving spouse, to the children.

   b. Major sections of the simple will include:

   1. Declaration and Revocation;
   2. Family and Guardian;
   3. Executor;
   4. Disposition of Property;
   5. Powers of Executor;
   6. Statement of Witnesses;

6. a. A codicil is a separate written document that amends or revokes a prior will.

   b. It is mentioned in the revocation clause to prevent needless litigation over the construction of two or more wills.

7. a. The will nominates two guardians, one for the person and one for the estate, because each has a different responsibility. In the uncomplicated trust-will, the estate guardian has a smaller role because the trustee manages the client's property to be held in trust for a minor child.

   b. The judge need not follow the testator's nominations if, in his or her judgment, they do not reflect the best interests of child.

8. Not waiving the bond can protect the estate from breaches of trust by the executor. This may be important when the testator nominates or anticipates that the probate judge may appoint a non-professional, who is not related to the decedent, to be executor.

9. The purpose of the residue tax clause is to relieve non-residuary (and

nonprobate) beneficiaries from having to pay their share of the death taxes. It may be the fairest provision, particularly when other beneficiaries receive illiquid assets. It also can speed up the probate process.

10. A survival clause avoids the risk of 1) double probate, and 2) unintended disposition to in-laws, etc., when one spouse survives the other a short period.

11. The "statement of witnesses" section of a will includes an attestation by the witnesses, made under penalty of perjury and in the presence of the testator, of the following facts:

- they were over age 21 and competent to witness the will;
- the testator, in their presence, said that the document was his or her will, and asked them to act as witnesses, and signed the will;
- they believe the testator was of sound mind, and was not acting under duress, fraud, or undue influence.

12. a. A living trust takes effect during the trustor's lifetime, while a testamentary trust takes effect after the testator's death. The latter is funded through the probate process.

b. Yes, by definition, all testamentary trusts are established in wills.

13. a. Two of the documents are wills: Exhibit 3-1 (simple will) and Exhibit 3-3 (trust-will).

b. Two of the documents create trusts: Exhibit 3-2 (living trust) and Exhibit 3-3 (testamentary trust, a.k.a. trust-will).

14.		**3-2 living trust**	**3-3 testamentary trust**
a.	takes effect?	upon execution & funding	upon probate order
b.	nominated trustees?	John C. Jones (trustor and trustee)	children over the age of 25, if none, then James A. Reliable.
c.	probated?	no, probate avoidance	yes, the funding mechanism is the probate process
d.	income beneficiaries?	initially the trustor, John C. Jones, then children, if wife does not survive the four month survivorship period	none, if wife survives, otherwise the children until they reach the ages set for termination of the trust
e.	remaindermen?	wife, if she survives the 4 month survivorship period, otherwise the children.	the children, but only if the trust is funded. This happens if wife does not survive the 4 month survivorship period.

15.		**3-2 living trust**
a.	income beneficiaries	initially the trustor, John C. Jones, then children, if wife does not survive four month survivorship period
b.	principal beneficiaries	initially the trustor, John C. Jones, then his wife (actually, the trustee of her living trust) or their children, if wife does not survive the four month survivorship period. Thus both wife and children are contingent remaindermen.

c.　vesting of
　　future interests

wife's remainder interest vests if she survives 4 months beyond her husband, each child's interests vests only if wife does not so survive and the child reaches age 21, the children's issue are also contingent remaindermen whose interests vest if a parent (trustor's child) dies before age 21.

16. Sections common to all witnessed wills:

   1. Declaration and Revocation,
   2. Family and Guardian,
   3. Executor,
   4. Disposition of Property,
   5. Powers of Executor,
   6. Statement of Witnesses.

   Sections found only in trust wills:

   1. Designation of Trustee,
   2. Powers of Trustee.

17. Distribution of Finnegan's estate in accordance with the trust-will in Exhibit 3-3:

   1. All *tangible personal property* (except vehicles and boats) will transfer immediately outright - equally to Joe and Gary.

   2. The *residue* goes into trust, with income to Joe and Gary as the trustee sees fit. In four years, when Gary attains age 21 (or sooner, if Gary dies), the corpus will be divided into shares, which are not necessarily equal, for Joe, Gary, Floyd, Fred and Kitty. At that time, Joe and Gary's shares will be distributed to them outright. Floyd's, Fred's, and Kitty's shares will be distributed to them when they each reach age 21.

ANSWERS TO QUESTIONS AND PROBLEMS - APPENDIX 3A

1. The purpose of the Rule is to prevent a transferor of property from controlling the disposition of property for an unreasonably long period after making the transfer.

2. Neither disposition violates the Rule. Both interests will vest at Helen's death, which is clearly within 21 years after the death of some life in being.

3. Both Holly and her children are lives in being insofar as this will is concerned. The income interests of the children and the grandchildren vest within the Rule's outer limits but the remainder over to the great grandchildren both violate the Rule. The great grandchildren's interest fail because there is a chance that a grandchild will give birth to a great grandchild more than 21 years after Holly's death (the time when lives in being is fixed), hence that grandchild would not be "in being" within the Rule's outer time limit. The remote interests of the great grandchildren are cut off and the grandchildren would end up with remainder interests instead of just income interests.

4. The Rule is frequently avoided today by

   a. statutes, such as the "wait and see" rule, that limit application of the Rule or invalidate it entirely, and
   b. perpetuities saving clauses in trust documents requiring that the trust terminate no later than the outer limits of the Rule

ENDNOTES

1. Alabama, Alaska*, Arizona*, California, Colorado*, District of Colombia, Florida, Hawaii, Idaho*, Indiana, Kentucky, Maine, Maryland, Michigan, Minnesota*, Missouri*, Montana*, Nebraska*, New Mexico*, New Jersey*, North Dakota*, Pennsylvania*, South Carolina, Tennessee*, Texas*, Wisconsin, Wyoming and Utah*. (States marked with * have adopted the UPC entirely or nearly entirely.)

2. *Estate of Muder*, 751 P. 2d 986 (Ariz. 1988).

3. *Estate of McEod*, 206 Cal. App.3d 1325 (1988).

4. Uniform Probate Code §2-507.

5. *Wolfe's Will*, 185 NC 563, (1923).

6. Cal. Probate Code §6402.5.

7. *Knupp v. District of Columbia*, 578 A. 2d 702 (D.C. Ct. App., 1990).

8. *Lucas v. Hamm*, 56 Cal. 2d 583.

— 4

Introduction to Property Transfers II: The Transfer Process

OVERVIEW

This is the second of two chapters that introduce the principles of property transfer. Chapter 3 examined the documents employed in the planning of property transfers. Documents covered included joint tenancy arrangements, property dispositions by contract, the will and the trust instrument. This chapter will look at the actual *process* of transfer of the property disposed of by these documents, emphasizing transfers taking effect at death.

The most common planning document disposing of property *during lifetime* is the living trust instrument. It directs the trustee to make the distributions, if any. The procedure is uncomplicated and usually unsupervised by the state. Thus, our study of the property transfer process will focus mainly on probate.

RATIONALE FOR PROBATE DISTRIBUTION

When a person dies, steps must be taken to transfer ownership of his or her property interests to the proper beneficiaries. Authorized agents try to undertake these transfers as well as possible, hopefully in accordance with the deceased's prior wishes. The documents covered in Chapter 3 are the legal embodiments of those wishes, and are used as the basis for transferring the property.

Historically, each of the 50 states and the District of Columbia has assumed a significant role in the estate distribution process. Each has chosen to protect the decedent's property in two basic ways. First, each state has enacted succession or intestacy laws that specify *who is to receive* property in the event that the decedent died owning property not disposed of by formal transfer documents. Succession laws are designed to reflect the probable disposition preferences of decedents.

The second way in which the states have sought to protect the decedent's property is by developing probate administration procedures designed to ensure that the beneficiaries, the creditors, and the taxing authorities, *receive* their rightful share of the estate property with a clear title.

Transfers at death are subject to far greater state supervision for property that is held in title in a manner which does not itself indicate a method of transfer. Where title to property itself provides for transfer, it will not ordinarily be subject to state supervision. Examples of the latter are *tenancy by the entirety* and title in *joint tenancy* with right of survivorship. The automatic ownership by the surviving co-tenants without any right held by the decedent-owner's estate is said to be a transfer by *operation of law*. The state does not "oversee" this title transfer. It occurs automatically and instantly. An additional step may be necessary to clear title to joint tenancy property; the decedent's name will need to be removed from the actual document. Fortunately, this is usually processed quickly by those authorities (banks, motor vehicle bureau, etc.,) keeping record of the title when a surviving cotenant appears before them with a certified copy of the death certificate.

In contrast with title held in joint tenancy, title that had been held by a decedent either as an *individual*, as a *tenant in common*, or as a spouse owning an interest in *community property*, in themselves indicate no procedure for title transfer. As a result, the states have established a process to transfer title by reference to an independent, acceptably drafted document. The state-administered process of transferring such title is called *probate*. The transfer document to which the probate process refers is called, of course, the will.

NONPROBATE VERSUS PROBATE ASSETS

At this point, the reader might be asking where *trusts* fit into this transfer scheme. The answer is that it depends on the type of document creating the trust. Property that, at the decedent's death, is held in a revocable or irrevocable *living trust,* is not held in the decedent's name. Legal title is in the name of the trustee. Since probate administration is concerned with transfer of property held in the decedent's name (individually or concurrently), property held by a trustee is not subject to probate administration. If, in accordance with the underlying trust document, the trustor's death triggers a transfer out of trust, to the remainderman, the transfer process is uncomplicated and not supervised by the court. The trustee simply makes the distribution by deed or assignment, depending on the nature of the assets.

Suppose the decedent created a living trust naming herself as sole trustee during her lifetime and naming a successor trustee to take over at her incapacity or death. Will probate administration be required at her death so that a court can ensure that the proper successor trustee is in fact appointed? In most states, the answer is no; the trustee change is considered a private matter, not one requiring court supervision.

Property owned by the decedent to be transferred *at death* into, rather than out of, a trust will be subject to probate administration. In such instances the probate process is the funding mechanism for the trust. This will occur for all testamentary trusts because no separate trust exists prior to the death of the testator. Near the conclusion of the probate, the court order for distribution to the trustee has a dual purpose: (1) it serves as the trust funding mechanism, and (2) it serves as the trust document since the terms of the trust, taken from the will, are repeated as part of the order. Generally, when a living trust is used, a probate is unnecessary. Nevertheless, the trustor will have created a pour-over will, so called because it scoops up assets left out of the trust and "pours" them into it. This "pouring" is done through the probate process which concludes with an order for distribution to the trustee of the living trust. In this case, the order does not include the language of the trust because the trust is already in existence as a separate document.

Property disposed of by contract, including *life insurance proceeds* on the life of the decedent, and *retirement benefits*, are not subject to probate administration because title to those assets is not actually held by the decedent. Instead, title is held by the insurance company or the pension fund, respectively, and each has agreed to transfer title directly to the named beneficiary at the death of the decedent; the insurance company or pension fund pays the named beneficiary in accordance with the payout option selected by the decedent or by the beneficiary.

One study found that 40 percent of adults die intestate. In such circumstances, the state's intestate succession laws will determine proper distribution. Intestate distribution is carried out by the probate process. In fact, probating an intestate decedent's estate might be even more important than for a testate decedent, to ensure correct identification of heirs, as well as to ensure distribution to them.

Figure 4-1 diagrams the probate and nonprobate interests of a decedent at the moment of death. The right side contains the nonprobate property including interests in living trusts that are revocable by the decedent, jointly owned

---

FIGURE 4-1   A Decedent's Property Interests

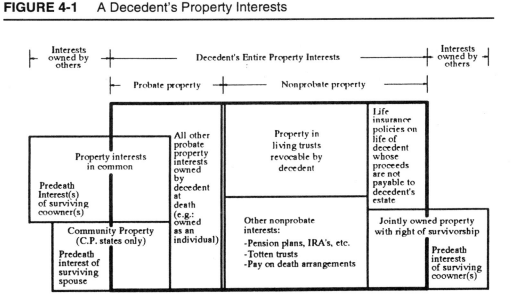

---

property, life insurance policies on the decedent's life other than those payable to the decedent's estate, and certain other nonprobate interests. Life insurance proceeds payable to the decedent's (probate) estate must, by definition, be a probate asset, since the probate estate will collect the proceeds and hold them pending an order for distribution. Policies issued since World War II are not likely to be paid into the insured's probate estate. In addition to the having several layers of alternate beneficiaries, the policy will have a provision very similar to intestate succession designating the order of beneficiaries in the event that the named beneficiaries predecease the insured, and only as a very last resort have the proceeds payable to the decedent's estate.

The left side contains probate assets, including the decedent's one-half interest in community property, the decedent's interests in probate held in common with others, and the catchall-- all other probate property owned individually by the decedent. Of course, the portion of interests held *by others,* whether as tenants-in-common, joint tenants, or as community property, are not part of the decedent's probate or nonprobate estate. One should also note that some community property states, such as California, no longer require a probate for property going to a surviving spouse, whether by virtue of the decedent's will or by intestate succession. Those states may require a simple filing of a request for confirmation by the court of the survivors right to take the property, followed by notice to interested parties, then a hearing, and, finally, a court order granting the confirmation.

The logic of Figure 4-1 suggests a relatively straightforward *procedure* to determine the assets of a decedent that will be subject to probate administration. First, list all of the decedent's property interests held immediately prior to death, including all insurance policies. Then delete from the list all assets for which there is a nonprobate mechanism of transfer, such as property in living trusts, joint tenancy property, and interests payable to a designated beneficiary, such as life insurance, pensions, and finally miscellaneous nonprobate interests such as Totten trusts. What is left should be the decedent's property interests subject to probate administration, mostly property in the decedent's name alone or held with others as tenants-in-common, and for states that still require probate for community property even when it goes to the surviving spouse, the decedent's half of the community property .

So far, we have seen how the decedent's probate property is determined. The next logical step is to decide who will receive this property. To do this, one first looks to the will. If there is no will, the state laws of intestate succession are applied. Details of these succession laws are covered next.

STATE LAWS ON INTESTATE SUCCESSION

We have seen that a decedent who dies leaving probate property not disposed of by a valid will is said to die intestate, and that property will pass under the state's laws of intestate succession. Further, a person receiving property under these laws is called an heir and is said to inherit the property.

In determining who should inherit, state laws are designed primarily to dispose of a decedent's estate in a manner similar to the probable intent of the typical decedent. Thus, they usually give priority to the decedent's spouse, next to the decedent's issue, and, if there is no spouse nor issue, then to the decedent's other blood relatives, with higher priority given to closer relatives. A more detailed description of the Uniform Probate Code's intestate succession priority arrangement will be examined shortly, but first, let's explore two important underlying concepts in the area of inheritance.

Degrees of Consanguinity

Let's examine a family tree. Figure 4-2 depicts *degrees of consanguinity*, or blood relationship, between a decedent and the decedent's relatives. As we have said, descendants (issue) of the decedent include children, grandchildren, great-grandchildren, and so on. Ascendants (ancestors) include parents, grandparents, and the like. Descendants and ascendants of a person are said to be in the person's *lineal*, or vertical line. The other relationships shown are *collateral*, meaning that they share with the person a common ancestor, but they are neither ascendants nor descendants of the person, and thus are not in the person's lineal or vertical line. For example, a nephew of a person is not his or her issue, but shares a common ascendant with the person, namely the person's parent. Since a relative's share of a person's intestate estate is determined by the closeness of the relationship, the person at the "center" of Figure 4-2 is shown as the "decedent."

The most common method of measuring degree of consanguinity to the decedent is the civil law procedure of counting blocks along degree lines. For example, the decedent's uncle is three steps from the decedent, because we first count upward to the common ancestor and then laterally, or diagonally down to the box where the uncle is located. Figure 4-2 can be helpful in determining relative closeness to the decedent of distant surviving relatives, especially in those states that have not adopted the more restrictive succession rules of the Uniform Probate Code.

FIGURE 4-2 Degrees of Consanguinity

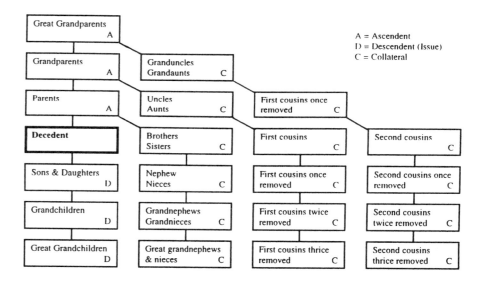

Per Stirpes Versus Per Capita

If an intestate decedent's only heirs are one living son and two grandchildren who are the daughters of the decedent's predeceased daughter, how much will each one inherit? Will they each inherit one-third of the estate, or will the son be entitled to a larger proportion because he is a closer descendant? To answer questions like this, we must distinguish between a per capita and a per stirpes distribution. A *per capita* distribution requires that all descendants receive an equal share of the property, or "share and share alike." On the other hand, a *per stirpes* distribution, also known by the more descriptive term *by right of representation,* may result in an unequal distribution, with larger distributions to descendants of a closer degree of affinity to the decedent than to those of a further degree. In the examples below, we'll contrast two different types of per stirpes rules, called 'traditional' per stirpes and 'per capita at each generation' per stirpes. Per capita is Latin for "by the head" and per stirpes comes from the Latin for "by the roots."

For a better understanding of the difference between per stirpes and per capita, consider the following description of the family tree illustrated in Figure 4-3. Cross-marks in the diagram indicate descendants who have predeceased the decedent.

FIGURE 4-3   Example Illustrating Distribution by Per Stirpes and Per Capita

---

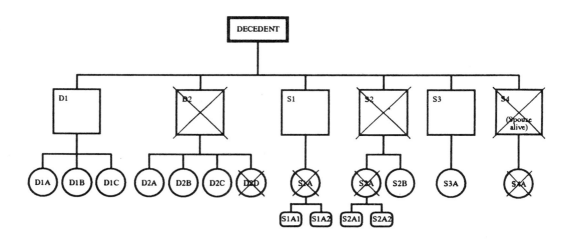

The decedent had the following descendants: Two daughters, D1 and D2, and four sons, S1, S2, S3 and S4. Only D1, S1 and S3 survived the decedent. D1 has three children, D1A, D1B and D1C, all alive. D2 is survived by three children, D2A, D2B, D2C, all alive, but the fourth child, D2D, predeceased the decedent, leaving no issue. S1 had only one child, S1A, who is deceased, but is survived by two children, S1A1 and S1A2. S2 had two children, S2A and S2B. S2A is deceased, but is survived by two children, S2A1 and S2A2. S2B is alive. S2 has no other descendants. S3 and his son S3A both survived the decedent. S4 and his daughter D4A predeceased the decedent, leaving a spouse but no descendants.

All three rules of distribution, described next, share one basic characteristic: the same people receive a share of the estate. Only the various portions change depending on which rule is applicable. Under all three rules, as one goes down the line of descent, only the surviving members of the *closest generation level* receive a share. In other words, if an ancestor is alive those in line below do not receive a share.

Thus, in our illustration, only the following nine descendants will receive property under any of the three rules: D1, D2A, D2B, D2C, S1, S2A1, S2A2, S2B and S3. Why won't the others receive anything? Either because they did not survive the decedent (D2D, S1A, S2, S2A, and S4), or because one of their ancestors (who were descendants of the decedent) survived the decedent (applies to D1A, D1B, D1C, S1A1, S1A2, and S3A).

It follows then also that no property will be allocated to any family line if all descendants in that line have predeceased the decedent. For example, S4's blood line, including D4A, and S4's spouse, receive nothing.

The three distribution rules differ, however, with regard to *how much* property each descendant will receive. The discussion below will analyze each rule separately.

Per capita. A per capita distribution simply requires that all eligible descendants receive an *equal amount* of the property. Thus, in the example, D1, D2A, D2B, D2C, S1, S2A1, S2A2, S2B and S3 would each receive a one ninth share.

Per stirpes. A per stirpes distribution would produce a larger distribution to those descendants who are closer to the decedent than to those who are further removed. Historically, two different forms of per stirpes have evolved: traditional per stirpes and per capita at each generation per stirpes. *Traditional per stirpes,* also referred to as by *right of representation,* has been used for hundreds of years. Under it, surviving descendants of predeceased children may take unequally depending upon how many in their family survive. *Per capita at each generation per stirpes*, which treats all members of each generational level equally, has become more common since it replaced traditional per stirpes in the 1990 revision of the Uniform Probate Code.[1]

Determining heirs' interests under either form of per stirpes requires a two step process. First, as in a per capita distribution, the property is divided into shares, one share for each of the decedent's predeceased children having living issue (two in our example-- D2 and S2), and one share for each surviving child (three in our example-- D1, S1 and S3). How these five shares are distributed for each per stirpital rule under the second step is described next.

Traditional per stirpes. Traditional per stirpes would pass each child's share of property to the closest surviving descendant(s) of the decedent. Thus, in our illustration, each living child, D1, S1 and S3, will receive a one fifth share and their descendants receive nothing. The surviving descendants of a deceased child share equally in their deceased parent's share. Thus, D2's living children, D2A, D2B, and D2C, will share equally in D2's one fifth share. They are said to "represent" their mother. Further, with regard to the one fifth share of the estate that goes to S2's descendants, S2A1 and S2A2 will share equally in what S2A would have received had S2A been alive at decedent's death. Thus, S2B will receive one tenth (one half of the S2 one fifth share) and S2A1 and S2A2, representing their father, each will receive one twentieth.

Summarizing, a traditional per stirpes distribution of the decedent's estate will be divided as follows: D1: 1/5; D2A, D2B, and D2C: 1/15 each (= 1/5 x 1/3); S1: 1/5; S2A1 and S2A2: 1/20 each (= 1/5 x ½ x ½); S2B: 1/10 (= 1/5 x ½); S3: 1/5.

Per capita at each generation per stirpes. Application of per capita at each generation per stirpes would distribute property similar to traditional per stirpes, except that at each generational level, the shares of those entitled to receive a portion of the estate (generally, because all lineal ancestors between the decedent and the heir are dead) are combined, and then divided equally amongst them. Thus, in the illustration, similar to traditional per stirpes, first, each living child, D1, S1, and S3 would receive a one fifth share. Next, unlike traditional per stirpes, because there are an unequal number of eligible children of two of the decedent's children (three from D2 and two from S2), the distribution to the grandchildren and great grandchildren will be different. The two one-fifth shares meant for the grandchildren D2A, D2B, D2C, S2A (for representation purposes) and S2B are combined and distributed equally to D2A, D2B, D2C and S2B, and S2A1 and S2A2 will split equally S2A's share, by representation. Thus each of the four eligible grandchildren will receive two twenty-fifths (= 2/5 x 1/5), and each of the two eligible great grandchildren will receive one half of their parent S2A's two twenty-fifths share, or one twenty-fifth (= ½ x 2/25).

Summarizing, a per capita at each generation distribution of the decedent's estate will be divided as follows: D1: 1/5; D2A, D2B and D2C: 2/25 each; S1: 1/5; S2A1 and S2A2: 1/25 each; S2B: 2/25; S3: 1/5. Notice that each eligible grandchild inherits the *same amount* (2/25s), rather than different amounts (i.e., not 1/15 each to D2A, D2B and D2C, and 1/10 to S2B, as in the case of traditional per stirpes). Whew!

Comparison of the three rules. One advantage of the per capita at each generation form of per stirpes rule is that it gives equal shares to those who are equally related. One advantage of the traditional per stirpes rule is that it passes the same share that the descendants would receive had their ancestors survived, and then died bequeathing the property to the next generation. One advantage of the per capita rule is that it treats everyone equally. This issue is important in planning because clients may strongly prefer one of these schemes over the others, and their will or trust document should reflect that preference. One survey revealed that most *clients* prefer the per capita at each generation per stirpes method. In contrast, most client's *attorneys* believe that their clients prefer the traditional per stirpes distribution rule. Most state intestate succession laws, including those that have adopted the UPC, do not use per capita, choosing instead for intestate succession, one or the other types of per stirpes distribution.

As mentioned, all three distribution rules are similar in that they dispose of an intestate estate to the same descendants. For each, all descendants who are more remotely related to the decedent will not inherit if an ascendant in a generation closer to the decedent is alive. Preventing inheritance by more remote descendants has the advantages of reducing the number of heirs, thereby making inheritable property more marketable, and minimizing the likelihood of inheritance by minors and the need for court-appointed guardians to care for their inherited property.

Finally, answering the question posed at the beginning of this section, under either per stirpes distribution rule, the son would inherit one half and the granddaughters would each inherit one quarter of the estate. Under per capita distribution, each would inherit one third.

Intestacy in UPC States

We are now ready to look at the rules of intestate succession used by those states which have adopted the Uniform Probate Code. Note that the UPC uses the term descendant rather than issue, reflecting a modern trend to avoid a biological connotation and extend inheritance rights to adopted children.

The Code's principal intestate sections, revised in 1990, are reproduced in Exhibit 4-1. In general, Section 2-101 prefaces the next four sections, which specify actual succession. The intestate share of the surviving spouse is determined by referring to §2-102 for common law states, or to §2-102A for community property states. The intestate share of heirs, other than the surviving spouse, is determined by referring to §2-103. §2-104 covers survival situations. Finally, if there are no "takers" under the above sections, §2-105 requires a procedure called "escheat" whereby the property ends up going to the state of domicile. A more specific analysis follows the Code.

EXHIBIT 4-1 Intestate Succession under the Uniform Probate Code

---

2-101 Intestate Estate

(a) Any part of a decedent's estate not effectively disposed of by will passes by intestate succession to the decedent's heirs as prescribed in this Code, except as modified by the decedent's will.

(b) A decedent, by will, may expressly exclude or limit the right of an individual or class to succeed to property of the decedent passing by intestate succession. If that individual or a member of that class survives the decedent, the share of the decedent's intestate estate to which that individual or class would have succeeded, passes as if that individual or each member of that class had disclaimed his (or her) intestate share.

2-102 Share of Spouse (Common Law States)

The intestate share of a decedent's surviving spouse is:
(1) the entire intestate estate if:
    (i) no descendant or parent of the decedent survives the decedent; or
    (ii) all of the decedent's surviving descendants are also descendants of the surviving spouse and there is no other descendant of the surviving spouse who survives the decedent;
(2) the first ($200,000), plus three fourths of any balance of the intestate estate, if no descendant of the decedent survives the decedent, but a parent of the decedent survives the decedent;
(3) the first ($150,000), plus one half of any balance of the intestate estate, if all of the decedent's surviving descendants are also descendants of the surviving spouse, and the surviving spouse has one or more surviving descendants who are not descendants of the decedent;
(4) the first ($100,000), plus one half of any balance of the intestate estate, if one or more of the decedent's surviving descendants are not descendants of the surviving spouse.

EXHIBIT 4-1 *(continued)*

2-102A Share of the Spouse (Community Property States)

(a) The intestate share of a surviving spouse in separate property is:
   (1) the entire intestate estate if:
      (i) no descendant or parent of the decedent survives the decedent; or
      (ii) all of the decedent's surviving descendants are also descendants of the surviving spouse and there is no other descendant of the surviving spouse who survives the decedent;
   (2) the first ($200,000), plus three fourths of any balance of the intestate estate, if no descendant of the decedent survives the decedent, but a parent of the decedent survives the decedent;
   (3) the first ($150,000), plus one half of any balance of the intestate estate, if all of the decedent's surviving descendants are also descendants of the surviving spouse and the surviving spouse has one or more surviving descendants who are not descendants of the decedent;
   (4) the first ($100,000), plus one half of any balance of the intestate estate, if one or more of the decedent's surviving descendants are not descendants of the surviving spouse.
(b) The one half of community property belonging to the decedent passes to the surviving spouse as the intestate share.

2-103 Shares of Heirs Other than Surviving Spouse

Any part of the intestate estate not passing to the decedent's surviving spouse under Section 2-102, or the entire intestate estate if there is no surviving spouse, passes in the following order to the individuals designated below who survive the decedent:
   (1) to the decedent's descendants by representation;
   (2) if there is no surviving descendant, to the decedent's parents equally if both survive, or to the surviving parent;
   (3) if there is no surviving descendant or parent, to the descendant of the decedent's parents or either of them by representation;
   (4) if there is no surviving descendant, parent, or descendant of a parent, but the decedent is survived by one or more grandparents or descendants of grandparents, half of the estate passes to the decedent's paternal grandparents equally if both survive, or to the surviving paternal grandparent, or to the descendants of the paternal grandparents or either of them if both are deceased, the descendants taking by representation; and the other half passes to the decedent's maternal relatives in the same manner; but if there be no surviving grandparent

---

EXHIBIT 4-1 *(continued)*

---

or descendant of a grandparent on either the paternal or the maternal side, the entire estate passes to the decedent's relatives on the other side in the same manner as the half.

2-104 Requirement that Heir Survive Decedent for 120 Hours

An individual who fails to survive the decedent by 120 hours is deemed to have predeceased the decedent for purposes of...intestate succession...

2-105 No Taker

If there is no taker under the provisions of this Article, the intestate estate passes to the state.

Intestate share to surviving spouse. In *common law states*, under §2-102, the surviving spouse is entitled to all of the decedent's intestate estate if the decedent leaves no parent or descendant, or if the decedent does leave descendants, but neither the decedent nor the surviving spouse have other descendants (e.g., child of a former marriage). Alternatively, the spouse takes the first $100,000 to $200,000, plus a fraction of the rest ranging from one half to three fourths depending upon whether parents or descendants of the decedent and/or spouse survive. An example of §2-102(3) is where the decedent and surviving spouse leave a child and the surviving spouse has a child from a former marriage. An example of §2-102(4) is where the decedent leaves a child from a former marriage.

Under §2-102A, the surviving spouse's intestate share in *community property states* is identical to that for common law states, except for an additional provision for the distribution of the community property. Thus, that spouse takes the same share of the decedent's separate property as he or she would take in a common law state. In addition, the surviving spouse is entitled to the decedent's entire half of the community property.

Intestate share to others. According to §2-103, other relatives of the decedent are divided into a hierarchical list of classes, corresponding to the degree of blood relationship to the decedent. Thus, to determine which class is entitled to succession of an intestate decedent's property, one would move down the list, stopping at the first class containing at least one living member.

Distribution would be made only to members within that class. A summary of this prioritized list follows:

1. Surviving descendants, per stirpes.
2. Parents
3. Descendants of parents, per stirpes.
4. Paternal and maternal grandparents, and their descendants, one-half to each side, per stirpes.

UPC §2-106, not quoted above, requires a 'per capita at each generation' form of per stirpes whenever descendants inherit by right of representation.

Under §2-104, any heir must survive the decedent by 120 hours to take by intestate succession. This state-imposed survival requirement has the effect of avoiding double probate in some common accident situations.

Finally, under §2-105, if none of the above relatives survive, then the decedent's intestate property passes to the state, under the doctrine of *escheat*. In English feudal law, escheat meant that the feudal lord received a reversion in the property, either because the tenant died without issue or because the tenant committed a felony. In American law, escheat has come to mean a reversion of the decedent's property to the state because no individual is "competent" to inherit. In most states, including California, there will be no escheat unless the decedent is not survived by *any* kin, no matter how remote the relationship. The UPC, on the other hand, limits inheritance to the closer relatives, under the arguable premise that more remote "laughing heirs" would be receiving a windfall not ever intended by the decedent. One wonders whether the typical decedent really would have preferred leaving property to the state rather than to distant relatives. Because many people die leaving no close relatives, "heir hunting" firms use probate court files to help locate missing heirs, in exchange for a sizable contingent fee, usually based on a percentage of the inherited property.

The examples listed next should help to illustrate these principles. In each case, assume that D is a decedent who died a resident of a common law UPC state, and owned $300,000 in property. Relevant UPC sections are cited parenthetically.

EXAMPLE 4 - 1. D is survived only by spouse and a cousin. Spouse will inherit all. [§2-102(1)(I)].

EXAMPLE 4 - 2. D is survived by spouse and their five children, one of whom has a daughter. Spouse will inherit all. [§2-102(1)(ii)].

EXAMPLE 4 - 3. Facts similar to Example 4-2, above, except that spouse also has a child of a former marriage. Spouse inherits $150,000 plus one half of the rest, or a total of $225,000. Each of the five children inherits an equal share of the rest, or $15,000. D's granddaughter inherits nothing. [§2-102(3) and §2-103(1)].

EXAMPLE 4 - 4. Facts similar to Example 4-2, above, except that decedent also has a child of a former marriage. Spouse inherits $100,000, plus one half of the rest, or a total of $200,000. Each of the children inherits an equal share of the rest, or $16,667 ($100,000 / 6). D's granddaughter inherits nothing. [§2-102(4) and §2-103(1)].

EXAMPLE 4 - 5. Facts similar to Example 4-2, above, except that spouse survived decedent by only 5 hours. Spouse will not inherit. Each of the five children will inherit one-fifth of the total, or $60,000. D's granddaughter still inherits nothing. [§2-104 and §2-103(1)].

EXAMPLE 4 - 6. D is survived by parents and two children. The children take all. [§2-103(1)].

EXAMPLE 4 - 7. D is survived by spouse, a parent, and a sister. Spouse inherits $275,000 and parents inherit $25,000. Sister receives nothing. [§2-102(2) and §2-103(2)].

EXAMPLE 4 - 8. D is survived by a sister, and two nephews, the sons of D's deceased brother. Based on the required per stirpes distribution, sister inherits $150,000, and each of the nephews takes $75,000. [§2-103(3)].

EXAMPLE 4 - 9. D's closest surviving relative is a second cousin. All property will escheat to the state. [§2-105].

If the decedent had been a resident of a community property state, each of the above dispositions of the decedent's individually owned property would still be correct. In addition, the decedent's half of the community property would pass to the surviving spouse, with the result that the surviving spouse would end up owning all of what had been the couple's community property.

Intestacy in Non-UPC States

The intestate succession laws in non-UPC states vary considerably, but all have a common thread; they are all more or less determined by degrees of consanguinity. For example, if an intestate decedent is survived by children but no spouse, the children usually take all. If the decedent leaves a spouse and children, the spouse and the children will usually share the property, with the spouse receiving from one third to one half. If the decedent is survived by a spouse but no children, the spouse usually receives all. If, in addition to the spouse, the decedent's parents are still alive, then in some states the spouse gets all, and in others, the spouse shares with the parents. Since state's intestate succession laws do vary, the reader is urged to make an independent investigation of the succession laws in his or her own state.

Advancements

Sometimes, an advancement will reduce an heir's intestate share. An *advancement* is a lifetime gift to an heir intended by the donor to represent all or a part of that heir's intestate share.

> EXAMPLE 4 - 10. Mom died intestate, survived by her three children, A, B, and C. Her estate consists of $120,000 in property, not including her $30,000 cash gift to A three months before she died. If Mom's gift is treated as an advancement, the children will inherit the following amounts: $20,000 to A and $50,000 each to B and C. If Mom's gift is not treated as an advancement, each of the children will inherit $40,000. In either outcome, A will keep the $30,000 gift.

Whether or not a gift is treated as an advancement depends primarily upon evidence of the donor's intent. Nearly all states have statutes spelling out what is needed to prove this intent. Some, like those adopting the UPC, require that the donor's intent be in writing. Some presume that gifts are not advancements, and others presume that gifts are advancements. These presumptions are rebuttable by contrary evidence. The rules apply only to intestate succession, since the law assumes that a testator wishing to reduce a beneficiaries' share will do so in the will itself.

LEGAL RIGHTS OF OMITTED AND ADOPTED CHILDREN

After-born, Omitted Child

Occasionally, a parent will die leaving a will that was executed prior to the birth of a child. Will that after-born child receive anything? Most often, yes, although the amount can range between nothing and a significant portion of the estate. In most states, including UPC states,[2] an after-born child is entitled to take the share he or she would have received had the decedent died without a will, unless any one of the following is true: (a) the omission was intentional; (b) the will left substantially all of the estate to the other parent; or (c) the testator made some other provision for the child.

The child's intestate portion can be the entire estate where the child has no brothers or sisters and the decedent-parent was unmarried, or it might be nothing as in community property states where the surviving spouse inherits all the community property. Of course, in a community property state, the omitted child might have a claim to a share of the decedent's separate property.

An Omitted Child

An after-born child is one of two common examples of an omitted child, which is defined as any living child (or living issue of any deceased child), who was not provided for in the will. The second common example of an omitted child is one not named in the will, although alive at the time the will was executed. While some states still permit this latter type of omitted child to take an intestate share, others, including UPC states, do not. An omitted child or omitted spouse is referred to as a *pretermitted* heir.

The most common planning strategy to avoid an excessive inheritance by after-born children is to treat them similar to other children by using class gift terminology. For example, by using the terms "descendants" or "issue" in the will or trust to designate the persons who will inherit, rather than specifically naming children, pretermitted child situations will probably be avoided, and thus property left to someone other than the children will be kept from being reduced by an omitted heir's claim.

Adopted Children

With regard to *adopted children*, many states, including those that have incorporated the UPC,[3] treat adopted children similar to natural children, so that an adopted child can inherit from the *adoptive parents* (and their blood relatives), and the adoptive parents (and their blood relatives) can inherit from the adopted child. Conversely, most states give the *natural parents* of a child adopted by another no rights to inherit by intestate succession from their natural child. Similarly, adopted children usually have no succession right to the interests of their natural parents. Called the "fresh start" policy, this rule, breaking inheritance rights between adopted children and their natural parents, reflects public policy belief that implementing a complete substitution of the adoptive family for the natural family is in the child's best interest.

> EXAMPLE 4 - 11. Sam and Sue placed their infant child, Gloria, up for adoption. Sometime later, Gloria was adopted by Kevin and Kay. If Sam later dies intestate, in many states, Gloria cannot inherit any of Sam's property. If Kay then dies intestate, Gloria will inherit equally with Kay's natural children. If Gloria subsequently dies intestate, Kevin and Kay's issue can inherit, but neither Sue, her issue, nor Sam's issue will inherit. Of course, any of these individuals may receive property if they are named in a given decedent's will.

The rule does not usually apply in the case of a "stepparent adoption," where an adult child is adopted by a stepparent, usually after divorce, or after death of a natural parent. An exception is made, allowing inheritance by these adopted children from both their natural parents and their stepparents, reflecting public policy belief that such children will be better off maintaining contact with their biological relatives.

> EXAMPLE 4 - 12. Mike was six years old when his natural parents, Edith and Frank divorced. Edith subsequently married Archie, who adopted Mike. In many states, Mike will be able to inherit from both Edith and Frank, and from Archie, his stepparent.

Stepparent adoptions appear to be growing in popularity, concomitant with the rising rates of divorce and remarriage. Although direct data is not available, one study determined that 48 percent of all adoptions in 1984 were of children at least five years old. Many of these were likely to have been stepparent adoptions.

Omitted heir situations have a peculiar consequence. They result in the limited application of the intestacy laws to a decedent who actually died testate (i.e., with a valid will). Another example of the need for intestacy proceedings when a valid will exists is the situation called *partial intestacy*, in which a will does not dispose of all the decedent's probate property, as when it fails to contain a residuary clause. The latter is more likely to occur when a lay-person does a holographic will, than when one has an attorney draft the will.

LEGAL RIGHTS OF OMITTED, DIVORCED, AND DISINHERITED SPOUSES

Omitted Spouse

An omitted, "after acquired" spouse whom the testator marries *after* executing a will is usually treated in the same manner as an omitted child. In most states, the spouse takes an intestate share, unless the omission was intentional or unless the spouse was otherwise provided for. And, as in the case of omitted children alive at the execution of the will, an omitted spouse whom the testator married *before* executing the will may or may not take an intestate share, depending upon the state. In UPC states, that spouse would not take an intestate share.

> EXAMPLE 4 - 13. Prior to Claude and Betty's engagement, Claude prepared his only will. Then the couple married, and Claude subsequently died. Assuming no other relevant contract exists, if Claude's premarital will *does not provide* for Betty and the omission appears unintentional, the will can be admitted to probate and in many states, Betty will receive her intestate share of Claude's property. If, on the other hand, the will *has provided* for Betty, in some states she will receive just the amount devised to her, which could range between very little to the entire estate. But in other states, Betty can choose to take an intestate share instead of what the will has provided for her.

Effect of Divorce

In most states, a *dissolution of marriage* will ordinarily revoke a will executed before the dissolution with regard to the surviving ex-spouse's share. In effect, the surviving ex-spouse is treated as having predeceased the testator. Thus, in most situations, the property will pass to a named alternate taker, or, if none, to the residuary beneficiary.

In some states, divorce revokes the entire will. In contrast, for life insurance policies and retirement contracts, a divorce in itself will not usually have the effect of invalidating an existing provision designating the ex-spouse as a beneficiary. Nor will it invalidate a bequest to relatives or friends of the ex-spouse (unless the bequest is conditional on continued marriage).

Protection against Disinheritance of Spouse

Can one spouse totally "disinherit" the other? Most states have laws designed to prevent this. States handle the potential problem of a penniless widow (or widower) by enforcing one or more of the following concepts: community property, dower and curtesy, the spousal right of election, family allowance, and homestead property.

Community property. As we have seen, *community property states* protect spouses by attributing to each spouse, ownership of one half of property acquired by their efforts during the marriage while domiciled in a community property state. Thus many, perhaps most, spouses in community property states own a nearly equal amount of property. Recently married spouses, however, will own little community property and the laws of the community property states do not require the decedent to leave the survivor any of the decedent's half of the community property. Nevertheless, some protection may be available under the Retirement Equity Act of 1984, which provides that after a person is married for one year to an employee who is a participant in a retirement plan, the only payment option is a joint annuity unless the nonparticipant spouse consents in writing to some other option.

Dower and curtesy. Originating in English common law, a *dower* represents a surviving wife's life estate interest in a portion of the real property owned by her deceased husband. A *curtesy* represents a surviving husband's life estate in a portion of the real property owned by his deceased wife. In the few states still recognizing dower and curtesy rights, the surviving spouse would be able to exercise that right against the deceased spouse's property.

Spousal right of election. All common law states, except Georgia, have enacted legislation replacing dower and curtesy with a spousal right of election, which essentially gives a surviving spouse the right to a choice. Either the spouse can "take under the will," that is, accept the provisions of the deceased spouse's will, if any, or the spouse can "take against the will," that is, elect instead to receive a statutorily specified minimum "elective share." In most states, the "elective share" is equal to that share the spouse would have inherited had the decedent died intestate.

The elective share statues are not foolproof, however, for at least two reasons. First, spouses may be encouraged to execute premarital and post-marital agreements *waving* their elective share rights. Such agreements are recognized in most states, provided that they are entered into freely, that they fully disclose both spouses finances without misrepresentation, and that they clearly spell out those elective rights to be waived. Second, lifetime giving strategies, either outright or in trust, may be successful in circumventing forced share litigation. While the courts in many states have tried to overcome these transfers, success has been spotty.

The elective share provisions of the Uniform Probate Code were revised in 1990 in an attempt to overcome these deficiencies by being more equitable and less arbitrary than elective share statutes predicated solely on intestacy. They allow the surviving spouse a sliding scale elective share amount equal to a "percentage of the augmented estate," which includes the probate estate plus the decedent's interest in property characterized by right of survivorship (joint tenancy, etc.) held with a nonspouse, proceeds on certain life insurance on the decedent's life payable to a nonspouse, and many transfers of property by the decedent during the two year period preceding death if the decedent retained certain interests in the property transferred (such as assets transferred to a revocable trust). The percentage allowed ranges from 3 percent, if the spouses were married less than one year, to 50 percent for marriages of 15 years or more, with a minimum share of $50,000. These provisions tend to reduce the significance of the manner in which the decedent held title on the share the pretermitted surviving spouse is allowed to claim.

Family allowance. All states give the probate court legal authority to grant a family allowance; funds awarded by the court to support the decedent's spouse and minor children during the period of estate administration. This special award is needed because the court will ordinarily delay property distributions until it can determine that all debts can be paid. In fact, the family allowance takes precedence over claims by taxing authorities and unsecured creditors. Even a disinherited spouse or child might be given a family allowance. The size of the family allowance, which is usually paid in installments, will vary, depending on the survivor's needs and the size of the estate.

Homestead and other exempt property. Finally, most states protect surviving family members from being dispossessed of certain property by the decedent's unsecured creditors or by the terms of the decedent's will. The *homestead*, as it is called, usually includes the family home and adjacent property, subject to maximum acreage limitations. Some state statutes may also exempt other property, such as household furnishings, a vehicle, wearing apparel, and the like. Depending on the state, such assets are offered the following protection: Exemption from forced sale while the surviving spouse and the decedent's descendants are minors, restriction from inter vivos alienation, testamentary disposition and intestate descent, and exemption from certain taxation. These statutes vary greatly from state to state. The UPC also grants a monetary homestead allowance of $15,000 for the spouse and $15,000 divided among all dependent minor children.[4]

Thus, most states have laws which prevent the death of one spouse from impoverishing the surviving spouse, however, surviving children are generally not afforded the same protection. In some other countries, such as France and Switzerland, most of a parent's estate must be left to the spouse and children. It may seem unfair that children in the USA are not similarly protected, since spouses have the ability to protect themselves when they marry but children have no choice when they enter the parent-child relationship. In addition, young children generally cannot support themselves. However, our society's refusal to protect children likely stems from a policy interest in discouraging expensive guardianships on the assumption that the protected spouse will support the minor children. Nonetheless, this is not an ideal solution in a world filled with second and third marriages, where the surviving spouse and the decedent's children may not be related.

Next, we direct our study to the final major subject in this chapter: probate administration process.

PRINCIPLES OF PROBATE ADMINISTRATION

The principles underlying probate administration of an American decedent's estate originated in Old England, where public officials and the Church of England commonly took control of a decedent's property, or at least supervised those individuals taking control, and then distributed it to the heirs and devisees. The word *probate* stems from the Latin word *to prove*, meaning to certify the validity of a will. When a will is "approved," it is admitted to probate. Today, attorneys seldom use probate in this restrictive sense. In modern usage, probate refers to the entire process of the administration of a decedent's estate, including those estates of people who die intestate, and thus have no will to prove.

Probate has been said to have three main *purposes*. First, it *protects creditors* by mandating that valid debts of the decedent be paid. Second, it implements the dispositive wishes of the testator by *supervising the distribution* of estate assets to beneficiaries. And third, probate serves to *transfer clear title* to property, that is, it enables survivors to receive property in a form which is marketable.

Presenting a comprehensive overview of the principles of probate administration in the United States requires generalization since each state has its own set of laws, however, there are many similarities. Nearly all have at least one set of *formal probate* procedures characterized by the following four attributes:

1. Appearance in *court* before a judge.
2. Presentation of at least two *petitions* and at least two court *hearings*, for which written *notice* has been given to all interested parties. (Interested parties are those who could be influenced by the probate process, including beneficiaries, creditors, and fiduciaries nominated in the will.) Notice to creditors is usually done through newspaper publication.
3. Issuance, by the court, of signed *orders* as a precondition to the performance by the personal representative of certain major steps, such as the sale of real property.
4. Review and approval, by the court, of one or more financial *accountings* and *reports* on significant matters of concern to the interested parties.

These commonly found requirements reflect the strong interest each state has in protecting creditors and beneficiaries from mistakes in estate administration.

In addition to providing these elaborate procedures, about half of the states offer the option of other, *less formal* settlement procedures. These states have adopted all or most of the provisions of the Uniform Probate Code. Flexibility under the UPC enables the estate's interested parties to choose whether to be extensively supervised by the court in the usual manner, to be supervised only with regard to certain specific acts, or to be almost totally unsupervised. While the states that do not allow for less formal administration might still allow for some degree of informality, most of their estates must follow the traditional formal procedures.

This section will examine the traditional approach and the flexible approach to estate administration, partly to show that their underlying philosophies are very different, and partly to give the reader an indication of the current trend in probate reform. Actually, this reform has influenced all states to some degree, including those offering much less flexibility. The traditionalist states are deregulating, but in a more fragmentary manner, as we shall see.

Substantial Formal Supervision: The Non-UPC Model

A somewhat detailed study of the formal probate procedures imposed by a typical non-UPC state, such as California, can give the reader a reasonable grasp of the major requirements of a *formal* probate found in all states, although the details will vary from state to state. In UPC states, the executor has the option of using the formal or informal unless another interested party objects, in which case the formal process is mandatory. Sections of the California Probate Code are cited parenthetically.

The formal probate process. After a person has died, the executor is expected to start the formal probate process as soon as is reasonably possible.

Petition for probate. The executor, nominated in the will, is required to petition the court for probate of the will within 30 days from the date of knowledge of the nomination (§8001). During that time, the will is also taken to the clerk of the superior court of the county where the decedent resided. California law currently recognizes a cause of action in tort for fraudulent destruction, concealment, or "spoilation" of a will.

In addition, any person "interested" in the estate may make a similar petition (§8000). Where there is no will, hence no executor, the interested person is likely to be a close relative. Rarely is more than one petition filed. Upon filing the petition, the county clerk must schedule a hearing on the petition within 45 days (§8003). Ordinarily, the person nominated in the will to be executor files the petition, requesting (1) probate of the will, (2) letters testamentary, and (3) authorization to administer under the Independent Administration of Estates Act. Each request will be described briefly.

1. *Probate of the will:* If, after the hearing, the will is "admitted to probate," that will is thereby considered to be the only valid will and, except in the most unusual circumstances, it will serve as the blue print for distribution.

2. *Letters testamentary* or *letters of administration:* Also known as "letters,"

this document, usually just one page long, contains the court's formal authorization of the person selected as the personal representative of the estate. A court certified copy of the letters testamentary, or letters of administration in cases where the selected personal representative was not named in the testator's will, empowers the personal representative to deal with third parties on behalf of the estate.

3. *Independent Administration of Estates Act*: The California Probate Code allows a somewhat simplified formal probate administration. Essentially, it eliminates the requirement of obtaining court approval for many of the common transactions undertaken by the personal representative. However, some actions are not exempt and require either express court approval or written notice to all beneficiaries of a proposed course of action, with a period in which to lodge an objection before the action is taken (§§10,400-10,600).

In addition to making these requests, the petition also makes several representations, including facts about the bond, the heirs, and the beneficiaries. A *probate bond* is required unless the will waives it or unless all potential beneficiaries agree to waive it (§8481). The bond protects the estate from a financial loss in the event of wrongful conduct by the personal representative. If the personal representative misappropriates estate property or loses it due to negligence, the bonding company must make the estate whole and then has the right to pursue the personal representative. This right of the bonding company to seek to recover the money it had to pay the estate from the personal representative is call a *right of subrogation*. Some planners do not consider a bond to be worth the cost. Ordinarily, the bond amount will be set equal to the total value of the personal probate property plus one year's estimated income from all of the probate property; the idea being that the personal representative cannot run off with the real property (§8482). The bond premium, typically one-half to one percent of the amount of the bond, is charged to the estate. The petition for probate must state either that the will waived the bond or that the requirements for a bond will be met. Where a bond is required, evidence that it has been issued is required before the court will issue letters. As a second representation, the petition for probate is required to identify all beneficiaries named in the will and any heirs at law even though not named as beneficiaries.

Two other forms are ordinarily filed with the county clerk at the time of filing the petition for probate. First, a *Proof of Subscribing Witness* is submitted, in which at least one witness to the will declares that he or she signed the original document, that the decedent appeared to be of sound mind and over age 18 at the time of the signing, and that the witness knows of no evidence that the will was signed under duress, menace, fraud or undue influence. If a witness cannot be found, or if all witnesses have died, proof can be offered by handwriting analysis. To make this task unnecessary, in the spirit of probate simplification, most states now recognize a *self-proved* will, also called a *self executing* will, that is, a will containing a formal affidavit as part of the original attestation portion of the will, wherein the witnesses state that all formalities were followed. This statement will stand unless an interested party challenges the validity of the will. At a minimum, this generally eliminates the need to locate witnesses to attest to the will's validity many years after the execution of the will, and in some states, such the affidavit creates a presumption that all formalities were complied with, putting the burden on the challenger to prove that such was not the case. The "Statement of Witnesses" sections in the wills in Exhibits 3-1 and 3-3 are self-proving.

The second form ordinarily filed along with the probate petition is the *Notice of Petition to Administer Estate*. This form contains essentially the same information as the announcement notice that must be published (three times prior to the hearing) in a newspaper of general circulation in the city in which the decedent resided. A replica of the published notice is shown in Exhibit 4-2.

The filed notice, and the published notice, are intended to announce the following to the public:

1. That a petition for probate has been filed.
2. That a hearing will be held.
3. That interested parties may attend the hearing to object to the granting of the petition.
4. That creditors must file claims against the estate within four months after the issuance of letters.
5. That anyone may examine the probate file kept by the county clerk.
6. That the petitioner is requesting authority to administer the estate under the Independent Administration of Estates Act.

Copies of the filed notice must be mailed to all heirs and potential beneficiaries at least 10 days prior to the date of the hearing.

EXHIBIT 4-2 Replica of a Newspaper Notice of Petition to Administer Estate

---

NOTICE OF PETITION TO ADMINISTER ESTATE OF
JOHN PAUL JONES, a.k.a. J. P. JONES
CASE NUMBER: 111111

To all heirs, beneficiaries, creditors, contingent creditors, and persons who may otherwise be interested in the will or estate, or both, of JOHN PAUL JONES, a.k.a. J. P. JONES.

A PETITION has been filed by Mary Jones in the Superior Court of Anystate, County of Anycounty.

THE PETITION requests that Mary Jones be appointed as personal representative to administer the estate of the decedent.

THE PETITION requests the decedent's WILL and codicils, if any, be admitted to probate. The will and any codicils are available for examination in the file kept by the court.

A HEARING on the petition will be held on 03-19-99 at 8:30 a.m. in Department 1 located at Superior Court of Anystate, County of Anycounty, 25 County Center Drive, Anycity, Anystate 99999.

IF YOU OBJECT to the granting of the petition, you should appear at the hearing and state your objections or file written objections with the court before the hearing. Your appearance may be in person or by your attorney.

IF YOU ARE A CREDITOR or a contingent creditor of the deceased, you must file your claim with the court and mail a copy to the personal representative appointed by the court within four months from the date of first issuance of letters as provided in Section 9100 of the Anystate Probate Code. The time for filing claims will not expire before four months from the hearing date noticed above.

YOU MAY EXAMINE the file kept by the court. If you are a person interested in the estate, you may file with the court a formal Request for Special Notice of the filing of an inventory and appraisal of estate assets or of any petition or account as provided in Section 1250 of the Anystate Probate Code. A Request for Special Notice form is available from the court clerk.

Attorney for petitioner: Gordon C. Brown, BROWN, AND BROWN, P.O. Box 0000, Anycity, Anystate, 99999-1111.

PUBLISH: February 19, 22, and 26, 1999.

The hearing. The "hearing" for any particular probate estate may last only a few seconds. The judge gives anyone in the court the opportunity to object, but objections are rarely raised. Grounds for objection include the allegation that there exists a more recently executed will, or that even though the will in question is the only one or the most recent one, it is invalid due to a serious mistake in drafting, or that it was not properly executed due to the testator's lack of capacity, or to undue influence, fraud, or mistake. If there are objections, the judge will set the matter for further proceedings to settle the dispute, which, if not resolved, can turn into a *will contest* in civil court. If the petition for probate is granted, the judge signs an *Order for Probate* that first states the court's findings, specifically:

1. All notices have been filed.
2. The decedent died on the specified date.
3. The will in question should be admitted to probate.

Then, the Order usually mandates that:

1. The will is admitted to probate.
2. The named personal representative is appointed.
3. Letters will be issued.
4. The personal representative is given authority to administer the estate under the Independent Administration of Estates Act.
5. A bond is or is not required.

Upon issuance of the Order for Probate, the executor secures his or her letters from the probate clerk. As we have noted, letters testamentary is the formal court document, usually just one page long, that identifies the person appointed as the personal representative of the estate.

This completes the first stage of formal dealings between the personal representative and the court.

After the hearing. After letters are issued, the personal representative, usually in conjunction with the executor's attorney, undertakes the marshaling of estate assets and expected claims. Within three months of appointment, the personal representative must file with the probate court a formal document called *Inventory and Appraisement.* This form lists all probate assets showing their fair market value. The personal representative is permitted to determine the value of cash items (bank deposits, etc.) but other assets must be appraised by a "probate referee," generally a court appointed independent appraiser.

The Inventory and Appraisement performs several important functions. First, it delineates those assets for which the personal representative is responsible. Second, as a public document available for public inspection at the court house, it describes the contents of the probate estate to all interested parties, including potential heirs, legatees, devisees, and creditors. Third, it provides information to the court to determine, among other things, the proper bond amount, the amount of the family allowance, and, if property is sold, the minimum bid that the court will approve. Finally, it may influence the taxing authorities with regard to valuation of assets included on the estate tax returns.

During the *creditors' claim period*, which lasts for four months after the date letters are issued, each creditor is expected to file with the court or personal representative a document called a *creditor's claim form*. Failure to file within the claim period will bar later collection, unless an exception is allowed (§9100). Exceptions include:

1. Certain creditors who did not have actual knowledge of the proceedings (§9103).
2. Taxes owed (taxing authorities are not subject to the creditor's period (§9201)).

Availability of a shortened creditor's period is said to be a major advantage to the probate process for estates that anticipate potential problems with creditors.

During estate administration, the personal representative is responsible for handling the financial affairs of the estate, such as:

1. Paying bills (rent, utilities, property insurance premiums).
2. Accumulating liquid assets so that large bills can eventually be paid (e.g., taxes and legal fees).
3. Protecting estate assets from exposure to loss by insuring and safe-guarding them.

Distribution of estate assets. The net estate will be distributed to the beneficiaries only after all matured debts and taxes, except the federal estate tax, have been paid. However, a partial distribution to beneficiaries may be made upon court approval of a *Petition for Preliminary Distribution*. Ordinarily, this petition is filed only after the end of the creditor's period. Further, the court must be satisfied that the distribution can be made "without loss to creditors or injury to the estate or any interested person." No more than 50 percent of the estate can be distributed in a preliminary distribution (§§11,620-24).

"Final Distribution" is made upon approval of a petition at a hearing, after the court determines that all current debts and taxes have been paid (§11,640). At the same time, the judge normally approves a final estate accounting, attorney's fees, and executor's commissions (§§12,200-252). The accounting may be avoided by waiver of all of the beneficiaries (§933). After distribution and the payment of fees, the executor requests and receives a final discharge (§§12,200-252).

The entire formal probate administration procedure takes from 6 to 24 months, in most cases.

Attorneys fees for California probate administration work are determined by statute, in the absence of a different agreement by the parties. Statutory probate fees are summarized in Table 4-1.

TABLE 4-1 California Statutory Probate Fees

	Probate Estate	Rate
First	$15,000	4.0%
Next	$85,000	3.0%
Next	$900,000	2.0%
Next	$9,000,000	1.0%
Next	$15,000,000	0.5%
Over	$25,000,000	Reasonable amount set by the court

California Probate Code §10810.

These fees are based on the *gross* probate estate, not net of liabilities. California executors are entitled to the same amount (§10800) as shown above for attorneys. California is one of many states that have statutory fees but for most states, probate administration fees simply must be "reasonable;" specific amounts or percentages are not mandated. In other states, probate fees must be "reasonable," but not in excess of a certain percentage (e.g., Iowa sets an upper limit of 2 percent times the value of the probate estate). One attorney in that state has indicated that local courts in Iowa typically and automatically grant the 2 percent ceiling, if the executor signs a "waiver of attorney's fee" (routinely done), without making any effort to determine reasonableness, resulting in a universal 2% rate regardless of time spent.

> EXAMPLE 4 - 14. The attorney's fee on a $500,000 California probate estate is $11,150 [($15,000)*(0.04) + ($85,000)*(0.03) + ($400,000)*(0.02)]. Additional fees will be allowed for "extraordinary services," such as sale of real property, estate litigation, and preparation of tax returns. The executor's commission will also be $11,150, resulting in a combined charge of 4.5 percent of the probate estate.

Sometimes, attorneys are asked by survivors to act as both estate attorney and executor. Whether they will receive a full double fee will depend upon several factors, including state law and the attitude of the specific probate judge. Some states, including California and New York, have made this 'double dipping' illegal, in the absence of prior court approval. In other states, probate judges frequently reduce the fee in such situations. A possible solution is for clients to negotiate probate fees before death makes them unavailable to stand up for the grieving survivors.

Summarizing the essential components of formal supervision: Formal probate in most non-UPC states requires at least four document filings (petition for probate, notice of death, inventory and appraisement, and final distribution), it also requires at least two formal court hearings (prior to admission of will to probate and appointment of letters, and prior to final distribution), one newspaper publication of notice, and at least one and possibly two accountings (inventory and appraisement, and final accounting). With these detailed legal formalities in mind, it is not surprising that many states have acted to simplify probate administration, a major example of which is outlined next.

We turn to the second major type of state probate supervision, the flexible approach under the Uniform Probate Code. A discussion of one non-UPC state's less comprehensive attempt at simplifying probate procedures can be found in Appendix 4A.

Estate Administration in UPC States: A Study in Flexibility

Except for their ability to utilize summary probate procedures for smaller estates and for property passing outright to the surviving spouse, personal representatives in California and other states usually must use formal probate. In contrast, probate procedures in a UPC state are much more liberal, allowing interested parties to largely select the degree of supervision they desire. The basic choices are three: completely court supervised administration, totally unsupervised (informal) administration, or a combination of unsupervised and supervised administration. The UPC also provides a simple summary procedure for estates worth less than $5,000. It is basically similar to that of California's affidavit-of-right procedure, described in Appendix 4A. Thus, very small estates will often be able to be settled without any administration.

Complete court supervised administration. Some estates in UPC states will be subject to supervised administration in essentially the same manner as California's formal continuing court supervision model, such is available in nearly all states. UPC supervised administration is a bit less regulated, however, because the personal representative is given greater freedom to act independently. Usually, there is no court involvement between the time letters are issued and the time that the personal representative petitions the court for closing of the estate. In contrast, probate administration in non-UPC states, as we have seen, requires court approval of all major transactions. Most personal representatives of estates in UPC jurisdictions choose not to be subject to supervised administration. Occasionally, another interested party will request it because he or she does not fully trust the estate's personal representative and believes that supervision is necessary to ensure notice as to what the personal representative is doing.

Informal and formal administration. In addition to supervised administration, which is pretty much a court-supervised process, UPC jurisdictions allow two other types of procedures, called informal and formal administration.

Informal administration procedures usually require no court appearances and very little notice. The application for informal appointment is the simplest way for a personal representative to be appointed. The prospective personal representative files an application with a court registrar, whose role is administrative rather than judicial. Once appointed, the personal representative has the powers needed to perform the job, including the power to deal with creditors and distributees. The personal representative is required to give notice of the appointment to all heirs and devisees by ordinary mail within 30 days of appointment. Within three months, the personal representative must prepare an inventory of the estate and mail it to all parties requesting it. The entire inventory can be valued by the personal representative unless an interested party objects.

Even with informal administration, the personal representative must give formal newspaper notice, similar to the procedure for a formal probate, in order to limit the creditor's claim period to four months from date of first publication.

Without published notice to creditors, the limitations period usually runs to three years after the date of the decedent's death.

Six months after appointment, the personal representative can apply to the registrar to close the estate, then after another six months, assuming no one has lodged an objection, the personal representative is discharged from all liability, except due to fraud and other major offenses. Unless the newspaper notice was given, distributees of estate property will continue to be liable for estate debts until the later of three years after date of the decedent's death or one year after the date of the distribution,

Formal administration procedures under the UPC include the petition for *formal testacy* (proving the will), petition for formal appointment of the personal representative, and petition for formal closing. Each is undertaken in a manner similar to that for supervised administration and requires giving proper notice to interested parties, filing a petition with the court, and appearing at a court hearing.

The UPC's unique method of settling disputes has been described as an "in and out" method. During informal proceedings, a dissatisfied interested party can petition the court for a formal resolution of a controversy, whereupon the matter will be taken up "in" court. Once the dispute is settled, administration can resume in informal proceedings "out" of court.

In addition to the right to petition the court, interested parties have other protective remedies, including the right to request that the personal representative obtain a bond even though it was waived in the will, the right to request a restraining order to keep the personal representative from doing some act (such as selling a family heir-loom), and the right to demand notice; that is, to receive a copy of any filings or orders in connection with the estate. With the exception of the right to notice, the requests are subject to the court's discretion.

We can now see the relationship between informal and formal proceedings under the UPC. At each significant step in the probate process, the interested parties can elect a different degree of supervision. For example, the probate process may begin with an application for informal appointment of the personal representative. Then a controversy may arise that requires court resolution. Finally, the personal representative may feel compelled to file a formal petition for closing. Only in the unusual case will an interested party early-on petition for complete supervised administration, making the informal process unavailable. The underlying premise throughout, is the desire on the part of all beneficiaries of the estate to minimize judicial supervision because it tends to delay distribution.

The movement toward reduced court involvement in estate administration has spread to many non-UPC states, due in part to the influence of the UPC. As illustrated in Appendix 4A, traditional states have moved to reduce court supervision by adopting summary procedures, set-asides, and procedures to reduce the personal representative's court reporting requirements. The overall effect of all state deregulation has been to reduce court congestion considerably.

The next chapter will require a change of focus, from the qualitative to the quantitative. It will be the first of four to introduce the principles of taxation.

QUESTIONS AND PROBLEMS

1. True or false: A decedent's intestate property does not go through the probate administration process. Explain.

2. Harry, who is single, has an interest in a house, some furniture, a car, some common stock, and a life insurance policy on his life. The *car* is in joint tenancy with his mother. The *house* is in trust, and the trust instrument says "for Harry's use for life, then to cousin Joe." The life insurance policy names his cousin, Joe, as the beneficiary. Harry owns the *furniture* and the *policy* as an individual. With regard to the *stock*, Harry is an equal tenant in common with Sam. Harry's (valid) will says "I leave my car, my stock, my life insurance proceeds and my house to Betty." It has no other dispositive provisions.
   a. Assuming that Mother and Joe are Harry's only living relatives and that Betty is a close friend, who will receive what if Harry dies?
   b. What will be included in Harry's probate estate? His non-probate estate? His testate estate? His intestate estate?
   c. Who will be an heir? A legatee? A devisee?
   d. In your state (or under the UPC, if state law is unavailable), will your answers to the above questions change if Harry was also survived by a son? Why or why not?

3. Describe your state's laws covering inheritance by intestate succession. They are usually found in a chapter of that state's probate or estates and

trusts code. If unavailable, describe the UPC rules.

4. Mary and John are married residents of your state, and own the following property: As joint tenants, they own their home and a car. They own 1000 shares of ABC Corporation stock, worth $28,000, as equal tenants in common (assume community property if you are in a community property state). As individuals, Mary owns $350,000 in a money market fund and a life insurance policy on her business partner's life, having a current (terminal) value of $22,000. John owns an apartment house. How will this property be distributed, in accordance with your state's laws on intestate succession (if unavailable, use UPC rules), if Mary dies without a will, leaving only the following surviving relatives (unless otherwise specified, assume that all surviving children are descendants of both John and Mary):
   a. Only John
   b. John and one child
   c. John and one child, who is the child of Mary and her first husband, Kirk. Does it matter whether the child had been adopted, either by Kirk's second wife or by John, and does it matter when this adoption occurred?
   d. John and three children
   e. John, Mary's mother and three children
   f. John and Mary's mother
   g. John and Mary's sister
   h. John, Mary's mother and Mary's fifth cousin
   i. John and Mary's fifth cousin
   j. John dies, then Mary dies survived by Mary's fifth cousin (Note: What happens to the home, the car, and the stock?)
   k. There are no surviving relatives.

   How would your answers to the above questions change if Mary died with a valid will containing a residuary clause?

5. Assume that Mary and John own property as stated in the previous problem, that Mary and John are childless, and that Mary's and John's sole surviving relatives are their parents. In a UPC state, who will inherit Mary's money market fund account if John and Mary both die intestate

and, alternatively,

a. John predeceased Mary by one year
b. John and Mary died in a car accident and the order of deaths cannot be determined
c. John survived Mary by six hours
d. John survived Mary by six days

6. Frank and Joan, husband and wife, had two living children, C1 and C2, four years ago when Frank executed his only will. The will leaves half of his property each to C1 and Joan. A year later, C3 was born. Today Frank tells you that he would like to leave all his property (owned as an individual and worth $180,000) to Joan when he dies. Advise Frank, being sure to tell him who would get how much of his property if he died now. Apply your state law or, if unavailable, the UPC.

7. Ten years ago George, who was single, executed his first and only will, leaving everything to his mother. Two years later, George married Karla. Today, George is in your office telling you that he would still like his mother to receive all his property at death. Based on your state law, or the UPC if unavailable, advise George.

8. Who is closer to you, your first cousin or your niece? Why?

9. Imagine that a close friend has died, and that you believe she named you executor in her will. Based on the laws of your state, or the UPC if necessary, what steps would you need to undertake before and during probate?

10. List the purposes of the form "petition for probate."

11. Find, cut out or photocopy, and bring to class a newspaper published "notice of petition." What is its purpose?

12. Attend a hearing for probate. Give the date of attendance, and a brief summary of what you observed.

13. A client of yours shows you an "inventory and appraisement." What are its uses?

14. What is the purpose of the creditor's claim? Who files it?

15. Ordinarily, what must the personal representative accomplish before a judge will permit final distribution under supervised probate?

16. Summarize the minimum legal procedures which are involved in supervised probate in most states.

17. Why is probate in UPC states considered so flexible?

18. Describe the informal probate administration procedures under the UPC.

19. a. To what extent do you think the laws of intestate succession in your state (or the UPC, if unavailable) are inefficient for parents of minor children?
  b. To what extent does a will leaving everything outright to the surviving parent solve the problem? To what extent do you think such a will fails to solve it?
  c. Can you recommend a better disposition?

20. Denise died recently, having many different ownership interests in property. Determine how much, if any, of each property below will be a probate asset in Denise's estate.
  a. An automobile, held jointly with Jake.
  b. A money fund account, owned by Denise as an individual.
  c. A life insurance policy (L1) on Denise's life, owned by Denise. Herb is beneficiary.
  d. A life insurance policy (L2) on Denise's life, owned by her. James, the sole beneficiary, died three years ago.
  e. A life insurance policy (L3) on Herb's life, owned by Denise, who is also beneficiary.
  f. Common stock, owned by the trustee of a living trust. At the moment of her death, Denise was trustor, trustee, and one of the beneficiaries.
  g. Commercial real estate owned in common by Denise (40%) and Herb (60%).

h. Defined benefit pension plan. Denise was participant, and Bob is named surviving beneficiary.

i. Residence, owned by Denise and Herb as community property.

Summary Probate Proceedings in California: One Non-UPC State's Alternatives to Formal Probate

As we have seen, formal probate typically requires at least four document filings, two formal court hearings, one newspaper publication of notice, and at least one and possibly two accountings. Although these procedures were allegedly designed to protect estate assets and ensure their proper distribution, many are considered unnecessary in rather simple estate situations. Over the years, non-UPC states have also simplified probate procedures for less complicated estates.

This Appendix will summarize the progress of probate simplification in California. Presently, California has two major types of "summary probate," as it is called, neither of which require newspaper notice, and both of which require not more than one petition and hearing. The two types, discussed next, are the affidavit of right and the summary distribution to the surviving spouse. As you read this, keep in mind that many UPC states, perhaps your own, have procedures similar to these.

AFFIDAVIT OF RIGHT [5]

The affidavit of right is a procedure that acknowledges a valid will (or the application of the laws of intestacy), and permits a settlement of the decedent's affairs more rapidly than formal probate. This action speeds up the transfer of property to the named heir. Essentially, an affidavit signed by the heir, is presented to the person or institution holding the property or title to it. That party is then required to turn ownership of the property over to the heir, who becomes liable on the assets for any liens, etc. The affidavit, of right for *personal property,* can only be used if the decedent's total estate does not exceed $60,000, an amount that does not include joint tenancy property, life estate interests, a motor vehicle or mobile home, $5,000 in salary, and any property subject to a summary distribution which is described below. The affidavit of right for *real property* can only be used if the decedent owned no more than $10,000 in California real property. A court-certified affidavit is issued by the county clerk to the county recorder.

SUMMARY DISTRIBUTION TO SURVIVING SPOUSE [6]

Married spouses in California frequently own separate and community property which, at death, will wind up passing outright to the surviving spouse, either because the spouse was named in the will, or by the operation of the laws of intestate succession. In two important ways, California probate law has simplified the administration requirements of such property.

Spousal Set-Aside

First, the surviving spouse may elect to have separate or community property "set aside," that is, pass to him or her without formal probate administration.

Summary Distribution Petition

Second, the surviving spouse can also elect, under a summary distribution, one court hearing for the purpose of obtaining written confirmation by the court that such property has in fact passed to him or her. This may be helpful to clear title and to distinctly isolate that property which is not subject to formal probate administration. Essentially, at the hearing the judge confirms that the property is, in fact, either community or separate property, and that it should, in fact, pass to the surviving spouse. The judge will sign an order confirming these findings. A summary distribution petition may be filed regardless of the amount or type of other property owned by the decedent at death, and therefore, formal probate may be required for other assets. Further, an affidavit of right and a summary distribution petition may both be used in the same estate, provided that all of the requirements are met.

Attorney fees for summary distribution legal work are not set by statute, but in practice, these fees are substantially less than those for formal probate. One third of the statutory fee is an amount commonly charged and many attorneys will do this for an hourly fee that is substantially cheaper for large estates. Even less is charged for a spousal set-aside without the petition for summary distribution.

ANSWERS TO QUESTIONS AND PROBLEMS

1. False. To be intestate is to die leaving probate property that is not disposed of by a valid will. Thus, by definition, intestate property is probate property. Logically, one could argue that intestate property needs probating even more than property disposed of by will, since a legal process is needed to help determine who is to receive the property, as well as to ensure that the intended beneficiaries *will actually receive* it.

2. a. Based on the procedure described in the text, first the <u>nonprobate assets</u> should be considered. Disposal instruments for them supersede the will. Accordingly, the <u>life insurance proceeds</u> will go to Joe, as named beneficiary. The <u>house</u> will pass to Joe, under the terms of the trust. The <u>car</u> will go to Mom, by right of survivorship under joint tenancy. The remaining assets (interest in the common stock, furniture) are <u>probate assets</u>. The <u>stock</u> will pass to Betty, under the will. And finally, the <u>furniture</u> will pass by intestacy to Mom, Harry's closest surviving relative.

   b. In Harry's probate estate: furniture and stock.
      In Harry's nonprobate estate: house, car, and life insurance proceeds.
      In Harry's testate estate: stock.
      In Harry's intestate estate: furniture.

   c. Mother is the only heir. An heir is a beneficiary who would receive property that passes by intestacy.
      Betty is the only legatee. A legatee is a beneficiary, under a will, of a gift of personal property.
      Technically, no one is a devisee; that is, a recipient, by will, of real property.

   d. If Harry is also survived by a son, in most states, including those adopting the UPC, *descendants will inherit before parents*. Thus, the son, rather than Mom, will likely inherit the furniture. Also, in some states, the son would receive the stock, under the rule that an omitted child takes an intestate share of the entire probate estate.

3. Under the UPC, as in non-UPC states, succession is determined by degree of affinity. Thus, surviving spouse takes all if there is no surviving issue or parent of the decedent. If there is surviving issue or parent, spouse shares with them. And if there is no surviving spouse, issue, parent, issue of parent, grandparent or issue of grandparents, then the property escheats to the state.

4. First, regardless of who besides John survives Mary, John will receive Mary's joint interest in the home and the car, by right of survivorship. In parts j and k, if we assume that John predeceased Mary, then Mary would become sole owner of the home and car, both of which would pass as probate property, by intestate succession in the same manner as all the other property (below).

The following analysis disposes of the $400,000 in probate property, consisting of Mary's individual $350,000 interest in the money fund, her $28,000 tenancy in common/community interest in the 500 shares of stock, and the life insurance policy, worth $22,000. We will assume probate in a pure UPC state:

a. Only John survives: John gets all (§2-102(1)(i)).
b. John and one child survive: Common law and community property states: John gets all. (§2-102(1)(ii).
c. John and one child, who is also the child of Mary's first husband, Kirk:

Common law states: John gets the joint tenancy items (home & car) by operation of law. Note that Mary's intestate estate = $14,000 + $350,000 + $22,000 = $386,000. Only her half of the tenants in common stock is in her estate. According to §2-102(4), John gets the first $100,000 plus 50% of the rest of the intestate estate, i.e., $100,000 + 0.5*(14,000 + 350,000 + 22,000 -100,000) = $243,000. Mary's child gets the balance: 14,000 + 350,000 + 22,000 - 243,000 = $143,000. (§2-103(1)).

Community property states: The main difference is that John gets all of the stock (her $14,000 half in addition to the half he already owns), the first $100,000 of the separate property plus 50% of the rest of the intestate estate, i.e., $14,000 + $100,000 + 0.5*(350,000 + 22,000 -100,000) = $250,000. The child's share is the balance: $386,000 - $250,000 = $136,000.

It may matter whether the child had been adopted. If he or she had been adopted as an infant, the *fresh start rule* would probably apply and, in most cases, all inheritance rights between the child and the non-custodial natural parent would be broken. Thus, if Kirk's second wife adopted the child as an infant, the child would probably not inherit from Mary. In this case, the answer to this part would be similar to part "a" and John would inherit all of Mary's estate.

On the other hand, if the child had been adopted as a non-infant (step-parent adoption), then in most states he or she could still inherit from both sets of parents, including Mary (and John).

d. John and three children survive: All states, John gets all. (§2-102(1)(ii)).
e. John, Mary's mother and three children survive: Same answer as part d, since mother won't share. (§2-102(1)(ii)).
f. John and Mary's mother survive:

Common law states: According to §2-102(2), John gets the first $200,000 plus 75% of the rest of the intestate estate, i.e., $200,000 + 0.75*(14,000 + 350,000 + 22,000 -200,000) = $339,500. Mary's mom gets the balance: $386,000 - 339,500 = $46,500. (§2-103(2)).

Community property states: John gets all of the stock ($14,000 represent's Mary's half), and $329,000 of the rest (= $200,000 + .75* ($372,000 - $200,000)) for a total of $343,000. Mary's mom gets the balance: $386,000 - $343,000 = $43,000 (§2-102A(a)(2) & §2-103(2)).

g. John and Mary's sister survive: John takes all (§2-102(1)(i) & §2-102A(1)(i)).
h. John, Mary's mother and Mary's fifth cousin survive: Same answer as part f. The fifth cousin receives nothing.
i. John and Mary's fifth cousin survives: Same answer as part a; Mary's fifth cousin takes nothing.
j. Only Mary's fifth cousin survives:

All probate property escheats to the state (§2-105), including the home, the car, and the stock, which Mary presumably received after John's earlier death. Note that the UPC intestate succession only extends upward to the grandparents and downward to their issue, hence the reach only extends out to second cousins and their issue.

k. There are no surviving relatives: All probate property escheats to the state.

If Mary died with a valid will, there would be no intestate property, and all probate property would be disposed of in accordance with the terms of the will.

5. a. John predeceased Mary by one year: Mary's parents will inherit the property (§2-103(2)).
   b. John survived Mary by 10 minutes, but there is no evidence of this: Mary's parents will inherit, as in part a, §2-104 does not apply, since John and Mary seem to have died simultaneously.
   c. John survived Mary by six hours: Mary's parents will take the property, as in part b, because §2-104 requires survivorship by at least 120 hours.
   d. John survived Mary by six days: John's estate, and, ultimately, his parents, will take the property. Under §2-104, John met the survival requirement of 120 hours.

6. Under Frank's current will, C2 is an omitted child not protected under the UPC. Therefore, C2 would receive . C3, an after-born child is protected by the UPC, and would take an intestate share. However, under §2-102(1)(ii), C3's intestate share would be zero because all children are from their marriage, thus Joan and C1 would split equally the entire $180,000. You should advise Frank to see an attorney to write a new will leaving everything to Joan.

7. If George died today, based on the UPC, unless Karla was otherwise provided for or unless the omission was intentional, Karla would likely take her intestate share. You should advise George to see a lawyer to write a new will explicitly omitting Karla.

8. Measured by the degrees of consanguinity, your niece, three steps away, is closer to you than your first cousin, who is four steps away.

9. This question is designed to have the student review the steps in the probate process, whether UPC on non-UPC. Steps for typical formal probate in non-UPC states:

   Petition court for probating of will, and file with court a <u>proof of subscribing witness</u> statement and a <u>notice of petition</u> statement.
   Purchase a probate bond.
   Publish notice in newspaper.
   At probate hearing, have issued:
   <u>Order for probate</u>
   <u>Letters testamentary</u>
   Manage the estate.
   Develop and file an <u>inventory an and appraisement</u>.
   File, if desired, a <u>petition for preliminary distribution</u>
   File an estate accounting.
   At final hearing, have issued an order for <u>final distribution</u>.
   Pay debts and distribute estate assets.

10. The petition for probate requests:

    1. probate of the will;
    2. letters testamentary;
    3. authorization to administer under the Independent Administration of Estates Act, if any.

11. The notice of death clipping should be available from any local newspaper that is recognized by the county in question.

12. The purpose of the hearing for probate is to give anyone in the court the opportunity to object to the petition for probate.

13. Uses of the inventory and appraisement:

    1. delineate the assets for which the personal representative is responsible;
    2. describe the estate to all interested parties;
    3. determine the proper bond amount; and
    4. possibly influence death tax return valuation.

14. Filed by a creditor, the creditor's claim is the method of formally presenting a claim against the estate.

15. Before a judge will permit final distribution under supervised probate, all current debts must be paid.

16. Minimum legal procedures in formal or supervised probate in most states:
    - four document filings (petition for probate, notice of death, inventory and appraisement, and final distribution);
    - two formal court hearings (request for probate and final distribution);
    - one newspaper notice; and
    - one accounting (inventory and appraisement).

17. UPC probate is considered so flexible because of its many options, and because the parties can elect different degrees of supervision at each stage of the process.

18.   Informal probate administration procedures under the UPC:

    a. application for informal appointment by the personal representative, filed with a court register;
    b. informal preparation of an inventory;
    c. notice to creditors;
    d. payment of debts; and
    e. application for informal closing after six months after appointment.

19.   a. Parents of minor children may find the UPC intestacy laws undesirable if a guardian must be appointed because a minor child has inherited property. Happily, this will occur under the UPC only if one or both of the parents have children of a former marriage. In many non-UPC states, children will inherit even if there are no children of a prior marriage.

      b. A will leaving everything outright to the surviving spouse may prevent guardianship proceedings, but its assumption that the surviving spouse will take care of all children may not be correct if the spouse is not the parent of the decedent's children or has children by a prior marriage. Further, the spouse could remarry, diverting assets intended for the children. Finally, the surviving spouse could die before the children reached adulthood, thus creating the need for a guardianship.

c. A better alternative would be providing for a trust for the benefit of the children. Trustees often are subject to less court supervision, and can use discretion in sprinkling trust assets unequally according to the children's needs. Guardians are required to treat each child equally. Finally, trustees are usually granted broad powers and great autonomy in managing trust assets, making a trust more efficient than a guardianship.

20. General rule: Probate assets include:
    i.   property owned by the decedent as an individual;
    ii. decedent's share of interests held in common with others;
    iii. in some states, the decedent's one half community property interests.

a. Automobile, held jointly with Jake: Non probate asset. Will pass to Jake by automatic survivorship, by operation of law.
b. Money fund account, owned by Denise as an individual: Probate asset.
c. Life insurance policy (L1) on Denise's life, owned by Denise. Herb is beneficiary: Non-probate asset.
d. Life insurance policy (L2) on Denise's life, owned by her. James, the sole beneficiary, died three years ago: Probate asset, since proceeds will be paid to (policy owner) Denise's estate, by default.
e. Life insurance policy (L3) on Herb's life, owned by Denise, who is also beneficiary: Probate asset, policy is owned by Denise as an individual.
f. Common stock, owned by trustee of a living trust. Denise is trustor, trustee, and one of the beneficiaries: Non probate asset. Not owned by Denise, as an individual.
g. Commercial real estate owned in common by Denise (40%) and Herb (60%): Denise's 40% interest is probate asset.
h. Defined benefit pension plan. Denise is participant, and Bob is named surviving beneficiary: Non-probate asset.
i. Residence, owned by Denise and Herb as community property: Denise's one half community interest is probate asset.

ENDNOTES

1. UPC §2-106.

2. UPC §2-302.

3. UPC §2-114(b).

4. UPC §2-402.

5. California Probate Code §§13,100-209.

6. California Probate Code §§13,500-660.

— 5

Introduction To Federal Unified Wealth Transfer Taxation

OVERVIEW

This chapter is the first of three covering Federal taxation of wealth transfers. Since wealth is transferred during life and at death, we examine the tax imposed on both types of transfers, i.e., on gifts and on estates. Because individuals may be able to save taxes by transferring wealth directly for the benefit of grandchildren, we also consider the generation-skipping transfer tax. It will be introduced at the end of Chapter 7 and covered in more detail in Chapter 12. It is important to understand that these taxes are *excise* taxes, not property taxes. An excise tax is a tax on a transaction. In this case it is levied on the transfer of wealth, with the tax based upon the value of property transferred. We begin with the basics of gift tax and estate tax law by showing how these two taxes are really part of a unified transfer tax system, even though it is not perfectly unified.

BRIEF HISTORY

Congress created a wealth transfer tax during the Civil War with the enactment of an inheritance tax. It was repealed shortly after the war. In 1916, Congress passed an estate tax with rates ranging between 1 and 10 percent. As a tax only on transfers at death, it was relatively easy to circumvent through the use of gifts which had the effect of reducing the size of the donor's taxable estate. In 1924, Congress plugged this loophole by enacting a gift tax. The gift tax was repealed in 1926 and reenacted in 1932, applicable to gifts made after June 5 of that year.

Prior to the gift tax and estate tax being unified in 1977, there were a number of imperfections in the system that could be exploited to reduce the taxes on the transfer of wealth. Because the gift tax *rates* were only 75% of the estate tax rates, gift giving reduced taxes for the very wealthy. For any given size taxable estate, the fact the decedent had made prior taxable gifts in no way increased the decedent's estate taxes. Estates of decedents who had made taxable gifts still started at the lowest marginal rates and had the same estate tax exemption as estates of persons who had not made taxable gifts. They were said to "take two trips up the rate ladder" since the estate tax is a progressive one. Before the 1977 unification of the estate and gift taxes, there was an annual exclusion of $3,000 per donee, a $30,000 lifetime gift exemption for each donor, and a $60,000 estate exemption which was undiminished by the decedent's use of the gift exemption. Although learning to calculate the taxes on pre-1977 transfers is no longer necessary, the following examples will help your understanding of the dramatic change brought about by unification of the two taxes.

EXAMPLE 5 - 1. In 1970, Adele made a gift worth $1,000,000 to her friend Lance. She used her $30,000 lifetime exemption and the $3,000 annual exclusion to bring the taxable gift down to $967,000. Adele paid gift tax of $235,118.

EXAMPLE 5 - 2. When Adele died in 1975, her net estate was left in equal shares to five friends. The gross estate was worth $1,150,000. There were debts and expenses of $150,000 which, combined with the $60,000 estate exemption, resulted in a taxable estate of $940,000. Adele's estate paid estate tax of $303,500. Even though Adele had made the earlier gift to Lance, it did not affect the amount of the estate tax. Notice that for estates there is no per-beneficiary exclusion comparable to the gift tax annual exclusion.

EXAMPLE 5 - 3. Brian also died in 1975 and has an estate identical to Adele's. It also was left to five friends. The gross estate was worth $1,150,000. There were debts and expenses of $150,000, which combined with the $60,000 estate exemption, resulted in a taxable estate of $940,000. Brian's estate paid estate tax of $303,500. Brian's estate tax is exactly the same as Adele's, even though Adele had made a huge taxable gift during her life time and Brian had not made any taxable gifts.

With the passage of the Tax Reform Act of 1976, a single "unified" rate schedule was adopted taxing lifetime gifts and death transfers at the same rate. With the implementation of the "unified" system, the transfer of the estate at death is treated almost as though it is just another gift. The adjusted taxable gifts, the value of the gifts with the annual exclusions subtracted boost the taxable estate into its appropriate marginal rates. Furthermore, the donor's taxable gifts (post-76) reduced the amount of unified credit (comparable to the old law's exemptions) available to shelter transfers at death. Before we get into the details of the calculations, compare the tax result in the following examples that repeat the facts of the three prior situations in the current estate tax era. We are using the current estate tax rates, the unified credit of $192,800 (appropriate for years after 1985), and an annual exclusion of $10,000 (increased from $3,000 to $10,000 for gifts after 1981).

EXAMPLE 5 - 4. In 1990, Catherine made a gift worth $1,000,000 to her friend Nathan. She used the $10,000 annual exclusion to bring the taxable gift down to $990,000. Catherine paid gift tax of $149,100. Notice that there is no donor lifetime exemption after 1976.

EXAMPLE 5 - 5. When Catherine died in 1995, her net estate was left in equal shares to five friends. The gross estate was worth $1,150,000. There were debts and expenses of $150,000, which resulted in a taxable estate of $1,000,000. Notice, there is no estate exemption for decedents dying after 1976. Because of her earlier gift, $990,000 is added back to Catherine's estate to determine the marginal rate and her unified credit has already been used up against the taxable gift. Catherine's estate paid estate taxes of $434,400. Compare Catherine's estate tax amount to that of Edward's estate in the example that follows.

EXAMPLE 5 - 6. Edward also died in 1995, with an estate identical to Catherine's, but Edward had never made any post-1976 taxable gifts. His estate was also left to five friends. The gross estate was worth $1,150,000. There were debts and expenses of $150,000, which resulted in a taxable estate of $1,000,000. Edward's estate paid estate tax of $153,000. Catharine's estate tax is $434,400, which is $281,400 more than Edward's estate, because it is being taxed at higher marginal rates and her unified credit was used up on the 1990 gift to Nathan. Also notice that Edward's estate tax on his taxable estate of $1,000,000 is $3,900 more than the gift tax on Catherine's $1,000,000 dollar gift. *** *Query 5 - 1. How do you account for the $3,900 difference? What is the transfer tax marginal rate just below $1,000,000?*

EXAMPLE 5 - 7. Suppose Catharine had not made the 1990 gift and that her estate was worth $2,150,000 when she died in 1995. Assume that debts and expenses stayed at $150,000 resulting in a taxable estate of $2,000,000. The estate tax would be $588,000. Compare this to the total paid when there was a gift of $1,000,000 (taxable gift of $990,000) followed by the donor's taxable estate of $1,000,000. The $4,500 difference is explained by the fact that the gift was reduced by the $10,000 annual exclusion. *** *Query 5 - 2. What is the marginal rate just below $2,000,000?*

In spite of unification, there is still room for using gifts as part of estate planning. We shall explore later in the text how gifts save transfer taxes by utilizing the annual exclusion, avoiding grossing up, and freezing the estate tax value.

UNIFIED TRANSFER TAX FRAMEWORK

The basic model of the present system is to tax wealth transfers cumulatively, allowing the donors of smaller gifts and estates to escape the payment of transfer taxes through a combination of annual exclusions (for gifts only) and the unified credit (applicable to both gifts and estates). There has been a phase-in of both the unified credit and the present top marginal rates. Before we go into details on the phase-in, peek ahead if you like, we will take this transfer tax step-by-step. The examples used to explore the fundamentals of the transfer tax system will use years between 1988 and 1996 because the rates, the unified credit, and the annual exclusion were unchanged for that period. We start with simple gifts, ones where the donor made no prior taxable gifts, then move to gifts with prior gifts. Next we go to a simple taxable estate, one where the donor made no prior post-76 taxable gifts. Finally, we look at an estate where the decedent had made post-76 taxable gifts.

Appendix D at the end of the text includes a copy of the Federal Gift Tax Return, Form 709, which should help to illustrate the gift tax scheme. The *donor* is responsible for filing the return and paying the tax. If the donor fails to do so, however, the donee is secondarily liable for payment of the tax.

Gift taxes for the first time donor. The steps for calculating the gift tax for a donor who has made no prior taxable gifts are summarized as follows: Subtract the annual exclusions ($10,000/donee), the marital deduction, and any attached mortgages or lien from the fair market value of the gift on the date of transfer. On this net amount, referred to as the *taxable gift*, use the transfer tax rate table to calculate the tentative tax. Finally, the gift tax that must be paid is determined by subtracting the unified credit from the tentative tax.

TABLE 5-1   Federal Gift Tax (Form 709) Basic Model - **No** Prior Gifts

---

Total current year's gross gifts	$xxx,xxx
Less: Annual exclusion(s) and deductions	(xxx,xxx)
Equals: Total taxable gifts	$xxx,xxx
Calculate: Tentative tax on total taxable gifts	xxx,xxx
Less: unified credit (not to exceed tentative tax)	(xxx,xxx)
Equals: Current gift tax	$xx,xxx

EXAMPLE 5 - 8. In 1989, Deborah made a gift of GnueCo stock worth $430,000 to her sister, Ophelia. Deborah had never made a taxable gift before. The tentative tax on a $420,000 taxable gift (remember the annual exclusion) is $128,600. When $128,600 of Deborah's unified credit was applied (up to $192,800 unified credit was available), no gift taxes were due.

EXAMPLE 5 - 9. In 1993, Edward made a gift of 1,000 shares of PlehCo stock worth $850,000 to his sister, Gloria. Edward had never made a taxable gift before. The tentative tax on a $840,000 gift is $283,400 which, when reduced by the $192,800 unified credit resulted in Edward paying gift taxes of $90,600.

EXAMPLE 5 - 10. In 1993, Francis made gifts of 1,000 shares of RenCo stock worth $850,000. His brother, Peter, received 500 shares and his sister, Patricia, received the other 500 shares. The tentative tax on taxable gifts of $830,000 (two annual exclusions this time) is $279,500 and the gift tax, after the $192,800 unified credit, is $86,700.

*** *Query 5 - 3. Given the following information, what gift tax did Martha pay? In 1990, Martha gave Quin an apartment building worth $750,000. It was free and clear of debt and liens. Martha was new to making large gifts.*

Gift taxes for the experienced donor. Where there have been prior gifts, calculating the gift tax for additional gift is as follows: The annual exclusions and deductions (marital, charitable, and mortgages or liens attached to the property transferred) are subtracted from the current year's gross gifts to arrive at current taxable gifts. Add to the current taxable gifts the taxable gifts for prior years to determine the total taxable gifts. Then, using the tax rate table, a tentative tax is calculated on both the prior years' cumulative taxable gifts and on the total taxable gifts. From the tentative tax on the total taxable gifts is subtracted the tentative tax on prior taxable gifts, leaving the tentative tax on current taxable gifts. The unused unified credit is determined by subtracting the unified credit used against the tentative tax of prior years' post-76 taxable gifts from the total unified credit allowable. Finally, the unused unified credit (credit still available) is subtracted from the tentative tax for current gifts to arrive at the gift tax that must be paid.

TABLE 5-2 Federal Gift Tax (Form 709) Overview Model - **With** Prior Gifts

Total current year's gross gifts	$xxx,xxx
Less: Annual exclusion(s) and deductions	(xx,xxx)
Equals: Current taxable gifts	$xxx,xxx
Plus: Total prior taxable gifts	xx,xxx
Equals: Total (current and prior) taxable gifts	$xxx,xxx

Calculate: Tentative tax on total taxable gifts	$xxx,xxx
Less: Tentative tax on total prior taxable gifts	(xx,xxx)
Leaves: Tentative tax on current taxable gifts	$xxx,xxx
Less: Unused unified credit (not to exceed tentative tax)	(xx,xxx)
Equals: Current gift tax	$xxx,xxx

For each example below, refer back to the earlier examples to see how they boost the later transfers into high marginal rates. Notice that it is the taxable amount that does the boosting and that we take into account that the earlier transfers already used up some (or all) of the unified credit.

EXAMPLE 5 - 11. In 1991, Deborah gave additional GnueCo stock worth $730,000 to her friend, Gerry. The gift tax was calculated as follows:

Total current year's gross gifts	$730,000		
- Annual exclusions	($10,000)		
= Current taxable gifts		$720,000	
+ Total prior taxable gifts		$420,000	
= Total taxable gifts			$1,140,000
Tentative tax on total taxable gifts			$403,200
- Tentative tax on prior taxable gifts			($128,600)
= Tentative tax on current taxable			$274,600
- Unused unified credit	$192,800	($128,600) =	($64,200)
Equals: Current gift tax			$210,400

Notice that it was not necessary to recalculate the tentative tax on the prior taxable gifts since that figure was already available.

EXAMPLE 5 - 12. In 1992, Deborah gave gold bars worth $650,000 to George, her favorite former teacher, and bonds worth 380,000 to her friend, Samantha. The gift tax was calculated as follows:

Total prior taxable gifts	$1,030,000		
- Annual exclusions	($20,000)		
= Current taxable gifts		$1,010,000	
+ Prior period gifts		$1,140,000	
= Total taxable gifts			$2,150,000
Tentative tax on total taxable gifts			$854,300
- Tentative tax on prior taxable gifts			($403,200)
= Tentative tax on current taxable gifts			$451,100
- Unused unified credit	$192,800	($192,800) =	$0
Equals: Current gift tax			$451,100

Again, notice that it was not necessary to recalculate the prior taxable gifts since both figures were already available. The prior taxable gifts were the last taxable period's total gifts reduced by the allowable annual exclusions.

*** *Query 5 - 4. On the gifts described next, taking into account Martha's earlier gift, what gift tax did she have to pay? In 1993, Martha gave three more gifts: a new car costing $36,000 to Jake; cash in the amount of $43,000 to Marilyn; and PontoCo common stock worth $88,000 to Eddie.*

Estate taxes for the stingy decedent. Sorry, didn't mean stingy, frugal is better. The steps for calculating the estate tax for a decedent who never made any post-76 taxable gifts are summarized as follows: From the decedent's gross estate (generally, all that the person owned at death), subtract the marital deduction and any debts, mortgages, liens and the expenses of the decedent's estate (i.e., executor's fees, appraiser's fees, and attorney's fees) to arrive at the *taxable estate.* The transfer tax rate table is used to calculate a tentative tax on the taxable estate. Finally, the death taxes that must be paid are determined by subtracting the unified credit from the tentative tax.

TABLE 5-3 Federal Estate Tax (Form 706) Basic Model - **No** Prior Gifts

---

Gross estate	$xxx,xxx
Less: Total deductions	(xx,xxx)
Leaves: Taxable estate	xxx,xxx
Calculate: Tentative estate tax	$xxx,xxx
Less: Unified credit	(xxx,xxx)
Less: State death tax credit	(xxx,xxx)
Less: Other credits	(xx,xxx)
Equals: Federal estate tax	$xxx,xxx

EXAMPLE 5 - 13. When he died in early 1997, Gregg left his entire estate to his three children. The gross estate was valued at $5,840,000. Total debts were $315,000 and expenses of administration were $55,000. He had made no post-1976 taxable gifts. His estate tax is as follows:

Gross Estate	$5,840,000	
- Debts & expenses	($370,000)	
= Taxable estate = Estate tax base	$5,470,000	
Tentative tax on estate tax base		$2,649,300
- Unified credit		($192,800)
= Total Death taxes (for most estates)		$2,456,500

*** *Query 5 - 5. Given the following information, what death tax did Georgine's estate pay? Georgine died in 1996, leaving her $800,000 estate to her children by right of representation. Debts totaled $150,000 and expenses were $50,000. Calculate her estate's death tax.*

*** *Query 5 - 6. Given the following information, what death tax did Harold's estate pay? Harold died in 1996, leaving his $980,000 estate to his brother. Debts totaled $65,000 and expenses were $20,000. Calculate his estate's death tax.*

Estate taxes for the generous decedent. Here, we put it all together. The estate taxes for an estate with prior post-76 gifts are calculated taking those gifts into account. These post-76 gifts are referred to as *adjusted taxable gifts.* They are adjusted in the sense that the annual exclusion has been subtracted, as has any marital or charitable deduction. The sole purpose of the adjusted taxable gifts coming into the estate tax equation is to move the decedent's taxable estate up into the appropriate marginal rates. The rates are appropriate in the sense that we now have a unified transfer tax system and the earlier gifts have already occupied the lower marginal rates. The steps are as follows: Start, as before, with the gross estate; subtract debts, expenses, and other deductions to arrive at the taxable estate. Add the adjusted taxable gifts to determine the total estate tax base. Use the tax rate table to determine the tentative tax on the total tax base.

From the tentative tax, subtract the gift taxes payable on post-76 gifts. For most estates, the gift taxes payable will be the same as the total of the gift taxes paid on the post-76 gifts. We will cover the exceptions later. Please note, this gift taxes payable credit is the amount after application of the unified credit for those earlier gifts, it is not the tentative tax on those gifts. Because we subtract as a credit only the gift taxes payable (i.e., the amount by which the tentative tax on those gifts exceeded the unified credit), we take the full unified credit to arrive at the death taxes.

TABLE 5-4 Federal Estate Tax (Form 706) Overview Model - **With** Prior Gifts

Gross estate	$xxx,xxx
Less: Total deductions	(xxx,xxx)
Leaves: Taxable estate	xxx,xxx
Plus: Adjusted taxable gifts (post-76)	xx,xxx
Equals: Estate tax base	$xxx,xxx
Calculate: Tentative estate tax	$xxx,xxx
Less: Gift taxes payable on post-76 taxable gifts	(xxx,xxx)
Less: Unified credit	(xxx,xxx)
Less: State death tax credit	(xxx,xxx)
Less: Other credits	(xx,xxx)
Equals: Federal estate tax	$xxx,xxx

The state death tax credit does not reduce the total estate taxes for most estates since it merely causes a division of the death taxes between the Federal and state governments. Every taxable estate large enough to pay Federal estate taxes will use the unified credit and the state death tax credit. The former will apply to every estate to keep the smaller ones (or cumulative transfers, if you will) from being taxed, and the latter is used because every state in the nation collects death taxes that are at least equal the Federal state death tax credit. Other credits will be introduced later.

In the example that follows, you need to refer back to the example where Deborah made gifts in 1989, 1991, and 1992 to see how all of those prior gifts affect her estate taxes. You may wish to tag those pages to allow you to flip back and forth before you tackle this problem.

> EXAMPLE 5 - 14. Deborah died in early 1997 and left her estate to her four children. Her estate was worth $5,840,000, debts were $315,000, and expenses totaled $55,000. Taking into account the gifts she made in 1989, 1991, and 1992, her estate tax is as follows:

Gross Estate	$5,840,000	
- Debts & expenses	($370,000)	
- Marital & charitable deductions	$0	
= Taxable estate	$5,470,000	
+ Adjusted taxable gifts (post-76)	$2,150,000	
= Estate tax base	$7,620,000	
Tentative tax on estate tax base		$3,831,800
- Gift tax payable on post-76 taxable gifts		($661,500)
- Unified credit		($192,800)
= Total Death taxes (for most estates)		$2,977,500
- State death tax credit	(we're jumping ahead)	($447,200)
- Other credits		$0
= Federal Estate Tax		$2,530,300

Notice that to calculate the gift tax payable credit one must add up all the taxes paid, NOT the tentative tax on those prior gifts, because the gift taxes paid (payable) were an amount in excess of the available unified credit. Because the entire prior adjusted taxable gifts (post-1976) are included in the tax base, the full $192,800 unified credit is used in the calculation. *** *Query 5 - 7. Given the following information and taking into account her earlier gifts, what death tax did Martha's estate pay? Martha died in 1996 leaving her $2,550,000 estate to her children. There were debts of $240,000 and expenses of $60,000.*

UNIFIED RATE SCHEDULE

Table 5-5 shows the Federal Unified Tax Rate Schedule presently in effect.

TABLE 5-5 Federal Unified Transfer-Tax Rates - Since 1/1/88

If the Amount is:		Tentative Tax		
Over	But Not Over	Base Amount +	Percent	On Excess Over
$0	$10,000	$0	18%	$0
10,000	20,000	1,800	20%	10,000
20,000	40,000	3,800	22%	20,000
40,000	60,000	8,200	24%	40,000
60,000	80,000	13,000	26%	60,000
80,000	100,000	18,200	28%	80,000
100,000	150,000	23,800	30%	100,000
150,000	250,000	38,800	32%	150,000
250,000	500,000	70,800	34%	250,000
500,000	750,000	155,800	37%	500,000
750,000	1,000,000	248,300	39%	750,000
1,000,000	1,250,000	345,800	41%	1,000,000
1,250,000	1,500,000	448,300	43%	1,250,000
1,500,000	2,000,000	555,800	45%	1,500,000
2,000,000	2,500,000	780,800	49%	2,000,000
2,500,000	3,000,000	1,025,800	53%	2,500,000
3,000,000	10,000,000	1,290,800	55%	3,000,000
10,000,000	21,040,000	5,140,800	60%*	10,000,000
21,040,000		11,764,800	55%	21,040,000

* For post-1987 transfers between $10,000,000 and $21,040,000 there is a 5% surcharge.

A more complete table showing the changes in maximum rates since 1977 appears as Table 1 in Appendix A at the end of the book.

As a result of the Economic Recovery Act of 1981 (ERTA), revised by the Tax Reform Act of 1984 and the Revenue Act of 1987, rates on amounts over $3 million have been decreasing periodically. Hence, the schedule shown as Table 1 at the end of the book is divided into five parts. The first part shows rates for *all* transfer years after 1976 for taxable amounts up to $3 million. The next four parts represent transition rates, on amounts over $3 million, that apply for transfers during 1977-81, 1982, 1983, and 1984 and thereafter.

The Revenue Act of 1987 phased out the transfer tax benefits of the lower rates and the unified credit (described below) for amounts exceeding $10 million transferred after December 31, 1987. The net effect is a "recapturing" of the taxes saved by the lower rates and the unified credit. This recapture is implemented with the imposition of an additional 5% tax ("bubble") on amounts between $10 million and $21,040,000.[1] Thus, the effective marginal FET rate for all transfers of between $10 million and $21,040,000 is 60 percent.

A few examples will demonstrate the application of the unified rates. The facts in these examples are intended to be sufficiently general to apply to both lifetime gifts and transfers at death.

> EXAMPLE 5 - 15. The *tentative tax* on the taxable amount $600,000 is $192,800. This represents the sum of $155,800 plus $37,000, which is 37% of $100,000, the excess of $600,000 over $500,000. Since the same rate table applies to all years for amounts up to $3 million, $192,800 would be the tentative tax on the amount $600,000 for all years after 1976.

> EXAMPLE 5 - 16. The *tentative tax* on the taxable amount $3,250,000 in any year after 1983 is $1,428,300. This represents the sum of $1,290,800 plus $137,500, which is 55 percent of $250,000, the excess of $3,250,000 over $3,000,000.

> EXAMPLE 5 - 17. The *tentative tax* on the taxable amount $21,040,000 in 1995 is $11,764,800. This amount represents the sum of *a*) $5,140,800 [the tentative tax on $10,000,000] and b) $6,624,000 [which is 60 percent of $11,040,000, the excess of $21,040,000 over $10,000,000]. $11,764,800 - $192,800 = $11,572,000 which is exactly 55% of $21,040,000.

Thus, Federal unified transfer tax rates are progressive. Marginal rates range from 18% to as high as 60% for amounts in excess of $10 million. The *marginal rate* is the rate levied on the next taxable dollar. The *average rate*, on the other hand, is the result obtained by dividing the tax by the total taxable amount. For estates over $21,040,000, the marginal and the average rate are both 55%.

UNIFIED CREDIT

In Federal estate and gift tax law, a *credit* is a dollar-for-dollar reduction in the *tentative tax*. A *deduction* is a dollar-for-dollar reduction in the *amount taxable* and provides only a fractional reduction in the tentative tax. The fraction is determined by the particular estate's marginal tax rate. In the next two chapters, we will study several credits, but the most significant one, the unified credit, will be introduced now.

Prior to 1977, the first year of the unified credit, estate and gift tax law permitted a deduction of $30,000 (in addition to the $3,000 per donee annual exclusions) on the gift tax return for total lifetime gifts and a deduction of $60,000 on the estate tax return for decedent's estates. These had the effect of eliminating taxation of small amounts of lifetime gifts and small estates. These two deductions were called the $30,000 lifetime gift exemption and the $60,000 estate exemption. Using the gift exemption did not reduce the estate exemption. Thus, the first $60,000 of taxable estate was tax free regardless of the amount of life time taxable gifts by the decedent. The Tax Reform Act of 1976 (TRA 76) eliminated the two exemptions and substituted a single *unified credit* applicable to both taxable gifts and taxable estates after 1976. The unified credit has increased over the years, as shown in Table 5-6.[2]

TABLE 5-6 Federal Unified Credit Amounts Effective Beginning In 1977

Year		Amount of Credit	Credit Shelter Amount
1977		$30,000	$120,667
1978		$34,000	$134,000
1979		$38,000	$147,333
1980		$42,500	$161,563
1981		$47,000	$175,625
1982		$62,800	$225,000
1983		$79,300	$275,000
1984		$96,300	$325,000
1985		$121,800	$400,000
1986		$155,800	$500,000
1987	and after	$192,800	$600,000

Indeed, Congress and the President have agreed in principle to increase the amount that can pass tax free by increasing the unified credit. The amount and timing of the increase were not agreed upon when this text went to press in May of 1997, but a unified credit equivalent of $1,200,000 has been proposed by some legislators. The third column in the table shows the *unified credit equivalent* estate, or the *credit shelter amount*, for each year's unified credit. This represents the amount by which the taxable amount can exceed zero and still have the tentative tax be completely sheltered (offset) by the unified credit.

Some people incorrectly refer to the present credit shelter amount as an "exemption" of $600,000. Clearly this is wrong, we don't subtract $600,000. We calculate the tentative tax on the taxable transfer, and then apply the appropriate unified credit. The present unified credit of $192,800 shelters $600,000 in taxable transfers because the tentative tax on that amount is $192,800.

> EXAMPLE 5 - 18. After the unified credit is subtracted, the *net tax* on the amount $600,000 in 1983 is $113,500, which is the tentative tax of $192,800, reduced by the 1983 unified credit of $79,300.

> EXAMPLE 5 - 19. Facts as in the prior example, except the applicable year is any year after 1986. After the unified credit is subtracted, the net tax on $600,000 is zero, which is the tentative tax of $192,800, reduced by the post-1986 unified credit of $192,800. Thus, since the starting of 1987, the first $600,000 in taxable transfer is totally sheltered by the unified credit.

> **Warning:** *Do NOT deduct the unified credit shelter amount. You must subtract the unified credit from the tentative tax in all of these transfer tax calculations. The major use of the unified credit equivalent is in giving general advice to clients, such as "the first $600,000 in transfers are tax free."*

In many situations, the allowable unified credit will be less than the amount in Table 5 - 6. The actual amount of the allowable unified credit is the *lesser of either* the unused unified credit in the year of the transfer *or* the amount of the tentative tax. For example, the allowable unified credit for a 1990 taxable amount of $250,000 (assuming no prior taxable gifts) is $70,800 which is the lesser of $192,800, the unused unified credit, and $70,800, the tentative tax on $250,000.

UNLIMITED MARITAL DEDUCTION

Since 1982, virtually all transfers to a *spouse*, whether made during lifetime or at death, have been tax free; the amount of the transfer is treated as a "marital" deduction from the total gross estate or gross gifts. A brief history of the gift tax and estate tax marital deductions is described next.

The *gift tax marital deduction* was first enacted in 1948 to equalize tax treatment for married taxpayers in common law and community property states. It allowed a deduction for up to 50 percent of the value of noncommunity property gifts made to a spouse. TRA 76 changed this limit to 100 percent of the first $100,000, no deduction for the next $100,000, and 50 percent for all amounts exceeding $200,000.

The *estate tax marital deduction* was also first enacted in 1948, also to equalize tax treatment across the states. Its amount was limited to one half of the adjusted gross estate. TRA 76 changed this limit to the greater of $250,000 or one half of the adjusted gross estate, subject to further adjustments for any gift tax marital deduction taken and for property held as community property. The *adjusted gross estate* was defined essentially as the decedent's separate property, reduced by deductions for funeral and administration expenses, claims against the estate, and losses during administration.

The *present* 100% "unlimited" gift and estate tax marital deductions became effective in 1982.[3]

> EXAMPLE 5 - 20. Last year, Wildcard gave property worth $10 million to his wife, Simba, a U.S. citizen. Although Wildcard's "gross gift" was $10 million, his taxable gift will be reduced to zero by the unlimited marital deduction. Thus, there will be no tentative tax.

> EXAMPLE 5 - 21. Based on the facts in prior example, assume instead that Wildcard died last year leaving his entire $10 million estate to his wife. His taxable estate and tentative tax will also be zero, as a result of subtracting the $10 million marital deduction from the $10 million gross estate.

The current unlimited marital deduction will be examined in greater detail in the chapters that follow. Wealth transfer taxes incorporate other significant deductions, but their examination will also be deferred.

UNLIMITED CHARITABLE DEDUCTION

When determining transfer taxes there is a 100% deduction for gifts or bequests made to qualified charities. Contrast this with income tax law which limits the amount that can be deducted based upon the type of gift, the nature of the charity (e.g., private foundations versus public charities), and the donor's adjusted gross income.

$10,000 ANNUAL EXCLUSION FOR LIFETIME GIFTS

The first $10,000 of total post-1981 lifetime gifts by any donor to each donee in a given year is treated as a deduction. Technically, it is called the annual exclusion.

> EXAMPLE 5 - 22. In 1982, Dad gave $21,000 cash to both son, Bob, and Uncle Bill. Assuming no other deductions and that Dad made no other gifts in that year, he would file only one gift tax return, and his current taxable gifts for 1982 would equal $22,000. The first portion of Dad's gift tax return would look as follows:

Total current year's gross gifts	$42,000
Less: Annual exclusions and deductions	20,000
Equals: Current taxable gifts	$22,000

> EXAMPLE 5 - 23. Mary gave husband, Karl, $200,000 in 1983. Assuming that it was her only gift in 1983, Mary's "total taxable gifts" for 1983 equals zero, which is $200,000, the amount of the gross gift, reduced by $200,000, the amount of the marital deduction. For intra-spousal gifts, the annual exclusion is not really needed to reduce the tax to zero.

Prior to 1982, the annual exclusion amount was $3,000. To qualify for the annual exclusion, the gift must be one of a present interest, meaning that the donee has immediate access to the gift for use and enjoyment. Thus, a gift to an irrevocable trust giving one person a life estate and another the remainder creates two gifts. The value of the life estate qualifies for the annual exclusion because it is a gift of a present interest, but the remainder does not qualify because it is a future interest.

WEALTH TRANSFERS ARE UNIFIED AND TAXED CUMULATIVELY

In wealth transfer taxation, succeeding transfers are unified, in part because they are taxed cumulatively. Under the *cumulative gift doctrine*, all past and present gifts are accumulated; that is, prior taxable gifts are added to current taxable transfers (whether lifetime gifts or the donor's estate at death) to determine the transfer tax base. There is one purpose, and only one purpose, to having adjusted taxable gifts as part of the estate tax calculation, and that is to boost the decedent's estate into higher marginal rates. These are the appropriate marginal rates when the net estate is seen as just another in a series of transfers.

As we have seen, TRA 76 created the *unified transfer tax*, combining gift and estate taxation into a single tax structure having one rate schedule. Thus, the transfer at death is treated as just the last in a series of transfers. However, TRA 76 did not achieve complete unification, for instance the annual exclusion is available only for lifetime gifts. Unification did not produce a tax system that makes planners indifferent as to the timing of transfers; that is, whether one would recommend gifts over holding property until death or vice versa depends on the circumstances. In some cases there are trade-offs. For instance, lifetime gifts use up less unified credit because of the annual exclusion, but appreciated property transferred at death receives a step-up in basis.

Let's recapitulate the points demonstrated in the earlier series of examples before we go on to cover several of the other credits.

First, regarding taxable gifts, in calculating the gift tax one includes in the item called "total prior taxable gifts" all taxable gifts made *since 1932*, the year of enactment of the gift tax. On the other hand, as we have said, in calculating the federal estate tax base, one includes in the item called "adjusted taxable gifts" only the taxable gifts made since January 1, 1977, i.e., since unification.

Second, in the *gift tax* model, the "unused unified credit" is the amount of the current unified credit reduced by the unified credit amount already used up to offset tentative gift taxes on gifts in prior years. It is based on the premise that once the amount of the (lifetime) unified credit is used up, each additional dollar of taxable gift is fully taxable. By way of contrast, in the *estate tax* model, the entire unified credit is subtracted from the tentative tax, because the "gift tax payable" credit for prior gift taxes is limited to the amount of gift taxes that would have been paid on the post-1976 gifts using the rates in effect at the date of death. This means that the gift taxes payable credit might be less than what was actually paid. This occurs where there were pre-1977 taxable gifts that pushed the post-1976 taxable gifts into higher marginal rates, or where very large post-1976 gifts were given at a time when the top marginal rates were higher than those in effect when the donor died. For instance, a $7,000,000 (after deducting the annual exclusion amount)gift made in 1981 (when the top marginal rate was 70%) would have resulted in gift tax of $3,903,800. Applying post-1984 rates to the 1981 transfer, the gift tax would be $3,443,800. Since the purpose of using adjusted taxable gifts as part of the estate tax calculation is solely to move the taxable estate into its appropriate (taking into account cumulative transfers) marginal rate, the gift tax payable credit would be $3,443,800 even though $3,903,800 was paid.

Fortunately for most estates, the gift taxes payable credit will equal the gift taxes paid because most decedents did not make taxable gifts both before and after the change in the law (1/1/77). Few people that made gifts so large (above $3,000,000) between 12/31/76 and 12/31/83 that the marginal rate for the gift was higher than the rate in effect at the donor's death. Notice that the tentative tax has remained the same since 12/31/76 for cumulative transfers up to $3,000,000 and has not decreased for transfers over $3,000,000 since 1983.

Third, the top marginal rates have decreased over the years until they reached their current level in 1984, while the unified credit increased every year after its introduction in 1977 until it reached its present $192,800 level in 1987. It is very likely that Congress will increase the unified credit to $248,300 sometime in the next two years. *** *Query 5 - 8. What will the unified credit equivalent estate be, if the unified credit becomes $248,300?*

Fourth, gifts are valued as of the day given and estates are valued as of the day of the decedent's death. However, estates are allowed to elect an alternate valuation date of 6 months after the date of death if certain results would follow. If the election is made, any property still held by the estate will be valued as of the six month date, rather than as of the date of death. Assets sold, distributed, or otherwise disposed of during the six month period, are valued as of the date transferred. An estate is allowed to make this election only if doing so will decrease (1) the gross estate and (2) the estate tax. It must also decrease the generation skipping transfer tax, if said tax is also applicable.

THE CREDITS

There are five basic estate tax credits: the unified credit, credit for state death taxes, credit for gift tax, credit for tax on prior transfers, and the credit for foreign death taxes. We have already covered the unified credit. The only other credits which is certain to enter into the calculation of the taxes if the estate exceeds the UCE (i.e., the unified credit equivalent estate, presently above $600,000) is the state death tax credit. The other three credits just mentioned occur less frequently and will be covered briefly at the end of the next chapter. The prior transfer credit will be introduced in Chapter 6 and covered again in conjunction with life estates in the chapter that describes advanced planning for wealthy couples.

Credit for State Death Taxes

§2011 allows a credit for *state* inheritance or estate taxes actually paid. The maximum credit is calculated using the State Death Tax Credit Table shown below and also reproduced in Appendix A.

TABLE 5-7 Federal Credit for State Death Taxes - Based upon federal adjusted taxable estate*

Adjusted Taxable Estate *		Credit is the Total of		
Over	But Not Over	Base Credit	+ Percent	On Excess Over
$40,000	$90,000	$0	0.8%	$40,000
$90,000	$140,000	$400	1.6%	$90,000
$140,000	$240,000	$1,200	2.4%	$140,000
$240,000	$440,000	$3,600	3.2%	$240,000
$440,000	$640,000	$10,000	4.0%	$440,000
$640,000	$840,000	$18,000	4.8%	$640,000
$840,000	$1,040,000	$27,600	5.6%	$840,000
$1,040,000	$1,540,000	$38,800	6.4%	$1,040,000
$1,540,000	$2,040,000	$70,800	7.2%	$1,540,000
$2,040,000	$2,540,000	$106,800	8.0%	$2,040,000
$2,540,000	$3,040,000	$146,800	8.8%	$2,540,000
$3,040,000	$3,540,000	$190,800	9.6%	$3,040,000
$3,540,000	$4,040,000	$238,800	10.4%	$3,540,000
$4,040,000	$5,040,000	$290,800	11.2%	$4,040,000

TABLE 5-7 (continued)				
$5,040,000	$6,040,000	$402,800	12.0%	$5,040,000
$6,040,000	$7,040,000	$522,800	12.8%	$6,040,000
$7,040,000	$8,040,000	$650,800	13.6%	$7,040,000
$8,040,000	$9,040,000	$786,800	14.4%	$8,040,000
$9,040,000	$10,040,000	$930,800	15.2%	$9,040,000
$10,040,000		$1,082,800	16.0%	$10,040,000

* Adjusted taxable estate is the taxable estate less $60,000.

Use of the table requires calculation of the "adjusted taxable estate," defined as the taxable estate reduced by $60,000. It is important to keep in mind that this taxable estate is the gross estate reduced by all deductions (e.g., debts, marital, etc.) and *before* prior taxable gifts are added into the tax base. Keep in mind that all states, even those with an inheritance tax, collect state death taxes at least equal to the federal state death tax credit. This maximizes their fiscal self-interest. Practitioners call this provision in the states' laws a "pickup," "soak-up," or "sponge" tax.

> EXAMPLE 5 - 24. D died in 1996 leaving a gross estate of $755,000 and total deductions of $46,000. The state-calculated inheritance tax was just $15,000. The Federal credit for state death tax for a taxable estate of $649,000 is $18,432 as determined using the table. To arrive at this latter figure, we obtain the *adjusted* taxable estate which equals $649,000 (i.e., $755,000 less $46,000 less $60,000) and apply the rates. The bracket that covers this estate starts at $640,000. The credit at $640,000 is $18,000, and just above is at a rate of 4.8 percent, hence 4.8 percent of $9,000 (i.e., $649,000 less $640,000) gives another $432, for a total credit of $18,432. Since the state-calculated inheritance tax is only $15,000 the state's "sponge" tax law would require the estate pay another $3,432.

In the above example, the state collects an extra $3,432 at no extra cost to the estate since it is merely a shift of this amount out of the Federal pocket into the state's pocket. If the state collects more than the credit, then it really does cost the estate's beneficiaries.

> EXAMPLE 5 - 25. Suppose in the prior example, the state's inheritance tax caused state death taxes of $20,000. Since the federal state death tax credit would still be $18,432, the extra $1,568 [$20,000 - $18,432] does come out of the beneficiaries' pockets.

In the states imposing *only* a pickup tax, no state death tax will be owed by estates that owe no FET. The following states (and District of Columbia) impose only a pickup tax: Alabama, Alaska, Arizona, Arkansas, California, Colorado, Florida, Georgia, Hawaii, Idaho, Illinois, Maine, Missouri, Minnesota, North Dakota, New Mexico, Nevada, Oregon, Texas, Utah, Virginia, Vermont, Washington, West Virginia, Wyoming. Among the states that actually have their own death tax rates, the state death tax will usually be *higher* than the Federal state death tax credit. Nonetheless, the estate is permitted a credit against the Federal tax of only the amount determined as the Federal state death tax credit. Thus, except for "pick-up tax" states, the state tax may be only partially covered by the credit.

EXAMPLE 5 - 26. Kevin lived in a pick-up tax state where the only death taxes were simply defined as being equal to the Federal state death tax credit. When Kevin died in 1995, his gross estate was $1,500,000. He left $300,000 to his church. There were debts and expenses of $200,000. The taxable estate is $1,000,000 and the adjusted taxable estate for calculating the state death tax credit is $940,000 [$1,000,000 - $60,000]. The credit (and the state's death tax) is calculated as follows: At the $840,000 bracket break, the credit is shown as $27,600 plus 5.6% for the amount above that level, another $5,600 [5.6% * ($940,000 - $840,000)], for a total credit of $33,200. Recall from earlier examples that the total death taxes (in a pick-up tax state) for a taxable estate of $1,000,000 is $153,000. Hence, the state will collect $33,200 and the Federal Government will collect $119,800 [$153,000 - $33,200].

EXAMPLE 5 - 27. Nicki was also domiciled in a pick-up tax state. When Nicki died her gross estate was $1,500,000. She left $300,000 to her mosque. There were debts and expenses of $200,000. Five years before, Nicki had made taxable gifts equal to $175,000 to help out her brother and his family. As in the prior example, the taxable estate is $1,000,000 and the adjusted taxable estate for calculating the state death tax credit is $940,000, even though Nicki made significant taxable gifts. Her tax base for calculating the tentative tax is $1,175,000, but this does not affect the state death tax calculation. The state death tax is $33,200.

*** *Query 5 - 9. Using the information in the last query, calculate Martha's state death tax assuming her state of domicile was a "pick-up" tax state.*

This chapter has introduced Federal wealth transfer taxation, emphasizing the tax calculations. The next two chapters cover the estate tax, the gift tax, and the generation-skipping transfer tax, with regard to other important characteristics that are generally a little less quantitative in nature.

QUERIES ANSWERED

1. The annual exclusion reduced the gross gift of $1 million down to $990,000. The marginal rate just below $1 million is 39%.

2. The marginal rate just below $2 million is 45%.

3. The gift tax on a gross gift of $750,000 (taxable gift of $740,000) is $51,800 [tentative tax of $244,600 minus unified credit of $192,800].

4. The three gifts (all over $10,000) total $167,000. The taxable gift is $137,000. Tentative tax on the total gifts ($877,000) is $297,830, less the tentative tax on prior period gifts ($244,600) results in tentative tax on the current taxable gifts of $53,230. Since the unified credit was used against the tentative tax on the 1990 gift, $53,230 is the gift tax due.

5. Georgine's taxable estate is $600,000. The tentative tax of $192,800 less the unified credit of $192,800 result0s in zero tax. Notice that you do NOT subtract $600,000. There is no $600,000 exemption. There is no $600,000 exclusion.

6. Harold's taxable estate is $895,000. The tentative tax of $304,850 minus the $192,800 unified credit gives estate taxes of $112,050.

7. Martha's estate, taking into account her earlier gifts:

Gross Estate	$2,550,000
- Debts & expenses	($300,000)
- Marital & charitable deductions	$0
= Taxable estate	$2,250,000
+ Adjusted taxable gifts (post-76)	$877,000
= Estate tax base	$3,127,000

Tentative tax on estate tax base	$1,360,650
- Gift tax payable, post-76 gifts	($105,030)
- Unified credit	($192,800)
= Total Death taxes	$1,062,820

8. The tentative tax on $750,000 is $248,300, so that would become the new unified credit equivalent estate. However, it is expected to be indexed for inflation, so it will change from time to time.

9. Martha's state death tax (also the amount her estate pays to the state) and the federal amount.

= Total Death taxes		$1,062,820
- State death tax credit	*Use the taxable estate less	*($118,800)
- Other credits	$60,000 before going to	$0
= Federal Estate Tax	the table.	$944,020

QUESTIONS AND PROBLEMS *[For all estate tax problems in this textbook, assume the decedent was domiciled in a pick-up tax state.]*

1. Outline the history of Federal wealth transfer taxation with emphasis on the changes that took place in 1977 and 1982.

2. Why would the imposition of an estate tax at death without an accompanying gift tax be largely ineffective?

3. (*a*) Describe the chronological progression of the amounts of the unified credit. (*b*) What is the meaning of the term 'exemption equivalent'?

4. Describe the unlimited marital deduction.

5. What is the annual exclusion? Is it available for transfers to non-relatives? When did it increase to $10,000? What was it immediately before the increase?

6. Determine the tentative tax and the amount of gift tax for the following transfers by rock star, Denise:

a. In 1989, she gave friend, Gilbert, shares of stock worth $350,000 and her friend, Janie, stock worth $140,000.
b. In 1990, she gave Roger municipal bonds worth $125,000, Max a vacant lot valued at $50,000, and Iris cash in the amount of $35,000.
c. In 1992, she gave her church stock worth $200,000, her mother, Marlene, a new Cadillac valued at $55,000, and her boyfriend a sailboat worth $180,000.

7. Determine the tentative tax and the amount of gift tax for the following transfers by wealthy mutual fund manager, Martin:

a. In 1987, he gave his daughter, Caroline, mutual fund shares of stock worth $550,000 and his son, Jon, additional shares worth $380,000.
b. In 1989, he gave his sister, Dori, tickets for an around-the-world, first class cruise valued at $60,000 plus spending money of $40,000.
c. In 1991, he gave another $45,000 to Caroline and $95,000 to Jon.

8. Determine the tentative tax and the amount of gift tax for the following transfers by CEO of SoftWearables, Shannon:

a. In 1993, she gave her husband, Henry, shares in SoftWearables that were worth $850,000 and her daughter, Cheryl, shares in the company worth $130,000. [No split gifts. We will do these in a later chapter.]
b. In 1995, she gave additional shares to Henry worth $90,000, a car to Cheryl worth $9,000, and to her son, William, and his wife, Ruby, cash in the amount of $100,000 so they could put it as a down payment on a house.

9. When Karla died in 1993, her gross estate was worth $1,980,000. Debts and expenses were $130,000. She left her estate to her four children. Determine: (a) the total death taxes; (b) the state death tax; and (c) the federal estate tax. [Remember, total death taxes is the amount after subtraction of the unified credit.]

10. When Faustino died in 1995, his gross estate was worth $1,150,000. Debts and expenses were $40,000. He left his $500,000 home to his wife, Rosa, a cash bequest of $30,000 to his church, and the rest of his estate to his seven children by a prior marriage. Determine: (a) the total death taxes; (b) the state death tax; and (c) the Federal estate tax.

11. When Margaret died in 1996, her gross estate was worth $850,000. Debts and expenses were $210,000. She left her estate to her best friend, Diane. Determine: (a) the total death taxes; (b) the state death tax; and (c) the Federal estate tax.

12. When Stephen died in 1996, his gross estate was worth $19,750,000. Debts and expenses were $1,340,000. He left his estate in equal shares to his brother, Mark, and his sister, Leilani. Determine: (a) the total death taxes; (b) the state death tax; and (c) the Federal estate tax. [Remember the 5% surcharge.]

13. When rock star Denise (see earlier problem) died intestate in 1997, she left an estate valued at $4,890,300. Debts and expenses were $1,348,900. The entire estate went by intestate succession to her mother. Take the earlier gifts into account as you determine: (a) the total death taxes; (b) the state death tax; and (c) the Federal estate tax.

14. When Martin (see earlier problem) died in 1995, his will left $200,000 to his sister, and the residue of his estate to his issue, by right of representation. His estate was valued at $13,840,500 and debts and expenses were $310,740. Take the earlier gifts into account as you determine: (a) the total death taxes; (b) the state death tax; and (c) the Federal estate tax.

15. When CEO Shannon (see earlier problem) died in early 1997, her will left half of her net estate (i.e., after debts and expenses but before taking marital or charitable deductions into account) to her husband, $100,000

to her temple, and the rest to her children. She left an estate valued at $14,460,600. Debts and expenses were $2,940,400. Take the earlier gifts into account as you determine: (a) the total death taxes; (b) the state death tax; and (c) the Federal estate tax. [Neither the marital share, nor the charitable share, are charged with any of the death taxes.]

Answer to Question: "Why Not Subtract only the *Unused* Unified Credit in Calculating the Federal Estate Tax?"

This Appendix has been written to explain why the full unified credit, rather than just the remaining unused unified credit, is subtracted on the Federal estate tax return. Consider a highly abstract example which, for ease of comprehension, makes the following assumptions:

- the tax rate on all transfers is a flat 50 percent;
- the unified credit is $30;
- there is no annual exclusion;
- there are no deductions.

Assume Marie's total wealth consists of $200 in cash. If our basic Federal unified transfer tax scheme is working properly and consistently, this wealth should incur a total tax of $70, regardless of whether she makes her transfers during her lifetime or at her death. Proof:

Total transfer taxes = $200 times .50, less $30 = $70

Now suppose Marie makes post-1976 lifetime gifts of $40 and $20 in two different years. Her gift tax returns are shown thus:

	First Gift	Second Gift
Current taxable gifts	$40	$20
Plus total prior taxable gifts	$0	$40
Equals total taxable gifts	$40	$60
tentative tax on total taxable gifts	$20	$30
Less tentative tax on prior taxable gifts	$0	($20)
Equals tentative tax on current taxable	$20	$10
Less unused unified credit	($20)	($10)
Leaves net gift tax	$0	$0

Next, assume that when Marie dies, her taxable estate will be $140, which is the amount of her original wealth, $200, reduced by $60, the amount of the lifetime gifts. Marie's FET, assuming that the full unified credit is taken, will be $70, as shown below:

Taxable estate	$140
Plus adjusted taxable gifts	$60
Equals estate tax base	$200
Tentative estate tax	$100
Less gift taxes payable credit	$0
Less unified credit	($30)
Leaves FET	$70

Thus, total lifetime plus death time transfer taxes are $70, as they should be. The average tax rate is 35% (=$70/$200). Had we mistakenly subtracted only the "unused" unified credit on the FET return (which, because of the gifts, would have been reduced to $0 at death), total transfer taxes would have been $100, resulting in an average tax rate of 50%. The upshot would have been the total failure to utilize the unified credit.

The critical reason that the full unified credit is subtracted on the estate tax *return is that the tentative estate tax is reduced not by the entire <u>tentative</u> gift tax on lifetime gifts, (as we did for the second gift, above), but only by the <u>net</u> gift tax on lifetime gifts which is lower than the tentative tax on lifetime gifts by the amount of the unified credit taken during lifetime. (These items are marked with asterisks above). Since we have not yet received the benefit of the already used portion of the unified credit, we must take it now by subtracting the entire unified credit.*

The estate tax return subtracts the gift taxes paid on lifetime gifts from the tentative estate tax only because it reflects a *prepayment of the transfer tax*; not to do so would result in a double tax payment for the gifts. The gift tax return, on the other hand, subtracts the tentative gift tax on prior gifts for a totally different reason. It subtracts it to consistently implement the law's intent to push current gifts into a (potentially) *higher tax bracket*. Since the gift tax return subtracts the full tentative gift tax on prior gifts, it must deduct only the unused unified credit; to subtract the full unified credit on the gift tax return would double count the benefit of the unified credit.

It would have been simpler to understand the unified scheme if the gift tax were calculated like the estate tax by figuring a tentative tax on *all* taxable gifts-- current and prior--and then subtracting from it the entire unified credit, as well as any gift tax paid on prior gifts. Such a scheme would truly make the two transfer taxes appear more similar. Although the gift tax and the estate tax schemes appear to produce inconsistent results, their effect on net transfer taxes, as we have seen from the above, is the same.

ANSWERS TO QUESTIONS AND PROBLEMS

1. History of federal wealth transfer taxation:

    Civil War: Inheritance tax enacted; repealed shortly thereafter.
    1916: First estate tax.
    1924: First gift tax; repealed in 1926; reenacted in 1932.
    1948: First marital deduction = 50% AGE.

1977: Unified rate schedule in effect. Unified credit replaces only $30,000 gift exemption and $60,000 estate exemption. Transfers are unified, i.e., cumulative.

1982: The 100% marital deduction & the QTIP election. Annual exclusion increased to $10,000

1984: The loss of the marital deduction for non-US spouses unless QDOT.

2. The imposition of a transfer tax at death without an accompanying gift tax would be largely ineffective because individuals could circumvent the tax by making lifetime transfers.

3. a. The unified credit increased annually from $30,000 in 1977 to $192,800 in 1987 and after.

   b. The exemption equivalent is the amount of the deduction needed to produce the same net tax as that produced by a given credit amount.

4. The unlimited marital deduction allows a deduction for all transfers to a spouse, whether during lifetime or at death. As we'll see later, the property must be included in the transferor's gross estate, it must actually "pass" to the spouse, and the transfer cannot be subject to a terminable interest, unless it falls into one of the exceptions described in the chapter.

5. The annual exclusion is an amount that can pass gift tax free without using up any of the donor's unified credit. It only applies to gifts of a present interest, with the one exception of gifts that qualify under §2503(c) discussed in a later chapter. It is available even for gifts to non-relatives, get me on your gift list. It went from $3,000 in 1981 to $10,000 in 1982.

6. Gifts by Denise:

   a. In 1989 [tt $145,600; gtx $0]
   b. In 1990 [tt current $65,700; gtx $18,500]
   c. In 1992 [tt current $81,850; gtx $81,850]

7. Gifts by Martin:

    a. In 1987 [tt $310,700; gtx $117,900]
    b. In 1989 [tt current $35,100; gtx $35,100]
    c. In 1991 [tt current $49,200; gtx $49,200]

8. Gifts by Shannon:

    a. In 1993 [tt $29,800; gtx $0]
    b. In 1995 [tt current $25,000; gtx $0] Watch your annual exclusions.

9. 1993 estate of **Karla** (a) the total death taxes [$520,500]; (b) the state death tax [$88,800]; and (c) the Federal estate tax [$431,700].

10. 1995 estate of **Faustino** (a) the total death taxes [$0; the tt is $185,400 < UCr]; (b) the state death tax [$0]; and (c) the Federal estate tax [$0].

11. 1996 estate of **Margaret** (a) the total death taxes [$14,800]; (b) the state death taxes [$14,800]; and (c) the Federal estate taxes [$0].

12. 1996 estate of **Stephen**(a) the total death taxes [$9,994,000]; (b) the state death taxes [$2,412,400]; and (c) the Federal estate taxes [$7,581,600].

13. 1997 estate of **Denise**, with earlier gifts (a) the total death taxes [$1,771,170]; (b) the state death taxes [$233,174]; and (c) the Federal estate taxes [$1,537,996].

14. 1995 estate of **Martin**, with earlier gifts (a) the total death taxes [$7,535,656]; (b) the state death taxes [$1,631,562]; and (c) the Federal estate taxes [$5,904,094].

15. 1997 estate of **Shannon**, with earlier gifts (a) the total death taxes [$2,671,055]; (b) the state death taxes [$470,012]; and (c) the Federal estate taxes [$2,201,043].

ENDNOTES

1. §2001(c)(2). For noncitizen nonresidents, the additional five percent tax is applied only to the extent necessary to phase out the graduated rates and unified credit actually allowed (generally, $13,000) by statute or treaty. §2101(b)

2. In 1992, H.R.4848, sponsored by Congressmen Waxman and Gephart, and S.2571 sponsored by Senators Mitchell, Rockefeller and others (both bills relating to long-term health care), proposed to reduce the tax free estate to $200,000, but the proposal generated so much opposition it was deleted when the House bill was reintroduced as H.R. 6076.

3. Although there is no marital deduction covering outright gifts to a noncitizen spouse, Congress created a special annual exclusion of $100,000 per year.

− 6

The Federal Estate Tax

OVERVIEW

In general, a federal estate tax return must be filed for all decedents who are *citizens or residents* of the United States and die with a total gross estate (regardless of where the property is situated[1]) plus adjusted taxable gifts equaling or exceeding the amount of the unified credit equivalent for the year of death.[2] For example, the estate of a decedent-citizen who died after 1987 having a gross estate of $550,000 and adjusted taxable gifts of $100,000 must file a return because the sum of the two transfers exceeds $600,000. Filing is still required even if the entire estate is left to a surviving spouse or where the gross estate exceeds $600,000 but recourse mortgages and other debts reduce it below that level.[3]

Once the taxable (net) value of the property transferred is determined, the unified transfer tax rate schedule is used to calculate a tentative tax. The same rate table is used whether the transfer is a taxable gift or a taxable estate. Credits are subtracted from the tentative tax to arrive at the net tax liability.

In addition, a Federal estate tax return must be filed even for a decedent *noncitizen, non resident* if the person died owning property situated in the United States that was worth more than $60,000.[4] Only the U.S. situs property is taxed,[5] but the estate is entitled to a maximum unified credit of only $13,000.[6] Special rules, beyond the scope of this text, apply for decedents who are citizens of both a U.S. possession and of a country having special treaties with the U.S.

The executor is responsible for paying the tax.[7] If there is no executor, persons in actual or constructive possession of any of the decedent's property are liable for the tax to the extent of the value of that property.[8] That includes surviving joint tenants[9] and the trustee of a decedent's revocable living trust.[10]

TABLE 6-1 Federal Estate Tax (Form 706) Comprehensive Outline

Gross estate (§§2031-2045)		$xxx,xxx
Less deductions:		
Debts & expenses (§2053)	xx,xxx	
Losses during administration (§2054)	xx,xxx	
Charitable bequests (§2055)	xx,xxx	
Marital bequests (§§2056-2056A)	<u>xx,xxx</u>	<u>(xxx,xxx)</u>
Leaves: Taxable estate (§2051)		xxx,xxx
Plus: Adjusted taxable gifts (post-76) (§2001)		<u>xx,xxx</u>
Equals: Estate tax base (§2001(b)(1)(A) & (B))		$xxx,xxx
Calculate: Tentative tax (§2001)		$xxx,xxx
Less Credits:		
Gift taxes payable (post-76) (§2001(b)(2))	xx,xxx	
Unified credit (§2010)	xx,xxx	
State death tax credit (§2011)	xx,xxx	
Prior transfer credit (§2013)	xx,xxx	
Other credits (§§2014-2015)	<u>xx,xxx</u>	<u>(xxx,xxx)</u>
Equals: Federal estate tax (§2001)		$xxx,xxx

This chapter is divided into three major parts. Each part will examine one of the three principal items found on the estate tax return: components of the gross estate, allowable deductions, and allowable credits. All code sections (e.g., §2033) included in this chapter refer to those found in the Internal Revenue Code. Many of these sections are included in Appendix B. The section numbers are frequently in the text because they are commonly used by estate planners as short-hand to convey a concept such as the attributes that cause a trust or other transfer to be taxed or not taxed. While studying this chapter, the reader is urged to look over Form 706, the U.S. Federal Estate Tax Return (Appendix C). Notice that the first page has the calculation of the estate tax and that the first two lines (the gross estate and allowable deductions) draw from page three, the recapitulations in Part 5. As discussion begins to focus on a particular Internal Revenue Code section, take the time to read the section, then read it again at the before you go on to the next topic.

THE GROSS ESTATE

There is no short definition for the term *gross estate*. Of course, it includes all that one owns in the usual sense of ownership. One should not be surprised that it also includes some property that the decedent did not own at death. Inclusion of property not owned is rare, but occurs where the decedent had sufficient control and beneficial interest in property at death that the control was so similar to ownership that inclusion just seems reasonable; e.g., property held in a revocable trust whereby the trustee holds legal title, but the decedent controlled beneficial interest. In developing the rules, Congress has added Code sections that specify a number of situations where property must be included in a decedent's gross estate even though the decedent lacked title to the property. Indeed, in some circumstances property is included even though the decedent no longer had a beneficial interest in the property; e.g., gift taxes paid on any gift made within three years of death must be included in the gross estate.

Another example involves retained interests. In the past, property owners attempted to reduce taxes by making lifetime gifts with "strings attached" by retaining some power to control beneficial enjoyment. For example, parents might transfer title to the family residence to their adult son with an agreement that the parents could continue to live there. Congress enacted the precursors to present day Code §§2036, 2037, and 2038 requiring such property be included in the transferor's gross estate.

Analysis of the components of the gross estate will be divided into three parts. The first part covers interests owned at death (§§2033-4, 2039-42). The next part covers transfers where the transferor retained an interest or control over beneficial enjoyment of the property transferred (§§2036, 2037, and 2038). Finally, those few types of transfers made within three years of death (§2035(d)(2)) that still require inclusion even though the decedent-transferor retained neither a beneficial interest nor control of the property. The latter includes only transfers of life insurance policies or the relinquishments of retained interests within three years of the donor's death. *For most gifts (cash, land, stock, bonds, jewelry, etc.), there is no three year rule.*

§2033: Basic Interests Owned at Death

The gross estate includes all property in which the decedent had a beneficial interest.[11] Common examples are fee simple interests such as ownership interests typically held in assets such as a house, furniture, personal effects, business interests, investments, and intangible property such as patent rights. However, many less obvious interests, including those less encompassing than fee simple interests, are also included. In principle, if the property had some value and the decedent had some beneficial interest in it at death, it is probably included. A few not-so-obvious examples follow:

EXAMPLE 6 - 1. Decedent died on June 18 owning 100 shares of XYZ stock, worth $10,000. On May 26, a *dividend* of $1.50 per share was declared, payable to stockholders of record on June 14, with payment on June 22. Included in the gross estate will be $10,150, representing the value of the stock plus the dividends declared.

EXAMPLE 6 - 2. The same facts apply as in the prior example, except that the holder-of-record date was June 24. The value of the dividends is not included in the decedent's gross estate because at date of death, decedent was not legally .entitled to the dividend.

EXAMPLE 6 - 3. Winnie created a life income trust for her brother Charlie, with a vested remainder interest for her nephew Max. When Max died, Charlie was still going strong at age 85 and the trust was worth $1,000,000. Max's gross estate includes the present value of the *remainder interest* in the trust. Due to his death, Max will never possess the trust property, but his will determines who will eventually have the property. Had he died without a will, then his heirs, according to the laws of intestate succession, would eventually receive the property. *** *Query 6 - 1. If the rate for valuing remainder interests was 8% when Max died, what is the included value?*

EXAMPLE 6 - 4. At her death, decedent owned local *municipal water district bonds.* Although income from such bonds is exempt from Federal income tax, the value of the bonds, plus the accrued interest on them, is included in her gross estate.

EXAMPLE 6 - 5. A couple lived and worked in a community property state. Stock was purchased using the wife's wages. They had no agreement, or special understanding, that the stock would be her separate property. When the husband died, the stock was worth $100,000. Even though it was held in the wife's name, it was community property, therefore, one-half of its value [$50,000] must be included in his gross estate.

Section 2033 would also cover the present value of a *joint and survivor annuity*, one which continues to be payable in whole or in part to another after the decedent's death, if the decedent purchased the annuity. Its value would be the present discounted value of the survivor's expected income payments. Code §2039, covered shortly, specifically calls for the inclusion of survivorship annuities in a decedent's gross estate. Overlapping Code sections are not at all unusual. An interest may be included by virtue of a broadly written section, such as §2033, and by virtue of a narrowly written but more detailed Code section, such as §2039.

> EXAMPLE 6 - 6. Movie star Jenny filed a law suit against a major studio for breach of contract, seeking four million dollars in damages because, according to her claim, it had failed to cast her in a movie that she understood was hers. The movie was a hit, and she sued for a percentage of the gross profits. After the discovery phase of the trial, it looked as though her claim had merit and the studio started talking seriously about settlement. Unfortunately, Jenny died when her Harley hit a palm tree. The studio is now refusing to settle so her estate is proceeding to trial. The estimated value of her claim is included in her estate even though the value is quite speculative.[12]

> EXAMPLE 6 - 7. Jim created an irrevocable trust that gave his daughter Jodi income for her life; after which the corpus would revert to Jim, if living, otherwise to his estate. Jodi was 40 years old, and the trust was worth $100,000 when Jim died. His gross estate includes the value of the vested reversionary interest. *** *Query 6 - 2. If the §7520 rate was 10% when he died what is the dollar of the trust corpus included in Jim's estate?*

Finally, consider the consequences of current transfer tax laws on the estates of people who engage in certain illegal activities.

> EXAMPLE 6 - 8. Decedent died when the plane he was piloting crashed. On board was a load of marijuana and a fair amount of "drug money." His gross estate had to include the cash and the street value of the dope because he had "exclusive possession and control" over both when he died. Further, his estate was not entitled to deduct that value of cash and marijuana forfeited under state drug enforcement laws either as a claim against the estate or a loss during administration. The IRS rationale was that such deductions would "frustrate the sharply defined state and Federal public policy against drug trafficking." Thus, decedent's other assets had to be used to pay the estate taxes.[13]

As said earlier, Code sections overlap. Some of the overlap is due to an effort by Congress to provide additional detail in its requirements for what property arrangements cause property to be included in the gross estate. Sometimes a seemingly redundant section is there to avoid taxpayer suits that would raise as an issue the question of whether more general language, such as is found in §2033, was really intended to cover some attenuated property interest.

§2034: Dower and Curtesy Interests

A dower interest is a surviving wife's life estate in a portion of the real property owned by her deceased husband, and a curtesy interest represents a surviving husband's life estate in a portion of the real property owned by his deceased wife. The extent of these statutory interests varies from state to state. Some states grant surviving spouses dower and curtesy interests in a percentage of the deceased spouse's real and personal property. As we have seen, one purpose of these laws is to prevent a decedent from entirely disinheriting the surviving spouse. Dower or curtesy interests are included in the gross estate of the first spouse to die.[14]

From an estate tax point of view, dower and curtesy interests and community property interests of the surviving spouse have the same effect. Dower and curtesy interests that can be claimed in fee (e.g., a specific percentage of the estate is set aside in fee for the surviving spouse) are included in the gross estate but are fully deductible using the marital deduction, as interests passing to the surviving spouse. Estates in those states that still define these interests as life estates for the surviving spouse can still have the property qualify for the marital deduction by use of what is called a qualified terminable interest property election.[15] This special election, called a QTIP election will be covered later in the chapters dealing with marital deduction planning. In community property states, the surviving spouse's half interest in the community property is excluded from the decedent's gross estate because it does not belong to the decedent spouse. Whether deductible or excludable, these interests are not taxed at the first spouse's death but are generally taxed at the second death.

§2039: Survivorship Annuities

An annuity is a series of two or more periodic payments, usually received by the annuitant monthly, quarterly or annually. Annuities are commonly used in retirement planning, often in conjunction with pension and insurance contracts. Ordinarily, an employee-"participant," upon retirement, will begin receiving a monthly annuity, possibly for as long as the retiree lives or, perhaps more commonly, for as long as the retiree and the retiree's spouse live. §2039 includes in the decedent's gross estate the date of death value of an annuity "receivable by any beneficiary by reason of surviving the decedent."

From the above description and from earlier examples, it should be clear that a single life annuity for the decedent's life is not part of the decedent's gross estate under §2039, since it ends with the decedent's death. Even if it was considered property owned at death under §2033, the date of death value would be zero.

Inclusion in participant's gross estate. Most survivorship annuities are fully included in the decedent-participant's gross estate. How much is included, and how that amount is calculated, depends on several factors. If the payments are not the result of a qualified pension plan, or even if they are the result of a qualified pension plan but the participant separated from service (retired) after 1984, the pension is fully included. If it is fully included, the amount included is either the lump sum amount, if the survivor has the right to take the lump sum, or the present value of the future payments, if the survivor is to receive periodic payments. Whether one uses Table S or Table B (see the Appendix) depends on whether the payments will continue for the life of the survivor (Table S) or for a fixed number of years (Table B). Prior to 1985, plans that were "qualified" under §401(a) were either partially or fully excluded from the participant's estate. The section is complex as it details the requirements for plan qualification. The tax advantages of qualified plans are that employer contributions are tax deductible to the employer and are not taxable income to the employee until paid, usually after retirement. In addition, periodic earnings on contributions are tax-deferred. Generally, nonqualified plans do not enjoy all these advantages.

The following summarizes the complex rules for qualified plan annuities. As stated earlier, the rule for decedents who retired after mid-1984 is quite simple, the annuity, whether qualified or not, is included.

1. *Fully included annuities.* With regard to any annuity whose payments began after July 17, 1984, or for which prior to that date the decedent had not made an irrevocable election to designate the beneficiaries, the *entire value* of the annuity is included in the gross estate.

2. *Partially excluded annuities.* Retirees who were in pay status (retired and receiving payments) before January 1, 1985, and had made an irrevocable election, after December 31, 1982 and before July 18, 1984, as to the form of benefits that would be paid to the beneficiary, can exclude up to $100,000 of the combined value of survivorship annuities from qualified plans.

3. *Totally excluded annuities.* Retirees that separated from service prior to January 1, 1983, and who had irrevocably elected the form of benefits before that date, can exclude all of his or her qualified annuity.

The exclusions just described are available only if the proceeds are not payable to the decedent's estate, and if the decedent could not change the form of benefit. Annuities qualifying for this exclusion include the following:

a. Tax-sheltered annuities or tax deferred annuities (TSAs, TDAs, also called 403(b) plans).

b. Individual retirement accounts (IRAs).

c. A portion of the value of the periodic payments under pension plans that have been "qualified" under §401. The amount qualifying for the exclusion is that portion attributable to the employer's contributions.

d. A lump-sum payment to a surviving beneficiary if that beneficiary elects to forego "5-year averaging." Five-year averaging is a method of reducing the beneficiary's tax burden by enabling the lump sum to be taxed at favorable tax rates in the year of receipt. In effect, the lump sum is divided by 5. Then, using income tax rates and assuming no other income, the calculated tax is multiplied by 5. The possible result is avoidance of a higher rate bracket.[16]

EXAMPLE 6 - 9. The decedent died this year, after retiring from work in 1985. At death, decedent had three joint and survivor annuities: one from her former employer's qualified retirement plan, one from a tax-sheltered annuity, and another from an individual retirement account. She had started drawing from all three after her retirement. The value of her gross estate will include the entire value of all three annuities.

EXAMPLE 6 - 10. During his employment, Stan contributed $25,000 to his qualified pension plan, and his employer contributed $75,000. The plan provided Stan and his wife with a joint and survivor annuity upon his retirement which started in 1983. Stan died in 1986, and the value of his spouse's survivorship annuity was $300,000. The amount excluded is the value of the annuity attributable to the employer's contributions up to a maximum of $100,000. The amount attributed to the employer is $225,000 [$300,000*($75,000 / ($25,000+$75,000))]. Thus the amount excluded is $100,000 and $200,000 is included in his gross estate.

EXAMPLE 6 - 11. In the Example immediately above, had Stan retired before 1983, his estate would have excluded $300,000, the entire annuity value, and had he retired after July 17,1984 the entire value would have been included.

In summary, a simple rule applies to decedents who retired after July 17, 1984, and that is that the *full* value of all annuities earned through employment or acquired by purchase is included in the gross estate. For decedents retiring between January 1, 1983 and July 17, 1984, up to $100,000 is excludable. Finally, for those retiring prior to 1983, the *entire* value of all qualifying retirement annuities is excludable.

Inclusion in gross estate of retiree's spouse. When the *participant-retiree's spouse dies first*, inclusion of a portion of the value of the participant's annuity in that nonparticipant spouse's gross estate will depend upon local property law. In community property states, the nonparticipant spouse's community interest in the annuity will be included in his or her own gross estate. That value could be as much as one-half of the total annuity value. On the other hand, in common law states, nothing will usually be included. Regarding property rights to the remaining benefits, case law has held that at the nonparticipant spouse's earlier death, any community interest passes 100% to the participant; the Retirement Equity Act precludes the nonparticipant decedent spouse from making any disposition of it.[17]

Tax on excess retirement accumulations. Designed to recoup part of the benefit of income tax-free accumulation of earnings during the decedent's lifetime, tax law imposes an additional 15 percent excise tax on an individual's "excess retirement accumulation." This excess is calculated by determining the value of the decedent's combined interests in qualified plans, including IRAs, then subtracting the present value of an life annuity for a person decedent's age at the time of death, if said annuity paid annually the greater of $150,000 or $112,500 indexed since 1986. The indexed value reached $155,000 in 1996, and thus the $150,000 amount was superseded. The additional tax is a deduction for calculating the Federal estate tax but it cannot be offset by the unified credit, and the excess accumulation cannot be reduced by the marital deduction; however, if the surviving spouse is the sole beneficiary of the pension interests, he or she can make a special election to have the interest avoid, or more probably delay, the tax by having the interest treated as though it was the surviving spouse's pension.

Thus, the tax may be levied when the survivor draws the funds out or upon her death, using her age at death and any other pensions that belonged to her to determine whether there still exists an excess accumulation. The accumulation is also subject to income tax (as "income in respect of a decedent") and, unless a marital deduction applies, to the regular estate tax. Some of the excess accumulation, determined as of August 1, 1986, could have been "grandfathered" (i.e., exempt from later tax), if an election was made by 1989.

EXAMPLE 6 - 12. In 1994, Dave who had retired in 1988 died at the age of 80. His entire estate worth over $3 million was left to his four children. It included his pension and his IRA. His qualified pension plan balance was $945,884 and his IRA account balance was $48,300. The §7520 rate for valuing periodic payments was 8% when he died. Table S is used to determine the annuity factor. For a person at age 80, when the rate is 8%, the annuity factor is 5.1710. Thus the amount that is not subject to the excess accumulations tax is: 5.1710 x $150,000 = $775,650. The amount subjected to the excess accumulations and the resulting excise tax is: $945,884 + $48,300 - $775,650 = $218,534; and $218,534 x 0.15 = $32,780, respectively. The $32,780 excess accumulations tax is a deduction in calculating Dave's estate tax. The tax is computed using Schedule S of the estate tax return and, like the rest of the estate tax, is due nine months after the date of death.

EXAMPLE 6 - 13. Suppose Dave died in 1996, but everything else was as in the prior example. Because the index amount was $155,000, it would be used instead of $150,000. Thus, the amount that is not subject to the excess accumulations tax is: 5.1710 x $155,000 = $801,505. The amount subjected to the excess accumulations and the resulting excise tax is: $945,884 + $48,300 - $801,505 = $192,679; and $192,679 x 0.15 = $28,902, respectively.

§2040: Joint Tenancy and Tenancy by the Entirety

There are two rules for determining the portion of joint tenancy property in the gross estate of a deceased joint owner:

♦ Spousal Rule: If a married couple are the only joint tenants, when the first spouse dies his or her gross estate must include one-half the property's fair market value as of the date of death (DOD FMV).

The Code refers to spousal joint tenancies and tenancies by the entirety as "qualified joint interests." For these, *one-half* of the total value is included *regardless* of the spouses' original contributions. Prior to 1977 the consideration furnished rule also applied to joint tenancies held by husbands and wives. Surviving spouses in several recent cases have successfully argued that it still applies where the joint tenancy was created pre-1977.[18] By having the property fully included in the first spouses estate a full step-up in basis, for income tax purposes, was obtained. The IRS disagrees with this position. As we move further away from 1977 there will be fewer decedents dying as owners of pre-1977 jointly held property, so the issue will become less important. Unless stated otherwise, assume spousal joint tenancies were created after 1976.

> EXAMPLE 6 - 14. At his death in 1995, Joel and his wife, Susan, held their home in joint tenancy. Susan paid $100,000 when she bought the house in 1980 using her separate funds. It was worth $400,000 when Joel died. Since the house is a *qualified joint interest*, his gross estate will include $200,000. Susan's new basis is half the old basis plus half the date of death value, i.e., $250,000.

> EXAMPLE 6 - 15. In the example immediately above, had Susan died first with Joel the survivor, the results would have been exactly the same.

♦ Consideration Furnished Rule: Include that portion of the DOD FMV of the property attributable to that portion of the consideration (money or money's worth) contributed by the decedent.

With the second rule, applicable to non-qualified joint interests (i.e., those where the joint tenants include non-spouses) one must used what is called the *consideration furnished test*. With even one non-spouse as a joint tenant, all interests are non-qualified, e.g., husband, wife, and adult child take title as joint tenants, all three are holders of non-qualified interests. The law starts with the presumption that the decedent co-owner contributed all of the consideration (or was initially the sole owner). To overcome this presumption, the estate has the burden of establishing that the surviving joint tenants contributed to the acquisition of the property. Generally, this is not as difficult as it seems. The IRS is not likely to challenge the contributions where the co-owners would not appear to have had a motive for trying to avoid taxes, nor to make gifts when the joint tenancy was established, and each of the co-owners had sufficient resources to pay his or her own way.

EXAMPLE 6 - 16. In 1955, two brothers, Jake and Ned, prior to either of them marrying purchased a fishing cabin on a lake, taking title in joint tenancy. Jake died this year. The records as to how much each paid as a down payment have been lost. But Ned can show that he and his brother were both earning about the same amount of money at the time of the purchase and were both about equally wealthy such that one making a gift to the other would not have made much sense. This would probably be sufficient to establish equal consideration.

EXAMPLE 6 - 17. Similar to the prior example, but change it such that Jake was Ned's father and Jake, although wealthy, already owned his own home whereas Ned was just starting out. Even if Ned claims to have paid an equal share of the purchase price, the circumstances do not support the claim and, without better evidence, it would be difficult to overcome the presumption that Jake furnished all of the consideration. Even a canceled check from Ned payable to the seller of the cabin might not be sufficient evidence, since a gift from Jake of the cash followed by Ned's use of the money as his share of the consideration would be treated as if all the funds came from Jake. Ned would need to establish a reasonable explanation for the source of the funds to establish that they came from a source other than a gift from his father.

There is a special rule where a donee (one of the surviving joint tenants) uses funds traceable to a gift from the decedent joint tenant as part of the purchase price. Those funds are treated as being part of the donor-joint tenant's consideration rather than that of the donee. Income from a gift is not traced back to the donor, but capital gain is.

EXAMPLE 6 - 18. Calvin gave his daughter, Deirdre, 100 shares of XYZ stock when they were worth $50,000. She sold the stock for $70,000 and placed the proceeds of the sale in a bank account in which she already had $30,000. The source of the $30,000 was $10,000 from XYZ dividends and $20,000 from money she saved out of her wages. Calvin and Deirdre purchased a house for $200,000, each putting up half of the purchase price, Deirdre's half share coming from her bank account. The house, held in joint tenancy, was worth $300,000 when Calvin died. His estate included 85% of the DOD FMV, i.e., $255,000. The percentage is calculated by taking Calvin's contribution of $100,000, adding the contribution of Deirdre that is traceable to Calvin's gift to her (another $70,000) and dividing the total ($170,000) by the $200,000 purchase price. Note that the gain is included in the numerator, but not the dividends.

Full inclusion in the decedent-donor's estate is preferred when it results in a step-up in basis without an increase in estate taxes.

EXAMPLE 6 - 19. Virginia put her home in joint tenancy with her only son,

Scott. At the time of the transfer the home was worth $200,000. She filed a gift tax return, reporting a $90,000 gift. Years later when it was worth $500,000 she died. The entire $500,000 is included in her estate and Scott's basis in the house is $500,000. Her other property was worth $75,000 and her estate paid debts and expenses of $30,000, so her taxable estate was $545,000 and therefore, no taxes were owed. *** *Query 6 - 3. Why didn't the $90,000 gift push the estate over the $600,000 mark? See the definition of "adjusted taxable gift" found in §2001(b).*

EXAMPLE 6 - 20. At her death, Rose owned a farm worth $100,000 jointly with her brother Tom. The farm was originally acquired for $50,000, with Rose paying $10,000 and Tom paying $40,000. Assuming the contribution of the survivor can be established, under the consideration-furnished test her estate includes only one fifth of the farm's value, i.e., $20,000, [($10,000/$50,000)*$100,000]. Tom's basis in the farm will be his contribution plus the amount included in Rose's estate, i. e., $60,000 [$40,000 he contributed and $20,000 included in Rose's estate].

EXAMPLE 6 - 21. At her death, Dottie owned $90,000 ABC common stock jointly with her husband and her son. The survivors know that Dottie actually contributed only $10,000 to the original $50,000 purchase price, (and the two of them paid $20,000 each) but they are not sure they can prove it. If they cannot, Dottie's gross estate will include the full $90,000. If they can, her gross estate will include only her proportional share, or $18,000, which is $90,000 reduced by the survivor's proportional share, or $72,000. This is not a qualified joint interest because a non-spouse was also a surviving co-owner.

The consideration furnished rule applies only at the death of a co-owner. There is a gift when different amounts of consideration are used to purchase property and the title is taken in joint tenancy because, by property law rules, all joint tenants interests must be equal. For gift or sale purposes, the "donee" co-owner has a basis in his or her share that is either carry-over or partly carry-over and partly purchase.

EXAMPLE 6 - 22. Edith and June purchase a vacation condominium in South Florida for $100,000, taking title as joint tenants. Edith paid $90,000 and June paid $10,000. Edith made a $40,000 gift [$30,000 taxable] to June since June has a 50% interest. June's basis would be $50,000 [$40,000 carried over with the gift and the other $10,000 is her consideration]. If they later sell the property for $150,000, each would recognize a gain of $25,000. If, instead of selling the property when it was worth $150,000, June made a gift of her half to her son, Tommy, she would report a gift of $75,000 [$65,000 taxable gift] and Tommy would have a carry-over basis of $50,000. This transfer would break the joint tenancy, so Tommy and Edith would be tenants in common, each as to a 50% share. Regardless of which one died first, Tommy or Edith, 50% of the value would be included in the person's estate.

For purposes of §2040, "joint interests" encompass only two forms of concurrent ownership: joint tenancy and tenancy by the entirety. In contrast, the two other major forms of co-ownership, tenancy in common and community property, are included in the decedent's gross estate based upon the decedent's interest.[19]

§2041: Power of Appointment

Powers of appointment were introduced in an earlier chapter so this is just a brief review. A power of appointment is a power that allows a person to name someone to receive a beneficial interest in property, even though the person directing the transfer does not own the property. The creator or grantor of the power is called the donor of the power. The person receiving the power is called the holder or donee. The parties to whom the holder may appoint the property are called the permissible appointees. The parties to whom the holder actually appoints are called the appointees, and the persons who will get the property if no appointment is made are called the takers by default.

For Federal estate tax purposes, a power of appointment is either a general power or it is a limited (or special) power. A *general* power of appointment is the power of the holder to appoint to the holder, the holder's estate, the holder's creditors or the creditor's of the holder's estate. All other powers are "special" or "limited" powers of appointment, which usually designate as permissible appointees either specific individuals (e.g., the donor gives the holder the power to appoint to the donor's brother Sam or sister Sue) or a class of people (e.g., appoint to any of my issue).

A decedent's gross estate will include the value of any property subject to a *general* power of appointment held by the decedent-holder at death. General powers are included in the gross estate regardless of whether the decedent-holder *exercised* the power at death, or, alternatively, did not exercise it and permitted the power to *lapse* at death. The key is that at the moment of death, the decedent was the holder of a general power.

EXAMPLE 6 - 23. At her death, decedent was trustee of an irrevocable trust created by her uncle. She had the power to invade the corpus of the trust for the benefit of anyone. In her will, she appointed her son to receive the entire corpus.

Her gross estate will include the entire value of the trust corpus, since it was subject to a general power which she *exercised* at her death.

EXAMPLE 6 - 24. The facts are similar to the prior example, except that decedent did not exercise the power at her death. The entire trust corpus is still included in her gross estate even though the power *lapsed* at her death.

EXAMPLE 6 - 25. The facts are similar to the prior example, except that the power to invade was on behalf of *anyone except* herself, her creditors, her estate, or the creditors of her estate. This is a "limited" power, not a general power, and thus the property is not included in her gross estate.

Notice that §2041 focuses on decedent *holders* of general powers, not on the donors or the appointees.

Exceptions. There are two major exceptions to the basic rule that being able to appoint to oneself makes the power a general one. Each exception so greatly restricts the circumstances that would allow appointment that the Code quite rightly defines them as not being general powers. Under the first exception, if the decedent's right to exercise a power is limited by an *ascertainable standard*, that is, limited for reasons of "health, education, support or maintenance," it is not a general power. Under the second exception, if the decedent's right to exercise the power requires the *approval* of either the creator of the power or an *adverse party*, it is not a general power. An adverse party is "a person having a substantial interest in the property, subject to the power, which is adverse to exercise of the power in favor of the decedent."[20]

EXAMPLE 6 - 26. During his lifetime, decedent was the income beneficiary of a trust created by his father. The trust gave him the right to invade corpus for reasons of his "health, education, support, or maintenance." Since the power is limited by an *ascertainable standard*, this right to invade is not a general power and the trust is not included in the decedent's gross estate even if decedent was the trustee.

EXAMPLE 6 - 27. Same facts as Example 2041-4, except decedent could invade corpus for reasons of his "health, education, support, maintenance, *or happiness*". The power is not limited by an ascertainable standard, and, therefore, the invasion right constitutes a general power of appointment and the entire value of the trust will be included in the decedent's estate even though he never exercised the right to invade.

EXAMPLE 6 - 28. During her lifetime, decedent had been an income beneficiary under a trust, which provides that upon her death, corpus was to be distributed to her son. Decedent could invade corpus for any reason provided she could get the written approval of her son. Since her son was an *adverse party*, i.e., his remainder interest would be reduced in value if the decedent had exercised the power in her own favor, the power is not a general power.

A general power of appointment over property will cause the property to be included in the holder's estate because the power creates rights considered equivalent to ownership rights. Thus, this estate tax rule makes sense even though under *property law* the holder is not the legal owner of the property regardless of whether the power is general or limited. Given that the holder does not have legal title, even if the property subject to the power is included in the holder's gross estate, it is not included in the holder's probate estate unless the holder transfers it there, an event not likely to happen.

§2042: Insurance on Decedent's Life

There are three circumstances that cause life insurance to be included in a decedent's estate:

♦ the proceeds are paid to the executor of the decedent's estate,
♦ the decedent at death possessed an incident of ownership in the policy, or
♦ the decedent transferred an incident of ownership within three years of death.

Receivable by executor. Very seldom is the executor of the decedent's estate named as a beneficiary, not even as an alternate beneficiary. Rarely, it happens that at the insured's death no named beneficiaries are living and the proceeds are payable to the estate by default. Modern policies generally have a default clause that allows the company to pay the proceeds directly to the decedent's heirs if named primary and alternate beneficiaries predecease the insured. The default clauses read something like intestate succession laws, starting with close family members, moving to more remote relatives if no close family members survive, and to the insured's estate only as a last resort.

Decedent possesses incidents of ownership. Policy ownership gives the owner numerous rights, including: to assign, to terminate, to borrow against the cash reserves (if any), to name beneficiaries, and to change beneficiaries. Possession by the decedent of these rights are called *incidents of ownership,* which result in the proceeds being included in the decedent's estate. The payment of premiums is not considered an incident of ownership and payment will not, by itself, cause inclusion. Nonetheless, barring some agreement, the law may create an incident of ownership due to the payment of premiums. This is especially true in community property states. A policy purchased by the decedent, but paid for entirely with community property, would be only half included in the decedent's gross estate.

Life insurance transferred within three years of death. Both §2042 and §2035(d)(2) require inclusion of the proceeds in the insured's gross estate, if the insured transferred an interest in the policy within three years of his or her death.

> EXAMPLE 6 - 29. On June 12, 1995, Marty transferred a $200,000 policy on his life to his son Joseph. Because the policy was a term policy, its value was under $10,000 and Marty did not have to report it as a gift. On January 1, 1997, Marty died in a car accident. Joseph collected the $200,000. Marty's gross estate included the $200,000 even though, when he died, he had no incident's of ownership nor were there any strings attached to the transfer. The insurance company must issue IRS Form 712 which shows the date the policy was transferred, and this form must be attached to Marty's 706, the U.S. Estate Tax Return.

§2042 versus §2033. It is important to distinguish between policies on the decedent's life and policies on the lives of others. Policies on the *decedent's life* are covered by §2042, but what if the decedent owned a policy on someone else's life? The policy is included in the decedent's estate under §2033 as a beneficial interest in property owned at death. Generally the value is the cost of replacement rather than the cash surrender value. Cost of replacement is what an insurance company would charge to put the policy in force (with the existing cash surrender value) given the insured's age and health. Where premiums are still being paid on the policy, its value is equal to its interpolated terminal reserve plus that portion of the premium paid that covers the period extending beyond the owner's date of death.

> EXAMPLE 6 - 30. At decedent's death, decedent's wife owned a policy on *his life*, with the proceeds payable to his estate. Decedent's gross estate will include the value of the proceeds, under §2042.

> EXAMPLE 6 - 31. Decedent died owning a $60,000 life insurance policy on his mother. The policy had a value of $14,000 at decedent's death. Although §2042 does not apply because the insurance is not on decedent's life, decedent's estate will include the $14,000 value under §2033.

EXAMPLE 6 - 32. At the moment of his death, decedent *owned* a $100,000 life insurance policy *on his own life*. Under §2042 (incidents of ownership), $100,000 will be included in his gross estate. However, if all premiums had been paid for with community property, it is presumed to be community property and only $50,000 would be included. This result could be overcome if the couple had a written agreement stating that the policy was the separate property of one spouse.

After one spouse dies, if the surviving spouse continues to own a policy on his or her own life, the entire proceeds are included in the surviving insured's estate when he or she dies, regardless of whether or not community property funds were the original source of the premiums.[21]

So far, we have studied §§2033, 2034, 2039, 2040, 2041 and 2042, all of which cover interests owned, held, or controlled by the decedent at death such that the interests are included in the decedent's estate. The next section examines a group of Code sections that make interests included in the gross estate even though the property is no longer owned, and sometimes not even controlled, by the decedent at the time of death. The property is included because the decedent transferred property but kept some control, sometimes just a *little string* attached, such that Congress thought the string justified including the property in the gross estate as if no transfer had taken place.

TRANSFERS WITH RETAINED INTEREST OR CONTROL

Where a person transfers property, usually into a trust, and retains the right to control who enjoys it, even if the retained right cannot really benefit the transferor economically, the retained interest will cause the transferred property to be included in the transferor's estate, if the retained interest is still present when the transferor dies,[22] or if the transferor releases the retained interest within three years of his or her death.[23] If a "string" exists it will be as if the decedent never made the transfer and, instead, continued to own the property until death. Thus, if one of the retained interest Code sections apply, the property is valued in the gross estate at the DOD FMV. It will not be treated, for estate tax purposes, as an adjusted taxable gift even though it was a taxable gift when the transfer occurred. The latter sounds bad but it is actually good, because it keeps the transfer from being taxed twice, since any gift tax payable on the earlier transfer is allowed as a credit even though the adjusted taxable gift goes to zero. These transfers are the subject of §2036, Transfers with Retained Life Estate; §2037, Transfers Taking Effect at Death; and §2038, Revocable Transfers.

Characteristics common to all three sections. The three "strings" sections (§§2036, 2037, and 2038) have these characteristics in common:

▸ The transfer must have been made by the *decedent*.
▸ The transfer was a gift, that is, a transfer "for less than full and adequate consideration in money or money's worth."
▸ The amount included in the gross estate is the value as of the *date of death* (or alternate valuation date), rather than the value at date of transfer.
▸ If the string pertained to only a specific portion of the property transferred, then only that *portion* of the transferred property is included. For example, if the retained control was only over one third of the property, then only one third of its value will be included in the gross estate. However, note that §2036 requires the entire property be included even if only the income interest was retained.
▸ A trust is almost always involved.

The sections often overlap. If more than one section applies, and each would cause a different amount to be included, the amount included is the greatest value.

§2036: Transfer with Retained Life Estate

A transfer with retained life estate arises when a decedent has made a transfer, by trust or otherwise, for less than full and adequate consideration, and has retained either (1) the possession or enjoyment of, or the right to *income* from, the property transferred, or (2) the right, either alone or in conjunction with any person, to *designate* who will enjoy or possess the property or its income.

Period of retention. In addition to the above retained control, §2036 applies only if the decedent-transferor retained that control for: (1) life, (2) any period that does not in fact end before the decedent's death, or (3) any period not ascertainable without reference to the decedent's death. In the following §2036 examples, assume that decedent D, before death, made a transfer for less than full consideration.

EXAMPLE 6 - 33. At a time when D's vacation home was worth $110,000, D said, while handing over a quit-claim deed, "Son, here's title to my vacation home. It's yours now, but I will expect you to let me use it occasionally." When D died the home was worth $200,000. The date-of-death value of the home will be included in D's gross estate because at the time of D's death D still retained the *right to enjoy* the property.

EXAMPLE 6 - 34. D transferred property into an irrevocable trust, retaining the right to the income for his lifetime, with the remainder to go to C. The property's value at date of death is included in D's gross estate because D retained the right to the income for his lifetime. Although the remainder value was treated as a taxable gift when the trust was established, it is not an adjusted taxable gift for estate tax purposes since the entire trust has been included in D's gross estate.

EXAMPLE 6 - 35. D transferred property into an irrevocable trust, with income to go to D for 20 years, then the remainder to go to C. D died 18 years after establishing the trust. The property's value is included because the *period of retention* did not, in fact, end before D's death. Again, the adjusted taxable gift would be zero insofar as D's estate and this trust is concerned.

EXAMPLE 6 - 36. The facts are in the prior example, except D lived beyond the 20 year term. D's gross estate would not include the trust property. There would be an adjusted taxable gift equal to the amount reported when the trust was funded, that would boost the rest of D's taxable estate into higher marginal rates. The adjusted taxable gift was the remainder value when the trust was funded.

EXAMPLE 6 - 37. D transferred property into an irrevocable trust, with income to go to D for up to one month before D's death, then remainder to go to C. The fair market value of the property, as of D's death, is included because the retained period is *not ascertainable without reference* to D's death.

When Is a Gift Complete? Generally, unless the owner releases dominion and control over the property, there is no gift. With an outright gift it is easy to determine when this takes place, but it is less obvious with gifts in trust where the donor retains some interest. Indeed, the IRS Regulations at §20.2511-2 are less than clear on this matter. We will not cover this completely, but will give you the basics. Bear in mind that a gift may be complete enough to cause a gift, but still result in the property being included in the donor's gross estate due to a retained interest. Obviously, if the donor has the right to revoke the gift, then no gift has really occurred, even if the donee has taken possession of the property; no gift would occur unless the right to take back the transfer ended.

EXAMPLE 6 - 38. Shane created a trust, transferring assets worth $100,000 to the trustee. The trust terms give Richard income for life, so long as the trust remains in existence, and upon Richard's death the trust terminates, with distribution to Shane's daughter Catherine. The terms of the trust state that it is revocable until the earlier of Richard or Shane's death. The first year the trustee distributed income of $5,000 to Richard, the second year $6,000 was distributed. At the beginning of the third year, when the trust was worth $120,000, Shane died. No gift occurred and, of course, the trust is included in Shane's estate. While Shane was alive, all income is reported on his income tax return and is treated as a gift from him to Richard. Given the amounts, and Richard's present interest (as each amount is distributed to him), the annual exclusion would cover the amounts Richard received before Shane's death. Distributions after Shane's death are from an irrevocable trust, taxable income for Richard (the trust would have an income distribution deduction) and would not be considered gifts. Note, while Shane was alive, the gifts of income are from him, not from the trust. Only people make gifts, not trusts nor trustees.

In some cases where just control is retained, even though it cannot benefit the donor, no gift is deemed to have occurred. Once the control ceases, either by release, death, or by the terms that established the trust, the transfer occurs. The following examples are based upon Reg. 25.2511-2(c) and (f).

EXAMPLE 6 - 39. Using assets worth $400,000, Abel creates an irrevocable trust for the benefit of Benito and Consuelo, remainder to their children when both are deceased. So long as both are alive, the Trustee is given the power to allocate the income between Benito and Consuelo in such proportions as the trustee thinks is appropriate, when one beneficiary dies, the survivor is to receive all income. Abel serves as the initial trustee. During the first year the trust has income of $30,000, which Abel distributes $25,000 to Benito and $5,000 to Consuelo. No gift occurred when the trust was created, even though it was irrevocable. The income is taxed to Abel, and he has made a gift of $25,000 ($15,000 taxable) to Benito and $5,000 to Consuelo (not taxable because it is completely covered by the annual exclusion).

EXAMPLE 6 - 40. At a time when the trust was worth $500,000, Abel resigned as trustee, giving the successor trustee a letter (with copies to both beneficiaries) that stated his resignation was irrevocable. At that time, Abel has made a $500,000 gift (both gross and taxable). From that moment on, income was no longer taxed to Abel, and distributions were not considered new gifts, but merely distributions of income from the irrevocable trust. *** *Query 6 - 4. Why is the taxable gift $500,000? What happened to the annual exclusion(s)?*

EXAMPLE 6 - 41. Suppose, instead of releasing his retained control by letter of resignation, Abel died while still serving as trustee, at a time when the trust assets were valued at $700,000. The $700,000 would be included in his gross estate and, from that moment onward, the income distributions would be from the trust, not from Abel (nor from his estate).

EXAMPLE 6 - 42. Suppose the terms of the trust created by Abel required him to get Benito's approval for anything other than a 50-50% split of the income, otherwise the income had to be divided equally between Benito and Consuelo. The trust's value is still included because Abel retained the right to designate the recipient "alone or *in conjunction with* any other person." There is no "adverse party" exception in §2036 like the one found under §2041.

Because these rules are based upon transfers with retained interests by the donor, we must bear in mind that a transfer of a community property asset is treated as coming one-half from each spouse.

EXAMPLE 6 - 43. The facts are similar to any of the above examples, except that the transfer was of property held prior to the transfer as community property, 50-50 tenancy in common, or spouses as joint tenancy. Only half the value of the property would be included in the transferor's estate, because only half is traceable to a transfer by the decedent.

EXAMPLE 6 - 44. D transferred property into an irrevocable trust, with one quarter of the income retained by D, and the rest distributed to C. After D's death, C is to receive all of the income. After C's death, the remainder will go to R. Only *one quarter* of the trust's value is included, since D retained an interest over only that portion.

EXAMPLE 6 - 45. D transferred property into an irrevocable trust, authorizing the trustee, a bank, in its sole discretion, to distribute trust income to X or Y in such amounts as the bank trust officer thinks appropriate. D retained the power to replace the bank with another corporate trustee. The value of the property is not included in D's gross estate under §2036 because D's right to replace trustees does not amount to the right by D to change or control the enjoyment of the property. However, the property would be included if D kept the right to appoint herself as successor trustee.

In the following example, a basic assumption is changed, so that decedent is not the transferor:

EXAMPLE 6 - 46. G transfers property into an irrevocable trust, with income to D for life, remainder to R. The value of the property is not included in D's gross estate under §2036, because D was *not the transferor*. This arrangement is referred to as a bypass trust because the trust assets "bypass" the income beneficiary's estate.

The *reciprocal trusts doctrine*, illustrated in the next example, was established by the courts to apply §2036 to family planning situations which in form avoid the literal terms of that section, but in substance do not. In essence, the transferor has made a transfer of property, and at about the same moment has received the right to enjoyment of other property arising from a separate but related transaction.

> EXAMPLE 6 - 47. A husband transfers $100,000 in property into an irrevocable trust H, with income payable to his wife for her life and the remainder to their children. At about the same time, his wife transfers $100,000 into trust W, with income payable to her husband for his life and the remainder to their children. Under §2036, the corpus of trust H will be included in husband's gross estate and the corpus of trust W will be included in wife's gross estate. These interrelated trusts leave the spouses in essentially the same economic position that they would have been had they created trusts naming themselves life beneficiaries.[24]

Clients willing to take aggressively anti-tax positions may engage in transfers designed to appear complete but that involve an implied *understanding* that the transferor has a retained life estate. The IRS has at times successfully attacked such schemes. Consider the following situation, in which a court found §2036 to apply to facts that had been structured to appear as a completed sale.

> EXAMPLE 6 - 48. Mom, age 82 and in poor health, transferred title to her home to her son and his wife in exchange for $270,000, which was the home's fair market value. The terms of this "sale-leaseback" called for a $20,000 down payment and a five year mortgage loan of $250,000. Mom immediately forgave the down payment of $10,000 by each of the spouses. In the next two years, in payment of rent, Mom gave son and his wife $10,000 each, and they promptly returned these amounts in payment of the mortgage. Two days after the sale, Mom executed her last will, which contained a provision forgiving any of the remaining debt at the time of her death. The date of death value of the home was included in her gross estate under §2036. In spite of a total lack of direct evidence, circumstances strongly suggested an understanding that decedent was permitted to live in the house until death, which she did, and that none of the consideration offered in exchange was ever really going to be paid. Thus, all consideration was disregarded. The following circumstantial factors, all taken together, indicate a strings attached transfer: decedent's age and her health concerns, her forgiveness of the mortgage both during her life and by her will, the fact that the rent payments approximated the interest payments on the note, and the fact that the son was the decedent's only heir and the natural object of her bounty. As a result, Mom was treated as having

made a transfer of property for less than full and adequate consideration in which she retained, for a period which did not in end before her death, the right to possess or enjoy the property.[25]

§2037: Transfers Taking Effect at Death

A "transfer taking effect at death" will arise when (1) possession or enjoyment of the property through ownership can be obtained only by surviving the decedent and (2) the decedent, at the time of the transfer, retained a reversionary interest, which, at the decedent's death, exceeded 5 percent of the value of the property. Such reversionary interest is defined as the possibility that the property may return to the decedent or may be subject to a power of disposition by him.

> EXAMPLE 6 - 49. D transfers property into trust, with income to B for B's life, with a reversion to D if he survives B, otherwise the remainder to go to R, or R's estate. Assume that D dies at age 70, predeceasing B, who is then 60 years old, and that on the date of D's death the value of the trust property was $1 million and the Federal §7520 rate was 8%. Using actuarial tables, it was determined that given D and B's ages, D's contingent reversionary interest (ignoring the fact of his death) was worth more than 5% of the value of the trust. The amount included in D's gross estate is the full value of the trust less the value of B's remaining life estate, i.e., the value of the reversionary interest without discounting it for the contingency that it might not return despite the fact that the property can no longer revert to D. Since B is 60 years old and the rate was 8% the amount included will be $283,790 [.28379 * $1,000,000; see Table S, 8% rate].

In the preceding example, D had a chance of surviving B at D's death, and based on that a value is calculated for what amounts to a contingent reversion for D. The reader might find this strange given that D, *in fact,* did not outlive B. However, as in certain other valuation situations, this calculation is made without regard to the fact of D's death. Thus, the calculation assumes that at the moment of D's death, both D and B were in normal health for their ages.

§2038: Revocable Transfers

Although §2038's title is "revocable transfers," this section covers much more. Transferred property will be included in the decedent-transferor's estate if, at the time of death, the decedent retained the right to change another's enjoyment of the property. The Code refers to this retained right as one to *alter, amend, revoke or terminate* the enjoyment of the property transferred.

> EXAMPLE 6 - 50. D transferred property into a *revocable living trust* designed mainly to avoid probate at D's death. D retained the power to revoke the trust. D's gross estate includes the value of this property under §2038.

> EXAMPLE 6 - 51. D transferred property into an irrevocable trust that gave B the right to all income. The trust was to last for a term of twenty years, but would terminated earlier in the event of B's death. At such time as the trust terminates it is to be distributed to B, if living, or to B's issue, but if B leaves no issue, then to C, or C's estate. D retained the right to have the trust terminate earlier than at the end of twenty years, if D thought such was in B's best interest. The trust property will be included in D's gross estate because D retained the power to alter the "enjoyment interests"of others in the property. *** *Query 6 - 5. Why does §2036 also apply?*

> EXAMPLE 6 - 52. The facts are the same as in the prior example, except D died 21 years after establishing the trust, which had terminated at the end of the 20th year. The corpus had been distributed to C upon the trust's termination. The value of the trust assets are not included in D's estate, even though D died within three years of the trust's termination, because D did not release a retained interest. The retained interest had simply expired according to the original terms of the trust.

> EXAMPLE 6 - 53. D transferred five bonds to C under the state's *Uniform Gift to Minors Act* and appointed herself custodian. D dies before C reached majority; therefore, the value of the bonds is included in D's gross estate. Under the *Uniform Act*, D had the power to liquidate some, or all, of the bonds and distribute the proceeds to the minor, thus both §§2036 and 2038 apply.

> EXAMPLE 6 - 54. Same as prior example, except that, shortly before D's death, D turned the bonds over to C because C became an adult. Even though D died within three years of transferring the bonds, they are not included in D's estate. §2035(d)(2) doesn't apply because it applies only to "releases" of retained interests. D did not release a retained interest, rather it ended by law as a result of C becoming an adult.

An interesting concept developed at common law is called *gifts causa mortis.* It is applied when a donor, thinking that imminent death is very likely, gives property with the understanding that if the donor survives the property will be returned. Obviously, §2038 applies to gifts *causa mortis.*

EXAMPLE 6 - 55. Elderly Tom, just before entering the hospital, gave Jim his coin collection (worth $150,000) with the understanding that if the heart operation was unsuccessful, the collection would be Jim's. Tom died three days after surgery. The collection was included in Tom's estate. Had Tom lived, Jim would have returned the coins.

EXAMPLE 6 - 56. Suppose, in the preceding example, that Tom gave Jim his coin collection to keep no matter what the outcome of the surgery, and that Tom died three days after the surgery. The collection would not be included in Tom's estate. Of course, the adjusted taxable gift value ($140,000) would boost his estate into higher marginal rates and the executor of Tom's estate would be responsible for filing a gift tax return showing the gift.

§2035(d)(2): Certain Transfers within Three Years of Death

Under §2035(d)(2), a property interest is included in the gross estate if the decedent made one of two fairly uncommon types of completed transfers (i.e., no strings attached) within three years of death. First, gratuitous relinquishments or transfers of a property interest that would have been included in the decedent's gross estate under §§2036, 2037, 2038, or 2042 (had the relinquishment or transfer not been made) are included in the gross estate under §2035(d)(2). Second, §2035(c) includes in the gross estate the gift tax paid for *any gift* made within three years of death. The following material on the three-year inclusionary rule is subdivided into these two parts: relinquishment or transfer of certain retained interests and gift tax paid on any gift made within three years of death.

Relinquishment or transfer of certain retained interests. A decedent's gross estate includes the value of property under which a relinquishment or transfer had been made within three years of death and which would have been included in the decedent's gross estate under Sections 2036, 2037, 2038, or 2042, had the relinquishment or transfer not been made. This sounds tricky, but it is not, provided you do not try to apply the rule to every transfer made within three years of death. Keep in mind the inclusionary rule applies *to two, and only two,* types of transfers, a gift of *life insurance* or the *severance of a retained* interest.

EXAMPLE 6 - 57. D transferred property worth $750,00 into a trust, with income to S or C for S's life, then remainder to B. D retained the right to allocate the income between the two income beneficiaries. The trust terms also stated that the trustee was to allocate income equally between the two income beneficiaries in any year in which D failed to give written directions concerning the allocation. Because of D's retention of control over the property, no gift is deemed to have occurred. When D died the trust was worth $1,340,000. D died possessing this right to "sprinkle" the trust income, therefore the entire value of the trust property as of D's DOD was included in D's gross estate by virtue of both §2036 and §2038.

EXAMPLE 6 - 58. Same as prior example, except that when the trust was worth $1,000,000, D relinquished his right to make the income allocation by writing a letter to the trustee stating that he irrevocably released his right to allocate the income. This act caused the gift to be complete, but note that the taxable gift is the full $1,000,000 because neither S nor C have a identifiable present interest. D paid gift taxes of $153,000. From that moment onward, D had no retained interest in the trust; however, §2035(d)(2) applies. If D dies within three years of the relinquishment, the property is included at the DOD value and the adjusted taxable gifts would be zero; the $153,000 credit would still be available. On the other hand, if D lived more than three years after the relinquishment, the property would not be included. The adjusted taxable gifts would be $1,000,000 for estate tax purposes, and the gift taxes payable credit of $153,000 would be available.

Enough trust stuff, time for a life insurance example.

EXAMPLE 6 - 59. Within three years of death, D assigned his ownership interest in a *life insurance* policy on his life. The value of the proceeds are included in his gross estate because the transfer occurred within three years of death, and the proceeds would have been included in D's gross estate under §2042 had the assignment (transfer) not been made.

Until recently, the IRS took the position that §2035(d)(2) would apply even if the decedent-insured never owned a life insurance policy, if he or she nonetheless either paid the premiums directly or provided the funds with which to pay the premiums. In 1991, to the relief of many estate planners, the IRS announced that it would no longer litigate this issue. To avoid the three year rule, planners make every effort to see a wealthy client never possess any incident of ownership in a newly issued policy. Thus, while the insured will usually have to sign the policy application *as insured*, he or she should never sign *as owner*. If the policy is owned by the trustee of an irrevocable trust, the insured should not be granted any power to change beneficial ownership of the policy or its proceeds.

Finally, the three year rule of §2035(d)(2) does not apply to *premiums* paid by the insured-transferor, even if paid within three years of death. Therefore, such payments do not cause the insurance to be included in the insured's estate. Thus, the *premiums* may themselves be treated as adjusted taxable gifts, but no portion of the *proceeds* are included in the gross estate just because premiums were paid by the decedent-insured.[26] The premiums will be adjusted taxable gifts if they exceed the annual exclusion amount or are transferred in such a manner that no one has a present interest in them, i.e., to an irrevocable life insurance trust which does not contain a Crummey power. There will be more on life insurance trusts later.

Most transfers are not subject to §2035(d)(2)'s three year rule. Thus transfers of stocks, bonds, cash, gold, jewelry, land, and other *garden variety* transfers, even if within three years of the transferor's death, are not brought into the gross estate; they are, and remain, adjusted taxable gifts. Had the gift not been made, the property, if still owned by the decedent at death, would only be included in the gross estate under §2033, not one of those four sections specified in §2035. *Thus, except in the case of life insurance, single transaction gifts, even those made within three years of death, are **not** included in the transferor's gross estate.* Accordingly, to understand this material fully, the reader must distinguish a single transaction gift from an indirect (generally through a trust) strings attached transfer, followed by the transferor later relinquishing the retained interest.

> EXAMPLE 6 - 60. Leslie gave her son $18,000 in common stock. She died one year later, at which time the stock was worth $200,000. Hey, it was a good investment. *Nothing*, insofar as this gift is concerned, is included in Leslie's gross estate. It is an adjusted taxable gift of $8,000. It is not a §2035(d)(2) gift because it would not have been included under §§2036, 2037, 2038, or 2042 had the gift not been made.

The facts in the example immediately above demonstrate that just because a lifetime gift is not included in the gross estate (at date of death value) does not necessarily mean that it will not be included, at least partly, in the estate tax base since adjusted taxable gifts (at date of gift value reduced by annual exclusions) do boost the taxable estate into higher marginal rates. The distinction between a transferred property being included in the *gross estate* versus its inclusion in *adjusted taxable gifts* is important for valuation reasons. All items in the gross estate are included at their date-of-death (or alternate valuation date) value, while adjusted taxable gifts are included in the tax base (not the gross estate) at date-of-gift value and are reduced by the annual exclusion, if such was applicable at the time of the gift. Also, the state death tax credit is based on the taxable estate (line

3 of the Estate Tax Return), not the tax base (line 5 of the Estate Tax Return) that results when adjusted taxable gifts are added to the taxable estate.

> EXAMPLE 6 - 61. Continuing the prior example, assume that Leslie transferred a life insurance policy, on her life, instead of stock. At the time of the transfer the policy's terminal value was $18,000 and its face value was $200,000. If Leslie died more than three years after the transfer, the gross estate would be unaffected, and adjusted taxable gifts would include $8,000 (the $18,000 terminal value reduced by the $10,000 annual exclusion). On the other hand, if Leslie died within three years of the transfer, the gross estate would include the entire $200,000 *face value*, and the adjusted taxable gifts would be zero.

Congress singled out life insurance because of its unique characteristic of suddenly, and radically, increasing in value when the insured dies; a feature that strongly motivates taxpayers to avoid subjecting that increase to transfer taxes. In the absence of §2035(d)(2), a deathbed gift of a policy on the life of the donor could cause a quick, relatively large avoidance of FET, at little or no gift tax cost. For example, without §2035(d)(2), a deathbed gift of a $1 million term policy could avoid FET on the entire face value with no gift tax consequences.

"Grossing up." Section 2035(c) requires that the gift taxes paid on *any* gift made within three years of death be included in the donor's gross estate. This is referred to as "grossing up" the gross estate. The two examples that follow are themselves followed by a table that compares the results of making gifts where the gift taxes are not grossed up versus circumstances where they are.

> EXAMPLE 6 - 62. X died owning property worth $10 million. X's estate paid death taxes of $4,948,000. X's only child received $5,052,000.

> EXAMPLE 6 - 63. Y also owned $10 million, but he gave his child $5 million and paid gift tax of $2,192,500. Y died more than three years after making the gift, still owning $2,807,500 [$10 million - ($5 million gift and gift tax paid)]. Y's estate tax base was $7,797,500, and his death tax was $1,544,125. Therefore, Y's child received $6,263,375 [the gift plus the estate property less the death taxes]. Thus Y's child received $1,211,375 more than did X's child [$6,263,375 - $5,052,000]. The $1,211,375 difference is explained partly by the $10,000 gift tax annual exclusion, but mostly by the exclusion from the tax base of the gift taxes.

	X	Y
Gross Gifts	N.A.	$5,000,000
Less annual exclusions, if any	N.A.	($10,000)
Taxable gifts	N.A.	$4,990,000
Tentative tax (gifts)	N.A.	$2,385,300
Less unified credit	N.A.	($192,800)
Gift tax	N.A.	$2,192,500
Taxable estate	$10,000,000	$2,807,500
Plus adjusted taxable gifts, if any	$0	$4,990,000
Estate tax base	$10,000,000	$7,797,500
Tentative tax (estate)	$5,140,800	$3,929,425
Less gift tax payable credit	$0	($2,192,500)
Less unified credit	($192,800)	($192,800)
Estate tax	$4,948,000	$1,544,125
Total transfer taxes (gift + estate tax)	$4,948,000	$3,736,625
Net to the children	$5,052,000	$6,263,375

Compare the preceding example to the one that follows where Z, who also owned $10 million, died within three years of making the $5 million gift, and Z's estate had to "gross up."

EXAMPLE 6 - 64. Same facts as before except Z died within three years of making the gift and the gift tax was included in Z's gross estate, bringing it up to $5,000,000 [$2,807,500 owned + $2,192,500 gift taxes], resulting in an estate tax base of $9,990,000 [$5,000,000 gross estate + $4,990,000 adjusted taxable gift]. The tentative tax of $5,135,300 was reduced by the credit for gift tax payable and the unified credit to result in death taxes of $2,750,000. Thus, Z's child received a total of $5,057,500 [$10 million minus $2,192,500 minus $2,750,000], which exceeds the total $5,052,000 received by X's child by only $5,500, the amount of the tax advantage of the $10,000 gift tax exclusion at the marginal rate of 55%.

	X	Z
Gross Gifts	N.A.	$5,000,000
Less annual exclusions, if any	N.A.	($10,000)
Taxable gifts	N.A.	$4,990,000
Tentative tax (gifts)	N.A.	$2,385,300
Less unified credit	N.A.	($192,800)
Gift tax	N.A.	$2,192,500
Taxable estate	$10,000,000	$5,000,000
Plus adjusted taxable gifts, if any	$0	$4,990,000
Estate tax base	$10,000,000	$9,990,000
Tentative tax (estate)	$5,140,800	$5,135,300
Less gift tax payable credit	$0	($2,192,500)
Less unified credit	($192,800)	($192,800)
Estate tax	$4,948,000	$2,750,000
Total transfer taxes (gift + estate tax)	$4,948,000	$4,942,500
Net to the children	$5,052,000	$5,057,500

The fact that gift taxes paid more than three years before death can result in significant tax savings is an important estate planning tool, provided clients are willing to act early enough to avoid the "gross up" rule of §2035(c). Most people, even the very wealthy, are unwilling to generate a gift tax even if it will save substantial transfer taxes.

Tax exclusive versus tax inclusive calculations. A different way of describing the grossing up rule is that the gift tax is generally calculated on a tax exclusive basis, i.e., the amount of the gift tax is not included in the base. The taxes paid are not "taxable gifts" even though they are paid by the donor, nor are they part of the estate tax base, provided the donor lives for three years after making the gift that generated the gift taxes. On the other hand, the estate tax is calculated on a tax inclusive basis, i.e., the tax is levied on the "taxable estate" out of which the estate tax is paid, and the tax itself is not a deduction. Grossing up converts a tax exclusive gift into a tax inclusive one. As we shall see in our later discussion of the generation-skipping transfer tax, on certain transfers ("direct skips") one computes the tax on a tax exclusive basis, thereby reducing the effective tax rate.

Comparing Powers of Appointment to Retained interests. When considering what can be done to make an estate plan more flexible when trusts are used, consider the following statements. Almost any retained interest by the creator (the settlor or trustor) of a trust will cause the trust to be included in the settlor's estate regardless of how innocuous that retained interest might be. A power can be very broad and, so long as it is not a general power, it will not be in the holder's estate. So, when trying to determine whether a trust that is connected in some manner to a decedent should be included in the decedent's estate it is helpful to use a decision tree:

1. Did the decedent create or fund the trust? If no, go to #5, if yes, go to #2.

2. Did the decedent retain an interest in the trust that either gave the decedent an economic benefit or the ability to control enjoyment? If no, then it is not in the decedent's estate. If yes, go to #3.

3. Did the decedent release the retained interest? If no, it is in the decedent's estate. If yes, go to #4.

4. Was the release within three years of decedent's death? If yes, the property is in the decedent's gross estate at the date of death value. If no, it is not in the gross estate, but it is an adjusted taxable gift.

5. Did someone give the decedent a power to appoint property such that the decedent would be considered the holder of a power? If no, then the trust property is not in the decedent's estate. If yes, go on to #6.

6. Could the decedent, at any time, have appointed the property to decedent's self, decedent's creditors, decedent's estate, or the creditors' of the estate? If yes, it was a general power, go on to #7. If no, it was a limited power, and as such it is not included in the gross estate, nor is was it an adjusted taxable gift. *** *Query 6 - 6. Why doesn't a lapsed or exercised limited power create an adjusted taxable gift?*

7. Was the general power still there when the holder died? If yes, the property subject to the power (whether exercised or lapsed) is included in the holder's estate. If no, go on to #8 if it lapsed during the holder's lifetime, or go to #9 if it was exercised during life.

8. Was the general power greater than the lesser of $5,000 or 5% of the trust (i.e., a 5 & 5 power)? If no, it is not in the gross estate, only because it was not in effect when the holder died. If yes, it did exceed the 5 & 5 limits before it lapsed *and* the holder continue to have an interest in the trust, go back to #1 [the lapsed % that exceeded 5% (or $5,000) is probably included as a

retained interest]. If yes, but the holder had no continuing interest in the trust after the lapse, nothing is included, but the lapsed % that exceeded 5% (or $5,000) is an adjusted taxable gift.

9. When the general power was exercised, was the property given to the decedent or the decedent's creditors, or did the decedent exercise the power in favor of someone else? If exercised in the holder's favor, then there is no taxable gift (but presumably the property increased the holder's estate). If exercised in favor of someone else (i.e., trustee, give $25,000 to my friend Betty), it would be treated as a gift from the holder, and, if over the annual exclusion amount, it will be treated as an adjusted taxable gift.

Use the decision tree above as you work through these examples (assume all trusts are irrevocable unless it is stated otherwise).

EXAMPLE 6 - 65. Sandra created an irrevocable trust for her brother Duane. Duane received all income each year, and he could appoint up to 5% of the corpus of the trust to whomever he might choose each year. Duane's children were the remaindermen. When he died, he had never exercised the power and the trust was valued at $1,000,000. Because this is a general power, even though it lapses unexercised, $50,000 is included in his gross estate, [$50,000, i.e., 5%*$1,000,000]. Note that the $50,000 remains in the trust. It is not part of Duane's probate estate, and that the trustee of the trust will have to pay its proportionate share of Duane's estate taxes (i.e., the pro rata amount of this portion compared to the rest of Duane's taxable estate), unless his estate plan calls for some special allocation of the estate taxes.

EXAMPLE 6 - 66. David created a trust for Keith. The trustee could distribute as much of the income or trust as the trustee thought would be good for Keith. The trustee never exercised the special power, other than to give Keith income from time to time. The trust gave Keith the unrestricted power to appoint up to 25% of the corpus at his death through specific mention of the power in his will; Lillian or her estate was the remainderman. Keith died with a will that made no mention of the trust. The trust was worth $1,000,000 when Keith died. Since this is a general power, even though it is restricted to exercise at death, Keith's estate will include $250,000 [25% * $1,000,000].

EXAMPLE 6 - 67. Curtis created a trust to benefit Donna for life, with remainder to her children. Roberta was the initial trustee, with Koala National Bank as the successor trustee. The trustee had the power to appoint, each year, as much of the trust to Donna as the trustee thought Donna should have to keep Donna happy. The power was never exercised and the trust was worth $1,000,000 when Donna died.

Since Donna was not a holder and did not create the trust, none of the trust is included in her estate. What if Roberta dies before Donna? Is any of the trust included in her estate? No, Roberta is a holder, but a holder of a limited power. And Curtis? Nothing is in his estate; he created the trust, but he did not retain any interest.

EXAMPLE 6 - 68. The same facts apply as in the prior example, except Curtis served as the initial trustee. If Curtis died while serving as trustee, or even if he was not serving as trustee but still had the right to appoint himself trustee, the entire trust would be included since Curtis retained the power to determine who would enjoy the property, even though he could not benefit himself.

EXAMPLE 6 - 69. At a time when the Federal rate for valuing split-interest gifts was 12%, Melinda, aged 65, established an irrevocable trust funded with all her worldly possessions and investments worth $1,000,000. The independent trustee was to pay her income for life with the remainder paid to her friend Dianne. The value of the gift (the remainder) using Table S is $242,540. Since this is a gift of a future interest there is no annual exclusion. Six years later, when Melinda died the trust was worth $1,125,000. The amount included in Melinda's gross estate insofar as this trust is concerned is the date of death value, i.e., $1,125,000. In calculating the estate tax, the adjusted taxable gift amount is zero because property that is drawn back into the gross estate is not also counted as an adjusted taxable gift for estate tax purposes.

EXAMPLE 6 - 70. Alejandro, aged 80, established an irrevocable trust funded with investments worth $750,000, just a small portion of his vast wealth. The independent trustee was to pay income to such individuals as Alejandro each year directed, and any year Alejandro failed to direct the trustee, the income had to be accumulated. At the end of ten years, the trust was to terminate and the remainder was to be paid to Alejandro's sister Irene, or to her issue. Even though the settlor did not retain any economic interest, the retention of control causes this to be an incomplete gift. Five years later, when Alejandro died the trust was worth $1,375,000, which is also the value included in his gross estate. After ten years, when the trust was worth $1,500,000, it terminated and the property was distributed to Irene. No new gift or transfer taxes occur as a result of this termination.

EXAMPLE 6 - 71. Suppose, in the preceding example, Alejandro died two years after the trust terminated, the results would be quite different. The trust would not be included in his gross estate because he did not have any retained interests when he died. But, upon the termination of the trust, his right to direct income ceased, therefore at that time the gift was complete. Alejandro had to pay gift taxes of $358,700 on a gift of $1,490,000. What about the fact that the retained interest ceased within three years of his death? Since he did not "release" the retained interest and it merely ended as per the terms of the original trust, §2035(d)(2) does not apply. However, §2035(c) does apply. The "gift" within three years of Alejandro's death resulted in gift taxes of $358,700 being paid, therefore that amount must be included in his gross estate. Of course, since the trust property itself is not included in the gross estate, an adjusted taxable gift in the amount of $1,490,000 is part of the estate tax calculation. There is also a $358,700 gift tax payable credit.

For the next four alternative examples the common facts are as follows: Melanie created an irrevocable trust funding it with assets worth $750,000. The trust required income be paid to Carol or Sean in such amounts as Melanie allocates each year, but if she failed to advise the trustee, and after her death, the payments were to be made equally. Once one of the income beneficiary dies, the income must be paid to the sole survivor; after both income beneficiaries die, the trust terminates and is to be distributed to Ruben or to his estate. Because of Melanie's retained control, no taxable transfer of the corpus will occur until that right to allocate income ends and each distribution of income will be treated as if it came from her.

> EXAMPLE 6 - 72. Suppose two years after establishing the trust, Melanie died. The trust was then worth $1,180,000. Her estate includes that date of death amount, not because she died within three years of establishing the trust, but because she retained a §2036 interest.

> EXAMPLE 6 - 73. Suppose that seven years after establishing the trust, Melanie died. The trust was then worth $1,585,000. The date of death amount is included; again, this has nothing to do with a three year rule.

> EXAMPLE 6 - 74. Suppose, Melanie released her right to decide who gets the income (i.e., she writes a letter to the trustee, irrevocably giving up the right to make any further income allocations) in year thirteen when the trust was worth $2,100,000, and died in year fifteen, when the trust was worth $2,250,000. The release was a taxable gift, resulting in her payment of gift taxes in the amount of $637,000. Because of §2035(d)(2), her gross estate includes the date of death value of the trust, i.e., $2,500,000. Because her gift within three years of death resulted in gift taxes, the $637,000 must also be included. Her adjusted taxable gifts are zero and, of course, the credit of $637,000 is available.

> EXAMPLE 6 - 75. Suppose Melanie released her right to allocate income in year ten when the trust was worth $1,800,000, and died in year fifteen, when the trust was worth $2,250,000. Nothing, insofar as the trust corpus is concerned, is in her

gross estate since her death was more than three years after she released her retained interest. There was a taxable gift, resulting in gift tax of $498,000, when she released the right to allocate income because she had kept control until then. Her estate will report $1,800,000 as an adjusted taxable gift and claim a gift tax payable credit of $498,000.

RULES

THE CONNECTION BETWEEN GIFTS & THE DONOR'S ESTATE

The following rules should help you understand how post-76 gifts relate to the donor's estate:

One: Generally, gifts given are simply "adjusted taxable gifts" to the extent such gifts exceed the annual exclusion. §2001(b)(2).

Two: Gift taxes paid (or payable) are generally allowed as a credit against the tentative tax to offset the fact that the adjusted taxable gifts are used to boost the estate into its appropriate marginal rate. §2001(b)(2).

Three: Gift taxes paid on <u>any</u> gift within three years of death are added to the gross estate. §2035(c).

Four: Retained interests in transfers (usually transfers in trust) will cause the property transferred to be included in the transferor's estate as though the transfer never took place. §§2036 - 2038.

Five: There are only three exceptions to rule number one:

a. Transfers of an interest in **life insurance** within three years of death will result in the date of death value being included in the transferor's estate. §2035(d)(2).

b. The **release** of a **retained** interest within three years of death will result in the date of death value of the trust assets being included in the settlor's estate as though no release occurred. §2035(d)(2).

c. Where an interest that was given away upon the creation of a joint tenancy is included in a deceased joint tenant's estate because of the "consideration furnished test," it will be included at the date of death value. §2040.

§2043: Part-Sale, Part-Gift Transfers

Many clients wrongly believe that a transfer will not be treated as a gift if the transferor receives some token amount of consideration in exchange. They think that a small receipt from the donee will shelter the transaction from gift taxation. The correct result is that, unless the transaction is at arms length, a gift occurs measured by the *difference* between the respective values of the consideration exchanged.

However, when §§2035-2038, or §2041 apply to a transfer, there are likely to be consequences not anticipated by the transferor. Section 2043 provides that the amount included in the gross estate under §§2035 - 2038, or §2041, is the date-of-death value of the property reduced only by a "consideration offset." Meaning the estate can subtract only the value of the consideration received.

> EXAMPLE 6 - 76. D "sold" his son his $20,000 vacation home, reserving the right to use the home from time to time. D was "paid" 200 shares of very speculative stock then worth just $1,000. When D died, the stock was worth $17,000 and the vacation home was worth $30,000. His gross estate will include the date-of-death value of the home [$30,000], less only the $1,000 date of gift value of the consideration received. The post-gift appreciation on both the stock received (because D owns it) and the vacation home (because of the retained interest) are in D's estate. Note that there is no three year rule involved here.

The example immediately above illustrates relatively uncommon estate-planning transfers. Most bargain-sale-type transfers are treated differently because they generally do not include a retained interest or a general power of appointment. Therefore, since the transferred property is not included in the gross estate, the §2043 offset rule does not apply. However, a simple bargain sale will be included in the *estate tax base* as an adjusted taxable gift equal to the original gross gift value, less both the annual exclusion(s) and the consideration received by the donor.

> EXAMPLE 6 - 77. In 1984, Jessie "sold" her son Charles a parcel of land worth $18,000 for $200. As a completed transfer, there are no strings attached; it is not a transfer involving a general power of appointment. Thus, this sale is not subject to §§2035 - 2038, or 2041; therefore, §2043 does not apply. Jessie will be treated as having made a gross gift of $17,800 and a taxable gift of $7,800. The latter amount is an adjusted taxable gift that will boost Jessie's estate into higher marginal rates

when she dies.

It should be kept in mind that §2043 applies only to transfers included in the gross estate under §§2035(d)(2), 2036-2038, or 2041. Section 2043 does not specifically mention §2042 but §2035(d)(2) does. So, if life insurance is "sold," other than in an arms length transaction, within three years of the insured's death, §2043 will apply.

> EXAMPLE 6 - 78. Four years before he died, Hissing sold Rita a $100,000 face-value policy on Hissing's life that had a terminal reserve value of $1,800. Rita paid just $500. Since more than three years have past, his gross estate does not include this policy. However, the transfer-for-value rule will render the proceeds in excess of the purchase price taxable as income to Rita.

> EXAMPLE 6 - 79. Based on the facts in the prior example, if Hissing died within three years of the "sale," his estate would be increased by $99,500, based on §2043 (a $500 offset) with reference to §2035(d)(2) that makes reference to §2042.

TWO: ESTATE TAX DEDUCTIONS

Estate tax deductions include funeral expenses, expenses in administering the estate, claims against the estate, debts of the decedent, certain taxes including the excise tax on excess retirement accumulations,[27] losses incurred during estate administration,[28] charitable bequests,[29] and the marital deduction.[30] In this section, we will introduce the marital deduction and charitable deduction, both of which are developed in detail in later chapters.

§2056: Marital Deduction

In calculating the taxable estate, the gross estate may be reduced by the value of any qualifying interest in property passing from the decedent to the surviving spouse. Thus, essentially an "unlimited" amount of property passing to the surviving spouse can avoid estate taxation, provided that certain requirements are met.

Requirements for the unlimited marital deduction. Subject to several exceptions, a property transfer to a spouse will qualify for the unlimited marital deduction if it meets the following three requirements:

1. *Included in decedent's gross estate.* The property must be *included* in the decedent's gross estate.

2. *Must "pass" to surviving spouse.* The property must actually *pass* to the surviving spouse.

> EXAMPLE 6 - 80. When she died, Orca left a $5 million estate. Her will left a pecuniary bequest of $2 million to Walter, her son by a prior marriage, and the residue to her husband Martin. Unfortunately, she used a will form that had the clause "all estate taxes shall be paid from the residue of my estate." Because the tax on the transfer to Walter reduces Martin's interest in the estate, it also reduces the marital deduction which in turn further increases the tax, etc., with the final result that the tax is $1,217,778 and Martin receives just $1,782,222. *** *Query 6 - 7. What is the death tax on $2 million? Would charging her son Walter's share with the estate taxes, but increasing that share such that he still nets $2 million result in an increase in Martin's share given that there would no longer be an interrelated calculation?*

Thus, to qualify for the full marital deduction, most planners will plan for taxes and other expenses to be paid from property *not* qualifying for the marital deduction. An additional problem of paying estate taxes out of the marital share is the need to make interrelated computations. In order to calculate the amount of the marital deduction, one needs to know the amount of the net tax; however, in order to calculate the net tax, the amount of the marital deduction must be calculated. A solution is determinable, but it requires an interrelated sequence of calculations.

3. *Not a terminable interest.* Third, to qualify for the unlimited marital deduction, the interest passing to the surviving spouse cannot be a terminable interest. A *terminable interest*, defined at §2056(b)(1), is one that *might* terminate or fail on the happening of some occurrence or event or contingency or on the failure of some event or contingency. The terminable interest rule was created to ensure that property will be subject to estate taxation in at least one of the two spouses' estates. Without it, property could qualify for the marital deduction in the estate of the first spouse and not even show up in the gross estate of the surviving spouse.

> EXAMPLE 6 - 81. In his will, decedent transfers property into a trust, with income to his wife for her life, then remainder to his child. The value of the life interest to the wife will not qualify for the marital deduction because it will "terminate ... on the occurrence of an event or contingency." Her interest will terminate at her death.

In general, a *life estate interest* passing to a surviving spouse does not qualify for the marital deduction and it is not included in the surviving spouse's estate, unless a special election is made.

Because of the way the Code defines a terminable interest, a transfer to a surviving spouse will not be considered a terminable one if no other person will possess or enjoy any part of the property after the interest passing to the surviving spouse terminates.

> EXAMPLE 6 - 82. At her death, Mrs. Carrie, an inventor, was receiving annual payments from several companies using one of her patented ideas. Her husband received her entire estate, including the patent rights (good for 17 years when first issued) that still had 14 years left. The value of the patent is included in Mrs. Carrie's estate and it qualifies for a marital deduction because *no other person* will enjoy any part of the property after the patent is finished.

Exceptions to the terminable interest rule. There are several exceptions to the terminable interest rule that will be covered in detail in the chapter that introduces estate plans for wealthy couples. We will just introduce three of the major ones here.

First, the rule will not be violated if decedent-testator conditions a spousal bequest upon surviving no more than *six months* after the decedent's death.[31] Thus, the survival clauses specifying "thirty days" or "four months" often included in the wills do create terminable interests, but they qualify for the marital deduction. Some states, such as California, have enacted *marital deduction saving* statutes for those wills and trusts that show a clear intention to qualify for the marital deduction but which, due to poor drafting, include a survivorship period in excess of six months. The statutes reduce the survivorship period to six months or they may provide a more generic solution, such as declaring void any provision which would cause the loss of the marital deduction.[32] Unfortunately, judicial reaction to these statutes has been less than enthusiastically supportive.

Second, a transfer in which the surviving spouse receives a life estate in all of the income, payable at least annually, plus a *general power of appointment*, exercisable during life and/or by will, is allowed to qualify for the marital deduction.[33] This arrangement is used in what is called a *power of appointment trust*, which is one type of marital trust explained in the later chapters on estate planning for wealthy couples.

Third, if the decedent's executor elects to treat certain property as "qualified terminable interest property," or "QTIP," it will qualify for the marital deduction despite the fact that the surviving spouse will not own the property and might have at most a limited power over the property.[34] A further discussion of this important estate planning tool is postponed until we study estate plans for wealthy couples.

Special rules for transfers to non-U.S. citizen spouse. Property passing at death to a *surviving spouse* who is not a U.S. citizen will qualify for the marital deduction only if it passes to a "qualified domestic trust," commonly called a QDT or a QDOT, created for the benefit of that spouse or if the surviving spouse becomes a U.S. Citizen.[35] The rationale for requiring the creation of this trust is to ensure collection of the estate tax on the death of a surviving spouse who might otherwise remove the wealth from the United States. The QDOT requirements are covered in greater detail in the chapter on advanced estate planning for wealthy married couples.

§2055: Charitable Deduction

The charitable deduction is evidence of Congressional encouragement of philanthropy. Compared to the various rules limiting the amount of deduction for income taxes, the charitable deduction is quite simple insofar as the transfer tax system is concerned. Outright transfers to qualified charities (most U.S. based religious organizations, publicly funded educational institutions, organizations for the disabled, for health research, etc.) are 100% deductible for both estate and gift tax purposes. The main issue for outright transfers is that the deduction is based on the value of the gift at the moment of transfer, whether this is by way of a lifetime gift or a bequest. If a bequest is left to the discretion of the executor or a beneficiary then no estate tax deduction will be allowed, even if the executor decides to leave a portion of the estate to a charity. Thus, precatory words in a decedent's will such as, "I leave $100,000 to Reverend Teagarden with the hope that he will use it for the ministry of the Church," would not result in a charitable deduction.

Transfers made to charities through the use of trusts must meet certain requirements specified in Code §2055. The special requirements for charitable giving through the use of trusts are designed to give reasonable assurance that the charity will actually receive a benefit that is reasonably close to the amount of tax deduction allowed, whether the deduction is an income tax deduction in the case of lifetime gifts or an estate tax deduction for transfers that take place at the death of the donor. Gifts to charities using trusts are classified either as charitable lead trusts, if the charity's interest precedes that of the non-charity beneficiary, or as charitable remainder trusts, if the charity's interest is that of remainderman, following the term or life estate interest of one or more non-charity beneficiaries.

These are further broken down into either charitable annuity trusts, if the periodic payments are fixed at the outset, or uni-trusts, if the payments are a fixed percentage of the value of the trust calculated annually. The latter requires an annual revaluation of the trust corpus. Thus, one speaks of a charitable remainder unitrust (CRUT), a charitable remainder annuity trust (CRAT), a charitable lead annuity trust (CLAT), or a charitable lead uni-trust (CLUT). In general, §2055 requires charitable remainder trusts to provide annual fixed payments of at least 5% of the corpus value whether such is fixed at the outset, an annuity trust, or revalued annually, a unitrust.

The reason the law requires the pay-out be fixed (i.e., either as a dollar amount or as a fixed percentage of the annually re-valued amount) is that if the law allowed a deduction for a trust that simply required "all income" be paid each year the charities might actually receive very little benefit. Persons more interested in the income tax deduction than the charity could flaunt the purpose of the law by having the trustee invest in low yield (or non-dividend paying) growth stock for a charitable lead trust; or in high yield, wasting (or risky) investments for a charitable remainder trust. Charitable lead trusts do not have an annual payment restriction. The reason for requiring a minimum 5% payout is less clear since the committee reports, related to this part of the law, do not address the issue. Some people have suggested that Congress felt that there should a purpose for delaying the charity receipt of the gift. A reason for a delay, such as the need of the donor for the retained income, should exist; otherwise, a gift in trust for a charity should not qualify for a charitable deduction. Setting up a charitable remainder trust retaining a mere 1% income interest would seem to have little purpose, other than delaying the charity's use of the trust property.

EXAMPLE 6 - 83. Anne Scheiber died in January 9, 1995, at the age of 101. She had worked for the IRS. Her salary was just $3,150 per year when she retired in 1943. In 1944, she used her life savings of $5,000 to open an investment account. By living frugally, investing, and reinvesting, her stock and bond investments grew to over $20 million when she died. Except for $50,000 that went to a niece, the balance of her estate (over $22 million by the time it was distributed) went to

Yeshiva University, a small co-ed university in New York City. The bequest specified that it be used for women's scholarships. The estate paid no estate taxes.

EXAMPLE 6 - 84. When he was 60 years old, Barry Barns transferred property worth $500,000 to establish a §2055 qualified CRUT that would make an annual payment for the rest of his life equal to 5% of the value of the corpus as determined on January 1st of each year. Upon his death Easter Seals would receive the remainder. Barry was allowed an income tax deduction based on the remainder value of the trust; and, since the only gift was the remainder interest given to a qualified charity, there was no taxable gift. Because Barry retained a life estate in the trust corpus, it is included in his estate when he dies, but, since it will then go outright to Easter Seals, it is 100% deductible for estate tax purposes.

EXAMPLE 6 - 85. Suppose Barry established a trust that did not provide fixed payments, but merely gave him all trust income for life. This arrangement would not meet §2055 requirements, therefore, Barry would not be allowed an income tax deduction. Even though the income tax deduction is lost, the only gift beneficiary is a charity, therefore there would be no gift tax. When Barry dies, the trust is included in his estate (§2036) but is fully deducted, since the trust property then goes outright to Easter Seals.

EXAMPLE 6 - 86. David Marine had been a doctor. At the time of his death in 1984, he had accumulated considerable wealth, but very few friends and no close relatives. His executors were given the limited power to appoint his estate to such "persons who have contributed to my well-being or who have been otherwise helpful to me during my lifetime...." The bequest to anyone of these persons was limited to no more than 1% of his estate, with a provision that it "may be considerably less." The residue of the estate was left in equal shares to Princeton University and John Hopkins University. The net estate was worth $2,130,081, of which the executors appointed $10,000 to Dr. Marine's housekeeper and another $15,000 to a friend of his. The balance of the estate was divided between the two universities and the executor claimed a $2,105,081 charitable deduction. The IRS successfully challenged the deduction on the grounds that at the time of the doctor's death the amount that would eventually go to the universities was unascertainable. The court stated that, although the amount of each bequest was limited to one percent of the corpus, since "the number of such bequests was unlimited and a standard for determining the amount of a bequest was uncertain, the amount of the charitable bequest could not be ascertained at the time of death and the deduction is not available."[36] The tax on $2,130,081 is $748,240. *** *Query 6 - 8. What limits, placed on the power of the executors, would have avoided taxes but still maintained significant flexibility?*

Additional material on charitable gifts and the charitable deduction is found in latter chapters.

THREE: ESTATE TAX CREDITS

As mentioned in the last chapter, there are five main estate tax credits: the unified credit, credit for state death taxes, credit for gift taxes payable, credit for tax on prior transfers, and the credit for foreign death taxes. Since the unified credit and the state death tax credit were covered in the last chapter, the following material discusses only the other three. Each of these credits represent Congress' attempt to take the sting out of the fact that some transfers may be twice taxed.

Credit/Offset for Gift Taxes Payable

To help prevent double taxation, the unified transfer tax system allows some level of offset for gift taxes on all gifts included in the decedent's estate tax base. Without this offset, the FET would be calculated on all accumulated transfers whether at death or as gifts, unfairly disregarding the fact that a transfer tax had already been paid on some of them. The law allows offsets for two different categories of gift taxes: those paid on pre-1977 gifts, and those paid on post-1976 gifts.

      Credit for gift taxes (pre-1977 gifts). The credit for gift tax, line 17 on page 1 of the Federal estate tax return, technically includes only gift taxes paid on pre-1977 gifts which are required to be included in the decedent's gross estate.[37] More exactly, the amount of the credit is limited to the lesser of the gift tax attributable to that property subject to the gift tax, or the estate tax attributable to that property. Thus, if in the year of the gift decedent paid a total combined gift tax of $30,000 for gift A, worth $100,000 and gift B, worth $200,000, the gift tax attributable to B is $20,000 [= $30,000 x ($200,000/$300,000)]. At death, if decedent's total FET was $300,000, based on a total gross estate (reduced by marital and charitable deductions) of $5 million, of which gift B was included at a value of $500,000, the FET attributable to gift B is $30,000 [=$300,000 x ($500,000/$5,000,000)]. Thus, the allowable credit for gift taxes paid for gift B is $20,000 (lesser of $20,000 or $30,000). The reader might be wondering what pre-1977 gifts could possibly show up in the gross estate. Ordinarily, pre-1977 gifts will not affect the estate tax return of post-1981 decedents, since §2035(d)(2) includes in the gross estate only certain transfers made within *three years* of death, and §2001 includes in "adjusted taxable gifts" (not the gross estate) only *post-1976* taxable gifts. However, a pre-1977 gift can wind up in the gross estate under §2036, §2037, §2038, or §2035 if the donor-decedent had made a pre-1977 transfer with a retained interest at the time of his or her death or had relinquished such an interest within three years of death.

> EXAMPLE 6 - 87. In 1962, decedent, then age 50, created an irrevocable trust, funding it with $2 million in property. Under the terms of the trust, income was payable to the decedent for life, with remainder to his descendants. Decedent paid a gift tax of $235,118 on the gift of the *remainder* interest. If decedent dies today, his gross estate will include today's value of the entire trust corpus, under §2036. A credit for gift tax paid will be allowed based on the lesser of the gift tax paid in 1962 that is attributable to the gift (pro rata share if more than one gift that year), or the amount of estate tax attributed to having the trust included in his taxable estate, (i.e., the pro rata share of the federal estate tax attributable to including the trust is the taxable estate).

Offset for gift taxes (post-1976 gifts). Based upon material covered earlier, it should be clear that two categories of post-1976 gifts will be included in the decedent's estate tax base. First, similar to the pre-1977 gifts described in the previous section, post-1976 gifts also subject to §2036, §2037, §2038, or §2035(d)(2) will be included in the transferor's gross estate. Second, the taxable portion of other completed post-1977 gifts ("adjusted taxable gifts") will be added to the estate tax base. Again, to prevent double taxation, the law allows an offset to the tentative tax for gift taxes paid on these gifts.[38] This offset is calculated by determining the amount that would have been "payable" had the tax rates in effect at the decedent's death been applicable at the time of the gift. Since rates for taxable amounts up to $3 million have been the same for all years after 1976, generally, the tax *payable* is different from the actual gift tax *paid* only for very large total taxable gifts, i.e, whose level exceeded this amount. Although the return does not call this offset a "credit" it has the effect of reducing the tentative tax dollar for dollar to an amount called the "gross estate tax," and it clearly is a credit. This credit is placed at line 9 on the estate tax return (Form 706).

THE PRIOR TRANSFER CREDIT

It seems inequitable to tax property twice on those occasions when it passes swiftly through two estates such that the second owner only had a limited opportunity to enjoy the inherited property. Congress obviously agrees. It has given some tax relief in the form of a prior transfer credit (PTC) if the two deaths occur within ten years of each other.[39]

Background on the PTC. As originally enacted, double taxation was avoided by allowing a deduction in the second estate equal to the value of property traceable to the first estate.[40] The relief was available only if the two deaths occurred within five years of one another and the old law required the executor claiming the deduction to trace the property from the first estate into the second. If the inherited property was sold and the proceeds were commingled with other funds, out of which both investments and consumables were purchased, it was difficult and sometimes impossible to trace the property. There was a fair amount of litigation between estates and the IRS over the tracing issue.

The PTC today. Present law allows a tax credit where property is included in the transferor's taxable estate and the transferee dies within ten years of the transferor. Actually, the credit is available even if the transferee dies two years before the transferor, but the circumstances, involving vested remainder interests, are so rare that they will not be covered. Since the credit is intended to reduce the unfairness of taxing property that passes quickly through two estates, a time factor affects the amount of the credit available, decreasing the maximum available by 20% two years after the transferor's death, and it drops another 20% each additional two year period, until the credit disappears altogether at the end of ten years. The credit, before applying the time factor, is based upon the amount of additional tax the inclusion of the transferred property generates in each estate. Since this is relief from double taxation, the credit is equal to the lesser of the two amounts.

The above overview greatly simplifies the law. The actual calculation is a three step process. In the explanation that follows, D1 represents the first decedent and D2, the second.

▸ **Credit Limit One**. Compute the portion of the Federal estate tax which bears the same ratio to D1's estate tax as the transferred property bears to D1's taxable estate.

$$CL1 \; = \; \frac{\textit{adjusted value of transferred property}}{\textit{adjusted value of D1's taxable estate}} * D1\textit{'s federal estate tax}$$

► **Credit Limit Two**. Compute the increase in estate tax at D2's death caused by inclusion of the net value of the transferred property. The net value is the value of the transferred property reduced by all death taxes (Federal and state) attributed to it at D1's death. The Federal estate tax is determined with the net value of the property included, then again with it excluded. The difference in the two tax amounts is credit limitation two.[41]

Federal tax on D2's taxable estate (including transferred property)	XXXX
Federal tax on D2's reduced estate (reduced by the adjusted value of the transferred property)	(XXXX)
Credit Limit Two	XXX

► **Time Factor**. The prior transfer credit is the *lesser of* limit one or limit two, times the appropriate time factor percentage based on how many years D2 lived after D1 died.

Years	Percentage
1-2	100%
3-4	80%
5-6	60%
7-8	40%
9-10	20%

An Extended PTC Example.

As we go through each of the three PTC steps, we will start each with some general comments. For limit one, the numerator is the value of the transferred property, adjusted by deducting liens, mortgages, and the property transferred's proportionate share of Federal and state death taxes. The denominator is D1's taxable estate, adjusted by deducting all death taxes. If the net value of the property (property less liens and mortgages) is used in this step of the calculation, and all death taxes were allocated pro rata, there is no need to make any adjustments for the taxes since the adjusted values (above and below the line) will be in the same ratio as the unadjusted values. If the property in D2's estate is the result of a bequest made "free of estate tax," which probably means the residue of the estate paid the death taxes, the transferred property's value (the numerator) would not be adjusted for taxes but the taxable estate (the denominator) would have to be reduced by all death taxes.

The Federal estate tax is adjusted only if a credit for certain gift taxes had been allowed for D1's estate under §2012 (pre-1977 transfers with a retained interest, such that the property is included in the decedent's estate), or if D1's estate also benefitted from a prior transfer credit. For most PTC computations, no adjustments need to be made to the denominator to adjust the value of D1's taxable estate, other than for death taxes, and, as pointed out earlier, even then an adjustment is not necessary for the numerator or the denominator if the death taxes were proportionately assessed and paid.

> EXAMPLE 6 - 88. D1 died January 1, 1988, leaving a taxable estate of $2,500,000. D1's friend D2, received XYZ stock worth $500,000. The total D1 estate taxes were $833,000. D's state was a pick-up tax state, so it collected an amount equal to the Federal state death tax credit ($138,800) and the balance of $694,200 went to the Federal Treasury. D2 died June 10, 1991, leaving a taxable estate of $1,500,000. D2 had sold the XYZ stock when it was worth $580,000, investing some of the proceeds and spending the rest. In both estates the death taxes were allocated pro rata. Credit limit one is calculated as follows:

$$CL1 = \frac{\$500,000}{\$2,500,000} * \$694,200 = \$138,840$$

The value of the stock in D2's estate is irrelevant to the PTC calculation. In fact, the assets transferred need not be part of D2's estate, so no tracing of assets is required. The theory is, that if the property had been sold, and the proceeds consumed, the money from the sale allowed D2 to retain other property. Presumably, the other property is taxed in D2's estate. Notice that the value of D2's estate is not used in calculating credit limit one.

Calculating limit two has three steps which have as their goal determining the Federal tax attributable to the net value of the transferred property. We do this by figuring the Federal estate tax both with the net value of the transferred property included and again with it excluded, and the difference is the additional tax caused by the inclusion. First, calculate D2's Federal estate tax without the PTC. This means, determine the Federal amount that would have been paid on D2's taxable estate, i.e., reduce the tentative tax by the unified credit and the state death tax credit. Second, determine the Federal estate tax on D2's estate with the net value of the transferred property removed. We will call this D2's *reduced* taxable estate. To arrive at the reduced D2 taxable estate one must subtract the net value of the property transferred from D2's (regular or full) taxable estate. To determine the net value of the transferred property, subtract from the value of the property transferred (as of D1's DOD) its *share* of **all** death taxes (yes, including state death taxes) and any debts, liens, or other obligations which reduced the value of the property when it was transferred from D1 to D2.

Continuing with this example, limit two is calculated as follows:

Federal Estate Tax on D2's $1,500,000 taxable estate	$298,600
Less Federal Estate Tax on D2's reduced taxable estate. This is $1,166,600, i.e.,	
$1,500,000 - (5/25 * ($2,500,000 - $833,000))	(178,244)
Credit limit two	$120,356

The figure $298,600 is the Federal estate tax on an estate of $1,500,000 after subtracting the unified credit and the Federal state death tax credit, [$555,800 (tentative tax) - $192,800 (unified credit) - $64,400 (state death tax credit)]. The figure (5/25 * ($2,500,000 -(833,000)) in the above example is the value of the property transferred, adjusted for its pro rata share of *all* death taxes. In this hypothetical situation, the decedent's state death taxes are equal to the Federal state death tax credit. Where the state death taxes are greater than the Federal state death tax credit, the actual state death tax paid must be used to make the adjustment. This would not affect limit one if the state death taxes were also allocated pro rata, but it would affect the calculation of limit two since the property transferred must be reduced by all death taxes charged against it. The figure $178,244 is the Federal tax on a taxable estate of $1,166,600, meaning the amount that would actually be paid on that size estate after taking the unified credit and the state death tax credit, [$414,106 (tentative tax) - $192,800 (unified credit) - $43,062 (state death tax credit)].

To finish this example the time factor adjustment must be made. Since D2 died in the fourth year following D1's death, the allowable credit is 80% of the lesser of the two credit limits. Therefore:

$$80\% * \text{ the lesser of } \begin{cases} \text{\textit{limit one}: } \$138,840 \\ \text{\textit{limit two}: } \$120,356 \end{cases} = \$96,285$$

The two year time brackets start with the actual date of D1's death through midnight of the anniversary two (or four, six, etc.) years later. It is easiest to visualize this (and to be assured of selecting the correct percentage) by drawing a time line, marking off the appropriate two year anniversaries, and then indicating with a slash the date of D2's death. Indicate on the time line "100%" for the first two years following D1's death, "80%" for the next two years, etc., until you have covered the period that includes D2's death.

The chapter on advanced marital deduction and bypass trust planning goes into detail as to how the PTC is used with marital deduction trusts to reduce taxes, even where no transfer of corpus takes place.

Credit for Foreign Death Taxes

A credit is allowed for most, but not all, foreign death taxes paid on property which is (*a*) included in the U.S. gross estate, and (*b*) situated in that foreign country.

This chapter has examined the principal items found on the estate tax return, including components of the gross estate, FET deductions, and FET credits. The next chapter examines the components of the gift tax return, covers certain special tax valuation rules, and introduces the Federal generation-skipping transfer tax.

QUESTIONS AND PROBLEMS

1. Distinguish between the gross estate, taxable estate and probate estate.

2. When Morton died in 1996, he left his estate to his three children. He left stock worth $560,000, a home worth $345,000, a car worth $9,000, home furnishings worth $23,000, and a bank account with $3,500 in it. The total of his debts and expenses was $45,000. He also had a $200,000 life insurance policy on his life that was paid out to his three children and a vacation cabin worth $150,000 held in joint tenancy with his brother. The brothers had each paid half of the purchase price on the vacation cabin. Calculate : (a) the gross estate, (b) the taxable estate, (c) the probate estate, (d) the total death taxes, (e) the state death tax credit, and (f) the Federal estate tax.

3. (a) What is a dower interest? (b) How is it taxed?

4. When Jack died, his 65 year old wife was entitled to receive a survivor's pension of $1,800 per month for her lifetime from a fully qualified plan (his employer had made all contributions). The §7520 rate used for valuing annuities was 8%. Determine how much is included in his estate if Jack retired in (a) 1986; (b) 1983; or (c) 1980. Use Table K to adjust for the fact that the payments are made monthly.

5. Frank and Kathleen co-owned a home. Frank contributed $25,000 and Kathleen contributed $75,000 of the $100,000 purchase price. When the first co-owner died the value of the property was $360,000. In each independent case determine: (1) how much is included in the decedent's estate and (2) the survivor's new basis.

   a. They held the property as joint tenants. Frank died first. They were just good friends.
   b. They held the property as joint tenants. Frank died first. They were married.
   c. They held the property as joint tenants. Kathleen died first. They were just good friends.
   d. They held the property as community property. Frank died first.

e. They held the property as tenants in the entirety. Frank died first.

f. They held the property as tenants in common. Frank died first, leaving his 25% share to Kathleen. (Does it matter for inclusion and basis whether they were married? Does it matter for estate taxes?)

6. (a) What is a general power? (b) What is the significant tax difference between a general power and a limited one? (c) When will a power to appoint to one's self not be a general power?

7. At his death, decedent-trustee was the holder of a power of appointment over property held in a trust created by his rich brother. Determine whether any portion of the trust principal is included in decedent's gross estate given each of the following alternative trustee powers. If a power is exercised in favor of someone other than the holder, state the gift and estate tax consequences that follow.

a. The unrestricted power to appoint property to his surviving descendants by specific mention of the power in his will. Decedent appointed the entire corpus to his grandson.

b. Same as part a, except decedent did not appoint property to anyone at his death.

c. The unrestricted power to appoint property to himself or his descendants. In his will, he appointed property to his grandson.

d. Same as part c, except decedent did not appoint to anyone at his death.

e. The power to appoint property to himself for "health" reasons.

f. The power to appoint property to himself for his "comfort."

g. The power to appoint property to himself, but only with the approval of his son, who was also the remainderman.

For h - i, the following power was included in the trust: The power to appoint to himself or to his children each calendar year and at his death, if the power was unexercised during that year, the greater of $5,000 or 5 percent of the trust property.

h. In his will, decedent exercised the power, naming his son to receive $50,000 of the $1 million trust corpus.

i. Decedent never exercised this power during his lifetime nor at his death.

For j - m the following 5 & 5 power was involved: The power to appoint to himself or to his children each calendar year up to the greater of $5,000 or 5% of the trust property. At his death the power lapsed, i.e., it could not be exercised through his will or by any other means once he died.

j. Shortly before he died, he exercised the power and had the trustee transfer 5% ($50,000) of the trust to himself.
k. Shortly before he died, he exercised the power and had the trustee transfer 2.5% of the trust ($25,000) to his son and another 2.5% to his daughter.
l. Shortly before he died, he had the trustee transfer 5% to his university to be used for scholarships.
m   Shortly before he died, he exercised the power by having the trustee transfer 3% of the trust to United Way.

8. Identify two situations where a limited power of appointment might be the right answer to an estate planning problem.

9. True or false? A gift of life insurance within three years of the insured-donor's death is the *ONLY* circumstance were a completed gift (i.e., one with no strings attached) is included in the gross estate of the donor.

10. What do §§2033, 2034, 2039, 2040, 2041, and 2042 have in common?

11. What do Sections 2036, 2037, and 2038 have in common?

12. Under §2036, two very different circumstances will cause a trust to be included in the settlor's estate. (a) Describe the one in which the settlor retains an economic benefit. (b) Describe the one in which the settlor retains no economic benefit.

13. Use the language of the IRC to describe the three common retained powers or rights that will cause a trust to be included in the settlor's gross estate under §2038.

14. Explain the impact of §2035(d)(1) and §2035(d)(2) by giving specific examples of:

   a. a single transaction lifetime gift where the property transferred is not included in the gross estate.
   b. a single transaction lifetime gift where the property transferred is included in the gross estate.
   c. a relinquishment of a "string" where the trust property is not included in the gross estate.
   d. a relinquishment of a "string" where the trust property is included in the gross estate.

Facts for problems 15 - 18: Gary transferred property worth $60,000 to his sister Pamela. Because of the unified credit, Gary paid no gift taxes when he made the transfer. When Gary died the property was worth $100,000. For each case state (insofar as the transfer goes and his estate) what is (a) in his gross estate; and (b) the adjusted taxable gift.

15. Gary transferred stock two years before he died.

16. Gary transferred stock four years before he died.

17. Gary transferred life insurance ($60,000 was its terminal reserve value) two years before he died. Pamela collected the $100,000 proceeds.

18. Gary transferred life insurance ($60,000 was its terminal reserve value) four years before he died. Pamela collected the $100,000 proceeds.

Facts for 19 - 23: Settlor Sam created an irrevocable trust, funding it with $1,000,000 of his own assets. The remaindermen of the trust were Sam's two children. For each independent case that follows calculate the following: (a) the gross gift; (b) the taxable gift; (c) the amount of the trust included in Sam's gross estate; (d) the adjusted taxable gift; (e) the amount of gift tax credit allowed.

19. Sam retained a life estate in the trust. At the time of funding, the Federal rate for split interest gifts (i.e., for valuing remainders, etc.) was 6% and Sam was 60 years old. He died ten years after establishing the trust. The trust was then worth $1,700,000.

20. Sam retained no economic interests in the trust, but the terms of the trust gave him the right to allocate income between his brothers Daniel and James. If he failed to allocate (whether due to inaction or his own prior death), then the trustee was to distribute the income equally, and once one brother died, the surviving brother was to receive all of the income each year. Sam died ten years later, without ever directing the trustee as to how to allocate. Both brothers survived him and the trust was worth $1,700,000.

21. Same facts as the prior example, except in year five, Sam had sent the trustee a letter stating that he forever released his right to make the allocation. The trust was worth $1,350,000 when Sam released his right. Again, when he died in year ten the trust was worth $1,700,000.

22. Same facts as the prior example, except the release occurred in year nine, when the trust was worth $1,600,000. As before, it was worth $1,700,000 in year ten when Sam died.

23. Under what circumstances would the gift taxes paid by Sam be included in his gross estate? Is this a special rule that relates only to transfers into trust?

24. When she died, Roxanna was serving as the trustee of an irrevocable trust that allowed her to distribute corpus or income to her children or the children of her sister Laurie. The trust was worth $700,000 when she died. For each of the following alternatives, determine whether the trust is included in her estate: (a) The trust had been established by the mother of Roxanna and Laurie, many years before. (b) The trust had been established by Laurie, many years before, and at the same time, Roxanna had established and funded a similar trust with Laurie as trustee. (c) Roxanna had established the trust, but kept no economic benefit for herself. (d) Roxanna's rich uncle had established the trust at his death.

Initially, Roxanna was also included as a permissible appointee, but she irrevocably released the right to appoint to herself seven years before she died.

25. Identify by number or schedule letter, the two pages of Form 706 where the amount of the total marital deduction must be shown.

26. When Craig died, he left is $14,000,000 estate to his wife, Rebecca. There were debts and expenses of $500,000. Craig and Rebecca were both USA citizens. (a) What is Craig's gross estate? (b) His taxable estate?

27. Florence left her net estate (after debts and expenses) of $1,000,000 to her husband, Juan Carlos. They were both residents of the USA for most of their adult lives. How much U.S.A. estate tax would be paid given each of the following circumstances? (a) Both were citizens of the USA. (b) Florence is a citizen of the USA and Juan Carlos is a citizen of Mexico. (c) Florence is a citizen of Mexico and Juan Carlos is a citizen of the USA. (d) Both were citizens of Mexico.

28. Guy had created a revocable probate-avoidance trust, fully funded before he died. Upon his death, the trust gave 50% of the corpus to the university where he received his bachelor's degree and 50% to United Way. A life insurance policy that he owned paid out $500,000 to a favorite niece. The trust had assets worth $4 million, and debts and expenses totaling $300,000. Determine Guy's (a) probate estate; (b) gross estate; (c) taxable estate; and (d) estate tax.

29. When Ruby died on August 12, 1994, her taxable estate in the amount of $1,400,000 was left to her only son, Thomas. Ruby's estate paid total death taxes of $320,000, of which $58,000 went to the state and $262,000 went to the Federal Government. When Thomas died on February 8, 1996, most of his $1,000,000 taxable estate was comprised of what was left of the estate that he had inherited from his mother. The estate taxes on Thomas's estate, before application of the PTC, would have been $33,200 paid to the state and $119,800 paid to the Federal Government. Calculate the following: (a) limit one; (b) limit two; (c) the PTC; and (d)

the Federal and state taxes after applying the PTC.

30. When Vaughan died on May 5, 1993, his taxable estate in the amount of $4,500,000 was left equally to his three children. Vaughan's estate paid total death taxes of $1,923,000, of which $335,600 went to the state and $1,587,400 went to the Federal Government. When Vaughan's oldest child, Stephanie, died on July 4, 1996, her taxable estate of $2,000,000 was left to her two children. The estate taxes on Stephanie's estate before application of the PTC would have been $99,600 paid to the state and $488,400 to the Federal Government. Calculate the following: (a) limit one; (b) limit two; (c) the PTC; and (d) the Federal and state taxes after applying the PTC.

QUERIES ANSWERED

1. Using Table S, the remainder factor, using an 8% rate, following an 85 year old's life estate is .66693. Hence, Max's estate would include:

    .66693 x $1,000,000 = $666,930

2. Using Table S, the remainder factor (also used for a reversionary interest), using a 10% rate, following a 40 year old's life estate is .07055. Hence, Jim's estate would include:

    .07055 x $100,000 = $7,055.

3. Because of the consideration-furnished test of §2040 the entire property is included in Virginia's estate, even though half was reported as a gift. The definition of "adjusted taxable gifts" found in §2001(b), excludes any gifts that are included in the gross estate; therefore, the $90,000 taxable gift to her son is removed from the estate tax calculation.

4. Because the trustee still will allocate income between Benito and Consuelo, neither beneficiary has an identifiable present interest. A present interest is a requirement for the annual exclusion.

5. This is another example of an overlap of Code sections. §2036(b)(2) requires inclusion where the decedent retains the right to "designate who shall possess or enjoy the property or the income therefrom." By being able to terminate the trust early, D was able to designate who would possess the property, hence, §2036(b)(2) applies as well as §2038.

6. Because the holder of a limited power never made a transfer (but is merely the donee) the exercise or lapse will not cause the holder to be treated as having made a taxable transfer. The exercise or the lapse of a limited power during the holder's lifetime will not create a taxable gift.

7. The death taxes on $2,000,000 are $588,000. Charging Walter's share with the taxes, but increasing the share so that he nets $2,000,000 will not increase Martin's share because estate taxes are calculated on a tax inclusive basis. It would take a bequest of $3,217,778 to Walter for him to net $2,000,000. This means that Martin would receive $1,782,222, the same as if the taxes were charged to his $3,000,000 share.

8. Instead of limiting the amount that could be given to each appointee to 1%, the limit could have been stated as, "all such appointments cumulatively shall not to exceed an amount that will produce a tentative tax equal to the decedent's available unified credit." Or, "cumulatively not to exceed" either some dollar amount, such as $200,000, or some small percentage of the net estate, such "as not to exceed 10% of the adjusted gross estate." Even though these limits do not set an exact amount going to charity, they do produce a minimum amount that must go to charity and the charitable deduction would be based upon that minimum amount. Thus, the first limit (not to exceed the UCE) would result in a charitable deduction of the net estate in excess of the UCE, thus producing a taxable estate of $600,000 with no tax due.

ANSWERS TO QUESTIONS AND PROBLEMS

1. Gross estate is an estate tax concept that includes all that one owned, controlled, and in some instances, transferred with retained interests. It even includes gift taxes paid on gifts made within three years of death. The taxable estate is the gross estate less debts, expenses, and deductions, such as the marital and charitable deduction. The probate estate consists of that property owned by the decedent for which there is no other mechanism of transfer other than the court process. Generally, it is made up of things owned by the decedent, plus property co-owned as a tenant in common.

2. Morton's estate. (a) GE $1,215,500 [50% of cabin]; (b) the TxE $1,170,500; (c) the probate $940,500; (d) the total DTx $222,905; (e) the S D Tx Cr $43,312; and (f) the FET $179,593.

3. (a) A dower interest is a surviving wife's statutory interest in her deceased husband's estate. At common law, generally a life estate in a portion of the real property. Today it may be a fee interest in a portion of the estate. (b) The property is included in the decedent's gross estate but generally there is a marital deduction available. If it is just a life estate, it can qualify for the marital deduction through the QTIP election. If it is an interest in fee in a percentage of the estate, that portion going outright to the surviving spouse qualifies for the marital deduction.

4. Annuity. Wife @ 65, $1,800/mo, rate 8%. Retired in (a) 1986 full value: $1,800*12*8.136 = $1175,738 (b) 1983: full value, less $100,000 = $75,738; (c) 1980: zero.

5. Frank $25,000 and Kathleen $75,000; at 1st death $360,000. 1) Included and 2) new basis.

   a. Joint tenants. Frank died. Friends. 1) consideration furnished rule, 25%*$360,000 = $90,000; 2) New basis = $90,000 + $75,000 = $165,000.
   b. Joint tenants. Frank died. Married. 1) 50%, $180,000 2) ½ + ½ = $180,000 + $50,000 = $230,000.
   c. Joint tenants. Kathleen died. Friends. 1) $270,000 2) $295,000.

    d. Community property. Frank died. 1) 50%, $180,000 2) FMV @ DOD, $360,000.

    e. Tenants in the entirety. Frank died. Same as for married joint tenants: 1) $180,000 2) $230,000.

    f. Tenants in common. Frank died, his 25% to Kathleen. 1) 25%*$360,000 = $90,000; 2) New basis = $90,000 + $75,000 = $165,000. (Is married important? Not for inclusion, still 25%. For estate taxes? Sure, 100% marital deduction)

6. (a) General power? See Code §2041, i.e., power to appoint to holder, holder's creditors, holder's estate, or creditors of holder's estate. (b) Difference? General power you include and a limited one you don't. (c) When will a power to appoint to one's self not be a general power? When it is limited by an ascertainable standard (HSEM) i.e., the health, support, education, or maintenance standard, or when the consent of the creator or of an adverse party must be obtained.

7. Note, the trust was created by someone else; therefore, these are all powers, not retained interests.

    a. Limited not included, exercise does not matter.

    b. Limited not included, exercise does not matter.

    c. Can appoint to self, therefore general, all included. That it was exercised will not increase the transfer tax.

    d. As in part c, all included, exercise or no exercise.

    e. Limited by an ascertainable standard, the H in HSEM.

    f. All included, no ascertainable standard for comfort.

    g. Not included, the adverse interest exception.

    h. This is a general power if it is there at the time of death, exercised or not, it is included. The exercise does not increase the inclusion, it will still be $50,000, i.e., 5%.

    i. Same as h.

    j. At the time of death the power had been exercised for the year, so it was not there, so nothing insofar as the trust is concerned is included. However, the $50,000 might still be in a bank account, unless he gave it away or spent it.

    k. Again, nothing to include. But he has made two gifts of $25,000 each;

thus, after the annual exclusions there will be an adjusted taxable gift of $30,000.

l.   Again, nothing to include. The gift qualifies for the charitable deduction, so not even an adjusted taxable gift to worry about.

m.   He still could have exercised a power over 2% of the trust before he died, so 2% times the value of the trust is included.

8.   There are many. Here are two: To allow a relative to pay-out money to help a mentally disabled adult child long after the parents are dead. To allow a surviving spouse to re-allocate the remainder interests of children in a bypass trust that was established when the first spouse died.

9.   True, although students of estate planning keep trying to add others.

10.   All cover beneficial interests in property held or controlled by the decedent at death, which are included in the decedent's gross estate.

11. a.   Transfer made by decedent...
    b.   ...for less than full consideration.
    c.   Included in the decedent's gross estate at date of death value; and
    d.   amount included is only that portion of the transferred property over which decedent retained control.
    e.   Some retained control or interest by decedent.
    f.   Usually arising in the context of a trust.

12.   (a) A retained life estate. (b) Retained power to decide who (other than the settlor) enjoys the income or the property.

13   The Code refers to the power to revoke, alter, or amend. Three examples:
    - Totten trusts;
    - revocable living trusts;
    - gifts to minors under the Uniform Gifts to Minors Act where the donor serves as custodian.

14. a.   Any outright transfer, other than life insurance, avoids inclusion in the gross estate.
    b.   Transfer of life insurance on the donor's life within three years of death.

      c. If the string is cut more than three years before the transferor dies, the property will not be included.

      d. If the string is cut within three years of the transferor's death, it is as though the string had not been cut; therefore, the property is included at its date of death value.

15. (a) GE zero; (b) Adj.TxG $50,000. Stock, no three year rule.

16. (a) GE zero; (b) Adj.TxG $50,000.

17. (a) GE $100,000; (b) Adj.TxG zero. Life insurance, special three year rule.

18. (a) GE zero; (b) Adj.TxG $50,000. Life insurance, but beyond the three year reach.

19. (a) GG $366,674 [0.36674 * $1,000,000]; (b) TxG $366,674 [no annual exclusion for future interest gifts]; (c) GE $1,700,000; (d) Adj.TxG zero; (e) GTxCr zero, no taxes paid, ten.tx covered by the unified credit.

20. (a) GG zero, retained control; (b) TxG zero; (c) GE $1,700,000; (d) Adj.TxG zero; (e) GTxCr zero.

21. (a) GG $1,350,000; (b) TxG $1,350,000 [no one with an identifiable present interest]; (c) GE zero; (d) Adj.TxG $1,350,000; (e) GTxCr $298,500.

22. (a) GG $1,600,000; (b) TxG $1,600,000 [no annual exclusion except for identifiable present interests]; (c) GE $2,108,000, both §2035(d)(2) and §2035(c) apply; (d) Adj.TxG zero; (e) GTxCr $408,000 [the gift tax on $1,600,000].

23. If Sam died within three years of any gift that triggers the actual payment of gift tax. [A special rule that relates only to transfers into trust?] No, any gift whether in trust or not and whether life insurance, diamonds, land, stocks or bonds, or whatever can be given, is governed by this rule. If taxes are paid and death occurs within three years of the gift, the gift taxes are part of the gross estate.

24. (a) Limited power, do not include. (b) Include, the trusts were reciprocal trusts, and Roxanna is considered the settlor with a retained power to control enjoyment. §2036 applies. (c) This would be a retained interest, therefore include even though Roxanna retained no economic benefit. (d) Include, since at one time she held a general power. When she released it, it was as though she was the transferor of the property into the trust. Since she is treated as the transferor, the fact that she controls enjoyment of the income and property causes §2036 to apply, and the trust is included in her estate.

25. The marital deduction amount must be shown on page 3 (line 18 of recapitulation and on page 25 (schedule M).

26. (a) GE? $14,000,000; (b) TxE? Zero

27. (a) Zero estate tax, 100% marital deduction. (b)$153,000 estate taxes, no marital deduction. (c) Zero estate tax, 100% marital deduction. (d) $153,000 estate taxes, no marital deduction.

28. (a) No probate estate; (b) GE $4,500,000; (c) TxE $500,000; and (d) estate tax. None, covered by the unified credit.

29. (a) limit one [$262,000]; (b) limit two [$119,800]; (c) the PTC [$119,800]; and (d) the Federal [zero] and state taxes [$33,200] after applying the PTC.

30. (a) limit one [$529,133]; (b) limit two [$319,014]; (c) the PTC [$255,211 i.e., 80%*$319,014]; and (d) the Federal [$233,189] and state [$99,600] taxes after applying the PTC.

ENDNOTES

1. §2031(a).

2. §6018(a)(1).

3. Reg. §20.2053-7, Deduction for unpaid mortgages.

4. §6018(a)(2).

5. §2103.

6. §2102(c)(1).

7. §2002; *Fleming v. Commissioner*, No. 90-2576, 7th Cir. 1992.

8. §2002, §2203.

9. *Estate of Guide v. Commissioner*, 69 T.C. 811 (1978).

10. LR 8335033.

11. §2033.

12. *Davis*, T.C. Memo 1993-155.

13. TAM 9207004.

14. §2034.

15. §2056(b)(7)

16. §402(a).

17. *Ablamis v. Roper*, 937 F2d 1450 (9th Cir. 1991).

18. See *Gallenstein* 975 F. 2d 286 (CA6, 1992) affg. 68 AFTR 2d 91-5721.

19. §2033.

20. §2041(b)(1)(C)(ii).

21. *Estate of Cavenaugh*, 100 TC, CCH ¶12,927 (1993).

22. §2036, 2037, and 2038.

23. §2035(d)(2)

24. *Estate of Grace*, 395 US 316 (1969).

25. *Maxwell*, 3 F. 3d. 591, affirming 98 T.C. 594 (1992).

26. *Estate of Morris R. Silverman*, 61 TC 338 (1973), acq., 1978-1 CB 2.

27. §2053.

28. §2054.

29. §2055.

30. §2056.

31. §2056(b)(3)(A).

32. E.g., CA Probate Code §21,525.

33. §2056(b)(5).

34. §2056(b)(7).

35. §2056A(a).

36. *Estate of Marine*, 990 F2d 136 (4th Cir. 1993).

37. §2012.

38. §2001(b)(2).

39. §2013.

40. 812(c) of the 1939 Code.

41. Reg. §20-2013-3.

— 7

The Federal Gift Tax; Basis Rules; §2701-04 Special Valuation Rules; The Federal Generation-Skipping Transfer Tax

OVERVIEW

Chapter 5 introduced the gift tax by outlining how it is calculated and how it is unified with the estate tax. This chapter will examine more qualitative factors, such as the requirements for a valid gift, types of taxable gifts, how gifts qualify for the annual exclusion, and how certain specific transfers are subject to gift tax. The chapter will also introduce Internal Revenue Code Chapter 14's special transfer tax valuation rules found in §§2701-2704, and the generation-skipping transfer tax. While reading the chapter, the reader is urged to review both the overview of the gift tax scheme in Tables 5-1 and 5-2, plus the United States Gift Tax Return, Form 709, included in Appendix D.

FEDERAL GIFT TAX

We begin by resolving a semantics problem, stemming from the fact that planners use the word "gift" in two different ways. Chapter 2 defined a gift as a completed transfer of an interest in property by an individual in exchange for any amount that is less than full and adequate consideration. This definition is accurate, gifts include transfers at *death*. Thus, planners correctly say, "...in his will he *gave*..."

However, the subject of this chapter is the federal gift tax, and here planners mean only *lifetime* gifts. Consequently, to avoid the necessity of always using the modifier "lifetime," as in "lifetime gift," whenever the word gift is mentioned *in this chapter*, all references to gifts will be to lifetime gifts.

Requirements for a Valid Gift: Influence of Local and Federal Law

Whether or not a transfer is treated as a gift is important for two reasons in estate planning. First, it will influence the respective property rights of the parties. Second, it will determine whether a federally taxable event has occurred. In deciding these issues, two different sets of rules must be examined: local property law and federal gift tax law.

Local property law. To be valid under local property law, a gift must ordinarily meet four requirements.

1. The donor must be capable of transferring property.
2. The donee must be capable of receiving and possessing the property.
3. There must be delivery to, and some form of acceptance by, the donee or the donee's agent. A gift of money by check is not complete until the funds are *paid* by the donor's bank; until then the donor has not totally relinquished dominion and control. Thus, certain last minute deathbed gifts may not work. An example of an agent would be an escrow agent who is holding the property on behalf of the donee.
4. Finally, under local law, a valid gift ordinarily requires donative intent on the part of the donor.

Federal gift tax law. To be subject to taxation under federal gift tax law, a gift must meet all of the above local property law requirements, subject to two major federal modifications.

a. Federal tax regulations explicitly state that *donative intent is not required* for a transfer to be subject to gift tax. The first series of examples depicted shortly will illustrate this point. Although not required for a gift, the existence of donative intent would be strong evidence that a gift had actually been made.
b. Under the unique language of federal law, the gift tax applies only to a

completed gift, which arises when "...the donor has so parted with dominion and control as to leave him no power to change its disposition, whether for his own benefit or for the benefit of another..."[1]

Ordinarily, completed gifts are made either outright or in trust. *Outright transfers* made beyond the donor's dominion and control are virtually always complete for gift tax purposes. Transfers in trust, on the other hand, may be totally complete, totally incomplete, or partially incomplete. An example of a *totally complete transfer in trust* is a transfer to an irrevocable trust with no retained interests or controls; the entire transfer is subject to gift taxation. An example of a *totally incomplete transfer in trust* is a transfer to a typical revocable trust; it is not at all subject to gift taxation because the trustor has retained the power to demand return of the trust property. An example of a *partially incomplete transfer in trust* is one to an irrevocable trust over which the trustor has retained an interest in (or control over) the income but not the remainder, in which case the only gift is of the remainder interest. Or, the trustor could give away the income interest for a period of time with the corpus reverting to the trustor when the time is up, e.g., another is given the income for ten years after which the trust terminates and the corpus is returned to the trustor or to the trustor's estate. Thus, for transfers in trust in which more than one property interest is created, gift tax law requires that each interest be examined independently to determine whether a completed gift of that interest has been made.

Thus, federal tax law and local property law both influence gift taxation. Summarizing, the relationship between federal law and local law in regard to the requirements for a valid gift may be stated as follows: Local law dictates whether a transfer of *property rights* has in fact been made, irrespective of taxability. On the other hand, federal tax law, in conjunction with local law, specifies whether a gift subject to taxation has been made. Federal law also spells out rules relating to the taxation of specific types of gifts, such as those in connection with powers of appointment, life insurance, joint ownership, and disclaimers. Gift tax aspects of each of these dealings is discussed later in this chapter. Issues related to who is subject to gift tax and what is the value of the gift are described next.

Who Is Subject to Gift Tax?

Under federal law, a gift subject to gift taxation applies to *individual U.S. citizens or residents*, regardless of where the property is located, whether the transfer is direct or indirect, real or personal, intangible or tangible. U.S. gift tax law also applies to *nonresident aliens* but only with regard to transfers of real property and tangible personal property situated within the U.S.[2]

Aspects of Taxable Gifts.

Valuation of gift. The value of the gift for tax purposes is its fair market value at the date of the gift. Any consideration received in exchange is subtracted in determining the gross value of the gift.

EXAMPLE 7 - 1. If Mom "sells" to son a $25,000 automobile for $1, Mom has made a gross gift in the amount of $24,999 and a taxable gift of $14,999.

Measuring the consideration received in exchange. To be recognized, consideration received in exchange must be measurable in money or money's worth. If it is not reducible to money or money's worth, it will be disregarded.

EXAMPLE 7 - 2. In the prior example, consideration received by Mom is still only $1, even though son gave her incredible amounts of love and affection before and after the gift, and even though son had graduated college and quit smoking, achievements Mom required as conditions for the gift.

The above example illustrates a situation where a gift is subject to gift taxation despite the fact that local law may view the exchange of consideration to be equal, and donative intent, therefore, to be nonexistent.

Some gifts are difficult to value. Gifts may be extremely difficult to value.

EXAMPLE 7 - 3. Last year, Dad guaranteed a bank loan made to Son. The IRS takes the position that by transferring a valuable economic benefit on behalf of Son, Dad made a completed gift, measured by the value of the guarantee, an amount that clearly would be difficult to value.[3] Moreover, if Son defaults on the loan, any amounts which Dad pays on the obligation will *also* be gifts subject to gift tax, without any offset for the earlier gift. Thus, the total of taxable gifts could exceed the amount of the guarantee.[4]

Fortunately, in the case of property settlements between divorcing spouses, federal law no longer requires a determination of the total value of the consideration exchanged by each spouse. Transfers of property subject to a written divorce or separation agreement are deemed to be made for full and adequate consideration even when it is clear that the "exchange" is not for money or money's worth.[5]

Gifts versus sales. Practically speaking, larger sales between *related parties* may be treated with suspicion by the Internal Revenue Service Its agents may contend that a gift rather than a sale has been made. However, larger sales made in the ordinary course of business and/or between unrelated parties are presumed not to be gifts.

EXAMPLE 7 - 4. Herb, owner of a retail drugstore, sells his aging delivery pickup truck to Karl, a *stranger*, who read about the truck in the classified section of the newspaper. Karl paid Herb $4,200 and promptly took out a similar ad and sold the truck three days later for $6,700. Herb has made a bad bargain, but not a gift, because the truck was sold in an *at arms-length* transaction.

EXAMPLE 7 - 5. Same facts as the prior example, except that Herb, who had already made gifts in excess of $10,000 to his son, Jerry, sold him the car for $4,200. Jerry then advertised and sold the car for $6,700. Herb may have great difficulty establishing to the satisfaction of the IRS that the deal was at arm's length, inasmuch as it was transacted between relatives.

Below-market dividend yield results in gift. Gifts can arise in the context of family oriented closely held business settings. Consider this fairly involved situation.

EXAMPLE 7 - 6. Two years ago MacKay created the MCK Inc., transferring assets to it in exchange for 300 shares of voting common stock, and 6,000 shares of voting convertible preferred stock that pays a $3 dividend on a par value of $900. The $3 dividend is a yield of only one third of one percent. Preferred dividend yields are generally much higher than that. MacKay gave the common stock to his children. He has continued to hold voting control of MCK. He will be deemed to have made annual gifts to his children of the difference between the dividends paid and the amount commensurate with the prevailing market rate, assuming MCK was capable of making those higher payments. MacKay could have prevented these gifts, either by initially issuing higher yielding preferred, liquidating the corporation, or by converting his preferred shares into common shares.[6] The first year, the comparable rate for preferred stock was 12% and MCK was capable of paying this rate. That year MacKay's gift to his children is deemed to be $630,000 [6,000 * ((12% * $900) - $3)].

Filing and Payment Requirements

When a return must be filed. In general, a gift tax return is due when the donor's income tax return is due (or if the donor is not required to file an income tax return, then when it would have been due had the donor been so required). Usually, this means April 15 of the year following the gift. An extension to file one's income taxes is also an automatic extension to file one's gift taxes. A gift tax return must be filed by any donor who, in any calendar year, gives:

- more than $10,000 to *any* donee (other than to a spouse or charity), or
- a gift of a *future interest* regardless of how small the value, or
- total gifts exceeding $100,000 to a *non U.S. citizen spouse*, or
- a gift for which spouses want to elect *gift splitting* even if after the split each gift is less than $10,000.

The terms *future interest* gift and *gift splitting* will be described shortly.

Who files. Only *people* file gift tax returns. For example, if a partnership or a corporation makes a gift, the individual partners or stockholders are ordinarily considered the donors, liable for filing the return and paying the tax. In the case of a gift subject to gift taxation of property from an irrevocable trust or an estate, the donor would ordinarily be the person acting as trustee or executor, but only in exercising a general power of appointment. On the other hand, in the case of a revocable living trust that makes a gift subject to taxation, the grantor would be treated as the donor. If a donor dies before filing a return, the donor's executor must file. The return is due April 15 of the year following the calendar year in which the gift occurred.

Who pays. The donor is responsible for paying the gift tax;[7] the *donee* is not subject to either gift tax or income tax on the gift.[8] However there is transferee liability if the donor fails to pay the tax. This means that any donee can be forced to pay the gift tax, up to the value of the gift received, if the donor fails to pay.

Net gift. Some clients, however, might wish to make a *net gift*, that is, to arrange in advance for the *donee* to be responsible for paying the gift tax. The

Supreme Court has ruled such a transaction to be part sale, part gift, causing the donor to realize taxable income to the extent that the gift tax paid by the donee exceeds the donor's adjusted basis.[9] However, other advantages may still make the net gift attractive.

Deductible Gifts

Two types of gifts are fully deductible, and three that are excluded from being treated as gifts, with the result in either case (whether deductible or excluded) of avoiding their inclusion as taxable gifts.

Charitable gifts. First, gifts to qualified charities are fully deductible from gross gifts for donors who are U.S. citizens or residents.[10] We'll see in Chapter 14 that gifts to charity in any one year are also deductible from *income tax*, but only up to certain percentages of adjusted gross income. Chapter 14 will discuss strategies for charitable gifting in detail.

Interspousal gifts. Second, under the unlimited marital deduction, gifts to a *U.S. citizen spouse* are fully deductible, provided that they are not terminable interests.[11] However, even terminable interest gifts might qualify for the marital deduction by using a gift QTIP election.[12] For an analysis of terminable interests, see the discussion on the estate tax marital deduction in Chapter 6, and the material on marital trusts in Chapter 11 and 12. Lifetime gifting between spouses is analyzed in Chapter 13.

Since 1988, only the first $100,000 per year in gifts to a *non U.S. citizen spouse* escape gift taxation.[13] In addition, all amounts of future interest gifts (see below) to a noncitizen spouse are subject to tax. Thus there is no marital deduction for gifts above $100,000 per year to a non U.S. citizen spouse. The annual exclusion and the concept of present and future interest gifts are discussed in the next section.

Gifts for tuition and medical care. Third and fourth, qualified payments in any amount made directly to an educational institution for tuition and payments in any amount made directly to a provider of medical care on behalf of any individual are fully excluded from being taxable gifts. Two things to emphasis here: the transfers must be *directly* to the providers, and not to the individuals themselves, and the person benefitting by the payments does *not* have to be related to the donor.[14]

Gifts to Political Organizations. Fifth, gifts are not taxable if made to a "political organization (within the meaning of section 527(e)(1)) for the use of such organization."[15]

Gift Tax Annual Exclusion and the Present Interest Requirement

The first $10,000 of the total annual value of gifts of a *present interest* to each donee is excluded from the donor's taxable gifts.[16] Note that the donor and donee do not have to be related. Present interests are those where "enjoyment" can start immediately whereas future interests, by the terms of the transfer, have the possession and enjoyment delayed.

> EXAMPLE 7 - 7. This year, Mom, a widow, gave Daughter a corporate bond valued at $24,300. Even though Daughter may not collect the par value until maturity, and even though the periodic interest income is payable in the future, the gift is of a present interest and qualifies for the annual exclusion. Daughter has a *present right to enjoy* the bond, for example, by selling it. Assuming that Mom, made no other gifts to Daughter during the year, the taxable value of the gift is $14,300, i.e., $24,300 - $10,000.

> EXAMPLE 7 - 8. Suppose, Mom transferred the $24,300 bond to an irrevocable trust, whereby the trustee was to deliver the bond, and any accrued income, to Daughter in one year. The gift, which is reportable for the year the bond is transferred into the trust, is a gift of a future interest. It will not qualify for the annual exclusion because, by the terms of the transfer, the enjoyment is delayed for a period of time. The taxable gift is $24,300.

Congress in 1932 chose to deny the annual exclusion for gifts of future interests for three reasons: (1) future interests are often difficult to value; (2) the number of donees of a future interest is often indeterminable at date of gift; and (3) future interests are often created to avoid taxes.

Gifts into trust. Most problems regarding future interest gifts arise in the context of trusts.

> EXAMPLE 7 - 9. T creates an irrevocable living trust, funding it with dividend-paying common stock worth $8,000. Under the terms of the trust, the trustee may *accumulate or distribute the income* to B for 10 years. At the expiration of 10 years,

the trust terminates and all principal and accumulated income is payable to B, or if B is dead, to B's estate. Assuming B is currently an adult, T has made a gift of a future interest of $8,000, for which no annual exclusion will be available because B's possession and enjoyment may be delayed.

No annual exclusion means, of course, that absent any deductions, the gift will be entirely taxable, such that part or all of the donor's unified credit will have to be used. Further, at the donor's death, the value of the taxable gift is added to the estate tax base, which may raise the donor's marginal estate tax rate. Thus, the client may prefer a disposition that, as in the next example, is at least partly sheltered by the annual exclusion.

EXAMPLE 7 - 10. Altering the facts of the prior example a little bit, assume that instead of being allowed to accumulate the income, the trustee is required to *pay all income* to B, an adult, at least annually, and the remainder goes to R at the end of the 10 year term. Upon creation of the trust, two interests arose: a *present interest in the income* for 10 years and a remainder interest. At ten percent, the present value of an income interest for a 10 year period equals .614457 times the value of the stock. The product of .614457 * $8,000 is $4,916, which represents the portion of the gift that is considered a present interest qualifying for the annual exclusion up to a maximum for any one donee of $10,000. Hence, the total taxable gift equals $3,084 [$8,000-$4,916], the value of the future (remainder) interest which does not qualify for the annual exclusion.

2503(c) Trusts. There is an exception to the present interest requirement for gifts in trust of future interests on behalf of minors found in IRC §2503(c). This Code section allows the annual exclusion even though there is no present interest provided the trust follows all the requirements of the section. In the absence of §2503(c), grantors might be encouraged to make outright gifts to minors, a practice which many argue would run contrary to public policy. A further discussion of gifting to minors will be found in Chapter 13. These trusts are referred to as *2503(c) trusts.* To qualify for §2503(c), the provisions of the trust must specify that (1) the income and principal may be spent for the benefit of the minor before age 21, and (2) any amount not so spent will either pass to the minor when he or she reaches age 21, and (3) if the minor dies before age 21, the corpus and accrued income must either be payable to the minor's estate or be subject to the minor's general power to appoint.

EXAMPLE 7 - 11. Stephanie transfers $10,000 in property into an irrevocable trust whose trustee is permitted to expend principal and income for the benefit of her minor son. When son reaches age 21, the trust terminates and all principal and accumulated income will be distributed to him. If he dies before the trust terminates the principal and accumulated income is subject to his general power to appoint it, but if he fails to appoint it, then the corpus will go to his sister Sue's trust if it has not then terminated, and if it has terminated, then directly to Sue. Although Stephanie has actually made a gift of a future interest, under the exception of §2503(c) the entire value of the property will qualify for the annual exclusion.

The Kiddie Tax

There is really no appropriate time to discuss a nasty little wrinkle that Congress added to the law several years ago, but having introduced one kind of trust (§2503(c) Trusts) for minors, this is as good as any. All unearned income of children under age 14 in excess of a statutory amount is taxed at the parent's marginal rate. The amount was originally $1,000 but, due to indexing, it has climbed to $1,300 in 1995. Of that amount, the first $650 a standard deduction for one claimed by another (e.g., claimed as a dependent on the parents' income tax return) and the next $650 is taxed at the child's base rate of 15 percent.[17]

The amounts $650 and $1,300 (indexed, but not necessarily annually) are reported on a separate return, using IRS Form 8615. For convenience, the parent's return may include the income of a child under 14 having only dividend and interest income less than $5,000. "Piggyback" reporting on the parent's return (attaching Form 8614) has some drawbacks. First, instead of the above $650 and $1,300 amounts, a lower unindexed $500 and $1,000 must be used. Second, the child can't take advantage of certain other deductions, such as charitable donations and the additional standard deduction for being blind. Finally, using the parent's return increases their adjusted gross income, which in effect raises the threshold amount used to determine cutbacks in itemized deductions and personal exemptions, as discussed earlier.

The source of the child's unearned income is immaterial; excess unearned income is taxed at the parent's rate even though they were not the original source of the property producing that income.

EXAMPLE 7 - 12. Dale and Josette's joint taxable income in the current year is $60,000, putting them in the 28 percent marginal rate bracket. Their 12-year-old daughter Lara has $2,100 in unearned income, including $1,300 in dividends from stock received as a gift from Dale's parents, and $800 in interest from a bank savings account, the deposits of which originated from earned income (compensation) to Lara when she was a newspaper delivery girl. Dale and Josette elect to report Lara's income on a separate return. Of the first $1,300 of unearned income, $650 will be tax-free, and $650 will be taxed at 15%. The amount $800, which is the excess of $2,100 over $1,300, will be taxed at the parents' marginal rate of 28%. Lara's total tax will be $321.50.

EXAMPLE 7 - 13. Based on the facts of the example immediately above, if Dale and Josette report Lara's income on their own return, Lara's total tax will be $383. The first $500 will be tax-free, and $500 will be taxed at 15 percent, the remainder, $1,100, will be taxed at 28 percent, for a total tax of $383. Therefore, using reporting Lara's income on the parents' return increases the tax by $61.50.

This tax has come to be called the "kiddie tax," and has the effect of moving the federal government a step closer toward taxing the family as a single economic unit.

EXAMPLE 7 - 14. Continuing the prior examples, if Lara turns age 14 the following year during which time she has exactly the same income, her total tax will drop to $217.50, since the $800 will also be taxed at her own rate of 15%.

Gift Splitting

Gift splitting treats a gift of the property owned by one spouse as if it were made one-half by each spouse. It is conceptually similar to federal spousal income splitting on a joint income tax return. For example, if one spouse earns taxable *income* of $48,000 and the other spouse only earns $2,000, higher income taxes will be paid if each spouse files a separate return reporting their respective amounts than if both file a joint return reporting $50,000. In effect, a joint return will result in a tax which approximates applying the rate schedule to one-half of their combined income (i.e., $25,000), and then multiplying the tax by two. Total income taxes are lower for several reasons, including the fact that progressively higher marginal rates may be avoided and, that more importantly, the spouse with the lower income amount might not otherwise be able to use the full benefits of the standard deduction and the personal exemption.

Under federal gift tax law, spouses may also *split a gift*. By making an election, with the consent of the non-donor spouse, on the gift tax return, a gift by the donor spouse of his or her *individually owned property* will be treated as if made one-half by each of them.[18] Thus, one spouse can enjoy the benefit of two annual exclusions (and two unified credits, if needed) to cover what is really just one gift.

EXAMPLE 7 - 15. Wife wishes to give $18,000 of her own money to a nephew. Assuming no other gifts and no gift splitting, wife's taxable gift, after the annual exclusion, will be $8,000. Thus, she may either have to pay a gift tax, or at least use up a portion of her unified credit. Alternatively, wife can *split* this gift with her husband, if he is willing, and each will then be considered to have made a gross gift of $9,000. After each donor's annual exclusion, there will be no taxable gift by either spouse.

To make the split gift election the consent of the non-donor spouse is required and two gift tax returns (one by each spouse) must be filed by spouses if, after the split, the values exceed the annual exclusion. Only the donor spouse needs to file a gift tax return if the split brings the gifts below the annual exclusion. There is a place on the donor spouse's tax return for the non-donor to sign, affirming his or her consent to the election.

EXAMPLE 7 - 16. Billy and Millie are married parents. This year Millie gave $20,000 of her individually owned property to their son. Assuming no other gifts, if the couple agree to gift splitting, only Millie will be required to file a gift tax return; Billy's consent will appear on Millie's return.

Gift splitting is used only for individually owned property since co-owned property is, by its nature, already "split," making the election unnecessary. This is especially true of community property which is always owned in equal shares (i.e., 50% each) by the spouses.

EXAMPLE 7 - 17. In prior example, had the $20,000 been community property, jointly held property, or an in-common interest in property (here assume 50%-50%), the gift would be considered made one-half by each spouse. Since the value of each spouse's half interest is $10,000, neither has to file a gift tax return.

EXAMPLE 7 - 18. If a couple gave $28,000 in 50%-50% concurrently held property to their nephew, each will have made a gross gift of $14,000 and a taxable gift of $4,000. Again, there is no gift splitting. Each spouse must file a gift tax return because each gift exceeds the annual exclusion.

Somewhat oddly, if a split gift results in the payment of a gift tax and the donor-spouse dies within three years of the gift, the *entire* gift tax paid, not just the one-half, is grossed up in the donor's gross estate.[19]

EXAMPLE 7 - 19. This year, from his property, Charles gave cash worth $150,000 to the couple's son and stock worth $150,000 to their daughter. Charles' wife, Susan, gave $9,000 of her property to their son. The effects on reportable gross gifts, annual exclusions, and taxable gifts of the decision whether to split the gifts or not is shown in the table below. If no split gift election is made, Susan will not have to file a Form 709, since her gift is covered by the annual exclusion. If gift splitting is elected, the taxable amount on both returns will be identical.

| | Without Gift Splitting | | With Gift Splitting | |
	Charles' Form 709	Susan's Form 709	Charles' Form 709	Susan's Form 709
Gross Gifts:		*(not filed)		
To Son	$150,000	$9,000	$79,500	$79,500
To Daughter	$150,000	$0	$75,000	$75,000
Total per return	$300,000	$9,000	$154,500	$154,500
Total per family	$309,000		$309,000	
Gift to Son	$10,000	$9,000	$10,000	$10,000
Gift to Daughter	$10,000	$0	$10,000	$10,000
Total per return	$20,000	$9,000	$20,000	$20,000
Total per family	$29,000		$40,000	
Total per return	$280,000	$0	$134,500	$134,500
Total per family	$280,000		$269,000	

Electing gift splitting reduces the family taxable gifts by $11,000 [$280,000 - $269,000]. The reduction is the result of the additional $11,000 in total family annual exclusions, since with the election Susan is allowed $20,000, rather than just $9,000. Gift splitting can mean lower gift taxes, or, as in this example, it may just result in using up less of the parent's total unified credit.

Completing the analogy with income splitting, gift splitting of individually owned property can lower gift taxes because it can permit the deduction of two full annual exclusions each year, even though just one gift is given and, for large gifts, it utilizes both spouses' unified credits.

Powers of Appointment

General power holders and taxable events. Gift taxation of powers of subject to gift tax, and only the *donee-holder* of the power will be taxed.[20] Of course, when the general power was created, the donor of the power (if created by gift) or the donor's estate (if created at death by will or trust) may have paid transfer taxes, unless the transfer was not subject to tax because of the annual exclusion, a marital deduction, or the application of the unified credit. For instance, if a donor placed property in an irrevocable trust which gives the income beneficiary a general power over 25% of the trust corpus, it would be the entire property placed in trust that would be the gift, not just the 25% subject to the general power.

Three events during the holder's lifetime can trigger gift tax to the holder of a general power of appointment: exercise by the holder in favor of someone else, release by the holder, or lapse of the holder's right to exercise or release the power.

> EXAMPLE 7 - 20. Dad transfers property into an irrevocable trust, with income to Mom for her life, then remainder to anyone Mom chooses during her lifetime or in her will. The trust provides that their three children will share the remainder if Mom does not exercise her power to appoint. Although Dad, as donor, created a general power of appointment in Mom, the holder, he did not make a §2514 transfer because he did not exercise, release, or let lapse, a power. Only the holder of a power can exercise, release, or let a power lapse.

In the above example, Dad would be treated as having made a gift (completed transfer for less than full consideration) because his transfer was into an irrevocable trust.

Exercise and release by holder. Exercise of a general power in favor of someone other than the holder, or the release by the holder of a general power, will be treated as a transfer subject to taxation.

> EXAMPLE 7 - 21. Continuing the prior example, Mom died recently. Since Mom held a general power at the time of her death, the value of the trust is included in her estate, whether she exercised the power by appointing it to a friend or failed to exercise it and allowed the remainder to go to the children as the takers by default.

Lapse and 5 & 5 powers. The general rule is that the lapse of a general power is treated as a transfer from the holder to whomever is the taker by default. However, §2041(b)(2) creates an exception that allows the lapse, *during the life* of the holder of certain general powers to occur without the lapse being deemed a taxable gift. The exception applies to the lapse during the holder's lifetime of a power, but only to the extent that what could have been transferred (but for the lapse) did not exceed the greater of $5,000 or 5% of the value of the property out of which the exercise of the power could have been satisfied. Powers which are drafted to make use of this exception permit the holder to withdraw property from a trust up to the greater of $5,000 or 5% of the value of the trust corpus. These are referred to as "5 & 5" powers. Usually the right is given such that it can be exercised annually, but failure to exercise the right in any year will not increase the dollar amount or the percentage for the next year. In other words, it is a noncumulative annually lapsing right.

Lapsing powers are often placed in irrevocable trusts created for the benefit of minors in order to obtain the annual exclusion for the parent-donor. The power of the child to withdraw an amount each time the parents add to the trust creates a present interest for the child-donee even though the power to withdraw lapses after a short time, as set forth in the trust, and even though there is a strong expectation that the child will not exercise the right to withdraw. This demand right is referred to as a "Crummey demand right" or as a "Crummey power." Trusts for this type of provision are called *Crummey Trusts,* and when established for minor children, they may be called *Minors' Demand Trusts.*

EXAMPLE 7 - 22. Grantor has set up a minors' demand trust for three grandchildren. Each grandchild can claim up to the lesser of one third of the amount transferred into the trust that year or the annual exclusion amount. If a grandchild does not demand out his or her share, the right to claim the gift lapses at the close of the year (with demand rights for gifts made late in the year extended to a minimum of thirty days). If no demand is made during the demand period, the transfer is locked into corpus and by other trust terms stays there until the youngest of the three grandchildren reaches age thirty. If a grandchild dies before termination of the trust, his or her share goes to the other grandchildren who do survive. If initially the trust is funded with less than $15,000 and none of the beneficiaries demand their share, no gift from the beneficiaries is deemed to have been made by the lapse because of the §2041(b)(2) exception.

EXAMPLE 7 - 23. If the initial transfer was $24,000, then each child would be deemed to have made a transfer to the extent his or her share lapsed and exceeded the "5 & 5" limits. Thus, each grandchild will be deemed to have transferred $3,000 to the trust. Since there are the two other grandchildren who will be the remaindermen if a grandchild dies, each grandchild will be deemed to have made a gift of a contingent future interest that vests when the youngest child reaches age thirty. The value of the gift from each grandchild can be determined actuarially. For each child, it would be based upon the probability of that grandchild dying before the termination of the trust. Obviously, the gift is very small in value considering the unlikelihood of the event which would cause the gift to vest in the other children (the death of a child before the youngest turns thirty) and the fact that the gift is one of a future interest, since enjoyment upon lapse is postponed until the termination of the trust. Because the gift is one of a future interest, no annual exclusion is available and a gift tax return would have to be filed for each grandchild.

The adverse result of creating lapsing powers of appointment which exceed the "5 & 5" limit is not the gift tax generated, since the gift value is usually extremely small, but rather the retained life estate implications. If a beneficiary has a retained life estate in any property that the beneficiary has previously transferred, whether into trust or otherwise, §2036 causes it to be included in his or her estate at death. The Regulations make it clear that the lapsing of powers which exceed the 5% limit are simply cumulated,[21] there is no attempt to apply sophisticated mathematics to take into account the fact that each subsequent release of a power includes a release of a portion of the trust previously released. Thus the mathematics are kept simple but this works against the taxpayer (the holder of a power, greater than 5%, who lets the power lapse) in that it causes greater inclusion in the estate of a beneficiary-holder who dies before the trust terminates.

One other comment before an example to further clarify, the "5 & 5" exception does not apply to lapses which take place at the death of the holder. Hence, a noncumulative annually lapsing power, to annually claim up to 5% of the corpus of a trust, which was not exercised during the holder's last year of life, would cause 5% of the DOD value of said trust to be included in the holder's estate.

EXAMPLE 7 - 24. Upon his death in 1984, Benny's father established a trust which gave Benny income for life, and a noncumulative annually lapsing general power of appointment over a portion of the trust. At Benny's death, the trust terminates and the remaining corpus goes to Benny's sister, Rachael. At all times relevant to this example the value of the trust remained constant at $1,000,000. Benny died in 1988, never having exercised the power. If the power was exercisable over 5% of the trust, then 5% ($50,000) of the trust value would be included in Benny's estate, even though none of the lifetime lapses of the power were deemed to be transfers.

EXAMPLE 7 - 25. If the power had been over 8% of the trust (instead of 5%), then for the years 1984, 1985, 1986 and 1987 each lapse is treated as though 3% (that which exceeded 5%) was transferred by Benny to the trust with Benny retaining a life estate in the transfers. §2036 would cause 12% of the trust to be included in Benny's estate and, since Benny died with an unexercised general power over 8% of the trust, §2041 causes another 8% to be included. Thus, a total of 20% of the value of the trust is included in Benny's estate. *** *Query 7 - 1. How much would be included if Benny had been given a 15% annually lapsing power?*

Ascertainable standard, adverse party exceptions. Similar to estate tax law, a power of appointment to name oneself, one's creditors, one's estate or the creditors of one's estate are not treated as a general powers if the power is subject to an ascertainable standard of health, education, maintenance or support, or if it is exercisable only in conjunction with either the creator of the power or an adverse party. Ascertainable standard language is commonly used in trust instruments to give flexibility, yet keep a trust out of the holder's estate.

Life Insurance

A taxable gift of life insurance can arise either during the insured's lifetime or at the insured's death.

Assignment. During the insured's *lifetime*, an assignment of ownership rights in the policy may constitute a taxable gift equal to the value of the rights assigned. Ordinarily, a donor will assign all rights to a policy, and their total value is considered to be the policy's terminal value.

> EXAMPLE 7 - 26. Joe assigns his life insurance policy to his son. The policy has a face value of $600,000 and a value for gift tax purposes of $87,000. Joe has made a present interest gross gift of $87,000 and a taxable gift of $77,000.

In contrast to the assignment of ownership interests, the simple *naming of a beneficiary* by the owner does not constitute a taxable gift since no property rights are transferred; the beneficiary receives a "mere expectancy," contingent upon the owner's keeping the policy in force and not changing the beneficiary designation.

At insured's death: the unholy trinity. A taxable gift of life insurance can arise at an insured's *death*. This will occur when the insured, owner, and beneficiary are all different parties. Sometimes this arrangement is referred to as the unholy trinity.

> EXAMPLE 7 - 27. Wife purchases with separate property a $100,000 life insurance policy on husband's life, naming son beneficiary. Upon husband's death, wife will be held to have made a $100,000 gift to son. Solution, wife should have given the policy to son prior to the husband's death.

> EXAMPLE 7 - 28. Changing the facts in the preceding example, assume that husband purchased and owned the policy until his death, paying the premiums entirely with jointly owned funds (or with community property). At husband's death, wife will be held to have made a $50,000 gift to son, reflecting her one-half interest in the proceeds. In some community property states, the wife may be able to legally claim half of the proceeds, especially if she can show that she was unaware of the policy's existence or unaware that her husband had named someone, other than herself, the beneficiary.

In the above example, the other $50,000 will be includable in husband's gross estate under §2042. Can you see why? Because husband/decedent/ insured had a $50,000 incident of ownership in the policy at his death. We will see in Chapter 15 that estate planners typically avoid this tax trap by selecting the same person to be both owner and beneficiary on a life insurance policy held on the life of another.

Gifts of Property in Joint Tenancy Ownership

Ordinarily, gifts are made when a fee simple owner of property transfers his or her entire interest to the donee. Sometimes, however, a donor transfers only a fraction of the total interest owned. For example, a donor can transfer his or her property into joint tenancy ownership with others.

General rule. The actual moment that a gift into joint tenancy occurs for gift tax purposes depends upon the nature of the property. In general, ownership and possession of most types of property are considered transferred when documents evidencing a transfer of title are *executed* and *delivered* or *recorded*. Where there are co-owners the donee need not physically take possession of the document of title but need only acknowledge acceptance of the gift. Thus, acquisition of a joint interest by the donee usually arises when the donor simultaneously acquires the asset and names the donee co-owner, or when the donor adds the donee's name as a co-owner of property already owned by the donor. Either way, a gift will occur at that time, and the value of the gift will be the net value of the property interest transferred at the time of the gift. In the examples that follow assume that the donee accepts the gift.

EXAMPLE 7 - 29. Uncle Charlie buys an automobile for $30,000 cash, *taking title* in joint tenancy with his nephew Brad. Charlie has made a gift of $15,000 to Brad in the year of purchase.

EXAMPLE 7 - 30. Changing the facts in the prior example just a bit, assume that Charlie bought the car two years ago for $48,000, taking title as an individual. This year, when the car is worth $30,000, Charlie instructs the motor vehicle bureau to *change the title* to read: "Charlie Jones and Brad Smith, as joint tenants." This year, Charlie has made a gift to Brad of $15,000.

EXAMPLE 7 - 31. This year, Dad purchased a building for $120,000, taking title in joint tenancy with his five adult sons. This year, Dad has made a gift of $20,000 to each son.

Two exceptions. There are two principal exceptions to the rule that the inclusion of others as co-tenant for less than full consideration results in an immediate gift. First, in the case of a *joint tenancy bank account*, in most states a gift arises upon withdrawal of the funds by the donee, not upon creation of the donee's interest. The statutes of a few states, such as New York, however, presume that a gift into a savings account arises at time of deposit, thereby giving rise to immediate federal gift taxation. Second, for a joint tenancy *U.S. government savings bond*, a gift, if any, arises when the bond is redeemed. Thus, if the initial purchaser redeems the entire bond, no gift has occurred.

EXAMPLE 7 - 32. On June 1 of last year, Mom deposited $40,000 in a savings account held jointly with Son. He withdrew $6,800 on February 1 of this year. In most states, Mom will be considered to have made a gift to Son, but not until February 1, this year. The gross gift amount is $6,800.

EXAMPLE 7 - 33. Dad purchased a $20,000 EE savings bond years ago, taking title with his son as joint tenants. At the bond's maturity next month, if Dad redeems the entire bond, there will be no gift. If son redeems the entire bond, Dad will have made a gift this year to son of $20,000. If both redeem $10,000 each, Dad will have made a gift this year to son of $10,000.

Disclaimers

Suppose, for some reason, that the intended donee does not want to accept a sizable gift made under a will, trust instrument, or other document. Inasmuch as the unified transfer tax system will often include in the donee's transfer tax base any gift property received by the donee and later transferred to another during lifetime or at death, a donee might wish to refuse the gift, to minimize his or her own future transfer taxes. Section 2518 allows the donee, was to "disclaim" a gift in such a way that it will be as though the gift was never made, and in the case of a bequest, as though disclaimant predeceased the decedent-donor. In order to disclaim and have this favorable result, the following requirements must be met:

1. The disclaimer must be "an irrevocable and unqualified refusal...to accept" the interest,
2. The refusal must be in writing,
3. The refusal must be received within nine months after the later of:
   a) the date on which the transfer creating the interest was made, or
   b) the day on which the person disclaiming reaches age 21,
4. The intended donee cannot have accepted any interest in the benefits; and
5. As a result of the refusal, the interest will pass, without the disclaiming person's direction, to someone else.

With regard to requirement 4, acts indicating "acceptance" include using the property, accepting dividends, interest or rents from the property, and directing others to act with regard to the property. However, acceptance will not be found in cases where the disclaimant merely accepted title to property, or merely because title vested immediately in the disclaimant on death of the decedent, as in the case of survivorship under joint tenancy. Requirement 4 is not applicable to benefits received by a person under 21 years of age. Section 2518(b)(4)(A) creates a special privilege for the spouse of a donor or decedent, she may disclaim and still retain benefits in the disclaimed property. This is used in estate plans that call for property disclaimed by the surviving spouse to be place in a trust that gives her (the disclaimant) a life estate and the power to withdraw limited by an ascertainable standard.

Meeting all of these requirements is particularly important because failure to meet any one could result in two completed gifts subject to taxation.

EXAMPLE 7 - 34. Dad gives his adult Son his vacation bungalow, completing the necessary transfer of title. After spending a weekend there, Son transfers title back to Dad, refusing the gift. Dad resumes vacationing there. Son's act is not a valid disclaimer because he *had already accepted* a benefit. Therefore, two successive completed gifts were actually made, first by Dad and then by Son.

EXAMPLE 7 - 35. During their life, husband and wife owned their home in joint tenancy. Within nine months of husband's death, wife acts to disclaim her survivorship interest. Her disclaimer is not invalid merely because her survivorship interest vested immediately at his death and she continued to live in the house and pay all expenses and related taxes prior to making the disclaimer, provided that while husband was alive the tenancy could be unilaterally partitioned.[22]

EXAMPLE 7 - 36. Mom died, disposing of her entire $1.8 million estate by will. It read, "to Dad if living, and if not then to our children." Within nine months of Mom's death, Dad, before receiving any interest or benefit in the property, presented a written refusal of $600,000 of the gift to the executor of Mom's estate. Dad has made a valid disclaimer, and he will not be considered to have ever owned that portion of the property, which will pass by the terms of the will to the children. This will utilize Mon's unified credit and reduce Dad's taxable estate.

Some commentators have maintained that a disclaimer should be taxed as a completed gift for the same reason that the lapse of a power of appointment by the holder is treated as a taxable gift. They contend that by disclaiming, the disclaimant in effect relinquished a vested right to receive property, which passed instead to someone else. Others support the disclaimer's favorable tax treatment on policy grounds, saying that it is a sufficiently valuable method for correcting inefficient transfers in wills and trust instruments to justify special tax treatment. Fortunately, current law is on the side of the latter group.[23]

Chapters 12 and 18 will demonstrate several other ways that disclaimers used in estate planing.

Miscellaneous Gift Tax Applications

Reciprocal trusts revisited. In Chapter 6, in the section on §2036, we saw that *reciprocal trusts* were subject to estate taxes. They may also be subject to gift taxation.

EXAMPLE 7 - 37. Mr. Garbanzo gives $10,000 to his son and $10,000 to Mrs.

Ceci's daughter, and at the same time Mrs. Ceci gives $10,000 to her daughter and $10,000 to Mr. Garbanzo's son. The IRS will treat the "mirror images" cross-family transfers as if they were made to each donor's own child. Thus, each parent will be treated as having made a $20,000 gross gift to their own child.[24]

Multiple taxation of transfers. Certain transfers may be subject to both gift tax and estate tax.

EXAMPLE 7 - 38. Pope, age 55, transfers $100,000 in property into an irrevocable trust, retaining a life estate in the income at a time when the §7520 rate is 8%. Pope's son is the remainderman. Pope has made a completed gross gift this year of $22,601, the current value of the remainder (based on Table B (8%), i.e., .22601 x $100,000). As a gift of a future interest it does not qualify for the annual exclusion. At Pope's death, the date of death value of the entire trust corpus will be includable in his gross estate under §2036(a). The adjusted taxable gift is reduced to zero and a credit for any gift tax payable is allowed to prevent double taxation. Of course, if Pope's taxable gifts never exceeded the unified credit shelter amount, no gift taxes would have been paid during his lifetime.

Where transferred property comes back into the gross estate because of a string being attached or because of the transfer falls under one of the §2035(d)(2) exceptions (transfer of life insurance or the severing of a string), the earlier gift will not be considered an adjusted taxable gift for purpose of calculation of the donee's estate tax. The last sentence of §2001(b) defines "adjusted taxable gifts" as being post-1976 taxable gifts "other than gifts which are includable in the gross estate of the decedent." The gift tax payable credit (§2001(b)(2)) is still available because the gift taxes would indeed have been paid on such gifts (if the tentative tax exceeded the available unified credit) and the property subject to the prior gift does enter into the estate tax calculation by being included in the gross estate as if no gift had ever taken place. The credit is the amount of gift taxes payable, not the gift taxes actually paid, see subparagraph (2) of §2001 for the wording that limits the credit to the amount of taxes that would have been paid if the rate schedule at the time of the gift had been the same as the rate at the time of death.

Basis Rules

The manner in which one acquires property determines the owner's basis in the property. Basis, of course, is important for two reasons: 1) basis is the starting point for determining depreciation for depreciable property; and, 2) upon sale, it is the difference between the price (net amount realized) and the adjusted basis that determines the amount of gain or loss for income tax purposes;

Gain and Loss The gain or loss realized from the sale of property is calculated by subtracting an asset's *adjusted basis* from the *amount realized*:

Gain or Loss = Amount Realized - Adjusted Basis

EXAMPLE 7 - 39. The realized gain on sale of 100 shares of common stock having an adjusted basis of $13,000 and sold for $16,000, net of selling commissions, equals $3,000. Had the stock been sold for $11,000, a loss in the amount of $2,000 would be realized.

Amount realized is defined as the fair market value of all money or property received, less selling expense such as commissions.

EXAMPLE 7 - 40. In the prior example, the $16,000 and $11,000 sales proceeds could have been in the form of cash or in kind. Alternatively, the buyer could have canceled an existing debt owed by the seller. Hence, if the buyer actually paid $6,000 cash and assigned to the seller title to his $8,000 automobile and also tore up a $2,000 IOU held on the buyer-debtor, the total amount realized is still $16,000.

Adjusted basis is defined in the Code as the "basis" that is "adjusted." The initial basis for an asset that is *purchased* is its cost. Adjustments to basis include items that reduce basis, such as allowance for depreciation, depletion, and obsolescence. Adjustment items that increase basis include capital expenditures for improvement.

EXAMPLE 7 - 41. In the earlier example, the adjusted basis of $13,000 was probably simply the original purchase price of the stock, net of the trading commission. However, had the asset been a machine used in the taxpayer's business, adjusted basis would likely reflect its current book (depreciated) value, including all capital improvements made subsequent to its acquisition. Hence, the $13,000 adjusted basis for the machine could, for example, be the net result of a $27,000 original purchase price, less $17,000 in accumulated depreciation, plus

$3,000 in capital improvements.

Recapture of depreciation, which arises when a depreciable business asset is sold for greater than its adjusted basis, is beyond the scope of this text.

Intangible assets such as stocks and bonds, and personal use assets such as a personal residence or personal automobile cannot be depreciated, therefore fewer adjustments to basis are likely, although they may occur, such as when one makes capital improvements to one's home.

Holding period. A gain or a loss can be either short term or long term, depending upon the length of the holding period, that is, how long the asset was held by the seller and, in the case of property acquired by gift, by prior owners, too. A gain or a loss is *short-term* if the holding period is not more than one year; it is *long-term* if the property is held more than one year.

By repealing the 60 percent deduction for long-term capital gains, TRA 86 made the short-term versus long-term distinction far less significant, however, long term capital gain has a top federal marginal rate of 28% and there is considerable sentiment in Congress for lowering it even further.

Realized versus recognized gains and losses. A gain or loss is *realized* when the basic transaction, typically a sale, has occurred. On the other hand, a gain or loss is *recognized* when the taxpayer reports the gain or loss on a tax return. Recognition will commonly occur either because tax law requires recognition in that year or because the taxpayer elects a Code-permitted option to report it that year. Common examples of gains or losses that may be recognized in tax years *after* the year of realization include installment sales,[25] tax-deferred exchanges of like kind property,[26] rollover of gain on sale of a principal residence,[27] involuntary conversion[28] (e.g., destruction of a house by fire with insurance proceeds used to purchase a replacement home), and certain capital transactions between corporations and their shareholders.

Property acquired by gift. As described above, the initial basis for property acquired by *purchase* is its cost, which is later adjusted by such items as depreciation and capital improvements, if any. In this section we will cover the somewhat more complex rule for determining the basis of property which has been acquired by *gift*. In the next section we will examine the rule for the basis of property acquired by transfer at *death*.

Date of gift value equaling or exceeding donor's basis. A simple rule applies for gift property whose date of gift value is equal to or greater than the donor's adjusted basis at the date of gift: the donee's basis will equal the amount of the donor's adjusted basis (herein, we will just use "basis") at the date of the gift. This is called the donee's *carryover basis* (COB for short).

EXAMPLE 7 - 42. Ten years ago, donor purchased common stock for $10,000. Two years ago, donor gave donee the stock when it was worth $11,500. At that date, donor's basis was still $10,000. This year, donee sold the stock for $14,500. Since date-of-gift value was greater than donor's basis, donee has realized a gain of $4,500, the difference between the amount realized ($14,500) and donee's basis ($10,000), which is donor's basis at date of gift.

EXAMPLE 7 - 43. As in the prior example, except that donee sold the stock for $7,000. Since date-of-gift value is greater than donor's basis, donee's basis is still $10,000, the donor's basis at date of gift. Therefore, donee has realized a loss of $3,000, the difference between the amount realized and donee's basis.

Date of gift value less than donor's basis. If a donee receives gift property with a date-of-gift value that is less than the donor's basis, then for purposes of calculating a *loss* only, donee's basis will be date-of-gift value. For purposes of calculating a gain, though, the COB rule applies; i.e., the donee's basis is the donor's basis at the date of the gift.

EXAMPLE 7 - 44. Donor acquired property several years ago for $6,000. Last year, when it was worth $4,200, donor gave it to donee, who this year sold it for $3,600. Since date-of-gift value is less than donor's old basis, donee's *basis for loss* is the $4,200 date-of-gift value, and hence donee has realized a loss of only $600.

In effect, the donee is not permitted to recognize the portion of the loss resulting from the property's decline in value while owned by the donor.

EXAMPLE 7 - 45. As in the prior example, except that donee sold the property for $7,100. Although date-of-gift value is less than donor's basis, donee's *basis for gain* is the donor's basis at the date of the gift. In this case, donee's basis is $6,000, and donee has therefore realized a gain of $1,100.

Occasionally, gift property having a date-of-gift value less than the donor's basis will be sold by the donee for an amount that is less than donor's basis but more than date-of-gift value, in which case the donee realizes neither gain nor loss.

EXAMPLE 7 - 46. Several years ago, donor acquired an asset for $2,000 and later gave it to donee when it was worth $1,450. If donee sells the asset for $1,800, no gain or loss will be realized. Since date of gift value ($1,450) is less than donor's basis at the date of the gift ($2,000), for purposes of calculating a *loss*, donee's basis will be date-of-gift value. There is no loss because the amount realized is greater than donee's basis (i.e., $1,800 minus 1,450 is not negative). On the other hand, for purposes of calculating a *gain*, donee's basis will be donor's basis at the date of the gift ($2,000).

Summary. A donee's basis for calculating a potential gain is the donor's old basis, whereas the donee's basis for calculating a loss is the lesser of (*a*) donor's old basis, or (*b*) date-of-gift value. Thus, in situations where date of gift value exceeds donor's old basis, basis for both gain and loss will be the same; both will be derived from donor's old basis.

For comparison purposes, Table 7-1 summarizes the results of the above five examples.

TABLE 7-1 Summary of Examples

##	Donor's old Basis	Date of Gift value	Amount Realized	Basis for Gain	for Loss	Gain or (Loss)
41	$10,000	$11,500	$14,500	$10,000	$10,000	$4,500
42	$10,000	$11,500	$7,000	$10,000	$10,000	($3,000)
43	$6,000	$4,200	$3,600	$6,000	$4,200	($600)
45	$6,000	$4,200	$7,100	$6,000	$4,200	$1,100
46	$2,000	$1,450	$1,800	$2,000	$1,450	$0

Two additional refinements. Two additional points should be made with regard to the sale of gift property.

First, in determining whether the donee's gain or loss is short term or long term, the length of the donor's *holding period* is added or "tacked on" to the length of the donee's holding period.

Second, if the donor pays gift tax on the gift, a portion of that tax is added to the donor's adjusted basis at the date of the gift to determine the donee's new basis. The amount added is that portion of the tax attributable to appreciation. Appreciation is considered to be the difference between the FMV on the date of gift and the property's basis. Hence:

New Basis = Old Basis + ((FMV Gift - Old Basis)/ FMV Gift)) * Gift Tax

EXAMPLE 7 - 47. Donor gave stock purchased for $400,000 twenty years ago to Donee when the stock was worth $1,010,000. Donor paid $153,000. Donee's new basis equals $492,406, i.e., $400,000 + (($1,010,000 - $400,000) / $1,010,000) * $153,000.

The following example incorporates many of the basis principles we have been considering.

EXAMPLE 7 - 48. Fourteen months ago, donor paid $22,000 for a personal computer for use in her business. After spending $1,000 in capital improvements and after depreciating it by $9,000, donor gave it to donee. It was then worth $21,300. Donor paid no gift tax. Today, donee sold it for $12,400. Donee's basis is $14,000, which is donor's old basis ($14,000 = $22,000 - $9,000 + $1,000). A loss of $1,600 is realized since this is the amount by which donee's basis for loss exceeds the amount realized (-$1,600 = $12,400 - $14,000). The $1,600 loss is long-term because donee's holding period is the length of time the computer was held by both the donee and the donor, a period exceeding one year. Since no gift tax was paid, no basis adjustment was made.

Inherited property. The general rule: when a person inherits (i.e., bequest, devise or inheritance, or surviving joint tenant) property from a decedent, all or a portion of the property's basis for both gain and loss is the value of the property included in the decedent's gross estate.[29] There are several exceptions to this rule that we will discuss as we go.

Notice that the change in the basis of property acquired by another's death can be a "step-up" or "step-down" in the basis depending on whether the decedent's pre-death basis was lower or higher than the value at death. However, common usage is to refer to this change at death as a *step-up* in basis. Furthermore, if the alternate valuation date is elected,[30] it is the alternate value that determines basis, but to simplify our discussion "date of death" (abbreviated DOD) should be understood to include the alternate valuation if such is applicable.

If an Estate Tax return (Form 706) is filed, there is a rebuttable presumption that the Form 706 values are correct.[31] However, the change in basis occurs whether or not there is a tax, and whether or not a return is filed. Thus, when a person dies, even if he or she leaves a very small estate, a change in basis will likely occur.

How much of the basis of the property acquired by death is stepped-up will depend upon whether or not the property was individually owned at date of death, and, if not, how the property was co-owned.

Individually owned property. Generally, Individually owned property acquired by death is entitled to a full step-up in basis. Thus, seller's entire basis for both gain and loss is the entire value of the property at date of the donor's death.

> EXAMPLE 7 - 49. Frank recently sold a vacant parcel of land for $75,000. The land had been purchased by Frank's dad for $500 in 1930 and was worth $40,000 in 1990 when it passed to Frank by inheritance. Dad's total estate was about $200,000, so no estate tax was owed and no return was filed. Frank has a realized gain of $35,000, the difference between the sale price and the basis established at date of death.

Concurrently owned property. If, at death, the decedent was sharing ownership in property, usually only the decedent's share will be stepped-up. The factor that determines whether any *surviving* co-owner can also enjoy a step-up in basis for his or her share depends upon the legal form of concurrent ownership. In general, no surviving co-owner's share will enjoy a step-up in basis unless the asset is either owned as community property or is includable in the predeceased co-owner's gross estate.

The rules for co-owner basis change at death are as follows:

Community property. The new basis is the FMV at date of death for both halves of the community property even though only half is included in the decedent spouse's estate. This is referred to as a full step-up in basis.

Joint tenancy. What is included in the decedent estate and the surviving co-owners new basis will follow one of two rules which depend on the relationship between the decedent and the surviving co-owner's.

Husband and wife rule. Where the only joint tenants (or tenants by the entire) are husband and wife, then half of the FMV at date of death is included in the decedent's estate and the surviving spouse's new basis will equal half the total pre-death basis and half the FMV at date of death.

New Basis = (DOD FMV + Old Basis) / 2

Consideration Furnished Rule. Where the joint tenants include nonspouses the rule is that the decedent's gross estate includes that portion of the property as the decedent's share of the consideration (price paid for the property) bears to the total consideration. Decedent's consideration includes any gifts given to other joint tenants and any share acquired by another person's death.

Include = (Decedent's Consideration / Total Consideration) * FMV DOD

The new basis for each surviving co-owner's interest is his or her old basis plus an increase for his proportional share of the amount included in the decedent's estate. The examples that follow demonstrate both rules.

EXAMPLE 7 - 50. At Ricky's death, he and his wife Victoria owned common stock as *joint tenants*. Ricky had paid $5,000 and Victoria paid $11,000 of the original $16,000 purchase price. When Ricky died, the stock was worth $22,000, and Victoria acquired Ricky's interest by right of survivorship. Four months later, she sold the stock for $29,000. Victoria will realize a gain of $10,000. Victoria's basis is $19,000, the sum of $8,000 (half of the original basis) plus $11,000 (Ricky's one-half interest included in his estate).

Consider the very different outcome for *community property*.

EXAMPLE 7 - 51. Same facts as in the prior example, except that at Ricky's death, he and his wife Victoria owned the common stock as *community property*. Once again half would be included in Ricky's estate but Victoria's basis would be the FMV DOD amount, $22,000.

Thus, ordinary community property states have a decided advantage over common law states with regard to basis adjustments at death, and estate planners often recommend that clients residing in community property states hold appreciated, or appreciating, property in community property form, if possible. On the other hand, estate planners anticipating a *step-down* in basis will advise clients to convert community property to some other form of ownership to avoid a double step-down.

The IRS takes the position that states recognizing the concept "community property with right of survivorship" (e.g., Nevada and Wisconsin) will not have the advantage of a double step-up in basis, but will be treated as husband and wife joint tenants.

EXAMPLE 7 - 52. Years ago, brothers Steve and Stan purchased stock for $10,000, taking title as joint tenants. Steve paid $6,000 and Stan paid $4,000 towards the purchase. At Steve's death the stock was worth $20,000. Included in Steve's gross estate is 60% of the stock's value because that corresponds to his share of the consideration paid for the stock, even though property law recognized that he owned 50% of the stock immediately before death. Stan's new basis would be $16,000 which is $12,000 (the amount included in Steve's estate) plus Stan's $4,000 basis in his pre-death interest in the property.

EXAMPLE 7 - 53. Three friends purchased a vacation cabin in 1980. Abe paid $20,000, Betty paid $30,000, and Cathy paid $50,000 of the $100,000 purchase price. In 1985, when the cabin was worth $160,000, Abe died. His estate included 20% of the DOD FMV, i.e. 20% * $160,000 = $32,000. Betty's new basis in her 50% interest in the cabin became $46,000 (½ * $32,000 + her original consideration of $30,000) and Cathy's new basis is $66,000 (½ * $32,000 + her original consideration of $50,000).

EXAMPLE 7 - 54. Continuing from the last example, in 1990, Cathy died, leaving Betty as the sole surviving joint tenant. The cabin was then worth $224,000. The amount included in Cathy's gross estate is based on her portion ($66,000) of the combined (hers and Betty's) predeath bases of $112,000. Therefor, included in her estate is $132,000 (($66,000 / $112,000) * $224,000), and Betty's new basis would be $178,000 (the $132,000 included in Cathy's estate plus Betty's old basis of $46,000).

It should be noted that a gift from one prospective co-joint tenant to another is treaded as consideration from the donor not the donee.

EXAMPLE 7 - 55. Martin gave his son, Andy, $50,000 shortly before they purchased a vacation condo for $150,000. Martin paid $100,000 on the purchase and Andy paid $50,000. When Martin died the condo was valued at $200,000, all of which had to be included in his estate because Andy's contribution was traceable to Martin's gift.

Tenants in Common Rule. Tenancy in common is the preferred form of ownership for nonrelatives. It does not have the survivorship feature found in joint tenancy, thus the co-owners control the disposition of their respective shares. Unlike joint tenancy, tenants in common can have unequal undivided shares, meaning that you could have one owner owning 20%, another owning 30%, and the third owning 50%. When a tenant in common owner dies his or her share of the total FMV DOD of the property is included in the gross estate. The disposition of a deceased tenant in common's interest depends on the decedent's will or, if there is no will, interstate succession laws.

EXAMPLE 7 - 56. Friends Arthur, Tony and Maria purchased property as tenants in common. They took title in equal shares even though Arthur generously paid $40,000, and Tony and Maria each paid only $30,000 of the $100,000 purchase price. Years later when Tony died the property was worth $240,000, and his estate included $80,000 since he owned a one-third interest. If Tony left his one-third interest to his wife, her basis would be $80,000. If he instead left his interest to co-owner Maria, her total basis in the two-thirds interest she would then own would be $110,000 ($80,000 + her $30,000 contribution).

Note, in the preceding example, because the interests were held as tenants in common property law recognizes unequal shares. Therefore, had the three agreed to hold percentage interests in proportion to each person's consideration, then Tony's share would have been 30% and only $72,000 would have been included in his estate.

The Rubber Band Rule of §1014(e). Internal Revenue Code §1014(e) provides that where a person gifts "appreciated property" within one year of donee-decedent's death, and then inherits the property (it comes bouncing back as if it had a rubber band attached when it was given), the adjusted basis of the property to the donor will be donee-decedent's adjusted basis immediately before the donee-decedent's death. Appreciated property means property worth more *at the time of the gift* than its basis. Since the donee had a carry-over basis, the donor will also get the property back with the basis unchanged.

EXAMPLE 7 - 57. Husband gives his terminally ill wife his interest in land, purchased many years ago for $400, and currently worth $10,000. Wife, who dies two months later, devises the land back to husband, who then sells it for $11,000. Husband, because the property was appreciated at the time he gave it to his wife, must now realize a gain of $10,600, not $1,000. The wife's adjusted basis just before her death was a carryover basis of $400.

Hence, there is an advantage of gifting low-basis property, in the case of a donor-devisee, if the donee-decedent lives *at least one year* after the date of gift. This strategy will work even if the original donor is not the spouse of the decedent but the original gift might use up the donor's unified credit if it is not covered by the annual exclusion. §1014(e) does not apply if the donee-decedent leaves the property to someone other than the original donor or the donor's spouse. Thus, A can give an appreciated asset to D, who can then transfer it at death to B; and the asset will have a stepped-up basis even if D's death occurs within one year of A's transfer of the asset to D.

Holding period. The holding period for property acquired from a decedent will be considered to have been *long term*, no matter how long the decedent and the devisee have held it. Thus, a decedent could have purchased the asset shortly before death and the devisee could have sold it shortly after death, and any gain or loss will be long term.

Income in Respect to a Decedent. One major exception to the step-up in basis rule has to do with what is called income in respect to a decedent. This "income in respect of a decedent" (IRD) technically consists of income to which the decedent was entitled at death but which had not been actually received prior to death. Examples of IRD include the gain portion of an installment sale promissory note where the gain is being recognized only as principle is collected, the vested amount in a qualified retirement plan, IRA accounts (the value in excess of basis, since IRA's can now have a basis), dividends declared but not received at the time of death, commissions earned, and business accounts receivables. IRD is subject to both estate tax and, when collected, to income tax. It is reported by the actual recipient of the income (executor, trustee or beneficiary). And because an estate tax is paid IRD which later is subject to income taxes, the recipient of IRD is allowed an income tax deduction for estate tax attributable to the IRD.[32] The deduction is basically the portion of the estate tax attributable to the IRD collected.

SPECIAL VALUATION RULES: §2701-§2704

Historical Background

Pre- §2036(c) transactions. Based on the material in Chapters 5, 6, and 7, the reader will probably assume that any gift-type transfer of property in which the client retains a valuable interest is not recommended by planners attempting to save estate taxes. After all, it may constitute a gift subject to immediate gift taxation, and will eventually subject the date of death value of the property to estate tax at the client's death.

EXAMPLE 7 - 58. Twenty-five years ago, Gustavson transferred $100,000 in stock in a closely held business into an irrevocable trust, with all income payable to

Gustavson for life, and then remainder to Gustavson's son. Based on Gustavson's age, $38,000, the value of the gifted remainder, was subject to gift taxation, with no annual exclusion available for this gift of a future interest. At Gustavson's death this year, his gross estate will include $388,000, the date of death value of the stock, under §2036(a). The estate will be allowed a credit for any gift tax actually paid on the original gift and it will not be treated as an adjusted taxable gift.

Clearly, Gustavson gained no estate tax savings from this particular transaction. However, prior to 1987, certain *other types* of transfers with retained interests were known to be less vulnerable to transfer taxation, and until then, estate planners were able to fashion strategies that succeeded in both avoiding any gift taxation and substantially lessening the estate tax. The most common transfers have been in the corporate recapitalization and grantor retained trust areas.

EXAMPLE 7 - 59. Twenty years ago Weiner, sole shareholder of the common stock of his $1 million closely held corporation, redeemed all shares in a transaction in which the corporation issued three new classes of stock: 1) 100 shares of nonvoting, noncumulative preferred stock, all to Weiner. Based on the sizable amount of the estimated annual dividend, this stock was appraised at a total value of $1 million; 2) 20 shares of voting common stock, all also to Weiner; and 3) 480 shares of nonvoting common stock, all to Weiner's son Ted. Since the value of the preferred stock equaled the total value of the firm, the value of all common shares was determined to be zero. Each year for the succeeding 20 years, Weiner gave Ted one share of his voting common. At Weiner's death this year, the corporation was worth a total of $6 million. Because of a decline in prevailing interest rates the value of the preferred stock had risen to $1,200,000. Weiner's gross estate will include only $1,200,000, the current value of the preferred stock owned at death. This transaction generated no gift tax whatsoever, and saved about $2.64 million in estate tax (= ($6,000,000 - $1,200,000) x .55).

EXAMPLE 7 - 60. Eighteen years ago, Warschauer transferred $200,000 in property into an irrevocable trust, retaining the right to all trust income for fifteen years. According to the terms of the trust instrument, had Warschauer died during this period, the trust would have terminated and all principal would have reverted to his estate. If he survived the period, the trust would continue until his death, with all principal passing to his daughter. Based on market rates eighteen years ago, the initial value of the income interest was exactly $200,000, which meant that the value of the gifted remainder was zero. Thus, Warschauer did not even need to file a gift tax return. Warschauer did in fact survive the fifteen year period, and his gross estate will now include nothing in connection with this property, which is worth $600,000. At his death, Warschauer had no interest in it. Warschauer's estate has saved $330,000 in estate tax (= $600,000 x .55).

Advent of §2036(c) and Chapter 14. The last two examples illustrate two of several types of popularly discussed "estate freezing" transactions involving gift tax-free completed transfers producing outstanding estate tax savings in which a client had retained a significant interest in property. As one might imagine, their predominant success in the courts over the years was immensely frustrating to both the IRS and certain members of Congress, who saw such schemes as tax abusive. Attempting to restrict them, Congress in 1987 first enacted §2036(c), which took an *estate tax approach.* Using very general language, §2036(c)required inclusion in the decedent's gross estate of the *entire* date of death value of virtually all property in which the transferor retained significant interests. Incredibly confusing and sweeping, §2036(c) created such taxpayer opposition that it was repealed retroactively in 1990 and replaced by the more limited special valuation rules of §2701-04, also called "Chapter 14" after their location in the Internal Revenue Code.

Chapter 14: §2701-§2704

In adopting Chapter 14, Congress abandoned the estate tax approach, and instead focused on *gift taxation*, which means subjecting certain transfers to gift taxation when the initial transfer is made, rather than later taxing the property at the transferor's death. In essence, Chapter 14 rules require that certain transfers of property incorporating retained interests must be valued in their entirety, reduced only by the value of "qualified" retained interests. Thus, any retained interests that do not qualify under the Code are disregarded, with the result that the entire value of the transferred property is subject to immediate gift taxation. Thus, for gift tax purposes, Chapter 14 treats the nonqualified retained interests as if they had, in fact, not been retained.

EXAMPLE 7 - 61. Had Weiner, in the earlier example, undertaken his corporate recapitalization today, under Chapter 14 he would be required to report a gift subject to taxation of $990,000 (= $1 million less one $10,000 annual exclusion). Thus, Weiner would be forced to use up all of his unified credit and pay some gift tax, and any future gifts would be sheltered only by the annual exclusion. Later, at his death this year, Weiner's gross estate would include the date of death value of the preferred stock, but adjusted taxable gifts would not include the $990,000. A credit for gift taxes would be available. From a transfer tax point of view, the result under the Chapter 14 rules is no different than had Weiner made a simple outright gift of the original common stock.

EXAMPLE 7 - 62. Had Warschauer, in the earlier example, made his transfer today, he would probably be required to report a taxable gift of $200,000, i.e., the entire value of the property transferred into the trust. The non-qualifying retained income interest would be given zero value.

Now let's examine each of the sections within Chapter 14 individually, in some greater detail.[33] Please keep in mind this analysis constitutes only a brief survey of a very technical area.

§2701: Transfers of corporate or partnership interests. In essence, under §2701, the value of a gift of an interest in a corporation or partnership to a family member will not be reduced by any interests retained by the donor unless certain specific conditions are met.

Stated in the broadest terms, the §2701 valuation rules apply to:

any post-October 8, 1990 transfer by an individual of certain junior equity interests in a corporation or partnership to a member of the transferor's family, if the transferor or an applicable family member retains an applicable retained interest in the corporation or partnership immediately after the transfer.

Since this is a complicated rule with many technical terms having very specific meaning, each of the terms will be defined or described, although briefly. After that, the rule will be summarized with an example.

"Transfer." A transfer of a business interest can be direct or indirect. Examples of an indirect transfer include a contribution to capital, a redemption and a recapitalization or other change in capital structure.[34]

"Junior equity interest." A junior equity interest includes common stock, or, in the case of a partnership, any interest in which the rights to income and capital are junior to the rights of all other equity interests.

"Member of the transferor's family." Family members of the transferor include the transferor's spouse, descendants of the transferor and the transferor's spouse, and any spouse of such descendants.[35]

"Applicable family member." An applicable family member of the transferor includes the transferor's spouse, *ancestors* of the transferor or the transferor's spouse, and any spouse of such ancestor.[36]

"Applicable retained interest." An applicable retained interest is any interest (except publicly traded stock) having either (*a*) a *distribution right*, but only if the

transferor and applicable family members hold control (50 percent or more) of the business immediately before the transfer, or (*b*) a liquidation, put, call or conversion right, irrespective of the degree of control held by the parties.[37] A distribution right is a right to a distribution from either a corporation with respect to its stock, or from a partnership with respect to the partner's interest. Two distribution rights are excepted from this definition: (*a*) a right to a distribution with respect to a junior equity interest (e.g., transferor gives preferred stock and retains common stock), and (*b*) a right to receive a "guaranteed payment" (as described in §707(c)) of a "fixed amount." A liquidation, put, call or conversion (LPCC) right is any LPCC right, the exercise or nonexercise of which affects the value of the transferred interest.[38] The Code lists certain exceptions.

> EXAMPLE 7 - 63. If undertaken today, the Weiner corporate recapitalization, described earlier, would fall within the valuation rules of §2701. Rationale: Weiner, an individual (indirectly) transferred a junior equity interest (common stock) in a corporation to a member of his family (his son), and retained an applicable retained interest (a nonmarketable distribution right with respect to preferred stock, which is not a junior equity interest or a right to receive guaranteed payments of a fixed amount), with respect to a business over which Weiner had control immediately before the transfer.

Section 2701 does not apply when the transferred interest is of the same class as the retained interest, or if market quotations are "readily available" for retained interest, or if the retained interest is proportionally the same as the transferred interest.[39]

> EXAMPLE 7 - 64. Up to now, Rocky has been the sole owner of RR Corporation, which has issued only one class of stock. Today, Rocky gives 10 percent of his common stock to his daughter, retaining the remaining 90 percent. §2701 does not apply, and the traditional rules would be used to value the transferred shares.

Effect of valuation treatment under §2701. When §2701 applies, three specific valuation rules must be observed:

1. The junior equity must be assigned a value of at least ten percent of the value of the business,[40]
2. The transferred interest must be valued by the "subtraction method," and
3. Retained rights other than "qualified payments" must be assigned a value of zero.[41] This is the so-called "zero valuation rule."

Regarding the second rule, the Treasury has interpreted §2701 to require use of the subtraction method to determine the amount of the gift.[42] A simplified application of the subtraction method would start with the value of all family held equity interests in the entity immediately after the transfer. Then, the value of all family held senior equity interests (with nonqualifying retained interests valued at zero) are subtracted. This leaves the gift amount that must be allocated pro rata to the transferred interests.

EXAMPLE 7 - 65. Based on the Weiner recapitalization in the preceding examples, the value of Weiner's gift equals $1 million, which is $1 million, the value of all family held equity interests after the transfer, reduced by zero, the value of Weiner's nonqualifying retained interest. Since Weiner's son receives all transferred interests, the entire $1 million is allocated to him. Thus, Weiner will have made a $1 million gross gift to his son.

Regarding the third rule, retained rights to *qualified payments* do not fall within the zero valuation rule. A qualified payment is a cumulative preferred dividend payable on a periodic basis determined at a specific rate.[43]

EXAMPLE 7 - 66. Had Weiner in the above examples retained a right to 12 percent *cumulative* preferred stock, the payment might be treated as a *qualified payment* if publicly traded stock of a similar quality had a dividend rate of 12 percent. The upshot would be that the value of the retained preferred stock could be subtracted from the value of all family held senior equity interests in determining the value of Weiner's gift. Thus, if the value of the qualifying preferred stock was $700,000, Weiner would have made a gross gift of $300,000. If the preferred was worth $950,000, Weiner's gift would be $100,000, because the "junior equity interest" must be assigned a minimum value of 10 percent of the entire business.

This discussion has merely highlighted the valuation rules under §2701. Additional analysis will be undertaken in Chapter 16, in planning for corporate recapitalizations.

§2702: Transfers of interests in trusts. While §2701 deals specifically with transfers of corporate or partnership interests to family members, §2072 addresses certain types of transfers of *any* kind of property to *trusts*. The sections are similar, however in that both treat nonqualifying retained interests as having a value of zero. They also both use the subtraction method of valuation to determine the tax value of the gift. In general terms, under §2702, the special valuation rules apply when:

> *a transfer is made in trust for the benefit of a member of the transferor's family and an interest is retained by the transferor or an applicable family member.*

Again, the key terms will first be defined or described.

"Member of transferor's family." A member of the transferor's family, more inclusive than under §2701, includes the transferor's ancestors, descendants, spouse and siblings, ancestors and descendants of the transferor's spouse, and spouses of the transferor's ancestors, descendants and siblings.[44]

"Applicable family member." An applicable family member includes the same members included under §2701.[45] These are the transferor's spouse, ancestors of the transferor or the transferor's spouse, and any spouse of such ancestor.[46]

Exceptions to §2702. §2702 does not apply (*a*) to retained interests in a personal residence in which the term holder resides, and *b*) possibly for certain tangible property, such as undeveloped real estate or art. In addition, the zero valuation rule under §2702 does not apply to two types of qualified retained income interests, called a "qualified annuity interest" and a "qualified unitrust interest." Among other requirements, the income must be payable at least annually, and must be stated as a fixed dollar amount (annuity interest) or a fixed percentage of the fair market value of the trust property, determined annually (unitrust interest).

> EXAMPLE 7 - 67. In the earlier example, had Warschauer made his transfer this year, and had his fifteen year income interest been structured to qualify as either an annuity interest or a unitrust interest, the full value of that interest could be deducted from the value of the transfer in calculating the value of Warschauer's immediate taxable gift resulting in a taxable gift of far less value.

Additional discussion of the valuation rules of §2702 will be found in Chapter 14 of the text, which also describes the specific techniques planners have developed to exploit these exceptions. We shall see that the trusts incorporating these techniques have come to be called grantor retained trusts, or GRITs, for short.

§2703: Valuation of property subject to rights and restrictions. Section 2703 requires that the value of any property subject to rights and restrictions on that property held by anyone shall be valued for transfer tax purposes without regard to the reduced valuation effect of those rights or restrictions.

> EXAMPLE 7 - 68. Shortly before his death this year, Hansen, sole shareholder of the common stock of his $1 million closely held corporation, executed a contract with his daughter, who is obligated to purchase all of Hansen's stock at Hansen's death for $600,000. Under §2703, Hansen's gross estate will include the stock at a value of $1 million; the reduction in actual value attributable to the obligation to sell the stock must be disregarded.

More specifically, the rights and restrictions that must be disregarded under §2703 include:

1. Any option, agreement, or other right to acquire or use the property as a price less than the fair market value of the property (without regard to such option, agreement, or right), or
2. Any restriction on the right to sell or use the property.[47]

Section 2703 does not apply to any agreement, option, right, or restriction, which meets all of the following requirements:

- It is a bona fide business arrangement,
- It is not a device to transfer such property to members of the decedent's family for less than full and adequate consideration in money or money's worth, and
- Its terms are comparable to similar arrangements entered into by persons in an arm's length transaction.[48]

> EXAMPLE 7 - 69. Shortly before his death this year, Trafalgar, sole owner of the common stock of his $1 million closely held corporation, executed a contract with a non-relative business associate, who is obligated to purchase all of Trafalgar's stock at Trafalgar's death for $960,000. The valuation rules under §2703 are not likely to prevent the inclusion of Trafalgar's stock in his gross estate at a value of $960,000.

Planning under §2703 for business buyout agreements, as they are called, will be discussed further in Chapter 16.

§2704: Taxation of lapse of voting and liquidation rights and restrictions in a corporation or partnership. §2704, of relatively limited application, will only be briefly summarized here. It addresses the influence on federal transfer taxation of the lapse of a voting or liquidation right in a corporation or partnership.

In general, if there has been a lapse and the person holding the right before the lapse and the members of that person's family hold control of the entity both before and after the lapse, then the lapse is treated as gift or a transfer at death, as the case may be, subject to tax. The value of the transfer subject to taxation is equal to the excess of the value of all interests held by that person before the lapse (determined as if the rights were nonlapsing) over the value of such interests immediately after the lapse.

Clearly, properly applying the Chapter 14 valuation rules to client situations requires considerable expertise and careful thought, and should be undertaken only with the help of a tax expert. However, all planners should have a general understanding of this commonly discussed topic.

FEDERAL GENERATION-SKIPPING TRANSFER TAX

One fundamental policy objective of federal wealth transfer taxation is to tax all individual wealth in excess of a certain amount each time it passes to the next generation. Can the unified estate and gift tax laws completely achieve that goal? They cannot. It is true that they can ensure that property is subject to tax once when it is transferred. But since they both fail to distinguish between transfers made to the next generation and transfers made to more distant generations, they cannot possibly meet that goal.

> EXAMPLE 7 - 70. Grandpa died last year leaving most of his large estate to his *granddaughter*. An estate tax will be imposed on this amount now, but not at the death of any of his children.

Only a tax that explicitly addresses the generational relationship between transferor and transferee can consistently tax wealth as it passes to succeeding generations. The generation-skipping transfer tax is designed to meet that objective.

The generation-skipping transfer tax (GSTT) is levied when a transfer is made (by gift or by bequest) to a person two or more generations below the donor. Persons in these lower generations are called *skip persons*. Every donor has a $1 million GSTT exemption, so most donors and most estates are not concerned with this tax. Gifts directly to grandchildren (or any other skip person) that qualify for the annual exclusion are not subject to the GSTT, so they do not use up any of the exemption. There is also a special rule called the predeceased ancestor exception that is applicable only for direct skips. For now think of direct skips as gifts or bequests that go directly to a grandchild or great-grandchild without being held in trust. In general, this rule "moves up" lower generations if a lineal descendant dies before the transfer. However, where transfers to grandchildren exceed the exemption amount (and the predeceased ancestor exception doesn't apply), the tax is horrendous since it is at the highest transfer tax marginal rate (presently 55%) and is in addition to the gift or estate tax.

The GSTT is discussed in much more detail in Chapter 12.

This chapter has focused on certain qualitative aspects of the federal gift tax and a very brief introduction to the federal generation-skipping transfer tax. The next chapter will present an overview of the federal fiduciary income tax.

QUERIES ANSWERED:

1. Total of 55%, i.e. $550,000.

QUESTIONS AND PROBLEMS

1. List the common law requirements for a valid gift.

2. Addie sells her empty lot, fair market value $22,000, to a stranger for $19,500. Is there a gift? Why or why not?

3. Would your answer to Question 2 change if the donee was, in fact, Addie's son? One of her employees?

4. (a) If Jones gives Smith 200 shares of a non-dividend-paying stock, is this a gift of a present or a future interest? Why? (b) Why might it matter?

5. Today Lois transfers $10,000 to an irrevocable trust that is required to distribute all income annually to her son, age 55, for his life. Then, remainder outright to his issue. Assuming 10 percent, calculate the amount of Lois' taxable gift.

6. Explain the public policy reason for the exception under §2503(c).

7. Two years ago, John gave his daughter $300,000, consisting of 300 shares of the closely held corporation that he owned as an individual. Last year, John gave his daughter $400,000 more of this stock.
   a. Assuming neither John nor his wife Jenny had ever made any other taxable gifts, calculate the total amount of gift taxes from these gifts, and also calculate John's and Jenny's remaining unused unified credits, available for this year, if
      1. No gift splitting was employed.
      2. John and Jenny split both year's gifts.
   b. Explain the advantages and disadvantages of gift splitting in this situation.

8. Wayne and his wife Sharon own a parcel of land worth $20,000 as equal tenants in common. This year they gave the land to their daughter Christina. Can this gift be split?

9. Assume that one of your wealthier clients is the reluctant holder of a general power of appointment and is not charitably inclined. What action on her part, if any, might minimize total unified transfer taxes?

10. Ralph established a trust in 1985 which gave Linda income for life, remainder to Linda's three children by right of representation. What would be the effect on Linda's estate at her death of each clause (considered independently) if such is part of the trust: (Explain your answer).

a. The Trustee is given absolute discretion to transfer the principal of the trust to Linda, if doing so would be in her best interest.
b. I give Linda the power to appoint, by direct reference to this power in her Will, the remainder of the trust amongst her children in such portion as she deems appropriate.
c. I give Linda the right to invade the corpus up to a maximum of 3% of the trust in any one year. This right shall be noncumulative.
d. I give Linda the power to invade the corpus of the trust, up to the whole amount, if such be necessary for her health, education, maintenance or support.

11. Rachel establishes a trust (worth exactly $1,000,000 at all times relevant here) for the benefit of Arthur during his lifetime, with remainder to Sarah upon Arthur's death. Arthur was 50 years old when the trust was established. The terms of the trust give Arthur the right to demand up to the greater of 5% or $5,000 from the trust in any year, but the right is noncumulative. In years 1, 2, 3, 5, and 6, he did not exercise the right. In year 4, he took out the maximum allowed. With appreciation in the remaining assets, the trust quickly returned to $1,000,000, which was its value in the 6th year when Arthur died.

a. In the first year the power lapsed, what was the gift to Sarah?
b. How much of this trust would be included in Arthur's estate?
c. If the demand right had been the greater of 7% or $7,000, what would be the gift to Sarah in the first year? Would a gift tax return have to be filed?
d. If the demand right had been the greater of 7% or $7,000, how much would be included in Arthur's estate?

12. Five years ago, Frank purchased a $280,000 face value life insurance policy on his own life. A year later he assigned (gave) the policy to his son, when it had a terminal value of $110,000. Four months after making this gift, Frank died. Frank's wife had always been beneficiary. Explain all gift and estate tax consequences. (Hint: there are at least three.) Does

the marital deduction come into play?

13. A client asks you to explain when the acquisition by gift of joint tenancy property is taxed.

14. Today, Karen and Sal buy 100 shares of ABC Corp. stock for $21,000, writing a check on their joint (or community) checking account and taking title in joint tenancy. Has a gift occurred? Why or why not?

15. Give an example of a way in which a qualified disclaimer can be a valuable estate planning tool.

16. Explain three reasons why gift splitting can be a valuable estate planning tool.

17. This year, Joe gave $1 million cash to his daughter Mary, who gave it to her son Sal, who gave it to his sister Sue. (a) How many gifts subject to taxation have been made? (b) Can §2518 (disclaimers) help? (c) How about §2013 (estate tax credit for tax on prior transfers)?

18. Congratulations! You have just won the state lottery, entitling you to $2 million cash a year for the next 20 years. You direct that your winnings be shared equally with your spouse and your 28-year-old daughter.
    a. Are there any tax consequences?
    b. Could there have been any way to avoid them?

19. Five years ago, Francisco and Dagny executed a "joint and mutual will", which is a single will, revocable only by mutual consent. Essentially, it provided that the first to die leaves his or her property to the survivor, who then leaves everything to their children at his or her death. 0.Francisco died today. (a) Can you think of any possible immediate tax consequences to Dagny? (b) If Francisco and Dagny wrote two different wills leaving everything to each other, and also executed an enforceable contract not to change these wills, would the result be any different from the result in part a? (Answer: No).

20. (a) Describe the GSTT. (b) What are its exceptions?

21. During the last ten years of her life, Queenie, a widow, undertook each of the following independent transactions. Explain whether or not each constituted a gift subject to taxation.

a. Purchased a life insurance policy on her life, naming her son beneficiary.
b. Transferred title to her personal residence to her daughter and continued to live there, rent-free, for two years, at which time she moved out and formally relinquished all rights to the property.
c. Funded a revocable living trust.
d. Funded an irrevocable living trust, under which her daughter was the sole beneficiary.
e. Purchased some land, taking title in the names of herself and her son as joint tenants. Queenie paid $90,000 of the $100,000 purchase price, and son paid $10,000.
f. Purchased common stock, taking title in the names of herself and her husband as joint tenants.
g. Purchased life insurance on the life of her uncle, naming her daughter beneficiary. Two years later, uncle died and daughter was paid the proceeds.
h. Paid $21,000 in tuition and $8,000 in room, board, and other fees each year for five years for her son's college education.
i. Opened a joint checking account with her daughter, depositing $26,000 of her own funds.

ANSWERS TO THE QUESTIONS AND PROBLEMS

1. Customary local law requirements for a valid gift:

   a. A donor capable of transferring property.
   b. A donee capable of receiving and possessing the property.
   c. Delivery to the donee, and some form of acceptance.
   d. Donative intent (not required for a taxable gift).

2. There is probably no gift, since Addie sold the property to a stranger, at arm's length. Probably a bad bargain.

3. If the donee was Addie's son, Addie probably made a gift of $2,500, since intent was probably donative.

   On the other hand, if the donee was Addie's employee, the difference in values is probably compensation, taxable to Addie's employee.

4. a. This gift of non-dividend paying stock is a gift of a present interest because, on the whole, enjoyment is not postponed. Smith can still presently enjoy the stock in other ways, such as by selling it.
   b. It might matter because gifts of future interests do not qualify for the annual exclusion.

5. This transfer represents a gift of a present interest to son of a life estate in the trust income for son's life, and a gift of a future interest in the remainder to son's issue. The former gift qualifies for the annual exclusion, while the latter does not.

   The value of the life estate, based on Table S, is $10,000 times .82550, or $8,255. It will qualify for the annual exclusion. The value of the remainder, $10,000 minus $8,255, or $1,745 is a future interest and will not qualify for the annual exclusion. Thus, the total taxable portion of the gift is $1,745

6. The public policy reason for the exception under Section 2503(c) is to avoid encouraging sizable present interest gifts to minors.

7. a. Calculation of gift taxes and the remaining unused unified credits:

	No Gift Splitting John's 709		Gift Splitting Identical returns x 2	
	2 yrs ago	last year	2 yrs ago	last year
Current yr gross gifts	$300,000	$400,000	$150,000	$200,000
- Annual exclusions	($10,000)	($10,000)	($10,000)	($10,000)
= Current tx gifts	$290,000	$390,000	$140,000	$190,000
+ Total prior tx gifts	$0	$290,000	$0	$140,000
= Total taxable gifts	$290,000	$680,000	$14,000	$330,000
Ten. tax total gifts	$84,400	$222,400	$35,800	$98,000
- Ten. tax prior gifts	$0	($84,400)	$0	($35,800)
= Ten. tax current	$84,400	$138,000	$35,800	$62,200
- Unused unified	$84,400	$108,400	($35,800)	($62,200)
Equals: Current gift	$0	$29,600	$0	$0

Total gift taxes	$29,600		$0

Unused unified		
John	$0	$94,800
Jenny	$192,800	$94,800
Total	$192,800	$189,600

b. Advantages: 1) Two additional annual exclusions were utilized (assumes Jenny didn't want to use them herself). 2) No Gift tax was due, by either spouse. 3) Remaining total unused unified credits of $189,600 are nearly equal to Jenny's unused unified credit of $192,800 without gift splitting, despite the fact that $29,600 in gift tax was saved.

Disadvantages: 1) Jenny's annual exclusions for both years were used up. Actually, this is not a problem unless she also wanted to make gifts to her daughter. 2) Jenny's remaining unused unified credit was reduced by 51 percent. However, this also should not be considered a significant problem. If Jenny wishes to make large gifts of her own property, she could make part of the gifts by way of John, to use his unused credit.

8. This gift cannot be split. Gift splitting requires that the gift property not be owned equally. In the typical situation, the gift property is owned totally by one spouse, as an individual.

9. Doing almost anything will subject the property to transfer taxation.

Exercising the power in favor of another or releasing the power are taxable transfers to the extent they exceed the annual exclusion. Thus, by releasing or exercising annual exclusion amounts each year, the holder may be able to reduce her future estate size and avoid transfer taxation on future appreciation of the underlying property.

10.   a.   Assuming the trustee is independent of Linda and did not transfer any of the corpus to her, the trustee is the holder of a limited power therefore nothing is included in Linda's estate.

   b.   Linda is the holder of a limited power and nothing is included whether or not she exercised the power.

   c.   This is a general power and 3% of the trust's value on her death will be included in her estate, assuming she did not exercise the power that last year. If she did exercise it to the full 3% then none of the trust would be included but the property taken out would be in her estate unless she gave it away or consumed it.

   d.   This is a power limited by an ascertainable standard as such is defined in §2041 and is therefore considered a limited power, therefore, nothing is included.

11.   a.   Because the gift (the lapse of the right to withdraw $50,000) is covered by the 5 and 5 exception no gift taxes place.

   b.   The 5 & 5 exception does not apply to lapses at death, therefore $50,000 would be included in Arthur's estate. Note, nothing is actually taken out of the trust due to this inclusion in Arthur's estate, it is included for calculation purposes only. Any estate tax attributed to this inclusion is charged to the trust.

   c.   Each year that a lapse occurred (years 1, 2, 3, and 5) due to a year ending without a withdrawal a gift occurred as to the amount not sheltered by the 5 & 5 exception. Thus for each of those years a gift of a remainder interest in $20,000 must be reported. Thus in the first year, if the federal rate f or future interest gifts was 8% the gift would be: 0.17697 * $20,000 = $3,539 [Table S (8%), 50 yr old, remainder factor].

   Each year that a lapse occurred, a gift tax return would have required since the amounts over 5% would be deemed gifts of future interests (no annual exclusion) discounted because of Arthur's retained life estate.

d. For each year a right to withdraw lapsed at the end of a year, it would be as if Arthur had transferred 2% of the corpus into trust and retained a life estate in the property transferred. Life time lapses occurred four years (years 1, 2, 3, and 5), thus for these years 8% of the trust is included. In the last year the entire 7% lapse is included because there is no 5% shelter for lapses at death. So the total of 15% time the value of the trust at his death is included in his estate. Note, the adjusted taxable gifts become zero even though gift tax returns were filed. This is because adjusted taxable gifts do not include gifts that end up being included in the donor's gross estate.

12. *Gift tax*: a. Frank made a taxable gift four years ago of $100,000 (= $110,000 terminal value minus $10,000 taxable gift value). b. Frank's son made a taxable gift to Frank's wife of $270,000 at Frank's death. *Estate tax*: Frank's gross estate will include $280,000 under Section 2035. There will be a marital deduction of $280,000. In addition, grossing up may be necessary.

13. Normally a gift in joint ownership is taxed when the transfer is made. However, in the case of a joint bank account, in most states a gift arises when the donee withdraws funds. In the case of U.S. Government bonds, a gift arises at redemption.

14. No gift has occurred because there is no transfer of consideration between them. Each owned the same amount before and after the purchase.

15. One example of the use of disclaimers in estate planning is to reduce a donee's future taxable estate.

16. Advantages of gift splitting: 1) It can sometimes subject gifts to a lower marginal rate of tax. 2) It can possibly shelter the entire gift (of between $10,000 and $20,000) by the annual exclusion, where otherwise a portion of the gift might be taxable, thereby using up the unified credit, or worse, incurring a gift tax. 3) It enables the family to use two unified credits, rather than just one, for large gifts.

17. a. Three taxable gifts have been made, unless some of the parties are married.

   b. Section 2518 (disclaimers) cannot help since the question implies that each person has accepted the money.

   c. The Section 2013(a) credit for tax on prior transfers cannot help because it applies only to estate taxes, not gift taxes.

18. a. The IRS could contend that you have made a present interest gift of one third of the commuted value of the annuity each to your spouse and daughter.

   b. The controversy could have been avoided by sharing the purchase of the lottery ticket with them, or giving them each, prior to winning, a one-third interest on the tickets, possibly by putting their names on it, too. However, the IRS has indicated it will probably challenge oral agreements as having been concocted after the lottery was won.

19. a. Dagny may be deemed today to have made a gift to the children of the remainder interest in her property. At Francisco's death the transfer provisions became irrevocable for Dagny, since at that moment Francisco, who was one of the parties to the agreed upon will, is no longer able to revoke them. Thus, the provisions of the will are now binding on Dagny. In fact, some jurisdictions such as Illinois would consider Dagny's interest to be simply a life estate, which would deny the marital deduction in Francisco's estate and make Dagny obligated to conserve the property for the benefit of the children. TAM 9023004; *Grimes v. Commissioner* 82-2 USTC (1988).

   Since Dagny's gift is not one of a present interest, it would not qualify for the annual exclusion. For these reasons, joint and mutual wills are not recommended by estate planners.

   b. If Francisco and Dagny executed an enforceable contract not to change these wills, the answer would be essentially the same. The will in part a, in effect, became an irrevocable, enforceable contract at the moment of Francisco's death.

20. a. The Generation Skipping Transfer Tax is a tax on three types of transfers, including direct skips, taxable terminations and taxable distributions. The attempt is to tax property as it passes from one generation to the next. The tax rate is at the highest marginal estate tax in a given year (presently 55%)..

b. Exceptions to the GSTT include:

1. $10,000 GSTT annual exclusion;
2. Predeceased ancestor exception for direct skips; and
3. $1 million lifetime exemption for all skips.

21. a. Not a gift. Queenie's powers to change the beneficiary and permit the policy to lapse means that son received only a (discretionary) contingent future interest, not a completed gift.

b. Probably a gift of at least the remainder subject to tax at time of title transfer. Definitely a gift subject to taxation by the time she relinquished all retained rights.

c. Never a gift subject to taxation, since revocable.

d. A gift subject to taxation. And only present interests, if any, will qualify for the annual exclusion.

e. $40,000 gift to son. It is the difference between the consideration given and the property received ($50,000 - $10,000).

f. A gift to husband, but not subject to taxation. Ordinarily, no form 709 need be filed, and the gift is totally sheltered by the unlimited marital deduction.

g. Assuming that Queenie owned the policy at uncle's death, gift of proceeds to daughter, since at moment of uncle's death, Queenie could have named herself beneficiary.

h. A gift of $29,000, subject to taxation. However, $21,000 would be excludable if a qualified tuition payment. The remaining $8,000 should qualify for the annual exclusion.

i. Gift subject to taxation will occur either upon deposit of money or upon daughter's later withdrawal, depending upon the law of Queenie's residence state.

ENDNOTES

1. Reg. §25.2511-2(b).

2. §2501(a)(2), §2511(a).

3. At Dad's death, none of this contingent claim is likely to be deductible against his gross estate, if Son has not defaulted. Reg 20.2053-4.

4. LR 9113009; Rev. Rul. 84-25 1984-1 C.B. 191.

5. §2516.

6. TAM 9301001.

7. §2502(c)

8. §102(a)

9. *Diedrich* 457 U.S. 191 (1982).

10. §2522(a).

11. §2523.

12. §2056(b)(7)

13. §2523(i).

14. §2503(e).

15. §2501(a)(5)

16. §2503(b).

17. §63(c)(5), §1(g)(7)(B)(i).

18. §2513.

19. TAM 9128009; §2035(c).

20. §2514(b).

21. Reg. 20.2041-3(d)(5), see also Reg. 20.2041-3(d)(4).

22. Reg. §25.2518-2 (d)(1); LR 9135043; LR 9135044; TAM 9208003.

23. Reg. §25.2518-1(b).

24. T.A.M. 88717003.

25. §453.

26. §1031.

27. §1034.

28. §1033.

29. §1014(a).

30. §2032.

31. Revenue Ruling 54-97, 1954-1 C.B. 113

32. §691(c)(3).

33. Omission of the remaining parts of this section should not significantly impede a general understanding of the estate freezing material, particularly the grantor retained trust (Chapter 14) and the corporate recapitalization (Chapter 16).

34. §2701(e)(5).

35. §2701(e)(1).

36. §2701(e)(2).

37. §2701(b).

38. §2701(c)(2).

39. §2701(a)(2).

40. §2701(a)(4).

41. §2701(a)(3)(A).

42. Reg. §25.2701-3(b).

43. §2701(a)(3)(A).

44. §2702(e).

45. §2702(a)(1).

46. §2701(e)(2).

47. §2703(a).

48. §2703(b).

— 8

Fiduciary Income Taxation

OVERVIEW

An estate or trust is a separate legal entity created to transfer property from one party to another. Since both are separate legal entities, each must file a tax return, Form 1041 (the Fiduciary Income Tax return), annually with the Internal Revenue Service (IRS) to report the trust's or estate's taxable events for the year. Fiduciary income taxation is unique because the fiduciary entity can be both a taxable entity and a conduit. As a taxable entity, the estate or trust must pay the required tax due within the prescribed time or be subject to various tax penalties. As a conduit, the entity reports to the beneficiaries how much of the taxable income is included on the beneficiaries' individual income tax returns. All of the entity's taxable events are classified and reported to the IRS by the entity.

The fiduciary is responsible for filing the decedent's final 1040 (the regular Income Tax return) and the 1041's for the trust or estate. If an amount is properly recorded on the final 1040, it will not also be reported on the first 1041. Death forms a wall between the two tax entities. Once a person dies, his or her tax year ends; therefore, any item collected or paid after death is generally not includable on the deceased's final income tax return. Do not confuse income taxation and transfer taxation. These are two independent tax systems and certain items are taxable for both purposes.

FIDUCIARY ACCOUNTING

Before a fiduciary tax return can be prepared, the income and expenses, for book purposes, must be determined, which mandates an understanding of fiduciary accounting. Further, an understanding of fiduciary accounting is needed to comprehend the tax terminology of Subchapter J (Estates, Trusts, Beneficiaries, and Decedents) of the Internal Revenue Code (IRC). The IRC uses many concepts from fiduciary accounting in determining the taxation of income from a fiduciary entity.

Goals of Fiduciary Accounting

It has long been recognized that fiduciary accounting has a purpose different from financial or tax accounting, and that fiduciary accounting standards are not well defined. Unlike financial accounting, fiduciary accounting must rely on the entity's controlling document (e.g., the will or trust) and state law. A fiduciary entity results from the division of legal and beneficial interests in property. The fiduciary is responsible for managing assets placed under his or her care for the benefit of the beneficiaries. The managerial process places on the fiduciary various duties and obligations. Determining how well the fiduciary carried out his or her duty is one of the primary the goals of fiduciary accounting. Through the preparation of certain reports, the fiduciary can describe to the beneficiaries the results of his or her activities and allows the beneficiaries to judge if the fiduciary has been a good steward. These reports should provide maximum clarity, full disclosure, and a complete description and explanation of all events during the accounting period. Fiduciary accounting uses the cash method for recording transactions.

Allocation between Corpus and Income

Fiduciary accounting income (FAI) represents the claims of the income beneficiaries against the various inflows and outflows of the entity. Computing the exact amount each beneficiary is entitled to receive is part of the fiduciary's responsibilities. Fiduciary accounting rules provide the mechanism for the accurate allocation of assets between the beneficiaries. Although most preparers would record inflows as income, this treatment would adversely affect the remainderman. Further recording all outflows as expense would adversely affect the income beneficiaries. Therefore, a system has been developed to protect the interests of both beneficiaries by allocating the inflows and outflows between income and corpus to compute the correct amounts available to the particular beneficiaries.

The *Uniform Principal and Income Act* (UPIA) was drafted to compute a fair allocation between income and corpus. The UPIA was revised in 1962 and is currently being reviewed for a new revision. Since most states have adopted some version of the UPIA, a review of the Act is helpful in understanding how items should usually be allocated. According to the UPIA, a fiduciary allocates receipts and expenditures using the following steps:

1. The governing document determines how the allocation is to be made;
2. If the document does not provide for the allocation, then state law controls; or
3. If neither allocates the particular item, the fiduciary (executor or trustee) is to use his or her best judgment according to what is reasonable and equitable in view of all beneficiaries' interests in the entity.

The grantor has considerable flexibility in determining how the income from the trust will be determined. When creating the trust, the grantor is allowed to state what items will be attributed to the income beneficiaries and what amounts should remain for the remaindermen. This latitude gives the grantor the ultimate responsibility for determining what property should go to which beneficiary. If the grantor wants every inflow to increase income and every outflow to reduce corpus, then his or her wishes should be followed, since it is the grantor's property that is being allocated. The intent of the grantor is paramount in the allocation of items between income and corpus. Due to the flexibility given the grantor, various items that are income/expense under financial accounting might not be so categorized under fiduciary accounting.

Two additional rules should be remembered while computing fiduciary accounting income:

1. Specific statutes control over general statutes, and
2. Directly related expenditures reduce the related type of receipt.

EXAMPLE 8 - 1. Under the UPIA, rental income is expressly stated to be income; therefore, the provisions applying to sole proprietorships cannot be used to allocate rental income between beneficiaries. Further, all rental expenses would be deducted from rental income in computing FAI.

What an income beneficiary is entitled to receive from the trust is based on the computation of fiduciary accounting income. The income beneficiary is not allowed to receive any item that is not an income item. If the trust did not receive any income items during the accounting period, the income beneficiary would not receive any distributions. Incorrect allocation results in the wrong beneficiary believing he or she has a claim to a given amount of assets. The fiduciary cannot show favoritism between income beneficiaries and remaindermen or between beneficiaries within the same classification. While the UPIA allows the grantor to give the trustee discretion in determining what amounts are allocated to income and corpus, the trustee's discretion is not as broad as that of the grantor.[1] When discretion is given in the trust document, the trustee must use reasonable discretion in his or her allocations, basing them on the intent of the grantor when construing the entire trust instrument aided by the surrounding circumstances.[2] Terms like "absolute" or "full authority" does not alter the trustee's responsibility to impartially act for the benefit of all beneficiaries.[3]

Effect of Fiduciary Accounting Income on Taxable Income

On the income tax return, the fiduciary is allowed a deduction for income distributions. The amount of this deduction is based on the distributions allowed by the fiduciary entity (the trust or estate) determined under applicable state law. Once the appropriate distribution has been determined, the deductible amount may be limited by federal tax laws. This interrelationship between the Code and state law applies throughout this area of the law, so understanding the state law in this area is very important to determining the correct amount of trust accounting income.

Section 643(b) of the IRC states:

For purposes of this subpart and subparts B, C and D, [§§641-668] the term "income," when not preceded by the words "taxable," "gross," "distributable net," or "undistributable net," means the amount of income of the estate or trust for the taxable year determined under the terms of the governing instrument and applicable local law.

Knowing how to compute FAI for the year is vital to preparation of a correct tax return. Furthermore, the taxation of the beneficiaries is based on the amount of distribution to which each is entitled, which in turn is generally controlled by the trust documents or the state's principal and income laws.

FIDUCIARY INCOME TAXATION

The primary purpose of Subchapter J is to allocate income and deductions between the fiduciary entity and the beneficiaries. Form 1041 is the only tax form designed to serve in a twin capacity. A fiduciary entity can be a taxpaying entity and/or a conduit, flowing various income and expense items out to the beneficiaries. To complicate matters further, proper preparation of Form 1041 requires the preparer to integrate fiduciary accounting income into the computations, so the correct allocation can be determined.

Subchapter J: An Overview of Fiduciary Taxation

Throughout our discussions, always remember that *Subchapter J was written not to compute taxable income specifically, but to allocate taxable income to the appropriate party, either the fiduciary entity or the beneficiary.*

Section 641 (b)

Section 641 (b) is the key section used to compute the taxable income of the fiduciary entity. Section 641 (b) states:

The taxable income of an estate or trust shall be computed in *the same manner as in the case of an individual*, except as otherwise provided in this part. The tax shall be computed on such taxable income and shall be paid by the fiduciary.

Since a fiduciary entity is recognized as a separate legal entity, remembering that it is taxed like a person is difficult; however, unlike a partnership or a corporation, a fiduciary entity has been created for managing and eventually transferring property. Due to its unique characteristic, operating a fiduciary entity has more similarities with an individual and his or her handling of property than any other tax entity; therefore, it is logical that the IRC uses the tax rules applicable to individuals in computing the taxable income of a fiduciary entity. If the preparer cannot find a different treatment of any income or expense item in the IRC or regulations, he or she should report the item as one would on a Form 1040.

Tax Accounting Method

A fiduciary entity can use any tax accounting method available to individuals. Selection of accounting method is made on the first Form 1041 filed. Once selected, any change in method is subject to the limitations found in §446. The choice of methods is not limited or determined by the accounting methods used by either the grantor, decedent or the beneficiaries.

Selecting a Fiduciary Income Tax Year

For trusts there is really no choice, they must use a calendar year.[4] Estates do not have the same restriction, so the estate's fiduciary can elect any year that ends on the last day of any month that is not more than 12 months from the date of death.[5] An estate begins on the day after the person dies. Providing the first year does not end more than 12 months after the decedent died, the executor's choice of year end will be acceptable. Beneficiaries must report on their income tax returns income from the fiduciary entity, based not on when the beneficiary received it, but rather as if it was all distributed to the beneficiary on the last day of the *fiduciary entity's tax year.*

> EXAMPLE 8 - 2. Joe died March 23, 1995. The executor elected January 31, 1996, as the end of the estate's first taxable year. In November 1995, the executor made distributions. Any taxable income allocated to the beneficiaries, based on those distributions, is reported by them on their 1996 tax returns.

Regulation §1.641(b)-3 holds that the IRS can terminate the estate for Federal tax purposes and begin taxing the estate as a trust. If the period of administration is unreasonably prolonged,[6] even if a probate court sanctions the continued existence of the estate, the IRS will begin taxing the estate as a trust, if the Service determines that all of the acts generally conducted by an executor have been (or should have been) completed.[7] Taxing the estate as a trust requires the estate to adopt a calendar year-end, forcing it to file a short year return. The provisions of §§446 and 481 (pertaining to adjustments that must be made when a taxpayer changes accounting methods and/or tax year) will be applied to the short year return.

An Overview of the Computations

Step one: Determine *adjusted total income*, using the tax rules for individuals, with certain modifications.

Step two: Determine the *income distribution deduction.*

Step three: Subtract the income distribution deduction (this amount is taxed to the beneficiaries) from adjusted total income.

Step four: The amount remaining is subject to tax at the fiduciary level.

The nature of income and of deductions is determined at the fiduciary level. If any income is distributed, it has the same characteristics it would have had if the fiduciary had retained it. Unless the trust document calls for some other allocation, amounts distributed to the beneficiaries consist of a proportional amount of every type of income received by the fiduciary, except capital gains are considered part of corpus and therefore are not generally allocated to beneficiaries unless the governing document requires it, or the entity terminates and all corpus (including, of course, the capital gains for the year) is distributed to the beneficiaries.

Exemptions. While a fiduciary entity is not allowed a standard deduction or a personal exemption, §642(b) allows an exemption depending on the nature of the entity. An estate is allowed a $600 deduction. If a trust must distribute all of its trust accounting income (TAI) currently, it is allowed a $300 deduction. All other trusts are allowed a $100 exemption.

> EXAMPLE 8 - 3. Trust Z's governing document requires Trust Z to distribute all of its TAI currently. For the year, Trust Z makes an additional $20,000 corpus distribution. Trust Z is allowed a $300 exemption.

> EXAMPLE 8 - 4. Trust X is not required to distribute all of its TAI currently, but the Trustee makes actual distributions exceeding its current year's TAI. Trust X is allowed a $100 exemption only, since the Trust was not required to distribute 100% of its TAI.

Tax rates. Trusts and estates have their own tax rates. Notice that it does not require very much taxable income to make it into the highest tax bracket.

TABLE 8-1 Federal Income Tax Rates: Estates and Trusts - **1997**				
Taxable Income				
Over	But not over	Base amount	+ percent	On excess over
$0	$1,650	$0.00	15.0%	$0
$1,650	$3,900	$247.50	28.0%	$1,650
$3,900	$5,950	$877.50	31.0%	$3,900
$5,950	$8,100	$1,513.00	36.0%	$5,950
$8,100	----	$2,287.00	39.6%	$8,100

Capital Gains. The capital gain and capital loss rules that apply to individuals also apply to estates and trusts.

Filing requirements. Generally, a decedent's estate must file a Form 1041 if: (a) the estate has annual gross income of $600 or more, or (b) the estate has a beneficiary who is a nonresident alien. A trust must file a Form 1041 if: (a) the trust has any taxable income, or (b) the trust has gross income of $600 or more, or (c) the trust has a beneficiary who is a nonresident alien

The return is due by the 15th of the 4th month following the entity's year end and is filed with the Service center for the region in which the fiduciary resides or has its principal place of business. An extension can be obtained by filing Form 8736 for trusts and Form 2758 for estates. Additional time is obtained by filing Form 8800. Fiduciary returns may be filed electronically.

Form 56, Notice Concerning Fiduciary Relationship, should be filed when the trust or estate is created. Form SS-4 must be filed to obtain the fiduciary entity's employer identification number. Although it is called an employer identification number, it is the tax identification number used for income tax reporting, regardless of whether the fiduciary entity has employees.

Taxable Income of a Fiduciary Entity

As we consider some of the different types of income that trusts and estates might receive, we will compare the treatment of these various types of income in the hands of the fiduciary with how it is treated when received by an individual taxpayer.

Interest and dividend income. Individual income tax rules apply to a fiduciary entity in the reporting of interest and dividend. Interest that would have been tax-exempt to an individual, is tax-exempt when received by a trust or estate. The fiduciary is not required to list separately the sources of dividend and interest income. Capital gain distributions received by the fiduciary entity are reported on Schedule D, Form 1041, just as capital gain distributions received by an individual are reported on Schedule D, Form 1040.

Net business and farm income. If an entity operates a sole-proprietorship or a farm, a Schedule C, Form 1040, Schedule C-EZ, Form 1040 or a Schedule F, Form 1040 must be prepared and attached to the Form 1041. The same rules that apply to individuals, when preparing the Schedule C, C-EZ, or F, apply to the entity.

Rents, royalties, partnerships, other estates and trusts, etc. All income from rents, royalties, partnerships, S corporations, other fiduciary entities, and Real Estate Mortgage Investment Conduits are recorded on Schedule E, Form 1040, and the net amount is reported on Form 1041. While preparing Schedule E, all directly related expenses are netted against the gross income from the particular activity. Only the net income is recorded on Form 1041. Interest, dividends, capital gains/losses and ordinary gains or losses from partnerships and other flow-through entities are shown on the appropriate lines on Form 1041 and not on Schedule E. Only estates, grantor trusts and qualified Subchapter S trusts can be S Corporation shareholders.

Net rental and royalty income. In reporting the net income or loss from rent and royalties, the fiduciary must attach Schedule E, Form 1040, to the Form 1041. The amounts shown on Schedule E reflect the total amount of income and expenses directly related to the property but only the entity's share of the depreciation or depletion.

Passive Activities. Trusts and estates are subject to the passive activity loss rules and the at-risk rules. In determining the deductible amount of any loss, the at-risk rules are applied first and then the passive activity rules.

A passive activity is a trade or business in which the taxpayer does not materially participate. Based on the Senate Finance Report, the participation of the fiduciary, not the grantor, decedent or beneficiaries, is used to decide if the activity is passive. Currently, no regulations exist establishing a material participation standard for a fiduciary, to help in determining if the activity is active or passive.

> EXAMPLE 8 - 5. Sue was a partner in a computer retail store. The partnership did not have a buy-sell agreement, so when she died, her share of the partnership was transferred to her estate. The executor does not participate in the store's operations. Even if Sue materially participated in the store's operations, her partnership interest will be treated as a passive activity in the hands of the executor and on the Form 1041.

Passive activities - rental real estate offset. A rule limiting the effect of the passive loss limitation rules is the rental real estate offset.[8] If an individual owner of rental real estate actively participates in the management of the rental property, he or she can offset against other income up to $25,000 of net losses. The offset is phased out once his or her modified adjusted gross income exceeds $100,000 and is eliminated once his or her modified adjusted gross income exceeds $150,000.

A trust is not allowed to use the offset. The characterization of property in the hands of the grantor does not carry over to the trust. Even if the trustee or a beneficiary actively participated in the management of the rental real estate, the trust is prevented from using the offset. The character of the loss is determined at the fiduciary level.

An estate is allowed to use the offset for taxable years ending within two years of the decedent's death, providing the *decedent* actively participated in the management of the rental property before his or her death. The offset available to the estate is reduced by how offset used when preparing the surviving spouse's tax return or the decedent's final 1040.[9]

Concluding remarks about passive activities. If a partnership's year end falls within the taxable year of the entity, the fiduciary entity is entitled to receive the partnership allocation for the entire year.[10] Passive losses are not deductible for alternative minimum tax purposes. Net losses from passive activities cannot be transferred to beneficiaries, but are suspended at the entity level, used by the entity to reduce future passive income and become basis adjustments at distribution of the activity. If a passive activity is sold by an entity, any suspended losses could become either a capital loss or a NOL. The rules applicable to allocation of capital losses or a NOL at termination would then govern the loss allocation.

Capital gains and losses. Capital gains and losses are reported on Schedule D, Form 1041. This is one of the few support schedules unique to fiduciary taxation. Parts I and II of Schedule D, Form 1041, are similar to Schedule D, Form 1040. The difference between the two forms is Part III of Schedule D, Form 1041. Part III reflects the allocation of gain or loss between the beneficiaries and the entity. All capital transactions are recorded on Part I and II, Form 1041, with the net gain or loss being reported on Form 1041. The sole purpose of Part III is to record the gain included in distributable net income (DNI).[11]

Sections 1211-1212 (limitations on capital losses and their carryover) and §§1221-1223 (general rules related to capital gains and losses) apply to trusts and estates, just as they do for individuals. The maximum rate at which long term capital gains can be taxed is 28%[12]. Individual holding period rules apply when determining if the capital gain or loss is either short or long term, however one of those rules is that property received from a decedent is automatically long term.[13] If the entity acquired the asset from a decedent, §1014 is followed to compute the entity's basis, while §1015 is used if the asset was acquired in an inter vivos transfer.

If an entity has a net capital loss, the maximum deduction in a single tax year is $3,000, with no limitation on the length of time the loss is carried forward. Capital losses cannot be allocated to beneficiaries while the entity exists and capital losses never reduce DNI, just as capital gains do not increase it. Section 642(h)(1) provides that in the entity's final year, a net capital loss or loss carry forward can be allocated to the beneficiaries using the same rules applicable to allocation of a NOL.

Section 643(e)(3) election. Normally, the entity recognizes no gain or loss when non cash property is distributed to a beneficiary. Each year, the entity may elect, under §643(e)(3), to treat the distribution as a sale to the beneficiary and recognize any gain or loss on the appropriate schedule, subject to §267 related party rules.[14] If the election is made and the distributed property is a capital asset, the distribution is recorded as a sale of a capital asset, subject to the general capital transaction rules. The election must be made each year, applies to all non cash distributions for the elected year and once elected cannot be revoked without IRS consent. Unless the distribution meets the requirements of §663(a), i.e, it's a specific or pecuniary bequest, the distribution is included in any DNI allocation, subjecting the beneficiary to taxation.

> EXAMPLE 8 - 6. Dottie's estate distributes 50 shares of stock to Helen, the residuary beneficiary of Dottie's estate. The estate's basis is $100 and the FMV of the stock is $150. If the §643(e)(3) election is made, the estate must recognize a gain of $50 on the "sale" of stock. Since the stock was received from a decedent, the gain will be long term. The distribution draws out DNI to Helen.

> EXAMPLE 8 - 7. If, by her will, Dottie had left the XYZ stock specifically to Helen, §663(a) would apply and no DNI would be drawn out by the distribution.

Ordinary gain or loss. The fiduciary will prepare Form 4797 and report any ordinary gain or loss from the sale of property, other than capital assets, and from involuntary conversions, other than casualty or theft. If the entity sells a depreciated asset, Form 4797 (Sales of Business Property) is completed to compute the ordinary gain and any depreciation recapture. Gains from casualty and theft are also included on this form. Sales of business assets subject to §1231 are reported on this form, whether the property was owned by the entity or by a partnership in which the entity had an interest. The rules applicable to an individual, when completing Form 4797 apply to a fiduciary entity, also.

Deductions Allowed in Computing Taxable Income

Generally, the rules for individual taxpayers claiming a deduction carry over to fiduciary income taxes. However, there are some special rules concerning deductions for fiduciary income taxes, such as those that come into play when the fiduciary entity has tax-exempt income.

Interest expense. A fiduciary entity is allowed to deduct interest expense in the same manner as an individual.[15] The fiduciary must classify the interest according to type and then apply any special rules in determining if the interest is deductible. If the interest expense directly relates to a passive activity, trade or business or other type of income, the interest should be deducted against the specific income type, not as a separate item. The main types of indirect interest are: qualified residence interest and investment interest expenses. Interest expense directly related to tax-exempt income is not deductible, nor is personal interest.

If the trust or estate pays interest owed at death, but due to the decedent's accounting method was not deductible before his or her death, the entity may deduct the interest as a deduction in respect of a decedent when the expense is paid. Interest accruing after the death of the decedent is subject to the double deduction rules under §642(g), which are discussed below. Only interest that the trust or estate is obligated to pay may be deducted.

Expenses related to tax-exempt income. No deduction is allowed for any expense attributable directly or indirectly to tax-exempt income.[16] On Form 1041 only the deductible share of such expenses are recorded. Form 1041 requires an allocation support schedule, showing how the figures were obtained and the gross amount of tax-exempt income. The purpose of allocating the expenses is to reduce the deductible expenses, so that only those related to taxable income are actually deducted.

Any expense directly related to taxable income can be fully deducted. If the fiduciary incurs $5,000 of rental expenses, these can be deducted in full. The problem occurs when the fiduciary incurs expenses associated with trust income as a whole. Most often these indirect expenses are nonbusiness expenses deductible under §212, e.g., trustee and attorney fees. Interest and taxes should be fully deductible, since they are deductible under specific IRC sections. The IRS and the courts paint a broad stroke when defining what is an indirect expense. The fiduciary must be prepared to defend his or her position if he or she excludes a particular indirect expense from reduction. If the trust or estate makes a distribution to a charity, the charitable contribution deduction must also be reduced, since the charity is deemed to receive part of the tax-exempt income.

Indirect expenses of the entity must be reduced by a proportionate share of the tax-exempt income. The fiduciary is allowed to use any reasonable method, based on the facts and circumstances.[17] However, two methods are provided for in the regulations. Under both methods, the net income or the gross income method, the fiduciary computes a ratio to figure out how much of the indirect expenses are not deductible.

With the *net income method*, the fiduciary computes the amount of gross FAI and then subtracts the expenses directly related to each particular income item. Then for each specific type of income, a ratio is computed, with the numerator being the net amount of that specific type of income and the denominator being the total net FAI.

With the *gross income method*, the fiduciary uses gross FAI as his or her denominator and gross income from the activity as his or her numerator. The only difference between the net income method and the gross income method is that with the gross income method directly related expenses are not subtracted before the allocation is made. Normally, direct expenses have a larger impact on taxable income; therefore, use of the gross income method will increase deductible expenses, since a smaller amount of the indirect expenses is being allocated to tax-exempt income.

Unless capital gains are included in FAI or in DNI, none of the expenses are allocated to capital gains, since expenses cannot be allocated against income that is excluded from DNI. If the amount of expenses directly attributable to tax-exempt income exceeds the total amount of tax-exempt income, the excess cannot be allocated to taxable income.[18]

EXAMPLE 8 - 8. Trust Z has rental income of $15,000, dividends of $10,000 and tax-exempt income of $5,000. The Trust had rental expenses of $4,000 and accounting fees of $2,000. Using both methods, accounting fees would be allocated as follows:

Fiduciary accounting income:

	Gross	Net
Rental income	$15,000	$11,000
Dividends	$10,000	$10,000
Tax-exempt income	$5,000	$5,000
Trust accounting income	$30,000	$26,000

Allocation of accounting fees: Net income method

($11,000/$26,000)	X	$2,000	=	$846
($10,000/$26,000)	X	$2,000	=	769
($5,000/$26,000)	X	$2,000	=	385
		Total		$2,000

Allocation of accounting fees: Gross income method

($15,000/$30,000)	X	$2,000	=	$1,000
($10,000/$30,000)	X	$2,000	=	667
($5,000/$30,000)	X	$2,000	=	333
		Total		$2,000

Under the gross income method, only $333 of accounting fees would not be deducted, whereas the net income method results in $385 not being deducted.

Depreciation. If a fiduciary entity owns qualified property, it is allowed to deduct depreciation, depletion and amortization (after this called depreciation), using the same rules applicable to individuals. Estates and trusts are not allowed a §179 deduction. The fiduciary selects the appropriate depreciation method, prepares Form 4562 and attaches it to Form 1041 to show the total amount of deductible depreciation. While the deductible amount is computed at the fiduciary level, the fiduciary entity **may not** be eligible to take any depreciation deduction. Depreciation must be apportioned between the entity and its beneficiaries under special rules. Deductible depreciation allocated to the entity from a partnership, trust, or estate is allocated under the same rules. The asset's basis is computed using the rules in §1014, for testamentary transfers, or §1015, for inter vivos transfers.

If the entity is entitled to take all or part of the deduction, depreciation directly related to a particular activity is reported on the specific support schedule (Schedules C, E or F), while all other depreciation is reported on Line 15a, Form 1041. If the entity is **not** entitled to a depreciation deduction, **no** deduction is recorded on Form 1041 nor on any support schedule. Tax depreciation not reported on Form 1041 is allocated to the income beneficiaries is reflected on their Schedule K-1, Lines 4 b, c, d or Lines 5 b, c, d.

Depreciation Apportionment rules. Apportionment of depreciation is covered in §642(e), which states:

> An estate or trust shall be allowed the deduction for depreciation
> and depletion only to the extent not allowable to beneficiaries
> under §§167(d) and 611(b).

Section 167(d) applies to depreciation, while §611(b) pertains to depletion. The general rule for allocating depreciation between the entity and its beneficiaries is:

1. To the extent there is a reserve for depreciation for FAI purposes, allocate the tax depreciation to the entity, and
2. If tax depreciation exceeds accounting depreciation or if there is no depreciation reserve for accounting purposes, allocate the tax depreciation

between the entity and the beneficiaries based on the allocation of FAI between the parties.[19]

The key to apportioning the tax depreciation between the entity and its beneficiaries is determined by how depreciation is handled for FAI purposes. Whether a reserve exists for FAI purposes is based on the terms of the document and state law. Generally, a reserve exists when FAI is reduced by some amount of depreciation. The fiduciary may reduce FAI for depreciation when the entity operates a sole proprietorship or general partnership and when the document requires a depreciation deduction or the fiduciary makes an improvement that would be depreciated under generally accepted accounting principles (GAAP). Depending on the state, income from rental property and natural resources may be reduced by depreciation. To the extent FAI is reduced by depreciation, the tax depreciation is allocated to the entity.

> EXAMPLE 8 - 9. Trust X owns a drug store, which is operated as a sole proprietorship. GAAP depreciation equals $10,000 and net income from the store is $50,000. If tax depreciation is equal to or less than $10,000, all of the tax depreciation will be reported on Schedule C, Form 1041. If tax depreciation is $15,000, the extra $5,000 is allocated under the set of rules discussed next.

When tax depreciation exceeds the reserve or there is no reserve for FAI purposes, tax depreciation follows FAI. Any beneficiary who receives FAI receives the "excess" tax depreciation, also. For accounting purposes, a charity is treated as any other beneficiary, so if the charity receives FAI, the charity would receive its share of tax depreciation, too. If no reserve exists and the entity is required to distribute all the FAI, the beneficiaries would be entitled to the entire depreciation deduction, and no depreciation deduction would taken on Form 1041.

> EXAMPLE 8 - 10. Trust Y has rental property. Under state law, no depreciation is allowed and the document is silent concerning a reserve. Since FAI is not reduced by depreciation, the allocation of tax depreciation follows the allocation of FAI. For tax purposes, rental depreciation is $20,000. FAI is $50,000. By the terms of the trust, FAI was allocated as follows: Allan - 50%; Bea - 25%; Charity - 10% and Trust Y - 15%. The tax depreciation would be allocated as follows: Allan - $10,000; Bea - $5,000; Charity - $2,000 and Trust Y - $3,000. Trust Y would file Form 4562 (Depreciation and Amortization) to report the $20,000 of depreciation and it would include $3,000 on Schedule E, Form 1041. The depreciation allocated to Allan and

Bea would be recorded on their Schedules K-1, Line 5b and the trustee would inform the Charity of the $2,000 depreciation allocation. Charities do not receive a Schedule K-1, since Schedule K-1 is reserved for beneficiaries who receive distributable net income.

EXAMPLE 8 - 11.   Trust Z owns rental property. For FAI, depreciation of $10,000 is deducted. Tax depreciation is $25,000. By the terms of the trust, FAI is allocated as follows: Art - 60%; Beth - 30% and Trust Z - 10%. The first $10,000 of tax depreciation must be allocated to Trust Z. Of the remaining $15,000, Art receives $9,000, Beth $4,500 and Trust Z $1,500. On Schedule E, Form 1041, Trust Z would report depreciation of $11,500 and on Art's Schedule K-1, Line 5b $9,000 would be reported while on Beth's Schedule K-1, Line 5b $4,500 would be recorded.

The existence or absence of a reserve for FAI does not alter the amount of deductible depreciation for tax purposes. All an accounting reserve does is determine who gets the deduction. If the depreciation is directly allocable to the beneficiaries, the depreciation is ignored for DNI purposes and has no impact on its computation or allocation. To the extent depreciation is deductible on Form 1041, depreciation reduces adjusted total income, which reduces the DNI allocated to the beneficiaries.

An exception for depletion.   Under fiduciary accounting rules, 27½% of income from natural resources, other than timber, must be allocated to corpus. Several courts have labeled this allocation as a set aside to fund a depletion reserve to protect the corpus.[20] As a reserve, the tax depletion is first allocated to the reserve. Since the amount allocated under fiduciary accounting (27½%) is greater than the allowable tax percentage depletion (15%), all the tax depletion should be allocated to the entity. Timber has no fixed percentage, but does require an allocation of inflows to corpus.

EXAMPLE 8 - 12.   Trust Y owns oil royalty property. In 1995, Trust Y had $10,000 of royalty income and $1,500 of tax depletion. Although the trust required all FAI to be distributed, the entire $1,500 of tax depletion would be reported on Schedule E, since the $1,500 (tax depletion) is less than the $2,750 of royalty income (accounting reserve) allocated to corpus. The beneficiary would receive a distribution of $7,250 with no depletion allocation. Trust Y would report the entire $10,000 less the $1,500 depletion, but of the net $8,500, $7,250 would be taxable to the beneficiaries, leaving $1,250 taxable to Trust Y.

Taxes.   A trust or estate can deduct any taxes allowed under §164. These taxes normally include: state, local and foreign income taxes and property taxes.

Sales tax is not deducted, but is added to the cost-basis of the item purchased. If the taxes are attributable to a specific type of income, they should be deducted in arriving at the net income from that income type. If any generation-skipping transfer tax (GSTT) is paid on income distributions, the entity may deduct these taxes, providing they were not deducted in determining the GSTT.[21] Other Federal income, excise, and custom taxes are not deductible.

Double deductions. Section 642(g) provides that estate expenses under §§2053 or 2054 can be deducted on Form 1041. This is allowed only if the expenses were not deducted on Form 706 and a statement waiving the right to deduct the expenses on Form 706 should be filed with Form 1041. This election is not an "all or nothing" election. The fiduciary has the discretion to deduct all, part, or none of the expenses on Form 1041 or on Form 706. These expenses do not include deductions in respect of a decedent, which can be deducted on both returns. Deductions in respect of a decedent are expenses that accrued prior to the decedent's death such that they are deductible as debts on the estate tax return (Form 706) and, when paid, are deductible as expenses on the fiduciary income tax return (Form 1041). Property taxes that became a lien before the decedent's death, and were paid by the executor, are an example of a deduction in respect of a decedent. Since the top income tax rate is 39.6%, an additional computation must be made to decide where the greater tax savings can be achieved. Due to the unified credit, the first dollar of taxable estate will be taxed at 37%. The marginal estate tax rate above $3,000,000 is 55% and within the "bubble" (between $10,000,000 and $21,040,000) it is 60%.

Charitable deduction. Section 642(c) details the rules covering a permitted charitable contribution deduction and computation of the allowed deduction is recorded on Schedule A, Form 1041 and carried over to Line 13, Form 1041. Section 642(c) states:

> "...there shall be allowed as a deduction in computing its taxable income...any amount of the *gross income*, without limitation, which *pursuant to the terms of the governing instrument* is, during the taxable year, paid for a purpose specified in §170(c)...."

Before a deduction is allowed, the following requirements must be met:

1. The will or trust document must authorize the contribution,

2. The amount of deduction is limited by gross income, and
3. Only those amounts actually paid during the year or during the following year may be deducted.[22]

For purposes of the deduction, gross income includes any amount earned on the trust's or estate's assets, any IRD, and any current year capital gains paid, permanently set aside or credited to the charity. All other amounts paid from corpus or tax-exempt income are not deductible. Specific and pecuniary bequests and non-cash contributions are customarily paid out of corpus, so no deduction is allowed. The amount the charity actually receives is determined by FAI and the document, so the actual distribution may be less than gross income. Only amounts actually paid can be deducted, even if gross income is higher. Of the amount distributed to the charity, it consists of every type of FAI received by the entity, subject to the special allocation rules. If the entity has tax-exempt income or depreciation, then these items must be allocated to the charity, just like to any other beneficiary.

The entity must actually distribute the property to the charity before a deduction is allowed. A special election can be made to treat distributions made during the following year as made in the current year, so the entity is allowed a current year deduction. If the fiduciary so elects, any payment made after the close of the current taxable year (year one), and before the close of the second taxable year (year two), may be treated as paid in year one for tax purposes. The election is irrevocable and must be made in the timely filed tax return for year two (including extensions). Failure to make the actual distribution before the due date of the year one tax return will require the fiduciary to forego the deduction and file an amended return for year one once the distribution is made during year two. This election is unique for charitable contributions and is separate from the 65-day rule.[23]

> EXAMPLE 8 - 13. Trust X is allowed to distribute 10% of TAI to the local cancer society. The Trustee cannot compute the available deduction until after the close of the current year (1995). The Trustee can elect to treat any distribution made at any time during 1996 as made in 1995, so he can get a charitable deduction for 1995.

Estates and pre-October 9, 1969 irrevocable trusts are allowed a deduction for amounts permanently set-aside for future payment to a charity. While funds do not have to be placed in a separate account, some bookkeeping entry must be made to show the set-aside. For an amount to be considered permanently set-aside, there must exist no more than a remote possibility that another beneficiary could receive the funds.

> EXAMPLE 8 - 14.   Estate Y requires the Executor to accumulate 50% of each year's capital gains for future distribution to Big Brothers. In 1995, Estate Y had capital gains of $10,000, so Estate Y can take a charitable deduction of $5,000 in 1995, even though the $5,000 might not be distributed for several years.

No deduction is allowed unless the document allows the entity to make a charitable contribution. Where the document does not provide for a charitable contribution, any payment made by the fiduciary is nondeductible and could subject the fiduciary to a surcharge. If a beneficiary authorizes the fiduciary to make the beneficiary's payment to a charity, the beneficiary will be allocated the income and take any charitable deduction on his or her individual Form 1040. The law is uncertain on whether a fiduciary entity can deduct charitable contributions made by a partnership or S corporation and passed through to the entity. Unless the document specially grants the fiduciary the authority to make charitable contributions, there appears to be no authority for allowing a deduction.

Administration expenses. Administration expenses unique to the operation of a fiduciary entity are deductible to the extent:

1. They are reasonable in amount;
2. incurred in the ordinary and necessary administration of the entity;
3. not allocable to the production or collection of tax-exempt income; and
4. have not been deducted for federal estate tax purposes.[24]

Administrative expenses that would fit this definition are:

1. fiduciary fees and commissions;
2. attorney fees;
3. accounting fees including fees for the preparation of any tax returns and for both court and informal accounting;
4. miscellaneous administrative expenses including court costs, fiduciary bonds, appraisals, advertising, investment advisory fees etc.; and
5. non-business casualty and theft losses.

Net operating loss (NOL). In fiduciary accounting, losses from business operations are added to corpus, resulting in no loss carry back or carry forward. Further, a loss from operations does not reduce the FAI available for distribution to the beneficiaries.

> EXAMPLE 8 - 15. Trust X operates a drug store as a sole proprietorship. In 1995, the store had a net loss of $5,000. 1995 FAI would not be reduced by any of the $5,000 loss. If the drug store has net income in 1996 of $3,000, the entire $3,000 would be allocated to FAI, and FAI would not be reduced by any part of the prior year's loss.

For tax purposes an NOL creates a different tax situation. Estates and trusts are allowed a net operating loss deduction under §172.[25] The entity's NOL is computed following individual income tax rules, except for two main changes. A NOL cannot be increased by the charitable contribution deduction or the income distribution deduction. If a trust or estate has a NOL, the NOL must be carried back three years, unless waived, and carried forward fifteen years. Except in the entity's final year, a NOL can only be used by the trust or estate. If a NOL exists in the termination year, the NOL is allocated to the corpus beneficiaries, who may use it on their personal returns and only carry forward any unused portion. The beneficiaries do not get a new fifteen year carry forward period. In computing and determining the tax treatment of a NOL, only the rules under §§172, 642(d) and 642(h)(1) apply. Any other rules applicable to losses do not apply.

Personal expenses. Fiduciary entities may not deduct personal expenses. Personal expenses are expenses not associated with the management, conservation or maintenance of property, e.g., interest/ expense on the decedent's credit cards paid by the executor. If a house is used as the personal residence of a beneficiary, the expenses related to the house, like utilities, repairs and yard maintenance, are not deductible. Qualified residence interest and property taxes would remain deductible. A beneficiary's temporary use of a house, before the sale or disposition of the house, should not disallow the deductions, since the expenses are of an investment nature and not personal.

Section 67(a) subjects trusts and estates to the limitation on deductibility of miscellaneous itemized deductions. Only to the extent these deductions exceed 2% of adjusted gross income are they deductible. The expenses must be reduced by tax-exempt income before applying the 2% floor. Section 67(b) lists various expenses that are not subject to the limitation and include the charitable deduction, interest expense, taxes, and deductions in respect of a decedent. Examples of expenses subject to the limitation are: safe deposit box rental, collection fees, and appraisal fees.

Section 67(e)(1) makes a special exception for fiduciary entities. Deductions, which are incurred concerning the administration of an estate or trust, which would not have been incurred if the property were not held in the trust or estate, are not subject to the 2% floor. Most administrative expenses should qualify for the exception; however, the IRS and the Tax Court have applied a harsh definition as to which expenses can be excluded. In the 1993 case, *O'Neill, Jr. v. Commissioner*,[26] the Sixth Circuit overruled the Tax Court and held that investment advisory expenses are not subject to the 2% floor. In the *O'Neill* case, nonprofessional trustees incurred substantial advisory fees in the management of a $4.5 million trust. Since state law placed a fiduciary duty on the trustees to manage the trust corpus properly, the trustees argued that the advisory expenses were unique to the trust's administration. The IRS and the Tax Court found that investment advisory fees were not unique to the administration of a fiduciary entity, since individuals incurred investment advisory fees, also. Only those expenses not payable by individuals could be unique to a fiduciary entity and subject to the exception. The Sixth Circuit disagreed. The Court accepted the trustees' arguments and found that advisory fees incurred by nonprofessional trustees are unique to the administration of a trust. The IRS has indicated it will not follow *O'Neill* outside the Sixth Circuit.[27]

Adjusted gross income (AGI) of a fiduciary entity is computed in the same manner as it is for an individual. Section 67(e) allows the fiduciary to deduct all administrative expenses, the income distribution deduction, and the entity's exemption in arriving at AGI. The instructions to Form 1041 contain an algebraic formula to compute AGI if DNI is less than the income distributed. If the amount distributed is less than DNI, the instructions recommend using the income distributed to compute AGI; however, the distribution deduction must be reduced by any amount attributed to tax-exempt income.

Funeral and medical expenses. Funeral and medical expenses deserve special attention because funeral expenses can only be deducted on the estate tax return and medical expenses can never be deducted on Form 1041. Medical expenses paid within one year of death can be deducted on the decedent's final return or on the estate tax return. An election is filed with the decedent's final return electing to take the medical deductions against income. If the medical expenses are deducted on the decedent's final 1040, they are subject to the 7.5% adjusted gross income limitation.

THE EFFECT OF TRANSFERS AND DISTRIBUTIONS

In this section we consider the income tax implications of making asset transfers to and from estates, trust, and beneficiaries. Generally, non-cash distributions (in-kind distributions) are subject to the same rules as cash distributions. The beneficiaries must include in income distributions of property if DNI is allocated to the distribution. This results in the beneficiaries having to pay tax, though they might not have the cash. Further, the type of income that comprises DNI determines the taxability of the distribution, not the type of property received as a distribution.

Property Transfers - General Rule

If the transfer of property is not considered a sale by the fiduciary entity (§643(e)(3) election or pecuniary bequest), the basis of the property in the hands of the beneficiary is the entity's adjusted basis in the property immediately before distribution.[28] The beneficiary can tack the entity's holding period to his holding period. The entity can only consider the lesser of the property's basis or its FMV when computing the income distribution deduction. This can result in the beneficiary having a basis greater than her taxable income.

Transfers Subject to §663(a)

If the transfer qualified under Section 663(a)(1), the beneficiary does not have any taxable income and the entity has no distribution deduction, since this type of distribution does not qualify for the distribution deduction. The beneficiary's basis is the entity's basis, if the beneficiary sells the property at a gain, or the FMV of the property at distribution, if the property is sold at a loss.[29] The entity's holding period is tacked onto the beneficiary's holding period.

Transfers Subject to a §643(e)(3) Election

If the entity elects to treat the distribution as a sale under §643(e)(3), the beneficiary's basis equals the entity's basis immediately before distribution, adjusted for any gain or loss recognized. Since the entity's basis is used to determine the beneficiary's basis, the beneficiary can probably tack on the entity's holding period. The entity can consider the FMV of the property when computing the income distribution deduction.

> EXAMPLE 8 - 16. Trust X has DNI of $50,000. Trust X distributes stock valued at $50,000 to June. The trust's adjusted basis in the stock is $10,000. Effect of no election: (1) No gain on transfer; (2) DNI is reduced by $10,000, so trust pays tax on $40,000; and (3) June has income of $10,000 and her basis is $10,000. If the election is made: (a) Trust has gain of $40,000; (b) DNI is reduced to zero; the gain does not increase DNI and the distribution deduction is increased to $50,000; and (c) June has income of $50,000 and her basis is $50,000.

Transfers to Satisfy a Pecuniary Bequest

A capital gain or loss is recognized when a trust or estate transfers property to satisfy a pecuniary gift, bequest, or claim, which is defined as a required distribution of a specific sum of money or specific property. The gain or loss is determined by the difference between the FMV of the property on the date of transfer and the entity's basis in the property. The entity is considered to have distributed cash and the beneficiary turned around and bought the property.[30] If the distribution does not meet the requirements of §663(a), the gain will be included in any DNI allocation, subjecting the beneficiary to taxation. The beneficiary's basis is the FMV of the property at the time of distribution and he must begin a new holding period. The distribution deduction equals the FMV of the property, providing sufficient DNI exists.

> EXAMPLE 8 - 17. Norm's will requires a $10,000 distribution to Keith. Instead of distributing cash, the Executor distributes stock valued at $10,000. The estate's basis in the stock is $7,000. The estate must report a $3,000 long-term gain on its Form 1041, but can include the full $10,000 when computing the income distribution deduction. Keith's basis in the stock is $10,000 and he must hold the stock for 12 months before being eligible for long term gain treatment on sale.

EXAMPLE 8 - 18. Norm's estate has estate accounting income (EAI) of $15,000. The Executor decides to distribute a car valued at $15,000, instead of cash, to Ann. Since EAI is not a pecuniary bequest, no sale occurs, unless §643(e)(3) is elected. If the car's basis is $9,000, Ann's basis is $9,000 and she can tack the estate's holding period to her's on any future sale. When computing the income distribution deduction, the Executor must use $9,000.

Transfers of Passive Activities

There are some fairly specific rules concerning transfers of passive activity investments between the grantor/ decedent and the fiduciary entity and between the fiduciary entity and the beneficiaries. These rules are in addition to the rules that apply to in-kind property distributions.

Lifetime Transfers from a Grantor to a Trust. If a grantor has any suspended losses when he or she transfers the investment to a trust, the losses are added to the basis. While the grantor is treated as disposing of the asset, according to the passive activity rules, he or she cannot recognize any of the suspended losses on his or her personal return.[31]

EXAMPLE 8 - 19. Harry owns a partnership interest in an office building. His basis in the partnership is $100,000; however, he has $20,000 in suspended losses. The trust's basis in the partnership will be $120,000, and Harry cannot use the suspended losses in the future to reduce his passive income.

Transfers from a Decedent to an Estate. The death of a person is treated as a distribution of his or her entire interest in the asset, so on the decedent's final return, the suspended losses can be used to reduce other income, subject to one limitation. The recipient's basis of property received at death is its fair market value (FMV) at date of death.[32] When the suspended losses exceed the increase in basis, the loss can be deducted on the decedent's final return.[33]

EXAMPLE 8 - 20. Mary died on 11/12/95. Her basis in a partnership was $20,000. The FMV of the partnership interest was $50,000. Mary had $100,000 of suspended losses. On Mary's final return, $70,000 of the losses may be deducted. ($50,000 - $20,000 = $30,000; $100,000 - $30,000 = $70,000)

EXAMPLE 8 - 21. Martin died on 12/31/95. His basis in a partnership was ($200,000). The FMV of the partnership interest was $30,000. His suspended losses totaled $150,000. None of the suspended losses will be recognized on Martin's final

Form 1040 and the estate's basis will be $30,000. Since the increase in basis, $230,000, exceeded the total suspended losses, neither Martin nor the estate can deduct the losses.

Transfers from Trust/Estate to a Beneficiary. Transfers of passive activities to a beneficiary are treated in the same manner as transfers from a grantor to a trust. Any suspended losses incurred by the entity are added to the basis and the entity is prevented from using the losses in the future.[34] If the distribution of a passive activity by an executor is considered a sale under §643(e)(3) or Reg. §1.1014-4, the estate can use the suspended losses on Form 1041. Related party rules (§267) prevent a trust from making a similar option.[35]

INCOME DISTRIBUTION DEDUCTION AND THE TAXATION OF BENEFICIARIES

As said earlier in the chapter, the main focus of Subchapter J is to allocate taxable income between the fiduciary entity and the beneficiaries. The trust or estate receives a deduction based on the taxable income distributed to the beneficiaries during the year. The deductible amount is computed on Schedule B, Form 1041 and recorded on Line 18, Form 1041. Since a fiduciary entity can distribute income and corpus, depending on the terms of the fiduciary document, an amount called distributable net income (DNI) must be calculated. Section 643(a) defines DNI. DNI limits the amount of taxable income allocated to the beneficiaries. Any amount distributed greater than DNI will be considered either undistributed net income (UNI) or corpus.

Key Definitions

Simple trust. The IRC establishes two types of trusts for calculating the income distribution deduction. Sections 651-652 are used to compute the distribution deduction for simple trusts and §§661-663 are used to compute the deduction for complex trusts. The terms "simple" and "complex" are not found in the Code, but are used throughout the regulations. The definition of a trust can change from year-to-year; however, in its final year, a trust will always be complex.

Section 651 defines a simple trust as a trust that:

1. is required to distribute all of its trust accounting income (TAI) currently;
2. no amount from the trust can be used for charitable purposes;
3. there are no distributions in excess of TAI for the year.

The trust document determines if the first two requirements are met. The word income in §651(a)(1) refers to trust accounting income.[36] If the document requires the trustee to distribute all the current year's TAI, the beneficiaries are deemed to have received the TAI for taxation purposes, whether it is actually distributed or not. If the document does not require all the TAI to be distributed currently, the trust cannot be classified as a simple trust, even if the trust actually distributes all of its TAI for the year.

A simple trust is limited in the type of distributions it can make. If the trust could have made a distribution that would qualify for a charitable deduction, the trust cannot be classified as a simple trust, even if no charitable distributions are actually made.[37] Further, if the trust makes distributions greater than TAI, it cannot be a simple trust. Although corpus distributions are allowed under the trust document, the trust will be a simple trust, unless distributions greater than current year's TAI are actually made. In years the trust does not make any corpus distributions, it will be a simple trust, and in years it makes a corpus distribution it will be a complex trust.

A simple trust is allowed a deduction for the TAI distributed limited by DNI.[38] The amount of the deduction must be reduced by any amount not included in gross income less any applicable expenses. This requires the fiduciary to reduce the available deductions by any amount of tax-exempt income, net of related expenses, included in TAI.

Complex trusts. If a trust does not meet the definition of a simple trust, it is a complex trust. The income distribution deduction for complex trusts and all estates is determined under §§661-663. A trust, which can accumulate income, can make charitable contributions or makes a corpus distribution will be a complex trust. Since a trust must distribute all remaining corpus in its final year, a trust will always be a complex trust in its final year. The main difference between the computation of the income distribution deduction for simple and complex trusts is the use of a tier system for complex trusts. The tier system results in a greater amount of DNI being allocated to beneficiaries who receive required TAI distributions.

Distributable Net Income (DNI). DNI is the statutory limit for the income distribution deduction. DNI determines the maximum distribution deduction. If actual distributions exceed DNI, the entity gets no deduction for the excess; however, if distributions are less than DNI, only the amount actually distributed can be deducted.[39] Section 643(a) defines DNI as the entity's net taxable income modified as follows:

1. No deduction for the income distribution;
2. No deduction for the personal exemption;
3. Net undistributed capital gains allocated to corpus are subtracted;
4. Net capital losses are added back;
5. Net tax-exempt income is added back; and
6. For simple trusts only, subtract any undistributed extraordinary dividends or taxable stock dividends that the fiduciary allocated to corpus in good faith.

DNI is reduced by all tax deductible expenses. Whether these expenses are deducted from income or corpus for accounting purposes is ignored. DNI is a tax computation; therefore, accounting allocations of expenses is disregarded, unless the Code specifically requires the allocation to be considered. This treatment of corpus expenses allows income beneficiaries to benefit, from a tax standpoint, from corpus expenses paid during the year, since DNI limits the taxable income allocated to the income beneficiaries, thereby, reducing how much income they must pay taxes on.

To visualize the allocation of FAI and DNI, think about Neapolitan ice cream. Unlike swirl ice cream, each flavor of Neapolitan is separate from the other flavors. If a person wanted only vanilla ice cream, he or she could remove vanilla from the "block of ice cream" leaving the other flavors. Gross accounting income, net accounting income and DNI form our "blocks of ice cream." Each block is composed of various "flavors" of income. When the fiduciary "scoops" the beneficiaries their share of FAI or DNI, each beneficiary receives some of every flavor. Exactly how much of each flavor a beneficiary receives is determined by the total composition of the block. If 50% of the total block is rental income, the beneficiary's "scoop" is 50% rent. Although there are many similarities in the configuration of each block, each block is different. In most situations, the FAI and DNI blocks contain the same flavors/income, but the percentage of flavors that comprise each block changes, based on the different rules used to build the blocks.[40] The construction of these "blocks of income" is the crux of computing the beneficiaries' allocation.

The composition of DNI is unique for each year. If DNI is not fully allocated to the beneficiaries during the particular year, the remaining block of DNI ice cream is stored in the freezer for distribution in later years. When distributions in a future year exceed that year's DNI, the fiduciary will look in the freezer for any prior year's DNI. When prior year's DNI, otherwise known as undistributed net income (UNI), is found in the freezer, the fiduciary must distribute the old DNI ice cream, based on the current year's accumulation distribution. If there remains either current year DNI or prior years' DNI, the beneficiary will be subject to some form of taxation for the particular year. Once all of the ice cream has been totally distributed, no further taxation can occur for the beneficiaries. By following the ice cream, the fiduciary will know if the beneficiaries are subject to taxation.

> EXAMPLE 8 - 22. In 1995, Trust X had DNI of $20,000. The composition of DNI was: 50% rent, 25% dividends, 15% taxable interest and 10% exempt interest. Distributions for the year were $15,000, so $15,000 of DNI was allocated to the beneficiaries and $5,000 remained with Trust X. Since $500 of the retained DNI was exempt ($5,000 * 10%), Trust X had taxable income of $4,400 ($4,500 - 100) and taxes of $1,051.50. UNI for 1995 was $3,448.50 ($4,500 - 1,051.50). If 1996 distributions exceed 1996 DNI, all or part of the 1995 UNI will be distributed in 1996. Of the $15,000 distributed to the beneficiaries, $10,000 was allocated to Harry and the rest to Terri. Of Harry's DNI, $5,000 was rent, $2,500 was dividends, $1,500 was taxable interest and $1,000 was exempt. Of Terri's DNI, $2,500 was rent, $1,250 was dividends, $750 was taxable interest and $500 was exempt. Once the composition of DNI is calculated, it remains the same for all beneficiaries and the entity.

Computation of DNI and the Income Distribution Deduction

Since the purpose of DNI is to compute the income distribution deduction, the best place to begin in calculating DNI is with the entity's adjusted total income (Line 17, Form 1041). Adjusted total income (ATI) is the total amount of taxable income for the year that must be taxed to someone, either the entity or the beneficiaries. If ATI is negative, the entity has a net capital loss, a NOL and/or excess deductions. Then, DNI will be zero, since DNI can *never* be negative. ATI is modified by two adjustments: one for tax-exempt interest and one for capital transactions.

Tax-exempt interest. Net tax-exempt interest is gross exempt interest less any expenses not deductible due to the exempt interest limitation. When calculating the deductible expenses for ATI, direct and indirect expenses related to tax-exempt income are not deductible. These nondeductible expenses reduce gross exempt interest and the net amount is added to ATI when computing DNI. DNI is net income, so the final amount is a composite of each type of income net of expenses.

The income distribution deduction is the amount of taxable income allocated to the beneficiaries. If the entity has any net tax-exempt income, it must be removed from both DNI and the distributions before calculating the income distribution deduction. Once the net exempt income is removed, the lesser of DNI or the distributions becomes the income distribution deduction.

> EXAMPLE 8 - 23. Trust Z has DNI of $30,000 of which $2,500 is exempt interest. Distributions for the year are $45,000. DNI and the distributions must be reduced by $2,500, since the entire amount of exempt interest is distributed. The income distribution deduction is $27,500, which is the lesser of deductible DNI ($27,500) and deductible distributions ($42,500). If distributions were $21,000, $1,750 ($2,500 * ($21,000/$30,000)) of exempt interest would be removed from distributions, since the entire amount of exempt interest is not distributed. Here, the income distribution deduction would be $19,250, since deductible distributions ($19,250) would be less than deductible DNI ($27,500).

Capital transactions. Capital transactions rarely affect DNI. Only capital gains can be added to DNI and this occurs infrequently. DNI is determined as if no capital transactions occurred during the year, so the net effect of all capital transactions is initially removed from ATI. Only net gains are added back to ATI. Capital gains are included in DNI when:

1. Capital gains are included in fiduciary accounting income;
2. The entity's final tax year;
3. The entity is required to distribute a specific amount each year and an insufficient amount of accounting income exists to meet the required distribution;
4. The fiduciary is required to distribute the proceeds from the sale of a specific asset; and

5. The fiduciary establishes a practice of using the capital gains to determine the entity's distributions and actually distributes the capital gains.

These specific incidents are narrowly interpreted, so capital gains are not included in DNI very often. Once the net tax-exempt interest and the allowed capital gains are added to ATI, the result is DNI for purposes of computing the income distribution deduction.

Allocation of DNI. The DNI allocated to the beneficiaries determines the income distribution deduction. DNI is allocated to beneficiaries who receive a distribution from the entity. The type of distribution, income or corpus, is irrelevant. If the entity made a distribution, DNI is allocated to it. Not all distributions are considered when allocating DNI to the beneficiaries. The following distributions are ignored when allocating DNI and computing the income distribution deduction:

1. Charitable distributions;
2. Distributions under §663(a) (explained below); and
3. Distributions in the current year that were considered when computing the income distribution deduction in a previous year.

Required ATI distributions are considered made whether a check was written or not. All other distributions must have been made before they can be considered. If an in-kind distribution was made, instead of cash, the lesser of the entity's basis or the fair market value (FMV) of the property is used to figure out the distributed amount. The distributed value can be increased if the transfer of property was considered a sale by making either a §643(e)(3) election or transferring property to satisfy a pecuniary bequest.

Section 663(a). Section 663(a) allows certain distributions to be free of any DNI allocation. The terms of the governing document establish if the gift or bequest meets the requirements. Unless the money or identity of the property are ascertainable under the document, the distribution will be included when allocating DNI for the income distribution deduction. To meet the test for a specific sum of money, the amount to be distributed must be fixed by the document and ascertainable at the date of death or inception of the trust. The amount cannot be subject to the fiduciary's discretion, a fraction of the taxable estate or determinable after subtracting administrative expenses. Most formula bequests do not meet the test, since the amount of the bequest is not determinable at death.[41] Specific property must be fixed as to kind and amount in the document. Certain pecuniary bequests meet the requirements of §663(a), while others do not.

The 65 day rule. The trustee can elect to treat all or part of the distributions made within 65 days after the end of the trust's year as made in the current year.[42] The election is filed with the current year's tax return and prevents the amounts actually paid from being deducted in the year actually paid. Only amounts necessary to remove any remaining current year's DNI can be distributed under the 65 day rule. The 65 day election does not apply to estates.[43]

Taxation of Beneficiaries

According to Regulation §1.652(b)-3, the character of the income and deductions:

> ... shall have the same character in the hands of the beneficiary as in the hands of the estate or trust. For this purpose, the amounts shall be treated as consisting of the same proportion of each class of items entering into the computation of DNI as the total of each class bears to the total DNI of the estate or trust unless the terms of the governing instrument specifically allocate different classes of income to different beneficiaries.

The composition of DNI determines the type of income distributed and taxed to the beneficiaries. If 80% of DNI is taxable income and 20% is tax-exempt interest, then 80% of the DNI allocated to the beneficiaries will be taxable income. The other 20% will be tax-exempt interest. Remember the Neapolitan ice cream analogy discussed earlier. For tax purposes, the "scoops" (distributions) received by the beneficiary are based on the composition of DNI. Anytime a "scoop" is made; the beneficiary partakes in each flavor. The fiduciary is not allowed to "pick and choose" which flavor a beneficiary gets, unless the document provides for a special allocation. Special allocations are discussed later.

Schedule K-1. The fiduciary records on Schedule K-1 the amounts taxable to the beneficiaries. The K-1 is shown on a net basis. Any amounts recorded on the Schedule are net of any expenses, so the beneficiaries report the net effect of any allocation only. Only net income can be allocated to the beneficiaries, except in the final year, when losses can be allocated to the corpus beneficiaries. Negative numbers are not shown on the Schedule K-1, except in the final year.

In determining the amounts reported on the K-1, the fiduciary must first compute the composition of DNI. This is done by allocating the entity's expenses against its income. Only income included in DNI can be reduced by the entity's expenses. The allocation of expenses follows a prescribed pecking order, and can result in DNI consisting of only one type of income, although the entity might have had four different classes of income originally. These rules apply to both simple and complex trusts and estates.

Allocation expenses against income. The order of allocating expenses against income is as follows:

1. All deductions directly attributable to a particular class of income are deducted from that income, e.g., all rental expenses reduce rental income.
2. All deductions not directly attributable to a specific type of income may be allocated to any type of income, as long as some deductions are allocated to tax-exempt income.[44] This rule provides some flexibility to the fiduciary. Depending on the needs of the beneficiaries, the fiduciary can allocate the indirect deductions against any type of income included in DNI. If the beneficiaries need a larger amount of portfolio income, to deduct some personal investment interest expense, for example, the fiduciary can allocate a larger amount of indirect costs to passive income, provided the fiduciary does not create a passive loss. If the reverse is true and the beneficiaries need passive income, none of the expenses have to be allocated to passive activities, but can be allocated solely to portfolio income.
3. Passive losses can only be deducted to the extent of passive income. Net passive losses cannot be allocated against any other type of income and are retained (suspended) by the entity. If directly related tax-exempt expenses exceed tax-exempt income, excess expenses cannot be deducted against any other type of income.
4. Any excess deductions (directly related expenses exceed the specific income), excluding passive losses and tax-exempt expenses, can be allocated against any type of income, just like indirect expenses discussed above. The income must be included in DNI before expenses can be allocated against it.

If a charity is included as an income beneficiary, then some DNI must be allocated to it. Unless a specific allocation in the fiduciary document prescribes otherwise, the charity is deemed to receive some of each type of income included in DNI.[45] This rule prevents an improper shifting of taxable income to the charity. Use of the gross income method, discussed above under "Expenses related to tax-exempt income," normally results in more taxable income being allocated to the charity reducing the taxable income allocable to the beneficiaries.

Special allocations. Sometimes the fiduciary document provides for a specific allocation of income to certain beneficiaries. These specific allocations can take many forms.

> EXAMPLE 8 - 24. Trust X is to distribute all the income from an apartment house to Sam. This is a specific allocation allowed under the Regulations; therefore, Sam is taxed on any taxable income attributable to the apartment house. Sam's distribution is solely dependent on that specific type of income.

> EXAMPLE 8 - 25. Trust X is to distribute $10,000 to Kathy, to be paid from tax-exempt income to the extent possible and the rest from taxable income. This would not be recognized as a specific allocation, so Kathy is allocated some of each type of income included in DNI, even if the fiduciary actually pays the $10,000 entirely from tax-exempt income. Kathy's distribution is fixed whatever the amount of tax-exempt income earned by the entity, so the only effect of the allocation is an attempt to apportion more of the tax-exempt income to her, which is not allowed under the Code.

> EXAMPLE 8 - 26. Trust X is to distribute one-half of the tax-exempt interest to Anita. This is an allowable specific allocation, since Anita's distribution is determined solely by the amount of tax-exempt interest earned by the trust.

For a specific allocation, such as the one in the prior example, to be effective in allocating the entity's DNI, the document must not give the trustee any discretion in how the allocation is made. The special allocation rule applies to charitable distributions also. In drafting, if the grantor wants a certain beneficiary to receive a specific type of income, he or she can include a provision in the fiduciary document requiring the fiduciary to allocate that type of income to the beneficiary; however, he or she must make sure to draft the provision to comply with the requirements of the Code. The fiduciary cannot make a special allocation on his or her own.

Specific allocations will be given effect in the allocation of DNI from a fiduciary entity, providing they have an economic impact independent of the income tax consequences.[46]

Excess deductions. In years when interest, taxes, and administrative expenses exceed income, the entity has excess deductions. Since these expenses cannot be included in a NOL under §172 and cannot be allocated to the beneficiaries, the entity has wasted excess deductions, because they are lost forever. Only in the final tax year can the entity allocate these excess deductions to the corpus beneficiaries following the same rules used for allocating a NOL or net capital loss. The beneficiaries may take the allocated deductions as miscellaneous itemized deductions on their personal returns. If the beneficiary does not itemize, or if the 2% AGI floor is too great, the beneficiary cannot carry back or carry forward any unused amount.

Tiers, Tiers, Too Many Tiers

Tiers are only applicable to complex trusts and to estates, and are used to allocate DNI among the beneficiaries. Section 662(a) defines the tiers. A complex trust or estate may or may not have tiers; the fiduciary must look to the governing instrument. A simple trust does not have tiers, since only one type of distribution exists, and DNI is allocated totally to that distribution.

First tier distributions. Section 662(a)(1) defines the first tier distributions as:

> the amount of income for the taxable year required to be distributed currently to such beneficiary, whether distributed or not.

If the governing instrument requires a certain amount of FAI to be distributed currently, the beneficiaries must pay taxes on that amount, limited by DNI. Section 662 applies if any part of the FAI is subject to a required distribution. The beneficiaries must pay taxes on the income, even if a distribution is not actually made.

DNI is recalculated if the entity has charitable *and* first tier distributions. DNI is computed as if no charitable contribution was made and is allocated to the beneficiaries to the extent they received first tier distributions. DNI for first tier distributions is called "modified DNI." Modified DNI applies to first tier distributions only and exists only when the trust has a charitable contribution and first tier distributions. Beneficiaries of first tier distributions have a potentially larger tax liability, since they lose some or all of the benefit resulting from the charitable contribution deduction.

EXAMPLE 8 - 27. Trust A had the following income for the year:

Taxable interest	$20,000
Tax-exempt interest	$10,000
Total income	$30,000

Trust A is required to distribute $24,000 of its current income to Alberta. The rest of the income can be distributed to Beth or the Red Cross or accumulated, and the trustee can make corpus distributions to Beth or to the Red Cross. The trustee made the following distributions:

Beth	$10,000
Red Cross	$18,000

DNI is computed as follows:

Taxable interest	$20,000	
Charitable deduction	(12,000)	[$6,000 exempt]
Tax-exempt interest	4,000	[$10,000-$6000]
DNI	$12,000	

Modified DNI is computed as follows:

Taxable interest	$20,000
Tax-exempt interest	10,000
Modified DNI	$30,000

Alberta is allocated $24,000 of modified DNI, which would consist of $16,000 taxable and $8,000 tax-exempt. Beth would not have any taxable income, since DNI would be zero ($12,000 - $24,000).

The effect of modified DNI, as reported on Form 1041:

Taxable interest	$20,000	
Charitable deduction	(12,000)	[$6,000 exempt]
Income distribution	(8,000)	[$4,000 exempt]
Taxable income	$ 0	
Taxable to Alberta	$16,000	[$8,000 exempt]
Taxable to Beth	$ 0	

Second tier distributions. Section 662(a)(2) defines second tier distributions as follows:

> All other amounts properly paid, credited, or required to be distributed to such beneficiary for the taxable year.

The main difference between first and second tier distributions is the provision that first tier distributions must come from current income, while second tier distributions can come from current income, accumulated income or corpus. If none of the distributions *must* be paid from current income, all distributions will be considered a second tier. *Any* income that must be paid is included in the beneficiary's income, to the extent of DNI, even if not actually paid. All other amounts must actually be paid to the beneficiaries before included in their income. Examples of second tier distributions under Regulation §1.662(a)-3(b) are:

1. Distributions made to a beneficiary in the discretion of the fiduciary.
2. Distributions required by the terms of the governing instrument upon the happening of a specified event.

EXAMPLE 8 - 28. Trust Y requires one-half of the trust corpus be distributed to Yolanda on her thirtieth birthday. When Yolanda turns 30 and receives the distribution, the distribution will be classified as a tier two distribution.

The amount of second tier distributions taxable to the beneficiaries is determined by DNI less any amounts allocated to first tier distributions. If more than one beneficiary receives distributions, each beneficiary must include his or her proportionate share in gross income. A beneficiary's proportionate share is an amount that bears the same ratio to DNI, less any first tier distributions, as the beneficiary's distribution bears to the total second tier distributions.

EXAMPLE 8 - 29. Trust Z has TAI and DNI of $30,000. The trust is required to distribute $15,000 of current income to Adams. The fiduciary has discretion to distribute the remaining income to either Bea, Charles or Dan or accumulate it. The fiduciary also can invade corpus for all four beneficiaries. Trust Z distributes $5,000 each to Bea, Charles and Dan and distributes an additional $5,000 to Adams. DNI would be allocated to each beneficiary as follows:

	Distribution	DNI
Adams	$20,000	$18,750
Bea	5,000	3,750
Charles	5,000	3,750
Dan	5,000	3,750
Totals	$35,000	$30,000

Adams is allocated a greater part of DNI, since he is received a first tier distribution of $15,000. The other $15,000 distribution was second tier, and the extra $5,000 would either be a distribution from corpus or from accumulated income.

No modifications of DNI are made in determining the taxation of second tier distributions. While the charitable contribution deduction is ignored in determining the DNI allocated to first tier distributions, no similar adjustment is made in allocating DNI to second tier distributions. As was shown in the example above, the adjustment for the charitable deduction made to first tier distributions results in a larger portion of DNI being allocated to first tier distributions; thereby, reducing the benefit of the charitable deduction to first tier distributions and reducing the DNI allocated to second tier distributions. Although income is allocated to a charitable contribution before any other expense, the larger the first tier distributions, the less benefit the beneficiaries, as a group, will receive from the charitable gift. To prevent this impact, as much of the distributions as possible should be allocated to the second tier. Since the governing document determines if a distribution will be first or second tier, careful drafting is needed to achieve the desired result.

Income in Respect of a Decedent

Section 691 details the tax treatment of income in respect of a decedent (IRD). Treasury Regulation §1.691(a)-1(b) defines IRD in these terms:

> In general, the term "income in respect of a decedent" refers to those amounts to which a decedent was entitled as gross income but which were not properly includable in computing his taxable income for the taxable year ending with the date of his death or for a previous taxable year under the method of accounting employed by the decedent.

IRD is income to which the decedent was entitled, but due to his or her death was not includable in his or her taxable income. An example of an IRD is salary earned but not paid to a cash basis taxpayer. Although the taxpayer had earned the salary, since it was not paid until after his or her death, it could not be included on his or her final income tax return. Since the income was never subject to income tax, upon the receipt of the income, someone must pay income taxes on it. Section 691 provides the rules concerning the taxation of this type of income. No step-up in basis exists for IRD at death.

IRD must be included in the income of the party that receives the IRD in the year of receipt. Therefore, if an estate receives the IRD, it must include it in income; however, if the beneficiary receives the IRD directly, the beneficiary is taxed on it. Whoever collects the IRD is entitled to any deductions associated with the IRD. The character of IRD is the same as if the decedent had received the property before death.

The unique characteristic about IRD is its dual taxation. IRD is included in the gross estate of the decedent, so it is subject to estate taxes. Further, IRD is subject to income tax on receipt. The recipient of an IRD is entitled to an income tax deduction attributable to the estate taxes paid on the net value of the IRD. This reduces the effect of dual taxation. Examples of IRD:

1. If the decedent completed all events sufficient to close a sale but did not collect the proceeds before death, on collection the proceeds will be IRD.

2. If the decedent had a contingent claim to sales proceeds, the completion of the agreement after death will result in IRD.[47]

3. The forgiveness of debt at death on an installment note is IRD. If the decedent had any unrecognized gain from the sale, the forgiveness of debt would trigger the recognition of the entire unreported gain and the gain would be IRD to the estate.[48]

4. Distributions from a qualified plan or an IRA made after death are IRD. Any distribution representing a nondeductible contribution is not taxed, since the decedent paid taxes on this amount before death.

Certain expenses are deductible for both estate and income tax purposes if they are related to IRD and have accrued prior to the decedent's death. The types of expenses are limited to:

1. Business expenses - §162
2. Interest deductions - §163
3. Deduction for taxes - §164
4. Expenses to produce income - §212
5. Depletion deduction - §611
6. Foreign tax credit - §27

Medical expenses, alimony, capital losses, net operating losses and charitable contributions are expressly excluded and cannot be deducted for income tax purposes by the recipient of IRD.

Estate Tax Deduction

IRD is included on both the estate tax and income tax returns. To reduce the tax burden, since the *recipient* of IRD is entitled to an income tax *deduction* for that portion of the estate taxes attributed to including IRD in the gross estate.[49] Further, an income tax deduction is allowed for generation skipping transfer taxes ascribed to IRD items included in a taxable termination or direct skips caused by the transferor's death.[50] The deduction must be allocated among the recipients of IRD, based on their proportionate share of the gross IRD received. No deduction is allowed for taxes paid on excess retirement accumulations, although the tax is a deduction on the estate tax return (Form 706).

The deduction is allowed each year IRD is included in income. To compute the deduction, all items treated as IRD in the gross estate are aggregated. The total is reduced by all DRD to arrive at a net value. The value of IRD is the lesser of the amount included in the gross estate or the amount included in income. Once the net value is determined, estate taxes are recomputed by excluding the net value from the gross estate. The difference between the original estate tax and the recomputed estate tax is the IRD deduction. The deduction is allocated among the various IRD items. All deductions and credits must be adjusted to reflect the elimination of the net IRD values. If a specific bequest of IRD is made to a surviving spouse or a charity, the deduction is eliminated.

EXAMPLE 8 - 30.   The Estate is the beneficiary of Decedent's IRA. At the Decedent's death, the IRA was valued at $2,000,000 and the Decedent's taxable estate was $5,000,000. With the IRA, Decedent's FET was $2,390,800, and without the IRA, Decedent's FET would have been $1,290,800. As the IRA is distributed to the Estate, the Estate can reduce any income taxes payable by the $1,100,000 of FET paid on the IRA.

EXAMPLE 8 - 31. The Decedent was entitled to salary of $5,000, dividends of $3,750 and rental income of $1,250 at his death. Decedent owed real estate taxes of $2,500 on the rental property. S2 (decedent's spouse) inherited the stock portfolio, his daughter, Jane, was entitled to the real estate, and the Estate received the salary. S_2 inherited ½ of the Decedent's estate and the Estate's marginal rate is 55%. The marginal rate is applied to the net IRD of $7,500 ($10,000 less $2,500) less the net IRD deemed allocated to the marital deduction ($3,750). The $2062.50 deduction ($7,500 - $3,750 * 55%) is allocated as follows:

	IRD Received	Percentage	Deduction
Estate	$5,000	50.0%	$1,031
S2	$3,750	37.5%	$773
Jane	$1,250	12.5%	$258
Total	$10,000	100.0%	$2,063

Throwback Rules

If all of the current year's DNI ice cream is not scooped, the trust pays taxes on the remaining amount and stores the difference in the freezer. The stored taxable income (DNI) turns into what is called undistributed net income (UNI). In 1969, Congress added IRC §§665-668, called the throwback rules. Congress enacted these laws to prevent a perceived abuse. People were saving taxes by having the trust pay taxes on the trust's taxable income and then distributing it in a later year, free of any additional taxes. Now, if a trust has any leftover DNI, it must keep a record of the retaining amount and "distribute it" when later years' distributions exceed that particular year's DNI. Once distributed, the beneficiary must recompute his or her prior years' taxes, as if the amount was distributed in the year originally earned. To simplify this computation, the beneficiary uses an averaging approach and only has to recompute taxes for three years. With the compressed tax rate brackets, the throwback rules cause an excessive amount of paperwork, but rarely cause additional taxes for the beneficiaries.

CONCLUSION

Some main points to remember:

1. Trusts and estates are taxed like individuals, with a few modifications.
2. The primary purpose of Subchapter J is to allocate income and expenses between the fiduciary entity and the beneficiaries.
3. Knowing the fiduciary document, state law, and fiduciary accounting is important to the successful completion of a fiduciary tax return.
4. There are two primary parts to preparing a fiduciary income tax return:
   a. Computing adjusted total income; and
   b. Allocating the income and deductions between the entity and the beneficiaries, which requires determining DNI and the income distribution deduction.

QUESTIONS AND PROBLEMS

1. What is the purpose of fiduciary accounting?

2. Explain the general rules for allocating between income and corpus.

3. The document is silent on how to allocate rental income and expenses. Under state law, rental receipts are allocated to income, but state law provides that net business income is allocated to corpus. The deceased owned several rental properties, which were reported by the deceased on his income tax return as a business activity. How should the executor account for the rental properties on the estate's books?

4. How does fiduciary accounting impact fiduciary income taxation?

5. Explain the purpose of Subchapter J.

6. Explain the main rule concerning the computation of fiduciary taxable income.

7. Which of the following statements are **true**?

   1. Trusts must use a calendar year end.
   2. Estates must use a calendar year end.
   3. The fiduciary must file a special notice to elect its tax accounting method.
   4. The fiduciary's tax return is due on the 15th day of the 4th month following its year end.
   5. Fiduciary returns can be filed electronically.

a.	1, 2 and 4 only	d.	2, 3 and 5 only
b.	1, 4 and 5 only	e.	1, 3 and 5 only
c.	2, 3 and 4 only		

8. Explain the general rule concerning the deductibility of depreciation for fiduciary entities.

9. All of the following apply to the taxation of capital transactions, EXCEPT:

   a. The maximum net capital loss deduction for any year is $3,000.
   b. Net capital losses do not decrease DNI.
   c. Transferring assets to satisfy a pecuniary bequest is considered a sale.
   d. Capital gains are included in DNI, normally.

10. Explain how the deceased's suspended passive activity losses are handled.

11. What are the three methods available for computing the allocation of indirect expenses to tax-exempt income?

12. Which of the following statements are **false**?

   1. Trusts cannot take the rental real estate offset.
   2. Income in respect of a decedent receives a "stepped-up" basis.
   3. The character of IRD is the same as if the decedent had received the property.

4. Medical expenses can be deducted on both the fiduciary income tax and estate tax returns.
5. Net operating losses are deductions in respect of a decedent.

    a. 2, 4 and 5 only   d. 1, 3 and 4 only
    b. 1, 3 and 5 only   e. 2 only
    c. 2, 3 and 4 only

13. What are the three requirements of §642(c) concerning the deductibility of charitable contributions?

14. State the rule that determines if a trust gets a $100 or $300 exemption.

15. State the three requirements for a trust to be classified as a simple trust.

16. Describe the "sweet" composition of FAI and DNI.

17. How is DNI allocated?

18. Which of the following statements are **true**?

1. DNI can never be negative.
2. DNI can include tax-exempt income.
3. The executor can elect the 65 day rule for estate distributions.
4. DNI is allocated to specific bequests.
5. Charities never receive DNI.

    a. 1, 3 and 5 only   d. 1, 4 and 5 only
    b. 2, 3 and 4 only   e. 2 only
    c. 1, 2 and 5 only

19. Explain how DNI is taxed to the beneficiaries.

20. What are the rules concerning allocating expenses between the various types of income?

ANSWERS TO THE QUESTIONS AND PROBLEMS

1. Fiduciary accounting allocates the annual inflows and outflows between income and corpus. Income beneficiaries are entitled to the fiduciary accounting income while the remaindermen are entitled to the remaining corpus once the entity ends. Fiduciary accounting apportions the various receipts and distributions between income and corpus, so the fiduciary will know the correct amount to distribute to the appropriate beneficiaries.

2. According to the UPIA, a fiduciary allocates receipts and expenditures using the following steps:
   1. First, the creating document determines how the allocation is to be made;
   2. Second, if the document does not provide for the allocation, then state law controls; or
   3. If neither allocates the particular item, the trustee is to use her best judgment according to what is reasonable and equitable in view of all beneficiaries' interests in the entity.

3. The deceased's use is ignored when determining the proper accounting method for fiduciary purposes. Specific statutes control over general statutes. Since a specific statute exists for rental receipts, all rental receipts and directly related expenses are allocated to accounting income.

4. §643(b) holds that the unmodified word "income" means fiduciary accounting income. Throughout the IRC, the word "income" is used frequently; therefore, knowing how to compute FAI for the year is vital, so a correct tax return can be prepared. Furthermore, the taxation of the beneficiaries is based on the amount of their distributions, which is controlled by the fiduciary documents and accounting.

5. Subchapter J was written not to compute taxable income specifically, but to allocate taxable income to the appropriate party, either the fiduciary entity or the beneficiary.

6. Section 641 (b) provides that the taxable income of an estate or trust shall be computed in <u>the same manner as in the case of an individual</u>, except as otherwise provided in this part. Due to its unique characteristic, operating a fiduciary entity has more similarities with an individual and his handling of property than any other tax entity; therefore, it is logical that the IRC uses the tax rules applicable to individuals in computing the taxable income of a fiduciary entity. If the preparer cannot find a different treatment of any income or expense item in the IRC or regulations, she should report the item as she would on a Form 1040.

7. B - 1, 4 and 5 only. §645 requires trusts to use a calendar year end. Estate can elect a fiscal year end. No special election must be filed to elect an accounting method, because one is elected when the first return is filed. Trusts and estates have the same filing deadline as individuals. Also, fiduciary entities can file electronically, like individuals.

8. The amount of depreciation is computed following the same rules that apply to individuals, except no §179 deduction is allowed. To the extent there is a reserve for depreciation for accounting purposes, the entity takes the tax deduction for computation of its taxable income. If any tax depreciation remains, it is allocated between the entity and its beneficiaries according to the allocation of accounting income.

9. D - capital gains are rarely included in DNI. Except in the final year or when the fiduciary establishes a practice of distributing the capital gains, capital gains do not increase DNI.

10. The death of a person is treated as a distribution of his entire interest in the asset, so on the decedent's final return, the suspended losses can be used to reduce other income, subject to one limitation. The recipient's basis of property received at death is its fair market value (FMV) at date of death. When the suspended losses exceed the increase in basis, the loss can be deducted on the decedent's final return.

11. The three methods for allocating indirect expenses to exempt income are: the gross accounting income method, the net accounting income method and any defensible, reasonable method.

12. A - 2, 4 and 5 only. Trusts cannot take the rental real estate offset. Estates can for the first two years, providing the decedent actively participated and the surviving spouse does not take the entire offset. IRD does not receive a stepped-up basis, which causes its dual taxation. IRD retains its character in the hands of the estate or its beneficiaries. Medical expenses cannot be take on Form 1041. Net operating losses expire with the deceased and cannot be deducted by either the estate or its beneficiaries.

13. Before a deduction is allowed, certain requirements must be met. These requirements are:
    1. The will or trust document must authorize the contribution,
    2. The amount of deduction is limited by gross income, and
    3. Only those amounts actually paid during the year or during the following year may be deducted.

14. Section 642(b) allows an $300 exemption if the trust must distribute all of its TAI currently. All other trusts are allowed a $100 exemption.

15. Section 651 defines a simple trust as a trust that:
    1. Is required to distribute all of its TAI currently;
    2. No amount from the trust can be used for charitable purposes; and
    3. There are no distributions in excess of TAI for the year.

16. The "sweet" composition of FAI and DNI is similar to Neapolitan ice cream. Unlike swirl ice cream, each flavor of Neapolitan is separate for the other flavors. If a person wanted only vanilla ice cream, he could remove vanilla from the "block of ice cream" leaving the other flavors. Gross accounting income, net accounting income and DNI form our "blocks of ice cream." Each block is composed of various "flavors" of income. When the fiduciary "scoops" the beneficiaries their share of FAI or DNI, each beneficiary receives some of every flavor. Exactly how much of each flavor a beneficiary receives is determined by the total composition of the block. If 50% of the total block is rental income, the beneficiary's "scoop" is 50% rent. Although there are many similarities in the configuration of each block, each block is different. In most situations, the FAI and DNI blocks contain the same flavors/income, but the percentage of flavors that comprise each block changes, based on the

different rules used to build the blocks. The construction of these "blocks of income" is the crux of computing the beneficiaries' allocation.

17. DNI is allocated based on its composition and the current year's distributions. The composition of DNI is unique for each year. If DNI is not fully allocated to the beneficiaries during the particular year, the remaining block of DNI ice cream is stored in the freezer for distribution in later years. When distributions in a future year exceed that year's DNI, the fiduciary will look in the freezer for any prior year's DNI. When prior year's DNI, otherwise known as undistributed net income (UNI), is found in the freezer, the fiduciary must distribute the old DNI ice cream, based on the current year's accumulation distribution. If there remains either current year DNI or prior years' DNI, the beneficiary will be subject to some form of taxation for the particular year. Once all of the ice cream has been totally distributed, no further taxation can occur for the beneficiaries.

18. C - 1, 2 and 5 only. DNI can never be negative. If it is, the entity has a net capital loss, a net operating loss or excess deductions, which are not negative DNI. While DNI can include tax-exempt income, the income distribution deduction dose not include adjusted tax-exempt income. The §663(b) 65 day rule is available for complex trusts only. §663(a) prevents DNI from being allocated to specific bequests. Only non-charity beneficiaries receive DNI.

19. Sections 652 and 662 state the character of the income and deductions shall have the same character in the hands of the beneficiary as in the hands of the estate or trust. The amounts shall be treated as consisting of the same proportion of each class of items entering into the computation of DNI as the total of each class bears to the total DNI of the estate or trust unless the terms of the governing instrument specifically allocate different classes of income to different beneficiaries. The composition of DNI determines the type of income distributed and taxed to the beneficiaries. If 80% of DNI is taxable income and 20% is tax-exempt interest, then 80% of the DNI allocated to the beneficiaries will be taxable income. The other 20% will be tax-exempt interest. Remember the Neapolitan ice cream analogy discussed earlier. For tax purposes, the

"scoops" (distributions) received by the beneficiary are based on the composition of DNI. Anytime a "scoop" is made; the beneficiary partakes in each flavor. The fiduciary is not allowed to "pick and choose" which flavor a beneficiary gets, unless the document provides for a special allocation.

20. Expenses are allocated against income in the following order:
    1. All deductions directly attributable to a particular class of income are deducted from that income.
    2. All deductions not directly attributable to a specific type of income may be allocated to any type of income, as long as some deductions are allocated to tax-exempt income. This rule provides some flexibility to the fiduciary. Depending on the needs of the beneficiaries, the fiduciary can allocate the indirect deductions against any type of income included in DNI. If the beneficiaries need a larger amount of portfolio income, to deduct some personal investment interest expense, for example, the fiduciary can allocate a larger amount of indirect costs to passive income, provided the fiduciary does not create a passive loss. If the reverse is true and the beneficiaries need passive income, none of the expenses have to be allocated to passive activities, but can be allocated solely to portfolio income.
    3. Passive losses can only be deducted to the extent of passive income. Net passive losses cannot be allocated against any other type of income and are retained (suspended) by the entity. If directly related tax-exempt expenses exceed tax-exempt income, excess expenses cannot be deducted against any other type of income.
    4. Any excess deductions (directly related expenses exceed the specific income), excluding passive losses and tax-exempt expenses, can be allocated against any type of income, just like indirect expenses discussed above. The income must be included in DNI before expenses can be allocated against it.

ENDNOTES

1. The court may interfere with the trustee's discretionary power in the event of fraud, misconduct or a clear abuse of discretion. *Beaty v. Bales*, 677 S.W.2d 750 (Tex App - San Antonio 1984). However, absolute or uncontrolled discretion may not be given to a trustee in Texas.

2. *Thorman v. Carr*, 408 S.W.2d 259 (Civ. App. 1966) ref. n.r.e.

3. Id. The presence or absence of such words as "absolute," "full" or "uncontrollable" in describing discretionary powers is of no significance.

4. IRC §645.

5. Congress is considering limiting the estate's year end to October, November or December.

6. Reg §1.641(b)-3(a)

7. *Earl A. Brown, Jr.*, 890 F2d 1329 (5th Cir, 1989).

8. IRC §469(i)

9. IRC §469(i)(4)(B)

10. Reg. §1.706-1(c)(2)(ii), (v), and (vi).

11. Rules covering allocation of capital gains to DNI will be discussed later in the Chapter.

12. Congress is considering reducing the capital gain tax rate for individuals. Any change would apply to trusts and estates.

13. IRC §1223(11).

14. Currently, estates are not subject to the related party rules. Congress has proposed to subject §643(e)(3) transfers of estates to the related party rules under §267.

15. IRC §163

16. IRC §265

17. Rev. Rul. 63-27, 1963-1 CB 57

18. Reg.§1.652(b)-3(d)

19. Reg. §1.167(h)-1(b)

20. See *Interfirst Bank of Fort Worth, N.A. v King*, 722 S.W.2d 18, (App. 12 Dist 1986) and *Hay v US*, 263 F.Supp. 813 (D.C. 1967)

21. IRC §164(a)

22. IRC §642(c)

23. IRC §642(c)(1) and Reg. §1.642(c)-1

24. Reg. §1.212-1(i)

25. IRC §642(d)

26. 994 F2d 302 (CA-6, 1993).

27. 1994-38 IRB 4

28. §643(e)(1)

29. IRC §§1014, 1015

30. Rev Rul 67-74, 1967-1 CB 194 and Regs. §1.651(a)-2(b)

31. IRC §469(j)(6)

32. IRC §1014

33. IRC §469(g)(2)

34. IRC §469(j)(12)

35. See endnote 12, *supra*

36. IRC §643(b)

37. Reg. §1.651(a)-4

38. IRC §§651(a) and (b)

39. IRC §§651(b) and 661(a)

40. For accounting purposes, 50% of the block might be rent, while for DNI purposes, only 25% of the block would be rent.

41. Rev. Rul. 60-87, 1960-1 CB 286; Reg.§1.663(a)-1(b)

42. IRC §663 (b)

43. IRC §663(b). Congress is considering allowing estates to elect §663(b)

44. Reg. §1.652(b)-3.

45. Reg. §1.662(b)-2

46. Reg §1.652(b)-2

47. Let. Rul. 9023012

48. IRC §691(a)(5)(A)(iii); Let. Rul. 9108027; *Estate of Frane*, 998 F2d 567 (CA-8, 1993)

49. IRC §691(c)

50. IRC §691(c)

PART 3

The Techniques of Planning

9

Introduction to Part 3:
The Goals of Estate Planning

OVERVIEW AND CAUTION

This chapter is an introduction to the many specific estate planning techniques to be covered in the remainder of the text. It will isolate the general goals that these techniques have in common. The goals can be categorized into two broad groups, nonfinancial and financial. Within the financial group, they can be further subdivided into tax and non-tax goals.

In reading this chapter, it would be well to keep in mind that the client invariably has a very fundamental goal, one far more general than saving taxes or attaining any other specific goal. The client's primary goal is *happiness and peace of mind*, and specific estate planning strategies may conflict with it. For example, gift giving reduces client wealth, and may jeopardize happiness by imperiling financial security and comfort. The planner should be especially attuned to the client's emotional and psychological preferences, and be sure not to persist in recommending techniques that appear inconsistent with them. Planning strategies are not ends in themselves; they are means to an end: greater happiness.

NONFINANCIAL GOALS

Some specific objectives in estate planning are not strictly financial in nature; they cannot be measured in dollars and cents. These nonfinancial goals, often called "personal planning," will be examined first. They include caring for future dependents, attaining privacy and speed in the property transfer process, and maintaining control over assets.

Caring For Future Dependents

One of the client's objectives should be to provide care for family members affected by client's disability or death. For example, *disability* of the client may trigger the need to select others to care for the client and the client's property. In addition, *death* of a client who was the single parent of a minor child will require court selection of one or more persons to care for that child. In either case, prior planning can permit the eventual selection process to more likely reflect the current wishes of the client, the individual who is currently in the best position to arrange for future care. Methods of planning for care at death and disability are examined in Chapter 17, covering miscellaneous lifetime planning.

Accomplishing Fair and Proper Distribution of Property

Good estate planning seeks to dispose of the client's property to the proper parties in the proper amounts at the proper time. Many factors will influence the choice of the best succession and distribution techniques, and every ensuing chapter will discuss them.

Attaining Privacy in the Property Transfer Process

Other things equal, clients would prefer that their wealth be transferred as privately as possible. They realize that their intended beneficiaries will experience less stress by avoiding public scrutiny. We have seen in Chapter 4 that the methods of property transfer are characterized by different degrees of privacy, with the probate process considerably more public than the process of transferring property by trust. Of course, if privacy were the only criterion, no one would consciously prefer the probate alternative. Probate may, however, offer unique advantages, and the client should weigh them against its disadvantages. The decision whether or not to avoid probate is the main focus of Chapter 10.

Attaining Speed in the Property Transfer Process

Similar to privacy, speed in property transfer is desired by most clients and is often less attainable with the probate alternative. The decision to avoid probate requires weighing the benefits against the drawbacks, as outlined in Chapter 10.

Maintaining Control Over Assets

As we shall see in later chapters, many lifetime estate planning strategies require that the client relinquish beneficial interests in property by making actual transfers. Few clients relish this; other things the same, they would rather hold on to their property. They usually seek to protect their economic interests, and wish to prevent their children from gaining unrestricted control over their wealth. But other goals may change their mind. Their desire to accomplish other estate planning goals, such as saving estate tax, can motivate them to make lifetime transfers.

Further, different lifetime transfer strategies require different degrees of transfer. Usually, the more complete the transfer, the more likely other goals can be accomplished. As you cover the remainder of the text, you should contemplate the degree of transfer involved in the various strategies covered, and ask what kind of clients would be most willing to undertake them.

FINANCIAL GOALS

Financial goals include non-tax and tax considerations and will be covered in that order.

Non-tax Financial Goals

Financial goals that are not tax-related include acquiring adequate liquidity, minimizing non-tax estate transfer costs, maintaining a satisfactory standard of living, ensuring proper disposition by careful drafting, preserving business value, and attaining pre- and postmortem flexibility.

Acquiring adequate liquidity. Death usually triggers the need for liquidity to pay taxes, administration expenses, claims, and the needs of the surviving family. Many if not most wealthier estate planning clients inherently lack sufficient liquidity, probably because the source of most of their wealth originated from investment in two types of illiquid assets: real estate and closely held business interests. Chapter 15 is devoted entirely to liquidity planning, and will describe in detail the major methods of increasing liquidity, including sale of assets during lifetime, acquiring life insurance and flower bonds, anticipating valuation discounts, and undertaking several tax-related elections available only to business owners.

Minimizing non-tax estate transfer costs. Non-tax estate transfer costs include attorney and trustee fees, executor commissions, court costs, and several other probate fees, such as the bond premium. Chapter 10 will examine these costs while exploring the decision to avoid probate.

Maintaining a satisfactory standard of living. We shall see that many tax objectives can be achieved with lifetime transfers. The planner should ensure, however, that clients will retain sufficient assets and income to maintain a satisfactory standard of living. This may require foregoing certain tax-saving transfers, such as outright gifts, in favor of retaining property. Or it may call for making other less complete or less costly transfers, such as an installment sale, which, in return, can generate valuable consideration. These alternatives will be explored in detail in Chapters 13 and 14, covering lifetime transfers.

Ensuring proper disposition by careful drafting. In the planning process, clients normally assume that no matter what happens, their intended beneficiaries will in fact receive their accumulated wealth. Clients trust the attorney to draft transfer documents properly. However, attorney drafting skill varies greatly, and poor drafting can frustrate a client's dispositive preferences in many ways. The examples below are merely illustrative.

EXAMPLE 9 - 1. A simple will fails to include a survival clause, creating the risk that a client's property will be inherited by her *in-laws* rather than by her parents.

EXAMPLE 9 - 2. Unaware of QTIP trust planning, an attorney drafts a simple will for Francis which leaves all of his property outright to his second wife, running the risk that she may neglect to adequately provide for her *stepchildren* (Francis' children of the former marriage), who are living with Francis' first wife.

EXAMPLE 9 - 3. A trust-will is drafted for a client, in which estate property will be held in trust until the youngest of the client's grandchildren reaches age 25. The disposition may be ruled invalid for violation of the *rule against perpetuities*.

EXAMPLE 9 - 4. Donald's attorney drafts a tax-saving testamentary trust into which nearly all of Donald's estate is intended to pass. However, because much of Donald's property is still held in *joint tenancy* with his wife, that property will not pass to the trust at his death but will go outright to his wife by automatic right of survivorship. At that point, the only way for her to move the property into the trust will be by making a taxable gift. And, a §2036 problem can arise if the gift is made into a trust *for her benefit*. An example is the bypass trust that we will cover in Chapter 11.

In each of these situations, more careful planning and drafting could have eliminated the risk of these unintended dispositions without significantly altering the client's objectives. Careful planning and drafting is an essential prerequisite to the achievement of dispositive goals. The client should be assisted in locating an attorney experienced in drafting estate planning documents.

Preserving business value. Death of an active closely held business-owning client can precipitate a serious decline in the amount of wealth receivable by the client's survivors. In Chapter 16, we shall see that *pre-arrangements by the client* can minimize this decline and increase the survivor's likelihood of receiving the full material fruits of the client's productive career.

Attaining pre- and postmortem flexibility. Flexibility in estate planning means that as circumstances change, the client or the client's surrogates can intelligently alter arrangements to accomplish desired goals. While the client is still alive and mentally competent, flexibility can fairly easily be maintained by the client periodically reviewing the estate plan and revising it when necessary. After the client either loses mental capacity or dies, flexibility, although not entirely impossible, is more difficult to sustain. Yet, as we shall see next, considerable flexibility can be maintained if the client anticipates the problem by providing in advance for *surrogate decision makers*.

The critical need for flexibility by naming surrogate decision makers emerges often in the context of providing for young adult children in the event that both parents die prematurely. For example, without planning, the parent's property is usually required by law to be held by a legal guardian, and transferred outright to the children when they reach legal adulthood at age 18. But most parents would prefer to delay outright distribution until the children are older and more mature. We shall see that they can accomplish this by designating responsible parties, such as trustees and attorneys-in-fact, to act on their behalf, parties who can make such an important decision after the parents are gone. Examples of written directives providing for extended flexibility through the use of surrogate decision makers include the trust power of appointment (Chapters 11 and 12), the durable power of attorney (Chapter 17), and the disclaimer (Chapter 18).

Maximizing benefits for the surviving spouse. Tax factors may impel a client to arrange future transfers to minimize the transfer tax bite to the surviving spouse. Different transfer devices accomplish this goal with different degrees of success. As the next example demonstrates, poor planning can result in an inefficient transfer, one that risks foregoing other benefits which could otherwise be enjoyed by the surviving spouse.

> EXAMPLE 9 - 5. Realizing that any property owned by Mom at her later death will be subject to transfer taxation, Dad *writes his own will*, one that will transfer a substantial amount of property outright to their middle-aged children in the event that he predeceases Mom. Dad has succeeded in arranging for some property to bypass Mom's taxable estate, but in so doing, he has unnecessarily denied to her all legal rights to the property.

> EXAMPLE 9 - 6. Continuing the prior example, an estate planner might instead recommend that Dad leave the property in *trust* for the benefit of Mom and the children. The trust would give Mom the following rights, without precipitating any greater transfer tax: (1) the right to income from the property for her life; (2) the right to invade the trust corpus for reasons of health, education, support or maintenance; and (3) the right to determine how much of the property to distribute outright to the children, and when to distribute it, at her death or sooner.

As we'll see in Chapters 11 and 12, careful planning for the spouse's welfare often maximizes tax saving, without sacrificing other important objectives.

Tax Saving Goals

Income taxes and transfer taxes represent the largest cause of estate shrinkage to medium and larger sized estates. Most of the specific planning strategies covered in this text will seek to reduce these taxes. Next, let's isolate the general tax goals they share in common.

Income tax saving goals. The goals of those planning strategies designed to save income taxes include obtaining a stepped-up basis, shifting income to a lower bracket taxpayer, and deferring recognition of income.

Obtaining a stepped-up basis. Achieving a step-up in income tax basis on transferred property can be especially important to a transferee who wishes to sell a rapidly appreciating asset. As we have seen in Chapter 7, a step-up is the normal tax consequence when a transferee makes an ordinary *purchase* for full consideration. However, much of estate planning favors lifetime *gifts*, that is, lifetime transfers for less than full consideration, and, as we have seen, the basis rule for them is quite different: The donee-transferee receives not a step-up, but a carryover basis. On the other hand, a step-up is normally available for gifts received at death. Thus, other things the same, planners are sometimes inclined to recommend deferring the transfer of an appreciating asset until death. This is just one of many basis considerations involved in making lifetime transfers, a subject that will be more thoroughly explored in Chapters 13 and 14.

Shifting income to a lower bracket taxpayer. Estate planning clients are often in the highest income tax bracket, while other family members, such as parents and children, are in lower brackets. As we have seen, under our progressive income tax rate structure, marginal and average rates of tax generally increase with increasing taxable income. Although somewhat reversed by the '93 tax act, tax reform since 1986 has lessened the significance of this, as well as other factors that once strongly encouraged income shifting.

Congressional tax reform directed a three-pronged attack on the popular methods of shifting of income to a lower-bracket family member. First, it adopted the *kiddie tax*, described in Chapter 7. The kiddie tax virtually eliminates any successful shifting of income to children who haven't reached age 14 by the end of the calendar year. Second, by lowering the maximum marginal income tax *rate* from 50 percent to 39.6 percent, tax reform has made income shifting relatively less attractive. And third, as will be described in Appendix 14A, two major lifetime *incomplete* transfer devices, the short-term trust and the spousal remainder trust, have been all but destroyed by two brief but sweeping revisions to the *grantor trust rules*. However, *completed* transfers (gifts) can still shift some income effectively, subject to the first two factors mentioned above.

Figure 9-1 illustrates the progression of maximum marginal federal income tax rates since 1952.

FIGURE 9-1 Maximum Marginal Federal Income Tax Rates, 1952-Present

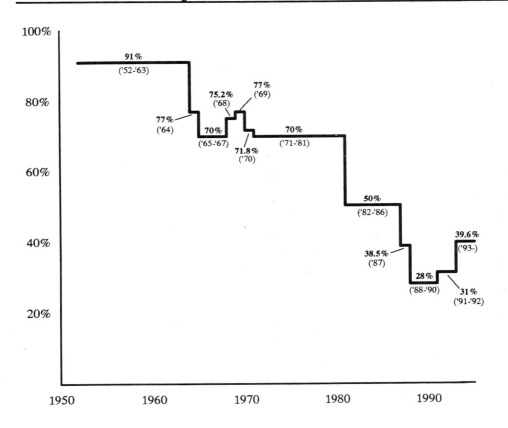

Many of the examples in the remainder of this book will assume a 50 percent "combined" marginal income tax rate (MTR) for wealthier clients, based on the premise that state and local taxes are commonly in the low double digit range. Thus, for each $1 more in taxable income, a high income taxpayer will incur 50 cents in tax. Likewise, every deduction of a dollar will save 50 cents in tax.

The following material answers several commonly asked questions related to income shifting.

What *transferors* are currently most suited to making income shifting transfers? Of course, taxpayers in the highest tax bracket. Married couples with joint taxable income in excess of $250,000 are taxed at the top (39.6 percent) federal marginal rate.

Which *transferees* will be most able to benefit tax-wise from income shifting? Those whose additional unearned income will be taxed at the zero or 15 percent marginal tax bracket. They include minor children over age 13, young adults in college, and, perhaps, the client's parents.

How much income can be shifted to another (dependent) *person* over age 13 and still be taxed at no more than the 15 percent marginal rate? For 1996, up to $24,000 (rate bracket) plus $650 (maximum standard deduction for a dependent), assuming that the donee has no other taxable income. On the other hand, any taxable income earned by a *trust* in excess of $1,650 plus its personal exemption will be subject to the higher 28, 31, 36 and 39.6 percent rates.

> EXAMPLE 9 - 7. Dad, a surgeon, projects before-tax earnings from two sources next year: $120,000 from his surgical practice, and $64,000 from dividends on common stock. He wishes to use some of this income to help support a daughter in college. Assuming that Dad will have a combined marginal income tax rate of 50 percent, and that daughter's rate is 15 percent, each dollar of Dad's income up to $24,000 (plus $650) that can instead be taxed to daughter will save (at least) 35 cents in tax per year.

Can all income potentially receivable by one person be taxed to another? The answer is no, because tax law distinguishes two types of income: personal service income and other income. Under the *assignment of income doctrine*, earnings from services performed will always be taxable to the person performing those services. However, income from something other than services, such as property, can be taxed to another if the underlying property is satisfactorily transferred for their benefit before the income is realized.

> EXAMPLE 9 - 8. Continuing the prior example, Dad will not be able to tax shift his surgical services income to anyone. However, by properly transferring beneficial interest in some of the common stock to daughter, the stock's dividend income can be shifted to her, making it taxable at her lower rate.

Can a client gain by shifting income to a *spouse*? Not ordinarily, because most spouses file a joint income tax return, which subjects both of their income to taxation at the same marginal rate. Filing separately will usually result in a higher combined income tax. Thus, spousal income shifting will not usually save income taxes.

Must a transfer of property be complete and outright, such as by gift or sale, to effect a valid tax shift? Usually, but with some techniques, not entirely. Examples of partially incomplete devices (covered in later chapters) that can successfully shift income include the custodial gift and the irrevocable trust.

We shall also see in Chapter 18 that income shifting to save income taxes can be arranged between estates and beneficiaries. And occasionally multiple taxpaying entities can be created to spread income around, thereby possibly subjecting some or all taxable income for each entity to lower marginal rates.

> EXAMPLE 9 - 9. Andy's will created three *trusts*, one for each of his three children, who are all over 13, transferring a total amount of property worth $450,000 ($150,000 in each trust) and generating approximately $30,000 ($10,000 per trust) in taxable income a year. For 1994, assuming that each trust is taxed as a separate entity and that all of the first year's income is *accumulated*, each trust will pay an income tax of $3,072.40, for a combined total tax of $9,217.20. If, instead, only one trust had been created, and if that trust was taxed as a single taxpaying entity, its income tax would total $10,992.40, which is $1,775.20.50 higher than the combined tax on the three trusts.

Estate planners describe this rate splitting technique as taking "three trips up the rate ladder," rather than one.

> EXAMPLE 9 - 10. Continuing the three trust situation in the prior example, instead of accumulating all income, let's consider two alternatives. First, assume that each trust *distributes all income* to the children, who are also in relatively low brackets. Rates and income will still be split among the children, with similar tax savings.
>
> As a second alternative to complete accumulation, assume that each trust *accumulates one-half* of the income and distributes the other half to the children. Rate splitting will be further enhanced, since the income will be divided among six rather than three taxpayers. However, because of the throwback rule, discussed briefly in Chapter 8, this bonus will work only in special circumstances, such as when the income is being accumulated for beneficiaries under age 21, or when the distributing entity is an estate. However, multiple taxpaying *estates* for one decedent are not possible.

Tax reform since 1986 has particularly restricted the benefits of shifting income to trusts and estates. In addition to radically lowering its maximum marginal tax rate, Congress greatly reduced the tax bracket amounts that are subject to the lower rates. Thus, incremental income taxed to estates and trusts get pushed up the rate ladder far more quickly than for income taxed to individuals.

Deferring recognition of income. When a property transaction results in the realization of a gain, that gain will usually be subject to immediate recognition, that is, includable in that year's taxable income. However, careful planning can defer the gain to later years. By exploiting the time value of money, deferral of the tax enables the taxpayer to temporarily earn greater income. Examples of transfers that defer taxable gain are the installment sale and the private annuity, covered in Chapter 14. And in Chapter 18 we will see that an estate can defer income by carefully choosing its fiscal year end.

Transfer tax saving goals and planning. As with income tax saving techniques, devices designed to reduce transfer taxes all seek to accomplish just a few general goals. They include reducing and freezing the estate tax base, leveraging the use of exclusions, exemptions and the unified credit, delaying the payment of the transfer tax, and minimizing the GSTT. This section will first briefly describe those goals, each with a specific example. Then it will explore, with an ongoing example, the aspects of transfer tax theory underlying transfer tax saving goals by examining the meaning of transfer tax unification and how current imperfections in our unified transfer tax system give rise to tax planning.

To better understand the next two sections, it would be well to remember that we have defined the estate tax base as the sum of the taxable estate (gross estate minus deductions) plus adjusted taxable gifts. These techniques will therefore accomplish one of the following objectives: reduce or freeze the gross estate or adjusted taxable gift values, or, less commonly, freeze or increase deductions.

Reducing the estate tax base. Certain planning arrangements can actually reduce the estate tax base. Estate reduction subjects less of the client's wealth to transfer taxation. Dollar for dollar, it offers the greatest estate tax payoff.

EXAMPLE 9 - 11. Sharon, a widow, gave her son James $10,000 cash outright last year. Due to the annual exclusion, the gift was not taxable and no gift tax was owed. Sharon's taxable estate is now $1 million rather than $1,010,000, which means that if she were to die today, her estate tax will be lower by $4,100, which is the product of 41 percent, her marginal estate tax rate, times the value of the gift.

Other techniques of estate reduction to be examined in later chapters include gifts into trust (Chapter 13), judicious use of the unlimited marital deduction (Chapters 11 and 12), bypass planning (Chapters 11 and 12), establishment of a grantor retained trust (Chapter 14), election of the alternate valuation date (Chapters 15 and 18), and special-use valuation of farm or closely held business property (Chapter 15).

Freezing the estate tax base. In contrast with techniques that can reduce the estate tax base, certain property arrangements can *limit the future increase* in the estate tax base by freezing the taxable value of a portion of the client's wealth at its *current value.* Thus, all future appreciation in this portion is excluded from transfer taxation.

> EXAMPLE 9 - 12. Nicky, a single parent, makes a *gift* of one of his vacation homes, worth $128,000, to his son Donny. Assuming Nicky has made no other taxable gifts this year, he will file a gift tax return and report a taxable gift of $118,000. Assuming no prior taxable gifts, no gift tax will be due because of the shelter of the unified credit. If Nicky dies 20 years later when the value of the vacation home is $500,000 (or, for that matter, any amount), Nicky's estate tax base will include the home at its (historical) taxable gift value, $118,000. With regard to that particular asset, Nicky's estate tax base has been frozen at its taxable date-of-gift value.

The estate tax benefit of freezing is illustrated in Table 9-1.

TABLE 9-1 Illustration of Estate Tax Savings from Estate Freeze on One Half of Total of Four Hypothetical Estates After 10 Years

	Assuming No Estate Freeze		
Present Estate Size	Estate Tax Base, i.e., 10 years @ 8% growth	Estate Tax in 10 Years	Tax as % of the Estate Tax Base
$1,000,000	$2,158,925	$665,873	30.8%
$2,500,000	$5,397,312	$2,416,522	44.8%
$5,000,000	$10,794,625	$5,424,775	50.3%
$10,000,000	$21,589,250	$11,874,088	55.0%

TABLE 9-1 (continued)

Assuming Estate Freeze over One-Half of the Present (starting) Estate

Present Estate Size	Estate Tax Base, i.e., 10 years @ 8% growth on just half of the estate	Estate Tax in 10 Years	Tax as % of the Estate Tax Base	Taxes Saved as a Result of the Freeze
$1,000,000	$1,579,460	$398,758	18.5%	$267,115
$2,500,000	$3,948,650	$1,619,758	30.0%	$796,764
$5,000,000	$7,897,300	$3,791,515	35.1%	$1,639,260
$10,000,000	$15,794,600	$8,424,760	39.0%	$3,449,328

The first half of the table shows the estate tax for each of four hypothetical estate sizes, assuming no freeze. The second half shows the effect of an estate freeze of one-half of each of these estates. Both parts of the table assume an annual growth rate for all estate assets of 8 percent per year over a period of 10 years. Both halves also show the total estate tax as a percent of the appreciated estate tax base values, if no freeze is undertaken. For example, at 8 percent per year, a present estate of $1 million will grow to about $2.16 million in 10 years. Assuming no estate freezing technique is used, the estate tax on $2.16 million will be $665,873, or 30.8 percent of the total estate tax base. Instead, assume a present estate freeze on one-half of that $1 million, or $500,000. Although the total inheritable estate in 10 years will still be $2.16 million, the estate tax base will be only $1.579 million, or the sum of $500,000, the frozen half, plus $1,079,460, the appreciated date-of-death value of the other unfrozen half. Thus, estate tax will be only $398,758, which is only 18.5 percent of the total inheritable estate. Estate freezing saved over $267,000. As Table 9-1 indicates, larger estate sizes will save correspondingly larger amounts of estate tax. The reader might keep in mind that estates between $10 million and $21,040,000 are subject to an additional 5 percent estate tax.

FIGURE 9-2 Graphical Portrayal of Estate Freeze Illustration

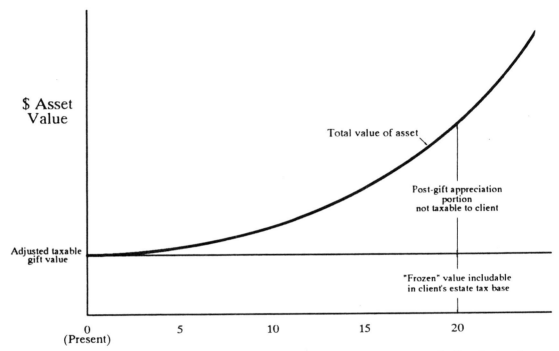

Number of years between date of transfer and date of client's death

The effect of an estate freeze can also be illustrated graphically. In Figure 9-2, the curved line represents the total appreciating value of a gifted asset subject to the freeze, from the present until the clients death, hopefully many years from now. It also represents the amount includable in the client's gross estate if no freeze is undertaken and the asset is owned at death. The slope of this curve is a direct function of the asset's rate of appreciation. The unchanging, frozen value of the asset includable in the client's future estate tax base is represented by the horizontal line, depicting the asset's future adjusted taxable gift value. The section above this line represents the increasing, (unfrozen) postgift appreciation portion of the asset's value, i.e., the amount not includable in the client's future estate tax base. The longer the client lives, the larger will be this portion, assuming ongoing appreciation.

Gifting is not the only available estate freezing technique. As we'll see later, some wealthier clients will prefer, instead of an outright gift, some type of incomplete estate-freezing asset transfer, i.e., one that either involves the client's receiving *consideration* in return, or enables the client to retain some rights or control over the transferred property. Such techniques include the private annuity, installment sale, grantor retained trust (all in Chapter 14), and the corporate recapitalization (Chapter 16).

As mentioned in Chapter 7, Congress, using two very different approaches since 1986, has attempted to impose greater limits on those estate freezing techniques that involve certain retained interests. First, Congress enacted Section 2036(c) in 1987, taking an *estate tax* approach. Very sweeping in nature, it required inclusion in the decedent's gross estate of the fair market value of all property in which the decedent had made a lifetime transfer of appreciating assets under which the transferor retained many significant interests not falling within the scope of §2036(a). But because the rules of §2036(c) were so complex and all-encompassing, and generated so much negative reaction from taxpayers, Congress in 1990 retroactively repealed this subsection. In its place, it enacted Sections 2701-2704.

In contrast to the estate tax approach of §2036(c), the provisions of §2701-04 take a *gift tax* approach. As described in Chapter 7, the new rules attempt to treat certain incomplete transfers as completed gifts, and in the process seek to impose a more conservative gift tax valuation of any retained interests, many of which are mandated under the rules to have no value at all. Thus, in many cases, the gift tax value of an estate freezing transfer (with retained rights) will wind up representing the entire value of the property transferred, reduced only by the value of legislatively permitted "qualifying" retained interests. As a result, estate planners, in attempting to keep gift taxes low, will structure these transfer techniques to specify only retained interests that "qualify" under the new law. Chapters 14 and 16 will briefly explore more how that can be done. In addition, Chapter 12 will discuss estate freezing techniques undertaken at the client's death that are not the subject of Sections 2701-2704.

Leveraging the use of exclusions, exemptions, and the unified credit. In business academics, to leverage means to magnify a benefit by engaging in one of a few special business transactions. Thus, one can *borrow* to magnify profitability (and loss) potential. Similarly, in estate planning, one can *gift appreciating assets* to magnify the tax saving benefit of the gift tax annual exclusion, the $1 million GSTT exemption, and the unified credit. Gifting appreciating assets can leverage these tax breaks by sheltering a larger future amount from estate taxation. And carefully done, it winds up eliminating an asset's entire value from the future taxable estate.

> EXAMPLE 9 - 13. Jacob makes a lifetime gift of a $100,000 face value insurance policy on his life having a current value of $10,000 for gift tax purposes. Since the current gift tax value of $10,000 is covered by the annual exclusion, Jacob has *leveraged the annual exclusion* with a leverage factor of ten: Each $1 in annual exclusion has potentially sheltered $10 from estate tax.

> EXAMPLE 9 - 14. Ainge makes a lifetime gift of $50,000 of appreciating property into an irrevocable trust for the benefit of his granddaughter. Ainge allocates $50,000 of his $1 million lifetime GSTT exemption to this transfer. If this property appreciates in value to $300,000 at his death, Ainge has *leveraged the GSTT exemption* with a leverage factor of six: Each $1 of exemption has sheltered $6 from GSTT.

> EXAMPLE 9 - 15. Five years ago, Julie, a successful entrepreneur, gave her son $610,000 of her corporation's closely held stock. No gift tax was due because the gift was totally sheltered by the annual exclusion and the unified credit. This year, Julie died when the value of that stock was $3,000,000. Julie's estate tax base will include only $600,000, the adjusted taxable gift value of the stock. It will now be totally sheltered by the unified credit. Had Julie died owning the stock, her estate tax base would have included $3,000,000. By making the gift, Julie was able to *leverage the gift tax unified credit* fivefold.

Which types of appreciating assets lend themselves to the highest rates of leveraging? Perhaps the best example is life insurance, it often starts with little value when leveraging is undertaken, but attains a relatively huge value (i.e., face value) at the time the asset finally escapes taxation, after the insured dies.

Reducing, freezing, and leveraging contrasted. It may be helpful to contrast these three very important concepts. *Reducing* takes advantage of exclusions and deductions to actually drive down the future estate tax base below what it would have been had the client done nothing and died today. Reducing would lower the horizontal line in Figure 9-2. In contrast, *freezing* itself will not reduce the future estate tax base; although some estate freezing transactions incorporate the use of exclusions and deductions to reduce the tax base, others do not. The unique contribution of 'freezing' is to keep the amount includable in the future estate tax base *equal or nearly equal to* its current level, even though assets may continue to appreciate. In Figure 9-2, freezing is represented by the vertical distance between the horizontal line and the curved line. Finally, by focusing on the potential magnification of the tax savings, *leveraging* connotes a 'multiplier' effect. It compares the amount of the exclusion, deduction or credit exemption equivalent that has been taken to reduce or freeze the estate with the future magnitude of the appreciated transferred assets that would have been includable in the estate tax base had the transfer not been made, and consequently, the exclusion, deduction or credit had not been taken.

EXAMPLE 9 - 16. The situation in the prior example actually incorporates all three of the goals under discussion. Here's why. It involves reducing, because the transfer has driven down the future estate tax base $10,000 below what it would have been had Julie made the gift and died today. It involves freezing because gifting the stock ensured that the amount includable in Julie's future estate tax base will be exactly $600,000, even though the stock may continue to appreciate. And it involves leveraging because the amount that will avoid taxation is a multiple of the transferred amount. When comparing $600,000, the amount of the credit exemption equivalent used to freeze the estate with $3,000,000, the magnitude of the value of the appreciated transferred stock that would have been includable in Julie's estate tax base had she not made the transfer, the upshot is a fivefold leveraging of the unified credit.

Delaying payment of the transfer tax. In certain situations, transfer taxes can be deferred, even though a completed taxable transfer has taken place.

EXAMPLE 9 - 17. Danny is contemplating several transfers of property from his large estate. His wife, Barbara, has an equally large estate, and can live very comfortably off her own wealth. If Danny gives his wealth to Barbara at his death, there will be no immediate estate tax on that property, since the transfer will be totally sheltered by the unlimited estate tax marital deduction. But the estate tax will only be deferred, not eliminated, since the property will probably be taxed at Barbara's later death. In fact, the gift to her will probably increase the overall estate tax on that property (compared to the amount of tax that Danny's estate would pay if he left the property outright or in trust to the children) since the gift (*a*) foregoes the use of the unified credit at Danny's death; and (*b*) will increase the size of Barbara's gross estate, possibly subjecting it to a higher tax rate. Thus, Danny faces the alternative of either deferring a potentially larger tax or, more immediately, incurring a (smaller) estate tax on his wealth.

Factors to consider in answering the question whether or not to defer the estate tax by means of the unlimited marital deduction are examined in Chapters

11 and 12. Those chapters also discuss the interrelationship of the marital deduction and the unified credit. Other transfer tax deferral devices covered in later chapters include the application of §6166, dealing with the payment of the estate tax in future installments for a decedent-owner of a closely held business (Chapter 16), and the simple practice of delaying property transfers (Chapter 13).

Minimizing the generation-skipping transfer tax. Chapter 7 described the nature of the GSTT, including its 55 percent tax rate and its exemptions. Failure to plan for this tax could prove costly.

> EXAMPLE 9 - 18. Vaguely aware that federal GSTT law includes a $1 million GSTT exemption for each spouse, a general practicing attorney feels safe in drafting wills for most of his married clients that do not explicitly refer to the exemption. This attorney may never realize that more careful drafting to properly allocate these exemptions to certain of his client's property could have saved considerable GSTT.

Efficient allocation of the GSTT exemption, a complex subject, is surveyed in Chapter 12. Now, let's examine in some detail the theory underlying these basic transfer tax saving goals.

The meaning of unification. Many transfer tax saving techniques take advantage of the fact that our "unified" transfer tax system is imperfect, that is, not completely unified. To appreciate fully how these strategies work, the reader must clearly understand both how perfect unification might function, and how the planner can exploit the imperfections inherent in our unified system. The following material will first portray what a tax world of perfect unification could be like, and then describe our present, imperfectly unified system. An ongoing example will illustrate the major points.

Perfect unification. According to this author, perfect unification of gift and estate taxes would imply a situation in which an individual would be *indifferent*, from a total transfer tax planning point of view, between making lifetime gifts and bequests. Under perfect unification, total transfer taxes would be the same whether an individual owned property at death, or whether that person gifted the property away during lifetime. This view of perfect unification would require all of the following conditions:

1. A uniform system of *deductions and credits* for all gift and estate transfers. Otherwise, individuals would prefer to make that transfer which enjoyed the shelter of higher deductions or credits.

2. A *tax on all completed transfers*, whether made during lifetime or at death, no matter the size of the transfer and no matter how long ago the transfer was made. Otherwise, individuals would seek to make that transfer which would be tax-free. This would require complete imposition of the *cumulative gift doctrine*, described in Chapter 5, and would entail the following specific procedures:

   a. *All prior gifts* made by the transferor would be added to the transferor's current transfer tax base. No gifts would be excluded, including gifts of very small value (even less than the annual exclusion amount) and gifts made many years ago.

   b. All prior gifts would be included in the estate tax base at their *current market value*, not date-of-gift value.

   c. All *gift taxes* paid would be grossed up; that is, added to the estate tax base.

3. A world in which the *time value of money* is negligible. Otherwise, individuals would prefer to pay the same (or even greater) transfer tax later rather than sooner.

4. Finally, only *one tax rate schedule* applicable to all lifetime and estate transfers. Otherwise, individuals would seek to make transfers that would be subject to the lower tax rates.

To see the operation of perfect unification, consider the following numeric example, which incorporates all of the above assumptions. While reading it, please keep in mind that the present tax system does not reflect all of these assumptions; these calculations are made for illustration purposes only. All transfers will be assumed to be made after 1987.

> EXAMPLE 9 - 19. Howard, a widower, died owning $2 million in property, consisting of $1 million in land and $1 million in cash. Ignoring all deductions and credits except the unified credit, Howard's estate tax is $588,000, calculated as follows:

Gross estate	$2,000,000
Less: Deductions	0
Taxable estate	$2,000,000
Tentative tax	$780,800
Less: Unified credit	(192,800)
Net estate tax	$588,000

Continuing the example, assume that instead of dying owning all of his wealth, Howard *gave* the land to his son four years before his death. At that time the land was worth $800,000. Under perfect unification, Howard's total combined transfer taxes would still be $588,000. First, Howard would have paid a gift tax of $75,000, calculated as follows:

Current gross gift	$800,000
Less: Exclusions and deductions	0
Taxable gift	$800,000
Tentative tax	$267,800
Less: Unified credit	(192,800)
Net gift tax	$75,000

Howard's estate tax and total transfer taxes would be $513,000 and $588,000, respectively, calculated as follows:

Gross estate (includes gift tax paid)	$1,000,000
Less: Deductions	0
Taxable estate	$1,000,000
Plus: Prior gifts (death value)	1,000,000
Estate tax base	$2,000,000
Tentative estate tax	$780,800
Less: Gift tax paid	(75,000)
Less: Unified credit	(192,800)
Net estate tax	$513,000
Total transfer taxes	$588,000

The gross estate of $1 million is the sum of property owned at death plus the gift tax paid. At death, Howard owned $925,000 in cash, which is the difference between the $1 million cash initially owned and the $75,000 gift tax paid. Grossing up then increases the gross estate back to $1 million. Note that for prior gifts we would use the date of death value.

Summarizing, under perfect unification, total transfer taxes would be the same whether an individual retained all property until death or whether he or she had made lifetime gifts. In Example 9 - 19, the gift tax plus estate tax equals $588,000, the same total tax as with no lifetime gifts.

Our present imperfectly unified system. Comparing our present transfer tax world with the list of conditions required for perfect unification, we see one similarity and several differences. They are similar with regard to item 4 (the existence of one transfer tax rate schedule applied to both gift and estate transfers). However, the two "worlds" are different with regard to all other conditions; our present transfer tax scheme does not fully reflect any of them. The dissimilarities are described in the following outline which, for ease of comparison, is numerically structured to parallel the previous list.[1]

1. Some *deductions and credits* are not uniformly applied to all transfers. For example, the $10,000 annual exclusion applies only to lifetime gifts. And the estate tax credit for tax on prior estate transfers (PTC discussed in chapter 6) is not allowable for the tax on prior gifts.

2. The *cumulative gift doctrine* has not been completely incorporated into our transfer tax system. Major omissions include the following:

   a. Not all prior gifts made by the transferor are added to the transferor's current transfer tax base. In fact, some gifts are not included at all.

      (1) Except in unusual situations, only *post-1976* gifts are added to the estate tax base. (Recall that Internal Revenue Code §2001 defines "adjusted taxable gifts" as only the total of all *post-1976* taxable gifts.) Pre-1977 gifts are usually totally excluded from the estate tax base. The major exception applies to pre-1977 transfers subject to retained interests and control under Code sections 2036, 2037, and 2038 or the relinquishments within three years of death of one of those retained interests, i.e., §2035(d)(2) would capture it even if the original transfer was pre-1977.

      (2) Ordinarily, only the *taxable* gift value, not the value of the entire gift, is added to the gift tax or estate tax base. Taxable gift value is the net gift value after subtracting deductions and exclusions, including the $10,000 annual exclusion. In contrast, property owned and transferred at death is entirely includable in the estate tax base; there is no annual exclusion for a decedent's estate. Hence, the estate tax base will be lower by the amount of any annual exclusions taken, creating an advantage to making lifetime transfers.

   b. Prior gifts that are includable in the estate tax base reflect the *value of the transfer at the date of the gift*, not the current, date of death value. In many, perhaps most, circumstances, date-of-gift value will be lower than current value, thereby enabling individuals to make gifts of appreciating assets and thereby freeze the taxable value by eliminating estate taxation on their subsequent appreciation.

    c. Not all *prior gift taxes* paid are grossed up, that is, added to the estate tax base. Only gift taxes paid on gifts made within three years of death are so included. Thus, certain gifts will be taxed on a tax-exclusive basis. In Chapter 6 there are examples that illustrate the tax advantage of gift taxes not being included in the transfer tax base.[2]

3. Finally, our transfer tax structure can not ever be perfectly unified because we live in a world having a significant *time value of money*. Thus, other things the same, individuals will prefer to delay the payment of transfer taxes.

To see how real-world imperfections 2a(2), 2b, and 2c affect the unified transfer tax, let's rework the numbers in Example 9 - 19. First, assuming no lifetime gifts, Howard's net estate tax will be $588,000, as previously shown. However, the lifetime gift alternative under today's imperfect unification has markedly different results.

Howard's gift tax, at the time of the gift, will be $71,100, rather that $75,000, calculated as follows:

Current gross gift	$800,000
Less: annual exclusion	(10,000)
Taxable gift	$790,000
Tentative tax	$263,900
Less: Unified credit	(192,800)
Net gift tax	$71,100

Howard dies owning $928,900 cash ($1 million less gift tax paid of $71,100). Because the gift tax is not in the gross estate, Howard's net estate tax will be $390,405, rather than $513,000, calculated as follows:

Gross estate	$928,900
Less: Deduction	0
Taxable estate	$928,900
Plus: Adjusted taxable gifts	790,000
Estate tax base	$1,718,900
Tentative estate tax	$654,305
Less: Gift tax paid	(71,100)
Less: Unified credit	(192,800)
Net estate tax	$390,405
Total transfer taxes	$461,505

Howard's total transfer taxes will be $461,505, the sum of $71,100 (gift tax) and $390,405 (estate tax). Hence the use of the lifetime gift has saved $126,495 in transfer taxes. Imperfect unification has enabled Howard to *freeze* the tax value of the land at its taxable gift value and to *reduce* his taxable estate by the amount of the annual exclusion and the gift tax paid. Thus, a total of $281,100 escaped transfer taxation. This represents the sum of three amounts: the $10,000 annual exclusion, the $71,100 gift tax paid, and the $200,000 in postgift appreciation in the land. We can check our result, since the total tax saved will be 45% (the marginal estate tax rate) of $281,100, which equals the tax saving of $126,495.

The effect of not grossing up can be interpreted in a different way: As mentioned in Chapter 6, the federal gift tax is calculated on what is called a *tax exclusive basis* (assuming no grossing up), since it is levied on the amount of the net gift not including the tax. On the other hand, the estate tax is calculated on a *tax inclusive basis*, since it is levied on the entire estate, including the amount that will be used to pay the estate tax. The requirement of grossing up in effect converts part of the federal gift tax from a tax exclusive calculation to a tax inclusive one. In contrast, not grossing up keeps the entire gift tax computation on a tax exclusive basis, enabling gifts to lower overall transfer tax costs.

Thus, careful exploitation of the present system's failure to completely unify estate and gift taxes can yield substantial transfer tax savings for clients owning medium to larger amounts of wealth. Further discussion of these issues will be deferred to the chapters on planning for lifetime transfers.[3]

This chapter has introduced the specific techniques of estate planning by presenting the main goals underlying them. The next chapter begins our detailed study of these techniques with an examination of the decision to avoid probate.

QUESTIONS AND PROBLEMS

1. (a) What is probably the typical client's principal goal in estate planning? (b) Give your own example of how a more specific goal described in this chapter can conflict with it.

2. List and briefly describe a client's nonfinancial estate planning goals.

3. List and briefly describe a client's non-tax financial estate planning goals.

4. Describe the advantage of selecting a surrogate decision maker in the estate planning process.

5. List and briefly describe a client's income tax saving goals.

6. For the years in question, Mom and Dad are in the combined 50 percent marginal income tax bracket and the standard deduction for a minor claimed as a dependent is $650. How much income tax can the family save each this year if they can shift $20,000 in taxable income to the following alternate taxpayers whom, we will assume, have no current gross income? Both children (12-year-old daughter and 16-year-old son) are claimed as dependents. Also, for each taxpayer, state the maximum potential total income not taxable at all, and taxable at 15 percent.

   a. Shift to their daughter.
   b. Shift to their son.
   c. Shift to an irrevocable trust that distributes all the income annually to their daughter. (See Table 8-1 in chapter 8 for trust income tax rates.)
   d. Shift to an irrevocable trust that accumulates all income annually for the benefit of their old son.
   e. Shift to an irrevocable trust that accumulates $1,650 and distributes the balance annually to their son.

7. List and briefly describe a client's transfer tax saving goals.

8. (a) What is the meaning of perfect unification? (b) Why is our present unified transfer tax system imperfect?

9. Compare the *gift* tax calculations for Howard in Example 9-19 in the text, contrasting perfect unification with our present tax system.
   (a) On a piece of paper, list the major numerical gift tax calculations, in side-by-side columns.
   (b) Which lines are different in amount? Why?

10. Now let's compare the *estate* tax calculations for Howard's estate in Example 9-19 of the text, contrasting perfect unification with our present tax system, under both the no-gift and the gift alternatives.
    a. On a piece of paper, list the major numerical calculations, in side-by-side columns.
    b. Which lines are different in amount? Why?

11. Diana and her husband Bill have an estate worth $4 million. Each would like to give their only grandson a 40% interest in the stock of their wholly and equally owned closely held business. It is currently worth about $3,050,000. Assuming no prior taxable gifts by either spouse, if the business triples in value by the time of their deaths, explain whether the major gift (or a series of gifts) would -
a. Reduce their estate tax base.
b. Freeze their estate tax base.
c. Leverage anything.

ANSWERS TO QUESTIONS AND PROBLEMS

1. a. The client's principal goal is happiness and peace of mind. Estate planning deals principally with property transfer decisions, many of which may be fundamentally unsettling for clients.
   b. Answers will vary but an example might be making a large lifetime gift to a young adult child.

2. Nonfinancial estate planning goals:

   a. Caring for future dependents, including the client and the client's minor children.
   b. Attaining privacy in the property transfer process.
   c. Attaining speed in the property transfer process.
   d. Maintaining control over assets.

3. Non-tax financial estate planning goals:

   a. Minimizing non-tax estate transfer costs.
   b. Maintaining a satisfactory standard of living.
   c. Ensuring proper disposition.
   d. Preserving business value.
   e. Attaining pre- and postmortem flexibility.
   f. Maximizing benefits for the surviving spouse.

4. The advantage of selecting a surrogate decision maker is flexibility in planning after the client becomes incapacitated or dies.

5. Income tax saving goals:

   a. Obtaining a stepped-up basis.
   b. Shifting income to a lower bracket taxpayer.
   c. Deferring recognition of income.

6. Without income shifting, the parent's tax would be: $20,000 *.50 = $10,000

   a. Shift income to daughter: kiddie tax applies.

   The first $650 of unearned income to the daughter would be tax free. The next $650 would be taxed at daughter's 15% rate. Based on the Kiddie tax, the remaining $18,700 would be taxed at the parent's 50% rate.
   Tax = $650* .15 + $18,700 * .50 = $97.50 + $9,350 = $9,447.50
   Total tax savings = $10,000 - $9,447.50 = $552.50
   Maximum not taxable at all and taxable at 15% = $650 at 0% plus $650 at 15%.

   b. Son would be taxed on all but $650 of the income.

   Tax = .15 * $19,350 = $2,902.50
   Total tax savings = $10,000 - $2,902.50 = $7,097.50
   Maximum not taxable at all and taxable at 15% = $650 at 0% plus $19,350 at 15%.

   c. Same answer as part "a," based on the combined effect of the conduit principle and the kiddie tax.

   d. Trust would be taxed on all but $100 (its personal exemption) of the income. Tax = $2,287 + .396 * ($19,900 - $8,100) = $2,287 + $4,672.80 = $6,959.80; total tax savings = $10,000 - $6,959.80 = $3,040.20
   Maximum not taxable at all and taxable at 15% = $100 at 0% plus $1,650 at 15%.

   e. Trust would be taxed on $1,650. Trust tax = $1,650 * 15% = $247.50
   Son would be taxed on $17,600 of the $18,250 amount actually distributed. Son's tax = $17,600 * 15% = $2,640.
   Tax savings = $10,000 - ($247.50 + $2,640) = $7,112.50
   Maximum total combined trust and individual income that is not taxed at all and is taxable at 15% is $750 ($100 for the trust and $650 for Son) and $19,250, respectively.

7. Transfer tax saving goals:

    a. Reducing the taxable estate.
    b. Freezing the taxable estate.
    c. Delaying payment of the transfer tax.
    d. Leveraging the use of exclusions, exemptions, and the unified credit.
    e. Minimizing the generation-skipping transfer tax.

8. a. Perfect unification means a transfer tax system under which individuals would be indifferent, from a total transfer tax planning point of view, between making lifetime or estate gifts.

    b. Our system is imperfect because of:

        1. the nonuniform application of some deductions and credits,

        2. the failure to completely incorporate the cumulative gift doctrine in the area of the inclusion of pre- 1977 gifts, the annual exclusion, gift valuation, and grossing up of gift taxes

        3. the time value of money.

9. a. Example 9-19 Calculations: (Differences are marked with an asterisk)

	Perfect unification	Our present law
gross gift	$800,000	$800,000
(exclusion)*	$0	$10,000
taxable gift	$800,000	$790,000
tentative tax	$267,800	$263,900
(unified credit)	$192,800	$192,800
gift tax	$75,000	$71,100

    b. The difference lies in the subtraction of the $10,000 exclusion under the present tax system. The imperfect unification of our present system with regard to the annual exclusion saved Howard $3,900 in gift taxes.

10. a.   Example 9-19 Estate Tax Calculations

No gift alternative	Perfect	Present Law	Difference
Taxable estate	$2,000,000	$2,000,000	$0
+ Adjusted taxable gifts (post-76)	$0	$0	$0
= Estate tax base	$2,000,000	$2,000,000	$0
Tentative tax on estate tax base	$780,800	$780,800	$0
- Gift tax payable credit	$0	$0	$0
- Unified credit	($192,800)	($192,800)	$0
= Total Death taxes	$588,000	$588,000	$0
Gift alternative			
Taxable estate	$1,000,000	$9,289,000	$71,100
+ Adjusted taxable gifts (post-76)	$1,000,000	$790,000	$210,000
= Estate tax base	$2,000,000	$1,718,900	$291,100
Tentative tax on estate tax base	$780,800	$654,305	$126,495
- Gift tax payable credit	($75,000)	($71,100)	$3,900
- Unified credit	($192,800)	($192,800)	$0
= Total Death taxes	$513,000	$390,405	$122,595

b.   The estate tax calculations under the 'no gift' alternative are the same. With regard to the gift alternative, the following factors explain the difference under our present system:

1. The gross estate excludes $71,100, the gift tax paid

2. "Prior taxable gifts" omit the $10,000 annual exclusion and the $200,000 post-gift appreciation.

An estate tax saving of $122,595 results from these three "imperfections," that have the effect of sheltering a total of $281,100 from taxation.

11. a.   The total transfer would be equal to $1,220,000. Each would use up his or her unified credit and would take advantage of the annual exclusion. There would be no GSTT because each would apply $600,000 of his or her $1 million exemption. It would reduce the tax base by the two annual exclusions.

b. Since the adjusted taxable gifts are valued as of the date of gift if the value of the stock triples then $3,600,000 - $1,200,000 = $2,400,000 has been sheltered from taxation, in essence frozen.

c. Since the stock triples in value the two annual exclusions, the unified credit equivalent amount. and the GSTT exemption have all been leveraged.

ENDNOTES

1. For a description of an additional imperfection based on the ability to obtain certain valuation discounts for lifetime gifts (but not gifts at death) of minority business interests by controlling owners, see Chapter 15.

2. Examples 2035-5 and 2035-7.

3. Chapters 13 and 14.

—10 ———————————————

The Decision to Avoid Probate

OVERVIEW

As we have seen, the term probate has come to mean the entire court process by which the state supervises the orderly distribution of a decedent's probate property. Since probate has significant drawbacks, most clients prefer to avoid it by planning the disposition of property with one of its two major alternatives, joint tenancy or the living trust. These are referred to as *will substitutes* because they supersede any provisions that might be in the deceased co-owner or trustor's will. This chapter surveys the advantages and disadvantages of all three mechanisms of transfer. To some degree the choice is subjective, what is best depends on the client's personal assessment of the pros and cons in the light of his or her personal circumstances. Although generalization can be risky, we will conclude the chapter with a summary of various client circumstances which are apt to favor probate, joint tenancy, or the living trust.

Several other limited alternatives to probate will not be discussed. Contracts such as life insurance and retirement plans can avoid probate but have limited general application for two reasons. First, the decision whether or not to utilize these contracts is usually independent of the decision whether or not to avoid probate. For example, life insurance is purchased for reasons other than avoiding probate-- such as the need for cash at someone's death; acquiring it is not influenced by the method chosen to transfer property. Second, these limited alternatives to probate are "asset specific;" that is, they cannot be used to help other client assets avoid probate. For example, a Totten trust only avoids probating of that particular bank account. In contrast, the will (via probate) and the living trust each are means of transferring virtually any asset owned by the client. Joint tenancy also applies only to specific assets held in that form of title but almost any property can be held in this form. In this chapter, we'll use the term joint tenancy generically to include tenancy by the entirety keeping in mind that the latter is available only to married couples.

Another type of asset specific alternative to probate is the *pay-on-death* account, which is a bank or savings account controlled by the depositor so long as living but with a provision that the account is payable to another if it is still open when the depositor dies. Pay-on-death accounts may be used with checking and savings accounts, money market accounts, and certificates of deposit. Although such avoid probate, they are includable in the depositor's gross estate.[1] A few states require that they comply with the formal execution requirements of a valid will. If not, they become an intestate asset.

We begin our comparative study of probate and its two major alternatives by examining the pros and cons of probate.

THE BENEFITS AND DRAWBACKS OF PROBATE

Below, we describe probate's major benefits and drawbacks. For a more thorough understanding of the probate process, the reader is urged to first review the section called Principles of Probate Administration in Chapter 4.

The Benefits of Probate

The major benefits of probate include fairness promoted by court supervision, orderly administration of assets, greater protection from creditors, and income tax savings.

Court supervision promotes fairness. Formal probate requires substantial court supervision, a process which, at its best, promotes fairness. Through the use of petitions, accountings, hearings, and court orders, probate seeks to ensure that asset distribution is fair. No other estate transfer procedure is so controlled by public authorities.

The public-forum nature of probate encourages *review and evaluation* by numerous observers. Judges and official clerks are called on to approve major estate activities. In addition, other interested, private parties such as beneficiaries and creditors have an opportunity to object to perceived inequities in estate administration. For example, they can object to many court rulings, including admission of a certain will to probate, appointment of a certain personal representative, payment of a certain creditor, and distribution of estate assets to a certain individual. They can raise these objections in the probate court itself; the parties need not seek a remedy elsewhere, and they can often do it without hiring a lawyer. In contrast, objections to disposition by joint tenancy and by the living trust require a different, procedurally more complicated legal action.

Critic's response. Critics of probate contend that the additional degree of equity fostered by probate administration is, at best, minimal. They argue that judges and other public officials too often give only superficial *rubber-stamp approval* of estate activities, and even occasionally dispense with certain onerous procedural requirements of their state's probate code. Supporters of probate respond to this criticism saying that judges implicitly and successfully rely on the interested parties, who are formally notified of the proceedings, to speak up in court if they feel they are being treated unfairly. Critics contend, however, that the average interested person would not be aware of the occurrence of many types of subtle or technical inequities.

The claim that probate encourages fairness is also subject to challenge because of the recent trend in the direction of *reduced supervision.* In Chapter 4, we learned that many states permit "informal" or "summary" probate procedures that can greatly reduce court surveillance. Also, we saw that UPC states permit the estate's interested parties to select the degree of supervision they desire. If they choose "informal probate," the estate will receive no direct supervision by the court. Thus, in many states, the risk of misadministration in probate is similar to that for trusts because of the opportunity to avoid the public forum. Of course, the ability in UPC states to request greater formal supervision later in probate reduces the risk of mismanagement.

In conclusion, through supervision, probate promotes fairness. However, the strength of this generalization has been weakened by the degree to which the courts only superficially oversee administrative activities, and by the recent movement of the states to reduce the degree of mandatory court supervision.

Orderly administration of assets. Probate offers an orderly administration of estate assets. Supervision by the court and by other public officials ensures further that property transfers and title clearance will be done correctly. Once again, however, this advantage is less pronounced to the extent that court approval is given only perfunctorily.

Greater protection from creditors. As we saw in Chapter 4, probate procedures typically require creditors to formally file their claims against probate assets within a certain period of time, such as four months from date of issuance of letters testamentary. Failure to timely file a creditor's claim can forever bar collection from those assets. Nonprobate assets, on the other hand, may only be protected by the state's general limitations period, which can be several years. Thus, asset disposition by probate can offer distributees greater protection from creditors much sooner, at least by the time of distribution.

Actual notice: the Tulsa decision. Recently, however, the U.S. Supreme court lessened this advantage, ruling in *Tulsa* that creditors who are "known or reasonably ascertainable" to the personal representative must be given "actual" notice of the limited creditor's period, rather than just "constructive" notice, by publication.[2] Notice by mail is considered acceptable actual notice.

The following is a partial listing of creditors who are usually known or reasonably ascertainable to the personal representative:

- Hospital where decedent died, all treating physicians, ambulance company and paramedics,
- Landlord or mortgage company,
- Pool-man, gardener, maid, newspaper delivery service,
- Installment payment creditor,
- Creditors who have already sent decedent unpaid bills,
- Credit card issuers,
- Creditors receiving interest that was deducted on decedent's last four years local, state, and federal income tax returns,
- Creditors for whom decedent has prepared financial statements in the last four years,
- Ongoing creditors determined from decedent's correspondence and canceled checks,

- Persons given a guarantee by decedent as owner of a closely held business.

Under *Tulsa*, actual notice need not be given to potential creditors whose claims are a matter of "conjecture," i.e., deduced by surmise or guesswork. An example of a conjectural claim would be a malpractice claim against a professional that has not yet resulted in a demand. The creditors' claim period does not affect the rights of secured creditors to the extent that the debt is covered by the collateral.

Clients who anticipate difficult to identify claims after their death may find the shorter limitations period a significant advantage. For example, professionals such as, doctors, lawyers, architects, engineers and accountants are potentially vulnerable to malpractice claims which, if instituted after their death, stand a greater chance of succeeding, partly because the defense's best witness, the decedent, is not available to testify. The shorter creditors' period can sometimes minimize this undesired outcome.

If there is insurance to cover a claim it will not be barred by the short probate creditors' period. The estate may be named as a party to the suit, but the real party in interest is the insurance company that will have to pay the claim. Generally, unless the injured party files a creditor's claim within the regular creditor's claim period, state probate statutes limit the recovery to the amount of insurance coverage. Although most malpractice insurance is issued on a "claims made" basis, meaning that the insurance covers only errors that occur while the policy is in force and only if a claim is submitted while it is in force. However, when a professional retires, he or she can purchase what is called "tail coverage" that will continue to cover latter claims for errors that were made during the period covered by insurance. There are several reasons why a person might miss the creditors' claim period, yet have a valid claim but for the tortfeasor's death. First, where there is *delayed discover*, the limitation does not begin to run until the wrong doing is discovered or should have been discovered, e.g., negligence by a doctor may not be discovered until long after an operation. Second, where there is *delayed injury or damage*, the limitations period does not begin to run until the injury or damage actually occurs, e.g., legal malpractice situations, such as errors in will drafting that prevent an estate from claiming a marital or charitable deduction, no damage occurs until the testator's death.

Many nonprofessional clients, especially those not litigation prone, will find the benefit of the shorter creditors' period to be of little value. And, in view of the fact that probate publicly exposes a pot of assets for creditors to reach, some clients may prefer more private and more decentralized methods of asset distribution.[3]

In UPC states, clients' estates can have the same claims protection without supervised probate. For example, informal UPC probate offers the four-month creditors' period because its provisions allow for the filing of a legal notice to creditors. As mentioned in Chapter 4, if the notice is not issued, the UPC imposes a three-year creditors' limitations period, starting at date of death. Certain other forms of summary probate in non-UPC states do not offer this protection. For example, in California, the creditors' period is not available under summary distribution to the surviving spouse, described in Appendix 4A.

Income tax savings. As we saw in Chapter 8, the probate estate is considered a separate tax entity during its existence, taxable at its own rates. Hence, some modest income shifting with an additional taxpaying entity is possible. For example, during estate administration, undistributed income (FAI) earned on estate property will be taxed to the estate rather than to the beneficiaries. This can reduce total income taxes if the estate is in a lower tax bracket than its beneficiaries. However, as mentioned in Chapter 9, the advantage has been somewhat undercut by tax reform since 1986, which generally lowered and compressed the income tax rate brackets.[4] Income tax planning for estates is described in Chapter 18.

The Drawbacks of Probate

Probate has several distinct disadvantages, including complexity, cost, lack of privacy, delay, and danger of unintended disposition.

Complexity. As we saw in Chapter 4, probate can be a complex process, requiring petitions, accountings, hearings, and other complicated legal procedures. Most laypersons understand neither their purpose nor their operation, and are forced to hire specialists to meet their requirements. Critics argue that supervised probate is usually an unnecessary, clumsy process offering considerable make-work for the legal profession, especially paralegals and legal secretaries. Others respond that the movement by many states toward less formal probate procedures has nearly made probate, in those states, no more complex than administration for a decedent whose assets had been placed in a living trust.

Cost. The cost of legal supervision under probate can be high. Studies have found that total probate administration expenses range between about 2 and 10% of gross estate assets, with larger estates and those subject to informal UPC administration experiencing the lowest rates.

The *personal representative's commission* usually constitutes the largest probate expense. Of course, a surviving beneficiary who acts as personal representative may wish to waive the commission. The statutes of most states either provide for "reasonable" compensation of the personal representative, or make no provision at all. Quite a few states have enacted statutory commissions based on a percentage of estate assets, such as the one included in Table 4-1, where the fee can reach as high as 4%. In general, personal representatives' commissions for formal probate range between 3 and 5%.

The next largest probate administration expense is usually the *attorney's fee*. Most states' statutes do not set attorneys' fees leaving it to the judge for each case to decide and approve a *reasonable* fee. In general, attorneys' fees usually range between 2 and 4% of the value of the probate estate. Other administration expenses unique to probate include fiduciary bond fees, accountants' and appraisers' fees, and court costs, including filing fees.

Probate administration costs will be higher for estates containing real property located in other states. Under what is called *ancillary administration*, that property is probated in the state in which it is located. This usually required hiring an attorney who practices in the other state to handle the ancillary administration.

Other factors that will affect the level of probate administration costs include the nature of the estate property (e.g., closely held business interests, expensive artwork, etc., versus marketable securities), the complexity of the estate distribution plan, the risk of a will contest, and the general economic conditions prevailing during estate settlement.

Contrary to popular belief, probate does *not* increase a estate tax. Indeed, since probate costs are deductible, probate may actually reduce estate tax. However, increasing costs in order to decrease estate tax is not wise planning. As previously discussed in Chapters 4 and 6, the probate estate and the gross estate are independent (although not mutually exclusive) concepts.

Lack of privacy. Probate is a public process; all probate proceedings are subject to public scrutiny. For example, any person can inspect a decedent's probate file, which eventually includes the decedent's will, the estate inventory and appraisement, and the order for final distribution. Those particularly interested in inspecting a file would include survivors who are fighting and members of the press seeking a story about a newsworthy decedent. Commonly cited examples of celebrities receiving embarrassing publicity which arguably could have been avoided include the estates of Amanda Blake, Greta Garbo, Natalie Wood, John Wayne, Darryl Zanuck, and the controversy surrounding the conservatorship for Groucho Marx.

The probate files of most decedents are not seen by anyone other than court officials. Interested parties, such as the decedent's relatives and the executor can have the attorney for the estate send them copies of every document that is filed, and many probate attorneys do this as a matter of practice without any request that they do so, thus the most interested parties have no reason to review the court's file unless one harbors suspicion that not everything is being sent. Keep in mind, however, that clients receiving estate planning advice are typically the wealthier, more prominent citizens, who are likely to arouse greater than average curiosity.

In some situations, a client may actually prefer the lack of privacy inherent in probate. For example, the public aspects of probate might discourage or uncover fraudulent dealings undertaken by unscrupulous survivors.

Delay. Even for smaller estates, probate administration takes considerable time, ranging from nine months to several years before final distribution is made. In any particular case, the delay can be quite unpredictable. Delay can be especially hard on grieving survivors, partly because it can increase or prolong tension and conflict among them. As a specific example of delay in probate, payment of proceeds of life insurance on the decedent's life to the decedent's testamentary trust will be delayed until the trust takes effect, which usually can be no sooner than the expiration of the creditor's period, several months after date of death. Thus, complete, immediate liquidity cannot be provided to the decedent's survivors. However, preliminary distributions of significant amounts can usually be made earlier if the executor can make a good faith representation that doing so will not jeopardize creditors.

Danger of unintended disposition. The nature of probate may in some cases increase the risk of an undesired *will contest*, one which may be settled with a distribution of assets in a manner that conflicts with testator intent. For example, a person named only in a prior will might contest the decedent's last will on a technicality. The person might, for example, claim that the decedent failed, at the time of execution, to verbally request that the witnesses sign the will. In contrast with probate, other nonprobate documents of transfer are more difficult to contest, partly because execution requirements are less stringent; thus a mistake in execution formality that would invalidate the transfer is less likely occur.

With a better understanding of the pros and cons of probate, let us now consider the two principal alternatives to probate. We first turn to the simpler alternative, disposition by joint tenancy.

ONE ALTERNATIVE TO PROBATE: JOINT TENANCY

Disposition by right of survivorship under title held in joint tenancy is one major alternative to probate. It, too, has several advantages and disadvantages, which we consider next.

Advantages of Joint Tenancy

Joint tenancy has a number of distinct advantages, including low administrative cost; convenience, speed and privacy; clear, undisputed disposition; the ability to reduce creditors' claims; and income shifting.

Low administrative cost. Joint tenancy is inexpensive, both to create and to terminate. Both actions typically involve simply adding or deleting names on a certificate of ownership. Financial institutions and others holding record of title will usually aid the survivors in doing this, eliminating the need for an attorney. The removal of the deceased cotenant's name from title usually requires the presentation of a death certificate and the completion of a short, preprinted form signed by one or more of the surviving joint tenants.

Convenience, speed, and privacy. The simplicity inherent in creating and terminating joint tenancies makes them a convenient, easily understood, and speedy dispositive device. And since joint tenancy combines a method of disposition at death with a method of holding title, the property owner will not need to execute a relatively complex document, such as a will or a trust, to dispose of property held jointly. In fact, at time of disposition, any existing will or trust will be disregarded as irrelevant to the automatic survivorship inherent in joint tenancy. Finally, unlike probate property, which is a matter of public record, joint tenancy property will pass to the surviving co-tenants in relative privacy. Compared to the ease of "pulling a file" at the probate court, it is more difficult for the public to obtain information about jointly held stock, bank accounts, and the like, although real estate, including that held in joint tenancy, is usually recorded in the county recorder's office.

Clear, undisputed disposition. Ordinarily, surviving joint tenants need not worry about not succeeding to ownership of the deceased cotenant's interest. Suits contesting joint tenancies are rare, partly because the legal formality requirements for taking title in joint tenancy are clear and minimal. There is little to challenge. In addition, the method of holding title in joint tenancy is usually clearly indicated. For example, some states require the words, "joint tenancy with right of survivorship and not as tenants in common," a title description that further minimizes confusion. In contrast, interested parties are more able to challenge the validity of a will, in part because its execution requirements and dispositive provisions are far more complex.

A few joint tenancies, however, have been successfully challenged. In some cases, courts have held that the decedent created a joint tenancy *for convenience only*, and did not intend to leave his or her interest to the surviving co-tenants. For example, an elderly person may create a joint tenancy solely to seek assistance in property management. A younger individual may be named as a cotenant simply to help write checks on the elder's bank funds. As another example, consider the facts of an actual court case, in which a husband took title to his own stock in joint tenancy with his wife, in order to avoid probate. At their later divorce, the wife was required to release her interest in the stock. The court reasoned from the facts of this case that the husband had not created the joint tenancy with donative intent. To safeguard against any controversy over unintended gifts in these types of situations, the client might wish to write and keep a letter clearly stating actual intent.

Ability to reduce creditors' claims. Property held in joint tenancy is not subject to the claims of a *deceased cotenant's* unsecured creditors, because death results in an instantaneous and automatic transfer of ownership to the surviving co-tenants. However, a creditor may be able to recover under the theory that the deceased cotenant made a transfer considered to be "fraudulent" as to creditors. In addition, the property will be subject to claims resulting from debts incurred by the *surviving co-tenants*, whether or not incurred jointly with the decedent.

Thus, joint tenancy can be one method of insulating property from some creditors.

EXAMPLE 10 - 1. Three years ago, Starfield financed the purchase of a car, which was used as collateral against the loan. Starfield died this year owning, among other things, the car (a probate asset), and some securities held in joint tenancy with his sister. If the bank loan goes into default, the bank will be able to recover the car. If proceeds from the sale of the car are not sufficient to pay off the loan, the bank may be able to reach other assets in Starfield's probate estate but it would not be able to seize the securities that now belong to the sister.

Income shifting. By placing property in joint tenancy with other family members, the client is able to shift income to lower-bracket taxpayers. Ownership interest of their share is usually immediately transferred to them (exceptions: bank accounts in some states and EE savings bonds), and, consequently, income generated by the transferred share belongs to them, too. If the cotenant is in a lower tax bracket than the creator, the combined tax on generated income may be reduced. However, we shall see shortly that the relinquishment of so much control can be a serious drawback to joint tenancy.

Disadvantages of Joint Tenancy

The disadvantages of joint tenancy as a dispositive device include non-tax factors such as inflexible, uncontrolled and inefficient disposition, surrender of ownership and control, incomplete probate avoidance, as well as tax disadvantages, including the basis problem and the risk of higher transfer taxes. After studying them, the reader will probably conclude that joint tenancy is of limited use for most wealthy clients.

Inflexible, uncontrolled, and inefficient disposition. Joint tenancy is an inflexible, uncontrolled, and inefficient dispositive device. Disposition is clear but rigid: The surviving co-tenant take outright, pro rata, the deceased cotenant's interest, and the last surviving cotenant winds up with an individual, fee simple interest in the property. In addition, all joint tenancies terminate at the death of the next-to-last surviving cotenant; thus right of survivorship cannot control disposition of property when the last cotenant dies. Several major disposition problems, discussed next, arise from these characteristics.

Danger of uncontrolled, undesired disposition. Joint tenancies can result in uncontrolled and undesired dispositions in three major ways.

First, by taking title in joint tenancy, clients risk distribution of their property to *unintended beneficiaries*, either as a result of chance, or by the intent of surviving co-tenant. For example, consider a joint tenancy between a childless couple. If both were to die in fairly rapid succession, such as in a common accident, all of the property could wind up in the hands of the surviving cotenant's heirs or beneficiaries. If the survivor regained mental capacity, he or she would have the right to direct disposition of this property to anyone, by will, trust, or other document. As illustrated in Chapter 3, the risk to the unlucky cotenant of uncontrolled disposition can be avoided with a will or a trust, documents that can control asset disposition after the survivor's death with a survival clause and other provisions, such as giving the survivor only a life estate and leaving the remainder to someone else, but such planning will not apply to assets held in joint tenancy. By taking title in joint tenancy, spouses leave ultimate disposition to chance, empowering the survivor to disregard the other's dispositive wishes.

> EXAMPLE 10 - 2. Cheryl remarries after the death of her first husband, and wishing to have her estate avoid probate, names her new husband Donny as co-joint tenant of her residence. Although Cheryl's will leaves all of her property to her children, Donny will become the sole owner of the house if he survives Cheryl.

Second, disposition by joint tenancy, when not coordinated with other planning, can result in an unintended *disproportionate distribution* of the client's estate.

> EXAMPLE 10 - 3. Coco owned the following assets several months before her death: Common stock in her name as an individual worth $29,000; a bank account in joint tenancy with her sister worth $1,000; and the rest of her property in her name as an individual, worth $970,000. Her will leaves her entire estate to her children, and directs that all taxes be paid out of the probate estate. Shortly before her death, Coco sold the stock, depositing the proceeds in her bank account. Assuming that debts, expenses, and taxes amounted to $200,000 at her death, Coco's children will receive property worth $770,000 (= $970,000 - $200,000), which is 79% of the before-tax bequest, and her sister will receive $30,000, which is 100% of the before-tax bequest. Although Coco intended to leave her sister a small sum, her inadvertent mistake wound up passing to her sister thirty times as much, free of all debts, expenses and taxes, which were paid entirely out of the children's share.

Third, joint ownership *prevents* the client from making other, less direct but *more desirable types* of transfers at death, such as giving an interest to a nonowner or splitting the interest by giving an income interest to one person and a remainder interest to another. Most planning arrangements to be discussed in the remaining chapters of this book require types of transfers not possible with joint tenancy.

Danger of inefficient disposition. Even if joint tenancies are expected to dispose of the client's assets to the right parties in the right amounts, they may do so inefficiently, generating delay and asset shrinkage. Three inefficiencies will be explored.

First, the property passing to the surviving cotenant will not be subject to those *protective provisions* often included in wills and trusts regarding responsible asset management. As a consequence, by selecting joint tenancy, clients often risk asset depletion by inexperienced co-tenant who will enjoy complete discretion over care and management of the property.

> EXAMPLE 10 - 4. In Example 10 - 2 above, if Cheryl had named her oldest child to be cotenant, disposition to Cheryl's husband could have been avoided, but that child would become the sole owner of all property, to the exclusion of the other children. If that lucky but generous child later splits the property with the siblings, he or she will have made one or more gifts subject to taxation. These two problems could have been avoided by naming all children as co-tenant, but Cheryl may not have wished to make an immediate gift of all her property to the children.

Second, creating joint tenancies may expose those assets to the *claims of the creditors of the other cotenant* even though the client, merely seeking an inexpensive way to avoid probate, did not really intend the cotenant to have an interest until the client died. For example, if son, who is named cotenant on property owned by Mom, incurs a court judgment due to an auto accident, the son's half interest in the joint tenancy asset may be subject to a judgment claim that could force partition and sale of the property.

Third, joint tenancies can result in *probate administration* and, possibly, intestacy. Joint tenancy does not in itself avoid probate administration at the death of the last surviving cotenant, nor in the case of simultaneous death situations.

> EXAMPLE 10 - 5. While alive, Russ and his wife Patti were advised to avoid probate by creating joint tenancies. After Russ died, Patti survived only a few years,

never realizing that at her death all of their property would be subject to probate administration. As the last surviving cotenant, Patti owned all of this property as an individual.

EXAMPLE 10 - 6. Based on the facts in the prior example, above, if Russ and Patti instead died in a common accident where there was no sufficient evidence as to who survived the other, under the Uniform Simultaneous Death Act each cotenant will be presumed to survive the other, resulting in each cotenant's half interest in the property being subject to probate administration.

The living trust, discussed in the next major section, does not have this drawback; it is designed to avoid probate administration at the death of both spouses.

Surrender of ownership and control. As discussed in Chapter 7, creating an interest in joint tenancy will usually constitute an immediate, completed *gift* to any cotenant who has not contributed an equal share of the consideration. Thus, each donee-cotenant will become the legal owner of an equal portion of the property. By receiving a (vested) present interest, each has the right to convert his or her share of the property into a tenancy-in-common interest, capable of being sold or devised to non-co-tenant. This might not be a problem for joint tenancies between people who contribute equal shares of property, nor for happily married spouses. Furthermore, tenancy by the entire cannot be unilaterally changed, sold or encumbered. Between others, however, the probate avoidance of joint tenancy may not be worth the client's immediate surrender of significant property interests.

Creating an immediate vested present interest in the donee-cotenant can give rise to other problems. The donee may be unable to later disclaim the gift to save transfer taxes. If the donee becomes incompetent, a guardianship may have to be appointed. The donor may need the donee's permission to sell the asset. Finally, the asset may be subject to the claims of the donee's creditors.

In contrast with joint tenancy, other documents of transfer such as the will and the trust instrument can *delay* the making of an outright gift at least until the client's death. Instead of creating present interests, they provide for *future interests*, ones that are *contingent* upon future events, such as the client's not later revoking those interests. Most clients do not wish to make outright gifts at the time they are planning to avoid probate.

The basis problem. As we have seen earlier, the rule for basis adjustment for appreciated joint tenancy property at the death of one spouse results in a "one-half'' step-up. Avoiding joint tenancy may open up one or two of the opportunities described next to achieve a step-up in basis for the entire value of the property.

Gift-death-devise strategy. First, the property could be *given to a donee* who is expected to die before the donor. At the donee's death, the entire property, which is then devised back to the donor, will receive a full step-up in basis. This strategy will be certain to work satisfactorily only in situations where the donee can be trusted to actually devise the property to the donor, such as where the parties are happily married. It will also succeed only if the donee's death occurs at least one year after the initial gift. Under Internal Revenue Code §1014(e), failure of the donee to survive by at least a year will cause the gift to be treated, for purpose of basis adjustment, as if the original transfer never occurred.

Community property ownership. The second way in which avoiding joint tenancy can open up an opportunity for a step-up in basis for the entire value of property involves the ownership of community property between spouses. As we saw in Chapter 7, unlike joint tenancy property, both halves of community property receive a step-up in basis at the death of the first spouse. Thus, married clients in *community property* states (even those of modest wealth) may be especially interested in avoiding joint tenancy arrangements, choosing instead to dispose of community property by will or trust instrument.

When step-up not necessary. For some clients, however, a basis step-up may not be important. For example, their property may not have appreciated substantially, indeed, if it has depreciated, then the strategies mentioned above would actually result in a full step-down in basis. Basis is not important if the survivor is not expected to sell the property. Or if any gain from sale of the property will be sheltered by certain provisions of the Internal Revenue Code. Common methods of sheltering an otherwise taxable gain on a *principal residence* include the rollover (postponement) of the gain on sale,[5] and the one-time exclusion of $125,000 of gain by an individual who has attained age 55.[6]

Possible higher estate tax. Joint tenancies can increase estate tax for two reasons: because of the somewhat harsh provisions of §2040 and because of their effect on the size of the surviving cotenant's gross estate.

§2040 consequences. When we first studied §2040, we learned that the *entire value* of property held in joint tenancy by a decedent is includable in the decedent's gross estate, except in two situations. First, if the joint tenancy was held solely with the surviving spouse, exactly one half is included. Second, if the joint tenancy was held by the decedent and at least one person who is not the decedent's spouse, the decedent's gross estate will include the entire value of the property, reduced only by an amount attributable to that portion of the consideration which can be shown to have been furnished by the survivors. Thus, a higher than necessary estate tax can result if a joint tenancy has a nonspouse cotenant and if the surviving co-tenant are unable to fully prove contribution. This may be a blessing in disguise. If the deceased joint tenant's taxable estate is less than the UCE there will be no transfer tax and yet the surviving joint tenants will have a new basis equal to the date of death fair market value.

> EXAMPLE 10 - 7. Clarissa and her brother, Scott, purchased a condo on the Florida coast for $100,000. They took title in joint tenancy. The condo was worth $300,000 when Scott died. Scott's other worldly possessions were worth approximately $180,000. Because Clarissa and Scott failed to keep adequate records concerning the purchase of the condo, it was deemed to be 100% in Scott's gross estate. As a consequence, Clarissa's basis in the condo is $300,000. Scott's estate paid no estate tax because the net value was less than the UCE.

Larger survivor's gross estate. Joint tenancies between spouses and other co-tenant can also result in a higher than necessary estate tax for the estates of *surviving co-tenant* because their gross estates will be quite large, having been loaded up with the predeceased cotenant's property passing to them by automatic right of survivorship. We shall see in Chapter 11 that in the case of some spouses, total spousal estate tax can be reduced by rejecting such a "100% marital deduction" plan, and instead passing less property outright to the surviving spouse. This principal also applies to unmarried couples in nontraditional relationships, as detailed in Chapter 17. Such an estate tax saving "bypass" of the surviving partner's estate can only be arranged satisfactorily with a will or a living trust. And, as mentioned above, neither document can dispose of property held in joint tenancy.

Possible gift taxation. Creation of joint tenancies between non-spouses can result in a taxable gift if an unequal contributions are made and if the value of the gift exceeds the annual exclusion. In contrast, disposition by will or by the typical living trust instrument produces no immediate gift during the client's lifetime because, as we have said, the documents generally do not create vested interests.

Finally, the client may not be able to avoid joint tenancy with regard to certain property. For example, some bank lenders may require that spouses hold title in their home in joint tenancy rather that in trust as a condition to granting a loan secured by the property. As living trusts become more popular as an estate planning device and lending institutions become more familiar with them, this requirement by lenders is less likely to occur, although the spouses may be asked to either personally guarantee the loan or give their written assurance that there is nothing in the trust document that would prevent them from using the property as collateral.

In view of the many significant drawbacks to joint tenancy, especially for clients with medium or large estates, planners generally recommend the other major alternative to probate, the living trust, discussed next.

THE OTHER ALTERNATIVE TO PROBATE: THE LIVING TRUST

The more popular alternative to probate for many estate planning clients is the living trust. As described in Chapter 3, it is a trust created during the trustor's lifetime and funded with some or all of the family wealth. While the trustor is alive, the living trust is usually revocable, which means that its terms are amendable and, if later desired, its assets can be retransferred to the trustor's name. Most trustors name themselves trustee of their living trust during their lifetime. However, under a doctrine called *merger*, a few states do not recognize trusts that name the same person to be trustor, trustee, and beneficiary.

At the trustor's death, the revocable trust becomes irrevocable and either terminates with the corpus distributed to the remaindermen, or continues in existence until a later date. In the case of a typical "joint" revocable living trust created by a husband and wife, all assets are placed in one trust, which is revocable by either of them during their lifetimes. At the first spouse's death, different things can happen, depending on the plan. A commonly used estate plan for smaller estates has the decedent's share of the trust property left in trust to the spouse, so that the trust becomes one large pot belonging entirely to the surviving spouse. Then, at his or her later death, the trust, which has avoided two probates, is either terminated or continued for the benefit of the children. Other distribution arrangements, particularly those designed to reduce estate tax at the surviving spouse's death, will be discussed in Chapter 11.

Taxation of a living trust depends on whether or not it is revocable. A *revocable* living trust usually has no additional transfer or income tax consequences during the trustor's lifetime. A transfer to it does not constitute a taxable gift since the transfer is not complete. And under the grantor trust rules, all income earned by a revocable trust is taxable to the grantor, that is, the trustor. In contrast, an *irrevocable* living trust is usually a separate income-taxpaying entity; all transfers into it usually constitute completed gifts, and, except when either the grantor trust rules or the kiddie tax apply, all undistributed FAI is taxed to the trust, while all distributed FAI is usually taxed to the beneficiaries.

Funded irrevocable living trusts also avoid probate. Not as commonly used as the revocable living trust because they involve gifting, they will be discussed at length in Chapters 13 and 15, in the context of gift giving and life insurance planning.

Advantages of the Living Trust[7]

The living trust has several distinct advantages over other transfer devices. They include greater organization, greater assurance of probate avoidance, lower total costs, greater privacy and speed, opportunity to test the future, ability to use the trust as an alternative to a conservatorship, and possible reduced litigation.

Greater organization. Establishing a living trust in effect requires the client to organize his or her property during lifetime, thereby enhancing efficient personal financial planning.

Greater assurance of complete probate avoidance. Compared with joint tenancies, the living trust offers greater certainty that probate will be avoided at the death of the surviving partner.

> EXAMPLE 10 - 8. Kim and Chris wish to provide for asset disposition in a manner similar to that directed in a simple will, but also wish to avoid probate on all property. Their planner makes it clear to them that joint tenancies will not achieve the latter goal because the surviving cotenant may wind up owning the property as an individual, making it subject to probate administration. Instead, they execute a living trust instrument, funding the trust with all of their property. The trust will continue to exist for both their lifetimes. At the survivor's death, the assets will pass from the trusts to their designated beneficiaries, free from probate.

The above example was intentionally unclear about both the clients' sex and marital status. In this context, neither is material; unmarried individuals, including members of the same sex, may legally take title in joint tenancy and may legally co-execute a single trust instrument.

Lower total cost than probate. Compared to will preparation and probate, the combined cost of preparation and administration of the living trust is usually significantly less. The following material discusses both preparation costs and total cost.

Preparation costs. Oddly, the cost of preparing the living trust instrument may be a bit higher than the cost of preparing a will for at least two reasons. First, the trust instrument is usually a more complicated document. Its provisions must arrange for the immediate receipt of property, for management of that property, and for the proper distribution of the property and its income for a period that might span several generations of beneficiaries. However, if the probate alternative to a living trust is a *testamentary trust*, the difference in drafting costs may not be as large; the cost of the probate alternative of will drafting will be higher.

Second, the cost of preparing the living trust instrument is also higher than for planning for probate with a will because in addition to drafting a trust instrument, the attorney must *also* draft a type of will. Unfortunately, the establishment of the living trust does not totally eliminate the need for a will. Because clients often fail to continue to take the additional step necessary to completely fund the trust in a manner to be explained shortly, most clients will die owning some property in their own name, rather than in the name of the trustee. Planners provide for disposition of this probate property with what is called a *pourover will*, specifying that any of the testator's assets not in the trust shall be distributed or "poured over" into the trust at the client's death. Because it disposes of all property outright to only one party (the trustee), the pour-over will is usually a brief, simple document, adding little to the preparation cost of avoiding probate with the living trust. But, as a true will, it disposes of probate assets, hopefully few. Thus, some probate administration costs may be incurred on assets passing under the pour-over will.

Total cost. While the specific cost of preparing the living trust may be higher, the total cost of the living trust alternative is usually lower, due to the relatively high cost of formal probate *administration* at death. In contrast with formal probate, administration of a living trust at the client's death involves minimal or no legal work in court. The pour-over will may not need to be probated, depending upon the size of the probate estate and the scope of the state's informal or summary administration rules. However, some *other postmortem legal duties* that are required under the probate alternative may also have to be performed under the trust alternative. They include

- Obtaining appraisals
- Marshaling and safeguarding assets
- Preparing an informal inventory of the assets
- Preparing and filing death tax returns
- Paying creditors
- Instituting litigation to protect assets
- Changing title to assets
- Distributing assets to beneficiaries
- Obtaining receipts from beneficiaries

While the costs of these actions usually do not add up to anywhere near the total cost of formal probate administration, they are not insignificant.

But the total cost of probate isn't always greater. The efficiency of *informal* probate administration in *UPC states* can make probate an attractive alternative to the living trust, measured by the criterion of cost.

Other factors influencing the relative costs of probate versus the living trust include whether someone other than the grantor or the grantor's spouse will serve as trustee or executor, the ability to deduct these costs as an income tax miscellaneous itemized deduction, and the schedule of local court costs.

At this point it should be reiterated that avoiding probate with the revocable living trust does not save additional transfer taxes. Chapter 12 will make it clear why the same amount of estate tax can be saved by disposing of property with a carefully drafted will.

As mentioned earlier, a detailed analytical model for comparing the costs of the living trust versus formal probate is presented later in the chapter.

Greater privacy. A trust instrument is usually very private, not subject to public inspection. Although property transfers into and out of a living trust may require *examination of the trust instrument* by financial and other institutions, the document usually need not be made publicly accessible. County recorders may require a filing of the trust in the public records, but usually only brief sections of the document need be submitted. In fact, many attorneys in the estate planning process draft a separate brief document called "memorandum of trust" or "confirmation of trust," available for examination by such institutions, in lieu of the trust instrument itself. At a minimum, it will contain sections describing the identity of trustee and successor trustee, and the trustee powers. It should be formally executed by trustor and trustee, and notarized. In this way critical parts of the trust, including dispositive provisions, may be kept completely secret.

However some states, such as New York which impose an inheritance tax on trust property, may require the public *filing of an inventory*, which can reveal the nature and value of the trust's assets and the names of its beneficiaries. In addition, in the litigation process, a determined contestant can gain access to the contents of a living trust through legal "discovery."

As mentioned earlier, privacy may be especially desired by particularly wealthy or prominent clients. They may wish to avoid any additional publicity and any inspection by disinherited or contentious survivors, who may be seeking the opportunity to initiate a will contest.

Speed. Property can usually be transferred out of a trust somewhat more rapidly than out of a probate estate because the transfer process is not ordinarily subject to supervision and approval by the courts. However, failure to perform certain postmortem legal duties (detailed above) can subject the trustee to significant personal liability and can trigger costly and avoidable litigation for the beneficiaries. Thus, for example, in those states where creditors' claims can be made against trust assets, the trustee will want to delay distribution. And for larger trusts owing a sizable estate tax, the trustee may delay major distributions of trust assets until an estate tax "closing letter" from the IRS is received, about one to two years after date of death.

Speed of disposition of real property located in a *different state* can be more rapid if that property is held in a living trust rather than disposed of by will, because ancillary administration can often be avoided. Real property held in a living trust is considered by most states to be intangible personal property, not subject to ancillary administration. However, some states require reporting procedures quite similar to the probate administration process.

Opportunity to test the future. By placing assets into a revocable living trust, the client has the opportunity to test the future by making the estate plan largely operational during lifetime. The client can obtain a preview of how the assets will be *managed* after death and how the beneficiaries can be expected to react to the receipt of family property. By naming another party trustee, the client can observe firsthand how well the assets are being managed and can make needed adjustments in management provisions before death. In addition, the trustee can be given the opportunity to become *familiar* with the trust assets during the client's lifetime, thus increasing the likelihood of both more efficient future management and a more smooth transition period after the client's death. Finally, by initiating a predictable pattern of asset distributions to beneficiaries during lifetime, the client can help a family member *learn to use assets* more maturely. Of course, a program of gifting is possible without a living trust, but having the terms of distribution in writing further ensures a continuous and consistent transfer program. It is these reasons why a few commentators have loosely called the revocable living trust a form of "living will." But this should not be confused with the universally known "living will," discussed in Chapter 17, which is a popular document containing directions regarding health care decisions.

Alternative to guardianship or conservatorship. We shall see in Chapter 17 that a client who becomes physically or mentally incapable of managing assets will need someone to provide that management. Just as a guardianship may have to be established to manage a minor's estate, a guardianship or conservatorship may be necessary to manage the estate of an incapacitated adult. Like probate administration, guardianships and conservatorships are carefully supervised by the court, which usually requires periodic accountings and formal court approval for many acts of asset management.

Used in lieu of a guardianship or conservatorship, the living trust can thus be seen as a vehicle to also avoid the expense, delay and publicity of probate-type administration before the client's death. The typical living trust begins with the client acting as trustee. Subsequently, a successor trustee takes over when the client relinquishes the role, becomes incapacitated, or dies. Thus, the living trust instrument has an additional application not directly available with a will: It can be easily structured to provide for the client's incapacity. Some commentators consider this *the major advantage* of the living trust for older clients, making the will alternative seriously deficient by comparison.

Another less expensive alternative to the guardianship or conservatorship is the durable power of attorney for property, discussed in Chapter 17. It does not avoid probate.

Possible reduced litigation. As we have seen, the probate process can offer a relatively convenient opportunity for a dissatisfied survivor to initiate a will contest. Such disputes over disposition of the client's property may be minimized with a living trust for two reasons. First, the client, as trustor and beneficiary, is able to live with the trust, receiving and making distributions and transferring property to it. All of these acts can constitute additional evidence of a well thought out estate plan. In contrast, a will ordinarily is simply a document, one not perceived to have much impact on the testator's day-to-day life. Thus, disappointed parties may be more successful in showing that the testator's will does not reflect his or her actual intent.

Second, disputes over the client's estate plan may be minimized with a living trust to the extent that the actual litigation may be more difficult to accomplish. However, commentators are in disagreement over how difficult a trust is to contest. Some maintain that the living trust is quite difficult to contest since it requires a separate legal action in a different court, one often with more onerous legal requirements and perhaps the absence of a sympathetic jury. In addition, transfers from a trust do not require notice to the testator's heirs. In contrast, probating the will, as we have seen, does involve formal notice, and act which may in itself trigger a contest. Other commentators argue that a trust can be contested on substantially the same grounds that are used to contest a will. Common grounds, it will be recalled, include fraud, undue influence, lack of capacity and improper execution.

Other advantages of living trusts. Living trusts are normally simpler to revise than wills. While a *codicil* to a will requires certain execution formalities (described in Chapter 3), an *amendment* to a living trust needs no formalities or witnesses, and may be in the trustor's handwriting. However, if the trustee is someone other than the trustor, he or she should at least be notified of the revision, and most attorneys also have the trustee sign the amendment.

Use of a living trust eliminates any hiatus or time gap in the management of the decedent-client's assets immediately after death. While the trustee (or successor trustee) of a living trust is empowered to carry on immediately, no one is authorized to act with regard to probate property until the court appoints a personal representative, at least several days after the testator's death. Of course, most assets do not require immediate attention.

Disadvantages of the Living Trust

The living trust has several disadvantages, including the burden of funding, possibly greater legal uncertainty, and some minor tax factors.

Funding burden. Establishment of a joint tenancy is a one-step process. The very act of creation of the joint interest creates the appropriate title. On the other hand, establishment of a living trust to avoid probate is a two-step process. First, the trust document must be executed, somewhat like that of a two party contract. Second, the trust must be *funded*; that is, legal title to the property intended to avoid probate must be formally transferred from the trustor to the trustee. Some trustor-clients never do the latter, because they are unaware that the additional step of funding is necessary. Others are aware of it but simply never get around to it. Most find it downright inconvenient, because it requires trips to the bank and to other places where title is officially kept. And clients who actively trade their property, such as those involved in frequent real estate deals and securities transactions, may especially dislike the greater complexity inherent in continually keeping property in trust name. However, for securities held in street name and traded in the typical brokerage account under the trustee's name, proper title will automatically be taken with each purchase without further work by the trustee.

Failure to fund the trust will cause that property not to be subject to the trust's terms.[8] As a result, at the client's death the property will usually pass through probate, under the (pour over) will or by intestate succession. Some attorneys carefully avoid this undesired outcome by insisting on initially funding the living trust themselves, rather than leaving the responsibility to the client. This may increase somewhat the legal cost of setting up the living trust. However, in at least one court decision, a trustor's written declaration stating the holding of certain specific property as trustee was held to be sufficient, even though the trustor had not made a legal *conveyance*, title change by deed. In the specific facts of the case, the trustors listed a specific item of real property held as a tenant in common on "Schedule A," at the end of his living trust. The court ruled the property to be held in trust and not subject to probate. A footnote to the ruling said "We hasten to note, however, that to be effective as to strangers, the declaration of trust must be recorded."

On an ongoing basis, planners may be able to help the client spot non-trust assets by paying particular attention to the client's tax forms, such as 1099s and K1s, which are issued by partnerships, S corporations, banks and other asset account holders. Forms that do not indicate the trust as record owner of the account may imply that a title change is in order.

To eliminate the funding burden for married couples with joint tenancy property, one commentator has suggested executing a "joint declaration of trust ownership," designed to instantly convert all jointly owned property into trust owned property without having to change record title to any jointly held assets. Other suggested advantages of this largely untested "magic wand" type document include maximizing use of each spouse's unified credit and GSTT exemption,[9] greater privacy, possible additional protection from creditors, and no need to change title to all assets whenever there is a change in trustees.

Greater legal uncertainty. Unlike the will, the living trust has not had the benefit of centuries of testing by the courts to resolve the inevitable conflicts that can arise. In the future, we can expect some continuing litigation in the area of the living trust, a prospect that raises a small degree of uncertainty over the outcome of any unresolved issues.

Longer creditor's period. As described in considerable detail earlier, probate can offer a shorter creditor's limitations period than can the living trust, which is often subject to the usual limitations period of from one to three years.

Living trust arrangements may be able to indirectly take advantage of the shorter creditor's period under probate. One commentator, an advocate of the living trust, includes in her trust forms a "pour-up" provision, giving the trustee discretion to distribute trust assets to the client's estate at the client's death. In this way, the living trust, with all of its advantages, may be used, unless a creditor's problem is anticipated later on. This arrangement is still considerably untested.

A second way that living trusts can (arguably) take advantage of the shorter creditor's period involves simply probating a small but significant portion of the client's property, under the assumption that the probate notice to creditors will be effective in barring later claims against trust property, as well as probate property. Largely untested, this strategy rests on the premise that formal notice serves to inform creditors that they should seek recourse *in general*, because the debtor has died. Some critics, however, argue that a probate notice cannot be effective against a pot of property that is in no way identified in the notice. Others believe that such notice will be effective only if the claims are smaller than the value of the probate estate. At least one state statute makes revocable living trust assets subject to creditor's claims and probate administration expenses to the extent that the probate estate can not pay them.[10] This tie-in should lend support to the argument that the limited creditors period should also bar collection against living trust assets. In the future, as more and more trustors die, case law should decide this issue.

Tax factors. There are a number of minor tax disadvantages to the living trust.

- Compared to the $600 available to an estate, a trust, after the grantor's death, has a smaller personal income tax *exemption*: either $100 or $300.
- A trust is subject to the income tax *throwback rules*, while an estate is not. However, the rapidly rising rate brackets for estates virtually destroy the benefit of avoiding the throwback rules. In addition, most trust income beneficiaries will probably prefer receiving income sooner rather than later, making the application of the throwback rules to most trusts unlikely.
- For income tax purposes, the trustee of a trust cannot select the close of the trust's *taxable year*, while the executor of an estate can. The advantage of selecting a fiscal tax year is illustrated in Chapter 18.
- As mentioned earlier, real property held in trust and located in states other than the client's residence state is usually considered by the client's residence state to be intangible personal property. Most states impose a death tax on such *distantly owned property*, which might otherwise escape taxation if it were disposed of by will, since "real property" located outside a state is not ordinarily subject to its tax. Of course no additional tax would be incurred in states imposing only a "pick-up" type death tax. And such real property may still escape death tax if it is owned by a corporation, rather than directly by a decedent-shareholder.
- Finally, the IRS has taken the position that property transferred by the trustee of a revocable trust within three years of the grantor's death will be included in his or her gross estate under *§2035*. The service argues that the property would have been included under §2038 had the "relinquishment" not been made.[11]

To avoid §2035 application under the last item, above, for *existing trusts*, planners recommend a two-step transfer: first the grantor should withdraw the amounts from the trust; second, he or she should directly make the gift. Rationale: when the grantor withdraws the property, there is no relinquishment since the grantor has control over it. To avoid §2035 application for *new trusts*, planners recommend that the instrument provide that during the trustor's lifetime, the trustor shall be the only permissible appointee, so that distributions to anyone else would have to be "characterized" as withdrawals by the trustor followed by later transfers to donees.[12]

Miscellaneous disadvantages. There are several other disadvantages to the living trust, all of which can be considered relatively minor for most clients.

Financing problems. In some states, property held in a living trust may not be secured as collateral against a loan by the trustor. In addition, if the trustor wishes to refinance property after it has been placed in trust, lenders may require that the trustor reassume title to it until the refinancing is completed. And some lenders may not finance trust property if they fear that the trust instrument may prohibit its sale.

Divorce. In some states, divorce may result in an improper distribution of assets from a living trust. As mentioned in Chapter 4, in most states, a dissolution of marriage will revoke a disposition to an ex-spouse in a *will* executed prior to the divorce. In contrast, these state statutes often do not apply to provisions in a living trust. However, in states adopting Uniform Probate Code §2-804(b), divorce revokes *any* revocable disposition or appointment of property for an ex-spouse or relative of an ex-spouse.

Other disadvantages. Living trusts may have disadvantages in certain special situations, two of which will be mentioned briefly without additional explanation. First, beneficiaries of a living trust may lose a defense against liability for *environmental clean-up* of real property held in the trust. In contrast, that defense is available to persons *acquiring* the property "by inheritance or bequest.[13] "Second, use of a living trust may reduce allowable *Medicaid benefits* for the beneficiary-spouse of a decedent who establishes a discretionary living trust. The problem will not arise for testamentary trusts.[14]

Not included among these disadvantages of a revocable living trust is any loss of a *basis step-up* at the grantor's death. Property held in a revocable living trust *will* receive a step-up because it is treated, from an income tax point of view, as owned by the grantor.

Living trusts require careful analysis, planning and preparation. Clearly, the decision whether or not to create a revocable living trust requires the planner's critical evaluation of many challenging issues, and drafting a living trust requires the knowledge of an experienced estate planning attorney. The tasks of evaluation and careful drafting require a skill level far above those of any practicing generalist, let alone someone lacking even rudimentary training in the issues. Nonetheless, recently, casual salespersons, sometimes traveling door-to-door, have been approaching the elderly in large numbers, offering to prepare living trusts. Tactics alleged by opponents include using high pressure sales pitches, imposing high prices, making misrepresentations and mistakes about the relative costs and advantages of living trusts, naming themselves as trustees, carelessly failing to ensure that property is transferred to the trust, producing an ineffective document, and making false claims of endorsement by legitimate nonprofit organizations. Some states have taken legal action against these organizations, but these unprofessional practices will probably continue as long as some uninformed elderly persons, overly fearful of probate and guardianships and distrustful of lawyers, naively reach out for help from outwardly friendly "advisors."

QUANTITATIVE MODEL FOR COMPARISON OF COSTS OF PROBATE VERSUS LIVING TRUST

This section applies the principles of finance to develop a model for comparing the costs of probate with the costs of the living trust. The technique used will incorporate the *time value of money* concept known as present value.

> EXAMPLE 10 - 9. Patty is evaluating the decision whether to avoid probate of her assets, worth $1 million, by setting up a revocable living trust. Her life expectancy is 10 years. With regard to costs, she has made the following estimates:
>
> Under the probate alternative: drafting her will, $600; probate administration, $25,000; other costs at death, including accountant's fees, $1,000.
>
> Under the trust alternative: drafting the trust and the pour-over will, $1,600; annual record-keeping until death,[15] $300 per year; nonprobate administration cost at death, $2,500; costs in higher income taxes due to inability to use a probate estate as a separate taxpayer, $1,100; other costs at death, including accountant's fees, $1,000.
>
> In calculating the total cost for each alternative, Patty could simply add up the expenses. That would result in a forecasted total cost under the probate alternative of $26,000, and a forecasted total cost under the trust of $11,100.

Simply adding up the costs, however, does not take into account the time value of money. To correctly compare amounts incurred at different points in time, we must make adjustments to reflect the fact that money not payable today can be invested profitably until the time that it is payable. We can do this by calculating the sum of the *present values of the costs for each alternative*. The present value of a cost is the amount that would have to be invested today to accumulate the actual amount of that cost payable in the future.

To better understand the present value concept, consider an intuitively simple illustration. At an assumed annual rate of investment of 10%, one would need to invest $100 today to accumulate the amount $110 payable in one year. In other words, at 10%, the present value of $110 payable in one year is $100. Present values of any amount can be derived from present value tables such as Table B for a term of years and Table S for amounts payable for life or at the end of a person's life. These tables are in Appendix A at the end of the text. Table B (10%) depicts the present values of a single $1 amount to be paid in the future, assuming an investment rates of 10%. Thus, the present value of $1 in one year at 10% is $0.909091, or a bit less than 91 cents. Since we have been calculating the present value of the amount $110, not $1, our answer must be the product of $110 and 0.909091, or $100.

How can we calculate the present value of the amount $300 payable each year for the next 10 years, with the first payment due in one year? Described in other words, we must calculate the total amount to be invested today which will enable us to fund this annuity, that is, to fund this entire progression of equal payments. To do this, we calculate the present value of the annuity. Table B in Appendix A shows the present values of a $1 annuity for specified periods, assuming certain investment rates.

> EXAMPLE 10 - 10.   With regard to Patty's actual figures, at 10%, the present value of $1 to be paid in 10 years is $0.386. We will use this lump-sum discount factor in the calculations that follow. The "annuity factor," as it is called, corresponding to 10 years and 10%, can be seen to 6.145. Since we wish to determine the present value of an annuity of $300, not $1, the answer must be the product of $300 and 6.145, or $1,844.

We are now ready to calculate Patty's total costs for the two alternatives in a manner which adjusts for the time value of money. The figures are shown in Table 10-1 and Table 10-2.

TABLE 10-1 Present Value of Costs of Probate

Items	Years	Amounts	Discount Factor	Present Value
Drafting	Now	$600	1.000000	$600
Administration	10	$25,000	0.385543	$9,639
Other costs	10	$1,000	0.385543	$386
		Total present value of probate costs		$10,625

TABLE 10-2 Present Value of Costs of Living Trust

Items	Years	Amounts	Discount Factor	Present Value
Drafting	Now	$1,600	1.000000	$1,600
Administration	10	$2,500	0.385543	$964
Record keeping	1-10	$300	6.144600	$1,864
Higher estate tax	10	$1,100	0.385543	$424
Other costs	10	$1,000	0.385543	$386
		Total present value of living trust costs		$5,238

Thus the sum of the present values of the costs are $10,625 for probate and $5,238 for the trust. These represent the total amounts that Patty would have to invest today, at 10%, to properly accumulate and pay all of the individual forecasted costs when they are due.

The analysis could be refined slightly to include the tax deductibility of these expenses. For example, as we shall see in Chapter 18, administration costs may be deducted on the estate tax return. Thus, if T represents the marginal estate tax rate, the after-tax cost of an estate tax deductible expense is the product of that expense times the expression one minus T.

The estimates in the above example have been made for illustration purposes only and should not be used as a general indicator of costs. Actual costs will vary considerably, depending on specific factors, such as the laws of the decedent's particular residence state and the cost of professional services in the decedent's locale. However, to generalize, the present-value cost of formal probate is usually higher than the present-value cost of the living trust by at least 20%.

WHICH ALTERNATIVE IS BEST?

From all of the material covered so far, the reader can gather that the decision whether or not to avoid probate is not always a simple one. It requires that the client examine and subjectively weigh the advantages and disadvantages of each, in the context of the laws and procedures of his or her state. It should be clear that there is no one absolutely correct answer for all situations. In fact, some clients owning larger estates may be advised to execute a will to probate certain assets and transfer the remaining assets by living trust, in order to obtain the unique benefits of both arrangements. Perhaps we can conclude with a description of a few of the circumstances in which clients are most likely to favor a particular alternative.

Probate

Clients who will be inclined to lean toward the probate alternative include:

1. *Professionals*, such as self-employed engineers and accountants, who stand to gain additional security from the short creditors' limitations period.
2. Those who have *large, complicated estates* or who expect family *disharmony* after their death may benefit from the extra protection potentially available through greater court supervision.
3. Wealthier residents of *UPC states* where the cost advantage to avoiding informal probate is minimal.
4. Young, healthy clients who expect to be acquiring numerous assets and would find onerous the constant *funding* requirement of the living trust.

Joint Tenancy

Since joint tenancy has some very significant disadvantages, clients are inclined to prefer it only if one, or perhaps all, of the following circumstances apply:

1. The client wants the property to pass *outright* to the surviving joint

tenants. This implies that there is no need for trusts, to save income or transfer taxes, to avoid guardianships, to delay distributions to younger survivors, or to provide for multiple beneficiaries over time by creating life estate and remainder interests.

2. A complete *step-up* in income tax basis at the client's death is *not needed*, or is not available by other means.
3. The creation of the joint tenancy interest does *not* result in an immediate *gift*.

These circumstances usually apply only to smaller estates.

Living Trust

Clients who will tend to prefer a living trust typically include those who want to avoid probate but do not like joint tenancy because of its significant disadvantages. For example:

1. Those with *larger estates* who wish to avoid the estate tax consequences of joint tenancy.
2. Those who place high priority on *privacy and speed* in the property transfer process.
3. Clients for whom the *total cost* of the living trust is expected to be considerably lower than the cost of probate; reasons include the following:
    a. Probate administration expenses are expected to be high, perhaps because the client is a resident of a non-UPC state, or because an independent executor must be named.
    b. Nonprobate administration fees are low, perhaps because a private individual can be named as trustee, and that trustee will not need to pay for outside record keeping.
4. Clients who do *not* anticipate a trust *funding burden* associated with numerous acquisitions of property.
5. Finally, clients who wish to avoid the publicity and cost of court appointed *guardians or conservators* if and when they become incapacitated.

HOW FREQUENTLY ARE THEY USED?

Based on the results of a survey of experienced estate planning attorneys conducted by Chris Prestopino, the revocable living trust was the most popular dispositive document used, with 45.1% of clients using them as the principal method of asset disposition. Complex wills were almost as popular (36.6%), followed by simple wills (13.8%) and joint tenancies (4.5%). Interestingly, while clients in general clearly chose to avoid joint tenancies, more than one half chose not to avoid probate.

QUESTIONS AND PROBLEMS

1. Discuss the validity of the claim that probate promotes fairness.

2. (a) Why isn't probate private? (b) Is the living trust always private?

3. (a) How has the advantage of probate's limited creditor's period been undermined recently? (b) Will any clients still prefer probate to minimize creditor's problems?

4. (a) Who might wish to contest a will by claiming the execution was invalid? (b) Why might it be easier to do than to challenge a living trust?

5. You wish to advise client Paxton about the income tax advantage to probate. Assuming that all of Paxton's survivors will be in the 28% marginal rate bracket, (a) how much income in the future Paxton estate could be subject to a lower rate? (b) what is the maximum amount of tax that could be saved by using the Paxton estate as a separate tax entity? (c) answer parts (a) and (b) this time assuming a 39.6% marginal rate for all survivors.

6. One of your clients asks you to summarize the advantages and disadvantages of using joint tenancies to avoid probate.

7. (a) Why should the living trust cost less than the formal probate alternative? (b) Are all cost components lower?

8. Wes has just received his lawyer's bill for developing a plan that avoids probate with a living trust. Included is a charge for drafting a will. Did the law firm make a billing mistake?

9. Today Dennis executed a living trust, with his sister as the only remainder beneficiary. Upon driving home from the lawyer's office, Dennis is killed in an auto accident. All of his property is still held in joint tenancy and tenancy in common form with his brother, Elmer. Is there a problem? Why or why not?

10. Evaluate the cost factor in the decision whether or not to avoid formal probate with a living trust, under the following assumed set of facts. For the probate alternative: drafting the will, $1,300; formal probate administration, $60,000; other costs at death, including accountants' and appraiser's fees, $2,300.

    For the trust alternative: drafting costs, $2,200; record-keeping until death, $500 per year; nonprobate administration costs at death, $3,100; costs in higher income taxes due to the inability to use a probate estate as a separate taxpayer, $1,000 (assume a one year probate); other costs at death, including accountants' fees, $3,600.

    Also assume an investment rate of return of 10%, and that the client will live 12 years.

11. Now evaluate the cost of *informal* probate versus the living trust. Assume all facts given in the problem immediately above, except that informal probate administration will cost $25,000.

12. (a) What types of clients are most likely to prefer probate? (b) To avoid probate with joint tenancies? (c) To avoid probate with the living trust?

13. For each of the following individuals, explain which of the three major types of asset disposition would probably best suit them.

    a. A 19 year old single college student owning only personal effects totaling $6,000.

   b. A former stockbroker who spent two years in prison for securities fraud.

   c. Michael Jackson, the entertainer.

   d. A plumber and his wife who own only a house, two cars and some other personal property. They have two middle aged, financially responsible children.

14. For each of the individuals listed in the question immediately above, invent an additional hypothetical fact or circumstance that would move you to recommend a method of asset disposition *different* from your original choice.

ANSWERS TO QUESTIONS AND PROBLEMS

1. Supporters of probate claim that court supervision in a public setting promotes fairness. Critics claim that judges and other officials offer only rubber stamp approval of administration acts, and that the trend of probate reform towards reduced supervision minimizes the credibility of this contention.

2. a. Probate isn't private because:

    1. All probate documents are available for inspection by the public.
    2. Probate proceedings are public.

   b. By and large, the living trust is truly private, except in cases where the trust (or portions of it) must be filed with the county recorder, or shown to a financial institution, or where an inventory of trust assets must be filed for inheritance tax purposes.

3. a. The advantage of probate's limited creditor's period has been undermined recently by the U.S. Supreme Court's decision in *Tulsa*, holding that creditors "known or reasonably ascertainable" to the personal representative must be given "actual" notice of the limited creditor's period, rather than just "constructive" notice, by publication. Actual notice need not be given to potential creditors whose claims are a matter

of "conjecture," i.e., deduced by surmise or guesswork. An example of a conjectural claim would be a malpractice claim against a professional that has not yet resulted in a demand. The *Tulsa* decision has generated great uncertainty among probate lawyers, who fear that dilatory creditors may flood the courts arguing that they were known or reasonably ascertainable. The upshot is that the creditors limitations period now offers far less certainty that all claims will be barred.

b. Clients who anticipate more claims after their death may still find the shorter limitations period a significant advantage. For example, professionals such as lawyers and accountants are potentially vulnerable to malpractice claims which, if instituted after their death, stand a greater chance of succeeding, partly because the defense's best witness, the decedent, is not available to testify. The shorter creditors' period can sometimes minimize this undesired outcome.

4. a. Disinherited and contentious survivors and others who may stand to gain may wish to contest the execution of a will.

b. Some commentators contend that since a will contest is initiated in probate court, it is a simpler process than contesting a trust, which requires separate legal action. Others say that a trust can be contested on substantially the same grounds that are used to contest a will. Common grounds include fraud, undue influence, lack of capacity and improper execution.

5. a. Based on the tax rates for estates and trusts (Table 8-1 of Chapter 8), only $1,650 (1997) will be subject to the 15% tax rate. The first $600 will be tax free.

b. The maximum amount of tax that could be saved using the Paxton estate as a separate tax entity is $382.50, calculated as follows:

$1,650 taxed at 15% rather than at 28%: $1,650*(.28-.15) = $214.50
$600 estate personal exemption not taxed (rather than at 28%): $600*.28 = $168
Total savings: $214.50 + $168.00 = $382.50

c. Assuming instead a 39.6% marginal rate for all survivors; the estate would have lower tax brackets of 15%, 28%, 31%, and 36%, thereby partially sheltering the first $8,100 (1997): tax on the first $8,100 = $2,287. Tax on $8,100 at 39.6% = $3,207.60; therefore, tax saved: $3,207.60 - $2,287 = $920.60.

6. Advantage of Joint tenancies to avoid probate

   a. Low administrative cost
   b. Convenience and speed
   c. Clear, undisputed disposition
   d. Reduced creditor's claims
   e. The possibility of income shifting.

   Disadvantage of joint tenancies:

   a. Inflexible disposition
   b. Incomplete probate avoidance (at death of surviving cotenant).
   c. Loss of ownership and control
   d. Loss of step-up in basis in part of the property
   e. Possible higher estate tax
   f. Possible gift tax.

7. a. The living trust should cost less than the formal probate alternative because of the typically large executor commissions and attorney fees in probate administration.

   b. Not all costs of a living trust are lower. The cost of *drafting* a trust might be higher, however, because:

      1. The trust is usually a more complex document than the will.
      2. A pour-over will must be drafted.

8. No, the lawyer didn't make a billing mistake. The higher cost reflects the need to draft a pour-over will, as well as a trust.

9. There is a problem. The trust will not control disposition over any of the assets. Elmer will receive Dennis's property interests, because joint tenancy disposition normally supersedes disposition by trust. Regarding the tenancy in common interests, which will go through probate, if the attorney included

a pourover will, Dennis' sister will receive them. With out a pour over will, the laws of intestate succession will determine who inherits those interests. Conclusion: living trusts must be funded to be effective.

10.

PRESENT VALUE COST OF FORMAL PROBATE

	Year	Amount	Factor	Present value
Drafting	now	$1,300	1.000	$1,300
Administration	12	$60,000	0.319	$19,140
Other costs	12	$2,300	0.319	$734
Total Present Value of Formal Probate				$21,174

PRESENT VALUE COST OF LIVING TRUST

	Year	Amount	Factor	Present value
Drafting	now	$2,200	1.000	$2,200
Record keeping	1-12	$500	6.814	$3,407
Higher tax	12	$3,100	0.319	$989
Administration	12	$1,000	0.319	$319
Other costs	12	$3,600	0.319	$1,148
Total Present Value of Living Trust				$8,063

11.

PRESENT VALUE COST OF INFORMAL PROBATE

	Year	Amount	Factor	Present value
Drafting	now	$1,300	1.000	$1,300
Administration	12	$25,000	0.319	$7,975
Other costs	12	$3,600	0.319	$1,148
Total Present Value of Informal Probate				$10,009

12. a. Clients most likely to prefer probate include:

1. Professionals, such as self-employed lawyers, engineers, and accountants, who stand to gain additional security from the short creditors' limitations period.

2. Those who have large, complicated estates or who expect family disharmony after death, may benefit from the extra protection potentially available through greater court supervision.
3. Wealthier residents of UPC states where the cost advantage to avoiding probate is minimal.
4. Young, healthy client who expect to be a acquiring numerous assets and would find onerous the constant funding requirement of the living trust.

b. Clients most likely to avoid probate with joint tenancies:

1. The client who wants the property to pass outright to the surviving joint tenants. This implies that there is no need for trusts after death, to save taxes or to provide for multiple beneficiaries.
2. Those who anticipate that a complete step-up in income tax basis at their death is not needed, or not available by other means. This may include situations where property has not appreciated substantially, or where the survivors do not plan to sell the property, or where they expect any gain from sale of the property to be sheltered by provisions of the Internal Revenue Code.
3. Those living in states where the creation of the joint tenancy interest does not result in an immediate gift.

c. Clients most likely to avoid probate with the living trust:

1. Those with larger estate who wish to avoid the estate tax consequences of joint tenancy.
2. Those who want greater privacy and speed in the property transfer process.
3. Clients for whom the total cost of the living trust is expected to be considerably lower than the cost of probate. Reasons include the following:

   i. Probate administration expenses are expected to be high, perhaps because the client is a resident of a non-UPC state, or because an independent executor must be named.
   ii. As trustee, the client will not need to pay for record-keeping.
   iii. Nonprobate administration fees are low, perhaps because private

individual can be named trustee.

4. Clients who do not anticipate a trust funding burden associated with numerous acquisitions of property.

5. Clients who wish to avoid the publicity and cost of court appointed guardians or conservators if and when they become incapacitated.

13. a. 19 year old college single student owning only personal effects totaling $6,000: Probate with a will. In virtually all states, formal administration would not be necessary because of the minimal size of the estate.

b. Former stockbroker who spent two years in prison for securities fraud: Probate, to avoid the longer creditor's limitations period. (Former clients and others may wish to institute civil claims.)

c. Michael Jackson, the entertainer: A revocable living trust, to retain privacy.

d. Plumber and wife: Probably joint tenancy, because it is inexpensive, and, because of the family's modest wealth, joint tenancy will not have the tax disadvantages normally inherent in that form of asset distribution.

14. a College student: Receives large inheritance or wins lottery-- living trust.
b. Stockbroker: leaves prison for a totally new career and survives 30 years and wants the privacy of a living trust.
c. Michael Jackson: Has contentious relatives and wishes the probate court to oversee distribution of his estate.
d. Plumber: house is worth $700,000 and wife wants to sell it at husband's death. Lives in a community property state so can enjoy full step-up in basis with a will or a living trust.

ENDNOTES

1. IRC §§2036 and 2038.

2. *Tulsa Professional Collection Services v. Estate of Pope* 485 US 478, 108 S.Ct. 1340 (1988).

3. For a discussion of the protection from creditors of a deceased cotenant's property under joint tenancy agreements, see below in the section "advantages of joint tenancy"-- "reduced creditor's claims."

4. See Figure 9-1.

5. §1034

6. §121.

7. Throughout the rest of this chapter, we will often use the shorthand "living trust" to mean *revocable* living trust.

8. *Heggstad v. Heggstad*, 20 Cal. Rptr. 2d 433 (1993).

9. To be discussed in Chapter 12.

10. CA Probate Code §18201.

11. In early 1993, a bill was introduced in the House of Representative that would treat a transfer from a revocable trust as having been made by the grantor. It did not pass.

12. TAM 9226007; TAM 9016002; TAM 9018004; TAM 9018004; TAM 9117003; *Jalcut Estate* 96 TC 675 (1991). Acquiesced by IRS in AOD 1992-002.

13. 42USC §9601(35)(A)(iii).

14. 42USC §1396a(k).

15. Fees incurred for the production of income, such as trustee fees of a living trust, income tax preparation fees and record keeping fees, are miscellaneous itemized deductions, subject to the 2% deduction floor.

Common Estate Plans: Using Bypass and Marital Deduction Trusts

OVERVIEW

This chapter will demonstrate how bypass planning and the marital deduction are used by wealthy couples to reduce estate taxes. More advanced application of these techniques, including use of the prior transfer credit, special estate plans, and trusts that obtain the marital deduction for non-U.S. spouses are the subject of Chapter 12.

Once the unified credit reached $192,800 in 1987, anyone could transfer an estate of up to $600,000 completely free of estate taxes. Any married couple with a combined estate as high as $600,000 can transfer it to their survivors, free of estate taxes just by using simple wills.[1]

> EXAMPLE 11 - 1. Husband (H) and Wife (W) together own property with a net worth of $600,000. By the terms of their simple wills, the children will receive the full $600,000 free of tax, no matter how ownership of the property was originally divided between the spouses, and no matter which spouse dies first. The surviving spouse will die owning property worth $600,000, the amount that generates a tentative tax fully covered by the unified credit.

Minimizing estate taxes is a concern mainly for families whose taxable estates are expected to exceed $600,000 at the second spouse's death. With lifetime gifts within the annual exclusion amount and various estate tax deductions (such as administration expenses and debts) gross estates over $600,000 will be transferred tax free if the gifts and deductions reduce it to $600,000 or less. Thus, our focus is on those married couples whose estate *tax base* exceeds the exemption equivalent by a substantial amount.

> EXAMPLE 11-2. S2's gross estate is $650,000; debts are $80,000; administration expenses are $30,000. Lifetime taxable gifts total $40,000 [gifts less any annual exclusion]. Her taxable estate is $540,000 and the estate tax base is $580,000. Thus, there would be no estate tax because the estate tax base does not exceed $600,000, the unified credit equivalent.

> EXAMPLE 11-3. H and W have a family estate with a net value of $800,000. Under a simple will arrangement, the marital deduction will entirely shelter the first estate from estate taxes. The second spouse to die will have a taxable estate of $800,000, and it will pay estate tax of $75,000.

ABBREVIATIONS, SIMPLIFICATIONS, AND ASSUMPTIONS

The term "transfer" refers to lifetime gifts and transfers at death. ET will mean the total estate tax. The calculations in examples will be for those states using the "pick up" tax as their only death tax. The pick up tax is an estate tax equal to the Federal Credit for State Death Taxes. Lifetime gifts and all deductions, except the marital deduction, will be excluded from the calculations and discussions as well. The Unified Credit of $192,800 equals the tax on transfers of $600,000, thus this amount will be referred to as the unified credit equivalent or UCE.

We often refer to the "first spouse to die" and the "second spouse to die" as S1 and S2 respectively. As a practical matter, wives outlive their husbands by an average of almost 10 years, hence it is not unusual in estate planning discussions to refer to S1 as the husband and S2 as the wife. From a tax standpoint, the crucial factor is not whether the husband or the wife dies first, but what property each owns when S1 dies and the structure of the estate plan. For example, order of death might have very significant implications if one spouse is working and the other is not, or if there is a great disparity in their incomes or in their individual net wealth.

Starting in 1984, the marital deduction was eliminated for property going to any non-US citizen spouse unless complex requirements are met to assure the property transferred stays in the US where it is likely to be taxed as it passes to the next generation. Because there is a different marital deduction structure for non-citizen spouses, our examples are for U.S. citizens until we specifically address planning for the non-citizen spouse in the next chapter.

THE MARITAL DEDUCTION: THEN AND NOW

It is helpful to understand the history of the marital deduction before getting into an extended discussion of the basic estate plans.

Today's gift and estate tax law allows a 100% marital deduction for transfers between spouses. There are certain restrictions which we will discuss later. In general, the law allows one spouse to transfer any amount of property to the other spouse without gift or estate taxes.

As hard as it is to believe, there was no marital deduction until several years after World War II. Then, for almost 30 years, the marital deduction for property passing from one spouse to the other was limited to 50% of the net value of S1's estate. Only since 1982 has the 100% marital deduction been part of the law.

The first marital deduction applied to estates of decedents dying after April 2, 1948. It set the maximum marital deduction at 50% of the adjusted gross estate (AGE), i.e., the gross estate less the deductions allowed for expenses, indebtedness, taxes, and losses[2]. Of course the maximum marital deduction was achieved only if at least half the estate was left to S2, since the marital deduction claimed could not exceed the value of the property passing from S1 to S2. Its purpose was to eliminate disparate treatment originating from differences in the two state property law systems adopted by the states.

Some states, like California and Texas, are community property states that trace their property law to early Roman law. In a community property state, each spouse owns half of all property acquired by the labor of either spouse while married and domiciled in a community property state. Other states are common law states, tracing their property law to English property law. In common law states, the husband generally held title to all property acquired during the marriage. Husbands tend to die before their wives, thus, before the change in 1948, for any given amount of combined wealth, a family in a common law state was likely to pay a higher estate tax when the first spouse died than would have been paid had the family resided in a community property state.

Years	Maximum Marital Deduction
1917 - 1947	▸ no marital deduction allowed
1948 - 1976	▸ 50% of AGE, except no marital deduction for community property.
1977-1981	▸ Greater of 50% of AGE or $250,000
1982 to present	▸ 100% of amount S1 ----> S2 with no limit.

During the early period from 1948 through 1981, the marital deduction was designed such that, if the husband died first, the resulting taxable estate would probably be the same regardless of the couple's domicile. No marital deduction was allowed for S1's half interest in community property. To have allowed a marital deduction for community property would have resulted in a "quartering" of the estate, which in turn would have perpetuated the inequality between the two property law systems.

> EXAMPLE 11-4. Guilliano died in 1960 domiciled in Kentucky, a common law state. He left his entire estate to his wife Cheryl. During the entire marriage they lived in Kentucky and acquired property with a net worth of $1,000,000. Because Kentucky is a common law state, 100% of the property was included in Guilliano's gross estate. The marital deduction removed half, leaving $500,000. The $60,000 death exemption reduced the taxable estate to $440,000. If Guilliano had lived and died domiciled in Texas, a community property state, the $1,000,000 would have been community property. Only his half would have been included in his estate. There would have been no marital deduction, and after the exemption, the taxable estate would have been $440,000, the same as Kentucky.

Of course, there were still inequalities. For instance, if the non-owning spouse (usually the wife) died first in a common law state there would be no estate, hence no tax. In a community property state, half of the property would be included. Since no marital deduction was allowed for community property, it would be subject to tax.

A Blip in the Law

From 1977 through 1981, the law allowed a marital deduction equal to the greater of $250,000 or 50% of the adjusted taxable estate. For large estates, those with an AGE in excess of $500,000, the maximum was 50% of AGE (just as it would have been pre-1977) but, for estates under $500,000 the maximum was $250,000. Thus, for estates between $250,000 and $500,000 the marital deduction became proportionally large; with smaller estates and for estates equal to, or below $250,000, it became a 100% marital deduction.

To keep community property states on a par with common law states, Congress allowed a marital deduction for small estates with community property to assure that the estate received at least the $250,000 alternative maximum marital deduction. The formula for calculating the amount allowed started with $250,000. This amount was reduced by half of the decedent's separate property (because the separate property was allowed a 50% marital deduction), then it was reduced further by the community property included in the decedent's estate (since the half belonging to the survivor already escaped taxation). The resulting number was the maximum alternative marital deduction for an estate with community property.

EXAMPLE 11-5. Mac died in 1977 leaving his half of the couple's $400,000 community property estate to his wife Tina, his adjusted gross estate was $200,000. Subtracting the $200,000 community property included in his gross estate from the $250,000 results in a $50,000 alternative marital deduction. $200,000 less the marital deduction results in a taxable estate of $150,000. If the couple had lived in a common law state, the result would have been the same. The entire $400,000 estate would have belonged to Mac. It would have been reduced by the full $250,000 alternate maximum marital deduction to result in a taxable estate of $150,000.

EXAMPLE 11-6. June died in 1980 leaving her estate to her husband Brian. She owned separate property worth $60,000 and held $300,000 as community property with Brian. Her gross estate would be $210,000 less a marital deduction of $100,000, leaving a taxable estate of $110,000. The marital deduction was calculated by subtracting half of the separate property ($30,000) and half of the community property ($150,000) from $250,000. The result ($70,000) when added to the marital deduction ($30,000, which is 50% of the $60,000 separate property) produces the available marital deduction. Once again, the $110,000 figure is the same as would have been taxed if June had owned $360,000 (her separate and all of the community property) and received a $250,000 marital deduction.

Being able to compute this alternative marital deduction has no usefulness and probably won't be useful even to entertain friends. Your time would be better spent working in the garden or teaching your dog to shake hands.

THE TERMINABLE INTEREST RULE

When the marital deduction first became part of the law, any transfer to a surviving spouse of what is called a *terminable interest* failed to qualify for the marital deduction.[3] A transfer was a terminable interest if the interest transferred to S2 ended at, or before, S2's death or upon the happening of some event, i.e., S2's remarriage. The reason for this limitation on the marital deduction is that to do otherwise might allow most estates, even those of the wealthy, to completely escape taxation. This would occur because the marital deduction would reduce or eliminate tax at S1's death on property that would later skip S2's estate (and the estate tax) when S2 died because S2 did not own the property. The most commonly encountered terminable interest is a trust created by S1 that, at his death, reserves a life estate for S2 with the remainder to the couple's children. S2's interest is a terminable interest because, even though she enjoys the property for her lifetime, she never owns it. At S2's death, the interest shifts to the remainderman S1 chose (according to the terms established by S1).

For purposes of the marital deduction, a *terminable interest*[4] is defined as a property interest with these three characteristics:

- It is subject to some future absolute or *contingent* termination of S2's interest;

- the possibility of termination was created by S1 and, if it occurs, there will be a shift in the interest; and

- some other person or entity (other than S2 or her estate) will enjoy (i.e., possess or own) the property.

The Elements of the Terminable Interest Rule

The question is not whether a termination must occur, but whether, viewed as of the moment of S1's death, a termination *might* occur. The second and third requirements of the rule exclude situations where the terminable nature was not created by S1, or those unique interests that simply end by their very nature. An example of the first would be a bequest conditioned on the surviving spouse living for nine months beyond S1's death (a terminal interest, even if she does survive); of the second would be a contingent ownership interest granted to S1 by a third party; and of the third, a lease or a patent.

> EXAMPLE 6-7. Mark's will stated: "I leave the residue of my estate to my wife, Gloria, provided she survives to the close of probate, and if she does not so survive then it shall be divided amongst my issue by right of representation." His $1 million dollar estate was transferred by probate to Gloria in just five months after his death. Nevertheless, the bequest did not qualify for the marital deduction, since Gloria *might* have died before the close of the probate, in which case her interest, created by her husband, would have terminated, satisfying the first requirement. He created the terminable character of the interest coupled with a shift. The interest would have gone to Mark's issue who would have enjoyed the property. Because it meets all three elements of the rule, it is a terminable interest and no marital deduction is allowed for the property, even though Gloria received the property, and it will be in her estate unless she consumes it or gives it away.

> EXAMPLE 11-7. When Lori died, she left her patent for turning base metals into gold to her husband Earl. The patent still had eleven years before it expired. Even though a patent by its very nature must terminate, the interest does not shift to someone else, therefore, it is not considered a terminable interest. Further, even though Lori invented the process and obtained the patent, she did not create the termination. Therefore, the value of the patent qualifies for the marital deduction.

> EXAMPLE 11-8. Selina owned a strip mall. She did not own the land, but was the lessee under what was originally a 99 year land lease. At the time of her death the land-lease still had 63 years remaining. Even though the mall was built on leased land, Salina's interest was very valuable. (It is not uncommon to find commercial property on leased land. At the end of the lease, the land, together with any structures, reverts to the lessor.) When she died, she left her entire estate to her husband, Duane. Since Selina never owned any more than a leasehold, the shift in interest back to the lessor at the end of the lease is not one that she created. Thus, the value of her interest in the leasehold qualifies for the marital deduction. If, however, she had left the mall to Duane for ten years and then to her son, it would have been a terminable interest and would not have qualified for the deduction.

Why Have a Terminable Interest Rule?

Consider what would happen if the law allowed a marital deduction for a terminable interest, such as a life estate for a surviving spouse, without requiring inclusion of the terminable interest property in S2's estate. The value of the property would be split into two parts; the life estate and the remainder interests. There is no denying that a life estate can be a valuable interest and that the interest can be valued using actuarial methods. For example, the value of a life estate would be measured based on the value of the property and the expected life span of the person with the life estate. The value of the remainder would be whatever is left after the value of the life estate is subtracted from the present value of the entire property.

When the interest is created at S1's death, the marital deduction for the life estate might swallow up most of the value of the transfer, leaving very little (the remainder interest) subject to the transfer tax. The tentative tax on this might be covered by S1's unified credit. Normally, the beneficiary of a life estate is not treated as a transferor when the life estate terminates at the beneficiary's death. Therefore, none of the property held by S2 as a life estate would be included in S2's estate.

> EXAMPLE 11-9. Suppose the law did allow a marital deduction based upon the value of a life estate (remember it never has, and probably never will). S1 died in 1988 leaving a life estate in a trust worth $2,000,000 to S2, his 59 year old widow. Since the Federal rate for split interests was 10% when S1 died, the value of S2's life estate was .78449 x $2,000,000 = $1,568,980. Thus, the value of the remainder was $431,020. The tentative tax on a $431,020 transfer is $132,347 which was covered by S1's unified credit, hence, no tax was due at S1's death. S2 died in 1990 and the property, then worth $2,400,000, passed to S1's children. On S2's death no part of this trust was included in S2's estate. Thus, an estate of $2,400,000 would have passed to the next generation tax free.

TERMINABLE INTEREST RULE EXCEPTIONS

Why have exceptions to the terminable interest rule? The law creates a number of exceptions to the terminable interest rule, each of which allows the marital deduction even though the interest is technically a terminable interest. Congress certainly did not want a loophole that would allow large estates to avoid estate taxes, however, there are policy and/or practical reasons for each of the exceptions. Additionally, all of the exceptions are ones in which the property qualifying for the marital deduction is ultimately included in S2's estate, unless S2 consumes it or gives it away. If S2 gives it away in large chunks (greater than the $10,000 annual exclusion), her gifts will be subject to the gift tax laws.

Six months or common disaster rule:§2056(b)(3). Almost from the start of the marital deduction and its terminable interest rule, Congress created an exception to the rule for "six months or common disaster" survivorship clauses, so long as S2 survived long enough to satisfy the contingency and receive the property. Typically, these clauses make a bequest contingent upon the beneficiary actually out living the decedent by six months or some other period shorter than six months. The law also allows the marital deduction for a marital bequest conditioned upon S2 surviving a common accident. A "common disaster" clause might state, "if my wife and I are injured in the same accident, and I die, I leave her my estate provided she recovers from said accident." Even though recovery might take longer than six months, this bequest would qualify for the marital deduction so long as recovery did occur. Therefore, a survivorship clause, as part of the decedent's will or living trust, can be part of the estate plan, and a marital deduction will be allowed provided the survivor actually survives to receive the property.[5]

A survivorship clause may be specific, relating just to certain bequests or to a bequest to a particular beneficiary, or it may cover all beneficiaries, e.g., *"For purposes of this Will, a beneficiary shall not be deemed to have survived me if that beneficiary dies within six months of my death."*

The clause avoids a double probate in situations where the beneficiary does not live long enough to really utilize the bequest. It also allows the testator to determine the alternate beneficiary of the bequest, rather than allowing it to be governed by the disposition of the beneficiary's estate. Without a survivorship clause the property goes into the beneficiary's estate even if the beneficiary lives just a moment longer than the testator.

Whether a bequest is a terminable interest is determined as of the death of S1; it does not depend upon whether the interest in fact terminates. Therefore, without the §2056(b)(3) exception, no marital deduction would be allowed for estates that actually passed to the surviving spouse if the bequest was subject to a survivorship clause.

Qualified Terminable Interest Property (QTIP): §2056(b)(7)

There are valid reasons for creating terminable interests whereby a surviving spouse is given income from a decedent spouse's estate for life, and yet the surviving spouse is given little or no control over the ultimate disposition of the property. With the population living longer, and with the high rate of divorce, remarriages with one or both spouses coming to the union with children by prior marriages are very common. It is natural for a person with considerable wealth when entering into a second (or third) marriage to desire to take care of the new spouse, yet also desire to assure that his or her wealth does not go to the other spouse's family after both are deceased.

Prior to 1982, the maximum marital deduction for a large estate was equal to 50% of the estate's net value. To qualify for the marital deduction, the surviving spouse had to receive the property, or at least be given a general power of appointment over it. To obtain the maximum marital deduction, at least half of S1's estate had to be transferred to the surviving spouse. Thus, S1 was forced to choose between obtaining the maximum marital deduction and losing control over who would ultimately own the property, or retaining control and giving up the marital deduction. Fortunately, the QTIP election is now part of the law. It allows the marital deduction without forcing S1 to give up control as to whom will eventually receive the property.

Prior to 1982, leaving more than half S1's estate to S2 did not increase the marital deduction for large estates, therefore, the most common plan left S2 only so much of S1's estate as qualified for the marital deduction. This could be either outright or in a trust that gave S2 a life estate and a general power to appoint the corpus.[6] The rest of S1's estate was transferred to a bypass trust, usually (but not in all cases) one giving the income of that trust to the surviving spouse for her life, with the remainder going to S1's family after her death. This arrangement did not sacrifice estate tax dollars on the first death and avoided having that bypass trust included in S2's estate.

Without a new exception to the terminable interest rule, the change allowing a 100% marital deduction would have created a dilemma for every couple who had kept their wealth separate because they each had children by prior marriages.

They would have been forced to choose between providing for the surviving spouse or insuring their estates passed to their children. The planner would have been forced to either transfer control of everything in excess of the unified credit equivalent to the surviving spouse, or else pay an estate tax on the first death, even though such taxes could have been avoided by the use of the marital deduction.

Fortunately, an option known as the QTIP election was added to the law.[7] This election allows the executor of S1's estate to obtain a marital deduction for what is called "Qualified Terminable Interest Property," referred to by the acronym QTIP. To be qualified for the marital deduction, the terminable interest property must meet these requirements:

- the surviving spouse must receive all income from the property for life;
- the right to the income cannot be contingent; and
- during the surviving spouse's life, the property cannot be appointed to anyone other than to the surviving spouse.[8]

The executor must make an election to claim the marital deduction for the QTIP property when the estate tax return is filed. The law allows the executor to make the QTIP election on less than 100% of the terminable interest property. This is done by electing to QTIP a fraction of the property. Thus, if the terminable interest property is in the form of a trust with a life estate for the surviving spouse, remainder to their children, and the trust is funded with property exceeding the applicable UCE, the executor may elect to QTIP only that portion of the trust which exceeds $600,000 in value.

There is no free lunch. That fraction of the QTIP property which receives a marital deduction at S1's death must be included in S2's estate at the time of S2's death.[9] Hence, the choice in making a QTIP election is how much of the terminable interest property to tax at S1's death versus how much at S2's death.

EXAMPLE 11-10. Fernando died in 1988 leaving his entire estate, $1,127,452, less debts & expenses of $197,420, in an irrevocable trust for his wife, Arcela. She was given a life estate and a limited power to appoint corpus at her death amongst their three children. Arcela had a modest estate of her own. Since the executor of Fernando's estate wanted to postpone all taxes until after Arcela's death, he QTIP'ed that portion that exceeded the unified credit equivalent estate, i.e., that fraction above $600,000.

Since the net value of the trust was $930,032, the QTIP fraction is:
When this fraction is multiplied by the net value of the trust, the marital deduction is $330,032 resulting in a taxable estate of exactly $600,000.

$$\frac{\$930,032 - \$600,000}{\$930,032}$$

The QTIP fraction serves a dual role; it determines how much of the QTIP property qualifies for the marital deduction on the first death, and just as importantly, it determines how much of that property (valued at the second death) must be included in S2's estate.

EXAMPLE 11-11. When Arcela died in 1998, the trust Fernando had established for her had grown from its initial net worth to $2,854,372, with debts of $420,870, for a net value of $2,433,502. Arcela had her own property worth $780,450 and her estate had debts and expenses that totaled $110,400, for a net value of $670,050. She too left her estate to their children. In determining her taxable estate her executor would have to add to what she owned the portion of the trust that had previously been QTIP'ed:

$$\frac{330,032}{930,032} * \$2,433,502 = \$863,555$$

Adding this amount to $670,050 results in a taxable estate of $1,533,605. ***
Query 1. What would the QTIP fraction have been if the net value of the trust at Fernando's death had been $1,789,373? What dollar value of the trust would be included in Arcela's estate given that change?

The QTIP fraction equation given above utilizes S1's unified credit equivalent and defers all taxes to the second death. The UCE in the formula must be adjusted to take into account any use of the unified credit elsewhere, either because S1 made taxable gifts during life or left part of the estate to someone other than the surviving spouse or a charity. Such transfers use up unified credit, hence, the UCE in the numerator should equal the unified credit equivalent that remains.

EXAMPLE 11-12. Suppose Fernando also owned a $250,000 life insurance policy that named his daughter by a prior marriage as the beneficiary. Now his gross estate would be $1,377,452. The net value after debts and expenses would be $1,180,032 [$250,000 life insurance plus the $930,032 in the trust]. The life insurance would utilize $250,000 of the unified credit equivalent, hence, the QTIP fraction in the above example would be ($930,032 - $350,000) divided by $930,032. The portion of the QTIP property, expressed in dollar amount, elected for the marital deduction would be equal to $580,032. Thus, after the marital deduction, the taxable estate would again be $600,000, comprised of the $250,000 life insurance policy plus the $350,000 portion of the QTIP property which was not covered by the marital deduction. [$1,377,452 - $197,420 -$580,032 = $600,000]

Of course, 100% of the QTIP property in the above example could have qualified for the marital deduction, but electing to QTIP 100% of the trust would have reduced S1's taxable estate below $600,000, thus wasting part of S1's unified credit, and needlessly increasing the amount of the property which would eventually be included in S2's estate.

There are times when it is advantageous to generate a tax on the first estate by using a QTIP fraction which is less than that necessary to defer all taxes. For instance, if S1 left QTIP property worth $5,000,000 in trust for S2, and S2 has no estate of her own, it might be advantageous to QTIP half of the $5,000,000 trust. By doing so, the QTIP half will qualify for the marital deduction, leaving a taxable estate of $2,500,000. Upon S2's death, half of the trust will be included in her estate. The tax on two estates worth $2,500,000 each is considerably less than the tax on a $600,000 estate and an estate worth $4,400,000. Two shorter trips up the rate ladder are cheaper than one long one. Furthermore, as will be discussed in the next chapter, generating a tax in both estates sometimes allows the second estate to utilize a prior transfer credit,[10] further reducing the total estate taxes.

Although most of our examples, and most real life QTIP trusts, concern decedent's estates, the QTIP election is available for lifetime transfers of terminal interest gifts.[11] This most likely to be done to allow the wealthier spouse to bring the less wealthy spouse's estate up to at least the UCE level. The use of the QTIP trust allows the wealthier spouse to keep the property in his or her family, whereas an outright gift surrenders that control. Of course, to utilize the less wealthy spouse's unified credit, the wealthy spouse must be willing to part with some property even if the other spouse (the donee spouse) dies first.

EXAMPLE 11-13. Eighty year old Ellen has a net worth of $4,500,000. Last year, after ten years of widowhood, she married Thomas, a kindly gentleman of modest means. Because Ellen wanted to take care of Thomas, should she died before him, and because she was willing to have that portion of her estate equal to the UCE go immediately to her children if Thomas died before her, she established a lifetime

QTIP trust. The trust was funded with stocks and bonds worth $600,000. The terms give Thomas a life estate. If Thomas dies first, the children receive only so much of the corpus as will generate a tentative tax equal to that available for Thomas' estate, after taking into account his own property and any taxable gifts he might have made, the balance reverts back to Ellen.

EXAMPLE 11-14. When Thomas died, the QTIP trust established for his benefit had a net worth of $850,000 and his own property had a net worth of $75,000. Since Ellen was still living, Ellen's children received $525,000 from the trust and she received the balance of $325,000. Thus, Thomas's taxable estate was $600,000 which produces a tentative tax equal to $192,800, which in turn is completely covered by his unified credit. If Ellen was dying at the time of Thomas' death she could reduce overall taxes by disclaiming the reversion amount (the $325,000), which would keep it out of her estate and allow it to be taxed at the lower marginal rates of Thomas' estate, rather than at the top marginal rates of her estate. With a disclaimer, the property would still go to her children.

General Power of Appointment Exception:§2056(b)(5)

A power to appoint property is the right to tell the owner of the property to transfer it to someone else. Powers of appointment were discussed in greater detail in Chapter 6. As a reminder, the Code defines a general power as "a power which is exercisable in favor of the decedent, his estate, his creditors, or the creditors of his estate. . . ."

EXAMPLE 11-15. Fred creates an irrevocable trust for Jerry's benefit. The terms of the trust provide Jerry with all the income from the trust and give her the right, when she reaches age twenty-five (25), to have the trustee terminate the trust and transfer all assets to anyone that Jerry designates (including herself). From the moment Jerry reaches age twenty-five (25), she has a general power of appointment.

The holder of a general power must include in his or her estate the value of property which could have been transferred by the exercise of a general power of appointment, regardless of whether it is ever exercised. It is enough that it merely could have been exercised. Limited powers do not result in inclusion of the property in the estate of the holder, provided the holder of the power did not create the power. Where the holder also created the power, the Internal Revenue Code treats it as a retained interest, rather than as a power to appoint.

A marital deduction is allowed for property passing in trust from S1 to S2, provided S2 is given income for life in the property and has a general power of appointment over the property, exercisable during life and/or at death.[12] Since S2 is a holder of a general power, the property will be included in S2's estate, or if she appoints it during life to someone else, it will be a gift from her to that person. Thus, although the transfer into a general power of appointment trust may technically be a transfer of a terminable interest, it is allowed to qualify for the marital deduction because (unless consumed) it will eventually be either given away by S2 or in S2's estate. Since Congress is allowing a marital deduction based upon S2 receiving a life estate, the trust must either require the trustee to make the trust assets productive, or state law (and most states have such laws) must give S2 the power to require the trustee to make them productive. If the trust document gives the trustee absolute investment power, especially if it includes a statement allowing investment in unproductive assets, the marital deduction may not be available even thought S2 is given a life estate.[13]

> EXAMPLE 11-16. Upon her death, Geraldine creates a trust for her husband Bob. It is funded with assets having a net value of $950,714. Bob is given a life estate in the trust and the power, exercisable only by specific mention of the power in his will, to appoint the corpus to whomever he chooses. If he fails to exercise the power, the property is to be distributed by right of representation to their issue. The trust will qualify for the marital deduction because of §2056(b)(5). Therefore, although it is in Geraldine's gross estate is not in her taxable estate. But when Bob dies, because the power is a general one, the entire trust will be included in his gross estate, whether or not he exercises the power.

> EXAMPLE 11-17. Upon his death, Gerry creates a trust for his wife Betty's life. It is funded with property worth $1,000,000. The terms of the trust give Betty the power to appoint the corpus to any of their five children when she dies. If she does not appoint the corpus, it will be distributed by right of representation at her death. Because Betty only has a limited power to appoint, §2056(b)(5) does not apply, and there is no automatic marital deduction. Assuming no QTIP (discussed later) election is made, the trust will be taxed at Gerry's death (resulting in $153,000 in death taxes), but no additional taxes would be owed when the trust terminates at Betty's death. The latter is true no matter how much the trust has grown, and no matter how unevenly Betty exercises her limited power to appoint the property among the children.

Pensions for the Benefit of S2: §2056(b)(7)(C)

In the case of an annuity included in S1's estate that is payable to S2 alone during S2's life, the QTIP election is automatic unless the executor of S1's estate affirmatively elects to have the annuity taxed in S1's estate. Electing to have it taxed will avoid having any value that remains at S2's death taxed as part of S2's estate, whereas allowing the automatic QTIP results in inclusion.

Charitable Remainder Trusts with a Life Estate for S2: §2056 (b)(8)

Property transferred to a qualified charitable remainder trust,[14] which has the surviving spouse as its only non-charitable beneficiary, qualifies for the marital deduction, even though it is a terminable interest. This is a special rule and no QTIP election is necessary. It is not included in S2's estate, although it would make no difference if it were included since it would then qualify for a charitable deduction. If the executor is in doubt as to whether the trust is a "qualified charitable" remainder trust, he or she should make a protective QTIP election, i.e., list it as part of the QTIP property on Schedule M of the 706.

THE BASIC ESTATE PLANNING PATTERNS

Planning to minimize the ET with the marital deduction and the bypass arrangement generally involves some variation of one of three basic planning options, described in considerable detail in this chapter. They are the **100% marital deduction**, the **AB Trust**, and the **ABC Trust**. These options do not depict precise will or trust arrangements, instead they trace the overall flow of property after S1's death. Our concern is with the timing of estate tax payments, the amount of those taxes, and which spouse (S1 or S2) controls who will eventually receive the couple's estate. First, we will take up the simplest plan, where S1 transfers all his estate to S2. Next, we will cover the bypass trust because it is common to almost all multiple trust plans. Lastly, we will take a look at the basic multiple trust plans, before going back to the QTIP election and how it is used in conjunction with the ABC Trust plan.

PLANNING OPTION 1: SIMPLE 100 PERCENT MARITAL DEDUCTION

Often, the unlimited marital deduction provides a simple and practical estate planning strategy. It entirely shelters all property S1 transfers to S2 from gift tax and ET. In the simple 100% marital deduction strategy, S1 leaves all property to the surviving spouse. The transfer is protected from transfer tax by the 100% marital deduction. Outright transfers by S1 to S2 that qualify for the 100% marital deduction include: gifts, transfers by will, transfers by right of survivorship when title is held solely by the spouses in joint tenancy or tenancy by the entirety, plus insurance on S1's life payable to S2. Transfers in trust for the benefit of S2 qualify too if they meet certain criteria.

> EXAMPLE 11-18. Tom and Gerri each have estates of $300,000. Gerri leaves her entire estate to Tom by a simple will. There is no ET because the estate is sheltered by the 100% marital deduction. At Tom's death, he leaves the combined estate of $600,000 to their child. There is no ET because of the unified credit equivalent.

Advantages of the 100 Percent Marital Deduction

The main attraction of the simple 100% marital deduction strategy is its simplicity. It is very easy to understand and inexpensive to establish. More elaborate estate planning may not be necessary for clients whose combined estates are less than the unified credit equivalent. Some clients may not be concerned about whether taxes will be due after the second death, i.e., where the couple leaves no issue or where the plan has the entire estate going to a charity at the second death.

Of course, these simple plans give S2 total dispositive control over all of both spouses' property. This may be an advantage or a disadvantage, depending on the circumstances. S2 will receive full ownership of the property, a fee simple interest. S2 can use it, consume it, gift it, or sell it. If she still owns it at her death, she can leave it to whomever she chooses, in such manner as she chooses.

Not all marital deduction plans confer full dispositive control to S2. S1 may retain dispositive control by placing the property in a trust known as a qualified terminable interest property (QTIP) trust. These are most commonly found in multiple trust plans known as ABC trust plans. (Patience, we will get to this soon.) However, a QTIP trust can be used alone where S1 wants dispositive control but sees no need for multiple trusts.

Disadvantages of the 100 Percent Marital Deduction

The 100% marital deduction that transfers all control to S2 has several significant drawbacks for large estates.

Higher total ET. The first drawback for wealthier couples is a higher total ET due to two factors. First, each spouse has the protection of the unified credit, but when S1 gives his entire estate to S2 protected by the marital deduction, his unified credit is unused. Unless S2 consumes or gives away S1's property using the annual exclusion or charitable gifts, it will become part of S2's transfer tax base, subject to either gift tax or estate tax to the extent that the combined value exceeds S2's unified credit equivalent. Second, because the two estates are combined and subject to ET as one estate, there is only one "run up the rate ladder." Marginal rates increase with the size of the estate. The larger the estate, the higher the rate of tax on the last dollar. Even if there were no unified credit, two $1 million estates would pay less tax than one $2 million estate.

> EXAMPLE 11-19. H and W own a family estate of $2 million with each owning one-half. They have simple wills leaving property to one another, or to the children if the other is deceased. At S1's death there will be no ET because the entire $1 million passing to S2 will be sheltered by the marital deduction. If S2 neither transfers nor consumes the property before dying, S2 will have a $2 million taxable estate subject to an ET of $588,000.

The simple 100% marital deduction planning is said to have the effect of "over qualifying" or "overusing" the marital deduction, resulting in a "loading up" of the taxable estate of S2, and subjecting a greater amount of the couple's wealth to tax at the second death than would occur with a more complex plan. In summary, two negative results can occur as a result of pouring the first estate into the second; the unified credit of S1 is wasted, and a portion of the combined estate may be subjected to higher marginal rates than would have been encountered with a more complex estate plan.

May not avoid probate. If a couple uses simple wills to carry out their 100% marital deduction planning, or if they hold everything in joint tenancy, there will be a probate, at least at the second death. Some states do not require a probate for property left from one spouse to the other. Of course, the use of living trusts as part of the estate plan overcomes this problem.

Not available for non-citizen spouses. The marital deduction only applies to property left to citizen spouses. The property of U.S. citizens is subject to estate taxation anywhere in the world. However, the property of non-citizens is only subject to estate tax if it is located in the U.S. Because a non-citizen spouse could take the property and leave the country (preventing estate taxation at S2's death), the marital deduction does not apply to property left to non-citizen spouses unless special trusts (with U.S. trustees) are used. This will be discussed in the next chapter.

BYPASS PLANNING

The common theme of most bypass planning is the division of S1's estate into a bypass portion and a marital deduction portion. The bypass portion is transferred to someone other than S2 in a way that bypasses S2's estate. The bypass portion is taxed at the first death. However, it may be that it is protected by the unified credit such that no tax is due. The marital deduction portion is transferred to S2 in a way that qualifies it for the marital deduction. Bypass planning thus avoids the two major problems with simple marital deduction planning. It makes use of S1's unified credit, and it potentially provides two runs up the rate ladder, depending on the details of the bypass plan chosen.

There are many variations on the bypass planning theme including the way the bypass property is transferred (whether outright or in trust), the number of trusts used and their characteristics, the proportion of S1's property in the bypass portion, and whether it will equal the unified credit equivalent (so no tax will actually be paid) or exceed it (and cause some tax at the first death). Usually, the bypass portion is eventually transferred to the couple's children, but there are many other possibilities. Remember, it is called bypass planning because it bypasses S2's estate (or some other income beneficiary's estate) for tax purposes. It is taxed in S1's estate whether taxes are paid or not, e.g., the tentative tax may be fully absorbed by the decedent's unified credit.

Simple outright bypass. The simplest form of bypass is the outright bypass where the UCE is left directly to someone other than S2.

EXAMPLE 11-20. Herbert has a $1.2 million estate. He leaves property worth $600,000 to his daughter, Denise, protected by his unified credit. He leaves $600,000 to his wife, Wilma, protected by the marital deduction. When Wilma dies, she leaves $600,000 to Denise protected by her unified credit equivalent. There is no estate tax paid at either death. If Herbert had left the entire $1.2 million to Wilma, it would have been protected at his death by the marital deduction. At Wilma's death, however, there would have been ET of $235,000 on her estate of $1.2 million, protected by only her unified credit.

Bypass share: outright or in trust. The couple might have strong reservations about the bypass plan if, at S1's death, it caused an immediate, outright transfer to the children. The children may be too young to be responsible for the property. S2 may need either the income from the property, or the property itself, for support. S2 might prefer to retain control over the management of those assets ultimately intended for the children. These are common and legitimate objections to the use of an immediate, outright transfer to the children to effect a bypass. Fortunately, the bypass can be arranged, and these objections overcome, by means of a transfer into a trust.

Recall that by limiting the powers given to the beneficiary of a life estate, the trust is excluded from the holder's gross estate. The beneficiary may have the right to take the income and a power of appointment that does not rise to the level of a general power of appointment. It may give S2 the income from the property and the right to take principal in accord with an ascertainable standard. S2 may also manage the property.

Generally, bypass property is taxed at the time it is initially transferred for the benefit of the income beneficiary, but not again when the income beneficiary dies. The amount transferred in this fashion might be just enough to create a tentative tax equal to the unified credit. Thus, although technically the transfer is taxed, the donor, or in the case of a bequest, the decedent's estate, does not have to pay any transfer tax.

For most of our discussion we will assume that the income beneficiary in question is S2, and that the bypass property is a bypass trust established by S1. We make this assumption because it is the most frequently encountered bypass arrangement, but there are other possibilities. The bypass plan works because the transfer of an amount sufficient to use S1's unified credit to someone other than S2 can be arranged to conform to both spouses' overall estate planning objectives.

In a typical bypass trust, the children of the marriage are the ultimate beneficiaries, or remaindermen. Neither spouse is likely to object to the children as the remaindermen of the bypass trust created at S1's death, since in all likelihood, both spouses expect their combined estates to eventually go to their children. S2 usually has the income from the bypass property as well as access to the principal for purposes of health, education, support or maintenance, without the property being included in her estate.

MULTIPLE TRUSTS IN ESTATE PLANNING: BASIC PATTERNS

Each of the three plans (including the 100% marital deduction plan discussed earlier) can be set up with a will or a trust instrument. Due to the costs and lack of privacy associated with probate, most wealthy couples that spend the time, energy, and money to have one of these more complex estate plans written choose the living trust over the testamentary trust (although either will accomplish the tax savings discussed in this chapter). For the most part, we will assume a living trust for these multi-trust plans.

The documents that implement the process usually separate it into three phases. This is true whether the estate plan uses a living trust or a testamentary trust.

The first phase can be described as the family trust phase. There is usually only one living or inter vivos trust in this phase. In such a trust, the property is transferred to the trustee while the trustors are alive. Most married couples serve as the initial trustees of their own family trust. They generally reserve the power to revoke or amend the trust.

The second phase starts with the death of one of the spouses, S1. The family trust is usually divided into multiple trusts after the first spouse dies. The multiple trusts are funded from the family trust at that time. It is not known which spouse will be the first to die at the time the plan is being drafted. Hence, the distribution of assets into the various trusts is based on the order of the two deaths. Generally, in these complex estate plans, Trust A receives all of S2's property. Sometimes some of S1's property goes into Trust A too, depending upon the size of S1's estate and the type of estate plan. Trust B will be funded from S1's estate. Whether Trust B receives all of S1's estate, or only part of it, will again depend upon the size of S1's estate and the type of estate plan. If there is a Trust C, it too will be funded from S1's estate. The funding of these trusts is fixed by the plan and the trustee generally has very little flexibility to change the plan (other than by using disclaimers).[15] After S1's death, Trusts B and C become irrevocable. S2 can control the distribution of assets only according to the terms of those trusts, e.g., she may or may not be given a limited power to appoint corpus when she dies or she may have a power to withdraw limited to an ascertainable standard. Usually, these plans allow S2 to amend (or even revoke) Trust A, since corpus is principally from S2's property.

The third phase commences with S2's death. If the plan has been properly carried out, the different trusts will already be funded. The executor, filing the estate tax return, must determine which trusts (or portions thereof) are included in S2's estate. After paying the estate tax, the trustee distributes the remaining trust property outright to the children if they have reached the specified age specified in the trust document, commonly 25, 30, or 35. On the other hand, if the children are much younger, then the two trusts (AB plan) or three trusts (ABC plan) are likely to be merged into a single "pot" trust until the children reach the age specified in the trust, at which time the trust is subdivided into equal shares for the children. The subdivision (creating separate trusts) is usually specified as when either the youngest reaches a certain age (i.e., twenty-one) or when the oldest reaches some age, although the trust can set a specific date after which division should be made, such as, "as soon after January 1, 2005 as the division can be accomplished."

Sometimes a testamentary trust arrangement is used for these complex estate plans, although it is less common than using the living trust. The testamentary trust is a lengthy will that incorporates a trust. With the testamentary trust, there is a probate after the testator dies. At the conclusion of the probate, the trust is funded by a court order, which incorporates into the order the trust language from the will. The order directs the distribution of the probate property to the trustee, who is charged with managing the trust estate in keeping with the terms of the trust. There may be several trusts depending upon the specific estate plan. Once the probate is completed and the trust or trusts are funded, the process is just like plans that start with an inter vivos family trust.

When you work with these complex estate plans, at the first death start by determining the property (and its value) included in S1's estate to arrive at S1's gross estate (net estate before the marital deduction if the values given are net values). At the same time, you will have determined the value of S2's estate as it is at S1's death. The next step is to review their estate plan to determine how the property is to be allocated to each of the trusts. At the second death, the trusts are already funded, therefore, after determining the net value of each trust, the task is merely to determine what portion of each trust is included in S2's estate. The portion included may depend upon the trust's characteristics (i.e., because of S2's general power to appoint the corpus of Trust A, it is always included) or it may depend upon what was done at S1's death (i.e., whether a QTIP election was, or was not, made on a terminable interest trust).

Definitions. In the discussions that follow, we will be using the shorthand terms "AB Trust" and "ABC Trust." Attorneys who draft trust documents and estate planners may choose different titles for the component trusts, although the terms AB Trust or ABC Trust are frequently used short hand designations and will effectively convey the general pattern to those familiar with estate planning. The naming of trusts seems to be as variable as the naming of neighborhood cats. The same cat may have a different name in each house he visits. The following names are frequently used, but there are many others possibilities:

- Trust A may be called the Survivor's Trust, the Marital Trust, or the General Power of Appointment Trust.
- Trust B may be called the Bypass Trust, the Credit Equivalent Trust, the Credit Shelter Trust, the Family Trust, or the Nonmarital Trust.
- Trust C may be called the QTIP Trust, the QTIP Marital Trust, and even Trust Q.

Depending on the plan and how Trusts B and C are defined, either may be called the Residuary Trust. Thus, if in an ABC Trust plan Trust B is defined in terms of the amount necessary to utilize the available unified credit and the residue of S1's estate flows into Trust C, the latter may be called the Residuary Trust. On the other hand, if Trust C is defined as the minimum amount that when qualified for the marital deduction would reduce S1's taxable estate to the UCE with the balance flowing into Trust B, the latter trust may be called the Residuary Trust.

PLANNING OPTION 2: THE AB TRUST

The modern AB Trust plan is based on using the marital deduction and both spouses' unified credits. We say "modern" because the unlimited marital deduction has only been available to estates of decedents dying after 1981. The "B" Trust is the bypass component. The "A" Trust is the surviving spouse's trust. The two components are structured and funded so as to leave the maximum amount possible to the surviving spouse while still utilizing both spouses' unified credits. Payment of transfer taxes is deferred until S2's death. For large estates, which ever spouse lives longest, thus becoming S2, will ultimately control who receives the bulk of the couple's estate. Only Trust B, the unified credit equivalent trust, has the remainder interest fixed by S1 at S1's death. *This plan makes sense for wealthy couples whose children are solely from their present marriage since the plan may give S2 ultimate control over the greater portion of the couple's combined estate.*

> EXAMPLE 11-21. The combined value of Hal and Wanda's property at S1's death, in 1997, is $5,000,000. It doesn't matter whether Hal or Wanda dies first because the trusts are set up so that Trust A becomes S2's trust and Trust B, the UCE, receives assets with a net value of $600,000. The balance of the estate, in the amount of $4,400,000, would go into Trust A. Trust B would have the remaindermen fixed (probably the couple's children) while Trust A would be subject to the control of S2. There is no requirement that the couple's children ultimately receive the property from Trust A. If S2 remarries, or for any reason, decides they are not deserving, she can change the remaindermen for that trust.

The Character of Trust A

Trust A receives all of S2's property plus all S1's property that exceeds S1's available unified credit equivalent ($600,000, unless S1 made lifetime taxable gifts reducing the available credit, or Congress changes the unified credit). To obtain the marital deduction at S1's death for property transferred from S1's estate into Trust A, it must have two characteristics: (1) S2 must receive all the income for life, paid at least annually; and (2) S2 must be given a general power of appointment exercisable during life and/or at S2's death.

The Character of Trust B

The funding for Trust B is usually defined in terms of S1's available unified credit equivalent. It usually receives exactly enough of S1's estate to cause a tentative tax equal to S1's available unified credit after taking into account property passing to someone other than S2 and any prior taxable transfers. Methods for achieving the right amount of funding are described at the end of this chapter under the heading "Allocating Assets to the Trusts." For most estates the initial value of Trust B will be $600,000 under present law, since this will cause a tentative tax of $192,800 which will be canceled out by the unified credit of $192,800.

Since the purpose of this trust is to utilize S1's unified credit and avoid inclusion in S2's estate, any characteristics that would cause inclusion (such as giving S2 a general power of appointment over trust corpus) must be avoided. The marital deduction is not sought for Trust B, so while it is common to give S2 all income for life, such is not required. The terms could call for sprinkling the income amongst S2 and the children, or it could even allow the trustee to accumulate income. Most AB plans give S2 all of the income from Trust B, probably for psychological reasons because it is not necessary for tax reasons. A general power to appoint would cause inclusion in S2's estate, so it is to be avoided. However, S2 may be given a power to invade the corpus limited by ascertainable standards or S2 may be given a special power to allocate the remainder. A special power, in those plans using one, is likely to be limited to the couple's children, adding flexibility to the plan within limits without causing the trust property to be included in S2's estate.

AB Trust Plan's Benefits

The AB Trust plan provides the opportunity for S2 to manage the assets from both estates, enjoy all of the income, and have access to all of the principal, even though that in Trust B can be reached only as needed within ascertainable standards. In the event both spouses die while their children are young, the plan allows disbursement to the children to be delayed until they are old enough to manage the property. An AB Trust can provide flexibility so that S2 can change the distribution plan in response to changed circumstances, it makes use of the marital deduction to delay taxation until the second death, and it uses S1's unified credit.

> EXAMPLE 11-22. The following table compares the resulting estate taxes applicable to an estate under the unlimited marital deduction and the AB Trust plans. The estate, with a net value of $2,000,000, all belongs to S1. S2 owns no property. In an AB Trust plan, even though S2 has no assets, the plan calls for S2's property to go into trust A since, before either spouse dies, no one can be certain which spouse will be S1 and which S2, or whether a spouse with little or no property might acquire a substantial estate before S1's death.

	100% Marital Deduction		**AB Trust**	
	S1 dies 1987	S2 dies 1997	S1 dies 1987	S2 dies 1997
GE	$2,000,000	$2,000,000	$2,000,000	$1,400,000
MD	($2,000,000)	$0	($1,400,000)	$0
TE	$0	$2,000,000	$600,000	$1,400,000
TT	$0	$780,800	$192,800	$512,800
UC	$0	($192,800)	($192,800)	($192,800)
ET	$0	$558,000	$0	$320,000

A tax savings of $238,000 results. This is partly due to $600,000 being "taxed" at S1's death with S1's $192,800 unified credit resulting in no tax owed. The reason that the ultimate savings is more than $192,800, is that the $600,000 sheltered by S1's unified credit (and held in Trust B) would otherwise be in S2's highest marginal rates, those between $1,400,000 and $2,000,000. Avoiding those higher marginal rates results in the $600,000 sheltered at S1's death, saving $45,200 over and above S1's unified credit.

EXAMPLE 11-23. This example shows results when both spouses have community property and separate property. The total net value stays at $2,000,000. S1 has separate property worth $350,000, S2 has separate property worth $700,000. They own community property worth $950,000. The plans and timing of the deaths are the same as the two prior examples. Remember, S2's property goes into trust A for management purposes and is not part of S1's estate. Upon S2's death, both trusts terminate and go to the children.

	100% Marital Deduction		AB Trust	
	S1 d1987	S2 d1997	S1 d1987	S2 d1997
GE	$825,000	$2,000,000	$825,000	$1,400,000
MD	($825,000)	0	($225,000)	0
TE	0	$2,000,000	$600,000	$1,400,000
TT	0	$780,800	$192,800	$512,800
UC	0	($192,800)	($192,800)	($192,800)
ET	0	$558,000	0	$320,000

Notice the gross estate at S1's death is the same for both plans. S1's estate consisted of separate property ($350,000) plus one-half of the community property, i.e., $350,000 + .5 * 950,000 = $825,000. Of course, our assumption, for simplicity, that the values will remain the same between S1's death and S2's death is unrealistic. Trust B will not be taxed at S2's death regardless of its value at that time, even if it greatly exceeds $600,000. The use of S1's unified credit is not being postponed until S2's death, since Trust B is actually taxed at S1's death, but the tentative tax is completely covered by the unified credit. Trust B is not taxed at S2's death because it entirely bypasses S2's estate. This is true, even if Trust B has grown to well over $600,000 at that time.

If either spouse is uncomfortable with the control given to S2 by the AB Trust plan, they should consider the ABC Trust plan which reduces the amount of property over which S2 exercises ultimate control, yet still allows estate taxes to be postponed until the second death.

PLANNING OPTION 3: THE ABC TRUST

The ABC Trust plan is like the AB Trust plan except that S1's net estate in excess of the unified credit equivalent goes into Trust C, instead of passing to Trust A. The terms of Trust C qualify it for the marital deduction through the QTIP election, thus, making it possible to defer all estate taxes until the second death. The real advantage of this plan when compared to the AB Trust is that S1's estate in excess of the UCE goes into Trust C which cannot be changed by S2. Since Trusts B and C are irrevocable, S1 can rest in peace, knowing that the remaindermen for these two trusts are fixed. S2 may be given the power, limited by an ascertainable standard relating to health, education, support, or maintenance, to invade the corpus of Trusts B and C. This invasion right can even be limited such that it only becomes available to S2 when Trust A has less than a certain value remaining, e.g., only if Trust A is worth less than the UCE. S1 can also give S2 a limited power of appointment, exercisable only by will, over Trusts B and C. Remember, neither a limited power to appoint, nor a power to invade limited by an ascertainable standard, will cause inclusion of the property in the holder's estate. Even though S2 is given these powers, it is S1 who defines their limits.

The Character of Trust A

This Trust A is likely to have the same characteristics as Trust A in the AB Trust plan. Trust A receives all of S2's separate property and S2's one-half interest in community property. S2 has a general power to appoint or to revoke this trust. Unless property actually passes from S1's estate into Trust A, there is no marital deduction for property in this trust because it holds property that already belongs to S2. It is not unusual for S1's plan to leave some property, such as all the tangible personal property, to S2's Trust A. The transfer of that property would automatically qualify for the marital deduction in addition to the property receiving the marital deduction through the QTIP election. Of course, there is also an automatic marital deduction for property (such as cars and the household bank account) held in joint tenancy by the couple.

The Character of Trust B

Trust B will have the same characteristics of Trust B in the AB Trust plan, including being defined in terms of S1's available unified credit. Thus, in most instances the value of the trust will initially be the lesser of $600,000 or S1's available unified credit (see "Allocating Assets to the Trusts" at the end of this chapter for details). When Congress eventually increases the unified credit such that it shelters a higher amount (such as $750,000), the "available unified credit" language automatically takes care of that contingency as well. Again, the trust can be a sprinkling trust without harming the planning objectives, but more commonly, S2 is given all income for life. As will be discussed in the next chapter, giving S2 income for life (also referred to as a life estate) in this trust may, under certain circumstances, allow a larger prior transfer tax credit. This is a bypass trust, in that it will be taxed at S1's death and escape tax (regardless of its growth) at S2's death.

The Character of Trust C

Trust C must meet all the Code QTIP requirements[16] to ensure the marital deduction is available should S1's executor decide that it is in the estate's best interest to make the QTIP election. The general requirements are that S2 must receive the income for life, and that no one can hold a power to appoint the property to anyone but S2 during S2's life. This trust usually receives that portion of S1's estate that exceeds the UCE. When a QTIP election is made for Trust C, the executor of S1's estate is claiming a marital deduction and, in effect, making a pact with the IRS that the property will eventually be subject to transfer tax triggered by S2 making a gift of her interest in the trust or by her death.[17] If the QTIP election is not made, Trust C will be taxed at S1's death and will not be taxed again when S2 dies, even though S2 enjoyed a life estate. Thus, Trust C is a marital deduction trust if the election is made, and a bypass trust if it is not.

Typically, S2 enjoys a life estate (a requirement for the QTIP) in the trust property, having the use of any tangible property that is part of this trust (such as the home and its contents) plus taking the income from investment property and placing it in her own personal accounts, or in her Trust A accounts.

If the QTIP election is not made, S2 must not allow income to accumulate in the trust. Doing so will be treated as a gift from her into the trust over which she has a retained life estate, creating a §2036 retained life estate problem. Of course this is only a problem if the QTIP election is not made, since if it is made over the whole trust, the trust will be included in S2's estate anyway.[18]

The QTIP election is made on Schedule M of S1's U.S. Federal Estate Tax Return, Form 706. Once the election is made (or not made) on a return, and the time for filing the estate tax return has passed, the executor cannot change the decision. Fortunately, the QTIP election can be made even on a late filed return.

Trust C cannot be a sprinkling trust since S2 must receive all income from the trust for life. The income must be distributed at least annually, and S2 must have the right to require the Trustee to change unproductive assets (ones that produce little or no income) into reasonably productive income producing assets. Even if some required terms are not in the trust, state laws frequently remedy the deficiency. Most states have statutes which require such simple trusts to distribute income at least annually, and give income beneficiaries the right to require the trustee to make unproductive assets productive (unless the trust instrument clearly gives the trustee authority to hold unproductive assets). These statutes satisfy the QTIP requirements even if the trust instrument is silent on the timing of income distributions, or if at the time of S1's death, a significant portion of the trust estate is made up of unproductive assets (such as undeveloped land) and the trust terms say nothing about the Trustee being obligated to make them productive. Note, as long as S2 has the right to require unproductive assets be made productive, the trustee need not make the assets more productive for the QTIP election to be made. Of course, if S2 makes the request and a significant portion of the corpus is comprised of very low yield assets, the trustee must comply with the request and seek a higher return.

S2 can be given a power to invade corpus, limited by an ascertainable standard and/or a limited power to appoint corpus so long as the latter is exercisable only at her death. The limited power to appoint is usually limited to allocation amongst the couple's children.

The trust instrument can also add flexibility by giving S2 a 5 & 5 power; however, S1 would be giving up some certainty as to who will ultimately receive the corpus. If one of the reasons for choosing the ABC plan was to assure that S1's property would go to S1's children by a prior marriage, a 5 & 5 power might not be desirable since each exercise by S2 takes property out of the trust.

Calculating the QTIP Election and the QTIP Fraction

When a QTIP election is available after S1's death, the executor must determine how much of the QTIP property to QTIP, i.e., the optimal portion of S1's estate to have taxable at S1's death. Subtracting that optimal amount from S1's total estate gives the marital deduction desired. The marital deduction is obtained by making a QTIP election of part (or all) of the QTIP property. If the document allows a division of the QTIP trust into two or more trusts, one of which the executor (the trustee) elects to completely QTIP and the other for which no election is made (let's call them Trust CQ and Trust CNQ, respectively) some additional planning opportunities exist. With the division, the trustee can "spend down" Trust CQ if S2 needs to utilize corpus. Since a QTIP'ed trust is in S2's estate, reducing a Trust CQ is better than reducing a single partially QTIP'ed Trust C since, in the later case, any reduction to the trust would reduce pro rata both the QTIP and the non-QTIP portion of the trust. However, if the document is silent as to the trustee's power to create separate trusts, the default rules of the Regulations require that the QTIP election be a specific portion or a fractional basis of the full value of the property. A fraction is created with the QTIP marital deduction amount as the numerator and entire value of the QTIP property as the denominator. This is the fraction of the QTIP property that is protected by the marital deduction at S1's death. This fraction also determines how much of the QTIP property will be taxed at S2's death. To determine the taxable part at S2's death, the value of the QTIP property at S2's death is multiplied by the QTIP fraction. Before applying this to specific estate plans let us break this process down into six steps.

Step by Step: Determining and Using the QTIP Fraction

Step 1. Determine the desired taxable estate for S1: Usually, the executor wants to postpone all taxes to the second death, but use S1's unified credit. This means using the marital deduction to bring the taxable estate to the UCE, i.e., $600,000. However, it might be advantageous to bring the taxable estate to some higher number, if generating some taxes at the first death saves taxes in the long run.

Step 2. Determine the QTIP marital deduction (QTIP MD) amount necessary to arrive at the desired taxable estate: Total Estate – Desired Taxable Estate = MD amount. If the only marital deduction is by way of a QTIP election, this will also be the QTIP MD amount. If some property passes to S2 immediately by joint tenancy, or by being transferred from S1's estate into a trust that S2 controls (Trust A), such will qualify for an automatic marital deduction (automatic MD). The automatic MD must be subtracted from the MD amount to arrive at the needed QTIP MD.

Step 3. Determine the value of the QTIP property: This is the property, almost always a trust, that meets the QTIP Code requirements, and to which the QTIP election will apply to give us the QTIP MD. Which trust is the QTIP trust depends upon the particular estate plan, e.g., with the ABC plan it is the value of Trust C, usually S1's estate less the UCE (the UCE having been transferred into Trust B). Generically, we will refer to it as the QTIP Trust. .

Step 4. The fraction: Create a fraction with the QTIP MD (Step 2) over the QTIP Trust (Step 3) to arrive at the QTIP fraction.

$$\frac{QTIP\ MD}{QTIP\ Trust} = QTIP\ Fraction$$

Step 5. S1's taxable estate: S1's taxable estate is S1's total estate less any automatic MD and less the product of the QTIP fraction and the QTIP Trust. Check your calculation, the result should match the desired taxable estate (Step 1).

$$S1\ Taxable\ Est. = Total\ Est. - automatic\ MD - (\frac{QTIP\ MD}{QTIP\ Trust} * QTIP\ Trust)$$

Step 6. S2's taxable estate: At S2's death, to determine S2's total estate, the QTIP Trust (*as it is then valued*) is multiplied by the QTIP fraction to determine the amount of the QTIP Trust included in S2's estate. This in turn is added to the rest of S2's estate (generally, Trust A).

$$S2's\ Taxable\ Est. = Trust\ A + (\frac{QTIP\ MD}{QTIP\ Trust[S1's DOD]} * QTIP\ Trust[S2's DOD])$$

Changes to the steps if the trust document allows the trustee to divided Trust C into Trust CQ (to be QTIP'ed) and Trust CNQ (which won't be QTIP'ed). One would still go through steps 1 - 2 as before, then at step 3, Trust CQ would be allocated the marital deduction amount and Trust CNQ the balance of the QTIP property. The fractions at step 5 would be 100% (1/1) for Trust CQ and zero for Trust CNQ. Finally, step 6 would have S2's estate equal to all of S1's property, plus all of Trust CQ. Since Trusts B and CNQ were fully included in S1's taxable estate, they would not be part of S2's estate.

Extended Example

The extended example set that follows is designed to increase your understanding of the QTIP election. Using a modern ABC plan, the example compares the result of death taxes for a 100% QTIP election, to what happens where there is no QTIP election. Later, we will explore what happens when S1's executor makes a partial QTIP election where the trustee does not have authority to divide Trust C into separate trust. For examples in this chapter we will ignore the prior transfer credit, as it will be covered in connection with multiple trust plans in the next chapter. We will assume that Trust C meets all of the QTIP requirements. *** *Query 2. Why not include the modern AB Trust plan as part of this QTIP example?* The assumption is also made that S2 does not remarry, therefore, there is no marital deduction for S2's estate. To simplify this first set of examples, all figures are given net of debts and expenses, and the value of the trusts increase modestly each year during the ten years between the two deaths. The assumption that the two deaths occur ten years apart avoids having to tackle the prior transfer credit as part of the example, but it also requires the assumption that the unified credit and the tax rates will not change during the time period chosen for this hypothetical situation. Even if they do change, the concepts are likely to remain valid.

Step by Step as it Applies to the ABC Trust Plan

Step 1. Determine the desired taxable estate for S1, e.g., equal to the UCE so as to postpone all taxes, or have S1 and S2's estates equal as of S1's death, or some dollar amount as determined by the executor to be optimal in reducing overall taxes for the two estates.

Step 2. Total Estate – Desired Taxable Estate = QTIP MD amount.

Step 3. Trust C is the QTIP Trust, defined as being S1's estate in excess of the UCE (Trust B):

      S1's Total Estate – Trust B = Trust C

Step 4. Create a fraction with the QTIP MD amount (Step 2) over the QTIP Trust (Step 3) to arrive at the QTIP fraction:

$$\frac{QTIP\ MD}{Trust\ C} = QTIP\ Fraction$$

Step 5. S1's taxable estate is S1's total estate less the product of the QTIP Trust and the QTIP fraction. Hopefully, the result matches the desired taxable estate (Step 1).

$$S1\ Taxable\ estate = Total\ estate - (\frac{QTIP\ MD}{Trust\ C} * Trust\ C)$$

Step 6. At S2's death, the amount **then** in Trust C is multiplied by the QTIP fraction in order to determine the amount of Trust C that must be included in S2's estate. Add that amount to the rest of S2's estate (e.g., Trust A) to determine S2's total estate.

Facts for this Extended Set: Henry (S1) and Wilma (S2) lived, and died, in a community property state. Their estate plan was an ABC Trust plan as described above. When Henry died in 1987, they owned property valued as follows:

S1's separate property	$1,500,000
Their community property	$1,800,000
S2's separate property	$2,000,000
Total	$5,300,000

Note: If Henry and Wilma lived in a common law state, the outcome would be exactly the same if we simply divide the community property equally between them:

S1's separate property	$2,400,000
S2's separate property	$2,900,000
Total	$5,300,000

In fact, the property laws for common law and community property states will result in ownership rights for each spouse that depend largely on how the spouses acquired their property.

After Henry's death the trusts were funded with assets having a net value as shown here:

Trust A		$2,900,000
Trust B		$600,000
Trust C		$1,800,000
	Total	$5,300,000

The values for these three trusts as of Wilma's death in 1998 will be given in Step 6.

PART ONE: The executor of Henry's estate elects to postpone all taxes until Wilma's death but desires to utilize Henry's unified credit. This means the optimal taxable estate is equal to the UCE, i.e., $600,000.

Step 1. The desired taxable estate for S1 = $600,000.

Step 2. $2,400,000 - $600,000 = $1,800,000

Step 3. The QTIP property: S1's Total Estate – Trust B = Trust C.

$$\$2,400,000 - \$600,000 = \$1,800,000$$

Step 4. Create a fraction with the QTIP marital deduction amount from Step 2 divided by the Trust C amount from Step 3 to arrive at the QTIP fraction.

$$\frac{QTIP\ MD}{Trust\ C} = QTIP\ Fraction$$

$$\frac{\$1,800,000}{\$1,800,000} = 100\%$$

Step 5. S1's taxable estate is S1's total estate less the product of Trust C and the QTIP fraction:

$$S1\ Taxable\ Estate = \$2,400,000 - ((\frac{\$1,800,000}{\$1,800,000}) * \$1,800,000)$$

$$= \$600,000$$

Step 6. At S2's death, the amount **then** in Trust C is multiplied by the QTIP fraction to determine the amount of Trust C that must be included in S2's estate. Add that amount to Trust A to determine S2's total estate. Assume that in the ten years the values for the three trusts increased to the following:

Trust A	$4,700,000
Trust B	$975,000
Trust C	$3,100,000
Total	$8,775,000

Note: The entire amount of Trust C (appreciated) is included in S2's estate. In this case, since *all* of Trust C was QTIP'ed, S2's estate is:

$$\$4,700,000 \text{ [Trust A]} + \$3,100,000 \text{ [Trust C]} = \$7,800,000$$

Trust A was not part of Henry's taxable estate because it contains Wilma's property only. Trusts B and C, combined, equal Henry's gross estate because all of Henry's property is allocated to these two trusts. Regardless of the whether a QTIP election is made, the value of Trust B will be taxed as part of Henry's estate, although there might be no tax due because of the unified credit. While Trust C's value is always part of the *gross* estate, it need not be taxed if the QTIP election is made to cover the entire trust because it then is protected by the marital deduction and will be taxed in S2's estate.

When Wilma dies, Trust A is included in her estate because she holds a general power over it, and because she transferred her property into it and retained the right to revoke it. Trust B is excluded from Wilma's estate because it is a bypass trust. Wilma did not create, nor fund, Trust B, therefore, she could not have a retained interest that would cause inclusion in her estate, nor did she hold a general power of appointment that would cause this trust to be included. Trust C is included in her estate only because of the QTIP election after Henry died. This was a trade-off; it escaped tax when he died, so it must be included in her estate.

Notice that the QTIP election, or the failure to elect, does not change the amount of property going into each trust. Of course, if no QTIP election is made, taxes must be paid at S1's death because property in excess of the unified credit equivalent will be taxable at S1's death.

PART TWO: Change the facts. Suppose the executor of Henry's estate decided that it was best NOT to postpone any taxes on Henry's share of the property, and therefore, elected NOT to make a QTIP election. This means the optimal taxable estate is equal to all of Henry's property, i.e., $2,400,000. Even though it's obvious that the amounts going into Trusts B and C (all of Henry's estate) will be the amount taxed at his death, and Wilma's property (all of Trust A) will be the only property taxed at her death, the steps are set forth here so that it will be apparent that we are following the same format, an important lesson before we start working on partial QTIP elections.

Step 1. The Desired Taxable Estate for S1 = $2,400,000.

Step 2. Total Estate − Desired Taxable Estate = QTIP Election amount.

$$\$2,400,000 - \$2,400,000 = \$0$$

Step 3. Trust C is the QTIP property.

$$S1's\ Total\ Estate - Trust\ B = Trust\ C = \$1,800,000$$

Step 4. Create a fraction with the QTIP MD from Step 2 over Trust C (Step 3) to determine the QTIP fraction.

$$\frac{\$0}{\$1,800,000} = zero$$

Step 5.
$$S1's\ Taxable\ estate = Total\ estate - (\frac{QTIP\ MD}{Trust\ C} * Trust\ C)$$

$$S1\ Taxable\ Estate = \$2,400,000 - ((\frac{\$0}{\$1,800,000}) * \$1,800,000)$$
$$= \$2,400,000$$

Step 6. In this case, since none of Trust C was QTIP'ed, S2's estate is just $4,700,000 [The value of Trust A only].

In all of these plans that we are considering, Trust A is included in S2's estate because it holds S2's property and, as to any property that flows into Trust A from S1's estate, S2 holds a general power of appointment over this trust. Where

S1's executor forgoes the QTIP election, Trust C is taxed at S1's death and then escapes tax at S2's death. Trust B is not included in S2's estate because it is a bypass trust, already taxed in S1's taxable estate, but bypassing the estate of S2. When possible, Trust B is funded with property expected to appreciate because it escapes tax at S2's death, even if its value greatly exceeds the UCE.

OPTIMAL ALLOCATION: THE PARTIAL QTIP ELECTION

Trust C has the chameleon character of being like a marital deduction trust if the QTIP election is made, or a bypass trust if the QTIP election is not made. However, the law allows still more flexibility by allowing partial QTIP elections. This allows a portion of the QTIP trust (Trust C in the ABC plan) to qualify for the marital deduction at S1's death. When the executor of S1's estate makes such an election, a portion of the QTIP trust, the QTIP fraction portion, acts like a marital trust and the rest of the trust is like a bypass trust. The QTIP election portion of Trust C escapes taxes at S1's death because of the marital deduction, but that same fraction of the QTIP trust, valued at S2's death, is included in S2's estate when S2 dies. The non-QTIP election portion is taxed at S1's death but not at S2's death.

A partial QTIP may be desirable to lower the overall estate taxes by taking advantage of lower marginal rates in both estates and utilizing the prior transfer credit (discussed in conjunction with the marital deduction in the next chapter). Generally, executors choose to postpone all taxes until S2's death even though the absolute amount of total taxes paid will almost always be greater when this is done. Given the time value of money, this makes sense rather than paying taxes at the first death. Besides, if taxes are paid at the first death, they will come out of property intended to produce income for the surviving spouse; whereas, postponing the taxes takes them out of the property going to the children (or others, if there are no children).

The picture changes dramatically if it is known at the time S1's estate tax return is being prepared that S2 is quite certain to die soon. In that case, paying taxes for both estates, rather than just at S2's death, will not only utilize both estates' lower marginal rates, but S2's estate will be able to use a prior transfer credit which substantially reduces taxes on the second death.

Where S2's death is likely to occur within two years of S1's death, the optimal allocation between the two taxable estates depends upon such factors as the age of S2 at the time of S1's death, the Federal rate for valuing split interests, and the size of the combined estates. Generally, the lower the Federal rate, the older the surviving spouse, and the larger the estate, the higher the percentage that should be allocated to S1's taxable estate and the lower to S2's. For instance, if the §7520 rate is 8%, S2 is 68 years old, dies within two years of S1, and the combined estate value is $10 million at the time of S1's death, the tax bill is lowest if $7,350,000 is taxed in S1's estate and only $2,650,000 is taxed in S2's estate. However, if all taxes are deferred until the second death, whether through a QTIP or regular marital deduction, with only the UCE amount being sheltered at S1's death, the estate taxes would be about $1,000,000 more than they would be with the optimal allocation.

Several competing factors must be considered when deciding whether and how much QTIP election to make. One consideration is the time value of money. If the deaths are not expected to occur close together, taxes paid a long time in the future are less burdensome than taxes paid today. However, if the property appreciates substantially between the deaths, the total tax bill will be higher. If property is appreciating very rapidly, sometimes it makes sense to get the tax paid sooner on a smaller amount. Another consideration is the prior transfer credit which substantially reduces taxes at the second death, but only if the deaths are close together in time. One must also consider the relative size of the two estates. A QTIP election can only shift the taxable estate in S2's direction, so optimization by QTIP election works only when S1's estate is larger than S2's, and only if it is large enough to equal the optimal S1 taxable estate.

Where the second death is likely to occur within a few years after the first occurred, and the estates have a combined value of over $1.2 million, the optimal allocation usually has S1's taxable estate slightly larger than that of S2, thus when the two estates are about equal in size, or when S2 has the larger estate, there should be no QTIP election because doing so would only further increase S2's taxable estate.

Since deductions other than the marital deduction are generally beyond the executor's control,[19] the focus in the examples to follow is on the marital deduction, which can be increased or decreased depending on how it is used in conjunction with the QTIP election. For simplicity, we will continue to ignore other deductions.

Partial QTIP Election Examples

While it seems more complex, the process for calculating estates with a partial QTIP election is the same process discussed earlier for the "all or nothing" QTIP elections. Where it was "all," the QTIP fraction was equal to one[20] and where it was "nothing," it was equal to zero[21].

> EXAMPLE 11-24. Sam has an estate of $2 million and his wife Susan has an estate of $700,000. His executor elects to have $1,100,000 taxed at Sam's death. The value of the three trusts at Sam's death would be: Trust A, $700,000; Trust B, $600,000; and Trust C, $1,400,000.
>
> Step 1. Sam's desired taxable estate is $1,100,000.
>
> Step 2. Sam's Total Estate – Desired Taxable Estate = QTIP MD
>
> $2,000,000 - $1,100,000 = $900,000.
>
> Step 3. Trust C is the QTIP property: $1,400,000.
>
> Step 4. $\dfrac{QTIP\ MD}{Trust\ C} = \dfrac{\$900,000}{\$1,400,000} = QTIP\ Fraction$
>
> Step 5. $Sam's\ Taxable\ estate = Sam's\ Total\ Estate - (\dfrac{QTIP\ MD}{Trust\ C} * Trust\ C)$
>
> $\$2,000,000 - (\dfrac{\$900,000}{\$1,400,000} * \$1,400,000) = \$1,100,000$
>
> Step 6. At Susan's death, Trust A has grown to $875,000; Trust B has grown to $750,000; and Trust C to $1,800,000. The portion of Trust C included in her estate:
>
> $\dfrac{\$900,000}{\$1,400,000} * \$1,800,000 = \$1,157,143$

Thus, $1,157,143 of Trust C is included in Susan's estate. When added to Trust A, this gives a total estate of: $875,000 + $1,157,143 = $2,032,143. Notice that Trust B is not taxed at Susan's death, even though it exceeded $600,000 when she died.

Equalizing Estates

Compared to the 100% QTIP option, most estates in the $1.2 million to $10 million range by equalizing the taxable estates will save almost as much tax as is saved with the optimal allocation. This example assumes that the executor seeks to have both taxable estates equal. Equalizing estates will only work if S1's estate is larger, because the QTIP marital deduction can only "move" property in one direction: out of S1's taxable estate and into S2's taxable estate.

Equalizing the estates uses the six step process that we have been using. If S1's estate is larger than S2's, the two are averaged and the average is the desired taxable estate for Step 1.

> EXAMPLE 11-25. Using the facts from the prior Sam and Susan example, suppose Susan is in extremely poor health at Sam's death and, therefore, the executor chooses to equalize the estates. The desired taxable estate would be determined as follows:

Step 1. Sam's desired taxable estate:

$$\text{Average: } \$2,000,000 + \$700,000 = \frac{\$2,700,000}{2} = \$1,350,000$$

Step 2. Sam's Total Estate – Desired Taxable Estate = QTIP MD:

$$\$2,000,000 - \$1,350,000 = \$650,000.$$

Step 3. Trust C = $1,400,000.

Step 4. $\qquad \dfrac{QTIP\ MD}{Trust\ C} = \dfrac{\$650,000}{\$1,400,000} = QTIP\ Fraction$

Step 5. $\quad Sam's\ Taxable\ estate = Sam's\ Total\ estate - (\dfrac{QTIP\ MD}{Trust\ C} * Trust\ C)$

$$\$1,350,000 = \$2,000,000 - (\frac{\$650,000}{\$1,400,000} * \$1,400,000)$$

Step 6. Suppose at Susan's death Trust A has grown to $875,000, but because taxes were paid out of Trust B and C, they had grown to just $610,000 and $1,425,000, respectively. The portion of Trust C that would be included in her estate would be:

$$\frac{\$650,000}{\$1,400,000} * \$1,425,000 = \$661,607$$

Susan's estate would be $1,536,607 [Trust A $875,000 + $661,607 from Trust C].

There is a shortcut to equalize the estates that reaches the same result. S2's estate is subtracted from S1's estate and half the difference is the amount of the QTIP election (Step 2):

$$\frac{Sam's\ estate\ -\ Susan's\ estate}{2} = QTIP\ MD$$

$$\frac{\$2,000,000\ -\ \$700,000}{2} = \$650,000$$

Notice that this is the same result as Step 2. *** *Query* 3. *The QTIP election in the above example was calculated to equalize the estates, why are they not equal?*

Allocating Assets to the Trusts

Estate planning involves planning for an uncertain future. The planner and client must guess how much and what kind of property will be in the estate. They must also guess whether the intended beneficiaries will be alive, and what their circumstances will be at the time the estate is distributed. Because of this uncertainty, planning documents are drafted to deal with uncertainty. Two drafting techniques for structuring disposition clauses in wills or trusts are pecuniary bequests and fractional share bequests.

A *pecuniary bequest* passes property to various shares such that the value of the assets adds up to the dollar value needed to satisfy the pecuniary bequest. For example, the clause funding Trust B might read: *"assets equal in dollar value to the amount which will generate a tentative tax exactly equal to S1's available unified credit, and all assets above that amount are given to the trustee of Trust A."*

Or, the marital bequest going to Trust A of an AB trust plan (or Trust C, in an ABC trust plan) could be defined in dollars: *"assets equal in dollar amount to the marital deduction necessary to reduce S1's taxable estate such that it generates a tentative tax exactly equal to S1's available unified credit are allocated to Trust A, all other assets are allocated to Trust B."*

Using a *fractional share bequest*, both bypass and marital shares will receive a fractional interest in each and every asset in the estate: *"Trust C shall consist of the smallest fractional share of S1's estate that, when added to all other interests in property that pass from S1 to S2, and qualify for the marital deduction, will eliminate, or reduce to the maximum possible extent, any estate tax. The balance of S1's estate shall be allocated to Trust B."*

The factors involved in deciding which type of provision to use are beyond the scope of this text.

QUESTIONS AND PROBLEMS - Use the ETAX program to do the problems that require calculation of estate or gift taxes.

1. What is the largest estate size that an *individual* can transfer, ET free, with a *simple will* to (a) a spouse; (b) any other individuals? Explain, and state any assumptions made.

2. (a) What is the largest net estate that a *husband and wife* can transfer, ET free, with *simple wills* to their children? (b) Does it make any difference how much is owned by each spouse? Explain.

3. (a) What is the largest net estate that a *husband and wife* can transfer to their children, ET free, with a *credit shelter bypass plan*? (b) Does it make any difference how much is owned by each spouse? Explain.

4. One spouse has considerable wealth and the other very modest wealth.
   a. Why is a credit shelter bypass plan a "hit or miss" arrangement?
   b. What is the minimum amount of property that each spouse must own to assure a bypass plan will work?
   c. What change could the couple make that would remove the "hit and miss" aspect of the plan?
   d. Regarding the change in part c, how much should be involved?
   e. What factors help determine whether a bypass should entail an outright transfer or a transfer into trust? Is ET savings a factor? Why

or why not?

5. For the 100% marital deduction describe (a) the major advantages and (b) the major disadvantages.

6. Assuming a wealthy couple has a simple 100% marital deduction plan, explain how each of the following defer or reduce the ET for S2: (a) remarriage; (b) consumption; or (c) gifts. (d) Explain the drawbacks to each of these estate planning devices.

7. Draw a time-line showing the changes in the marital deduction. Be sure to include the start of the QTIP marital deduction and the elimination of the marital deduction for non-citizens who don't use trusts.

8. Briefly state the reason for the terminable interest rule. Then explain why Congress allows each of the following exceptions to the rule:
a. The six months survivorship clause.
b. The transfer to a general power of appointment trust.
c. The transfer to a QTIP trust, with a QTIP election.
d. The pension to the surviving spouse automatic QTIP election.
e. The life estate for S2, with remainder to a charity exception.

9. Explain why each of the following bequests to a surviving spouse would or would not qualify for a marital deduction:

a. A bequest of a sum, not to exceed $100,000, that she could use to purchase a residence, provided she relinquish her dower (life estate) rights to decedent's home. She did relinquish the right within two months of S1's death, and the executor immediately paid $100,000 towards her purchase of a $160,000 home.
b. Decedent's will gave S2 the right to elect either a life estate in S1's home or to take $100,000 outright. She chose the $100,000.
c. Decedent's living trust left his entire estate in trust for S2. She had a power to appoint the trust to anyone, even to her estate at her death. The remainder went to their children if she did not exercise the power to appoint. The trustee could accumulate income if such was not

needed for S2's reasonable support and maintenance. The trust had a corpus valued at $950,000. Decedent's pourover will left his property, in trust, to the trustee of his living trust. They also held $300,000 in a joint bank account; the source of this money was money inherited from the decedent's parents. S2 did not re-marry and did survive beyond the year. Consider both the trust, specifically §2056(b)(5), and the bank account, §2040. With the latter, what effect does the pourover will have?

d. Decedent's will left his entire $1,000,000 estate to his only son, with a provision that if his son died it would go to his son's issue by right of representation. Because of a pre-nuptial agreement, S2 could not claim a dower interest. The son, who had no issue, disclaimed so much of the estate as exceeded the UCE estate, by writing a letter to S1's executor stating, "My father should not have disinherited my mother. I hereby refuse to accept any of my father's estate that is in excess of $600,000 and I assign that excess to my mother." The probate court accepted this as a valid assignment of the son's interest in the probate property that exceeded $600,000 in value and, at the conclusion of the probate, ordered the excess ($400,000) distributed to S2. Review §2518 to determine whether this qualifies as a tax effective disclaimer and therefore, for the marital deduction. Would your answer change if the son had issue at the time of his father's death and when he wrote the letter to the executor?

10. Explain why each of the following would or would not qualify for the QTIP election.

a. An estate plan executed before 1982 created, at S1's death in 1997, a trust holding S1's entire estate worth a net of $2,500,000. The trust required that all income be distributed at least annually to S2, and after S2's death the property was to be distributed to the couple's issue by right of representation. The independent trustee was given the power to distribute corpus to S2, if the trustee thought the income was insufficient for her happiness.

b. The same facts as in (a) except the trustee could also distribute funds to pay medical bills or educational expenses of the couple's children.

c. The couple's estate plan was an ABC Trust plan. Decedent's estate had a net worth of $4,000,000 consisting mainly of undeveloped land. Terms of the trust, that also applied to Trust C, said that the trustee would not be liable for failing to diversify investments, nor for continuing to hold property that was in trust at the time of the settlor's death, nor for failing to make such property productive. In giving an answer, you should consider both how this "absolution from liability" clause might be interpreted and state marital deduction-savings statutes that might help state law. A weaseling answer would be good.

d. The couple had an ABC Trust plan. S1's estate was worth $2,000,000 and S2's estate was worth about the same. Although Trust C had a provision giving S2 income for life, it also said, that in the event S2 became mentally incompetent, the trustee could directly pay S2's bills for living expenses and accumulate any moneys not needed. The executor of S1's estate QTIP'ed all of Trust C. S2 died eleven months after S1's death. S1's executor has filed an amended 706, that states the QTIP was claimed in error because Trust C could not qualify for the QTIP election. The executor attached a check for the estate tax. Was the executor right? What benefits are sought by the executor?

11. In multi-trust estate plans, why is Trust A often called the survivor's trust?

12. In a multi-trust plan, when and why is Trust B likely to be called the credit shelter trust? Under what circumstances are taxes likely to be paid from it? Why is it unlikely that taxes will be paid from it at S2's death, even if it exceeds the UCE amount?

13. In the AB Trust plan and the ABC Trust plan, why not simply define the funding of the trust in terms "of property worth $600,000" instead of using something like "property that uses up the available unified credit?" Given that unified credit of $192,800 covers exactly $600,000 in net value transferred, why would it make any difference?

14. H and W own a family estate worth $3 million, with H owning $2,700,000 and W owning $300,000. Assuming there is no estate growth between the two deaths, and that no prior transfer credit is available, use the ETAX program to complete the following table showing the amount and timing of estate tax payments for each of the following alternatives Also determine the amount that passes to their children. On the left side we assume H dies first and on the right side that W dies first. Assume that, if taxes are paid at the first death, they are paid out of Trust B. (a) a 100% marital deduction; (b) an AB Trust; (c) an ABC Trust, where the executor postpones all tax by making 100% QTIP election for Trust C; and (d) an ABC Trust where the executor equalized the estate by use of a partial QTIP election. Start by showing the value of each trust for the two multi-trust plans:

H dies first - AB Trust plan: Trust A _____ Trust B _____
ABC Trust plan: Trust A _____ Trust B _____ Trust C _____

W dies first - AB Trust plan: Trust A _____ Trust B _____
ABC Trust plan: Trust A _____ Trust B _____ Trust C _____

$3 M, less ET = net	H dies first		W dies first	
	H's ET	W's ET	W's ET	H's ET
100%MD	_____	_____	_____	_____
	net to children = _____		net to children = _____	
AB Trust	_____	_____	_____	_____
	net to children = _____		net to children = _____	
ABC 100%	_____	_____	_____	_____
	net to children = _____		net to children = _____	
ABC equal	_____	_____	_____	_____
	net to children = _____		net to children = _____	

15. (a) Re-work Question 14, assuming that between the first and second deaths all property doubles in value. (b) What conclusions can be drawn?

$6 M, less ET = net	H dies first		W dies first	
	H's ET	W's ET	W's ET	H's ET
100%MD	———— ———— net to children = ———————		———— ———— net to children = ———————	
AB Trust	———— ———— net to children = ———————		———— ———— net to children = ———————	
ABC 100%	———— ———— net to children = ———————		———— ———— net to children = ———————	
ABC equal	———— ———— net to children = ———————		———— ———— net to children = ———————	

FACTS FOR 16 - 20: S1 and S2 lived in a common law state. S1 owned property having a net value of $2,325,780 and S2 owned property having a net value of $1,451,700. Assume debts and expenses are zero, and that no prior transfer credit is available because the two deaths are more than 10 years apart. First determine S1's estate before the marital deduction, and the values for trusts A and B for the AB Trust, and trusts A, B, and C for the ABC plan. Those numbers won't change regardless of what S1's executor does insofar as the QTIP election. For the second part of each problem you will need to know the value of the Trusts when S2 died: For the AB Trust plan, when S2 died Trust A was worth $5,525,638 and Trust B was worth $1,086,000. For the ABC Trust plan, when S2 died Trust A was worth $2,524,506, Trust B was worth $1,086,000, and Trust C was worth $2,778,506.

16.1   The couple had an AB Trust estate plan. Determine: (a) S1's gross estate and taxable estate; (b) the values of Trust A and Trust B.

16.2   Determine S2's taxable estate.

17.1   The couple had an ABC Trust estate plan. S1's executor elected to postpone all taxes until S2 died, but fully utilize S1's unified credit. Determine: (a) S1's gross estate; (b) the values of Trust A, Trust B, and Trust C; (c) the QTIP fraction; and (d) how the fraction is applied to arrive at the taxable estate.

17.2   Determine S2's taxable estate.

18.1   The couple had an ABC Trust estate plan. S1's executor elected to pay all taxes at S1's death, so no QTIP election was made. Determine: (a) the QTIP fraction and (b) show how it is applied to arrive at the desired taxable estate. [The value of S1's gross estate and values of Trust A, Trust B, and Trust C at S1's death will be the same as previously determined, since they are not dependent upon whether or not a QTIP election is made.]

18.2   Determine S2's taxable estate.

19.1   The couple had an ABC Trust estate plan. S1's executor elected to make a QTIP election that would equalize the two estates, at least as of S1's death. Determine: (a) the QTIP fraction and (b) show how it is applied to arrive at the desired taxable estate.

19.2   Determine S2's taxable estate.

20.1   The couple had an ABC Trust estate plan. S1's executor elected to make a QTIP election such that S1's taxable estate would equal $1,456,000. Determine: (a) the QTIP fraction and (b) show how it is applied to arrive at the desired taxable estate.

20.2   Determine S2's taxable estate.

FACTS FOR 21 - 25: S1 and S2 lived in a community property state. S1 owned property having a net value of $1,897,560, S2 owned property having a net value of $466,048, and they owned community property worth $893,200. Assume debts and expenses are zero and that no prior transfer credit is available because the two deaths are more than 10 years apart. Again, you must start by determining S1's estate before the marital deduction, and the values for trusts A and B for the AB Trust, and trusts A, B, and C for the ABC plan. Those numbers won't change regardless of what S1's executor does insofar as the QTIP election. For the second part of each problem you will need to know the value of the Trusts when S2 died: For the AB Trust plan: When S2 died Trust A was worth $4,620,189 and Trust B was worth $1,086,000. For the ABC Trust plan: When S2 died Trust A was worth $1,587,095, Trust B was worth $1,086,000, and Trust C was worth $2,808,098.

21.1 The couple had an AB Trust estate plan. Determine: (a) S1's gross estate and taxable estate; (b) the values of Trust A and Trust B.

21.2 Determine S2's taxable estate.

22.1 The couple had an ABC Trust estate plan. S1's executor elected to postpone all taxes until S2 died, but fully utilize S1's unified credit. Determine: (a) S1's gross estate; (b) the values of Trust A, Trust B, and Trust C; (c) the QTIP fraction; and (d) how the fraction is applied to arrive at the taxable estate.

22.2 Determine S2's taxable estate.

23.1 The couple had an ABC Trust estate plan. S1's executor elected to pay all taxes at S1's death, so no QTIP election was made. Determine: (a) the QTIP fraction; and (b) show how it is applied to arrive at the desired taxable estate. [The value of S1's gross estate and values of Trust A, Trust B, and Trust C at S1's death will be the same as previously determined, since they are not dependent upon whether or not a QTIP election is made.]

23.2 Determine S2's taxable estate.

24.1 The couple had an ABC Trust estate plan. S1's executor elected to make a QTIP election that would equalize the two estates, at least as of S1's death. Determine: (a) the QTIP fraction; and (b) show how it is applied to arrive at the desired taxable estate.

24.2 Determine S2's taxable estate.

25.1 The couple had an ABC Trust estate plan. S1's executor elected to make a QTIP election such that S1's taxable estate would equal $1,900,000. Determine: (a) the QTIP fraction; and (b) show how the fraction is applied to arrive at the desired taxable estate.

25.2 Determine S2's taxable estate.

QUERIES ANSWERED

1. The QTIP fraction and the marital deduction that result in a $600,000 taxable estate when applied to the trust at Fernando's death are as follows:

$$\frac{\$1,789,373 - \$600,000}{\$1,789,373} * \$1,789,737 = \$1,189,373$$

If the trust was worth $2,334,220 at Arcela's death, the amount included in her estate would be:

$$\frac{\$1,189,373}{\$1,789,373} * \$2,334,220 = \$1,551,526$$

2. Trust B in the modern AB trust is equal to the available unified credit equivalent, and everything above the unified credit equivalent is transferred to Trust A; hence, S1's estate receives a marital deduction equal to the value of that property. With this plan there is no terminable interest property to QTIP.

3. Sam and Susan's taxable estates are not equal because Trusts A and C changed in value between the two deaths. Trust B has no effect on the estate value at the second death because it is a bypass trust.

ANSWERS TO THE QUESTIONS AND PROBLEMS:

1. Estate size: (a) a spouse - no limit if S2 is a US citizen, otherwise, only $600,000 (decedent still gets the UCr, even if S2 isn't a citizen); (b) others? Explain. $600,000 assuming UCr has not been used up during life with post-76 taxable gifts. No limit if giving to a charity.

2. (a) $600,000. Only the last-to-die's UCr means anything. (b) No, the last gets it all anyway.

3. (a) $1,200,000 since both UCr's will be used. (b) Yes, each must have an estate at least equal to the UCr to have both fully utilize their respective UCr's.

4. Spouses with unequal wealth.
   a. If the poor spouse dies first, less than a full $600,000 will be sheltered.
   b. $600,000.
   c. Transfer some of the rich spouse's property to the less wealthy spouse.
   d. Enough so that the less wealthy spouse has at least a UCE estate.
   e. Outright transfers are most likely where there are children by a prior marriage, and S1 has sufficient wealth to both take care of S2 (a QTIP trust) and still leave some significant portion of the estate to his children. The children by the first marriage don't have to wait until S2 dies to inherit part of the estate (UCE). If children are only from this marriage or if S2 will need the income from S1's entire estate, an AB or ABC arrangement is more likely, since S2 can have all the income for life. With the ABC, S1 can assure that his or her property will eventually go to S1's family. ET is not a major consideration as to which bypass plan to use, however, for very large estates, the ABC when coupled with the prior transfer credit is preferred over the outright bypass or the AB trust. We take up this combination in the next chapter.

5. (a) Simple. See the chapter discussion for details. (b) Loss of utilization of S1's UCr & the UCE amount that goes into S2's estate is taxed at the

highest marginal rates insofar as her estate goes.

6. (a) Remarriage: another marital deduction, including possibly using a lifetime QTIP gift, if the new spouse is old & poor. (b) Consumption: spend it and it isn't there for the taxman. (c) Gifts: using annual exclusion and/or unified credit of the survivor gets some portion of the estate transferred tax free (annual exclusion amounts) and any future appreciation avoids tax. (d) Explain the drawbacks to each of these estate planning devices. It's obvious, but still worth thinking about. Remarriage: S2 might disinherit he children of the first marriage, or at least make them wait until the new spouse dies before they come into their inheritance. Consumption: Well unless it is spent on the kids, they hate to see too much of that wealth disappear. Generally, no-one likes to see his or her wealth decrease. Gifts: parallel comments as to consumption.

7. Show the big changes as starting in 1977 (unification, same rates, etc.), 1982 (100% marital deduction, QTIP, & $10,000 annual exclusion), and 1984 (QDOT).

8. No marital deduction is allowed unless S2's interest is vested. (a) The six months survivorship clause. If S2 makes it, the property is in S2's estate. If S2 doesn't make it, then no MD. (b) The transfer to a general power of appointment trust. The GPA causes the trust to be included in S2's estate. (c) The transfer to a QTIP trust, with a QTIP election. If no election is made, no MD. If it is made, then the QTIP portion is taxed at S2's death. (d) The pension to the surviving spouse automatic QTIP election. The surviving spouse collects the pension for his or her life, and the PV of the remaining payments are included in S2's estate when S2 dies. (e) The life estate for S2, with remainder to a charity exception. The only beneficiaries are S2 and the charity.

9. Explain why certain bequests do or don't qualify for a marital deduction:
    (a) No marital deduction for two reasons: (1) whether she would get the money was uncertain; and (2) the amount was uncertain (Est. of Edmonds, 72 TC 970). Notice that had she claimed her dower rights, those would have qualified for a QTIP election since they were a vested

life estate in QTIP property.

(b) The $100,000 does qualify. S2 has alternate bequests, vested at S1's death, wherein she makes the choice. This should qualify even if the other alternative was one that did not qualify, so long as the one she chose did qualify. Est. of Tompkins, 68 TC 912

(c) The property in trust won't qualify since §2056(b)(5) requires income for life for S2 and the trustee's power to accumulate spoils this. The title to the joint bank account controls regardless of the pourover will, therefore, $150,000 is included in S1's estate and is removed from his taxable estate by a marital deduction of $150,000.

(d) The property "assigned" is transferred to S2 just as if it had been left to her or had passed to her by intestate succession, therefore, it qualifies for the marital deduction. Notice that the last part of §2518 allows even an "assignment" to qualify so long as the assignee is the person that would have received the property as a result of the disclaimer without the assignment language. That last statement tells us that had the son had issue, his issue would have received the property as a result of a disclaimer absent the assignment language, therefore, had he had issue, this would have been treated as a gift from the son, and would not have qualified for the marital deduction. Indeed, the son would have to file a gift tax return.

10. Explain why certain bequests qualify (or don't) for the QTIP election.

(a) Even pre-QTIP law trusts can qualify for the QTIP election, provided they meet the QTIP requirements; This one does. Note that the power to distribute to S2 is alright; the trust just can't allow distributions to anyone other than S2 during S2's life-time.

(b) It won't qualify as written, for the reasons given for the last question. Perhaps the children will make a tax effective disclaimer (see §2518) of this potential benefit, in which case it would qualify.

(c) If the language is interpreted to mean that the trustees need not invest in productive property even if S2 so requests, then by being allowed to retain unproductive property deprives S2 of an income interest, therefore, a QTIP election is not available. If the language merely protects the trustee from liability in the event the value of the property goes down (or fails to keep up with other reasonable investments), even though prudence would have suggested diversification, the QTIP should be available. Many states have laws that give the surviving spouse the right to compel the trustee to make the property productive in the absence of language to the contrary in the trust document. Those states that have such laws generally compel interpretation of vague language, such as discussed here, in such a way as to obtain the marital deduction if it is clear from the overall estate plan that such was the intent of the estate plan. Since this language is applied to Trust C, a trust intended to qualify for the marital deduction, the clause would be given the interpretation that S2 could compel the trustee to make the property productive, e.g., develop it or sell it and re-invest in income earning investments.

(d) Probably so. S2 did not have a vested life estate since, under some circumstances, the trustee had authority to accumulate income. The executor seeks to undo the QTIP and pay some taxes on S1's death (in light of S2's death so soon), thereby using the lower rates of S1's estate and setting S2's estate up for the benefit of a prior transfer credit.

11.   It generally is funded with S2's property, and even if some of the corpus has as its source property from S1, S2 has a GPA over the trust.

12.   In the two multi-trust plans studied in this chapter, it (Trust B) is defined in terms of S1's available UCr. For those plans that use the UCE to define the value for funding this trust, credit shelter is a good descriptive name for the trust. However, we will see in the next chapter that some plans define trust B such that it does not equal the UCE. If Trust C is not 100% QTIP'ed, Trust B may have to pay its share of the estate tax. If it is a UCE trust, no tax is paid out of it at the second death because it is not part of S2's estate (i.e., none of her property went into it so no retained interests, there is no general power of appointment over it, and it won't have been QTIP'ed).

13.   Because, even with plans that have Trust B as a credit shelter trust, it might be more or less than $600,000. If S1 has made taxable gifts post-76, some of the UCr will have been used up. Likewise, if some of S1's estate is left to someone other than S2 or a charity, that bequest will use up UCr. Finally, the amount could be more than $600,000 if Congress

increases the UCr to more than $192,800. The latter is likely to happen soon.

14. Taxes, with various plans, varying the who (H or W) dies first.
   (a) 100%MD: H $0, $1,098,000, $1,902,000; W the same.
   (b) AB: H $0, $784,000, $2,216,000; W $0, $939,000, $2,061,000.
   (c) ABC(100%): H $0, $784,000, $2,216,000; W $0, $939,000, $2,061,000.
   (d) ABC =: $363,000, $363,000, $2,274,000; W $0, $939,000, $2,061,000.

15. (a) Rework Question 14, between the 1st and 2nd deaths property doubles.
   1. 100%MD: H $0, $2,748,000, $3,252,000; W the same.
   2. AB: H $0, $2,088,000, $3,912,000; W $0, $2,418,000, $3582000.
   3. ABC(100%): H $0, $2,088,000, $3,912,000; W $0, $2,418,000, $3,582,000.
   4. ABC equal: H $363,000, $1,098,000, $4,539,000; W $0, $2,418,000 $3,582,000.

   (b) Conclusion: not making the QTIP election often lowers overall taxes, but it ignores timing of the payments and the fact that waiting until both spouses are dead means that neither S1 or S2 really pay the taxes. Finally, if S1 is insurable, rather than paying the taxes at S1's death, use some of the money "saved" by postponing the payment to buy life insurance on S2's life, holding it in an irrevocable life insurance trust.

16.1 AB Trust estate plan: (a) S1's gross estate [$2,325,780] and taxable estate [$600,000]; (b) Trust A[$3,177,480] and Trust B[$600,000].

16.2 S2's taxable estate:[$5,525,638; just Trust A].

17.1 ABC Trust estate plan. (postpone taxes): (a) S1's gross estate [$2,325,780]; (b) Trust A [$1,451,700], Trust B [$600,000], Trust C [$1,725,780]; (c) QTIP fraction [$1,725,780/$1,725,780 = 1]; and (d) taxable estate: $2,325,780 - ($1,725,780/$1,725,780) * $1,725,780 = $600,000

17.2 S2's taxable estate: [Tr A + QTIP fraction * Tr C] $2,524,506 + (1) * $2,778,506 = $5,303,012

18.1 ABC Trust estate plan (pay all taxes): (a) QTIP fraction [0/$1,725,780 = 0]; and (b) taxable estate: $2,325,780 - (0) * $1,725,780 = $2,325,780

18.2 S2's taxable estate: $2,524,506 + (0) * $2,778,506 = $2,524,506

19.1 (a) QTIP fraction [$437,040/$1,725,780] and (b) taxable estate: $2,325,780 - ($437,040/$1,725,780) * $1,725,780 = $1,888,740

19.2 S2's taxable estate: $2,524,506 + ($437,040/$1,725,780) * ($2,778,506) = $3,228,141

20.1 (a) [(Step 2) $2,325,780 - $1,456,000 = $869,780. Step 3 is the value of Trust C, therefore Step 4: QTIP fraction $869,780/$1,725,780] and (b) taxable estate (Step 5): $2,325,780 - ($869,780/$1,725,780) * $1,725,780 = $1,456,000

20.2 Determine S2's taxable estate (Step 6): $2,524,506 + ($869,780/$1,725,780) * ($2,778,506) = $3,924,852

21.1 (a) S1's gross estate [$2,344,160] and taxable estate [$600,000]; (b) the values of Trust A [$2,656,808] and Trust B [$600,000].

21.2 Determine S2's taxable estate. Just Trust A: [$4,620,189]

22.1 (a) S1's gross estate [$2,344,160]; (b) the values of Trust A [$912,648], Trust B [$600,000], and Trust C [$1,744,160]; (c) the QTIP fraction [$1,744,160 /$1,744,160 = 1]; and (d) the taxable estate: $2,344,160 - (1) * $1,744,160 = $600,000

22.2 Determine S2's taxable estate: [Tr A + QTIP fraction * Tr C] $1,587,095 + (1) * $2,808,098 = $4,395,192

23.1 (a) the QTIP fraction [0/$1,744,160 = 0]; and (b) taxable estate: $2,344,160 - 0 * $1,744,160 = $2,344,160

23.2 Determine S2's taxable estate. Trust A only [$1,587,095].

24.1 (a) the QTIP fraction [$715,756/$1,744,160]; and (b) taxable estate: $2,344,160 - ($715,756/$1,744,160) * $1,744,160 = $1,628,404

24.2 Determine S2's taxable estate: $1,587,095 + ($715,756/$1,744,160) * $2,808,098 = $2,739,462

25.1 (a) the QTIP fraction; and (b) taxable estate: $2,344,160 - ($444,160/$1,744,160) * $1,744,160 = $1,900,000.

25.2 Determine S2's taxable estate: $1,587,095 + ($444,160/$1,744,160) * $2,808,098 = $2,302,193.

ENDNOTES

1. IRC §2011.

2. §§2053 and 2054.

3. IRC §812(e)(1)(B) of the 1939 Code.

4. IRC§2056(b)(1).

5. IRC §2056(b)(3).

6. IRC §2056(b)(5).

7. IRC §2056(b)(7).

8. IRC §2056(b)(7)(B).

9. IRC §2044.

10. IRC §2013 and Reg. §20.2013 - 4, Example (2).

11. IRC §2523(f).

12. IRC §2056(b)(5).

13. Reg. §20.2056(b)-5(f)(5)

14. IRC §664.

15. IRC §§2518 & 2046 concerning disclaimers will be discussed in the next chapter.

16. IRC §2036(b)(7).

17. IRC §2044.

18. IRC §2044.

19. Deciding whether to claim deductions as estate tax or income tax deductions may be within the executor's control.

20. $\dfrac{Trust\ C}{Trust\ C} = 1$

21. $\dfrac{0}{Trust\ C} = 0$

−12 ——————————————————————

Advanced Bypass and Marital Deduction Planning

————————————————————

OVERVIEW

This chapter continues the discussion of marital deduction and bypass planning, starting with variations on the basic trust plans described in the last chapter, followed by a review of a couple older plans seen now only in estate planning museums. The calculation of the prior transfer tax credit is explained, as is its rather surprising application to bypass trusts. The chapter concludes with an examination of the generation-skipping transfer tax; and its impact on marital deduction and bypass planning.

VARIATIONS ON A THEME

There are variations on the AB Trust and the ABC Trust plans that may better suit certain families, yet utilize both unified credits, and like the ABC plan, keep the option of deferring estate taxes or paying them on the first death.

THE ASUPERB TRUST PLAN

The AsuperB Trust has Trust A defined as receiving all S2's property and Trust B defined as receiving all S1's property. It is simpler than the ABC plan as there is one less trust, and given the absence of any reference to a separate credit shelter trust, it may be more readily understood by clients. The AB Trust plan takes an automatic marital deduction for the property in excess of the UCE because that excess is transferred from S1's estate into Trust A; however, the AsuperB plan allows the executor of S1's estate to decide (via QTIP) whether to pay taxes at the first death or to postpone them until the second death.

Trust B must have all the QTIP attributes that allow a QTIP election if it is desired, i.e., mainly income for life for S2 and no power to appoint to anyone other than S2 during S2's lifetime. Of course utilization of S1's unified credit is important so, even if one wished to pay no taxes, the executor would use that QTIP Fraction for Trust B that would reduce S1's taxable estate to the available UCE. Once again, the six step process is used, starting with determining the optimal taxable estate at S1's death.

> EXAMPLE 12-1. When S1 died in 1995, the couple's AsuperB Trust plan gave S2 a life estate in Trust B, plus a power to withdraw corpus that was limited to an ascertainable standard. At S2's death, Trust B property is distributed to S1's children by a prior marriage. Trust A is revocable by S2 and her children by a prior marriage are the remaindermen. Their combined net worth was $3,877,250; of which S1's property, worth $2,843,760, was allocated to Trust superB; and S2's property, worth $1,033,490, was allocated to Trust A. To postpone all taxes until S2's death, the executor of S1's estate wants to QTIP Trust B to bring S1's taxable estate to $600,000.
>
> Step 1. The desired taxable estate for S1 = $600,000.
>
> Step 2. Determine the QTIP MD: Total Estate – Desired Taxable Estate = QTIP MD.
> $$\$2,843,760 - \$600,000 = \$2,243,760$$
>
> Step 3. For the AsuperB plan there is no separate UCE Trust, therefore Trust B is the QTIP Trust, i.e., S1's Estate = Trust B (the superB) = the QTIP Trust = $2,843,760.
>
> Step 4. Create a fraction with the QTIP MD (Step 2) over the QTIP Trust (Trust superB) to arrive at the QTIP Fraction.

$$\frac{QTIP \ MD}{Trust \ B} = QTIP \ Fraction$$

$$\frac{\$2,243,760}{\$2,843,760} = QTIP \ Fraction$$

Step 5. S1's taxable estate is S1's total estate less the product of the QTIP Trust and the QTIP Fraction.

$$S1 \text{'s Taxable estate} = Total \ estate - (\frac{QTIP \ MD}{Trust \ B} * Trust \ B)$$

Therefore, S1's TxE = $2,843,760 - $2,243,760 = $600,000.

Step 6. Assume that when S2 died in 1998, Trust A was worth $1,137,642 and Trust B was worth $3,117,970. As before, at S2's death, the total estate is equal to all of Trust A plus the QTIP Fraction multiplied by the amount **then** in the Trust B.

$$S2 \text{'s Taxable estate} = Trust \ A + (\frac{QTIP \ MD}{Trust \ B} * Trust \ B)$$

S2's taxable estate would be:

$$S2 \text{'s TxE} = \$1,137,642 + \frac{\$2,243,760}{\$2,843,760} * \$3,117,970$$

$$= \$3,597,757$$

Of course, S1's executor can make a partial QTIP that equalizes the estates if that produces a better result than either partial QTIP to defer all taxes, or complete taxation of Trust B. If S1's executor was very certain that S2 was going to die shortly after S1, or if S2 had already died when S1's executor was preparing the S1 estate tax return, the QTIP might be made to equalize the two estates.

EXAMPLE 12-2: Using the same values from the previous example, equal estates at S1's death would be:

Step 1.

$$\frac{S1 \text{'s } E + S2 \text{'s } E}{2} = \frac{\$2,843,760 + \$1,033,490}{2} = \$1,938,625$$

Step 2. Determine the QTIP MD: Total Estate – Desired Taxable Estate = QTIP MD amount = $2,843,760 - $1,938,625 = $905,135

Step 3. Trust B is the QTIP Trust, i.e., S1's Estate = Trust B (the superB) = the QTIP Trust = $2,843,760.

Step 4. Create a fraction with the QTIP MD (Step 2) over the QTIP Trust (Trust superB) to arrive at the QTIP Fraction.

$$\frac{\$905,135}{\$2,843,760} = QTIP \ Fraction$$

Step 5. S1's taxable estate is S1's total estate less the product of Trust B and the QTIP Fraction.

$$S1\text{'s Taxable estate} = \$2,843,760 - (\frac{\$905,135}{\$2,843,760} * \$2,843,760)$$

$$= \$2,843,760 - \$905,135$$

$$= \$1,938,625$$

Step 6. S2's estate includes all of Trust A plus the QTIP fraction times Trust B valued at S2's death:

$$S2\text{'s TxE.} = \$1,137,642 + \frac{\$905,135}{\$2,843,760} * \$3,117,970 = \$2,130,055$$

There are several reasons a couple might prefer the AsuperB plan over the AB plan. *S1 may not want to have property in excess of the UCE pass into S2's control, as must happen with the AB plan, yet their total estate might be just approaching, or be just slightly greater than, the UCE. For a couple in that situation, an ABC plan, with the complicating factor of the third trust, might be over planning.* For instance, if S1's net estate is $625,000 with an ABC plan, the B Trust would be funded with assets worth $600,000 and the C Trust with assets worth a mere $25,000; both trusts would have to file state and Federal income tax returns each year and the trustees would have to maintain separate accounts for each trust. With the AsuperB plan, Trust B would be funded with assets worth $625,000 and there would be no Trust C. If the executor chose to postpone estate taxes the QTIP fraction would be $25,000/$625,000. At the time an estate plan is drafted for an elderly couple whose combined estate is over $600,000 but less than $1,200,000, the planner, recognizing that there is a high probability that S1's estate will be under the UCE amount, may recommend the simpler but equally effective AsuperB plan over the ABC plan, knowing that if the superB Trust is slightly, or even greatly, above the UCE a partial QTIP can be used to defer taxes.

Even for large estates there is at least one advantage in the AsuperB as compared to the ABC Trust, but it comes with a trade-off. The funding provisions of most ABC plans define either the B Trust or the C Trust as a pecuniary bequest, e.g., "After the death of the first Settlor, the trustee shall allocate to Trust B property equal in value to that amount which will be needed to increase the taxable estate to the largest amount that will not result in a Federal estate tax being imposed on the deceased Settlor's estate after allowing for available unified credit." The "equal in amount" language usually translates into $600,000 in value and, since it is defined in dollar terms, it is a pecuniary bequest. Where, as usually happens, it takes months, and occasionally years, for the trustee to allocate the assets in the family trust (or for the probate estate to obtain an order for distribution) to the separate trusts, the values are likely to be very different from those at the date of death. Where a pecuniary bequest is funded with assets that have appreciated in value, the difference between the basis (the date of death value or alternative date value) and the fair market value on the date of funding is a capital gain to the family trust (or the probate estate) making the transfer. Since the gain occurs when the family trust (or probate estate) is terminating, the gain is passed on to the pecuniary trust which must then pay taxes on the gain. Of course, the trust would have a basis in those assets equal to their fair market value at the time of funding. If property used to fund the trust has decreased in value between S1's death and funding, no loss is recognized because the family trust and the pecuniary trust (B or C) are considered related parties. The superB Trust avoids this problem of gain recognition because it is not defined in pecuniary terms but rather in terms of "all of S1's property not specifically bequested."

Many plans using multiple trusts give all tangible personal property (cars, furniture, etc.) to S2, or to the trustee of S2's Trust A. Since such property is not investment property, it might be best to allow S2 to control these assets without any need to account for them to the remaindermen.

THE AB WITH DISCLAIMER INTO C TRUST PLAN

A wealthy couple with a long and trusting marriage, with no children by prior marriages, might prefer that each transfer his or her entire estate to the survivor; trusting the survivor to take care of the children and the grandchildren. Nevertheless, they would most likely want to at least use the shelter of a bypass trust to utilize S1's unified credit, thus the AB Trust plan would seem ideal. However, because the marital deduction is automatic for property from S1's estate transferred into Trust A, it does not allow sophisticated postmortem planning, such as the equalization of estates or some other apportionment between the two taxable estates. The AB with disclaimer into C (ABdC) Trust plan may be the answer for these couples. This plan begins by defining Trust B as a UCE trust, with S1's estate in excess of the UCE left to Trust A, which also holds S2's property. So far this sounds just like the modern AB Trust plan, however this one adds the provision that any of S1's property in excess of the UCE that is disclaimed by S2 goes into Trust C, a QTIP trust. The general rule of §2518 disqualifies a disclaimer from being tax effective if the disclaimant takes any benefit from the property disclaimed. However, §2518(b)(4)(A) allows an interest disclaimed that passes "to the spouse of the decedent, ..." to still qualify as a tax effective disclaimer. Thus, the surviving spouse (S2) can receive income from the trust, even have a 5 & 5 power (used for herself only), and can be the holder of a power to withdraw limited by an ascertainable standard. None of these "benefits" cause the disclaimer trust to be included in S2's estate. However, a 5 & 5 power will cause inclusion in S2's estate of that portion of the trust that could have been withdrawn by S2.

A disclaimer is considered to be tax effective if it avoids being treated as a taxable transfer from the disclaimant (S2 in this case) to whomever receives the property as a result of the disclaimer. To be tax effective, the person making the disclaimer cannot "direct" to whom the property goes, therefore, *this Trust C*, unlike the one in the ABC plan, must *not* give S2 even a limited power to appoint the property at her death. Remember, for the typical ABC, the limited power to appoint was an option for Trust C that creates flexibility.

The disclaimer is most likely to be used where, due to S2's poor health or extreme old age, S2 is not likely to live for very long after S1's death. Since the decision to disclaim is not made until after S1's death, the assessment of S2's health need not be made until then. However, §2518 requires that the decision of whether or not to disclaim be made within the nine months following S1's death.

EXAMPLE 12-3. When S1 died in 1994, the couple had an ABdC Trust. It gave S2 a life estate in Trust B, plus a power to withdraw corpus limited to an ascertainable standard, and she was given a limited power to appoint Trust B corpus amongst their children. In the absence of exercise of the power the remainder would be distributed to their issue by right of representation. Trust A was revocable by S2, and, to the extent she did not appoint it otherwise, it would also go to their issue by right of representation. Their combined net worth was $5,831,010; with S1's property worth $4,360,790 and S2's property worth $1,470,220. No disclaimer was made. Trust B received $600,000 from S1's estate; and the rest, plus all of S2's property, was added to Trust A, giving it a value of $5,231,010. Since the property in excess of the UCE went to Trust A, the estate automatically received a $3,760,790 marital deduction, thereby reducing S1's taxable estate to $600,000.

EXAMPLE 12-4. Suppose, S1 and S2 were in a fatal car accident in which S2 died just a couple of days after S1. The executor of S2's estate disclaimed all of S1's estate in excess of the UCE with the result that it went into Trust C instead of into Trust A, resulting in three trusts valued as follows: Trust A $1,470,220; Trust B $600,000; and Trust C $3,760,790. S1's executor could then QTIP all of Trust C to postpone all taxes to S2's death, but doing so would create very unequal estates. This would be foolish given that the tax on S2's estate would be due just a few days after the tax on S1's estate. Therefore, the executor of S1's estate QTIP'ed to equalize the two estates. You should be able to identify the 6 step process even though some steps are combined.

$$\frac{S1's\,E + S2's\,E}{2} = \frac{\$4,360,790 + \$1,470,220}{2} = \$2,915,505$$

The QTIP election necessary to reduce S1's estate from $4,360,790 to $2,915,505 is:

$$QTIP\ MD = \frac{\$1,445,285}{\$3,760,790} * \$3,760,790 = \$1,445,285$$

Therefore, taxable estates of S1 and S2 are:

$$S1's\,E = \$4,360,790 - \$1,445,285 = 2,915,505\ and$$
$$S2's\,E = \$1,470,220 + \frac{\$1,445,285}{\$3,760,790} * 3,760,790 = \$2,915,505$$

With the ABdC plan the equalization (or some other allocation between the two estates) can be accomplished by S2 (or S2's executor) making a partial disclaimer sufficient to equalize the two estates; and S1's executor forgoing the QTIP election.

EXAMPLE 12-5. S2's executor in the preceding example would simply disclaim that portion of S1's estate that would result in the two estates being equal in value as of S1's death. This requires a disclaimer by S2 (or the executor of S2's estate since S2 died soon after S1) of all of S1's estate that *exceeds* $1,445,285 (what is disclaimed won't go to S2, what is not disclaimed will). Trust A is then worth

$2,915,505 [$1,470,220 + $1,445,285)], Trust B is worth $600,000, and Trust C is worth $2,315,505 [$3,760,790 - $1,445,285]. S1's estate equals the combined value of trusts B and C [$2,915,505]; and S2's estate equals the value of Trust A, also $2,915,505.

It may be easier to grasp how just using a disclaimer (without a QTIP) can equalize the two estates (assuming S1's E > S2's E) if one simply divides the combined estates into two equal shares, places one share in Trust A, and spreads the balance between Trust B [UCE] and disclaimer Trust C. The amount in Trust C is the disclaimed amount. Of course, actual equalization works only when S1's estate is larger than S2's estate. If equalization is desired, and S1's estate is smaller than S2's estate, S2 should disclaim all of S1's estate that would otherwise come to her (or to her trust) because failure to do so would simply increase S2's estate, resulting in an even greater inequality.

> EXAMPLE 12-6. Using the facts in the prior example, let's calculate the disclaimer by the divide and allocate method. The combined value is $5,831,010, divided by two gives a desired taxable estate of $2,915,505. This is the value of Trust A. The sum of Trusts B (valued at $600,000) and C (the balance at $2,315,505) equal S1's total taxable estate, which is also equal to the desired taxable estate of $2,915,505. Since Trust C is "filled" by the disclaimer, the amount to be disclaimed is $2,315,505. It is simple algebra: Desired taxable estate = Trust B + Trust C. Therefore, Trust C = Desired taxable estate - Trust B. Since Trust B is equal to the UCE, it is easy to solve for Trust C. Finally, Trust C also equals the amount disclaimed.

A tax effective disclaimer must be delivered to S1's executor within nine months after S1's death, therefore, if S2's state of health is uncertain as that deadline approaches, S2 can make the disclaimer, and the decision as to whether to QTIP Trust C can be delayed a further six months by S1's executor obtaining a six month extension to file the tax return, together with an extension to pay the tax. S2's poor health and the need for additional time to assess the wisdom of making the QTIP election is sufficient justification for the six month extension. Six months is the longest allowed extension for filing the estate tax return if the executor is within the country.[1] Although it is possible to make a QTIP election on a late filed return, the penalties for late filing (if one decided against making the election) might out-weigh any benefits derived by splitting the tax between the two estates.

Choosing between the ABC plan and the ABdC plan is like choosing between varieties of apples rather than between apples and oranges. The main difference being that, with the ABdC plan, S2 decides whether to take control of S1's estate that exceeds the UCE, whereas S2 has no such option with the ABC plan. Although a limited power may be part of the ABC plan for both Trusts B and C, it can only be used with Trust B in the ABdC plan. Also, the ABdC Trust is a much more complicated plan to explain to clients. In those situations where a tax should be generated at the first death, it may be more difficult to carry out with the disclaimer plan due to S2's poor health, whereas, with the ABC plan, it is S1's executor who makes the QTIP election.

For large estates using the ABC plan where there is a possible savings by making only a partial QTIP election but, because of the time-value of money, the executor wants to defer the tax until the second death, the executor is always well advised to obtain the six-month extension to allow the longest possible time to evaluate S2's heath before making (or foregoing) the QTIP election. With the ABdC, the disclaimer must be made within nine months of S1's death or it is not tax effective so it is not possible to get an extra six months "wait-and-see" period.

True, with an ABdC plan, S2 can always make a disclaimer that would accomplish the optimal split between the two taxable estates, and the executor of S1's estate could then wait until the six month extension period is almost up to file the return, making or not making the QTIP election at that time (depending upon S2's health), but that is a much more complicated way to create an ABC plan. Besides, as stated earlier, the ABdC plan must also have a more restrictive Trust C, i.e., S2 must be denied a limited power of appointment. Furthermore, S2 might be too ill to make a disclaimer, a circumstance that might indicate that generating a tax in S1's estate would be wise. A court is likely to rule that the right to disclaim is personal to S2, so long as she is alive, whereas the decision to make a QTIP election rests with S1's executor. Even if S2 is nominated as executor of S1's estate, but is too ill to serve, the successor executor can make the appropriate election.

A durable power of attorney, discussed later in this book, could be written for S2 with enough specificity to allow the holder of the power to make a disclaimer if S2 is too ill to do it herself. Most durable powers, as presently written, are too general to accomplish this and, unless there is specific language authorizing the agent to make a disclaimer, it might not withstand challenge by the IRS. Of course, if S2 dies before the nine months are up, S2's executor can make the disclaimer, assuming he or she can be quickly appointed by the court. Given that S2 is dead, the probate court is not likely to object to a disclaimer that is made to save death taxes, especially if the remaindermen of all trusts are the same people.

NONCITIZEN SURVIVING SPOUSES: THE QDOT TRUST

All property passing outright to the surviving spouse qualifies for the marital deduction, unless that spouse is not a U.S. citizen. In that case, to qualify, the property must pass instead to a "qualified" domestic trust, (QDOT). The intent is to ensure collection of ET on marital deduction property intended for the benefit of a spouse who may have less secure ties with the U.S. than exist for most citizens.

According to the requirements of IRS §2056A(a), at least one of the trustees of a QDOT must be a U.S. citizen or domestic corporation. Trusts exceeding $2 million at S1's death must either have a bank as trustee (or co-trustee), or else the trustee must furnish a bond or security of at least 65% of the value of the corpus.

Estate tax is imposed (once S1's unified credit is exhausted) on any corpus distributed prior to the spouse's death, and on the value of the corpus remaining at the spouse's death (or sooner, if the trust ceases to qualify as a QDOT). However, distribution of income, and distribution of principal on account of "hardship," are exempt from the tax.[2] The tax is the amount that would have been imposed, after all credits, had the property subject to the tax been included in S1's taxable estate.

The trust need not have been created by the decedent prior to death; either the executor or the surviving spouse may create the QDOT prior to the due date of the S1's U.S. estate tax return including extensions. For a QDOT created after S1's death, the surviving spouse must irrevocably assign marital deduction property to the trust before the due date of the return.

The surviving noncitizen spouse's choice of whether or not to transfer S1's property into a QDOT trust may be based on the decision to defer or to equalize their estates. If S2 creates and funds a QDOT trust, S1's estate will get a marital deduction for the property, but the property will be subject to ET at S2's death (or earlier, if trust property is transferred to S2 during her lifetime). Alternatively, if S2 accepts the property without transferring it to a QDOT, the property will be subject to S1 estate taxation immediately, but may avoid ET later to the extent S2 can convert the property into "non-U.S. situs" assets. Some noncitizen S2s may prefer to pay the tax up-front, then take the property, and disappear. S1's estate will have $600,000 sheltered by the unified credit even if the estate is left to a non-U.S. citizen spouse.

ESTATE PLANS SELDOM SEEN

We cover next several estate plans that you are not likely to see in your practice, but are of interest because they will come up from time to time at continuing education seminars or in discussions with colleagues. The Estate Trust was never popular because of its limitations; the Traditional AB Trust was very popular until 1982, when the 100% marital deduction and the QTIP election made it obsolete. The QTIP election and the lowering of the top marginal rates made the inflexible Estate Equalization Trust less desirable than ABC Trusts, since the latter can accomplish the same tax savings but gives S1 greater control over who will be the remaindermen and gives S1's executor more options.

ESTATE TRUST

An unusual type of marital trust called the Estate Trust is almost never used. Its unique feature is that during S2's lifetime the terms of the trust allow the trustee discretion as to how much income to distribute to S2, but at S2's death all accumulated income and corpus must be distributed to S2's probate estate. Consequently, trust income can be accumulated and taxed at trust rates, but given the compressed nature of those rates, there is little reason to use this trust in an attempt to save income taxes. The reason this plan qualifies for the marital deduction is that it is not considered a terminable interest since the interest of S2 does not shift to someone else (see the definition of a terminable interest at §2056(b)(1)). Given the greater flexibility of the QTIP trust, which allows the marital deduction while letting S1 control the remainder interest, it is difficult to imagine a reason to use one of these trusts.

THE TRADITIONAL AB TRUST

The Traditional AB Trust (TAB) is the name for those estate plans, drafted during the period from 1948 through 1981, that were designed to use the maximum marital deduction then available. For large estates, the maximum marital deduction was 50% of the adjusted gross estate (AGE). That amount was "given" to S2 by way of a marital deduction trust, and that portion of S1's estate that could not escape taxation at S1's death was left to a bypass trust, thus avoiding S2's estate. The tax savings for these old plans came not at the first death but at the second death. The idea was to transfer into Trust A, in addition to S2's property, so much of S1's estate as exactly equaled the maximum marital deduction available to S1's estate, and to pass the rest of S1's estate (the taxed portion) into Trust B. Smaller estates (those under $500,000) could use the alternate minimum marital deduction of $250,000 for decedents dying between 1977 and 1981, inclusive, but for larger estates, even during that time-frame, the 50% AGE was the controlling factor. Because the pre-1982 marital deduction was limited to 50% of AGE, the property going into Trust B would have been taxed even if it passed directly to S2, therefore, placing it in Trust B did not increase the estate tax at S1's death, but doing so did allow it to avoid S2's estate when S2 died.

As with the more modern plans, Trust A generally held all of S2's property; in addition it received from S1's estate the maximum marital deduction amount. In common law states this would be equal to 50% of S1's net estate. In community property states, because the marital deduction was not allowed for the community property, the marital deduction was 50% of S1's separate property.

The names given the two trusts are similar to the names now used for the modern AB Trust plan. Trust A might have been called the Survivor's Trust, the Marital Deduction Trust, or General Power of Appointment Trust. S2 had to receive all income for life and hold a general power of appointment over it.[3] The names and characteristics of Trust B were similar to those for the Trust B of the modern AB trust except instead of being equal to the UCE amount, the trust was funded with all that property which would not qualify for the martial deduction, hence, 50% of S1's separate property and S1's half of the community property. The trust was likely to be called the Trust B or the Bypass Trust. Like the credit shelter trust of the modern AB plan, it could be a sprinkling trust benefitting the children as well as S2, but it was much more commonly created with all income being given to S2. A sprinkling trust with S2 as both trustee and one of the potential beneficiaries has all the trust income taxed to S2 anyway. This defeats one of the primary reasons for having a sprinkling provision in a trust, namely the ability to lower over-all income taxes within a group of beneficiaries by distributing more income to the lower tax bracket members. It was very common to give S2 invasion rights limited to an ascertainable standard. Also common were B Trusts in which S2 had limited powers to appoint amongst the children, and, less commonly, S2 was given a 5 & 5 power.

EXAMPLE 12-7. Compare two pre-1982 estate plans. The first one is referred to as the 100% S1 to S2 plan, one where S1 leaves everything to S2 and, upon S2's death, everything goes to their children. The second one is a TAB in which, after S1's death, S1's taxable estate goes into a bypass trust (Trust B) and the maximum marital deduction amount, plus all of S2's property goes into Trust A, a general power of appointment trust. Upon S2's death, Trusts A and B terminate and go to their children. When S1 died in 1965, S1 owned separate property worth $1,800,000 and S2 owned separate property $200,000; in addition they had community property worth $300,000. S2 died in 1976 and between deaths the assets had doubled in value. Pre-1977 tax rates are used.

With plan one, all of S1's estate, less estate tax is transferred to S2 and doubles in value. With plan two, Trust A was funded with property worth $1,250,000 [the ½ of S1's separate that qualifies for the marital deduction, plus S2's separate property and S2's half of the community property] and Trust B with property out of S1's estate worth $1,050,000 [½ S1's separate property plus S1's half of the community property].

	100% S1 ---> S2		TAB Trust	
	S1 d1965	S2 d1976	S1 d1965	S2 d1976
GE	$1,950,000	$3,956,000	$1,950,000	$2,500,000
MD	(900,000)	0	(900,000)	0
EstEx	(60,000)	(60,000)	(60,000)	(60,000)
TxE	$990,000	$3,896,000	$990,000	$2,440,000
Tax	$322,000	$1,776,800	$322,000	$968,800

The entire estate tax savings of $808,040 [$1,776,800 - $968,800] occurred at the second death; the bypass trust kept Trust B property from being taxed again in S2's estate. The value of Trust B [$1,050,000 - $322,000 = $728,000] doubled; therefore, $1,456,000 avoided the second tax. The tax saved is equal to 55.5% of the latter figure, corresponding roughly to the pre-1977 average marginal rate between $2,500,000 and $4,000,000.

Notice that with a TAB, the marital deduction for Trust A is in terms of dollar amounts (not as a QTIP Fraction), because part of S1's separate property is transferred from S1's estate into Trust A, the trust over which S2 has a general power of appointment; therefore, the marital deduction is automatic, unlike the QTIP trust for which an election must be made in order to claim a marital deduction. Furthermore, at S2's death, all of Trust A is included in S2's estate, not just a fraction of it. Some plans written prior to 1981 still exist, and as demonstrated in the above example, Trust B may exceed the UCE amount. Even though it makes little sense today to have S1's separate property split equally between Trusts A and B, neither the executor nor the trustee can rewrite the decedent's estate plan. However, the tax laws allow the executor to obtain a marital deduction on Trust B, by making the QTIP election provided S2 has the requisite income interest. Fortunately, most of these old TAB plans do give S2 a life estate in Trust B. As discussed before, the QTIP'ed portion is expressed as that fraction of Trust B necessary to bring S1's taxable estate down to the desired taxable estate (most commonly the UCE). It is that same fraction that determines the amount of Trust B includable in S2's estate, therefore, it must be expressed as a fraction rather than as a dollar amount. *** *Query 1. What would be the QTIP fraction for the above example had S1 died in 1995 instead of 1965 and the executor wanted to postpone all tax?*

THE ESTATE EQUALIZATION AB TRUST

The funding of the two trusts created at S1's death required the executor of S1's estate to have S2's property valued too. Trust B was funded such that it exactly equaled half of the combined values. These plans enjoyed some popularity for very large estates when the maximum marginal rate was 77% for estates over $10 million. With the QTIP trust and the possibility of using a partial QTIP election there is much greater flexibility in allocation between the two estates, and if S2 is healthy at the time S1's estate tax return is prepared it is likely that Trust C will be fully QTIP'ed, therefore there is no need to have S2's property valued, whereas with the old Estate Equalization AB Trusts, all assets had to be valued to determine the funding amount for Trust B. With an ABC plan, an AsuperB plan, or an ABdC plan, S2's property needs to be appraised at S1's death only if the executor of S1's estate desires to use the QTIP election to equalize (or optimize) the two taxable estates.

General Comments on Estate Planning Using Trusts

From an estate planning standpoint, almost anything that can be described in words, with or without examples, that one can get a trustee to agree to carry-out, can be accomplished through the use of trusts, so long as it is legal and not against public policy. Any of the plans discussed here can be accomplished by a testamentary trust just as well as through a living trust with the exception of avoiding probate at the first death. With a testamentary trust the funding process at the first death is the probate court's order for distribution.

State death tax. For the most part, we have ignored the influence of state death taxes. Generally, their effect is relatively small compared to the impact of the Federal tax, and in most states are of no consequence due to the Federal credit for state death taxes. As explained earlier, a slight majority of the states, plus the District of Columbia, impose only a pickup tax, that is, an amount exactly equal to the Federal credit for state death taxes. Consequently, in these states, no additional taxes are paid as a result of the state death tax. The remaining states impose a death tax that may be larger than the pickup amount, but usually is not unless the estate is going to non-family members.

Revocable living trust versus the testamentary trust. The main advantage to the living trust is that it avoids probate of the settlor's assets to the extent they are held in trust at the time of the settlor's death. The testamentary trust is funded through the probate process and does have the advantage that in most states the probate process considerably shortens the period during which creditors can assert their claims.

One living family trust or separate trusts for each spouse. A one trust document plan for both spouses, called a *joint spousal grantor trust*, will work as long as the assets of each spouse are carefully identified and distinguished. It does not have the gift tax danger and dispositive restrictions of the joint and mutual will, which generally is irrevocable as to all probate assets at the first spouse's death. In contrast, the most usual pattern in the joint trust is for the surviving spouse's assets, plus any assets from S1's estate that are added to Trust A, to remain subject to S2's control.

If commingling of spousal assets (individually owned property) is a significant risk, each spouse could execute his or her *own* living trust document. Another reason for two trusts is that a poorly drafted joint spousal grantor trust document could give rise to estate or gift tax consequences for wealthier clients, particularly when the spouses fund the trust with different amounts of individually owned property. For example, the spouse contributing the greater amount may be deemed to have made a taxable gift of a terminable interest in a portion of the trust to the other spouse, if the terms of the trust do not qualify the transfer for the marital deduction. The latter is not likely to occur with a well drafted joint trust because they are usually revocable so long as both spouse's are alive, and the portions that are irrevocable after the first death are designed to either use the unified credit or to qualify for the marital deduction.

Debts and expenses. Of course, any estate will have deductible debts and expenses, which will alter the calculations. Expenses in administering a decedent's probate estate typically range between 5 and 10% of the total estate. Ordinarily, estate planners handle debts and expenses in the following manner: Regarding *debts*, in performing the calculations, planners use net worth as the value of the estate property; regarding *expenses*, planners either estimate the expenses or simply ignore them because they are not likely to have a significant influence on the choice of estate plans. Given the complexity of multiple trust plans, most planners want to keep the calculations used as examples as simple as possible without misleading the client. Perhaps making a gift of a copy of this book is a good idea.

THE PTC AND BYPASS TRUSTS[4]

Illogical though it might be, the prior transfer credit (PTC) is available for D2's interest in a life estate created by D1. What is deemed to have been transferred from D1 to D2 is the value of the life estate, measured as of the date of D1's death. Valuation is based upon the life table factors published by the Treasury, even though, due to the PTC time factor, this credit would seldom be available to anyone who lived out the life expectancy stated in the table. In the example that follows, D1 is D and B (the income beneficiary) is D2.

> EXAMPLE 12-8. On March 4, 1992, when D died, her net estate, worth $2,359,985 went into a Trust, with income for life to B (age 60) with a remainder to R (age 40). D's estate paid death taxes of $764,393, of which $127,599 was paid to D's state and the balance, $636,794 was paid to the Federal Government. B died on August 10, 1994, leaving an estate with a net value of $1,850,775 to three nephews. The trust established by D was distributed to R a few months after B's death. Although the trust's value was then in excess of $4 million, no additional taxes were paid because the trust was not included in B's estate.

PTC Step 1. The value of the property *transferred* to B before adjustment for taxes is the value of B's life estate. The Federal rate for valuing split interest gifts for the month of March, 1992, was 8%, therefore, the life estate factor for a 60 year old income beneficiary was .71621, and the value of the property deemed to be "transferred" is $1,690,245. Limit one is:

$$LT1 \; = \; \frac{\$1,690,245}{\$2,359,985} \; * \; \$636,794 \; = \; \$456,078$$

Of course, the fraction reduces to the life estate factor since we used the factor in the first place to arrive at the value of the life estate. Therefore, limit one in this case can be calculated by multiplying the factor times the Federal tax, as follows:

$$LT1 = .71261 * \$636,794 = \$456,078.$$

PTC Step 2. The tax on B's $1,850,775 taxable estate without a PTC is $520,849, of which $88,856 is state death tax and $431,993 is the Federal estate tax. To determine the second limit, the Federal tax on the reduced estate must be calculated and subtracted from the Federal tax on B's taxable estate. The reduced estate is $1,850,775 less the amount deemed transferred and subtracted from the Federal tax on B's taxable estate net of its share of the total death taxes:

Federal Estate Tax on B's $1,850,775 taxable estate.	$431,993
Less Federal Estate Tax B's reduced estate of $707,996	
i.e., $1,850,775 - .71621 * ($2,359,985 - $764,393)	(21,575)
Credit limit two	$410,418

Remember, the amounts shown as Federal estate tax, $421,993 for the full estate and $21,575 for the reduced estate, is the actual Federal tax (after the unified credit and the state death tax credit) on taxable estates of $1,850,775 and $707,996, respectively. To arrive at the *reduced taxable estate*, B's taxable estate is reduced by the net value of what was deemed to have been transferred to B. What was deemed transferred is the value of B's life estate in the B and C trusts, after all the estate taxes generated at S1's death have been removed from them, i.e., 0.71621*($2,359,985 - $764,393). Note that $764,393 is the total tax at D's death, not just the Federal tax.

PTC Step 3. Since B died more than two years, but less than four years, after D, the time factor is 80% and the actual PTC is:

$$80\% \; * \; \textit{the lesser of} \begin{cases} \textit{limit one}: \$456,078 \\ \textit{limit two}: \$410,418 \end{cases} = \; \$328,334$$

Therefore, B's estate pays taxes as follows:

Death taxes before PTC & State D Tx Cr	$520,849
less State Death Tax Credit	(88,856)
less Prior Transfer Credit	(328,334)
Federal Estate Tax	$103,659

Total taxes = $88,856 + $103,659 = $192,515

The state death tax credit is not changed by the presence of a PTC. In the above hypothetical, the PTC eliminates over three-quarters of the second tax even though none of the corpus of the trust was actually transferred into B's estate.

If the remainderman dies after the income beneficiary, but still within ten years of the settlor (D1), there will also be a PTC for the remainderman's estate based on the remainder value at D1's death of the remainderman's interest. If the remainder is vested, and remainderman dies before the income beneficiary, the remainderman-decedent's interest in the remainder must be valued for inclusion in the remainderman's estate. This value is based upon the beneficiary's age (B's age), the value of the trust, and the Federal split-interest gift rate (§7520 rate) at that time. R in the above example would become D2 for purpose of computing the PTC for his estate. Obviously, the income beneficiary will be older than he or she was when the trust was established, therefore the remainder factor (from Table S) is likely to be higher, however this depends upon the Federal §7520 rate at R's death. Thus, the amount included in R's estate insofar as the trust is concerned would be the remainder factor (based B's age) times the trust's value as of R's death. These changes are taken into account when calculating the value of the remainder in R's (D2) gross estate, but in calculating the value of what was transferred for determining the PTC limits, one must continue to use the value of the remainder as of D1's death. Remember, any change in value, insofar as the *property transferred* is concerned, is irrelevant to the PTC calculation. What is deemed to have transferred, is based on the values at D1's death, and that is the value used in calculating R's reduced estate. To the extent the value of a trust (or a vested remainder in a trust) is actually part of D2's estate, any change will change the value of D2's taxable estate.

THE PTC AND THE QTIP ELECTION

The PTC has its greatest estate planning potential when utilized in conjunction with the ABC, AsuperB, or ABdC estate plans, because the partial QTIP election gives S1's executor some control in the allocation of the couple's total estate between the two taxable estates. For large estates, if the surviving spouse is diagnosed as terminally ill before S1's estate tax return is filed, it may be better to make either no QTIP election or only a partial QTIP election, so that some taxes are generated in the first estate, which in turn will generate a PTC for the second estate. The optimal QTIP election is one where the QTIP fraction used is one that will best utilize lower marginal tax rates for both estates and the PTC for S2's estate in such a way that the greatest amount possible passes to the children. This is demonstrated in the example set that follows. Keep in mind that the maximum extension to file is six months, therefore, the maximum period after S1's death to assess S2's health is 15 months.

FACTS FOR THE EXAMPLE SET: At the time of S1's death on October 11, 1993, S1 and S2 had community property worth $843,760, S1 owned separate property worth $4,450,920, and S2 owned separate property worth $975,688. Their estate plan was a modern ABC Trust plan, with S2 having a life estate in Trusts B and C. S1 died at age 75, survived by 65 year old S2. The Federal rate for valuing split interest gifts for October of 1993 was 6%. The net value going into each trust after S1's death was: Trust A $1,397,568; Trust B $600,000; and Trust C $4,272,800. When S1 died, S2 was in extremely poor health, but had a greater than 50% probability of living at least a year.

EXAMPLE 12-9. S1's executor was very diligent at assembling the information and valuations necessary to file the estate tax return by its due date of July 11, 1994. He elected to QTIP all of Trust C so as not to pay any tax. Unfortunately, S2 died December 27, 1994. The assets in the three trusts had increased in value by 10%. As a result, the three trusts at S2's death were worth: Trust A $1,537,325; Trust B $660,000; and Trust C $4,700,080; for a total value of $6,897,405. S2's taxable estate was the combined value of Trusts A and C, so, although this strategy resulted in zero taxes at S1's death, S2's executor paid $2,878,573 at S2's death. The net amount going to the children was the total of the three trusts, less the tax:

$$\$6,897,405 - \$2,878,573 = \$4,018,832$$

EXAMPLE 12-10. In this alternative version, S1's executor was very cautious.

Although she had also diligently assembled the information and valuations necessary to file the estate tax return by its due date of July 11, 1994, she obtained an extension to file and to pay until January 11, 1995; intending to re-assess S2's health as that latter date approached. S2's death on December 27, 1994 made re-assessment unnecessary. The assets in the three trusts had increased in value by 10%. S1's executor chose the optimal QTIP election, even though it meant Trusts B and C would have to paid their pro rata share of the S1 estate taxes about a year earlier than if they were postponed until S2's return was due, and some interest would have to be paid for the six month extension period. The interest amount for both the Federal and state death taxes would also be deductible on S1's return (the interest deduction is an interrelated calculation). Since she had obtained an extension to file and to pay, no penalties had to be paid. To work through to the amounts paid at each death we will follow the six step QTIP calculations (combining some of the steps in the interest of brevity). At Step 5, we will calculate S1's taxes. To simplify, interest is not taken here as a deduction although in a real situation it would be. Step 6 is followed by the three step PTC calculation for S2's estate to determine S2's taxes. From the value of the three trusts at S2's death, we will subtract the amount of taxes for both estates, and also subtract the estimated interest on S1's late paid taxes to come up with the net amount going to the children. Finally, we compare the net amount going to the children with this alternative to the net amount with the 100% QTIP alternative.

Step 1. By trial and error the executor determined that the best result (the largest after tax transfer to the children) was accomplished when S1's taxable estate equaled $3,811,009.

Step 2. The marital deduction necessary to achieve the desired taxable estate:

$$\$4,872,800 - \$3,811,009 = MD = \$1,061,791$$

Step 3. Trust C is the QTIP property, therefore the QTIP Fraction is:

$$\$1,061,791/\$4,272,800$$

Steps 4 & 5. S1's taxable estate equals S1's estate less the marital deduction that results from the QTIP election. Therefore, S1's taxable estate equals:

$$\$4,872,800 - \$1,061,791 = \$3,811,009$$

This results in Federal taxes of $1,283,310 and state death taxes of $260,745, for a total of $1,544,055.

Step 6. S2's estate equals Trust A plus the QTIP fraction times Trust C's value at S2's death. Therefore, S2's taxable estate equals:

$$S2'sE = \$1,537,325 + (\frac{\$1,061,791}{\$4,272,800}) * \$4,700,080 = \$2,705,295$$

Having determined S2's taxable estate, we turn our attention to calculating the PTC and the estate taxes that will have to be paid.

PTC Step 1. Limit one: Since the Federal rate for October of 1993 was 6% and S2 was 65 years old, the factor for computing her life estate value was .56599.

$$.56599 * \$1,283,310 = \$726,314$$

PTC Step 2. Limit two: The total taxes on an estate of $2,705,295 before taking the PTC is $941,806, of which $156,066 is the state death tax and $785,740 is the Federal death tax.

Federal Estate Tax on $2,705,295	$785,740
Less Tax on S2's reduced Taxable Estate of $821,258, i.e.,	
$2,705,295 - .56599 * ($4,872,800 - $1,544,055)	(59,470)
Credit limit two	$726,270

Again, a reminder that the Federal tax amounts, used to arrive at limit two, are the tax on the S2's taxable estate and on S2's reduced taxable estate, calculated by taking both the unified credit and the state death tax credit into account.

PTC Step 3. Since S2 died within two years of S1's death, the time factor is 100% and the actual PTC is:

$$100\% * \text{ the lesser of } \begin{cases} \text{limit one: } \$726,341 \\ \text{limit two: } \$726,270 \end{cases} = \$726,270$$

Therefore, S2's estate pays taxes as follows:

Death taxes before PTC & State D Tx Cr	$941,806
less State Death Tax Credit	(156,066)
less Prior Transfer Credit	(726,270)
Federal Estate Tax	$59,470

The total death tax for both estates using the optimal QTIP election is $1,759,591 [$1,544,055 + $156,066 + $59,470] compared to $2,878,573 when the 100% QTIP election is made. The difference in tax is $1,118,976 of which $726,470 is attributable to the PTC and the balance is due to the utilization of lower marginal rates in the first estate rather than "loading upon" the second estate by making a 100% Trust C QTIP election. S1's estate would have to pay approximately $70,000 in interest (about 4.5% because it for just six months) on the late paid taxes. Compare the value going to the children using the optimal QTIP election with what was previously calculated. In both cases we are assuming the total value of the three trusts at S2's death to be the same since S1's taxes were not paid until after S2 died. Therefore, the value of the trusts (at S2's death) less the taxes and the interest (estimated to be $70,000) would be as follows:

$$\$6,897,405 - \$1,759,591 - \$70,000 = \$5,067,814$$

The optimal QTIP results in $1,048,982 [$5,067,814 - $4,018,832] more to the children than with the 100% QTIP election.

This potential savings that comes from using the PTC with multiple trust plans is obviously just as important as the utilization of both unified credits. It results form the phantom transfer from S1's estate to S2, (the fact that an estate is allowed a PTC based upon the hypothetical value of S2's life estate) even though, due to S2's death, very little is actually transferred. Of course it is limited in usefulness to those times when the two deaths are close enough in time to utilize the PTC.

The optimal QTIP fraction depends on the following factors:
  ▸ the Federal rate for valuing split interest gifts such as life estates;
  ▸ the age of S2;
  ▸ the combined value of the couple's estates; and finally,
  ▸ whether S1's estate equals, or exceeds, the amount necessary to make the optimal mix.

Given the multiple factors (age, rate, values) and the fact the fact that only a portion of S1's estate is deemed to have been transferred, the optimal QTIP fraction tends to be one that taxes more of the combined total in S1's estate. However, for combined estates between $1,200,000 and $6,000,000, if the second death is very likely to occur within two years of the first, the optimal result will generally require a QTIP election that brings S2's estate almost equal to that of S1. With very large estates, the optimal QTIP fraction is likely to be one that causes S1's taxable estate to be considerably larger than S2's. For instance, with combined estates over $20,000,000, the optimal allocation between the two estates is likely to require a taxable estate for S1 that is significantly larger than that of S2. For these large estates, as much as 75% to 80% of the combined values should taxed at S1's death, with only 20% to 25% at S2's death, if the goal is to pass the greatest amount possible to the children or other heirs. The exact ratio can be determined by trial and error - or by using a computer program. Even for very large estates, a QTIP election that equalizes the two estates generally produces results fairly close to those achieved by the optimal QTIP election; and certainly very superior to the 100% QTIP alternative. *** *Query 2. Using the facts from the above example set, what is the QTIP fraction that equalizes the two estates as of S1's death? Remember, the fraction is applied only to Trust C.*

THE GENERATION SKIPPING TRANSFER TAX

Up to now, we have focused our tax planning discussion on how gifts and trusts are used to reduce transfer taxes for the nuclear family, i.e., S1, S2, and their children. Similar planning works for transfers to more remote family members. For example, a childless couple could develop a bypass plan for nephews and nieces. A bypass trust plan works well for any survivors who belong to the same, or to the next generation.

Complexity arises when a bypass trust (or of an outright transfer) skips the estates of the transferor's children. The Generation-Skipping Transfer Tax (GSTT) is designed to capture additional taxes, such that the total transfer tax approximates that which would have been collected had the property passed through the estates of the children. It is imposed on direct skips, taxable terminations, and taxable distributions to, or for the benefit of, a skip person. A skip person is a beneficiary who is at least two generations younger than the transferor. For this discussion, think in terms of grandparent, parent, and grandchild, with the grandchild being the skip person vis-a-vis the grandparent. Keep in mind that this GSTT is not appreciably "unified" with gift and estate taxes; it is a separate tax having its own unique rules. The tax is reported on Form 706 (for transfers at death) and Form 709 (for gifts), shown in Appendices C and D, respectively.[5]

Purpose of the GSTT

The purpose of the GSTT is to assure that large estates, as they pass from one generational level to the next, are subjected to a transfer tax. Prior to the mid-1980's, a common method for the very wealthy to pass their estates through many generations was to create trusts that would benefit first the children for their lives, then the grandchildren, and then the great-grandchildren for as long as the rule against perpetuities would allow. Transfer tax (either the estate tax or the gift tax) would be levied only upon the establishment of the trust. No new taxes would be levied as the interests passed from one generation to the next. These were the ultimate bypass trusts designed to last over a hundred years.

The first generation-skipping transfer tax was enacted in 1976. Although planners found it quite complicated, they quickly learned that the tax was easy to circumvent. In fact, there is widespread belief among planners that no one ever filed a return under the 1976 Generation-Skipping Transfer Tax. As a result, in 1986, Congress acknowledged its error by repealing it retroactively, and at the same time, enacting the new, more comprehensive law described below. Trusts that became irrevocable prior to September 25, 1985 are grandfathered, that is, not subject any generation-skipping transfer tax.

Overview of the Current GSTT

The solution devised by Congress is to tax transfers that skip a generation, and to tax such transfers even if they are (or have been) subject to the regular transfer tax (whether gift or estate). The tax levied on a generation skipping transfer (GST) is called the Generation Skipping Transfer Tax (GSTT). A GST is a transfer to a "skip person," defined as a person two or more generations below the transferor or a trust whose beneficiaries are all skip persons.[6] The basic rule, simple enough to state but complicated in the application, is as follows:

GSTT = the Taxable Amount x the Applicable Rate[7]

Think of the taxable amount as the value of the gift or estate that is given to a skip person or to skip persons. Complications set in because the taxable amount depends upon whether the transfer is a direct skip, a taxable termination, or a taxable distribution. The *applicable rate* is the maximum Federal estate tax rate multiplied by the inclusion ratio. The *inclusion ratio* is determined by the amount of the $1 million dollar per donor GST exemption that is allocated by the donor to the transfer. We will start by covering the calculation of the tax for each of the three types of skips, but to keep this as simple as possible, the initial examples will assume no allocation of the exemption. Later we will consider the allocation of the exemption and look at examples were it is a factor.

Calculating the GSTT

The taxable amount depends upon whether the transfer is a direct skip, a taxable termination or a taxable distribution. Keep in mind that the goal is to approximate the transfer tax that would be levied if the property passed through each generational level. Generally, unless the governing instrument by specific reference to the GSTT provides otherwise, the GSTT must be charged to the property transferred.

Direct skips. A direct skip is a transfer to a skip person that is subject to an estate or gift tax.[8] Generally, these are outright gifts or bequests from grandparents to grandchildren. For all direct skips, other than a direct skip *from* a trust, the liability for the GSTT is placed upon the transferor.[9] The taxable amount, in the case of a direct skip, is the value of the property received by the transferee.[10] This means that in the case of a bequest, the taxable amount is net of its share of debts, expenses, etc., and its share of the death taxes (both Federal and state). Alternate valuation and special use valuation elections are available to reduce the taxable amount of direct skips that meet the requirements of §§2032 and 2032A, respectively. For gifts of a present interest, the annual exclusion also reduces the taxable amount for GST purposes.

> EXAMPLE 12 - 11. Barry makes a gift of Bucky Company common stock worth $750,000 to his granddaughter Julie. He had used his $1 million exemption on earlier gifts to other grandchildren and his $10,000 annual exclusion on an earlier gift to Julie. Because of those earlier gifts Barry pays gift taxes of $322,500 and a GSTT of $412,500 [$750,000 x 0.55].

Things get a little more complicated with direct skips from a decedent. The GSTT is paid by the estate (the transferor) and the GSTT should not itself be subjected to the GSTT, therefore multiplying the net estate by 55% will produce a tax that is too high. The result for an estate should be the same as if the transfer was a direct skip gift. Let's look at the last example, after the regular gift tax had been paid, Barry (the donor) parted with assets worth $1,162,500 to make a gift to Julie of $750,000. The $1,162,500 is the gift of $750,000 plus the GSTT of $412,500. In order to leave a skip person $750,000 by way of a bequest (instead of a gift) would require a net estate (before the GSTT) of $1,162,500. The GSTT of $412,500 divided by $1,162,500 equals 0.3548387, which is the GSTT rate for direct skips from a decedent.

EXAMPLE 12 - 12. During her life, Tisha had used up her $1 million exemption on gifts to grandchildren. Her net estate, after payment of the Federal estate tax and the state death tax was $1,162,500. She left her entire estate to Frank, her favorite grandson. The estate paid $412,500 in GSTT [0.3548387 x $1,162,500]. Frank actually received just $750,000.

Part 2 of Schedule R of the U.S. Estate Tax Return (Form 706) shows the steps for calculating the GSTT for direct skips. Notice that after subtracting debts, regular death taxes, and the exemption the net amount left is divided by 2.818182 to determine the GSTT (see line 8 of Schedule R). How does this number relate to the 0.3548387 rate given above? Dividing "1" by 0.3548387 equals 2.818182, therefore the result will be the same whether one divides the net estate (net after regular tax) by 2.818182 or whether one multiplies it by 0.3548387.

Taxable terminations. A taxable termination means that a shift in interest from one generation to the next has occurred as a result of the death of a person, the release of an interest, the passage of time, or otherwise. The trustee is liable for the GSTT in the case of a taxable termination and in the case of a direct skip from a trust. The taxable amount is the value of the property with respect to which the taxable termination has occurred, reduced by any expenses or indebtedness that would be deductible under §2053. If the taxable termination is the result of the death of an interested party, the alternate valuation election may be made in accordance with §2032.

Just because a GST trust terminates, does not mean that a taxable termination has occurred. Whether it is also a taxable termination depends on whether the termination resulted in a shift from one generation to another. Furthermore, as shown in the examples that follow, a taxable termination may occur without the trust itself terminating.

EXAMPLE 12 - 13. When grandpa Xuyen died in 1990 his estate plan created a trust which gave income for life to his son Ha, remainder to Ha's issue by right of representation, except that if any of Ha's children were under age 35, the assets were to remain in trust until the youngest reached age 35. Because the executor allocated the $1 million exemption to direct skips, none of the exemption was allocated to the trust. When Ha died in 1995 the trust was worth $2,000,000 and Ha's youngest child, Yi Yun, was 32 years old. Because the death of Ha causes the interest to shift to a younger generation, even though the trust does not terminate, a taxable termination has occurred. The tax payable by the trustee is $1,100,000, leaving just $900,000 in the trust.

EXAMPLE 12 - 14. Continuing the prior example: In 1998, shortly after Yi Yun's 35th birthday, the trust corpus, valued at $1,090,000, was distributed to him and his brother Sui-on. Since this is not a shift in generations, there is no new GSTT (nor any other transfer tax) as a result of the trust terminating. Had Yi Yun died after his father, but before his 35 birthday, with the result that his interest went to his children, there would be a GSTT on his share. On the other hand, if he died before his 35th birthday, but left no issue with the result that Sui-on received his share, there would be no additional GSTT because the two brothers are in the same generation.

Taxable Distributions. The Code gives a functional definition for a *taxable distribution*: "the term 'taxable distribution' means any distribution from a trust to a skip person (other than a taxable termination or a direct skip)."[11] This covers situations where a trust has beneficiaries in two or more generations and the trustee distributes to one of the beneficiaries in one of the lower generations. The transferee (i.e., distributee-beneficiary) is liable for the GSTT. The taxable amount is the value of the property received by the transferee, reduced by any expenses or indebtedness that would be deductible under §2053.

EXAMPLE 12 - 15. Using the facts from the prior two examples, if while Ha (the son of the trustor) is still alive, the trustee, using powers given to her by the terms of the trust, makes a $500,000 distribution to grandson Yi Yun it would be a taxable distribution. The GSTT in the amount of $275,000 is charged to Yi Yun with the result that he only gets $225,000.

Because the GSTT liability is placed upon the transferee, if the trustee pays the GSTT, it is treated as a taxable distribution. The amount that must be "distributed" to achieve a net desired distribution can be solved algebraically. Let the gross distribution be Dg and the net distribution be Dn, then solve for Dg as follows:

Dg - GSTT = Dn; and since GSTT = 0.55 x Dg,

Dg - 0.55 x Dg = Dn. Therefore, (1- 0.55) x Dg = Dn; and finally,

Dg = Dn/0.45.

EXAMPLE 12 - 16. Suppose in the prior example, the trustee was willing to pay the tax so that Yi Yun would receive $500,000. This will require the trustee parting with $1,111,111 whether the trustee pays the GSTT of $611,111[0.55 x $1,111,111] and distributes $500,000 to Yi Yun or the trustee distributes $1,111,111 and lets Yi Yun pay the tax on it.

EXAMPLE 12 - 17. Suppose the trustee distributed $500,000 in corpus to Siu-on (Yi Yun's brother) after Ha had died (i.e., after the taxable termination had occurred) but before the trust had terminated. This distribution is not a taxable distribution for GSTT purposes, because by that time the two brothers were in the oldest generation with an interest in the trust.

Applicable Rate

The applicable rate is made up of two components: the maximum Federal estate tax rate and the inclusion ratio. Remember, the GSTT is equal to the taxable amount (a reference to the transferred property) times the applicable rate (a tax rate modified to take into account the allocation of the $1 million exemption).

Maximum Federal estate tax rate. The term maximum Federal estate tax rate is the maximum imposed by §2001 which presently is 55%.[12] Notice it does not include the 5% surcharge that tosses estates between $10,000,000 and $21,040,000 into a 60% marginal rate. The purpose the surcharge is to "take back" the benefits of the unified credit and the lower marginal rates and, as a surcharge, it is not deemed to increase the maximum Federal rate above 55%.

The inclusion ratio. Think of this as that portion of the transfer that is *not saved* from the dreaded GSTT by the $1 million exemption. The inclusion ratio is defined as the value one minus the "applicable fraction,"[13] or

$$1 - \frac{GSTT\ exemption\ allocated}{Net\ FMV\ of\ property\ tranferred}$$

The net FMV value of the property transferred means net of debt, expenses, and liens, as well as any charitable deduction and any Federal estate taxes and state death taxes charged to the property. Generally, the allocation of the exemption is an elective one made by the donor in the case of gifts and by the executor in the case of estates. It is not unusual to make allocations in a multiple trust estate plan such that some of the GST trusts have inclusion ratios of either zero or one. We will get into this allocation of the exemption to various trusts a little bit more in the section on efficient utilization of the exemption.

EXAMPLE 12 - 18. When Ruben died $3,000,000 of his estate (net of regular death taxes) was left to his grandchildren. The executor allocated the entire $1 million exemption to this bequest, resulting in an applicable fraction of one-third ($1,000,000/$3,000,000) and an inclusion ratio of two-thirds (1 - 1/3). The GSTT would be $3,000,000 x 0.55 x .6666667, which is $1,100,000.

EXAMPLE 12 - 19. When Josephine died she left her $3,000,000 estate (this was net of regular death taxes) in trust for her son Albert, with remainder to his issue. Since this was her entire net estate, the exemption was allocated to this trust. While Albert was still alive, the trustee made a distribution out of corpus in the amount of $360,000 to Albert's daughter, Martha. This, of course, was a taxable distribution. Given the inclusion ratio, the applicable rate would be 0.55 x .6666667. Therefore, the tax on the distribution would be: $360,000 x 0.55 x .6666667 = $132,000.

EXAMPLE 12 - 20. When Albert died the trust was worth $4,500,000. His death caused a taxable termination. The applicable rate is as before: 0.55 x .6666667. The GSTT is: $4,500,000 x 0.55 x .6666667 = $1,650,000.

Timing the Exemption Allocation

As indicated earlier in this discussion, the allocation of the exemption is not automatic. Generally, at the death of a transferor, one should allocate in a manner that is most likely to reduce the GSTT, taking into account the present value of money. Because most taxpayers would prefer to postpone taxes of whatever variety, the Code has as a default position the automatic allocation of the exemption to lifetime direct skips unless the donor elects not to have the automatic allocation apply.[14]

Discretionary allocations. Given a choice the person making the decision would like to accomplish two or three things, some of which may be in opposition or which may require the use of a functioning crystal ball. Consider the following examples:

EXAMPLE 12 - 21. Eunice never trusted her two boys to wisely handle investments. The oldest, Jimmy, she had given up on. The youngest, Billie, she wanted to provide a good living, but make sure he couldn't squander the estate she had put together. She loved her grandchildren, who have turned out to be fine adults. She left her estate in equal shares, one share immediately to Jimmy's children by right of representation and the other in trust for Billie for his lifetime, the remainder, free of trust, to Billie's children by right of representation. The plan specifically gave her executor authority to allocate the exemption as the executor deemed appropriate. Her estate, after payment of all Federal estate and state death taxes, had a net value of $1,500,000. Her executor could allocate $750,000 of the exemption to the direct skip and $250,000 to the trust, or vice-versa, or equally between the two transfers, or in any other proportion. If it is fully allocated to the trust, the trust will have a zero inclusion ratio such that even if it is worth more than $1 million when it terminates no GSTT will be due. However, doing so will cause an immediate GSTT for the portion of the direct skip not covered by the exemption. Allocation $750,000 to the direct skip will post-pone all GSTT until the trust ends, but the trust will have an inclusion ratio of two-thirds.

Forced delay of allocations. In the case of inter vivos gifts, if the property would be included in the donor's estate due to a retained interest (§§2036 - 2038), the allocation cannot be made until the close of the *estate tax inclusion period* (ETIP). The ETIP is the point at which the retained interest either ends (released or ends by the terms of the transfer) or the donor dies.

EXAMPLE 12 - 22. Stacie funds a ten-year qualified personal residence trust (QPRT) with her $550,000 home. The remaindermen are her three grandchildren. At the end of the ten-year term the house is worth $750,000. At that time the ETIP ends and she can allocate $750,000 of the exemption to the transfer.

EXAMPLE 12 - 23. Suppose, in the prior example, that Stacie died in year seven when the home was worth $625,000. At that time the ETIP would end, and her executor could allocate $625,000 of the exemption to the transfer. In both cases, Stacie would have preferred to have made the allocation at the beginning of the trust, when the initial transfer was made so as to use only $550,000 of her exemption.

Special Rules Pertaining to Generations & the GSTT

There are a number of special rules related to GSTT, some of which we will cover here, others which we will just warn you that they exist, but that are beyond the scope of this text.

Generation assignment. Where transferees are related to the transferor the assignments are fairly straight forward. The Code requires that one start with the transferor's grandparents and count down generations to the transferee and compare the number to the number of generations between the grandparent and the transferor, if the difference is greater than one, the transferee is a skip person.

EXAMPLE 12 - 24. Jack wishes to leave half of his multi-million dollar estate to his brother's daughter Alice and the other half to Alice's two children, Martin and Paula. Are any or all of these skip persons? Jack's grandfather is two generations above him. From the grandfather to Alice is three generations. Three minus two equals one, so Alice is not a skip person. It is four generations from the grandfather to Martin and Paula. Four minus two equals two, therefore, both Martin and Paula are skip persons.

Predeceased ancestor exception. A special rule (called the *predeceased ancestor exception)* allows a direct skip person to "move up" a generation if his or her parent is a lineal descendent of the transferor (or the transferor's spouse) and the parent dies before the transfer occurs (i.e, the date of the gift or the date the transferor dies).[15] The move up exception also applies if the parent dies within 90 days of the transfer, provided the parent is treated as having predeceased the transfer either because of a survivorship clause in the transferor's estate planning documents (i.e., the grandparent's will or trust) or because of applicable state law.

EXAMPLE 12 - 25. Sarah's will left her multimillion dollar estate to her issue by right of representation. All three children survived her, but one child, named Richard, died 75 days after her. Richard left two children who were entitled to inherit his entire estate. Sarah's will had a 60 day survivorship clause. Since Richard lived beyond the 60 days, he was entitled to a one third share of Sarah's estate. Richard's executor disclaimed Richard's share so that it could pass directly to his children. This share is subject to the GSTT because insofar as Sarah's will (and her state of domicile) is concerned he did not predecease her. Had her will included a 90 day survivorship clause (or an even a longer one) Richard would have been considered to have predeceased Sarah and there would be no GSTT.

The usual disclaimer rules do not work for GSTT, at least they do not work in the sense that a disclaimer will not move the disclaimant's children up a generation. Thus in the above example, even though the disclaimer worked for other purposes (e.g., avoiding Richard's gross estate for regular estate tax and avoiding his probate estate), for GSTT purposes the disclaimer did not cause Richard to be treated as though he had predeceased Sarah. In the typical estate plan for wealthy couples that use multiple trusts, it is very likely that the contingent remaindermen are skip persons, this may cause a GSTT problem.

Common facts for the *alternative* examples that immediately follow: S1 and S2 had four children all of whom had children of their own. The estate plan included a bypass trust, carved out of S1's estate. The trust gave S2 a life estate, with the remainder to the couple's issue, by right of representation. When S1 died, the trust was worth $4,000,000. When S2 died, the trust was worth $6,000,000.

> EXAMPLE 12-26. All four children survived their mother (S2) and took equal shares of the trust estate. The GSTT did not apply because the children of the transferor are not skip persons.

> EXAMPLE 12-27. All four children outlived their father (S1), but one of them died before S2, leaving two adult children (grandchildren of S1 and S2). When S2 died the three living children each received a one-fourth share, and the two grandchildren a one-eight share. The portion of the trust going to the grandchildren is subjected to the GSTT even though their parent is deceased. The predeceased ancestor exception applies only to direct skips, so the grandchildren do not move up even though their parent died before the parent's interest in the trust vested.

Marital relationships. A transfer to one who is related to the transferor's spouse is in the generation level determined as if the transfer was from the spouse rather than from the transferor. The counting up (and down) from the spouse to her (or his) grandparent is just for the purpose of determining whether a donee is a skip person. For all other purposes the transfer is treated as coming from the transferor, unless the couple elect to "split the gift"[16] in which case both spouses are treated as being donors.

A spouse or ex-spouse of a transferor is treated as in the same generation as the transferor, regardless of age difference. This "same-generation-treatment" will continue even if a marriage ends due to the transferor's death or ends by divorce, which some people say is a little like death. Likewise, anyone married to a lineal descendant of the transferor's grandparents (or a lineal descendant of the transferor's spouse's grandparents) is in the same generation as that person's spouse (i.e., the lineal descendent) even if the marriage ends.

> EXAMPLE 12 - 28. Jennifer wishes to leave a portion of her estate to the widow of her uncle's grandson. Would this be a generation skipping transfer? The widow of the grandson is in the same generation as was the grandson. The parent of the grandson is at the same generation level (count up and count back down) as Jennifer. Therefore, the grandson was (and his widow is) just one generation below Jennifer and no generation skipping transfer will occur.

Transferees who are not lineal descendants. If the linear descendent rules and spouse rules don't apply, then assignment to generations is based upon the difference in age between the transferor and the transferee. A person older than, or not less than 12.5 years younger than, the transferor is considered to be in the same generation as the transferor. A person 12.5 to 37.5 years younger is in the next generation below, and similar rules apply to assign individuals to still younger generations based upon 25 year increments. Obviously, a person 40 years younger is a skip person and a person 30 years younger is not.

Planning Considerations: Efficient Utilization of the Exemption.

Generally, one would like the exemption to reduce GSTT sooner, rather than later, cover completely a GST trust which is likely to grow, and to limit its allocation to trusts that will actually go to skip persons.

These are facts for the extended set of examples that follow: Andre and Mary have three children, Tom, Carol, and Whitney. Their ABC Trust plan allows Trust C to be divided into as many as three trusts after the first spouse's death. The division will depend on how much is QTIP'ed and the best allocation of the GSTT exemption. There is a provision for a Trust C_E to hold such property as is to be GSTT exempt (in addition to Trust B), a Trust C_Q to hold the QTIP'ed non-exempt portion, and Trust C_{NQ} to hold that portion not QTIP'ed. The terms of the trust provide that after the surviving spouse's death (S2), any distribution to a skip person should be satisfied first from GSTT exempt property, next to the extent possible from property included in S2's estate, and last from other trust property; with the distributions from all trusts adjusted to allow overall distribution to Andre and Mary's issue by right of representation. It also provides that if Trust C_E is QTIP'ed, estate tax charged to the QTIP property at S2's death is to be first charged to Trust C_Q before any is charged to Trust C_E.

When Andre died in 1994, his property was worth $3,000,000 and Mary's property was worth $800,000. Trust A was funded with all of Mary's property (i.e., $800,000), Trust B with assets worth $600,000, and Trust C, before division, with the $2,400,000 balance.

> EXAMPLE 12 - 29. The executor of Andre's estate decided to postpone all taxes until Mary's death, therefore, a QTIP election was made covering all $2,400,000 allocated to Trust C. To fully utilized Andre's $1 million exemption, a $400,000

reverse QTIP election was made. Thus the Trustee divided Trust C into Trust C_E holding assets worth $400,00 and Trust C_Q holding assets worth $2,000,000. Both C trusts were QTIP'ed (i.e., an election was made to qualify both for the marital deduction) and Trust C_E was reverse QTIP'ed. The executor allocated Andre's exemption to Trust B and to Trust C_E.

EXAMPLE 12 - 30. How would things change if the executor decided to equalize the two estates by a QTIP election covering just part of the Trust C property? Again Trust A would have Mary's property and Trust A would be funded with $600,000. However, to equalize the two estates as of Andre's death, the non-QTIP (NQ) portion of Trust C plus Trust B must equal the value of the combined estates divided by two. Since both the combined value of the estates and Trust B's value are known, one simply solves for NQ, i.e., NQ = ($800,000 + $3,000,000)/2 - 600,000 = $1,300,000. Now what? The trustee divides this amount between Trust C_E (which this time won't be QTIP'ed) and Trust C_{NQ} (which also won't be QTIP'ed), and the balance goes into Trust C_Q which will be QTIP'ed. Trust C_E receives $400,000, which together with Trust B, is allocated the exemption. Trust C_{NQ} receives $900,000 [$1,300,000 - $400,000] and the balance of Trust C is allocated to Trust C_Q. Thus Trust C_Q (and the marital deduction) will be $1,100,000 [$2,400,000 - $1,300,000]. Recap: Andre's estate: $3,000,000 - $1,100,000 = $1,900,000. And, Mary's estate as of Andre's death: $800,000 + $1,100,000 = $1,900,000.

Where does all this take us? Why so many different trusts? First, the combination of the Trust B and the Trust C_Q assure that S1's full exemption will be utilized even if all of the Trust C property is QTIP'ed. Remember, a QTIP tosses the QTIP'ed property into S2's gross estate, where for GSTT (and estate tax, too) it is treated as a transfer from S2. The reverse QTIP allows QTIP'ed property to be treated as if it came from S1, but only for the purpose of using up S1's GSTT exemption. It does not affect the QTIP marital deduction. Then why have a separate Trust C_E if no QTIP election is made, after all the Trust C property will be taxed only in S1's estate and the exemption (to the extent not allocated to Trust B) can be allocated to it? When the plan was designed all Andre and Mary's children were alive. If the children outlived their parents no GST would occur. However, since the remaindermen's interests in Trusts B and C do not vest until after S2's death, a GST may occur as to property in those trusts even if all three children are alive when S1 dies. A GST may occur if any children die, leaving issue, before S2 dies. The predeceased ancestor rule applies only to direct skips, and since S2's interest in these trusts intervenes, a grandchild would not move up a generation even if his or her parent dies before the grandchild's interest vests. By creating trusts with zero inclusion ratios (Trust B and Trust C_E) and requiring that distributions to skip persons be made first from those trusts, with all trusts used to adjust distributions to accomplish a "by right of representation" distribution, the GSTT will be kept to a minimum. By having Trust C_Q charged with the taxes at S2's death rather than taking them out of Trust C_E also serves the purpose of reducing the GSTT impact.

EXAMPLE 12 - 31. Consider what happens at Mary's death, assuming that the executor at Andre's death QTIP'ed to postpone all taxes, and between the two deaths Tom died, leaving two adult children. At the time of Mary's death the four trusts had the following net values:

	FMV		Tax		Net to Distribute
Trust A	$1,100,000	-	$194,000	=	$906,000
Trust B	$700,000	-	$0	=	$700,000
Trust C_E	$500,000	-	$0	=	$500,000
Trust C_Q	$2,300,000	-	$1,399,000	=	$901,000
Totals	$4,600,000	-	$1,593,000		$3,007,000

S2's taxable estate is equal to the combined values of Trust A and both Trust C's. The tax on an estate of $3,900,000 is $1,593,000. Trust A is charged with the amount of estate tax it would have paid had it alone been taxed, and since the estate tax on a taxable estate of $1,100,000 is $194,000, said amount is charged to Trust A. The balance of the estate tax, in the amount of $1,399,000 [$1,593,000-$194,000], is charged to Trust C_Q. Since the two living children receive one-third of the after tax value of the trusts, each "share" is $1,002,333. Tom's two children will divide a $1,002,333 share. Because they are skip persons, their share comes first from Trusts B and C_E. These two trusts have sufficient assets to satisfy their share and, because of the trusts have a zero inclusion ratio, the bequest to them is completely sheltered from GSTT. Indeed, since the rest of the estate is treated as coming from Mary (S2) no distributions would be hit with a GSTT even if all three of the children had died before Mary.

EXAMPLE 12 - 32. Next consider what happens at Mary's death assuming that it occurs more than ten years after Andre's death (no PTC to worry about) and that Trust C had been QTIP'ed to equalize estates. Again, between the two deaths Tom died leaving two adult children. At the time of Mary's death, the five trusts had the following net values:

	FMV		Tax allocated		Net to Distribute
Trust A	$1,100,000	-	$194,000	=	$906,000
Trust B	$700,000	-	$0	=	$700,000
Trust C_E	$500,000	-	$0	=	$500,000
Trust C_{NQ}	$900,000	-	$0	=	$900,000
Trust C_Q	$1,400,000	-	$639,000	=	$761,000
Totals	$4,600,000		$833,000		$3,006,000

S2's taxable estate is equal to the combined values of Trust A and Trust C_Q, i.e., $2,500,000. The tax on $2,500,000 is $833,000. Trust A is charged with taxes of $194,000 and the balance of $639,000 [$833,000- $194,000] is charged to Trust C_Q. Since one-third of the after-tax value of the trusts is $1,002,000, with the grandchildren's share coming completely from Trusts B and C_E completely sheltered from GSTT.

EXAMPLE 12 - 33. Finally, consider what would have happened if the facts were as described in the prior example, except that Carol had also died leaving one child. Now two-thirds of the estate is left to skip persons (insofar as Andre is concerned). The Trusts and the allocation of the regular death estate taxes remains the same. The grandchildren's total after-tax share (before GSTT) is worth $2,004,000; of which $1,200,000 is drawn from Trusts B and C_E. The balance of $804,000 can be drawn from trusts taxed in Mary's estate. Mary is the transferor of the $804,000. Since Tom and Carol pre-deceased Mary, the predeceased ancestor rule moves the grandchildren up a generation vis-a-vis Mary, and no GSTT is due. Only distributions from Trust C_{NQ} are neither sheltered by the exemption nor treated as transfers from Mary. However, all distributions from Trust C_{NQ} will be to children, thus no GSTT. Hence, only if all three children predeceased Mary would there be a GSTT and the taxable amount would be the amount in Trust C_{NQ}.

Credit for Certain State Taxes

If a generation-skipping transfer (other than a direct skip) occurs at the same time as, and as a result of, the death of an individual, there is allowed a credit against the Federal GSTT equal to the lesser of the state GSTT or 5% of the Federal GSTT.[17] Most states have simply adopted a state GSTT "pickup" tax equal to 5% of the Federal GSTT for such indirect skips.

Certain Transfers Excluded from the GSTT

The annual exclusion applies to GST present interest inter vivos gifts. Those inter vivos gifts that would not be treated as taxable gifts because of §2503(e) (payments directly to educational institutions or to medical providers) are also excluded from the definition of a GST.[18]

Grandfathering in Some Grand Old Trusts

Some generation-skipping trusts that were around when the GSTT laws went into effect are exempt from the GSTT. To be grandfathered, a trust had to be irrevocable as of September 25, 1985; or the skip must be caused by a will, a testamentary trust, or a trust in existence on October 21, 1986 that became irrevocable as a result of the testator or trustor's death before January 1, 1987. A grandfathered trust will lose its exempt status if the trustee accepts additions of property, or if modifications are made to it, after the dates just mentioned.

The Need for GSTT Planning

It should be evident by now that planning for the $1 million lifetime GSTT exemption requires careful thought and attentive drafting of complex will or trust clauses, and can add considerably to the expense of estate planning. It also forces the planner to openly discuss with the client an unpleasant fact: the eventual death of the client's children.

No GSTT planning necessary for some clients. Which wealthier clients most probably *do not need* GSTT planning? First, clients with estates not expected to exceed $1 million when combined with taxable gifts need not ever worry about a GSTT. They may, however, wish to do some trust planning to skip a generation by transferring some property for the benefit of their grandchildren, confident that GSTT law will automatically allocate the $1 million exemption at their death, so that all trusts created will have an inclusion ratio of zero.

Second, those who do not wish to directly include grandchildren in their plan may not need GSTT planning. For example, clients preferring a 100% marital deduction plan, as in a simple will, probably want their property to pass entirely to the surviving spouse and the children, all of whom are nonskip persons. Even clients anticipating a bypass may have no wish to provide for grandchildren. Of course, with either plan the property may wind up passing under the instrument to grandchildren (i.e., "descendants" or "issue") if a child predeceases a grandchild. However, the property involved may be sheltered from the GSTT under the *predeceased ancestor exception*, with the help of some careful drafting, to ensure that a direct skip will in fact occur or that the interest is covered by the $1 million exemption.

Third, in some situations, GSTT trust planning should be avoided because it could result in more, not less, total transfer taxes. If the client is willing to leave the estate *outright to the children*, perhaps satisfied with only a hope that they will preserve the property for ultimate disposition to the grandchildren, a greater amount may wind up, GSTT-free, in the grandchildren's hands. The savings is based on two factors: (1) the unified credit can reduce the estate tax but not the GSTT; and (2) effective marginal estate tax rates begin at 37% (first $150,000 in excess of $600,000), while the GSTT rate is higher, at a flat 55%.

> EXAMPLE 12-34. Suppose Caesar left his entire $2 million estate (after estate tax) *outright* to his five *children*. The combined GSTT and estate tax incurred later would be zero, under simple assumptions, after the property finally passes to the grandchildren. Assuming an overall 50% rate of appreciation on the property, each child's $400,000 share would grow to $600,000, and, at each child's death, would be entirely sheltered from estate tax by the unified credit. No GSTT would result because there would be no transfer to a skip person. Thus, by using the children's five unified credits, Caesar's entire $3 million estate could pass to the grandchildren, transfer tax-free.

Clients needing GSTT planning. Which wealthier clients are most likely to need careful GSTT planning?

- "dynastic"-oriented clients wishing to perpetuate their wealth,
- clients with wealthy children,
- clients who believe that their children cannot handle large amounts of money maturely, and
- clients who wish to give to their grandchildren things that their children cannot or will not give.

Summary. There are several methods of at least partially circumventing the GSTT, particularly through the use of the $1 million GSTT exemption. In general, only family estates exceeding $2 million in total value at the first spouse's death are prevented from arranging totally GSTT-free generation-skipping transfers.

Generation-skipping planning is modestly popular to clients today. However, interest in generation-skipping estate planning should grow in the years to come, if only because clients will be living longer and will be more likely to know their great grandchildren. A recent U.S. Census Bureau report concluded that by 2040, the nation could have more people over 65 than under 21, and that the *four-generation family* will become common.

QUESTIONS AND PROBLEMS

FACTS FOR 1 - 9: S1 and S2 lived in a common law state. S1 owned property having a net value of $4,487,287 and S2 owned property having a net value of $1,321,980. Assume debts and expenses are zero, and that no prior transfer credit is available because the two deaths are more than 10 years apart. The numbers for the AsuperB at S1's death won't change regardless of what S1's executor does insofar as the QTIP election, but the A and dC trusts in the ABdC plan depend upon what S2 does insofar as the amount disclaimed. The second part of each problem asks you to determine S2's taxable estate. For that calculation you will be given the value of the trusts as of when S2 died; of course, these are made up numbers that factor in some growth between the first and second death.

1.1 The couple had an AsuperB Trust estate plan. S1's executor elected to postpone all taxes until S2 died, but fully utilize S1's unified credit. Determine: (a) S1's gross estate; (b) the values of Trust A and Trust B; (c) the QTIP fraction; and (d) how the fraction is applied to arrive at the taxable estate.

1.2 Determine S2's taxable estate given that Trust A was then worth $2,298,923 and Trust B $7,045,041.

2.1 The couple had an AsuperB Trust estate plan. S1's executor elected to pay all taxes at S1's death. Determine: (a) the QTIP fraction; (b) show how it is applied to arrive at the desired taxable estate.

2.2 Determine S2's taxable estate given that Trust A was then worth $2,298,923 and Trust B $4,555,008.

3.1 The couple had an AsuperB Trust estate plan. S1's executor elected to make a QTIP election that would equalize the two estates, at least as of S1's death. Determine: (a) the QTIP fraction; (b) show how it is applied to arrive at the desired taxable estate.

3.2 Determine S2's taxable estate given that Trust A was then worth $2,298,923 and Trust B $5,400,535.

4.1 The couple had an AsuperB Trust estate plan. S1's executor elected to make a QTIP election such that S1's taxable estate would equal $2,330,000. Determine: (a) the QTIP fraction; (b) show how it is applied to arrive at the desired taxable estate.

4.2 Determine S2's taxable estate given that Trust A was then worth $2,298,923 and Trust B $5,868,012.

5.1 The couple had an ABdC Trust estate plan. The widow chose not to disclaim any property. Determine: (a) S1's gross estate; (b) the values of Trust A, Trust B, and Trust C; and (c) S1's taxable estate.

5.2 Determine S2's taxable estate given that Trust A was then worth $6,641,322 and Trust B $875,400.

6.1 The couple had an ABdC Trust estate plan. S2 and the executor for S1's estate worked together. S2 disclaimed all property that would otherwise have flowed into Trust A; S1's executor elected to pay all taxes at S1's death. Determine: (a) S1's gross estate; (b) the values of Trust A, Trust B, and Trust C [remember that Trust C is equal to the value of the property disclaimed]; (c) S1's taxable estate.

6.2 Determine S2's taxable estate given that Trust A was then worth $2,298,923, Trust B $597,883, and Trust C $3,873,571.

7.1 The couple had an ABdC Trust estate plan. S2 and the executor for S1's estate worked together, S2 disclaimed all property that would otherwise have flowed into Trust A; S1's executor elected to make a QTIP election that would equalize the two estates, at least as of S1's death. Determine: (a) the values of Trust A, Trust B, and Trust C; (b) the QTIP fraction and (c)show how it is applied to arrive at the desired taxable estate.

7.2 Determine S2's taxable estate given that Trust A was then worth $2,298,923, Trust B $799,842, and Trust C $5,182,024.

8.1 The couple had an ABdC Trust estate plan. S2 and the executor for S1's estate worked together. S2 disclaimed just enough property to equalize the estates, at least as of S1's death; S1's executor made no QTIP election. Determine: (a) the values of Trust A, Trust B, and Trust C; (b) show how this disclaimer works to bring about the desired taxable estate.

8.2 Determine S2's taxable estate given that Trust A was then worth $5,051,157, Trust B $667,134, and Trust C $2,562,798.

9.1 The couple had an ABdC Trust estate plan. S2 and the executor for S1's estate worked together, S2 disclaimed just enough property to bring S1's taxable estate to $1,500,000; S1's executor made no QTIP election. Determine: (a) the values of Trust A, Trust B, and Trust C; (b) show how this disclaimer works to bring about the desired taxable estate.

9.2 Determine S2's taxable estate given that Trust A was then worth $7,493,815, Trust B $790,897, and Trust C $1,186,346.

FACTS FOR 10 - 18: S1 and S2 lived in a community property state. S1 owned property having a net value of $2,220,480 and S2 owned property having a net value of $800,660, and they owned community property worth $1,596,400. Assume debts and expenses are zero and that no prior transfer credit is available because the two deaths are more than 10 years apart.

10.1 The couple had an AsuperB Trust estate plan. S1's executor elected to postpone all taxes until S2 died, but fully utilize S1's unified credit. Determine: (a) S1's gross estate; (b) the values of Trust A and Trust B; (c) the QTIP fraction; and (d) how the fraction is applied to arrive at the taxable estate.

10.2 Determine S2's taxable estate given that Trust A was then worth $2,845,970 and Trust B $$5,373,250.

11.1 The couple had an AsuperB Trust estate plan. S1's executor elected to pay all taxes at S1's death. Determine: (a) the QTIP fraction; (b) show how it is applied to arrive at the desired taxable estate.

11.2 Determine S2's taxable estate given that Trust A was then worth $2,845,970 and Trust B $3,400,523.

12.1 The couple had an AsuperB Trust estate plan. S1's executor elected to make a QTIP election that would equalize the two estates, at least as of S1's death. Determine: (a) the QTIP fraction; (b) show how it is applied to arrive at the desired taxable estate.

12.2 Determine S2's taxable estate given that Trust A was then worth $2,845,970 and Trust B $4,057,301.

13.1 The couple had an AsuperB Trust estate plan. S1's executor elected to make a QTIP election such that S1's taxable estate would equal $1,500,000. Determine: (a) the QTIP fraction; (b) show how it is applied to arrive at the desired taxable estate.

13.2 Determine S2's taxable estate given that Trust A was then worth $2,845,970 and Trust B $4,727,110.

14.1 The couple had an ABdC Trust estate plan. The widow chose not to disclaim any property. Determine: (a) S1's gross estate; (b) the values of Trust A, Trust B, and Trust C; and (c) S1's taxable estate.

14.2 Determine S2's taxable estate given that Trust A was then worth $7,151,221 and Trust B $1,068,000.

15.1 The couple had an ABdC Trust estate plan. S2 and the executor for S1's estate worked together, S2 disclaimed all property that would otherwise have flowed into Trust A; S1's executor elected to pay all taxes at S1's death. Determine: (a) S1's gross estate; (b) the values of Trust A, Trust B, and Trust C [remember that Trust C is equal to the value of the property disclaimed]; (c) S1's taxable estate.

15.2 Determine S2's taxable estate given that Trust A was then worth $2,845,970, Trust B $675,896, and Trust C $2,724,627.

16.1 The couple had an ABdC Trust estate plan. S2 and the executor for S1's estate worked together. S2 disclaimed all property that would otherwise have flowed into Trust A; S1's executor elected to make a

QTIP election that would equalize the two estates, at least as of S1's death. Determine: (a) the values of Trust A, Trust B, and Trust C; (b) the QTIP fraction and (c)show how it is applied to arrive at the desired taxable estate.

16.2 Determine S2's taxable estate given that Trust A was then worth $2,845,970, Trust B $806,439, and Trust C $3,250,862.

17.1 The couple had an ABdC Trust estate plan. S2 and the executor for S1's estate worked together. S2 disclaimed just enough property to equalize the estates, at least as of S1's death; S1's executor made no QTIP election. Determine: (a) the values of Trust A, Trust B, and Trust C; (b) show how this disclaimer works to bring about the desired taxable estate.

17.2 Determine S2's taxable estate given that Trust A was then worth $4,109,611, Trust B $726,013, and Trust C $2,067,648.

18.1 The couple had an ABdC Trust estate plan. S2 and the executor for S1's estate worked together. S2 disclaimed just enough property to bring S1's taxable estate to $1,500,000; S1's executor made no QTIP election. Determine: (a) the values of Trust A, Trust B, and Trust C; (b) show how this disclaimer works to bring about the desired taxable estate.

18.2 Determine S2's taxable estate given that Trust A was then worth $5,549,221, Trust B $809,544, and Trust C $1,214,316.

FACTS FOR 19: S1 died May 7, 1994, survived by S2 who was then 70 years old. The Federal rate for valuing split interests (life estates, etc.) was 8%. They had an ABC plan that named their children as remaindermen of all trusts. At S1's death their holdings had the following net value:

S1's separate	$3,450,090
S2's separate	$1,970,400
Total value	$5,420,490

S1's executor QTIP'ed Trust C to equalize the two estates and paid estate taxes of $944,430; of which $787,928 was Federal tax and $156,502 was state.

S2 died August 23, 1995 and the trusts had the following values:

Trust A	$2,246,256
Trust B	$496,761
Trust C	$2,359,691

S2's taxable estate was $2,858,800. The estate would have had to pay state taxes of $169,574 and Federal taxes of $853,590 without the PTC credit.

19.1 Determine, as of S1's death: (a) the value of Trust A, Trust B, and Trust C; (b) the QTIP Fraction necessary to equalize the two estates; and (c) S1's taxable estate.

19.2 Given the information on the values for the three trusts at S2's death, show how one arrives at S2's taxable estate.

19.3 Determine: Limit one.

19.4 Determine: Limit two.

19.5 Determine: (a) the PTC after adjusting for time; (b) the state death tax; and (c) the Federal estate tax.

19.6 Had S1's executor postponed all taxes to the second death, the value of the three trusts, given the same percentage growth, would have been as follows: Trust A $2,246,256; Trust B$684,000; and Trust C $3,249,103. This would have resulted in state death tax of $450,243 and Federal tax of $2,020,204. (a) How much more total tax would have been paid? (b) What is the net value going to the children in each case. [In both cases, subtract the death taxes at S2's death from the value of the trusts at that time, since any taxes at S1's death had already been paid (and removed) from the trusts.] (c) Why doesn't the difference in tax equal the difference in the amount going to the children?

FACTS FOR 20: S1 died on September 15, 1994, survived by S2 who was then 80 years old. The Federal rate for valuing split interests (also called the §7520 rate) was 6%. They had an ABC plan that named their children as remaindermen of all trusts. At S1's death their holdings had the following net value:

S1's separate	$2,549,000
community property	$864,500
S2's separate	$1,284,600
Total value	$4,698,100

S1's executor QTIP'ed Trust C to equalize the two estates and paid estate taxes of $759,035, of which $632,311 was Federal tax and $126,724 was state.

S2 died December 10, 1997 and the trusts had grown about 11%, having the values as follows:

Trust A	$1,905,704
Trust B	$496,435
Trust C	$1,970,225

S2's taxable estate was $2428780, the estate would have had to pay state taxes of $133102 and Federal taxes of $665000 without the PTC credit.

20.1 Determine, as of S1's death: (a) the value of Trust A, Trust B, and Trust C; (b) the QTIP Fraction necessary to equalize the two estates; and (c) S1's taxable estate.

20.2 Given the information on the values for the three trusts at S2's death, show how one arrives at S2's taxable estate.

20.3 Determine: Limit one.

20.4 Determine: Limit two.

20.5 Determine: (a) the PTC after adjusting for time; (b) the state death tax; and (c) the Federal estate tax.

20.6 Had S1's executor postponed all taxes to the second death, the value of the three trusts, given the same percentage growth, would have been as follows: Trust A $1,905,704; Trust B$666,000; and Trust C $2,643,188. This would have resulted in state death tax of $341,076 and Federal tax of $1,608,814. (a) How much more total tax would have been paid? (b) What is the net value going to the children in each case. (c) Why doesn't the difference in tax equal the difference in the amount going to the children?

FACTS FOR 21: S1 died April 15, 1992, survived by S2 who was then 60 years old. The Federal rate for valuing split interests was 12%. They had an AsuperB plan with their children named as the remaindermen. At S1's death their holdings had the following net value:

S1's separate	$3,900,700
S2's separate	$480,640
Total value	$4,381,340

S1's executor QTIP'ed Trust B so as to equalize both estates, at least as of S1's death, and paid estate taxes of $681,428; of which $567,375 was Federal and $114,054 was state.

S2 died November 18, 1993. The trusts had grown by about 9% [the tax at S1's death was paid from trust B], therefore the trusts had the following values:

Trust A	$523,898
Trust B	$3,509,006

Since S2's taxable estate was $2,062,213, the estate would have had to pay state taxes of $104,079 and Federal taxes of $514,707 without PTC credit.

21.1 Determine as of S1's death: (a) the value of Trust A and Trust B; (b) the QTIP Fraction necessary to equalize the two estates at S1's death.

21.2 Given the information on the values for the two trusts at S2's death, show how one arrives at S2's taxable estate.

21.3 Determine: Limit one.

21.4 Determine: Limit two.

21.5 Determine: (a) the PTC after adjusting for time; (b) the state death tax; and (c) the Federal estate tax.

FACTS FOR 22: S1 died May 5, 1996, survived by S2, who was then 75 years old. The Federal rate was 10%. They had an AsuperB plan. At S1's death their holdings had the following net value:

S1's separate	$3,798,400
community property	$945,050
S2's separate	$1,304,500
Total value	$6,047,950

S1's executor QTIP'ed Trust B such that S1's taxable estate was $3,425,282 and paid estate taxes of $1,331,905; of which $1,109,878 was Federal and $222,027 was state.

S2 died October 10, 1996. The trusts had grown by about 5% [remember S1's estate taxes were paid out of Trust B], therefore the trusts had the following values:

Trust A	$1,865,876
Trust B	$3,085,971

S2's taxable estate was $2,476,899. The estate would have had to pay state taxes of $136,952 and Federal taxes of $684,728 without the PTC credit.

22.1 Determine as of S1's death: (a) the value of Trust A and Trust B; (b) the QTIP Fraction necessary to have a taxable estate equal the desired S1 taxable estate.

22.2 Given the information on the values for the two trusts at S2's death, show how one arrives at S2's taxable estate.

22.3 Determine: Limit one.

22.4 Determine: Limit two.

22.5 Determine: (a) the PTC after adjusting for time; (b) the state death tax; and (c) the Federal estate tax.

23. Reserved for a QDOT question.

24. Reserved for an estate trust question.

25. The Drexlers own a total of $2 million in assets, with one-half owned by each spouse. Their simple wills pass property from S1 to S2, then at S2's death all property passes outright to their *grandchildren* (rather than to their children). They believe that there property will not be subjected to the GSTT because they each have a $1 million GSTT exemption. Explain what would happen with their present arrangement and how they could effectively avoid the GSTT.

26. A bypass trust provides for income to the trustor's wife for her life, then remainder outright to his daughter, if she survives her mother; otherwise, to the daughter's *issue*.

a. Could there be a potential GSTT problem?

b. Is the size of the trust a factor?

c. Can you suggest a solution to the problem?

27. Burdick, a widower, wanted his grandchildren, Diana and Chris, to ultimately receive the bulk of his estate. So, at his death he created two irrevocable trusts, which, after payment of estate taxes, each had a net worth of $1 million. Burdick's daughter, Heather, will receive all income from each trust for her lifetime, after which the trusts will terminate, and be distributed to the grandchildren. Diana's trust contains only fixed income securities and Heather's trust only common stock. The corpus of Diana's trust remained unchanged, while the corpus of Heather's trust tripled between Burdick's death and Heather's death.

a. Calculate the GSTT due at Heather's death for Diana's trust, for Heather's trust, and for both trusts combined. Assume, alternatively, that at his death, the executor for Burdick's estate allocated the $1 million GSTT exemption in the following manner:

1. Entirely to Diana's trust.

2. One-half to Diana's trust and one-half to Heather's trust.

3. Entirely to Heather's trust.

b. What conclusions can be drawn?

28. (a) How does the reverse QTIP election work? (b) Is it needed to obtain a marital deduction?

29. Which clients do not need to worry too much about GSTT planning and which ones do need to worry about it?

30. Explain the GSTT exemption.

QUERIES ANSWERED

1. Since Trust B is valued at $1,050,000 and the desired taxable estate in 1995 to postpone taxes until S2's death is $600,000, S1's estate needs an additional marital deduction of $450,000. The QTIP fraction [applied to Trust B] is

$$QTIP \ fraction \ = \ \frac{\$450,000}{\$1,050,000}$$

2. The numerator of the fraction is the amount necessary to bring S1's estate equal to S2's, and the denominator is the value of Trust C. Total value of their combined estates divided by two [$6,270,368 ÷ 2 = $3,135,184] gives the desired taxable estate at S1's death. Subtract that amount from S1's estate to arrive at the needed marital deduction [$4,872,800 - $3,135,184 = $1,737,616]. Therefore the QTIP fraction is $1,737,616/$4,272,800 which, since the value of Trust C is the same as the denominator of the fraction, results in a taxable estate for S1 of:

$$\$4,872,800 - \$1,737,616 = \$3,135,184$$

ANSWERS TO THE QUESTIONS AND PROBLEMS:

FOR 1 - 9: common law state. S1 $4,487,287 & S2 $1,321,980.

1.1 AsuperB Postpone: (a) S1's GE [$4,487,287]; (b) Tr A [$1,321,980] and Tr B [$4,487,287]; (c) the QTIP [$3,887,287/$4,487,287]; and (d) applied to arrive at the TxE [fraction times Tr B = MD, GE - MD = TxE = $600,000].

1.2 S2's TxE [Tr A + QTIP x Tr B = $8,401,964],Tr A $2,298,923 and Tr B $7,045,041.

2.1 AsuperB Trust. pay taxes: (a) the QTIP [no QTIP or 0% or 0/Tr B]; (b) TxE [Tr B only,$4,487,287].

2.2 S2's TxE [Tr A only, $2,298,923];Tr A $2,298,923, Tr B $4,555,008.

3.1 AsuperB. QTIP to equalize: (a) the QTIP [$1,582,654/$4,487,287]; (b) TxE [(Tr A + Tr B)/2 = $2,904,634].

3.2 S2's TxE [Tr A + QTIP x Tr B = $4,203,677]; Tr A $2,298,923 and Tr B $5,400,535.

4.1 AsuperB. QTIP so S1's TxE equals $2,330,000. (a) the QTIP [GE - desired taxable estate = MD (numerator); MD/Tr B = QTIP Fraction, i.e., $2,157,287/$4,487,287]; (b) arrive at the desired TxE [S1's GE - (QTIP x Tr B), i.e., $2,330,000].

4.2 S2's TxE [Tr A + QTIP x Tr B = $5,120,001]; Tr A $2,298,923 and Tr B $5,868,012.

5.1 ABdC. no disclaimer (a) S1's GE [$4,487,287]; (b)Tr A [$5,209,267], Tr B [$600,000], and Tr C [zero]; and (c) S1's TxE [$600,000].

5.2 S2's TxE [$6,641,322]; Tr A $6,641,322 and Tr B $875,400.

6.1 ABdC. S2 disclaimed all property, S1's exe. paid all taxes. (a) S1's GE [$4,487,287]; (b) Tr A [$1,321,980],Tr B [$600,000],Tr C [$3,887,287]; (c) S1's TxE [$4,487,287].

6.2 S2's TxE [$2,298,923], Tr A $2,298,923, Tr B $597,883, Tr C $3,873,571.

7.1 ABdC. S2 disclaimed all property, QTIP to equalize: (a)Tr A [$1,321,980], Tr B [$600,000], Tr C [$3,887,287]; (b) the QTIP [$1,582,654/$3,887,287]; (c) TxE [$2,904,634].

7.2 S2's TxE [$2,298,923 + $2,109,788 = $4,408,711; notice that Trust B exceeds UCE but is not taxed @ S2's death] Tr A $2,298,923, Tr B $799,842, Tr C $5,182,024.

8.1 ABdC. S2 disclaimed just enough to equalize, no QTIP: (a)Tr A [$2,904,634], Tr B [$600,000], Tr C [$2,304,634]; (b) show works to TxE [$4,487,287 - $1,582,654 = $2,904,634; notice that Tr A = Tr B + Tr C].

8.2 S2's TxE [$5,051,157]. Tr A $5,051,157, Tr B $667,134, Tr C $2,562,798.

9.1 ABdC. Disclaimed to bring S1's TxE to $1,500,000: (a) Tr A [S2's estate

+ (S1's estate > $1,5000,000) = $4,309,267], Tr B [$600,000],Tr C [$900,000]; (b) show works to TxE [S1's estate > $1,5000,000 = MD = $2987287; TxE = S1's estate - MD = $1,500,000].

9.2 S2's TxE [Tr A only; $7,493,815] Tr A $7,493,815, Tr B $790,897, Tr C $1,186,346.

FOR 10 - 18: community property state. S1 $2,220,480; S2 $800,660; community $1,596,400.

10.1 AsuperB. Postpone: (a) S1's GE [$3,018,680]; (b) Tr A [S2 + ½ * cp = $1,598,860] & Tr B [S1 + ½ * cp = $3,018,680]; (c) the QTIP [MD/Tr B = $2,418,680/$3,018,680]; and (d) applied to arrive at the TxE [fraction times Tr B = MD; and GE - MD = TxE = $600,000].

10.2 S2's TxE [7151220]; Tr A $2,845,970 and Tr B $5,373,250.

11.1 AsuperB. Pay all taxes: (a) the QTIP [zero]; (b) applied to arrive at TxE [No marital deduction, therefore TxE = Tr B = $3,018,680].

11.2 S2's TxE [Tr A = $2,845,970]; Tr A $2,845,970 and Tr B $3,400,523.

12.1 AsuperB. QTIP to equalize: (a) the QTIP [$709,910/$3,018,680]; (b) applied to arrive at the desired TxE [GE - MD = $2,308,770].

12.2 S2's TxE [$3,800,135] Tr A $2,845,970 and Tr B $4,057,301.

13.1 AsuperB. QTIP S1's TxE equals $1,500,000. (a) the QTIP [(Tr B-$1,500,000)/Tr B]; (b) applied to arrive at the desired TxE *Notice that S1's GE goes into Tr B; the MD is that QTIP fraction times Tr B that produces a number that when subtracted from Tr B results in the desired taxable estate.* [TxE = Tr B - (Tr B*(Tr B - $1,500,000)/Tr B)) = $1,500,000.]

13.2 S2's TxE [$5,224,151]; Tr A $2,845,970 and Tr B $4,727,110.

14.1 ABdC. No disclaimer. (a) S1's GE [$3,018,680]; (b)Tr A [$4,017,540], Tr B [$600,000], and Tr C [zero]; and (c) S1's TxE [$600,000].

14.2 S2's TxE [$7,151,221]; Tr A $7,151,221 and Tr B $1,068,000.

15.1   ABdC. Disclaimed all & pay all taxes at S1's death. (a) S1's GE [$3,018,680]; (b) Tr A [$1,598,860], Tr B [$600,000], and Tr C [$2,418,680]; (c) S1's TxE [$3,018,680].

15.2   S2's TxE [$2,845,970] Tr A $2,845,970, Tr B $675,896, &Tr C $2,724,627.

16.1   ABdC. Disclaimed all & elected QTIP to equalize (a)Tr A [$1,598,860], Tr B [$600,000], and Tr C [$2,418,680]; (b) the QTIP [$709,910/$2,418,680]; and (c) to arrive at the desired TxE [$3,018,680 - $709,910 = $2,308,770].

16.2   S2's TxE [$3,800,135]; Tr A $2,845,970, Tr B $806,439, and Tr C $3,250,862.

17.1   ABdC. Disclaimed to equalize (a) Tr A [$2,308,770], Tr B [$600,000], and Tr C [$1,708,770]; (b) disclaimer works to bring about the desired TxE

17.2   S2's TxE [$4,109,611]; Tr A $4,109,611, Tr B $726,013, and Tr C $2,067,648.

18.1   ABdC. Disclaimed to bring S1's TxE to $1,500,000 (a) Tr A [$3,117,540], Tr B [$600,000], and Tr C [$900,000]; (b) disclaimer brings about the desired TxE [GE - MD = TxE = $1,500,000].

18.2   S2's TxE [$5,549,221]; Tr A $5,549,221, Tr B $809,544, and Tr C $1,214,316.

19.1   (a) Tr A [$1,970,400], Tr B [$600,000], and Tr C [$2,850,090]; (b) the QTIP to equalize [$739,845/$2,850,090]; (c) S1's TxE [$2,710,245].

19.2   S2's TxE [$2,858,800].

19.3   Limit one. [$455,044; factor .57752 x $787,928].

19.4   Limit two. [$587,296; S2's "reduced taxable estate" = $1,411,731 and the Federal tax on it is $266,294].

19.5   (a) the PTC [$455,044; death within 2 years, therefore, 100% of the lower of the two limits]; (b) the St D Tx [$169,574; notice that it is as given, it did not change]; and (c) the FET[$853,590 - $455,044 = $398,545].

19.6 Compares postponing to above: Tr A $2,246,256, Tr B$684,000, and Tr C $3,249,103 and St D Tx $450,243 and FET $2,020,204. (a) tax difference? [equalized: postpone; ($169,574 + $398,545) - ($450,243 + $2,020,204) = $1,902,328]; (b) different net to the children [$5,102,708 - $568,119 = $4,534,589 versus $6,179,359 - $2,470,447 = $3,708,912; $4,534,589 - $3,708,912 = $825,677]; (c) Why doesn't the difference in tax equal the difference in net to the children? *Some of what is lost by not using the PTC and the lower marginal rates(equalizing estates) is made up by the fact that postponing allows the amount that would have otherwise been paid at S1's death to grow between the two deaths.*

20.1 (a) Tr A [1716850], Tr B [$600,000], and Tr C [2381250]; (b) the QTIP to equalize [632200/2381250]; and (c) S1's TxE [2349050].

20.2 S2's TxE [2428780].

20.3 Limit one.[215940; .34151 x 632311].

20.4 Limit two. [301388].

20.5 (a) the PTC [80% x 215940 = 172752]; (b) the St D Tx [133102]; and (c) the FET.[492248].

20.6 Compares postponing to above: Tr A $1,905,704, Tr B$666,000, and Tr C $2,643,188 = $5,124,892. St D Tx of $341,076 and FET of $1,608,814. (a) tax difference? [equal: postpone; $1,384,385 - $1,949,890 = $565,505; for equal don't forget to add in tax at S1's death]; (b) different net to the children? [$4,372,364 - ($1,331,020 + $492,248) = $3,747,014 versus $5,124,892 - $1,949,890 = $3,265,002, therefore: $3,747,014 - $3,265,002 = $482,012]; (c) Why doesn't the difference in tax equal the difference in net to the children? [See answer at 19.6.]

21.1 (a) Tr A [$480,640] and Tr B [$3,900,700]; (b) the QTIP to equalize. [$1,710,030/$3,900,700].

21.2 S2's TxE [Tr A + Tr C x ($1,710,030/$3,900,700) = $2,062,213].

21.3 Limit one. [.81376 x $567,375 = $431,707].

21.4 Limit two. [reduced S2 estate = zero, therefore zero tax & difference = $514,405].

21.5 (a) the PTC [lesser limit @ 100% (less than two years), i.e., $461,707]; (b) the St D Tx [$107,079, as given]; and (c) the

FET.[$514,405 - $461,707 = $52,698].

22.1 (a) Tr A [$1,304,500 + ½ x $945,050 = $1,777,025] and Tr B [$3,798,400 + ½ x $945,050 = $4,270,925]; (b) QTIP to TxE equal desired S1 TxE [desired estate = $3,425,282 (given); (Tr B x $845,643/$4,270,925) = MD of $845,643; S1's E - MD = $4,270,925 - $845,643 = $3,425,282].

22.2 S2's TxE [Tr A + QF x Tr B = $1,865,876 + ($845,643/$4,270,925) x $3,085,971 = $2,476,899].

22.3 Limit one. [.56144 x $1,109,878 = $623,130].

22.4 Limit two. [Reduced S2 estate = $826,815; Fed tax on reduced estate = $61,371 & the difference = limit two = $623,358].

22.5 (a) the PTC [less than two years, 100% of the lower of the two limits = $623,130]; (b) the St D Tx [$136,952]; and (c) the FET.[$61,599].

23. Reserved for a QDOT question

24. Reserved for an estate trust question.

25. If S2 is survived by his or her grandchildren's parents, the Drexlers' property will not pass totally GSTT-free, under a simple will. At S2's death, S2's $1 million exemption will be allocated to the entire $2 million transfer to the grandchildren. The result will be an inclusion ratio of 0.5 [$1 million/$2 million] and a GSTT on one-half of the property. In addition, asset values could appreciate before S2's death.

26. a. GSTT problem? There could be a potential GSTT problem if daughter fails to survive her mother. In that event, a transfer out of trust to the daughter's issue (e.g., a grandchild of the trustor) could be a taxable distribution subject to the GSTT. The predeceased parent direct skip exception rule would not apply. As a taxable distribution, it is not a direct skip.

   b. Size of the trust can be a factor because of the $1 million lifetime GSTT exemption, which can exempt part or all of the distribution.

   c. The commonly used solution is to allocate a portion of the $1 million exemption to the bypass trust assets.

27. a. Calculation of GSTT for different GSTT allocation arrangements. The GSTT will be incurred at Heather's death, because there will then be taxable distributions to the grandchildren. General rules:

Inclusion ratio = 1 minus (Amount of GSTT exemption allocated to transfer/Total value of property transferred)

GSTT = Taxable amount x .55 x Inclusion ratio.

1. Entirely to Diana's trust.

   GSTT on Diana's trust:
   Inclusion ratio = 1 minus ($1 million/$1 million) = 0
   GSTT = $1 million x .55 x 0 = $0

   GSTT on Heather's trust:
   Inclusion ratio = 1 minus ($0/$1 million) = 1.0
   GSTT = $3 million x .55 x 1.0 = $1,650,000

   GSTT on Both trusts combined:
   GSTT = $0 + $1,655,000 = $1,655,000

2. One-half to Diana's Tr And one-half to Heather's trust.

   Inclusion ratio for each trust = 1 - ($500,000/$1 million) = .5

   GSTT on Diana's trust:
   GSTT = $1 million x .55 x .5 = $275,000

   GSTT on Heather's trust:
   GSTT = $3 million x .55 x .5 = $825,000

   GSTT on Both trusts combined:
   GSTT = $275,000 + $825,000 = $1,100,000.

3. Entirely to Heather's trust.

GSTT on Diana's trust:
Inclusion ratio = 1 minus ($0/$1 million) = 1
GSTT = $1 million x .55 x 1 = $550,000

GSTT on Heather's trust:
Inclusion ratio = 1 minus ($1 million/$1 million) = 0
GSTT = $3 million x .55 x 0 = $0

GSTT on both trusts combined:
GSTT = $550,000 + $0 = $550,000

  b. What conclusions can be drawn? Allocating the GSTT exemption entirely to Heather's trust, the trust containing the appreciating assets, saved the most GSTT. In general, one should allocate the exemption:
1. so that each trust has an inclusion ratio of either exactly one or exactly 0, but not in between; and
2. to the trust whose assets are most likely to appreciate by a greater amount.

28. a. Reverse QTIP? The property in the reverse QTIP trust is treated as if it came from S1 for GSTT purposes, therefore S1 is able to use the entire $1 million GSTT exemption.
    b. No, the QTIP election obtains the marital deduction but creates the problem that the QTIP trust is then treated as if it came from S2. The reverse QTIP allows dual treatment, both the marital deduction and treatment as if in S2's estate for regular estate taxes, and treatment as if it was only from S1 for GSTT purposes.

29. Clients whose estates are not expected to exceed $1 million, and those who do not wish to directly include grandchildren in their plan, do not need to worry too much about the GSTT. For example, clients preferring a 100% marital deduction plan, as in a simple will, probably want their property to pass entirely to the surviving spouse and then to the children. Even clients anticipating a bypass may have no wish to provide for grandchildren. Of course, with either plan the property may wind up passing under the instrument to grandchildren (i.e., "issue") if a child predeceases a grandchild. However, the property involved can usually be

sheltered from the GSTT under the predeceased parent direct skip rule, with the help of some careful drafting, to ensure that a direct skip will in fact occur.

Clients who should do some GSTT planning include: "dynastic" oriented clients wishing to perpetuate themselves through multi-generation trusts; clients with very wealthy children; clients who believe that their children cannot handle large amounts of money maturely; and clients who wish to give to their grandchildren significant amounts of wealth.

30. Explain the GSTT exemption. It is a $1 million per donor exemption from the GSTT tax. It is allocated automatically to direct skips and can be allocated systematically to generation skipping trusts.

ENDNOTES

1. §6081

2. Reg. 20.2056A-2(d).

3. §2056(b)(5)

4. The reader may wish to review the basic prior transfer credit material presented earlier in the text before tackling this material.

5. The GSTT applies to nonresident aliens to the extent that the transferred property is situated in the United States for purposes of the estate tax or the gift tax.

6. §2613(a).

7. §2602.

8. §2612(c)(1).

9. §2603(a)(3).

10. §2623.

11. §2612(b).

12. §2641(b).

13. §2642(a)

14. §2632(b)(1) - (b)(3).

15. §2612(c)(2)

16. §2513.

17. §2604.

18. §2611(b)(1).

−13 ————————————————

Lifetime Transfers I: Overview and Survey of Gift Planning

OVERVIEW

The last two chapters focused on property transfers at death. This chapter will introduce lifetime transfers of property, examining the techniques utilized in *giving gifts*, the most popular type of intra-family lifetime transfer. The techniques of planning for other lifetime transfers, including incomplete transfers, intra-family sales, and charitable gifts will be described in Chapter 14.

Lifetime transfers take many forms and are made for many reasons. They are made to individuals and to charities. They are made outright or to a fiduciary such as a trustee or custodian. They can take the form of a completed transfer, such as a sale or a gift, or they can remain incomplete, as in the case of a transfer with a retained interest. They can be a transfer of a total interest in property or just a partial interest.

While you read this chapter and the next, you will want to keep in mind two important principles. First, different types of transfers are designed to accomplish different types of goals. Second, the less complete the transfer, the less likely the transfer will achieve desired *tax* goals. This latter point cannot be over emphasized because clients often prefer to retain some control over the transferred property. By definition, every lifetime transfer requires the relinquishment of some control. Gifts mean loss of access, control and flexibility, and clients who are especially reluctant to give this up are more likely to feel uncomfortable with their estate plan, no matter what the magnitude of the financial rewards. Planners should be sensitive to this issue.

To minimize loss of access, control and flexibility, some clients may contemplate gifts to family members who in turn secretly agree to always make the assets available to the donor. This arrangement is, of course, a retained interest which, if it came to light after the donor died, would cause the property to be included in the donor's estate. There are other problems with this arrangement: First, the donees may have a "change in attitude," later disposing of the gift asset or refusing to share it or return it. Second, the gift assets are subject to the claims of the donee's creditors.

We begin our discussion of lifetime transfers with an examination of completed lifetime gifts, hereafter simply called *gifts*. For present purposes, we shall define a gift as any transfer that gives rise to potential gift taxation. As explained in Chapter 7, a gift is *complete* for tax purposes when there is surrender of dominion and control and delivery of an interest in property by a donor capable of transferring that property to an accepting donee capable of receiving and possessing it.

Essentially, a gift may be made outright, or it may be made to another party, usually a fiduciary, for the benefit of the donee. An *outright* gift results in the receipt by the donee of a fee simple interest in the gift property, yielding to the donee all of the rights that accompany that interest. Thus, an outright gift extends to the donee the greatest flexibility of ownership and control. However, the donor may not wish to bestow that degree of flexibility. For example, a donor may wish to make a sizable gift to help his or her child finance *future* college expenses but is reluctant to make an outright gift.

The usual alternative to an outright gift is the transfer to a *fiduciary*, who is responsible for managing the property and distributing its income and principal in accordance with the legal conditions either contained in the underlying document or established by local law. Significant gifts for a minor are especially likely to be in the name of a fiduciary, such as a custodian, a trustee, or occasionally a guardian. Gifts to adult donees are usually outright but are sometimes made in trust.

The next two sections will describe the major non-tax and tax considerations in making substantial gifts. The discussions will assume an outright gift unless some other type of gift (e.g., one in trust) is specifically mentioned.

NON-TAX MOTIVES FOR MAKING GIFTS

Consider the many non-tax motivations that encourage clients to make gifts. Common examples include the desire by parents or grandparents to provide for an expensive education, to help children finance a home or an automobile, to help establish or expand a business, to encourage a child to work in the client's business, to help a child who has experienced a significant loss or who is unemployed, to care for elderly parents, and the simple desire to witness a donee's enjoyment over the benefits that a gift can bring. Clients will be most willing to make gifts for the *tax* advantages to be described next when they are also motivated by one or more of these *non-tax* objectives.

TAX CONSIDERATIONS IN MAKING GIFTS

There are death tax and income tax advantages and disadvantages of making gifts that must be considered.

Tax Advantages of Gifting

Gifts are commonly made to save federal, state and local death taxes, GSTT, and federal, state and local income taxes. In the examples that follow, look for two common tax threads. First, many gifts can be made at no gift tax cost. Second, even if a gift tax is incurred, gifts may still be desirable because they often have the potential of reducing total transfer taxes and income taxes.

    Death tax and GSTT advantages. Death tax and GSTT advantages include the ability to reduce or freeze the taxable estate in three ways: using the shelter of the annual exclusion and the unified credit, avoiding grossing up, and excluding postgift appreciation. Each will be discussed next.

    1. Shelter of annual exclusion and unified credit. Most clients about to embark upon a program of gifting will be able to transfer a significant portion of their estate, free of gift tax, death tax and GSTT. The gift tax and GSTT annual exclusions enable a donor to gift, free of tax, $10,000 per donee per year. Spousal gift splitting doubles this amount to $20,000.

EXAMPLE 13 - 1. Mom wishes to gift maximum equal amounts of her own property to her three children and three grandchildren. Each of the six donees can receive $10,000 each year, gift tax and GSTT free, adding up to a current aggregate annual tax-free gift total of $60,000.

In the above example, because total gross gifts to any one donee during a given calendar year will amount to no more than the annual exclusion, the donor need not even file a gift tax return.

EXAMPLE 13-2. Altering the facts in Example 13-1 a bit, assume that Dad also wishes to make similar annual exclusion gifts of *his own* property interests. Each of the six donees can now receive $20,000 each year for a current annual gift total of $120,000. Neither Mom nor Dad need file a gift tax return.

EXAMPLE 13 - 3. In the $120,000 total gift example immediately above, if greater than $60,000 of the gift property belonged to one of the two donors, they would have to *split* the gifts and file two gift tax returns each year. However, the tax outcome would be unchanged; of the total of $120,000 in gifts per year, no gift tax or GSTT would be due because taxable gifts would still equal zero.

Generalizing from these examples, the total number of annual exclusions available over time equals the number of donors times the number of donees times the number of years of gifting. Thus, in the above examples, if the donors engaged in gifting each year for the next eight years, they could make 96 annual exclusion gifts totaling $960,000 [= (2 x 6 x 8) x $10,000].

Actually, a donor can gift a much larger amount, gift tax (and GSTT) free, but only if the donor is willing to use up some unified credit (and, if applicable, the GSTT exemption).

EXAMPLE 13 - 4. In Example 13 - 2, if Mom and Dad gave $50,000 to each person, they will have made six taxable gifts of $30,000, or total taxable gifts for the year of $180,000. Assuming that the donors had made no prior taxable gifts, the tentative gift tax on their joint gift-tax return will be $48,400. Although the application of the unified credit would result in a zero gift tax, the amount of the spousal combined unused unified credit would be reduced by $48,400, from $385,600 (two times $192,800) to $337,200. Each donor would be able to gift an additional $510,000 in excess of all annual exclusions, without paying any gift tax since each has used up only $90,000 of the $600,000 unified credit equivalent.

Thus, spouses with five suitable donees can give away, tax free, a total of $2.2 million over a span of 10 years. Of course, the couple would totally use up their unified credits, making the lifetime or death time transfer of the next dollar in excess of the annual exclusion subject to tax at the marginal rate of 37%. Regarding *GSTT*, spouses can gift, GSTT free, a total of $2 million (two $1 million lifetime exemptions), plus $20,000 times the number of suitable beneficiaries per year.

EXAMPLE 13 - 5. Corey, a bachelor, has already made total lifetime taxable gifts of $600,000. This year, he makes a single gift of a painting Corey appraised at $20,000. His gift tax will be $3,700, determined as follows:

Gross Gift	$20,000
Less annual exclusion	($10,000)
Current taxable gift	$10,000
Plus prior taxable gifts	$600,000
Total Taxable gifts	$610,000
Tentative tax on total	$196,500
Less tentative tax on prior taxable gifts	($192,800)
Tentative tax on current gifts	$3,700
Less unused unified credit	$0
Gift tax payable	$3,700

Since the annual exclusion applies only to lifetime transfers, a somewhat different tax result would occur if the most recent transfer was made at death.

EXAMPLE 13 - 6. Assume the same basic facts as in Example 13-5, except that Corey dies owning the $20,000 painting, and therefore transfers it at death. The estate tax due will be $7,400, calculated as follows:

Taxable estate	$20,000
Adjusted taxable gifts	$600,000
Estate tax base	$620,000
Tentative tax	$200,200
Less unified credit	$192,800
Estate tax	$7,400

The $3,700 difference in the tax for the two prior examples is due to the absence of a per donee exclusion in calculating the estate tax.

Summarizing, the making of annual exclusion gifts and gifts sheltered by the unified credit and the $1 million lifetime GSTT exemption represents a simple estate planning technique that enables clients to substantially reduce their gross estate prior to death without having to pay gift taxes or GST tax.

2. No grossing up. The second death tax and GSTT advantage of gifting derives from the ability to exclude from the gross estate the amount of any *gift tax* paid on gifts given more than three years before death. As mentioned, unlike the estate tax, the gift tax is calculated on a tax exclusive basis. At this point, please take a few minutes to review the examples in the grossing up section of Chapter 6, that illustrate the estate tax advantage to paying a gift tax.

One additional point, grossing up can be avoided even for gift tax paid on gifts made within three years of death if the decedent and spouse elect gift splitting and the surviving spouse paid the entire gift tax.

3. Postgift appreciation. The third death tax and GSTT advantage of gifting is the ability to exclude postgift appreciation of the gifted property from future estate tax and GSTT. It can accomplish this tax saving in two different ways. First, gifting will usually *freeze* estate tax values by limiting the estate tax value of the transferred asset to its adjusted gift value. Second, gifting can *leverage* the use of exclusions, exemptions and the unified credit by transferring assets whose present low value is totally sheltered by these tax breaks, thereby excluding from estate tax and GSTT the entire value of the asset, including all future appreciation. The unique effects of freezing and leveraging have been amply demonstrated with numerous examples in Chapter 9. The following illustrates the use of both techniques in a single fact situation.

> EXAMPLE 13 - 7. Eighty-two year old Jeanne's estate consists of $2 million in municipal bonds and $1 million in common stock. More than able to live well on the bond income, Jeanne gifts all of the stock to an irrevocable trust paying the income to her three children for their lives with the remainder going to her grandchildren. Jeanne allocates her $1 million GSTT exemption to this transfer. In this simple but effective estate freeze, Jeanne has virtually ensured that she will die with an estate tax base at about $3 million (assets owned at death plus adjusted taxable gifts), no matter how much the value of the stocks rise. And Jeanne has leveraged the use of her $1 million GSTT exemption. For example, if the stock is eventually worth $4 million when it passes to the grandchildren, each $1 in current GSTT exemption will have sheltered $4 from GSTT.

Comprehensive example. By way of a complete review of these three major tax advantages of making lifetime gifts, consider the following comprehensive example. Assume that all transfers occur after 1987, when the unified credit is $192,800. While the numbers focus solely on estate tax savings, please keep in mind that substantial GSTT savings would also occur if the gift was to a skip person.

> EXAMPLE 13 - 8. Burt, a widower, has a net estate of $5 million. His estate planner predicts that the property will double in value to $10 million in 10 years, the length of Burt's expected life span. While a planner would likely advise a number of gifts to take advantage of multiple annual exclusions over the years, for simplicity, we will assume that Burt agrees to make just one really big gift this year: $2,000,000 to his only child. Burt's total transfer taxes will be $3,200,650, assuming this is the only gift made, rather than the $4,948,000 that would be paid if the gift is not made, a difference of $1,747,350.
>
> *Suppose Burt makes the gift:* Assuming that he has made no prior taxable gifts, Burt will pay a gift tax of $583,500, calculated as follows:

Gross Gift	$2,000,000
Less annual exclusion	($10,000)
Taxable gift	$1,990,000
Tentative tax	$776,300
Less unified credit	($192,800)
Gift tax payable	$583,500

Burt dies in 10 years, owning property worth $4,833,000. He started with $5,000,000, but gave away $2,000,000 and paid gift taxes of $583,500. What remained was worth $2,416,500, which doubled over the decade to $4,833,000. Burt's estate tax will be $2,617,150, calculated as follows:

Taxable estate	$4,833,000
Adjusted taxable gifts	$1,990,000
Estate tax base	$6,823,000
Tentative tax	$3,393,450
Less gift tax payable credit	($583,500)
Less unified credit	($192,800)
Estate tax	$2,617,150

Burt's child will receive a total of $6,215,850, which is the sum of $2,215,850, the value of Burt's after tax estate, plus $4 million, the date of death value of the gift property.

Burt does not make the gift: Alternatively, if Burt does not make the gift, his beneficiaries will receive only $5,052,000, which is the $10 million value of the estate, reduced by estate tax of $4,948,000, calculated as follows:

Taxable estate	$10,000,000
Adjusted taxable gifts	$0
Estate tax base	$10,000,000
Tentative tax	$5,140,800
Less unified credit	($192,800)
Estate tax	$4,948,000

Burt's child will receive a total of $5,052,000, which is the estate of $10 million less the estate tax. This is $1,163,850 [$6,215,850 - $5,052,000] less than achieved by making the $2,000,000 gift.

Let's analyze the increased wealth to the next generation that results from making this large gift. As a result of Burt's gift, his son will have, by the time Burt dies, $1,163,850 more than he would have had if no gift was made. We have deliberately kept the taxable amounts in the 55% marginal tax range, so that changes between the two alternatives will be affected by that marginal tax rate. Here, is a summary of elements (three positive and one negative) that cause the difference:

♦ appreciation on $2 million avoided tax	$1,100,000
♦ the gift tax ($583,500, doubled) avoided tax	$641,850
♦ annual exclusion avoided tax	$5,500
♦ less the appreciation on the gift tax	($583,500)
Net increase to Burt's son	$1,163,850

This example assumed that Burt made only one lifetime gift to just one person, thereby reaping the benefit of only one annual exclusion. Substantially more transfer tax would be saved if Burt made many smaller gifts to several persons *each year* until his death, utilizing the shelter of multiple annual exclusions.

Must gifts be made more than three years before death to keep the assets out of the gross estate? No, except for gifts of life insurance or relinquishments of §2036, §2037 or §2038 retained interests.[1] In fact, donors can make deathbed gifts to take advantage of the annual exclusion. Chapter 17 will describe the use of the durable power of attorney for property, that enables even an incapacitated client's agent to make gifts on the client's behalf. However, the IRS has ruled that the document creating the power must expressly authorize the attorney-in-fact to make gifts,[2] otherwise, any transfers will be treated as revocable, therefore incomplete.

In conclusion, a program of gifting can result in substantial estate tax and GSTT savings and, commonly, the ultimate transfer of a larger amount of wealth, tax free, to succeeding generations. The gifts can be tax sheltered by the annual exclusion as well as by the exclusion of both the gift tax and postgift appreciation from the donor's taxable estate.

Income tax advantages. The making of gifts also offers some income tax advantages, including shifting income.

Shifting income. As we saw in Chapter 9, gifts can result in some income shifting. In general, since the donee (or trustee, for gifts into an irrevocable trust) becomes the owner of gifted property, any income earned on that property will be taxed to the donee (or trustee or trust beneficiary), who is usually subject to a lower marginal income tax rate. Further, the reduced taxable income to the donor might put her or him in a lower tax bracket.

As explained in earlier in the text, outright gifts to children under age 14 will not save much income tax due to the *kiddie tax*.

EXAMPLE 13 - 9. In 1994, the Gerards were in the 50%, Federal and state combined, marginal income tax bracket, and wished to shift taxable income to a custodial account for their 13-year-old son, Wayne, who had no other income. They transferred $12,000 in 10% coupon bonds to Wayne, who was taxed on the $1,200 interest received for the year. After subtracting $600, the maximum standard deduction amount allowable against unearned income of a dependent, Wayne's income tax for the first year on the remaining $600 was $90, which is $510 less than the $600 tax that would have been owed by the Gerards. The Gerards realized that it would not make any income tax sense to shift additional income to Wayne by transferring additional income producing securities since the additional income would be all taxed at their rate, not Wayne's.

Beginning in the taxable year that a child reaches age 14, the kiddie tax will not apply and all of the child's income will be taxable to the child.

> EXAMPLE 13 - 10. Continuing Example 13-9 above, in the following year Wayne turned 14, and the Gerards transferred an additional $48,000 in 10% coupon bonds for Wayne's benefit. Wayne's income tax on the total 1995 taxable income of $6,000 was $810 (= ($6000 - $600) x .15). This is $2,190 less than the tax of $3,000 that would have otherwise been payable by the Gerards (i.e., .50 x $6,000 = $3,000).

The example immediately above involved the shifting of $6,000 in 15% taxable income. At the limit, as much as $24,000 in 1996 income could be shifted to a 15% income tax bracket for an *individual* (age 14 or older) reporting no other income, assuming a standard deduction of $650.[3] On the other hand, a *trust's* 15% bracket ends at $1,650, reflecting Congress's strong interest in discouraging the use of trusts to shift income.

As these examples suggest, parents anticipating paying their children's college expenses may wish to transfer assets to the children to reduce the income tax bite. However, tax law may help them to acquire certain investments to finance college expenses without transferring assets and at no tax cost. Interest on certain U.S. EE Saving Bonds purchased and owned by one or both parents themselves (or by the student, if at least 24 years old) after 1989 and redeemed to pay tuition and fees will not be subject to income tax. However, this interest exclusion is phased out for taxpayers having "modified" 1996 adjusted gross income (indexed) between $65,250 and $95,250 for joint returns, and between $43,500 and $58,500 for single and head of household returns.[4] According to §135, modified adjusted gross income is adjusted gross income without regard to §911, §931 or §933 (foreign income exclusions), and after application of §86 (taxable social security income), §219 (retirement contribution deductions), and §469 (limit on deductibility of passive losses).

Obtaining a step-up in basis. In Chapter 7 the reader learned that the income tax basis of any property owned by a decedent at death will be stepped-up to date of death value. This step-up is particularly valuable for people wishing to sell rapidly appreciating property. Unfortunately, the property owner must *die* to accomplish the step-up. Astute readers may wonder whether gifting may be able to accelerate the timing of this step-up. For example, could A, owner of a low basis asset and in excellent health, gift the asset to B, who dying, to achieve an earlier basis step-up in the asset, which A will later sell after having received the asset back by way of B's will or trust? As we'll see in two examples later in the chapter, the answer is yes, as long as B doesn't die within one year of the gift date.

Tax Disadvantages of Gifting

There are several tax dangers and disadvantages in making lifetime gifts, including prepaying the transfer tax, adverse §2035 consequences, the danger that the gift is later ruled incomplete, and loss of step-up in basis.

Prepaying the transfer tax. A *large gift* can result in a gift tax liability that must be paid by April 15 of the following year, thereby reducing the client-donor funds available for investment. Nonetheless, as we have seen, prepayment of the transfer tax is justifiable if it has the effect of substantially reducing the client's estate tax. This will happen if the gift property appreciates greatly before the client's death or if it appreciates modestly and the client can avoid grossing up by surviving at least three years after making the gift. On the other hand, gifting property and prepaying the transfer tax may turn out to have been a costly mistake, particularly in situations where the property actually *declines* in value and the client *dies within three years* of making the gift. Then no transfer taxes will have been saved, the client lost the use of the gift tax money, and the donee has a carry over basis on the property. Thus, to assess the likelihood of financial success resulting from a large gift, the planner should consider factors such as the life expectancy of the client-donor, the expected appreciation potential of the property, the different basis rules, and the utility of the property to the donor and to the donee.

Even if a large gift is totally sheltered by the unified credit, it will have the effect of reducing the amount that can be transferred at death free of tax since it will be included in the estate tax base as an adjusted taxable gift. Before recommending large gifts or a gift giving plan, one must determine whether the gifts will also be subjected to state gift taxes since there is no federal state gift taxes credit, whereas there is a federal state death tax credit.[5]

An additional adverse §2035 consequence: unsheltered postgift appreciation. We mentioned in the preceding discussion that if a gift is made within three years of death, §2035(c) requires the gift tax paid be included in the donor's gross estate under the grossing-up rule. In addition to this adverse consequence, recall the discussion in Chapter 6 that the entire *date-of-death value* of the gift property is included in the donor's gross estate if the retained interest rules of §§2036, 2037, 2038 apply, or an incident of ownership in life insurance was retained, §2042, at the date of death; and of course §2035(d)(2) causes inclusion if a transfer of a retained interest or of an incident of ownership in life insurance occurs within three years of death.

As mentioned in Chapter 10, another potentially common pitfall under §2035(d)(2) can arise when a trustee of a revocable living trust makes a gift within three years of the trustor's death. The IRS has been very aggressively taking the position that the gift constitutes a relinquishment of revocability that under §2038 will subject the date-of-death value of the gift to inclusion in the trustor's gross estate. To avoid this result, either the gift should be made directly by the trustor, after withdrawal from the trust, or the trustee should be empowered to make distributions only to the trustor.

In summary, §2035(c) and §2035(d)(2) can have the effect of taking back all three major advantages of gifting. These two sections require grossing up of gift taxes and, in the case of life insurance and transfers in which retained controls are relinquished within three years before death, including all postgift appreciation in the taxable estate. Remember that if a transfer is pulled back into the gross estate the benefit of the annual exclusion is lost. In essence, insofar as the death taxes are concerned, it is as though the gift never took place.

Gift later ruled incomplete. If it is later determined that a gift was not complete, the date-of-death value of the property will be included in the donor's gross estate in spite of the fact that the donor, in all good faith, paid a gift tax at the time of the gift. The estate will receive a credit for the gift tax paid, but from a transfer tax perspective the gift will be considered as not having been made. Common examples of defective gift schemes include giving stocks and bonds while retaining an interest, transferring title to the residence but continuing to live there rent-free, and transferring property to an irrevocable trust but retaining discretionary powers, or giving those powers to the trustee but reserving the right to serve as trustee. A different, timing problem is illustrated in the following example:

EXAMPLE 13 - 11. On her deathbed, decedent made a gift by writing a check on her bank account. She died before the check was cashed. In her state, because she had the power to revoke by stopping payment, the gift was not complete, and therefore includable in her gross estate under §2038.

Loss of step-up in basis. A major tax disadvantage of making lifetime gifts is the loss in the step-up in basis that would have been received on appreciated property had it been retained by the donor until death. This is a drawback for a donee who wishes to sell the appreciated property. On the other hand, if the donee has no plans to sell the property during his or her lifetime, or intends to trade the asset in a tax-deferred exchange, the problem might disappear since there will be a step-up in basis at the donee's death.

> EXAMPLE 13 - 12. Granny has always wanted to do something nice for her loving, adult grandson, and today she gives him some real property that she and her deceased husband acquired in the 1920's. When Granny dies, the gift property will not receive a step-up in basis, and grandson will own an asset with a sizable unrealized gain to be recognized if he sells it prior to his death. However, this potential taxable gain will vanish if grandson dies owning the property.

Other disadvantages. Two other tax disadvantages to consider are noted briefly.

Net gifts. First, a particular income tax disadvantage applies to net gifts, discussed in Chapter 7, whereby the donee agrees to pay the gift tax thus reducing the value of the gift, which in turn reduces the gift tax. A net gift can result in a taxable gain to the donor if the gift tax paid by the donee exceeds the donor's basis in the property.

Valuation disputes with IRS. Second, a significant valuation problem can arise with gifting. The IRS will sometimes successfully challenge the value of a gift in both gift tax and estate tax audits, even many years after the gift was made because of the lack of an effective statute of limitations.

Estate and Gift Tax Statute of Limitations. The statute of limitations for both estate tax returns and for gift tax returns is three years after the return is filed, except for an early filed return the three years starts from the due date of the return.[6] There are exceptions to the three year rule; for instance, if the return under reports the value of the gross estate or the total gifts by more than 25% the statute of limitations is increased to six years after the return is filed, and there is no time limit if the return is filed with an intent to commit fraud or to willfully evade taxes. Finally, there is no time limit if no return is filed.[7]

Because Corey, in Example 13-5, had an appraisal of the painting he gave away, and he was not trying to evade gift taxes, the IRS is limited by the three year statute of limitations in challenging the value of the painting for gift tax purposes. However, the IRS may challenge the adjusted taxable gifts value of this gift on the estate tax return at Corey's death, even if his death occurs many years later. This later challenge would serve only to boost the taxable estate into higher marginal rates and would not result in any more gift tax being paid, in fact the gift tax payable credit would have to be recalculated based on the higher value of the gift. Thus, the gift tax period of limitation is not increased but the estate tax will be higher if the revaluation of the gift boosts the estate into a higher marginal rate.[8]

Another major consideration in giving is the selection of the best assets to gift.

TYPES OF ASSETS TO GIVE

In giving, the client usually has a wide selection of assets from which to choose. From an estate planning perspective, some assets make better gifts than others. The following constitutes a basic set of guidelines for selecting gift property. As the examples will illustrate, the choice of the best asset will usually depend on the specific family situation.

Basis Considerations

An asset's basis will influence its potential gift appeal.

Gifting high-basis assets to reduce taxable gain. Other things being the equal, a high-basis asset makes a better gift than a low-basis asset, if the donee is likely to sell the asset soon after receiving it. As we have seen, the general rule is that the donee retains the donor's basis. Sale by the donee at a price above this basis results in a taxable gain, thus, the higher the basis the lower the taxable gain.

EXAMPLE 13 - 13. Donor wishes to give donee $100,000 in marketable securities. Donor owns stock A, now worth $100,000, which she purchased two years ago for $95,000; and stock B, also worth $100,000, which was acquired 15 years ago for $20,000. The donee plans to sell the stock he receives when it reaches $110,000 in value. The donee will realize a gain of only $15,000 on the sale of stock A but a gain of $90,000 on the sale of stock B. Needless to say, the donee would prefer to receive stock A.

Although a high-basis asset usually makes a good gift from an income tax point of view, it will make an unattractive gift if its basis is too high, i.e., higher than its date-of-gift value. Property in which the owner has an *unrealized loss* is not a good asset to give because the donee, upon selling it, will not be able to recognize that loss. A better strategy would be for the donor to sell the property, realize the loss, and then give the cash to the donee.

Gifting low-basis assets for other reasons. On the other hand, giving low-basis assets makes more sense in some circumstances. For example, if for liquidity or other reasons a donor *plans to sell* a retained asset at the time of giving another asset, he or she should consider gifting a lower-basis asset and selling the higher-basis asset in order to personally incur a lower tax outlay. This strategy will be especially productive if the donee either is in a lower tax bracket or has no immediate plans to sell the property received as a gift. Gain realized upon later sale by the donee will at least be deferred, and may be totally eliminated due to the step-up-at-death principle, if the donee dies before the asset is sold. Keep in mind the Rubber Band Rule discussed in Chapter 7 whereby appreciated property that returns to the donor as a result of the donee's death has an adjusted basis to the donor the donee-decedent's adjusted basis immediately before the donee-decedent's death.

Assets having sentimental or utilitarian value are more likely to be kept by a donee. If a gift is going to be kept by the donee, basis considerations are unnecessary.

Postgift Appreciation

General considerations. If estate tax reduction is a major goal, the generous client should consider gifting *growth assets*, that is, assets expected to appreciate substantially, rather than assets whose value is likely to remain stable or to fall. Some assets have greater inherent appreciation potential than others, although in general this determination represents mere speculation. However, assets such as life insurance, or equity interests in either a closely held business or real estate may be likely growth prospects, while assets such as patent and royalty rights, whose value usually declines over time, would not make good gift assets in this context. Cash and cash equivalents are also less than highly desirable, because their values cannot be expected to rise. In general, from a transfer-tax point of view, assets having a combined low gift tax value and potentially high estate tax value make the best gifts.

Opportunity shifting. An excellent example of a type of gift of highly appreciating assets is called opportunity shifting. It involves the transfer of a wealth- or an income-producing opportunity before it is objectively ascertainable. For example, business clients may be able to recognize the prospect of a profitable commercial enterprise before it blossoms sufficiently into a verifiably valuable opportunity. By transferring ownership during its early stages, a value shift can occur without transfer-tax cost and before the income the venture generates is considered attributable to the client.

> EXAMPLE 13 - 14. Dad, owner of a successful computer component firm, has just established a new corporation to pursue the viability of a recently developed engineering idea. The new firm is capitalized at $50,000, and Dad gives an adult daughter 20% of the stock and places another 20% in an irrevocable trust for the benefit of his minor son.

This example demonstrates the creation of *additional taxpaying entities*, the new corporation and the trust, as well as the *splitting* income and wealth among more family members before the value of the enterprise has manifested itself. Similar techniques can be arranged for almost any asset that is expected to appreciate in value. Good hunches by savvy people are the major sources of intra-family opportunity shifting.

Administration Problems

Assets that are likely to create problems in estate administration can make good gift assets. For example, *art works*, especially those currently worth less than the annual gift tax exclusion, may not need to be valued if transferred by lifetime gift, but could create valuation disputes, a potentially higher estate tax, and additional costs of valuation if transferred at death. Further, *aliquot assets* such as real estate may need to be sold to pay death taxes, if transferred at death. Alternatively, a lifetime gift of these assets may avoid a later problem.

Other Asset Choice Considerations

Transfer income earning assets to shift income. Where income shifting is a planning goal, high income earning assets make better gifts. As we have seen, income tax law in general requires an actual transfer of the "tree" (asset) in order to transfer the "fruit" (income) of that tree.

Avoid gifting assets with tax benefits to donor. The well-heeled donor should ordinarily consider gifting assets that do not have *built-in tax benefits* such as income exclusions, deductions, or credits which would be of less value to a lower bracket donee. The client should consider retaining assets such as tax shelters, municipal bonds, and income-producing real property in his or her own portfolio. However, when a tax-shelter property reaches the "crossover point" and begins to throw off "phantom income" to the investor, it may be a good time to gift the property, to shift the income to a lower bracket.

Gift nonbusiness assets to qualify for §303, §2032A and §6166. Giving nonbusiness property may offer death and income tax advantages by virtue of reducing the decedent's taxable estate, thereby increasing the portion that is considered business in the estate retained such that specific provisions of the Internal Revenue Code that are favorable to business owners apply. These provisions allow the following tax saving opportunities:

a. **§303** - This section allows the estate to pay death taxes, funeral bills, and administrative expenses, with cash from a closely held corporation provided the corporation stock is valued at 35% or more of the decedent's adjusted gross estate (AGE). The corporation can buy back stock from the decedent's estate with the transaction being treated as a capital transaction instead of a dividend distribution. Since the stock held by the estate will have received a step-up in basis there should be very little, if any, capital gain.[9]

b. **§2032A** - This section allows the real estate used in a closely held business to be reduced by up to $750,000 based upon its special use valuation. The decedent's special use real estate must equal or exceed 25% of the decedent's AGE and the real estate combined with the rest of the special use business must be equal or exceed 50% of the AGE.[10]

c. **§6166 -** This section allows payout over 14 years (with a favorable 4%

late payment interest charge on $153,000 of the deferred tax) provided the business is equal to or greater than 35% of AGE.[11]

For clients with business interests that don't meet the percentage requirements, gifts of nonbusiness assets will increase the business percentage. However, IRC§2035(d)(3) requires that the percentage requirements for §303 and §2032A be met with any transfers within 3 years added back into the gross estate, and IRC§2035(d)(4) requires that for §6066 the business meet the 35% threshold with and without gifts made within three years of decedent's death. Note that this "adding back" is done to determine whether the estate still meets the percentage thresholds, it does NOT mean that the gifts are actually added into the gross estate for tax purposes.

EXAMPLE 13 - 15. Farmer Brown had the following assets immediately before and after he gave away his XYZ stock to his three children:

items	FMV @ DOG	2032A %	FMV @ DOG	2032A %
stock	$750,000			
farm land	$700,000	32.6%	$700,000	50.0%
farm equipment	$150,000	39.5%	$150,000	60.7%
other property	$550,000		$550,000	
	$2,150,000		$1,400,000	

To qualify for §2032A the business land must equal 25% or more of AGE, and the land and other business property (tractors, etc.) must equal 50% or more of AGE. The gift accomplishes this, provided the thresholds are still met when he dies.

EXAMPLE 13 - 16. Farmer Brown dies about three years after making the gift of stock. The stock has increased in value to $800,000 and the other items (still owned by him when he died) have the values shown in the table:

items	FMV @ DOD	2032A %	FMV @ DOD	2032A %
stock	$800,000			
farm land	$740,000	32.0%	$740,000	48.8%
farm equipment	$125,000	37.4%	$125,000	57.1%
other property	$650,000		$650,000	
	$2,315,000		$1,515,000	

If his death was just short of three years, the land percentage is met (i.e, 32% > 25%), but the total special use business percentage is not met (i.e., 37.4% < 50%), thus special use is not available. If his death is just beyond the three year reach of §2035(d)(3), then the gift is not added back to determine §2032A, and the two §2032A percentage limits are exceeded (i.e., 48.8% > 25% and 57.1% > 50%). Notice that the 35% threshold for §6166 (drawn-out payment schedule) is met both with and without the gift, therefore the §6166 election is available regardless of whether the death was just under or just over three years after the gift. One final comment, even if farmer Brown died within three years of the gift, the stock's appreciation is NOT being taxed, nor is the annual exclusion lost. The gift of the stock is still an adjusted taxable gift of $720,000 (three kids, three annual exclusions). It is not part of the gross estate. We were merely bring it back to test whether the elections (§§ 303, 2032A and 6166) are available.

Miscellaneous tax factors. Some assets should not be gifted if they may generate adverse tax consequences. For example, consider an asset for which the donor had taken the *investment tax credit*, which was repealed by TRA 86. If the donor gifts the asset before the end of its useful life, he or she will be required to "recapture" part of the credit, that is, repay part of the taxes saved from the credit.

In at least one situation, gifts to children can generate a tax benefit otherwise unavailable to the parents.

EXAMPLE 13 - 17. Because of their high income, the Piatts are not qualified to contribute before-tax dollars to an *Individual Retirement Account* (IRA). Their adult son, John, is qualified, he cannot afford to make the contributions. John enters into an informal agreement with his parents, who will give him $1,500 a year, to help contribute $2,000 to his own IRA. This annual arrangement is to continue indefinitely, so long as John adds $500 and does not make any premature withdrawals. Each year, John will save hundreds of dollars in income tax by taking the IRA deduction. The Piatts have the satisfaction of knowing that have increased the financial security of his later years.

As a result of the kiddie tax, generous parents may wish to transfer to their young children property that *does not generate taxable income*, at least not until the children reach age 14. Possible assets include U.S. government EE bonds, municipal bonds, interests in land, a closely held business, and growth stocks. In many situations, the parent can then determine the timing of the tax "hit" by choosing which year to liquidate the assets and, consequently, which year to realize the likely gain. It should be mentioned that the popular U.S. Government EE savings bonds are not transferable. An outright gift of them is considered a redemption. However, there is no restriction on an owner adding co-owners.

While the material up to now has centered on a discussion of the tax and non-tax aspects of gifting to individuals in general, the next section discusses gifts to a spouse followed by a section on gifts to minor children. We choose to focus on these donees because several tax and non-tax implications of gifts to them are unique and require further explanation. Gifts to spouses are different in part because of the additional tax saving available through the use of the marital deduction. Gifts to minors are unique in part because of the techniques by which the transfer is often arranged, usually with the assistance of a fiduciary.

GIFTS TO THE SPOUSE: TECHNIQUES AND CONSIDERATIONS

This section will explore the tax characteristics of lifetime gifts between spouses. We shall see that the gift tax marital deduction offers unique planning opportunities to reduce taxes, in some cases by an even greater amount than for gifts to a nonspouse. The following material discusses inter-spousal gift considerations involved in saving death taxes and income taxes.

Inter-spousal Gifts to Save Death Taxes

In the last two chapters, we examined in some detail several marital deduction techniques designed to minimize, or at least postpone, the estate tax for a married couple. We will now see that when one spouse is substantially wealthier than the other and there is a significant chance that the less wealthy spouse will die first, death taxes can sometimes be saved by means of bypass planning coupled with a program of inter-spousal gifts. However, this strategy will not work if the basic testamentary scheme involves the simple 100% marital deduction, as the following example shows.

> EXAMPLE 13 - 18. Husband has a $2 million estate and wife owns nothing. Their estate plan leaves everything to the survivor, who then leaves everything to their children. Without a change in their estate plan, restructuring the distribution of wealth between them by means of completed gifts will result in no estate tax saving. The first spouse to die, whether husband or wife, will leave an estate subject to no estate tax, either because there is no gross estate (wife dies first) or because the entire gross estate is sheltered by the 100% marital deduction (husband dies first or

gifts were made to balance the estates). Thus, either spouse, as S2, will wind up owning the entire $2 million at death no matter how much each spouse owned prior to their deaths, and inter-spousal gifts will not change the total estate tax. See Figure 13-1.

FIGURE 13-1 Based on Example 13-18: No Inter-spousal Gifts, 100% MD Plan

---

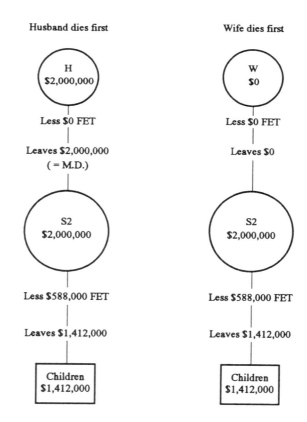

However, if the spouses use a bypass trust, estate tax may be saved by means of lifetime inter-spousal gifts, as the following two examples demonstrate. First we'll see the effect if no gift is made, and then we'll calculate the estate tax savings from an inter-spousal gift.

EXAMPLE 13 - 19. Let's assume that the couple in Example 13-18 creates a *credit shelter bypass*, but the husband makes *no lifetime gifts*. The family wealth will devolve in the following manner: S1 will incur no estate tax no matter which spouse dies first, either because that spouse owns no property or because of the combined shelter of the marital deduction and the unified credit. If husband dies first, wife will receive $1.4 million and $600,000 will pass to the bypass share. Upon wife's later death, her estate will incur an estate tax of $320,000, leaving a net combined amount to the children of $ 1,680,000, which is the sum of $1,080,000 from her, plus 600,000 from the bypass share. Alternatively, *if wife dies first*, husband's $2 million estate at his later death will incur an estate tax of $588,000, leaving a total of only $1,412,000 to pass to the children. No bypass would be created if wife died first since wife had no assets to put into a bypass trust. See Figure 13-2.

FIGURE 13-2 Illustration of Example 13-19: No Gifts, AB Trust Plan

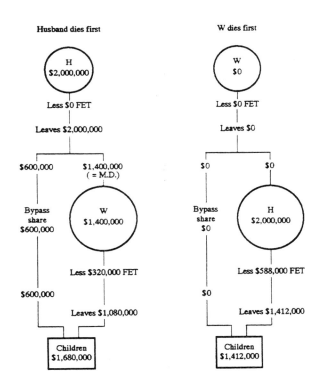

Now consider the effect of an *inter-spousal gift* upon this credit shelter bypass plan.

> EXAMPLE 13 - 20. Assume that the husband in Example 13-19 *gives* his wife one half of his wealth. The effects on estate tax under a credit shelter bypass plan are as follows. Since the gift was made between the spouses no gift tax will be due. The gift will not even be listed on husband's estate tax return as an adjusted taxable gift because the transfer tax scheme subtracts the marital deduction amount in arriving at adjusted taxable gifts.
>
> If the husband dies first, the results will be the same as in the 'no-gifts' Example 13-19: there will be no estate tax upon husband's death, and an estate tax of $320,000 upon wife's later death. However, if *wife dies first*, a markedly different result will occur as compared to when she had no estate. Wife's estate will still incur no estate tax, but on husband's later death there will be an estate tax of $320,000, an amount that is $268,000 less than the Example 13-18 result in which no gift had been made. Thus, the children will be able to receive a total of $1,680,000, rather than $1,412,000. Husband's gift of one half of his wealth to wife will, if wife predeceases husband, generate a transfer tax saving of $268,000. See Figure 13-3.

The inter-spousal gift saved estate tax because it enabled the less wealthy S1 to devise property into the bypass, thereby reducing S2's gross estate and estate tax. Similarly, other inter-spousal gifts can also generate large tax savings for other types of bypass arrangements.

Drawbacks. In spite of the large potential estate tax saving, the wealthier spouse may have some reservations about making a sizable gift to his or her spouse.

Relinquishment of control. First, for the transfer to be complete, the donor spouse must be willing to surrender complete dominion and control to his or her spouse. In this age of high rates of marital dissolution, planners should be mindful of the possibility of future marital strife and its effect on the overall plan. It could generate a bitter regret by the donor that the gift was ever made. Further, even if the spouses are happily married, the wealthier spouse may still be reluctant to relinquish control over so much wealth. As a possible solution, the donor spouse could instead transfer the property into a living QTIP trust that prevents the donee spouse from exercising dispositive control over the corpus. However, if the donee spouse does in fact die first, §2036 may require later inclusion of the corpus in the donor's (S2's) gross estate to the extent that the latter retained any benefits or controls (such as a life estate in the income).

FIGURE 13-3 Illustration of Example 13-20: Gift to Wife, AB Trust Plan

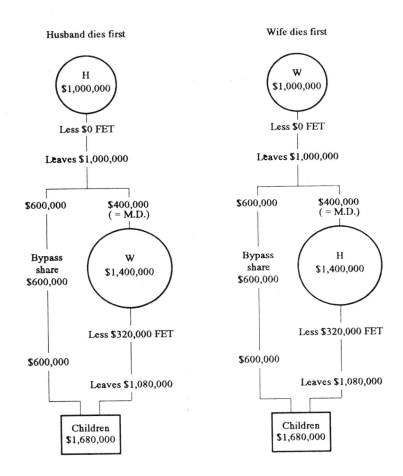

FET saving unlikely. Second, demographic statistics indicate two salient facts: many more wives survive their husbands than vice versa and husbands in noncommunity property states are likely to be wealthier than their wives. Thus, in the most common situations, where the wealthier spouse (husband) dies first, a prior lifetime gift to the less affluent spouse (wife) will have saved no estate tax, as Example 13-18 demonstrated. Thus, estate-leveling inter-spousal gifts designed to maximize estate tax saving through bypass plans will accomplish this goal in only a minority of family situations.

In conclusion, completed inter-spousal gifts, when added to an estate bypass plan, can occasionally result in estate tax savings. The strategy will work in situations where the less wealthy spouse is expected to die first and where the spouses are happily married, elderly, and reasonably confident in each other's ability to faithfully handle such an undertaking.

Inter-spousal Gifts to Save Income Taxes

Ordinarily, there is no *lifetime* income tax advantage to inter-spousal gifts. As we have seen, the joint income tax return, filed by the overwhelming majority of spouses, has the effect of combining spousal income and produces one tax, no matter which spouse earned the income. However, a completed gift from one spouse to the other can save income taxes if the donee spouse dies first, and the donor later sells it at a gain. The tax-saving results from the opportunity to experience a step-up in basis before sale and was illustrated earlier in this chapter. Of course one must avoid §1014(e)'s rubber band rule: if one gets gives appreciated property and the donee bequeaths it back within one year, there is no step-up in basis.

> EXAMPLE 13 - 21. Bob gave his wife stock that he had bought for $6,000. It was worth $50,000 when he gave it to her. She died seven months later, leaving the stock, then worth $55,000, to Bob. He was unable to obtain a step-up in basis due to the restriction in Code Section 1014(e). However, had wife *lived longer than one year*, Bob's basis would have been $55,000 (assuming that as the date of death value), because of the resulting step-up in basis.

> EXAMPLE 13 - 22. In the prior example, had Bob's wife bequeathed the property to her *bypass trust* for the benefit of husband, §1014(e) would not apply because the property would pass to a different party (the trustee) and not back to the donor-spouse. Thus, a step-up would have been available even if the donee spouse had not lived one year after the gift had been made.

As a result, the gifting strategy used by couples such as those in the example illustrated in Figure 13-3 will save estate tax and income tax, regardless when the first spouse dies.

In community property states, of course, since the surviving spouse receives a step-up in basis at S1's death for all community property owned, this gifting strategy need only be considered for the client's separate property.

Next, we turn to considerations in making gifts to minor children.

GIFTS TO MINORS: TECHNIQUES AND CONSIDERATIONS

Gifts to minor children are somewhat unique, not in their tax-saving potential so much as in the manner by which their transfer is usually arranged. As mentioned earlier in this chapter, gifts to minors are usually not made outright but are made instead through a *fiduciary* in the form of a guardianship, a custodianship, or a trust.

Outright gifts transfer the greatest amount of control to the donee, invite the least amount of challenge from the IRS, and are the least complicated to make. But an outright gift to a person, whether a minor or an adult, will only work satisfactorily when the donee has sufficient maturity to rationally possess, conserve, and enjoy the gift property. In other circumstances, the transfer should be made to a *fiduciary*. Many states have statutes that require gifts, above some set value, given to a minor be held for the minor by a fiduciary. The transfer to a fiduciary should be arranged to achieve the same tax advantages, use of the annual exclusion and shifting of income, available with an outright gift, yet protect the donee from the risks of his or her own immaturity, and, to conform to any restrictions state law places on the ownership and use of property by minors.

Before examining types of fiduciary gifts that meet these objectives, it will be helpful to review a tax issue that has bearing on the use of property given on for the benefit of a minor. If income from a gift is used to discharge the *obligation of support* of the donor-parent that income will be taxable to the parent.[12]

> EXAMPLE 13 - 23. Dad gives 14-year-old Junior $500 so that Junior can purchase lunches during his freshman year in high school. Junior deposits the money in his own savings account, subsequently withdrawing interest as well as principal to buy the lunches. The interest income will be taxable to Dad as income used in discharge of a support obligation.

This rule applies even if the source of the income is not from the parents, e.g., income from a trust.

Thus, in order to enjoy the full tax advantages of a completed gift to a minor, income from the gift must not be used to discharge support obligations. Ordinarily, parents are not obligated to support their adult children, so the issue does not usually apply to adult donees. But there are exceptions. In about fifteen states including Illinois and New Jersey, judges in divorce cases have imposed the duty of support for *higher education* for adult children. However, several factors limit the application of this exception. In 1992, Pennsylvania's supreme court ruled that divorcing parents will no longer be so obligated, reasoning that children become adults at age 18 and that the Legislature had not explicitly addressed the issue. No court has required parents in an *intact family* to pay for an adult child's higher education.[13]

Gifts under Guardianship

Individuals may make completed gifts to themselves or others as guardians for the benefit of minor children.

Drawbacks. Gifts under guardianships have some significant drawbacks. First, to be legally valid, the transfer must be made with local (probate) court supervision, which usually requires the expense of time and money in securing court approval, a bond, an annual accounting, and other legal necessities. State laws vary on specific requirements. Further, property held in a guardianship is difficult to manage efficiently because many actions, including the purchase and sale of property, often require court approval. Court supervision does afford the ward greater potential protection from misuse of the property by the adult fiduciary, but protection is rarely a major consideration. Finally, another disadvantage of guardianships is that the guardian must turn over the property outright to the ward at majority (age 18), an age donors usually consider too immature to receive a fee simple interest in most gift property.

Custodial Gifts

Uniform Gifts To Minors Act. The Uniform Gifts to Minors Act (UGMA), adopted in one form or other in all states, allows a relatively simple method of making fiduciary gifts to minors of certain property. No court supervision is required. The gift property is transferred in the name of someone, acting "as custodian for (minor's name) under the (state name) Uniform Gift to Minors Act." This type of titling serves to "incorporate by reference" all of the provisions of that Act, including broad investment powers under the "prudent person" standard, and the ability of the custodian to spend property on behalf of the minor without a court order. Further, a bond need not be given; and, unless the donor or donee request them, accountings are not necessary. Thus, custodial gifts have many advantages over guardianships.

Commonly permissible custodial gift property under UGMA includes securities, cash, life insurance, and annuities, but there is legislative movement by several states to greatly expand this list. In most UGMA states, real property cannot be held in custodial form.

Uniform Transfers To Minors Act. In 1983 the National Conference on Uniform Laws adopted the Uniform Transfers to Minors Act (UTMA) designed to replace the UGMA. Major changes include the following:

1. Allows *any property interests* to be transferred, including real estate, partnership interests, patents, royalty interests, and intellectual property,
2. Allows custodial gifts *at death* by permitting a fiduciary (executor or trustee) to establish a custodianship if authorized in a governing will or trust,
3. Authorizes transfers to a custodian from persons *other than* the transferor who are obligated to the minor (examples of situations include a personal injury recovery, life insurance proceeds payable to a minor beneficiary, and a joint bank account of which the minor is a surviving cotenant), and
4. Allows a transferor to revocably nominate a custodian to receive property *in the future*.

The following states have adopted UTMA without significant alterations: Arkansas, California, Colorado, Connecticut, Florida, Hawaii, Idaho, Illinois, Missouri, Montana, Nevada, New Hampshire, North Carolina, North Dakota, Oregon, Rhode Island and West Virginia.

Evaluation of custodial gifts. A custodial gift can save the time and expense involved in establishing a trust. They are considered completed gifts that qualify for the annual exclusion. Although custodianships are like trusts in many ways, they are more restrictive for the following reasons:

- A custodial gift may be *created for only one person*; a trust can provide for multiple beneficiaries, with unequal distributions among them.

- A custodianship is *not a separate legal entity*; all income is taxable to the minor. In contrast, an irrevocable trust is a separate taxpayer, enabling one additional "run up the rate ladder."
- Because the law gives the custodian the power to distribute income or principal to the minor, if the *donor serves as the custodian* and predeceases the minor, §2036/§2038 bring the custodial property into the custodian's gross estate. In contrast, some irrevocable trusts can avoid this estate tax problem by denying the trustee this power.
- Donees usually must receive custodial property outright *by age 21*; trust beneficiaries' distributions of principal may be delayed to a later age.
- Finally, a custodianship *does not have spendthrift provisions.*

To preserve the income shifting advantage of custodial gifts, UTMA provides that custodial property may not be used to satisfy any obligation to support for the minor, such as an obligation in a divorce decree. Thus, custodial gifts if properly structured can achieve essentially all of the tax advantages of completed outright transfers.

Gifts to Irrevocable Minors' Trusts

Although both gifts under guardianships and custodial gifts are usually an improvement over substantial outright gifts to minors, there are serious drawbacks, some of which have been mentioned above. They usually terminate at or shortly after the donee's age of majority, at which time the donee enjoys fee simple ownership of the property. And they may be restrictive, either in the red tape involved to create and continue them (gifts under guardianships) or in the type of property that usually may be given (custodial gifts) under the laws of many states. They are also inflexible in that the controlling state law usually is not or cannot be modified by private document. Thus, the donor under a guardianship arrangement usually cannot provide, by private document, that court supervision will not be required. The presence of these and other drawbacks lead many donors to use irrevocable trusts for gifts to minors.

In structuring gifts in trust for the benefit of minors, planners usually seek to obtain all of the tax benefits available to outright gifts. The four major tax objectives are:

1. Using the annual gift tax exclusion to avoid both gift taxes and the using up of the unified credit,
2. Excluding the gift from the donor's gross estate,
3. Excluding all postgift appreciation in the value of the gift property from the donor's estate tax base, and
4. Shifting the taxable income earned on the gift property to the trust or to the donee.

The irrevocable trust may also have the non-tax advantage of insulating the gift property from the parents' creditors and, in some cases, from the child's creditors.

Drafting an irrevocable trust takes great care because the nature of such transfers seem to invite scrutiny by the IRS. For example, the donor may wish to act as trustee and to restrict the minor child's enjoyment of the trust principal and income for some period of time. These requirements reflect the donor's desire to retain a considerable degree of control over the gift property. The problem is that a very fine line exists between harmless controls and controls that are deemed to be retained interests by the donor. Earlier in this chapter we saw some outright gift situations in which the transferor was penalized by income and estate tax provisions for retaining too much control. To this list we must add certain ill-designed transfers into trusts for the benefit of minors. The following discusses particular tax hurdles facing the planners of irrevocable minors' trusts and several methods for dealing with these problems. The discussion will include qualifying transfers into minors' trusts for the annual exclusion, a word of estate tax caution, the mention of an income tax concern, and finally a GSTT caveat.

Qualifying for the annual exclusion. As mentioned in Chapter 7, to qualify for the gift tax annual exclusion, the donee must be given a *present interest*, that is, an unrestricted right to the immediate use, possession, or enjoyment of property or the income from property. The reader might ask how a gift into trust for the benefit of a minor can qualify for the annual exclusion when, in fact, the minor is not typically given the unrestricted right to the immediate use of either the principal *or* the income. The answer lies in an exception carved out by the Internal Revenue Code, and two planning devices sanctioned by the courts, even if not loved by the IRS, that form the basis for added clauses in trust documents.

The three alternatives are called the 2503(c) Trust, the Crummey Trust, and the Mandatory Income Trust. The text of §2503 in included in Appendix B.

2503(c) Trust: Under §2503(c), a gift in trust is not considered a gift of a future interest (even though it really is one) if three conditions are met.

First, the trust must provide that the property and income may be expended by or for the benefit of the donee before the donee attains age 21.[14] This requirement creates the same potential §2036/§2038 problem for trustors wishing to be trustees as it does for custodial gifts.

Second, any portion of the property not so expended will pass to the donee at age 21. This is the most restrictive of the three conditions.

Third, if the donee dies before age 21, the property must either be payable to the donee's estate or the donee must hold a general power of appointment over the property. This is met even if the general power is exercisable only through the donee's will; and the trust contains a clause making siblings the takers by default. In many states, a minor may not legally execute a will. Thus, in the event of the death of the minor, the trust property would most likely go to his or her siblings.

As mentioned in Chapter 7, the 2503(c) exception was created to discourage the adoption of trusts which pay out income to presumably immature minors immediately upon the trustee's receipt, for the sole purpose of taking advantage of the annual exclusion. Thus, *2503(c) Trusts*, as they are called, normally terminate when the child reaches age 21. However, the §2503(c) trust need not terminate at this age, as long as the beneficiary can request a complete distribution at age 21.[15]

The Crummey Trusts and lapsing withdrawal powers. Crummey is the name of a taxpayer who succeeded in federal court in getting an annual exclusion for each year's transfer into a trust containing withdrawal rights for the benefit of minor children.[16] The typical *Crummey Trust* clause provides that the child has the right to withdraw, for a brief period (30 to 90 days) as set in the trust document, after each transfer of property into the trust, the *lesser* of the amount of the available annual exclusion or the value of the gift property transferred. Since the child has the right to withdraw that amount, the gift is considered a gift of a present interest satisfying the §2503(b) present interest requirement and the donor receives an annual exclusion for the gift. To be effective, the child must be given actual notice of the withdrawal right.

Use of a Crummey power can result in undesired gift tax and income tax consequences. For example, a beneficiary's failure to exercise a Crummey power in a given year may mean that the beneficiary has made a *taxable gift* by permitting a general power of appointment to lapse.[17] The gift tax value would be the amount that the value permitted to lapse exceeded the greater of $5,000 or 5% of the aggregate value of the property from which the exercise of the power could be satisfied. For example, suppose $120,000 was contributed as an initial gift in trust, with a child of the trustors having a $20,000 demand right that lapses 90 days after each addition. When the demand right lapses unexercised, the amount that $20,000 exceeds the greater of $5,000 or 5% of $120,000 (i.e., $14,000) is treated as a future interest gift to the remaindermen. As a gift of a future interest, it will not qualify for the annual exclusion. The taxable gift value will be very small since only the amount that goes to someone other than the person who let the withdrawal right lapse is considered a gift; and even that must be discounted since it is a future interest. Furthermore, if the person who let the withdrawal right lapse eventually receives the corpus of the trust, the gift will not be an adjusted taxable gift since the transfer (a contingent remainder) has reverted to the beneficiary.[18] The latter situation is the usual case, since the beneficiary with the withdrawal right is usually also the remainderman, especially for minors' trusts. Given the extremely small gift tax value and the likelihood that the transfer would not enter into the estate tax calculation most planners ignore this tax consequence. Some avoid the problem by limiting the annual withdrawal right to the 5 and 5 limits, i.e., the greater of *$5,000* (rather than the $10,000 annual exclusion amount) or 5%, or by giving the beneficiary a general testamentary power of appointment over the trust principal.

Mandatory Income Trust (MIT): A trust that requires mandatory distribution of income annually to the minor, either outright or to the minor's custodial account, as the way of entitling the donor to the annual exclusion is called a *mandatory income trust*. The gift is considered as comprising two parts, the income interest and the remainder or reversion interest. Tax law considers the former to be a present interest qualifying for the annual exclusion and the latter to be a future interest that does not so qualify. The alternative fractions making up the gift are derived from Tables S or B, depending upon the nature of the income interest.

> EXAMPLE 13 - 24. Gerry transferred $100,000 into an irrevocable trust established for his friend, Betty giving her income for life with the corpus to revert to Gerry, or to his issue, after Betty's death. Betty just turned 85 years old and the

rate for valuing split interest gifts was 8%, therefore, the factor would be .33307. This means that $33,307 represents the value of the income interest qualifying for the annual exclusion. Since the present value exceeds $10,000 the full annual exclusion is allowed. *** *Query - 1. Estimate old would Betty have to be before the annual exclusion is less than $10,000?*

Because §2503(b) requires the donee to have a present interest in order for a gift to qualify for the annual exclusion, and because this trust makes use of the present interest value of the income stream to satisfy that requirement, it is called a §2503(b) Trust by some estate planners. This is an unfortunate choice of terms since many other trusts qualify for the annual exclusion by creating a present interest, e.g., Crummey trusts, wherein the demand right satisfies that require- ment. We will use MIT instead of §2503(b), but be aware that the latter is still in common use.

Comparison of the three minors' trusts. By way of summary, Figure 13-4 highlights the differences between the three popular minors' trusts, tracing their evolution through the generations, with a focus on the rights of the beneficiaries and their taxation.

MITs and §2503(c) Trusts have become less attractive since the Crummey decision. Prior to Crummey, planners had to choose between an arrangement requiring annual distribution of all trust *income* to the minor [satisfying §2503(b)] or one effectively requiring distribution of the entire trust *corpus* at age 21 [satisfying §2503(c)]. Although some planners favored the MIT for larger gifts, the choice was not enthusiastically made, partly because the value of the income interest qualifying for the annual exclusion had to be discounted. The Crummey provision solved this dilemma by enabling the donor to give the child the *right to demand* a modest amount from the trust annually, without handing income or principal over to the child at age 21. Usually the child is made to realize that there is much to lose by exercising the demand right. For example, the child might lose a greater inheritance in the future, or the parent might simply refuse to make anymore gifts into the trust. However, the IRS takes the position that the child's power of withdrawal not be illusory, as it would be if there was an "understanding" or "agreement" not to exercise it.[19]

FIGURE 13-4 Evolution of Irrevocable Mandatory Income Trusts (MIT), §2503(c), and *Crummey* Minors' Trusts: Beneficiaries and Taxation

TIMELINE →

Key Events:	*Creation of Trust*	*Youngest child reaches age 21*	*Child reaches specified age*	*Death of child*	*21st birthday of youngest grandchild*

PrimaryBeneficiary	**MINOR CHILDREN**	**ADULT CHILDREN**	**ADULT CHILDREN**	**GRAND-CHILDREN**
Their property interests in income and principal of trust:	Income: MIT: all annually 2503(c): none Crummey: none Principal: MIT: none 2503(c): none likely Crummey: limited demand right	Income: MIT: all annually Crummey: depends on wishes of grantor Principal: MIT: none Crummey: limited demand right plus authorized distributions	Income: MIT: all annually Crummey: depends on wishes of grantor Principal: MIT: none Crummey: limited demand right plus authorized distributions	Income: As directed by instrument Principal: As directed by instrument
Trust name and characteristics:	*Grantor creates and transfers no more than $10,000 per beneficiary each year to:* **Irrevocable Minor's Trust**	*If 2503(c), usually terminates, with all assets distributed to the children. The other trusts continue as:* **Children's Trust**	**Childrens' Trust** *either terminates...*	*...or continues on as:* **GST Trust** *...which then terminates when youngest grandchild reaches age 21, or later, if allowed by local perpetuities law.*

TAX EFFECTS TO DONOR, OR BENEFICIARY NAMED ABOVE

Type of taxation

1. Taxable gift to donor-grantor? — Not in most cases. However, a 2503(b) provision would only shelter the value of the minor's income interest. Sheltered by annual exclusion under 2503(c), MIT (2503(b)), or Crummey provision (2503(b)).

2. Includable in beneficiaries' estate tax base at death?	No, except for 2503(c) trust, if a minor child dies	No, except for principal distributions that continue to be owned	No, except for principal distributions that continue to be owned	Yes, to extent of principal distributions that continue to be owned

3. Income taxable to grantor or beneficiaries?

Not to grantor (no rights to income or principal retained).

Yes to minor children, to extent distributed or to extent it could be withdrawn.	Yes to children, to extent distributed.	Yes to children, to extent distributed.	Yes to grand-children, to extent distributed.

Undistributed FAI and all capital gains taxable to trust.

4. Any GSTT incurred? — No, provided that grantor (and possibly grantor's children) allocated $1 million GSTT exemption(s) to the gift transfers. To extent not so sheltered, trust will have inclusion ratio, and a portion of any taxable termination or taxable distribution to a skip person will be subject to GSTT.

Income taxation has recently become a more important factor in choosing a minor's trust. The short tax rate "ladder" for trusts will encourage clients to seek to avoid trust taxation of income. A newly created Crummey-type trust may be able to avoid taxation at the trust level by giving the Crummey power holder a general power of appointment over trust income, as it is earned, causing it to be taxed to the holder even if the income is not withdrawn.

> EXAMPLE 13 - 25. Eight years ago, Knute created irrevocable Crummey-type trusts for his two sons, then ages 6 and 7. Each trust now contains assets valued at approximately $140,000, generating about $9,000 in accumulated income which is taxable to the trust, some at its marginal rate of 39.6%.

A recent court decision made Crummey powers even more attractive by sanctioning annual exclusions for the trustor's *grandchildren*, who were given a 15 day $10,000 demand right, but who were only contingent beneficiaries of the trust principal, because they stood to receive principal distributions *only* if their parents predeceased the termination of the trust. In *Cristofani*, the IRS unsuccessfully argued that it was so unlikely that the grandchildren would receive the principal, there was "no imaginable reason" why the grandchildren would not exercise their withdrawal rights unless there was, in fact, a prior *understanding* that they would not do so, hence they really had no present interests in the transfers. The court rejected this implied agreement argument, ruling that the test of a Crummey power is the legal right of the beneficiary to demand the property be turned over by the trustee, not the likelihood of actually receiving the property. The IRS intends to continue litigating the court's broad interpretation of *Crummey* in situations similar to *Cristofani*, but only in cases arising outside the Federal 9th Circuit.[20] While this case supports the use of Crummey type gifts to contingent beneficiaries, commentators are increasingly concerned that Congress may restrict or eliminate the Crummey withdrawal power as a means of creating a present interest. If Congress chooses to do so, it might grandfather (allow the annual exclusion) for existing irrevocable trusts, or perhaps eliminate it even for them unless there is an assurance that the beneficiary will eventually receive the property or at least, as in the §2503(c) Trust, that it will be taxable in the beneficiary's estate if her or she does not get to enjoy it.

> EXAMPLE 13 - 26. Christopher resides in the 9th Circuit. He creates an irrevocable trust to last for ten years. The trust provides for distribution of the

remainder to his two children, if surviving. A predeceased child's share shall go to his or her issue. One child has three children and the other has two, for a total of five grandchildren. All seven beneficiaries are given Crummey demand powers. Beginning this year, Christopher can fund the trust annually with $70,000 in property, entirely sheltered by seven annual exclusions even though the trust corpus will most likely go just to the two children.

Estate tax caution. In designing the irrevocable trust, the estate planner must be mindful of the dangers of letting the donor retain controls that would cause the property to be includable in the donor's gross estate. For example, as mentioned earlier in the chapter, naming the grantor to be trustee of a §2503(c) trust will cause estate tax inclusion of the trust assets at the grantor's death unless the trust has already terminated. The underlying Code provisions have been covered in Chapter 6, specifically: §2036, transfers with retained life estate, and §2038, revocable or amendable transfers. The reader is urged to review them at this point.

Income tax concern. The donor of a gift in trust for a minor child usually wishes to avoid being taxed on the income received by the trust, preferring instead to let the trust be taxed to the extent the income is accumulated, or to let the child be taxed to the extent that the income is paid to the child. However, the trust must be designed so as not to conflict with the numerous grantor trust rules. For example, reservation by the donor of the unlimited right to make withdrawals from the trust will cause the income to be taxed to the donor. This will not apply if the grantor retains a reversion that can only occur on the death of a beneficiary (before age 21) who is a lineal descendant of the grantor and holds all present interests in any portion of the trust.[21]

GSTT Caveat. As implied above, Crummey trusts often provide for transfer to the beneficiaries' *issue or descendants* if the beneficiary fails to survive. As a taxable termination or taxable distribution, this transfer will *not* be sheltered from the GSTT as an annual exclusion gift because its origin was not a direct skip gift. Planners recommend avoiding this GSTT consequence either by having the client allocate a portion of the $1 million exemption to transfers to the Crummy trust, or enjoying a GSTT exemption by setting up a separate trust for each skip person, with each trust conforming to certain requirements under §2642(c)(2).

HOW POPULAR ARE COMPLETED GIFTS?

Based on the results of a survey of experienced estate planning attorneys conducted by Prestopino, the most popular larger gifts are outright annual exclusion gifts, with 29.2% of clients of experienced estate planning attorneys undertaking them. Next in order of popularity are gifts in trust (19.1%), custodial annual exclusion gifts (12.1%), outright gifts of an amount greater than the annual exclusion (5.5%), and, finally, custodial gifts exceeding the annual exclusion (1.3%). Of the clients using gifts in trust, 60% incorporated a Crummey demand provision, 6% a §2503(b) provision, and 12% an §2503(c) clause.

This chapter has introduced the planning for lifetime transfers, devoting considerable detail to gifts. Chapter 14 will explore another group of lifetime transfers: ones different from gifts in that they are either incomplete, or are completed transfers to charity.

QUERY ANSWERED

1. Using the abbreviated table you can calculate that she would have to be between 105 (factor of .14110 * $100,000 = $14,110) and 109 where the value drops to $3,704. With the full table you would find that at age 108 she would have had a present interest determined by the factor .08319; this times $100,000 gives a present interest of $8,319, limiting the annual exclusion to that amount. Gerry's taxable gift would then be $91,681 instead of $90,000.

QUESTIONS AND PROBLEMS

1. Good planning requires that the client feel comfortable with a proposed lifetime transfer. How can lifetime transfers be a source of discomfort?

2. One of your clients explains to you that she'd like to make a lifetime transfer to her child, perhaps in the form of a gift. But she is not clear

on how gifts differ from other lifetime transfers. Inform her.

3. Now that your client is aware of the unique nature of a gift, explain to her the difference between an outright and a non-outright gift.

4. What is the approximate minimum net worth that (a) a single client and (b) married clients should own (or expect to own) before considering gifting amounts of $10,000 or more in order to save estate tax? Why?

5. Carrie, a rich elderly widow, expects to live 10 years. She would like to begin a program of lifetime gifting to her four children.
   a. What equal amount can Carrie give to each child, per year, without paying any gift tax, while fully using up her unified credit? In addition, calculate the combined value of all gifts 1) each year, and 2) over ten years. Assume no prior taxable gifts.
   b. How would your answers to part "a" change if Carrie created a trust naming her four children primary beneficiaries and her eight grandchildren contingent beneficiaries?
   c. Why might Carrie be willing to use up her unified credit?

6. In terms of estate tax savings, is a gift of $20,000 by an unmarried donor to one donee in one year necessarily twice as valuable as a gift of only $10,000? Why or why not? Discuss in terms of estate reduction and estate freezing.

7. Why is the ability to avoid grossing up a tax advantage to gifting?

8. Two years ago, Zack gave his daughter Luna a one acre plot of desert land in Nevada, then worth $9,000. Subsequently, oil was found, making the plot worth $900,000. Assuming no prior taxable gifts,
   a. How much attributable to this land will be includable in Zack's estate tax base if he dies today? Explain.
   b. How much would be includable if, instead, Zack made the gift four years ago and died today? Explain.
   c. How much would be includable if, instead, Zack made the gift in 1981 and dies today? Explain.

9. Describe the attributes of those clients who would be most willing to make sizable gifts.

10. Summarize the major tax disadvantages to gifting.

11. "Higher-basis assets make better gifts." From an income tax point of view, is this statement true, false, or uncertain?

12. Discuss any significant reasons why each of the following assets have particularly attractive or unattractive gift potential.
    a. Stock: donor's basis, $60,000; fair market value, $20,000.
    b. Stock: donor's basis, $20,000; fair market value, $800,000. Does age of the donor matter at all?
    c. Life insurance on the donor's life.
    d. Rights to a patent.
    e. Raw land.
    f. A junk bond.
    g. A corporate dividend check that the donor endorses over to the donee.

13. a. Under what circumstances can an inter-spousal gift save estate tax?
    b. Under what circumstances can an inter-spousal gift save income tax?

14. Contrast the advantages and disadvantages of the alternative methods of making gifts to minors.

15. Paradiso, a client, asks you to review the recommendation of one of your competitors. That planner proposed transferring $10,000 per year for life into an irrevocable trust, whose terms provide that all income will be accumulated until Paradiso's son Max (age 4) reaches age 35. At that time, all accumulated income will be distributed to Max, who will thereafter receive all income currently until Paradiso's death, at which time, the trust will terminate and all principal will be distributed outright to Max.
    a. Will the periodic transfers be free of gift tax? Why or why not?
    b. Will this arrangement reduce Paradiso's future estate tax or freeze any part of his estate? Why or why not?

c. If your answer to part "a" is no, suggest three alternative provisions in the trust that will change the result.

d. Which of the three provisions in part "c" probably most reduces the maximum life of the trust?

e. Which of the three provisions in part "c" will probably be most appealing to Paradiso, who is quite reluctant to allow distribution of either income or principal until Max reaches age 35?

f. How much income shifting per year, if any, will your answer in part "e" accomplish?

16. A client of yours needs some planning advice. She wants to start a college fund for her 8-year-old daughter. Her goal is to accumulate approximately $50,000 in 10 years, at which time equal monthly payments can be made to daughter over a period of the following 4 years.

a. If neither income shifting nor estate tax reduction are important, is a program of gifting really necessary? Why or why not?

b. If your client wishes to shift income to her daughter (who for simplicity, we'll assume, has no taxable income of her own), recommend strategies for each of the following alternative sets of assumptions:

(1) Client wishes to accumulate a fund that can revert to the client if her daughter later decides not to attend college. (The answer to this part will not be found in this book. Hint: EE bonds)

(2) Client would like an arrangement under which she can continue funding after her daughter's graduation.

c. In part "b" above, recommend suitable investments to purchase. (Hint: is the daughter a "kiddie"?)

17. Under simple assumptions, what is the largest family estate size that a husband and wife can own and transfer, estate tax and gift tax free, assuming all of the following: a credit shelter bypass plan; that S1 is expected to live five years and S2 fifteen years; and both spouses wish to make annual exclusion gifts each year to each of their four children?

ANSWERS TO THE QUESTIONS AND PROBLEMS

1. Lifetime transfers can be a source of discomfort if the client really doesn't want to relinquish the degree of control or beneficial interest in the property required to meet an estate planning goal.

2. A completed gift, as distinguished from other lifetime transfers (sales and incomplete gifts) has the following attributes:

    a. It has potential gift tax consequences.
    b. It can shift income.
    c. It results in the donor's total loss of beneficial control and enjoyment in the property.

3. An outright gift ordinarily results in the receipt by the donee of a complete interest (i.e., both legal and beneficial) in the gift property. A non-outright gift is usually made to a fiduciary, which means that any particular beneficiary receives only a beneficial interest. And usually, that beneficial interest is not in fee simple. For example, it may be a future interest, such as a remainder. Or it may be a present interest for a limited time, such as a life estate. And, as implied above, under most non-outright transfers, beneficiaries often have no management rights to the property.

4. a. $600,000; b. $1,200,000. Gifting to save estate tax by clients having less wealth is unnecessary, since (as shown in Chapters 5, 11, and 12) property transfers at death sheltered by the unified credit can reduce estate tax to zero without the necessity of lifetime gifting.

5. a. Total gifts over 10 years = $400,000 (= 4 children x $10,000 annual exclusion x 10 years) + $600,000 exemption equivalent of the unified credit = $1 million total gifts for all years. Total gifts per year = $1 million divided by 10 = $100,000. Therefore, equal amount of gifts per child per year = $100,000 divided by 4 = $25,000.
        Combined value of all gifts: 1) Each year: $100,000 (= 4 x $25,000).

2) Over ten years: the value is $1,000,000 (= 10 x $100,000).

b. Based on the *Cristofani* case, if Carrie gave all twelve beneficiaries Crummey withdrawal powers, she could gift a total of **$180,000** to the trust each year, or a total of $1,800,000 over ten years. She could give $600,000/10 = $60,000 per year sheltered by the unified credit, and $10,000 x 12 = $120,000 per year sheltered by the annual exclusion. By giving additional Crummey powers, Carrie will be able to gift an additional $800,000 (80% more), free of gift tax.

c. Carrie might be willing to use up her unified credit to be able to effect a small estate freeze, i.e., to exclude future asset appreciation of the gifted property from her estate tax base. Only $15,000, the *taxable gift* value of each $25,000 gift will be included at her death, rather than the entire date of death value of the $15,000 portion that would otherwise not be gifted.

6. No, a gift of $20,000 by an unmarried donor to one donee in one year is not necessarily twice as valuable, estate tax-wise, as a gift of only $10,000. The first $10,000 can truly *reduce* the estate tax base by causing the gross estate to be lower by that amount. The second $10,000 will not reduce the estate tax base any additional amount. While the gross estate will be an additional $10,000 lower, adjusted taxable gifts will be $10,000 higher, resulting in no further change in the estate tax base. But, although the second $10,000 amount can not reduce the estate tax base, it will *freeze* it at that $10,000 gift tax value. Both $10,000 gifts will keep all future appreciation in the value of the gift property out of the donor's estate tax base. Of course, this benefit is inherent in the notion of a freeze, but the two concepts are somewhat different.

7. Avoiding grossing up makes the gross estate lower by the amount of the gift tax paid, thereby saving estate tax.

8. a. & b. Regardless when Zack died, nothing related to the gift would be includable in his estate tax base if the gift was made after 1981. It is not includable in the gross estate, since §2035 includes only one kind of outright gift: life insurance. Not includable in adjusted taxable gifts because the taxable amount is zero, i.e., $9,000 value of gross gift minus $9,000 annual exclusion.

   c. On the other hand, if Zack made the gift before 1982, the amount of the adjusted taxable gift, $9,000 - $3,000 = $6,000, is includable in adjusted taxable gifts, and consequently, the estate tax base. However, as in parts "a" and "b," nothing is includable in Zack's gross estate.

 9. Attributes of clients most willing to make sizeable gifts: Wealthy, older, generous, having rapidly appreciating assets.

10. Major tax disadvantages to gifting:

   a. Time value of money is a drawback to prepaying the gift tax.
   b. Possible adverse §2035 consequences with certain transfers.
   c. The gift may later be ruled incomplete.
   d. Loss of step-up in basis.

11. Uncertain. A higher basis will make a better gift only if all of the three assumptions below can be made:

   a. The basis doesn't exceed the current value of the gift. Otherwise, the donor should prefer to realize the loss him/herself. If the donor doesn't realize the loss, no one else can, either.
   b. The donee is likely to sell the gift asset before his/her death.
   c. The donor, for other reasons, is not left in the position of having to sell another asset with a lower basis.

12. In each case, we consider only the significant conceptual points:

   a. Stock with $60,000 basis and $20,000 fair market value: This is an asset with a basis that is *too* high. Not a good gift asset - better for donor to sell; to deduct the loss.
   b. Stock with $20,000 basis and $800,000 fair market value: This asset has already appreciated greatly. From a basis point of view, not a good gift asset because of the carryover basis rule. However, if the donee is not likely to sell the asset before death, perhaps because he/she is very old, then basis considerations may not be important. Also, there will be gift

tax consequences. Finally, the above assumes that the asset is not expected to appreciate greatly in the future. If it is, then it may still have attractive gift potential.

c. Life insurance on the donor's life: An excellent gift asset, assuming donor is expected to live at least three years. It has a relatively low gift tax value and a high estate tax value. Basis considerations are not usually significant, unless the donee plans to surrender or sell the policy.

d. Patent rights: From a transfer tax point of view, not often a good gift because a patent usually depreciates over time. Thus, patents often have a higher gift tax value and a lower estate tax value.

e. Raw land: Assuming substantial post-gift appreciation, raw land is a good gift asset if it reduces estate tax.

f. A junk bond: No appreciation potential, but it may be able to shift some income (junk bonds ordinarily pay relatively large coupon interest amounts).

g. Cash dividend check, issued by a corporation, that is endorsed over to the donee: Cannot shift the dividend income because the stock itself wasn't transferred. Similar to a gift of cash.

13. a. An inter-spousal gift can save estate tax when the wealthier spouse transfers enough property to the poorer spouse, who dies first, so that the bypass share can be fully funded.

b. An inter-spousal gift can save income tax when a relatively low basis asset is transferred to the spouse dying first, who then retransfers it at death to the donor spouse. The donee spouse must live at least one year after the gift is made.

14. Gift under guardianship:

a. Is costly.

b. Requires court supervision.

c. Is difficult to manage efficiently.

d. Provides greater protection from abuses by guardian.

e. Must be turned over outright to donee at age of majority (age 18).

Custodial gifts:

a. Are simply arranged.
b. Are often limited to certain types of property.
c. Must be turned over outright to donee, usually by age 21.
d. Have adverse estate tax consequences if donor is custodian.

Gifts to an irrevocable trust:

a. Are more complex to set up.
b. Have much greater flexibility, especially regarding distribution of income and principal to the beneficiary.
c. Have potential adverse estate tax, gift, and income tax consequences if not structured correctly.

15. a. The periodic transfers will not be free of gift tax because they are transfers of future interests, since all income is accumulated and presumably the trust does not presently meet the requirements of either §2503(b), §2503(c) or Crummey. Of course, no gift tax will be owed until Paradiso's entire unified credit is used up.

b. This arrangement will not reduce Paradiso's estate because his gifts will not qualify for the annual exclusion. But it will *freeze* a portion of his estate by eliminating from the estate tax base the future appreciation in the trust assets.

c. The three alternative provisions are the following:

  1. 2503(b) provision: each year, all income distributed currently to Max.
  2. 2503(c) provision: principal distributed outright to Max when he turns 21 (the two other aspects are not described here).
  3. Crummey provision: annual withdrawal right of lesser of annual exclusion amount or amount actually transferred.

d. The §2503(c) provision probably most reduces the trust's life. Under its rules, when Max turns age 21, he must be able, at minimum, to request complete distribution.

e. The Crummey provision would probably be most appealing a Paradiso, since it would not require distribution of either income or principal until Max reaches age 35. Of course, Max would have the withdrawal right for a brief period each year, but most donors are successful in totally discouraging beneficiaries from exercising that right.

f. The Crummey trust can usually accomplish only a very modest degree of income shifting. In addition to the $100 personal exemption, only $1,500 in taxable income to a trust is taxed at the 15% rate. The excess will be taxed to the trust at 28%. If Paradiso is in the 28% bracket, this means an annual saving of only $223 [= $1,500*(.28 - .15) + $100*(.28)].

16. a. If neither income shifting nor estate reduction are important, the client need not make any gifts; she could simply accumulate a fund in her own name. Gifting to establish the fund would serve no purpose.

b. To shift income, the client will need to make gifts of income generating property.

1. By purchasing U.S. Government EE bonds in joint name with her daughter, client might be able to "have her cake and eat it." No taxable gift occurs until redemption. Reporting of income can be deferred until redemption. If daughter attends college, daughter can redeem and pay the income tax. If daughter chooses not to be a student, Mom may be able to redeem and pay the tax.

An additional alternative for tuition financing by middle income clients would be to have the client purchase EE bonds in her own name and later sign them over to the college directly in payment of tuition. Under recent tax legislation (§135), the bonds would be entirely exempt from federal income tax for families with a joint AGI of less than $61,850 (indexed). There is a gradual phase out of this exception above this AGI, with total phase-out at $91,850 (indexed).

2. Two possible alternatives to enable the arrangement to continue after graduation are the Crummey trust and the §2503(b) trust. Most planners prefer Crummey, partly because the entire gift amount qualifies for the annual exclusion and partly because income need not be payable or paid in any given year.

    c. (Yes, the daughter will be a "kiddie" until the tax year she reaches age 14). To avoid the kiddie tax, investments chosen should not throw off taxable income until that time. Client should consider EE bonds, municipal bonds, zero or low dividend paying growth stocks, etc.

17. From Chapter 11 we saw that without gifting, a married couple can pass $1.2 million under a credit shelter bypass plan, since each spouse can shelter $600,000 with his or her unified credit. With gifting, each spouse can shelter an additional amount equal to the product of his or her life expectancy times 4 (= # children) times $10,000. Thus S1 can shelter an additional 5x4x$10,000 = $200,000, and S2 can shelter an additional 15x4x$10,000 = $600,000. As a consequence, the largest family estate size that this couple can totally shelter from estate tax and gift tax is $2,000,000 (= $1,200,000 + $200,000 + $600,000).

ENDNOTES

1. See Chapter 6, under §2035 materials, for detailed explanations.

2. TAM 9231003.

3. An indexed amount, increased to $650 for tax years beginning in 1995. Rev. Proc. 94-72, IRB 1994-50, 14.

4. Due to a mistake in drafting the 1993 tax law, post-1992 rather than post-1989 inflation adjustments are currently being used as the index, unless Congress corrects the error.

5. §2011.

6. IRC §6501(a).

7. Exceptions to the three year rule, generally, see §6501(c), and the 25% under reporting, see §6501(e).

8. Estate of *Frederick R. Smith* (1990) 94 TC 872.

9. §303.

10. §2032A.

11. §6166.

12. IRC §677(b).

13. Wall Street Journal, November 19, 1992, p. B1.

14. Controls over the expenditures can disallow the annual exclusion. *Illinois National Bank of Springfield v. U.S.* 756 F.Supp. 1117 (1991).

15. LR 8507017

16. *Crummey v. Commissioner*, 397 F.2d 82 (9Cir. 1968).

17. §2514(e).

18. §2001(b)

19. Rev. Rul. 81-7, 1981-1 CB 474.

20. *Estate of Maria Cristofani* 97 TC 74 (1991).

21. §673(b).

— 14

Lifetime Transfers II: Other Intra-family Transfers; Charitable Transfers

OVERVIEW

Gift planning, the subject of the previous chapter, is often rejected by clients for two reasons. First, by their very nature, gifts generally mean nothing in return. They reduce wealth making the donor feel less financially secure, a feeling people would rather not experience. Second, making a gift means less control over the property, a difficult step for many potential donors.

This second chapter on lifetime transfers explores two types of intra-family arrangements. The first, those where the client receives *consideration*, as the installment sale and the private annuity. The second, the client retains some control over the transferred property, such as the grantor retained interest trust. The chapter will also cover the popular types of lifetime charitable transfers, including outright charitable transfers and split interest charitable transfers, such as the annuity trust, the unitrust, and the pooled income fund. With the charitable trusts, the client may be able to increase income and receive an income tax credit.

COMPLETED INTRA-FAMILY TRANSFERS FOR CONSIDERATION

In this section, we'll study lifetime transfers that are different from the others in two important ways. First, they differ from gifts because they *generate consideration* to the transferor. Second, they differ from the second type of lifetime intra-family transfer to be covered later in this chapter in that like gifts, they are *complete*, that is, they entail total transfer of (one or) all interests in the asset.

Intra-family Loan

Lending money or other property to family members is a simple method of transferring assets in exchange for consideration. Often, the financial benefits of an intra-family loan can be well worth the financial and emotional risks.

Financial benefits of intra-family loans. Loans work best when borrowing rates and investing rates of return are far apart. In 1992, when short-term borrowing rates were 9% or higher and one-year certificates of deposit earned about 3.5%, a short-term loan of $10,000 at 6% could save the borrower at least $300 per year and generate additional annual pretax income to the lender of about $250. Long-term loans could save far less per year because rate differentials were not nearly as pronounced, but over a thirty year period, the accumulated amounts are still significant. Additional advantages of intra-family home mortgages are the ability to both avoid or reduce up-front points and application fees charged by commercial lenders, reduce loan processing time, and parents (or other relatives) may make loans to children with credit histories that would not satisfy commercial lenders. In contrast, children wishing to make gifts to supplement their parent's income might borrow from them and pay an above-market rate of interest.

Financial risks of intra-family loans. In addition to the risk of unexpected taxation (to be described shortly), intra-family loans entail other financial risks. A child may not be a good credit risk, making the loan payments difficult to collect resulting in family friction. If the loan is secured, the lien must be properly filed to ensure the lien's priority over other creditors.

Nonfinancial risk of intra-family loans. The risks of an intra-family loan can also be partly emotional. Some parent-lenders later discover that their children have taken the immature attitude that since mom and dad have a lot of money they need not be repaid. Family loans can also engender jealousies and antagonisms between relatives and in-laws.

Taxation of non-gift intra-family loans. Taxation of intra-family loans that contain no gift element is relatively straightforward.

Income taxation. Interest paid by the borrower is, of course, taxable income to the lender. Interest is not tax deductible to the borrower unless the loan is secured by a principal or secondary residence or incurred in connection with a trade or business.[1] If the loan is in default, the lender will not be able to deduct the loss unless a businesslike effort is made to collect it.

Gift taxation. No gift will result if the borrower's note reflects an arms-length transaction. Thus, there must be provision for repayment and the interest rate charged must be reasonable.

The lender may elect to *forgive* loan payments under the shelter of the annual exclusion. However, if the IRS can establish that a prior agreement had been made to forgive all payments, it will contend that the entire loan constituted an immediate gift. To avoid this result, a lender might accept each payment, and later gift a somewhat different amount back to the borrower.

Estate taxation. The value of the note is included in the lender-decedent's gross estate at death.[2]

Taxation of gift-type intra-family loans. The income and gift tax effects discussed above assume a true loan, one that does not have a gift element; the borrower exchanges full consideration in the form of a note which when issued has a present value equal to the amount borrowed.

Other intra-family loans entail additional tax risks. Clients may wish to charge no interest, or an interest rate that is below market rates. Tax law treats these "below market" loans between family members as "gift loans," subjecting the client-lender to income taxation and gift taxation.

Income taxation. In subjecting these loans to income tax, the law[3] assumes a fiction: The forgone interest is treated as if it had been transferred by the lender to the borrower, and then retransferred by the borrower to the lender, thereby subjecting the client to income taxation on this imputed interest income. Whether or not a loan is "below market" will essentially depend upon whether the lender charged a rate at least equal to the appropriate applicable federal rate (AFR), as described in §1274(d) and announced by the U.S. Treasury each month.

There are two exceptions to the imputed interest rules. First, they do not apply to loans up to $10,000 used to purchase non-income producing property, such as an automobile. Second, they do not apply to loans up to $100,000 if the borrower's net investment income is less than $1,000. This might work well for investment-poor students needing large amounts to fund educational expenses, such as for law school or medical school, or for a child needing the money for a down payment on a house. If net investment income exceeds the $1,000 limit, the imputed interest is limited to the actual amount of that income.

Gift taxation. If the loan rate is below market, the client will also be treated as having made a gift. If the loan is a term loan, one with a specified maturity, the value of the gift is the difference between the amount loaned and the discounted present value of the note. If the loan is a demand loan, one with no specified maturity date and lender has right at any time to demand full repayment, at the end of each year the lender will be treated as having made a gift of the imputed interest for the portion of the year the loan was outstanding, less the amount actually charged. A more detailed discussion of the tax effects of below market "interest free" loans is contained in Appendix 14A that immediately follows this chapter.

Properly structured, intra-family loans can be beneficial to both lender and borrower, provided that both understand the terms, which should be reduced to writing.

Ordinary Sale

The client can sell property for cash to a family member at a fair market price. Under certain circumstances, an ordinary sale can be especially beneficial to both family members. The client may truly wish to sell at a fair price but would prefer to keep the asset in the family; the buyer will be spared the effort and expense of looking for similar property and commissions that might have been incurred are avoided. As a true sale, there may be income tax consequences to the seller. Careful records should be kept, since intra-family sales might receive greater IRS scrutiny than a sale between unrelated parties, especially if the transaction is sizable. The buyer, of course, has the burden of acquiring the cash or other acceptable property needed for the purchase. The seller is not allowed to deduct any loss incurred in the sale, due to the Code's prohibition against loss recognition on sales between related parties.[4]

Bargain Sale

If the client has mixed transfer motives, on the one hand wishing to gift a particular asset to a family member, and on the other hand not willing to completely forgo the receipt of all consideration in return, a bargain sale may be appropriate. As described in Chapter 2, under a bargain sale the client sells the asset for an amount less than what would be regarded full and adequate consideration. The difference between the consideration received by the client-donor and the value of the asset transferred is a gift, for tax purposes. Regarding income tax, the client would recognize a gain to the extent the consideration received exceeds the parent's basis.

> EXAMPLE 14 - 1. Mom owns property with a basis of $90,000 and a current value of $240,000, which she sells to her son for $110,000. Mom's taxable gain is $20,000, the difference between $110,000 and her $90,000 basis. Son's new basis is $110,000, his purchase price. Mom has also made a gift of $130,000, the difference between the FMV of the property she transferred to her son and the consideration he paid to her.

A taxable bargain sale may not be the best outcome, however, if a true tax-free gift was intended. Occasionally, an intended gift is treated as a bargain sale.

> EXAMPLE 14 - 2. La Croix borrows money from a bank to purchase a building. After claiming depreciation on the property for a number of years, he "gives" the property to his daughter, who assumes the debt. The transaction will be treated as a bargain sale, if his adjusted basis is less than the outstanding debt. La Croix will be considered to have received consideration in the amount of the debt assumed.[5]

As a compromise between a gift and a sale, the bargain sale can be arranged to closely reflect the client's degree of generosity.

Installment Sale

Instead of selling the asset to a family member for immediate cash, the client could sell it in exchange for an installment note, in which the buyer agrees to make periodic payments of principal and interest, based on a fair market rate of interest. This is referred to as seller financing; and the seller is said to *take back paper*, a reference to the seller receiving a note instead of cash. An installment sale can defer income tax on some or all capital gain while keeping post-sale appreciation out of the seller's gross estate.

Income taxation. Under income tax installment sales rules,[6] the seller may spread recognition of the gain over the collection period. Although it is presumed that the seller will use the installment method to recognize gain, the seller can make an election to recognize the entire gain in the year of sale, which would make good sense if the seller has offsetting capital losses for the year. The gain is recognized in proportion to the amount of each payment of principal. A percentage of each principal payment, measured by the gross profit (gain) divided by the selling price, is included as capital gain. There are restrictions on deferral of gain on an installment sale of certain trade or business inventory.[7] Losses are never reported on an installment basis.

> EXAMPLE 14 - 3. Mom, a widow, sells her rental house to her daughter for $80,000, payable with a down payment of $10,000. Interest is payable monthly, and principal will be payable in five equal annual $14,000 payments. Mom's current adjusted basis in the house is $20,000. Her gross profit is $60,000, and each year she will recognize a capital gain of $60,000/$80,000, or 75% of the principal amount received. Thus, in the year of sale, her reportable gain will be $7,500 of the total $10,000 received. In each of the succeeding five years she can expect to report a gain of $10,500 (=.75 x $14,000).

Any *interest* received on the balance due will also be taxable income. Interest paid will be fully deductible by the buyer if it is considered business interest, investment interest which is offset by net investment income, interest on a debt secured by a primary or secondary residence, or some other type of qualified interest.

At least two different events will trigger to the seller an *immediate recognition* of part or all of the remaining gain. If the seller sells or "otherwise disposes" of the installment note, or if the seller cancels the note, then he or she will have to report currently the remaining gain from the original transaction. Gain recognition will also be triggered if the buyer is a related party who resells the property within two years of the purchase.[8]

The buyer of the property, as in any valid sale, will enjoy a step-up in basis in the property to the amount of the purchase price. However, with regard to the seller's note, transfer of the note at the death of the seller *will not generate a step-up basis* in the note. The legatee-heir will continue to report installment gain in the same manner as the seller.

Gift taxation. If the installment transaction is a bona fide sale for full and adequate consideration, there will be *no gift tax* consequences to the lender. Lack of full consideration can arise when the interest rate specified in the note is considered inadequate.

EXAMPLE 14 - 4. Continuing with the above example, assume the installment note specifies an interest rate of 10%, which is equal to the current applicable mid-term federal rate (AMFR). Since the rules for installment sales under §7520(a)(2) require a minimum rate of *120%* of the current mid-term AFR to avoid the inference of a gift, the present value of the sum of all principal and interest payments, discounted at 12%, will be less than $80,000, the current value of the house. Thus, Mom will be treated as having made a gift of the difference. For a small loan the annual exclusion will cover the gift.

A parent may wish to *forgive* one or more of the purchaser's future payments. In the usual case, only the amount forgiven constitutes a taxable gift in the year forgiven. The gift will qualify for the annual exclusion.

EXAMPLE 14 - 5. Continuing the above series of examples, if daughter wants to use the money to buy a car so Mom forgives a $14,000 annual payment, Mom has made a gift of that amount. After the annual exclusion, Mom's taxable gift will be $4,000. If Mom is married and her husband agrees to split the gift, the taxable gift would be zero. However, from an income tax stand point, Mom will be treated as though she received the payment and then returned it to daughter.

The IRS quite correctly maintains that if the seller, at the time of the sale, had an understanding with the buyer that the seller would *not* collect on the note, then the *entire value* of the property is a taxable gift. However, an IRS challenge has rarely prevailed where the note has been correctly drafted and properly secured, so as to be legally enforceable.

Estate taxation. Ordinarily, when the holder of an installment note dies, only the present value of the installment note is included in his or her *gross estate*.

EXAMPLE 14 - 6. Continuing the prior example, if Mom dies just before the fourth payment is due, her gross estate will include the discounted value of the note. Of course, Mom's gross estate will also include any proceeds from receipt of earlier payments from daughter, to the extent retained by Mom, or any assets she purchased with those proceeds. However, her gross estate will not include the value of the installment asset sold.

If the seller made a partial gift and took back paper secured by the property transferred, and dies before the note is paid off, the date-of-death value of the property sold would be included in the seller's gross estate, less only the actual consideration paid.[9] That would be considered a transfer for less than full and adequate money, or money's worth, with a retained income interest.

Since family transactions are often scrutinized more carefully by the IRS, the client should be strongly advised to determine the value of the asset by qualified appraisal, and to use an adequate rate of interest.

Self-canceling provision. The client may seek to avoid inclusion of the value of the note in his or her gross estate by incorporating a self-canceling provision, specifying that no further payments will be made after his or her death. Since the initial value of a *self-canceling installment note* (called a "SCIN") is less than one whose payments cannot be prematurely canceled, the buyer will have to give additional consideration, usually in the form of a higher principal amount or a higher interest rate.[10] And, of course, the older the client, the greater the additional consideration. Otherwise, the IRS could assert the existence of a gift element in the transaction, again creating the risk of §2036(a) application.

> EXAMPLE 14 - 7. Marty, age 53, sells property currently worth $100,000 in exchange for a 20 year self-canceling installment note. The likelihood of Marty dying before reaching age 73 is .3129964 [1 minus (61673/89771)], see Table 80CNSMT. To reflect this additional consideration, Marty sets the face amount of the note at $131,300.

Case law has ruled that the value of the canceled notes under a SCIN are not includable in the note holder's gross estate.[11] However, cancellation of payments will trigger recognition of entire remaining gain on the decedent-note holder's *estate income tax* return (Form 1041).[12] While the gain will be income in respect of a decedent, no income tax deduction for its proportionate share of the estate tax is available because the note is not included in the decedent's gross estate. Because the tax on this gain is recognized by the estate it is not a debt at the time of death and therefore is not deductible from the gross estate. Planners may still wish to recommend the SCIN to wealthier clients whose potential estate tax rate exceeds their marginal income tax rate.

The SCIN represents aggressive planning and should be used only when the client is willing to be subject to potentially greater income tax exposure.

The appeal of installment sales. Tax deferral, through installment sales, is attractive for several reasons. First, it spreads the gain over a number of years, perhaps keeping it in lower marginal rates. Second, even though the Revenue Reconciliation Act of 1990 put a 28% ceiling on capital gains rate, Congress is expected to move, in the very near future, the capital gains rate even lower. Since the rate in effect when each installment is collected is the applicable rate, spreading the payments into a period of lower rates is an advantage.

On the other hand, there are restrictions on installment reporting for certain sales. The sale of publicly traded property (e.g., stocks and bonds) does not qualify for installment reporting. A portion of a sale might not qualify (under the so-called "proportional disallowance rule") if the sales price exceeds $150,000. Thus, the installment sale is available mainly for the occasional sale of real estate or tangible personal property.

Intra-family sales, whether of the ordinary, bargain, or installment variety, are significant value-shifting devices. The sale will freeze a portion of the client's estate, since post-sale appreciation will inure to the new owner, whose gross estate is probably far smaller than the client's and who will probably live considerably longer.

Private Annuity

Overview. A private annuity usually involves the sale of an asset by the client in exchange for the unsecured promise of a life annuity by another family member. It is distinguished from a commercial annuity, which is purchased from an insurance company or other financial institution.

> EXAMPLE 14 - 8. Schwab, age 65 and in poor health, agrees to transfer a $100,000 asset ($20,000 basis) to his son, under a private annuity arrangement when the federal rate for valuing annuities was 10%. Based on Table S (10%), Schwab will receive $14,042 a year for life ($14,042 = $100,000/7.1213).

The private annuity can generate periodic income for the client and can completely exclude the transferred property from his or her gross estate.

Taxation of private annuity. Tax aspects of the private annuity are as follows.

Gift taxation. If the transaction is designed properly, there will be *no taxable gift* as long as the value of the property transferred equals the discounted present value of the annuity promised. So long as, when the private annuity was established, the annuitant had a greater than 50% probability of living more than one year (or actually did live 18 months or more), the IRS generally accepts the use of the Alpha Tables (Treasury's actuarial tables) for valuing the private annuity.[13] If a gift element is present, there is the risk that it will be deemed a transfer for less than money's worth with a retained interest resulting in the date of death value of the asset being included in the annuitant's estate.[14]

Income taxation. *No gain* is immediately recognizable upon creation of a private annuity because the amount realized (i.e., the value of the unsecured promise to pay an annuity for someone's life) is not considered immediately ascertainable. Thus, as with the installment sale, gain is reported as the annuity payments are *received.* But unlike the installment sale, taxability of the payments is governed by the annuity rules of §72. A portion of each payment is treated as a tax-free return of the annuitant's basis, also called *investment in the contract.* The excluded fraction, called the *exclusion ratio*, is calculated by dividing the investment in the contract by the *expected return*, which is the total of all amounts the annuitant expects to receive under the annuity contract. In the typical case, the expected return equals the total of all expected payments over the annuitant's life expectancy obtained from the mortality table in IRS Reg. §1.72-9.

> EXAMPLE 14 - 9. Based last example, Schwab's tax-free portion of the payment is $1,000, which is the product of an annual payment, $14,042, and the exclusion ratio, of .07121. This ratio is calculated by dividing the investment in the contract, $20,000, by the expected return, $280,848, which is the product of $14,042 and 20, Schwab's life expectancy, derived from the regulations. Schwab will be required to report as gain $4,000, or one twentieth of his $80,000 total gain in each of the first twenty years. Thus, for the first twenty years, of the entire $14,042 payment, Schwab will report $4,000 as taxable gain and $9,042 as ordinary income. The remaining $1,000 will be an income tax-free return of capital. If Schwab outlives his 20 year life expectancy all subsequent payments constitute ordinary income. If he dies within 20 years, gain reporting stops and he will receive a loss deduction on his final income tax return for the unrecovered basis.

Estate taxation. Upon death of the client-annuitant, *nothing* connected with the transaction should be includable in the estate tax base, inasmuch as he or she no longer has an interest in the property transferred. As with any life estate based upon the life of its owner, the life annuity terminates, becoming valueless at the death of its owner.

EXAMPLE 14 - 10. Continuing the example above, if Schwab lives for two years, his son will have paid less than $30,000 for an asset worth $100,000. In connection with this transaction, Schwab's gross estate will include nothing more than the portion of the two payments that Schwab received, and still retained at death.

However, as with the installment sale, if the original transaction were to be ruled a *gift* because the value of the annuity promised the client is less than the value of the property transferred, the client's gross estate will include the *entire* date-of-death value of that property as a §2036(a) transfer with retained life estate. Such effect would wipe away the major tax appeal of the transaction, a danger that can be minimized by securing a qualified professional appraisal. For some additional protection, several commentators have suggested incorporating as a provision in the transaction a "valuation readjustment" or "savings"-type clause. One such clause would require the purchaser to pay additional consideration if the IRS determines that a gift had been made. The IRS has attacked these clauses, arguing that (1), as completed gifts, the transactions cannot be altered, and (2) they are contrary to public policy.

Analysis of private annuity. Advantages and disadvantages of the private annuity are described next.

Two advantages. First, from an estate tax point of view, the private annuity is even better than the installment sale: It can result in *complete* exclusion of the asset value from the annuitant's estate tax base. Second, as illustrated in the most recent example, the total amount eventually paid by the payor can be expected to be *relatively small* in situations where non-terminal clients have shorter than average life expectancies.

Disadvantages. The private annuity has three significant drawbacks. First, while the seller in an installment sale can, and usually does, require security, the annuitant under a private annuity cannot use the transferred property as security because doing so will result in it being included in the annuitant's gross estate.[15] Thus, private annuity arrangements are always unsecured, a distinct disadvantage to the annuitant-client. Lack of security will increase the risk of not being repaid, a result that could be unsettling, especially to an annuitant who is more or less depending on the payments for support. Second, while interest paid by the purchaser under an installment sale may be tax deductible, *no part* of the annuity payment under a private annuity is deductible.[16] Third, if the annuitant lives a very long life, the payor has made a *bad bargain.*

EXAMPLE 14 - 11. Continuing the example above, if, instead of dying, Schwab regains his health and lives 20 years, his son will have paid more than $280,000 for the $100,000 asset. Schwab's gross estate may have to include this amount (which is nearly three times the value of the asset transferred), plus its resulting income, if he doesn't consume or gift these receipts during his lifetime.

Since the private annuity can accomplish significant estate freezing without gift tax consequences, it can be a very attractive transaction if the parties are willing to assume the inherent risks. As we have seen, it works best when the client wants to save estate tax, is not expected to live more than a few years, anticipates a significant cash flow need for life, and has little or no worry that the payments won't be forthcoming. Unfortunately, all of these characteristics seem to apply to only a few clients. Private annuities are infrequently used, with less than one percent of clients of experienced estate planning attorneys adopting them.

INCOMPLETE INTRA-FAMILY TRANSFERS

This section briefly covers three currently used incomplete intra-family transfers, the intentionally defective irrevocable trust, gift-leaseback and grantor retained trust.

Intentionally Defective Irrevocable Trust

When a client wishes to make gifts to significantly reduce estate tax, has little interest in shifting income, and wishes to retain some control over the transferred assets, the planner may wish to consider recommending an intentionally defective irrevocable trust (IDIT). Taking advantage of the differences in tax rules between §2036 - 2038 (estate tax) and §671-677 (grantor trust income tax rules) with regard to retained powers, transfers to an IDIT are made complete for federal estate and gift tax but incomplete for income tax. Thus, the trust corpus is not included in the grantor's gross estate, similar to the treatment of any other completed gift; but, because the trust provides for grantor retained powers uniquely proscribed by the grantor trust rules, all trust income is taxable to the grantor. This result offers an additional opportunity to save estate tax since income tax paid by the grantor rather than by the trust beneficiary will have the effect of additionally reducing the amount of assets held by the grantor at death, at no gift tax cost.

> EXAMPLE 14 - 12. Maxwell transfers $610,000 to an IDIT for the benefit of his adult son, Kirk. Since Maxwell has made no prior taxable gifts, he can totally shelter the current gift from gift taxation with the annual exclusion and unified credit. Required to distribute all income to Kirk annually, the trustee distributes $50,000 income in the first year. Maxwell is obligated to pay an additional $17,500 income tax, based on his 35% combined marginal rate. This year Maxwell has effectively transferred an additional $17,500 for the benefit of his son, free of gift tax.

Powers that the grantor may wish to retain over an IDIT include acting as trustee and having the grantor's spouse as one of the trust beneficiaries. As trustee, the grantor can have the following powers: to invest, to allocate receipts between income and principal, to vote shares of stock held in the trust, and to distribute income or principal to trust beneficiaries for such reasons as "sickness," "emergency" or "disability." Naming the spouse to be one of the beneficiaries enables the grantor to retain indirect access to the trust. Of course, any distributions to the spouse could increase his or her estate, which may run contrary to the estate tax goals of the trust.

The IRS may argue that payment of income taxes by the grantor constitutes a gift. At least one commentator believes the IRS will not succeed, provided the trust instrument is worded carefully.

The advantages of the IDIT over a simple gift include retained control, and greater potential estate tax avoidance at little or no additional gift tax cost.

Gift-Leaseback

When a business-owning parent wishes to establish a program of gifting but is held back for lack of available assets, he or she might find the answer in a gift-leaseback arrangement. As its name suggests, the parent gives a business asset outright or in trust to a lower-bracket family member and leases the asset back for use in the business. The parent is able to continue using the asset, can take a deduction for the lease payment, and can still enjoy all the other advantages inherent in gifting.

The ability to *deduct* the lease payments under a gift-leaseback might depend in part on the location of the client's business, and in part on how carefully the arrangement is structured. In some circuits, the Federal appellate courts have disallowed the deduction, while other circuits have allowed it as a legitimate business expense. Even in circuits that allow the deduction, it will be denied if the transaction is poorly structured. Some requirements for success include having a legitimate business purpose, charging a reasonable lease payment, having a written and enforceable lease, and, if the gift is in trust, the trustee must be independent and not subservient to the donor.

Grantor Retained Interest Trust

With a grantor retained interest trust, the client transfers property into an irrevocable trust, retaining the right to income for a period of years, after which the trust ends and the remaindermen are usually relatives of the grantor. The acronym "GRIT" is used in this text to refer to all varieties of grantor retained interest trusts, including common law GRITs, GRATs, GRUTs, and others that fall under §2702. Who will eventually receive the corpus, and whether the corpus is includable in the client's gross estate usually depends upon the type of GRIT created, and how long the client lives. With all GRITs, if the client *does not survive* the income period, §2036(a) will apply, and the GRIT will have served no useful purpose. The date of death value of the trust will be included in the grantor's gross estate, and the adjusted taxable gift (insofar as the GRIT is concerned) is zero. In fact, some GRITs (i.e., all those except GRATS and GRUTS--see below) provide that the corpus will revert to the client-grantor's estate, if he or she does not survive. This is accomplished by granting the client a contingent testamentary power of appointment over the trust corpus. Reversion is made contingent upon the grantor not surviving the period. Putting the contingent reversion in the terms of the trust, reduces the remainder value. Since the remainder value is the taxable gift, the smaller it is, the less unified credit is used. If the client *does survive* the income period, the result is the same for all GRITs: the client's entire beneficial interest in the trust ceases, and the corpus vests in the remaindermen (usually the client's children), and the gift value will be an adjusted taxable gift when the grantor dies.

Tax consequences. A properly structured GRIT has gift tax, estate tax and income tax consequences worth knowing about.

Gift taxation. At the creation of the GRIT, the value of the gift equals the entire value of the property transferred into the trust reduced by the value of the retained interests. Whether the value of a retained interest is deemed to equal zero or some larger amount depends upon the facts of the GRIT and the provisions of §2702. If §2702 applies (e.g., the remaindermen are the grantor's children), all *retained* interests are valued at zero (called the *zero valuation rule*) unless the retained interest is a *qualified retained interest*, an interest in a personal residence trust, or an interest in a tangible personal property trust. From an estate planning stand point, one wants the retained interest to be valued at greater than zero (the higher the better), thereby reducing the gift tax valuation. It is said that §2702 uses the "subtraction method" to arrive at the value of the gift. One starts with the value of the property transferred into trust and subtracts the allowable value of the retained interest. Hence, if the retained interest is given zero value (because it doesn't meet §2702's requirements), the taxable gift value will be the total value of the property transferred into the trust.

Since the gift portion of a GRIT is one of a future (remainder) interest, it does not qualify for the annual exclusion. As a result, any resulting taxable gift must use some unified credit, if available, and will require payment of gift tax once all the donor's unified credit is used up. The basic rules for valuing the retained interest at greater than zero, assuming §2702 applies:

1. There is a qualified retained interest. The retained interest will be given its actuarial value if it is defined as fixed payments retained by the grantor, and paid at least annually.

    These payments can be fixed in dollar amount (the trust will be called a GRAT, grantor retained annuity trust). The trust can call for annual increases, but the valuation of the retained interest will consider these increase only to the extent that they do not exceed 120% of the prior year's payment.[17] A GRAT may state the initial payments in absolute dollar amounts (e.g., "$1,500 per month") or as a percentage of the initial amount placed in the trust (e.g., "6% times the initial value of the trust, payments to be made quarterly").

    These payments can be fixed as a percentage of the trust's value determined annually (the trust will be called a GRUT, grantor retained unitrust). As with the GRAT, the GRUT can provide for increasing percentages each year, but the retained interest will be valued only to the extent that the increase in the fixed percentage does not exceed 120% of the prior year's percentage.[18]

2. The zero valuation rules do not apply to Personal Residence Trusts and Qualified Personal Residence Trusts. These are valued under §7520, meaning we treat them as common law GRITS. More on this later.

3. The retained interest in a "Tangible Property" GRIT will be valued at the FMV of the term interest. The grantor has the burden of establishing what the price for which the term interest could be "sold."

Income taxation. As a grantor trust, all trust income is taxable to the trustor until the end of the stated period, if he or she lives that long.[19]

Estate taxation. If the client *survives* the income period, none of the corpus will be includable in the gross estate. However, the taxable gift value will be included in the estate tax base as an adjusted taxable gift.

If the client *dies before* the expiration of the income period, as mentioned, the date-of-death value of the corpus is included in the client's gross estate, as a transfer with retained income or enjoyment which did not in fact end before the transferor's death.[20] Thus, premature death of the client cannot reduce estate tax. Fortunately, this type of estate planning has very little downside risk; if the client had not set up the GRIT the property would have been in the client's gross estate at date of death values anyway. Therefore, if the client outlives the term much is accomplished in the way of estate planning but dying during the term has as its only downside the cost of establishing the trust (mainly attorney's fees) and the cost of maintaining it (mainly accountant's fees). Remember, since the corpus comes back into the gross estate the earlier gift disappears as an adjusted taxable gift for estate tax purposes.[21]

GST taxation. The ability to leverage the $1 million GSTT exemption to a GRIT transfer is limited by statutory law. Under §2642(f),[22] the GSTT exemption cannot be allocated to most GRITs until the close of the "estate tax inclusion period" (called ETIP), which occurs when the property would no longer be includable in the grantor's gross estate in the event the grantor died. In most GRIT situations, this would be the *end of the specified income period*, at which point §2036(a) no longer applies. The value of the property against which the allocation may be made will equal the value that is included in the grantor's gross estate, or the GRIT's value at the end of the term. Ordinarily, an allocation of the GSTT exemption for most non-GRIT transfers is made *at the time the GSTT trust becomes irrevocable, which has the effect of attaining* maximum leverage for appreciating assets. In the case of a GRIT, the exemption allocation is delayed until the end of the income period. This means that more of the client's GSTT exemption will have to be used up for two reasons: First, the allocation will have to be made to the *entire value* of the property, rather than just the present value of the remainder, excluding the income interest. Second, in the case of assets *appreciating* during the income period of the GRIT, the allocation amount will necessarily be higher. However, even though the advantage of leveraging the exemption under a GRIT is restrained, it is not eliminated, since any appreciation *after the term* [i.e., after the retained interest period] is sheltered from future GSTT. Thus, although allocating the GSTT exemption to a GRIT will not result in as much leveraging as with an ordinary lifetime gift, it generally will yield more leveraging than with a transfer at death because the leveraging period can also include a period during the grantor's lifetime.

GRIT Planning.

The following material explains how GRITs were structured before tax reform, and then describes planning opportunities currently available.

The "Common Law" GRIT. Prior to the passage of §2702, relatively uncomplicated GRITs were quite successful in freezing the value of appreciating property at little or no gift tax cost. The following example portrays what is now called a "common law GRIT." The following series of examples uses *current* IRS valuation tables (see Table B (10%) in Appendix A), so that the reader can validate first hand the calculations.

> EXAMPLE 14 - 13. In 1985, Haney, when he was 58 years old, created a GRIT, funding it with $500,000 in common stock. The trust terms retain for Haney all income from the trust, payable at least annually, for the lesser of 10 years or for Haney's life. If Haney dies before the end of the 10-year period, the trust will terminate and the corpus will revert to his estate. If Haney survives the period, the trust will terminate at the end of 10 years and the corpus will then be distributed outright to Haney's son. When the trust was established, Haney made a *taxable gift* of the remainder interest in the stock, which, at 10%, is valued at $161,996 [= $500,000 x .385543 x (72082/85776). As a future interest, the remainder does not qualify for the annual exclusion. Haney owed no gift tax, he simply used up some of his unified credit.

EXAMPLE 14 - 14. Continuing the above example, if Haney died four years after establishing the trust, the date of death value of the corpus would be included in his gross estate, and the trust would have gained no estate tax advantage, but instead of there being an adjusted taxable gift of $161,996 it would be zero. Thus the only disadvantage was the fees paid to establish and maintain the trust for the four years.

EXAMPLE 14 - 15. Examining the consequences of the alternative outcome, if Haney instead *dies twelve years later* when the corpus is worth $1 million, his gross estate will include nothing in connection with this property, although adjusted taxable gift would be $161,996. By surviving the income period, Haney would have succeeded in freezing the transfer tax value of this stock at $161,996, the original gift tax value of the remainder interest, less than the value of the stock when transferred and far less that its value when Haney died. Described in other terms, Haney would have leveraged the gift tax unified credit many times over.

Review of §2702. In general, §2702 applies when there is a transfer of an interest in a trust to, or for, the benefit of a member of the transferor's family, where the transferor (or an "applicable family member") has retained an interest in the trust. §2702 GRITs that fall under the zero valuation rule must treat the entire value of the transfer as a taxable gift unless the Code allows otherwise, e.g., the interest is qualified one.

EXAMPLE 14 - 16. In the ongoing example above, had Haney instead created his GRIT today, the entire value of the transfer, $500,000, would be treated as a taxable gift. §2702 applies because the trust was for the benefit of a member of the transferor's family. The zero valuation rule applies because the arrangement does not fall under one of the qualified retained interests. Thus, under the subtraction method of valuation, the gift tax value equals $500,000, the total value of the transfer, reduced by zero, the allowable value of the retained interest.

Careful GRIT planning will include one of two strategies: Either planners will structure a common law GRIT to avoid §2702 entirely. Or they will create a GRIT that is avoids the zero valuation rule. A GRIT transfer to a non-family member (described next) is a common example of the former strategy. Examples of the other approach will be explained shortly.

GRIT Transfers to non-family members. §2702 only apply if (1) the transferor (i.e., the grantor or settlor) or an "applicable family member" retains an interest, and (2) an interest is transferred to a "member of the transferor's family." Applicable family members are the transferor's spouse, an ancestor of the transferor or of the transferor's spouse, and the spouse of any ancestor.[23]

Members of the transferor's family are the transferor's spouse, any ancestor or lineal descendant of the transferor or the transferor's spouse; any sibling of the transferor; any spouse of the transferor's ancestors, lineal descendants, or siblings.[24] To clarify, think of the applicable family members as the older generation, who are likely to set-up one of these trusts. The older generation will retain an interest for a term of years, then the trust will terminate, and the corpus will go to the younger generation (the members of the transferor's family). Most likely, a parent (or parents) will establish a GRIT to eventually benefit children or grandchildren. Notice that, by these definitions, even though brothers and sisters are members of the transferor's family, nephews and nieces are not. Nor is a best friend or a "significant other." In other words, the common law GRIT is alive and well, if the remainderman is not a member of the transferor's family as such is defined in the Code.

> EXAMPLE 14 - 17. In the prior example, had the beneficiary of the transferred interest been Haney's *nephew* rather than his son, the entire actuarial value of the retained income interest could be subtracted in arriving at the gift tax value. It would be a common law GRIT.

Examples of common non-applicable family member situations (i.e., we can still use the common law GRIT that does not "fix" the amount of income), are trusts with unmarried partners and/or close friends as remaindermen. It should be clear now that we call the GRIT in the above example a common law GRIT, because it does not fall under the restrictive requirements of §2702. For it, we can use the remainder column of the appropriate Table B to determine the value of the gift. As you will see, when we get into the trusts that must comply with §2702, the income must be fixed in some manner (merely requiring "all income" for the income beneficiary is not good enough); and the valuation is based upon using the annuity column to determine the value of the retained income interest, and subtracting that from the initial value of the trust to determine the value of the gift (i.e., the remainder value).

The five types of §2702 GRITs described in the next few pages avoid the harsh zero valuation rule (for the retained interests) by falling satisfying one or more of the requirements found in the Code. They are the GRAT, GRUT, tangible personal property GRIT, and two types of personal residence GRITs.

GRAT and GRUT. The zero valuation rule of §2702 does not apply to "qualified" retained income interests, i.e., one of the two types of income interests that meet §2702(b)'s detailed technical requirements. Trusts must have either a *qualified annuity interest* or a *qualified unitrust interest,* and the trusts prepared with these interest in mind are called the *grantor retained annuity trust,* GRAT, and the *grantor retained unitrust,* GRUT. Among other requirements, the payment must be made at least annually. For a GRAT it must be stated as a *fixed dollar amount,* sometimes stated as a percentage of the initial value of the trust corpus, and for a GRUT the annual payment will be a *fixed percentage* of the fair market value of the trust property *determined each year.* In valuing the retained interest, the Code will take into account terms of the trust that increase the annual payments (however defined) but not by more than 120% of the prior year's payment.

> EXAMPLE 14 - 18. Jake creates a GRAT, transferring $200,000 in trust and retaining the right to an annual payment equal to 6% of the initial corpus; thus he will receive $12,000 each year.

> EXAMPLE 14 - 19. Pam creates a GRUT, transferring $200,000 in trust and retaining the right to six percent of the fair market value of the trust property, determined annually. The first year she will receive $12,000. If the trust is worth $210,000 on the valuation date of the second year, she will receive $12,600 for that year. On the other hand, if the value has dropped to $190,000, the payment will be only $11,400. The annual valuation day is likely to be set in the trust agreement as January 1 of each year, since most reporting and planning is done on a calendar year basis.

Clients choosing between a GRAT or a GRUT who would prefer to minimize their receipt of unneeded income that may someday augment their gross estate will probably prefer a GRAT, under which income payments are based on the *initial* value of the corpus. This is especially true if the corpus will be funded with assets expected to appreciate over the retained income period.

The detailed rules for GRATs and GRUTs are very similar to the rules for charitable remainder trusts (called CRATs and CRUTs), described later in this chapter.

"Zeroing out" a GRAT or a GRUT. If the payments to the grantor are high enough, the value of the retained interest could equal the value of the property transferred into trust. This is referred to as *"zeroing out"* a GRAT. That is the remainder interest is valued at zero.

> EXAMPLE 14 - 20. If the §7520 rate is 6% when Mark creates a 15 year GRAT

with assets valued at $1 million, he could zero it out if he retained an annuity of $103,963 per year.

Note that with a zeroed out GRAT, not only is there is no gift tax, the grantor does not use up any unified credit. Thus, the GRIT can result in a large estate tax base *reduction*, as well as a freeze, at no transfer tax cost. Although these were much the rage at estate planning seminars in the early 1990s, including excitement about one and two year term zeroed out GRATs (yes, the retained income amounts were huge), the IRS has taken the position that a GRAT cannot be successfully zeroed out. It claims that, for any GRAT whose annuity amount will exhaust the corpus precisely at the termination of the trust, the value of the retained interest can not equal the initial corpus because of the possibility that the grantor may die prior to the expiration of the trust term.[25] The IRS has taken the position that an intended zeroed out GRAT may not be adequately funded to make all the payments if: 1) the annual payment is set at a level that would exhaust the corpus before the end of the income period; or 2) the exercise of a trustee power to invest in highly speculative assets would substantially increase the chance of a loss.[26] For our examples we will assume a less aggressive position, with GRITs that last more than just a couple of years, and which leave some reasonable value allocated to the remainder interest.

Tangible personal property transfers. The zero valuation rule of §2702 does not apply to tangible personal property where: (*a*) the failure by a term interest holder to exercise his or her rights would not have a substantial effect on the value of the remainder interest, and (*b*) the property is of a type for which no depreciation deduction would be allowable. In such case, the value of the retained interest is set equal to the amount the interest could be sold for to an unrelated third party. One possible type of property is artwork, such as a painting.

EXAMPLE 14 - 21. Drew, age 65, gives his daughter a remainder interest in a painting, worth $1 million, and retains a 13 year term certain interest. The gift tax value is the million dollars reduced by the amount Drew can show that an unrelated third party would pay for the right to possess the painting for 13 years.

In view of the fact that the IRS requires evidence of "actual sales or rentals that are comparable" to sustain the value of the term interest, few clients will be able to successfully employ this strategy.

Qualified personal residence trust. Finally, the zero valuation rule of §2702 does not apply to a GRIT whose sole asset is a personal residence of the term interest holder. The details and restrictions are quite complex, probably discouraging all but the most ambitious planners and clients.

> EXAMPLE 14 - 22. Marcus, on his 60th birthday, creates a ten year GRIT, structuring it to contain only his $200,000 personal residence. The result is the same as that described for a common law GRIT. Thus, if the §7520 rate is 8%, we would use the remainder factor of 0.463193 from Table B (8%) to arrive at a remainder value of $92,639. Assuming that the terms of the trust create a contingent reversion should Marcus not live the ten year term, the probability that he will die reduces the gift value to $75,513 [i.e., (68248/83726) * $92,639]. See Table 80CNSMT.

Qualified personal residence trust. More planners will recommend a personal residence GRIT as a result of recent regulations which have outlined the conditions required for 'safe-harbor' residence trust called a qualified personal residence trust (QPRT).[27] Among the rules, the QPRT can hold an interest in only one residence. It can receive additions of cash to pay six months of mortgage payments, but any excess cash must be distributed to the term holder. The trustee may sell the residence, hold the proceeds, and buy another residence within two years from the sale. If the residence ceases to be a personal residence of the term holder, the trust corpus must be held for the balance of the term interest and must meet all of the requirements for functioning exclusively as a qualified annuity interest trust, similar to a GRAT. However, unlike a GRAT or a GRUT, a QPRT can provide for reversion of the corpus to the client's estate if he or she does not survive the term period. As with the traditional common-law GRIT, this contingent reversion will have the advantage of reducing the value of the remainder and thus the value of the taxable gift. The GRATs and GRUTs that are subject to the §2702 rules (i.e., the remaindermen are members of the transferor's family) can have a contingent reversion but, because it is not a qualified retained interest, it will be subject to the zero valuation rule, hence it will not decrease the remainder value the way it does with the common law GRIT and the QPRT.

Calculating the gift for a QPRT. The remainder value is the gift. Its value, when the grantor has contingent reversion, is calculated as follows:

$$\text{Remainder value} = R_t*(\#Y/\#X) * \text{FMV of the property}$$

Where:

R_t = Term of years remainder factor for given interest rate "t" [28]

#X = Number alive at starting age for grantor

#Y = Number alive at ending age for grantor [29]

> EXAMPLE 14 - 23. The 7520 rate is 8.0% and the grantor is 75 at start of a 10 year QPRT. The house being used to fund the trust is worth $500,000.
>
> R_t = .463193
> Value for 75 (1980 census) = 56799
> Value for 85 (1980 census) = 27960

Therefore, the remainder value for this QPRT is:

$$.463193 * (27960/56799) * \$500,000 = \$114,006$$

Remember if the grantor dies during the term of the trust, its fair market value will be included in the grantor's estate but the adjusted taxable gift value drops back to zero insofar as this gift goes because §2001(b) defines adjusted taxable gifts as being those post-1976 taxable gifts except for those "gifts that are includable in the gross estate...." Therefore, the QPRTs, like other qualified GRITs, carry very little downside risk, other than the attorneys' fees in establishing them and the accountants' fees in maintaining them.

Must a client who survives the term of the QPRT vacate the residence? No, since he or she can rent it from the remainderman. However, the agreement must be arms length, with lease payments equal to fair rental value, in order to avoid the risk of §2036(a) application.[30] At one time, planners thought that the settlor could purchase the home from the trustee just as the term of the trust came to an end, but regulations proposed by the Treasury prohibit purchase by the settlor, the settlor's spouse, or an entity controlled by either of them.[31] Clearly, some clients will not appreciate this aspect of the QPRT. Others, however, will welcome the ability to transfer property to their children at a greatly reduced transfer tax cost.

PLANNING FOR CHARITABLE TRANSFERS

We now shift gears and examine transfers designed to assist charitable institutions while providing significant benefits to the donor-client.

Introduction to Charitable Giving

Transfers to charity, whether lifetime or at death, are supported by several provisions of the Internal Revenue Code, which normally allows generous deductions on a contributor's income tax, gift tax, and estate tax returns. While charitable transfers can be made during lifetime or at death, lifetime transfers will be the primary focus of this section, partly for consistency with the chapter theme, partly because lifetime charitable transfers often are more complex and need greater elaboration, and partly because they have a significant income tax advantage over charitable transfers at death, as we shall see. Lifetime gifts to charity are of essentially two types (outright gift and split-interest gift), offering to clients considerable flexibility in the amount and type of interest in a given piece of property that can be donated.

At the outset, it should be noted that charitable gifts, unlike other lifetime transfers, will hardly ever result in no net decrease in wealth to the client's family unit as a whole. Thus, the client will usually need to possess a charitable motive to feel comfortable about making charitable transfers. The material presented below describes how to best minimize the decline in family wealth resulting from a charitable donation.

Tax Consequences of Charitable Transfers

Income tax consequences. To qualify for an itemized charitable income tax deduction, the donee charity must meet the requirements under the Code.[32] In addition, the Code contains rather complex *limitations* on the amount of charitable contributions deductible from income by individuals in any given tax year. As shown next, there are limitations on both the total amount deductible for all charitable gifts, and on the specific amount deductible for any particular gift.

Limitations on total amount deductible. In general, total deductible charitable contributions may not exceed 50% of a taxpayer's "contribution base" (CB), the name for an amount that is approximately equal to adjusted gross income.[33] However, there are some major exceptions with regard to this 50% limitation. Taxpayers are limited to a 30% of CB for contributions to private charities (includes most private foundations and organizations). In addition, deductible limits for both public and private charities are reduced to 30% and 20%, respectively, for contributions of most kinds of "capital gain property" (see below).[34] Contributions in excess of these limits may be carried over, to be deducted during the next five years.[35] To further complicate matters, since 1991 charitable deductions are part of the itemized deductions which for high income taxpayers are subject to a 3% overall floor.

> EXAMPLE 14 - 24. Fanny Superstar, prominent singer just donated her $15 million Malibu estate to charity. This year she has earned $20 million in income. She can deducted $5.4 million (30% times the donation, but subject to the 3% floor, i.e., 30% * $20 million - 3% * 20 million = $5.4 million). She can carry over the remaining $9 million to later years. Assuming her income remains about the same in the next two years, and that this is a combined marginal tax rate of 50 %, by making the donation, Fanny should save approximately $2.7 million in each of the first and second year, and $1.2 million the third year, for a total income tax savings of about $6.6 million.

This summary of the annual limitations has been merely a capsule overview; individuals wishing to make contributions of this relative size should consult a tax adviser specializing in this area.

Amount deductible for a particular gift. The amount deductible from adjusted gross income for any particular charitable gift is usually its *fair market value*, subject to the total annual limitation outlined above. However, there are two important *exceptions for noncash gifts*. First, if sale of the property would have resulted in ordinary income or in short-term capital gain, the asset is called "ordinary income property," and the donor is limited to deducting the *adjusted basis* of the property, with a 50% CB limit.

Second, if the property would have resulted in a long-term capital gain had it been sold instead of donated, the asset is called "capital gain property," and one of three alternative tax consequences will occur. If the property is tangible personalty given to a public charity which *uses it* in its activities, then the *fair market value* is deductible (with a 30% CB limit). If, on the other hand, the charity is a private foundation, or if it is a public charity which *cannot* use the donated property in its activities, then the amount deductible is limited to the donor's *basis*, with a CB limit of 50% for donations to public charities and a 30% limit for donations to private charities. An example of a "related use" is placing a donated painting on a wall of the donee art museum or the donee university. An example of an unrelated use would be the storage of the painting in the institution's basement or the immediate sale of the painting. Finally, if the donation to a public charity qualifies for a deduction based upon its fair market value, but with a 30% CB limitation, the taxpayer can elect to use the property's basis as the deduction and raise the CB limit to 50%.[36]

EXAMPLE 14 - 25. Charles, a real estate developer earning $380,000 in adjusted gross income this year, has four assets (each currently worth $100,000), one of which he is considering donating to a public charity. Besides *cash*, Charles has a parcel of *real estate* which his business purchased three years ago and which currently has an adjusted basis of $20,000. Charles also has two blocks of *common stock*, each of which cost $20,000. Stock A was purchased three years ago, and Stock B was acquired last month. The following describes (ignoring the 3% floor) the amount deductible if Charles contributes, alternatively, each asset to the charity which, for the moment we shall assume, can properly use any of the assets in its activities.

1.   Cash: $100,000 deduction.
2.   Business real estate: $20,000 deduction.
3.   Stock A: $100,000 deduction. This stock could be the stock of Charles' real estate development corporation. The charity could be given the right to redeem the stock for cash.
4.   Stock B: $20,000 deduction.

The charitable deduction for business real estate is limited to the developer's basis because the property represents his business inventory. A better alternative might be to sell the inventory and donate the after-tax cash proceeds. Assuming a 50% combined marginal tax rate, Charles could donate $60,000 cash ($100,000-($100,000-$20,000) * .50), yielding a tax saving of $30,000 ($60,000 *.50). In contrast, donating the property would save only $10,000 in tax (.50 * $20,000). Of course, the charity would be receiving only $60,000 (cash) rather than $100,000 (real estate).

Any charitable contributions of $250 or more must be substantiated contemporaneously in writing by the donee charity, which states the amount of cash donated, a description (but not value) of the property, and a good faith estimate of the value of any property it provided in consideration for the donation.[37] In addition, a charitable donor of property exceeding $5,000 in value is required to obtain a "qualified appraisal" and supply additional information detailing the transaction.

Income tax planning for outright gifts to charity. Several planning strategies evolve from these and other income tax rules.

In many cases, contributing *capital gain property* to a public charity is more advantageous than contributing cash.

> EXAMPLE 14 - 26. Jeff, who is in the 35% combined income tax bracket, wishes to contribute $5,000 to his favorite public charity. Jeff could give an original oil painting, acquired for $1,000 and now worth $5,000, or he could sell the painting and donate the cash proceeds. If Jeff contributes the painting, his after-tax cost will be $3,250 which is the $5,000 value of the painting, less the $1,750 tax savings from the deduction. Alternatively, if Jeff sells the painting and still donates the full $5,000, his after-tax cost will be $4,370, which is the $5,000 donated cash, plus the $1,120 tax on the gain ($4,000 * .28), minus the $1,750 tax saving from the deduction.

From 1987 to 1992, the appreciation portion of the charitable deduction ($4,000 in the above example) was treated as a tax preference item, meaning that it was subject to the *alternative minimum tax*. Fortunately, the 1993 tax act repealed this provision. When considering giving a large gift to a charity, a client should review his or her portfolio to see if there are appreciated assets which could easily be replaced in the security markets. Using the money to replace the property increases the basis in the investment to the purchase price and the charitable deduction is the same as it would have been had cash been given.

> EXAMPLE 14 - 27. Anderson has been planning to gift $10,000 cash to charity. He also owns shares of publicly traded ABC corporation stock, currently worth $10,000 and having a basis of $1,000. Although Anderson likes the stock as an investment, if he donates it to charity and immediately purchases an equivalent amount of ABC stock on the market, the new shares will now have a basis of $10,000. Anderson's taxable gain will be $9,000 less, if he later sells the stock.

Owners of nonmarketable property that they wish to sell may consider making a *bargain sale* of the property to charity. The income tax consequences of a bargain sale to a private individual were described earlier in the chapter. Bargain sales to charities are treated very differently. With the related party bargain sale no loss can be recognized and a gain is recognized only if the bargain price exceeds the seller-donor's basis. But for bargain sales to a charity the transaction is treated as though it is two transactions in one: a sale and a gift. The old basis is allocated to each part in direct proportion to the part's value when compared to the whole. Thus, where B represents the old basis, B_g represents basis allocated to the gift portion and B_s represents the basis allocated to the sale portion, G stands for the value of the gift, which is the difference between the amount paid (S for sale) by the charity and the fair market value (FMV) of the property transferred to the charity at a bargain price.

$$B_g = (G/FMV)*B$$
$$B_s = (S/FMV)*B$$
$$Gain = S - B_s.$$

EXAMPLE 14 - 28. This year, Margaret transferred her vacant city lot to her church. She inherited the lot from her mother. It was valued in her mother's estate at $100,000, which of course established Margaret's basis. At the time of transfer, the lot was worth $500,000. Since Margaret is cash poor and wants to purchase a $500,000 life insurance policy, so her son won't be too disappointed about her transferring the lot, the church has agreed to pay Margaret $150,000 for the lot. Margaret's gain:

Gain = $150,000 - ($150,000/$500,000)*$100,000 = $120,000

Of course Margaret will have a charitable deduction of $350,000, the difference between the FMV and the amount paid to Margaret. If Margaret has modest income, she and the church might wish to structure this as an installment sale whereby the church pays the price in five $30,000 annual installments, since Margaret's excess income tax charitable deduction can be carried forward, and the installment reporting will avoid bunching up the capital gain in the first year.

As in a private sale, an outright gift of *mortgaged property* to charity is treated as a bargain sale, resulting in taxable gain to the donor. However, the bargain sale may be a simpler way to sell difficult to market assets, such as an interest in a closely held business.

Gift tax consequences. Similar to the unlimited marital deduction, an unlimited gift tax deduction is allowed for the present value of gifts to qualifying charities.[38] The rules covering the charitable deduction require that a gift tax return must be filed if total gross gifts, including those to charity, exceed the amount of the annual exclusion.

Estate tax consequences. Similar to lifetime outright inter-spousal gifts, *lifetime* gifts to charity are not included in the donor's estate tax base. They are not includable in the gross estate because they are not owned by the decedent at death. And they are not an adjusted taxable gift because they were deducted in arriving at that amount. The estate taxation of lifetime charitable gifts *in trust* will be described in the next major section, which details gifts of split interests.

Outright bequests to charity are totally deductible from the gross estate.[39] Thus, a multimillionaire could give all (or all but $600,000) of his or her entire estate to charity and ensure total avoidance of the estate tax. Of course, he or she could also accomplish this goal by making a series of lifetime charitable transfers. In fact, lifetime charitable transfers are preferable to donations at death, as the next example illustrates.

> EXAMPLE 14 - 29. Sampson wishes to make an outright gift of $100,000 to his church which has been a source of continuous spiritual support to him and his family for many years. Sampson's estate planner recommends a lifetime transfer over a similar transfer at death, reasoning as follows: If Sampson donates the property at his death, his gross estate will be reduced by the amount of the gift, but he will enjoy no income tax benefit.[40] Alternatively, if Sampson makes the gift during his lifetime (even a deathbed gift), not only will his gross estate and estate tax base be lower by the date-of-death value of the gift property, but Sampson will also be able to save income taxes by deducting some or all of the value of the gift from his income.

Other tax planning for outright gifts to charity. Several other strategies include inter-spousal transfers, redemption bailout of corporate stock, gifts of life insurance, and the gift annuity.

Inter-spousal transfers. If a client insists on making a bequest to charity, the planner might urge the client to plan making an outright marital deduction gift to the surviving spouse, who could then donate the property to charity. While the estate tax consequences are the same, the income tax results will improve, since S2 will be able to enjoy a charitable income tax deduction. Of course, S2, as fee simple recipient of the property, could later refuse to make the donation. QTIP'ing the property will ensure receipt by the charity, but not until S2's death. Finally, the client may be encouraged to make a lifetime gift to the spouse of property destined for charity if more time is needed by that spouse to make full use of a charitable deduction carryover which arose as a result of the restrictive percentage limitations on total amounts deductible in a given tax year (discussed earlier).

Redemption bailout of corporate stock. A client owning stock in a closely held corporation may wish to gift some stock to a charity, which will later tender the stock for redemption by the corporation. Advantages include saving income tax, "bailing out" corporate earnings and profits without incurring dividend income, helping younger family shareholders concentrate their ownership, and enabling the charity to receive cash. This arrangement should be undertaken with great caution, however, and may be challenged if the IRS believes it can prove the existence of an "understanding" between donor and charity that the charity would surrender the shares for redemption. In that case, the donor would be forced to incur a taxable gain.

Charitable gifts of life insurance. Lifetime gifts to charity of life insurance policies are popular. The client can transfer an existing policy to charity, or purchase a new policy naming the charity as beneficiary and then assigning to the charity all ownership rights in the policy. The client may agree to continue to pay the premiums. The client should be able to take income tax and gift tax charitable deductions for the policy's terminal value at date of gift (or adjusted basis, if less, in the case of income tax) and take additional income tax deductions for all premiums paid.

Gift annuity. As a way of increasing income during retirement, some clients arrange a gift annuity with a charity. A gift annuity involves the transferring of assets to charity, which agrees to pay a guaranteed annuity for life. If the starting payment date is delayed, such as until the client's retirement, the arrangement is called a *deferred payment gift annuity*. In states allowing it, the gift annuity may be funded with real property, such as the personal residence with the client gifting only a *remainder* interest, enabling the client to continue to live there.

Under the bargain sale rules, the client will report the proportional gain ratably over his or her life expectancy, upon commencement of the annuity payments. A portion of each annuity payment will be taxable income, under the annuity rules of §72. Besides augmenting retirement income with a guaranteed, partially income tax-free payment, advantages of the gift annuity include a sizable current income tax deduction, lower estate tax and probate costs, and reduced asset management worries.

Gifts of Split Interests

Despite the added income tax advantage of lifetime charitable gifts, clients with strong charitable motives are often reluctant to make outright, present interest gifts to charity because they are not willing to *relinquish total control* of an asset. For example, they may be relying on an asset as a source of income or enjoyment, or they may have been planning to pass the asset on to the children. Reluctant clients may be more willing, however, to make what could be called a compromise charitable gift; that is, a split-interest gift in which only part of an interest in property is given to charity. The client will often be able to accomplish *three objectives:* retain a much-desired portion of the interest, transfer the less-needed part, and still enjoy substantial income tax and death tax savings.

A split interest arrangement divides the asset into two separate property interests, the income interest and the remainder interest. The client has the ability either to retain the right to the income from the asset, and presently gift the remainder interest to charity, or to gift the income interest to charity and designate a private party to take the remainder.

Arrangements for donating remainder interests to charity. Three devices recognized by tax law are commonly used by clients to retain an income interest in an asset and to gift the remainder interest to charity. Two of them, broadly called *charitable remainder trusts*, are the annuity trust and the unitrust. The third is called the *pooled income fund*. For each, the charity receives an irrevocable (vested) remainder interest in the asset. These 'strings-attached' arrangements will cause the date of death value of the property to be included in the donor's gross estate.[41] Fortunately, an equivalent charitable deduction will reduce the taxable amount to zero.[42]

Charitable remainder annuity trust. Under the charitable remainder annuity trust (CRAT), the client receives a fixed annuity income of at least 5% of the *original value* of the assets transferred into trust, payable at least annually, usually for life. The value of the deductible interest is calculated from IRS valuation Table S.

EXAMPLE 14 - 30. Carrie, age 75, creates a CRAT, funding the trust with $100,000 cash. The trust provides for a 5% annual payment to Carrie for her life. At an assumed rate of 10%, the value of Carrie's retained income interest, derived from Table S, is $28,072, the product of the table value (5.6144) and $5,000, the annual trust income. Therefore, Carrie's deductible remainder interest is $71,928, the difference between the total value of the property and the value of the retained income interest.

Charitable remainder unitrust. The charitable remainder unitrust (CRUT) is much like the CRAT, above, except that the annual income depends on a fixed percentage of the *current fair market value* of the assets in the trust, re-determined annually. Thus, the amount of the annual income paid to the client will vary (hopefully upward) from year to year.[43]

The CRUT can provide for the income to be the *lesser* of the unitrust amount or the amount actually earned on the trust property, with any deficiencies payable in later years when earnings are higher. Thus, the owner of a rapidly appreciating, low-dividend-paying corporation can contribute stock to a CRUT and enjoy a large stream of income years later, after retirement, when the stock starts paying dividends. This "net income with make-up" unitrust (NIMCRUT) represents risky planning; the IRS has challenged these arrangements.

Calculation of the amount of the deductible remainder interest for a CRUT is complex and will not be derived in the examples that follow.

EXAMPLE 14 - 31. Bob and Jeanne Ferrell, both age 65, wish to establish a CRUT to supplement their income and to benefit their favorite charity. They fund the trust with $100,000 of rental real estate having a tax basis of $20,000. The rental property is appreciating at an average annual rate of 8% but has paid them only 2% a year in income ($2,000 this year). The trust provides that they will be paid an annual amount equal to 6% of the value of the trust corpus, determined annually. It will cost the Ferrells $4,000 in legal fees to establish the trust. If the trust corpus can grow by three percent annually (10% overall return less 6% to the Ferrells less one percent trustee fee), the Ferrells will receive the following pre-tax amounts during the first five years: $6,000, $6,180, $6,365, $6,556, and $6,753. Assuming that the surviving spouse dies in 20 years, the last annual income payout in that year will be $10,521. Based on the IRS valuation tables, at 10%, the Ferrells will be able to deduct a charitable remainder interest of approximately $36,000, which at their 50% combined tax rate will immediately save them $18,000 in income tax. The Ferrells have, of course, relinquished the right to transfer the remainder interest, which is projected to be $209,743 ($100,000 stock growing at 10% - 6% - 1% = 3% annually for 20 years, reduced by 55% estate tax at S2's death). This arrangement has significantly supplemented the Ferrell's income. However, the plan has modestly improved their wealth position. At 10%, the net present value of this strategy, compared with doing nothing, is $9,853. Present value of benefits: tax savings from charitable deduction: $18,000; twenty years of new increasing after-tax income: $45,135. Present value of costs: preparation fees: $4,000; loss of old forfeited 2% rental income on appreciating asset: $18,105; after tax value of forfeited remainder: $31,177.

EXAMPLE 14 - 32. In the example immediately above, if the Ferrells like everything about the proposed CRUT except having to forfeit their disposition of the remainder interest, they may consider adopting what has been called a "wealth replacement plan," funding an *irrevocable life insurance trust* with a joint life (second death) insurance policy in the amount of approximately $210,000, naming their children as trust beneficiaries.

The facts in the two examples above make many favorable assumptions about the clients, and probably represents the 'best case' scenario. At the other extreme, consider the following:

EXAMPLE 14 - 33. It is five years later, and the Ferrells have had some terrible luck. First, because of their poor health, Bob and Jeanne were able to acquire life insurance on their lives only at a *very high premium*. Second, market investment rates of return have declined significantly, generating far less income to the Ferrells than the amounts projected by the planner. In fact, the income generated has been far below the required trust distributions, and each year the Ferrells have had to report the amount of these deficiencies as a *taxable capital gain*. Third, lower market rates have caused the quarterly life insurance premiums to rise, and have delayed substantially how soon the "vanishing" premiums will actually end, which means the Ferrells can expect to pay far more in total for the policy than the planner's computer-forecasted "illustrations" initially projected. Fourth, due to sizable investments in junk bonds and unprofitable real estate, the life insurance company is in danger of *insolvency*, with its remaining assets being seized by the state Department of Insurance. Fifth, the Ferrells were unable to deduct the entire $36,000 in the first tax year, due to the *AGI limitations*. The nondeductible portion had to be carried over to the next tax year. Sixth, because the rental real property was subject to a mortgage, the transfer of it constituted a bargain sale, resulting in a *taxable capital gain* to the Ferrells,[44] and creating the risk of disqualification of the trust as a charitable remainder trust.[45] Seventh, the trust invested in a spaghetti factory, a trade or business considered not substantially related to the performance of its exempt purpose, causing the trust to *lose its tax exempt status* and making all undistributed trust income taxable.[46] Eighth, the land under the spaghetti factory was found contaminated with toxic waste, making the Ferrells potentially liable under federal law for clean-up costs. Finally, Bob and Jeanne have always been quite confused about this *complex* arrangement. For example, they are not able to fully understand why two trusts had to be created. They are now seeking another attorney to determine if they can recover damages from their once enthusiastic financial advisors.

Of course the above hypothetical depicts a "worst case" scenario, with certain trust assets encumbered, contaminated, and producing unrelated business income. Ordinarily, trustees will want to avoid acquiring such difficult assets, even when offered by the client. A charitable remainder trust can be funded with the client's personal residence, provided that all trust beneficiaries vacate the premises before the transfer.

At their best, charitable remainder trusts offer to the client the advantages of higher cash flow during lifetime, lower investment risk and greater portfolio diversification. At their worst, they can be a confusing financial burden. Recent case law involves many planners battling with the IRS or attempting to reform their client's defective charitable trusts. In one recent case, a $25 million estate was not entitled to an $18 million deduction because its charitable trust was not in the form of an annuity trust, a unitrust or a pooled income fund.[47] Although the IRS Regulations are exceedingly complex, requiring the drafting of long and technical documents, the Treasury has issued safe harbor sample documents which may be suitable for most client's needs. However, this is an area where very experienced counsel is needed.

Disillusioned clients will become more prevalent if financial planners continue to aggressively promote these trusts primarily as a means of increasing retirement income and avoiding capital gains tax. In one quarter page advertisement in a local newspaper observed by this author, a planner's main pitch was "stop paying unnecessary taxes." The fact that a sizable charitable contribution would be required was not mentioned anywhere in the ad.

Charitable trusts is one area where clients need the advice of a truly rare breed: a highly skilled tax advisor and drafter particularly adept at time value of money/cash flow analysis.

Figure 14-1 reviews the above material by illustrating the evolution of charitable remainder trusts, depicting the successive beneficiaries (grantor, spouse and charity) over time, and their taxation.

FIGURE 14-1 Evolution of Charitable Remainder Trust: Beneficiaries and Taxation

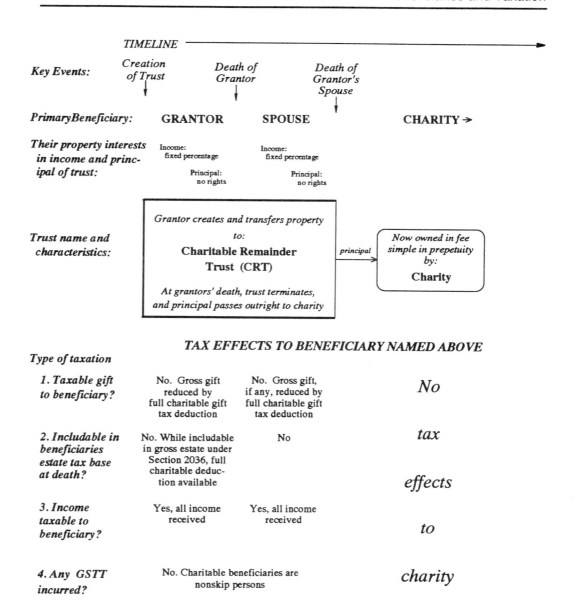

Pooled income fund. Instead of a separate trust created by the client and advisors, a pooled income fund is an investment fund created and maintained by the *target charity*, which "pools" property from many similar contributors. Thus, the client is spared the expense of planning and drafting a trust, an arrangement which would be considered 'overkill' when the charitable donation is relatively small (e.g., $10,000 to $100,000).

Many pooled income funds limit donations to cash and cash equivalents. The pooled income fund ordinarily provides that the charity will pay to the grantor an income for life and, if desired, for the life of the grantor's spouse, based on the rate of return actually earned by the fund as a whole. At their death, the property passes to the charity. Valuation of the charitable deduction is calculated using Treasury tables available from the IRS.

Comparison of the three techniques. All three techniques have the advantages of providing an income for life, reducing estate tax and obtaining a relatively immediate income tax deduction. The CRAT may appeal to clients who desire the certainty of a fixed income, even in a declining market. The CRUT may be preferred by those willing to risk fluctuating income for the opportunity to realize higher income payments. Thus the CRUT can offer a hedge against inflation. Assets in a CRUT do require an annual valuation, a possible extra trust cost. The pooled income fund may be preferred by those who would like to avoid having to establish and maintain a trust. Pooled income funds, however, are not permitted to invest in tax-exempt securities.[48] Not all qualifying charities have created pooled income funds. Most colleges, however, use them to encourage charitable contributions by well-heeled alumni.

Arrangement for donating income interests to charity: The charitable lead trust. Instead of contributing a remainder interest, the client can donate an asset's income interest for a period of years to charity, with the remainder interest then passing to a private party (either reverting to the grantor or spouse, or passing to another person, such as a child or grandchild). The client or the client's estate will receive an income tax deduction for the value of the income interest, based on Treasury valuation tables. However, to get the charitable deduction, the trust must be set up as a grantor trust, making the income taxable to grantor.[49] This is not necessary if the trust is created in the client's will, and charitable lead trusts are therefore often designed to take effect after the client's death.

In a manner similar to a zeroed out GRAT, a charitable lead trust may be structured to generate an immediate charitable deduction equal to almost 100%

of the current value of property transferred by way of the trust. If done successfully, the value of the remainder interest (probably given to the settlor's children) will approximate zero, resulting in very little use of the settlor's unified credit. Further, nothing (or very little) is included in the client's taxable estate. Either the client will not own the property at death (because it was a lifetime charitable gift), or, if this is done as part of a testamentary plan, the estate will be entitled to a charitable deduction that offsets most of the value of the property going into the charitable lead trust. The goal is for the property to not only benefit the charity for a period of years, but to grow in value such that the remaindermen eventually receive a sizable distribution at the end of the term, all without incurring transfer taxes insofar as said property is concerned. As the examples below show, success of the charitable lead trust depends upon the actual rate of future asset appreciation.

> EXAMPLE 14 - 34. Reed creates a lifetime charitable lead trust, funding it with $100,000 in stock of his closely held corporation. The trust is obligated to pay a "guaranteed annuity" of $11,750, or 11.75% of the initial value of the corpus annually to the charity for a period of 20 years. Then, the trust will terminate and the remaining corpus, if any, will be distributed outright to Reed's surviving children and grandchildren. Assuming a 10% discount rate, the IRS Table annuity factor is 8.5136. The value of the charity's 20 year income interest is $100,034.80, the product of $11,750 and 8.5136. Reed's deduction is limited to $100,000, the value of the property. Since the value of the present income interest is no less than the entire value of the property, the value of the remainder interest must be zero, which means that Reed has made no taxable gift.

> EXAMPLE 14 - 35. Continuing the example immediately above, assume 20 years have passed. The closely held stock in the trust has performed so far in excess of 10% that its annual income has been more than ample to pay the annuity. And, as a result, the trust corpus and accumulated income is now worth $800,000. This amount will pass outright to Reed's descendants completely transfer tax free.

> EXAMPLE 14 - 36. Altering the projected outcome in the example above, assume again that 20 years have passed, but the closely held stock has earned only a 10% annual average rate of return, forcing the trustee to use trust corpus to satisfy in part the $11,750 annual distribution requirement. The corpus is now worth nothing (just as the IRS tables anticipated) and Reed's descendants, as remaindermen, will receive no trust distribution.

The outcomes in the preceding examples represent the two extremes of very good and very bad fortune; for most clients the likely result will be somewhere in between. Thus, the gift tax value of the remainder will not likely be zero, which means the grantor will have to partially use up his or her unified credit on a future interest gift that does not qualify for the annual exclusion. In addition, at eventual distribution date, the corpus will have appreciated somewhat, but not greatly.

Charitable lead annuity trusts are more attractive when interest rates are relatively low. A low (discount) rate results in a higher valuation of the deductible charitable interest donation, and a lower valuation of the taxable remainder interest gift.

> EXAMPLE 14 - 37. Charlie established a charitable lead trust for a 20 year term with assets worth $1,000,000. The trust must pay the charity $70,000 per year. If the §7520 rate is 6% the "lead" interest for the charity is worth $802,833 [$70,000 * 11.4699], but if the rate is 12% the lead interest is just $522,858 [$70,000 * 7.4694]. Thus the higher the rate, the better is Charlie's tax deduction.

The charitable lead trust works best for wealthier, estate tax-avoiding clients who can afford to forego substantial income and own a significant amount of highly appreciating assets that also generate considerable income. Few clients can be expected to qualify.

This chapter has focused on viable non-gift lifetime intra-family transfers and charitable gifts. Appendix 14A that follows immediately after this chapter examines six defective incomplete transfers. The first five were once popular, but have been rendered ineffective by changing tax law. The sixth has always been defective. They are: the interest-free loan, short-term trust, spousal remainder trust, sale of a remainder interest, joint purchase, and family estate trust. You are urged to read this appendix, partly to gain a historical perspective, partly because some clients will still be involved in prior-consummated transfers of this kind, and partly to be aware of formerly popular devices about which clients will inquire for some time to come. The next chapter will survey the principles of liquidity planning.

QUESTIONS AND PROBLEMS

1. Why are many planning-minded clients disinclined to make gifts?

2. How can a bargain sale add flexibility to gift planning?

3. (a) Describe the installment sale. (b) What tax advantage does it have over the ordinary sale?

4. Summarize the major advantages and disadvantages of the private annuity.

5. Crucible, a wealthy 60-year-old, asks you for advice on lifetime transfers. His daughter is interested in acquiring his antique car, which is worth $40,000 and has a basis of $10,000. In each of the following alternatives, calculate Crucible's taxable gain for each future year.
   a. Ordinary sale.
   b. Installment sale, over 10 years (no down payment), with equal annual payments on principal, plus interest at a rate of 10% on the outstanding balance. (Query - will there be any other taxable income?)

6. The Platos are a husband and wife in their 70s, with an adult daughter age 45. They wish to make a lifetime transfer of a considerable amount of wealth to her, and you recommend four alternatives for consideration:
   Large outright gift.
   Installment sale.
   Private annuity.
   Grantor retained annuity trust.
   a. Which transfer would probably involve the greatest present value of expected total costs to daughter? Why?
   b. Which one will probably save the most estate tax? Why?
   c. Which is probably the safest, in terms of IRS challenge? Why?
   d. In which have the Platos retained the greatest interest? Why?
   e. Name several other factors that will influence which transfer, if any, the Platos will ultimately select.

7. Under what circumstances will a gift-leaseback work well?

8. Discuss the income-shifting and estate tax-reducing ability of the grantor retained interest trust.

9. In this question, please compare the advantages of the lifetime transfers

you have studied. In each box on the next page, place the code number which you think describes how well that transfer accomplishes each goal. Use a range if the outcome is uncertain and be prepared to explain why you choose a number or a range. Code: 3 = excellent; 2 = good; 1 = fair; 0 = poor. (See Table 14-1.)

10. Explain the reason for the advantage of each of the following *charitable* transfers.
    a. Gift of appreciated property rather than cash derived from sale of the property.
    b. Lifetime gift rather than gift at death.
    c. Gift of a split interest rather than a whole interest.

11. Stover is 70 years old and is currently in the 35% combined state and federal marginal income tax bracket. He wishes to gift to charity his block of ABC Corp. stock, currently worth $20,000. His adjusted basis in the stock is $2,000.
    a. Calculate Stover's "after (income) tax cost" if he bequeaths the stock to the charity and dies shortly thereafter.
    b. Perform the same calculation as in part a, above, assuming that Stover sells the stock and gives the entire $20,000 cash to charity during his lifetime.
    c. Calculate Stover's after-tax cost, assuming instead that he makes a lifetime gift of the stock to charity.
    d. What should Stover plan to do?

12. Compare the advantages of the CRAT, the CRUT, and the pooled income fund.

TABLE 14-1 Comparative Advantages of Lifetime Transfers										
Types of Transfers	Goals									
	Ability to Retain		Ability to Avoid		Step up in Basis	Shift income	Estate Tax Base		Avoid Probate	Low risk of IRS attack
	Control	Income	Income Tax	Gift tax			Reduce	Freeze		
Annual exclusion gifts										
Large out-right gifts										
Ordinary sale										
Bargain Sale										
Installment sale										
Private annuity										
Gift-lease back										
Grantor retained interest trust (GRIT)										
Irrevocable Life Insurance Trust										

Defective Incomplete Transfers

OVERVIEW

This appendix will describe six defective transfer devices that, for one of two reasons, are presently not recommended by planners. The first five have been virtually legislated out of existence by Congress between 1984 and 1990. And the sixth has always been riddled with tax defects, making it inherently defective.

The evolution of income tax law in the last few years has resulted in depriving taxpayers of the major tax benefits earlier available through the use of the *interest free loan*, the *short-term trust*, the *spousal remainder trust*, the *sale of a remainder interest* and the *joint purchase*. The interest-free loan was first to go with the passage of TRA 84. The next two were killed by TRA 86. The last two were rendered ineffective by Case law and by the Revenue Reconciliation Act of 1990. They were all vulnerable to attack because, unlike the transfers covered in Chapter 13 and 14, each was able to accomplish, in a very large way, at least two of the following: shift large amounts of income; enable the transferor to retain a substantial interest in or control over the property; or freeze large estate tax values at little or no gift tax cost.

The *family estate trust* has never worked, since its operation clearly violates major holdings of case law and provisions of the Internal Revenue Code.

This appendix has been written for three reasons. First, it will give the reader a better historical perspective on lifetime transfers. Second, these strategies may have been employed by some clients in the past, and may still be in use. The reader should be aware of their operation since questions will be raised about their efficacy. Finally, the planner can expect even uninvolved clients to be curious about these formerly popular devices, for years to come.

INTEREST-FREE LOAN

Until 1984, the interest-free loan was considered to be an attractive, although somewhat tax-risky, device to shift income to a lower-tax-bracket family member. However, the Tax Reform Act of 1984 all but destroyed its appeal. The following material presents and overview of the major tax and non-tax considerations in making IFLs and describes the few areas in which IFLs still might be put to use.

An arm's-length loan, in which the lender charges a fair market rate of interest, does not achieve many estate planning objectives. It does not shift income significantly, although it may provide for the borrower an otherwise unavailable loan opportunity. An interest-free loan (IFL) of cash, on the other hand, may be able to shift taxable income from the lender to the borrower. Since the borrower is free to use the loaned property to generate income without incurring a financing charge, the loan may put the borrower in a higher standard of living. Further, the income generated may be taxed at a significantly lower rate. Unfortunately, other tax consequences often render IFLs largely unattractive.[50] As the following material suggests, tax controversy has highlighted their brief history.

Gift Tax Consequences

In 1984, the U.S. Supreme Court settled a longstanding conflict between taxpayers and the IRS by ruling that an IFL constitutes a taxable gift of the reasonable value of the use of the money loaned.[51] In calculating the taxable gift value, the taxpayer is required to use a federal rate of interest, which is published and revised semiannually by the IRS and set approximately equal to the rate that had been paid by the U.S. Treasury on securities of similar maturity several months earlier.

IFLs can be made for a fixed term, or they can have a demand provision. If the loan is made for a *fixed term*, the gift is considered as having been made as of the loan inception, with the gift amount equal to the difference between the amount loaned and the discounted present value of the note.

> EXAMPLE 14 - 38. Dad and Mom lend $100,000 cash, interest-free, to Mary who has just graduated dental school and wishes to start a practice. Mary signs a 10-year note, with no principal payable until maturity. Assuming that the current federal long-term rate is 10%, the present discounted value of the note is approximately $38,500, and Mom and Dad are deemed to have made a gift of approximately $61,500, the difference between the amount transferred and the value received.

If, on the other hand, an interest-free loan incorporates a *demand loan*, with the loan callable by the lender at any time, then at the end of each year the lender will have made a gift of one year's imputed interest.

> EXAMPLE 14 - 39. Assume the facts in Example 14- 35, except that the note is a demand loan, having no maturity. If the loan is still outstanding at the end of their first taxable year, Mom and Dad will have made a gift of one year's interest, imputed to be $10,000, calculated on the basis of the assumed 10% short-term federal rate. For every year that the loan remains outstanding, a similar gift computation will have to be made.

Thus, in order to minimize the gift tax, an IFL must have no maturity. And, to prevent the entire transfer from being treated as an outright gift, the loan must have a demand provision.

If an interest-free demand loan becomes unenforceable, a more significant taxable event will have occurred.

> EXAMPLE 14 - 40. Assume the facts in Example 14-36. Four years go by, and the state's statute of limitations on collection on the original note expires. In that year, a taxable gift of the entire loan principal is triggered.

Thus, IFLs must be redrafted periodically to prevent this unfortunate tax consequence.

Despite the court decision subjecting interest-free loans to gift taxation, many client-lenders will not owe any gift tax because of the combined shelter of the annual exclusion and the unified credit. Thus, the parents in the above examples will incur no gift tax liability, unless they have already made taxable gifts large enough to have fully used up their unified credits. In general, the gift tax issue should not discourage many from the use of interest-free loans as a method of shifting income to a lower tax bracket. However, the income tax issues, discussed next, usually will.

Income Tax Consequences

The IRS has argued, in a business context, that the interest forgone by a corporate lender constitutes taxable income to an employee-executive borrower. To date, the IRS has had little success in the courts, and unless it can influence Congress to act, imputed interest income on an interest-free loan will not likely be taxed to the *borrower*.

In 1984, Congress did act, however, to tax to the *lender* the amount of the interest forgone under an IFL.[52] This forgone interest is treated as if it had been received by the lender and paid by the borrower. Thus, the lender is deemed to have received taxable interest, which is includable in gross income. Similarly, the borrower is deemed to have paid interest, which, under TRA 86, ordinarily would not be tax deductible, unless it is considered business interest, investment interest which is offset by investment income, or interest on a debt secured by a primary or secondary residence. The upshot will usually be greater taxable income without the corresponding deduction. And the compression of tax rates under TRA 86 further reduced the income shifting attractiveness of the IFL.

> EXAMPLE 14 - 41. Dad, in the 31% income tax bracket, makes a $20,000 interest-free demand loan to his son, who is in the 15% bracket and is able to invest the proceeds in a bank time deposit yielding an annual return of 8%. Assuming a federal rate of 10%, the tax consequences in the first full year are as follows:
>
> *Gift tax treatment*: At the end of each year, Dad will be deemed to have made a gross gift of $1,600, the amount of the forgone interest. Because of the annual exclusion, there will be no taxable gift.
>
> *Income tax treatment in the absence of the 1984 Act*: Each year, son would earn $1,600 taxable income on the deposit, paying a tax of $240. Instead, had Dad invested the loan money, he would have paid a tax of $496. Thus, in the absence of the 1984 act, under TRA 86 tax rates the family would have saved $256 in income tax.
>
> *Income tax treatment under the 1984 Act*: If son does not itemize, he will still pay a tax of $240, and in addition, Dad will pay a tax of $496 on the $1,600 of imputed interest, for a total of $736. On the other hand, if son itemizes, the $1,600 imputed interest payment is an investment interest expense which he can deduct. In this case, the son's tax would effectively be zero, the Dad's tax would still be $496, so the family as a whole would not have any tax savings from the loan.

The 1984 Act incorporated four exceptions, which may provide the basis for a very modest degree of income shifting. First, where the proceeds of an IFL between individuals are invested by the borrower to yield less than $1,000 income in any given year, forgone interest will not be imputed. Thus, at an assumed 8% investment return, the client could lend $ 12,500 interest free, without being subject to income taxation.

The second exception to the 1984 Act applies to a loan balance of $10,000 or less to any individual, which is not subject to imputed interest unless it is used to purchase income-producing assets.

Third, the amount of the imputed interest is limited to the borrower's net investment income for the year in cases where the aggregate amount of outstanding loans between two individuals does not exceed $100,000, provided that one of the principal purposes of the loan is not federal tax avoidance.

The fourth exception to the 1984 Act applies to loans to employees and to corporate shareholders, who are permitted to owe up to $10,000 without imputing forgone interest, provided that one of the principal purposes of the loan is not federal tax avoidance.

Interest-free demand loans should be made in the form of cash, rather than other property. A transfer of noncash in exchange for a note might be treated as a taxable *sale* to the extent of the consideration received.

Estate Tax Consequences

At the lender's death, the gross estate will include the current value of the note. The market value of a *demand note* will equal the face amount of the note, since the decedent, just prior to death, could have demanded full repayment.[53] On the other hand, the market value of a *term note* will usually be different from the face amount and is calculated by using a market rate of interest to discount the value of the future payments. In executing either kind of note, the lender has not really been able to reduce his or her gross estate significantly. The interest-free loan was never designed to reduce death taxes.

In conclusion, because of its serious tax consequences and the compression of income tax rates, the IFL will no longer be used much.

SHORT-TERM TRUST

Prior to March 2, 1986, the short-term trust was a very popular device to shift income to a lower-bracket taxpayer. Also called the Clifford trust, after the taxpayer whose court case originally set the standards for satisfactory construction, it is arranged in the following manner.[54] The transferor creates and funds a living trust, irrevocable for at least 10 years, for the benefit of a lower-bracket beneficiary, who will receive all of the income earned on the trust property during that time. In this discussion, we'll assume 10 years. At the end of 10 years, the principal reverts to the transferor and the trust terminates.

Gift Tax Consequences

The transferor in a short-term trust is irrevocably parting with a 10-year income interest in the property, and the actuarial value of this income interest is taxable as a gift. Its calculation is derived by multiplying the total value of the property by a fraction representing the proportion of the total value of the property constituting that income interest. The fraction is obtained from Table B, found in Treasury Regulations 25.2512-5, see Table B of the Appendix. If the §7520 rate was 10% when a 10-year short-term income trust was established, the factor for determining the gift 0.614457. Thus, a little more than 61% of the transfer represents the income interest. The other 39% represents the reversionary interest, which is not a gift since it reverts back to the trustor.

> EXAMPLE 14 - 42. Dr. Jones and his wife set up a short-term trust for the benefit of their daughter, who is 11 years old, to defray her future college expenses. They fund the trust with high-income stock, worth $32,000. The trust provides that all income will be accumulated until daughter reaches her 18th birthday. Then daughter will receive approximately equal amounts each year for the next four years, with all remaining accumulated income payable to her on her 21st birthday. At that time all principal will revert to the parents. Upon creation of the trust, the Joneses have made a gift of an income interest worth $19,662.62, which is $32,000, the total value of the stock, multiplied by 0.614457. However, no gift tax is owed, due to the annual exclusion of $20,000 available to spouses making a split gift.

The annual exclusion is available to the parents, above, despite the fact that technically the gift of the income to be accumulated is a future interest, because the short-term trust is structured to meet an exception under Section 2503(b) or 2503(c), mentioned in the discussion of trusts for minors in Chapter 13.

Income Tax Consequences

Grandfathered trusts. Income earned on the property placed in a 10-year short-term trust on or before March 1, 1986, will not be taxable to the transferor-grantor, except when the kiddie tax applies. Instead, the income will be taxed to the trust or to the beneficiary, depending on whether it is accumulated or distributed. And the accumulated income later distributed to the beneficiary could be subject to some additional tax, under the throwback rules, unless the beneficiary is under age 21.

The failure to avoid the grantor trust provisions of the Internal Revenue Code will cause income received by the trust to be taxable to the grantor. Thus, the short-term trust had to be carefully drafted to avoid running afoul of the grantor trust rules. For example, the trust had to be irrevocable for at least 10 years from the date the trust was *funded* with the property, not from the date the document was executed.

Nongrandfathered trusts. TRA 86 destroyed the income tax benefit of the short-term trust by deleting the 10-year exception under Internal Revenue Code (IRC) Section 673. Thus, for any transfers into trust after March 1, 1986, the grantor will be treated as the owner of any portion of a trust in which the grantor has any *reversionary interest which exceeds 5%* of the value of such portion. Based on the present values in Table B of Appendix A, the grantor of a 10-year short-term trust has a reversionary interest that is about 38.55% of the value of the trust. Thus, the typical new short-term trust will be treated as a grantor trust. Nonetheless, the new kiddie tax will apply even to these trusts, subjecting most or all trust income for the benefit of a child under age 14 to taxation at the parent's marginal rate.

How long must a short-term trust created after March 1, 1986, last so that the present value of the remainder interest does not exceed 5% of the corpus? IRS tables indicate that the reversion can't occur for at least 32 years! Although several commentators are suggesting that there may be situations where this period is acceptable, in most cases, grantors will not wish to make an irrevocable transfer of property for such a long time. Most clients will no longer wish to shift income with the short-term trust. Thus, the short-term trust is no longer able to save significant income tax by shifting income.

Estate Tax Consequences to the Grantor

Several estate tax consequences may occur when the grantor dies. First, if creation of the trust resulted in a "taxable gift," that is, the transfer of an amount in excess of the annual exclusion and other deductions, then that taxable value will be added to the estate tax base, as an "adjusted taxable gift." Of course, a credit will be applied for any gift tax paid, but the taxation of adjusted taxable gifts along with the rest of a decedent's estate may subject the gift to a higher marginal rate of taxation than that incurred when the gift tax was calculated.

A second estate tax consequence at the grantor's death will be the addition to the gross estate of the actuarial value of the decedent-grantor's interest in the trust property. Determination of that amount will depend on when the decedent dies, as explained next.

If the grantor of a short-term trust dies *before the trust reverts*, the value of the gross estate will include the value of the grantor's reversionary interest at death. Derived from the U.S. Treasury estate tax valuation table found in Treasury Regulations 20.2031-7. The value depends on the assumed rate of interest and the number of years remaining to reversion. For example, assuming a 10% discount rate, if a grantor dies exactly five years prior to reversion, the gross estate will include 62.0921 percent of the decedent's share of the trust property.

If the grantor of a short-term dies *after reversion*, the value of the gross estate will include the date of death market value of the property that had reverted, if still owned, or the value of any other assets acquired with the property.

From the above we can see that the value of the grantor's taxable estate may exceed the value of the trust principal, a decided estate tax disadvantage to the short-term trust. This will always happen when the grantor outlives the trust and the funding of the trust has created a taxable gift. It should be clear now why, the short-term trust was never designed to reduce death taxes.

As an income tax planning device, the short-term trust was often used for two common types of beneficiaries: children and elderly parents. Both are individuals whom many clients wish to assist, and who are often in a lower income tax bracket. Unfortunately, due to tax reform, the short-term trust will hardly ever be used in the future.

SPOUSAL REMAINDER TRUST

A popular income-shifting device prior to TRA 86 was the spousal remainder trust (SRT). As in the case of the short-term trust, the grantor, typically a high-income-tax-bracket parent, transferred income-earning property to an irrevocable trust, which for a specified period paid all income to a low-income-tax-bracket family member, typically a young adult child, and remainder to the grantor's spouse. Properly arranged, the value of the income interest, which is valued in a manner similar to the short-term trust, would qualify for the annual gift tax exclusion. However, unlike the short-term trust, whose property reverted to the grantor, the SRT corpus then passed to the grantor s spouse. Although the value of the remainder interest will not qualify for the annual exclusion, it will not be subject to gift tax, due to the unlimited gift tax marital deduction.

> EXAMPLE 14 - 43. In 1985 Dad created an SRT, funding it with $30,000 in bonds. Income is required to be paid annually to daughter, a college freshman, for the next four years. At the end of the fourth year, the corpus will pass outright to Mom. Based on the valuation tables, the value of a gift of an income interest for a four-year term certain represents 31.6987 percent of the total value of the property transferred. Thus, Dad has made a gross gift to daughter of $9,510. There will be no taxable gift, since the gift of the income interest is sheltered entirely by the annual exclusion, and the gift of the remainder interest is sheltered entirely by the marital deduction.

Prior to TRA 86, the SRT had several advantages over the short-term trust. First, because the corpus does not revert to the grantor, the trust was not required, under the grantor trust rules, to remain in existence for at least 10 years. Thus, the trust could terminate at any time, and if it terminated sooner than 10 years, the relative value of the transferred income interest would be less than that for the short-term trust. This meant that a greater amount of property could be transferred to the SRT free of gift tax. Further, earlier termination might have encouraged grantors to make successive annual gift tax-free transfers into the trust, unimpeded by the requirement of waiting 10 years after date of the most recent transfer to terminate the trust.

The SRT often facilitated the client's estate tax planning objectives. It helped to equalize the spouses' estates in order to minimize the combined estate tax, and remainder interests were transferred to the less wealthy spouse by means of the SRT.

Compared with the short-term trust, the SRT had one potentially major disadvantage: At the termination of the trust, the property passes to the grantor's spouse, rather than the grantor. Thus, the SRT worked best in a harmonious family setting. And any SRT having an agreement in which the remainderman spouse agreed to immediately retransfer the remainder interest to the grantor was attacked by the IRS, which claimed that the grantor in fact retained a reversion, thereby destroying all income and transfer-tax benefits.

TRA 86 destroyed the usefulness of the spousal remainder trust by amending Section 672 to treat any power or interest held by a spouse (who lives with the grantor) as if that interest were held by the grantor. Thus, the traditional spousal remainder trust funded after March 1, 1986 will be treated as if it will revert to the grantor, making it a *grantor trust*, and thereby preventing the shifting of income to the lower-bracket-income beneficiary. Few clients will now choose this once appealing transfer strategy.

SALE OF A REMAINDER INTEREST AND JOINT PURCHASE

The ordinary sale, bargain sale, installment sale, and private annuity may all be unacceptable to some clients, who, during their lifetimes, do not want to surrender the present enjoyment of property. All of these sales techniques involve the immediate transfer of the right to possession and enjoyment. Prior to 1986, another type of sale, however, the *sale of a remainder interest*, did not have this drawback, and, although it was coming under increasing attack from the IRS, it was an attractive alternative. Like the other devices, it was able to freeze estate tax values, generate cash flow, and assist family members. But unlike the others, it also permitted the client to retain the right to possession and enjoyment of the property "sold" until death.

> EXAMPLE 14 - 44. In 1982, 60-year-old parent had some valuable jewelry and had a physician-son who agreed to purchase the remainder interest in the gems. Assuming 10%, the son paid 22.674% of the current value of the jewelry for the right to receive it outright at the client's death. The client was able to own and enjoy the jewelry for life. And the estate tax value of the asset was still effectively frozen, since the client's gross estate would include only the amount of the sale proceeds

that has been retained at death. Of course, the son would not receive possession of the jewelry until the client's death, but he probably would have received it no sooner anyway.

With an installment sale, the client could occasionally forgive a payment, which constituted a taxable gift, but one that qualified for the annual exclusion. Use of the installment sale also postponed recognition of the client's gain. In determining gain or loss, the client's tax basis is apportioned between the remainder interest and the retained life estate. Thus, in our example, the client's tax basis became 22.674% of the former basis.

Exclusion of the remainder interest from the seller's gross estate was not guaranteed, however, as the IRS may have contended that the only way to escape the trap of §2036 is for the purchaser to have paid the full value of the property, not just the value of the remainder interest. Of course, this would have made the transaction even less attractive to the buyer than an ordinary sale.

The passage of §2036(c) in the Revenue Act of 1987 (and a subsequent court decision) increased the likelihood of inclusion, due to the emphasis of that section on estate freezing transfers.[55] But the risk of §2036 could have been greatly minimized if, instead of making a transfer of property, the client and the family member joined in purchasing property from a *third party*, with the client purchasing a life interest and the family member acquiring the remainder interest. As a result, this "joint purchase","split purchase" or split agreement rapidly replaced the sale of a remainder interest as the preferred transfer after 1986.

Finally, the passage of §2702 in 1990 entirely killed both the sale of a remainder interest and the joint purchase. In either case, the client will be treated as having made a gift to the extent that the value of the underlying property exceeds the price paid by the other purchaser. Planners no longer recommend these two techniques to any of their clients.

THE FAMILY ESTATE TRUST: A TRAP FOR THE UNWARY

The reader should be cautioned against recommending one so-called estate planning device, the family estate trust. Also called a constitutional trust, an equity trust, and an ABC trust, the family estate trust is an arrangement fraught with tax danger. Many variations have been created, but they all have the following characteristics:

1. The same person acts in four different capacities: grantor, trustee, trust employee, and beneficiary.
2. The grantor transfers assets into the trust in exchange for "certificate units." The trustee leases the employees' services to others (typically including the individual's current employer), who pay a salary directly to the trustee.
3. The certificate units entitle the grantor to share in the income "earned" by the trust.
4. Upon the grantors death, the trust assets pass to others, not to the grantor's estate.

The family estate trust has been touted as a great tax saver. It is said to be able to reduce income tax by shifting income to a lower bracket (the trust and other family members), and to reduce the client's death taxes by shifting assets before death to other beneficiaries. In fact, just the opposite is true. The IRS has been aggressively and successfully challenging family estate trusts in the courts, which have regularly upheld the following tax consequences:

1. Under the *assignment-of-income doctrine*, explained in Chapter 9, wages assigned to the trust are still taxable to the client-wage earner, not to the trust.
2. Personal living expenses are not deductible.
3. Fees to set up the trust are not deductible.
4. The date of death value of the property owned by the trust is subject to inclusion in the *gross estate* of the client-trustor as an incomplete transfer.
5. At least two tax *penalties* may be imposed. First, if negligence is proven against the taxpayer, a negligence penalty of 5% of the additional tax due will be assessed. Second, tax preparers will be charged penalties of hundreds of dollars for each return found to exhibit negligent or willful attempts to understate the tax liability.

In view of the tax exposure, clients would do well to steer clear of the family estate trust.

ANSWERS TO THE QUESTIONS AND PROBLEMS

1. Planning-minded clients are often unwilling to make outright gifts because they don't want to relinquish: 1) dominion and control over assets; and 2) income earning capacity derived from assets.

2. A bargain sale can add flexibility to gift planning because it can be structured to reflect the degree of generosity that the client feels. The sale can require any amount of consideration in payment for the transferred asset.

3. a. Under an installment sale, the client transfers an asset in exchange for a note which obligates the buyer to make periodic payments of income and principal.
   b. Compared to the ordinary sale, it has the tax advantage of spreading recognition of the client's taxable gain over the collection period.

4. Advantages of the private annuity:

   a. Hopefully, there is no gift tax on the transfer.
   b. Hopefully, the asset is not included in the client's estate tax base. Thus, is can reduce or freeze the gross estate.

   Disadvantages of the private annuity:

   a. The contract cannot be secured.
   b. No part of the annuity payment is deductible by the payor.
   c. If the annuitant lives a very long life, the payor will have made a bad bargain.
   d. There is a §2036 danger, if the value of the property transferred is greater than the value of the annuity received.

5. a. Ordinary sale: Gain = $40,000 - $10,000 = $30,000. Entire tax is due in year of sale.
   b. Installment sale: Gross profit = $30,000. Seventy-five percent of each principal payment is taxable in the year received (= $30,000 gross profit ÷ $40,000 selling price). Thus, each year, taxable capital gain is

.75*$4,000 = $3,000. Any interest received, of course, is taxable, too.

6. a. A gift and a GRAT require no payments by the daughter. On the other hand, both the *installment* sale and the *private annuity* obligate the daughter to pay the entire present actuarial value of the asset transferred. Which of the two would in fact cost more will depend on how long the client lived. For example, if the donor lived an unusually long life, the private annuity would cost more, because the payments will have to be made for the annuitant's entire life.

    b. The *private annuity* will probably save the most estate tax. At the annuitant's death, nothing in connection with the transaction (except any annuity payments not spent) will be includable in the annuitant's estate tax base. The large outright gift and the GRAT (unless it is zeroed out) will probably require inclusion of an adjusted taxable gift in the estate tax base, which could increase estate tax by raising the tax bracket. The value of the note under an installment sale would be includable in the grantor's gross estate.

    c. The *large outright gift* is probably safest, assuming that the valuation is acceptable to the IRS. It is the least aggressive and least controversial strategy. The installment sale, quite established in the law, is almost as safe. On the other hand, the IRS challenges private annuities and GRATs frequently.

    d. The Platos will retain the greatest interest with the GRAT, since they will retain an estate for years in the asset, and, likely, a reversion right if they die within the income period. They would retain no interest in the large outright gift, and only an income interest in the installment sale and the private annuity.

    e. Other factors include:
        Client's health
        Desire to retain control
        Daughter's financial status
        Client's need for income
        Appreciation potential of the asset
        Income tax bracket of daughter
        Daughter's maturity
        Adjusted basis of the asset

7. A gift-leaseback will work well for a business-owning client who wishes to shift income to a lower bracket family member, and has business assets that can be transferred.

8. Income shifting: As a grantor trust, the GRIT cannot shift income during the period when the grantor retains the right to income.

   FET reduction: By transferring appreciating assets directly to a younger generation family member, the GRIT can avoid estate tax in both spouses' estates. Of course, any taxable gift will be included in the grantor's taxable estate.

9. Numbers are somewhat subjective and may depend upon the particular fact situation and/or assumptions made. Good for class discussion or several students should compare their answers.

10. a. A gift of appreciated property will eliminate the need to recognize the unrealized gain on the property, thereby reducing the net, after tax cost of the charitable expense.
    b. A lifetime gift will reduce income tax (charitable deduction) and exclude the gift from the gross estate. A gift at death will only reduce the taxable estate but not reduce income tax.
    c. Gift of a split interest can enable the donor to retain a highly desired portion of the property, such as a life estate in the income.

11. a. Gift of stock at death: After (income) tax cost = $20,000, since no income tax deduction will be available.
    b. Sale of stock and lifetime gift of cash proceeds: Stover will pay income tax of $6,300 (=.35*18,000). If he gives the entire gross proceeds of $20,000, his charitable deduction will generate a tax savings of $7,000 (=.35*$20,000). Thus, Stover's after-tax cost will be $19,300 (=$20,000 + $6,300 - $7,000).
    c. Lifetime gift of stock: Stover's charitable deduction will generate a tax saving of $7,000 (=$20,000*.35). Thus, his after-tax cost will be **$13,000** (=$20,000 - $7,000).
    d. All things the same, Stover should seriously consider making a lifetime

gift of the stock, to minimize the after-tax cost of the contribution.

12. All of the techniques offer clients an opportunity for a large current charitable deduction, coupled with a (potentially high) income stream for the rest of their lives.

> CRAT: Offers the certainty of a fixed income for life.
> CRUT: Offers possibly higher income payments in future years, because income is based on a fixed percentage of current value.
> Pooled Income Fund: Offers opportunity for a split interest charitable gift without the need to set up and maintain a private trust.

ENDNOTES

1. §163.

2. §2033.

3. §7872(a)(1).

4. §267.

5. *Juden* 89-1 USTC 9142; 63 ¶ AFTR 2d 89-595 (CA-8, 1989)

6. §453

7. §453(b)(2) & §453(l)

8. §453(e)(1).

9. §2043.

10. For an example of a successful SCIN involving a $12 million note, see *Wilson* TCM 1992-480.

11. *Estate of Moss* 74 TC 1239 (1980).

12. *Frane v. Commr.* 998 F. 2d 567 (8 Cir. 1993) in part reversing *Estate of Frane* 98 TC 26 (1992); §691(a)(5).

13. Reg. §25.7520-3(b)(3)

14. §2036(a).

15. IRC Section 2036. See also *Bell Estate v. Commr.* 60 TC 469 (1973).

16. §453(b)(1); *Rye v. United States* 92-1 USTC ¶50,186.

17. Reg. §25.2702-3(b)(1)

18. Reg. §25.2702-3(c)(1)

19. §677(a)

20. §2036(a)

21. §2001(b)

22. §2642.

23. §2701(e)(2); Reg. §25.2701-1(d)(2)

24. §2701(e) and §2704(c)(2); Reg. §25.2702-2(a)(1)

25. LR 9239015.

26. Regs. §25.2702-3(e), Exs. 1 & 5; LR 9248016, relying on RR 77-454.

27. §25.2702-5

28. Table B, term of years remainder values.

29. 80CNSMT, 1980 census survival values.

30. LR 9249014.

31. Prop. Reg. §25.2702-5(c)(9)

32. §170(c).

33. §170(b)(1)(F).

34. §170(b)

35. See §§170(b)(1)(B), 170(b)(1)(C), 170(b)(1)(D), & 170(d)(1)(A)

36. §170(b)(1)(C)

37. §170(f)(8).

38. §2522(a).

39. §2055(a).

40. *U.S. Trust Co. v. U.S.*, 803 F. 2d 1363 (5 Cir., 1986).

41. §2036(a).

42. §2055.

43. Valuation of unitrust interests are calculated based on §7520 applicable federal rates released monthly by the IRS, along with unitrust valuation factors derived from the Treasury department's *Actuarial Values-- Beta Volume* (IRS Pub. 1458), available from the U.S. Government Printing Office ((202) 783-3238).

44. Reg. §1.1011-2(a)(3); LR 7908016.

45. In LR 9015049, the IRS disqualified a proposed unitrust funded with mortgaged property.

46. §681(a). The rules on unrelated business taxable income are found in §511, et. seq.

47. *E. La Meres Estate*, TC CCH 12,880.

48. §642(c)(5)(C).

49. Attaining grantor trust status without subjecting the corpus to estate taxation under §2036-2038 can be a challenge, see LR 9224029 and LR 9247024.

50. Actually, any loan made at a rate of interest below an acceptable market rate will be subject to taxation. However, we will continue to use the term *IFL* to refer to all below-market loans.

51. *Dickman v. Commissioner*, 104 S. Ct. 1086.

52. §7872.

53. If the executor is not a family member, he or she (or it, in the case of a bank) may choose to call the note due and payable after the death of the lender in order to properly manage the estate.

54. Clifford lost the case, however. *Helvering v. Clifford* 309 U.S. 331 (1940). Subsequent to the Clifford decision, Congress added the 10-year requirement to the Code, under Section 673, et. seq.

55. One court held that consideration for purposes of §2036 must equal the entire value of the property. *Gradow* 897 F.2d 516 (1990).

LIQUIDITY PLANNING

OVERVIEW

This chapter will explore the role of liquidity in estate planning. It will summarize the liquidity needs at death, examine the sources of liquidity available to the estate before and after death, and describe the planning techniques commonly undertaken with these sources. Planning devices covered include sale of assets during lifetime, iife insurance, flower bonds, valuation discounts and control premiums, and several strategies unique to business owners, including sale of the business and three liquidity enhancing techniques arising from specific provisions of the Internal Revenue Code.

SUMMARY OF CASH NEEDS AT DEATH

Types of cash needs. Death will usually trigger the need for liquidity. Cash may be needed to pay a variety of obligations, which can be subdivided into three categories: last expenses, funds for the readjustment period, and liquidity needs for the dependency period.

With regard to last expenses, there may be *taxes*, including federal and state income and transfer taxes. There may be *expenses of (estate and trust) administration*, payable to lawyers, executors, accountants, appraisers, and trustees. There may be *debts and claims* against the decedent's estate, including last illness and funeral expenses. There may be immediate cash *needs* for the maintenance and welfare of the *surviving family*. And there may be *cash bequests* and other transfers that must be made to the decedent's heirs and beneficiaries.

Funds may be needed during the readjustment period as the surviving family members struggle to rearrange their lives.

Perhaps the largest amount will be needed to support the dependency period, determined by the number of surviving *dependents* and the length and nature of their needs, which will usually include *education*. Finally, there may be the need for funds to continue *running the family business*.

Cash needs for larger estates. Cash needs can be influenced by estate size and family situation. In general, cash needs rise with increasing estate size. For larger family estates, the estate tax usually constitutes the greatest cash need at the death of the surviving spouse. Most wealthier clients will probably choose an estate plan incorporating either a 100% marital deduction or a credit shelter bypass, both of which will result in a zero estate tax for S1. This delay in cash needs can influence the choice of the liquidity source, as we shall see.

Cash needs for smaller estates. In contrast with clients having larger estates, young families with smaller estates will often have *relatively* large cash needs at the death of *either* spouse. Although transfer taxes may not be due, there will be the need to replace the economic value of the income or services that had been provided by the deceased spouse in the role of parent or breadwinner. As the children get older, the total present value of this cash need should decline.

Next, we turn our attention to the major sources of estate liquidity.

SALE OF ASSETS DURING LIFETIME

We will begin our discussion of the sources of estate liquidity with one of the simplest liquidity-generating devices. During lifetime, the client might be able to sell particularly illiquid assets. Relatively *high basis assets* are preferable, of course, because they result in little or no taxable gain. In fact, assets that have a built-in loss make the best assets for sale, because only the client can use the loss to offset other taxable gains or to reduce taxable income. Death eliminates this potential tax benefit by *stepping down* the basis to date-of-death value.

Relatively *low basis assets*, on the other hand, do not make the most desirable assets for sale because of the resulting tax on the sizable gain (a prospect which can be largely eliminated if the client dies owning the assets). However, the client might be able to offset the gain with losses, whether incurred during the present taxable year or carried over from previous years. Or a sale may be practical in situations where other factors justify paying a tax whose maximum marginal rate on long-term capital gains is 28%. For example, for reasons detailed in the next chapter, an interest in a *closely held business* will often command a substantially higher price if it is sold prior to the owner's death.

Thus, sale of assets during the client's lifetime can provide liquidity by converting an illiquid asset into cash in anticipation of the cash need.

LIFE INSURANCE

Next, we turn our attention to perhaps the most commonly used estate liquidity source, life insurance.

Introduction

Let's first review the basic terminology. In its simplest form, a life insurance policy is a contract owned by the person called the *owner*, which pays an amount called the *face value* to the person called the *beneficiary*, upon the death of the person called the *insured*. Life insurance has several uses, but in estate planning its major purpose is to provide funds to cover cash needs arising at the client's death.

We'll cover three major topics in this section. First, we'll survey the various types of insurance policies commonly used.[1] Next, we'll review the major concepts in the income, gift, and estate taxation of insurance. Finally, we'll examine the insurance planning techniques frequently used to provide needed liquidity.

Types Of Insurance

Hundreds of different insurance policies are sold in the United States today.

However, most are simply minor variations of each other, and the number of really different types, for our purposes, are two. They are term insurance and cash value insurance. Each is briefly described next.

Term insurance. The simplest form of insurance is a one-year policy whose *increasing periodic premium* is based on the likelihood of death in that year. If the insured dies, the beneficiary is paid the face value. If the insured does not die, the company owes nothing and the contract terminates. This is the essence of term insurance; whether or not the company is financially obligated to pay depends solely on whether or not the insured dies during the contract period.

Most term insurance is *renewable*; that is, the company is obligated to sell another year's insurance at a previously agreed-upon price, at the option of the policy owner. Evidence of insurability, such as a physical exam, cannot now be required. Most term policies are renewable to ages 65 or 100. The premium, or cost of *annually renewable* term insurance policies rises annually with increasing age, reflecting the continuing increase in the likelihood of death. Other term insurance policies have premiums that remain constant for 5, 10, or 20 years, and then rise to a new plateau for another similar period, etc., until termination date. Most *illustrated* term insurance premiums are guaranteed for one, three, five, or ten years. Thereafter, premiums can be raised, up to a guaranteed maximum. Regardless of how often the premium rises, all term insurance is characterized by rising premiums and by the uncertainty as to whether the company will ever be legally obligated to pay the face value.

Cash value insurance. In contrast with term insurance, cash value insurance is characterized by a *constant* ("level") *periodic premium*. It is also characterized by certainty: When a cash value insurance contract ends, either because the insured dies or because the policy owner no longer wants coverage, the company will ordinarily be obligated to pay a significant amount of money. If the insured *dies*, the company will pay the face value, of course, as it does on its term insurance policies. If, on the other hand, the owner *surrenders* a cash value policy before the insured's death, the company will be obligated to pay an amount called the *cash surrender value*, described later. Actuarially, insurers can afford to do this because they charge a much higher premium for cash value insurance.

Cash value insurance, which is typically renewable to ages 65, 95 or 100, originated as a solution to a problem of early lapse perceived to be inherent in term insurance. Many years ago, when term insurance was just about the only policy sold, agents found that policy owners frequently terminated their insurance as it got more and more expensive with advancing age. To retain clients, companies started offering cash value insurance, charging a constant premium over time. Evidence has since shown that such policies are not as frequently surrendered by policyholders, despite advancing age. Essentially, the earlier year's premiums are more than the company actuarially needs to fund death and other claims, and the later years' premiums are less than the company needs. The overcharge in early years enables the company to accumulate a type of actuarial reserve, some of which is made contractually available as a cash value to the policyholder, either to borrow, to pledge, or in the event of surrender prior to the insured's death, to receive outright.

Today's cash value policy premiums typically range between three and five times the initial premium charged for annually renewable term insurance for a given policyholder. This is a substantial difference, and today all states have what are called *nonforfeiture laws*, which specify how to calculate the minimum cash surrender value that the company must legally make available to the policy owner at the end of each policy year. Competition usually compels carriers to offer more than the minimum statutory requirement. Guaranteed cash surrender values are listed, year by year, in the policy itself.

> EXAMPLE 15 - 1. Audrey, an insurance salesperson, offers Gerard, age 45, a choice of two policies, each having a face value of $100,000. First, she describes a cash value *whole life* policy, sold by the ABC Co., which has a level annual premium of $2,700. Its cash surrender value at the end of the fifth policy year will be $7,500. At the end of the 20th policy year, the cash value will be $43,500. Audrey then describes an annually renewable to age 100 term policy that is sold by the XYZ Co. The policy's first five years of premiums will be $500, $550, $610, $680, and $750. The premiums, which will be listed in the policy, rise annually until age 100. For example, Gerard's annual premiums will rise to $1,735, $4,620, $13,100, and $31,400 at ages 60, 70, 80, and 90 respectively.

Whole life policy. All cash value policies have a maturity date, that is, a date at which, if the insured reaches it alive, the face value will be paid. A whole life cash value policy, as its name implies, has a maturity date that extends beyond the "whole life" of most insured, typically the insured's 95th or 100th birthday.

> EXAMPLE 15 - 2. In Example 15-1, above, if Gerard purchases the whole life policy and keeps it in force, under simple assumptions ABC will send him a check for $100,000 if he reaches age 100 alive.

Universal life Policy. During periods of high rising interest rates, traditional cash value policies such as whole life and endowment are not as attractive because the contractually guaranteed cash values are typically designed to appreciate at a relatively modest rate of growth in comparison with returns available on other short-term, interest-sensitive investments. Naturally, applicants are then more attracted to other products, including term insurance, where the cash saved from the significantly lower initial premiums can be separately invested with other financial institutions to earn higher yields.

In response, the insurance industry developed a product called universal life insurance, which is essentially a third type of cash value insurance that offers the policyholder greater flexibility and, sometimes, greater investment yield. It offers greater *flexibility* because the policyholder is permitted to vary the amount of the face value and the premium payments from time to time to meet changing financial conditions. It can sometimes offer greater investment *yield* because the insurer invests premium dollars in a portfolio of securities having a shorter average maturity. Thus, during periods of greater inflation (especially when yield curves are downward sloping), the insurer can usually earn greater income, which it can pass on to the policyholder in the form of higher cash values. The typical universal life policy offers a guaranteed rate of appreciation of some low amount, commonly 4%, with the provision that a higher rate will be earned if the investments are more profitable. Thus, during periods of relatively high short-term rates, universal life insurance stands to gain in popularity. In contrast, in today's low rate-normal yield curve markets, universal life's popularity has not been as strong. For example, in 1990, the amount of universal life insurance purchased dropped 5% from the year earlier, and the number of universal life policies issued fell by 11%.[2]

Some commentators dislike universal life insurance because its complexity, flexibility, and uncertain future premium makes it virtually impossible to evaluate numerically and undertake cost comparisons with term policies and traditional cash value policies.

Split dollar cash value insurance arrangements. More a unique method of paying cash value insurance premiums than a different type of insurance, a split dollar arrangement is most commonly found as a nonqualified employee fringe benefit. In the typical plan, the employer pays to the insurer a portion of the premium equal to the lesser of the total premium or the increase in the cash value. The employee pays the balance of the premium. When the insured dies, or when the policy is surrendered, if earlier, the employer ordinarily receives an amount equal to the premiums it paid and the remainder is paid to the policy owner (if surrendered) or the beneficiary (if the insured dies). Split dollar insurance enables the employee to purchase cash value insurance less expensively than if purchased alone.

Taxation of Life Insurance

This section will survey the major concepts in the federal income, gift, and estate taxation of insurance. Many of these topics were covered in greater detail in Part 2 of the text, and the reader is referred there for elaboration and clarification.

Income taxation. Two major income tax aspects of life insurance are the taxation of the cash value accumulation and the taxation of the policy proceeds. To qualify for the two favored tax treatments described next, an insurance policy must meet the requirements under §7702, recently enacted to discourage the popularity of certain universal life and endowment type policies containing an unusually large investment element relative to the size of the death protection component.

Income taxation of cash value accumulation. Increases in cash value buildup will not ordinarily be subject to income taxation while the policy is in force, primarily because the taxpayer-policyholder is not considered able to actually or constructively receive these amounts without surrendering the policy.[3] When a cash value policy is surrendered, any excess of the cash surrender value (amount realized) over the total premiums paid (adjusted basis) will be includable in the owner's gross income. Usually this difference, if positive, will be quite small and not a significant tax burden.

An exception to the rule that loans from the cash build-up in a policy are not taxable unless what is withdrawn exceeds the amount paid into the policy occurs if the policy is "a modified endowment contract" as such is defined in IRC §7702(A). A modified endowment contract is a life insurance policy entered into on, or after, June 21, 1988, that fails the "seven pay test." Failure occurs anytime the cumulative premiums paid into the policy in the first seven years exceeds the total of net level premiums which would have been sufficient to provide a paid-up policy, based upon the initial death benefit, after seven annual payments. Congress set out to plug a loop-hole whereby insurance companies were selling single premium life insurance policies, with very little life insurance protection, as tax free investment vehicles rather than as life insurance. With a modified endowment contract withdrawals and distributions, even as loans, are treated as taxable income to the extent of any cash value accumulation. The portion of a withdrawal or distribution which is included in the policy owner's gross income (i.e., the amount equal to the accumulated cash build up at the time of withdrawal) is subject to an additional ten percent income tax unless the owner is over 59 ½, is disabled, or is receiving the payment as part of series of equal annuity payments for life.

Income taxation of policy proceeds. Section 101 generally excludes from gross income all proceeds received from a life insurance policy paid by reason of the insured's death. The Code has carved out an exception to the proceeds exclusion rule for policies that have been transferred for valuable consideration. The amount included in the transferee-owner's gross income in the year of the transfer will equal the policy proceeds, reduced by the amount of consideration paid and the total premiums paid by the new owner. This *transfer for value rule*, as it is called, does not apply to policy transfers to the following parties:

- The insured (or to a grantor trust[4] of the insured)
- A partner of the insured.
- A partnership in which the insured is a partner.
- A corporation in which the insured is a shareholder or officer.
- A transferee whose basis will be determined by reference to the transferor's basis.[5]

EXAMPLE 15 - 3. For over 15 years, Terry had been the owner of a $10,000 face value insurance policy on his life. Last year, he *gave* the policy to his beneficiary-son Ralph, who began to pay the premiums. Terry died last month. No portion of the proceeds will be includable in Ralph's gross income because Ralph did not give valuable consideration for the policy.

EXAMPLE 15 - 4. If, in the prior Example, we assume instead that Terry *sold* the policy to Ralph for $100, and that the premiums paid by Ralph totaled $400, Ralph's gross income will include $9,500.

EXAMPLE 15 - 5. Ulysses and Zeno are *business partners*. For years, each had owned an insurance policy on his own life. Now, their attorney is drafting a "cross purchase business buyout" contract, and the partners have agreed to exchange policies, with some cash also included as part of the transaction. Thus, Ulysses will become owner and beneficiary of the policy on the life of Zeno, and Zeno will become owner and beneficiary of the policy on the life of Ulysses. Upon the death of either partner, no part of the proceeds will be includable in the other's gross income.

The last example illustrates the use of existing insurance policies to fund a business buyout agreement, which is discussed further in the next chapter.

In late 1992, the IRS issued regulations detailing how insurance companies may design policies to offer "living" or accelerated benefits for terminally ill insureds without subjecting the beneficiary to income taxation of a lump-sum benefit. Under the rules, the insured must be expected to die within twelve months, and the death benefit can be discounted by an amount consistent with a life expectancy of no more than one year. The discount rate must be based on a formula that takes into account the greater of the applicable mid-term federal rate or the policy loan rate.[6] Living benefits insurance can help clients whose liquidity needs begin before death, such as to pay final medical expenses and to replace lost income.

Gift taxation. There are two common situations where insurance can be the subject of gift taxation. First, a taxable gift will arise when the owner *assigns* the ownership to another person without receiving consideration in return. Ordinarily, the gift of an insurance policy will qualify for the annual exclusion, unless it is made to an irrevocable trust. Even then, if a beneficiary of the trust is given a Crummey demand power, the annual exclusion is available. Second, a taxable gift of the policy proceeds will arise when the policy matures, at the *death* of a decedent-insured, if the insured, owner, and beneficiary are all different parties. The effect of this rule, as we shall see shortly, is to compel planners to recommend that the same (noninsured) party be both owner and beneficiary.

Estate taxation. Life insurance is most commonly included in a decedent's federal estate tax base under Code §§2033, 2042, 2001, or 2035. Since this material was covered in detail in Chapter 6, each section will be reviewed only briefly here.

Under §2033 (property owned at death), the terminal value of a life insurance policy on the *life of someone other than the decedent* will be includable in the decedent's gross estate to the extent of the decedent's date of death ownership interest in the policy.

Under §2042, proceeds on the *life of the decedent* will be includable in the decedent's gross estate if, at the insured's death, either the proceeds were receivable by the decedent's executor, or the decedent possessed any incidents of ownership in the policy. Interestingly, the entire proceeds under split dollar arrangements will still be includable, even though part of the proceeds is payable to a third party, such as the employer.

Under §2035, the proceeds of a life insurance policy on the *life of the decedent* will be includable in the decedent's gross estate if, within three years of death, the non owning decedent made a completed transfer of incidents of ownership in the policy.

Finally, under §2001, the decedent's *adjusted taxable gifts* will include the date-of-gift taxable terminal value of *any* life insurance policy for which the decedent made a completed transfer more than three years before death.

With these tax rules in mind, let us turn to the techniques of insurance planning.

Life Insurance Planning

The fundamental goal in using life insurance in liquidity planning is to provide for cash needs while minimizing income, gift, and estate taxation, as well as other costs. This multifaceted criterion will be employed next to help determine who should be chosen to be the insured, the owner, and the beneficiary of a proposed life insurance policy. For simplicity, throughout this section we will assume an estate's need for cash will be met with insurance, rather than some other source of liquidity.

Selecting the insured. Proper family planning would provide for insurance on the life of that spouse whose death is expected to trigger a cash need. For *smaller estates*, this could occur at the death of either or both spouses, depending upon certain factors, such as the size of their economic contribution to the family.

For *larger estates*, we have seen that effective planning with the use of the marital deduction and the credit shelter bypass will usually eliminate the need for cash to pay estate tax at the death of the first spouse, but will create a relatively large need at the surviving spouse's death. Thus, ordinarily, little or no insurance will be required on S1's life to pay estate tax. The real insurance need will be on S2's life. However, some insurance may be needed to meet nontax "capital" needs, such as to cover certain last expenses, readjustment needs, and cash requirements during the dependency period. This will be particularly important for parents with a large amount of earned income who are supporting younger children.

Insurance arrangements for the second death. Since most clients do not know for certain whether the husband or the wife will be the surviving spouse, both may need to be insured. Several commonly used purchase arrangements are discussed next.

1. *Full coverage for both spouses.* One simple but costly plan would be to insure both spouses for the full amount of protection needed at the surviving spouse's death. Because of needless extra cost, this plan is seldom recommended.

2. *Minimal coverage for both spouses.* An alternative method of insuring the spouses is to purchase immediately a small amount of insurance on both spouses which, upon the death of either, can be used to purchase a "fully paid up" larger policy on the life of the survivor. This can eliminate the cash flow drain on the surviving spouse's assets that would otherwise be used to pay the premium.

3. *Second to die insurance.* A third method of insuring both spouses for cash needs at the survivor's death is to purchase a joint life policy of second to die insurance, also called survivorship life insurance. It pays the proceeds only upon the death of the second spouse. This alternative should save premium dollars in two ways: First, only one policy need be purchased. Second, the contingency insured against is more remote in time than that insured against under a single-life policy; the policy proceeds are not payable until both of the insured spouses have died.

Second to die insurance may be particularly economical if one of the spouses is uninsurable. Medical underwriting standards are eased because the life expectancy of the healthier spouse becomes paramount. Unfortunately, many uncompetitive second to die policies can wind up costing nearly as much as a single-life policy, especially if the premiums have to be paid for a much longer period. Careful cost comparison is necessary.

4. *Full coverage for wife only.* A final alternative is to insure only the wife, usually the probable survivor, for the required liquidity. If she survives her husband, the contract becomes, de facto, a second-death policy. If she predeceases him, the proceeds can be invested and then made available to pay the

estate tax at his later death. The cost of insuring only the wife should be more expensive than the cost of a second to die policy; the latter will more likely pay the proceeds at a later date, since the wife may predecease the husband.

Selecting the owner and beneficiary. The amount of planning effort needed in choosing who will be owner and beneficiary will usually depend on the size of family estate, because transfer tax cost is the primary criterion. In the case of married clients, selecting the owner and beneficiary for a *smaller estate* is rather simple, since little or no transfer taxes will result from any selection alternative. The client and the client's spouse will be able to own policies on their own lives, making the proceeds payable to the other without generating any estate tax. The contingent beneficiary could be the client's children, if sufficiently mature, or it could be the trustee of a trust, perhaps the trustee of the couples probate avoidance living trust.

On the other hand, selecting the owner and beneficiary of insurance on the lives of the spouses of *larger estates* requires greater precautions, in order to minimize the effects of transfer tax costs. We consider next the effect of naming various parties as owners and beneficiaries.

Spouse as owner and beneficiary. Naming one or the other spouse as owner or beneficiary will not minimize transfer costs. It will usually subject the proceeds either to a transfer tax, or to probate administration, or to both, depending upon which spouse dies first. Consider the somewhat complicated tax and probate consequences for each of the possible outcomes.

First, if the *insured spouse dies first and is the owner,* the proceeds will be includable in his or her gross estate under §2042. If the proceeds qualify for the marital deduction, thereby avoiding S1 taxation, they will be included in *S2's gross estate*, barring consumption, gifting, or remarriage. If the *insured spouse dies second and is the owner* then the proceeds will be includable in his or her *gross estate*, again under §2042 and no marital deduction will be available.

Second, if the *insured spouse dies first and the noninsured spouse is the owner and beneficiary*, then the proceeds will be included in *S2's gross estate*, barring gifting, remarriage or consumption. From the discussion of gift taxation of insurance earlier in the chapter, it should be clear that if the noninsured spouse is named *owner* and someone other than a spouse is named beneficiary, then that spouse will be deemed to have made a *taxable gift* to the beneficiary of the proceeds upon the death of the insured spouse. Thus, in the usual larger family estate, even the noninsured spouse should not be named either owner or beneficiary.

Conclusions. Two important conclusions can be drawn from the above. First, naming *either spouse* as owner or beneficiary of a policy on the life of a spouse will subject the proceeds to transfer taxation at least at the second death. Thus, to minimize transfer costs, *neither spouse of a larger estate should be designated as either owner or beneficiary* of an insurance policy on the life of either. Second, since a taxable gift will occur whenever the insured, owner and beneficiary are all different parties, *whoever is selected should be named both owner and beneficiary*, to avoid gift consequences. Designation of other possible parties, including a child and two types of trusts, is evaluated next.

Child as owner and beneficiary. Instead of a spouse, one of the client's children could be named owner and beneficiary. The child could be *requested* to use the proceeds to provide liquidity to the estate upon the death of the insured. This alternative will work best when the child is sufficiently *mature* to handle such a responsibility. Nonetheless, there will always be a risk that the child may permit the policy to lapse. Or the child, having received the policy proceeds upon the death of the insured parent, may be *unwilling* to provide the funding needed by the estate. Since the child will become the legal owner of the proceeds, any gratuitous transfer of the funds to the estate or to the surviving spouse will be treated as a *taxable gift*. However, as will be mentioned later, the child could purchase estate assets or lend money to the estate. Additionally, the proceeds, or at least their value, may inevitably wind up in the child's own gross estate.

Revocable trust as owner and beneficiary. To eliminate any doubts over whether a named beneficiary will cooperate to make the proceeds available to the estate and to remove the chance that the insurance proceeds will be subject to probate in a spouse's estate, the wealthy client could name a revocable trust to be the owner and beneficiary. However, a power to revoke the trust if held by the client or the client's spouse will cause the proceeds to be *includable in the insured's gross estate*. Thus, although avoiding probate of the proceeds, a revocable insurance trust offers no transfer tax advantage over the insured-owner arrangements considered so far.

Irrevocable trust as owner and beneficiary.[7] The irrevocable life insurance trust (ILIT) offers what most commentators consider to be the solution.

Organization and structure of an ILIT. The client-insured creates the ILIT and names the trustee to be owner and beneficiary of the policy. The grantor must not be named a trust *beneficiary*, because of possible §2036(a) problems; and since the uninsured spouse is usually one of the beneficiaries of an ILIT, he or she should not be a grantor. This will require greater care in preparation in community property states.

Upon the death of the insured, the trustee is authorized to lend the proceeds to the insured's estate or to purchase assets from the estate. If the insured is S1, then the trust corpus usually continues to provide benefits to S2 in the form of a bypass trust, similar to the one discussed in Chapters 11. At the death of S2, the trust is again authorized to lend cash to the S2 estate, or to purchase estate assets. Then, the trust is either terminated, with corpus payable to the children, or it is continued, distributing income to the children until either they reach a specified age or, in the case of a generation-skipping trust qualifying for the $1 million lifetime exemption, until the grandchildren reach a specified age, usually not later than 21.

Ownership of insurance by an irrevocable trust requires that the clients be willing to surrender all interest in the policy. However, insurance having little or no cash value is usually one of the least distasteful assets to gift, for three principal reasons. First, the *gift tax value* is minimal. The typical policy will have little or no terminal value, either because it is a term policy or because it is a cash value policy that has been recently purchased or has a sizable outstanding loan. The gross gift value of a newly issued policy is simply the first year's premium. Second, in contrast with its gift tax value, its *estate tax value* will be very large, making it a desirable asset to exclude from the estate. Third, because it is merely a document that does not produce income, clients generally do *not experience loss* in the pleasure of ownership commonly felt when they gift tangible property or intangible income earning property.

A ILIT is likely to be used as a source of funds to pay estate taxes therefore it is important to choose a policy that the client knows will be there when it is needed. Since term insurance becomes increasingly expensive as the client gets older, it is a poor choice for a ILIT. For a single client a whole life policy makes sense. If another type of cash value insurance, such as universal life is considered, the client must make sure that there is a guaranteed proceeds amount sufficient to pay the taxes. A married couple has two choices, if the sole purpose is to create a fund to pay estate taxes at the second death, then a second to die policy would be least expensive for any given level of coverage. With a sophisticated estate plan incorporating bypass and marital trusts, the taxes are most likely to be postponed until the second death. But what about those rare situation where S2 is dying at the time of S1's death the executor will want to generate a tax at S1's death, will use of a second to die policy cause hardship or force the executor to postpone the taxes to the second death even though it means more overall estate taxes? The answer is no. These situations anticipate the death of the second spouse shortly after the first death. §6161 allows the executor to postpone payment of the estate tax for reasonable cause, thus the executor of S1's estate would not be forced to sell assets, but would file the return, report the estate tax owed and request a one year extension with an explanation as to why cash is presently unavailable.

A second to die policy is not advisable if the primary purpose is to provide income to the surviving spouse. The income earners (one or both) should be separately insured taking into account the amount of insurance needed to replace the insured's earning capacity. For any given family wealth level (until we reach the very wealthy), a young couple with dependent children will need greater amounts of insurance than an older couple with grown children, therefore term insurance may be recommended so as to cover the years when children will be dependent. This will give the greatest coverage possible at the least cost. If the couple can afford additional insurance and are concerned about covering estate taxes in the event both die young, then they should consider another ILIT to purchase a significant whole life second to die policy.

Who should pay the premiums on the trust-owned policy? One alternative is to fund the trust with sufficient income-earning assets to enable the trust to pay them. Unfortunately, the grantor trust rules will make that income taxable to the client-grantor rather than the trust.[8] A preferred alternative has the client making annual gifts to the trust in amounts sufficient to pay the premiums. The insured-spouse in community property states should make the periodic gifts from his or her separate property to keep the proceeds out of the estate of the noninsured spouse, who is beneficiary of the trust. By having a Crummey demand right held by the insured's children, these gifts can qualify for the annual exclusion.

Impressive goals of ILIT. With regard to a *married client* owning an estate whose value exceeds $600,000, the exemption equivalent of the unified credit, only the designation of an irrevocable trust as owner and beneficiary can achieve all of the following goals:

1. Exclude the insurance proceeds from *income taxation* and from the *taxable estates* of both spouses and, perhaps, the children.

2. Exclude the insurance proceeds from the *probate estates* of both spouses.
3. Enjoy the shelter of the gift tax *annual exclusion* for transfers to the trust of both the policy and the funds needed to pay policy premiums.
4. Ensure that a *responsible party* will in fact provide the needed post-death liquidity.
5. Make the *proceeds available* to the surviving spouse, for health or certain other reasons.

The following is an extended discussion of how a carefully structured ILIT can implement these goals.

1. Income tax, estate tax and GSTT issues. Regarding the first goal, an ILIT will not ordinarily fall within the grip of §2036(a). However, because they are not direct skips, annual exclusion transfers into the trust will not insulate the corpus from GSTT, and thus planners may elect to allocate the $1 million exemption to such transfers, anticipating that premature death of a child can give rise to a taxable distribution to, or a taxable termination for, the benefit of a skip person.

Excluding the insurance proceeds from the gross estate of a decedent can have an additional benefit: preventing the beneficiary's exposure to transferee liability for payment of the estate tax. In one case, the decedent died possessing incidents of ownership on a $50,000 policy. The IRS was unable to collect $62,378 in estate tax from the decedent's assets which were then owned by his nonresident alien widow, living in Venezuela. However, the policy beneficiary, a U.S. citizen, was held liable for the estate tax up to $50,000, the amount of the proceeds includable in the gross estate.[9]

The ILIT can also be effectively used by a *single person* to achieve similar tax and nontax goals.

Whether an existing policy is transferred to the trust, or whether a new policy is created and transferred when the trust is established, the client-trustor-insured must live *three years* after the policy is transferred to ensure the avoidance of inclusion of the proceeds in the gross estate under §2035(d)(2). Because of the drawbacks, and in spite of the life underwriter's frequent eagerness to sell the policy (perhaps in part because he or she thinks the attorney could kill the deal!), the policy should be purchased by the trustee, not the insured client, after creation of the trust, to completely avoid the three year rule. If the client transfers an existing policy, the annual exclusion will not be available unless the trust gives the beneficiaries a Crummey invasion power.

The trust can include a *contingent marital deduction clause*, so that if the three-year rule caused the proceeds to be includable in the insured's gross estate, then the proceeds would be paid outright to the spouse (or to a marital trust). This would save the marital deduction and avoid estate tax. On the other hand, if the insured lived longer than three years, causing the three-year rule not to apply, then the proceeds would be used to fund the ILIT; which then is called a bypass trust because the proceeds will be excluded (bypass) from the estates of both spouses.

If each spouse is an insured, then two trusts will have to be established, with each trust owning one policy. These trusts must be drafted very carefully to avoid §2036(a) problems and the reciprocal trust doctrine discussed in Chapter 6.

If the trust is *required* to use insurance proceeds to pay the decedent's estate debts, including taxes, the proceeds will be includable in the decedent's gross estate, under §2042. Thus, as we have said, the trustee should instead be simply *advised* that it may *lend* the proceeds to the estate or *purchase* estate assets to achieve funding.

Transfers into an ILIT can be structured to avoid the GSTT. To the extent that gift transfers for premium payments qualify for either the annual exclusion or the lifetime exemption, they and any appreciation resulting will avoid GSTT. Thus a life insurance trust can greatly leverage the transfers, creating a potentially large body of assets that are GSTT-free.

> EXAMPLE 15 - 6. Dorfman and his wife establish an irrevocable trust, funding it with $40,000 cash each year to pay the premium on a $4 million second-to-die policy. The first $20,000 is sheltered from gift tax by a Crummey provision, and the remaining $20,000 by the unused unified credit. In addition, Dorfman and his wife each allocate $10,000 of their $1 million GSTT exemptions to these transfers.[10] Thus, the entire $4 million proceeds will also be sheltered from any future GSTT, thus, a one hundredfold leveraging of the GSTT exemption is accomplished.

Although recent GSTT rules prevent annual exclusion gifts to a single trust for the benefit of both nonskip and skip persons from also being sheltered from the GSTT, planners achieve complete shelter from GSTT in one of two ways. Either they create one trust, and use the client's $1 million GSTT exemption to shelter these gifts, or they create two trusts, one for the benefit of only nonskip persons (e.g. spouse and children) and the other for the benefit of only skip persons (grandchildren, etc.).[11]

Figure 15-1 illustrates the single trust approach, depicting the evolution of an

ILIT from its creation to its typical termination, when the youngest grandchild reaches age 21. As time passes and key events occur, the trust's descriptive name changes, from *ILIT* to *bypass trust* to *children's trust* to *GST trust*. Figure 15-1 also highlights the identity of primary beneficiary during each period, that beneficiaries typical property interests in trust income and principal, and the gift, estate, income and GST tax effects to that beneficiary.

2. Avoiding probate. Regarding the second goal for the ILIT, the policy proceeds will avoid probate at both spouses' deaths because neither S1, S2, or their estates, will ever own the proceeds.

3. Shelter of annual exclusion. With regard to the third goal of the ILIT, the gift of a policy to an irrevocable trust will not ordinarily qualify for the *annual exclusion* because it is not considered a gift of a present interest. However, both that transfer and the payments into a trust to fund the insurance premiums can be made to qualify with the use of a Crummey demand provision held by the children.

4. Selection of trustee as responsible party. An insured spouse who is also grantor should not be named trustee, since this could constitute an incident of ownership in the policy. The other spouse could be named trustee, without this adverse result.

Most corporate trustees are extremely reluctant to become trustees of an insurance trust prior to the insured's death, if the trust is unfunded. And even if it is funded, the advent of higher risk, higher return life insurance policies and growing insurance company insolvency problems have made more and more trustees, particularly corporate trustees, increasingly concerned about possible *liability* if expected policy death benefits are not entirely paid or if the policy turns out to be relatively uncompetitive. In addition, an ILIT may not be profitable for a corporate trustee even after the proceeds are received, particularly if they must be allocated in one of two all too common ways: proceeds immediately distributed to trust beneficiaries, or used to acquire closely held business stock, an asset considered difficult to manage.

To overcome the liability concerns and encourage a fiduciary to act as trustee of a client's life insurance trust, the planner may have to take one or more of the following steps. First, the planner can include language in the trust instrument

FIGURE 15-1 Evolution of Irrevocable Life Insurance Trust: Beneficiaries and Taxation

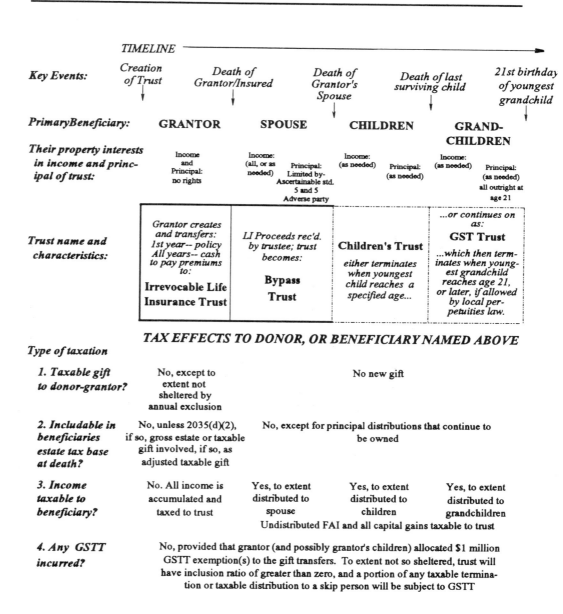

Type of taxation

1. Taxable gift to donor-grantor?
No, except to extent not sheltered by annual exclusion

No new gift

2. Includable in beneficiaries estate tax base at death?
No, unless 2035(d)(2), if so, gross estate or taxable gift involved, if so, as adjusted taxable gift

No, except for principal distributions that continue to be owned

3. Income taxable to beneficiary?
No. All income is accumulated and taxed to trust

Yes, to extent distributed to spouse

Yes, to extent distributed to children

Yes, to extent distributed to grandchildren

Undistributed FAI and all capital gains taxable to trust

4. Any GSTT incurred?
No, provided that grantor (and possibly grantor's children) allocated $1 million GSTT exemption(s) to the gift transfers. To extent not so sheltered, trust will have inclusion ratio of greater than zero, and a portion of any taxable termination or taxable distribution to a skip person will be subject to GSTT

that *exculpates* the trustee from liability in connection with life insurance policy acquisition and ownership. Exculpatory clauses are enforced by the courts, but are strictly construed against the trustee, and offer no protection from acts of "bad faith," "reckless indifference," "gross negligence," and "willful misconduct."

Second, the beneficiaries may have to send a "letter of agreement," consenting to, and releasing the trustee from liability for, investments in life insurance. Obviously, investing in just one asset violates the prudent investor rule so the beneficiaries consent is needed.

Third, the grantor can agree to indemnify the trustee, i.e., reimburse the trustee for any related loss.

Finally, the planner can arrange a non-corporate fiduciary, such as a family friend, to act as initial trustee, with the corporate fiduciary succeeding as trustee only after the insured(s) have died and the proceeds have been paid.

Life insurance is an important liquidity source because it supplies cash exactly when it is needed: at death of the client. Planned carefully, it can also be structured to avoid all transfer taxes.

FLOWER BONDS

This topic could come under the heading: Sometimes Congress does the darnedest things. In the 1950s and early 1960s the federal government issued Treasury bonds with set maturity dates that could be used at their par value, plus accrued interest, to pay the federal estate tax, provided the bonds were part of the decedent's estate. Since the bond yields, while reasonable when issued, were quite low (3% to 5%) compared to other safe investments in the 1970s and 1980s, they began selling at deep discounts. This created some estate planning opportunities for persons with terminal illnesses to purchase bonds at as little as 85% of par shortly before death; and the decedent's executor could turn them in to the government at par to pay the estate tax, achieving a guaranteed 15% increase in value in a short time span. Of course, to the extent the bonds could be used to pay estate taxes their value in the estate was the par value, thus some of that 15% increase in value would be lost to increased estate taxes.

Discounts have decreased as the bonds still in circulation are reaching maturity, the last ones (yield of 3.5%) will come due November 15, 1998, thus the estate planning opportunities are generally very limited, especially when one weighs the opportunity cost of holding a low yielding bond for at least nine months.

LIQUIDITY PLANNING DEVICES UNIQUE TO BUSINESS OWNERS

Many owners of closely held businesses can anticipate a severe liquidity problem for their estates. Not infrequently, the largest portion of the estate consists of the interest in the business, that, almost by definition, is quite illiquid. The need to pay the estate tax in cash within nine months after date of death acts as a cloud that can force survivors to sell the business at distress prices, probably to outside parties. The business owner should plan in advance to minimize future liquidity problems. However, if certain conditions are met, the tax attributable to the business portion of the estate can be delayed four years, and then made payable in installments over the next ten years. See the discussion of §6166 in the next section. The following presents several liquidity generating or tax lowering devices that only apply to business-owning clients.

Sale Of the Business

First, consideration should be given to the predeath *sale* of the business to one or more individuals, or to a *merger* with a publicly held firm, as a means of converting a relatively illiquid asset into a liquid one. A pre-death sale will ordinarily trigger a capital gains tax, and a client who for that reason chooses not to sell or merge before death should consider executing a funded *buyout agreement* with the other owners, triggered at the client's death. The buyout contract, discussed in some detail in the next chapter, will obligate the other owner(s) to pay the client's estate a predetermined cash amount in exchange for the client's interest in the firm. Since the sale will occur after death, the resulting step up in basis of the decedent's interest will eliminate or substantially reduce any capital gains tax.

Three other liquidity generating devices created by Congress, and incorporated into the Internal Revenue Code, for business-owning clients are discussed next. Their sections numbers will be quoted frequently because that's how many in the industry identify the techniques.

§6166, §6161 and §6163: Estate Tax Deferral

§6166: Installment payment of the estate tax. To help reduce the risk of an immediate liquidity crisis at the business owner's death, Congress enacted §6166, which permits the estate of a decedent-owner of a closely held business to elect to defer payment of the estate tax attributable to the business, with interest owing at only 4% per year on the first $153,000 in deferred federal estate tax. The estate then can pay that estate tax in 10 installments starting in the fifth year.

The deferred taxes in excess of $153,000 is subject to whatever is the current applicable federal long-term rate, (AFLTR), which is approximately equal to the long-term rate at which the U.S. Treasury recently borrowed.[12] The executor has the option of deducting the interest paid on §6166 debt on either the estate tax return or the estate (fiduciary) income tax return. If deducted on the fiduciary return, deductibility is not subject to the personal interest limitations.[13] However, deducting the interest on the estate tax return may save more tax, because the estate tax rate is likely to be higher. In order to take advantage of the interest as a deduction one must file a claim for refund (Form 843) and recalculate the estate tax with the interest as a deduction. Since the deduction can only be taken after the interest is paid,[14] most estates wait until after the seventh or eighth principal payment (out of the ten scheduled) on a 6166 extension to do the recalculation as it will usually reduce the estate taxes so much that the last two payments do not have to be made. The estate might even be owed a refund. Because the interest paid reduces the estate tax, less interest is owed and some of what was paid as interest becomes principal payment, which in turn reduces the interest deduction thereby increasing the tax, etc., which is obviously a complex interrelated calculation.[15]

Three conditions must be met for qualification under §6166. First, the value of the decedent's interest in the business must be at least *35%* of the value of the *adjusted gross estate*, which is the gross estate reduced by debts, expenses, losses, and certain taxes.[16] Second, the decedent's interest must have been in a *closely held business*, which is defined as: (1) a sole proprietorship; or (2) a partnership in which at least 20% of the capital interest is included in the decedent's gross estate, or that has 15 or fewer partners; or (3) a corporation in which at least 20% of the voting stock is included in the decedent's gross estate, or that has 15 or fewer shareholders. Third, to qualify, the sole proprietorship, partnership, or corporation must have been actually engaged in carrying on a *trade or business* at the time of the decedent's death.

> EXAMPLE 15 - 7. Decedent died owning 40% of the stock in a corporation, with the decedent's interest worth $600,000. Decedent had a gross estate of $1 million and an adjusted gross estate of $900,000. Assume that the estate tax is $120,000. Under the above rules, the estate will qualify under §6166, since the business qualifies as a closely held business, and decedent's interest is at least 35% of the adjusted gross estate. The amount of the tax that may be deferred is calculated to be $80,000, which is the amount of the estate tax ($120,000) times the ratio of the value of the business interest ($600,000) divided by the adjusted gross estate ($900,000).

Estate tax deferral under §6166 can be a source of estate liquidity by reducing the amount of the decedent's estate's immediate cash needs. However, it will offer only limited benefit to many clients because of three of the Section's restrictions. First, as shown in the example above, only a *portion* of the estate tax can be deferred, measured by the proportion of the estate consisting of the qualifying business. Second, while the tax can be deferred, the *interest* on the tax starts accruing nine months after death. Finally, the interest on the deferred estate tax in excess of $153,000 will be at *current market rates*, not 4%. Since this is a relief provision designed to avoid a forced sale of the business it should not come as a surprise to learn that the sale, redemption, or other disposition of all, or a significant portion, of the business, or the failure to make timely interest or principal payments, will result in immediate *acceleration* of the deferred payments. However, §6161, discussed next, can be used to defer an installment, provided a timely request is made.

§6161: Extension to pay tax for reasonable cause. The IRS has discretion under §6161 to grant an extension to any estate of up to 10 years to pay the estate tax upon a showing of "reasonable cause." Examples of situations satisfying this requirement include:

- The estate has liquid assets but they are located in other states, not immediately available to the executor.
- A large part of the estate is in the form of assets which consist of rights to receive payments in the future (royalties, accounts receivables, etc.).
- The estate includes a claim to substantial assets which cannot be collected without litigation.
- The estate does not have sufficient funds to pay taxes and provide for a

family allowance and claims.

• The estate cannot borrow except at rates that would constitute a hardship.

Ordinarily, reasonable cause will not be found merely because liquid assets (listed securities) must be sold at distress prices. However, in the last few years, the IRS, well aware of the difficulty of selling illiquid assets (land) in a recessionary market, has readily granted extensions for reasonable cause under §6161. Of course, there will be interest charged (at the late payment rate), but the good news is that it is deductible on the estate tax return. Generally, claiming the interest is done by way of a claim for refund after the tax and the interest are paid. Warning, a request for an extension must be made before the due date of the return; and subsequent requests must be made before the last extension has expired. Failure to timely file the request will result in it being denied regardless of how meritorious the reason.

Estates may use §6166 or §6161 installments to pay the *generation-skipping transfer tax*, but in the case of §6166, only if the tax results from a direct skip.[17]

§6163: Deferral of estate tax for reversion, remainder. Section 6163 allows estate tax deferral for tax attributable to a reversionary or remainder interest includable in a decedent's gross estate. The tax can be postponed until six months after the termination of the "precedent" interest, i.e., the interest immediately preceding the reversion or remainder. That termination could be many years after the decedent's death.

> EXAMPLE 15 - 8. Exactly two years ago, Jake created an irrevocable living trust, with all income payable to Jake's son (or his estate) for five years. Then, remainder will be payable to Jake's daughter D (or her estate). If D dies today, the present value of her remainder interest in the trust will be includable in her gross estate. Under §6163, payment of the estate tax attributable to that interest may be delayed until three years and six months from today.

§303 Redemption

The Internal Revenue Code provides another method to lessen the impact of taxes on the estates of business-owning decedents. §303 permits the estate of a decedent-shareholder of a corporation to redeem the decedent's shares with favorable *income tax* treatment. Specifically, the transaction will be treated as a disposition of a capital asset rather than the receipt of a dividend.

EXAMPLE 15 - 9. Decedent's estate redeemed decedent's 1000 shares of stock in a closely held corporation. Immediately before death, each share had an adjusted basis of $100. The date-of-death value of each share was $150. Upon redemption, the estate received $158,000 cash. If the redemption does not qualify for capital gains treatment, the estate will be deemed to have received a dividend of $158,000, that is treated as ordinary income. Alternatively, if the redemption qualifies under §303, the estate will have a taxable long-term gain of only $8,000, reflecting the step-up in basis at date of death.

Federal tax reform since 1986, by taxing most capital gains at not much less than ordinary income rates,[18] reduced somewhat the tax advantage of the §303 redemption. But given that the stock owner's death will have stepped-up the *adjusted basis* of the stock, very little, if any, gain is likely, as is demonstrated in the above example.

There are three major requirements to qualify under §303. First, as with the §6166 deferral, the value of the decedent's interest in the stock must be at least *35%* of his or her adjusted gross estate. Second, the *amount paid* by the corporation in redemption of the shares *may not exceed* the sum of federal and state death taxes, generation skipping transfer taxes and funeral and administration expenses. Third, the shareholder (usually the estate) must be obligated to pay the taxes and/or expenses.[19]

Regarding distributions, if a cash distribution exceeds the amount of the corporation's earnings and profits, the excess is considered a nontaxable return of capital. But if the firm distributes appreciated property instead of cash, the distribution will probably be considered a sale by the corporation, with the gain subject to immediate taxation.

Thus, a §303 redemption can provide liquidity to the estate by encouraging a postdeath cash-generating transaction which might otherwise produce very undesirable income tax consequences.

By means of lifetime planning, §§6166 and 303 may be made available to a client who had anticipated not qualifying because he or she did not expect the estate to meet the 35% test. The client can be urged to acquire additional interest in the firm, or to reduce the size of the nonbusiness estate by *gifting* in order to reduce the adjusted gross estate and thereby increase the proportion represented by the business.

§2032A: Special Use Valuation

One other liquidity source explicitly provided by the Code is available to the business owner's estate. Its purpose might be best explained with a hypothetical fact situation.

Suppose a client has owned a farm for many years, one that had originally been located well outside of the city limits. But with the progress of urban growth, the farm is presently in the heart of one of the high-rent districts. Although the general value of the land is considerably greater than the capitalized value of the farm as a business, the client has no interest in selling; she and her survivors are determined to remain working the farm in the indefinite future.

The reader might be wondering which value will be includable in the client-owner's gross estate at her death. Will it be the value of the farm in its *present use* or the value of the property in its *highest and best use*, available, for example, for construction of a high-rise building? Valuation at its highest and best use might force the survivors to sell the land to pay the large estate tax. On the other hand, valuation at its present use might enable the survivors to carry on the business.

§2032A permits qualifying estates to value at least a portion of real property in such situations at its *present, "qualified use" value*, as a farm or other trade or business.

Requirements. The five major requirements and conditions under §2032A are briefly described next.

1. The property must have been held for "qualified use" and actively managed by the decedent or the decedent's family for *five out of the eight years* prior to the decedent's death. For example, *passive leasing* for cash by the decedent of the property for farming by others will later disqualify the estate from §2032A.[20] However, the surviving spouse may later rent the property to a family member.[21]

2. At least *50%* of the value of the gross estate, reduced by liens, must consist of real or personal property devoted to the qualifying use.[22]

3. The value of the real property portion must constitute at least *25%* of the gross estate as adjusted.[23]

4. The qualifying property must pass to a qualifying heir and must continue to be used as a *qualified use* for at least *10 years* after the decedent's

death. A qualified heir is a member of the decedent's family who acquired the property from the decedent.[24] A qualified use requires use of the property for farming or other trade or business.[25]

5. Perhaps most significant, the maximum amount by which the value of the special use *real estate* can be reduced by this election is $750,000.[26] Thus, assuming a 55% marginal estate tax rate, the greatest estate tax saving will be $412,500. While this is no small amount, very large disparities between highest and best use value and qualified use value may create too sizable a liquidity crisis for §2032A to solve, and may still force survivors to sell out involuntarily.

The §2032A election can reduce the need for liquidity by reducing the size of the gross estate and, therefore, the amount of the estate tax cash requirement. Since it applies only to real property and has some onerous requirements, it is not used very frequently. Generally, if §2032A is available, the estate will also qualify for §6166 deferral since §2032A had a 50% threshold and §6166 has a 35% threshold.

VALUATION DISCOUNTS AND CONTROL PREMIUMS

Over the years, the courts have offered taxpayers the ability to generate liquidity by significantly discounting the transfer tax value of closely held business interests, real property and securities subject to special market circumstances. The most common discounts are the minority discount, lack of marketability discount, and fractional interest discount.

Minority Interest Discount for Business Interests

A *minority interest* is an interest in a business that, in terms of voting, is not a controlling interest. It lacks the power to effect changes in policy, structure, or strategy.

EXAMPLE 15 - 10. Jack owns 50.1% of a corporation worth $1 million, and Jill owns 49.9%. Jill owns a minority interest. Alone, Jill cannot run or control the business, set compensation levels, sell or encumber business assets, elect herself an officer, or control corporate policy. Jill would most certainly have difficulty selling her interest to a third party for $499,000.

Ownership of a partnership interest may also qualify for a minority interest discount. Common law allows each partner one vote, regardless of his or her capital (investment), unless the partnership agreement provides to the contrary.

For transfer tax valuation, minority discounts of between 15 and 50% are obtainable for such interests. Factors influencing the size of the discount include overall quality of management, composition of other share holdings, size of the business and its history of profitability, existence of business opportunities not currently being exploited by management, and degree of the company's financial leverage.[27]

In some situations, minority interest discounts are not available. The IRS contends that a gross estate including two separate minority interests in the same property which add up to a majority interest should be denied the benefits of minority interest discounts.[28]

> EXAMPLE 15 - 11. Dad's estate plan will leave his 40% business interest at his death to a marital trust. At Mom's later death, her gross estate will include Dad's interest in the marital trust, as well as her own 40% business interest. The IRS will disallow a minority discount for either interest.

Planners should be able to circumvent this problem by either having S1 dispose of his or her interest to the bypass trust, which is not taxed to S2, rather than to the marital trust, or having one or both spouses make a lifetime transfer of the interest (by gift, installment sale, etc.).

Minority interest discounts are not available to stock subject to a §2032A special use valuation election.

A donor holding a majority stock position who gifts some of the shares can reduce both the retained shares and the gifted shares to a minority position.

Valuation discounts and imperfect unification. Chapter 9 described several factors explaining why our federal "unified" transfer tax system is not perfectly unified. Those factors included the allowance of an annual exclusion for lifetime gifts, failure to include postgift appreciation in the estate tax base, and ability to avoid grossing-up gift taxes on gifts made more than three years before death. To this group we may now include another factor, one whose tax saving potential rests on the ability to obtain valuation discounts for certain gifts made during lifetime but not at death.

EXAMPLE 15 - 12. Fiore owns 100% of the stock in a closely held corporation worth $300,000. This year, he gave each of his three children one third of the stock. Taking a 25% minority interest discount on each transfer, Fiore will report on Form 709 three gross gifts of $75,000 (= $100,000 - .25 x $100,000), totaling $225,000. Thus, in addition to saving taxes by taking three annual exclusions, Fiore has reduced his future gross estate by an extra $75,000 (= 3 x ($100,000 - $75,000)). Had Fiore planned instead to bequeath the stock to the children at his death, these minority discounts would not be available.

Revenue rulings have stated that a minority interest will not be disallowed solely because a transferred interest, if combined with interests held by family members, would be part of a controlling interest.[29] Valuation discounts for such gifts are allowed because the gift tax is computed on a *per gift* basis. They are not allowed for transfers at death, where after distribution none of the beneficiaries have control, because the estate tax is computed on *per estate* basis. Thus, valuation discounts create a fourth instance of imperfect unification.

Control premium. Fairly recently, case law has come to recognize that a fractional interest in property can actually be worth *more* than its proportional share.[30] For example, the value of a 51% interest in a particular closely held firm has been ruled to be worth greater than 51% of that firm, reflecting a premium in value for the benefit of majority controlling interest. In one case a decedent owned about 52% of voting stock in a corporation which gave him, among other things, the power to elect all directors. The court approved a 38% control premium, raising the value of the decedent's interest from $372,152 to $514,000.[31]

Thus, the control premium is essentially the 'flip side' of the minority discount. While including property subject to a control premium in the gross estate will ordinarily increase estate tax, careful planning can actually reduce estate tax, to the extent that the majority interest is bequeathed to the surviving spouse.

EXAMPLE 15 - 13. Anderson was the sole owner of a $1 million closely held corporation. At his death, he bequeathed 51% of the stock to his surviving widow and 49% to his son. In connection with this business interest, based on a control premium of 10%, Anderson's gross estate will include $1 million, and his marital deduction will include $561,000 (= 110% of 51% of $1 million). The control premium has reduced Anderson's taxable estate by $51,000.

In community property states, control premiums cannot apply to stock held as community property since neither spouse can have majority control.

Lack of Marketability Discount for Business Interests

Due to lack of an established market, restricted stock, stock in a closely held business, and partnership interests are invariably more difficult to sell than business stock that is publicly traded. Thus, discounts for lack of marketability ranging from 15 to as high as 50% for lack of marketability are obtainable, and apply to both minority and majority interests. Factors influencing the size of the discount include extent of resale restrictions and SEC restraints on marketability, size and dollar value of the stock, the firm's growth expectations, and size of the company's total assets and equity.

Use of minority interest and lack of marketability discounts can leverage the benefit of the gift tax annual exclusion.

> EXAMPLE 15 - 14. Crabb gives his daughter a $20,000, two percent interest in his $1 million closely held business. After applying minority interest and lack of marketability discounts, the value of Crabb's reportable gross gifts should be less than $10,000.

Some courts have allowed taxpayers both a minority discount and a lack of marketability discount, while others have collapsed the two into one discount. Whether collapsed or not, a combined discount of 30 to 40% is generally considered safe.

Fractional Interest Discount for Real Property

Undivided interests in real property can generate a fractional interest discount because they are neither easily partitioned nor readily marketable. In addition, they may be noncontrolling.

> EXAMPLE 15 - 15. Jones died owning a 58% interest in common in real property that was leased. His estate was allowed a 15% fractional interest discount.[32]

The fractional interest discount for real property, strongly opposed by the IRS, is analogous to the minority interest and lack of marketability discounts for stock. The IRS has taken the position that the only discount allowed should be the cost of a partition action.[33] It should be noted, however, that the problem of control premiums in real estate cannot arise because all realty owners must agree about significant property decisions.

Other Valuation Discounts

Worth mentioning briefly are three other valuation discounts.

- Securities, even those publicly traded, that are subject to special *securities laws restrictions* can be discounted. Restrictions include lack of registration, and the need to sell the stock by private placement.
- Large quantities of a stock listed on an exchange can receive a *blockage discount* if its sale all at one time could have a depressing effect on the market price. However, if the block represents a controlling interest in the corporation, possibly triggering an even higher price, a *premium* may be attached to its value. Blockage discounts may be available for other property, such as a large number of paintings left in the estate of a prominent artist.[34]
- A discount may be allowed for a business that lost a *key person* (e.g., the decedent) who was responsible for its good will.

Valuation discounts can generate liquidity by reducing the value of property subject to transfer tax, thereby saving transfer taxes.

FAMILY LIMITED PARTNERSHIPS

Family limited partnerships (FLPs) have been used by families in agricultural areas for decades as a means of getting children involved in running the ranch or farm, but only recently have they become a popular planning tool for any family run business. FLPs offer many attractive estate planning advantages over most other business forms and transfer devices. However, due to the costs of establishing them and appraisal costs associated with making multiple transfers of the limited partnership interests they usually are not recommended unless the parents owning the business have a net wealth in excess of two or three million dollars. For those that qualify, an FLP has numerous advantages: (1) the parents can give away wealth and still retain control; (2) transfers can be made at substantial discounts as compared to the value of underlying assets, thus saving unified credit and gift taxes; (3) restrictions can be placed on transfers by children; and (4) there is some protection from creditors.

Family partnerships are sanctioned by IRC with certain requirements set forth in §704(e). Among other things, the income and tax benefits must be distributed or allocated according to each owner's percentage in the partnership. The general partners may be paid for their personal services to the partnership. Also, capital must be "a material income-producing factor." A family partnership cannot be used to redistribute income generated from personal services by the general partner.

Establishing a Family Limited Partnership. To establish a family limited partnership one must follow the requirements of the state's limited partnership act, which will probably require publication of the names of the general partner and the limited partners. The Uniform Limited Partnership Act requires that there be at least one general partner and one limited partner. With an FLP, one, or both parents, serve as the general partner. They may start by owning all but a very small portion of the limited partnership units. Over time the parents transfer by gift a significant portion of the limited partnership units to the children. Given the wealth of the parents, it is unlikely that this transfer can be accomplished utilizing gifts covered by annual exclusions alone; thus to make this work usually requires using up both parents' unified credit, and perhaps even incurring some gift taxes.

Under unusual circumstances, such as the death or bankruptcy of the general partner, most limited partnership agreements give the limited partners the right to elect a new general partner. As with most real estate limited partnerships a limited partner cannot take assets from the partnership or otherwise force liquidation of the partnership before its term is up. The term is likely to be set at 50 years, however once both general partners are dead, a vote by the limited partners could liquidate the partnership. Whether this would take a super majority depends upon the terms of the partnership agreement.

FLP Costs. The major cost are attorney's fees to establish the partnership, probably between $2,000 to $7,000 depending on the nature of the business assets, and appraisal fees to establish both the underlying value and the appropriate discounts, probably in the range of $5,000 to $15,000. In addition, when partnership shares are transferred as gifts, an appraisal will again have to be made. This is one reason that the parents should consider large initial gifts right after the partnership is established, however, subsequent appraisal fees by the same appraisal firm should be considerably lower than the first ones, since the company will be familiar with the business. There will also be annual accounting fees for preparation of the partnership returns and the K1s that must be distributed to all partners. The state may also charge an annual fee for the right to do business as a limited partnership in the state.

Discounts. The two types of valuation discounts discussed earlier in the chapter play a significant role, limited partnership units can be transferred at a huge discount because the units have limited marketability, being a business enterprise closely held by just a handful of owners, and the owners of limited partnership units have extremely limited control since the general partners manage the partnership assets.

> EXAMPLE 15 - 16. The Jackson family wants to create a family limited partnership with Jack and Lilly Jackson as general partners. The net value of their combined estates is $17,600,000 which includes their ranch valued at $9,000,000. The limited partnership interests will represent 95% of the total value of the ranch, the other 5% being allocated to the general partnership interest. The limited partnership portion will be divided into 95 limited partnership units. This year the parents wish to transfer 20 units to each of their three children. If the lack of marketability discount is 30% and the minority interest discount is 25%, then the transfer of each 20 unit share to a child results in the following gift:
>
> Calculation: $9,000,000 *.70 *.75*.20 = $945,000
> [FMV ranch x (1 - .3) x (1 - .25) x .20 = discounted value of the share]

Each gift is from both parents, therefore both unified credits are used and each gift is entitled to two annual exclusions, making the total taxable transfers from each parent $1,387,500 [3 * (($945,000/2) - $10,000)]. The total gift tax for both parents is $629,250. The Jacksons have removed 60% [$5,400,000 at FMV] of the ranch to their children. Because of the size of their combined estate, assuming the plan calls for postponing all estate taxes until the second death, the estate of the last parent to die will be in the 60% marginal rate bracket. If that death occurs at least three years after the gifts so as to avoid grossing up, the discounted transfers and the reduction of the estate by the gift taxes paid will have saved total transfer taxes of $2,110,425.

Tax on $17,000,000 [S1's bypass holds $600,000] $9,148,000

Tax on $11,570,750 [17,600,000 - 5,400,000 - 629,250]* $6,408,325
     Plus gift taxes on the two gifts $ 629,250
     Total transfer taxes $7,037,575

Taxes saved: $9,148,000 - $7,037,575 = $2,110,425

In addition, any postgift appreciation escapes estate taxes. *Only the second to die owes taxes, but his or her estate must take into account the adjusted gifts of $1,387,500 and the gift taxes paid credit of $314,625.

Appraisals. Despite numerous attempts by the IRS to disallow discounts in a family setting, it has lost numerous times in the tax court and finally conceded the existence of the discounts, provided the client can back them up by creditable professional appraisals using current market data for the discounts. These discount appraisals are in addition to the appraisal of the underlying assets owned by the partnership.

Ability to control gifted assets. In addition to the discounts, the most attractive feature of the FLP is the ability of the donor to retain control over the assets. While key rights of a limited partner must be recognized, the general partner maintains all the managerial control over the partnership assets, determining when and whether to make income distributions to all the partners or to reinvest the income into additional assets. For most wealthy clients, the biggest roadblocks to making substantial gifts are the donor's reluctance to lose control of his or her business, or other important valuable assets, and concern about how well the donee-children will use the gifts. The control offered to the parent-general partner makes this an acceptable vehicle to give assets now, especially when one can utilize the tax benefits of valuation discounts and low values on appreciating assets.

Getting the children involved. Once the children have a vested interest in the business they should take a greater interest in how it works. Annual reports must be given to all partners and formal partnership meetings with all the family partners present are a good time to discuss the family investments and why they performed well or poorly. To avoid having the children liable as though general partners, they cannot be involved in the actual management of the business and they must not appear to outsiders as general partners.

Using the children's lower tax brackets. One benefit of a family limited partnership is that it is possible to shift income into the lower tax brackets of the children. This applies to the percentage interest the child actually owns in the partnership. When a parent is in the 39.6% federal income tax bracket, this can make a significant difference if the child is only in the 15% tax bracket. For children under 14, however, they will be subject to the kiddie tax for annual unearned income over $1,300 and thus subject to the parents' higher tax brackets.

Protection against failed marriages of children. One nice protection is the assets can be held as the separate property of each of the children. While the income distributed is usually commingled with the child's other assets, the partnership interest is usually clearly identified as the child's separate property. In community property states, only the community property is divided in a divorce proceeding, and while everything is presumed to be community property unless it can be traced to a gift, an inheritance, or to property owned prior to the marriage, it should be easy to establish the units as gifts, therefore, they can stay in the family. Of course, the child can change them into joint tenancy or into community property by written agreement with his or her spouse.

Loss of step-up in basis on gifted assets. One disadvantage in gifting assets is the donees (the children) lose the ability to get a step up in basis at the death of the parent of the part of the partnership that was given to the children. When the assets have a very low tax basis, this can reduce the tax benefits of the family limited partnership. Of course, if the children do not intend to sell the business, then the low basis is a price worth paying to avoid the transfer tax costs.

Limited asset protection. Often touted is the FLP's asset protection capabilities. It is true that limited partnership units given several years before the parents have financial difficulty should not be subject to levy by the parents' creditors. Most states have some form of fraudulent transfers act that allows creditors to attach property transferred by debtors for inadequate consideration when such transfer takes place in the face of mounting financial pressure. However, if sufficient time has passed, the parent is generally the only one liable to his or her personal creditors, and as general partner the only one liable to the creditors of the partnership.

In the past, creditors of limited partners collected by using a court issued *charging order* that allows creditors to collect the money distributed to a partner. Unfortunately for the creditor, the partnership income tax liability of the partner whose interest was seized was also passed on to the creditor. All limited partners must be treated the same insofar as distributions are concerned, and those distributions are controlled by the general partner. The idea in using the FLP as an asset protection device has been to starve out a creditor by not making distributions even though FLP profits force the limited partners and the creditor with the charging order to recognize taxable income. In theory the tax liabilities put the creditor in the mood to greatly discount the debt to avoid additional tax liability. Some recent state court decisions have held that if a charging order, because of the conduct of the general partner, does not allow a reasonable chance for the payment of the debt, the creditor can foreclose on the debtor's partnership interest, forcing the liquidation of some of the underlying assets sufficient to pay the creditor, provided the foreclosure does not unreasonably interfere with the partnership business. If other courts adopt this course, then a charging order can delay the creditors of a child-limited partner but it would eventually allow them to be fully paid by means of foreclosure if the income distributions were being withheld such that the creditors were not being paid timely. The partnership agreement should give the family a first right of refusal for any attempted sale by the limited partners.

If asset protection is crucial to family members involved in a business enterprise, they should consider the newest business organization to gain widespread acceptance, the limited liability company, discussed next.

THE LIMITED LIABILITY COMPANY

The limited liability company (LLC) is strictly a creature of the various state legislatures. Unlike the partnership it does not have common law roots but since the LLC first statute, Wyoming, 1977, almost every state has adopted one, bringing the total to 46 states and the District of Columbia. Legislation is pending in Hawaii, Massachusetts, Pennsylvania and Vermont. Why the sudden popularity? When done correctly, it offers business owners the chance to have the limited liability of a corporation with the tax pass-through advantages of a partnership. Each owner-investor is called a *member* and his or her ownership share is called a *membership interest*.

Creating an LLC. Of course one must comply with the state statute. But one must also consider the IRS rules concerning taxation of business entities. Regardless of state law, for federal income tax purposes an entity will be taxed as a corporation if it has *more than four* of the six characteristics of a corporation. Those characteristics are:

1. Associates or co-owners
2. Intent to make a profit & divide income
3. Continuity of life
4. Centralized management
5. Entity alone liable for business debts
6. Ownership interests freely transferrable

Since the LLC is made up of co-owners intent on making a profit, and since the point of the LLC is to limit liability, three of the characteristics are already in place. It is easy to avoid at least two of the other three by limiting the life of the LLC to a definite, even if long, term of years, restricting the sale of the membership interests by requiring they be offered first to the entity and next to the other members before a sale can take place to an outside third party, and requiring that all members agree on significant management decisions. The latter will work well for businesses with only two or three owners. If the owners intend to take on additional members it would be best to put a definite term into the agreement and restrict transferability.

Advantages compared to corporations. Both LLCs and corporations enjoy limited liability for the owners. An owner is liable only for torts in which he or she is actually involved. If one drives the company car on business and causes an accident in which others are injured, only the business and the owner-driver are liable. Other co-owners are not. Furthermore, none of the co-owners are liable for contracts entered into in the company's name. Of course, for either of these business forms the owners may be asked to personally guarantee certain contracts, such as leases and loans, which will create personal liability but contractual liability is not characteristic of these two business forms. LLCs have the single level of taxation at the membership level. Of course, S corporations also have this characteristic, but LLCs do not have the restrictions on stock ownership that S corporations have. Trusts, foreign individuals, and other corporations can be members. Although LLCs are most likely to be closely held, there is no restriction on the number of owners, whereas federal law limits to 75 the number of S corporation shareholders. S corporations are limited to one class of stock whereas LLCs can have membership interests with different rights such as income, capital preferences, or voting.

Advantages compared to partnerships. Both share the advantage of single level taxation but partnerships have the disadvantage of all partners being fully liable for all contracts taken in the partnership name and any torts that arise out of the partnership business whether committed by other partners or by partnership employees. Both allow withdrawal of assets, subject to the partnership or LLC agreement, without such withdrawals being deemed income. Of course, withdrawals do affect the owners' capital accounts. Some states require LLCs to pay some minimal annual fee (less than $1,000) whereas general partnerships are not charged any fees.

Advantages compared to limited partnerships. The advantages and disadvantages are similar to those stated for the general partnership, except limited partners enjoy limited liability. Unlike LLCs the limited partnership must have at least one person, the general partner, exposed to unlimited personal liability. Furthermore, limited partners must not be involved in the day to day management of the partnership or they will lose their limited liability insofar as third parties rely on their appearance as general partners in extending credit to the partnership.

Disadvantages. Not all states presently have LLC statutes, although that will probably cease to be a disadvantage within the next year or two as the last four states are considering adoption of LLC statutes. There is considerable variation among the LLC statutes already adopted.

OTHER LIQUIDITY SOURCES

Two other sources of liquidity to the estates of both nonbusiness and business owners also deserve brief mention.

Employee Retirement Benefits

As an employee, the client may have accumulated substantial retirement benefits on the job. If some of these benefits are payable after the client's death, the estate or the employee's spouse could be made beneficiary to provide a degree of needed liquidity.

Postmortem Liquidity Planning Techniques

There are a host of techniques that can be undertaken after death over which the client has little or no control during lifetime. Postmortem devices, such as disclaimers and the alternate valuation date election, will be examined in Chapter 18, which surveys postmortem tax planning.

This chapter has examined the planning for liquidity. Chapter 16 will present the principles of planning for the closely held business.

QUESTIONS AND PROBLEMS

1. How will the following factors influence liquidity needs at death?
   a. Size of the family estate.
   b. Whether the decedent is S1 or S2.
   c. Age of the family members.

2. "High-basis assets make desirable assets for a predeath sale designed to generate liquidity." True, false or uncertain? Explain.

3. (a)What traits distinguish cash value insurance from term insurance? (b) Universal life insurance from other types of cash value insurance?

4. Is life insurance ever subject to income taxation? Explain.

5. Explain the two primary ways in which life insurance can be subject to gift taxation.

6. Life insurance can be subject to estate taxation under §§2001, 2033, 2042, and 2035(d)(2). Briefly explain the application of each.

7. Who, if anyone, should be the *insured* of a policy designed to provide liquidity to a family estate of $250,000, assuming the following alternative facts?
   a. Spouses in their 30s; husband working; wife at home with two young children.
   b. Spouses in their 30s; both working; no children.
   c. Spouses in their 50s; both working; children are self-supporting adults living elsewhere.
   d. Single adult; no children.
   e. Single parent of one six-year old child.
   f. Retired couple; self-supporting adult children living elsewhere.

8. Re-answer part a, d, and f of Question 7, assuming instead a $2 million family estate owned by spouses who wish to set up a credit shelter bypass plan. In each case, would it matter how liquid the family wealth was?

9. What factors influence the selection of the owner and primary and contingent beneficiary of an insurance policy on the life of a spouse in a small family estate situation?

10. (a) Describe the characteristics of the irrevocable life insurance trust. (b) What are its advantages?

11. A rich client of yours is about to acquire a $500,000 life insurance policy on his life, naming his wife owner and beneficiary. They each have a net worth of $1 million. Advise him.

12. Would any of your answers to Question 11 change if the net family estate was worth about $800,000? Why or why not?

13. Five years ago, Mary assigned ownership of an insurance policy on the life of her husband, Bud, to the trustee of Bud's living trust. The trustee is beneficiary, and terms of the trust provide that at Bud's death Mary is entitled to a life estate in the trust income. If Mary survives Bud, could there be an estate tax problem?

14. April, age 40, is a recently divorced single mother of two young children. She is not on friendly terms with her ex-husband who, in her opinion, is a "selfish spendthrift." April owns few assets, and asks your estate planning advice to help achieve her goal of financial security for her children.

15. How are the arrangements based on §§6166, 303, and 2032A each designed to provide estate liquidity?

16. At his death recently, Silva owned a successful farm, which, over the years, continued to be approached by an expanding metropolitan area. As a farm, the land is worth $350,000, but a real estate developer is now willing to pay Silva's estate $1,200,000 for it. If the rest of the estate amounts to $400,000, what should Silva's total gross estate be if the property (a) does not qualify, and (b) does qualify for special use valuation?

17. Minnie and Mark, both age 68, are married parents of two adult children, Betty and Bryan. They own a $500,000 interest in a closely held business and $100,00 in other assets. Betty pretty much runs the business and would like to continue to do so after her parents are gone. Bryan has no interest in owning or running the business. If Minnie and Mark wish to leave all their property equally to their children after their own deaths, is there a distribution problem? Can life insurance help solve it?

ANSWERS TO THE QUESTIONS AND PROBLEMS

1. a. Generally speaking, cash needs will rise with increasing estate size, due to the estate tax.

   b. In most cases, the death of S1 will result in no estate tax, due to the shelter of the marital deduction and the unified credit. On the other hand, the death of S2 can result in a significant estate tax for families with medium to large estates.

   c. The younger the minor children, the greater the typical amount of liquidity need to fund the economic loss provided by that deceased spouse for the remainder of the children's period of dependence. Also, the older the client, the less time there is to accumulate liquidity.

2. True. They will result in little or no taxable gain, or will produce a loss, which in the usual case will be deductible only by the client.

3. a. The traits that distinguish cash value insurance from term insurance are:

      1. The pattern of the *premiums* over time (cash value: constant premiums; term: increasing premiums).
      2. Whether or not the proceeds are *certain* to be paid (cash value: certain; term: uncertain).

   b. The traits that distinguish universal life (UL) insurance from other types of cash value insurance are:

      1. *degree of flexibility,* UL policies permit the policy holder to vary the face value and premium payments, and
      2. *investment yield,* UL policies offer a variable yield, based on shorter-term investment rates.

4. Life insurance can be subject to income taxation in the following ways:

   a. Income taxation of cash value accumulation: Not taxable during accumulation period. When surrendered for cash value, the excess of the cash value over total premiums paid will constitute taxable income.

b. Income taxation of policy proceeds: Generally excluded unless the policy was transferred for valuable consideration.

5. Gift taxation of life insurance can arise either when a policy is assigned, or at the insured's death, whenever the insured, owner and beneficiary are all different parties.

6. Estate taxation can arise under Code§§2033, 2042, 2001, 2035, as described in detail in Chapter 6. The following is a summary.

Under §2001, the decedent's *adjusted taxable gifts* will include the date-of-gift taxable terminal value of *any* life insurance policy for which the decedent made a completed transfer more than three years before death.

Under §2033 (property owned at death), the terminal value of a life insurance policy on the *life of someone other than the decedent* will be includable in the decedent's gross estate to the extent of the decedent's date of death ownership interest in the policy.

Under §2042, proceeds on the *life of the decedent* will be includable in the decedent's gross estate if, at the insured's death, either the proceeds were receivable by the decedent's executor, or the decedent possessed any incidents of ownership in the policy. Interestingly, the entire proceeds under split dollar arrangements will still be includable, even though part of the proceeds is payable to a third party, such as the employer.

Under §2035, the proceeds of a life insurance policy on the *life of the decedent* will be includable in the decedent's gross estate if, within three years of death, the decedent made a completed transfer of incidents of ownership in the policy.

7. The major question in deciding whom to insure is whose death will result in financial loss that should be replaced.

a. *Spouses in their 30's; husband working; wife at home with two young children:* Both spouses may need insurance: for the husband to replace his lost income; for the wife to finance day care services, etc., while the widower is working.

b. *Spouses in their 30s; both working; no children:* Often, neither spouse needs coverage, because the (modest) loss from the death of either is assumable. However, this depends on their relative current standard of living and desired standard of living when the first one dies. Spouses who live modestly and save a lot may not need life insurance if the survivor can live on one salary and the expected investment income. On the other hand, spouses who save little and live expensively (costly home, cars, lifestyle, etc.) and want the surviving spouse to continue enjoying this lifestyle will probably need a considerable amount of insurance on the lives of both spouses.

c. *Spouses in their 50's; both working; children are self-supporting adults living elsewhere:* Essentially same answer as part b, except less insurance usually necessary because surviving spouse expected life span is lower and expected investment income is often greater.

d. *Single adult; no children:* No insurance usually necessary.

e. *Single parent of one six-year old child:* Considerable insurance would ordinarily be needed for the parent, to provide funds needed to raise the child.

f. *Retired couple; self-supporting adult children living elsewhere:* Answer depends on surviving spouse's other expected sources of income. To the extent that retirement benefits will continue and investment income will be high, less insurance is needed.

8. With a larger estate size, death taxes might be an estate expense. In each case, the clients may wish to pay the taxes out of liquid estate property, making insurance unnecessary. On the other hand, if not, or if there are insufficient liquid assets, then insurance would often be needed.

a. Possibly a *joint life policy* on the death of the second spouse. See text for discussion of other alternatives, which include insuring *both spouses* for the full amount, insuring *both spouses* for only a small amount that can be used to purchase a fully paid up policy on the life of the survivor, and insuring the *wife only*.

d. No insurance usually necessary. Most clients would probably let the relatively unrelated estate beneficiaries worry over paying the estate tax on what could be a $2 million windfall.

f. Same as part a. It might matter how liquid the family wealth was. As mentioned above, liquid assets could be used to pay part or all of the estate tax, thus reducing the need for insurance.

9. In the small family estate, convenience and other non-tax factors would influence the decisions as to who should be the owner and primary and contingent beneficiaries. The insured's spouse could be named owner and primary beneficiary, to avoid probate in the insured's estate. The contingent beneficiary could be a child or a trustee, under a trust for the benefit of the child.

10. a. Characteristics of the irrevocable life insurance trust:

     1. It is created by the insured.
     2. Trustee is owner and beneficiary of the policy.
     3. Trust terminates at or after S2's death.

    b. Advantages:

     1. There is no transfer taxation of proceeds at either spouse's death.
     2. It is not included in either spouse's probate estate.
     3. It qualifies gifts of the policy and the policy premiums for the annual exclusion.
     4. It qualifies for the gift tax annual exclusion for gifts to the trust.
     5. It ensures that a responsible party will provide the needed liquidity.
     6. Proceeds are available to S2, subject to an ascertainable standard.

11. Naming the insured's spouse to be owner or beneficiary will usually either cause the proceeds to be subject to estate or gift tax at that spouse's death, and/or to be included in that spouse's probate estate. The preferred plan is an irrevocable life insurance trust, for the reasons discussed in the answer to the previous question. Even in the case of a single client, the trust would be preferred because it would avoid estate taxation and probate, and would insure that a responsible party is managing the policy and, later, the proceeds.

12. The answers to the above question would very likely change. A family estate size of $800,000 owned by two spouses who developed a credit shelter

bypass plan would enable as much as $400,000 in insurance to be owned by the spouses without being subject to transfer taxation or probate administration.

13. As indicated in the chapter, Mary may be considered to have made a Section 2036(a) transfer with a retained life estate, which would include the entire policy proceeds in her gross estate.

14. To establish an asset base to provide income to her children in the event of her premature death, April should establish an irrevocable life insurance trust, a device that can function reasonably free from the control of her ex-husband. The trustee would be the policy beneficiary, directed to provide for the children's needs. And the trustee ought to be instructed to pay funds, wherever possible, directly to provider.

15. §6166: By deferring tax payments, note that the interest is deductible.
    §303: By reducing income tax on stock redemption
    §2032A: By reducing the gross estate, and thus the estate tax.

16. a. If the property does not qualify for special use valuation, the land will probably be valued at about $1,200,000, its highest and best use value, making the gross estate equal to $1,600,000.
    b. If the property does qualify for special use valuation, the land will probably be valued at about $450,000, which is the $1,200,000 highest and best use value, reduced by $750,000, the maximum amount allowed by law. Thus, Silva's gross estate will equal about $850,000.

17. The problem is that an equal distribution of the $600,000 estate will mean leaving to Bryan at least a $200,000 interest in the business, an asset he does not want. A survivorship (second death) life insurance policy in the amount of $400,000 could result in Betty receiving the entire $500,000 business and Bryan receiving $400,000 in cash proceeds and the remaining $100,000 in other assets. Thus, life insurance can simplify distribution of "lumpy" estate assets to survivors with widely different lifestyles and preferences.

ENDNOTES

1. In this chapter, the word *insurance* will be used as shorthand to mean life insurance.

2. 1991 *Life Insurance Fact Book Update,* American Council of Life Insurance.

3. *Theodore H. Cohen*, 39 TC 1055 (1963), acq. 1964-1 CB 4.

4. *Swanson*, 33 TCM. 296 (1974), aff'd. 518 F2d. 59 (8 Cir., 1975); Rev. Rul. 85-13 1985-1 CB 184

5. §101(*a*)(2).

6. Reg §1.7702-2(d).

7. For a summary comparison of the income, estate, and gift taxation of the irrevocable life insurance trust versus other popular trusts in estate planning, see Table 17-1 in Chapter 17.

8. §677(a)(3).

9. *Baptiste*, TCM 1992-198; §6324(a)(2).

10. Each must allocate the excess of their $20,000 share of the premium gift over their $10,000 annual exclusion amount.

11. IRS §2642(c)(2).

12. §6601(j).

13. §163(h)(2)(E).

14. Rev. Rul. 80-250 1980-2 CB 278.

15. Cecil Cammack, Jr., at Cammack Computations Co., 1-800-594-5826, will do these computations at a very reasonable price.

16. §6166(b)(6); §2053(d)

17. LR 9314050.

18. Currently, 28% for capital gains versus 31, 36, or 39.6% for ordinary income. For a long time prior to 1987, the maximum effective federal marginal rate on long-term capital gains was 20%, while maximum ordinary rates were either 70% (1971-81) or 50% (1982-86). See Figure 9-1.

19. §303(b)(3).

20. *J. Fisher*, TC CCH 12,923 (1993).

21. §2032A(b)(5)(A).

22. §2032A(b)(1)(a).

23. §2032A(b)(1)(B).

24. §2032A(e)(1).

25. §2032A(b)(2).

26. §2032A(a)(2).

27. *John and Viola Moore v. Commissioner*, 62 TCM 1128 (1991) (35% discount on gift of partnership interest); *Estate of Winkler v. Commissioner*, 62 TCM 1514 (1991) (20% discount on nonvoting stock); *Estate of Catherine Campbell v. Commissioner*, 62 TCM 1514 (1991) (56% discount); *Estate of Lenheim v. Commissioner*, 60 TCM 356 (1990); *Nancy Moonyham v. Commissioner*, TC Memo 1991-178.

28. TAM 9140002.

29. Rev. Rul. 93-12, 1993-7 IRB 13.

30. *Estate of Chenowith v. Commissioner* 88 TC 1577 (1987).

31. *Estate of Salsbury v. Commissioner* 34 TC Memo (CCH) 1441 (1975).

32. *Smythe v. U.S.* 86-1 U.S. Tax Cases (CCH)

33. See TAM 9336002.

34. *G.O'Keeffe Estate* TC ¶12,886(M) (50% blockage discount allowed).

− 16

Planning for Closely Held Business Interests

OVERVIEW

A closely held business is a firm privately owned by one or a few individuals who actively participate in its management. Unique estate planning problems can arise for owners of a closely held business. Typically, the firm generates the major source of its owner's *income* and represents the single largest part of his or her *family wealth*. Too often, however, the firm can sustain or increase that level of income and value only if the owners continue to be actively involved in its management. For example, a closely held corporation is rarely in a position to start paying a dividend after the client-owner dies if it wasn't paying them before.

This income and value can be jeopardized by two events, each of which is certain to occur. First, each owner's *involvement* with the firm is destined to end, and the enterprise will lose his or her economic contribution. Second, the ownership interest in the business must eventually be *transferred*, subjecting it to transfer costs, including taxes.

Estate planning seeks to minimize the adverse impact of these significant events by attempting to achieve four basic objectives:

1. To generate sufficient *income* for the owner and the owner's family after

the owner's active involvement in the business ends.

2. To transfer to the owner's chosen beneficiaries the maximum *value* attributable to that business.

3. To minimize the *costs* of transferring the business interest to the owner's chosen beneficiaries.

4. To provide sufficient *liquidity* to pay the transfer costs.

This chapter will focus on how closely held business interests accomplish these goals. Shares in publicly traded corporations require far less attention from estate planners. Their owners can easily accomplish these objectives, for two reasons: First, withdrawal of any one owner will have a far less depressing effect on business value and income, making continuity more assured. Publicly traded firms usually employ far more personnel, making business success much less dependent on the efforts of any one individual. In contrast, studies indicate that only 30-35% of successful closely held family businesses survive in the second generation, and only 10-20% survive in the third generation. In many cases, this is due to unresolved family conflicts. Second, the goal of liquidity is invariably easier to achieve for owners of publicly held firms because the client's survivors receive readily marketable securities.

However, liquidity problems can arise for wealthier clients owning publicly traded stock that is either a large block, or "restricted" under federal securities law. Large block holdings (i.e., tens of thousands of shares) may give rise to the problem of *blockage*, which is the temporarily depressing effect on the market price that results from selling a large block all at once. While federal tax law will allow some valuation discount for blockage effects, overall liquidity is nonetheless reduced. *Restricted stock* is usually acquired either from an affiliate of the issuing company, or in a private, unregistered transaction. Federal securities law prohibits restricted stock from being sold without either registering it under the Securities Act of 1933, or meeting an exemption from registration. The most common methods of disposing of such stock is by a secondary offering, a private placement, or by "Rule 144 sales," none of which are simple transactions. Although blockage and restricted stock can constitute significant liquidity problems, their consequences will be felt by a only a handful of estates, and their impact on overall liquidity is not nearly as great as the depressing effect of death or withdrawal of the owner on the value of a closely held business interest.

Thus, the many owners of closely held businesses have relatively unique problems, and this chapter will survey the major principles and techniques of estate planning devoted to assisting them. The chapter will first present an overview of general planning in this area, and then examine in greater detail the business buyout agreement, the corporate recapitalization and the partnership capital freeze.

PLANNING IN GENERAL FOR CLOSELY HELD BUSINESS INTERESTS

All estate planning for closely held business interests is premised on the fact that the client-owner cannot carry on forever. As mentioned, we are certain of the occurrence of two future events: that the client's active *involvement* in the management of the firm will terminate, and that the client's *ownership* interest will have to be transferred. Since these events have major economic implications for the four objectives mentioned earlier, we shall begin with a further discussion of them.

Withdrawal from the Firm: Minimizing Decline in Income and Value

Client-owners have the ability to choose when to terminate their active management of the firm. Some elect to remain active until disability or death. The rest withdraw sooner, for any number of reasons, including the desire to adopt a new lifestyle, to consume more of the wealth that time and hard work have created, and to step aside to provide a business opportunity for a son or daughter. No matter when the client plans to withdraw, if the departure is expected to reduce the value and income derived from the business, the client can take several steps to minimize the decline.

Delegate responsibility. First, the owner can plan early to "share the entrepreneurial spirit" by passing on knowledge of the business and by delegating greater and greater responsibility to those who one day may be able to replace his or her contribution. To provide an *incentive* to assume this responsibility, the business can contribute to certain tax-favored fringe benefit plans, including medical insurance contracts, group term life insurance, and retirement plans. In general, contributions to these plans are income tax deductible by the firm and are either tax free or tax deferred to the employee.

Execute contracts for future income. Second, the owner can use current business value to raise his or her own future *income* by executing certain *contracts*, such as a nonqualified deferred compensation plan, disability income insurance, and a qualified retirement plan. Nonqualified deferred compensation is a custom-tailored agreement under which the employer agrees to pay the employee in the future for services rendered presently. Tax law ordinarily permits the income tax to be similarly deferred. The professional athlete, a person with a brief but often lucrative career, is a frequent party to the deferred compensation contract.

Freeze the estate. Third, the firm may be able to undertake a corporate recapitalization or create a partnership capital freeze. These are intricate transfer devices which, in addition to sustaining value and income, can *reduce transfer taxes*. Each can offer additional employment incentives to family members, and each may be able to freeze the value of the client's interest in the business, and still continue to provide him or her with rights to substantial income and voting power in the business affairs. However, as we shall see later, recent tax legislation has severely restricted their potential value, and the client should be advised to seek expert tax counsel when exploring these techniques.

Maintain a list of instructions. Fourth, the client can place in a safe deposit box a list of business instructions for the surviving family. The list could include recommendations as to whether to sell the firm or continue running it, the name of the chosen successor, a list of business advisors, and the location of key company documents. These arrangements can reduce stress and risk of failure, particularly after the sudden death of the client-owner.

Execute a buyout contract. Finally, if an abrupt departure by the owner is likely to result in a significant decrease in the value (and in the income) of the business, the client might consider selling the business or negotiating a contract for its future sale. By staying on as a consultant during a transition phase, the decrease in value may be avoided. Selling a business will be explored later in the chapter.

In summary, by planning early, the client can usually take one or more significant steps to forestall a large decline in the future income from, and the value of, interests that will pass to his or her chosen beneficiaries.

Transferring the Business Interest

As well as minimizing the decline in business value resulting from withdrawal from the firm, the client will want to choose *when* and *to whom* to transfer the business interest. Planning for the transfer will depend in large part on whether the client wishes to transfer the equity interest itself to a family member, or whether the client intends to sell it to an unrelated party and later transfer the sale proceeds to the chosen beneficiaries. The next two sections will probe these alternatives.

Transfer of an equity interest to a family member. Some clients will want to make a transfer of some or all of the business to a particular family member who is willing and able to take over its management. Many transfer devices are available, and the most common ones are discussed next.

Lifetime strategies. As mentioned earlier, to encourage the family member to adopt a long-term commitment and to prevent deterioration in business value and income, the client should consider starting a program to prepare a family member for eventual ownership and control. In addition to delegating increasing amounts of responsibility, the owner can offer incentives, such as *gifts* of ownership interests in the business, possibly in the form of stock or stock options. The transfers can be outright, or they can be in trust, with the client and family member acting as co-trustees. Transfers into trust can promote a more orderly transition by enabling the client to monitor and develop the family member's interest, abilities, and commitment.

Instead of making a completed gift, the client may wish to arrange a gift-leaseback, installment sale, sale-leaseback, or private annuity. In fact, an installment sale can be a simple, inexpensive, and relatively tax-safe estate freezing alternative to the corporate recapitalization or the partnership capital freeze. The latter two are discussed later in the chapter. In general, most aspects of gifts and other transfers of business interests can be analyzed in a manner similar to lifetime transfers of business interests that are not closely held. The reader is referred to Chapters 13 and 14 for greater detail.

Transfer at Death strategies. Instead of making a lifetime gift of the business interest to a family member, the client, to retain complete control, may prefer to delay and pass it on at death. However, there are several drawbacks to waiting until after the owner dies to transfer a closely held business.

Liquidity problems. First, estate liquidity problems may arise if a nonspouse survivor winds up owning a relatively illiquid asset having a substantial taxable value. For a discussion of several methods of handling liquidity problems, review the material on liquidity planning in Chapter 15.

> EXAMPLE 16 - 1. Keith, a widower, died two years ago, the very successful owner of a business whose going concern value was $6 million. The estate tax attributable to this value was $3,300,000 (= .55 x $6 million). Due to lack of succession planning, Keith's children were forced to sell the business last month to a competitor for the firm's $3 million liquidation value, with the unfortunate result that the IRS became a larger "beneficiary" than the children.

Unprepared survivors. Second, transfers at death of closely held business interests to unprepared survivors who subsequently decide to carry on the business can generate severe problems. The combined tasks of dealing with grief and assuming new business duties can cause panic, guilt, exhaustion, family squabbles, and finally, failure. Adverse parties such as customers, employees and creditors may be tempted to take advantage of the new owner's naivete. While careful planning can reduce this risk, it cannot entirely eliminate it, particularly if the successors are not very experienced in business. Realistically, only a minority of client-owners will actually plan for this outcome. A 1988 Laventhal & Horwath poll of family business owners found that only 45% had selected successors, and only one in three had developed a strategic plan.[1]

Uncertainty and friction. Third, transfers at death of closely held business interests to beneficiaries not involved in the business but who do not intend to sell may be ill-advised if the beneficiaries have no desire to manage the firm. By its nature, the closely held business requires active cooperation among its owners, cooperation which usually requires constant interaction. Unaware of the firm's precise manner of operation, uninvolved owners can precipitate uncertainty and friction among the manager-owners and other employees, especially if they disagree with how the business is being run.

Hard for survivors to sell. Fourth, transferring business interests at death can create problems for surviving transferees who do wish to sell out. In structuring the terms of the sale, survivors will not be able to take advantage of the client's knowledge and experience. The business may no longer be as productive, a fact that could substantially lower the bid price. The bidders may not be willing to pay the surviving beneficiaries a fair value for the client's interest, particularly if it is a minority interest. The survivors may have little bargaining power in view of both their probable (and perhaps apparent) need for cash and usually the uniqueness of the business limits the prospective buyers. Its not like selling the home or publicly traded shares of stock.

Legal and tax complexities. Fifth, legal and tax complexities may arise. If a client's interest in S corporation stock is to be distributed at death to a trust, such as a bypass or a marital trust, that trust must be designed to qualify as a "Qualified Subchapter S Trust" in order not to jeopardize the corporation's Subchapter S status. Requirements include the naming of only one income beneficiary.[2] Essentially, an S corporation is a corporation that is treated by federal income tax law as if it were a partnership; income is taxed to the individual shareholders rather than to the corporation.

Valuation disputes with IRS. Finally, *disputes with the IRS* over the estate tax valuation of a closely held business are common and often result in litigation or settlement at higher than expected values. And the Code imposes an estate tax penalty of 20% of the tax underpayment for *valuation understatements* at less than 50% of the correct value. The penalty applies only if the additional tax owed exceeds $5,000.[3] A pre-death sale can at least more ensure that the owner will be available to intelligently confront the IRS.

For these and many other practical reasons, the client would normally be well-advised not to delay until death the gifting of a business interest to a family member.

Sale to a unrelated party. Instead of transferring an ownership interest to the surviving beneficiaries, the client could arrange the sale of the business interest to a unrelated party. Potential buyers include the client's key employees, individual strangers, and other firms, including competitors. In addition to eliminating potential friction, this alternative can yield to the beneficiaries other far more liquid assets (cash or publicly traded stock), assets requiring less income generating effort. The following material explores several aspects of the sale option, including timing and tax effects.

Timing. The business could be sold before or after the client withdraws from active management. *While the client is still active*, the entire firm could be sold outright, or some of its assets could be sold and then leased back to the firm. Or prearrangement could be made to sell the firm when the client withdraws at retirement, disability, or death. Actual timing of the sale will often depend largely on the personal, non-economic preferences of the client. The material below discusses the economic and tax factors influencing that decision.

In general, the greater the expected decline in the value of the firm resulting from the client's withdrawal, the greater the economic motive to sell it while it is still being actively run by the client. Value will fall most for single-owners, especially those offering professional services, such as physicians, accountants, and attorneys. Often, the primary business assets of these firms are the personal customer relationships which, in may cases, are not transferable. Other closely held businesses, such as product-oriented firms and service firms with more than one owner, may be more able to retain their value after departure of the owner-client.

Sale of the business interest prior to the owner's withdrawal will often bring a *higher price* since potential buyers can currently observe that the business is operating successfully under the direction of an active owner-client. Further, the client's astute awareness of the firm's identity and its earnings potential will provide additional bargaining power during the negotiations. And if the sale is completed while the client is alive, the agreement may include an obligation of the new owner to retain the client as an "adviser" or "consultant," as a way of increasing the client's future income. Finally, sale of a closely held business prior to the client's death can minimize unsettling disputes with the IRS over the firm's actual estate tax fair market value.

In the alternative, the business interest could be sold at or after *the client's withdrawal* from the firm. If the sale is structured in advance to take effect at the client's disability or death, it is called a *business buyout agreement*, an arrangement to be discussed shortly.

Taxable gain. Selling the business for cash prior to the owner's death will give rise to the *immediate recognition* of a taxable gain, unless the transaction is an installment sale or other tax-deferred exchange. On the other hand, transferring the interest at death can eliminate most or all of the taxable gain because of the *step-up* in basis that the interest will receive at death. However, at a maximum tax rate of 28%, the tax impact of a pre-death sale for cash may turn out to be a reasonable price to pay to achieve substantial estate liquidity, in view of the high costs of alternate liquidity sources, such as insurance on the life of an elderly client. In addition, many commentators expect the Congress to enact a lower maximum rate on capital gains, perhaps down as low as the 20% maximum capital gains rate in effect prior to TRA 86.

Form of the transaction. Sale of the business can take one of several forms. It can be for *immediate cash*, either to one or a few individuals, to many individuals, as in a public offering, or to a corporation. It can be in the form of an installment sale with any of these parties, with the client's recognition of the taxable gain spread over the collection period. Or the sale can be for *stock*, in a tax-deferred exchange with a publicly held firm. And the capital gains tax may be eliminated entirely by a step-up in basis if the transfer is after the owner's death.

A common planning device employed to sell a closely held business to one or a few individuals is the *business buyout agreement*, also called a buy-sell agreement, in which the firm, one or more owners, employees, or other parties contract in writing with the client in advance to purchase the client's interest in the business, usually at the client's death or disability. The buyout agreement offers many advantages, including future liquidity, a guaranteed market, and possibly greater certainty over the selling price. Often, the purchase is funded with life and disability insurance.

If a client whose business is not incorporated plans to retain it for an indefinite period, consideration should be given to *incorporating*. Incorporating will generate divisible shares of ownership which may be easier to transfer or liquidate when the need arises. Incorporating will also enhance continuity, since a corporation has an indefinite existence, one that might be more able to survive the client's departure. One disadvantage of forming a typical C corporation is that almost any distribution of corporate property to the shareholders will be taxed to them as dividend income and thus subject to double taxation, once at the corporate level and again to the shareholder. Two exceptions are the §303 redemption to pay death taxes, covered in Chapter 15, and a complete redemption of the deceased shareholder's stock.

The Need for Early Planning

When should planning for closely held business interests begin? For many reasons, planning should begin early, when the client is still active and in good health. First, the client can more clearly express specific estate planning *objectives* at this point, and the client's knowledge and expertise can provide professional planners with greater help in reaching these objectives. Second, the client will be able to take advantage of planning concepts that are available only to *healthy* clients, including relatively inexpensive life and disability insurance. Third, as implied earlier, if the business will eventually have to be sold, *careful planning* can eliminate the need for a sudden forced sale at the client's incapacity or death, both times when the business, having lost the client's services, is clearly less valuable.

With these general principles in mind, let's examine the specific legal arrangements to which we have been referring.

BUSINESS BUYOUT AGREEMENT

Earlier we learned that placing upon one's survivors the burden of selling the business after the client's death can create problems. These problems can be eliminated or minimized by the client's careful preparation of a business buyout agreement. Executed by the client and one or more prospective purchasers, the buyout agreement obligates the other parties to purchase the interest of the client upon the occurrence of specific future events, such as the client's death and, often, the onset of his or her permanent disability.

Types of Agreements: Cross Purchase, Entity-Redemption, or Mixed

The three most common types of buyout agreements are distinguished by the identity of the contracting parties. The first type, called the *cross-purchase* agreement, provides that the owners, usually all of them, purchase the interest of a particular owner. In many contracts between owners, a reciprocal type of cross purchase agreement is undertaken, in which each owner agrees to purchase a pro rata share of the interest of any owner that dies. The second type, called the *entity* or *redemption* agreement, has the business itself purchase the interest of one or more owners. The third type, called the *mixed* agreement, usually gives the business an option to purchase an owner's interest, and gives the other owners the option or obligation to purchase the balance. As a hybrid of the other two, the mixed agreement has the characteristics of both cross purchase and entity-redemption, and is often considered the most flexible arrangement.

Taxation of Buyout Agreements

As we shall see, the most critical issues in taxation of buyout agreements arise in the estate tax area.

Gift taxation. Generally, the execution of a buyout agreement does not result in a taxable gift. However, an agreement having a contract price below fair market value will, if it gives a purchaser an unqualified present purchase right.

Income taxation. Income tax effects of buyout agreements will depend on the type of the agreement.

Cross-purchase agreement. The *selling owner*, usually the estate of a decedent-business owner, will be selling a capital asset subject to capital gain treatment. However, in view of the *step-up* in basis at decedent's death, the only recognizable gain will be on any appreciation above estate tax value. The *buyer's* new basis will be the purchase price of the business interest acquired.

Entity-redemption agreement. The *acquiring business's* new basis will be its purchase price, which is not a tax deductible expense. If the business has been paying premiums on life insurance to fund the arrangement (see below) it will not be allowed a tax deduction for those premiums; they must be paid with after-tax dollars.[4] Further, any cash value buildup on a policy, and any receipt of proceeds, while not includable as ordinary income, may be subject to the alternative minimum tax.[5]

The *selling party*, again usually the decedent-owner's estate, will be taxed on the sale proceeds as a dividend, to the extent of the corporation's earnings and profits. Dividend treatment can be avoided if the sale can qualify for favorable redemption treatment under §302 or §303, both sections permit the redeeming party to treat the sale as a disposition of a capital asset rather than the receipt of a dividend. This means that there will be little or no taxable gain, due to the step up in basis at death. Without this favorable treatment, the entire receipt would be taxable at ordinary income rates.

Mixed agreement. Tax aspects for contracting parties under a mixed agreement follows the patterns mentioned above, to the extent that it takes on the characteristics of both of the other two types.

EXAMPLE 16 - 2. Stan and Oliver, equal owners of a corporation, are trying to decide whether to arrange a cross-purchase or an entity-redemption buyout plan. The adjusted basis of each of their stock in the business is $20,000. They project that the business will be worth $200,000 when the first owner dies. Thus, under either arrangement, the purchase price is expected to be $100,000, and the total value of the surviving owner's stock will equal $200,000, the total value of the business. However, the survivor's basis will be different, depending on which arrangement is selected. If a cross-purchase plan is chosen, the surviving shareholder's basis in his stock will increase to $120,000, which is $20,000, the basis of the pre-owned stock, plus $100,000, the purchase price of the decedent's stock. Alternatively, if an entity-redemption arrangement is chosen, the basis of the surviving shareholder's stock will remain $20,000, because he will not have purchased any additional shares.

Estate taxation. The deceased owner's gross estate will invariably include some value attributable to the decedent's ownership interest held at the moment of death. Ordinarily, the estate executor will prefer avoiding a dispute with the IRS over this value. One method of avoidance has been to establish a selling price in the buyout agreement that will, by law, *fix the value* for estate tax purposes. Only half jokingly, one commentator has said that in the absence of a price "set" by a buyout agreement, the "value" of the business can be said to be the amount agreed upon by "a willing IRS agent and a willing executor, neither of whom has ever owned a business."

Agreements prior to §2703. Prior to October 9, 1990, the effective date of §2703, fixing the value of the business for estate tax purposes was far simpler because case law was quite generous in allowing fixed values that may have been substantially below fair market value. Three valuation methods are commonly included in buyout contracts:

First, a *specific dollar amount* has been specified, with a provision normally made for periodic review so the owners can agree to revise the amount as conditions change. Without provision for a review, if, for example, the value of the business subsequently increased, the purchasing owners would receive a windfall at the expense of the selling owner. Unfortunately, experience has shown that inertia reduces the likelihood of periodic reviews.

Second, the selling price can be determined by *appraisal*, the agreement specifying that a qualifying appraiser will determine the value of the business at the time of sale. The appraisal method has the advantage of ensuring that a current value will be used.

Third, business buyout agreements can use a *formula* method of valuing business interests, preferably with the appropriate formula determined by an expert appraiser. Its terms ordinarily call for valuation to be a specified percentage of book value, or a multiple of current earnings. A formula is more flexible and often more accurate than a specific amount, since the derived selling price can vary with economic conditions. However, because a formula is more arbitrary than an appraisal, it may later turn out not to be reflective of current economic conditions.

Impact of §2703. Currently, to fix the estate tax value of the business equal to the buyout agreement amount, agreements (executed after October 8, 1990) must meet specific statutory requirements under §2703(b)[6] and its final regulations:

1. The agreement must be a *bona fide* business arrangement.
2. The agreement *cannot be a device* to transfer property to members of the decedent's family for less than full and adequate consideration in money or money's worth.
3. The terms of the agreement must be *comparable* to similar arrangements entered into by persons in an arm's length transaction.

Some comments on these requirements: The thrust of these requirements is to ensure a value reasonably close to the value of the business interest at the moment of the transfer. Thus, an agreement under which the surviving owner, a son, is obligated to purchase the client's $1 million business interest (current value) for a fixed $300,000 (historical contract value) would be currently labeled a "disguised bequest," and not meet requirements 1 and 2. On the other hand, prices set between unrelated owners are not usually subject to intense scrutiny by the IRS if the transaction otherwise appears to be made at arm's length. And IRS regulations provide that a buyout agreement will meet all three requirements if more than 50% of the value of the property subject to the agreement is owned by persons who are not "natural objects of the transferor's bounty."[7]

Planners feel that the comparability requirement of item 3 will create considerable uncertainty and additional expense for difficult appraisals, in particular because typical buyout agreements are not public documents. However, for businesses in some industries, agreements may be able to specify a formula, such as a multiple of sales or earnings, if that formula is known to be the predominant valuation method for the industry.

Even though valuation discounts may be available, if valuation is not set for estate tax purposes, the estate could wind up owing more estate tax. Anticipating those possibilities, planners heed the §2703 valuation rules carefully, and also suggest that the agreement either require the buyer(s) to pay any additional state and federal death taxes resulting from this problem. Or they recommend including a "savings" clause increasing the selling price to estate tax values, however, such clauses have been ruled against public policy[8] if they are merely an attempt to pass the property to a family member at a below market price.

> EXAMPLE 16 - 3. Dad's will provided for a credit shelter bypass plan, leaving $600,000 to a bypass trust and the residue of his estate to a marital trust for Mom. Dad executed a business buyout agreement with his son, who was obligated to buy Dad's 1,000 shares of closely held business stock for $1 million. Dad died owning the stock and $800,000 in other property. Son paid Dad's estate $1,000,000 for the stock, and Dad's executor distributed $600,000 in property to the bypass trust and the residue of $1.2 million to the marital trust. After an IRS audit, Dad's executor was agreed that the stock's fair market value was $2 million. Thus, Dad's gross estate totaled $2,800,000. Since only $1.2 million went to Mom, only that amount qualified for the martial deduction, leaving a taxable estate of $1,600,000. This generates estate taxes of $408,000. The additional $1 million is considered as having been left to the son and, in the absence of a clause allocating taxes to the credit shelter trust, he must pay 10/16ths of the tax and the other 6/16ths would be charged to the credit shelter trust. This tax would have been avoided had the buyout agreement provided a more realistic selling price. The figures shown next detail the estate tax calculations for the two alternatives.

	Alternative Values Given the Stock				
	Sales Agreement $1 million		IRS & After Audit $2 million	
Gross Estate	$2,800,000	*1*	$2,800,000	
Less Marital Deduction	$1,200,000	*2*	$2,200,000	*3*
Taxable Estate	$1,600,000		$600,000	
Tentative Tax	$600,800		$192,800	
Less Unified Credit	($192,800)		($192,800)	
Estate Tax	$408,000		$0	

notes

1 $2,800,000 = stock @ $2 million & other property @ $800,000

2 marital deduction = $1,800,000 - UCE into Trust B

3 marital deduction = $2,800,000 - UCE into Trust B

Funding

A business buyout agreement can require that the survivors pay a cash lump sum at the triggering event, or it can require payment of cash in periodic installments. The choice sometimes depends upon the nature of the triggering event.

Cash lump-sum payment. Buyout agreements that require payment of a cash lump sum equal to the entire contracted price are most likely to be funded with life insurance and/or lump-sum disability insurance.

Life insurance. The principles of the acquisition of life insurance to fund a business buyout agreement will be influenced by the type of buyout chosen. Under an *entity* agreement, the firm purchases and acts as beneficiary of a policy on the life of each business owner, with each policy in the amount of money that is necessary to buyout that owner's interest. In a (reciprocal type) *cross-purchase agreement*, each contracting party purchases and acts as beneficiary of a policy on the life of each of the other contracting owners.

> EXAMPLE 16 - 4. Sol and Harry are equal shareholders of a corporation that has a net worth of $300,000. The men have executed an *entity* buyout arrangement. The corporation will own and be the beneficiary of two $150,000 face value policies, one on Sol's life and one on Harry's life. The men plan to review and update this amount periodically, as the value of the business changes.

> EXAMPLE 16 - 5. Facts essentially similar to those in the prior example, except that a *reciprocal cross-purchase* plan is adopted. Sol will own and be beneficiary of a $150,000 policy on Harry's life, and Harry will own and be beneficiary of a $150,000 policy on Sol's life.

A reciprocal cross-purchase arrangement funded with life insurance becomes *unwieldy* when the agreement includes numerous owners, because each other contracting party will have to purchase a policy on the life of each other contracting owner. For example, although only 2 policies would have to be purchased for a firm with two contracting owners, 6 policies would have to be purchased for three owners, and 12 policies for four owners. In general, the number of policies purchased under a cross-purchase plan would be $n(n - 1)$, where n equals the number of contracting owners. Under an entity plan, the business itself would simply purchase one policy on the life of each contracting owner. Thus, only n policies would have to be purchased.

The number of policies needed under a cross purchase arrangement can be reduced somewhat by using one of two specialized life insurance contracts. First, two contracting parties may be able to purchase a *first to die* joint lives policy, whose proceeds are payable only on the death of the first insured. The premium cost should be less than the total cost for two separate policies because only one life is insured. Second, some companies offer a policy covering more than two insured owners for different amounts based on the their respective ownership interests.

Besides the problem of purchasing numerous policies under a cross purchase agreement, an income tax problem can arise from the *transfer for value rule*, if on the death of one corporate owner the surviving owners purchase the remaining decedent-owned policies. At their later deaths, part of the proceeds may be subject to income taxation.[9]

Compared with the cross purchase agreement, the entity agreement may raise the client's estate tax, if the infusion of policy proceeds into the corporation increase the stock's value. And an entity agreement funded with life insurance can trigger a corporate *alternative minimum tax*, to the extent that the "book income" of the corporation, which will include the insurance proceeds, exceeds taxable income, which will not.

For any buyout agreement, insurance premiums are not deductible from income, even if paid by the firm.[10] Thus all premiums must be paid with after-tax dollars.

With a cross purchase agreement between owners who are not close in age (or who have unequal interests), a larger premium will likely be paid by the younger (or smaller) owner(s), who are usually less affluent.

Using the firm's assets. A second method of funding a lump-sum payment under an entity arrangement is with the firm's own *cash or noncash assets*. This can also make life insurance unnecessary, but too often the business will not own sufficient distributable assets, particularly the amount of cash that may be needed to pay estate debts.

Lump-sum disability insurance. Finally, in an attempt to accommodate buyout agreements, more and more insurance companies are offering disability policies promising to pay a lump sum at the onset of disability, rather than the usual income stream.

Certain triggering events not conducive to lump-sum agreements. Other, usually uninsurable events triggering the buyout could be retirement, divorce, insolvency of an owner, criminal activity, and loss of a professional license. However, since none of these other events can be reasonably expected to generate a sizable cash flow, a full-cash buyout under such circumstances may be financially difficult to consummate.

Installment payments. In lieu of choosing a lump-sum payment, the parties can agree to an *installment sale* of the business interest. The installment sale can make the purchase of life insurance unnecessary and can be a source of periodic income to the client and the client's family. However, installment payments carry the risk that the purchasers will be unable to make the payments, a situation that can lead to disaster if the family again winds up owning a business that is now failing. Further, a decedent owner's family may dislike receiving deferred payments if the estate has the need for immediate liquidity to pay a large estate tax or other outlay incurred at death. Finally, an installment note creates a potentially stressful creditor-debtor relationship between the decedent's surviving family and the successor business owners.

In conclusion, the advantages of the business buyout agreement include business continuity, liquidity, a guaranteed market, and possibly greater certainty over the selling price. The preceding overview material merely highlights the general principles of this complex subject. A business buy-out agreement should not be executed without the help of expert legal advice.

FREEZING THE VALUE OF THE BUSINESS INTEREST

Overview

The world contains more than a few outstandingly successful owners of closely held corporations. Some have amassed a degree of wealth that they themselves consider to be more than adequate to provide for their income and capital needs for the rest of their lives. To them, the prospect of acquiring more property may be relatively unimportant, perhaps in part because of the additional estate tax it will trigger. Few of them, however, look forward to relinquishing control of their business interests. They may be having too much fun, or they may have yet been unable to sufficiently groom a younger generation family member.

Prior to 1987, highly successful entrepreneurs had several relatively safe, although complicated methods of freezing the estate tax value of their business without losing effective control. The most common methods are called the corporate recapitalization and the partnership capital freeze. Through a reorganization of the firm's capital accounts, these techniques enabled the owner to retain complete voting control of the firm and continue to receive the same amount of income from the firm, yet freeze future transfer taxes by arranging for other family members to benefit from the future appreciation of the business.

As mentioned in Chapter 7, by enacting §2701 in 1990, the federal government has substantially restricted the use of business estate freezing. The material that follows first discusses the use of business estate freezing during its heyday, and then traces the influence of recent legislation. The reader might wish to review the material on §2701 in Chapter 7.

Corporate Recapitalization

Recapitalization prior to §2036(c).   Prior to §2036(c),[11] corporate recapitalization (recaps) were structured in varying manners. A commonly used variation has the following characteristics: Prior to the recap, the client possessed controlling interest in the firm through ownership of the voting common stock. After the recap, the client owned a combination of some voting shares, usually common, and some nonvoting preferred shares, which were entitled to a substantial dividend. The younger generation family members, to whom the client wished to transfer future wealth, were issued nonvoting common shares and, if the client approved, some voting shares. In the following three examples, assume the date to be prior to December 18, 1987.

> EXAMPLE 16 - 6. Alfred is the owner of a highly successful computer software corporation, owning all 1000 shares of the common stock, valued at $2,000 per share. Presently, this is the only class of stock. This year, the company will earn a net income of $260,000. Within the next six months, the company expects to be releasing a revolutionary new software package, one that can triple the company's sales and net worth. Alfred is divorced and has two children, Kyle and Maude. Kyle, age 32, has worked for the firm for ten years and shows great promise to take over when Alfred departs. Maude, age 28, a tenured biology professor, has never been interested in working for the company. At his death, Alfred wishes to leave his entire estate in approximately equal shares to the children.

A recapitalization of the firm is undertaken. In exchange for Alfred's 1,000 shares of common, the corporation issues three classes of new stock:

1. 20,000 shares of nonvoting, 13% *preferred stock*, all to Alfred. The stock is noncumulative, and has a par value of $100 per share.
2. 480 shares of nonvoting common stock, one-half to Kyle and one-half to Maude.
3. 20 shares of voting common stock, all to Alfred.

Both types of common stock will share, pro rata, in any income available after payment of the preferred dividend.

Assume that when Alfred dies (in about ten years), the business will be worth $6 million. The value of Alfred's business interest included in his gross estate is expected to be $2,160,000. This is the sum of $2 million, (the value of the preferred stock) plus $160,000 (the value of the 20 shares of voting common), derived in the following manner: Of the $6 million market value capitalization, since the preferred stock is still expected to be worth $2 million at Alfred's death, the total value of the common shares will be worth $4 million, or $8,000 per share. Thus, nearly all of Alfred's interest in the firm will be frozen at its value as of date of recapitalization, and nearly the entire post-recapitalization appreciation will inure to Kyle and Maude, free of transfer tax.

EXAMPLE 16 - 7. In the prior example, instead of passing the voting common shares at his death, Alfred could make periodic gifts of them to Kyle in amounts not exceeding the annual gift tax exclusion. In this way, Alfred would have both given additional incentive to Kyle to remain with the firm and, at the same time, reduced even further the value of the business interest taxable in his estate at his death.

The ideal recap was designed to have the following tax-related benefits:

1. No taxation to the corporation arising from the recap.
2. No taxable income to the client upon receipt of the new shares.
3. No taxable gift by the client.
4. At death, the amount included in the client's taxable estate attributable to the firm would approximately equal the value of the client's interest in the business at the date of the recap.

Even prior to the passage of §2036(c), one or more of these benefits could have been lost with an improperly structured recap. In fact, even a state-of-the-art recap may not have been able to achieve all of them, in view of the zeal with which the IRS was attacking them. For many years, the IRS took the position that the value of the common shares transferred could not possibly equal zero because the value of the preferred shares could not be made to equal the total value of the firm. Consequently, some positive value would have remained in the common stock, value which was therefore transferred as a taxable gift to the other family member. Referring to Example 16 -7, if the preferred stock was actually determined to be worth $1,600,000, rather than $2 million, the 500 shares of common would have had a total fair market value of $400,000. Under the simple assumption that each share was worth $800, Alfred would have been deemed to have made a gift of $384,000.

Former impact of §2036(c). Until is was repealed, §2036(c) virtually eliminated the use of the estate freezing recapitalization after December, 1987. Using very sweeping language, it included in the decedent's gross estate the date of death value of the entire business that had been the subject to the estate freezing recap. The reader will be spared a discussion of the specific application of this subsection, since it was repealed retroactively by the 1990 Act.

Current impact of §2701. As more fully described in Chapter 7, §2701 has taken a very different approach to throttling business estate freezes. While the thrust of §2036(c) was to impose an *estate tax* at the transferor's later death, §2701 is directed at imposing a *gift tax*, at the time of the transfer. Thus, instead of including the date of death value of the business in the transferor's gross estate, it seeks to subject the date of gift value of the transfer to gift taxation.

The value of the gift, under the new law, will likely be considerably greater than zero. §2701 limits the value of retained interests that can be subtracted in arriving at that taxable gift value. Thus, in the ongoing example shown earlier, Alfred's retention of preferred stock would be valued at zero under the new law, partly because the dividends were specified to be noncumulative, i.e., the corporation did not have an ongoing obligation to pay Alfred previously unpaid dividends. On the other hand, in planning situations where the dividends are made cumulative, payable on a periodic basis, and determined at a fixed "market" rate, the present value of these dividends, considered a "qualified payment," can be subtracted from the total value of the business in determining the value of the gift of the common stock. However, the new law sets a minimum value in the transferred common equal to at least *ten percent* of the value of the entire business. Thus, the corporate recap will likely result in the reporting of a sizable taxable gift. And another transfer tax could arise later. In situations where the corporation fails to make one or more preferred dividend payments to the transferor within four years of the due date, the new law imposes an additional transfer tax, at death or sooner if the retained interest is transferred during lifetime, on the accumulated value of those unpaid dividends.

One final drawback to the recap is that a *decline* in business value can result in an *inflated*, rather than a frozen, client gross estate.

When may recaps work? Estate freezing recaps of the type created prior to §2036(c) may still work for some *family members*, such as nieces and nephews, and between unrelated parties, since §2701 does not apply to recaps benefitting such transferees. The definition of "applicable family members" includes only the transferor's spouse, descendants, descendants of the spouse and all spouses of the above.[12]

Estate freezing recaps that are subject to §2701 may be attractive for smaller businesses, particularly those recaps giving rise to a gift that can be entirely sheltered by the spouses's unified credits. Preferred stock resulting from such a recap need not pay a dividend, and the taxable gift could be reduced by giving the preferred stock a valuable feature, such as voting rights or preemptive subscription rights. Risks abound, however, and expert tax counsel is needed.

In lieu of a recap, which is clearly a complex transaction, the client might consider a simple outright gift of the business. Gifting is simple, and control can be retained by transferring nonvoting stock.

Finally, there are available other types of business freeze techniques not affected by the antifreeze rules because no form of lifetime gifting is involved. They are discussed briefly next.

Testamentary freeze. This involves a bequest of common stock to younger generation beneficiaries and preferred stock to the spouse.

Postmortem recapitalization freeze. A recapitalization after the client's death, in which the marital trust receives the preferred stock and the bypass trust receives the common stock.

Postmortem funding freeze. The marital trust receives assets not likely to appreciate and the bypass trust receives appreciating assets.

Generation-skipping freeze. The children receive, by gift or bequest, the preferred stock and the grandchildren receive the common stock.

Notwithstanding these possible opportunities, the current limitations and restrictions are numerous, and commentators have been guarded about the extent to which corporate recapitalizations will be used in the future.

Partnership Capital Freeze

It may be possible to reorganize an unincorporated firm to achieve the same results as the estate-freezing recap. Conceptually similar to the recap, under the partnership capital freeze, two classes of partnership interests are created, one for the client and one for the younger family members. The client's interest could similarly be frozen at its present value, with future appreciation in the business accruing to the other share.

As with the recap, the partnership capital freeze deals in a complex, rapidly changing area of tax law, subject to the provisions of §2701 and also to frequent IRS attack. Again, planning should be approached carefully, with the help of competent counsel.

VALUING THE BUSINESS

The subject of the *value* of a closely held business has arisen in several contexts in this chapter. How is business valuation determined? Often, as we have seen, correct valuation is necessary for tax purposes, and the IRS and the courts have written much on the subject. The following briefly outlines the major influences on business value by summarizing the eight general factors invariably requiring careful consideration. These items are taken from Revenue Ruling 59-60,[13] the IRS' classic exposition on valuation of the shares of closely held stock.

1. Nature and history of the business.
2. Economic outlook and conditions of the economy and industry.
3. Book value of the stock and financial condition of the company.
4. Company earning capacity.
5. Company dividend-paying capacity.
6. Extent of company goodwill and other intangibles.
7. Recent sales of the company's stock and the size of the block to be valued.
8. Market price of publicly traded stock in the same industry.

The extent of use of each factor depends upon the underlying facts concerning the specific business interest.

This chapter has presented an overview of the objectives and techniques of estate planning for closely held business interests. The next chapter will examine miscellaneous planning techniques not covered in earlier chapters.

QUESTIONS AND PROBLEMS

1. What could you say to client owning a closely held business who respects your advice but seems to be stubbornly refusing even to consider estate planning?

2. What unique estate planning problems are common to owners of closely held businesses?

3. Identify the objectives of estate planning for owners of closely held business interests.

4. One of your clients is worried about the possible future decline in the value of his firm upon his departure. Recommend ideas that can help minimize that decline.

5. (a) Describe the inter vivos methods of transferring business interests to a family member. (b) Under what conditions will such transfers be ill-advised?

6. (a) You are trying to encourage one of your clients to consider selling her business to a third party while she is still alive. Describe the benefits of this strategy. (b) Is planning for a sale after death always unwise? Why or why not?

7. Horne, a closely held business-owning client, requests your advice. He has a simple will, but has done no other planning. Neither his wife nor his children have any interest in continuing the business after his death.

Horne does not wish to retire. Recommend a significant planning strategy for his consideration.

8. Describe the alternative methods for payment that can be arranged when a business is sold.

9. When should planning for closely held business interests begin? Why?

10. (a) Describe the essential characteristics of the typical business buyout agreement. (b) What are its advantages?

11. What is the tax advantage of including a method for determining the selling price in a properly drafted business buy-out agreement?

12. (a) Describe the three methods by which a business buyout agreement can be funded. (b) Why might types of funding influence the choice of whether a cross-purchase or an entity plan is adopted?

13. Why might income taxation influence the choice of whether a cross-purchase or an entity plan is adopted?

14. McQueen is the surviving shareholder of the M-C Corporation. Forty years ago, he and Cross acquired the business, and just prior to Cross's death two years ago each had a $46,000 basis in their stock. McQueen purchased Cross's shares from the Cross estate for $180,000, pursuant to a buyout agreement. Presently, McQueen is thinking of selling the firm. Analyze the overall economic desirability of each of the following alternatives. Be sure to consider all of the objectives of planning for closely held business interests, including income taxation. Assume a combined marginal tax rate of 50% for ordinary income, 35% for capital gains, and 55% for estate tax.
    a. McQueen presently sells his shares for $600,000 cash.
    b. McQueen presently exchanges his shares for 6,000 shares of the publicly traded XYZ Corporation, which is currently trading at $100 per share.
    c. McQueen continues to own the shares until death, which is actuarially expected to occur in five years. The shares, worth

$600,000 at death, will be bequeathed to his wife, who we believe may be able to sell them for $400,000 cash.

d. McQueen continues to own the shares until death (date of death value is still $600,000), at which time the KR Corporation, a competitor of M-C, purchases the shares from McQueen's estate for $700,000 cash, pursuant to a buyout agreement, executed presently.

e. Can you recommend any alternative methods of disposition? (Hint: the M-C Corporation currently has an ESOP.)

ANSWERS TO THE QUESTIONS AND PROBLEMS

1. You could describe to your stubborn client the problems he and his family may face if he were to involuntarily withdraw from management tomorrow, either as a result of disability or death. Problems include inability to generate sufficient future income, incurring significant unnecessary loss in the value of the business, facing excessive transfer costs, and failing to provide sufficient liquidity to pay these costs. For more detail, see the material in the early part of the chapter.

2. Unique estate planning problems common to owners of closely held businesses:

   a. The business typically represents the single largest part of its owner's wealth, and generates the major source of his or her income.

   b. Too often, that value and income can only be sustained by the client's active involvement in management.

   c. Therefore, this values or income can be jeopardized by the client's withdrawal from the firm and the subsequent transfer of the business interest.

3. Objectives of estate planning for owners of closely held businesses:

    a. Income continuation
    b. Transfer of maximum business value
    c. Minimum transfer cost
    d. Adequate liquidity.

4. Common methods for minimizing the decline in value of the firm upon client departure:

    a. Delegate greater responsibility; provide incentives
    b. Use current business value to raise future income
    c. Negotiate a contract for present or future sale

5. a. Types of inter vivos business transfers to a family member:

        1. Completed gifts of business interests
        2. Gift, installment sale, sale-leaseback, private annuity

    b. The client may insist on retaining complete control over the business, making these transfers ill-advised.

6. a. Benefits of sale to a third party while client-owner is still alive:

        1. Eliminate potential friction between survivors and other owners and managers
        2. Survivors receive more liquid assets
        3. A higher selling price

    b. Planning for a post-death sale may not be unwise if a buyout agreement is executed, since it enhances the potential proceeds from the business transferable to the client's survivors.

7. Horne should consider negotiating a buyout agreement with co-owners, executives, or competitors, to avoid the prospect of his survivors having to run the business, at least for a brief period, and to avoid the post-death sale at a substantially reduced price.

8. Alternative methods for payment when a business is sold include:

   a. Sale for present cash, publicly or privately
   b. Sale for future cash, under an installment sale
   c. Sale for stock, under a tax-deferred exchange with a publicly traded firm

9. Planning should begin when the client is active and in good health, to incorporate the client's expertise into the plan, to take advantage of planning concepts available only to healthy clients, and to avoid a sudden, forced sale.

10. a. Under a typical business buyout agreement, each party is obligated to purchase the interest of each other party at that party's earlier disability or death.

    b. Advantages include:

       1. Liquidity
       2. A guaranteed market
       3. Greater certainty over the selling price

11. The tax advantage of including a method for determining the selling price in a buyout agreement is that the price will set the value of the business that is included in the decedent-owner's gross estate.

12. a. The business buyout agreement can be funded with life insurance, by an installment sale, or, under an entity agreement, with the firm's liquid assets.
    b. Funding with life insurance can rule out a cross purchase plan because of the numerous policies which must be acquired if the contract has three or more parties.

13. Income taxation can influence choice of the plan because the cross-purchase plan can generate a step-up in basis of the acquiring owner's stock.

14. It should be mentioned at the outset that either estate tax is not a major issue, or it is an issue but conclusions based on estate tax projections are quite

speculative.

a.   Immediate sale for $600,000 cash:

Advantages:

1. Immediate liquidity
2. Complete withdrawal can be psychologically beneficial.
3. Elimination of worry for survivors.
4. Sale now, when the firm is (perhaps) peaking in value.

Disadvantage: Income taxation on capital gain:

Gain = $600,000 - ($180,000 + $46,000) = $374,000
Tax = $374,000 * .35 = $130,900
Net Proceeds = $469,100

b.   Stock for stock: exchange:

Advantages:

1. Immediate liquidity
2. No income taxation, either now or at death

Disadvantage: Client's ownership is not diversified.

c.   Sale by surviving spouse for $400,000:

Advantage: Step-up in basis at death

Disadvantages:

1. Sells for $200,000 less than stepped-up basis. However, the after-tax loss could be somewhat less. Assuming the entire loss is immediately deductible, the after-tax loss would be $200,000 times (1 - .35) = $130,000. Conversely, the taxes saved = $200,000 x .35 = $70,000.

Net proceeds = $470,000.

However, without offsetting gains this loss may be deductible only up to $3,000 per year, until her death (after that: no deduction). The above calculations ignore this important time value of money consideration.

Assuming that Mrs. McQueen has a 20 year life expectancy, and that she will be deducting only $3,000 per year for life, the present value of that annual $3,000 deduction at an assumed 8% is $29,454. The present value of the tax savings from the deductions is therefore $29,454 x .28 = $8,247. Net result: net present value of the proceeds = $408,247 (= $400,000 + $8,247), which is a lot less than the $456,000 based on the assumption of immediate deduction of the entire loss.

2. Risk that business is not sold, or sold for less. Probably the worst alternative of all.

Note: Mrs. McQueen may wish to list the gross estate value of the business on McQueen's estate tax return at $600,000, not $400,000, so as to achieve a larger basis step-up, inasmuch as the estate tax will still be zero. Conversely, the IRS may argue for a $400,000 value. Mrs. McQueen could succeed if she could show that the business interest dropped $200,000 after McQueen died.

d. Sale to competitor at death for $700,000, pursuant to buyout agreement:

Advantages:

1. Step-up in basis at death.
2. $100,000 greater proceeds. There will be no tax, assuming that the estate tax value of the business is fixed at $700,000. In that case, there will be a step-up in basis to that $700,000. If the estate tax value is $600,000, there will be a $100,000 capital gain and $35,000 in tax, so that net proceeds are $665,000.
3. Liquidity.

Disadvantage: If buyout agreement is not revised regularly, risk that the contract price is below fair market value.

e. Immediate sale to the company's ESOP:

§1042 permits a tax deferred roll-over of the proceeds from sale of employer securities to an ESOP, provided the employer is a closely held corporation and the proceeds are reinvested in the securities of any other active incorporated business. And the securities could get a step-up in basis at the client's later death. Thus, unlike a merger, the ESOP arrangement can enable a client to diversify his or her investment portfolio without incurring an immediate (or future) tax on the gain realized. This factor makes it superior to alternative b, stock for stock exchange.

ENDNOTES

1. *Wall Street Journal*, May 7, 1990, p. B1.

2. §1361(d)(3).

3. §6662(a) and (g).

4. §264(a)(1).

5. §56(g)(4)(B).

6. §2703.

7. Reg. §25.2703-1(b)(3).

8. In *Commissioner vs. Procter* 142 F.2d 824 (4th Cir. 1944).

9. The transfer for value rule was described in Chapter 15.

10. §264(a)(1).

11. Revenue Act of 1987.

12. §2701(e)(1).

13. 1959-1 C.B. 237.

— 17

Miscellaneous Lifetime Planning

OVERVIEW

In the past seven chapters, we have covered six major estate planning topics: avoiding probate, wise use of the marital deduction, bypass planning, lifetime transfers, liquidity planning and planning for closely held business interests. This chapter will cover other miscellaneous aspects of lifetime planning. First, it will explore a number of more narrow topics, many of which are interrelated only because they influence the preparation of a client's will or trust instrument. Examples include provisions for the care of minor children, that select the executor and trustee, and that deal with survival clauses and the allocation of death taxes. Next, the chapter will examine estate planning for unmarried couples in nontraditional relationships. Then, a final but in no way less important section focuses on documents and strategies used in planning for the client's own incapacity, and includes a discussion of two types of durable powers of attorney, and the living will.

WILL AND TRUST PLANNING

By now the reader should agree that the will and the trust instrument are the major documents used in estate planning. Both have been referred to in every chapter so far, especially those in Part 3 outlining the techniques of planning. The material below describes several other types of planning frequently undertaken in drafting the will and the trust instrument. In reading this material, the reader is urged to refer back frequently to the will and trust documents illustrated in Exhibits 3-1, 3-2 and 3-3.

Planning for the Care of Family Members: An Introduction

The occurrence of both disability and death of the client can require the making of important decisions as to how to care for affected family members who are unable to care for themselves. Disability of the client may require the selection of others to care for the *client* and the client's property, and death of the surviving client-parent of a minor child will require selection of one or more persons to care for that orphaned *child*. In either case, prior planning can enable the selection process to reflect the wishes of the client, whose direct input can better ensure that the proper care will be provided. Planning for care of minor orphaned children will be discussed in the next section. Planning for the disabled client's care will be surveyed at the end of the chapter. We begin, however, with a discussion of factors common to both.

Planning for the care of both the orphaned child and the incapacitated client have three factors in common. First, by not making arrangements in advance, clients force their local *court* to assume greater responsibility in arranging for this care. Without help from the client, the court, in its attempt to act in the dependent's best interest, must rely on *secondhand information* obtained from other family members and from friends. To best ensure that the court's decisions reflect his or her wishes, the client should plan to express those wishes in writing now, before it is too late.

Second, for both minors and incapacitated adults, the law distinguishes two types of care: care of the person and care of the property. An individual legally responsible for care of the *person* is charged with providing everyday physical and psychological needs. An individual legally responsible for care of the *property* of a minor or incapacitated person is charged with safeguarding, investing, and expending that person's income and wealth.

Third, because care of the person and care of the property entail such dissimilar responsibilities, *different parties* will often be nominated and appointed to perform each task, as we shall see.

Planning for the Care of the Client's Minor Children

The material below explores the arrangements that can be undertaken to provide care for the client's minor children in the event that both parents die prematurely.

Planning for the orphaned minor's personal care: The parental guardian. In the typical household, the married parents of a child are the *natural* and *legal guardians* of their children. Thus, upon the death of one parent, the surviving parent will continue as sole guardian. Only in the most unusual situations will the courts deny this right. On the other hand, when a minor child survives the death of *both* parents, the state must select a successor guardian. The selection process typically culminates in an order by a judge of the probate court after a noticed hearing. The court will usually appoint the person nominated in the parent's will, unless the nominee is unwilling, unable, or unsuitable to perform. If the will contains no nomination, or if there is no will, the court must examine the family situation more carefully, relying on other information, including a list of willing friends and relatives, as well as the expressed preferences of the child, if sufficiently mature to have and express an opinion. Since the court's main criterion is the best interests of the child, it seeks to appoint that person who is best capable of providing the minor with such basics as food, clothing, shelter, medical care, and schooling, as well as providing psychological well-being, love, and attention.

Since the court's eventual selection of a guardian may not reflect the deceased parent's unexpressed wishes, and to avoid guardianship "warfare," the client-parent should clearly assert that preference by nominating a personal guardian in the will. Considering the stakes, it can be the most important estate planning action made by young parents.

The ideal parental guardian. Whom should the client nominate? An ideal parental guardian will possess the following qualities:

1. The *integrity, maturity, physical stamina*, and *experience* needed to be a parent.
2. A strong *concern* for the minor's welfare.
3. The ability to provide a *stable personal environment* conducive to raising a child in a manner consistent with the client's particular moral, religious, social, and financial situation.

Of course, these attributes are ideals; the usual client will have difficulty identifying more than one or two capable and willing nominees, none of whom might be ideal. But however imperfect, a nomination greatly reduces the risk of an undesired appointment. Nominating more than one parental guardian will allow for an alternate/successor guardian who will serve in the event that the preferred person named is unwilling or unable to serve or continue to serve.

Once the choice is made, the client should be encouraged to review periodically the nomination in light of both the minor's changing needs and the nominee's changing personal and financial situation.

Planning for the orphaned minor's financial care: Three fiduciary choices. Anticipating the possibility that their spouse will not survive them, clients will usually want to provide for adequate financial care for their orphaned minor children. They will ordinarily want to transfer all or most of their probate and nonprobate property for the benefit of the children. Common nonprobate sources of property for the children include life insurance proceeds, survivorship under joint tenancy arrangements, trust property, and gifts from others.

While most states allow a minor to receive outright a modest amount of property, larger amounts will be required to be turned over to a *fiduciary* who is legally responsible for their care and custody. What legally acceptable fiduciary arrangements are available? While the law recognizes parental guardianships as the only legal arrangement for the minor's *personal* care, it recognizes several arrangements for the minor's *financial* care. The client may choose a financial guardianship, a trust, or a custodianship under one or the other Uniform Acts. Each is surveyed briefly.

Financial guardianship. A financial guardian, also called an estate guardian, is typically appointed by the court in a manner similar to the procedures used for appointment of a parental guardian. Usually required to file a formal accounting with the court every one or two years, the financial guardian must obtain written permission from the court to undertake transactions that are out of the ordinary, such as the sale of real property. Reflecting the general trend in probate reform, some states have enacted streamlined guardianship proceedings to minimize court involvement.

In general, the *criteria* for selecting a financial guardian are radically different from those used in selecting a parental guardian. As we have mentioned, while the primary consideration in selecting the parental guardian is parental ability, the primary focus in selecting the financial guardian is *skill in financial management*. Since skill in financial management is also the primary criterion used to select a trustee, we shall defer further discussion of its attributes to the sections on selecting the executor and the trustee.

Trust for the minor. Instead of a financial guardian, a trustee can be chosen to manage the client's property left for the benefit of a minor child. The trust can be created and funded during the client's life. Or it can be created by the client's will and funded with probate and nonprobate property.

The trust has sizable advantages over the financial guardianship. First, it is a *private* arrangement, not usually subject to court supervision and control. While a guardianship requires filing of a bond, periodic accountings and court approval for asset transfers, a trust can avoid these costly and time consuming activities. However, some states require ongoing probate court supervision of testamentary trusts after the trustor's death. But the trend has been to eliminate this requirement.

Second, the trust offers great *flexibility*; the client can tailor it to his or her personal wishes. For example, while guardianship property usually must be surrendered outright to the minor upon reaching age 18, the age of majority, trust property can be retained in trust until the age specified by the client. Further, while a separate guardianship must usually be established for each minor, a single trust can have multiple beneficiaries, as in the case of the family pot trust, described later in the chapter. And the trustee can be given discretion to distribute different amounts of trust assets to different beneficiaries at different times. For example, the trustee can be given the power to distribute principal to an income beneficiary, or to accumulate income and add it to principal, or to "spray" or "sprinkle" income among the beneficiaries. Finally, the trust is more flexible because it can include a spendthrift provision, a protective clause to be described later. Financial guardianships are not established with such refinements.

A third advantage of the trust over the financial guardianship rests on the fact that the *statutory and case law* of trusts is much more well defined. Thus, a trustee will often feel less uncertain than a guardian about the potential adverse consequences of a particular fiduciary act or decision.

A financial guardianship usually arises by default when the client dies having done no planning. Because it is expensive and cumbersome, it is rarely preferred over a trust.

Custodianship under the Uniform Acts. Finally, the client may wish to leave property to a custodian for the benefit of a minor child under the Uniform Gifts to Minors Act or the Uniform Transfers to Minors Act in the manner described in Chapter 13. Like trusts, custodianships offer far greater privacy than financial guardianships, since they are not subject to court supervision. However, like guardianships, custodianships are quite inflexible because they are usually controlled by statute. For example, in most states property held by the custodian must be turned over to the minor upon reaching age 21. Also, most states limit the kinds of property that can be transferred under the Uniform Gifts to Minor's Act, which is the only one of the two acts that has been adopted in many states.

Selection of Executor and Executor's Powers

As we have said, the executor is responsible for representing and managing a decedent's probate estate. Specific tasks of this multifaceted job include marshaling and valuing the decedent's assets, filing tax returns, paying taxes and debts, distributing assets, and accounting for the entire process. It also involves dealing with grieving family members, distributing personal effects, and resolving family conflicts, all of which can be emotionally taxing. Finally, the executor must keep assets invested, or sell them to pay taxes, and, possibly manage or liquidate the decedent's business. While most of these jobs can be performed by the estate attorney's office, total estate expenses may be higher due to a larger attorney fee, and the executor is still primarily responsible to the court for completing these acts.

Selection. Whom should the client consider nominating for the job of executor? An ideal nominee will possess the following qualities:

1. *Longevity,* that is, the likelihood of being able to serve after the death of the client, perhaps many years hence.
2. *Skill in managing* legal and financial affairs.

3. *Familiarity* with the testator's estate and the testator's wishes.
4. Strong *integrity*, coupled with *loyalty* to the testator and the testator's family.
5. *Impartiality*, and absence of conflicts of interest.

An ideal financial guardian will also possess these qualities.

Let us use these criteria to evaluate the types of potential candidates who are normally available to serve.

Family member or a friend. Nominating a family member or a friend to be executor might reduce administration costs paid to people who are not beneficiaries. Family members and friends usually possess a strong degree of familiarity and loyalty. However, they often have only modest legal and financial skills, which may compel them to incur expenses by hiring professional advice. While they can normally delegate some of their work to the estate attorney, they cannot delegate their legal responsibility, since the executor cannot avoid personal liability for certain types of mistakes that might occur in administration. Nonetheless, in small estates most mistakes are not costly, and, in general, nominating as executor the spouse, an adult child, or a good friend makes sense. Naming the spouse is probably the most popular choice.

Corporate executor. The testator may prefer to select a corporate executor such as a bank trust department. Reasons include inability to find and select a responsible family member or friend, conflict among family members, or a complex estate. Banks usually do a technically satisfactory job in managing estate assets. However, because they are usually unfamiliar with the decedent's family, they cannot offer much of a personal touch in the administration process. For example, they may have difficulty deciding to whom should be given minor personal effects of which the decedent made no specific mention. Finally, many banks will not agree to be executor if the estate is too small, if they dislike certain provisions of the will, or if they are not also nominated trustee under the estate plan's trust arrangements.

Attorney. Should an attorney, such as the testator's attorney, be considered for nomination as executor? Probate attorneys will usually do a satisfactory job in managing assets during the probate period, because they commonly possess a substantial degree of expertise acquired over the years by doing the work delegated by their many executor-clients. Nomination of the testator's attorney, however, may increase the risk of a *will contest*. Dissatisfied with the will provisions, an aspiring beneficiary might allege that the nomination is further evidence that the testator was subject to "undue influence" by over persuasion and intimidation, and might petition that the will not be admitted to probate. But it would be well to keep in mind that successful will contests are rare.

In addition, nominating an attorney might not reduce administration costs, since many attorney-executors hire other attorneys to represent the estate. Finally, and perhaps most significant, acting as an executor can create potential *conflicts of interest* for the attorney in the areas of drafting, confidentiality, and the duty to deal impartially with beneficiaries. For example, an attorney who anticipates becoming a fiduciary may be tempted to insert in the client's will an unconventional, self-serving exculpation (hold harmless) clause for all simple negligence acts. In fact, these ethical issues may compel an attorney to refuse the nomination. Based on EC5-6 of the attorney's Code of Professional Responsibility:

> *A lawyer should not consciously influence a client to name him as executor, trustee or lawyer in any instrument. In those cases where a client wishes to name his lawyer as such, care should be taken by the lawyer to avoid even the appearance of impropriety.*

However, not all attorneys so refuse. In a 1992 survey of 463 experienced estate planning attorneys, only 14% indicated they "never" accept fiduciary appointments when asked, while 38% "seldom" accept, 24% "sometimes" accept, 20% "often" accept, and 4% "always" accept.

In general, caution should be exercised when considering the nomination of an attorney.

Other considerations. The testator should also nominate an *alternate* executor to serve in case the primary nominee is unwilling or unable to serve. Many clients nominate a bank as the alternate because they are confident that a corporate executor will always be available to serve. Regardless of the choice of executor, the testator should always consult with the nominees to get their consent, and should periodically review the choice in light of changing circumstances.

Executor's powers. What powers should be explicitly granted to an executor? Most simple wills either do not delineate the powers of the executor, or list just a few powers. The will in Exhibit 3-1 explicitly grants to the executor the powers to distribute principal and income; to sell, lease, mortgage, pledge, assign, invest, and reinvest estate property; and to operate a business.

When a will "is silent" regarding a specific proposed action of the executor, we look for authority first to the provisions of the state's estates and trusts or probate code *statutes*, which usually delineate many executor's powers. If nothing pertinent is found, the executor may feel obliged to request permission from the *court*. For example, in the absence of explicit permission in the will, executors in many states must seek formal written permission to be able to sell real property. Thus, specifying powers explicitly in the will can offer the executor greater *flexibility* by minimizing unnecessary delays in probate. And enumerating powers in the will can reveal more to the survivors about the testator's *wishes*, especially with regard to the degree of court supervision originally envisioned by the testator.

Allocation of Death Taxes

Which beneficiaries should bear the burden of death taxes? All of them, or only some? If only some, which ones? If all, should the taxes be shared equally or in proportion to the amount bequeathed? A number of important considerations in determining how to allocate death taxes are examined next.

No clause in will usually means apportionment. In the absence of a provision in the will, both federal and state law determine which beneficiaries will share the cost of death taxes.

Federal law. Federal law controls the burden on a few types of assets. The Internal Revenue Code provides that the pro rata share of estate tax on life insurance,[1] property subject to a general power of appointment,[2] QTIP property[3] (usually at the second death), and property included in the gross estate because of a retained interest[4] is payable out of those assets.

State law. Under state law, with regard to all assets owned by the decedent, the old common law rule provided that death taxes were paid from the residuary probate estate. However, most states have changed this rule by enacting a type of *equitable apportionment statute*, which spreads the tax burden more or less proportionately among all of the beneficiaries receiving the taxed assets. Thus, even recipients of nonprobate assets, such as property held by the decedent in joint ownership, would owe a portion of the tax. Of course, *charitable recipients* and most *spouses* would not ordinarily incur a tax burden, since their distributions are deducted before one arrives at the taxable estate.

Tax clause in will. The client can override these federal and state directives by expressly including a tax clause in the will.

Residuary tax clause. Some attorneys do this by routinely drafting wills containing a tax clause embracing the old common law rule: all taxes will be paid out of the residuary estate. Payment of taxes from the residue can speed up the probate process by making it unnecessary to obtain reimbursement from non-residuary and nonprobate beneficiaries. In addition, recipients of specific non-residuary bequests of illiquid assets are not forced to search for the required cash. And paying the taxes out of the residue may be especially helpful if the will specifically bequeaths certain assets over which the testator does not wish the *tax burden* to fall. For example, if the testator leaves only one relatively illiquid asset, such as a piano, to a particular beneficiary, should that person have to pay any transfer taxes attributable to it? Most clients would probably say no unless that beneficiary is known to have considerable wealth, or at least access to a reasonable amount of discretionary liquid assets.

Problems with the residuary tax clause. Yet there are at least three situations where a residuary tax clause will conflict with the testator's wishes. First, the testator may specifically bequeath an asset such as a closely held business that comprises a very *large portion* of the entire estate. If the tax clause allocates the entire tax burden to the residue, the effect may be to radically reduce the total of net after-tax residuary gifts, or wipe them out entirely.

> EXAMPLE 17 - 1. Livingston's estate consists of a closely held business currently worth $800,000 and other assets also worth $800,000. He has two children: A, who works in the business, and B, who does not. Livingston would like to leave the business to A and other property of the same value to B. The attorney drafts a will bequeathing the business to A and the residue to B, and includes a conventional "boiler plate" residuary tax clause. At Livingston's death, B's after-tax share will be reduced to about $400,000, or one-half of the amount passing to A.

Second, many clients view their *residuary legatees* as the primary "objects of their bounty;" such clients often want them to receive as much wealth as possible. An apportionment tax clause would more closely meet this objective.

A third consideration is the effect of the tax allocation upon a bypass plan that provides for determination of the amount of the *marital deduction by formula.* To minimize estate tax, such plans invariably incorporate an allocation clause placing the burden of the tax on the property that is subject to the estate tax. Which clause is chosen, of course, will then depend on whether the marital share comes from a specific bequest (residuary tax clause preferred), or from the residue (apportionment clause preferred).

Whatever the provisions of state law, the client would be well advised to consider including a desired tax clause in the will for greater certainty. Determining the best tax clause can be a difficult job, particularly when there are several beneficiaries. An undesired provision can mean unnecessary delay, or a pattern of property distribution radically different from that envisioned by the testator. Yet rarely will the courts override the provisions of a will or the applicable statute to prevent an undesired result. Consequently, the client should consider the alternatives carefully.

Lapse Problem and Survival Clauses

The phrase "If A survives me, I give her. . ." is a survival clause and is commonly included in wills and trusts instruments, partly to avoid the consequences of a lapse.

Effect of a lapse. A lapse occurs when a beneficiary named in a will fails to survive the testator. Each state's probate code contains sections which determine, in the absence of a provision in the will, to whom a lapsed testamentary bequest will pass. A very common type of *antilapse statute*, as it is called, provides that bequests to one of the testator's *predeceased blood relatives* will instead pass to that relative's *surviving issue*. The UPC limits the antilapse to predeceased to grandparents and descendants of grandparents.[5]

> EXAMPLE 17 - 2. Rudolph died. His will left his car to his *brother*, Randall, and the residue of his estate to his friend James. Randall had predeceased Rudolph. Due to the state's antilapse statute, the bequest of the car will pass to Randall's only son, Jeremy.

Antilapse statutes expressly apply only to wills, not living trust instruments or property held in joint tenancy. However, some courts have applied their antilapse statutes to living trust instruments by analogy. On the other hand, the interests of predeceased co-joint tenants are always cut off by their death; thus, the surviving co-tenants will share a greater percentage of the property.

If the state has *no antilapse statute*, or if the particular statute does not apply, perhaps because the lapsed bequest was to a beneficiary not related to the deceased, or in a UPC state to a remote relative, then a lapsed specific bequest will ordinarily pass to the *residuary beneficiary*.

> EXAMPLE 17 - 3. In Example 17-2, if the car was left to Rudolph's predeceased *friend* Josef instead of Randall, the car will pass to James, the residuary beneficiary, because the state's antilapse statute applies only to relatives.

These last two results are unfortunate if the testator actually wished, in the event the named beneficiary predeceased the testator, to leave the property to certain of the named beneficiary's survivors who are not blood relatives. An example might be a son- or daughter-in-law, such as the dearly loved ex-spouse of the testator's child who is raising the testator's grandchild.

> EXAMPLE 17 - 4. Grandpa, a widower, died recently, and in his will he left his entire estate to his son. Because the son predeceased Grandpa the property will pass to son's children, based on the state's antilapse statute. Nothing will pass directly to Mary, who is son's ex-spouse and will be raising the children alone. This result could easily have been avoided if Grandpa's will had explicitly named Mary to receive a portion of his property in the event that his son predeceased him.

If a *residuary gift lapses* in the absence of a specific antilapse statute provision, the property will pass by *intestate succession*.

> EXAMPLE 17 - 5. In Example 17-3, if James had also predeceased Rudolph, the residuary bequest will lapse, and the estate will pass in accordance with that state's intestacy laws.

Avoiding a lapse with a survival clause. A lapse can usually be avoided with a *survival clause* designating an alternate taker.

> EXAMPLE 17 - 6. Continuing the series of examples above, if Rudolph's will instead left the car to Isaac "in the event that Randall fails to survive me," and Isaac survives Rudolph, then Isaac, the alternate taker, will receive the car.

Survival period. A survival clause may require survival for some *period* beyond the testator's death. An example would be the phrase, "...if she survives me *by 30 days*..." Extending the survivorship requirement reduces the likelihood that bequeathed property will be subject to two successive probates in situations when the beneficiary dies shortly after the decedent.

> EXAMPLE 17- 7. In Example 17-2, if Randall survived Rudolph by only one month, the car will still pass to Randall and also be subject to administration in his estate. If, instead, Rudolph's will bequeathed the car to Randall "if he survives me by six months, otherwise to Isaac," then Isaac will receive the car, which will be subject to administration only in Rudolph's estate.

Estate tax and survival periods. Bypass planning also influences the decision whether or not to use a survival period. One rule of thumb used is to insert a survival period requirement in the wills or trusts of both spouses unless their estates are substantially unequal in amount. In that case use it only in the document of the less wealthy spouse. The basic rationale is twofold: first, to take advantage of both unified credits, where practical; second, to avoid unnecessarily loading up a wealthier S2's gross estate.

In a common accident, there may be an estate tax reason for providing that the *beneficiary* will always be presumed to have survived the testator. For example, to achieve *estate equalization* (see Chapter 11) in a common accident situation, disposition of property can be based on a stated assumption that the wealthier spouse (W) predeceased the less wealthy spouse (L). In that event, W's estate will receive a marital deduction, reducing the taxable estate, while L's gross estate will increase by the amount of the bequest. And to prevent property from passing to L's named beneficiaries, W's bequest can be structured to qualify as a QTIP transfer.

> EXAMPLE 17-8 While alive, both William, owner of $1 million in property, and his wife Mary, owner of $200,000 in property, executed simple wills leaving all their property to the other spouse, if he/she survived by four months, otherwise to the children of each of their prior marriages. Mary survived William by 36 days. Thus, all of William's $1 million estate, reduced by an estate tax of $153,000, passed outright to his children, and all of Mary's $200,000 estate (no estate tax) passed outright to her children. The entire estate tax could have been avoided had William's will been different in two ways: first, if there had been no required survival period; and second, if the will passed $600,000 to a credit shelter bypass trust and $400,000 to a QTIP trust, with his children as the remaindermen of both trusts.

Selecting length of survival period. How long should the survival period be?

Making it at least several months in duration will provide for the multiple death event which, relatively speaking, probably occurs most frequently: death of the decedent and the intended beneficiary in a common accident. However, specifying too long a survival period can delay distribution of estate assets since the executor will be required to wait that long to determine whether or not the named beneficiary in fact survived that period. Further, as mentioned in Chapter 6, a marital bequest will not qualify for the marital deduction if it is contingent on the spouse's surviving the decedent by any period greater than six months.

Many planners use a survival period of about one month for tangible personal property and between four and six months for other property. The shorter period for tangible personal property reflects the usual testator's desire to permit the surviving beneficiary to be able to use such property almost immediately, if even for only a short while, and to avoid storage and other additional costs.

Selection of Trustee and Trustee's Powers

Below we consider the factors involved in selecting a suitable trustee, and in determining which trustee powers to include in the trust instrument. It should become clear that the factors are quite similar to those mentioned earlier, in the section dealing with selection of executor.

Selection. We saw that a good executor (and financial guardian) is characterized by longevity, skill in managing, familiarity, integrity, loyalty and impartiality. In general, these traits also apply to selecting a trustee, except that in the case of a trustee, greater weight is accorded to skill in ongoing financial management. Since the trustee's job is often long term, the trustee's ability to manage and invest property over a long period becomes a major criterion. As in the case of the executor, potential nominees include family members, friends, the family attorney, and a corporate fiduciary.

Family member, friend. Selecting a family member or friend to be trustee can minimize costs, maximize administrative speed, and may ensure a personal relationship with the survivors.

Disadvantage of family member as trustee. But selecting a family member to be trustee can also result in mismanagement, since few family members have much experience in maintaining, investing, and accounting for an investment portfolio, all critical responsibilities of the trustee. Thus, family members may feel compelled to hire professionals for advice. In addition, family conflicts can arise. For example, nominating the client's children of a former marriage to be trustees of a QTIP trust can create a difficult situation for the client's second and surviving spouse.

Selecting a trust beneficiary to be trustee can also cause problems of proper distribution. For example, in one case, the trustee, who was also a remainder beneficiary, was ordered by the court to make additional distributions to the decedent-trustor's disabled son, under a trust which allowed such distributions.[6] In this situation a conflict of interest resulted in a breach of fiduciary obligation that nearly frustrated the deceased trustor's dispositive intent to provide care for his disabled son.

Finally, selecting as trustee a family member having general invasion powers may result in undesirable income, gift and estate tax consequences. First, under the grantor trust rules, the trustee will be taxed on the trust income.[7] Second, exercise of a general power by the trustee during the trustee's lifetime will constitute a taxable gift.[8] Third, the trust corpus will be includable in the trustee's gross estate at the trustee's death.[9] Tax problems can also arise for interested trustees having less sweeping powers.

Attorney . Selecting an attorney to be trustee can create the same minor risk of a will contest as in nominating an attorney to be executor. In addition, since management of the trust may be a long-term assignment, the client should determine whether the attorney has the time and expertise required to perform effectively. Finally, anticipating trusteeship, the attorney may be tempted to include unconventional *self-serving clauses* in the trust instrument and be subject to other conflicts of interest, similar to the problems described earlier in the selection of the attorney as executor.[10]

Corporate trustee. Selecting a corporate trustee, such as a bank trust department or a trust company, will increase the likelihood that an impartial satisfactory job will be performed. Most corporate trustees try to match the investment strategy for the trust assets to the needs of the beneficiaries, balancing both the income beneficiary's needs with the interests of the remaindermen. The trust instrument can give some guidance as to the settlor's view of appropriate asset allocation. Most trust departments try to build long term personal relationships with the beneficiaries.

Cotrustees. A common choice is the cotrusteeship of family member and corporate trustee. It can combine the advantages of each: personal knowledge of the family situation and competent asset management. And naming the surviving spouse to be a cotrustee can be psychologically uplifting to that spouse.

Ordinarily, cotrusteeships do not save management fees, since the corporate trustee will probably charge its customary fee. There may be some situations where corporate trustees will turn down cotrustee arrangements, particularly when they anticipate that the other trustee may be difficult to accommodate. When cotrustees disagree, they may have to seek a resolution in court, unless the trust instrument authorizes a less formal method, such as giving the corporate trustee the final say.

Nominating an alternate trustee. As in nominating an executor, the client should always nominate a successor trustee and should consult with the proposed trustees to ensure that the job will be accepted. Many bank trust departments set minimum asset amounts, which creates the possibility that they may refuse to manage small trusts. Minimum amounts can range between $100,000 and $500,000, depending upon the bank and the ease with which the portfolio's assets can be managed.

Trustee's powers: three common options. The client has at least three commonly used options in deciding what trustee powers to confer in a trust document.

No explicit powers. First, the client can specify no powers, relying entirely on implied powers, and on that state's statutory and case-law framework, which explicitly confers some powers to trustees. Many states have adopted the Uniform Trustees Powers Act, which codifies numerous trustee powers. This approach is often used for clients having relatively small estates and no assets requiring difficult administration, such as a closely held business.

Some explicit powers. The second approach is to rely on the state's laws in general but also explicitly grant in the trust instrument some other desirable powers not found in the statute, ones that may facilitate asset administration. This is the approach used in Exhibit 3-2, the living trust, and in Exhibit 3-3, the trust-will.

Many, many explicit powers. A third approach is not to rely at all on state law and instead draft a document that exhaustively includes all powers that the trustee should be permitted to have. The resulting independent tailor-made document eliminates certain risks, such as future legislative and judicial revision of the law, and the uncertain consequence of a change in the client's residence state. On the negative side, a custom-drafted form will be a more complex document, more difficult to read and perhaps more prone to internal inconsistency.

Timing Trust Distributions

Age. All estate planning trusts specify a time when the corpus will be distributed outright to the beneficiaries. Determining in advance the best time can be difficult for a client with minor children, because the client cannot accurately predict their rates of maturation. A client may prefer to delay distribution of corpus to a later age, such as age 30 or 40. Others prefer staggered ages. For example, the client may specify that one third be distributed at age 21, half the balance at age 25, and the remainder at age 30. Other clients may prefer to delay distribution to beneficiaries until age 50 or so, by which time the beneficiaries will have fully established their own lives. Other clients, seeking an alternative to mandatory distribution and trust termination when a beneficiary reaches a certain age, simply give the beneficiary a power of withdrawal over the property. Thus, their trustee would be empowered to continue to manage the property indefinitely if the beneficiary became unable or unwilling to make a withdrawal request.

Finally, a few clients may prefer to leave the bulk of their wealth to charity. They may fear the potentially devastating impact the anticipation of inherited wealth can have on financially immature children. For example, a study by the National Bureau of Economic Research found that a single person inheriting more than $150,000 is four times as likely to quit working than one getting less than $25,000. Children of wealthier families may be prone to a malady one commentator had called "affluenza," characterized by the following symptoms: lack of connection between work and reward, inadequate self discipline, distorted view of money, lack of motivation, guilt, and low self esteem. Finally, some clients may feel their children simply do not deserve any inheritance.[11]

Single versus multiple trusts. For clients with more than one child, a separate trust can be established for each child, or a single trust can include all children. How much each child will receive may depend upon how many trusts are created.

Multiple trusts. Creating multiple trusts, i.e., a *separate trust* for each child, adds flexibility but increases administration costs. In addition, separate trusts may be considered unfair to the younger children for the following reason. If the client lives, expenses in raising all children will ordinarily come from family property in general and not from separate shares reserved for each child. Thus, expenses to raise even the youngest child will come from what could be called the family "pot" of wealth. On the other hand, if the client dies leaving orphan minor children, and if a separate trust is immediately created for each child, the pot will likely be split before all expenses in raising the children have been incurred. Thus, each child's remaining expenses will be financed out of his or her own separate share, rather than from the pot. Consequently, the younger children will receive a relatively smaller final distribution upon reaching adulthood because living expenses over a longer period of time will have been charged only to their shares. A single trust can solve this problem.

Single pot trust. The name given by some attorneys to a type of single trust created for more than one child, one that retains the "pot" characteristic, is the pot trust or family pot trust. Under its usual terms, the trust remains undivided until the *youngest child reaches age 21*, the age at which parental obligations are commonly perceived to terminate. At that time, the assets are divided into *equal separate shares*, one for each child. The assets are distributed outright, or they are held for distribution at some older age.

The choice of the age at which the assets in a pot trust are divided into separate shares or separate trusts involves a *trade-off* between inequality and delay. The younger that age, the more *unequal* will be the total cumulative amounts distributed to the children, but the *sooner* will the older children be certain of the size of their shares. Conversely, the older the age at which the assets are divided into separate shares, the less the inequality, but the later the share amounts will be determined.

> EXAMPLE 17 - 8. Mrs. Hunsaker, a widow, is pondering the type of distribution clause for her trust. She has two children, Colleen, age 20, and Nancy, age 15. Colleen is a senior in college and is engaged to be married, and Nancy, still in high school, is headed for college. One alternative would split the trust into two equal shares immediately upon her death, with outright distribution to each child at age 21. Another alternative would delay dividing the assets into equal shares until Nancy reaches age 21, at which time both children would equal shares outright. If Mrs. Hunsaker dies just after the trust is executed, with the first alternative, Colleen will receive her distribution in less than one year and none of it will have been used to finance Nancy's living expenses. With the second alternative, Colleen will have to wait until age 26 to receive her distribution, and the entire corpus will have been available to meet Nancy's living expense, including most of her college education.

Delaying division of the trust assets probably better reflects the financial condition that would have resulted had the client not died: One pot of wealth would have been the source for both children's needs. For this reason, most attorneys recommend delaying the division. However, some attorneys recommend dividing the corpus of a pot trust into separate shares sooner, when the *oldest child reaches age 18*, rather than age 21, reasoning that parents would probably prefer that each child bear subsequent (perhaps very unequal) costs (e.g., college, graduate school) only out of his or her own share. This, of course, reflects a very different philosophy of family financial planning. The planner should determine which best suits the preferences of each client rather than using boiler plate changes.

Restrictions against Assignment

As mentioned in Chapter 3, the client may wish to include a *spendthrift clause*, insulating the trust from the claims of the beneficiaries' creditors and restricting beneficiaries from transferring their interests in trust income or principal prior to their receipt. Spendthrift clauses are legally recognized in the majority of American jurisdictions, even if the beneficiary is not a "spendthrift." And they can help a financially prudent beneficiary (e.g., a professional) by protecting trust assets from most creditors. However, such clauses are not foolproof. Although they may deny a creditor the right to demand that the *trustee* directly hand a distribution over to it, they do not prevent the creditor from exercising the usual legal remedies (i.e., action in court) against a beneficiary *after* the beneficiary receives a distribution. In addition, all states will enforce a promise made by the beneficiary prior to a distribution that the beneficiary will hand it over to the creditor once it is received. Thus, while a spendthrift clause can discourage excessive spending, it cannot completely prevent the beneficiary from "spending" trust property prior to receiving it, as long as there are potential creditors around who are willing to risk having to seek payment from the beneficiary.

Several states, including California, have recently enacted exceptions to the general rule that spendthrift trust assets are not subject to the claims of beneficiaries creditors. Common exceptions apply, including the following:

- revocable trusts, if the trustor is a beneficiary,
- cases involving spousal and child support judgments, and
- creditors that are government agencies.

In addition, California has established a procedure similar to wage garnishment for judgment creditors of up to 25% of amounts distributable in excess of support needs.

Spendthrift clauses work best in a discretionary trust, one in which the beneficiary has no legally enforceable right to income or principal.

Special Needs Trust. One interesting application of the spendthrift concept is a discretionary spendthrift trust used for the benefit of a *developmentally disabled child* after the parent's death. Called a *special needs trust*, it may not work in some states, where courts have ruled it in violation of public policy. It seeks to insulate trust assets from governmental claims, and, at the same time, keep the child eligible for public benefits, including Supplemental Security Income (SSI), Medicaid, and Social Security Disability Insurance (SSDI). The special needs trust provides for the health, safety and welfare of the beneficiary in ways not provided by any public agency, that no part of the corpus may be used to replace public benefits, and that in the event that the trust renders the beneficiary ineligible for public benefits, the trustee is authorized (but not required) to terminate the trust and distribute the corpus to a "precatory trustee," who is requested (but not required) to provide for the disabled person's basic living needs. The word *precatory* originated from the word 'pray.' Precatory language is used in a will or trust when the writer wants to recommend a course of action but not impose an enforceable obligation on anyone.

Foreign trust. Clients owning substantial liquid assets and wishing to more completely protect them from *their own creditors* may consider creating a foreign "protection of assets" trust. Certain jurisdictions including the Bahamas, Bermuda and the Cayman Islands offer great protection from pre- and post-judgment remedies of future creditors. Drawbacks include setup costs in excess of $25,000, considerable reporting requirements, and ethical issues. However, at its best, such a trust will trigger no additional taxes.

Trust Taxation: A Summary

Now that the text has covered the major types of trusts used in estate planning, it might help to summarize and compare the gift, estate and income taxation of these trusts. See Table 17-1. In interpreting the comments, keep in mind that some of these trusts come into being under the terms of other trusts, often not

Table 17-1 Summary of Trust Taxation

Trust Type	Taxable Gift?	In Gross Estate?	Income Taxed to Grantor?
Revocable Living Trust	No, not a completed gift	Yes, in grantor's gross estate, (§2038) but may qualify for marital or charitable ded.	Yes, it is a grantor's trust (§676)
Bypass Trust	No, starts @ grantor's death	S1: yes S2: generally not, but QTIP & superB can also be bypass trusts	No, taxed to the trust or to the beneficiaries
Marital Trusts (QTIP, GPA, & Estate Trust	Generally not created until grantor's death. Can create QTIP during life & obtain marital ded.	S1: QTIP, not if election is made, other two automatic marital ded. S2: QTIP - it depends, other two yes	No, but generally taxable to S2 (QTIP & GPA required, Estate Trust if distributed)
Minor's Trusts (§2053(c), MIT, or Crummey)	Only to extent not sheltered by annual exclusion	Not unless grantor retained control over enjoyment (§§2036 or 2038), over ann. exc. would be adj. tax gift	No, taxable to trust or beneficiaries (so long as not used for support)
Intentionally Defective Irrevocable Trust	Only to extent not sheltered by annual exclusion	No, but if originally a gift, then it may be an adjusted taxable gift	Yes, by design. Taxes paid also reduce grantor's taxable estate
Irrevocable Life Insurance Trust	Only to extent not sheltered by annual exclusion	No, but if originally a gift, then it may be an adjusted taxable gift	Generally not. Usually not funded with income producing assets
Grantor Retained Income Trust	Yes, remainder value if retained interest is qualified, otherwise, whole trust	Yes, if dies before term ends, otherwise no, but if originally a gift, then it may be an adjusted taxable gift	Yes, to the extent of income interest. Trust may also pay taxes
Charitable Remainder Trust	Remainder is a completed gift, but not taxable (§2055)	Yes, in the gross estate, but it qualifies for charitable deduction	Yes, to extent of income interest. Trust doesn't pay taxes

until the client's death. Thus, the nature of a trust may change over time. For example, the bypass and marital trusts usually come into effect at the client's death under the terms of the client's revocable living trust instrument (or trust-will). Thus, the comments for the living trust above apply to tax effects during the client-grantor's lifetime or at his or her death, while the comments for the bypass and marital trusts refer to tax effects at, or after, the grantor's death.

In interpreting the comments, keep in mind that some of these trusts come into being under the terms of other trusts, often not until the client's death. Thus, the nature of a trust may change over time. For example, the bypass and marital trusts usually come into effect at the client's death under the terms of the client's revocable living trust instrument (or trust-will). Thus, the comments for the living trust above apply to tax effects during the client-grantor's lifetime or at his or her death, while the comments for the bypass and marital trusts refer to tax effects at, or after, the grantor's death.

Perpetuities Savings Clause

Appendix 3A discusses the *rule against perpetuities*, which is a common law principle invalidating a trust dispositive clause if a contingent interest transferred might vest in a transferee beyond a life being plus 21 years. The reader is referred to that appendix for a discussion of ways in which the rule can be violated, as well as a description of savings clauses that can be used in wills and trusts to prevent the operation of the rule.

PLANNING FOR NONTRADITIONAL RELATIONSHIPS

Recently, planners have been asked for advice from more and more *unmarried* clients involved in nontraditional, long term relationships with members of the same or opposite sex. These relationships present some unique planning challenges and can lead to a set of surprisingly different planning strategies. Two characteristics not applicable to married clients explain most of the differences. First, being unmarried, the partners *will not be entitled* to the advantages offered by law to married couples. Second, since unmarried partners usually do not have children in common, they usually have *totally different sets of surviving kin.*

Thus, while they may have a strong desire to leave most or all property for the benefit of the partner *for life*, they will not want the partner to be able to control disposition of their property at or after the partner's death. Underlying strategies based on these characteristics are discussed next.

Greater Need to Avoid Intestacy

Unmarried partners are not included as heirs in intestate succession statutes, making written estate planning documents even more important. Intestacy will have the undesired effect of *disinheriting* the surviving partner, who is hardly ever a blood relative.

Less Shelter from Estate Tax May Dictate Larger Bypass

In theory, the largest combined estate size that unmarried partners can transfer to survivors, estate tax free, with a credit shelter bypass is $1,200,000, just as for married clients. However, *in fact*, the true maximum is usually less, to the extent that one of the partners owns less than $600,000. While the first $600,000 owned by a partner will be sheltered by the unified credit, any excess amount cannot be sheltered by the marital deduction. Thus, estate planning cannot "zero out" the estate tax for any first partner to die (P1) owning greater than $600,000. Since P1 will incur an estate tax whether the excess is left to the surviving partner (P2) or to the bypass, P1 may prefer to leave the *entire* estate to the bypass, in order to minimize P2's estate tax, and to ensure that the property will ultimately pass to P1's surviving kin.

As a partial solution, the partners may agree to arrange separate wills leaving everything to one another, and agreeing that at P2's death, property originating from P1 will pass to P1's surviving kin. But, short of executing a joint and mutual will, P1 has no way to prevent P2 from revising the instrument later on. So the surest plan requires use of bypass trusts to minimize P2's estate tax and to ensure that each will have selected his or her own remaindermen as the ultimate beneficiaries of their respective estates.

Greater Need for Life Insurance at First Death

Since P1 estates exceeding $600,000 will usually owe an estate tax, liquidity planning will often require life insurance on P1 as well as P2. The proceeds can still be kept out of both partner's gross estates with irrevocable life insurance trusts.

Lifetime Giving More Important

Inability to save as much estate tax on transfers at death may prompt unmarried partners to engage in greater gift planning. Although unmarried partners will not be able to utilize the gift tax marital deduction, they can still take advantage of one annual exclusion per donee per year. Thus, they can still undertake an ongoing program of lifetime giving to reduce their estate tax base. Careful planning should *avoid outright gifts* to the partner, however, to enable the donor, as a potential P1, to retain final dispositive control. Instead, the planner should encourage gifting *in trust*, with provisions granting a life estate in the income to the partner and the remainder to the trustor's surviving relatives. As future interests, however, the remainder interest portion of such gifts in trust will not qualify for the annual exclusion and will either use up the client's unified credit or result in a actual gift tax.

Joint Tenancies in Community Property States May Be More Attractive

Finally, in community property states, joint tenancies as a means of disposing of property of unmarried decedents may be more attractive, relative to the will and the trust. Only married couples can own community property. Lacking the income tax advantage of a full step-up in basis, a uniquely community property characteristic, unmarried couples, especially those with smaller estates, may choose joint tenancies as a simple form of co-ownership. From a tax basis point of view, joint tenancies will be no worse than any other form of ownership of property. Furthermore, if the first partner to die is the one who owned the property before it was transferred into joint tenancy, this form of ownership also provides a full step-up in basis since the entire value would be included in his or her estate. However, from a control point of view, joint tenancies may still not be desirable. It does not keep dispositive control in the hands of the original owner, whereas a trust would do so.

We turn next to the second major topic of the chapter: planning for the client's own incapacity.

PLANNING FOR THE CLIENT'S INCAPACITY

More and more, disability is preceding death as people live longer and longer. To cite just two examples of demographic data, consider a 1992 U.S. Census Bureau report that the number of Americans 65 and older grew by 22% in the 1980's, more than twice the growth rate for the nation as a whole. It also found that two thirds of Americans 75 and older consider themselves "healthy".

A client's disability creates the need for care by a surrogate decision maker. Since the client will usually have specific preferences regarding care, planning for incapacity while the client is physically and mentally fit increases the likelihood of more satisfying final years.

As in the case of minors, the law recognizes two types of care for incapacitated adults: care for the client's property and personal care for the client. The final two sections of this chapter deal with planning for each.

Planning for the Care of the Incapacitated Client's Property

Four techniques are available to care for the property of an incapacitated client: the guardianship or conservatorship, revocable living trust, durable power of attorney for property, and the special needs trust. Only the last two will be described in detail.

1. Guardianship or conservatorship of the client's property. Similar to the guardianship of the estate of a minor, all states recognize a court-supervised arrangement to manage the property of an incapacitated client. Called a *guardianship* or a *conservatorship*, depending on the state, establishment of either normally requires a court hearing, and the appointee is ordinarily subject to continuing court supervision. The guardian or conservator is required to give periodic accountings to the court, and is typically required to obtain court permission before engaging in most property transactions. Most guardians and conservators have little or no discretionary authority. However, some states are reducing court involvement in guardianships and conservatorships in much the same way they are reducing court involvement for probate proceedings.[12]

For reasons similar to those for avoiding probate, many clients will plan to avoid the necessity of having a property guardian or conservator. Some clients, however, may prefer the protection offered from their closer court supervision. Clients owning larger estates, or those who cannot recommend a friend or relative to manage property, might prefer a court-administered alternative. Most clients will prefer one or both of the arrangements described next.

2. Revocable living trust. In planning for incapacity, the client could create a self-trusteed revocable living trust, funding it with family assets. The trust instrument could provide for a successor trustee when the client became unable to manage the trust's financial affairs. The successor trustee could be the spouse, an adult child, another relative, a trusted friend, or a corporate trustee. In comparison with a guardianship or conservatorship, a living trust offers the advantages of privacy, flexibility, and freedom from court appearances and accountings. On the other hand, since the trust is a private, unsupervised arrangement, there exists a greater potential for *undiscovered fraud and mismanagement* by the successor trustee.

One additional disadvantage of the trust arrangement to handle incapacity is the possible requirement of a *formal legal determination* of the trustee-client's *incapacity* before a successor trustee can take over the job. Embarrassing litigation can develop between the trustor and a family member who is attempting to establish that the trustor is incompetent. However, this conflict can also arise if a guardianship or conservatorship is being established. The trust can contain a clause providing for a *private* determination of incapacity, in the same manner provided by the springing durable power of attorney for property, discussed next.

3. Durable power of attorney for property. Creation of a trust can be relatively expensive. Clients owning smaller estates may prefer to execute a simpler document, known as a durable power of attorney for property. Popularized by the Uniform Probate Code, the durable power of attorney for property has been recognized by the statutes of every state. The durable power of attorney for property is different from the durable power of attorney for health care, described in the next section. Since state laws vary, the reader is strongly urged to examine the law of his or her particular state.

A power of attorney is a written document executed by one person, called the *principal*, authorizing another person, called the *attorney-in-fact* or the *agent*, to perform designated acts on behalf of the principal. A durable power of attorney for property (DPOA) creates an agency relationship that allows the agent to perform acts to protect the principal's property interests, even if the principal becomes incapacitated.

Durable versus nondurable powers of attorney. General powers of attorney can be either durable or nondurable. Nondurable powers of attorney are not practical alternatives for caring for the property of elderly clients because they become legally invalid at the onset of the client's incapacity, just when they are needed most. In one situation, an attorney-in-fact under a nondurable power of attorney gifted property after the principal became mentally incompetent and the IRS ruled that the gift was voidable under local law (by a court-appointed guardian or by the principal had he regained mental capacity), and therefore the gift was included in the principal's gross estate under §2038.[13]

The *durable* power of attorney was developed to overcome this deficiency. Thus, a DPOA is durable because it survives the client's incapacity. Exhibit 17-1 illustrates the common provisions of a DPOA. The italicized sentence makes it "durable."

EXHIBIT 17-1 Durable Power of Attorney (for property)[14]

TO WHOM IT MAY CONCERN:

I, John Jones, a resident of Anytown, Anystate, in the county of Anycounty, do hereby constitute and appoint Aaron Agent, a resident of Anytown, Anystate, to be my attorney-in-fact, with full power to name and stead and on my behalf and with full power to substitute at any time or times for the purposes described below one or more attorneys and to revoke the appointment of my attorney so substituted and to do the following:

1. To manage my affairs; handle my investments; arrange for the investment, reinvestment, and disposition of funds; exercise all rights with respect to my investments; accept remittances of income and disburse the same, including authority to open bank accounts in my name and to endorse checks for deposit therein or in any bank where I may at any time have money on deposit and sign checks covering withdrawals therefrom.
2. To endorse and deliver certificates for transfer of bonds or other securities to be sold for my account and receive the proceeds from such sale.

EXHIBIT 17-1 Durable Power of Attorney (for property) *(continued)*

---

3. To sign, execute, acknowledge, and deliver on my behalf any deed of transfer or conveyance covering personal property or real estate wherever situated (including transfers or conveyances to any trust established by me), any discharge or release of mortgage held by me on real estate or any other instrument in writing.

4. To negotiate and execute leases of any property, real or personal, which I may own, for terms that may extend beyond the duration of this power and to provide for the proper care and maintenance of such property and pay expenses incurred in connection therewith.

5. To subdivide, partition, improve, alter, repair, adjust boundaries of, manage, maintain, and otherwise deal with any real estate held as trust property, including power to demolish any building in whole or in part and to erect buildings.

6. To enter into a lease or arrangement for exploration and removal of minerals or other natural resources or to enter into a pooling or unitization agreement.

7. To hold securities in bearer form or in the name of a nominee or nominees and to hold real estate in the name of a nominee or nominees.

8. To continue or participate in the operation of any business or other enterprise.

9. To borrow money from time to time in my name and to give notes or other obligations therefore, and to deposit as collateral, pledge as security for the payment thereof, or mortgage any or all my securities or other property of whatever nature.

10. To have access to any and all safe deposit boxes of which I am now or may become possessed, and to remove therefrom any securities, papers, or other articles.

11. To make all tax returns and pay all taxes required by law, including federal and state returns, and to file all claims for abatement, refund, or other papers relating thereto.

12. To demand, collect, sue for, receive, and receipt for any money, debts, or property of any kind, now or hereafter payable, due or deliverable to me; to pay or contest claims against me; to settle claims by compromise, arbitration, or otherwise; and to release claims.

13. To employ as investment counsel, custodians, brokers, accountants, appraisers, attorneys-at-law, or other agents such persons, firms, or organizations, including my said attorney and any firm of which my said attorney may be a member or employee, as deemed necessary or desirable, and to pay such persons, firms, or organizations such compensation as is deemed reasonable and to determine whether or not to act upon the advice of any such agent

---

EXHIBIT 17-1 Durable Power of Attorney (for property) *(continued)*

---

without liability for acting or failing to act thereon.

14. To expend and distribute income or principal of my estate for the support, education, care, or benefit of me and my dependents.
15. To make gifts to any one or more of my spouse and my descendants (if any) of whatever degree (including my said attorney who is a spouse or descendant of mine) in amounts not exceeding $10,000 annually with respect to any one of them and gifts to charity in amounts not exceeding 20% of my federal adjusted gross income in any one year.
16. To renounce and disclaim any interest otherwise passing to me by testate or intestate succession or by inter vivos transfer.
17. To exercise my rights to elect options and change beneficiaries under insurance and annuity policies and to surrender the policies for their cash value.

In general I give to my said attorney full power to act in the management and disposition of all my estate, affairs and property of every kind and wherever situate in such manner and with such authority as I myself might exercise if personally present.

This power of attorney shall be binding on me and my heirs, executors, and administrators and shall remain in force up to the time of the receipt of my attorney of a written revocation signed by me.

This power of attorney shall not be affected by my subsequent disability or incapacity.

IN WITNESS THEREOF, I have set forth signature on March 19, 1999.

_____
(Signature)

STATE OF ANYSTATE

COUNTY OF ANYCOUNTY

On _March 19, 1999_ , the above named _John Jones_ appeared and acknowledged the foregoing instrument to be his/her free act and deed.

_____
(Signature)
Notary Public

My commission expires: January 1, 2001

This particular example of a DPOA form can be criticized for being simply a *unilateral authorizing instrument*, which means that the named attorney-in-fact would not be liable for failure to act. Some commentators recommend instead creating a *bilateral contract* between principal and attorney-in-fact, particularly if the latter is not the client's spouse, to eliminate this problem. This may require a signature by the attorney in fact, and the payment of some compensation.

Non-springing versus springing DPOAs. There are two common types of DPOAs. The first type becomes effective as soon as it is executed. The second type, called a "springing" DPOA, becomes effective *at* the principal's incapacity. It will contain the following clause, in addition to those found in Exhibit 17-1:

> *In the event that I have been determined to be incapacitated to provide informed consent for medical treatment and surgical and diagnostic procedures, I wish to designate as my surrogate for health care decisions:[followed by the identification of the agent].*

Some attorneys recommend that a physician or a "trusted committee" of three of the client's trusted friends and relatives should be empowered to determine when the power of attorney becomes effective.

Springing powers are authorized by about two-fifths of the states.[15] Clients in states not authorizing springing powers have no choice but to execute a non-springing DPOA while they are competent and then hope that their attorney-in-fact does not improperly act on their behalf prior to their incapacity. Delaying delivery of the document may help.

To be valid, of course, any DPOA must be *executed* prior to the principal's incapacity. To ensure competent execution, many advisers recommend the preparation of a DPOA for an older client at the time the will is being prepared.

Advantages of the DPOA. The DPOA has several advantages over the other devices designed to manage an incapacitated client's property. Compared to a guardianship or conservatorship, the DPOA is less expensive to create and to administer. The non-springing type can avoid the necessity of a court-held incompetency proceeding, an event that can be painful and embarrassing to all parties, especially the client. Compared with the living trust, the DPOA is also less expensive to create and administer. Some clients who refuse to set up a trust may be willing to executing a DPOA, because of its relative simplicity. Yet a trust can continue after the client's death, whereas a DPOA, being based on agency law, must terminate when the principal dies. It may be durable but it is not that durable.

However, the trust and the DPOA need not be considered alternatives; greater flexibility may result if a DPOA authorizes the attorney-in-fact to add newly acquired property (by gift, inheritance, etc) to the clients partially funded living trust, or to fund an existing unfunded revocable living trust (a "standby trust") with the client's assets, at the onset of incapacity. Upon funding, the assets could be managed by a skilled trustee. Thereafter, the attorney-in-fact may be permitted to perform other duties that were not given to the trustee, including establishing and funding other trusts, making gifts and disclaimers, and appearing at tax audits.

Regarding the power of the attorney-in-fact to make gifts, one court has ruled that failure to explicitly include that power in the document will totally frustrate gift planning. In that case, the attorney-in-fact did make gifts before the principal's death. Relying on Virginia's narrow construction of powers of attorney law, the appellate court treated the gift as revocable at the time of the principal's death, resulting in inclusion of gifted assets in the gross estate under §2036(a) and §2038.[16] However, in a more recent Virginia case, the tax court allowed gifts by an attorney-in-fact because Virginia law authorizes attorneys-in-fact to make gifts "in accordance with the principal's personal history of making or joining in lifetime gifts."[17]

Drawbacks of the DPOA. The DPOA has at least two potential estate tax drawbacks for the attorney in-fact, either of which might subject the principal's property to inclusion in the *attorney-in-fact's* gross estate in the event the attorney-in fact dies first. First, the attorney-in-fact may be deemed to have a general power of appointment over the principal's property. Eliminating this danger may require either prohibiting entirely the ability of the attorney-in-fact to make gifts to him or herself, etc., or limiting such gifts to an ascertainable standard, or to the greater of $5,000 or 5% of the value of the property.

One non-tax drawback to the DPOA concerns its *acceptance*. Certain financial institutions may be unwilling to honor the DPOA if they cannot satisfy themselves that it is currently valid. The power, they reason, may already have been revoked by the principal or the principal may be dead. Due to their uncertainty about the validity of custom drafted DPOAs they may insist on the execution on their own form. The industry's increasing use of the DPOA should substantially lessen these concerns. The attorney can minimize acceptance problems with careful and specific custom-drafting of enumerated powers, and by having the client periodically re-execute the DPOA to prevent it from appearing outdated. Nevertheless, some institutions refuse to accept a DPOA, and some banks and the IRS will, but might require the use of their own forms.

Other helpful techniques to maximize acceptability include a provision in the document that empowers the attorney-in-fact to bring legal action against a recalcitrant third party and indemnifies the third party when it acts in reliance on the document and the agent's instructions. However, pursuing legal action can be expensive and time consuming. Finally, the clients themselves, while competent, can show the document to banks, insurance companies, health care providers, etc., to find out whether it will be accepted, and to stop dealing with those institutions that refuse. New York has recently adopted a statute making it unlawful to refuse to recognize the New York statutory form DPOA and indemnifying a bank when it does. California's statute permits the filing of an action to compel the honoring of a statutory durable power and specifies that a refusal is unreasonable if the sole reason for the refusal is that it's not on a form prescribed by the reluctant party.[18]

The second non-tax drawback of the DPOA is that it can be *misused*. Lawyers will attest to situations where attorneys-in-fact, particularly the children of clients, have used the property in a manner clearly contrary to clients' best interests. Although such behavior is actionable, it is rarely challenged. Because the DPOA delegates very fundamental property rights, the client should first think long and hard about the possible consequences.

4. Special needs trust and other asset "spend-down" planning. A different kind of living trust may be capable of preserving assets owned by clients anticipating possible long-term disability.

The medical profession has been tremendously successful in prolonging the life of the seriously ill, often at great economic cost. Such patients often need *custodial care* for help with feeding, bathing, dressing and transportation. Later, they may need *skilled nursing care* provided in a licensed facility, and costing $3,000 per month or more. Their condition may finally require a lengthy period of *hospitalization*, costing far more. Private and public insurance can help pay these costs, but often not entirely. Long-term care insurance has recently become available, but policies usually are expensive and contain significant restrictions and exclusions, so few people are willing to buy it. Federal Medicare insurance for patients over 65 will pay for up to 150 days of hospitalization, with sizable deductibles after the first 50 days. Medicare pays for little or no post-hospitalization nursing facility care. These limitations in private and public insurance raise the possibility that a client will totally deplete the wealth acquired over a lifetime, thereby preventing any significant amount going to the children.

To prevent this, some clients are turning to attorneys who specialize in *elder law*. Many recommend "spending down" assets through the use of gifts and trusts. This action seeks to accomplish two goals. First, it strives to insulate the client's assets from the claims of health care providers and government agencies. Second, it attempts to impoverish the client sufficiently to qualify for certain types of federal and state assistance, including Supplemental Security Income, In-Home Supportive Services, In-Home Medical Care Services, and perhaps most importantly, Medicaid. Each state, in exchange for matching federal Medicaid grants, imposes federally influenced limits on both 1) assets (roughly $3,000 for spouses living together, and $70,000 if one spouse is in a nursing home, not counting the residence), and 2) income (income limit depends upon the actual cost of medical and custodial care).

Three common spending-down strategies will be compared. First, the client may wish to make *outright gifts* of property to children. However, outright gifts have the major drawback covered in earlier chapters: the client loses total control over the property. Second, the client could purchase a single premium annuity. Although distributions from the annuity do count for purposes of the income test, the overall value of the annuity does not count under the assets test. Finally, and perhaps most effective, the client could make substantial gifts to an irrevocable *special needs trust*, also called a *discretionary support trust*. Under this trust, the client-trustor retains the following powers and interests:

- While competent, the power to act as trustee.
- While *not* competent, or while completely disabled and subject to catastrophic health care costs, the right to invade principal on the basis of health, education, maintenance or support.
- The power to appoint an unlimited amount of trust property to family members other than the trustor.
- The power to change beneficiaries so as to reallocate the estate among the children, if desired.

In addition, a group of other persons, including children, advisors, and siblings (the more the better) are given a power to authorize the trustee to revest any trust property in the trustor. Any one of these persons may individually exercise this power.

The special needs trust will be incomplete for both estate tax and income tax purposes, and its assets will not be counted for purposes of eligibility under Medicaid. The trustee may also own the long-term health care insurance policy, if any, to further exclude payments from the income test. If the residence is in this grantor trust, it will qualify for the §121 one-time exclusion of $125,000 of gain, and for the §1034 rollover. In addition, all trust assets will obtain a basis step-up at the trustor's death. Under Medicaid rules, the client would be ineligible for public assistance for up to thirty six months (sixty months, in the case of certain transfers, including those from revocable trusts) after the date of the transfers into trust.[19] In addition, states may recover property after the beneficiary's death from the probate estate as well as other former assets of the beneficiary, including those conveyed to a survivor, heir or assign through joint tenancy, tenancy in common, survivorship, life estate and living trusts. Property in the estate of the surviving spouse is exempt.

Although the law prohibits nursing homes from charging patients greater than the amount paid under government assistance, the client's trust assets can be used to improve care by acquiring for the patient services not funded by public assistance. These could include an extra private nurse, physiotherapists, additional medication, or a paid companion who reads to the patient or takes the patient on special outings. However, even with these extras, wealthier clients will probably not be interested in spending down or in establishing a special needs trust. Most will want a higher overall quality of care, and may not like being regarded as a "welfare case."

Impoverishing a client owning sizable assets so as to qualify for public assistance funds is a controversial subject and raises ethical issues. Some planners will not recommend it, because they see it as taking unfair advantage of an imperfect system designed for truly needy people, and also encouraging children to treat Medicaid as if it were "their personal inheritance insurance." Others find no moral dilemma, and consider it no different from tax planning, such as when providing for a credit shelter bypass trust to minimize estate tax. Perhaps all planners might agree that clients should be encouraged to understand, at a minimum, other basic protective planning steps well in advance by purchasing an effective long-term care insurance policy and by carefully saving for their future care.

Planning for the Personal Care of the Incapacitated Client

Similar to the procedure for selecting the guardian of a minor child, the procedure for selecting the person who will care for an incapacitated adult is usually undertaken in the county probate court after a noticed hearing. Some states call this fiduciary a *guardian* or *committee*, while others use the name *conservator*. States define guardian, conservator, and committee differently. In some states, such as California, a conservator is one appointed by the court to manages the personal care, and the property of, an adult unable to provide for personal needs and/or unable to manage financial resources, whereas a guardian is appointed to perform such services for a minor. In other states, such as New York, a conservator concerns itself primarily with an "impaired" person's property, while a committee cares for both the person and the property of an "incompetent" person. The UPC parallels the New York terminology and, in addition, permits a guardian to be appointed to oversee the person and the property of an "incapacitated" person. In any case, the court chooses the party only after careful, formal consideration.

Selecting a personal care provider. Whom should the client recommend to provide personal care in the event of his or her incapacity? Ordinarily, the client has few choices.

Spouse, family members. The spouse is usually the best first choice. Next come other family members, especially adult children. However, the children may lead busy lives and may not be capable nor willing to do all the work required. This problem will be even more likely to arise for a client in an advanced stage of incapacity, such as at the onset of incontinence. Prior to this degree of impairment, the client may simply need home delivery of meals, other housekeeping services, or adult day care, all of which are often commercially available. While these services are often not inexpensive, some programs are government subsidized. Services can be arranged for a fee by a "private geriatric care manager," who is often a social worker or nurse. Helpful sources of information include: County and local departments for the aging, for referrals on services for elders; the National Association of Area Agencies on Aging (800-677-1116), which has an "elder care locator"; the National Association of Professional Geriatric Care Managers (602-881-8808); the National Academy of Elder Law Attorneys (602-881-4005); and the Children of Aging Parents, offering a clearing house of information including contacts for supports groups for adult children.

Nursing home. Older clients would be well advised to visit residential health care facilities for the elderly. Such facilities vary widely in cost, extent of services offered, and the degree of incapacity permitted. At one end of the spectrum is the traditional nursing home, which offers complete care, but is quite expensive and in general has a reputation, at worst, for offering "a life sentence to mental and physical imprisonment," where patients lose nearly all of their independence in a dehumanizing environment.

Assisted living. Other less structured facilities offer a new and increasingly popular style of housing called assisted living for elderly people without serious medical problems. Private apartments are provided, as well as meals, laundry, housekeeping, social activities and transportation, and regular visits by nurses. Such facilities usually cost considerably less than nursing homes, and offer the greatest degree of independence possible.[20]

Life care facility. Finally, one other type of organization called a life care facility offers seniors the right to occupy, for life, an apartment in a large residential health-care facility, which also provides, on the premises, all meals and round-the-clock nursing, medical, and hospital services. And many of them now permit the client or the client's estate to sell the apartment later on. Clients selling their personal residence to acquire a life care facility can more than likely enjoy the one time $125,000 exclusion on gain on sale under § 121, but probably will not be able to roll over any excess gain under § 1034, if the acquired interest is simply one for life.

Some figures from the U.S. Census Bureau regarding the elderly living in commercial facilities like the three described above plus long-term care rooms in hospital wards, and soldiers', fraternal or religious homes for the aged, may be helpful. In 1990, 1.8 million people lived in commercial facilities, with women outnumbering men almost 3 to 1. Residents 85 and older constituted 42%, up from 34% in 1980. Overall, only 5.1% of the nation's elderly occupy these facilities, but the figure was 24.5% for those 85 and older. Only one in seven was married, and 61% were widowed. These figures suggest that a significant minority of elderly clients will reside in a commercial facility prior to death.

Delegation of health care decisions. Until recently, people have not had the ability to delegate the power to make *medical* decisions. Today, almost all states recognize an individual's ability either to delegate to some degree important medical decisions, or at least to state in writing what those decisions should be.

Cruzan case. The need to state medical choices clearly and in writing is dramatically illustrated by the 1990 U.S. Supreme Court decision, *Cruzan v. Missouri.*[21] A victim of an automobile accident seven years earlier, 32 year old Nancy Cruzan had remained in a persistent vegetative state, with functioning respiratory and circulatory systems, but little else. She was unable to swallow or recognize her relatives. After it became clear that there was no reasonable hope of any improvement in her condition, her family sought to let her die by withdrawing her feeding tube. The state of Missouri would not allow it, despite the fact that a year before the accident, Nancy had told a friend that "if sick or injured she would not wish to continue her life unless she could live at least halfway normally." On appeal, the U.S. Supreme Court affirmed, approving the Missouri requirement that the family would have to show "clear and convincing evidence" of Nancy's wishes to remove life sustaining equipment, something the jury determined that the Cruzans did not establish.

After the Supreme Court decision and just after the Cruzans requested a new hearing in the local court claiming new evidence that Nancy would not wish to live, the state attorney general withdrew as a party to the case, which meant that there was no longer anyone to oppose removal of Nancy's feeding tube. Nancy died at age 33 on December 26, 1990, twelve days after the tube was removed.

Based on the Supreme Court's ruling, it would appear that standards of proof such as Missouri's "clear and convincing evidence" may be difficult to meet without a written statement by the incapacitated person. Estate planning has two common written documents for this purpose: the durable power of attorney for health care and the living will.

Durable power of attorney for health care. Like the durable power of attorney for property (DPOA), the durable power of attorney for health care (DPOAHC) appoints a person as attorney-in-fact to make decisions on behalf of the principal. However, the documents are different in three important respects.

Types of decisions. First, of course, the DPOAHC concerns *medical*, not property decisions. Examples of medical decisions listed in this type of "advance directive" include the power to secure the placement in or removal from a medical facility, to withhold future medical treatment, to use or not use medication, to perform or not perform surgery, and the power to use or not use artificial life-sustaining methods, such as respiration, nourishment, and hydration. As one might expect, this last power is quite controversial, and some legal commentators have defended it ardently. Reflecting an increasingly popular dissatisfaction with the zealous use of artificial life-sustaining methods, some have argued that rapid advances in medical technology combined with the implicit premise of medicine to "do everything" for patients, violates patients' rights, condemning the very sick to an existence void of relationship in antiseptic hospital-like settings, an existence worse than death.

Delegating a surrogate with the power to terminate life support can be helpful in situations where the physician in charge refuses to act. One study has shown that physicians are reluctant to terminate life support in cases where the patient would take a relatively long time to die, where the life support became necessary because of medical errors, and in cases where the patient has been on life support for a relatively long period of time.[22]

Springing power. Second, the DPOAHC differs from the DPOA in that the DPOAHC is always a springing power, whereas the DPOA can be non-springing. Thus the DPOAHC becomes effective only upon the principal's incapacity, that is, upon his or her inability to make health care decisions. The DPOAHC does not apply just to situations where the principal is terminally ill but to all situations where the principal is unable to give "informed consent" with respect to a particular medical decision.

Separate documents. Third, while it is possible to include the legal content of a DPOAHC within a DPOA document they are usually drafted as separate documents. They involving very different situations, different evolving law, and possibly different attorneys-in-fact. In addition, many attorneys prefer to use a preprinted state medical association form for health care because of its widespread acceptance by the medical profession. In contrast, a custom drafted form can generate decision making delay as, for example, when a hospital requires its own lawyers to carefully evaluate it. Appendix 17A shows an example of a statutory form of DPOAHC, that is, a form produced in a statute from a state that also permits custom instruments.

Acceptance of the document. The DPOAHC is statutorily recognized in almost every state. State law varies in terms of both the scope of the authority of the attorney in fact to act on behalf of the client and the protection afforded to health care providers who act on those instructions. Some states such as California have statutes permitting health care providers to *assume* that a DPOAHC is valid in absence of knowledge to the contrary. Offering some support, the American Medical Association has ruled that it is appropriate for doctors to withdraw life-supporting, artificial feeding systems from hopelessly comatose patients.

Drawback. One drawback of the DPOAHC concerns the fact that it is so powerful. It can place reluctant family members in the difficult position of having to make critical life or death decisions, ones they may regrettably relive in their minds over and over, long after the crisis has ended. Nevertheless, the durable power of attorney for health care has become one of the most popular estate planning devices.

Living will. The DPOAHC has become widely accepted in the United States. Before then, most states only recognized some variation of the living will, which typically addresses just one of the two features of the DPOAHC: it details those health care interventions that the person does or does not wish to be subjected to in situations when he or she is no longer capable of making those decisions.

Appendix 17B illustrates one example of a living will. The reader will notice that this particular one, reflecting the modern trend of about eight states, enables the signer to name another person, called a "proxy," to "act on my behalf" regarding these wishes. Living wills are recognized in the statutes of most states. Many attorneys in states where living wills are not yet officially recognized, nevertheless urge their clients to execute them, with the expectation that the courts will accept them if and when tested.

Disadvantages of living will. When compared to the DPOAHC, living wills have at least five limitations. First, a living will does not appoint a surrogate decision maker, which restricts its flexibility considerably, especially in view of the rapid advances in medical technology. Second, living wills are typically very brief, covering only a few possible outcomes, mostly in the area of life-sustaining treatment. No living will, no matter how detailed, can spell out all of the possible treatment decisions that may be needed. Third, most living will statutes apply only to terminal patients, not those who are just incurably ill, such as a person in a persistent vegetative state, and many states require that death be "imminent." Fourth, the language of living wills is usually quite vague, failing to define important terms, leaving the physician and the family to disagree over proper care. Finally, a number of states' living will statutes provide that a physician is obligated to comply with the directives in a living will concerning withdrawal or withholding of life-sustaining procedures. In the event the physician chooses not to comply, he or she must transfer the patient to another physician.

With regard to the second and fourth limitations, more and more attorneys are drafting quite specific living wills (and DPOAHCs, for that matter). For example, the client may be asked to enter preferences in writing in a matrix-table depicting alternative medical scenarios and procedures. The *rows* of the matrix might list ten to fifteen medical *procedures*, such as invasive diagnostic tests; CPR; pain medication; artificial nutrition and hydration; mechanical breathing, and the like. The *columns* of the matrix might list alternative physical *scenarios*, such as coma or persistent vegetative state with no chance of regaining awareness; irreversible brain damage or disease; irreversible brain damage or disease combined with terminal illness; coma with small chance of recovery and greater chance of surviving with brain damage, etc. Then, for each cell in the matrix-table, the client would insert one of several letters signifying a desired action, such as U = uncertain; N = do not want procedure; T = yes, try procedure but have it stopped if no clear improvement is shown; and Y = yes try procedure for as long as possible. The danger in documenting this detail is that the client may thoughtlessly and hastily fill in the blanks on a written instrument that may wind up being the only hard evidence available, thereby ruling out the possibility of an alternative choice which may reflect the careful contemplation of the client's sincere loved ones.

Miscellaneous factors. In some states, planners recommend that clients execute both a living will and a DPOAHC, particularly in states where DPOAHCs are not written to include the main characteristic of the living will. Finally, in their attempt at coordination, more and more states are adopting integrated statutes that deal with both types of advance directive.[23]

Several states, including Virginia, recognize a variation on the living will called the *directive to physicians*, giving instructions with regard to the use of life-sustaining treatment. The directive to physicians has been largely rendered obsolete in most other states by the common acceptance of the DPOAHC.

Whatever documents are used, they should be updated periodically, for three reasons. First, state law may require it. Second, the client's wishes may have changed. And third, the planner should make sure the documents remain consistent with the rapidly changing law in this area.

This chapter has described miscellaneous lifetime estate planning techniques not covered earlier. Chapter 18 will examine tax planning techniques which can be employed on behalf of the client after the client's death.

QUESTIONS AND PROBLEMS

1. (*a*) Describe the attributes of an effective parental guardian, executor, and trustee. (*b*) Why are they different?

2. One of your clients asks you to describe the legal alternatives available to provide for her young son's financial care. Be sure to mention the advantages and disadvantages of each.

3. What factors will influence which beneficiaries a testator should choose to bear the burden of death taxes?

4. (*a*) What is a survival clause? (*b*) How does it overcome the consequences of lapse?

5. Cassie's will simply says, "I leave all my securities to John, and everything else to Mary." If John predeceases Cassie, analyze the possible recipients of the securities, using the alternative assumptions made in the text about the contents of the will and the influence of state law. Apply the law of your state, if possible.

6. Describe the family pot trust and the trade-off involved in determining the age of distribution to young adult beneficiaries.

7. Hancock and his wife died on January 1, 1978, the victims of an auto accident. They were survived by two children, Tiffany and Thomas, who had just turned age 19 and 17, respectively, on that very date. All of the Hancock's property, totaling $1 million, passed to a single pot trust, whose terms were identical to those found in the trust-will in Exhibit 3-3, except that instead of receiving their remainder distributions at age 21, each child received one-half of the principal at age 25 and the balance at age 30. Over the years, the trustee made, in addition to mandatory

distributions, the following discretionary principal distributions (all on January 1) for education expenses:

1979: $50,000 to Tiffany.
1981: $40,000 each to the children.
1983: $10,000 to Thomas.

a. If all assets (i.e., *principal*, consisting entirely of low dividend paying stock) in the trust appreciated exactly 10% per year and all (dividend) *income* was distributed annually to the children, how much did each child receive, as the final, mandatory distribution of *principal*, and when did they receive it? (Assume no trustee fees or other expenses. Hint: Calculate chronologically the two share amounts at beginning and end of each year. Ignore all dividend income.

b. Would Tiffany's final distribution have been more or less if the trust was instead divided into separate shares when the *oldest* child reached age 18 rather than 21? (General answer can be inferred without making specific recalculations).

8. You are the creditor of a deadbeat who is a beneficiary under a trust containing a spendthrift clause similar to the one in Exhibit 3-2. What ability, if any, do you have at getting at the trust assets?

9. Pat and Kris, lovers for many years, do not ever wish to get married. They have no children. Pat owns $700,000 and Kris owns $900,000 in property.

a. Assuming Kris dies today and Pat survives by 10 years, calculate the total estate tax incurred at both deaths under the following plans:

1. Simple wills, naming each other as contingent beneficiaries, leaving all property to the partner, if surviving.

2. A *credit shelter bypass* using a will or a living trust, with the remaining share outright to Pat.

3. A similar bypass, but in the amount of Kris' *total net property* after payment of the estate tax.

b. Would your answers to part a change if Pat survived Kris by less than 10 years? Why or why not?

   c. How well can each of the plans listed in part a achieve both partner's desire to leave their property to their own relatives after the surviving partner dies? If none will succeed, recommend an alternative solution.

   d. How much can lifetime gifting help reduce estate tax in part a? Is it consistent with the client's goals?

10. What legal alternatives does a client have in property planning for his or her own incapacity? Describe the advantages and disadvantages of each.

11. Your 86-year-old mentally competent client wishes to plan for her incapacity but refuses to immediately transfer her assets to anyone. Is planning impossible, or does this refusal merely create a particular problem?

12. Your friend says, "I just signed four estate planning documents at my estate planning attorney's office." Name and briefly describe the likely four.

13. An attorney jokingly tells a client: "Today you'll be signing two documents, one for wealth and one for health. One gives someone the power to steal from you, while the other gives someone the power to kill you." (a) What two documents is she talking about? (b) Is there any truth to her cynicism?

14. Explain several reasons why you might urge a client to consider additional estate planning after each of the following events?
a. marriage
b. birth or adoption of a child
c. divorce of client

d. remarriage

e. death, separation or divorce of any child

f. family estate amount becomes medium sized

g. retirement

h. death of spouse

i. death of a parent

j. changes in tax laws

k. a change in the value of the client's business

l. a change in the client's state of residency

15. In view of your answers to the question immediately above, what do you think of mail-order type estate plans, or other marketing approaches for plans that render it difficult to revise the plans periodically?

ANSWERS TO THE QUESTIONS AND PROBLEMS

1. a. Attributes of a good parental guardian, executor and trustee.

Parental Guardian:

1. Integrity, maturity, physical stamina and experience needed to be a permanent parent
2. Strong concern for the minor's welfare
3. A stable personal situation

Executor:

1. Longevity
2. Skill in managing legal and financial affairs
3. Familiarity with the testator's estate and wishes
4. Integrity and loyalty

Trustee: Same as those for executor, except greater weight on skill in financial management.

b. The attributes are different because of the differing responsibilities. Parental skills are most important for a personal guardian. On the other hand, property management skills are most important for an executor and trustee, with even greater significance for the trustee, because of the possible time span of the job.

2. Legal alternatives available for a minor's financial care include guardianship, trust, and custodianship.

a. Guardianship: Advantage: Substantial court supervision

Guardianship: Disadvantages:

1. Expensive
2. Inflexible
3. Public
4. Limited duration

b. Trust: Advantages:

1. Private
2. Flexible
3. Potentially less expensive

Trust: Disadvantage: Not court supervised

c. Custodianship: Advantages:

1. Inexpensive
2. Private

Custodianship: Disadvantages:

1. Inflexible
2. Not court supervised
3. Limited duration
4. Property limitations

3. Factors in deciding who should bear the burden of death taxes include:

   a. How liquid is the bequest?
   b. How wealthy is the beneficiary?
   c. How much access to liquid assets does the beneficiary have?
   d. Is a large specific bequest being made?

4. a. A survival clause requires that the named beneficiary survive the client-testator to take a bequest. If not, the bequest is made to an alternate taker.
   b. A survival clause overcomes the consequences of lapsation by allowing the client, rather than state law, determine who is to be the alternate taker.

5. If we assume that Cassie's residence state has an antilapse statute similar to the one in the text, and if we assume that John is Cassie's relative, then John's surviving issue will receive the securities. Alternatively, if no antilapse statute applies, or if John is not a relative, then Mary, as residuary beneficiary, will receive the securities.

6. The family pot trust is a single trust originally for the benefit of two or more beneficiaries, at least one of whom is a minor. Corpus is typically not divided into separate shares for the beneficiaries until the youngest reaches a certain age, such as 21. Selecting that age involves a tradeoff between inequality and delay. The older the predetermined age, the more equitable will be the distribution, but the longer the older beneficiaries may have to wait for that distribution.

7. a. Calculation of amount received by each child as the final, mandatory distribution of principal. Note that all dates are as of January 1:

   1978: The $1 million trust corpus grew to $1.1 million.
   1979: The $1.1 million was reduced by the $50,000 discretionary distribution to Tiffany, and the remaining $1,050,000 was able to grow to $1,155,000 by the end of the year.
   1980: The $1,155,000 corpus grew to $1,270,500.
   1981: The initial $1,270,500 was reduced by the two $40,000

discretionary distributions, leaving $1,190,500 to grow to $1,309,550 by the end of the year.

1982: Thomas turned age 21 on January 1, and the trust was divided into two equal shares of $654,775 (=$1,309,550 ÷ 2), one for each of the children. Each share grew to $720,252 at the end of the year.

1983: Thomas' share, $720,252, was reduced to $710,253 by the discretionary distribution of $10,000. This corpus grew to $781,278 at the end of the year. Tiffany's $720,253 share grew to $792,278 at the end of the year.

1984: Thomas' share, $781,278, grew to $859,406 at the end of the year. Tiffany, who turned age 25, received a mandatory distribution of $396,139, or half of the $792,278 corpus. The trust balance, $396,139 grew to $435,753 at the end of the year.

1985: Thomas' share, initially $859,406, grew to $945,346 at the end of the year. Tiffany's $435,753 grew to $479,328 by years's end.

1986: Thomas, who turned age 25, received a mandatory distribution of $472,673, or half of the $945,346 corpus. The trust balance, $472,673, grew to $519,940 at the end of the year. Tiffany's $479,328 grew to $527,261 at the end of the year.

1987 - 1988: Thomas' share, initially $519,940, grew to $629,128 by the end of 1988. Tiffany's $527,261 grew to $637,986 by the end of 1988.

1989: Thomas' share, $629,128, grew to $692,041 at the end of the year. Tiffany, who turned age 30, received her final mandatory distribution of $637,986.

1990: Thomas' share, $692,041, grew to $761,245 by year's end year.

1991: Thomas, who turned 30, received his final mandatory distribution of $761,245.

Final answers:

Tiffany received $637,986 on January 1, 1989. (Note: she also received $50,000 on 1/1/79, $40,000 on 1/1/8/, and $396, 139 on 1/1/84.)

Thomas received $761,245 on January 1, 1991. (Note: he also received $40,000 on 1/1/81, $10,000 on 1/1/83, and $472,673 on 1/1/86.)

b. If the trust had been divided into separate shares when the oldest child reached age 18, Tiffany's final distribution would have been less, in part because her $50,000 distribution in 1979 would have come entirely out of her share, rather than just from the "pot."

8. You will probably have to wait until the beneficiary actually receives the asset distributions before you can legally act to seize them, unless your state has a statutory exception permitting you to require the trustee to turn over trust assets directly to you, as would be the case in some states for revocable living trusts and divorce situations.

9. a. 1. Simple will: At Kris' death, estate tax of $114,000 on a $900,000 gross estate results in Pat receiving the difference, $786,000. Thus, Pat's gross estate will total $1,486,000, on which an estate tax of $356,980 will be paid. The difference, $1,129,020 will presumably pass to Pat's relatives. Total combined estate tax: $470,980.
   2. Credit shelter bypass: s in part 1, above, Kris' estate will incur an estate tax of $114,000. If $600,000 of the $786,000 remaining passes to the bypass, Pat will receive outright $186,000. Thus, Pat will have a gross estate of $886,000 and an estate tax of $108,540, which leaves $776,460 to pass to Pat's surviving relatives. Kris' relatives receive $600,000. Total combined estate tax: $220,540.
   3. Total bypass: Again, as in parts 1 and 2, Kris' estate tax will be $114,000. Thus the bypass share can be $786,000. Pat's gross estate will be just $700,000, producing an estate tax of $37,000, which leaves $663,000 to Pat's surviving relatives. Kris' relatives receive $786,000. Total combined estate tax: $151,000.

b. The answers to parts *a-1*, *a-2*, and *a-3* would change if Pat survived Kris by less than ten years because Pat's estate could take the *credit for tax on prior transfers* (PTC), based on the fact that some property bequeathed by Kris to Pat was previously taxed in Kris' estate. Thus, the relative estate tax disadvantage of not arranging a total bypass would be reduced.

c. *Simple will/joint tenancy*: If both Kris and Pat wish to ultimately leave their property outright to their own surviving relatives, simple wills and joint tenancy arrangements will only succeed in doing that for P2, that partner who *winds up surviving* the other. In contrast, P1's property will pass outright to P2, who will have total dispositive control over it.

A *credit shelter bypass plan* without a trust will be partially effective, but only with regard to the bypass share. The share passing outright to P2 might ultimately pass to P2's surviving relatives.

A *bypass of Kris' entire net estate* is the only way to totally accomplish this objective. Happily, it also minimizes estate tax. Thus, because of the unavailability of the marital deduction, the deferral versus equalization tradeoff described in Chapter 11 does not apply to unmarried couples, making equalization relatively more desirable.

Provisions of this bypass would ordinarily include a life estate for the surviving partner, and remainder to surviving relatives.

d. Due to the unavailability of the marital deduction and the natural desire by each partner to ultimately leave all assets to their own surviving relatives, large outright *lifetime* gifts to the other partner would not save much estate tax, and would not be consistent with their objectives. However, the partners could gift assets to an *irrevocable trust* giving the partner a life estate in the income and naming their own surviving relatives remaindermen. In such a plan, a living irrevocable trust would be the bypass vehicle.

10. Alternative in property planning for incapacity:

a. Guardianship & Conservatorship: Advantage: Substantial court supervision

Guardianship & Conservatorship: Disadvantages:

1. Expensive
2. Inflexible
3. Public

b. Trust: Advantages:

1. Private

2. Flexible
3. Potentially less expensive

Trust: Disadvantage: Not court supervised

c. Durable Power of Attorney for property: Advantages:

1. Private
2. Flexible
3. Potentially less expensive

DP: Disadvantage: Not court supervised

NOTE: The trust and the durable power of attorney for property need not be considered alternatives; they can both be used for a client.

11. Planning is still possible for an aging mentally competent client who refuses to immediately transfer assets to anyone. She may execute a *"springing" durable power of attorney*, one that takes effect at her incapacity. She could also create a *living trust*, naming herself as trustee, with a successor trustee appointed when a private determination of incapacity is made by several physicians. The point is that planning for incapacity can and should begin when the client is still mentally competent.

12. - *Living trust:* A trust taking effect during the lifetime of the trustor. Also called an inter vivos trust.
    - *Pour over will:* A will that distributes, at the testator's death, probate assets to a trust that had been created during the testator's lifetime.
    - *Durable power of attorney for property:* A durable power of attorney granting to the attorney-in-fact the power to make decisions concerning the property of the principal.
    - *Durable power of attorney for health care (DPOAHC):* A durable power of attorney granting to the attorney-in-fact the power to make medical decisions on behalf of the principal.

13. a. She is talking about the durable power of attorney for property and either

the durable power of attorney for health care or the living will.

b. There is some truth to her cynicism. In a few cases, attorneys have reported that attorneys in fact, usually children, have "misappropriated" the client's property, and others likely have ended the client's life somewhat prematurely, against what they knew to be the client's expressed wishes. Of course, these are exceptional cases, but clients should be calmly apprised of these possibilities, particularly when the attorney in fact is someone other than a loving spouse.

14. a. Marriage:

-to include new spouse in will/trust document
-to undertake marital deduction planning
-to change life insurance and pension beneficiary designations
-to acquire life and disability insurance

b. Birth of a child:

-to prevent omitted child intestacy problems
-to provide for parental guardianship and trustee property management at death of surviving spouse
-to acquire more life and disability insurance
-to execute durable powers of attorney

c. Divorce of client:

-to ensure that the document will be recognized (in some states, divorce revokes an entire will, not just those provisions pertaining to the spouse)
-to remove ex-spouse's name from any and all beneficiary, or trustee, or attorney-in-fact designations

d. Remarriage:

-to include new spouse in documents
-to undertake marital deduction (QTIP) planning
-to provide for all of client's children of all marriages

-to consider a premarital agreement

e. Death, separation or divorce of any child: to review all documents for names of all beneficiary, or trustee, or attorney-in-fact designations

f. Family estate becomes medium sized: to undertake gift and estate tax planning

g. Retirement:

-if moving to a different state, to write new will/trust documents that conform to laws of the new state
-to execute durable powers of attorney
-to drop life and disability insurance coverages
-to discuss nursing home plans with children

h. Death of spouse:

-to encourage client not to make any drastic changes (e.g. sell home) for several months
-to revise will/trust
-to undertake post-mortem tax planning
-to remove spouse's name from all beneficiary, or trustee, or attorney-in-fact designations

i. Death of parent:

-to revise will/trust, based on changed wealth due to bequests from parent
-to revise other documents, deleting parent's name from planning

j. Changes in tax laws:

-to revise all tax related documents, including wills, revocable trusts, durable powers, and property agreements.
-to consider gifting in light of changed tax laws

k. A change in the value of the client's business:

-to adopt a business buyout agreement
-to consider revising the overall estate plan, in view of potential change in estate tax

l. A change in the client's state of residency: to consider revising all documents and planning strategies, in the light of changed local law

15. The answer, in two words: not much. Successful estate planning should involve an ongoing process of plan revision to reflect changed circumstances, in connection with both the client and the laws.

17A: Durable Power of Attorney for Health Care*

17B: Advance Directive: Living Will and Health Care Proxy*

* Reprinted by permission of Choice in Dying (formerly Concern For Dying/Society for the Right to Die), 200 Varick St., New York, NY 10014. Telephone 1-800-989-9455

APPENDIX 17A

INSTRUCTIONS

FLORIDA DESIGNATION OF HEALTH CARE SURROGATE

PRINT YOUR NAME

Name: _____

        (Last)   *(First)*   *(Middle Initial)*

In the event that I have been determined to be incapacitated to provide informed consent for medical treatment and surgical and diagnostic procedures, I wish to designate as my surrogate for health care decisions:

PRINT THE NAME, HOME ADDRESS AND TELEPHONE NUMBER OF YOUR SURROGATE

Name: _____

Address: _____

_____ Zip Code: _____

Phone: _____

If my surrogate is unwilling or unable to perform his duties, I wish to designate as my alternate surrogate:

PRINT THE NAME, HOME ADDRESS AND TELEPHONE NUMBER OF YOUR ALTERNATE SURROGATE

Name: _____

Address: _____

_____ Zip Code: _____

Phone: _____

I fully understand that this designation will permit my designee to make health care decisions and to provide, withhold, or withdraw consent on my behalf; to apply for public benefits to defray the cost of health care; and to authorize my admission to or transfer from a health care facility.

APPENDIX 17A *(concluded)*

FLORIDA DESIGNATION OF HEALTH CARE SURROGATE — PAGE 2 OF 2

ADD PERSONAL INSTRUCTIONS (IF ANY)

Additional instructions (optional):

I further affirm that this designation is not being made as a condition of treatment or admission to a health care facility. I will notify and send a copy of this document to the following persons other than my surrogate, so they may know who my surrogate is:

PRINT THE NAMES AND ADDRESSES OF THOSE WHO YOU WANT TO KEEP COPIES OF THIS DOCUMENT

Name: _____

Address: _____

Name: _____

Address: _____

SIGN AND DATE THE DOCUMENT

Signed: _____

Date: _____

WITNESSING PROCEDURE

TWO WITNESSES MUST SIGN AND PRINT THEIR ADDRESSES

Witness 1:

    Signed: _____

    Address: _____

Witness 2:

    Signed: _____

    Address: _____

© 1995
CHOICE IN DYING, INC.

Courtesy of Choice In Dying
200 Varick Street, New York, NY 10014 1-800-989-WILL

9/95

APPENDIX 17B

FLORIDA LIVING WILL

INSTRUCTIONS	
PRINT THE DATE	Declaration made this _____ day of _____, 19_____.
PRINT YOUR NAME	I, _____, willfully and voluntarily make known my desire that my dying not be artificially prolonged under the circumstances set forth below, and I do hereby declare:
	If at any time I have a terminal condition and if my attending or treating physician and another consulting physician have determined that there is no medical probability of my recovery from such condition, I direct that life-prolonging procedures be withheld or withdrawn when the application of such procedures would serve only to prolong artificially the process of dying, and that I be permitted to die naturally with only the administration of medication or the performance of any medical procedure deemed necessary to provide me with comfort care or to alleviate pain.
	It is my intention that this declaration be honored by my family and physician as the final expression of my legal right to refuse medical or surgical treatment and to accept the consequences for such refusal.
	In the event that I have been determined to be unable to provide express and informed consent regarding the withholding, withdrawal, or continuation of life-prolonging procedures, I wish to designate, as my surrogate to carry out the provisions of this declaration:
PRINT THE NAME, HOME ADDRESS AND TELEPHONE NUMBER OF YOUR SURROGATE	Name: _____ Address: _____ _____ Zip Code: _____ Phone: _____

APPENDIX 17B *(concluded)*

FLORIDA LIVING WILL — PAGE 2 OF 2

PRINT NAME, HOME ADDRESS AND TELEPHONE NUMBER OF YOUR ALTERNATE SURROGATE

I wish to designate the following person as my alternate surrogate, to carry out the provisions of this declaration should my surrogate be unwilling or unable to act on my behalf:

Name: _____

Address: _____

_____ Zip Code: _____

Phone: _____

ADD PERSONAL INSTRUCTIONS (IF ANY)

Additional instructions (optional):

I understand the full impor... ...is declaration, and I am emotionally and mentally competent to make t... declaration.

SIGN THE DOCUMENT

Signed: _____

WITNESSING PROCEDURE

Witness 1:

    Signed: _____

    Address: _____

TWO WITNESSES MUST SIGN AND PRINT THEIR ADDRESSES

Witness 2:

    Signed: _____

    Address: _____

Courtesy of Choice In Dying
200 Varick Street, New York, NY 10014 1-800-989-WILL   9/95

ENDNOTES

1. §2206.

2. §2207.

3. §2207A.

4. §2207B.

5. UPC §2-603.

6. *Pollock v. Phillips* 41 S.E. 2d 242 (W. Va., 1991).

7. §678.

8. §2514.

9. §2041(a)(2).

10. In *Marsman v. Nasca* 573 N.E. 2d 1025 (Mass. App. 1991, the court exonerated an attorney-trustee's "abuse of discretion," where a clause in the trust exculpated the trustee from liability except for willful neglect or fraud; for a contrary holding see, *First Alabama Bank of Huntsville v. Spraquins* 515 S. 2d 962 (Ala. 1987).

11. "How much sharper than a serpent's tooth it is to have a thankless child." *King Lear*, Act 1, Scene V.

12. For example, see California Probate Code §2590-95.

13. R 8623004

14. This is a slightly modified version of the sample form contained in Charles M. Hamann. "Durable Powers of Attorney," *Trusts and Estates*, February 1983, pp. 30-31.

15. Including AK, CA, DL, ID, KN, MA, MI, MT, NE, NJ, NY, NC, OK, TN, UT, VT, VA, WA, WI. Three state specifically prohibit it (CT, IL, SC).

16. *Estate of Casey v. Commissioner*, 948 F2d. 895 (1991). Also see LR 9231003.

17. *J. Ridenour Estate* 46 TCM 1850 (1992).

18. CA Civil Code §2480.5.

19. The Omnibus Budget Reconciliation Act of 1993, besides increasing the period from thirty months, made several other restrictive changes, reflecting Congressional interest in discouraging spend down planning. (Amendments made to 42 USC §1396).

20. Wall Street Journal articles on December 3 and 4, 1992. Both on page A1.

21. 110 S.Ct. 2841 (1990)

22. *Lancet*, Sept. 11, 1993, p. 645.

— 18

Postmortem Tax Planning

OVERVIEW

The estate planning process does not end at the client's death. Assets must still be marshaled, preserved, and distributed by the decedent's representatives, a group that includes executors, trustees, accountants, attorneys, and survivors. In the transmission process, tax law often enables these aides to recommend and make choices. This chapter focuses on the tax elections available to them as parties dealing in the decedent's property. The technical detail in this chapter is testimony to the claim that estate administration after the client's death can involve complex tax issues requiring the expert advice of an estate planning attorney, not one conducting a general law practice.

The chapter will begin with an overview of the principles of postmortem tax compliance, better known as the preparation of tax returns. Next, it will survey those planning devices primarily designed to reduce income taxes, including estate expense elections, choice of tax year, and distribution-planning strategies. Finally, the chapter will present those planning devices primarily designed to save death taxes, including the alternate valuation date, the use of disclaimers, and the decision to make the QTIP election.

TAX RETURNS AFTER DEATH

Overview of Tax Compliance After Death

We already know that death of an individual may trigger estate and inheritance taxes. Transfer of a decedent's property is often not a transfer tax-free procedure. But can the work be done free of income tax? Will the death of an income-earning individual terminate the obligation to pay taxes on all income received thereafter? Of course, the answer to both questions is no, because income ordinarily subject to taxation will be received by survivors, estates, and trusts. If income ordinarily subject to taxation is being received, you can be sure that the Internal Revenue Code imposes a tax on that income to one or another recipient in the year received.

Since death can create or continue the obligation to pay transfer and income taxes, we must first study the nature of these tax obligations and their effects on the survivors. This section will introduce principles of postmortem federal tax *compliance*, that is, the completion of federal tax returns and the payment of federal taxes on income and on property in connection with the death of a decedent.

Several transfer tax and income tax returns will usually be filed after the client's death.

Transfer Taxes

With regard to transfer taxes, the decedent's representatives may be required to file a state estate or inheritance tax return, and a Form 706, federal estate tax return, which is due within nine months after date of death. As mentioned in Chapter 6, a federal estate tax return must be filed for decedents dying with a total gross estate plus adjusted taxable gifts equaling or exceeding $600,000, the amount of the exemption equivalent of the unified credit for the year of death. For example, the estate of a decedent who died this year having a gross estate of $555,000 and adjusted taxable gifts of $100,000 must file a return because their sum exceeds $600,000. Unfortunately, filing is required even though no estate tax will be due, as in the case where the entire estate is left to a surviving spouse.

One further point regarding the estate tax return: Since evidence of a step-up in basis is essentially derived from the information on Form 706, many tax practitioners will recommend filing this return for smaller estates in order to ensure that the death value of appreciated property will be recognized as its new basis. However, the IRS is not bound by such estate tax values in an income tax dispute.

Income Taxes

With regard to income taxes, the representatives may be required to file state returns, and the following two types of federal returns. First, the *decedent's final income tax return* will be reported on Form 1040, covering all income for the last tax year up to date of death. Second, if the decedent leaves a probate estate, one *estate fiduciary income tax return*, Form 1041, will be filed for each tax year of the estate's existence. The fiduciary return for the first year will report all income from the decedent's date of death to the end of the first tax year. When the estate is terminated, usually by final distribution, the last estate income tax return will be filed for a "short" year, from the beginning of the tax year to date of distribution. After estate termination, the beneficiaries will report income from distributed estate property on their own tax returns.

The following example summarizes these federal income tax rules and assumes that all taxpayers report taxes on a *calendar year* basis; that is, their tax year begins January 1 and ends December 31. Actually, an estate needn't use a calendar year. Planning with the use of a fiscal rather than calendar year will be discussed later in the chapter.

EXAMPLE 18 - 1. Farley, a widower, died on May 12, 1990. In his will, Farley left 100 shares of Xerox stock outright to his son Jordan and the residue of his estate in trust for the benefit of his granddaughter Sheila. The date of final estate distribution to Jordan and the trust was February 25, 1992. The following post-death tax returns were filed. All income earned by the decedent from January 1 through May 12, 1990, was reported by the executor on the decedent's final income tax return, Form 1040. All income earned by the estate between May 13 and December 31, 1990, was reported by the executor on the first estate income tax return, Form 1041. The executor filed a second Form 1041 return for all estate income for the entire year 1991 and a third for income earned during the period from January 1 to February 25, 1992. Jordan reported on his Form 1040 all income received on the stock after

February 25, 1992. Trust property income, or DNI, earned after that date will be reported by the trust, on Form 1041, and by Sheila on her Form 1040, to the extent the income is actually distributed to her.

All capital gains income on trust property will be reported by the trust except in the trust's last year, when these gains will be "carried out" and reported by the beneficiaries. All non-grantor trusts must use a calendar tax year.

A *joint return* may be filed for a decedent and the surviving spouse for the year of death, covering income of the decedent to date of death and income of the spouse for the entire year.[1] In the alternative, returns may be filed for each spouse separately. In most situations, filing jointly will save total taxes in the same way it does when both spouses are alive. The greater the difference between the two spousal incomes, the greater the tax usually saved by filing jointly. The surviving spouse will also be permitted to enjoy the lower rates applicable to joint returns for *two years after the decedent's death*, provided that he or she (*a*) has not remarried and (*b*) maintains a home for one or more dependent children.[2]

Next, we turn to postmortem income tax planning ideas.

PLANNING DEVICES PRIMARILY DESIGNED TO SAVE INCOME TAXES

Some postmortem planning strategies are primarily undertaken to reduce the income tax bite. They include various expense elections, selection of probate estate tax year, and distribution planning. Before examining these techniques, let us survey three tax principles on which most of them will be based.

First, greater income tax can be saved when taxable income can be spread among more taxpaying entities. Proper pre-death planning can result in the creation of *additional taxpaying entities* after the client's death. These tax entities can include the estate, several trusts (with at least one trust for each beneficiary), and the beneficiaries themselves. After death, proper timing of distributions among these entities can often save significant tax dollars, as we shall see.

A second tax principle on which postmortem income tax planning is based is the notion of the *conduit*. The conduit principle prevents double taxation of estate or trust income. It is derived from the concept of distributable net income, or DNI, which is roughly equal to the estate or trust's fiduciary accounting income, and which constitutes the maximum amount of income taxable to the beneficiaries, as well as the maximum amount deductible by the estate or trust. The amount taxable to an estate or trust roughly equals its total income, including capital gains and losses, reduced by the distribution deduction, which roughly equals the lesser of the amount distributed or its DNI. Thus, a trust or estate that distributes all of its income will be taxed only on its capital gains. Consequently, under the conduit principle, DNI earned by an estate or trust which is distributed to the beneficiaries in the year earned will be taxed to the beneficiaries and not to the estate or trust, which simply acts as a conduit for delivering income from the source to the beneficiaries. Conversely, any DNI retained by the estate or trust will not be offset by a distribution deduction, which will make that DNI taxable to it rather than to the beneficiaries. Further, all capital gains are taxed to the estate or trust, except in the last taxable year.

A third tax principle on which postmortem income tax planning is based is that in the year in which an estate or trust makes its final distribution, all income, including capital gains, will be *carried out* to and taxable to the beneficiaries. Thus in its *termination year,* a trust or estate will have no taxable income.

These tax principles represent only the briefest summary of the principles of income taxation of estates and trusts detailed in Chapter 8. The reader is strongly urged to review that more comprehensive section before continuing.

Expense Elections Available to the Executor

During administration, the executor is able to make several informal elections with regard to estate expenses. We will refer to the executor's ability to make elections because the executor is the person having that legal authority. Of course, most executors rely on their attorney or accountant to apprise them of the tax alternatives. These include the medical expense election, the administration expense and losses election, and the election to waive the executor's commission. They are covered next.

Medical expense election. Any of the decedent's unreimbursed medical expenses which are unpaid at death may be deducted either on the decedent's final income tax return or on the federal estate tax return, but not on both.[3]

The choice of where to deduct unpaid medical expenses will depend on which alternative will yield the greater tax saving. The size of the tax saving will be a function of the marginal tax rate which, in turn, will be influenced by the size of the estate tax base. However, smaller estates may be unable to benefit from a deduction on either return. If deducted on the *income tax return*, only the excess of the medical expense amount over 7.5% of adjusted gross income is deductible, and any remaining nondeductible amount may not be deducted on the estate tax return. With regard to the *estate tax return*, no estate tax may be due for smaller estates, even without the deduction, either because no estate tax return need be filed or because other deductions, including the marital deduction, may independently reduce the taxable estate to zero.

Administration expense and losses election. Expenses in administering the decedent's estate, including executor's commission, attorney's fees, and casualty losses, are deductible either on the federal estate tax return or on the estate income tax return, or partly on each.[4] However, double deductions are not allowed.

Again, the choice of where to deduct these items will usually turn on which return will produce the greater tax saving. And again, smaller estates may be unable to enjoy a deduction on either return. Casualty losses are deductible against income only to the extent that they exceed 10% of adjusted gross income. And there may be no estate tax to save in the case of a small estate, or any size estate for that matter, which will essentially pass to the surviving spouse. Larger estates not incorporating a 100% marital deduction often will be able to choose because they can save taxes on either return, but there may be situations, as in the next example, when the deduction can and should be divided between the two returns.

EXAMPLE 18 - 2. Let's assume that Maggie, owning a gross estate of $5 million, will die later this year leaving everything to her husband, Earl. Expenses in administering Maggie's estate are expected to total $700,000. If the estate's marginal income tax rate exceeds the marginal estate tax rate, greater taxes would be saved by deducting the entire amount on Form 1041. On the other hand, if the marginal estate tax rate is higher, a greater tax saving would result if only $100,000, not the entire amount, is deducted on Form 706 and the rest is deducted on Form 1041. To see why, consider the effect of the expense outlay on the amount of the maximum marital deduction. Since the actual amount passing to Earl will be only $4.3 million, this amount will constitute the maximum allowable marital deduction. If the executor deducts all of the administration expenses on the estate income tax return, the estate will wind up incurring an estate tax, despite the fact that Maggie left her entire estate to her spouse, since the taxable estate of $700,000 will exceed $600,000, the exemption equivalent of the unified credit. Alternatively, if the executor deducts at least $100,000 of these expenses on the estate tax return, the estate tax will be zero since the taxable estate will have been reduced to the amount of the exemption equivalent. Since no more than $100,000 is needed to do this, the other $600,000 can be deducted on the income tax return.

Thus, if an amount is deductible on another return, it would be imprudent to deduct it on any estate tax return that can already shelter all taxable estate property with the unified credit or some other shield.

Election to waive executor's commission. The executor's commission, as a deductible administration expense, will be taxable as income to the executor. However, the executor may elect to waive (i.e., refuse) that commission. Waiver of the commission may be worthwhile if the executor is residuary beneficiary of the estate and if his or her personal marginal income tax rate exceeds the marginal tax rate for both the estate estate tax and the estate income tax. If the executor is not residuary beneficiary of the estate, a waiver of the commission will mean a complete forfeit of that amount. Thus, the non-residuary executor will usually prefer to receive the commission, no matter the tax cost.

EXAMPLE 18 - 3. An estate has been left entirely to the decedent's *daughter*, who is the executor. The executor's commission will be $10,000. The estate's marginal estate tax rate is 41% and its marginal income tax rate is 28%. The daughter's marginal income tax rate is 31%. *Not waiving* the commission will lower the estate tax by $4,100 and raise daughter's income tax by $3,100, for a net tax saving of $1,000.

EXAMPLE 18 - 4. Facts similar to the last example, except that decedent left his entire estate to his *spouse*, who is executor. Due to the unlimited marital deduction, the effective marginal estate tax rate is 0%. Regarding income tax rates, assuming that spouse's effective marginal rate is 31%, and the estate's marginal rate is 28%, *waiving* the commission will raise estate income tax by $2,800 and lower spouse's income tax by $3,100, for a net tax saving of $300.

EXAMPLE 18 - 5. Facts similar to EXAMPLE 18 -4, except that the entire estate has been left outright *to the decedent's children* of a former marriage. Waiving the executor's commission would mean totally forfeiting the receipt of that amount. As executor, spouse, not wishing to forfeit all cash flow from the estate, elects *not to waive* the commission. Instead of nothing, spouse will receive $6,900, after tax, from the estate.

Selection of Estate Taxable Year

The executor of a probate estate has considerable flexibility in choosing its taxable, or tax, year. Although all income tax years except the first and the last must be 12 months long, the executor can choose the estate's tax year to end on the last day of any month. If it ends on December 31, the estate is said to be on a *calendar year* with the first tax year running from date of death to December 31. All other tax years will then run from January 1 to December 31, except for the year of final distribution of the estate assets, which will run for a "short year," from January 1 to date of distribution. Alternatively, if the estate's elected tax year ends on the last day of any month other than December, it is said to be on a *fiscal year*.

Whether an estate is on a calendar year or fiscal year, two basic income tax benefits are available to it. First, it can be made a separate taxpaying entity, capable of *splitting income* with the other tax entities involved in the estate distribution process. By lowering tax rates and by radically lowering bracket amounts for estates, tax reform since 1986 has reduced the tax saving benefit of splitting income.

Second, further tax saving can be realized in the first and last tax years of an estate's life, since both years are usually shorter than 12 months. The first tax year is shorter because date of death does not usually coincide with the last day of the tax year. The last tax year is shorter than 12 months because date of final distribution doesn't usually coincide with the last day of the tax year. A *short tax year* produces income tax savings because proportionately less income will ordinarily be taxed in those years, at proportionately lower rates.

In contrast to the tax benefits available to all estates, some benefits are available only to estates having a carefully selected fiscal year. In each of the next two examples, assume that the decedent died on March 10, 1991.

> EXAMPLE 18 - 6. The estate of a decedent is planning the distribution of income to its beneficiary, the surviving spouse. It elects a fiscal year ending January 31. If the estate distributes income earned on March 15, 1992, to the spouse during the month of January, 1993, the spouse may not have to report the income until April, 1994, more than two full years after the income was initially received by the estate. This assumes that no quarterly estimated tax payments will have to be filed by the spouse.

EXAMPLE 18 - 7. An estate, which has a lower marginal income tax rate than its beneficiaries, expects to receive an income of $30,000 every three months starting in June 1992, until estate termination on November 30, 1994. To spread the income out over as many tax years as possible, the estate elects to have its fiscal year close just before the expected date of final distribution. Thus, it chooses a fiscal year ending September 30. Estate taxable income (DNI) for each year will be the following: first year, $60,000; second year, $120,000; third year up to September 30, 1994, $120,000. Thus, for each of the first three tax years, the estate will be taxed on all of this accumulated income, and DNI carried out to beneficiaries will be zero. In the final year, the beneficiaries will receive the after-tax accumulation, tax free. In contrast, more total tax would be owed if the estate elected a fiscal year that effectively prevented it from being a taxpaying entity in the third year. For example, had the estate elected a fiscal year ending November 30, the pattern of estate taxable income would be as follows: first year, $60,000; second and last estate taxable year ending November 30, 1991, $120,000. DNI to the beneficiaries would be $120,000. The beneficiaries would receive tax free the after-tax accumulation on $180,000 of income, but the last year's $120,000 would constitute taxable DNI to them, not to the estate. In the last taxable year of an estate, DNI is totally carried out to the beneficiaries.

If the executor of an estate expects an unusually large income receipt shortly after the period of administration begins, he or she may wish to elect a year end which would give it a rather short first year, so that other taxable income received later will be taxed during the following year rather than lumped with the large receipt and taxed at a higher rate.

EXAMPLE 18 - 8. Decedent Malley was an accountant who died on May 19 owning, among other things, account receivables amounting to $50,000. The estate elects a fiscal year ending July 31 to include most of this income in the first tax year, while causing most other income to be taxed in the second and later years.

On the other hand, a relatively long first tax year would be desirable if a large deduction is expected within 6 to 12 months from date of death.

EXAMPLE 18 - 9. Combined with a large amount of early income, as in example 18 - 8, the estate expects to make a large distribution to the beneficiaries in April of the following year. The estate instead elects a fiscal year closing on April 30, so that the deduction can be used to reduce estate taxable income.

Distribution Planning

Although federal tax reform since 1986 reduced income tax rates substantially for all tax entities, an estate or trust may be able to save some income tax for its beneficiaries by properly planning the amount and timing of beneficiary distributions. Much of distribution planning hinges on the existence of differentials in marginal tax rates, and thus one of the planner's tasks is to compare the tax rates of the various entities and allocate taxable income to those in lower brackets. In this section, we will consider situations where the beneficiaries are, alternatively, in a higher bracket and in a lower bracket in comparison with the distributing estate or trust. This section will also examine the income tax advantage of prolonging the estate's life.

Estate or trust in lower bracket than beneficiaries. When the estate or trust is in a lower income tax bracket than its beneficiaries, consideration should be given to distribution arrangements that will generate a greater taxable income to itself and a correspondingly lesser taxable income to its beneficiaries.

Accumulation of income. The most common device used accumulates income by reducing and delaying distributions of DNI. In some cases, excess accumulations will be subject to the *throwback rules*, which, as mentioned in Chapter 8, seek to prevent a trustee from delaying a distribution to a beneficiary in years when the beneficiaries' tax rate is high, only to distribute the income in later years when the rate is expected to be lower. The throwback rules require excess distributions to a beneficiary in later years to be taxed to the beneficiary as if they had been received in the years in which the trust actually received and accumulated them. However, the throwback rules do not apply to estates nor to any trust accumulations made for a beneficiary when under the age of 21.

> EXAMPLE 18 - 10. Jonathan died earlier this year, leaving his entire estate to his wife, Kathleen. The estate has earned some income this year but elects *not to distribute* it to Kathleen until next year. This year Kathleen, who has earned considerable income herself, is also recipient of a large lump-sum pension distribution from Jonathan's employer. Therefore, she is in the 31% marginal tax bracket. The estate, on the other hand, is subject to a 15% marginal tax rate, partly because the executor has elected a fiscal year that will give the estate a very short first taxable year. The accumulated income will be distributed to Kathleen in later years when her tax rate is likely to be lower. The throwback rules will not apply.

Non-application of the throwback rules to estates can constitute a reason not to avoid probate. Without probate, there is no taxpaying estate capable of accumulating income in one year and making an accumulation distribution in another. Since the probate-avoiding revocable living trust is usually subject to the throwback rules, it cannot usually exploit this tax strategy. With the lower rates brought about by tax reform, however, the decision to elect probate cannot rest solely on income tax savings. And the probate fees might substantially wipe out any tax saving.

Realization of a gain. Another way to benefit from the estate or trust having a lower tax rate than the beneficiaries is through the realization of a gain. If an estate asset has appreciated after death and is expected to be quickly sold upon receipt by the designated beneficiary, the executor of a lower-bracket estate should give consideration to *selling the asset* prior to distribution so that the estate can recognize the gain. The after-tax proceeds can be distributed to the beneficiary tax free, assuming all DNI has already been distributed. However, to be taxed to the estate, the sale will have to be made before its last taxable year so that the gain is not automatically "carried out" to the beneficiary.

Despite having a lower marginal tax rate, the executor of an estate may wish to distribute rather than sell the asset if the beneficiary has a *realized loss* that is presently unusable for lack of any offsetting gains. The beneficiary, who could sell the asset, then would not have to carry over an unused loss to future years.

Estate or trust in higher marginal tax bracket than beneficiaries. In cases where an estate or trust is subject to a higher marginal income tax rate than one or more of its beneficiaries, the executor or trustee may prefer to *distribute income* to them in the year the income is received, so that it is taxed at the beneficiaries lower rate. In addition, when the estate or trust's tax year overlaps those of the beneficiaries, the executor or trustee can time the distribution so that it is made in one of two years in which the beneficiaries' tax rate is lower.

EXAMPLE 18 - 11. It is the month of November, and the beneficiary of an estate just lost his job as a law firm associate and expects to be unemployed for about six months. Instead of distributing $50,000 of income to him in late December, the executor distributes it early next January, during a year in which the beneficiary's taxable income is expected to be substantially lower. The estate has a fiscal year ending February 28, so the choice to distribute in either December or January has no effect on its own taxation; both months are in the same tax year, the year in which the income is received.

Tax planning of distributions from estates and trusts are subject to some other tax constraints, one of which is described next.

Unduly prolonging the estate life. By now, the reader is aware of several potential income tax advantages to having a probate estate. This will encourage some executors to delay closing their estates. Since termination of an estate by final distribution cuts off the tax benefits available to this separate taxpayer, tax planning would suggest undertaking this ploy by delaying the estate's date of final distribution. Unfortunately, the IRS has authority to treat an estate as *terminated* for tax purposes if it concludes that the estate's life had been "unduly" prolonged.[5]

How long can an estate usually be kept open without generating IRS disapproval? Some authorities believe that a reasonable life is about 3 to 4 years for an ordinary estate, and as long as 15 years for an estate which elects to defer payment of taxes under Section 6166. However, the income tax benefit from prolonging an estate's life has been significantly curtailed in recent years due to tax reform's compression of income tax rates.

PLANNING DEVICES PRIMARILY DESIGNED TO SAVE DEATH TAXES

We turn now to an examination of several postmortem tax planning strategies which have their greatest impact on death taxes. They include the alternate valuation date election, disclaimers, QTIP election, and several miscellaneous other techniques discussed briefly in Chapters 15 and 16.

Alternate Valuation Date Election

The size of the estate tax for an estate will, of course, often be a direct function of the value of its interests includable in the gross estate. An intelligent executor or estate adviser will try to keep valuation as low as possible. Often, conflicts with the IRS arise regarding the correct valuation of particular estate assets and deductions. While such conflicts make the entire subject of estate valuation seem quite subjective, there is one specific rule in this field that offers some objective certainty. The Code allows the executor the option to value estate assets and deductions as of either one of two different points in time.

Under Section 2032, the value of the assets included in the gross estate (and corresponding liabilities) may be determined as of date of death, *or* they may be determined as of the alternate valuation date (AVD), which is *six months after date of death.* This section was enacted after the Great Depression to limit the adverse tax and liquidity effects that radical changes in market values could have on an estate. For example, consider a hypothetical decedent who died in mid- to late 1929 owning a considerable amount of stock, which had to be included in the gross estate at high, pre-crash date-of-death values. Such an estate could have wound up owing, nine months after death, an estate tax that was considerably larger than its total current market value!

Under AVD rules, the executor may not pick and choose which assets to value at which of the two dates. If the election is made, *all* assets (and deductions) must be valued at the AVD. However, any assets sold or distributed after death and before the AVD must be valued as of that sale or distribution date.

Prior to 1984, the AVD election was permitted in situations where it *increased* the gross estate, thereby resulting in greater step-up in basis for assets owned at death. This strategy was attractive for estates completely sheltered by the unified credit and/or marital deduction. §2032(c) now permits the AVD election only if it reduces both the value of the gross estate and the estate tax (and GSTT, if any).

As implied above, if the AVD is elected, assets valued at that date will be so valued for purposes of step-up (or step-down) in income tax basis. Thus, with a smaller step-up (or greater step-down), a lower estate tax value will save estate tax but will risk a larger income tax in the future. Since the minimum marginal estate tax rate is 37% while the maximum marginal income tax rate on capital gains is 28%, the AVD election should lower net taxes by at least nine cents for every dollar of reduced valuation. In addition, if the inherited asset is not sold, the AVD advantage increases to at least 37 cents per dollar. Finally, even if the heir chooses to sell the asset, a time value of money savings will result to the extent that the income tax can be paid after the estate tax is due.

Based on a survey of experienced estate planning attorneys conducted by this author, the alternate valuation date is being elected in the estate tax returns of approximately 11% of decedents.

Disclaimer Planning

A disclaimer is an unqualified refusal to accept a gift. We have already studied disclaimers in two earlier chapters. First, in Chapter 7, covering the federal gift tax, we examined the transfer tax aspects of disclaimers, including the requirements for a valid disclaimer. Second, in Chapter 12, surveying marital deduction and bypass planning, we saw how a disclaimer provision could be included in a bypass arrangement to add postmortem flexibility to the client's estate plan. That discussion also mentioned several disadvantages of the use of disclaimers. The purpose of the present discussion is to add additional detail to disclaimer planning, in the context of general postmortem planning.

Because of the requirement that the disclaiming donor cannot have accepted any interest in the benefits, the client's survivors must be told as soon as possible not to accept the decedent's property or income if a disclaimer is anticipated. The following material describes three general situations where disclaimers can be effectively utilized. They include spousal disclaimers to reduce the marital deduction, disclaimers by a nonspouse to increase the size of the marital deduction, and disclaimers to correct defective or inefficient dispositive documents.

Spousal disclaimer to reduce the marital deduction. We have seen how a spousal disclaimer of a marital deduction bequest can add postmortem flexibility by enabling the surviving spouse to choose the amount of the marital bequest to disclaim to the bypass share, thereby self-determining the amount of estate tax to defer to the second death. That section was described as Option 4, "100% marital deduction with disclaimer into bypass," in which the surviving spouse was bequeathed the entire amount of the decedent spouse's estate, subject to S2's ability to disclaim all or part of it in the event that a bypass eventually became desirable.

The marital deduction disclaimer can be used for any size estate but is probably most needed for certain rapidly appreciating *smaller estates*. For example, a plan for an estate that is currently too small to justify the use of a bypass could include a disclaimer provision, available in the event that the estate grew large enough to warrant a bypass distribution.

On the other hand, the disclaimer can also work well in *larger estates* in which S1 has under-utilized the million dollar GSTT exemption. The surviving spouse, at S1's death, may be able to disclaim assets being received outright *into* a GSTT exempt credit shelter bypass trust or QTIP trust.

Factors that may help the surviving spouse decide whether and how much to disclaim include S2's needs and his or her income tax bracket. First, the greater S2's perceived *need* for S1's assets to live comfortably, the less S2 will probably be willing to disclaim. This, in turn, will depend on the size of S2's estate. Of course, by disclaiming, S2 would not ordinarily be relinquishing all interests in the property, since the typical recipient bypass or QTIP trust provides for some invasion powers and for most or all income to be paid to S2. However, many S2s are still likely to react emotionally that by disclaiming, they are in reality making a complete relinquishment.

Second, S2's willingness to disclaim will also depend on his or her marginal *income tax rate*, since the higher S2's rate, the more desirable will be a disclaimer if it has the effect of redirecting taxable income to other beneficiaries.

For a further discussion of the benefits and drawbacks of providing for a spousal disclaimer into a bypass, see Chapter 12.

Disclaimer by a nonspouse to increase the marital deduction. A disclaimer can be used to raise a marital deduction that is subsequently found to be inadequate. For example, a client may have died with an estate plan that neither included a bypass nor took full use of the unlimited marital deduction. This can occur when a person dies intestate or dies owning a considerable amount of property in *joint tenancy* with someone other than a spouse. The nonspouse beneficiary may be encouraged to disclaim the interest so that it may qualify for the marital deduction by passing to the surviving spouse. However, problems in implementation may arise. First, only a *donee* of property held in joint tenancy may disclaim.[6] Thus, such a disclaimer will work only if the decedent was the original donor of the property. Second, courts may be unwilling to allow the guardian of a minor child (or unborn child) to disclaim rights to property, reasoning that full relinquishment of property is not in the child's best interest. However, since a disclaimer cannot be made by a person until he or she reaches age 21, a disclaimer that is delayed until the disclaimant reaches majority might be effective.

Third, until recently, the IRS had been taking the position that the disclaimer had to be made within nine months of the date the joint tenancy was *created*, rather than the date of death. Then, after losing in the courts, the Service acquiesced with regard to joint tenancies where state law gives the joint tenant the right to sever the joint tenancy or cause the property to be partitioned.[7] Thus, disclaimers of joint interests may not be valid in some states. For example, a qualified disclaimer is not permitted in states such as Arkansas where *tenancy by the entirety property* cannot be partitioned by one spouse without the permission of the other.[8]

Disclaimers to correct defective and inefficient dispositive documents. Occasionally, wills and trusts are drafted erroneously. One always hopes that these mistakes will be discovered during the client's lifetime. If not, they can still often be corrected by disclaimer. For example, a disclaimer may also be used to refuse an undesirable bequest of a general power of appointment.

> EXAMPLE 18 - 12. Barbara died seven months ago leaving a will that provides for a bypass trust for the benefit of her husband, Jake. The will gives Jake the right to invade the trust for reasons of "health or happiness." Since courts have consistently held that the term *happiness* does not constitute an ascertainable standard, Jake will be deemed to be the holder of a general power of appointment over the entire trust corpus, which will be includable in Jake's gross estate at his later death. Jake may be able to prevent this unfortunate result by properly disclaiming his power over the corpus.

A disclaimer can also be used to overcome an inefficient disposition, thereby increasing the size of a charitable contribution.

> EXAMPLE 18 - 13. Sally, a widow, was 90 years old when she died six months ago. She left one surviving relative, her son Abbott, who is aged 73 and in failing health. Sally's will, paraphrased somewhat, reads, "All to Abbott, but if he does not survive me by 30 days, then all to the Girl Scouts of America." Abbott, who should be able to live for 30 days but is not likely to live more than six months, has no issue and would not mind leaving all of the property inherited from his mother to the Girl Scouts. To avoid taxation of the property in Sally's estate, Abbott could disclaim all interest in Sally's bequest. Consequently, the property would pass to the Girl Scouts without being subject to taxation in Sally's estate.

A disclaimer may be made with respect to an undivided *portion* of an interest, which the IRS defines as a fraction or percentage of each and every substantial interest owned by the disclaimant extending over the entire term of the disclaimant's interest.[9]

> EXAMPLE 18 - 14. Lynn survived her husband, who bequeathed her 100 shares of stock outright and a life estate in $10,000 annual income in trust property. Lynn

may disclaim fewer than 100 shares of the stock, and she may disclaim a life estate in less than $10,000 annually of the trust property. But she may not disclaim only a remainder interest in the stock, or only a term for years portion of her life estate, such as for the first five years of the income.

Two other common examples of disclaimers include one allowing a married couple to fully utilize their $2 million GSTT exemption, and a disclaimer by a wealthier child in favor of a sibling who is more in need.[10] These examples are merely illustrative of the many situations where postmortem disclaimers can be used to alter estate dispositions to obtain more desirable results. Disclaimers are generally considered to be an extremely powerful estate planning tool. It should be noted that since the stakes can be quite high in this technical area of the law, the client is encouraged to seek competent counsel prior to attempting to make a qualified disclaimer.

QTIP Election Planning

Overview. As mentioned in Chapter 6, property normally can qualify for the marital deduction only if it "passes" to the spouse. In other words, the spouse cannot ordinarily receive an interest that might terminate; the interest cannot be terminable. Over the years, however, the Code has carved out several exceptions to this rule. Up to 1982, the most commonly used marital trust designed to take advantage of an exception was the power of appointment trust, i.e., the one giving the spouse a life estate in the income and a general power of appointment over the corpus.[11] Since then, the QTIP trust, based on the QTIP election exception, effective in 1982, has become far more popular. It is found in §2056(b)(7) and provides that property subject to a terminable interest can qualify for the marital deduction if it meets the following two requirements for "qualified terminable interest property:"

1. The surviving spouse must be entitled to receive all income from the property for life, payable at least annually.
2. No person may have the power to appoint the property to anyone other than the surviving spouse.

Why might clients wish to bequeath only a terminable interest to their spouse? Why wouldn't clients always prefer to give marital deduction property to the spouse outright, or in trust with the spouse receiving a general power of appointment over the property? Why restrict the spouse's ability to control disposition of the property? There are several possible reasons, including the desire to protect the estate from the consequences of S2's immaturity or senility, and the goal of protecting assets from the surviving spouse's creditors. But perhaps the most common reason is a desire by S1 to absolutely *guarantee the ultimate disposition* to an intended remainder beneficiary. The typical S1 choosing a QTIP arrangement has children of a former marriage and wishes to provide for the surviving spouse's income needs during lifetime, yet still absolutely ensure that his or her own children will eventually receive the property after the surviving spouse's death. Only a QTIP-type arrangement will do all this and still qualify the property for the marital deduction.

Some planners also recommend the QTIP plan for clients still married to their first spouse to eliminate the risk that their surviving spouse might remarry and leave substantial property to the new spouse rather than the children. Others disagree, pointing out that most S2's either do not remarry or act prudently when they do.

From the above, it should be clear that a QTIP type of marital trust inherently conflicts with the goal of maximum *dispositive* flexibility through the use of surrogate decision makers. More specifically, this approach is in direct contrast with the less popular power of appointment trust, discussed in Chapter 12, that grants to S2 a general power of appointment over the trust property. A QTIP plan, on the other hand, usually allows no discretionary distributions by S2 to others, relying instead on the "dead hand" control and directives of the immutable S1 will or trust instrument. Commentators strongly recommend that the QTIP trusts of more trusting clients grant the surviving spouse a limited power of appointment to distribute, at death, principal to permissible appointees named in the instrument. This power will add additional flexibility, for example, by allowing a surrogate decision maker to take greater advantage of GSTT exemptions under changing circumstances. Thus, while the effect of federal legislation was once to foster dispositive flexibility by requiring, as a condition for qualifying for the marital deduction, that the surviving spouse be granted a general power of appointment, its effect now is to discourage it by allowing a marital deduction for property over which the surviving spouse may have little

POSTMORTEM TAX PLANNING / 831

or no control. However, in contrast to dispositive inflexibility, the QTIP plan can offer some additional *estate tax planning* flexibility by means of the actual QTIP election. This will be shown in the next three examples, presented shortly.

Making the Election. "QTIP'able" property need not be included in the S1 marital deduction; to include it, an election must be made at S1's death.

Uniqueness of QTIP election. In contrast with the decision as to who will ultimately *receive* the property outright, the final decision whether to make that election to *include* QTIP property in the S1 marital deduction will not be up to the S1-transferor. And in contrast with the spousal disclaimer, that decision will not be up to S2. Instead, *S1's executor* will be required to make the choice on the S1's estate tax return.

Deferral versus equalization revisited. If the election is made, the QTIP property can qualify for the S1 marital deduction, and S1's taxable estate and estate tax will be reduced. However, at S2's death, the S2 date-of-death value of the qualifying property *must* be taxed as though it were includable in S2's gross estate.[12] The estate of S2 will receive reimbursement from the QTIP trust for the tax incurred by it.[13]

Thus, in considering the QTIP election, the S1 executor must choose one of the following two tax consequences: (1) making the election will defer the estate tax by reducing the S1 taxable estate and increasing the S2 taxable estate; and, alternatively, (2) not making the election will accelerate the estate tax by producing a larger S1 taxable estate, but can result in a smaller S2 taxable estate, via bypass.[14] The choice whether or not to make the election essentially boils down to a tax issue: whether to *defer or to equalize spousal* estate tax. The reader is directed back to Chapter 12 for an extended discussion of the factors influencing this decision.

As you study and review the present section, you might keep in mind that the S1 executor's QTIP election has nothing to do with determining who will receive the property; the trust terms decide that and, except for the possibility of disclaimer by a beneficiary, it is no longer subject to change by anyone.

EXAMPLE 18 - 15. Kenneth died three months ago. He is survived by his ex-wife, his second wife (S2), and D, E, and F, three adult children of the first marriage. There are no children from the second marriage. At his death, Kenneth owned $2 million in property. S2 owns $1 million in property, and she intends to leave it to X and Y, the children of *her* first marriage. Kenneth's will creates two trusts, trust B and trust A. Trust B is a bypass trust and will receive an amount equal to the exemption equivalent of the unified credit. Trust A will receive the residue of Kenneth's estate. The trustees of both trusts are required to pay all income monthly to S2 for her life. At S2's death, the amount of each corpus will pass outright in equal shares to Kenneth's three children. S2 is given a power to invade the corpus of trust B, subject to an ascertainable standard. S2 is given no power over the corpus of trust A. The property in trust A, which includes the decedent's residence, meets the requirements for qualified terminable interest property. As executor of Kenneth's estate, S2 *decides to elect* to include the value of this property in the S1 marital deduction. By so electing, S2 has made it certain that this QTIP property will be included in her gross estate at her death. During his lifetime, Kenneth created a plan which both ensures that the children of his first marriage will eventually receive all of his property, and preserves the marital deduction for his estate, as S1. Trust A is called the QTIP trust.

EXAMPLE 18 - 16. Modifying the facts in the preceding example a bit, assume that S2, as executor of the S1 estate, *does not elect* to include the A trust property in the S1 marital deduction. The property will still pass to the children upon S2's death, but will neither be deductible from S1's gross estate nor be includable in S2's gross estate. By not electing, S2 has chosen not to defer the estate tax. *Both trusts*, not just the B trust, will *bypass* S2's estate. Both are called bypass trusts.

EXAMPLE 18 - 17. Again modifying the facts in Example 2056(b)(7)-1 a bit, assume that S2, as executor of Kenneth's estate, makes a QTIP election as to only five fourteenths, or $500,000 of the trust A property. A partial bypass of the A trust property will result.

Tax law permits *partial QTIP elections* with regard to fractional asset shares.

EXAMPLE 18 - 18. In all three examples above, Kenneth's three children, as named remainder beneficiaries, will be certain to receive the entire corpus of each trust at S2's death. Making or not making the QTIP election will not alter this result. However, it can influence the size of each remainder distribution to the extent that it influences the size of the total estate tax.

Disclaimers and QTIP elections can partially raise the marital deduction for an S2 in spite of the forced application of the pre-1982 marital deduction rules for certain wills and trusts executed before September 12, 1981.

Thus, as an alternative to the power of appointment marital trust described in Chapter 12, the QTIP election, while offering less dispositive flexibility to S2, does give S2 some greater flexibility in marital deduction and bypass planning, while enabling S1 to retain total dispositive control over the property.

QTIP Election Versus Disclaimer. The astute reader will observe that the disclaimer and the QTIP election are *both* strategies that can enable a surrogate decision maker to decide on behalf of the deceased client whether or not to defer the estate tax. One advantage of the QTIP alternative over the disclaimer is the ability to delay the decision an additional six months. While a disclaimer must usually be made within 9 months after date of death, a QTIP election is made on the federal estate tax return which, when including an automatically granted 6-month extension to file, will be due 15 months after date of death. An advantage of the disclaimer over the QTIP election is that under the QTIP election, the spouse's right to income cannot be made contingent upon the election being made.[15]

Perhaps the most fundamental difference between the disclaimer and the QTIP arrangement concerns the amount of control S2 is given over the assets involved. Often, it is the single deciding factor in making the choice. Thus, if the client wishes the spouse to have complete control, an outright transfer anticipating the possibility of a disclaimer will be preferred. If, on the other hand, minimal S2 control is desired, a transfer to a QTIP trust will be the better choice.

Other Postmortem Death Tax-Saving Devices

Three other postmortem tax elections often available to the estates of business owners include the §6166 election to pay the estate tax in installments, the §303 redemption of stock, and the §2032A special use valuation election. These elections were covered in some detail in Chapter 15 and will not be discussed further here.

This chapter has focused on postmortem planning techniques designed to reduce income and death taxes. They have been the subject of this last chapter because they represent, conceptually, the final phase of planning undertaken on behalf of a client.

QUESTIONS AND PROBLEMS

1. List the federal tax returns that may have to be filed during a period of administration of a decedent's property.

2. Maxie, a widower, died recently, leaving his $2 million gross estate to his brother Morey. Maxie spent the last six months in a hospital, paying $50,000 of the $80,000 hospital bill before he died. Marginal tax rates for the taxpaying entities are as follows: Maxie's final Form 1040, 31%; the Form 1041, 28%; the Form 706, 41%. How much in tax will Maxie's estate save if the allowable expense is deducted, alternatively, on
   a. The Form 706?
   b. The final Form 1040?
   c. The estate's Form 1041?
   On which return should the deduction be made?

3. Moose died recently, leaving his entire $2 million gross estate to his wife, Trixie, who is named executor. Assume that the only estate expense is the executor's commission of $100,000. Marginal tax rates for the taxpaying entities are: Trixie's Form 1040, 31%; the final Form 1040, 15%; the Form 1041, 28%; the Form 706, 41%.

   a. Should Trixie accept or waive the commission? Why?
   b. Where, if at all, should the estate deduct the commission? Why?
   c. Would your answers to parts "a" and "b" change if Moose owned a $200,000 estate, and Trixie's Form 1040 marginal rate was 28%?
   d. Would your answers to parts "a" and "b" probably change if Trixie, the executor, was Moose's cousin to whom Moose left nothing by will or otherwise? Assume a $2 million gross estate.

4. Describe the income tax advantages available to all estates and those advantages available only to estates having a carefully chosen fiscal year.

5. How can the executor of an estate or the trustee of a trust reduce income taxes by planning the distributions to beneficiaries if the beneficiaries marginal tax rates are:
   a. Higher than that of the estate or trust?
   b. Lower than that of the estate or trust?

6. What is the benefit of prolonging an estate's life, and what is the tax consequence if it is "unduly" prolonged?

7. Explain. What two conditions must be met before an estate can make the alternate valuation date election? What is the tax advantage? When are assets valued?

8. Give two specific examples where a disclaimer can reduce the estate tax.

9. (a) Can "qualified terminable interest property" wind up not being part of the S1 marital deduction? (b) If yes, should the QTIP arrangement be considered a bust?

10. Describe the unique contribution of a QTIP arrangement to estate planning.

11. (a) Can a QTIP arrangement and a disclaimer provision be alternative methods of achieving a common objective? Why or why not? (b) Which will place greater property rights in the hands of S2? Why?

12. Brunk owned three assets at his death. Their description and appraised values at date of death, six months after death and nine months after death, respectively, are as follows: Home and furnishings, $300,000, $320,000, $340,000; securities, $800,000, $700,000, $600,000; and an interest in a closely held business, $500,000, $400,000, $300,000. Brunk bequeathed all assets to his son, who, as executor, sold the home for $310,000 four months after Brunk died, and sold the business for $320,000 eight months after Brunk died. Assuming no deductions, calculate Brunk's taxable estate.

13. (This question requires the ability to calculate present values). Assume that decedent, a widower, died owning only one asset, 10,000 shares of stock that she originally purchased for one dollar a share. The stock's total date of death value was $800,000 and its value six months after death was $750,000. Decedent's son stands to inherit all of the stock and he is considering selling it exactly 21 months from now. The estate tax will be paid exactly nine months from now, out of the son's own funds. Assume that the income tax on any capital gain, based on a combined marginal tax rate of 35%, will be paid on day of sale.

   a. Calculate the estate tax saved if the alternate valuation date (AVD) is elected. You'll need to determine the marginal estate tax rate.

   b. If son never sells the asset, how much combined income tax and estate tax will be saved if the AVD is elected?

   c. If son does sell the asset and has a combined marginal income tax rate of 50%, how much total income tax and estate tax will be saved if the AVD is elected?

   d. If the AVD is elected, at 10%, calculate both the present value of the reduced estate tax and the present value of the higher income tax, as of the estate tax due date (i.e. take present value back to a point that is 9 months after today).

   e. Compare the net difference between your two answers to part "d" with your answer to part "c."

14. With regard to the QTIP election:

   a. Who makes it?

   b. If the election is made, will it influence either the ultimate disposition of the property, or taxation of the qualifying property, or both? Explain.

   c. If the election is not made, how will the tax result change?

15. Dad died eight months ago. He and Mom operated a successful farm for 50 years. All of their assets, worth about $3 million, were held in joint tenancy. Ten years ago, the family lawyer drafted a revocable living trust which essentially left one-half of S1s estate to S2 and the balance to a

bypass trust for the benefit of S2, as life income beneficiary, and for Mom and Dad's three children (all adults), as remaindermen. This trust was never funded. The lawyer also drafted a pour over will, which Dad never signed.

    a. Describe the estate tax consequences of the current "plan."

    b. Recommend postmortem planning to reduce estate tax.

ANSWERS TO THE QUESTIONS AND PROBLEMS

1. Federal tax returns:

    a. Estate tax: Form 706, due nine months after date of death.

    b. Income tax:

        1. Form 1040: Decedent's final income tax return, for all income for the last year up to date of death.

        2. Form 1041: Estate income tax return (if there is a probate estate), for each tax year of the estate's existence.

        3. Form 1041: Trust income tax return for each tax year of any trust created by the decedent.

2. Taxes saved = amount deducted times the tax rate. $50,000 of the total must be deducted on the final 1040. The other $30,000 can be deducted on the 706 or the final 1040. To save the most taxes, the $30,000 should be deducted on the 706.

    a. 706: ($30,000 + $9,300) *.41 = $15,183 saved. Remember, the additional income tax due to not claiming these medical expenses on the 1040 is a debt that is deductible on the 706.

    b. Final 1040: ($30,000)*.31 = $9,300 saved.

    c. Estate's 1041: Not deductible.

3. a. If Trixie accepts the $100,000 commission, that amount will be taxable income to her, resulting in an income tax outlay of ($100,000)*.31 = $31,000. If the expense is deducted on the 706, estate tax will not be reduced, because the entire estate is already sheltered by the marital deduction and the exemption equivalent of the unified credit.

    If, alternatively, the expense is deducted on the estate's 1041, there will be an estate income tax saving of ($100,000)*.28 = $28,000. Thus, Trixie should *waive* the commission because it will result in a net increase in her after-tax proceeds of $31,000 - $28,000 = $3,000.

    b. The estate should not pay or deduct the commission, for the reasons mentioned above.

    c. The results would change. Trixie would be indifferent between waiving and accepting the commission. At equal marginal tax rates, the tax saved on the form 1041 would just equal the higher tax on Trixie's 1040. However, cutting the hypothetical gross estate to $200,000 would not in itself alter the results. For any size estate, a 100% marital deduction would prevent additional tax savings with other deductions. Thus, the effective marginal estate tax rate would still be 0%.

    d. The answers would very likely change. Trixie would probably rather accept the commission. Her after-tax proceeds would be $69,000, which is far better than receiving nothing.

4. a. Income tax advantages available to all estates:

    1. Estate can be a separate taxpaying entity, thereby splitting income and enjoying the benefit of deduction elections for administrative expenses and losses.
    2. Estate can take advantage of short tax years, which are the first and the last years of the estate's existence.

    b. Income tax advantages available only to estates having a carefully chosen fiscal year:

    1. Timing of distributions to delay the reporting of taxable income to beneficiaries (example 18-6).
    2. Selecting a fiscal year to spread income out over as many tax years as

possible (example 18-7, 18-8, and 18-9).

5. Tax planning for distributions to beneficiaries:

  a. When the estate or trust is in a lower bracket than the beneficiaries, it should consider accumulating income, realizing gains, and, if it is an estate, prolonging its life.
  b. When the estate is in a higher bracket, it should use the conduit principle to distribute income in the year received.

6. The benefit of prolonging an estate's life is subjecting estate income to a lower tax rate. The tax consequence of "unduly" prolonging it is that the IRS will treat the estate as terminated, taxing the income to the beneficiaries as if they received it.

7. The alternate valuation date election can reduce the value of assets in the gross estate (or raise deductions), and therefore the estate tax, if their total value 6 months after date of death is lower (higher) than date of death value.

8. Disclaimers to reduce the estate tax:

  a. Disclaimer into a bypass trust
  b. Disclaimer by a non-spouse to increase the marital deduction
  c. Disclaimer by a non-spouse to increase the charitable deduction
  d. Disclaimer of a taxable power of appointment

9. a. Yes, QTIP property can wind up not being part of the S1 deduction, if the executor for S1's estate chooses not to make the QTIP election .
  b. The QTIP arrangement can't be considered a bust if one of its purposes is to ensure that the property will pass to certain beneficiaries, such as the children of a former spouse. And it can become part of a bypass arrangement.

10. The unique contribution of a QTIP arrangement to estate planning is to enable property (remainder interest) which will not at all pass to S2 to qualify for the marital deduction.

11. a. Yes, a QTIP arrangement and a disclaimer provision can be alternative methods of achieving the same objective, which is estate tax minimization. Both typically enable S2 to decide whether or not to qualify certain property for the marital deduction and, consequently, to determine the size of the bypass share.

   b. The disclaimer provision will place greater property rights in the hands of S2 because if S2 doesn't disclaim, her or she will receive it. On the other hand, the QTIP election only influences estate taxation, not property disposition; disposition of the property is in complete control of S1.

12. Calculation of Brunk's taxable estate:

Estate assets	DOD Value	AVD Value
Home & furnishings	$300,000	$310,000
Securities	$800,000	$700,000
Business	$500,000	$400,000
Total	$1,100,000	$1,010,000

AVD values are determined 6 months after death; the nine month values, included as a 'red herring,' are inapplicable. For purposes of AVD values, all estate assets sold prior to the AVD are valued at selling price and assets distributed are valued as of date of distribution.

13. The main issue in this problem is whether to elect an AVD value which will lower estate tax but raise income tax (due to a lower step-up in basis) if the stock is later sold. A careful analysis requires consideration of the time value of money, which is done in part d.

   a. FET saved if AVD is elected: Since up to $250,000 of taxable amount exceeding $750,000 is subject to a 39% marginal estate tax rate, reducing the gross estate by $50,000 from $800,000 to $750,000 will save: 39 x $50,000 = $19,500

   b. Son never sells the asset: Son will incur no income tax. The combined taxes saved will be $19,500.

   c. Son sells the asset and AVD is elected: Since using AVD value makes stepped-up basis $50,000 lower than using date of death value, electing the AVD will increase son's taxable gain by $50,000. Thus, Son will incur an additional income tax of: 50 * $50,000 = $25,000

Combined with a lower estate tax of $19,500, son's combined net taxes saved is: $19,500 - $25,000 = -$5,500. In other words, electing the AVD will not save total taxes, they will be *greater* by $5,500 than if the AVD is not elected.

d. Time value of money analysis: Present value of reduced estate tax, as of estate tax due date = $19,500 x 1.0 = $19,500. Assume that income tax on the gain will be due exactly 21 months from now, which is exactly 1 year after the estate tax due date. Thus, present value of higher gains tax = $25,000 x .9091 = $22,727.50.

e. Difference in present values = $19,500 - 22,727.50 = -$3,227.50. This number is less negative than -$5,500, the answer in part "c," indicating a reduced monetary disadvantage to selecting the AVD because the additional income tax can be delayed (at least) one year. At 10%, only $22,727.50 is needed nine months from now to accumulate and pay the extra tax of $25,000 in 21 months.

Finally, it should be noted that the decision to elect the AVD will not always be disadvantageous. For example, the difference in present values will often be positive when the beneficiary is in a lower combined income tax bracket. And it will always be positive when the beneficiary does not intend to sell the estate asset(s).

14. a. The executor of the estate of S1 makes the election, since S1 is the decedent whose document qualifies for the QTIP election.

b. If the QTIP election is made, it will influence taxation of the qualifying property, but not its disposition. Except for adjustments for payment of estate tax, all named beneficiaries will still receive their designated shares. Tax-wise, the property will be deductible from S1's gross estate and includable in S2's gross estate at his or her later death.

c. If the QTIP election is not made, the qualifying property will be includable in S1's gross estate, and, hopefully, not includable (via bypass) in S2's gross estate. Thus, a greater bypass may increase S1 estate tax (but only if, under simple assumptions, the bypass becomes greater than $600,000). And a greater bypass will ordinarily reduce S2 estate tax.

ENDNOTES

1. §6013(a)(2).

2. §1(a)(2), §2(a)(1).

3. §213; §2053

4. Reg. 1.642 (g)-2.

5. Reg. §1.641(b)-3(a).

6. Reg 25.2518-2(c)(4)(I).

7. LR 9106016; TAM 9208003.

8. LR 9208003.

9. Reg. 25.2518-3(b).

10. For an example of an unsuccessful disclaimer to correct a defect in a trust intended to achieve QTIP treatment, partly because the court felt that the disclaimer would amount to nearly a complete rewrite of the trust, see *Estate of Bennett*, 100 TC No. 5 (1993).

11. §2056(b)(5).

12. §2044.

13. §2207(a).

14. However, the IRS and case law have ruled that the marital deduction will be disallowed in the case of a trust that is not to be funded if the QTIP election is not made, LR9104003; *Estate of Clayton*, 97 TC 327 (1991), or if failure to elect resulted in the property passing to a second trust that did not qualify for QTIP treatment. *J. Spencer Estate* TC CCH ¶12,908(M).

15. LR861106.

Three Study Aids:
Estate Planning Cases with Study Questions;
CFP Estate Planning Topics

OVERVIEW

This chapter features three study aids. The first two are hypothetical case studies, included for two primary reasons. First, estate planning is an intensely fact oriented and client oriented subject, and the more analysis of family situations studied, the better. Second, some readers may be preparing to take a final exam or a certification examination in estate planning, estate and gift tax, or financial planning. These questions should help in that preparation.

The first case is one used in at least one CFP certification examination.[1] The reader will notice it to be quite general in orientation, testing several other financial planning subjects besides estate planning, which is the subject matter of less than one third of the seventeen questions. The CFP Board of Examiners has indicated that it will continue to use cases that test a financial planners ability to intergrate various aspects of financial planning, hence numerous topic areas are likely to be covered.

The second case is far more estate planning oriented, and can be used to better test one's knowledge of numerous technical issues in estate planning.

The third part of the chapter includes that portion of the "Job Knowledge Requirements" of the Certified Financial Planner (CFP) that most relate to estate planning.

ONE: CFP CERTIFICATION EXAM CASE

Case Scenario And Multiple-Choice Questions

The following case scenario with multiple-choice questions appeared on a CFP certification examination. The answers are located on a separate page at the end of the case. The case has been approved for publication by the CFP Board of Examiners.

Instructions: Read the information provided about William and Marilyn Mathews and choose the best answer to the multiple choice questions that follow.

WILLIAM AND MARILYN MATHEWS

Your clients, Bill and Marilyn Mathews, have asked you to help them with a number of issues facing them as Bill prepares to sell his business and formally retire. Marilyn will also retire, having worked as the company bookkeeper for twenty years. Negotiations for the sale of Bill's business, Calculator City, are almost concluded, pending resolution of a number of questions Bill raised regarding installment payments for the business as well as a request from the proposed owner that Bill continue to provide consulting services.

Personal Information

	Age	Health	Occupation
William Mathews	65	Excellent	Business Owner
Marilyn Mathews	63		Bookkeeper
John Mathews (son)	32	Excellent	Engineer
James Mathews (son)	30	Excellent	CPA
Grandchildren	3,4,5, & 7	Excellent	

Neither son has any intention of becoming involved in the business. The Mathews file a joint tax return. Client and spouse have simple wills leaving all to each other.

The current economic environment exhibits low real short-term rates, high real long-term rates, little economic growth, and high unemployment.

Client Objectives

1. Maintain current lifestyle, including frequent travel.

2. Revise estate plan to minimize taxes, take advantage of opportunities in various elections available in the Internal Revenue Code, and maximize amounts passing to children and grandchildren.

3. Review investment portfolio and make changes as necessary to reflect different priorities and risk tolerance levels during retirement. Initial indications are that the clients are willing to take normal investment risks, desirous of adequate current income, reasonable safety of principal, inflation protection, tax advantage, and some modest long term appreciation, in that order of priority.

4. Review and revise total risk management and insurance situation as necessary to provide adequate protection, and eliminate gaps and overlaps.

5. Determine the most advantageous method of taking distributions from the 401(k) accounts.

WILLIAM AND MARILYN MATHEWS
Statement of Financial Position as of 12/31/92

Assets		Liabilities	
Invested Assets			
Cash/Cash Equivalents	$8,000	Auto Loan	$6,000
Marketable Securities[1]	1,580,000	Mortgage[2]	12,000
Business Interest[3]	1,500,000	Mortgage[4]	74,000
Life Ins Cash Value[5]	$60,000		$92,000
Annuity	120,000		
	$3,268,000		
Use Assets			
Primary Residence	$188,000		
Summer Home	126,000		
Personal Property	60,000		
Automobiles	26,000		
	$400,000		
Retirement Plan Assets[6]			
IRA (H)	$27,000		
IRA (W)	28,000		
401(k) (H)	280,000		
401(k) (W)	40,000		
	$375,000	Net Worth	$3,951,000
		Total Liabilities	
Total Assets	$4,043,000	& Net Worth	$4,043,000

---

[1] See separate Investment Portfolio Supplement

[2] Principal residence; originally, 30 years @ 7%

[3] Business is to be sold for $1.5 million. Purchase price was $700,000 in 1982. Terms of sale include $300,000 down payment on July 1, 1993, with the balance to be paid over 120 months starting August 1, 1993, at 10% interest.

[4] Summer home; originally, 15 years @9%

[5] Face Amount: $200,000; Bill is insured, Marilyn is beneficiary.

[6] Spouse is beneficiary for IRA and 401(k). The IRAs are invested in a common stock growth mutual fund. The 401(k) plans are invested in 3-year Treasury notes.

WILLIAM AND MARILYN MATHEWS
Projected Monthly Cash Flow Statement - (Incomplete)
1/1/93 through 12/31/93

*Cash Inflows

Social Security (H)	$820
Social Security (W)	$410
Installment Payments (120 pmts @ 10%)	?
Interest Income (tax-exempt)	$600
Dividend Income	$540
Interest Income (taxable)	?
Other Investment Income	?

Outflows

Savings and Investment	?
Mortgage (residence: PITI)	$600
Mortgage (summer home: PITI)	$1,100
Food	$300
Utilities	$400
Transportation (gas, oil, maintenance)	$200
Car Payment	$600
Clothing	$250
Entertainment	$450
Travel	$1,680
Family Gifts	$1,666
Charitable Gifts	$500
Life Insurance	$300
Hospitalization (Medigap/Medicare)	$100
Automobile Insurance	$150
Miscellaneous	?
Federal income Tax	$5,800
State Income Tax	$900
Other	?

WILLIAM AND MARILYN MATHEWS
INSURANCE AND ANNUITY INFORMATION

Whole Life Policy
Person Insured/Owner	Bill
Face Amount	$200,000
Dividend Option	Paid-Up Additions
Issue Date	2/13/77
Beneficiary	Marilyn
Current Cash Value	$60,000
Premium	$300 per month

Single Premium Deferred Annuity
Person Insured/Owner	Bill
Fixed or Variable	Fixed
Current Value	$120,000
Current Interest Rate	6.5%
Issue Date	1/1/81
Purchase Price	$40,000

Homeowners Policy
Type	HO-3
Amount on Dwelling	$175,000
Personal Property Coverage	$ 87,500
Personal Liability	$100,000

Automobile Policy
Type	Personal Auto policy
Bodily Injury/Property	$300,000 Combined Single Limit
Collision	$250 Deductible
Comprehensive	Full, with $100 Deductible
Uninsured Motorist	$300,000 Single Limit

WILLIAM AND MARILYN MATHEWS
INVESTMENT PORTFOLIO SUPPLEMENT

Common Stocks	Fair Market Value
AT&T	$30,000
Bell South	10,000
Bell Atlantic	9,000
Ameritech	8,500
NYNEX	7,000
Pacific Telesis	8,000
Southwestern Bell	8,000
US West	7,000
Canon	22,000
Comerica Bank	29,000
Danko	7,000
de Beers	8,000
du Pont	29,000
Disney	12,000
Dow Chemical	9,000
Detroit Edison	24,000
General Motors	8,000
GME	10,500
D&T, Inc.[*]	25,000
Common stock mutual fund (IRAs)	55,000
Municipal Bonds	
Franklin Intermediate Tax Exempt Fund	$100,000
Annuities and Insurance	
Cash value life insurance	$60,000
Single Premium Deferred Annuity	120,000
Bonds	
Treasury notes (401(k))	$320,000
US EE Savings Bonds	75,000
Cash and Equivalents	
Cash	$8,000
Cash equivalents, incl. Money Markets	134,000
Treasury Securities (T-Bills)	1,000,000
TOTAL	$2,143,000

[*]Small Business Corp. (§ 1244 stock) solely owned by Bill and originally purchased for $76,000 in 1/1/87.

QUESTIONS

1. The tax treatment of the down payment made to Bill for the sale of his business is:

    a. <u>not</u> taxable as a return of basis.
    b. fully taxable as a capital gain.
    c. partially a return of basis and partially taxable as ordinary income.
    d. partially a return of basis, partially a capital gain, and partially ordinary income.
    e. partially a return of capital and partially a capital gain.

2. How much will Bill receive from the monthly installment payments during 1993 (rounded to the nearest dollar)?

    a. $ 79,290   d. $379,290
    b. $ 95,149   e. $395,149
    c. $190,297

3. The amount of interest income from the installment sale for the year ending 12/31/93 is approximately:

    a. $ 49,000   d. $ 72,000
    b. $ 59,000   e. $120,000
    c. $ 60,000

4. How will Bill's receipt of installment payments for the sale of his business affect his Social Security benefits?

    a. His Social Security benefits will be reduced because of his installment payments.
    b. His Social Security benefits will <u>not</u> be taxable because installment payments are <u>not</u> wages.
    c. Receipt of installment payments will increase the amount of Modified Adjusted Gross Income, causing some of the Social Security benefits to be taxable.
    d. Because Bill is 65, his Social Security benefits will be subject to the

excess earnings test applied to the installment payments. Benefits will be reduced $1 for every $2 earned over the base amount.

e. Because Bill is 65, his Social Security benefits will be subject to the excess earnings test applied to the Installment payments. Benefits will be reduced $1 for every $3 earned over the base amount.

5. Bill and Marilyn both have account balances in the 401(k) Plan, and they want to determine what options they can pursue. Which of the following statements describe options available for Bill and Marilyn?

   (1) Bill can make an IRA Rollover with his account; Marilyn can elect 10-Year Special Averaging for hers.
   (2) Both Bill and Marilyn can make IRA Rollovers.
   (3) Bill can elect a partial rollover and use 5-Year Special Averaging on the balance; Marilyn can roll over her entire amount.
   (4) Both Bill and Marilyn can elect either 5-Year or 10-Year Special Averaging for their respective distributions.

   a. (1), (2) and (4) only   d. (2) and (3) only
   b. (1) and (3) only   e. (1), (2), (3) and (4)
   c. (2) only

6. The Mathews family is considering the purchase of a survivorship life insurance policy, payable on the second death of either Bill or Marilyn, for the primary purpose of providing liquidity for the payment of the federal estate tax. The ownership and beneficiary arrangements are being studied for the best overall result. Which of the following options for ownership and beneficiary arrangements are viable?

   (1) Bill and Marilyn can purchase the policy and retain ownership; the proceeds will <u>not</u> be includable in either estate because of the unlimited marital deduction.
   (2) Bill and Marilyn can purchase the policy, then transfer ownership to one or both of their sons, so that the proceeds avoid inclusion in either Bill's or Marilyn's estate <u>no</u> matter when death occurs because they do <u>not</u> have any incidents of ownership.

(3) Ownership can be vested immediately in an irrevocable life insurance trust, with appropriate "Crummey" provisions, to avoid inclusion of the proceeds in either estate.

(4) The Mathews family Revocable Living Trust can be the initial owner and beneficiary, in order to avoid estate taxes in either estate, because life insurance death proceeds retain their tax-free character in the trust.

   a. (1), (3) and (4) only   d. (2) only
   b. (2) and (4) only   e. (1) and (4) only
   c. (3) only

7. If Bill decides to make a partial withdrawal from his Single Premium Deferred Annuity, what income tax result will ensue?

   a. The withdrawal will be taxed as long-term capital gain, subject to a maximum rate of 28%.

   b. The withdrawal will be subject to ordinary income tax, since their is <u>no</u> preference for long-term capital gain.

   c. The withdrawal will be taxed according to the annuity rules, so that a portion will be taxable as ordinary income and the balance will be a tax-free recovery of capital.

   d. The withdrawal will be tax-free up to Bill's cost basis, since FIFO treatment applies to this annuity.

   e. The withdrawal will be taxable on a LIFO basis to the extent of earnings in the contract.

8. Bill is contemplating selling his D&T, Inc. stock for the fair market value. Assuming he sold D&T on 12/31/92, the tax impact would be:

   a. a fully deductible capital loss of $51,000.

   b. a capital loss limited to $3,000 assuming no other investment transactions; carryover $48,000 long-term capital loss.

   c. an ordinary loss of $50,000 with a $1,000 loss carryover.

   d. an ordinary loss of $51,000.

   e. a short-term capital loss of $51,000 because of Section 1244 status.

9. In view of the combined estate values for Bill and Marilyn, which of the following estate planning techniques may be appropriate?

    (1) placing life insurance in an irrevocable trust
    (2) making use of annual gift tax exclusion
    (3) establishing a revocable living trust, using the unlimited marital deduction and the full unified credit.
    (4) arranging for a preferred stock recapitalization for Bill's business interest

    a. (2) and (3) only   d. (1), (2) and (4) only
    b. (1), (2) and (3) only   e. (1), (2), (3) and (4)
    c. (1), (3) and (4) only

10. The Mathews currently own a number of tax-advantaged financial instruments. Which of the following statements is/are true with respect to these various instruments?
    (1) Interest income and capital appreciation from the municipal bond fund is federally tax exempt.
    (2) An initial partial withdrawal from the single premium deferred annuity is fully taxable.
    (3) When redeemed, the return on the savings bonds is not subject to state income taxes.
    (4) The Treasury bills are federally taxed only upon maturity.

    a. (1), (2) and (3) only   d. (3) and (4) only
    b. (2) and (4) only   e. (1), (2), (3) and (4)
    c. (3) only

11. If Bill and Marilyn wish to limit the growth of their combined estate, which techniques may be advisable?

    (1) use of the annual gift tax exclusion and split gift election
    (2) current use of both unified credits
    (3) payment of tuition for grandchildren
    (4) payment of direct medical expenses for children and grandchildren

a. (1) and (2) only
b. (2), (3) and (4) only
c. (1) only

d. (1), (2) and (3) only
e. (1), (2), (3) and (4)

12. Assume Bill provides consulting services for the new owner and is properly classified as an independent contractor. Which statements properly describe Bill's ability to shelter current taxable income?

(1) Bill may take a non-deductible IRA for $2,000
(2) Bill may set up a profit-sharing Keogh
(3) Bill can set up a money purchase plan.
(4) Bill can set up a combined money purchase and profit-sharing plan, but his contributions will be limited to 20% of Schedule C income.

a. (2) and (3) only
b. (1), (2) and (3) only
c. (2), (3) and (4) only

d. (1), (2), (3) and (4)
e. (1) and (3) only

13. In reviewing Bill and Marilyn's cash-flow projections as well as the investment portfolio supplement, you question the appropriateness of some of the holdings. Which combination of portfolio weaknesses best summarizes a valid critique of their investments?

a. excessive liquidity, inadequate tax advantage, marginal equity diversification
b. inadequate tax advantage, excessive growth orientation, marginal equity diversification
c. excessive liquidity, excessive growth orientation, inadequate tax advantage
d. excessive reliance on Treasury Bills, insufficient growth opportunities, inadequate current income
e. insufficient growth opportunities, inadequate liquidity, excessive tax advantage

14. Assuming that Bill reaches agreement with the new owner as to the installment payments for the business interest, what are the estate tax

ramifications if Bill dies at the end of the third year of the ten-year payout schedule?

a. The remaining value of the installments is not includable in Bill's estate, because the payments continuing to Marilyn qualify for the marital deduction.

b. Seventy percent of the original cash purchase price upon which the installments were based is includable in Bill's estate but qualifies for the marital deduction because payments will continue to Marilyn.

c. The present value of the future income stream to Marilyn in included in Bill's estate, but the continuing payments qualify for the marital deduction.

d. The present value of the future income stream to Marilyn is included in Bill's estate, but the continuing income payments do not qualify for the marital deduction because it is a terminable interest.

e. Nothing is included in the estate because the installment payments are not guaranteed.

15. The inadequacies in their estate planning can be summarized as follows:
    (1) failure to take full advantage of each unified credit.
    (2) failure to avoid probate.
    (3) lack of proper documents to address the potential problem of incapacity.
    (4) failure to coordinate titling of assets with documentation.

    a. (1) and (2) only
    b. (2) and (3) only
    c. (1) and (3) only
    d. (2) and (4) only
    e. (1), (2), and (3)

Regarding question 16 and given the current economic conditions, you recommend allocating the Mathews' investment funds into three asset categories: equity, debt, and cash.

16. In order to meet their goals, the Matthews should:
    (1) reduce cash level, expand fixed income securities,
    (2) expand fixed income securities.

(3) increase cash level, decrease equities.
(4) expand fixed income securities, decrease equities.

a. (1) only
b. (1) and (4) only
c. (2) and (3) only

d. (2), (3) and (4)
e. none of the above

17. You are considering liquidating the individual equity holdings and moving this amount into equity mutual funds. The following alternative allocations have been proposed:

Choice A		Choice B	
Market index fund	40%	Growth fund	33%
Growth fund	20%	International equity fund	33%
Value-oriented fund	20%	Value-oriented fund	34%
International equity fund	20%		
Choice C		Choice D	
Market index fund	30%	Small company fund	25%
Gold stock fund	50%	Aggressive growth fund	45%
Equity-income fund	20%	Growth fund	30%

a. Choice A is preferred because it includes multiple management styles and market diversification.
b. Choice B is preferred because it employs both active and passive funds.
c. Choice C is preferred because it best meets the Mathews' goals.
d. Choice D is preferred because it maximizes growth while meeting the Mathews' goal.
e. Do not liquidate the current portfolio.

ANSWERS TO CASE QUESTIONS

1.	E	6.	C	11.	E	16.	E
2.	A	7.	D	12.	C	17.	A
3.	A	8.	D	13.	A		
4.	C	9.	B	14.	C		
5.	A	10.	D	15.	E		

Since the release of the Mathews case, the CFP Board of Examiners has responded to candidates' questions regarding some of the exam items. Those responses, as they appear in the CFP Information Bulletin, are as follows:

Item #

2.   This is based on a sale price of $1.5 million with a down payment of $300,000, leaving a balance of $1.2 million. Payments are for 120 months at an interest rate of 0.83% per month (10% divided by 12). By the end of 1993, Bill will have received five payments. The answer to the question can be arrived through normal annuity calculations. I would agree that it probably should be calculated as an annuity due, in which case, the answer would have been slightly different, the amount of $78,635. Even if calculated this way, clearly the closest and best answer would be A.

7.   See IRS Publication 575 which is on point.

TWO: ESTATE PLANNING CASE
Sheila and Jerry Briggs

Chris Prestopino wrote the Briggs case, and accompanying questions, with a focus on estate planning. In that it has a specific focus, it is not that similar to CFP exam cases, which tend to cover several different areas of financial planning. However, many of the concepts (calculation of gross estate, the calculation of the estate tax, choice of trust type, etc) could be tested in a more general examination case; just one would not find so many estate planning questions. The answers are at the end of the chapter, just before the endnotes.

"I knew I should have talked with you first, I just knew it"..., exclaimed Jerry Briggs in your office one day last week. "...but our family attorney sounded so convincing..." Jerry had just finished showing you a copy of the wills that the attorney had just prepared for him and his wife, Sheila. You, of course, know them to be standard 'simple wills,' each document simply leaving everything outright to the spouse, if surviving, otherwise outright in equal shares to the children of their current marriage. After examining the wills, you pointed out some planning omissions and mistakes, and recommended that Jerry and Sheila set up an appointment for next week to discuss and develop an overall financial plan, with the assistance of an attorney specializing in estate planning. They agreed, and before they left filled out a questionnaire about their financial situation and objectives.

Jerry and Sheila Briggs, age 67 and 62 respectively, have been happily married for nearly 38 years. They have two children, Bob, 36 and Gail, 34. Jerry also has a son, Steve, 46, from a former marriage. While Sheila is in excellent health, the stress of Jerry's business has taken its toll. Jerry suffers from a heart condition, having experienced a mild attack three years ago.

Figure 1 depicts the Jerry and Sheila Briggs' financial statement. Jerry is a 50 percent stockholder in Gardens Unlimited, a rapidly growing mail order garden supply distributor. The sole co-owner is Craig Toft, an old college buddy. Sales last year were $23 million, making the firm's common stock worth approximately $1,800,000. The firm has a defined contribution profit sharing plan, and Jerry's account is currently worth $200,000. Sheila is named surviving beneficiary in this plan. Jerry thrives in his business environment, but because of his bad heart, realizes that he must slow down. Sheila entered the job market about 12 years ago, after Bob and Gail graduated college, and is presently enjoying work as a senior citizen's supervisor for the local recreation district. This year, Jerry will pay himself a salary of $90,000, and Sheila will earn $28,000. Their son Bob, a personal injury attorney for a large firm, has a wife, Mary, and two children, Chris and Cass. Bob has always been regarded by his parents as relatively mature and responsible. On the other hand, Gail, who is not married, has been a bit of a problem for her parents. She never finished college, and may now have a drug problem; for the past year she has acted confused at times, and has frequently asked Jerry for money. To date, Gail has received nearly $6,000 "to help pay the rent and other odds and ends".

The Briggs are living quite comfortably, but, considering their sizable income, have been strikingly unable to save much money. And currently, their monthly cash inflows just equal their outflows, with fixed outflows of $82,000 and variable outflows of $42,000.

As indicated in the accompanying financial statement, their principal asset is Jerry's interest in his company's stock. The profit sharing plan invests primarily in commercial real estate. Three years ago, just before he died, Sheila's father gave her one sixth of his interest in his closely held Uniform Company, which is a thriving industrial uniform supply distributor. Her dad's basis in this interest was $175,000 and its FMV at date of gift was $160,000. Sheila would have difficulty selling this stock, as there is no secondary market. At his death, Sheila's dad left her his 30 year high yield bond issued by Trigger Co.

Jerry has always handled the financial affairs for the family, and Sheila admits, quite frankly, to being terrified of being placed in the position of undertaking this role. The Briggs live in a common law, non-community property state, having a "pickup" or "sponge" inheritance tax equal to the amount of the federal credit for state death taxes. In your analysis, you have decided to make several simplifying assumptions. First, there will be no funeral or administrative expenses incurred at either Jerry's or Sheila's death. Second, there will be no future appreciation in asset values, unless otherwise specified.

Sheila and Jerry's objectives include the following:
- To plan for Jerry's complete withdrawal from the firm by age 70.
- To provide for adequate income during retirement.
- To incur no death taxes at the death of the first spouse.
- To minimize death taxes at the death of the second spouse.
- To ensure adequate liquidity at all times.
- To dispose of the Briggs family assets in the following manner:

- At the death of the first spouse, everything to the surviving spouse.
- At the death of the surviving spouse:
    - Sheila - all of her property to go equally to Bob and Gail.
    - Jerry - approximately one-half of his property to go to Steve and one quarter to Bob and Gail each.

JERRY AND SHEILA BRIGGS
Statement of Financial Condition (End of Last Year)

ASSETS[1]   LIABILITIES AND NET WORTH

Cash/Cash Equivalents		Liabilities[2]	
Checking account (JT)[3]	$10,000	Credit card balance	$5,000
Money market account (JT)	100,000	Auto note balance	13,000
Total Cash/Cash Equivalents	$110,000	Home mortgage bal.	32,000
Invested Assets		Total Liabilities	$50,000
Uniform Co. Common Stock (W)	$150,000		
Trigger Co. Bond (W)[4]	50,000		
Gardens Unlimited			
Com Stk (basis $50,000)(H)	900,000		
Profit sharing			
plan benefits (H)	200,000		
Total Invested assets	1,300,000		
Use Assets			
Personal residence (JT)	$280,000		
Personal Property (JT)	100,000		
Automobiles (JT)	60,000		
Total Use Assets	$440,000	Net Worth	$1,800,000
		TOTAL LIABILITIES	
TOTAL ASSETS	$1,850,000	& NET WORTH	$1,850,000

1. Presented at fair market value.
2. Principal only.
3. JT means: for assets owned by spouses in joint tenancy with right of survivorship and for liabilities it means the spouses are jointly liable
4. "W" means owned solely by wife Sheila and "H" means owned solely by husband Jerry.

Questions

1. If Jerry were to predecease Sheila and die today, without further planning, what would be the size of his federal gross estate, for estate tax purposes?

    a.   zero   b. $1,175,000   c. $1,375,000   d. $1,800,000
    e.   none of the above

2. If Jerry were to predecease Sheila and die today, without further planning, how much of his gross estate would pass under his present will?

    a.   zero (none)   b. $900,000   c. $1,100,000   d. $1,175,000
    e.   all of his gross estate

3. If when Jerry died the Uniform Company common stock was worth $168,000 and a year later Sheila sold it for $170,000, what would be her realized gain or loss? Negative number means a loss.

    a.   ($2,000)   b. ($7,000)   c. no gain or loss   d. $8,000
    e.   none of the above are correct

For all further questions, assume that the Jerry and Sheila each presently own one additional asset that is not shown on the financial statement: each was given a gift of a valuable painting from Jerry's dad. The gifts bring the value of Jerry's gross estate up to $1,600,000 and Sheila's gross estate up to $500,000.

4. If Jerry were to predecease Sheila and die today without further planning, what would be the federal estate tax due on behalf of Jerry's estate?

    a.   zero   b. $396,750   c. $408,000   d. $589,550
    e. $600,800

5. If Jerry died today and Sheila died, still unmarried, in ten years, without further planning, how much of the Briggs family assets would the children receive in total, after payment of death taxes? Assume no further savings or asset appreciation, no gifting or consumption of presently owned assets, and that all $50,000 of debts are paid off over time entirely with disposable income, not principal, prior to Sheila's death.

    a. more than $1,000,000 but no more than $1,400,000
    b. more than $1,400,000 but no more than $1,500,000
    c. more than $1,500,000 but no more than $1,600,000
    d. more than $1,600,000 but no more than $1,700,000
    e. more than $1,700,000

6. How much of the Briggs family estate would the children receive, after payment of estate taxes, if Jerry were to die today with an AB Trust plan?

    a. more than $1,000,000 but no more than $1,700,000
    b. more than $1,700,000 but no more than $1,800,000
    c. more than $1,800,000 but no more than $1,900,000
    d. more than $1,900,000 but no more than $2,000,000
    e. more than $2,000,000

7. In considering the amount of property passing to the bypass at the death of the first spouse, you are trying to determine the federal estate tax consequences of recommending a bypass of an amount <u>not</u> equal to the exemption equivalent of the unified credit. Assuming that the surviving spouse does not remarry and does not consume or make gifts of principal, which statement below is the most correct appraisal, in light of the Briggs' situation?

    a. When compared with a credit shelter bypass, a bypass of an amount smaller than the exemption equivalent would probably reduce the federal estate tax for the estate of the first spouse to die.
    b. When compared with a credit shelter bypass, a bypass of an amount smaller than the exemption equivalent would probably increase federal estate tax for the estate of the second spouse to die.
    c. When compared with a credit shelter bypass, a bypass of an amount smaller than the exemption equivalent would probably increase federal estate tax for the estates of both spouses.
    d. When compared with a credit shelter bypass, a bypass of an amount larger than the exemption equivalent would probably reduce federal estate tax for the estate of the first spouse to die.
    e. When compared with a credit shelter bypass, a bypass of an amount

larger than the exemption equivalent would probably increase federal estate tax for the estate of the second spouse to die.

8. In planning for the initial funding of the marital and bypass shares with specific assets, efficient estate tax planning for the Briggs would recommend funding Trust A (marital trust) with assets that are _____ likely to appreciate, and funding Trust B (UCE trust) with assets that are _____ likely to appreciate.

   a. more, less   b. more, more   c. less, more   d. less, less
   e. None of the above are true, relative appreciation has little bearing on trust funding.

9. In recommending a bypass for Jerry's plan, you are considering how to structure the marital deduction portion. Based on the facts, select the best disposition arrangement for Jerry, with regard to assets that qualify for the marital deduction.

   a. An outright bequest, partly because it is simple and tax effective.
   b. A power of appointment trust, partly because the limited power of appointment given to Sheila will ensure the preservation of trust assets for other beneficiaries.
   c. A bypass trust, partly to qualify bypass assets for the marital deduction.
   d. A QTIP trust, partly because of Steve.
   e. A charitable remainder unitrust (CRUT), partly because Jerry has a charitable motive and has been a member of the Uniform Denominational Church for many years.

10. For this question, assume that you recommend to the Briggs that Jerry's estate plan 1) contain a bypass, and 2) incorporate two trusts, a bypass trust and a QTIP trust. What type of control over these trusts would you want the instrument to grant to Sheila, as surviving spouse?

   a. A power of appointment over the principal of the bypass trust to invade for her benefit, subject to an ascertainable standard.
   b. A power of appointment over the principal of the bypass trust to

invade for her benefit, not subject to an ascertainable standard.

c. A power of appointment over the principal of the QTIP trust to invade for her benefit, not subject to an ascertainable standard.

d. A power of appointment over the principal of the QTIP trust to invade for her benefit, subject to an ascertainable standard.

e. A power of appointment over the principal of the QTIP trust, with only Sheila and the children as permissible appointees.

11. Regarding planning for the federal generation-skipping transfer tax (GST), which of the following best describes the Briggs' situation?

a. The Briggs do not need any planning for the GST since no GST, as we presently know it, could possibly be incurred, whether or not the Briggs do any further death tax planning.

b. The present arrangement will likely result in a GST at Sheila's death, if she survives Jerry.

c. No planning for the Briggs can prevent an inevitable GST from being incurred.

d. Based on the $1 million exemption, the Brigg's family assets are vulnerable to the GSTT on amounts in excess of $1 million, even with the most careful planning.

e. None of the above are true.

12. In recommending a bypass estate plan for the Briggs, you intend to suggest that their estate planning attorney include certain clauses in the final principal dispositive instrument, whether it turns out to be a will or a living trust. Which clause would you <u>not</u> want to recommend?

a. A perpetuities saving clause, to prevent a contingent gift from being ruled invalid because it vests too long after the decedent's death.

b. A residuary clause.

c. A survival clause, because of the danger of lapsation.

d. A clause allocating death taxes, because the alternative, state and federal law (by default), may be inefficient and undesirable.

e. You would recommend all of the above clauses for the Briggs.

13. In this question only, assume that five years have gone by, and that Jerry died of a second heart attack ten months ago. Sheila has not remarried. The Briggs never returned to your lawyer-associate's office to sign any documents, which means that no additional planning has been implemented. In administering the affairs of Jerry's estate, Sheila has permitted Steve to drive Jerry's sports car, which is currently worth $18,000. Sheila intends to let Steve have the car, in accordance with Jerry's deathbed statements. If Sheila writes a letter today "irrevocably and unqualifiedly" refusing to accept the bequest of the car, and transfers title of the car to Steve in two weeks,

    a. Steve will be legally entitled to at least part ownership in the car. Sheila will not have been considered to have made a "gross" or "taxable" gift to Steve because she will never have owned the car.

    b. Steve will be legally entitled to full ownership in the car. Sheila will have made a "gross" gift, but will not have been considered to have made a "taxable" gift to Steve because of the benefit of the annual exclusion and the unified credit.

    c. Steve will be legally entitled to full ownership in the car. Sheila will have been considered to have made a "taxable" gift because she will have owned the car.

    d. Steve will be legally entitled to full ownership in the car. Sheila will have been considered to have made a taxable gift because she will have owned the car and the gift is one of a future interest.

    e. Steve will not be legally entitled to any ownership interest in the car.

14. You are now attempting to decide whether to recommend that Jerry dispose of his assets with a will or with a living trust document. If you recommend a will, you intend to make sure that title to all assets in joint tenancy between Jerry and Sheila will be converted to equal tenants in common. The costs for the will alternative are: drafting- $2,000; probate administration costs- $20,000. The costs for the trust alternative are: drafting- $3,800; non-probate administration costs at death- $14,000. Assuming no other relevant costs, a discount rate of 11 percent, that any drafting costs will be incurred today, and that all administration costs in connection with Jerry's death will be incurred exactly 12 years from today, which answer below summarizes within five dollars a present value cost analysis taking into account the time value of money?

a. The net advantage of the living trust over a will is about $5,000.
b. The net advantage of the living trust over the will is greater than zero but less than $5,000.
c. The net advantage of the will over the living trust is greater than zero but less than $5,000.
d. The net advantage of the will over the living trust is equal to $5,000.
e. None of the answers above are correct

15. While in your office, Jerry and Sheila mentioned that their family attorney had made several questionable assertions regarding the selection of either joint tenancies (WROS), the will, or the living trust as the overall best type of dispositive instrument for them. Which of that attorney's comments, all listed below, is correct?

a. He said taking title to all assets in joint tenancy will prevent a step-up in tax basis of some or all property at the first spouse's death, thereby making joint tenancies distinctly disadvantageous in comparison with the other instruments of transfer.
b. He said that proper planning with a living trust can make will planning entirely unnecessary.
c. He said that a will is capable of disposing of all of the Briggs' present assets, except those held currently in joint tenancy form.
d. He said that if the Briggs execute a will, at either of their deaths the posting of notice to creditors in a legal newspaper will effectively insulate the decedent's estate from all known creditors who delay in filing claims beyond the creditor's period.
e. None of the above statements are true.

16. Jerry and Sheila (who have never made taxable gifts) are considering giving the Gardens unlimited stock to their children. If they were to arrange a split gift of $300,000 of this stock this year, with each child receiving shares worth $100,000, calculate the amount of Jerry's remaining unified credit that would be available for gifts in succeeding

years. Still available would be:

a. $108,400   b. $115,200   c. $157,000   d. $163,000
e. $192,800

17. What planning recommendations would be appropriate in connection with Gail's situation?

    1. In the event of both spouse's premature death, give an independent trustee of any trust created the discretionary power to sprinkle income and principal among beneficiaries.
    2. Provide for outright distribution of assets immediately at the death of the surviving spouse.
    3. Name Gail to be a surrogate decision maker during the remaining lifetime of the surviving spouse.
    4. Include a restriction against assignment in all trust documents.

      a. 1 only   d. 3 and 4 only
      b. 1 and 4 only   e. 1, 2, 3 and 4
      c. 2 and 3 only

18. You next turn to liquidity and life insurance planning for the Briggs. Based on the family situation, and assuming that the final plan will include a credit shelter bypass plan, which statement below represents the best analysis and recommendation for the Briggs?

a. The Briggs should consider an irrevocable life insurance trust having the following characteristics: trustee is owner and beneficiary of policy.
b. The Briggs should consider a irrevocable life insurance trust having the following characteristics: trustee is owner of policy and Bob and Gail are co-beneficiaries.
c. The Briggs should consider a irrevocable life insurance trust having the following characteristics: Jerry and Sheila are owners of policy and trustee is beneficiary.
d. The Briggs should consider a revocable life insurance trust having the following characteristics: trustee is owner and beneficiary of policy.

e. No liquidity problems can be reasonably anticipated in the future, since all expected future debts can be easily paid with available assets.

19. Continuing your planning for liquidity, you estimate that if Jerry were to die today, Sheila would need, among other funds, a cash lump sum of $122,000 exactly one year from today and an annual cash inflow of $43,000 per year for 24 years with the first inflow arriving in exactly four years. Ignoring other cash needs and other sources of liquidity, how much life insurance should the Briggs own to fund just these two needs? Assume a discount rate of 9 percent.

    a. $434,224   b. $529,311   c. $539,384   d. $1,154,000
    e. None of the above answers are within $1,000 of the correct answer.

20. In planning for Jerry's business interests, which of the following represents a preferred recommendation and correct analysis, given the facts?

    a. While still alive, Jerry's selling his entire interest in Gardens Unlimited sometime in the next two years for $900,000 would be attractive from the point of view of both income tax and the overall objectives of the family.
    b. An entity business buyout arrangement between Jerry and Craig funded with life insurance would be preferable to a cross purchase arrangement because it would mean fewer policies would be needed and because the surviving owner would incur less income tax if and when he finally sells the firm.
    c. Jerry should bequeath the stock to Sheila, either outright or in trust, to be able to obtain a step-up in basis.
    d. If Jerry and Craig immediately sell the business to a ABC Corp., a large mail order firm, in exchange for ABC stock, they will incur no immediate income tax liability and will be able to diversify their holdings free of income tax consequences.
    e. None of the above statements represents preferred recommendations or correct analysis.

21. In recommending planning for the Briggs' incapacity, which statement below is correct?

    a. A living trust can explicitly provide for expert management of Jerry's property in the event of his incapacity.

    b. A living trust can explicitly provide for Jerry's personal care in the event of his incapacity.

    c. A will can explicitly provide for expert management of Jerry's property in the event of his incapacity.

    d. A will can explicitly provide for Jerry's personal care in the event of his incapacity.

    e. More than one of the answers above is correct.

THREE: CFP ESTATE PLANNING TOPICS

In the process of developing appropriate examination questions for the CFP comprehensive exams, the Board of Standards and Practices for the Certified Financial Planner commissioned an extensive survey of practicing CFP licensees to determine the "job knowledge" requirements for persons wishing to practice personal financial planning. The following outline is just the estate planning section from the job knowledge topics list found in the CFP Board of Standards' General Information Booklet.[2] The Booklet is a manual that describes the certification requirements for the CFP license.[3]

The numbers in parentheses refer to ratings made by the panel. The first number describes relative importance: 1 = important, 2 = more important. The second number describes the target cognitive level: 1 = knowledge of facts/terms, 2 = comprehension/application, 3 = analysis/synthesis, 4 = evaluation.

JOB KNOWLEDGE REQUIREMENTS OF THE CERTIFIED FINANCIAL PLANNER: TOPICS, RELATIVE IMPORTANCE AND TARGET COGNITIVE LEVEL

The following topics become effective for certification examinations administered by the CFP Board of Standards after December 31, 1996

Estate Planning Benefits and Strategies

77. Estate planning overview (4)
    A. The meaning of "estate planning"
    B. Situations in which individuals need estate planning and consequences of integrated planning
    C. Steps in estate planning process
    D. The financial planner's role on the estate planning team

78. Estate planning pitfalls and weaknesses (4)
    A. Weaknesses in a client's existing estate plan
    B. Common pitfalls to avoid during estate planning

79. Methods for property transfer at death (4)
    A. The probate process (wills and intestate succession)
    B. Title (operation of law)
    C. Trusts
    D. Contracts (insurance/pensions)

80. Estate planning documents (4)
    A. Wills
    B. Trusts
    C. Personal care documents
    D. Marital agreements
    E. Durable power of attorney for property
    F. Business agreements

81. Overview of the federal unified tax system (4)
    A. Unified transfer tax system
    B. Generation-skipping transfer tax

82. Federal gift taxation (4)
    A. Basic concepts
    B. Techniques for managing gift tax liability
    C. Analysis and calculation of federal gift tax liability

83. Federal gross estate (4)
    A. Inclusions in a decedent's gross estate
    B. Exclusions from a decedent's gross estate

84. Valuation techniques and the federal gross estate (4)
    A. Valuation of specific property interests
    B. Valuation techniques

85. Federal estate tax deductions (4)
    A. Defining the gross estate
    B. Deductions (debts and expenses)
    C. Adjusted gross estate
    D. Deductions (marital/charitable)
    E. Taxable estate
    F. Adjusted taxable gifts
    G. Tax base

86. Calculation of federal estate tax liability (4)
    A. Steps to calculate the estate tax
    B. Various credits affecting the estate tax calculation (unified credit, state death tax, prior transfer, etc.)

87. Characteristics and tax aspects of property interests (4)
    A. Title forms
    B. Other interests
    C. Advantages and disadvantages of forms of property interests

D. Taxation aspects
E. Recommendation and justification of the most appropriate form of property interests

88. Probate (4)
    A. Probate process
    B. Advantages and disadvantages of probate
    C. Techniques of avoiding probate
    D. Recommendation and justification of the most appropriate probate avoidance techniques

89. Liquidity planning (4)
    A. Sale of assets
    B. Life insurance
    C. Special techniques for closely-held business owners (e.g., §§ 6166, 303, 2032A and buy-sell agreements)

90. Powers of appointment (4)
    A. Use and purpose in estate planning
    B. General and special (limited)
    C. "5 & 5" power (§ 2041(b)(2))
    D. Federal gift and estate tax implications

91. Features of trusts (4)
    A. Classification of trusts
    B. Characteristics of selected trust provisions
    C. Rule against perpetuities

92. Taxation of trusts and estates (4)
    A. Income tax implications of trusts
        1) Exemptions
        2) Simple and complex trusts
        3) Distributable net income
    B. Federal gift tax implications of trusts
    C. Federal estate tax implications of trusts
    D. Income tax implications of estates
    E. Recommendation and justification of the most appropriate trust
    F. Excise tax on retirement plans at death

93. Estate freeze issues
    A. Limitations on corporate and partnership freezes (§ 2701)
    B. Trust freezes (§ 2702 including qualified personal residence trusts)

94. Life insurance for estate planning (4)
    A. Advantages and disadvantages of specific life insurance techniques in estate planning
    B. Life insurance trusts
    C. Ownership, beneficiary designation and settlement options
    D. Gift and estate taxation of life insurance
    E. Recommendation and justification of the most appropriate life insurance technique

95. Gifts (4)
    A. Suitability of gifts for client and recipient
    B. Techniques for gift-giving

96. Taxation of gifts (4)
    A. Income taxation of lifetime transfers
    B. Federal gift taxation of lifetime transfers
    C. Circumstances causing inclusion of gifts in gross estate
    D. Calculation and analysis of the effect of a lifetime gift program

97. Recommendation and justification of the most appropriate property to give as a gift (4)
    A. Selection of the most appropriate property to give as a gift
    B. The most appropriate lifetime gift-giving techniques
    C. Justification of the lifetime gift-giving techniques selected for the client's situation

98. Marital deduction and bypass planning (4)
    A. Characteristics of the marital deduction
    B. Recommendation and justification of property interests that qualify for the marital deduction
    C. QTIP planning and the prior transfer credit
    D. Special planning for non-U.S. spouse

99. Federal estate tax implications of the marital deduction and bypass planning (4)
    A. Federal estate tax implications of using the marital deduction
    B. Calculation of increased wealth transfer generated from modifying a client's estate plan

100. Recommendation of the most appropriate marital or non-marital transfer (4)
    A. Factors to consider in selecting the optimum mix of marital and non-marital transfers
    B. Selection of the most appropriate single or combination of marital and/or non-marital transfers for a client's situation
    C. Justification of the marital and non-marital transfer techniques selected for the

client's situation

101. Estate planning for nontraditional relationships (4)
    A.   Children of another relationship
    B.   Cohabitation
    C.   Adoptions
    D.   Same sex relationships
    E.   Communal relationships

102. Charitable contributions and transfers (4)
    A.   Considerations for contributions and transfers
    B.   Requirements for a gift to qualify for a charitable deduction
        1)   Charitable remainder trusts
        2)   Charitable lead trusts
    C.   Tax and non-tax characteristics of specific forms of charitable transfers including alternative minimum tax considerations
    D.   Charitable income tax deduction limitations
    E.   Calculation of the maximum total and/or maximum current year income tax deduction for a client's situation
    F.   Recommendation and justification of the most appropriate property and form of charitable transfer

103. Intra-family business and property transfers (4)
    A.   Characteristics of intra-family transfers
    B.   Federal income, gift and estate tax implications of intra-family transfers
    C.   Recommendation and justification of the most appropriate intra-family business and property transfer technique

104. Postmortem planning techniques (4)
    A.   Characteristics of postmortem estate planning techniques
    B.   Determination of whether a client qualifies for special tax treatment
    C.   Recommendation and justification of the most appropriate postmortem planning technique

105. Planning for incapacity (4)
    A.   Definition of incapacity
    B.   Care of client's dependents
    C.   Personal care of incapacitated client
    D.   Care of incapacitated client's property

106. Special topics in estate planning (4)
    A.   Divorce/remarriage
    B.   Selection of fiduciaries and guardians

Answers for the Briggs case:

1. Answer "c"

Cash/MM/2 =	$55,000
Stock, Gardens Unlimited	$900,000
Pensions	$200,000
Residence/2	$140,000
Personal Property/2	$50,000
Autos/2	$30,000
Gross Estate	$1,375,000

2. Answer "b" Only Jerry's $900,000 Gardens Unlimited stock would pass by will. All joint tenancy assets pass by operation of law (the right of survivorship) and the profit sharing account would pass to the beneficiary designation according to the contract.

3. Answer "c" Sheila owns this stock so Jerry's will does not control. Since it was a gift from her father that had a higher basis that its FMV when he gave it to her the special rule for calculating her gain or loss applies. Since she sold it for more than the date of gift value but less than the carry over basis there is no gain or loss.

4. Answer "a" They have simple wills, therefore everything to the surviving spouse. With the 100% marital deduction the taxable estate would be zero, therefore no tax.

5. Answer "b" When Sheila dies she would own all of the property, $1,600,000 from Jerry and $500,000 of her own property for a total of $2,100,000. Debts and expenses assumed to be zero:

Taxable estate	$2,100,000
Tentative tax	$829,800
Unified Credit	($192,800)
Death taxes	$637,000
Net to the children	
Sheila's estate	$2,100,000
less death taxes	($637,000)
Net to the children	$1,463,000

6. Answer "b" Utilize a bypass to use Jerry's unified credit.

    Jerry's estate

Gross estate	$1,600,000
Marital deduction	($1,000,000)
Taxable estate	$600,000
Tentative tax	$192,800
Unified Credit	($192,800)
Death taxes	$0

    Sheila's estate

Gross & taxable estate	$1,500,000
Tentative tax	$555,800
Unified Credit	($192,800)
Death taxes	$363,000

    Net to the children

From Sheila	$1,500,000
less taxes	($363,000)
Plus bypass amount	$600,000
Net amount	$1,737,000

7. Answer "b" because a smaller bypass will increase the marital share at the first death, and thereby probably "load up" the estate of the second spouse to die. The other answers are wrong because:

    a. a credit shelter bypass plan already zeros out the tax; it can't be reduced any more.
    c. a smaller bypass will increase the marital share and therefore could not possibly increase the tax on the first estate.
    d. a larger bypass will unshelter some property from taxation at the first death, thereby probably increasing the tax.
    e. a larger bypass will reduce the marital share, thereby probably reducing the surviving spouse's estate and estate tax.

8. Answer "c" Funding the marital share with assets less likely to appreciate will avoid loading up the surviving spouse's estate. Funding the bypass share with assets more likely to appreciate will enable a greater amount of property to avoid (i.e., to bypass) taxation at the surviving souse's death.

9. Answer "d" The QTIP trust will enable Jerry to retain control over the eventual disposition of the corpus such that Steve will receive his full share. The other answers are incorrect because:
   a. Jerry does not want Sheila to have fee simple control over the property.
   b. A general power would cause this property to be included in Sheila's estate and she would control it.
   c. a bypass trust would not qualify for the marital deduction.
   e. A CRUT would not leave property to their children.

10. Answer "a" Sheila can invade based upon ascertainable standards, thus a limited power, the property is not included in her estate. The other answers are incorrect because:

    b. There would be no bypass and the property would be in Sheila's estate.
    c, d, & e: No one other than S2 can have any right to corpus so long as S2 is alive if the QTIP election is desired.

11. Answer "e" The other answers are incorrect because:

    a. A GSTT may be incurred if, due to any of their children predeceasing her, property then goes to grandchildren.
    b. Neither Sheila nor the children are skip persons.
    c. Gifts may keep the Briggs' assets below $2 million which can be sheltered by their GSTT exemptions.
    d. Each spouse has a $1 million dollar exemption that can shelter $2 million.

12. Answer "e" All of the clauses are standard estate planning provisions commonly included in estate planning documents.

13. Answer "c" Jerry's deathbed statements do not constitute a valid testamentary transfer. Thus, under the Briggs' simple will, Sheila was bequeathed the car. Because Sheila did not disclaim it within 9 months of his death, she will have made a gift of it to Steve. Thus, her transfer of title to Steve is a taxable gift to the extent the value of the car exceeded the annual exclusion amount.

14. Answer "c" Factor 11% for 12 years is .285841.

    With a will: $2,000 + $20,000*.285841 = $7,717.
    Living trust: $3,800 + $14,000*.285841 = $7,802
    Advantage of will: $7,802 - $7,717 = $85.

15. Answer "e" The other answers are incorrect because:

    a. a step-up as to one half of the value of the assets will occur whether in joint tenancy or will or living trust.
    b. need a pourover will.
    c. certain assets are not probate assets, such as the pension plan benefits.
    d. Tulsa requires actual notice to known creditors.

16. Answer "d"

Jerry's gift tax return	
Gross gifts	$150,000
Annual exclusion	$30,000
Current taxable gifts	$120,000
Tentative tax	$29,800
Unified credit	$29,800
Gift tax	$0

Remaining unused unified credit = $192,800 - $29,800 = $163,000.

    a. Assumes $300,000 gross gifts and a $10,000 total annual exclusion.
    b. Assumes $300,000 gross gifts and a $30,000 total annual exclusion.
    c. Assumes $150,000 gross gifts and a $10,000 total annual exclusion.
    e. Assumes a zero tentative tax.

17. Answer "b"

    1. Correct, an independent trustee can have a limited power of appointment, and based upon Gail's health can determine the appropriate distributions.
    2. incorrect Gail might receive too much money which she could use to support her drug habit.
    3. incorrect, Gail may not be capable of handling that task.
    4. correct because Gail cannot pledge trust assets to support a drug habit.

18. Answer "a" Only by naming the trustee of an irrevocable trust to be both owner and beneficiary of the policy will the Briggs be able to both avoid probate and federal estate tax on the proceeds.

19. Answer "a"

Present value of $122,000 in one year @ 9%: = $122,000 * .917431 = $111,927.
Present value of $43,000 annually for 3 years: $43,000*9.706612 = $322,297.

Total present value of the cash flows = $111,927 + $322,297 = $434,224.

    b. doesn't discount the $417,384 three years further back.
    c. same error as b, plus doesn't discount the lump sum.
    d. ignores the time value of money.

20. Answer "e" The other answers are incorrect because:

    a. An income tax on the $850,000 would be immediately incurred.
    b. The same number of policies (two) will have to be purchased under either plan.
    c. Sheila will have difficulty selling the business for a reasonable value.
    d. The only way to diversify is by selling the AVC stock, in the process incurring a capital gains tax.

21. Answer "a" because a successor trustee can be authorized to take over at

the onset of Jerry's incapacity. The other answers are incorrect because:

b. The trust authorizes property management not health care.
c. A will becomes a controlling document only after the testator is dead.
d. A will becomes a controlling document only after the testator is dead.
e. Only "a" is correct.

ENDNOTES

1. Reprinted with permission of the Certified Financial Planner Board of Standards.

2. Reprinted with permission of the Certified Financial Planner Board of Standards.

3. The General Information Booklet, revised annually, is available free from CFP Board, 1660 Lincoln Street (Suite 3050), Denver CO 80264-3001. Telephone (303) 830-7543. FAX (303) 860-7388.

Tax and Valuation Tables

TABLE 1 Federal Unified Transfer Tax Rates Since 1977

If the Amount is:		Tentative Tax		
Over	But Not Over	Base Amount...	+ Percent...	On Excess Over
All years after 1976-taxable amounts up to $2,500,000				
$ 0.	$ 10,000.	$ 0.	18.0%	$ 0.
10,000.	20,000.	1,800.	20.0	10,000.
20,000.	40,000.	3,800.	22.0	20,000.
40,000.	60,000.	8,200.	24.0	40,000.
60,000.	80,000.	13,000.	26.0	60,000.
80,000.	100,000.	18,200.	28.0	80,000.
100,000.	150,000.	23,800.	30.0	100,000.
150,000.	250,000.	38,800.	32.0	150,000.
250,000.	500,000.	70,800.	34.0	250,000.
500,000.	750,000.	155,800.	37.0	500,000.
750,000.	1,000,000.	248,300.	39.0	750,000.
1,000,000.	1,250,000.	345,800.	41.0	1,000,000.
1,250,000.	1,500,000.	448,300.	43.0	1,250,000.
1,500,000.	2,000,000.	555,800.	45.0	1,500,000.
2,000,000.	2,500,000.	780,800.	49.0	2,000,000.
2,500,000.	3,000,000.	1,025,800.	53.0%	2,500,000.
1977-1981				
$3,000,000.	$3,500,000.	$1,290,800.	57.0%	$3,000,000.
3,500,000.	4,000,000.	1,575,800.	61.0	3,500,000.
4,000,000.	4,500,000.	1,880,800.	65.0	4,000,000.
4,500,000.	5,000,000.	2,205,800.	69.0	4,500,000.
5,000,000.	-	2,550,800.	70.0	5,000,000.
1982				
$3,000,000.	$3,500,000.	$1,290,800.	57.0%	$3,000,000.
3,500,000.	4,000,000.	1,575,800.	61.0	3,500,000.
4,000,000.	-	1,880,800.	65.0	4,000,000.
1983				
$3,000,000.	$3,500,000.	$1,290,800.	57.0%	$3,000,000.
3,500,000.	-	1,575,800.	60.0	3,500,000.
1984 and later				
$3,000,000.	-	$1,290,800.	55.0%	$3,000,000.

(Amounts between $10 million and $21,040,000 are subject to an additional 5% tax)

TABLE 2 Federal Unified Credit and Unified Credit Equivalent (UCE)

Year		Credit	UCE
1977		$30,000	$120,667
1978		$34,000	$134,000
1979		$38,000	$147,333
1980		$42,500	$161,563
1981		$47,000	$175,625
1982		$62,800	$225,000
1983		$79,300	$275,000
1984		$96,300	$325,000
1985		$121,800	$400,000
1986		$155,800	$500,000
1987	& thereafter	$192,800	$600,000

TABLE 3 Maximum Credit against Federal Estate Tax for State Death Taxes

Adjusted taxable Estate*		Maximum Credit		
At Least	But Not Over	Base Amount	Plus Percent	On Excess Over
$40,000	$90,000	$0	0.8%	$40,000
$90,000	$140,000	$400	1.6%	$90,000
$140,000	$240,000	$1,200	2.4%	$140,000
$240,000	$440,000	$3,600	3.2%	$240,000
$440,000	$640,000	$10,000	4.0%	$440,000
$640,000	$840,000	$18,000	4.8%	$640,000
$840,000	$1,040,000	$27,600	5.6%	$840,000
$1,040,000	$1,540,000	$38,800	6.4%	$1,040,000
$1,540,000	$2,040,000	$70,800	7.2%	$1,540,000
$2,040,000	$2,540,000	$106,800	8.0%	$2,040,000
$2,540,000	$3,040,000	$146,800	8.8%	$2,540,000
$3,040,000	$3,540,000	$190,800	9.6%	$3,040,000
$3,540,000	$4,040,000	$238,800	10.4%	$3,540,000
$4,040,000	$5,040,000	$290,800	11.2%	$4,040,000
$5,040,000	$6,040,000	$402,800	12.0%	$5,040,000
$6,040,000	$7,040,000	$522,800	12.8%	$6,040,000
$7,040,000	$8,040,000	$650,800	13.6%	$7,040,000
$8,040,000	$9,040,000	$786,800	14.4%	$8,040,000
$9,040,000	$10,040,000	$930,800	15.2%	$9,040,000
$10,040,000		$1,082,800	16.0%	$10,040,000

* Adjusted taxable estate is taxable estate less $60,000.

TABLE 4 Federal Gift Tax Rates prior to January 1, 1977

Taxable Gift*		Gift Tax		
At Least	**But Not Over**	**Base Amount**	**Plus Percent**	**On Over**
$0	$5,000	$0	2.25%	$0
$5,000	$10,000	$113	5.25%	$5,000
$10,000	$20,000	$375	8.25%	$10,000
$20,000	$30,000	$1,200	10.50%	$20,000
$30,000	$40,000	$2,250	13.50%	$30,000
$40,000	$50,000	$3,600	16.50%	$40,000
$50,000	$60,000	$5,250	18.75%	$50,000
$60,000	$100,000	$7,125	21.00%	$60,000
$100,000	$250,000	$15,525	22.50%	$100,000
$250,000	$500,000	$49,275	24.00%	$250,000
$500,000	$750,000	$109,275	26.25%	$500,000
$750,000	$1,000,000	$174,900	27.75%	$750,000
$1,000,000	$1,250,000	$244,275	29.25%	$1,000,000
$1,250,000	$1,500,000	$317,400	31.50%	$1,250,000
$1,500,000	$2,000,000	$396,150	33.75%	$1,500,000
$2,000,000	$2,500,000	$564,900	36.75%	$2,000,000
$2,500,000	$3,000,000	$748,650	39.75%	$2,500,000
$3,000,000	$3,500,000	$947,400	42.00%	$3,000,000
$3,500,000	$4,000,000	$1,157,400	44.50%	$3,500,000
$4,000,000	$5,000,000	$1,378,650	47.25%	$4,000,000
$5,000,000	$6,000,000	$1,851,150	50.25%	$5,000,000
$6,000,000	$7,000,000	$2,353,650	52.50%	$6,000,000
$7,000,000	$8,000,000	$2,878,650	54.75%	$7,000,000
$8,000,000	$10,000,000	$3,426,150	57.00%	$8,000,000
$10,000,000		$4,566,150	57.75%	$10,000,000

* Taxable amount after the annual exclusion and the gift exemption.

WARNING:

THESE ARE **PRE-1977 GIFT** TAX RATES

TABLE 5 Federal Estate Rates prior to January 1, 1977

Taxable Estate*		Estate Tax		
At Least	But Not Over	Base Amount	Plus Percent	On Excess Over
$0	$5,000	$0	3.0%	$0
$5,000	$10,000	$150	7.0%	$5,000
$10,000	$20,000	$500	11.0%	$10,000
$20,000	$30,000	$1,600	14.0%	$20,000
$30,000	$40,000	$3,000	18.0%	$30,000
$40,000	$50,000	$4,800	22.0%	$40,000
$50,000	$60,000	$7,000	25.0%	$50,000
$60,000	$100,000	$9,500	28.0%	$60,000
$100,000	$250,000	$20,700	30.0%	$100,000
$250,000	$500,000	$65,700	32.0%	$250,000
$500,000	$750,000	$145,700	35.0%	$500,000
$750,000	$1,000,000	$233,200	37.0%	$750,000
$1,000,000	$1,250,000	$325,700	39.0%	$1,000,000
$1,250,000	$1,500,000	$423,200	42.0%	$1,250,000
$1,500,000	$2,000,000	$528,200	45.0%	$1,500,000
$2,000,000	$2,500,000	$753,200	49.0%	$2,000,000
$2,500,000	$3,000,000	$998,200	53.0%	$2,500,000
$3,000,000	$3,500,000	$1,263,200	56.0%	$3,000,000
$3,500,000	$4,000,000	$1,543,200	59.0%	$3,500,000
$4,000,000	$5,000,000	$1,838,200	63.0%	$4,000,000
$5,000,000	$6,000,000	$2,468,200	67.0%	$5,000,000
$6,000,000	$7,000,000	$3,138,200	70.0%	$6,000,000
$7,000,000	$8,000,000	$3,838,200	73.0%	$7,000,000
$8,000,000	$10,000,000	$4,568,200	76.0%	$8,000,000
$10,000,000		$6,088,200	77.0%	$10,000,000

* Taxable amount after the estate exemption.

WARNING:

THESE ARE **PRE-1977 ESTATE** TAX RATES

Federal Income Tax Rates: Estates and Trusts - 1997				
Taxable Income				
Over	But not over	Base amount	+ percent	On excess over
$0	$1,650	$0.00	15.0%	$0
$1,650	$3,900	$247.50	28.0%	$1,650
$3,900	$5,950	$877.50	31.0%	$3,900
$5,950	$8,100	$1,513.00	36.0%	$5,950
$8,100	----	$2,287.00	39.6%	$8,100

Note on the Valuation Tables that follow this page: The factors set forth in this book are taken from Department of the Treasury, Internal Revenue Service Publication 1457 (8-89), Actuarial Values Alpha Volume. The Mortality Table on the following page is drawn from the 1980 census. Once the 1990 census information is digested by the U.S. Department of Health and Human Services, Public Health Service, National center for Health Statistics, we can expect all of the tables (Table S, B, K, and 80CNSMT) to be updated.

TABLE S - SINGLE LIFE

PV of Annuity (A), Life Estate (LE), & Remainder Interests (REM)

	(6%) SIX PERCENT				(8%) EIGHT PERCENT		
Age	A	LE	REM	Age	A	LE	REM
0	16.0427	.96256	.03744	0	12.1984	.97587	.02413
5	16.1438	.96863	.03137	5	12.3137	.98510	.01490
10	15.9954	.95973	.04027	10	12.2492	.97994	.02006
15	15.7958	.94775	.05225	15	12.1534	.97227	.02773
20	15.5847	.93508	.06492	20	12.0581	.96465	.03535
25	15.3348	.92009	.07991	25	11.9452	.95562	.04438
30	14.9997	.89998	.10002	30	11.7796	.94237	.05763
35	14.5550	.87330	.12670	35	11.5402	.92321	.07679
40	13.9928	.83957	.16043	40	11.2168	.89734	.10266
45	13.3093	.79856	.20144	45	10.8011	.86409	.13591
50	12.5056	.75034	.24966	50	10.2879	.82303	.17697
55	11.5878	.69527	.30473	55	9.6749	.77399	.22601
60	10.5543	.63326	.36674	60	8.9526	.71621	.28379
65	9.4331	.56599	.43401	65	8.1360	.65088	.34912
70	8.2265	.49359	.50641	70	7.2190	.57752	.42248
75	6.9766	.41860	.58140	75	6.2305	.49844	.50156
80	5.6919	.34151	.65849	80	5.1710	.41368	.58632
85	4.5120	.27072	.72928	85	4.1633	.33307	.66693
90	3.5239	.21143	.78857	90	3.2953	.26362	.73638
95	2.7526	.16516	.83484	95	2.6006	.20805	.79195
100	2.2788	.13673	.86327	100	2.1694	.17356	.82644
105	1.8323	.10994	.89006	105	1.7638	.14110	.85890
109	0.4717	.02830	.97170	109	0.4630	.03704	.96296

TABLE **S** - SINGLE LIFE						
PV of Annuity (A), Life Estate (LE), & Remainder Interests (REM)						
(10%) TEN PERCENT				(12%) TWELVE PERCENT		
Age	A	LE	REM	Age	A	LE	REM
0	9.8078	.98078	.01922	0	8.1918	.98302	.01698
5	9.9138	.99138	.00862	5	8.2852	.99422	.00578
10	9.8806	.98806	.01194	10	8.2657	.99188	.00812
15	9.8262	.98262	.01738	15	8.2301	.98762	.01238
20	9.7771	.97771	.02229	20	8.2015	.98418	.01582
25	9.7216	.97216	.02784	25	8.1720	.98064	.01936
30	9.6329	.96329	.03671	30	8.1208	.97450	.02550
35	9.4937	.94937	.05063	35	8.0341	.96409	.03591
40	9.2945	.92945	.07055	40	7.9037	.94845	.05155
45	9.0264	.90264	.09736	45	7.7214	.92657	.07343
50	8.6818	.86818	.13182	50	7.4794	.89753	.10247
55	8.2550	.82550	.17450	55	7.1710	.86052	.13948
60	7.7326	.77326	.22674	60	6.7814	.81376	.18624
65	7.1213	.71213	.28787	65	6.3122	.75746	.24254
70	6.4093	.64093	.35907	70	5.7482	.68979	.31021
75	5.6144	.56144	.43856	75	5.0993	.61191	.38809
80	4.7295	.47295	.52705	80	4.3517	.52221	.47779
85	3.8608	.38608	.61392	85	3.5962	.43155	.56845
90	3.0929	.30929	.69071	90	2.9126	.34951	.65049
95	2.4638	.24638	.75362	95	2.3401	.28081	.71919
100	2.0696	.20696	.79304	100	1.9781	.23737	.76263
105	1.6997	.16997	.83003	105	1.6398	.19678	.80322
109	0.4545	.04545	.95455	109	0.4464	.05357	.94643

TABLE B -TERM CERTAIN

PV of Annuity (A), Income Interest (Inc. Int.), & Remainder Interests

	(6%) SIX PERCENT				(8%) EIGHT PERCENT		
Year	A	Inc.Int.	REM	Year	A	Inc.Int.	REM
1	.09434	.05660	.943396	1	0.9259	.074074	.925926
2	1.8334	.11000	.889996	2	1.7833	.142661	.857339
3	2.6730	.16038	.839619	3	2.5771	.206168	.793832
4	3.4651	.20790	.792094	4	3.3121	.264970	.735030
5	4.2124	.25274	.747258	5	3.9927	.319417	.680583
6	4.9173	.29503	.704961	6	4.6229	.369830	.630170
7	5.5824	.33494	.665057	7	5.2064	.416510	.583490
8	6.2098	.37258	.627412	8	5.7466	.459731	.540269
9	6.8017	.40810	.591898	9	6.2469	.499751	.500249
10	7.3601	.44160	.558395	10	6.7101	.536807	.463193
15	9.7122	.58273	.417265	15	8.5595	.684758	.315242
20	11.469	.68819	.311805	20	9.8181	.785452	.214548
25	12.783	.76700	.232999	25	10.674	.853982	.146018
30	13.764	.82589	.174110	30	11.257	.900623	.099377
35	14.498	.86989	.130105	35	11.654	.932365	.067635
40	15.046	.90277	.097222	40	11.924	.953969	.046031
45	15.455	.92735	.072650	45	12.108	.968672	.031328
50	15.761	.94571	.054288	50	12.233	.978679	.021321
55	15.990	.95943	.040567	55	12.318	.985489	.014511
60	16.161	.96968	.030314	60	12.376	.990124	.009876

TABLE B -TERM CERTAIN
PV of Annuity (A), Income Interest (Inc.Int.), & Remainder Interests

	(10%) TEN PERCENT				(12%) TWELVE PERCENT		
Year	A	Inc.Int.	REM	Year	A	Inc.Int.	REM
1	0.9091	.09090	.909091	1	0.8929	.107143	.892857
2	1.7355	.17355	.826446	2	1.6901	.202806	.797194
3	2.4869	.24868	.751315	3	2.4018	.288220	.711780
4	3.1699	.31698	.683013	4	3.0373	.364482	.635518
5	3.7908	.37907	.620921	5	3.6048	.432573	.567427
6	4.3553	.43552	.564474	6	4.1114	.493369	.506631
7	4.8684	.48684	.513158	7	4.5638	.547651	.452349
8	5.3349	.53349	.466507	8	4.9676	.596117	.403883
9	5.7590	.57590	.424098	9	5.3282	.639390	.360610
10	6.1446	.61445	.385543	10	5.6502	.678027	.321973
15	7.6061	.76060	.239392	15	6.8109	.817304	.182696
20	8.5136	.85135	.148644	20	7.4694	.896333	.103667
25	9.0770	.90770	.092296	25	7.8431	.941177	.058823
30	9.4269	.94269	.057309	30	8.0552	.966622	.033378
35	9.6442	.96441	.035584	35	8.1755	.981060	.018940
40	9.7791	.97790	.022095	40	8.2438	.989253	.010747
45	9.8628	.98628	.013719	45	8.2825	.993902	.006098
50	9.9148	.99148	.008519	50	8.3045	.996540	.003460
55	9.9471	.99471	.005289	55	8.3170	.998037	.001963
60	9.9672	.99671	.003284	60	8.3240	.998886	.001114

Table K

Adjustment Factors for Annuities Payable at the End of Each Interval

Interest Rate	Annually	Semi-Annually	Quarterly	Monthly	Weekly
6%	1.0000	1.0148	1.0222	1.0272	1.0291
8%	1.0000	1.0196	1.0295	1.0362	1.0387
10%	1.0000	1.0244	1.0368	1.0450	1.0482
12%	1.0000	1.0292	1.0439	1.0539	1.0577

The factors in this table are used to adjust the values for life estates, remainders, annuities, and interests for a term of years when the payments are made other than annually.

TABLE 80CNSMT

Age x	L(x)	Age x	L(x)	Age x	L(x)	Age x	L(x)
0	100,000						
1	98,740	31	96,350	61	82,581	91	11,908
2	98,648	32	96,220	62	81,348	92	9,863
3	98,584	33	96,088	63	80,024	93	8,032
4	98,535	34	95,951	64	78,609	94	6,424
5	98,495	35	95,808	65	77,107	95	5,043
6	98,459	36	95,655	66	75,520	96	3,884
7	98,426	37	95,492	67	73,846	97	2,939
8	98,396	38	95,317	68	72,082	98	2,185
9	98,370	39	95,129	69	70,218	99	1,598
10	98,347	40	94,926	70	68,248	100	1,150
11	98,328	41	94,706	71	66,165	101	815
12	98,309	42	94,465	72	63,972	102	570
13	98,285	43	94,201	73	61,673	103	393
14	98,248	44	93,913	74	59,279	104	267
15	98,196	45	93,599	75	56,799	105	179
16	98,129	46	93,256	76	54,239	106	149
17	98,047	47	92,882	77	51,599	107	78
18	97,953	48	92,472	78	48,878	108	51
19	97,851	49	92,021	79	46,071	109	33
20	97,741	50	91,526	80	43,180	110	0
21	97,623	51	90,986	81	40,208		
22	97,499	52	90,402	82	37,172		
23	97,370	53	89,771	83	34,095		
24	97,240	54	89,087	84	31,012		
25	97,110	55	88,348	85	27,960		
26	96,982	56	87,551	86	24,961		
27	96,865	57	86,695	87	22,038		
28	96,730	58	85,776	88	19,235		
29	96,604	59	84,789	89	16,598		
30	96,477	60	83,726	90	14,154		

Internal Revenue Code: Selected Edited Sections[*]

*Note: Omitted passages are marked with five asterisks (*****).

SECTIONS INCLUDED

CHAPTER 1J: SUBPART D: GRANTOR TRUST RULES

SEC. 671: TRUST INCOME, DEDUCTIONS, AND CREDITS ATTRIBUTABLE TO GRANTORS AND OTHERS AS SUBSTANTIAL OWNERS

Where it is specified in this subpart that the grantor or another person shall be treated as the owner of any portion of a trust, there shall then be included in computing the taxable income and credits of the grantor or the other person those items of income, deductions, and credits against tax of the trust which are attributable to that portion of the trust to the extent that such items would be taken into account under this chapter in computing taxable income or credits against the tax of an individual. Any remaining portion of the trust shall be subject to subparts A through D.

*****

SEC. 672: DEFINITIONS AND RULES

(a) ADVERSE PARTY.-For purposes of this subpart, the term "adverse party" means any person having a substantial beneficial interest in the trust which would be adversely affected by the exercise or nonexercise of the power which he possesses respecting the trust. A person having a general power of appointment over the trust property shall be deemed to have a beneficial interest in the trust.
(b) NONADVERSE PARTY.-For purposes of this subpart, the term "nonadverse party" means any person who is not an adverse party.
(c) RELATED OR SUBORDINATE PARTY.-For purposes of this subpart, the term "related or subordinate party" means any nonadverse party who is-

> (1) the grantor's spouse if living with the grantor;
> (2) any one of the following: The grantor's father, mother, issue, brother or sister, an employee of the grantor, a corporation or any employee of a corporation in which the stock holdings of the grantor and the trust are significant from the viewpoint of voting control; a subordinate employee of a corporation in which the grantor is an executive.

For purposes of sections 674 and 675, a related or subordinate party shall be presumed to be subservient to the grantor in respect of the exercise or nonexercise of the powers conferred on him unless such party is shown not to be subservient by a preponderance of the evidence.
(d) RULE WHERE POWER IS SUBJECT TO CONDITION PRECEDENT.- A person shall be considered to have a power described in this subpart even though the exercise of the power is subject to a precedent giving of notice or takes effect only on the expiration of a certain period after the exercise of the power.
(e) GRANTOR TREATED AS HOLDING ANY POWER OR INTEREST OF GRANTOR'S SPOUSE.-For purposes of this subpart. if a grantor's spouse is living with the grantor at the time of the creation of any power or interest held by such spouse. the grantor shall be treated as holding such power or interest.

SEC. 673: REVERSIONARY INTERESTS

(a) GENERAL RULE.-The grantor shall be treated as the owner of any portion of a trust in which he has a reversionary interest in either the corpus or the income therefrom, if, as of the inception of that portion of the trust, the value of such interest exceeds 5 percent of the value of such portion.

(b) REVERSIONARY INTEREST TAKING EFFECT AT DEATH OF MINOR LINEAL DESCENDANT BENEFICIARY.-In the case of any beneficiary who-

(1) is a lineal descendant of the grantor, and

(2) holds all of the present interests in any portion of a trust, the grantor shall not be treated under subsection (a) as the owner of such portion solely by reason of a reversionary interest in such portion which takes effect upon the death of such beneficiary before such beneficiary attains age 21.

SEC. 674: POWER TO CONTROL BENEFICIAL ENJOYMENT

(a) GENERAL RULE.-The grantor shall be treated as the owner of any portion of a trust in respect of which the beneficial enjoyment of the corpus or the income therefrom is subject to a power of disposition, exercisable by the grantor or a nonadverse party, or both, without the approval or consent of any adverse party.

(b) EXCEPTIONS FOR CERTAIN POWERS.-Subsection (a) shall not apply to the following powers regardless of by whom held:

(1) POWER TO APPLY INCOME TO SUPPORT OF A DEPENDENT.-A power described in section 677(b) to the extent that the grantor would not be subject to tax under that section.

(2) POWER AFFECTING BENEFICIAL ENJOYMENT ONLY AFTER OCCURRENCE OF EVENT.-A power, the exercise of which can only affect the beneficial enjoyment of the income for a period commencing after the occurrence of an event such that a grantor would not be treated as the owner under section 673 if the power were a reversionary interest, but the grantor may be treated as the owner after the occurrence of the event unless the power is relinquished.

(3) POWER EXERCISABLE ONLY BY WILL.-A power exercisable only by will, other than a power in the grantor to appoint by will the income of the trust where the income is accumulated for such disposition by the grantor or may be so accumulated in the discretion of the grantor or a nonadverse party, or both, without the approval or consent of any adverse party.

(4) POWER TO ALLOCATE AMONG CHARITABLE BENEFICIARIES.-A power to determine the beneficial enjoyment of the corpus or the income therefrom if the corpus or income is irrevocably payable for a purpose specified in section 170(c) (relating to definition of charitable contributions).

(5) POWER TO DISTRIBUTE CORPUS.-A power to distribute corpus either-

(A) to or for a beneficiary or beneficiaries or to or for a class of beneficiaries (whether or not income beneficiaries) provided that the power is limited by a reasonably definite standard which is set forth in the trust instrument: or

(B) to or for any current income beneficiary, provided that the distribution of corpus must be chargeable against the proportionate share of corpus held in trust for the payment of income to the beneficiary as if the corpus constituted a separate trust.

A power does not fall within the powers described in this paragraph if any person has a power to add to the beneficiary or beneficiaries or to a class of beneficiaries designated to receive the income or corpus, except where such action is to provide for after-born or after-adopted children.

    (6) POWER TO WITHHOLD INCOME TEMPORARILY.-A power to distribute or apply income to or for any current income beneficiary or to accumulate the income for him, provided that any accumulated income must ultimately be payable-

        (A) to the beneficiary from whom distribution or application is withheld, to his estate, or to his appointees (or persons named as alternate takers in default of appointment) provided that such beneficiary possesses a power of appointment which does not exclude from the class of possible appointees any person other than the beneficiary, his estate, his creditors, or the creditors of his estate, or

        (B) on termination of the trust, or in conjunction with a distribution of corpus which is augmented by such accumulated income, to the current income beneficiaries in shares which have been irrevocably specified in the trust instrument.

Accumulated income shall be considered so payable although it is provided that if any beneficiary does not survive a date of distribution which could reasonably have been expected to occur within the beneficiary's lifetime, the share of the deceased beneficiary is to be paid to his appointees or to one or more designated alternate takers (other than the grantor or the grantor's estate) whose shares have been irrevocably specified. A power does not fall within the powers described in this paragraph if any person has a power to add to the beneficiary or beneficiaries or to a class of beneficiaries designated to receive the income or corpus except where such action is to provide for after-born or after-adopted children.

    (7) POWER TO WITHHOLD INCOME DURING DISABILITY OF A BENEFICI-ARY.-A power exercisable only during-

        (A) the existence of a legal disability of any current income beneficiary, or

        (B) the period during which any income beneficiary shall be under the age of 21 years,

to distribute or apply income to or for such beneficiary or to accumulate and add the income to corpus. A power does not fall within the powers described in this paragraph if any person has a power to add to the beneficiary or beneficiaries or to a class of beneficiaries designated to receive the income or corpus, except where such action is to provide for after-born or after-adopted children.

    (8) POWER TO ALLOCATE BETWEEN CORPUS AND INCOME.-A power to allocate receipts and disbursements as between corpus and income. even though expressed in broad language.

(c) EXCEPTION FOR CERTAIN POWERS OF INDEPENDENT TRUSTEES.-Subsection (a) shall not apply to a power solely exercisable (without the approval or consent of any other person) by a trustee or trustees, none of whom is the grantor. and no more than half of whom are related or subordinate parties who are subservient to the wishes of the grantor-

    (1) to distribute, apportion, or accumulate income to or for a beneficiary or beneficiaries, or to, for, or within a class of beneficiaries; or

    (2) to pay out corpus to or for a beneficiary or beneficiaries or to or for a class of beneficiaries (whether or not income beneficiaries).

A power does not fall within the powers described in this subsection if any person has a power to add to the beneficiary or beneficiaries or to a class of beneficiaries designated to receive the income or corpus, except where such action is to provide for afte adopted children.

(d) POWER TO ALLOCATE INCOME IF LIMITED BY A STANDARD. Subsection (a) shall not apply to a power solely exercisable (without the approval or consent of any other person) by a trustee or trustees, none of whom is the grantor or spouse living with the grantor, to distribute, apportion, or accumulate income to or for a beneficiary or beneficiaries, or to, for, or within a class of beneficiaries, whether or not the conditions of paragraph (6) or (7) of subsection (b) are satisfied, if such power is limited by a reasonably definite external standard which is set forth in the trust instrument. A power does not fall within the powers described in this subsection if any person has a power to add to the beneficiary or beneficiaries or to a class of beneficiaries designated to receive the income or corpus except where such action is to provide for after-born or after-adopted children.

SEC. 675: ADMINISTRATIVE POWERS

The grantor shall be treated as the owner of any portion of a trust in respect of which-

(1) POWER TO DEAL FOR LESS THAN ADEQUATE AND FULL CONSIDERATION.-A power exercisable by the grantor or a nonadverse party, or both, without the approval or consent of any adverse party enables the grantor or any person to purchase, exchange, or otherwise deal with or dispose of the corpus or the income therefrom for less than an adequate consideration in money or money's worth.

(2) POWER TO BORROW WITHOUT ADEQUATE INTEREST OR SECURITY.-A power exercisable by the grantor or a nonadverse party, or both, enables the grantor to borrow the corpus or income, directly or indirectly, without adequate interest or without adequate security except where a trustee (other than the grantor) is authorized under a general lending power to make loans to any person without regard to interest or security.

(3) BORROWING OF THE TRUST FUNDS.-The grantor has directly or indirectly borrowed the corpus or income and has not completely repaid the loan, including any interest, before the beginning of the taxable year. The preceding sentence shall not apply to a loan which provides for adequate interest and adequate security, if such loan is made by a trustee other than the grantor and other than a related or subordinate trustee subservient to the grantor.

(4) GENERAL POWERS OF ADMINISTRATION.-A power of administration is exercisable in a nonfiduciary capacity by any person without the approval or consent of any person in a fiduciary capacity. For purposes of this paragraph, the term "power of administration" means any one or more of the following powers: (A) a power to vote or direct the voting of stock or other securities of a corporation in which the holdings of the grantor and the trust are significant from the viewpoint of voting control; (B) a power to control the investment of the trust funds either by directing investments or reinvestments, or by vetoing proposed investments or reinvestments, to the extent that the trust funds consist of stocks or securities of corporations in which the holdings of the grantor and the trust are significant from the viewpoint of voting control; or (C) a power to reacquire the trust corpus by substituting other property of an equivalent value.

SEC. 676: POWER TO REVOKE

(a) GENERAL RULE.-The grantor shall be treated as the owner of any portion of a trust, whether or not he is treated as such owner under any other provision of this part, where at any time the power to revest in the grantor title to such portion is exercisable by the grantor or a non-adverse party or both.

(b) POWER AFFECTING BENEFICIAL ENJOYMENT ONLY AFTER OCCURRENCE OF EVENT. Subsection (a) shall not apply to a power the exercise of which can only affect the beneficial enjoyment of the income for a period commencing after the occurrence of an event such that a grantor would not be treated as the owner under section 673 if the power were a reversionary interest. But the grantor may be treated as the owner after the occurrence of such event unless the power is relinquished.

SEC. 677: INCOME FOR BENEFIT OF GRANTOR

(a) GENERAL RULE.-The grantor shall be treated as the owner of any portion of a trust, whether or not he is treated as such owner under section 674, whose income without the approval or consent of any adverse party is, or, in the discretion of the grantor or a nonadverse party, or both, may be-
  (1) distributed to the grantor or the grantor's spouse;
  (2) held or accumulated for future distribution to the grantor or the grantor's spouse; or
  (3) applied to the payment of premiums on policies of insurance on the life of the grantor or the grantor's spouse (except policies of insurance irrevocably payable for a purpose specified in section 170(c) (relating to definition of charitable contributions)).
This subsection shall not apply to a power the exercise of which can only affect the beneficial enjoyment of the income for a period commencing after *the occurrence of an event* such that the grantor would not be treated as the owner under section 673 if the power were a reversionary interest; but the grantor may be treated as the owner after *the occurrence of the event* unless the power is relinquished.

(b) OBLIGATIONS OF SUPPORT.-Income of a trust shall not be considered taxable to the grantor under subsection (a) or any other provision of this chapter merely because such income in the discretion of another person, the trustee, or the grantor acting as trustee or co-trustee, may be applied or distributed for the support or maintenance of a beneficiary (other than the grantor's spouse) whom the grantor is legally obligated to support or maintain, except to the extent that such income is so applied or distributed. In cases where the amounts so applied or distributed are paid out of corpus or out of other than income for the taxable year, such amounts shall be considered to be an amount paid or credited within the meaning of paragraph (2) of section 661(a) and shall be taxed to the grantor under section 662.

SEC. 678: PERSON OTHER THAN GRANTOR TREATED AS SUBSTANTIAL OWNER

(a) GENERAL RULE.-A person other than the grantor shall be treated as the owner of any portion of a trust with respect to which:

   (1) such person has a power exercisable solely by himself to vest the corpus or the income therefrom in himself, or

   (2) such person has previously partially released or otherwise modified such a power and after the release or modification retains such control as would, within the principles of sections 671 to 677, inclusive, subject a grantor of a trust to treatment as the owner thereof.

(b) EXCEPTION WHERE GRANTOR IS TAXABLE.-Subsection (a) shall not apply with respect to a power over income, as originally granted or thereafter modified, if the grantor of the trust or a transferor (to whom section 679 applies) is otherwise treated as the owner under the provisions of this subpart other than this section.

(c) OBLIGATIONS OF SUPPORT. Subsection (a) shall not apply to a power which enables such person, in the capacity of trustee or co-trustee, merely to apply the income of the trust to the support or maintenance of a person whom the holder of the power is obligated to support or maintain except to the extent that such income is so applied. In cases where the amounts so applied or distributed are paid out of corpus or out of other than income of the taxable year, such amounts shall be considered to be an amount paid or credited within the meaning of paragraph (2) of section 661(a) and shall be taxed to the holder of the power under section 662.

(d) EFFECT OF RENUNCIATION OR DISCLAIMER.-Subsection (a) shall not apply with respect to a power which has been renounced or disclaimed within a reasonable time after the holder of the power first became aware of its existence.

*****

CHAPTER 11: ESTATE TAX

Subchapter A: Citizens or Residents

SEC. 2001: IMPOSITION AND RATE OF TAX

(a) IMPOSITION.-A tax is hereby imposed on the transfer of the taxable estate of every decedent who is a citizen or resident of the United States.

(b) COMPUTATION OF TAX.-The tax imposed by this section shall be the amount equal to the excess (if any) of-
   (1) a tentative tax computed in accordance with the rate schedule set forth in subsection (c) on the sum of-
      (A) the amount of the taxable estate, and
      (B) the amount of the adjusted taxable gifts, over
   (2) the aggregate amount of tax which would have been payable under chapter 12 with respect to gifts made by the decedent after December 31, 1976, if the rate schedule set forth in subsection (c) (as in effect at the decedent's death) had been applicable at the time of such gifts.
For purposes of paragraph (1)(b), the term "adjusted taxable gifts" means the total amount of the taxable gifts (within the meaning of section 2053) made by the decedent after December 31, 1976, other than gifts which are includable in the gross estate of the decedent.

(c) RATE SCHEDULE
   (1) (Editor's note: Transfer tax rates will be found in Table 4 of Appendix A.)
                              *****
   (2) PHASEOUT OF GRADUATED RATES AND UNIFIED CREDIT.--The tentative tax determined under paragraph (1) shall be increased by an amount equal to 5 percent of so much of the amount (with respect to which the tentative tax is to be computed) as exceeds $10,000,000 but does not exceed $21,040,000.

(d) ADJUSTMENT FOR GIFT TAX PAID BY SPOUSE.
                              *****

(e) COORDINATION OF SECTIONS 2513 AND 2035.

SEC. 2002: LIABILITY FOR PAYMENT

Except as provided in section 2210, the tax imposed by this chapter shall be paid by the executor.

SEC. 2031: DEFINITION OF GROSS ESTATE

(a) GENERAL.-The value of the gross estate of the decedent shall be determined by including to the extent provided for in this part, the value at the time of his death of all property, real or personal, tangible or intangible, wherever situated.

(b) VALUATION OF UNLISTED STOCK AND SECURITIES.-In the case of stock and securities of a corporation the value of which, by reason of their not being listed on an exchange and by reason of the absence of sales thereof, cannot be determined with reference to bid and asked prices or with reference to sales prices, the value thereof shall be determined by taking into consideration, in addition to all other factors, the value of stock or securities of corporations engaged in the same or similar line of business which are listed on an exchange.

(c) CROSS REFERENCE.

*****

SEC. 2032: ALTERNATE VALUATION

(a) GENERAL.-The value of the gross estate may be determined, if the executor so elects, by valuing all the property included in the gross estate as follows:

   (1) In the case of property distributed, sold, exchanged, or otherwise disposed of, within six months after the decedent's death such property shall be valued as of the date of distribution, sale, exchange, or other disposition.

   (2) In the case of property not distributed, sold, exchanged, or otherwise disposed of, within six months after the decedent's death such property shall be valued as of the date six months after the decedent's death.

   (3) Any interest or estate which is affected by mere lapse of time shall be included as its value as of the time of death (instead of the later date) with adjustment for any difference in its value as of the later date not due to mere lapse of time.

(b) SPECIAL RULES.

*****

(c) ELECTION MUST DECREASE GROSS ESTATE AND ESTATE TAX.- No election may be made under this section with respect to an estate unless such election shall decrease-

   (1) the value of the gross estate. and

   (2) the amount of the tax imposed by this chapter (reduced by credits allowable against such tax).

(d) ELECTION.

   (1) In General.-The election provided for in this section shall be made by the executor on the return of the tax imposed by this chapter. Such election, once made, shall be irrevocable.

   (2) Exception.-No election may be made under this section if such return is filed more than 1 year after the time prescribed by law (including extensions) for filing such return.

SEC. 2033: PROPERTY IN WHICH THE DECEDENT HAD AN INTEREST

The value of the gross estate shall include the value of all property to the extent of the interest therein of the decedent at the time of his death.

SEC. 2034: DOWER OR CURTESY INTERESTS

The value of the gross estate shall include the value of all property to the extent of any interest therein of the surviving spouse, existing at the time of the decedent's death as dower or curtesy, or by virtue of a statute creating an estate in lieu of dower or curtesy.

SEC. 2035: ADJUSTMENTS FOR GIFTS MADE WITHIN 3 YEARS OF DECEDENT'S DEATH

(a) INCLUSION OF GIFTS MADE BY DECEDENT.-Except as provided for in subsection (b), the value of the gross estate shall include the value of all property to the extent of any interest therein of which the decedent has at any time made a transfer, by trust or otherwise, during the three-year period ending on the date of the decedent 's death.
(b) EXCEPTIONS.-Subsection (a) shall not apply-
  (1) to any bona fide sale for an adequate and full consideration in money or money's worth, and
  (2) to any gift to a donee made during a calendar year if the decedent was not required by section 6019 [other than by reason of section 6019(2)] to file any gift tax return for such year with respect to gifts to such donee. Paragraph (2) shall not apply to any transfer with respect to a life insurance policy.
(c) INCLUSION OF GIFT TAX ON CERTAIN GIFTS MADE DURING 3 YEARS BEFORE DECEDENT'S DEATH.-The amount of the gross estate (determined without regard to this subsection) shall be increased by the amount of any tax paid under chapter 12 by the decedent or his estate on any gift made by the decedent or his spouse made after December 31. 1976, and during the three-year period ending on the date of the decedent's death.
(d) DECEDENTS DYING AFTER 1981-
  (1) IN GENERAL.-Except as otherwise provided in this subsection (a) shall not apply to the estate of a decedent dying after December 31, 1981.
  (2) EXCEPTIONS FOR CERTAIN TRANSFERS. Paragraph l of this subsection and paragraph (2) of subsection (b) shall not apply to a transfer of an interest in property which is included in the value of the gross estate under section 2036, 2037, 2038, or 2042 or would have been included under any of such sections if such interest had been retained by the decedent.
  (3) THREE-YEAR RULE RETAINED FOR CERTAIN PURPOSES.- Paragraph (1) shall not apply for purposes of-
    (A) section 303(b) (relating to distributions in redemption of stock to pay death taxes),
    (B) section 2032A (relating to special valuation of certain farm, etc., real property), and
    (C) subchapter C of chapter 64 (relating to lien for taxes).
  (4) COORDINATION OF THREE-YEAR RULE WITH SECTION 6166(a)(1). An estate shall be treated as meeting the 35 percent of adjusted gross estate requirement of section 6166(a)(1) only if the estate meets such requirements both with and without the application of paragraph (1).

SEC. 2036: TRANSFERS WITH RETAINED LIFE ESTATE

(a) GENERAL RULE.-The value of the gross estate shall include the value of all property to the extent of any interest therein of which the decedent has at any time made a transfer (except in case of a bona fide sale for an adequate and full consideration in money or money's worth), by trust or otherwise, under which he has retained for his life or for any period not ascertainable without reference to his death or for any period which does not in fact end before his death-

    (1) the possession or enjoyment of, or the right to the income from, the property, or

    (2) the right, either alone or in conjunction with any person, to designate the persons who shall possess or enjoy the property or the income therefrom.

(b) VOTING RIGHTS

    (1) IN GENERAL, For purposes of subsection (a)(1), the retention of the right to vote (directly or indirectly) shares of stock of a controlled corporation shall be considered to be a retention of the enjoyment of transferred property.

    (2) CONTROLLED CORPORATION.
        *****

    (3) COORDINATION WITH SECTION 2035.
        *****

(c) LIMITATION ON APPLICATION OF GENERAL RULE.

(Editor's note: In 1990, the anti-freeze provisions of old §2036(c) were repealed retroactive to inception, and old §2036(d) was relabeled new §2036(c).)
*****

SEC. 2037: TRANSFERS TAKING EFFECT AT DEATH

(a) GENERAL RULE.-The value of the gross estate shall include the value of all property to the extent of any interest therein of which the decedent has at any time after September 7, 1916, made a transfer (except in case of a bona fide sale for an adequate and full consideration in money or money's worth), by trust or otherwise, if-

    (1) possession or enjoyment of the property can, through ownership of such interest, be obtained only by surviving the decedent, and

    (2) the decedent has retained a reversionary interest in the property (but in the case of a transfer made before October 8, 1949, only if such reversionary interest arose by the express terms of the instrument of transfer), and the value of such reversionary interest immediately before the death of the decedent exceeds 5 percent of the value of such property.

(b) SPECIAL RULES.
        *****

SEC. 2038: REVOCABLE TRANSFERS

(a) IN GENERAL.-The value of the gross estate shall include the value of all property-
    (1) Transfers after June 22, 1936- To the extent of any interest therein of which the decedent has at any time made a transfer (except in case of a bona fide sale for an adequate and full consideration in money or money's worth), by trust or otherwise, where the enjoyment thereof was subject at the date of his death to any change through the exercise of a power (in whatever capacity exercisable) by the decedent alone or by the decedent in conjunction with any other person (without regard to when or from what source the decedent acquired such power), to alter, amend, revoke, or terminate, or where such power is relinquished during the three-year period ending on the date of the decedent's death.
    (2) TRANSFERS ON OR BEFORE JUNE 22, l936.
*****

(b) DATE OF EXISTENCE OF POWER.
*****

SEC. 2039: ANNUITIES

(a) GENERAL.-The gross estate shall include the value of an annuity or other payment receivable by any beneficiary by reason of surviving the decedent under any form of contract or agreement entered into after March 3, 1931 (other than as insurance under policies on the life of the decedent), if, under such contract or agreement, an annuity or other payment was payable to the decedent, or the decedent possessed the right to receive such annuity or payment, either alone or in conjunction with another for his life or for any period not ascertainable without reference to his death or for any period which does not in fact end before his death.

(b) AMOUNT INCLUDABLE.
*****

SEC. 2040: JOINT INTERESTS

(a) GENERAL RULE.-The value of the gross estate shall include the value of all property to the extent of the interest therein held as joint tenants with right of survivorship by the decedent and any other person, or as tenants by the entirety by the decedent and spouse, or deposited, with any person carrying on the banking business, in their joint names and payable to either or the survivor, except such part thereof as may be shown to have originally belonged to such other person and never to have been received or acquired by the latter from the decedent for less than an adequate or full consideration in money or money's worth; Provided, That where such property or any part thereof, or part of the consideration with which such property was acquired, is shown to have been at any time acquired by such other person from the decedent for less than an adequate and full consideration in money or money's worth, there shall be excepted only such part of the value of such property as is proportionate to the consideration furnished by such other person: Provided further, that where any property has been acquired by gift, bequest, devise, or inheritance, as a tenancy by the entirety by the decedent and spouse, then to the extent of one half of the value thereof, or, where so acquired by the decedent and any other person as joint tenants with right of survivorship and their interests are not otherwise specified or fixed by law, then to the extent of the value of a fractional part to be determined by dividing the value of the property by the number of joint tenants with right of survivorship.

(b) CERTAIN JOINT INTERESTS OF HUSBAND AND WIFE.-

    (1) INTERESTS OF SPOUSE EXCLUDED FROM GROSS ESTATE,- Notwithstanding subsection (a), in the case of any qualified joint interest, the value included in the gross estate with respect to such interest by reason of this section is one half of the value of such qualified joint interest,

    (2) QUALIFIED JOINT INTEREST DEFINED.-For purposes of paragraph (1), the term "qualified joint interest" means any interest in property held by the decedent and the decedent's spouse as-

        (A) tenants by the entirety, or

        (B) joint tenants with right of survivorship, but only if the decedent and the spouse of the decedent are the only joint tenants.

SECTION 2041: POWERS OF APPOINTMENT

(a) IN GENERAL.-The value of the gross estate shall include the value of all property.

    (1) POWERS OF APPOINTMENT CREATED ON OR BEFORE OCTOBER 21, 1942.

            *****

    (2) POWERS CREATED AFTER OCTOBER 21, 1942.-To the extent of any property with respect to which the decedent has at the time of his death a general power of appointment created after October 21, 1942, or with respect to which the decedent has at any time exercised or released such a power of appointment by a disposition which is of such a nature that if it were a transfer of property owned by the decedent, such property would be includable in the decedent's gross estate under section 2035 to 2038, inclusive. For purposes of this paragraph (2), the power of appointment shall be considered to exist on the date of the decedent's death even though the exercise of the power is subject to a precedent giving of notice or even though the exercise of the power takes effect only on the expiration of a stated period after its exercise, whether or not on or before the date of the decedent's death notice has been given or the power has been exercised.

    (3) CREATION OF ANOTHER POWER IN CERTAIN CASES.

            *****

(b) DEFINITIONS.-For purposes of subsection (a)-

    (1) GENERAL POWER OF APPOINTMENT-The term "general power of appointment" means a power which is exercisable in favor of the decedent, his estate, his creditors, or the creditors of his estate: except that-

        (A) A power to consume, invade, or appropriate property for the benefit of the decedent which is limited to an ascertainable standard relating to the health, education, support, or maintenance of the decedent shall not be deemed a general power of appointment.

        (B) A power of appointment created on or before October 21, 1942, which is exercisable by the decedent only in conjunction with another person shall not be deemed a general power of appointment.

        (C) In the case of a power of appointment created after October 21, 1942, which is exercisable by the decedent only in conjunction with another person-

(i) If the power is not exercisable by the decedent except in conjunction with the creator of the power-such power shall not be deemed a general power of appointment.

(ii) If the power is not exercisable by the decedent except in conjunction with a person having a substantial interest in the property, subject to the power, which is adverse to the exercise of the power in favor of the decedent-such power shall not be deemed a general power of appointment.

*****

(iii)

*****

For purposes of clauses (ii) and (iii), a power shall be deemed to be exercisable in favor of a person if it is exercisable in favor of such a person, his estate, his creditors, or the creditors of his estate.

(2) LAPSE OF POWER-The lapse of a power of appointment created after October 21, 1942, during the life of the individual possessing the power shall be considered a release of such power. The preceding sentence shall apply with respect to the lapse of powers during any calendar year only to the extent that the property, which could have been appointed by exercise of such lapsed powers, exceeded in value, at the time of such lapse, the greater of the following amounts:

(A) $5,000, or

(B) 5 percent of the aggregate value, at the time of such lapse, of the assets out of which, or the proceeds of which, the exercise of the lapsed powers could have been satisfied.

(3) DATE OF CREATION OF SUCH POWER

*****

SEC. 2042: PROCEEDS OF LIFE INSURANCE

The value of the gross estate shall include the value of all property-

(1) RECEIVABLE BY THE EXECUTOR.-To the extent of the amount receivable by the executor as insurance under policies on the life of the decedent.

(2) RECEIVABLE BY OTHER BENEFICIARIES.-To the extent of the amount receivable by all other beneficiaries as insurance under policies on the life of the decedent with respect to which the decedent possessed at his death any of the incidents of ownership, exercisable either alone or in conjunction with any other person.

*****

SEC. 2043: TRANSFERS FOR INSUFFICIENT CONSIDERATION

(a) IN GENERAL.-If any one of the transfers, trusts, interests, rights, or powers enumerated and described in sections 2035 to 2038, inclusive, and section 2041 is made, created, exercised, or relinquished for a consideration in money or money's worth, but is not a bona fide sale for an adequate and full consideration in money or money's worth, there shall be included in the gross estate only the excess of the fair market value at the time of death of the property otherwise to be included on account of such transaction, over the value of the consideration received therefore by the decedent.

(b) MARITAL RIGHTS NOT TREATED AS CONSIDERATION.
*****

SEC. 2044: CERTAIN PROPERTY FOR WHICH MARITAL DEDUCTION WAS PREVIOUSLY ALLOWED.

(a) GENERAL RULE.--The value of the gross estate shall include the value of any property to which this section applies in which the decedent had a qualifying income interest for life.

(b) PROPERTY TO WHICH THIS SECTION APPLIES.-- This section applies to any property if-

(1) a deduction was allowed with respect of the transfer of such property to the decedent--

(A) under section 2056 by reason of subsection (b)(7) thereof, or

(B) under section 2523 by reason of subsection (f) thereof, and

(2) section 2519 (relating to dispositions of certain life estates) did not apply with respect to a disposition by the decedent of part or all such properties.

(c) PROPERTY TREATED AS HAVING PASSED FROM DECEDENT For purposes of this chapter and chapter 13, property includable of the gross estate of the decedent under subsection (a) shall be treated as property passing from the decedent.

SEC. 2051: DEFINITION OF TAXABLE ESTATE

For purposes of the tax imposed by section 2001, the value of the taxable estate shall be determined by deducting from the value of the gross estate the deductions provided for in this part.

SEC. 2053: EXPENSES, INDEBTEDNESS, AND TAXES

(a) GENERAL RULE.-- For purposes of the tax imposed by section 2001, the value of the taxable estate shall be determined by deducting from the value of the gross estate such amounts--

(1) for funeral expenses

(2) for administration expenses,

(3) for claims against the estate, and

(4) for unpaid mortgages on, or any indebtedness in respect of, property where the value of the decedent's interest therein, undiminished by such mortgage or indebtedness, is included in the value of the gross estate,

as are allowed by the laws of jurisdiction, whether within or without the United States, under which the estate is being administered.

(b) OTHER ADMINISTRATION EXPENSES.--Subject to the limitations in paragraph (1) of subsection (c), there shall be deducted in determining the taxable estate amounts representing expenses incurred in administering property not subject to claims which is included in the gross estate to the same extent such amounts would be allowable as a deduction under subsection (a) if such property were subject to claims, and such amounts are paid before the expiration of the period of limitation for assessment provided in section 6501.

(c) LIMITATIONS.--

    (1) LIMITATIONS APPLICABLE TO SUBSECTIONS (a) AND (b).--

        (A) CONSIDERATION FOR CLAIMS.--The deduction allowed by this section in the case of claims against the estate, unpaid mortgages, or any indebtedness shall, when founded on a promise or an agreement, be limited to the extent that they were contracted bona fide and for an adequate and full consideration in money or money's worth; except that in any case in which any such claim is founded on a promise or agreement of the decedent to make a contribution or gift to or for the use of any donee described in section 2055 for the purposes specified therein, the deduction for such claims shall not be so limited, but shall be limited to the extent that it would be allowable as a deduction under section 2055 if such promise or agreement constituted a bequest.

        (B) CERTAIN TAXES.--Any income taxes on income received after the death of the decedent, or property taxes not accrued before his death, or any estate, succession, legacy, or inheritances taxes, shall not be deductible under this section. This subparagraph shall not apply to any increase in the tax imposed by this chapter by reason of section 4980A(d).

        (C) CERTAIN CLAIMS BY REMAINDERMEN.--No deduction shall be allowed under this section for a claim against the estate by a remainderman relating to any property described in section 2044.

    (2) LIMITATIONS APPLICABLE ONLY TO SUBSECTION (a).--In the case of the amounts described in subsection (a), there shall be disallowed the amount by which the deductions specified exceed the value, at the time of the decedent's death, of property subject to claims, except to the extent that such deductions represent amounts paid before the date prescribed for the filing of the estate tax return. For purposes of this section, the term "property subject to claims" means property includable in the gross estate of the decedent which, or the avails of which, would under the applicable law, bear the burden of the payment of such deductions in the final adjustment and settlement of the estate, except that the value of the property shall be reduced by the amount of the deduction under section 2054 attributable to such property.

(d) CERTAIN STATE AND FOREIGN DEATH TAXES--

*****

SEC. 2054: LOSSES

For purposes of the tax imposed by section 2001, the value of the taxable estate shall be determined by deducting from the value of the gross estate losses incurred during the settlement of estates arising from fires, storms, shipwrecks, or other casualties, or from theft, when such losses are not compensated for by insurance or otherwise.

SEC. 2055: TRANSFERS FOR PUBLIC, CHARITABLE, AND RELIGIOUS USES

(a) IN GENERAL.-- For purposes of the tax imposed by section 2001, the value of the taxable estate shall be determined by deducting from the value of the gross estate the amount of all bequests, legacies, devises, or transfers--

(1) to or for the use of the United States, any state, any political subdivision thereof, or the District of Columbia, for exclusively public purposes;

(2) to or for the use of any corporation organized and operated exclusively for religious, charitable, scientific, literary, or educational purposes, including the encouragement of art, or to foster national or international amateur sports competition (but only if no part of its activities involve the provision of athletic facilities or equipment), and prevention of cruelty to children or animals, no part of the net earnings of which inures to the benefit of any private stockholder or individual, which is not disqualified for tax exemption under section 501 (c)(3) by reason of attempting to influence legislation, and which does not participate in, or intervene in (including the publishing or distributing of statements), any political campaign on behalf of(or in opposition to) any candidate for public office;

(3) to a trustee or trustees, or a fraternal society, order or association operating under the lodge system, but only if such contributions or gifts are to be used by such trustee or trustees, or by such fraternal society, order, or association, exclusively for religious, charitable, scientific, literary, or educational purposes, or for the prevention of cruelty to children or animals, such trust, fraternal society, order, or association would not be disqualified for tax exemption under section 501(c)(3) by reason of attempting to influence legislation, and such trustee or trustees, or such fraternal society, order or association, does not participate in, or intervene in (including the publishing or distributing of statements), any political campaign on behalf of (or in opposition to) any candidate for public office; or

(4) to or for the use of any veterans' organization incorporated by Act of Congress, or of its departments or local chapters or posts, no part of the net earnings of which inures to the benefit of any private shareholder or individual.

For purposes of this subsection, the complete termination before the date prescribed for the filing of the estate tax return of a power to consume, invade, or appropriate property for the benefit of an individual before such power has been exercised by reason of the death of such individual or for any other reason shall be considered and deemed to be a qualified disclaimer with the same full force and effect as though he had filed such qualified disclaimer. Rules similar to the rules of section 501(j) shall apply for purposes of paragraph (2).

(Subsections b through g are omitted)

SEC. 2056: BEQUESTS, ETC., TO SURVIVING SPOUSE

(a) ALLOWANCE OF MARITAL DEDUCTION.-For purposes of the tax imposed by section 2001, the value of the taxable estate shall, except as limited by subsection (b), be determined by deducting from the value of the gross estate an amount equal to the value of any interest in property which passes or has passed from the decedent to his surviving spouse, but only to the extent that such interest is included in determining the value of the gross estate.

(b) LIMITATION IN THE CASE OF LIFE ESTATE OR OTHER TERMINABLE INTEREST-

    (1) GENERAL RULE.-Where, on the lapse of time, on the occurrence of an event or contingency, or on the failure of an event or contingency to occur, an interest passing to the surviving spouse will terminate or fail, no deduction shall be allowed under this section with respect to such interest-

        (A) if an interest in such property passes or has passed (for less than an adequate and full consideration in money or money's worth) from the decedent to any person other than such surviving spouse (or the estate of such spouse); and

        (B) if by reason of such passing such person (or his heirs or assigns) may possess or enjoy any part of such property after such termination or failure of the interest so passing to the surviving spouse; and no deduction shall be allowed with respect to such interest [even if such deduction is not disallowed under subparagraphs (A) and (B)]-

        (C) if such interest is to be acquired for the surviving spouse. pursuant to directions of the decedent, by his executor or by the trustee of a trust.

*****

    (2) INTEREST IN UNIDENTIFIED ASSETS.

*****

    (3) INTEREST OF SPOUSE CONDITIONAL ON SURVIVAL FOR LIMITED PERIOD-For purposes of this subsection, an interest passing to the surviving spouse shall not be considered as an interest which will terminate or fail on the death of such spouse if-

        (A) such death will cause a termination or failure of such interest only if it occurs within a period not exceeding six months after the decedent's death, or only if it occurs as a result of a common disaster resulting in the death of the decedent and the surviving spouse, or only if it occurs in the case of either such event; and

        (B) such termination or failure does not in fact occur.

    (4) VALUATION OF INTEREST PASSING TO SURVIVING SPOUSE.

*****

    (5) LIFE ESTATE WITH POWER OF APPOINTMENT IN SURVIVING SPOUSE-In the case of an interest in property passing from the decedent, if his surviving spouse is entitled for life to all the income from the entire interest, or all the income from a specific portion thereof, payable annually or at more frequent intervals. with power in the surviving spouse to appoint the entire interest, or such specific portion (exercisable in favor of such surviving spouse, or of the estate of such surviving spouse, or in favor of either, whether or not in each case the power is exercisable in favor of others), and with no power in any other person to appoint any part of the interest, or such specific portion, to any person other than the

surviving spouse-

(A) the interest or such portion thereof so passing shall, for purposes of subsection (a), be considered as passing to the surviving spouse, and

(B) no part of the interest so passing shall, for purposes of paragraph (1)(A), be considered as passing to any person other than the surviving spouse.

This paragraph shall apply only if such power in the surviving spouse to appoint the entire interest, or such specific portion thereof, whether exercisable by will or during life, is exercisable by such spouse alone and in all events.

(6) LIFE INSURANCE OR ANNUITY PAYMENTS WITH POWER OF APPOINTMENT IN SURVIVING SPOUSE.

*****

(7) ELECTION WITH RESPECT TO LIFE ESTATE FOR SURVIVING SPOUSE-

(A) IN GENERAL.-In the case of qualified terminable interest property-

    (i) for purposes of subsection (a), such property shall be treated as passing to the surviving spouse, and

    (ii) for purposes of paragraph (1)(A), no part of such property shall be treated as passing to any person other than the surviving spouse.

(B) QUALIFIED TERMINABLE INTEREST PROPERTY DEFINED.-For purposes of this paragraph-

    (i) IN GENERAL.-The term "qualified terminable interest property" means property-

        (I) which passes from the decedent,

        (II) in which the surviving spouse has a qualifying income interest for life, and

        (III) to which an election under this paragraph applies.

    (ii) Qualifying Income Interest For Life- The surviving spouse has a qualifying income interest for life if-

        (I) the surviving spouse is entitled to all the income from the property, payable annually or at more frequent intervals, or has a usifruct interest for life in the property, and

        (II) no person has a power to appoint any part of the property to any person other than the surviving spouse.

Subclause (II) shall not apply to a power exercisable only at or after the death of the surviving spouse. To the extent provided in regulations, an annuity shall be treated in a manner similar to an income interest in property (regardless of whether the property from which the annuity is payable can be separately identified).

    (iii) PROPERTY INCLUDES INTEREST THEREIN.- The term "property" includes an interest in property.

    (iv) SPECIFIC PORTION TREATED AS SEPARATE PROPERTY.- A specific portion of property shall be treated as separate property.

    (v) ELECTION.-An election under this paragraph with respect to any property shall be made by the executor on the return of tax imposed by section 2001. Such an election, once made, shall be irrevocable.

(8) SPECIAL RULE FOR CHARITABLE REMAINDER TRUSTS.

*****

(9) DENIAL OF DOUBLE DEDUCTION.

*****

CHAPTER 11: ESTATE TAX, CONTINUED

Subchapter B: Nonresidents Not Citizens

SEC. 2101: TAX IMPOSED

(a) IMPOSITION.--Except as provided in section 2107, a tax is hereby imposed on the transfer of the taxable estate(determined as provided in section 2106) of every decedent nonresident not a citizen of the United States.

(b) COMPUTATION OF TAX.-- The tax imposed by this section shall be the amount equal to the excess (if any) of--

    (1) a tentative tax computed under section 2001 (c) on the sum of--

        A) amount of the taxable estate, and

        B) the amount of the taxable gifts, over

    (2) a tentative tax computed under section 2001 (c) on the amount of adjusted taxable gifts.

For purposes of the preceding sentence, there shall be appropriate adjustments in the application of section 2001 (c)(2) to reflect the difference between the amount of credit provided under section 2012(c) and the amount of credit provided under section 2010.

(c) ADJUSTMENTS FOR TAXABLE GIFTS.--

    1) ADJUSTED TAXABLE GIFTS DEFINED.--For purposes of this section, the term "adjustable taxable gifts" means the total amount of the taxable gifts (within the meaning of section 2503 as modified by section 2511) made by the decedent after December 31, 1976, other than gifts which are includable in the gross estate of the decedent.

    2) ADJUSTMENT FOR CERTAIN GIFT TAX.-- For purposes of this section, the rules of section 2001 (d) shall apply.

CHAPTER 12: GIFT TAX

SEC. 2501: IMPOSITION OF TAX

(a) TAXABLE TRANSFERS.--

    (1) GENERAL RULE.-- A tax, computed as provided in section 2502, is hereby imposed for each calendar year on the transfer of property by gift during such calendar year by any individual, resident or nonresident.

    (2) TRANSFERS OF INTANGIBLE PROPERTY.-- Except as provided in paragraph (3), paragraph (1) shall not apply to the transfer of intangible property by a nonresident not a citizen of the United States.

    (3) EXCEPTIONS--Paragraph (2) shall not apply in the case of a donor who at any time after March 8, 1965, and within the 10-year period ending with the date of transfer lost United States citizenship unless--

        (A) such donor's loss of United States citizenship resulted from the application of section 301(b), 350, or 355 of the Immigration and Nationality Act, as amended (8 U. S. C. 1401 (b), 1482, or 1487), or

        (B) such loss did not have for one of its principal purposes the avoidance of taxes under this subtitle or subtitle A.

    (4) BURDEN OF PROOF.-- If the Secretary establishes that it is reasonable to believe that an individual's loss of United States citizenship would, but for paragraph (3), result in the substantial reduction for the calendar year in the taxes on the transfer of property by gift, the burden of proving that such loss of citizenship did not have for one of its principal purposes the avoidance of taxes under this subtitle A shall be on such individual.

    (5) TRANSFERS TO POLITICAL ORGANIZATIONS.--Paragraph (1) shall not apply to the transfer of money or other property to a political organization (within the meaning of section 527(e)(1)) for the use of such organization.

(b) CERTAIN RESIDENTS OF POSSESSIONS CONSIDERED CITIZENS OF THE UNITED STATES.--A donor who is a citizen of the United States and a resident of a possession thereof shall, for the purposes of the taxes imposed by this chapter, be considered a "citizen" of the United States within the meaning of the term wherever used in this title unless he acquired his United States citizenship solely by reason of, 1) his being a citizen of such possession of the United States, or 2) his birth or residence within such possession of the United States.

(c) CERTAIN RESIDENTS OF POSSESSIONS CONSIDERED NONRESIDENTS NOT CITIZENS OF THE UNITED STATES.--A donor who is a citizen of the United States and a resident of a possession thereof shall, for purposes of the tax imposed by this chapter, be considered a "nonresident not a citizen of the United States" within the meaning of the term wherever used in this title, but only if such donor acquired his United States citizenship solely by reason of (1) his being a citizen of such possession of the United States, or (2) his birth or residence within such possession of the United States.

(d) CROSS REFERENCES.--

    (1) For increase in basis of property acquired by gift for gift tax paid, see section 1015(d).

    (2) For exclusion of transfers of property outside the United States

SEC. 2503: TAXABLE GIFTS

(a) GENERAL DEFINITION.-The term "taxable gifts" means the total amount of gifts made during the calendar year, less the deductions provided in subchapter C (section 2522 and following).

(b) EXCLUSIONS FROM GIFTS.-In the case of gifts (other than gifts of future interests in property) made to any person by the donor during the calendar year, the first $10,000 of such gifts to such person shall not, for purposes of subsection (a), be included in the total amount of gifts made during such year. Where there has been a transfer to any person of a present interest in property, the possibility that such interest may be diminished by the exercise of a power shall be disregarded in applying this subsection, if no part of such interest will at any time pass to any other person.

(c) TRANSFER FOR THE BENEFIT OF A MINOR.-No part of a gift to an individual who has not attained the age of 21 years on the date of such transfer shall be considered a gift of a future interest in property for purposes of subsection (b) if the property and the income therefrom-
    (1) may be expended by, or for the benefit of, the donee before his attaining the age of 21 years, and
    (2) will to the extent not so expended-
        (A) pass to the donee on his attaining the age of 21 years, and
        (B) in the event that the donee dies before attaining the age of 21 years, be payable to the estate of the donee or as he may appoint under a general power of appointment as defined in section 2514(c).

(d) Repealed.

(e) EXCLUSION FOR CERTAIN TRANSFERS FOR EDUCATIONAL EXPENSES OR MEDICAL EXPENSES.-
    (1) IN GENERAL-Any qualified transfer shall not be treated as a transfer of property by gift for purposes of this chapter.
    (2) QUALIFIED TRANSFER.-For purposes of this subsection, the term "qualified transfer" means any amount paid on behalf of an individual-
        (A) as tuition to an educational organization described in section 170(b)(I)(A)(ii) for the education or training of such individual, or
        (B) to any person who provides medical care [as defined in section 213(e)] with respect to such individual as payment for such medical care.

SEC. 2513: GIFT BY HUSBAND OR WIFE TO THIRD PARTY

(a) CONSIDERED AS MADE ONE-HALF BY EACH.--

    (1) IN GENERAL.--A gift made by one spouse to any person other than his spouse shall, for the purpose of this chapter, be considered made one-half by him and one-half by his spouse, but only if at the time of the gift each spouse is a citizen or resident of the United States. This paragraph shall not apply with respect to a gift of an interest in property if he creates in his spouse a general power of appointment, as defined in section 2514 (c), over such interest. For purposes of this section, an individual shall be considered as a spouse of another individual only if he is married to such individual at the time of the gift and does not remarry during the remainder of the calendar year.

    (2) CONSENT OF BOTH SPOUSES.--Paragraph (1) shall apply only if both spouses have signified (under the regulations provided for its subsection(b)) their consent to the application of paragraph (1) in the case of all such gifts made during the calendar year by either while married to the other.

(b) MANNER AND TIME OF SIGNIFYING CONSENT.--

    (1) MANNER.--A consent under this section shall be signified in such manner as is provided under regulations prescribed by the secretary.

    (2) TIME.--Such consent may be so signified after the close of the calendar year in which the gift was made, subject to the following limitations--

        (A) The consent may not be signified after the 15th of April following the close of such year, unless before the 15th day no return has been filed for such year by either spouse, in which case the consent may not be signified after a return for such year is filed by either spouse.

        (B) The consent may not be signified after a note of deficiency with respect to the tax for such year has been set to either spouse in accordance with section 6212(a).

(c) REVOCATION OF CONSENT.--Revocation of consent previously signified shall be made in such manner as is provided under regulations prescribed by the secretary, but the right to revoke a consent previously signified with respect to a calendar year-

    (1) shall not exist after the 15th day of April following the close of such year if the consent was signified on or before such 15th day; and

    (2) shall not exist if the consent was not signified until after such 15th day.

(d) JOINT AND SEVERAL LIABILITY FOR TAX.--If the consent required by subsection (a)(2) is signified with respect to a gift made in the calendar year, the liability with respect to the entire tax imposed by this chapter of each spouse for such year shall be joint and several.

SEC. 2514: POWERS OF APPOINTMENT

(a) POWERS CREATED ON OR BEFORE OCTOBER 21, 1942.-- An exercise of general power of appointment created on or before October 21, 1942, shall be deemed a transfer of property by the individual possessing such power; but the failure to exercise such a power or the complete release of such a power shall not be deemed an exercise thereof. If a general power of appointment created on or before October 21, 1942, has been partially released so that it is no longer a general power of appointment, the subsequent exercise of such power shall not be deemed to be the exercise of a general power of appointment if--

(1) such partial release occurred before November 1, 1951, or

(2) the donee of such power was under a legal disability to release such power on October 21, 1942, and such partial release occurred not later than six months after the termination of such legal disability.

(b) POWERS CREATED AFTER OCTOBER 21, 1942.-- The exercise or release of a general power of appointment created after October 21, 1942, shall be deemed a transfer of property by the individual possessing such power.

(c) DEFINITION OF GENERAL POWER OF APPOINTMENT.--For purposes of this section, the term "general power of appointment" means a power which is exercisable in favor of the individual possessing the power (hereafter in this subsection referred to as the "possessor"), his estate, his creditors, or the creditors of his estate; except that--

(1) A power to consume, invade, or appropriate property for the benefit of the possessor which is limited by an ascertainable standard relating to health, education, support, or maintenance of the possessor shall not be deemed a general power of appointment.

(2) A power of appointment created on or before October 21, 1942, which is exercisable by the possessor only in conjunction with another person shall not be deemed a general power of appointment.

(3) In the case of a power appointment created on or before October 21, 1942, which is exercisable by the possessor only in conjunction with another person--

(A) if the power is not exercisable by the possessor in conjunction with the creator of the power--such power shall not be deemed a general power of appointment;

(B) if the power is not exercisable by the possessor except in conjunction with a person having a substantial interest in the property subject to the power, which is adverse to exercise of the power in favor of the possessor-- property subject to the power, which is adverse to exercise of the power in favor of the possessor-- such power shall not be deemed a general power of appointment. For the purposes of this subparagraph a person who, after the death of the possessor, may be possessed of a power of appointment(with respect to the property subject to the possessors power) which he may exercise in his own favor shall be deemed as having interest in the property and such interest shall be deemed adverse to such exercise of the possessor's power;

(C) if (after the application of subparagraphs(A) and (B) the power is a general power of appointment and is exercisable in favor of such other person--such power shall be deemed a general power of appointment only in respect of a fractional part of the property subject to such power, such part to be determined by dividing the value of such property by the number of such persons(including the possessor) in favor of whom such power is exercisable.

For purposes of subparagraphs (B) and (C), a power shall be deemed to be exercisable in favor of a person if it is exercisable in favor of such person, his estate, his creditors, or the creditors of his estate.

(d) CREATION OF ANOTHER POWER IN CERTAIN CASES.-- If a power of appointment created after October 21, 1942, is exercised by creating another power of appointment which, under the applicable local law, can be validly exercised so as to postpone the vesting of any estate or interest in the property which was subject to the first power, or suspend the absolute ownership or power of alienation of such property, for a period ascertainable without regard to the date of the creation of this first power, such exercise of the first power shall, to the extent of the property subject to the second power, be deemed a transfer of property by the individual possessing such power.

(e) LAPSE OF POWER.--The lapse of a power of appointment created after October 21, 1942, during the life of the individual possessing the power shall be considered a release of such power. The rule of the preceding sentence shall apply with respect to the lapse of powers during any calendar year only to the extent that the property which could have been appointed by exercise of such lapsed powers exceeds in value the greater of the following amounts:

   (1) $5,000, or
   (2) 5 percent of the aggregate value of the assets out of which, or the proceeds of
        which, the exercise of the lapsed powers could be satisfied.

(f) DATE OF CREATION OF POWER.--For purposes of this section a power of appointment created by a will executed on or before October 21, 1942, shall be considered a power on or before such date if the person executing the will dies before July 1, 1949, without having republished such will, by codicil or otherwise, after October 21, 1942.

SEC. 2518: DISCLAIMERS

(a) GENERAL RULE.-- For purposes of this subtitle, if a person makes a qualified disclaimer with respect to any interest in property, this subtitle shall apply with respect to such interest as if the interest had never been transferred to such person.

(b) QUALIFIED DISCLAIMER DEFINED.-- For purposes of subsection (a), the term "qualified disclaimer" means an irrevocable and unqualified refusal by a person to accept an interest in property but only if--

   (1) such refusal is in writing
   (2) such writing is received by the transferor of the interest, his legal representative,
        or the holder of the legal title to which the interest relates not later than the date
        which is nine months after the later of--
        (A) the date on which the transfer in such person is made, or
        (B) the day on which such person attains age 21.
   (3) such person has not accepted the interest or any benefits, and
   (4) as a result of such refusal, the interest passes without any direction on the part of
        the person making the disclaimer and passes either--
        (A) to the spouse of the decedent, or
        (B) to a person other than the person making the disclaimer.

(c) OTHER RULES.--For purposes of subsection (a)--
   (1) DISCLAIMER OF UNDIVIDED PORTION OF INTEREST.-- A disclaimer with
        respect to an undivided portion of an interest which meets the requirements of the
        preceding sentence shall be treated as a qualified disclaimer of such portion of the

interest.

(2) POWERS.-- A power with respect to property shall be treated as an interest in such property.

(3) CERTAIN TRANSFERS TREATED AS DISCLAIMERS.--A written transfer of the transferor's [*sic*] entire interest in the property--

(A) which meets requirements similar to the requirements of paragraphs (2) and (3) of subsection(b), and

(B) which is to a person or persons who would have received the property had the transferor [*sic*] made a qualified disclaimer (within the meaning of subsection (b)), shall be treated as a qualified disclaimer.

CHAPTER 13: GENERATION-SKIPPING TRANSFER TAX

SEC. 2601: TAX IMPOSED

A tax is hereby imposed on every generation-skipping transfer (within the meaning of subchapter B).

SEC. 2602: AMOUNT OF TAX

The amount of the tax imposed by section 2601 is--
    (1) the taxable amount (determined under subchapter C), multiplied by
    (2) the applicable rate (determined under subsection E).

SEC. 2603: LIABILITY FOR TAX

(a) PERSONAL LIABILITY.--
    (1) TAXABLE DISTRIBUTIONS.--In the case of a taxable distribution, the tax imposed by section 2601 shall be paid by the transferee.
    (2) TAXABLE TERMINATION.-- In the case of a taxable termination or a direct skip from a trust, the tax shall be paid by the trustee.
    (3) DIRECT SKIP.-- In the case of a direct skip (other than a direct skip from trust), the tax shall be paid by the transferor.
(b) SOURCE OF TAX.--Unless otherwise directed pursuant to the governing instrument by specific reference to the tax imposed by this chapter, the tax imposed by this chapter on a generation- skipping transfer shall be charged to the property constituting such transfer.
(c) CROSS REFERENCE.-- For provisions making estate and gift tax provisions with respect to transferee liability, liens, and related matters applicable to the tax imposed by section 2601, see section 2661.

SEC. 2611: GENERATION-SKIPPING TRANSFER DEFINED

(a) IN GENERAL.--For purposes of this chapter, the term "generation-skipping transfer," means--
    (1) a taxable distribution,
    (2) a taxable termination, and
    (3) a direct skip.
(b) CERTAIN TRANSFERS EXCLUDED.-- The term "generation-skipping transfer" does not include--
    (1) any transfer which, if made inter vivos by an individual, would not be treated as a taxable gift by reason of section 2503 (e) (relating to exclusion of certain transfers

for educational or medical expenses), and

(2) any transfer to the extent--

    (A) the property transferred was subject to a prior tax imposed under this chapter,

    (B) the transferee in the prior transfer was assigned to the same generation as (or a lower generation than) the generation assignment of the transferee in this transfer, and

    (C) such transfers do not have the effect of avoiding tax under this chapter with respect to any transfer.

SEC. 2612: TAXABLE TERMINATION; TAXABLE DISTRIBUTION; DIRECT SKIP

(a) TAXABLE TERMINATION.--

    (1) GENERAL RULE.--For purposes of this chapter, the term "taxable termination" means the termination (by death, lapse of time, release of power, or otherwise) of an interest in property held in a trust unless--

        (A) immediately after such termination, a non-skip person has an interest in such property, or

        (B) at no time after such termination may a distribution (including distributions on termination) be made from such trust to a skip person.

    (2) CERTAIN PARTIAL TERMINATIONS TREATED AS TAXABLE.-- If, upon the termination of an interest in property held in trust by reason of the death of a lineal descendant of the transferor, a specified portion of the trust's assets are distributed to 1 or more skip persons (or 1 or more trusts for the exclusive benefit of such persons), such termination shall constitute a taxable termination with respect to such portion of the trust property.

(b) TAXABLE DISTRIBUTION.-- For purposes of this chapter the term "taxable distribution" means any distribution from a trust to a skip person (other than taxable termination or direct skip).

(c) DIRECT SKIP.-For purposes of this chapter--

    (1) IN GENERAL.--The term "direct skip" means a transfer subject to a tax imposed by chapter 11 or 12 of an interest in property to a skip person.

    (2) SPECIAL RULE FOR TRANSFERS TO GRANDCHILDREN.-- For purposes of determining whether any transfer is a direct skip, if--

        (A) an individual is a grandchild of the transferor or the transferor's spouse or former spouse) and

        (B) as of the time of the transfer, the parent of such individual who is a lineal descendant of the transferor (or the transferor's spouse or former spouse) is dead,

such individual shall be treated as if such individual were a child of the transferor and all of that grandchild's children shall be treated as if they were grandchildren of the transferor. In the case of lineal decedents below a grandchild, the preceding sentence may be reapplied. If any transfer of property to a trust would be a direct skip but for this paragraph, any generation assignment under this paragraph shall apply also for purposes of applying this chapter to transfers from the portion of the trust attributable to such property.

    (3) LOOK-THRU RULES NOT TO APPLY.--Solely for the purposes of determining whether any transfer to a trust is a direct skip, the rules of section 2651 (e)(2) shall not apply.

SEC. 2613: SKIP PERSON AND NON-SKIP PERSON DEFINED

(a) SKIP PERSON.-- For purposes of this chapter, the term "skip person" means--
    (1) a natural person assigned to a generation which is 2 or more generations below the generation assignment of the transferor, or
    (2) a trust--
        (A) if all intents in such trust are held by skip persons, or
        (B) if--
            (i) there is no holding an interest in such trust, and
            (ii) at no such time after the transfer may a distribution (including distributions on termination) be made from such trust to a non-skip person.
(b) NON-SKIP PERSON.--For purposes of this chapter, the term "non-skip person" means any person who is not a skip person.

SEC. 2631: GST EXEMPTION

(a) GENERAL RULE.--For purposes of determining the inclusion ratio, every individual shall be allowed a GST exemption of $1,000,000 which may be allocated by such individual (or his executor) to any property with respect to which such individual is the transferor.
(b) ALLOCATIONS IRREVOCABLE.--Any allocation under subsection (a), once made, shall be irrevocable.

SEC. 2641:APPLICABLE RATE

(a) GENERAL RULE.--For purposes of this chapter, the term "applicable rate" means, with respect to any generation-skipping transfer, the product of--
    (1) the maximum Federal estate tax rate, and
    (2) the inclusion ratio to the transfer.
(b) MAXIMUM FEDERAL ESTATE TAX RATE.--For purposes of subsection (a), the term "maximum Federal estate tax rate" means the maximum rate imposed by section 2001 on the estates decedents dying at the time of the taxable distribution, taxable termination, or direct skip, as the case may be.

SEC. 2642: INCLUSION RATIO

(a) INCLUSION RATIO DEFINED.--For purposes of this chapter--
    (1) IN GENERAL.--Except as provided in this section, the inclusion ratio with respect to any property transferred in a generation-skipping transfer shall be excess (if any) of 1 over--
        (A) except as provided in subparagraph (b), the applicable fraction determined for the trust from which such transfer is made, or
        (B) in the case of a direct skip, the applicable fraction determined for such skip.

(2) APPLICABLE FRACTION.--For purposes of paragraph (1), the applicable fraction is a fraction--

   (A) the numerator of which is the amount of the GST exemption allocated to the trust (or in the case of a direct skip, allocated to the property transferred in such skip), and

   (B) the denominator of which is--

      (i) the value of the property transferred to the trust (or involved in the direct skip), reduced by

      (ii) the sum of-

         (I) any Federal tax or State death tax actually recovered from the trust attributable such property, and

         (II) any charitable deduction allowed under section 2055 or 2522 with respect to such property.

(b) VALUATION RULES, ETC.

*****

(c) TREATMENT OF CERTAIN DIRECT SKIPS WHICH ARE NONTAXABLE GIFTS.

   (1) IN GENERAL. In the case of a direct skip which is a nontaxable gift, the inclusion ratio shall be zero.

   (2) EXCEPTION FOR CERTAIN TRANSFERS IN TRUST. Paragraph (1) shall not apply to any transfer to a trust for the benefit of an individual unless--

      (A) during the life of such individual, no portion of the corpus or income of the trust may be distributed to (or for the benefit of) any person other than such individual, and

      (B) if the trust does not terminate before the individual dies, the assets of such trust will be includable in the gross estate of such individual.

      Rules similar to the rules of section 2652(c)(3) shall apply for purposes of subparagraph (A).

   (3) NONTAXABLE GIFT. For purposes of this subsection, the term "nontaxable gift" means any transfer of property to the extent such transfer is not treated as a taxable gift by reason of--

      (A) section 2503(b) (taking into account the application of section 2513), or

      (B) section 2503(e)

(d) SPECIAL RULES WHERE MORE THAN ONE TRANSFER MADE TO TRUST.--

*****

(e) SPECIAL RULES FOR CHARITABLE LEAD ANNUITY TRUSTS.--

*****

(f) SPECIAL RULES FOR CERTAIN INTER VIVOS TRANSFERS.-- Except as provided in regulations--

   (1) IN GENERAL. For purposes of determining the inclusion ratio, if--

      (A) an individual makes an inter vivos transfer of property, and

      (B) the value of such property would be includable in the gross estate of such individual under chapter 11 if such individual died immediately after making such transfer (other than by reason of section 2035),

any allocation of GST exemption to such property shall not be made before the close of the estate tax inclusion period (and the value of such property shall be determined under paragraph (2)). If such transfer is a direct skip, such skip shall be treated as occurring as of the close of the estate tax inclusion period.

(2) VALUATION. In the case of any property to which paragraph (1) applies, the value of such property shall be--

    (A) if such property is includable in the gross estate of the transferor (other than by reason of section 2035), its value for purposes of chapter 11, or

    (B) if subparagraph (A) does not apply, its value as of the close of the estate tax inclusion period (or, if any allocation of GST exemption to such property is not made on a timely filed gift tax return for the calendar year in which such period ends, its value as of the time such allocation is filed with the Secretary).

(3) ESTATE TAX INCLUSION PERIOD. For purposes of this subsection, the term "estate tax inclusion period" means any period after the transfer described in paragraph (1) during which the value of the property involved in such transfer would be includable in the gross estate of the transferor under chapter 11 if he died. Such period shall in no event extend beyond the earlier of--

    (A) the date on which there is a generation-skipping transfer with respect to such property, or

    (B) the date of the death of the transferor.

(4) TREATMENT OF SPOUSE. Except as provided in regulations, any reference in this subsection to an individual or transferor shall be treated as including a reference to the spouse of such individual or transferor.

(5) COORDINATION WITH SUBSECTION (d). Under regulations, appropriate adjustments shall be made in the application of subsection (d) to take into account the provisions of this subsection.

CHAPTER 14: SPECIAL VALUATION RULES

SEC. 2701. SPECIAL VALUATION RULES IN CASE OF CERTAIN INTERESTS IN CORPORATIONS OR PARTNERSHIPS.

(a) Valuation Rules.

    (1) IN GENERAL.--Solely for purposes of determining whether a transfer of an interest in a corporation or partnership to (or for the benefit of) a member of the transferor's family is a gift (and the value of such transfer), the value of any right--

        (A) which is described in subparagraph (A) or (B) of subsection (b)(1), and

        (B) which is with respect to any applicable retained interest that is held by the transferor or an applicable family member immediately after the transfer,

shall be determined under paragraph (3). This paragraph shall not apply to the transfer of any interest for which market quotations are readily available (as of the date of transfer) on an established securities market.

    (2) EXCEPTIONS FOR MARKETABLE RETAINED INTERESTS, ETC.-- Paragraph (1) shall not apply to any right with respect to an applicable retained interest if--

        (A) market quotations are readily available (as of the date of the transfer) for such interest on an established securities market,

        (B) such interest is of the same class as the transferred interest, or

        (C) such interest is proportionally the same as the transferred interest, without regard to nonlapsing differences in voting power (or, for a partnership, nonlapsing differences with respect to management and limitations on liability).

Subparagraph (c) shall not apply to any interest in a partnership if the transferor or an applicable family member has the right to alter the liability of the transferee of the transferred property. Except as provided by the secretary, any difference described in subparagraph (C) which lapses by reason of any Federal or State law shall be treated as a nonlapsing difference for purposes of such subparagraph.

    (3) VALUATION OF RIGHTS TO WHICH PARAGRAPH (1) APPLIES.--

        (A) IN GENERAL.--The value of any right described in paragraph (1), other than a distribution right which consists of a right to receive a qualified payment, shall be treated as being zero.

        (B) VALUATION OF QUALIFIED PAYMENTS.--If--

            (i) any applicable retained interest confers a distribution right which consists of the right to a qualified payment, and

            (ii) there are 1 or more liquidation, put, call, or conversion rights with respect to such interest,

the value of all such rights shall be determined as if each liquidation, put, call, or conversion right were exercised in the manner resulting in the lowest value being determined for all such rights.

    (4) MINIMUM VALUATION OF JUNIOR EQUITY.--

        (A) IN GENERAL.--In the case of a transfer described in paragraph (1) of a junior equity interest in a corporation or partnership, such interest shall in no event be valued at an amount less than the value which would be determined if the total value of all the junior equity interests in the entity were equal to 10 percent of the sum of--

      (i) the total value of all of the equity interests in such entity, plus

      (ii) the total amount of indebtedness of such entity to the transferor (or an applicable family member).

   (B) DEFINITIONS.--For purposes of this paragraph--

      (i) JUNIOR EQUITY INTEREST.--The term "junior equity interest" means common stock or, in the case of a partnership, any partnership interest under which the rights as to income and capital are junior to the rights of all other classes of equity interests.

      (ii) EQUITY INTEREST.--The term "equity interest" means stock or any interest as a partner, as the case may be.

(b) APPLICABLE RETAINED INTERESTS.--For purposes of this section--

   (1) IN GENERAL.--The term "applicable retained interest" means any interest in an entity with respect to which there is--

      (A) a distribution right, but only if, immediately before the transfer described in subsection (a)(1), the transferor and applicable family members hold (after application of subsection (e)(3)) control of the entity, or

      (B) a liquidation, put, call, or conversion right.

   (2) CONTROL.--For purposes of paragraph (1)--

      (A) CORPORATIONS.--In the case of a corporation, the term "control" means the holding of at least 50 percent (by vote or value) of the stock of the corporation.

      (B) PARTNERSHIPS.--In the case of a partnership, the term "control" means--

         (i) the holding of at least 50 percent of the capital or profits interests in the partnership, or

         (ii) in the case of a limited partnership, the holding of any interest as a general partner.

(c) DISTRIBUTION AND OTHER RIGHTS; QUALIFIED PAYMENTS.--For purposes of this section--

   (1) DISTRIBUTION RIGHT.--

      (A) IN GENERAL.--The term "distribution right" means--

         (i) a right to distributions from a corporation with respect to its stock, and

         (ii) a right to distributions from a partnership with respect to a partner's interest in the partnership.

      (B) EXCEPTIONS.--The term "distribution right" does not include--

         (i) a right to distributions with respect to any junior equity interest (as defined in subsection (a) (4)(B)(i));

         (ii) any liquidation, put, call, or conversion right, or

         (iii) any right to receive any guaranteed payment described in section 707(c) of a fixed amount.

   (2) LIQUIDATION, ETC. RIGHTS.--

      (A) IN GENERAL.--The term "liquidation, put, call, or conversion right" means any liquidation, put, call, or conversion right, or any similar right, the exercise or nonexercise of which affects the value of the transferred interest.

      (B) EXCEPTION FOR FIXED RIGHTS.--

         (i) IN GENERAL.--The term "liquidation, put call, or conversion right" does not include any right which must be exercised at a specific time and at a specific amount.

         (ii) TREATMENT OF CERTAIN RIGHTS.--If a right is assumed to be exercised in a particular manner under subsection (a)(3)(B), such right shall be treated as so exercised for purposes of clause (i).

(C) EXCEPTION FOR CERTAIN RIGHTS TO CONVERT.--The term "liquidation, put, call, or conversion right" does not include any right which--

   (i) is a right to convert into a fixed number (or a fixed percentage) of shares of the same class of stock in a corporation as the transferred stock in such corporation under subsection (a)(1) (or stock which would be of the same class but for nonlapsing differences in voting power),

   (ii) is nonlapsing,

   (iii) is subject to proportionate adjustments for splits, combinations, reclassification, and similar changes in the capital stock, and

   (iv) is subject to adjustments similar to the adjustments under subsection (d) for accumulated but unpaid distributions.

A rule similar to the rule of the preceding sentence shall apply for partnerships.

(3) QUALIFIED PAYMENT.--

(A) IN GENERAL.-- Except as otherwise provided in this paragraph, the term "qualified payment" means any dividend payable on a periodic basis under any cumulative preferred stock (or a comparable payment under any partnership interest) to the extent that such dividend (or comparable payment) is determined at a fixed rate.

(B) TREATMENT OF VARIABLE RATE PAYMENTS.--For purposes of subparagraph (A), a payment shall be treated as fixed as to rate if such payment is determined at a rate which bears a fixed relationship to a specified market interest rate.

(C) ELECTIONS.--

   (i) WAIVER OF QUALIFIED PAYMENT TREATMENT.--A transferor or applicable family member may elect with respect to payments under any interest specified in such election to treat such payments as payments which are not qualified payments.

   (ii) ELECTION TO HAVE INTEREST TREATED AS QUALIFIED PAYMENT.--A transferor or any applicable family member may elect to treat any distribution right as a qualified payment, to be paid in the amounts and at the times specified in such election. The preceding sentence shall apply only to the extent that the amounts and times so specified are not inconsistent with the underlying legal instrument giving rise to such right.

   (iii) ELECTIONS IRREVOCABLE.--Any election under this subparagraph with respect to an interest shall, once made, be irrevocable.

(d) TRANSFER TAX TREATMENT OF CUMULATIVE BUT UNPAID DISTRIBUTIONS.--

(1) IN GENERAL.--If a taxable event occurs with respect to any distribution right to which subsection (a)(3)(B) applied; the following shall be increased by the amount determined under paragraph (2):

(A) the taxable estate of the transferor in the case of a taxable event described in paragraph (3)(A)(i).

(B) The taxable gifts of the transferor for the calendar year in which the taxable event occurs in the case of a taxable event described in paragraph (3)(A)(ii) or (iii).

(2) AMOUNT OF INCREASE.--

(A) IN GENERAL.--The amount of the increase determined under this paragraph shall be the excess (if any) of--

    (i) the value of the qualified payments payable during the period beginning on the date of the transfer under subsection (a)(1) and ending on the taxable event determined as if--

        (I) all such payments were paid on the date payment was due, and

        (II) all such payments were reinvested by the transferor as of the date of payment at a yield equal to the discount rate used in determining the value of the applicable retained interest described in subsection (a)(1), over

    (ii) the value of such payments paid during such period computed under clause (i) on the basis of the time when such payments were actually paid.

(B) LIMITATIONS ON AMOUNT OF INCREASE.--

    (i) IN GENERAL.--The amount of the increase under subparagraph (A) shall not exceed the applicable percentage of the excess (if any) of--

        (I) the value (determined as of the date of the taxable event) of all equity interests in the entity which are junior to the applicable retained interest, over

        (II) the value of such interests (determined as of the date of the transfer to which subsection (a)(1) applied).

    (ii) APPLICABLE PERCENTAGE.--For purposes of clause (i), the applicable percentage is the percentage determined by dividing--

        (I) the number of shares in the corporation held (as of the date of the taxable event) by the transferor which are applicable retained interests of the same class, by

        (II) the total number of shares in such corporation (as of such date) which are of the same class as the class described in subclause (I).

A similar percentage shall be determined in the case of interests in a partnership.

    (iii) DEFINITION.--For purposes of this subparagraph, the term "equity interest" has the meaning given such term by subsection (a)(4)(B).

(C) GRACE PERIOD.--For purposes of subparagraph (A), any payment of any distribution during the 4-year period beginning on its due date shall be treated as having been made on such due date.

(3) TAXABLE EVENTS.--For purposes of this subsection--

(A) IN GENERAL.--The term "taxable event" means any of the following:

    (i) The death of the transferor if the applicable retained interest conferring the distribution right is includable in the estate of the transferor.

    (ii) The transfer of such applicable retained interest.

    (iii) At the election of the taxpayer, the payment of any qualified payment after the period described in paragraph (2)(C), but only with respect to the period ending on the date of such payment.

(B) EXCEPTION WHERE SPOUSE IS TRANSFEREE.--

    (i) DEATHTIME TRANSFERS.--Subparagraph (A)(i) shall not apply to any interest includable in the gross estate of the transferor if a deduction with respect to such interest is allowable under section 2056 or 2106(a)(3).

    (ii) LIFETIME TRANSFERS.--A transfer to the spouse of the transferor shall not be treated as a taxable event under subparagraph (A)(ii) if such transfer does not result in a taxable gift by reason of--

(I) any deduction allowed under section 2523, or

(II) consideration for the transfer provided by the spouse.

(iii) SPOUSE SUCCEEDS TO TREATMENT OF TRANSFEROR.--If an event is not treated as a taxable event by reason of this subparagraph, the transferee spouse or surviving spouse (as the case may be) shall be treated in the same manner as the transferor in applying this subsection with respect to the interest involved.

(4) SPECIAL RULES FOR APPLICABLE FAMILY MEMBERS.--

(A) FAMILY MEMBER TREATED IN SAME MANNER AS TRANSFEROR.--For purposes of this subsection, an applicable family member shall be treated in the same manner as the transferor with respect to any distribution right retained by such family member to which subsection (a)(3)(B) applied.

(B) TRANSFER TO APPLICABLE FAMILY MEMBER.--In the case of a taxable event described in paragraph (3)(A)(ii) involving the transfer of an applicable retained interest to an applicable family member (other than the spouse of the transferor), the applicable family member shall be treated in the same manner as the transferor in applying this subsection to distributions accumulating with respect to such interest after such taxable event.

(5) TRANSFER TO INCLUDE TERMINATION.--For purposes of this subsection, any termination of an interest shall be treated as a transfer.

(e) OTHER DEFINITIONS AND RULES.--For purposes of this section--

(1) MEMBER OF THE FAMILY.--The term "member of the family" means, with respect to any transferor--

(A) the transferor's spouse,

(B) a lineal descendant of the transferor or the transferor's spouse, and

(C) the spouse of any such descendant.

(2) APPLICABLE FAMILY MEMBER.--The term "applicable family member" means, with respect to any transferor--

(A) the transferor's spouse,

(B) an ancestor of the transferor or the transferor's spouse, and

(C) the spouse of any such ancestor.

(3) ATTRIBUTION RULES.--

(A) INDIRECT HOLDINGS AND TRANSFERS.--An individual shall be treated as holding any interest to the extent such interest is held indirectly by such individual through a corporation, partnership, trust, or other entity. If any individual is treated as holding any interest by reason of the preceding sentence, any transfer which results in such interest being treated as no longer held by such individual shall be treated as a transfer of such interest.

(B) CONTROL.--For purposes of subsections (b)(1), an individual shall be treated as holding any interest held by the individual's brothers, sisters, or lineal descendants.

(4) EFFECT OF ADOPTION.--A relationship by legal adoption shall be treated as a relationship by blood.

(5) CERTAIN CHANGES TREATED AS TRANSFERS.--Except as provided in regulations, a contribution to capital or a redemption, recapitalization, or other change in the capital structure of a corporation or partnership shall be treated as a transfer of an interest in such entity to which this section applies if the taxpayer or an applicable family member--

(A) receives an applicable retained interest in such entity pursuant to such contribution to capital or such redemption, recapitalization, or other change, or

(B) under regulations otherwise holds, immediately after the transfer, an applicable retained interest in such entity.

This paragraph shall not apply to any transaction (other than a contribution to capital) if the interests in the entity held by the transferor, applicable family members, and members of the transferor's family before and after the transaction are substantially identical.

(6) ADJUSTMENTS.--Under regulations prescribed by the Secretary, if there is any subsequent transfer, or inclusion in the gross estate, of any applicable retained interest which was valued under the rules of subsection (a), appropriate adjustments shall be made for purposes of chapter 11, 12, or 13 to reflect the increase in the amount of any prior taxable gift made by the transferor or decedent by reason of such valuation.

(7) TREATMENT AS SEPARATE INTERESTS.--The Secretary may by regulation provide that any applicable retained interest shall be treated as 2 or more separate interests for purposes of this section.

SEC. 2702: SPECIAL VALUATION RULES IN CASE OF TRANSFERS OF INTERESTS IN TRUSTS

(a) VALUATION RULES.-

(1) IN GENERAL.- Solely for purposes of determining- whether a transfer of an interest in trust to (or for the benefit of) a member of the transferor's family is a gift (and the value of such transfer), the value of any interest in such trust retained by the transferor or any applicable family member (as defined in section 2701(e)(2)) shall be determined as provided in paragraph (2).

(2) VALUATION OF RETAINED INTERESTS.-

(A) IN GENERAL.- The value of any retained interest which is not a qualified interest shall be treated as being zero.

(B) VALUATION OF QUALIFIED INTEREST.- The value of any retained interest which is a qualified interest shall be determined under section 7520.

(3) EXCEPTIONS

(A) IN GENERAL.- This subsection shall not apply to any transfer-

(i) to the extent that such transfer is an incomplete transfer, or

(ii) if such transfer involves the transfer of an interest in trust all the property in which consists of a residence to be used as a personal residence by persons holding term interests in such trust.

(B) INCOMPLETE TRANSFER.- For purposes of subparagraph (A), the term "incomplete transfer" means any transfer which would not be treated as a gift whether of not consideration was received for such transfer.

(b) QUALIFIED INTEREST.- For purposes of this section, the term "qualified interest" means-

(1) any interest which consists of the right to receive fixed amounts payable not less frequently than annually,

(2) any interest which consists of the right to receive fixed amounts which are payable not less frequently than annually and are a fixed percentage of the fair market value of the property in the trust (determined annually), and

(3) any noncontingent remainder interest if all of the other interests in the trust consists of interests described in paragraph (1) or (2).

(c) CERTAIN PROPERTY TREATED AS HELD IN TRUST.- For purposes of this section-

(1) IN GENERAL.- The transfer of an interest in property with respect to which there is 1 or more term interests shall be treated as a transfer of an interest in a trust.

(2) JOINT PURCHASES.- If 2 or more members of the same family acquire interests in any property described in paragraph (1) in the same transaction (or a series of related transactions), the person (or persons) acquiring the term interests in such property shall be treated as having acquired the entire property and then transferred to the other persons the interests acquired by such other persons in the transaction (or series of transactions). Such transfer shall be treated as made in exchange for the consideration (if any) provided by such other persons for the acquisition of their interests in such property.

(3) TERM INTEREST.- The term "term interest" means-
(A) a life interest in property, or
(B) an interest in property for a term of years.

(4) VALUATION RULE FOR CERTAIN TERM INTERESTS.- If the nonexcercise of rights under a term interest in tangible property would not have a substantial effect on the valuation of the remainder interest in such property-
(A) subparagraph (A) of subsection (a)(2) shall not apply to such term interest, and
(B) the value of such term interest for purposes of applying subsection (a)(1) shall be the amount which the holder of a term interest establishes as the amount for which such interest could be sold to an unrelated third party.

(d) TREATMENT OF TRANSFERS OF INTEREST IN PORTION OF TRUST.- In the case of a transfer of an income or remainder interest with respect to a specified portion of the property in a trust, only such portion shall be taken into account in applying this section to such transfer.

(e) MEMBER OF THE FAMILY.- For purposes of this section, the term "member of the family" shall have the meaning given such term by section 2704(c)(2).

SEC. 2703 CERTAIN RIGHTS AND RESTRICTIONS DISREGARDED

(a) GENERAL RULE.- For purposes of this subtitle, the value of any property shall be determined without regard to-
    (1) any option, agreement, or other right to acquire or use the property at a price less than the fair market value of the property (without regard to such option, agreement, or right), or
    (2) any restriction on the right to sell or use such property.
(b) EXCEPTIONS.- Subsection (a) shall not apply to any option, agreement, right or restriction which meets each of the following requirements:
    (1) It is a bona fide business arrangement.
    (2) It is not a device to transfer such property to members of the decedent's family for less than full and adequate consideration in money or money's worth.
    (3) Its terms are comparable to similar arrangements entered into by persons in an arm's length transaction.

SEC. 2704 TREATMENT OF CERTAIN LAPSING RIGHTS AND RESTRICTIONS

(a) TREATMENT OF LAPSED VOTING OR LIQUIDATION RIGHTS.--
    (1) IN GENERAL.--For purposes of this subtitle, if--
        (A) there is a lapse of any voting or liquidation right in a corporation or partnership, and
        (B) the individual holding such right immediately before the lapse and members of such individual's family hold, both before and after the lapse, control of the entity,
such lapse shall be treated as a transfer by such individual by gift, or a transfer which is includable in the gross estate of the decedent, whichever is applicable, in the amount determined under paragraph (2).
    (2) AMOUNT OF TRANSFER.-- For purposes of paragraph (1), the amount determined under this paragraph is the excess (if any) of--
        (A) the value of all interests in the entity held by the individual described in paragraph (1) immediately before the lapse (determined as if the voting and liquidation rights were nonlapsing), over
        (B) the value of such interests immediately after the lapse.
    (3) SIMILAR RIGHTS.--The Secretary may by regulations apply this subsection to rights similar to voting and liquidation rights.
(b) CERTAIN RESTRICTIONS ON LIQUIDATION DISREGARDED.--
    (1) IN GENERAL.--For purposes of this subtitle, if--
        (A) there is a transfer of an interest in a corporation or partnership to (or for the benefit of) a member of the transferor's family, and
        (B) the transferor and members of the transferor's family hold, immediately before the transfer, control of the entity,
any applicable restriction shall be disregarded in determining the value of the transferred interest.

    (2) APPLICABLE RESTRICTION.--For purposes of this subsection, the term "applicable restriction" means any restriction--

        (A) which effectively limits the ability of the corporation or partnership to liquidate, and

        (B) with respect to which either of the following applies:

            (i) The restriction lapses, in whole or in part, after the transfer referred t to in paragraph (1).

            (ii) The transferor or any member of the transferor's family, either alone of collectively, has the right after such transfer to remove, in whole or in part, the restriction.

    (3) EXCEPTIONS.--The term "applicable restriction" shall not include--

        (A) any commercially reasonable restriction which arises as part of any financing by the corporation or partnership with a person who is not related to the transferor or transferee, or a member of the family of either, or

        (B) any restriction imposed, or required to be imposed, by any Federal or State law.

    (4) OTHER RESTRICTIONS.-- The secretary may by regulations provide that other restrictions shall be disregarded in determining the value of the transfer of any interest in a corporation or partnership to a member of the transferor's family if such restriction has the effect of reducing the value of the transferred interest for purposes of this subtitle but does not ultimately reduce the value of such interest to the transferee.

(c) DEFINITIONS AND SPECIAL RULES.--For purposes of this section--

    (1) CONTROL. --The term "control" has the meaning given such term by section 2701(b)(2).

    (2) MEMBER OF THE FAMILY.--The term "member of the family" means, with respect to any individual--

        (A) such individual's spouse,

        (B) any ancestor or lineal descendant of such individual or such individual's spouse,

        (C) any brother or sister of the individual, and

        (D) any spouse of any individual described in subparagraph (B) or (C).

    (3) ATTRIBUTION.-- The rule of section 2701(e)(3) shall apply for purposes of determining the interests held by any individual.

CHAPTER 77: MISCELLANEOUS PROVISIONS

SEC 7520 VALUATION TABLES

(a) GENERAL RULE.- For purposes of this title, the value of any annuity, any interest for life or a term of years, or any remainder or reversionary interest shall be determined-
    (1) under tables prescribed by the Secretary, and
    (2) by using an interest rate (rounded to the nearest 2/10ths of 1 percent) equal to 120 percent of the Federal midterm rate in effect under section 1274(d)(1) for the month in which the valuation date falls.

If an income, estate, or gift tax charitable contribution is allowable for any part of the property transferred, the taxpayer may elect to use such Federal midterm rate for either of the two months preceding the month in which the valuation date falls for purposes of paragraph (2). In the case of transfers of more than 1 interest in the same property with respect to which the taxpayer may use the same rate under paragraph (2), the taxpayer shall use the same rate with respect to each such interest.

*****

Federal Estate Tax Return (Form 706)

Form **706** (Rev. April 1997) Department of the Treasury Internal Revenue Service	**United States Estate (and Generation-Skipping Transfer) Tax Return** Estate of a citizen or resident of the United States (see separate instructions). To be filed for decedents dying after October 8, 1990. For Paperwork Reduction Act Notice, see page 1 of the separate instructions.	OMB No. 1545-0015

Part 1.—Decedent and Executor

1a Decedent's first name and middle initial (and maiden name, if any)	1b Decedent's last name	2 Decedent's social security no.

3a Legal residence (domicile) at time of death (county, state, and ZIP code, or foreign country)	3b Year domicile established	4 Date of birth	5 Date of death

6a Name of executor (see page 2 of the instructions)	6b Executor's address (number and street including apartment or suite no. or rural route; city, town, or post office; state; and ZIP code)

6c Executor's social security number (see page 2 of the instructions)	

7a Name and location of court where will was probated or estate administered	7b Case number

8 If decedent died testate, check here ▶ ☐ and attach a certified copy of the will. | 9 If Form 4768 is attached, check here ▶ ☐

10 If Schedule R-1 is attached, check here ▶ ☐

Part 2.—Tax Computation

1	Total gross estate (from Part 5, Recapitulation, page 3, item 10)	**1**
2	Total allowable deductions (from Part 5, Recapitulation, page 3, item 20)	**2**
3	Taxable estate (subtract line 2 from line 1)	**3**
4	Adjusted taxable gifts (total taxable gifts (within the meaning of section 2503) made by the decedent after December 31, 1976, other than gifts that are includible in decedent's gross estate (section 2001(b)))	**4**
5	Add lines 3 and 4	**5**
6	Tentative tax on the amount on line 5 from Table A on page 10 of the instructions	**6**
7a	If line 5 exceeds $10,000,000, enter the lesser of line 5 or $21,040,000. If line 5 is $10,000,000 or less, skip lines 7a and 7b and enter -0- on line 7c. 7a	
b	Subtract $10,000,000 from line 7a 7b	
c	Enter 5% (.05) of line 7b	**7c**
8	Total tentative tax (add lines 6 and 7c)	**8**
9	Total gift tax payable with respect to gifts made by the decedent after December 31, 1976. Include gift taxes by the decedent's spouse for such spouse's share of split gifts (section 2513) only if the decedent was the donor of these gifts and they are includible in the decedent's gross estate (see instructions)	**9**
10	Gross estate tax (subtract line 9 from line 8)	**10**
11	Maximum unified credit against estate tax **11** 192,800 00	
12	Adjustment to unified credit. (This adjustment may not exceed $6,000. See page 7 of the instructions.) **12**	
13	Allowable unified credit (subtract line 12 from line 11)	**13**
14	Subtract line 13 from line 10 (but do not enter less than zero)	**14**
15	Credit for state death taxes. Do not enter more than line 14. Figure the credit by using the amount on line 3 less $60,000. See Table B in the instructions and attach credit evidence (see instructions) .	**15**
16	Subtract line 15 from line 14	**16**
17	Credit for Federal gift taxes on pre-1977 gifts (section 2012) (attach computation) **17**	
18	Credit for foreign death taxes (from Schedule(s) P). (Attach Form(s) 706-CE.) **18**	
19	Credit for tax on prior transfers (from Schedule Q) **19**	
20	Total (add lines 17, 18, and 19)	**20**
21	Net estate tax (subtract line 20 from line 16)	**21**
22	Generation-skipping transfer taxes (from Schedule R, Part 2, line 10)	**22**
23	Section 4980A increased estate tax (from Schedule S, Part I, line 17) (see page 20 of the instructions)	**23**
24	Total transfer taxes (add lines 21, 22, and 23)	**24**
25	Prior payments. Explain in an attached statement **25**	
26	United States Treasury bonds redeemed in payment of estate tax . **26**	
27	Total (add lines 25 and 26)	**27**
28	Balance due (or overpayment) (subtract line 27 from line 24)	**28**

Under penalties of perjury, I declare that I have examined this return, including accompanying schedules and statements, and to the best of my knowledge and belief, it is true, correct, and complete. Declaration of preparer other than the executor is based on all information of which preparer has any knowledge.

Signature(s) of executor(s) _____ Date _____

Signature of preparer other than executor _____ Address (and ZIP code) _____ Date _____

Cat. No. 20548R

Form 706 (Rev. 4-97)

Estate of:

Part 3.—Elections by the Executor

Please check the "Yes" or "No" box for each question. (See instructions beginning on page 3.)

		Yes	No
1	Do you elect alternate valuation?		
2	Do you elect special use valuation? . . . . If "Yes," you must complete and attach Schedule A–1.		
3	Do you elect to pay the taxes in installments as described in section 6166? . . . . If "Yes," you must attach the additional information described on page 5 of the instructions.		
4	Do you elect to postpone the part of the taxes attributable to a reversionary or remainder interest as described in section 6163?		

Part 4.—General Information (Note: *Please attach the necessary supplemental documents. You must attach the death certificate.)*
(See instructions beginning on page 6.)

Authorization to receive confidential tax information under Regulations section 601.504(b)(2)(i), to act as the estate's representative before the Internal Revenue Service, and to make written or oral presentations on behalf of the estate if return prepared by an attorney, accountant, or enrolled agent for the executor:

Name of representative (print or type)	State	Address (number, street, and room or suite no., city, state, and ZIP code)

I declare that I am the ☐ attorney/ ☐ certified public accountant/ ☐ enrolled agent (you must check the applicable box) for the executor and prepared this return for the executor. I am not under suspension or disbarment from practice before the Internal Revenue Service and am qualified to practice in the state shown above.

Signature	CAF number	Date	Telephone number

1   Death certificate number and issuing authority (attach a copy of the death certificate to this return).

2   Decedent's business or occupation. If retired, check here ▶ ☐ and state decedent's former business or occupation.

3   Marital status of the decedent at time of death:

☐ Married
☐ Widow or widower—Name, SSN, and date of death of deceased spouse ▶ ....
....
☐ Single
☐ Legally separated
☐ Divorced—Date divorce decree became final ▶

4a Surviving spouse's name	4b Social security number	4c Amount received (see page 6 of the instructions)

5   Individuals (other than the surviving spouse), trusts, or other estates who receive benefits from the estate (do not include charitable beneficiaries shown in Schedule O) (see instructions). For Privacy Act Notice (applicable to individual beneficiaries only), see the Instructions for Form 1040.

Name of individual, trust, or estate receiving $5,000 or more	Identifying number	Relationship to decedent	Amount (see instructions)

All unascertainable beneficiaries and those who receive less than $5,000 . . . . ▶

Total . . . .

(continued on next page)

Form 706 (Rev. 4-97)

Part 4.—General Information *(continued)*

Please check the "Yes" or "No" box for each question.

		Yes	No
6	Does the gross estate contain any section 2044 property (qualified terminable interest property (QTIP) from a prior gift or estate) (see page 6 of the instructions)?		
7a	Have Federal gift tax returns ever been filed? . . . . If "Yes," please attach copies of the returns, if available, and furnish the following information:		

7b Period(s) covered	7c Internal Revenue office(s) where filed

If you answer "Yes" to any of questions 8–16, you must attach additional information as described in the instructions.

		Yes	No
8a	Was there any insurance on the decedent's life that is not included on the return as part of the gross estate?		
b	Did the decedent own any insurance on the life of another that is not included in the gross estate?		
9	Did the decedent at the time of death own any property as a joint tenant with right of survivorship in which **(a)** one or more of the other joint tenants was someone other than the decedent's spouse, and **(b)** less than the full value of the property is included on the return as part of the gross estate? If "Yes," you must complete and attach Schedule E		
10	Did the decedent, at the time of death, own any interest in a partnership or unincorporated business or any stock in an inactive or closely held corporation?		
11	Did the decedent make any transfer described in section 2035, 2036, 2037, or 2038 (see the instructions for Schedule G beginning on page 11 of the separate instructions)? If "Yes," you must complete and attach Schedule G		
12	Were there in existence at the time of the decedent's death:		
a	Any trusts created by the decedent during his or her lifetime?		
b	Any trusts not created by the decedent under which the decedent possessed any power, beneficial interest, or trusteeship?		
13	Did the decedent ever possess, exercise, or release any general power of appointment? If "Yes," you must complete and attach Schedule H		
14	Was the marital deduction computed under the transitional rule of Public Law 97-34, section 403(e)(3) (Economic Recovery Tax Act of 1981)? If "Yes," attach a separate computation of the marital deduction, enter the amount on item 18 of the Recapitulation, and note on item 18 "computation attached."		
15	Was the decedent, immediately before death, receiving an annuity described in the "General" paragraph of the instructions for Schedule I? If "Yes," you must complete and attach Schedule I		
16	Did the decedent have a total "excess retirement accumulation" (as defined in section 4980A(d)) in qualified employer plans and individual retirement plans? If "Yes," you must complete and attach Schedule S		

Part 5.—Recapitulation

Item number	Gross estate	Alternate value	Value at date of death
1	Schedule A—Real Estate		
2	Schedule B—Stocks and Bonds		
3	Schedule C—Mortgages, Notes, and Cash		
4	Schedule D—Insurance on the Decedent's Life (attach Form(s) 712)		
5	Schedule E—Jointly Owned Property (attach Form(s) 712 for life insurance) . . .		
6	Schedule F—Other Miscellaneous Property (attach Form(s) 712 for life insurance) .		
7	Schedule G—Transfers During Decedent's Life (attach Form(s) 712 for life insurance)		
8	Schedule H—Powers of Appointment		
9	Schedule I—Annuities		
10	Total gross estate (add items 1 through 9). Enter here and on line 1 of the Tax Computation		

Item number	Deductions	Amount
11	Schedule J—Funeral Expenses and Expenses Incurred in Administering Property Subject to Claims . . .	
12	Schedule K—Debts of the Decedent	
13	Schedule K—Mortgages and Liens	
14	Total of items 11 through 13	
15	Allowable amount of deductions from item 14 (see the instructions for item 15 of the Recapitulation) . . .	
16	Schedule L—Net Losses During Administration	
17	Schedule L—Expenses Incurred in Administering Property Not Subject to Claims	
18	Schedule M—Bequests, etc., to Surviving Spouse	
19	Schedule O—Charitable, Public, and Similar Gifts and Bequests	
20	Total allowable deductions (add items 15 through 19). Enter here and on line 2 of the Tax Computation . .	

Page 3

Form 706 (Rev. 4-97)

Estate of:

SCHEDULE A—Real Estate

- *For jointly owned property that must be disclosed on Schedule E, see the instructions on the reverse side of Schedule E.*
- *Real estate that is part of a sole proprietorship should be shown on Schedule F.*
- *Real estate that is included in the gross estate under section 2035, 2036, 2037, or 2038 should be shown on Schedule G.*
- *Real estate that is included in the gross estate under section 2041 should be shown on Schedule H.*
- *If you elect section 2032A valuation, you must complete Schedule A and Schedule A-1.*

Item number	Description	Alternate valuation date	Alternate value	Value at date of death
1				
	Total from continuation schedules or additional sheets attached to this schedule . . .			
	TOTAL. (Also enter on Part 5, Recapitulation, page 3, at item 1.)			

(If more space is needed, attach the continuation schedule from the end of this package or additional sheets of the same size.)

(See the instructions on the reverse side.)

Schedule A— Page 4

Form 706 (Rev. 4-97)

Instructions for Schedule A—Real Estate

If the total gross estate contains any real estate, you must complete Schedule A and file it with the return. On Schedule A list real estate the decedent owned or had contracted to purchase. Number each parcel in the left-hand column.

Describe the real estate in enough detail so that the IRS can easily locate it for inspection and valuation. For each parcel of real estate, report the area and, if the parcel is improved, describe the improvements. For city or town property, report the street and number, ward, subdivision, block and lot, etc. For rural property, report the township, range, landmarks, etc.

If any item of real estate is subject to a mortgage for which the decedent's estate is liable, that is, if the indebtedness may be charged against other property of the estate that is not subject to that mortgage, or if the decedent was personally liable for that mortgage, you must report the full value of the property in the value column.

Enter the amount of the mortgage under "Description" on this schedule. The unpaid amount of the mortgage may be deducted on Schedule K. If the decedent's estate is NOT liable for the amount of the mortgage, report only the value of the equity of redemption (or value of the property less the indebtedness) in the value column as part of the gross estate. Do not enter any amount less than zero. Do not deduct the amount of indebtedness on Schedule K.

Also list on Schedule A real property the decedent contracted to purchase. Report the full value of the property and not the equity in the value column. Deduct the unpaid part of the purchase price on Schedule K.

Report the value of real estate without reducing it for homestead or other exemption, or the value of dower, curtesy, or a statutory estate created instead of dower or curtesy.

Explain how the reported values were determined and attach copies of any appraisals.

Schedule A Examples

In this example, alternate valuation is not adopted; the date of death is January 1, 1997.

Item number	Description	Alternate valuation date	Alternate value	Value at date of death
1	House and lot, 1921 William Street NW, Washington, DC (lot 6, square 481). Rent of $2,700 due at end of each quarter, February 1, May 1, August 1, and November 1. Value based on appraisal, copy of which is attached			108,000
	Rent due on item 1 for quarter ending November 1, 1996, but not collected at date of death			2,700
	Rent accrued on item 1 for November and December 1996			1,800
2	House and lot, 304 Jefferson Street, Alexandria, VA (lot 18, square 40). Rent of $600 payable monthly. Value based on appraisal, copy of which is attached			96,000
	Rent due on item 2 for December 1996, but not collected at date of death . . .			600

In this example, alternate valuation is adopted; the date of death is January 1, 1997.

Item number	Description	Alternate valuation date	Alternate value	Value at date of death
1	House and lot, 1921 William Street NW, Washington, DC (lot 6, square 481). Rent of $2,700 due at end of each quarter, February 1, May 1, August 1, and November 1. Value based on appraisal, copy of which is attached. Not disposed of within 6 months following death	7/1/97	90,000	108,000
	Rent due on item 1 for quarter ending November 1, 1996, but not collected until February 1, 1997	2/1/97	2,700	2,700
	Rent accrued on item 1 for November and December 1996, collected on February 1, 1997	2/1/97	1,800	1,800
2	House and lot, 304 Jefferson Street, Alexandria, VA (lot 18, square 40). Rent of $600 payable monthly. Value based on appraisal, copy of which is attached. Property exchanged for farm on May 1, 1997	5/1/97	90,000	96,000
	Rent due on item 2 for December 1996, but not collected until February 1, 1997 .	2/1/97	600	600

Schedule A— Page 5

Instructions for Schedule A-1.—Section 2032A Valuation

The election to value certain farm and closely held business property at its special use value is made by checking "Yes" to line 2 of Part 3, Elections by the Executor, Form 706. Schedule A-1 is used to report the additional information that must be submitted to support this election. In order to make a valid election, you must complete Schedule A-1 and attach all of the required statements and appraisals.

For definitions and additional information concerning special use valuation, see section 2032A and the related regulations.

Part 1.—Type of Election

Estate and GST Tax Elections.—If you elect special use valuation for the estate tax, you must also elect special use valuation for the GST tax and vice versa.

You must value each specific property interest at the same value for GST tax purposes that you value it at for estate tax purposes.

Protective Election.—To make the protective election described in the separate instructions for line 2 of Part 3, Elections by the Executor, you must check this box, enter the decedent's name and social security number in the spaces provided at the top of Schedule A-1, and complete line 1 and column A of lines 3 and 4 of Part 2. For purposes of the protective election, list on line 3 all of the real property that passes to the qualified heirs even though some of the property will be shown on line 2 when the additional notice of election is subsequently filed. You need not complete columns B–D of lines 3 and 4. You need not complete any other line entries on Schedule A-1. Completing Schedule A-1 as described above constitutes a Notice of Protective Election as described in Regulations section 20.2032A-8(b).

Part 2.—Notice of Election

Line 10.—Because the special use valuation election creates a potential tax liability for the recapture tax of section 2032A(c), you must list each person who receives an interest in the specially valued property on Schedule A-1. If there are more than eight persons who receive interests, use an additional sheet that follows the format of line 10. In the columns "Fair market value" and "Special use value," you should enter the total respective values of all the specially valued property interests received by each person.

GST Tax Savings

To compute the additional GST tax due upon disposition (or cessation of qualified use) of the property, each "skip person" (as defined in the instructions to Schedule R) who receives an interest in the specially valued property must know the total GST tax savings on all of the interests in specially valued property received. This GST tax savings is the difference between the total GST tax that was imposed on all of the interests in specially valued property received by the skip person valued at their special use value and the total GST tax that would have been imposed on the same interests received by the skip person had they been valued at their fair market value.

Because the GST tax depends on the executor's allocation of the GST exemption and the grandchild exclusion, the skip person who receives the interests is unable to compute this GST tax savings. Therefore, for each skip person who receives an interest in specially valued property, you must attach worksheets showing the total GST tax savings attributable to all of that person's interests in specially valued property.

How To Compute the GST Tax Savings.—Before computing each skip person's GST tax savings, you must complete Schedules R and R-1 for the entire estate (using the special use values).

For each skip person, you must complete two Schedules R (Parts 2 and 3 only) as worksheets, one showing the interests in specially valued property received by the skip person at their special use value and one showing the same interests at their fair market value.

If the skip person received interests in specially valued property that were shown on Schedule R-1, show these interests on the Schedule R, Parts 2 and 3 worksheets, as appropriate. Do not use Schedule R-1 as a worksheet.

Completing the Special Use Value Worksheets.—On lines 2–4 and 6, enter -0-.

Completing the Fair Market Value Worksheets.—*Lines 2 and 3, fixed taxes and other charges.*—If valuing the interests at their fair market value (instead of special use value) causes any of these taxes and charges to increase, enter the increased amount (only) on these lines and attach an explanation of the increase. Otherwise, enter -0-.

Line 6—GST exemption.—If you completed line 10 of Schedule R, Part 1, enter on line 6 the amount shown for the skip person on the *line 10 special use allocation schedule* you attached to Schedule R. If you did not complete line 10 of Schedule R, Part 1, enter -0- on line 6.

Total GST Tax Savings.—For each skip person, subtract the tax amount on line 10, Part 2 of the special use value worksheet from the tax amount on line 10, Part 2 of the fair market value worksheet. This difference is the skip person's total GST tax savings.

Part 3.—Agreement to Special Valuation Under Section 2032A

The agreement to special valuation by persons with an interest in property is required under section 2032A(a)(1)(B) and (d)(2) and must be signed by all parties who have any interest in the property being valued based on its qualified use as of the date of the decedent's death.

An interest in property is an interest that, as of the date of the decedent's death, can be asserted under applicable local law so as to affect the disposition of the specially valued property by the estate. Any person who at the decedent's death has any such interest in the property, whether present or future, or vested or contingent, must enter into the agreement. Included are owners of remainder and executory interests; the holders of general or special powers of appointment; beneficiaries of a gift over in default of exercise of any such power; joint tenants and holders of similar undivided interests when the decedent held only a joint or undivided interest in the property or when only an undivided interest is specially valued; and trustees of trusts and representatives of other entities holding title to, or holding any interests in the property. An heir who has the power under local law to caveat (challenge) a will and thereby affect disposition of the property is not, however, considered to be a person with an interest in property under section 2032A solely by reason of that right. Likewise, creditors of an estate are not such persons solely by reason of their status as creditors.

If any person required to enter into the agreement either desires that an agent act for him or her or cannot legally bind himself or herself due to infancy or other incompetency, or due to death before the election under section 2032A is timely exercised, a representative authorized by local law to bind the person in an agreement of this nature may sign the agreement on his or her behalf.

The Internal Revenue Service will contact the agent designated in the agreement on all matters relating to continued qualification under section 2032A of the specially valued real property and on all matters relating to the special lien arising under section 6324B. It is the duty of the agent as attorney-in-fact for the parties with interests in the specially valued property to furnish the IRS with any requested information and to notify the IRS of any disposition or cessation of qualified use of any part of the property.

Form 706 (Rev. 4-97)

Checklist for Section 2032A Election.—*If you are going to make the special use valuation election on Schedule A-1, please use this checklist to ensure that you are providing everything necessary to make a valid election.*

To have a valid special use valuation election under section 2032A, you must file, in addition to the Federal estate tax return, **(a)** a notice of election (Schedule A-1, Part 2), and **(b)** a fully executed agreement (Schedule A-1, Part 3). You must include certain information in the notice of election. To ensure that the notice of election includes all of the information required for a valid election, use the following checklist. The checklist is for your use only. Do not file it with the return.

1. Does the notice of election include the decedent's name and social security number as they appear on the estate tax return?

2. Does the notice of election include the relevant qualified use of the property to be specially valued?

3. Does the notice of election describe the items of real property shown on the estate tax return that are to be specially valued and identify the property by the Form 706 schedule and item number?

4. Does the notice of election include the fair market value of the real property to be specially valued and also include its value based on the qualified use (determined without the adjustments provided in section 2032A(b)(3)(B))?

5. Does the notice of election include the adjusted value (as defined in section 2032A(b)(3)(B)) of **(a)** all real property that both passes from the decedent and is used in a qualified use, without regard to whether it is to be specially valued, and **(b)** all real property to be specially valued?

6. Does the notice of election include **(a)** the items of personal property shown on the estate tax return that pass from the decedent to a qualified heir and that are used in qualified use and **(b)** the total value of such personal property adjusted under section 2032A(b)(3)(B)?

7. Does the notice of election include the adjusted value of the gross estate? (See section 2032A(b)(3)(A).)

8. Does the notice of election include the method used to determine the special use value?

9. Does the notice of election include copies of written appraisals of the fair market value of the real property?

10. Does the notice of election include a statement that the decedent and/or a member of his or her family has owned all of the specially valued property for at least 5 years of the 8 years immediately preceding the date of the decedent's death?

11. Does the notice of election include a statement as to whether there were any periods during the 8-year period preceding the decedent's date of death during which the decedent or a member of his or her family **(a)** did not own the property to be specially valued, **(b)** use it in a qualified use, or **(c)** materially participate in the operation of the farm or other business? (See section 2032A(e)(6).)

12. Does the notice of election include, for each item of specially valued property, the name of every person taking an interest in that item of specially valued property and the following information about each such person: **(a)** the person's address, **(b)** the person's taxpayer identification number, **(c)** the person's relationship to the decedent, and **(d)** the value of the property interest passing to that person based on both fair market value and qualified use?

13. Does the notice of election include affidavits describing the activities constituting material participation and the identity of the material participants?

14. Does the notice of election include a legal description of each item of specially valued property?

(In the case of an election made for qualified woodlands, the information included in the notice of election must include the reason for entitlement to the woodlands election.)

Any election made under section 2032A will not be valid unless a properly executed agreement (Schedule A-1, Part 3) is filed with the estate tax return. To ensure that the agreement satisfies the requirements for a valid election, use the following checklist.

1. Has the agreement been signed by each and every qualified heir having an interest in the property being specially valued?

2. Has every qualified heir expressed consent to personal liability under section 2032A(c) in the event of an early disposition or early cessation of qualified use?

3. Is the agreement that is actually signed by the qualified heirs in a form that is binding on all of the qualified heirs having an interest in the specially valued property?

4. Does the agreement designate an agent to act for the parties to the agreement in all dealings with the IRS on matters arising under section 2032A?

5. Has the agreement been signed by the designated agent and does it give the address of the agent?

Form 706 (Rev. 4-97)

Estate of:

	Decedent's Social Security Number

SCHEDULE A-1—Section 2032A Valuation

Part 1.—Type of Election (Before making an election, see the checklist on page 7.):

☐ **Protective election (Regulations section 20.2032A-8(b)).**—Complete Part 2, line 1, and column A of lines 3 and 4. (See instructions.)

☐ **Regular election.**—Complete all of Part 2 (including line 11, if applicable) and Part 3. (See instructions.)

Before completing Schedule A-1, see the checklist on page 7 for the information and documents that must be included to make a valid election.

The election is not valid unless the agreement (i.e., Part 3—Agreement to Special Valuation Under Section 2032A)—

● Is signed by each and every qualified heir with an interest in the specially valued property, and

● Is attached to this return when it is filed.

Part 2.—Notice of Election (Regulations section 20.2032A-8(a)(3))

Note: *All real property entered on lines 2 and 3 must also be entered on Schedules A, E, F, G, or H, as applicable.*

1 Qualified use—check one ► ☐ Farm used for farming, or

　　　　　　　　　　　► ☐ Trade or business other than farming

2 Real property used in a qualified use, passing to qualified heirs, and to be specially valued on this Form 706.

A	B	C	D
Schedule and item number from Form 706	Full value (without section 2032A(b)(3)(B) adjustment)	Adjusted value (with section 2032A(b)(3)(B) adjustment)	Value based on qualified use (without section 2032A(b)(3)(B) adjustment)

Totals . . . .

Attach a legal description of all property listed on line 2.

Attach copies of appraisals showing the column B values for all property listed on line 2.

3 Real property used in a qualified use, passing to qualified heirs, but not specially valued on this Form 706.

A	B	C	D
Schedule and item number from Form 706	Full value (without section 2032A(b)(3)(B) adjustment)	Adjusted value (with section 2032A(b)(3)(B) adjustment)	Value based on qualified use (without section 2032A(b)(3)(B) adjustment)

Totals . . . .

If you checked "Regular election," you must attach copies of appraisals showing the column B values for all property listed on line 3.

(continued on next page)

Schedule A-1— Page 8

Form 706 (Rev. 4-97)

4 Personal property used in a qualified use and passing to qualified heirs.

A Schedule and item number from Form 706	B Adjusted value (with section 2032A(b)(3)(B) adjustment)	A (continued) Schedule and item number from Form 706	B (continued) Adjusted value (with section 2032A(b)(3)(B) adjustment)
		"Subtotal" from Col. B, below left	....

Subtotal . . . .   Total adjusted value . . . .

5 Enter the value of the total gross estate as adjusted under section 2032A(b)(3)(A). ▶ _____

6 Attach a description of the method used to determine the special value based on qualified use.

7 Did the decedent and/or a member of his or her family own all property listed on line 2 for at least 5 of the 8 years immediately preceding the date of the decedent's death? . . . . ☐ Yes ☐ No

8 Were there any periods during the 8-year period preceding the date of the decedent's death during which the decedent or a member of his or her family:

	Yes	No
a Did not own the property listed on line 2 above?		
b Did not use the property listed on line 2 above in a qualified use?		
c Did not materially participate in the operation of the farm or other business within the meaning of section 2032A(e)(6)?		

If "Yes" to any of the above, you must attach a statement listing the periods. If applicable, describe whether the exceptions of sections 2032A(b)(4) or (5) are met.

9 Attach affidavits describing the activities constituting material participation and the identity and relationship to the decedent of the material participants.

10 Persons holding interests. Enter the requested information for each party who received any interest in the specially valued property. **(Each of the qualified heirs receiving an interest in the property must sign the agreement, and the agreement must be filed with this return.)**

	Name	Address
A		
B		
C		
D		
E		
F		
G		
H		

	Identifying number	Relationship to decedent	Fair market value	Special use value
A				
B				
C				
D				
E				
F				
G				
H				

You must attach a computation of the GST tax savings attributable to direct skips for each person listed above who is a skip person. (See instructions.)

11 Woodlands election.—Check here ▶ ☐ if you wish to make a woodlands election as described in section 2032A(e)(13). Enter the Schedule and item numbers from Form 706 of the property for which you are making this election ▶ ....

You must attach a statement explaining why you are entitled to make this election. The IRS may issue regulations that require more information to substantiate this election. You will be notified by the IRS if you must supply further information.

Schedule A-1— Page 9

Form 706 (Rev. 4-97)

Part 3.—Agreement to Special Valuation Under Section 2032A

Estate of:	Date of Death	Decedent's Social Security Number

There cannot be a valid election unless:

- The agreement is executed by each and every one of the qualified heirs, and
- The agreement is included with the estate tax return when the estate tax return is filed.

We (list all qualified heirs and other persons having an interest in the property required to sign this agreement)

_____

_____ ,

being all the qualified heirs and _____

_____ ,

being all other parties having interests in the property which is qualified real property and which is valued under section 2032A of the

Internal Revenue Code, do hereby approve of the election made by _____ ,

Executor/Administrator of the estate of _____ ,

pursuant to section 2032A to value said property on the basis of the qualified use to which the property is devoted and do hereby enter into this agreement pursuant to section 2032A(d).

The undersigned agree and consent to the application of subsection (c) of section 2032A of the Code with respect to all the property described on line 2 of Part 2 of Schedule A-1 of Form 706, attached to this agreement. More specifically, the undersigned heirs expressly agree and consent to personal liability under subsection (c) of 2032A for the additional estate and GST taxes imposed by that subsection with respect to their respective interests in the above-described property in the event of certain early dispositions of the property or early cessation of the qualified use of the property. It is understood that if a qualified heir disposes of any interest in qualified real property to any member of his or her family, such member may thereafter be treated as the qualified heir with respect to such interest upon filing a Form 706-A and a new agreement.

The undersigned interested parties who are not qualified heirs consent to the collection of any additional estate and GST taxes imposed under section 2032A(c) of the Code from the specially valued property.

If there is a disposition of any interest which passes or has passed to him or her or if there is a cessation of the qualified use of any specially valued property which passes or passed to him or her, each of the undersigned heirs agrees to file a **Form 706-A**, United States Additional Estate Tax Return, and pay any additional estate and GST taxes due within 6 months of the disposition or cessation.

It is understood by all interested parties that this agreement is a condition precedent to the election of special use valuation under section 2032A of the Code and must be executed by every interested party even though that person may not have received the estate (or GST) tax benefits or be in possession of such property.

Each of the undersigned understands that by making this election, a lien will be created and recorded pursuant to section 6324B of the Code on the property referred to in this agreement for the adjusted tax differences with respect to the estate as defined in section 2032A(c)(2)(C).

As the interested parties, the undersigned designate the following individual as their agent for all dealings with the Internal Revenue Service concerning the continued qualification of the specially valued property under section 2032A of the Code and on all issues regarding the special lien under section 6324B. The agent is authorized to act for the parties with respect to all dealings with the Service on matters affecting the qualified real property described earlier. This authority includes the following:

- To receive confidential information on all matters relating to continued qualification under section 2032A of the specially valued real property and on all matters relating to the special lien arising under section 6324B.
- To furnish the Service with any requested information concerning the property.
- To notify the Service of any disposition or cessation of qualified use of any part of the property.
- To receive, but not to endorse and collect, checks in payment of any refund of Internal Revenue taxes, penalties, or interest.
- To execute waivers (including offers of waivers) of restrictions on assessment or collection of deficiencies in tax and waivers of notice of disallowance of a claim for credit or refund.
- To execute closing agreements under section 7121.

(continued on next page)

Form 706 (Rev. 4-97)

Part 3.—Agreement to Special Valuation Under Section 2032A *(Continued)*

Estate of:	Date of Death	Decedent's Social Security Number

• Other acts (specify) ▶ _____

By signing this agreement, the agent agrees to provide the Service with any requested information concerning this property and to notify the Service of any disposition or cessation of the qualified use of any part of this property.

Name of Agent	Signature	Address

The property to which this agreement relates is listed in Form 706, United States Estate (and Generation-Skipping Transfer) Tax Return, and in the Notice of Election, along with its fair market value according to section 2031 of the Code and its special use value according to section 2032A. The name, address, social security number, and interest (including the value) of each of the undersigned in this property are as set forth in the attached Notice of Election.

IN WITNESS WHEREOF, the undersigned have hereunto set their hands at _____ ,

this _____ day of _____ .

SIGNATURES OF EACH OF THE QUALIFIED HEIRS:

Signature of qualified heir	Signature of qualified heir
Signature of qualified heir	Signature of qualified heir
Signature of qualified heir	Signature of qualified heir
Signature of qualified heir	Signature of qualified heir
Signature of qualified heir	Signature of qualified heir
Signature of qualified heir	Signature of qualified heir

Signatures of other interested parties

Signatures of other interested parties

Schedule A-1— Page 11

Form 706 (Rev. 4-97)

Estate of:

SCHEDULE B—Stocks and Bonds

(For jointly owned property that must be disclosed on Schedule E, see the instructions for Schedule E.)

Item number	Description including face amount of bonds or number of shares and par value where needed for identification. Give 9-digit CUSIP number.	Unit value	Alternate valuation date	Alternate value	Value at date of death
1					
	Total from continuation schedules (or additional sheets) attached to this schedule . . .				
	TOTAL. (Also enter on Part 5, Recapitulation, page 3, at item 2.)				

(If more space is needed, attach the continuation schedule from the end of this package or additional sheets of the same size.)
(The instructions to Schedule B are in the separate instructions.)

Schedule B— Page 12

Form 706 (Rev. 4-97)

Estate of:

SCHEDULE C—Mortgages, Notes, and Cash

(For jointly owned property that must be disclosed on Schedule E, see the instructions for Schedule E.)

Item number	Description	Alternate valuation date	Alternate value	Value at date of death
1				
	Total from continuation schedules (or additional sheets) attached to this schedule . .			
	TOTAL. (Also enter on Part 5, Recapitulation, page 3, at item 3.).			

(If more space is needed, attach the continuation schedule from the end of this package or additional sheets of the same size.)
(See the instructions on the reverse side.)

Schedule C— Page 13

Form 706 (Rev. 4-97)

Instructions for Schedule C.— Mortgages, Notes, and Cash

Complete Schedule C and file it with your return if the total gross estate contains any:

- mortgages,
- notes, or
- cash.

List on Schedule C:

- mortgages and notes payable **to the decedent** at the time of death.
- cash the decedent had at the date of death.

Do not list on Schedule C:

- mortgages and notes payable **by the decedent.** (If these are deductible, list them on Schedule K.)

List the items on Schedule C in the following order:

- mortgages,
- promissory notes,
- contracts by decedent to sell land,
- cash in possession, and
- cash in banks, savings and loan associations, and other types of financial organizations.

What to enter in the "Description" column:

For mortgages, list:

- face value,
- unpaid balance,
- date of mortgage,
- date of maturity,
- name of maker,
- property mortgaged,
- interest dates, and
- interest rate.

Example to enter in "Description" column:

"Bond and mortgage of $50,000, unpaid balance: $24,000; dated: January 1, 1980; John Doe to Richard Roe; premises: 22 Clinton Street, Newark, NJ; due: January 1, 1997; interest payable at 10% a year--January 1 and July 1."

For promissory notes, list:

- in the same way as mortgages.

For contracts by the decedent to sell land, list:

- name of purchaser,
- contract date,
- property description,
- sale price,
- initial payment,
- amounts of installment payment,
- unpaid balance of principal, and
- interest rate.

For cash in possession, list:

- such cash separately from bank deposits.

For cash in banks, savings and loan associations, and other types of financial organizations, list:

- name and address of each financial organization,
- amount in each account,
- serial or account number,
- nature of account--checking, savings, time deposit, etc., and
- unpaid interest accrued from date of last interest payment to the date of death.

Important: If you obtain statements from the financial organizations, keep them for IRS inspection.

Form 706 (Rev. 4-97)

Estate of:

SCHEDULE D—Insurance on the Decedent's Life

You must list **all** policies on the life of the decedent and attach a Form 712 for each policy.

Item number	Description	Alternate valuation date	Alternate value	Value at date of death
1				
	Total from continuation schedules (or additional sheets) attached to this schedule . .			
	TOTAL. (Also enter on Part 5, Recapitulation, page 3, at item 4.)			

(If more space is needed, attach the continuation schedule from the end of this package or additional sheets of the same size.)

(See the instructions on the reverse side.)

Schedule D— Page 15

Instructions for Schedule D.—Insurance on the Decedent's Life

If you are required to file Form 706 and there was any insurance on the decedent's life, whether or not included in the gross estate, you must complete Schedule D and file it with the return.

Insurance you must include on Schedule D.—Under section 2042 you must include in the gross estate:

- Insurance on the decedent's life receivable by or for the benefit of the estate; and
- Insurance on the decedent's life receivable by beneficiaries other than the estate, as described below.

The term "insurance" refers to life insurance of every description, including death benefits paid by fraternal beneficiary societies operating under the lodge system, and death benefits paid under no-fault automobile insurance policies if the no-fault insurer was unconditionally bound to pay the benefit in the event of the insured's death.

Insurance in favor of the estate.—Include on Schedule D the full amount of the proceeds of insurance on the life of the decedent receivable by the executor or otherwise payable to or for the benefit of the estate. Insurance in favor of the estate includes insurance used to pay the estate tax, and any other taxes, debts, or charges that are enforceable against the estate. The manner in which the policy is drawn is immaterial as long as there is an obligation, legally binding on the beneficiary, to use the proceeds to pay taxes, debts, or charges. You must include the full amount even though the premiums or other consideration may have been paid by a person other than the decedent.

Insurance receivable by beneficiaries other than the estate.—Include on Schedule D the proceeds of all insurance on the life of the decedent not receivable by or for the benefit of the decedent's estate if the decedent possessed at death any of the incidents of ownership, exercisable either alone or in conjunction with any person.

Incidents of ownership in a policy include:

- The right of the insured or estate to its economic benefits;
- The power to change the beneficiary;
- The power to surrender or cancel the policy;
- The power to assign the policy or to revoke an assignment;
- The power to pledge the policy for a loan;
- The power to obtain from the insurer a loan against the surrender value of the policy;
- A reversionary interest if the value of the reversionary interest was more than 5% of the value of the policy immediately before the decedent died. (An interest in an insurance policy is considered a reversionary interest if, for example, the proceeds become payable to the insured's estate or payable as the insured directs if the beneficiary dies before the insured.)

Life insurance not includible in the gross estate under section 2042 may be includible under some other section of the Code. For example, a life insurance policy could be transferred by the decedent in such a way that it would be includible in the gross estate under section 2036, 2037, or 2038. (See the instructions to Schedule G for a description of these sections.)

Completing the Schedule

You must list every policy of insurance on the life of the decedent, whether or not it is included in the gross estate.

Under "Description" list:

- Name of the insurance company and
- Number of the policy.

For every policy of life insurance listed on the schedule, you must request a statement on **Form 712,** Life Insurance Statement, from the company that issued the policy. Attach the Form 712 to the back of Schedule D.

If the policy proceeds are paid in one sum, enter the net proceeds received (from Form 712, line 24) in the value (and alternate value) columns of Schedule D. If the policy proceeds are not paid in one sum, enter the value of the proceeds as of the date of the decedent's death (from Form 712, line 25).

If part or all of the policy proceeds are not included in the gross estate, you must explain why they were not included.

Form 706 (Rev. 4 97)

Estate of:

SCHEDULE E—Jointly Owned Property
(If you elect section 2032A valuation, you must complete Schedule E and Schedule A-1.)

PART 1.—Qualified Joint Interests—Interests Held by the Decedent and His or Her Spouse as the Only Joint Tenants (Section 2040(b)(2))

Item number	Description For securities, give CUSIP number, if available.	Alternate valuation date	Alternate value	Value at date of death
Total from continuation schedules (or additional sheets) attached to this schedule				
1a Totals				
1b Amounts included in gross estate (one-half of line 1a)				

PART 2.—All Other Joint Interests

2a State the name and address of each surviving co-tenant. If there are more than three surviving co-tenants, list the additional co-tenants on an attached sheet.

Name	Address (number and street, city, state, and ZIP code)
A.	
B.	
C.	

Item number	Enter letter for co-tenant	Description (including alternate valuation date if any) For securities, give CUSIP number, if available.	Percentage includible	Includible alternate value	Includible value at date of death
Total from continuation schedules (or additional sheets) attached to this schedule					
2b Total other joint interests					
3 Total includible joint interests (add lines 1b and 2b). Also enter on Part 5, Recapitulation, page 3, at item 5					

(If more space is needed, attach the continuation schedule from the end of this package or additional sheets of the same size.)
(See the instructions on the reverse side.)   **Schedule E— Page 17**

Form 706 (Rev. 4-97)

Instructions for Schedule E.—Jointly Owned Property

If you are required to file Form 706, you must complete Schedule E and file it with the return if the decedent owned any joint property at the time of death, whether or not the decedent's interest is includible in the gross estate.

Enter on this schedule all property of whatever kind or character, whether real estate, personal property, or bank accounts, in which the decedent held at the time of death an interest either as a joint tenant with right to survivorship or as a tenant by the entirety.

Do not list on this schedule property that the decedent held as a tenant in common, but report the value of the interest on Schedule A if real estate, or on the appropriate schedule if personal property. Similarly, community property held by the decedent and spouse should be reported on the appropriate Schedules A through I. The decedent's interest in a partnership should not be entered on this schedule unless the partnership interest itself is jointly owned. Solely owned partnership interests should be reported on Schedule F, "Other Miscellaneous Property."

Part 1—Qualified joint interests held by decedent and spouse.—Under section 2040(b)(2), a joint interest is a qualified joint interest if the decedent and the surviving spouse held the interest as:

- Tenants by the entirety, or
- Joint tenants with right of survivorship if the decedent and the decedent's spouse are the only joint tenants.

Interests that meet either of the two requirements above should be entered in Part 1. Joint interests that do not meet either of the two requirements above should be entered in Part 2.

Under "Description," describe the property as required in the instructions for Schedules A, B, C, and F for the type of property involved. For example, jointly held stocks and bonds should be described using the rules given in the instructions to Schedule B.

Under "Alternate value" and "Value at date of death," enter the full value of the property.

Note: *You cannot claim the special treatment under section 2040(b) for property held jointly by a decedent and a surviving spouse who is not a U.S. citizen. You must report these joint interests on Part 2 of Schedule E, not Part 1.*

Part 2—Other joint interests.—All joint interests that were not entered in Part 1 must be entered in Part 2.

For each item of property, enter the appropriate letter A, B, C, etc., from line 2a to indicate the name and address of the surviving co-tenant.

Under "Description," describe the property as required in the instructions for Schedules A, B, C, and F for the type of property involved.

In the "Percentage includible" column, enter the percentage of the total value of the property that you intend to include in the gross estate.

Generally, you must include the full value of the jointly owned property in the gross estate. However, the full value should not be included if you can show that a part of the property originally belonged to the other tenant or tenants and was never received or acquired by the other tenant or tenants from the decedent for less than adequate and full consideration in money or money's worth, or unless you can show that any part of the property was acquired with consideration originally belonging to the surviving joint tenant or tenants. In this case, you may exclude from the value of the property an amount proportionate to the consideration furnished by the other tenant or tenants. Relinquishing or promising to relinquish dower, curtesy, or statutory estate created instead of dower or curtesy, or other marital rights in the decedent's property or estate is not consideration in money or money's worth. See the Schedule A instructions for the value to show for real property that is subject to a mortgage.

If the property was acquired by the decedent and another person or persons by gift, bequest, devise, or inheritance as joint tenants, and their interests are not otherwise specified by law, include only that part of the value of the property that is figured by dividing the full value of the property by the number of joint tenants.

If you believe that less than the full value of the entire property is includible in the gross estate for tax purposes, you must establish the right to include the smaller value by attaching proof of the extent, origin, and nature of the decedent's interest and the interest(s) of the decedent's co-tenant or co-tenants.

In the "Includible alternate value" and "Includible value at date of death" columns, you should enter only the values that you believe are includible in the gross estate.

Schedule E— Page 18

Form 706 (Rev. 4-97)

Estate of:

SCHEDULE F—Other Miscellaneous Property Not Reportable Under Any Other Schedule

(For jointly owned property that must be disclosed on Schedule E, see the instructions for Schedule E.)
(If you elect section 2032A valuation, you must complete Schedule F and Schedule A-1.)

		Yes	No
1	Did the decedent at the time of death own any articles of artistic or collectible value in excess of $3,000 or any collections whose artistic or collectible value combined at date of death exceeded $10,000? . . . . If "Yes," submit full details on this schedule and attach appraisals.		
2	Has the decedent's estate, spouse, or any other person, received (or will receive) any bonus or award as a result of the decedent's employment or death? . . . . If "Yes," submit full details on this schedule.		
3	Did the decedent at the time of death have, or have access to, a safe deposit box? . . . . If "Yes," state location, and if held in joint names of decedent and another, state name and relationship of joint depositor. If any of the contents of the safe deposit box are omitted from the schedules in this return, explain fully why omitted.		

Item number	Description For securities, give CUSIP number, if available.	Alternate valuation date	Alternate value	Value at date of death
1				
	Total from continuation schedules (or additional sheets) attached to this schedule . .			
	TOTAL. (Also enter on Part 5, Recapitulation, page 3, at item 6.)			

(If more space is needed, attach the continuation schedule from the end of this package or additional sheets of the same size.)
(See the instructions on the reverse side.)

Schedule F— Page 19

Form 706 (Rev. 4-97)

Instructions for Schedule F.—Other Miscellaneous Property

You must complete Schedule F and file it with the return.

On Schedule F list all items that must be included in the gross estate that are not reported on any other schedule, including:

● Debts due the decedent (other than notes and mortgages included on Schedule C)

● Interests in business

● Insurance on the life of another (obtain and attach **Form 712,** Life Insurance Statement, for each policy)

Note for single premium or paid-up policies: *In certain situations, for example where the surrender value of the policy exceeds its replacement cost, the true economic value of the policy will be greater than the amount shown on line 56 of Form 712. In these situations, you should report the full economic value of the policy on Schedule F. See Rev. Rul. 78-137, 1978-1 C.B. 280 for details.*

● Section 2044 property (see **Decedent Who Was a Surviving Spouse** below)

● Claims (including the value of the decedent's interest in a claim for refund of income taxes or the amount of the refund actually received)

● Rights

● Royalties

● Leaseholds

● Judgments

● Reversionary or remainder interests

● Shares in trust funds (attach a copy of the trust instrument)

● Household goods and personal effects, including wearing apparel

● Farm products and growing crops

● Livestock

● Farm machinery

● Automobiles

If the decedent owned any interest in a partnership or unincorporated business, attach a statement of assets and liabilities for the valuation date and for the 5 years before the valuation date. Also attach

statements of the net earnings for the same 5 years. You must account for goodwill in the valuation. In general, furnish the same information and follow the methods used to value close corporations. See the instructions for Schedule B.

All partnership interests should be reported on Schedule F unless the partnership interest, itself, is jointly owned. Jointly owned partnership interests should be reported on Schedule E.

If real estate is owned by the sole proprietorship, it should be reported on Schedule F and not on Schedule A. Describe the real estate with the same detail required for Schedule A.

Line 1.—If the decedent owned at the date of death articles with artistic or intrinsic value (e.g., jewelry, furs, silverware, books, statuary, vases, oriental rugs, coin or stamp collections), check the "Yes" box on line 1 and provide full details. If any one article is valued at more than $3,000, or any collection of similar articles is valued at more than $10,000, attach an appraisal by an expert under oath and the required statement regarding the appraiser's qualifications (see Regulations section 20.2031-6(b)).

Decedent Who Was a Surviving Spouse

If the decedent was a surviving spouse, he or she may have received qualified terminable interest property (QTIP) from the predeceased spouse for which the marital deduction was elected either on the predeceased spouse's estate tax return or on a gift tax return, Form 709. The election was available for gifts made and decedents dying after December 31, 1981.

If this election was made and the surviving spouse retained his or her interest in the QTIP property at death, the full value of the QTIP property is includible in his or her estate, even though the qualifying income interest terminated at death. It is valued as of the date of the surviving spouse's death, or alternate valuation date, if applicable. Do not reduce the value by any annual exclusion that may have applied to the transfer creating the interest.

The value of such property included in the surviving spouse's gross estate is treated as passing from the surviving spouse. It therefore qualifies for the charitable and marital deductions on the surviving spouse's estate tax return if it meets the other requirements for those deductions.

For additional details, see Regulations section 20.2044-1.

Schedule F— Page 20

Form 706 (Rev. 4-97)

Estate of:

SCHEDULE G—Transfers During Decedent's Life
(If you elect section 2032A valuation, you must complete Schedule G and Schedule A-1.)

Item number	Description For securities. give CUSIP number, if available.	Alternate valuation date	Alternate value	Value at date of death
A.	Gift tax paid by the decedent or the estate for all gifts made by the decedent or his or her spouse within 3 years before the decedent's death (section 2035(c))	X X X X X		
B.	Transfers includible under section 2035(a), 2036, 2037, or 2038:			
1				
	Total from continuation schedules (or additional sheets) attached to this schedule . .			
	TOTAL. (Also enter on Part 5, Recapitulation. page 3, at item 7.).			

SCHEDULE H—Powers of Appointment
(Include "5 and 5 lapsing" powers (section 2041(b)(2)) held by the decedent.)
(If you elect section 2032A valuation, you must complete Schedule H and Schedule A-1.)

Item number	Description	Alternate valuation date	Alternate value	Value at date of death
1				
	Total from continuation schedules (or additional sheets) attached to this schedule . .			
	TOTAL. (Also enter on Part 5, Recapitulation. page 3, at item 8.).			

(If more space is needed, attach the continuation schedule from the end of this package or additional sheets of the same size.)
(The instructions to Schedules G and H are in the separate instructions.)

Schedules G and H— Page 21

Form 706 (Rev. 4-97)

Estate of:

SCHEDULE I—Annuities

Note: *Generally, no exclusion is allowed for the estates of decedents dying after December 31, 1984 (see page 13 of the instructions).*

		Yes	No
A Are you excluding from the decedent's gross estate the value of a lump-sum distribution described in section 2039(f)(2)? . . . . If "Yes," you must attach the information required by the instructions.			

Item number	Description Show the entire value of the annuity before any exclusions.	Alternate valuation date	Includible alternate value	Includible value at date of death
1				
	Total from continuation schedules (or additional sheets) attached to this schedule . .			
	TOTAL. (Also enter on Part 5, Recapitulation, page 3, at item 9.)			

(If more space is needed, attach the continuation schedule from the end of this package or additional sheets of the same size.)

Schedule I— Page 22

(The instructions to Schedule I are in the separate instructions.)

Form 706 (Rev. 4-97)

Estate of:

SCHEDULE J—Funeral Expenses and Expenses Incurred in Administering Property Subject to Claims

Note: *Do not list on this schedule expenses of administering property not subject to claims. For those expenses, see the instructions for Schedule L.*

If executors' commissions, attorney fees, etc., are claimed and allowed as a deduction for estate tax purposes, they are not allowable as a deduction in computing the taxable income of the estate for Federal income tax purposes. They are allowable as an income tax deduction on Form 1041 if a waiver is filed to waive the deduction on Form 706 (see the Form 1041 instructions).

Item number	Description	Expense amount	Total amount
1	**A. Funeral expenses:**		
	Total funeral expenses		....
	B. Administration expenses:		
1	Executors' commissions—amount estimated/agreed upon/paid. (Strike out the words that do not apply.)		....
2	Attorney fees—amount estimated/agreed upon/paid. (Strike out the words that do not apply.) . . .		....
3	Accountant fees—amount estimated/agreed upon/paid. (Strike out the words that do not apply.) . .		....
4	Miscellaneous expenses:	Expense amount	
	Total miscellaneous expenses from continuation schedules (or additional sheets) attached to this schedule		
	Total miscellaneous expenses		
	TOTAL. (Also enter on Part 5, Recapitulation, page 3, at item 11.)		

(If more space is needed, attach the continuation schedule from the end of this package or additional sheets of the same size.)
(See the instructions on the reverse side.)

Schedule J— Page 23

Form 706 (Rev. 4-97)

Instructions for Schedule J.— Funeral Expenses and Expenses Incurred in Administering Property Subject to Claims

General.—You must complete and file Schedule J if you claim a deduction on item 11 of Part 5, Recapitulation.

On Schedule J, itemize funeral expenses and expenses incurred in administering property subject to claims. List the names and addresses of persons to whom the expenses are payable and describe the nature of the expense. **Do not list expenses incurred in administering property not subject to claims on this schedule. List them on Schedule L instead.**

The deduction is limited to the amount paid for these expenses that is allowable under local law but may not exceed:

1. The value of property subject to claims included in the gross estate, plus

2. The amount paid out of property included in the gross estate but not subject to claims. This amount must actually be paid by the due date of the estate tax return.

The applicable local law under which the estate is being administered determines which property is and is not subject to claims. If under local law a particular property interest included in the gross estate would bear the burden for the payment of the expenses, then the property is considered property subject to claims.

Unlike certain claims against the estate for debts of the decedent (see the instructions for Schedule K in the separate instructions), you cannot deduct expenses incurred in administering property subject to claims on both the estate tax return and the estate's income tax return. If you choose to deduct them on the estate tax return, you cannot deduct them on a Form 1041 filed for the estate. Funeral expenses are only deductible on the estate tax return.

Funeral Expenses.—Itemize funeral expenses on line A. Deduct from the expenses any amounts that were reimbursed, such as death benefits payable by the Social Security Administration and the Veterans Administration.

Executors' Commissions.—When you file the return, you may deduct commissions that have actually been paid to you or that you expect to pay. You may not deduct commissions if none will be collected. If the amount of the commissions has not been fixed by decree of the proper court, the deduction will be allowed on the final examination of the return, provided that:

- The District Director is reasonably satisfied that the commissions claimed will be paid;

- The amount entered as a deduction is within the amount allowable by the laws of the jurisdiction where the estate is being administered; and

- It is in accordance with the usually accepted practice in that jurisdiction for estates of similar size and character.

If you have not been paid the commissions claimed at the time of the final examination of the return, you must support the amount you deducted with an affidavit or statement signed under the penalties of perjury that the amount has been agreed upon and will be paid.

You may not deduct a bequest or devise made to you instead of commissions. If, however, the decedent fixed by will the compensation payable to you for services to be rendered in the administration of the estate, you may deduct this amount to the extent it is not more than the compensation allowable by the local law or practice.

Do not deduct on this schedule amounts paid as trustees' commissions whether received by you acting in the capacity of a trustee or by a separate trustee. If such amounts were paid in administering property not subject to claims, deduct them on Schedule L.

Note: *Executors' commissions are taxable income to the executors. Therefore, be sure to include them as income on your individual income tax return.*

Attorney Fees.—Enter the amount of attorney fees that have actually been paid or that you reasonably expect to be paid. If on the final examination of the return the fees claimed have not been awarded by the proper court and paid, the deduction will be allowed provided the District Director is reasonably satisfied that the amount claimed will be paid and that it does not exceed a reasonable payment for the services performed, taking into account the size and character of the estate and the local law and practice. If the fees claimed have not been paid at the time of final examination of the return, the amount deducted must be supported by an affidavit, or statement signed under the penalties of perjury, by the executor or the attorney stating that the amount has been agreed upon and will be paid.

Do not deduct attorney fees incidental to litigation incurred by the beneficiaries. These expenses are charged against the beneficiaries personally and are not administration expenses authorized by the Code.

Interest Expense.—Interest expenses incurred after the decedent's death are generally allowed as a deduction if they are reasonable, necessary to the administration of the estate, and allowable under local law.

If you elect to pay the estate tax in installments, you may deduct the interest payable as it accrues. For more information, see the instructions for Question 3, Elections by the Executor, on page 5 of the separate instructions.

Interest incurred as the result of a Federal estate tax deficiency is a deductible administrative expense. Penalties are not deductible even if they are allowable under local law.

Miscellaneous Expenses.—Miscellaneous administration expenses necessarily incurred in preserving and distributing the estate are deductible. These expenses include appraiser's and accountant's fees, certain court costs, and costs of storing or maintaining assets of the estate.

The expenses of selling assets are deductible only if the sale is necessary to pay the decedent's debts, the expenses of administration, or taxes, or to preserve the estate or carry out distribution.

Schedule J— Page 24

Form 706 (Rev. 4-97)

Estate of:

SCHEDULE K—Debts of the Decedent, and Mortgages and Liens

Item number	Debts of the Decedent—Creditor and nature of claim, and allowable death taxes	Amount unpaid to date	Amount in contest	Amount claimed as a deduction
1				

Total from continuation schedules (or additional sheets) attached to this schedule . . . .

TOTAL. (Also enter on Part 5, Recapitulation, page 3, at item 12.) . . . .

Item number	Mortgages and Liens—Description	Amount
1		

Total from continuation schedules (or additional sheets) attached to this schedule . . . .

TOTAL. (Also enter on Part 5, Recapitulation, page 3, at item 13.) . . . .

(If more space is needed, attach the continuation schedule from the end of this package or additional sheets of the same size.)
(The instructions to Schedule K are in the separate instructions.)

Schedule K— Page 25

Form 706 (Rev. 4-97)

Estate of:

SCHEDULE L—Net Losses During Administration and
Expenses Incurred in Administering Property Not Subject to Claims

Item number	Net losses during administration (**Note:** *Do not deduct losses claimed on a Federal income tax return.*)	Amount
1		
	Total from continuation schedules (or additional sheets) attached to this schedule	
	TOTAL. (Also enter on Part 5, Recapitulation, page 3, at item 16.)	

Item number	Expenses incurred in administering property not subject to claims (Indicate whether estimated, agreed upon, or paid.)	Amount
1		
	Total from continuation schedules (or additional sheets) attached to this schedule	
	TOTAL. (Also enter on Part 5, Recapitulation, page 3, at item 17.)	

(If more space is needed, attach the continuation schedule from the end of this package or additional sheets of the same size.)

Schedule L— Page 26   (The instructions to Schedule L are in the separate instructions.)

Form 706 (Rev. 4-97)

Estate of:

SCHEDULE M—Bequests, etc., to Surviving Spouse

Election To Deduct Qualified Terminable Interest Property Under Section 2056(b)(7).—If a trust (or other property) meets the requirements of qualified terminable interest property under section 2056(b)(7), and

   a. The trust or other property is listed on Schedule M, and

   b. The value of the trust (or other property) is entered in whole or in part as a deduction on Schedule M,

then unless the executor specifically identifies the trust (all or a fractional portion or percentage) or other property to be excluded from the election, the executor shall be deemed to have made an election to have such trust (or other property) treated as qualified terminable interest property under section 2056(b)(7).

If less than the entire value of the trust (or other property) that the executor has included in the gross estate is entered as a deduction on Schedule M, the executor shall be considered to have made an election only as to a fraction of the trust (or other property). The numerator of this fraction is equal to the amount of the trust (or other property) deducted on Schedule M. The denominator is equal to the total value of the trust (or other property).

Election To Deduct Qualified Domestic Trust Property Under Section 2056A.—If a trust meets the requirements of a qualified domestic trust under section 2056A(a) and this return is filed no later than 1 year after the time prescribed by law (including extensions) for filing the return, and

   a. The entire value of a trust or trust property is listed on Schedule M, and

   b. The entire value of the trust or trust property is entered as a deduction on Schedule M,

then unless the executor specifically identifies the trust to be excluded from the election, the executor shall be deemed to have made an election to have the entire trust treated as qualified domestic trust property.

		Yes	No
1	Did any property pass to the surviving spouse as a result of a qualified disclaimer?		
	If "Yes," attach a copy of the written disclaimer required by section 2518(b).		
2a	In what country was the surviving spouse born? _____		
b	What is the surviving spouse's date of birth? _____		
c	Is the surviving spouse a U.S. citizen?		
d	If the surviving spouse is a naturalized citizen, when did the surviving spouse acquire citizenship? _____		
e	If the surviving spouse is not a U.S. citizen, of what country is the surviving spouse a citizen? _____		
3	**Election Out of QTIP Treatment of Annuities.**—Do you elect under section 2056(b)(7)(C)(ii) **not** to treat as qualified terminable interest property any joint and survivor annuities that are included in the gross estate and would otherwise be treated as qualified terminable interest property under section 2056(b)(7)(C)? (see instructions)		

Item number	Description of property interests passing to surviving spouse	Amount
1		
	Total from continuation schedules (or additional sheets) attached to this schedule	
4	Total amount of property interests listed on Schedule M	**4**

5a	Federal estate taxes (including section 4980A taxes) payable out of property interests listed on Schedule M	**5a**	
b	Other death taxes payable out of property interests listed on Schedule M . . .	**5b**	
c	Federal and state GST taxes payable out of property interests listed on Schedule M	**5c**	
d	Add items a, b, and c	**5d**	
6	Net amount of property interests listed on Schedule M (subtract 5d from 4). Also enter on Part 5, Recapitulation, page 3, at item 18	**6**	

(If more space is needed, attach the continuation schedule from the end of this package or additional sheets of the same size.)
(See the instructions on the reverse side.)

Schedule M— Page 27

Examples of Listing of Property Interests on Schedule M

Item number	Description of property interests passing to surviving spouse	Amount
1	One-half the value of a house and lot, 256 South West Street, held by decedent and surviving spouse as joint tenants with right of survivorship under deed dated July 15, 1957 (Schedule E, Part I, item 1)	$132.500
2	Proceeds of Gibraltar Life Insurance Company policy No. 104729, payable in one sum to surviving spouse (Schedule D, item 3)	200,000
3	Cash bequest under Paragraph Six of will	100.000

Instructions for Schedule M.—Bequests, etc., to Surviving Spouse (Marital Deduction)

General

You must complete Schedule M and file it with the return if you claim a deduction on item 18 of Part 5, Recapitulation.

The marital deduction is authorized by section 2056 for certain property interests that pass from the decedent to the surviving spouse. You may claim the deduction only for property interests that are included in the decedent's gross estate (Schedules A through I).

Note: *The marital deduction is generally not allowed if the surviving spouse is not a U.S. citizen. The marital deduction is allowed for property passing to such a surviving spouse in a "qualified domestic trust" or if such property is transferred or irrevocably assigned to such a trust before the estate tax return is filed. The executor must elect qualified domestic trust status on this return. See the instructions on pages 28–30 for details on the election.*

Property Interests That You May List on Schedule M

Generally, you may list on Schedule M all property interests that pass from the decedent to the surviving spouse and are included in the gross estate. However, you should not list any "Nondeductible terminable interests" (described below) on Schedule M unless you are making a QTIP election. The property for which you make this election must be included on Schedule M. See "Qualified Terminable Interest Property" on the following page.

For the rules on common disaster and survival for a limited period, see section 2056(b)(3).

You may list on Schedule M only those interests that the surviving spouse takes:

1. As the decedent's legatee, devisee, heir, or donee;

2. As the decedent's surviving tenant by the entirety or joint tenant;

3. As an appointee under the decedent's exercise of a power or as a taker in default at the decedent's nonexercise of a power;

Page 28

4. As a beneficiary of insurance on the decedent's life;

5. As the surviving spouse taking under dower or curtesy (or similar statutory interest); and

6. As a transferee of a transfer made by the decedent at any time.

Property Interests That You May Not List on Schedule M

You should not list on Schedule M:

1. The value of any property that does not pass from the decedent to the surviving spouse;

2. Property interests that are not included in the decedent's gross estate;

3. The full value of a property interest for which a deduction was claimed on Schedules J through L. The value of the property interest should be reduced by the deductions claimed with respect to it;

4. The full value of a property interest that passes to the surviving spouse subject to a mortgage or other encumbrance or an obligation of the surviving spouse. Include on Schedule M only the net value of the interest after reducing it by the amount of the mortgage or other debt;

5. Nondeductible terminable interests (described below);

6. Any property interest disclaimed by the surviving spouse.

Terminable Interests

Certain interests in property passing from a decedent to a surviving spouse are referred to as *terminable interests.* These are interests that will terminate or fail after the passage of time, or on the occurrence or nonoccurrence of some contingency. Examples are: life estates, annuities, estates for terms of years, and patents.

The ownership of a bond, note, or other contractual obligation, which when discharged would not have the effect of an annuity for life or for a term, is not considered a terminable interest.

Nondeductible terminable interests.— A terminable interest is *nondeductible,* and should not be entered on Schedule M (unless you are making a QTIP election) if:

1. Another interest in the same property passed from the decedent to some other person for less than adequate and full consideration in money or money's worth; and

2. By reason of its passing, the other person or that person's heirs may enjoy part of the property after the termination of the surviving spouse's interest.

This rule applies even though the interest that passes from the decedent to a person other than the surviving spouse is not included in the gross estate, and regardless of when the interest passes. The rule also applies regardless of whether the surviving spouse's interest and the other person's interest pass from the decedent at the same time.

Property interests that are considered to pass to a person other than the surviving spouse are any property interest that: **(a)** passes under a decedent's will or intestacy; **(b)** was transferred by a decedent during life; or **(c)** is held by or passed on to any person as a decedent's joint tenant, as appointee under a decedent's exercise of a power, as taker in default at a decedent's release or nonexercise of a power, or as a beneficiary of insurance on the decedent's life.

For example, a decedent devised real property to his wife for life, with remainder to his children. The life interest that passed to the wife does not qualify for the marital deduction because it will terminate at her death and the children will thereafter possess or enjoy the property.

However, if the decedent purchased a joint and survivor annuity for himself and his wife who survived him, the value of the survivor's annuity, to the extent that it is included in the gross estate, qualifies for the marital deduction because even though the interest will terminate on the wife's death, no one else will possess or enjoy any part of the property.

The marital deduction is not allowed for an interest that the decedent directed the executor or a trustee to convert, after death, into a terminable interest for the surviving spouse. The marital deduction is not allowed for such an interest even if there was no interest in the property passing to another person and even if the terminable interest would otherwise have been deductible under the exceptions described below for life estate and life insurance and annuity payments with powers of appointment. For more information, see Regulations sections 20.2056(b)-1(f) and 20.2056(b)-1(g), Example (7).

If any property interest passing from the decedent to the surviving spouse may be paid or otherwise satisfied out of any of a group of assets, the value of the property interest is, for the entry on Schedule M, reduced by the value of any asset or assets that, if passing from the decedent to the surviving spouse, would be nondeductible terminable interests. Examples of property interests that may be paid or otherwise satisfied out of any of a group of assets are a bequest of the residue of the decedent's estate, or of a share of the residue, and a cash legacy payable out of the general estate.

Example: A decedent bequeathed $100,000 to the surviving spouse. The general estate includes a term for years (valued at $10,000 in determining the value of the gross estate) in an office building, which interest was retained by the decedent under a deed of the building by gift to a son. Accordingly, the value of the specific bequest entered on Schedule M is $90,000.

Life Estate With Power of Appointment in the Surviving Spouse.—A property interest, whether or not in trust, will be treated as passing to the surviving spouse, and will not be treated as a nondeductible terminable interest if: **(a)** the surviving spouse is entitled for life to all of the income from the entire interest; **(b)** the income is payable annually or at more frequent intervals; **(c)** the surviving spouse has the power, exercisable in favor of the surviving spouse or the estate of the surviving spouse, to appoint the entire interest; **(d)** the power is exercisable by the surviving spouse alone and (whether exercisable by will or during life) is exercisable by the surviving spouse in all events; and **(e)** no part of the entire interest is subject to a power in any other person to appoint any part to any person other than the surviving spouse (or the surviving spouse's legal representative or relative if the surviving spouse is disabled. See Rev. Rul. 85-35, 1985-1 C.B. 328). If these five conditions are satisfied only for a specific portion of the entire interest, see the section 2056(b) regulations to determine the amount of the marital deduction.

Life Insurance, Endowment, or Annuity Payments, With Power of Appointment in Surviving Spouse.—A property interest consisting of the entire proceeds under a life insurance, endowment, or annuity contract is treated as passing from the decedent to the surviving spouse, and will not be treated as a nondeductible terminable interest if: **(a)** the surviving spouse is entitled to receive the proceeds in installments, or is entitled to interest on them, with all amounts payable during the life of the spouse, payable only to the surviving spouse; **(b)** the installment or interest payments are payable annually, or more frequently, beginning not later than 13 months after the decedent's death; **(c)** the surviving spouse has the power, exercisable in favor of the surviving spouse or of the estate of the surviving spouse, to appoint all amounts payable under the contract; **(d)** the power is exercisable by the surviving spouse alone and (whether exercisable by will or during life) is exercisable by the surviving spouse in all events; and **(e)** no part of the amount payable under the contract is subject to a power in any other person to appoint any part to any person other than the surviving spouse. If these five conditions are satisfied only for a specific portion of the proceeds, see the section 2056(b) regulations to determine the amount of the marital deduction.

Charitable Remainder Trusts.—An interest in a charitable remainder trust will **not** be treated as a nondeductible terminable interest if:

1. The interest in the trust passes from the decedent to the surviving spouse; and

2. The surviving spouse is the only beneficiary of the trust other than charitable organizations described in section 170(c).

A "charitable remainder trust" is either a charitable remainder annuity trust or a charitable remainder unitrust. (See section 664 for descriptions of these trusts.)

Election To Deduct Qualified Terminable Interests (QTIP)

You may elect to claim a marital deduction for qualified terminable interest property or property interests. You make the QTIP election simply by listing the qualified terminable interest property on Schedule M and deducting its value. You are presumed to have made the QTIP election if you list the property and deduct its value on Schedule M. If you make this election, the surviving spouse's gross estate will include the value of the "qualified terminable interest property." See the instructions for line 6 of General Information for more details. **The election is irrevocable.**

If you file a Form 706 in which you do not make this election, you may not file an amended return to make the election unless you file the amended return on or before the due date for filing the original Form 706.

The effect of the election is that the property (interest) will be treated as passing to the surviving spouse and will not be treated as a nondeductible terminable interest. All of the other marital deduction requirements must still be satisfied before you may make this election. For example, you may not make this election for property or property, interests that are not included in the decedent's gross estate.

Qualified terminable interest property is property **(a)** that passes from the decedent, and **(b)** in which the surviving spouse has a qualifying income interest for life.

The surviving spouse has a *qualifying income interest for life* if the surviving spouse is entitled to all of the income from the property payable annually or at more frequent intervals, or has a usufruct interest for life in the property, and during the surviving spouse's lifetime no person has a power to appoint any part of the property to any person other than the surviving spouse. An annuity is treated as an income interest regardless of whether the property from which the annuity is payable can be separately identified.

The QTIP election may be made for all or any part of a qualified terminable interest property. A partial election must relate to a fractional or percentile share of the property so that the elective part will reflect its proportionate share of the increase or decline in the whole of the property when applying sections 2044 or 2519. Thus, if the interest of the surviving spouse in a trust (or other property in which the spouse has a qualified life estate) is qualified terminable interest property, you may make an election for a part of the trust (or other property) only if the election relates to a defined fraction or percentage of the entire trust (or other property). The fraction or percentage may be defined by means of a formula.

Qualified Domestic Trust Election (QDOT)

The marital deduction is allowed for transfers to a surviving spouse who is not a U.S. citizen only if the property passes to the surviving spouse in a "qualified domestic trust" (QDOT) or if such property is transferred or irrevocably assigned to a QDOT before the decedent's estate tax return is filed.

A QDOT is any trust:

1. That requires at least one trustee to be either an individual who is a citizen of the United States or a domestic corporation;

Form 706 (Rev. 4-97)

2. That requires that no distribution of corpus from the trust can be made unless such a trustee has the right to withhold from the distribution the tax imposed on the QDOT;

3. That meets the requirements of any applicable regulations; and

4. For which the executor has made an election on the estate tax return of the decedent.

You make the QDOT election simply by listing the qualified domestic trust or the **entire value** of the trust property on Schedule M and deducting its value. You are presumed to have made the QDOT election if you list the trust or trust property and deduct its value on Schedule M. **Once made, the election is irrevocable.**

If an election is made to deduct qualified domestic trust property under section 2056A(d), the following information should be provided for each qualified domestic trust on an attachment to this schedule:

1. The name and address of every trustee;

2. A description of each transfer passing from the decedent that is the source of the property to be placed in trust; and

3. The employer identification number for the trust.

The election must be made for an entire QDOT trust. In listing a trust for which you are making a QDOT election, unless you specifically identify the trust as not subject to the election, the election will be considered made for the entire trust.

The determination of whether a trust qualifies as a QDOT will be made as of the date the decedent's Form 706 is filed. If, however, judicial proceedings are brought before the Form 706's due date (including extensions) to have the trust revised to meet the QDOT requirements, then the determination will not be made until the court-ordered changes to the trust are made.

Line 1

If property passes to the surviving spouse as the result of a qualified disclaimer, check "Yes" and attach a copy of the written disclaimer required by section 2518(b).

Line 3

Section 2056(b)(7) creates an automatic QTIP election for certain joint and survivor annuities that are includible in the estate under section 2039. To qualify, only the surviving spouse can have the right to receive payments before the death of the surviving spouse.

The executor can elect out of QTIP treatment, however, by checking the "Yes" box on line 3. Once made, the election is irrevocable. If there is more than one such joint and survivor annuity, you are not required to make the election for all of them.

If you make the election out of QTIP treatment by checking "Yes" on line 3, you cannot deduct the amount of the annuity on Schedule M. If you do not make the election out, you must list the joint and survivor annuities on Schedule M.

Listing Property Interests on Schedule M

List each property interest included in the gross estate that passes from the decedent to the surviving spouse and for which a marital deduction is claimed. This includes otherwise nondeductible terminable interest property for which you are making a QTIP election. Number each item in sequence and describe each item in detail. Describe the instrument (including any clause or paragraph number) or provision of law under which each item passed to the surviving spouse. If possible, show where each item appears (number and schedule) on Schedules A through I.

In listing otherwise nondeductible property for which you are making a QTIP election, unless you specifically identify a fractional portion of the trust or other property as not subject to the election, the election will be considered made for all of the trust or other property.

Enter the value of each interest before taking into account the Federal estate tax or any other death tax. The valuation dates used in determining the value of the gross estate apply also on Schedule M.

If Schedule M includes a bequest of the residue or a part of the residue of the decedent's estate, attach a copy of the computation showing how the value of the residue was determined. Include a statement showing:

● The value of all property that is included in the decedent's gross estate (Schedules A through I) but is not a part of the decedent's probate estate, such as lifetime transfers, jointly owned property that passed to the survivor on decedent's death, and the insurance payable to specific beneficiaries.

● The values of all specific and general legacies or devises, with reference to the applicable clause or paragraph of the decedent's will or codicil. (If legacies are made to each member of a class, for example, $1,000 to each of decedent's employees, only the number in each class and the total value of property received by them need be furnished.)

● The date of birth of all persons, the length of whose lives may affect the value of the residuary interest passing to the surviving spouse.

● Any other important information such as that relating to any claim to any part of the estate not arising under the will.

Lines 5a, b, and c.—The total of the values listed on Schedule M must be reduced by the amount of the Federal estate tax, the Federal GST tax, and the amount of state or other death and GST taxes paid out of the property interest involved. If you enter an amount for state or other death or GST taxes on lines 5b or 5c, identify the taxes and attach your computation of them.

Attachments.—If you list property interests passing by the decedent's will on Schedule M, attach a certified copy of the order admitting the will to probate. If, when you file the return, the court of probate jurisdiction has entered any decree interpreting the will or any of its provisions affecting any of the interests listed on Schedule M, or has entered any order of distribution, attach a copy of the decree or order. In addition, the District Director may request other evidence to support the marital deduction claimed.

Form 706 (Rev 4-97)

Estate of:

SCHEDULE O—Charitable, Public, and Similar Gifts and Bequests

		Yes	No
1a If the transfer was made by will, has any action been instituted to have interpreted or to contest the will or any of its provisions affecting the charitable deductions claimed in this schedule? . . . . If "Yes," full details must be submitted with this schedule.			
b According to the information and belief of the person or persons filing this return, is any such action planned? If "Yes," full details must be submitted with this schedule.			
2 Did any property pass to charity as the result of a qualified disclaimer? . . . . If "Yes," attach a copy of the written disclaimer required by section 2518(b).			

Item number	Name and address of beneficiary	Character of institution	Amount
1			

Total from continuation schedules (or additional sheets) attached to this schedule . . . .

3 Total		**3**	
4a Federal estate tax (including section 4980A taxes) payable out of property interests listed above	**4a**		
b Other death taxes payable out of property interests listed above	**4b**		
c Federal and state GST taxes payable out of property interests listed above	**4c**		
d Add items a, b, and c		**4d**	
5 Net value of property interests listed above (subtract 4d from 3). Also enter on Part 5, Recapitulation, page 3, at item 19		**5**	

(If more space is needed, attach the continuation schedule from the end of this package or additional sheets of the same size.)
(The instructions to Schedule O are in the separate instructions.)

Form 706 (Rev. 4-97)

Estate of:

SCHEDULE P—Credit for Foreign Death Taxes

List all foreign countries to which death taxes have been paid and for which a credit is claimed on this return.

....

If a credit is claimed for death taxes paid to more than one foreign country, compute the credit for taxes paid to one country on this sheet and attach a separate copy of Schedule P for each of the other countries.

The credit computed on this sheet is for the ....
(Name of death tax or taxes)

.... imposed in ....
(Name of country)

Credit is computed under the ....
(Insert title of treaty or "statute")

Citizenship (nationality) of decedent at time of death

(All amounts and values must be entered in United States money.)

1 Total of estate, inheritance, legacy, and succession taxes imposed in the country named above attributable to property situated in that country, subjected to these taxes, and included in the gross estate (as defined by statute)	
2 Value of the gross estate (adjusted, if necessary, according to the instructions for item 2)	
3 Value of property situated in that country, subjected to death taxes imposed in that country, and included in the gross estate (adjusted, if necessary, according to the instructions for item 3)	
4 Tax imposed by section 2001 reduced by the total credits claimed under sections 2010, 2011, and 2012 (see instructions)	
5 Amount of Federal estate tax attributable to property specified at item 3. (Divide item 3 by item 2 and multiply the result by item 4.)	
6 Credit for death taxes imposed in the country named above (the smaller of item 1 or item 5). Also enter on line 18 of Part 2, Tax Computation	

SCHEDULE Q—Credit for Tax on Prior Transfers

Part 1.—Transferor Information

	Name of transferor	Social security number	IRS office where estate tax return was filed	Date of death
A				
B				
C				

Check here ▶ ☐ if section 2013(f) (special valuation of farm, etc., real property) adjustments to the computation of the credit were made (see page 17 of the instructions).

Part 2.—Computation of Credit (see instructions beginning on page 17)

Item	Transferor			Total A, B, & C
	A	B	C	
1 Transferee's tax as apportioned (from worksheet, (line 7 ÷ line 8) × line 35 for each column) . .				
2 Transferor's tax (from each column of worksheet, line 20)				
3 Maximum amount before percentage requirement (for each column, enter amount from line 1 or 2, whichever is smaller)				
4 Percentage allowed (each column) (see instructions)	%	%	%	
5 Credit allowable (line 3 × line 4 for each column)				
6 TOTAL credit allowable (add columns A, B, and C of line 5). Enter here and on line 19 of Part 2, Tax Computation				

Schedules P and Q— Page 32   (The instructions to Schedules P and Q are in the separate instructions.)

Form 706 (Rev. 4-97)

SCHEDULE R—Generation-Skipping Transfer Tax

Note: *To avoid application of the deemed allocation rules, Form 706 and Schedule R should be filed to allocate the GST exemption to trusts that may later have taxable terminations or distributions under section 2612 even if the form is not required to be filed to report estate or GST tax.*

*The GST tax is imposed on taxable transfers of interests in property located **outside the United States** as well as property located inside the United States.*

See instructions beginning on page 17.

Part 1.—GST Exemption Reconciliation (Section 2631) and Section 2652(a)(3) (Special QTIP) Election

You no longer need to check a box to make a section 2652(a)(3) (special QTIP) election. If you list qualifying property in Part 1, line 9, below, you will be considered to have made this election. See page 19 of the separate instructions for details.

1 Maximum allowable GST exemption	**1**	$1,000,000
2 Total GST exemption allocated by the decedent against decedent's lifetime transfers	**2**	
3 Total GST exemption allocated by the executor, using Form 709, against decedent's lifetime transfers	**3**	
4 GST exemption allocated on line 6 of Schedule R, Part 2	**4**	
5 GST exemption allocated on line 6 of Schedule R, Part 3	**5**	
6 Total GST exemption allocated on line 4 of Schedule(s) R-1	**6**	
7 Total GST exemption allocated to intervivos transfers and direct skips (add lines 2–6)	**7**	
8 GST exemption available to allocate to trusts and section 2032A interests (subtract line 7 from line 1)	**8**	

9 Allocation of GST exemption to trusts (as defined for GST tax purposes):

A Name of trust	B Trust's EIN (if any)	C GST exemption allocated on lines 2–6, above (see instructions)	D Additional GST exemption allocated (see instructions)	E Trust's inclusion ratio (optional—see instructions)

9D Total. May not exceed line 8, above	**9D**	
10 GST exemption available to allocate to section 2032A interests received by individual beneficiaries (subtract line 9D from line 8). You must attach special use allocation schedule (see instructions)	**10**	

(The instructions to Schedule R are in the separate instructions.)

Schedule R— Page 33

Form 706 (Rev. 4 97)

Estate of:

Part 2.—Direct Skips Where the Property Interests Transferred Bear the GST Tax on the Direct Skips

Name of skip person	Description of property interest transferred	Estate tax value

1 Total estate tax values of all property interests listed above	1	
2 Estate taxes, state death taxes, and other charges borne by the property interests listed above .	2	
3 GST taxes borne by the property interests listed above but imposed on direct skips other than those shown on this Part 2 (see instructions)	3	
4 Total fixed taxes and other charges (add lines 2 and 3).	4	
5 Total tentative maximum direct skips (subtract line 4 from line 1)	5	
6 GST exemption allocated	6	
7 Subtract line 6 from line 5	7	
8 GST tax due (divide line 7 by 2.818182).	8	
9 Enter the amount from line 8 of Schedule R, Part 3	9	
10 **Total GST taxes payable by the estate** (add lines 8 and 9). Enter here and on line 22 of the Tax Computation on page 1	10	

Schedule R— Page 34

Form 706 (Rev. 4-97)

Estate of:

Part 3.—Direct Skips Where the Property Interests Transferred Do Not Bear the GST
Tax on the Direct Skips

Name of skip person	Description of property interest transferred	Estate tax value

1 Total estate tax values of all property interests listed above	1	
2 Estate taxes, state death taxes, and other charges borne by the property interests listed above .	2	
3 GST taxes borne by the property interests listed above but imposed on direct skips other than those shown on this Part 3 (see instructions)	3	
4 Total fixed taxes and other charges (add lines 2 and 3).	4	
5 Total tentative maximum direct skips (subtract line 4 from line 1)	5	
6 GST exemption allocated	6	
7 Subtract line 6 from line 5	7	
8 GST tax due (multiply line 7 by .55). Enter here and on Schedule R, Part 2, line 9	8	

Schedule R— Page 35

SCHEDULE R-1 **(Form 706)** (Rev. April 1997) Department of the Treasury Internal Revenue Service	**Generation-Skipping Transfer Tax** Direct Skips From a Trust Payment Voucher	OMB No. 1545-0015

Executor: File one copy with Form 706 and send two copies to the fiduciary. Do not pay the tax shown. See the separate instructions.
Fiduciary: See instructions on the following page. Pay the tax shown on line 6.

Name of trust		Trust's EIN
Name and title of fiduciary	Name of decedent	
Address of fiduciary (number and street)	Decedent's SSN	Service Center where Form 706 was filed
City, state, and ZIP code	Name of executor	
Address of executor (number and street)	City, state, and ZIP code	
Date of decedent's death	Filing due date of Schedule R, Form 706 (with extensions)	

Part 1.—Computation of the GST Tax on the Direct Skip

Description of property interests subject to the direct skip	Estate tax value

1 Total estate tax value of all property interests listed above	**1**	
2 Estate taxes, state death taxes, and other charges borne by the property interests listed above .	**2**	
3 Tentative maximum direct skip from trust (subtract line 2 from line 1)	**3**	
4 GST exemption allocated	**4**	
5 Subtract line 4 from line 3	**5**	
6 **GST tax due from fiduciary (divide line 5 by 2.818182) (See instructions if property will not bear the GST tax.)**	**6**	

Under penalties of perjury, I declare that I have examined this return, including accompanying schedules and statements, and to the best of my knowledge and belief, it is true, correct, and complete.

Signature(s) of executor(s)	Date
	Date
Signature of fiduciary or officer representing fiduciary	Date

Form 706 (Rev. 4-97)

Instructions for the Trustee

Introduction	Schedule R-1 (Form 706) serves as a payment voucher for the Generation-Skipping Transfer (GST) tax imposed on a direct skip from a trust, which you, the trustee of the trust, must pay. The executor completes the Schedule R-1 (Form 706) and gives you 2 copies. File one copy and keep one for your records.
How to pay	You can pay by check or money order. ● Make it payable to the "Internal Revenue Service." (DO NOT abbreviate Internal Revenue Service.) ● Make the check or money order for the amount on line 6 of Schedule R-1. ● Write "GST Tax" and the trust's EIN on the check or money order.
Signature	You must sign the Schedule R-1 in the space provided.
What to mail	Mail your check or money order and the copy of Schedule R-1 that you signed.
Where to mail	Mail to the Service Center shown on Schedule R-1.
When to pay	The GST tax is due and payable 9 months after the decedent's date of death (shown on the Schedule R-1). You will owe interest on any GST tax not paid by that date.
Automatic extension	You have an automatic extension of time to file Schedule R-1 and pay the GST tax. The automatic extension allows you to file and pay by 2 months after the due date (with extensions) for filing the decedent's Schedule R (shown on the Schedule R-1). If you pay the GST tax under the automatic extension, you will be charged interest (but no penalties).
Additional information	For more information, see Code section 2603(a)(2) and the instructions for Form 706, United States Estate (and Generation-Skipping Transfer) Tax Return.

Schedule R-1 (Form 706)— Page 37

Form 706 (Rev. 4-97)

Estate of:

SCHEDULE S—Increased Estate Tax on Excess Retirement Accumulations
(Under section 4980A(d) of the Internal Revenue Code)

Part I Tax Computation

1 Check this box if a section 4980A(d)(5) spousal election is being made. . . . . ▶ ☐
  You must attach the statement described in the instructions.
2 Enter the name and employer identification number (EIN) of each qualified employer plan and individual retirement account in
  which the decedent had an interest at the time of death:

	Name	EIN
Plan #1		
Plan #2		
Plan #3		
IRA #1		
IRA #2		
IRA #3		

		A Plan #1	B Plan #2	C Plan #3	D All IRAs
3	Value of decedent's interest				
4	Amounts rolled over after death	▨	▨	▨	
5	Total value (add lines 3 and 4)				
6	Amounts payable to certain alternate payees (see page 20 of the instructions)				▨
7	Decedent's investment in the contract under section 72(f)				
8	Excess life insurance amount				▨
9	Decedent's interest as a beneficiary				
10	Total reductions in value (add lines 6, 7, 8, and 9) . . .				
11	Net value of decedent's interest (subtract line 10 from line 5)				

12 Decedent's aggregate interest in all plans and IRAs (add columns A–D of line 11) . . . . ▶ | **12** |

13 Present value of hypothetical life annuity (from Part III, line 4) . . . . . | **13** |

14 Remaining unused grandfather amount (from Part II, line 4) . . . . . | **14** |

15 Enter the greater of line 13 or line 14 . . . . | **15** |

16 Excess retirement accumulation (subtract line 15 from line 12) . . . . | **16** |

17 Increased estate tax (multiply line 16 by 15%). Enter here and on line 23 of the Tax Computation on
   page 1 . . . . | **17** |

(The instructions to Schedule S are in the separate instructions.)

Schedule S— Page 38

Form 706 (Rev. 4-97)

Part II   **Grandfather Election**

1   Was a grandfather election made on a previously filed Form 5329? . . . . ▶   ☐ Yes ☐ No
     If "Yes," complete lines 2–4 below. **You may not make or revoke the grandfather election after
     the due date (with extensions) for filing the decedent's 1988 income tax return.** If "No," enter
     -0- on line 4 and skip to Part III.

2 Initial grandfather amount	**2**	
3 Total amount previously recovered	**3**	
4 Remaining unused grandfather amount (subtract line 3 from line 2). Enter here and on Part I, line 14, on page 38	**4**	

Part III   **Computation of Hypothetical Life Annuity**

1 Decedent's attained age at date of death (in whole years, rounded down)	**1**	
2 Applicable annual annuity amount (see page 21 of the instructions)	**2**	
3 Present value multiplier (see page 21 of the instructions)	**3**	
4 Present value of hypothetical life annuity (multiply line 2 by line 3). Enter here and on Part I, line 13, on page 38	**4**	

Schedule S— Page 39

Form 706 (Rev. 4-97)

(Make copies of this schedule before completing it if you will need more than one schedule.)

Estate of:

CONTINUATION SCHEDULE

Continuation of Schedule _____
(Enter letter of schedule you are continuing.)

Item number	Description For securities, give CUSIP number, if available	Unit value (Sch. B, E, or G only)	Alternate valuation date	Alternate value	Value at date of death or amount deductible

TOTAL. (Carry forward to main schedule.) . . . .

See the instructions on the reverse side.

Continuation Schedule— Page 40

Form 706 (Rev 4-97)

Instructions for Continuation Schedule

When you need to list more assets or deductions than you have room for on one of the main schedules, use the Continuation Schedule on page 40. It provides a uniform format for listing additional assets from Schedules A through I and additional deductions from Schedules J, K, L, M, and O.

Please keep the following points in mind:

● Use a separate Continuation Schedule for each main schedule you are continuing. Do not combine assets or deductions from different schedules on one Continuation Schedule.

● Make copies of the blank schedule before completing it if you expect to need more than one.

● Use as many Continuation Schedules as needed to list all the assets or deductions.

● Enter the letter of the schedule you are continuing in the space at the top of the Continuation Schedule.

● Use the *Unit value* column <u>only</u> if continuing Schedule B, E, or G. For all other schedules, use this space to continue the description.

● Carry the total from the Continuation Schedule(s) forward to the appropriate line on the main schedule.

If continuing	Report	Where on Continuation Schedule
Schedule E, Pt. 2	*Percentage includible*	*Alternate valuation date*
Schedule K	*Amount unpaid to date*	*Alternate valuation date*
Schedule K	*Amount in contest*	*Alternate value*
Schedules J, L, M	*Description of deduction continuation*	*Alternate valuation date* **and** *Alternate value*
Schedule O	*Character of institution*	*Alternate valuation date* **and** *Alternate value*
Schedule O	*Amount of each deduction*	*Amount deductible*

For sale by the U.S. Government Printing Office
Superintendent of Documents, Mail Stop SSOP, Washington, DC 20402-9328

☆U.S. GOVERNMENT PRINTING OFFICE: 1997-426-052/70295

Printed on recycled paper

Federal Gift Tax Return (Form 709)

Form **709**	**United States Gift (and Generation-Skipping Transfer) Tax Return**			OMB No. 1545-0020
(Rev. December 1996)	(Section 6019 of the Internal Revenue Code) (For gifts made after December 31, 1991)			
Department of the Treasury Internal Revenue Service	**Calendar year 19** .... ▶ **See separate instructions. For Privacy Act Notice, see the Instructions for Form 1040.**			

Part 1—General Information

1 Donor's first name and middle initial	2 Donor's last name	3 Donor's social security number
4 Address (number, street, and apartment number)		5 Legal residence (domicile) (county and state)
6 City, state, and ZIP code		7 Citizenship

			Yes	No
8	If the donor died during the year, check here ▶ ☐ and enter date of death.......................... ▸			
9	If you received an extension of time to file this Form 709, check here ▶ ☐ and attach the Form 4868, 2688, 2350, or extension letter			
10	Enter the total number of separate donees listed on Schedule A—count each person only once. ▶			
11a	Have you (the donor) previously filed a Form 709 (or 709-A) for any other year? If the answer is "No," do not complete line 11b .			
11b	If the answer to line 11a is "Yes," has your address changed since you last filed Form 709 (or 709-A)?			
12	Gifts by husband or wife to third parties.—Do you consent to have the gifts (including generation-skipping transfers) made by you and by your spouse to third parties during the calendar year considered as made one-half by each of you? (See instructions.) (If the answer is "Yes," the following information must be furnished and your spouse must sign the consent shown below. **If the answer is "No," skip lines 13–18 and go to Schedule A.**)			
13	Name of consenting spouse	14 SSN		
15	Were you married to one another during the entire calendar year? (see instructions)			
16	If the answer to 15 is "No," check whether ☐ married ☐ divorced or ☐ widowed, and give date (see instructions) ▶			
17	Will a gift tax return for this calendar year be filed by your spouse?			
18	Consent of Spouse—I consent to have the gifts (and generation-skipping transfers) made by me and by my spouse to third parties during the calendar year considered as made one-half by each of us. We are both aware of the joint and several liability for tax created by the execution of this consent.			

Consenting spouse's signature ▶   Date ▶

Part 2—Tax Computation

1	Enter the amount from Schedule A, Part 3, line 15	1	
2	Enter the amount from Schedule B, line 3	2	
3	Total taxable gifts (add lines 1 and 2)	3	
4	Tax computed on amount on line 3 (see Table for Computing Tax in separate instructions). . .	4	
5	Tax computed on amount on line 2 (see Table for Computing Tax in separate instructions). . .	5	
6	Balance (subtract line 5 from line 4)	6	
7	Maximum unified credit (nonresident aliens, see instructions)	7	192,800	00
8	Enter the unified credit against tax allowable for all prior periods (from Sch. B, line 1, col. C) . .	8	
9	Balance (subtract line 8 from line 7)	9	
10	Enter 20% (.20) of the amount allowed as a specific exemption for gifts made after September 8, 1976, and before January 1, 1977 (see instructions)	10	
11	Balance (subtract line 10 from line 9)	11	
12	Unified credit (enter the smaller of line 6 or line 11)	12	
13	Credit for foreign gift taxes (see instructions)	13	
14	Total credits (add lines 12 and 13)	14	
15	Balance (subtract line 14 from line 6) (do not enter less than zero)	15	
16	Generation-skipping transfer taxes (from Schedule C, Part 3, col. H, Total)	16	
17	Total tax (add lines 15 and 16)	17	
18	Gift and generation-skipping transfer taxes prepaid with extension of time to file	18	
19	If line 18 is less than line 17, enter BALANCE DUE (see instructions)	19	
20	If line 18 is greater than line 17, enter AMOUNT TO BE REFUNDED	20	

Under penalties of perjury, I declare that I have examined this return, including any accompanying schedules and statements, and to the best of my knowledge and belief it is true, correct, and complete. Declaration of preparer (other than donor) is based on all information of which preparer has any knowledge.

Donor's signature ▶   Date ▶

Preparer's signature (other than donor) ▶   Date ▶

Preparer's address (other than donor) ▶

Attach check or money order here.

For Paperwork Reduction Act Notice, see page 1 of the separate instructions for this form.   Cat. No. 16783M   Form **709** (Rev. 12-96)

Form 709 (Rev. 12-96)   Page **2**

SCHEDULE A   **Computation of Taxable Gifts**

Does the value of any item listed on Schedule A reflect any valuation discount? If the answer is "Yes," see instructions . . . Yes ☐   No ☐

Part 1—Gifts Subject Only to Gift Tax. *Gifts less political organization, medical, and educational exclusions—see instructions*

A Item number	B • Donee's name and address • Relationship to donor (if any) • Description of gift • If the gift was made by means of a trust, enter trust's identifying number and attach a copy of the trust instrument • If the gift was of securities, give CUSIP number	C Donor's adjusted basis of gift	D Date of gift	E Value at date of gift
1				

Total of Part 1 (add amounts from Part 1, column E) . . . . ▶

Part 2—Gifts That are Direct Skips and are Subject to Both Gift Tax and Generation-Skipping Transfer Tax. You must list the gifts in chronological order. *Gifts less political organization, medical, and educational exclusions—see instructions. (Also list here direct skips that are subject only to the GST tax at this time as the result of the termination of an "estate tax inclusion period." See instructions.)*

A Item number	B • Donee's name and address • Relationship to donor (if any) • Description of gift • If the gift was made by means of a trust, enter trust's identifying number and attach a copy of the trust instrument • If the gift was of securities, give CUSIP number	C Donor's adjusted basis of gift	D Date of gift	E Value at date of gift
1				

Total of Part 2 (add amounts from Part 2, column E) . . . . ▶

Part 3—Taxable Gift Reconciliation

1	Total value of gifts of donor (add totals from column E of Parts 1 and 2)	**1**	
2	One-half of items . . . . attributable to spouse (see instructions)	**2**	
3	Balance (subtract line 2 from line 1)	**3**	
4	Gifts of spouse to be included (from Schedule A, Part 3, line 2 of spouse's return—see instructions) . .	**4**	
	If any of the gifts included on this line are also subject to the generation-skipping transfer tax, check here ▶ ☐ and enter those gifts also on Schedule C, Part 1.		
5	Total gifts (add lines 3 and 4)	**5**	
6	Total annual exclusions for gifts listed on Schedule A (including line 4, above) (see instructions) . . .	**6**	
7	Total included amount of gifts (subtract line 6 from line 5)	**7**	

Deductions (see instructions)

8	Gifts of interests to spouse for which a marital deduction will be claimed, based on items . . . . of Schedule A	**8**		
9	Exclusions attributable to gifts on line 8	**9**		
10	Marital deduction—subtract line 9 from line 8	**10**		
11	Charitable deduction, based on items . . . . less exclusions . .	**11**		
12	Total deductions—add lines 10 and 11		**12**	
13	Subtract line 12 from line 7		**13**	
14	Generation-skipping transfer taxes payable with this Form 709 (from Schedule C, Part 3, col. H, Total) .		**14**	
15	Taxable gifts (add lines 13 and 14). Enter here and on line 1 of the Tax Computation on page 1 . . .		**15**	

(If more space is needed, attach additional sheets of same size.)

Form 709 (Rev. 12-96)

SCHEDULE A **Computation of Taxable Gifts** *(continued)*

16 Terminable Interest (QTIP) Marital Deduction. (See instructions for line 8 of Schedule A.)

If a trust (or other property) meets the requirements of qualified terminable interest property under section 2523(f), and

  a. The trust (or other property) is listed on Schedule A, and

  b. The value of the trust (or other property) is entered in whole or in part as a deduction on line 8, Part 3 of Schedule A,

then the donor shall be deemed to have made an election to have such trust (or other property) treated as qualified terminable interest property under section 2523(f).

If less than the entire value of the trust (or other property) that the donor has included in Part 1 of Schedule A is entered as a deduction on line 8, the donor shall be considered to have made an election only as to a fraction of the trust (or other property). The numerator of this fraction is equal to the amount of the trust (or other property) deducted on line 10 of Part 3, Schedule A. The denominator is equal to the total value of the trust (or other property) listed in Part 1 of Schedule A.

If you make the QTIP election (see instructions for line 8 of Schedule A), the terminable interest property involved will be included in your spouse's gross estate upon his or her death (section 2044). If your spouse disposes (by gift or otherwise) of all or part of the qualifying life income interest, he or she will be considered to have made a transfer of the entire property that is subject to the gift tax (see Transfer of Certain Life Estates on page 3 of the instructions).

17 Election Out of QTIP Treatment of Annuities

  ☐ ◄ Check here if you elect under section 2523(f)(6) **NOT** to treat as qualified terminable interest property any joint and survivor annuities that are reported on Schedule A and would otherwise be treated as qualified terminable interest property under section 2523(f). (See instructions.) Enter the item numbers (from Schedule A) for the annuities for which you are making this election ►_____

SCHEDULE B **Gifts From Prior Periods**

If you answered "Yes" on line 11a of page 1, Part 1, see the instructions for completing Schedule B. If you answered "No," skip to the Tax Computation on page 1 (or Schedule C, if applicable).

A Calendar year or calendar quarter (see instructions)	B Internal Revenue office where prior return was filed	C Amount of unified credit against gift tax for periods after December 31, 1976	D Amount of specific exemption for prior periods ending before January 1, 1977	E Amount of taxable gifts

1	Totals for prior periods (without adjustment for reduced specific exemption)	**1**			
2	Amount, if any, by which total specific exemption, line 1, column D, is more than $30,000		**2**		
3	Total amount of taxable gifts for prior periods (add amount, column E, line 1, and amount, if any, on line 2). (Enter here and on line 2 of the Tax Computation on page 1.)		**3**		

(If more space is needed, attach additional sheets of same size.)

Form 709 (Rev. 12-96)   Page **4**

SCHEDULE C	Computation of Generation-Skipping Transfer Tax

Note: Inter vivos direct skips that are completely excluded by the GST exemption must still be fully reported (including value and exemptions claimed) on Schedule C.

Part 1—Generation-Skipping Transfers

A Item No. (from Schedule A, Part 2, col. A)	B Value (from Schedule A, Part 2, col. E)	C Split Gifts (enter ½ of col. B) (see instructions)	D Subtract col. C from col. B	E Nontaxable portion of transfer	F Net Transfer (subtract col. E from col. D)
1					
2					
3					
4					
5					
6					

	Split gifts from spouse's Form 709 (enter item number)	Value included from spouse's Form 709	Nontaxable portion of transfer	Net transfer (subtract col. E from col. D)
If you elected gift splitting and your spouse was required to file a separate Form 709 (see the instructions for "Split Gifts"), you must enter all of the gifts shown on Schedule A, Part 2, of your spouse's Form 709 here.	S-			
In column C, enter the item number of each gift in the order it appears in column A of your spouse's Schedule A, Part 2. We have preprinted the prefix "S-" to distinguish your spouse's item numbers from your own when you complete column A of Schedule C, Part 3.	S-			
	S-			
	S-			
	S-			
	S-			
In column D, for each gift, enter the amount reported in column C, Schedule C, Part 1, of your spouse's Form 709.	S-			
	S-			

Part 2—GST Exemption Reconciliation (Section 2631) and Section 2652(a)(3) Election

Check box ▶ ☐ if you are making a section 2652(a)(3) (special QTIP) election (see instructions)

Enter the item numbers (from Schedule A) of the gifts for which you are making this election ▶ ....

1	Maximum allowable exemption	1	$1,000,000
2	Total exemption used for periods before filing this return	2	
3	Exemption available for this return (subtract line 2 from line 1)	3	
4	Exemption claimed on this return (from Part 3, col. C total, below)	4	
5	Exemption allocated to transfers not shown on Part 3, below. **You must attach a Notice of Allocation.** (See instructions.)	5	
6	Add lines 4 and 5	6	
7	Exemption available for future transfers (subtract line 6 from line 3)	7	

Part 3—Tax Computation

A Item No. (from Schedule C, Part 1)	B Net transfer (from Schedule C, Part 1, col. F)	C GST Exemption Allocated	D Divide col. C by col. B	E Inclusion Ratio (subtract col. D from 1.000)	F Maximum Estate Tax Rate	G Applicable Rate (multiply col. E by col. F)	H Generation-Skipping Transfer Tax (multiply col. B by col. G)
1					55% (.55)		
2					55% (.55)		
3					55% (.55)		
4					55% (.55)		
5					55% (.55)		
6					55% (.55)		
					55% (.55)		
					55% (.55)		
					55% (.55)		

Total exemption claimed. Enter here and on line 4, Part 2, above. May not exceed line 3, Part 2, above . . . . .

Total generation-skipping transfer tax. Enter here, on line 14 of Schedule A, Part 3, and on line 16 of the Tax Computation on page 1 . . . .

(If more space is needed, attach additional sheets of same size.)   ♻ **Printed on recycled paper**   *U.S. Government Printing Office 1997 — 417-677/60033*

Federal Fiduciary Income Tax Return

(Form 1041)

Form **1041**	Department of the Treasury—Internal Revenue Service **U.S. Income Tax Return for Estates and Trusts**	1996

For calendar year 1996 or fiscal year beginning , 1996, and ending , 19 | OMB No. 1545-0092

A Type of entity:
- ☐ Decedent's estate
- ☐ Simple trust
- ☐ Complex trust
- ☐ Grantor type trust
- ☐ Bankruptcy estate–Ch. 7
- ☐ Bankruptcy estate–Ch. 11
- ☐ Pooled income fund

B Number of Schedules K-1 attached (see instructions) ▶

Name of estate or trust (If a grantor type trust, see page 7 of the instructions.)

Name and title of fiduciary

Number, street, and room or suite no. (If a P.O. box, see page 7 of the instructions.)

City or town, state, and ZIP code

C Employer identification number

D Date entity created

E Nonexempt charitable and split-interest trusts, check applicable boxes (see page 8 of the instructions):
- ☐ Described in section 4947(a)(1)
- ☐ Not a private foundation
- ☐ Described in section 4947(a)(2)

F Check applicable boxes: ☐ Initial return ☐ Final return ☐ Amended return ☐ Change in fiduciary's name ☐ Change in fiduciary's address

G Pooled mortgage account (see page 9 of the instructions): ☐ Bought ☐ Sold Date:

Income

1	Interest income	1
2	Dividends	2
3	Business income or (loss) (attach Schedule C or C-EZ (Form 1040))	3
4	Capital gain or (loss) (attach Schedule D (Form 1041))	4
5	Rents, royalties, partnerships, other estates and trusts, etc. (attach Schedule E (Form 1040))	5
6	Farm income or (loss) (attach Schedule F (Form 1040))	6
7	Ordinary gain or (loss) (attach Form 4797)	7
8	Other income. List type and amount	8
9	**Total income.** Combine lines 1 through 8 ▶	9

Deductions

10	Interest. Check if Form 4952 is attached ▶ ☐	10
11	Taxes	11
12	Fiduciary fees	12
13	Charitable deduction (from Schedule A, line 7)	13
14	Attorney, accountant, and return preparer fees	14
15a	Other deductions NOT subject to the 2% floor (attach schedule)	15a
b	Allowable miscellaneous itemized deductions subject to the 2% floor	15b
16	**Total.** Add lines 10 through 15b	16
17	Adjusted total income or (loss). Subtract line 16 from line 9. Enter here and on Schedule B, line 1 ▶	17
18	Income distribution deduction (from Schedule B, line 17) (attach Schedules K-1 (Form 1041))	18
19	Estate tax deduction (including certain generation-skipping taxes) (attach computation)	19
20	Exemption	20
21	**Total deductions.** Add lines 18 through 20 ▶	21

Tax and Payments

22	Taxable income. Subtract line 21 from line 17. If a loss, see page 13 of the instructions	22
23	**Total tax** (from Schedule G, line 8)	23
24	**Payments: a** 1996 estimated tax payments and amount applied from 1995 return	24a
b	Estimated tax payments allocated to beneficiaries (from Form 1041-T)	24b
c	Subtract line 24b from line 24a	24c
d	Tax paid with extension of time to file: ☐ Form 2758 ☐ Form 8736 ☐ Form 8800	24d
e	Federal income tax withheld. If any is from Form(s) 1099, check ▶ ☐	24e
	Other payments: **f** Form 2439 ; **g** Form 4136 ; Total ▶	24h
25	**Total payments.** Add lines 24c through 24e, and 24h ▶	25
26	Estimated tax penalty (see page 13 of the instructions)	26
27	**Tax due.** If line 25 is smaller than the total of lines 23 and 26, enter amount owed	27
28	**Overpayment.** If line 25 is larger than the total of lines 23 and 26, enter amount overpaid	28
29	Amount of line 28 to be: **a Credited to 1997 estimated tax** ▶ ; **b Refunded** ▶	29

Please Sign Here

Under penalties of perjury, I declare that I have examined this return, including accompanying schedules and statements, and to the best of my knowledge and belief, it is true, correct, and complete. Declaration of preparer (other than fiduciary) is based on all information of which preparer has any knowledge.

▶ Signature of fiduciary or officer representing fiduciary | Date | ▶ EIN of fiduciary if a financial institution (see page 4 of the instructions)

Paid Preparer's Use Only

Preparer's signature ▶	Date	Check if self-employed ▶ ☐	Preparer's social security no.
Firm's name (or yours if self-employed) and address ▶		EIN ▶	
		ZIP code ▶	

For Paperwork Reduction Act Notice, see page 1 of the separate instructions. | Cat. No. 11370H | Form **1041** (1996)

Form 1041 (1996)   Page **2**

Schedule A — Charitable Deduction. Do not complete for a simple trust or a pooled income fund.

1	Amounts paid for charitable purposes from gross income	1	
2	Amounts permanently set aside for charitable purposes from gross income	2	
3	Add lines 1 and 2	3	
4	Tax-exempt income allocable to charitable contributions (see page 14 of the instructions)	4	
5	Subtract line 4 from line 3	5	
6	Capital gains for the tax year allocated to corpus and paid or permanently set aside for charitable purposes	6	
7	**Charitable deduction.** Add lines 5 and 6. Enter here and on page 1, line 13	7	

Schedule B — Income Distribution Deduction

1	Adjusted total income (from page 1, line 17) (see page 14 of the instructions)	1	
2	Adjusted tax-exempt interest	2	
3	Total net gain from Schedule D (Form 1041), line 17, column (a) (see page 15 of the instructions)	3	
4	Enter amount from Schedule A, line 6	4	
5	Long-term capital gain for the tax year included on Schedule A, line 3	5	
6	Short-term capital gain for the tax year included on Schedule A, line 3	6	
7	If the amount on page 1, line 4, is a capital loss, enter here as a positive figure	7	
8	If the amount on page 1, line 4, is a capital gain, enter here as a negative figure	8	
9	**Distributable net income (DNI).** Combine lines 1 through 8. If zero or less, enter -0-	9	
10	If a complex trust, enter accounting income for the tax year as determined under the governing instrument and applicable local law 10		
11	Income required to be distributed currently	11	
12	Other amounts paid, credited, or otherwise required to be distributed	12	
13	Total distributions. Add lines 11 and 12. If greater than line 10, see page 15 of the instructions	13	
14	Enter the amount of tax-exempt income included on line 13	14	
15	Tentative income distribution deduction. Subtract line 14 from line 13	15	
16	Tentative income distribution deduction. Subtract line 2 from line 9. If zero or less, enter -0-	16	
17	**Income distribution deduction.** Enter the smaller of line 15 or line 16 here and on page 1, line 18	17	

Schedule G — Tax Computation (see page 16 of the instructions)

1	**Tax: a** ☐ Tax rate schedule or ☐ Schedule D (Form 1041)	1a	
	b Other taxes	1b	
	c Total. Add lines 1a and 1b	1c	
2a	Foreign tax credit (attach Form 1116)	2a	
b	Check: ☐ Nonconventional source fuel credit ☐ Form 8834	2b	
c	General business credit. Enter here and check which forms are attached: ☐ Form 3800 or ☐ Forms (specify) ▶	2c	
d	Credit for prior year minimum tax (attach Form 8801)	2d	
3	**Total credits.** Add lines 2a through 2d	3	
4	Subtract line 3 from line 1c	4	
5	Recapture taxes. Check if from: ☐ Form 4255 ☐ Form 8611	5	
6	Alternative minimum tax (from Schedule I, line 41)	6	
7	Household employment taxes. Attach Schedule H (Form 1040)	7	
8	**Total tax.** Add lines 4 through 7. Enter here and on page 1, line 23	8	

Other Information

		Yes	No
1	Did the estate or trust receive tax-exempt income? If "Yes," attach a computation of the allocation of expenses. Enter the amount of tax-exempt interest income and exempt-interest dividends ▶ $		
2	Did the estate or trust receive all or any part of the earnings (salary, wages, and other compensation) of any individual by reason of a contract assignment or similar arrangement?		
3	At any time during calendar year 1996, did the estate or trust have an interest in or a signature or other authority over a bank, securities, or other financial account in a foreign country? See page 17 of the instructions for exceptions and filing requirements for Form TD F 90-22.1. If "Yes," enter the name of the foreign country ▶		
4	During the tax year, did the estate or trust receive a distribution from, or was it the grantor of, or transferor to, a foreign trust? If "Yes," see page 17 of the instructions for other forms the estate or trust may have to file		
5	Did the estate or trust receive, or pay, any seller-financed mortgage interest? If "Yes," see page 17 of the instructions for required attachment		
6	If this is a complex trust making the section 663(b) election, check here (see page 17 of the instructions) ▶ ☐		
7	To make a section 643(e)(3) election, attach Schedule D (Form 1041), and check here (see page 17) ▶ ☐		
8	If the decedent's estate has been open for more than 2 years, check here ▶ ☐		

Schedule I   Alternative Minimum Tax (see pages 18 through 22 of the instructions)

Part I—Estate's or Trust's Share of Alternative Minimum Taxable Income

1	Adjusted total income or (loss) (from page 1, line 17)	**1**	
2	Net operating loss deduction. Enter as a positive amount	**2**	
3	Add lines 1 and 2	**3**	
4	**Adjustments and tax preference items:**		

a	Interest	4a	
b	Taxes	4b	
c	Miscellaneous itemized deductions (from page 1, line 15b)	4c	
d	Refund of taxes	4d (	)
e	Depreciation of property placed in service after 1986	4e	
f	Circulation and research and experimental expenditures	4f	
g	Mining exploration and development costs	4g	
h	Long-term contracts entered into after February 28, 1986	4h	
i	Amortization of pollution control facilities	4i	
j	Installment sales of certain property	4j	
k	Adjusted gain or loss (including incentive stock options)	4k	
l	Certain loss limitations	4l	
m	Tax shelter farm activities	4m	
n	Passive activities	4n	
o	Beneficiaries of other trusts or decedent's estates	4o	
p	Tax-exempt interest from specified private activity bonds	4p	
q	Depletion	4q	
r	Accelerated depreciation of real property placed in service before 1987	4r	
s	Accelerated depreciation of leased personal property placed in service before 1987	4s	
t	Intangible drilling costs	4t	
u	Other adjustments	4u	

5	Combine lines 4a through 4u	**5**	
6	Add lines 3 and 5	**6**	
7	Alternative tax net operating loss deduction (see page 21 of the instructions for limitations)	**7**	
8	Adjusted alternative minimum taxable income. Subtract line 7 from line 6. Enter here and on line 13	**8**	

Note: *Complete Part II before going to line 9.*

9	Income distribution deduction from line 27	9	
10	Estate tax deduction (from page 1, line 19)	10	
11	Add lines 9 and 10	**11**	
12	Estate's or trust's share of alternative minimum taxable income. Subtract line 11 from line 8	**12**	

If line 12 is:

- $22,500 or less, stop here and enter -0- on Schedule G, line 6. The estate or trust is not liable for the alternative minimum tax.
- Over $22,500, but less than $165,000, go to line 28.
- $165,000 or more, enter the amount from line 12 on line 34 and go to line 35.

(continued on page 4)

Part II—Income Distribution Deduction on a Minimum Tax Basis

13	Adjusted alternative minimum taxable income (from line 8)	13	
14	Adjusted tax-exempt interest (other than amounts included on line 4p)	14	
15	Total net gain from Schedule D (Form 1041), line 17, column (a). If a loss, enter -0-	15	
16	Capital gains for the tax year allocated to corpus and paid or permanently set aside for charitable purposes (from Schedule A, line 6)	16	
17	Capital gains paid or permanently set aside for charitable purposes from current year's income (see page 21 of the instructions)	17	
18	Capital gains computed on a minimum tax basis included on line 8	18	( )
19	Capital losses computed on a minimum tax basis included on line 8. Enter as a positive amount	19	
20	Distributable net alternative minimum taxable income (DNAMTI). Combine lines 13 through 19	20	
21	Income required to be distributed currently (from Schedule B, line 11)	21	
22	Other amounts paid, credited, or otherwise required to be distributed (from Schedule B, line 12)	22	
23	Total distributions. Add lines 21 and 22	23	
24	Tax-exempt income included on line 23 (other than amounts included on line 4p)	24	
25	Tentative income distribution deduction on a minimum tax basis. Subtract line 24 from line 23	25	
26	Tentative income distribution deduction on a minimum tax basis. Subtract line 14 from line 20	26	
27	**Income distribution deduction on a minimum tax basis.** Enter the smaller of line 25 or line 26. Enter here and on line 9	27	

Part III—Alternative Minimum Tax

28	Exemption amount	28	$22,500
29	Enter the amount from line 12	29	
30	Phase-out of exemption amount	30	$75,000
31	Subtract line 30 from line 29. If zero or less, enter -0-	31	
32	Multiply line 31 by 25% (.25)	32	
33	Subtract line 32 from line 28. If zero or less, enter -0-	33	
34	Subtract line 33 from line 29	34	
35	If line 34 is: • $175,000 or less, multiply line 34 by 26% (.26). • Over $175,000, multiply line 34 by 28% (.28) and subtract $3,500 from the result	35	
36	Alternative minimum foreign tax credit (see page 21 of instructions)	36	
37	Tentative minimum tax. Subtract line 36 from line 35	37	
38	Regular tax before credits (see page 22 of instructions)	38	
39	Section 644 tax included on Schedule G, line 1b	39	
40	Add lines 38 and 39	40	
41	**Alternative minimum tax.** Subtract line 40 from line 37. If zero or less, enter -0-. Enter here and on Schedule G, line 6	41	

 Printed on recycled paper

GLOSSARY

Abatement The legal process of reducing or eliminating the bequests of a decedent-testator who died owning insufficient assets to pay all bequests, debts and administration expenses.

Ademption The failure to fulfill a specific bequest in a will because the property bequeathed was sold, given away or lost before the testator's death.

Adjusted basis The amount subtracted from the amount realized to calculate gain or loss on sale or exchange of property.

Adjusted taxable gifts In federal estate tax (FET), the sum of post-1976 taxable gifts. It is added to the taxable estate on the federal estate tax return to arrive at the estate tax base.

Administrator A personal representative who was not nominated in the will.

Adverse party In the Internal Revenue Code, a person having a substantial interest in the property, subject to the power, which is adverse to exercise of the power in favor of the decedent.

After-born child A child who was born after the execution of a parent's will.

Alternate valuation date Under FET law, the date that is six months after date of death. Assets may be valued on this date or on date of death.

Annual exclusion Under the federal gift tax, a deduction, up to $10,000, from gross gifts for gifts by any donor to each donee in a given year.

Annual exclusion gift A gift of property worth no more than the annual gift tax exclusion. attorney as executor.

Antilapse statute A state statutory provision that specifies, in the absence of a provision in the will, to whom a lapsed testamentary bequest will pass.

Appointee (of a power of appointment) The party or parties whom the holder of a power of appointment actually appoints.

Apportionment statute See Equitable apportionment statute.

991

Ascertainable standard Wording in a will or trust intentionally limiting the freedom of holder of a power of appointment over property. The most common words of limitation are, "health," "education," "support," and "maintenance," derived from Section 2041. Use of the words avoid FET taxation to the holder of the power as a general power of appointment.

Assignment Any type of passing of property in which the transferor gives up some kind of interest to the transferee. See transfer.

Assignment of income doctrine Under income tax law, a doctrine holding that earnings from services performed will always be taxable to the person performing those services.

Bargain sale The part-gift, part-sale of an asset for some amount less than what would be regarded full and adequate consideration. The difference between the consideration received by the client-donor and the value of the asset transferred constitutes a gift, for tax purposes.

Beneficial interest An interest that carries an economic benefit. Examples of beneficial interests in property include the temporary or permanent right to possess, consume, and pledge the property.

Beneficiary A person who is receiving or will receive a gift of a beneficial interest in property. See Donee.

Bequest A gift, by will, of personal property. Also called a legacy.

Blockage discount A valuation discount given to a large quantity of a stock listed on an exchange, or certain other property, if its sale all at one time could have a temporarily depressing effect on the market price.

Bond In probate, an agreement under which an insurance company guarantees that the personal representative will faithfully perform required probate duties.

Business buyout agreement An agreement between one or more owners of a closely held business and one or more other persons that obligates one or more of the parties to purchase the interest of one of the others upon the occurrence of specific future events, such as the latter's death and, often, the onset of his or her permanent disability.

Buyout agreement See Business buyout agreement.

Buy-sell agreement See Business buyout agreement.

Bypass An arrangement under which property owned by a decedent and intended for the lifetime benefit of the surviving spouse does not actually pass to the surviving spouse, thereby avoiding inclusion in the latter's gross estate.

Bypass trust A trust designed to contain property that bypasses the surviving spouse's estate. See Bypass.

Cash value life insurance policy A policy that accumulates economic value because the insurer charges a constant premium that is considerably higher than mortality costs requires during the earlier years. Part of this overpayment accumulates as a cash surrender value which, prior to the death of the insured, can be enjoyed by the owner, basically in one of two ways. First, at any time the owner can surrender the policy and receive this value in cash. Second, the owner can make a policy loan and borrow up to the amount of this value.

Charitable lead trust A trust under which the client donates an asset's income interest to charity, at the end of which the remainder interest passes to a private party, typically children or grandchildren for a specified term of years. The client (or the client's estate) will receive an income tax deduction for the value of the income interest.

Charitable remainder annuity trust (CRAT) A trust into which the client transfers assets in exchange for a fixed annuity income of at least 5 percent of the original value of the assets transferred into trust, payable at least annually, usually for life. The value of the remainder is deductible on the income tax return.

Charitable remainder unitrust (CRUT) A trust that is much like the charitable remainder annuity trust, except that the annual income depends on a fixed percentage of the current fair market value of the assets in the trust, determined annually.

Chose in action A claim or debt recoverable in a lawsuit.

Closely held business A firm privately owned by one or a few individuals who actively participate in its management.

Codicil A separate written document that amends or revokes a prior will. It is executed if the testator wishes to change or add to the will.

Collateral A relative who shares a common ancestor with a person but who is neither a descendant nor an ascendant of that person. Contrast with issue.

Committee See Guardian.

Community property In the eight states recognizing it, all property that has been acquired by the efforts of either spouse during their marriage while living in a community property state, except property acquired by only one of the spouses by gift, devise, bequest or inheritance, or, in most of the community property states, by the income therefrom. The eight states are: Arizona, California, Idaho, Louisiana, Nevada, New Mexico, Texas, and Washington. In addition, Wisconsin has recently adopted a form of community property known as "marital partnership property."

Completed gift A gift in which the donor has so parted with dominion and control (in an interest in property) as to leave him no power to change its disposition, whether for his own benefit or for the benefit of another. (Rev. Rul. 67-396, 1969-2 C.B. 351).

Complex trust A nongrantor trust which, in a given year, either (a) accumulates some fiduciary accounting income (FAI) (i.e., does not pay out all FAI, which it has received, to the beneficiaries) or (b) distributes principal.

Conduit principle In the income taxation of estates and trusts, the rule that fiduciary accounting income distributed to beneficiaries will be taxed to them, rather than to the estate or trust.

Consanguinity Degrees of blood relationship between a decedent and the decedent's relatives.

Conservator A court-appointed fiduciary responsible for the person or property of an elderly incompetent person, or both.

Consideration furnished test Under the federal estate tax, the proposition that includes in a decedent's gross estate the entire value of property held by the decedent in joint tenancy, reduced only by an amount attributable to that portion of the consideration in money or money's worth which can clearly be shown to have been furnished by the survivors.

Contingent interest A future interest that is not vested; that is, an interest whose possession and enjoyment are dependent on the happening of some future event, not on just the passage of time.

Corpus The property in a trust. Also called principal.

Creator The person who creates the trust and whose property usually winds up in it. Also called grantor, settlor, or trustor.

Credit shelter bypass A bypass of an amount approximately equal to $600,000, the exemption equivalent of the unified credit.

Crummey provision A general power clause found in some trusts that give one or more beneficiaries the right to withdraw, for a limited period of time each year, the lesser of the amount of the annual exclusion or the value of the gift property transferred into the trust. Allows the donor to claim an annual exclusion. Often found in trusts for minors and in irrevocable life insurance trusts.

Cumulative gift doctrine The requirement that all lifetime gifts be accumulated; that is, that prior taxable gifts be added to current taxable transfers to determine the estate or gift tax base.

Curtesy A surviving husband's life interest in a portion of the real property owned by his deceased wife.

Custodial gift A gift to a custodian for the benefit of a child, under the Uniform Gifts to Minors Act or the Uniform Transfers to Minors Act.

Death tax A tax levied on certain property owned or transferred by the decedent at death. Either an estate tax or an inheritance tax.

Decedent In estate planning nomenclature, the person who has died.

Deferral A term used in this text to mean delaying payment of the FET until the death of S2 by taking the marital deduction in the estate of S1.

Descendant *See* issue.

Devise A gift, by will, of real property.

Devisee A beneficiary, under a will, of a devise, i.e., a gift of real property.

Direct skip Under federal generation-skipping tax law, a transfer to a skip person that is subject to the gift tax or the estate tax.

Disclaimer An unqualified refusal to accept a gift. In estate planning, a valid disclaimer must meet the requirements of both local law and IRC Section 2518.

Distributable net income (DNI) An amount more or less equal to fiduciary accounting income (FAI) that acts as the measuring rod for estate and trust income taxation.

Distribution deduction In the income taxation of estates and trusts, an amount equal to the lesser of distributable net income or the amount actually distributed to beneficiaries.

Distribution planning Planning the amount and timing of beneficiary distributions from an estate or irrevocable trust, usually with the objective of reducing income tax.

DNI See Distributable net income.

Donee A person who is receiving or will receive a gift of a beneficial interest in property. See Beneficiary.

Donor A person making a gift.

Dower A surviving wife's life interest in a portion of the real property owned by her deceased husband.

Durable power of attorney A power of attorney that does not become legally invalid at the onset of the principal's incapacity.

Durable power of attorney for health care (DPOAHC) A durable power of attorney granting to the attorney-in-fact the power to make medical decisions on behalf of the principal.

Durable power of attorney for property A durable power of attorney granting to the attorney-in-fact the power to make decisions concerning the property of the principal.

Equalization A term used in this text to mean a plan of property disposition by the spouses so that the taxable estates (or estate tax bases) of the two are more or less equal.

Equitable apportionment statute A state statute that spreads the death tax burden more or less proportionately among all of the beneficiaries receiving the taxed assets.

Escheat The reversion of an intestate decedent's property to the state, because either the decedent left no next of kin, or all surviving relatives are considered under state law to be too remote for purposes of inheritance.

Estate A quantity of wealth or property. See also Net estate, Gross estate, and Probate estate.

Estate tax A federal or state tax on the decedent's right to transfer property.

Estate planning The study of the principles of planning for the use, conservation, and efficient transfer of an individual's wealth.

Estate tax base This author's name for the sum of the taxable estate plus adjusted taxable gifts on the federal estate tax return. It more or less represents the sum of deathtime gifts plus lifetime gifts, and constitutes the amount used to calculate the tentative estate tax.

Estate trust One type of marital trust under which the corpus (and any accumulated income) is made payable to the estate of the surviving spouse at his or her death. Its unique feature is that it qualifies for the marital deduction even though the surviving spouse may not receive all of the income during his or her lifetime. However, income cannot be payable to anyone else.

Execute To complete a document (i.e., to do what is necessary to render it valid).

Executor A personal representative who was nominated in the will.

Exemption equivalent (of the unified credit) In federal estate taxation, the amount by which the taxable amount can exceed zero and still be sheltered by the unified credit.

Exercise a power of appointment To invoke the power by appointing a permissible appointee.

FAI See Fiduciary accounting income.

FET Used in this text to mean the net federal estate tax.

Family limited partnership A limited partnership meeting the requirements of §704(e) for the benefit of family members, generally with parents as the general partners and children as the limited partners. Used to take advantage of lack of control discounts and lack of marketability discounts as the parents transfer limited partnership units to the children.

Family pot trust See Pot trust.

Fee simple interest The greatest interest that a person can have over property, corresponding to the layperson's usual notion of full ownership.

Fiduciary A person in a position of trust and confidence; one who has a legal duty to act for the benefit of another. Examples include executor, trustee, attorney-in-fact, and custodian.

Fiduciary accounting income (FAI) In the income taxation of estates and trusts, most sources of federal gross income, including cash dividends, interest, and rent (reduced by certain expenses) but not including stock dividends and capital gains.

Fiscal year An income tax year that ends on the last day of any month except December.

Flower bonds Certain issues of long-term U.S. Treasury bonds which, if owned by the decedent at death, can be used at par value to pay the federal estate tax.

Fractional interest discount A valuation discount for real property that is neither easily partitioned nor readily marketable.

Freezing the estate tax value Using estate planning transfer techniques to effectively ensure that the future value of certain appreciating property includable in the estate tax base will not be significantly higher than its current value.

Future interest A beneficial interest in property in which the right to possess or enjoy the property is delayed, either by a specific period of time or until the happening of a future event.

General bequest A gift payable out of the general assets of the estate, but not one that specifies one or more particular items.

General power of attorney A document executed by one person called the principal, authorizing another person called the attorney-in-fact, to perform designated acts on behalf of the principal.

Generation-skipping transfer tax (GSTT) A federal or state tax on certain property transfers to a skip person, that is, someone who is two generations or more younger than the donor.

Gift A completed lifetime or deathtime transfer of property by an individual in exchange for any amount that is less than full consideration.

Gift tax A tax on a completed lifetime transfer of property for less than full consideration.

Grantor The person who creates the trust and whose property usually ends up in it. Also called creator settlor, or trustor.

Grantor retained annuity trust (GRAT) A grantor retained trust that pays the grantor a fixed income for a specified period and meets all other requirements of IRC §2702.

Grantor retained trust (GRT) An irrevocable trust into which the client transfers appreciating property in exchange for the right to receive income for a period of years. Under most GRTs, distribution of corpus at the end of the period depends upon whether or not the client survived this period. If not, the corpus reverts to the client-grantor's estate. If the client did survive the period, the corpus passes to a younger-generation beneficiary.

Grantor retained unitrust (GRUT) A grantor retained trust that pays the grantor a fixed percentage of the trust's principal for a specified period and meets all other requirements of IRC §2702.

Grantor trust A living trust in which the trustor, also called the grantor, has retained sufficient interest in the trust to make the income received by the trust taxable to the grantor, not to the trust or its beneficiaries.

Grantor trust rules The federal income tax rules concerning grantor trusts. They are located in Internal Revenue Code Sections 671-78.

Gross estate An FET term indicating property owned by the decedent at death, property transferred by the decedent under which the decedent retained an interest or control, and certain amounts in connection with property transferred within three years of death.

Grossing up Inclusion in the gross estate of gift taxes paid on any gifts made within three years of death.

GSTT See Generation-skipping transfer tax.

Guardian A court-appointed fiduciary responsible for the person or property of a minor or, in some cases, an incompetent adult, or both. In some states, a guardian is called a committee.

Heir A beneficiary who will receive property that passes by intestacy.

Holder (of a power of appointment) The person who has received the power of appointment, i.e., the one who has the right to appoint designated property to a permissible appointee. Also called the donee of the power.

Holding period In income tax law, the length of time that property is held. It determines whether a gain is short term or long term. The current threshold is one year.

Holographic will A will, recognized in many states, that is usually required to be written entirely in the hand of the testator. It need not be witnessed.

Incidents of ownership Powers and interests over an insurance policy on decedent's life that would subject the proceeds to inclusion in the decedent's gross estate under Section 2042.

Income beneficiary The beneficiary of a trust who has a life estate or estate for years in the trust income.

Income shifting See Shifting income.

Income tax A tax levied on income earned by a taxpayer during a given year.

Incomplete Not complete, i.e., rescindable or amendable, made without total relinquishment of dominion and control.

Inherit To receive property by intestate succession.

Inheritance tax A state tax on the right of a beneficiary to receive property from a decedent.

Installment sale The sale of an asset in exchange for an installment note, in which the buyer agrees to make periodic payments of principal and interest, based on a fair market rate of interest.

Intangible personal property Personal property that is not in itself valuable, but derives its value from that which it represents.

Intentionally defective irrevocable trust An irrevocable trust funded with gift assets that is complete for estate tax and incomplete for gift tax. Its objective is to give the grantor greater asset control and reduce FET by a greater amount than an outright gift.

Inter vivos transfer A transfer made while the transferor is alive.

Inter vivos trust A trust taking effect during the life of the trustor. Also called a living trust.

Interest by the entirety An interest in property similar to a joint interest; however, it can be created only between husband and wife. And unlike joint tenancy, neither spouse may transfer the property without the consent of the other.

Interest for years An interest in property giving the transferee the right to possess it for a fixed period.

Interest-free loan A demand loan, having no interest charge, usually to a family member in a lower income tax bracket. TRA 86 virtually eliminated its use.

Interest in common An interest in property held by two or more persons, each having an equal undivided right to possess property. Unlike a joint interest, however, an interest in common may be owned in unequal percentages, and when one owner dies the remaining owners do not automatically succeed in ownership. Instead, the decedent's interest passes through his or her estate, by will, by some other document, or by the laws of intestate distribution.

Intestate Having died leaving probate property not disposed of by a valid will.

Instrument Any legal document.

Inventory and appraisement A probate document that delineates all probate assets at their fair market value.

Irrevocable Subject to no right to rescind or amend (the terms of a transfer of one or more interests in property).

Issue A person's direct offspring, including children, grandchildren, great-grandchildren, and the like. Also called descendants. Contrast with Collaterals.

Itemized deductions In federal income tax law, deductions from adjusted gross income that are specifically listed, and taken in lieu of the standard deduction.

Joint interest A form of equal, undivided ownership in property that, upon death of one owner, automatically passes to the surviving owner(s). Also called joint tenancy.

Joint tenancy See Joint interest.

Kiddie tax In federal income tax law, the taxation of the unearned income of a minor child at the parent's marginal income tax rate.

Lack of marketability discount A valuation discount given stock in a business arising from the lack of an established market making the stock more difficult to sell.

Lapse The result when a beneficiary named in a will fails to survive the testator. Also, a power of appointment is said to lapse if the holder does not exercise it within the permitted period.

Leasehold An interest in property entitling the lessee to possess and use the properly for a specified time, usually in exchange for a fixed series of payments.

Legacy A gift, by will, of personal property. Also called a bequest.

Legatee A beneficiary, under a will, of a gift of personal property.

Letters testamentary A formal court document in probate indicating the court's authorization and empowerment of the estate's personal representative to deal legally with third parties.

Leveraging The process by which a given amount of exclusion, exemption, or credit can shelter a multiple of that amount from future transfer taxation.

Life estate An interest in property that ceases upon someone's death.

Life insurance policy A contract in which the insurance company agrees to pay a cash lump-sum amount (the face value or policy proceeds) to the person named in the policy to receive it (the beneficiary) upon the death of the subject of the insurance (the insured).

Limited liability companies A business organization in which the owners, called members, do not have personal liability for the contracts or the torts of the business, yet the organization is taxed like a partnership.

Living trust A trust taking effect during the lifetime of the trustor. Also called an inter vivos trust.

Living will A document detailing those health care interventions that a person does or does not want to be subjected to in situations when he or she is no longer capable of making those decisions.

Marital deduction In federal gift and estate taxation, the deduction for certain transfers to a spouse.

Marital trust A trust structured to receive property that will qualify for the marital deduction.

Minority discount A valuation discount given to an interest in a business that is not a controlling interest.

Net estate The net worth of a person; i.e., total assets minus total liabilities.

Omitted child See Omitted heir.

Omitted heir Any living spouse, child, or issue of any deceased child who is not provided for in a will.

Omitted spouse See Omitted heir.

Opportunity shifting The transfer of a rapidly appreciating wealth- or an income-producing opportunity to a family member before it is objectively ascertainable.

Outright transfer A transfer in which the transferee receives both legal interests and all beneficial interests, subject to no restrictions or conditions.

Partnership capital freeze Like a recapitalization, the reorganization of a partnership for the purpose of freezing the FET value of the client's partnership interest. Severely restricted by the

Revenue Reconciliation Act of 1990.

Permissible appointee (of a power of appointment) A party whom the holder may appoint by exercising the power.

Per capita A scheme of distribution from a will or trust requiring that issue of a decedent of all degrees share equally.

Perfect unification The author's theoretical set of conditions in which an individual would be indifferent, from a total transfer tax planning point of view, between making lifetime and deathtime gifts. It helps identify the factors that make our current system imperfect, which serves as the basis for transfer tax planning.

Per stirpes A scheme of distribution from a will or trust requiring that certain issue of a decedent, as a group, inherit the share of an estate that their immediate ancestor would have inherited if he or she had been living.

Perpetuities saving clause A clause in a will or trust that prevents interests from being ruled invalid under the rule against perpetuities.

Personal exemption In federal income tax law, amounts deductible on behalf of the taxpayer, the spouse, and each dependent, in calculating taxable income.

Personal property All property except fee simple and life estates in land and its improvements.

Personal representative The person appointed by the probate court to represent and manage the estate. If nominated in the will, called an executor.

Pickup tax A state death tax set at least equal to the federal credit for state death taxes.

Pooled income fund An investment fund created and maintained by the target charity, which "pools" property from many similar contributors. This arrangement ordinarily provides that the charity will pay to the grantor an income for life and, if desired, for the life of the grantor's spouse, based on the rate of return actually earned by the fund as a whole. At their death, the property passes to the charity.

Pot trust A trust established for the benefit of minor children which typically remains undivided until the youngest child reaches age 21 (or age 18). At that time, the assets are divided into equal separate shares, one for each child. The assets are distributed outright, or they are held for distribution at some older age. Also called a Family pot trust.

Pour-over will A will that distributes, at the testator's death, probate assets to a trust that had been created during the testator's lifetime.

Power of appointment A power to name someone to receive a beneficial interest in property.

Power of appointment trust A marital trust that gives to the surviving spouse the right to receive all income from the property for life, payable at least annually. It also gives him or her a general power of appointment over the principal, exercisable alone and in all events, at death or during life.

Power of attorney A document executed by one person, called the principal, authorizing another person, called the attorney-in-fact, to perform designated acts on behalf of the principal.

Precatory language Language in a will that does not direct or command, but merely expresses a wish, hope or desire. Precatory language is not given recognition by the courts in probate.

Present interest An immediate right to possess or enjoy property.

Pretermitted heir See omitted heir.

Principal The property in a trust. Also called corpus.

Private annuity A transfer of property under which the seller receives an unsecured promise of a life annuity.

Probate The legal process of administering the estate of a decedent. It focuses on the will and the probate estate, that is, property which will be disposed of by, and only by, either the will or by the state laws of intestate succession. More narrowly and less commonly, probate is used to mean certifying or proving the validity of the will after the death of the testator.

Probate estate All of the decedent's property passing to others by means of the probate process. This includes all property owned by the decedent except joint tenancy interests. In addition, the probate estate does not include property transferred by the decedent before death to a trustee, life insurance proceeds on the decedent's life, and the decedent's interest in pension and profit sharing plans.

QTIP election An election by the executor of the estate of the first spouse to die to treat certain property as QTIP property, thereby qualifying it for the marital deduction.

QTIP trust A marital trust for which a federal estate tax election is made. It provides that the surviving spouse is entitled to all of the income from the trust property, payable at least annually. In addition, the trust cannot give anyone a power to appoint any of the property to anyone other than the surviving spouse. Its uniqueness lies in the fact that its property need not pass to or be controlled by the surviving spouse.

Real property Fee simple or life estate interests in land and any improvements.

Recapitalization A reorganization of a closely held corporation for the purpose of freezing the value of the client's interest in the firm. Severely restricted by enactment of Revenue Reconciliation Act of 1990.

Reciprocal wills Two wills for two different people that are virtually identical; each leaves all (or substantially all) property to the other if the latter survives, otherwise to third persons. Sometimes called mirror wills. Reciprocal wills are usually simple wills; more complex wills are invariably unique in structure.

Remainder In the context of trusts, the future interest right to the remaining trust assets at the termination of all other interests. More technically, the right to use, possess and enjoy property after a prior owner's interest ends, in a situation where both interests were created at the same time and in the same document.

Remainderman The beneficiary of a trust who will receive the remainder at the termination of all other interests.

Residuary bequest A gift of that part of the testator's estate not otherwise disposed of by the will.

Reversion A future interest in property that is retained by the transferor; it will become a present interest when all other interests created at the same time have ended.

Revocable Subject to the right to rescind or amend (the terms of a transfer of one or more interests in property).

Rule against perpetuities A common law principle invalidating a dispositive clause in a will or a trust if the contingent interest transferred may vest in the transferee too long after the client's death.

S1 The author's nomenclature for the first spouse to die.

S2 The author's nomenclature for the second spouse to die.

Sale A transfer of property under which each transferor receives an amount of consideration that is regarded equivalent in value.

Self-canceling installment note (SCIN) An installment note which provides that no further payments will be made after the seller's death.

Self-proved will A will containing a formal affidavit by witnesses stating that all formalities have been complied with. It eliminates the need for the witnesses to later testify in probate.

Separate property In community property states, all property that is not community property. That is, all property acquired by a person not during marriage, and all property acquired during a marriage by gift, devise, bequest or inheritance, or, in most community property states, income earned on property so acquired.

Settlor The person who creates the trust and whose property usually winds up in it. Also called creator, grantor, or trustor.

Shifting income In estate planning, saving income tax by enabling income otherwise taxable to the client to be taxable to a family member in a lower tax bracket.

Short-term trust An irrevocable trust that reverts to the grantor sometime after 10 years. TRA 86, in subjecting this trust to the grantor trust rules, virtually eliminated its further use.

Simple will A will prepared for a family having a small estate, one for whom death tax planning is not a significant concern.

Skip person In federal generation-skipping transfer tax law, a beneficiary who is at least two generations younger than the transferor.

Soakup tax See Pickup tax.

Special use valuation A provision in federal estate tax law (Section 2032A) that permits qualifying estates to value farm or other trade or business property at its present "qualified-use value" rather than at its "highest and best use" value.

Specific bequest A gift of a particular item of property which is capable of being identified and distinguished from all other property. Contrasted with general bequest and residuary bequest.

Spendthrift clause A clause in a trust that restricts the beneficiary from transferring any of his or her future interest in the corpus or income. For example, a typical spendthrift clause would not permit the beneficiary to pledge the interest as collateral against a loan.

Splitting a gift Treating a gift of the property owned by one spouse, on the federal gift tax return, as if it were made one-half by each spouse.

Sponge tax See Pickup tax.

Spousal remainder trust An irrevocable trust providing for income for a period to a lower-income tax bracket family member, then remainder to the trustor's spouse. Future use of this trust was virtually eliminated by TRA 86, which subjected it to the grantor trust rules.

Springing durable power of attorney A durable power of attorney that becomes effective at the onset of the principal's incapacity.

Standard deduction In federal income tax law, a fixed amount that may be deducted from adjusted gross income. It may be used instead of specifically subtracting actual "itemized" deductions.

Standby trust An unfunded living trust whose principal financial management and control provisions do not come into effect until the grantor is determined to be incapacitated. At that point, the trust is usually funded by the grantor's attorney-in-fact, and, if the grantor had served as a trustee, management of the trust is taken over by a successor trustee.

Step-up in basis In income tax law, the upward adjustment in basis resulting from the acquisition of property from a decedent.

Surrogate decision makers Individuals capable of making decisions regarding a client's property and family at times when the client is unable, either due to incapacity or death. Examples include attorney-in-fact, trustee, and executor.

Survival clause A disposition provision in a will or trust naming an alternate taker of certain property if the donee fails to survive the donor.

Takers in default Persons who receive property subject to a power of appointment if the holder permits the power to lapse.

Tangible personal property Personal property which has value of its own.

Taxable estate In federal estate tax law, the gross estate reduced by total deductions.

Taxable distribution In federal generation-skipping transfer tax law, any distribution of property out of a trust to a skip person (other than a taxable termination or a direct skip).

Taxable gift In federal gift tax law, for a given year, total gross gifts reduced by total deductions and exclusions.

Taxable termination In federal generation-skipping transfer tax law, a termination of a nonskip person's interest in income or principal of a trust, with the result that skip persons become the only remaining trust beneficiaries.

Tax clause A provision in a will specifying which property bears the burden of paying taxes.

Tenancy by the entirety *See* interest by the entirety.

Terminable interest An interest which will terminate or fail on the lapse of time, on the occurrence of an event or contingency, or on the failure of an event or contingency to occur.

Property otherwise qualifying for the marital deduction will not qualify if the interest passing to the spouse is terminable, unless it is QTIP property, or otherwise excepted.

Terminal value Used in this text to indicate the value of a cash value life insurance policy that is currently in force. Formally called the policy's interpolated terminal reserve value, its amount is nearly equal to its cash surrender value.

Term life insurance A type of life insurance policy that has no value prior to the death of the insured because the premium charged, which increases over time with increasing risk of death. Term insurance simply buys pure protection: if the insured dies during the policy term, the company will pay the face value; otherwise, it will pay nothing.

Testamentary capacity The mental ability required of a testator to validly execute a will.

Testamentary transfer A transfer at death by will.

Testamentary trust A trust established by a trust-will into which probate property is transferred at the testator's death.

Testate Dying with a valid will.

Testator The person who executes a will.

Throwback rules In the income taxation of trusts, rules that subject income accumulated by a trust in one year and distributed to a beneficiary in another year to possible additional taxation to that beneficiary.

TRA 86 Tax Reform Act of 1986.

Transfer Any type of passing of property in which the transferor gives up some kind of interest to the transferee. Sometimes called an assignment.

Trust A legal arrangement between trustor and trustee that divides legal and beneficial interests in property among two or more people.

Trust beneficiary A person who is named to enjoy a beneficial interest in the trust.

Trust-will A will disposing of some or all of the testator's probate property to a trust, the terms of which are described in the document. The trust usually takes effect at the testator's death.

Trustor The person who creates the trust and whose property usually winds up in it. Also called creator, grantor, or settlor.

Undue influence Influence by a confidante which has the effect of impeding the testator's free will. A will can be denied probate (or at least certain clauses will be disregarded) if it can be established that the testator, at execution, was subject to undue influence.

Unification of gift and estate taxes Partially successful efforts by Congress in 1976 to tax lifetime and deathtime transfers equally, so that an individual would be indifferent, from a total transfer tax planning point of view, between making lifetime and deathtime gifts.

Unified credit Presently $192,800, a reduction in the tentative gift tax and tentative estate tax.

Uniform Gifts to Minors Act Like the Uniform Transfers to Minors Act, a statute in many states permitting custodial gifts for the benefit of a minor.

Uniform Probate Code (UPC) A complete set of probate laws originally promulgated by legal scholars and practitioners and currently adopted in whole or in part by about two fifths of the states.

Uniform Simultaneous Death Act (USDA) A statute providing that when transfer of title to property depends on the order of deaths, and that when no sufficient evidence exists that two people died other than simultaneously, the property of each is disposed of as if each had survived the other.

Uniform Transfers to Minors Act See Uniform Gifts to Minors Act.

Vested interest A nonforfeitable future interest whose possession and enjoyment are delayed only by time and not dependent on the happening of any future event.

Wait-and-see statute A provision in some state statutes that can overcome the effect of the rule against perpetuities by finding an interest void only if its turns out, in fact, not to vest within the required period.

Will A written document disposing of a person's probate property at death.

Witnessed will A written will, recognized in all states, that must be signed by two or more witnesses who acknowledge, among other things, that the testator asked them to witness the will, that they in fact did witness the testator's signing, and that the testator is mentally competent to execute a will (in accordance with state law).

Index